To Mr. & Mrs. Mickey Rooney   7500 Devista Dr.
                              Hollywood Calif. 90046

Dear Jan & Mickey

 Sorry you can't make it June 12ᵗʰ but you have an ongoing raincheck. While we'll miss you we're happy you are working cause that means pleasure for a lot of people.

 Mickey I'll bet you don't remember the 1ˢᵗ time we met. The year was 1937 ~~thereabouts~~ or thereabouts. I was new in Hollywood living in the Montecito apartments. Some one had run over a dog in the street outside. You came in to look for a phone book so you could find the nearest Veterinarian & take the dog to him. I figured this had to be a nice guy & I was right.

 Nancy sends her best & so did I.
                         Sincerely RR

To Rev. Paul T. Butler — Ozark Bible College
                              1111 No. Main, Joplin Mo. 64801

*f***P**

A LIFE IN LETTERS

Edited with an Introduction and Commentary by

Kiron K. Skinner

Annelise Anderson

Martin Anderson

WITH A FOREWORD BY GEORGE P. SHULTZ

FREE PRESS

NEW YORK • LONDON • TORONTO • SYDNEY • SINGAPORE

FREE PRESS
A Division of Simon & Schuster, Inc.
1230 Avenue of the Americas
New York, NY 10020

Designed by Dana Sloan

Manufactured in the United States of America

10   9   8   7   6   5   4   3   2   1

Library of Congress Cataloging-in-Publication Data

Reagan, Ronald.
    Reagan : a life in letters / edited with an introduction and
commentary by Kiron K. Skinner, Annelise Anderson, Martin
Anderson ; with a foreword by George P. Shultz.
        p.   cm.
    Includes bibliographical references and index.
    1. Reagan, Ronald—Correspondence.   2. Presidents—
United States—Correspondence.   3. United States—Politics
and government—1945–1989—Sources.   I. Skinner, Kiron K.
II. Anderson, Annelise Graebner.   III. Anderson, Martin.
IV. Title.
E877.A4 2003
973.927'092—dc21
    [B]   2003049249
ISBN 0-7432-1966-X

For information regarding special discounts for bulk purchases,
please contact Simon & Schuster Special Sales at 1-800-456-6798
or business@simonandschuster.com

For Ronald Reagan
Who wrote all the letters

CONTENTS

FOREWORD

by George P. Shultz

Ronald Reagan is widely known as "The Great Communicator." Well, we hardly knew how great a communicator he really was. We have read his handwritten stories, his essays written to be delivered as radio talks, and his public documents. Now we have this volume of letters, based on a stream of personal correspondence with a large, diverse set of people. Anyone who writes knows what an effort it is to assemble your thoughts and commit them to a piece of paper. Writing is an exercise in communicating with yourself as well as with others. A good writer is almost by necessity a good thinker.

I spent a lot of time with Ronald Reagan before and after his presidency, but most especially during our time in office together. I served him because I respected him and was honored to be a partner in what he was doing. Any close associate could see that Ronald Reagan was a deep and thoughtful man. People often speak about his steadfastness without quite realizing where it came from. He had steady purpose because he had deep convictions formed throughout his life.

These letters are extraordinary, showing us the development of Ronald Reagan's thinking. Some earlier presidents—Washington, Jefferson, Adams—were wonderful letter writers. They wrote at a time when the letter was the main method of recording views and communicating. By the time Ronald Reagan came along, the telephone, the dictating machine, and other devices made communication easy and convenient. Yet Ronald Reagan continued to write in his own hand.

We know from his wife, Nancy, that he was something of a workaholic. He spent hours at a desk in his bedroom in the White House writing letters, speeches, and draft statements of one kind or another. When spending the weekend with the Reagans at Camp David, I stopped by the president's cabin at Aspen several times and saw him seated at a table writing. He'd nod as I came in and say, "Please wait for just a minute while I finish this," and he'd continue writing.

When you read these letters, you see the personality and the character and the humor of Ronald Reagan—a real human being with many facets. I remember a trip to South America with the president during which we both worked hard. At the end of my last event, I got on *Air Force One,* had a drink and some supper, and went soundly to sleep. A couple of days later, over from the White House came an envelope. It contained a photograph of the president posing imploringly in front of me; my head was back and I was dead to the world. Reagan had written on the picture: "But George, I have to talk to you—the Russians are calling!!"

Writing is not only a process of communicating with yourself as well as with others but also a way of becoming more sensitive to other human beings. You can see this process in these letters, and I could see this human sensitivity in the way Ronald Reagan handled himself.

Whenever he met a head of government for the first time, his clear intent was less to develop the talking points and more to get a feeling for what kind of person this was. I remember vividly the visit of Samora Machel, president of Mozambique, a country that we thought could be weaned away from the Soviet bloc by common-sense talk and helpful action. Ronald Reagan had agreed to the meeting but, as the day approached, the press was full of stories about how odd a meeting this was and why in the world the president would meet with a person holding a degree from Moscow State University. The president was uneasy about his visitor at the start. When the two sat down together in the Oval Office, the first thing that happened was an engaging smile and then some talk back and forth. Pretty soon, the visitor was telling jokes about one ridiculous incident after another from his observations in Moscow. The president responded. They got along famously. Before long, they were on a first-name basis. The president judged this man, correctly as it turned out, to have a grip on reality and to be ready for some common sense and help. This process actually worked and we did help Mozambique make strides in a positive direction. The point is that Ronald Reagan had a capacity to sit down and engage with someone and in the process make a judgment about the character of the individual sitting opposite him.

In many ways, the most important relationship Ronald Reagan developed with a presumed adversary was with Mikhail Gorbachev. Reagan started with the same assumption: you could sit down with someone and through a personal exchange take the measure of the man.

We were waiting at Fleur d'Eau, the grand mansion we had rented when we were the hosts at the first big summit meeting between Ronald Reagan and the Soviet leader. Geneva was cold and snowy that morning. Ronald Reagan greeted Mikhail Gorbachev at 10:00 A.M. with an engaging smile. Flashbulbs lit the landscape. The image was dramatic: the hatless, coatless seventy-four-year-old who had bounded out in the bitter cold to greet the leader twenty years his junior. In the photos, Gorbachev—in topcoat and brown fedora—looked older than the president. President Reagan steered his guest into a side room for a meeting that was expected to last about twenty minutes. Thirty went by, then forty. The president's personal assistant and keeper of the schedule approached me asking whether he should go in and give the president an opening to break up the meeting. What did I think? "If you're dumb enough to do that, you shouldn't be in your job," I said.

After about an hour and a quarter, the leaders emerged, smiling. You could tell just by looking at them that the president and Gorbachev had hit it off well.

Once again Ronald Reagan had used personal diplomacy to take the measure of a man. As events unfolded over the next four years, that relationship developed in Geneva paid big dividends. There are many reasons for the turn in the Cold War. One of them was the relationship between Ronald Reagan and Mikhail Gorbachev, which was based on an underlying confidence that they could deal with each other.

Many of these letters reveal the beliefs and values held by Ronald Reagan. Perhaps that explains why the first deal he struck with the Soviet Union in 1983 had to do with human rights. The start was an informal, very private meeting between Ambassador Anatoly Dobrynin, who was a skilled diplomat, and President Reagan, with me present as the arranger. Initially, the president intended simply to deliver a brief message that he was ready for constructive discussion with a relatively new Soviet leader. The result was an extended conversation covering the full range of issues we had with the Soviet Union. President Reagan talked about all manner of things, but he came down hard on the importance of human rights, citing our lack of agreement on that as a fundamental impediment in our relationship. He used the plight of the Pentecostals who had been living in our embassy for several years as an example. They had rushed in to the embassy during the Carter administration. The Soviets had not allowed them to emigrate, and we could not send them out of the embassy because of concern for their lives. So there they sat. They were a continuing expression of human frustration with the Soviet system.

Ronald Reagan's advocacy and the depth and sincerity of the way he expressed it made an impact on Dobrynin. After lots of back and forth, we decided to try to persuade the Pentecostals to leave the embassy, with the expectation that they would eventually be allowed to emigrate. The president and I knew, and so did the Pentecostals, that we were taking a chance with their lives, but we felt that we had a deal. The deal was: "We'll let them out if you don't crow." A few months later, all of them—along with members of their families—were allowed to emigrate, some sixty people in all. Ronald Reagan never crowed.

Perhaps that experience convinced the Soviets that Ronald Reagan's concern for human rights was not politically driven but was an expression of his own personal attitude. If so, as these letters show, they were right. And the fact that he didn't crow may have said to them that here's a man who can keep his word even though the temptation to crow about this triumph must have been tremendous.

A certain integrity comes through in these letters, and you could see that integrity in Ronald Reagan's responses at critical moments. When he was warned that action to bring inflation under control early in his presidency might create difficulties in the economy, he quoted that well-known thought of Rabbi Hillel: "If not us, who? If not now, when?" And I recall a proposal made to a small group including the president for something that had little substance but was hot politics. When the presenter finished, Ronald Reagan said simply, "That's not what we came for." That was the end of it.

When I came to California after serving in three cabinet positions, including director of the Office of Management and Budget, Ronald Reagan, who was then governor, invited me to Sacramento for lunch. I found myself getting an intense grilling about how the federal budget worked—how did you put it together, what was the way you handled various department requests, how did the president weigh in, and so on. I came away with a clear sense that this man didn't want just to be president; he wanted to do the job right. And the letters show that his mind and his spirit were ready.

Ronald Reagan loved to negotiate and he enjoyed talking about the process. You can see this in some of his letters. I remember once discussing a complex proposal to the Soviets that originated in the Defense Department, including an understanding that we would not deploy a strategic defense for seven years. I recalled for the president a phrase I had used in my earlier life: "Mr. President," I said, "We don't have anything to deploy so you are giving them the sleeves from your vest." He loved the image. From time to time, considering other proposals, he would ask, "Where are the sleeves to your vest?"

I found this volume wonderful reading, at turns profound, inspirational, and fun. Here are my suggestions to the reader on how to handle this book. Start with the table of contents and pick out a subject that you are in the mood for. Then turn to that chapter and take a look at the introductory material provided by the editors. Then leaf through the letters and focus on one or two that really catch your attention. That will entice you to look for more. You can put this book down, pick it up and select another topic, and dig in once again.

This is a wonderful reference work that reveals Ronald Reagan's interests, his personality, his character, and how they developed over seventy years. So dig in for a wonderful read.

July 12, 2003

INTRODUCTION

"You specified that you wanted to hear from me personally, so here I am," Ronald Reagan wrote to a citizen in 1981. And here he is, in his own words, in over 1,000 letters—to family, friends, colleagues, and often to people he had never met.

This book presents letters by Ronald Reagan written during 72 years of his life, from 1922 to 1994. Reagan revealed himself—his beliefs, his values, his character, and his policies—through these private letters. He made candid, considerate, and tough statements that he rarely made in a public speech or an open forum. He enjoyed responding to citizens, and comforting or giving advice or encouragement to friends. Throughout some periods of his life, there are many thousands of surviving letters written in his own hand. We created a database of over 5,000 letters of interest for which we have a hand-written draft or which he dictated. We have found thousands of others of lesser interest, and we believe that there are still scores more in private collections. Over the course of his life, Reagan may have written upwards of 10,000 letters.

Reagan wrote to many people. He wrote to members of his family; to old friends from high school and college; to old friends from his years as a radio announcer, an actor, and a spokesman for General Electric. He wrote to Californians he came to know when he ran for and served as governor. He wrote to people who supported him financially, politically, and philosophically when he was running for president. He wrote to members of the media, some of whom were also friends; to movie fans who became friends and supporters; to heads of government; to civic and intellectual leaders; and to children and young people. Among Reagan's most unguarded correspondents were old friends such as Walter Annenberg, Laurence Beilenson, George Murphy, William F. Buckley Jr., Victor Krulak, and Barney Oldfield.

He also wrote to "uncommon" people, as he called them—typical Americans who wrote to him about his policies or their problems. Nancy Clark Reynolds, one of Reagan's secretaries during his governorship, reports that "Reagan was willing to talk to anybody. He was willing to write to anybody."[1]

Reagan reached out to people, including his critics, through letters. During the second year of Reagan's presidency, Deputy Chief of Staff Michael K. Deaver put it this way: "I don't think there's a day goes by that he doesn't appear with that yellow pad and say, 'Boy, did I let this guy know what I think.' "[2] Reagan also wrote many letters of sympathy and support. Lindy Fekety (then Lindy St. Cyr), a secretarial assistant at the White House, remembers that she would "sometimes tear up listening to the tapes [on the Dictaphone] and typing up the letters. They were heartwarming and gallant."[3] Chuck Donovan, deputy chief of the Correspondence Unit, saw thousands of Reagan's letters during his eight years at the White House. As he remembers, "It was emotion for emotion. . . . He could be sympathetic for someone who needed it."[4]

Reagan especially seemed to enjoy correspondence with children. At the beginning of his governorship, Reynolds took responsiblity for letters that came from children. Later, she began giving these letters to Reagan, and he continued corresponding with children who wrote to him even during his presidency. "Even though he had tough days," she recalls, "he had an optimistic view of life. I saved children's letters for tough days."[5]

It was not until 1967 when Reagan became governor of California that much of his correspondence was systematically saved. Many early letters survive, however, offering fascinating glimpses into his life.

During his years as governor, from 1967 to 1975, Reagan wrote letters in his office in the state capitol as well as in his home in Pacific Palisades, which he often visited on the weekend.[6] He dictated some of them.[7] It was in these years that Helene von Damm began a practice of giving Reagan a sample of letters drawn from the large pool of incoming correspondence so that he could have a sense of what people thought about his policies and what was happening in their lives—and he would often respond.

After his governorship and before his presidency, between 1975 and 1980, Reagan's offices were in Los Angeles, California, at the public relations firm started by Michael K. Deaver and Peter Hannaford, both of whom had worked for him as governor. Some of Reagan's letters were written by members of his staff (and therefore have been excluded from this volume). Reagan personally wrote a substantial number of letters during these years. As was the case in his governorship, he both dictated and wrote letters by hand.[8] Between 1979 and 1980, for example, Reagan dictated over 800 letters.

When a president assumes office, he inherits the Correspondence Unit, a White House department that assists with all facets of presidential correspondence. The Correspondence Unit has many sections, totaling some 60 people in the 1980s, but the office of the Director of Correspondence is the section that is most directly involved with the Oval Office. President Reagan appointed Anne Higgins to the directorship.

Only a small number of the 10,000 to 12,000 pieces of mail sent to President

Reagan each day ever reached his desk, and through several means. One was a special code. Family and friends were instructed to write on their envelope a sequence of numbers chosen by President Reagan. These letters bypassed normal White House channels. Letters from the public reached President Reagan through Higgins's office. Following the process established during Reagan's governorship, Higgins and her staff passed along letters that were "representative . . . of a large number of opinions." Every few weeks, Higgins would provide the president with between twenty and thirty of them. A cover sheet would be attached to the sample, and it would give a tally of positions on policy issues from the larger pool of letters being received.[9]

President Reagan also had extensive correspondence with American and foreign leaders. Even if some of these letters were sent to the Correspondence Unit, they were not typically answered by staff. Letters from leaders of closely allied countries, such as Canada, Great Britain, or Japan, might go to the National Security Council for review, but letters to leaders for whom President Reagan had developed a close personal relationship were sent to his office. Many of these replies were written by President Reagan himself.

President Reagan wrote wherever he was and whenever he had time to write. He wrote letters in the Oval Office, in his study at the White House, at Camp David, on the helicopter ride to Camp David, and on long trips on *Air Force One*. Some of these locations were listed on his stationery.

President Reagan often wrote letters during weekends at Camp David on yellow legal-size paper, ready for typing on official stationery. Higgins recalls that "he was a secretary's dream because he had all the information on the top [of the letter]: the name, the address, the zip code, and the telephone number if there was one. . . . [Reagan] didn't need editing. They [his letters] were fine. Everything was usually perfect." Higgins adds that President Reagan "would write on both sides of the yellow pad. He didn't waste the paper."[10] Reagan dictated 265 letters during his presidency, but discontinued the method in February 1982 because he preferred writing by hand.

It became immediately apparent to the Correspondence Unit staff that writing letters was important to President Reagan. A few days into his administration, the White House Post Office called Higgins to report that someone was using the president's stationery because sealed letters on his distinctive pale green stationery were arriving in the post office. It was discovered that President Reagan was writing letters and sealing them so that they could be mailed.[11]

After President Reagan left the White House in January 1989, the number of letters he wrote declined substantially. His methods, however, remained the same. He continued to write to family, friends, colleagues, and well-wishers by hand, though many were typed and some were written by staff. He wrote letters in his office in Los Angeles, at his home in nearby Bel Air, and at his ranch in the mountains near Santa Barbara.

In a letter dated November 5, 1994, Ronald Reagan informed his "fellow Americans" that he had Alzheimer's disease. Attention was focused on the message, but the medium was itself something of a statement. He might have used television or radio, but instead he said goodbye in a letter.

FREQUENT CORRESPONDENTS

Reagan wrote to many people over the years. Some of them were simply citizens who wrote a single letter to encourage or advise or criticize. Others wrote—and received answers—more frequently. When we know who they are, we identify them in the annotations to individual letters.

The following people appear, however, so frequently as to merit special introduction. They are a diverse group, including another president of the United States, a Hollywood fan, a young pen pal, and many friends and confidants acquired over the years with whom Reagan corresponded throughout much of his long career.

Walter Annenberg, a media magnate, was one of the wealthiest persons in America and a major philanthropist. He served as Ambassador to the United Kingdom 1969–74. He shared many of Reagan's views and contributed generously to Reagan's presidential library. Their long friendship began during Reagan's years with General Electric on one of his many train trips; Annenberg invited Reagan to have a drink with him.

Laurence Beilenson was an old friend of Reagan's from Hollywood. He was general counsel of the Screen Actors Guild during the years Reagan was president of that organization. He wrote *The Treaty Trap,* a 1969 book about how nations keep (or fail to keep) their treaty commitments. Reagan liked the book and welcomed Beilenson's ideas.

Roy Brewer, a liberal Democrat, was a labor leader in the Hollywood crafts union who fought alongside Reagan to prevent Communist infiltration of the Hollywood unions. Reagan respected Brewer, once describing him as "one labor leader who talked as much about labor's responsibility as he did about its privileges."

Alan Brown was a retired Navy officer who lived in Spain. He grew up in Los Angeles, attending the Harvard Military School, where many Hollywood figures sent their children. Politics was his hobby and he met Reagan when Reagan was a candidate for president.

William F. Buckley Jr., founded *National Review* in 1955 and was for years its editor. He and Reagan were close friends and corresponded from 1962 through the Reagan presidency about politics, policy, and personal matters.

Earl B. Dunckel traveled with Reagan on the General Electric tours during 1954 and 1955. A self-described conservative, Dunckel debated politics with Reagan on their travels. Dunckel sent policy and political suggestions to Reagan regularly.

Charles Grimm was the manager of the Chicago Cubs baseball team when Reagan announced their games and covered spring training in southern California in 1936 and 1937. After "Charlie" died Reagan remained friends with his wife, Marion.

Garth Henrichs graduated from Eureka College several years before Reagan entered. One of Reagan's classmates, Dick Crane, married Henrichs's sister. Henrichs began corresponding with Reagan in early 1938, congratulating him on his first movie, *Love Is on the Air*. Reagan's mother answered the first letters, but Reagan began writing his own replies in 1949 while confined to a hospital bed with a shattered thigh.

Ruddy Hines, Reagan's pen pal in the White House, was six years old when he and Reagan began exchanging letters in 1984. The correspondence continued through 1988.

Victor H. Krulak, a retired Marine general who became president of the Copley News Service, met Reagan at the Bohemian Grove, the redwooded retreat of the Bohemian Club in northern California. They were both members of the Owl's Nest camp at the Grove. While Reagan was president, Krulak was writing columns for the Copley News Service. Reagan often passed them around in White House staff meetings. They exchanged letters on policy issues and camp matters.

Helen Lawton lived next door to the Reagan family in Dixon, Illinois, and knew Reagan as a young boy.

William Loeb and his wife, Nackey, ran New Hampshire's most influential newspaper, the Manchester *Union Leader*. He was the publisher until his death in 1985; she took over as publisher until her death in 2000.

Douglas Morrow was a screenwriter and movie producer whom Reagan met in Hollywood. He set up Reagan's 1979 briefing on nuclear missile defenses at NORAD. Morrow died in 1994 at age 81.

George Murphy, Hollywood actor and producer, co-starred with Reagan in the 1943 film *This Is the Army;* Murphy played Reagan's father. Reagan and Murphy were close allies fighting the attempted communist takeover of the Hollywood unions in the 1940s; Murphy was president of the Screen Actors Guild 1944–46; Reagan replaced him in 1947. Murphy was elected senator from California in 1964 and served one term. Reagan said that he owed a great deal to this "cool, dapper guy" who had to deal with him in his early wide-eyed liberal days. Reagan wrote frankly to Murphy about politics.

Richard Nixon was the 37th president of the United States. He first wrote to Reagan in 1959 to compliment him on a speech. Their correspondence continued through early 1994. Nixon wrote Reagan memos and letters of advice during his presidential campaign, during the transition, and during the presidency on specific issues.

Barney Oldfield and Reagan met on the set of *Dodge City* on April 1, 1939. A press officer in World War II, Oldfield worked for Warner Brothers as Reagan's publicist in the late 1940s. Oldfield was later a consultant for Litton Industries, traveling often to the Soviet Union. He sent Reagan frequent letters with humorous stories or one-liners as well as commentary on more serious topics; Reagan used some of these letters in White House staff meetings. Oldfield's great-uncle was the legendary racing car driver of the same name. Oldfield died on April 26, 2003.

Ward Quaal, an innovator in radio and television broadcasting, was the retired president of Chicago's WGN Continental Broadcasting Company. WGN was the top radio broadcaster in the Midwest when Reagan was first looking for a job in radio; WGN turned him down. Quaal and Reagan met when the future president was acting in radio commercials for the WGN radio station in Chicago. Quaal and Nancy Reagan's father, Loyal Davis, were friends.

Nancy Davis Reagan, whom Reagan married in 1952, received many love letters from her husband, most written while he was traveling. Many were published in her book *I Love You, Ronnie: The Letters of Ronald Reagan to Nancy Reagan.* A few others are included in this volume.

Neil Reagan was Reagan's older brother. Both attended Eureka College. Neil appeared in four movies in the 1940s, including one in which Reagan starred, *Tugboat Annie Sails Again.* A top executive of the McCann-Erickson advertising firm, Neil handled the advertising for Reagan's first campaign for governor of California. He and his wife, Bess, kept in close touch with Ronald Reagan, and Neil and Ronald remained close until Neil died in 1996.

Ronald Reagan's children. Reagan wrote some long and very thoughtful letters to his children.

Samueline and Bertha Sisco were sisters whose correspondence with Reagan began in 1972 when Reagan was governor of California and continued until at least 1987. The Sisco sisters originally wrote to Reagan asking for financial assistance to care for their brother. They also wrote about experiences on their farm, and Reagan responded with stories of his own, and often with advice.

Paul Trousdale, a real estate developer in Southern California, was a Reagan supporter from the years Reagan served as governor of the state.

Lorraine Wagner was a movie fan of Reagan's who first wrote to him in 1946. Reagan's mother answered (in Reagan's name) early correspondence, but as of mid-1951, Reagan himself began answering Lorraine's letters, often about policy issues or the media. They corresponded until 1994.

Reagan

A LIFE IN LETTERS

CHAPTER ONE

The Early Years

"*I*WAS BORN *in Tampico Illinois," Ronald Reagan once wrote to a friend. "Besides the local records I have an older brother who remembers my birth. He wasn't happy, he wanted a sister."*

The event that made Neil Reagan less than happy occurred February 6, 1911, in a farming town of some 1,276 people about 125 miles west of Chicago. The Reagans moved to Chicago in December 1914, a few months before Ronald's fourth birthday, but moved a year later to Galesburg, Illinois. By late 1917 they were in Monmouth, Illinois. In August 1919 they returned to Tampico.

The Reagans moved to Dixon, population 8,191 and about 100 miles west of Chicago, in December 1920 when Reagan was nine years old; it would be Reagan's home until he became a radio announcer in Davenport, Iowa, in the fall of 1932. "All of us have to have a place we go back to," Reagan would later write. "Dixon is that place for me." [1]

In 1928 Reagan went to Eureka College in Eureka, Illinois, a small college affiliated with the Disciples of Christ, the church to which he, his mother, and his brother belonged; his father was Roman Catholic. Eureka was about 100 miles south of Dixon. "If I had it to do all over again," Reagan told an enthusiastic crowd at Eureka on October 17, 1980, "I'd come right back here and start where I was before. . . . Everything good that has happened to me—everything—started here on this campus in those four years that still are so much a part of my life." [2] *Reagan went job hunting after college in the depths of the Depression. He was hired as a radio announcer by a station in Davenport, Iowa, 76 miles southwest of Dixon.*

Reagan was English and Scottish on his mother's side, Irish on his father's side. His parents, Jack and Nelle, were Democrats; his father was a strong supporter of Franklin Delano Roosevelt. Reagan cast his first vote—in 1932, in Dixon—for FDR. He did not turn away from the Democratic Party until his experiences in Hollywood after World War II.

Few letters survive from Reagan's early years—perhaps because he did not write many. But he later wrote many letters recalling his early years.

GROWING UP

Reagan described growing up, in a letter written in the early 1980s, in these terms: "My boyhood was spent in the typical midwestern America melting pot. The schoolroom was a mix of races and creeds and so was my circle of friends. In fact, in my own home my father was Catholic and my mother was Protestant. He left our religious upbringing to my mother." [3]

In these letters Reagan tells about the places he lived, how he learned to read, the books that mattered to him, and some of the events of his childhood and teenage years.

———————

Ronald Reagan was 11 years old when he wrote this letter to Gladys Shippert, a senior at Whitewater College High School, and her sister Alma. They had known each other for more than five years, and all attended the First Christian Church in Dixon, Illinois. Reagan, Shippert, and some of their friends spent their free time listening to WOC radio, the station where Reagan would land his first job after college. When the Shippert family moved from Dixon in 1921, Reagan began writing letters to Gladys. He wrote her for a couple of years. *

In the letter below, Reagan mentions his school activities and John Garland Waggoner II, a Dixon High School student who graduated in 1922 and went to Eureka College, where he played football. His father, H. G. Waggoner, died five months before Reagan wrote this letter and was replaced by Reverend Ben H. Cleaver as the minister of the First Christian Church. Cleaver's daughter, Margaret, would become Reagan's high school and college sweetheart.

Written on the barbershop stationery of F. E. Morey of Minonk, Illinois, this is the only letter from Reagan that Gladys Shippert, later known as Mrs. Clarence Kaecker, saved. It is the earliest Reagan letter that the authors have found.

> Gladys Shippert
> Whitewater, Wisconsin
> November 21, 1922 [4]

To my Lady Fair and her Sister

I have been writing this letter since you sent yours. I have been trying to get those percentage problems. Dixon Highschool has played 10 games won 8 tied 1 and lost 1 they tied sterling. They cant have the thanksgiving game because of the

———————

* Reagan's letter and the envelope in which it was sent were reproduced in an Illinois newspaper article that tells the story of Reagan's friendship with Shippert and the history of the letter. See John E. Devine Jr., "A Letter from Lee County's First Citizen," *The Ashton Gazette*, November 20, 1980, pp. 4–5. The letter was subsequently reprinted in Norman E. Wymbs, *A Place to Go Back To: Ronald Reagan in Dixon, Illinois* (New York: Vantage Press, 1987). Copies of Reagan's letter to Shippert have been circulating in Dixon, Illinois, for many years. The original is held in Dixon by the family of Gladys Kaecker, who died in November 1999.

smallpox in Sterling. I play quarter back on the S.S.* team Sat we were going to play the N.S.† team but there captain got yellow and he wouldent play. Our class at S.S.‡ has got the janiters job at the church and we get $25 a month and were plastering our class room and were going to have scouts and our class took the banners for attendance and collection. Sat. Dixon went to Rochell and beat them 27 to 6 the game we lost was with dekalb. They beat us 6 to 0. Don't laugh at the paper I am using.

Heres my picture
Arent He
Darling:

Because a kid gave it to me to use for spelling and I ran out of another kind of paper Id had. I am writing it in school. monday we had a hygene test. monday mama got a letter from mrs. Wagnor and she said Garland has made the team at Eureka they played Illinois last week. Oh the little kids are having recess now and theres a fight I will have to wait and see the fight. well Its 5 min. later and the fights over.

I have 12 rabbits and I am going to kills and eat them. Tuesday we had a Geography test and oh say what are the college colors there. We have an allstate end playing on our highschool team his name is cowboy morrison I am drum magor of the boys band here We had a parade Sat. before last.

well I will have to close,

now Ronald Reagan

PS.
　　Smell that meat
　　Aint It good.

———————

Reagan replies to a request from the publisher of Avenue M, *a magazine about Chicago, to recall what he can about the year he lived there.*

Mr. Frank Sullivan
Chicago, Illinois
December 5, 1988 [5]

Dear Mr. Sullivan:
　　Thank you for your kind letter and most generous words. I'm deeply grateful.
　　You asked about my brief stay in Chicago. I'm afraid there isn't much to tell.

———————

* South Central school on the south side of Dixon, Illinois.
† North Central school on the north side of Dixon.
‡ Sunday school.

I was about three years old, my brother about two and a half years older than that. Our father worked at Marshall Field's. We lived in a ground floor flat on Cottage Grove for about a year and then moved to Galesburg.

I do have a few things I remember such as seeing the fire department coming down the street at a gallop. Yes the fire engines were horse drawn then and the sight of them made me decide I wanted to be a fireman. My brother tried to hitch a ride on a beer truck—also horse drawn—and fell underneath the wagon. He still bears the scar from knee to ankle where the steel-rimmed wheel ran over his leg.

My closest call was bronchial pneumonia. After I was older my mother told me I almost didn't make it. I don't remember that but I do remember the neighbor boy who loaned me his entire set of lead soldiers. I spent my convalescence lining them up in battle formation on the bed.

Last episode—we ran away one early evening. Our parents had gone out for groceries. We got scared there without them and went looking for them after blowing out the gas light without turning off the gas. They found us after quite a hike. We had crossed the Midway and by then were lost and didn't know the way home. That does Chicago. Next stop Galesburg where Dad got a job in the O.T. Johnson department store.

Again thanks for your letter and best regards.

Sincerely,
Ronald Reagan

————

Mrs. Lowe wrote to tell Reagan how her daughter, Becky, started reading when she was two and a half years old—in 1959. Becky heard Reagan on GE Theater *say, "At General Electric, progress is our most important product," and saw the words on the television screen at the same time. She soon recognized the words "General Electric" on a return address on an envelope. Now a mother, Becky was reading to her three-year-old son, Patrick, but thus far Patrick hadn't read anything to Becky. "Obviously Patrick doesn't have the great teacher his mommy had," Mrs. Lowe concluded.*

Reagan tells her that he enjoyed the letter and recalls how he learned to read. Sheila Tate worked for Nancy Reagan in the White House.

Mrs. Rose Ann Lowe
Akron, Ohio
February 6, 1985[6]

Dear Mrs. Lowe:

By way of Sheila Tate and Nancy I received your letter and you were right. I enjoyed hearing from you very much. I was very proud to learn I'd been such a successful English teacher.

Please give my regards to my pupil Becky and to Patrick. I have a tip for her. I have no memory of learning to read. I only know that one evening when I was five years old my father saw me with a newspaper and asked me what I was doing. I told him reading. He thought I was just pretending until I read him a few lines.

In thinking back I remembered that my mother used to read my brother and me to sleep and she did so sitting on the bed between us so we too could see the page. She followed the lines with her finger as she read. I don't know of anything else that could have resulted in my learning to read.

Thanks again and best regards,

Ronald Reagan

John Morley was a freelance writer who asked Reagan about his younger days. Reagan refers to his years in Tampico the second time the Reagans lived there as his "Huck Finn" years.

Mr. John Morley
Laguna Hills, California
May 22, 1984[7]

Dear John:

I'm afraid all I can come up with in the line of photos of the "younger" days is this shot of me as a lifeguard in Dixon. I'm returning the two you sent in case you need them. Everything we have is in storage with all our furniture in California and to tell you the truth I can't recall if there are any albums etc. We lost a number of things like that in the Bel Air fire.

If you meant other pictures—Hollywood, Sacramento, the ranch or here let me know. Those I can deliver.

You asked for more information: well we left Tampico while I was still a baby—around two years old. We lived in Chicago then Galesburg and Monmouth (both in Illinois). I started school in Galesburg, only went to first grade there. Then we returned to Tampico and lived above Pitney's store.

All this travel was because Jack's interest was shoes and he kept moving for promotions in the shoe departments of department stores. In Chicago it was Marshall Field's. Our move to Dixon was because Pitney opened a shoe store and Jack became top man.

But those few years back in Tampico became my Huck Finn years. Across the street living above their store was the Winchell family. Their youngest son and I (same age) became buddies. We used to do a lot of hiking out to the Hennepin Canal or to a large sandpit which had been created by a tornado.

One Saturday night when the stores were open so our folks were working downstairs he and I were upstairs at Winchell's. We found his father's shotgun. We put it butt down on the floor and he pulled the trigger. Nothing happened. Then I pumped it once and said now try it and he did. That produced the loudest bang we'd ever heard and a dishpan-sized hole in the ceiling.

When two white faced parents fearful of what they might find, pushed open the door the two of us were sitting on the couch studying our Sunday school lesson to beat h—l—a perfect picture of innocence.

Well I'd better stop or I'll be doing my life story.

It's good to hear from you and I enjoyed your article on "When."

Best regards,
Ron

When Reagan decided he wanted to be baptized, he chose his mother's church—the Disciples of Christ—which viewed baptism as an act of faith and did not baptize infants. He was baptized June 21, 1922. The book that brought Reagan to this decision, That Printer of Udell's, *is a story of a young man, Dick Falkner, hired as a printer by Udell. Falkner develops practical ways to help the poor, joins the Disciples of Christ church, and wins his true love. Harold Bell Wright was a minister who had told the unfolding story of Falkner to his congregation before he published it as a book in 1903.*[8]

Mrs. Jean B. Wright
Valley Center, California
March 13, 1984[9]

Dear Mrs. Wright:

It is true that your father-in-law's book, indeed books, played a definite part in my growing up years. When I was only ten or eleven years old I picked up Harold Bell Wright's book, *That Printer of Udell's,* which I'd seen my mother reading and read it from cover to cover. Perhaps I should tell you I became an avid reader at a very early age and had my own card for the Dixon Illinois Public Library. I made regular use of that card.

That book—*That Printer of Udell's*—had an impact I shall always remember. After reading it and thinking about it for a few days I went to my mother and told her I wanted to declare my faith and be baptized. We attended the Christian Church in Dixon and I was baptized several days after finishing the book.

The term, "role model," was not a familiar term in that time and place but looking back I know I had found a role model in that traveling printer Harold Bell Wright had brought to life. He set me on a course I've tried to follow even unto this day. I shall always be grateful.

Sincerely,
Ronald Reagan

Another book of his mother's that Reagan enjoyed was a book of poems by Robert Service, a poet who was born in England, grew up in Scotland, and emigrated to Canada. His first book of poems, including "The Shooting of Dan McGrew" and "The Cremation of Sam McGee," was published in the United States as The Spell of the Yukon.[10]

Simon Byrne and Neil Hollander
Lucky Films Productions Ltd.
London, England
During presidency[11]

Dear Mr. Byrne and Mr. Hollander:

Thank you very much for sending me the script and the posters for "The Shooting of Dangerous Dan McGrew." And may I add, thank you for going forward with this project. I've just begun to read the script so can't play critic except to say I'm fascinated and can't wait 'til I have time to read on. I'll be looking forward to the finished film.

I first discovered Dangerous Dan and Lou, as well as Sam McGee when I was only a boy. My mother had a small leather-bound volume of Robert Service. I was amazed to discover a few years ago that I could recite the two poems. I have no recollection of ever attempting to memorize them but memorize them I did.

Again my thanks to you and very best wishes.

Sincerely,
Ronald Reagan

Reagan's recollections of his childhood reading expressed in the following letter are similar to those he conveyed a few years earlier in a letter to Dallas O. Baillio, a librarian in Mobile, Alabama, which begins "There must be a little snob in each one of us because my first reaction was to try and think of examples of classic literature I could list as favorites in my younger years. None were forthcoming so I decided to 'come clean.' "[12]

Miss Helen P. Miller
Dixon, Illinois
September 3, 1981[13]

Dear Miss Miller:

My brother did see that your letter reached me and first of all, let me thank you for all that you did with the news people in my behalf. Thank you, also, for the snapshot. We were delighted to have it, but, really, you touched a nerve with your letter and opened the door on a great deal of nostalgia and warm memories.

You asked, what did the Dixon Library mean to me? I haven't seen the new addition to the building, I remember with great warmth the old stone building, and I believe I was probably as regular a patron as the library ever had. And I'm speaking about the time that began when I was about ten years old.

I can barely remember a time in my life when I didn't know how to read. As a matter of fact, I was a family mystery in that I had learned to read before entering the first grade. The joy of reading has always been with me. Indeed, I can't think of greater torture than being isolated in a guest room or a hotel room without something to read.

Beginning at about age ten, I would make what to me was a long trek on foot in the evening after dinner—we called it supper then—down Hennepin Avenue past South Central School, up the hill and across the street to the library. I would usually take out two books. I made those trips at least once a week and sometimes more often. I didn't go with a specific book in mind but would browse for lengthy periods.

I, of course, read all the books that a boy that age would like—The Rover Boys; Frank Merriwell at Yale; Horatio Alger. I discovered Edgar Rice Burroughs and read all the Tarzan books. I am amazed at how few people I meet today know that Burroughs also provided an introduction to science fiction with John Carter of Mars and the other books that he wrote about John Carter and his frequent trips to the strange kingdoms to be found on the planet Mars. Then came all of Zane Grey, Mark Twain, and others.* Every once in a while, a kindly librarian would nudge me into things she thought would be helpful—not only enjoyable, but profitable for me to read.

When we moved to the north side of the river, my walk was across the Galena Avenue bridge through town and to the library. The library was really my house of magic. Now and then I would take a foray upstairs to the Indian museum where I was fascinated by the artifacts and (at that time) the full length birch bark canoe. But mainly it was the books, and I can assure you the love of books still stays with me. I now have a library of my own and am very proud of it. But as I say—it all started there in my house of magic—the Dixon Public Library.

Thank you for your kind letter and best regards.

Sincerely,
Ronald Reagan

Reagan wrote in his own hand his memories of the Fourth of July and Christmas.

The Fourth of July
Circa April 1981 [14]

To one who was born and grew up in the small towns of the Midwest there is a special kind of nostalgia about the 4th of July. I remember it as a day almost as long anticipated as Christmas. This was helped along by the appearance in store windows of all kinds of fireworks and colorful posters advertising some with vivid pictures of those fireworks in action.

No later than the 3rd of July—sometimes earlier—Dad would bring home

---

*The letter to Baillio also mentions King Arthur stories, *The Count of Monte Cristo, The Last of the Mohicans,* Sherlock Holmes stories, and *Northern Trails* (William Joseph Long).

what he felt he could afford to see go up in smoke and flame. We'd count and re-count the number of firecrackers, display pieces etc. and go to bed determined to be up with the sun so as to offer the first thunderous notice of the 4th of July.

I'm afraid we didn't give too much thought to the meaning of the day. And yes there were tragic accidents to mar the day resulting from careless handling of the fireworks. I'm sure we are better off now that fireworks are largely handled by pro-fessionals in great displays. But there was a thrill never to be forgotten in seeing a tin can blown 30 feet in the air by a giant "cracker"—giant meaning it was about four inches long.

Enough of nostalgia. Somewhere in our growing up we began to be aware of the meaning of the day and with that awareness came the birth of patriotism. July 4th, the birthday of our nation. I believed then and even more so today—the great-est nation on earth.

In recent years I've come to think of that day as more than just the birthday of a nation. It commemorates the only true philosophical revolution in all history. Oh, there have been revolutions before and since ours, but those revolutions simply exchanged one set of rules for another. Ours was a revolution that changed the very concept of government. Let the 4th of July always be a reminder that here in this land for the first time it was decided that man is born with certain God given rights; that government is only a convenience created and managed by the people with no powers of its own except those voluntarily granted to it by the people.

We sometimes tend to forget that great truth and we never should.

Happy 4th of July.

Christmas
August 1981 [15]

I find it difficult to pick out a single Christmas I could call the most memo-rable. Christmas has always been a very special day for as long back as I can re-member. Maybe this was due to my mother and her joyous spirit about the day.

There were very few decorated trees in the years of my growing up. We couldn't afford them. But never defeated, my mother would with ribbon and crepe paper decorate a table or create a cardboard fireplace out of a packing box. And she always remembered whose birthday it was and made sure we knew the meaning of Christmas.

Since those times there are many warm memories of Christmas and our own children. I've always felt we should create a tradition that would set a pattern for them so that Christmas would be special and not just a holiday.

One Christmas is remembered because of a particular gift, a gift truly in keep-ing with the spirit of the day. I must have presented something of a problem to my brother after we were grown up and in our middle years. A problem with regard to what might be a suitable gift.

He solved the problem with a letter. In the letter he told me he had found a truly needy family with small children who wouldn't go to bed with dreams of Santa Claus in their heads. He changed that and became Santa himself, providing a Christmas from tree to turkey plus toys and gifts for all. My present was his letter describing in detail the joy of the children and the grateful happiness of their mother.

That was a memorable Christmas and a gift that will never grow old.

Ruth Graybill and her husband, Ed, ran the concession in Lowell Park on the Rock River in Dixon. In 1927 Reagan applied to them for a job as lifeguard, and they hired him. Several people had died in the Rock River's currents, but no one died in the six summers Reagan lifeguarded there. In this letter Reagan recalls his Lowell Park years and the origin of his horseback-riding hobby.

> Ruth Graybill
> Dixon, Illinois
> January 15, 1985 [16]

Dear Ruth:

It takes a while for letters to reach my desk so I've just received your letter of December 5th. I'll send all the Inaugural invitations you requested—too late of course to be used but I assume you wanted them as souvenirs. They'll be on their way shortly.

Your letter brought back a lot of memories of those wonderful Lowell Park days. That was a very important part of my life. Do you remember the day you provided spareribs and sauerkraut for lunch and Johnny Crabtree and I ate four pounds of spareribs. I wonder what would have happened if someone in the river had needed help just about then.

Do you remember my riding Jensen's old grey horse around the park now and then? That started me on a beloved hobby that has continued to this day. In fact I later became a cavalry officer in the reserve before WWII. Well the attached photo is of my present mount which happens to be a grey, but a little friskier than Jensen's horse.

Take care of yourself and all the best.

> Love,
> Dutch

In a letter written during the 1980 presidential campaign, Reagan remembers a double date in Dixon, Illinois; Margaret Cleaver was his high-school and college girlfriend. The closing, "Yours in the bond," is used by fraternities; Reagan was a member of Tau Kappa Epsilon (TKE) at Eureka and so, apparently, was Stanley Hamilton.

Mr. Stanley Hamilton
August 18, 1980 [17]

Dear Stan:

It sure was good to hear from you and to recall those meetings going all the way back to 1931.

You left out the summer night you spent in Dixon when I got you a blind date for after the beach closed at Lowell Park. As I recall, I was with Margaret Cleaver. With Kay still in the Canal Zone, I wonder what her impressions are since the treaty has been signed. Give Bob my best when you talk or write to him and thank you for being in my corner. I'm going to give it the best try I can.

Yours in the bond,
Dutch

Reagan writes to Mildred White, whom he taught to dive at Lowell Park. She was then Mildred Segner. Hazelwood was a 600-acre estate three miles outside of Dixon originally built by Alexander Charters. The house burned in 1905. The property was later bought by Charles Walgreen, founder of the drugstore chain, and developed as a country club. Reagan had caddied at Hazlewood and stayed there as a guest on later trips to Dixon. [18] Robert Michel of Illinois was minority leader of the U.S. House of Representatives.

Mrs. John B. White
Peoria, Illinois
October 5, 1982 [19]

Dear Mildred:

This will be a greeting from out of the past. Congressman Bob Michel told me of meeting your son and in the course of the conversation mentioned his mother who was taught diving by a lifeguard at Lowell Park, Dixon Illinois.

I remember very well. Your son was absolutely right. It doesn't seem that long ago does it? Back during the campaign (1980) I got to stay at Hazelwood and of course visited Lowell Park. I was saddened to learn there is no longer a beach or swimming there.

Thank your son for bringing back some happy memories. Just between us I think maybe lifeguarding at Lowell Park was the best job I ever had.

All the best to you and please give my regards to your husband.

Sincerely,
Dutch

The Dixonian *was the Dixon high school yearbook. Reagan graduated from high school in 1928. Here he thanks Marjorie Bidwell for a reproduction of the yearbook and recalls an early experience in the town of Franklin Grove, which was about ten miles from Dixon.*

> Mrs. Marjorie Cushing Bidwell
> Franklin Grove, Illinois
> September 26, 1985 [20]

Dear Marjorie:

Thanks to Katherine* I have your reproduction of the 1926 *Dixonian*. Please thank her for me and bless you for making it all possible. I've had a few days of warm nostalgia and happy memories. There will be more for I still have it on my desk so I can sneak another look every once in a while.

Speaking of memories I have one that has to do with Franklin Grove. When I was drum major of the YMCA boys band we were asked to lead the Decoration Day parade in Franklin Grove. The parade marshal on a big white horse rode back down the parade at one point which left me out in front. No one had told me the parade route so I kept on marching. He rode back up the line just in time to have the band turn a corner. I was left marching up the street all by myself. I didn't look around until the music began to sound faint and far away. Then I cut across back yards and got back in front again.

Well thanks again and

> Best regards,
> Ronald Reagan "Dutch"

———

Reagan's parents brought him up with a hatred of bigotry, as he explains in the following letters, one to a supporter and one to a critic.

> Mr. Freddie Washington
> Moss Point, Mississippi
> November 23, 1983 [21]

Dear Mr. Washington:

I'm sorry to be so late in answering your letter but it takes a while for mail to get sorted and letters to arrive at my desk. I can't tell you how much your letter means to me. I've been frustrated and angered by the attempts to paint me as a racist and as lacking in compassion for the poor. On the one subject I was raised by a mother and father who instilled in me and my brother a hatred for bigotry and prejudice long before there was such a thing as a civil rights movement. As for the poor, we were poor in an era when there were no government programs to turn to. I'm well aware of how lucky I've been since and how good the Lord has been to me.

———

* Kathryn Cushing, Marjorie's daughter, was a class ahead of Reagan at Dixon High School.

Forgive me for telling you all this but I want you to know and understand how very moved I was by your kind letter. Again my heartfelt thanks.

Sincerely,
Ronald Reagan

———————

A black, unemployed Vietnam veteran sent a telegram expressing support for Reagan's defense policy but calling him "a worse president than tricky Dick Nixon" and "a closet racist and friend of the rich." Reagan tries to explain.

Leonard Kirk
March 23, 1983 [22]

Dear Mr. Kirk:

I appreciate very much your support of my defense policy. I believe I also can understand why you think me a "closet racist." Certainly there has been a constant drumbeat of propaganda to that effect ever since I took office. Some leaders of black organizations have joined in this whether to enhance their own stature by arousing the membership to anger or not I don't know.

You of course would have no way of knowing the truth about me. May I point out a few things in my own behalf?

I was raised from childhood by my parents who believed bigotry and prejudice were the worst things a person could be guilty of. My father once slept in his car during an Illinois blizzard rather than stay in a hotel that wouldn't allow Jews. He was Irish Catholic.

As a sports announcer broadcasting Big League baseball in the middle '30s I campaigned against the rule that prohibited blacks from playing in organized ball. As governor of California I appointed more blacks to executive and policy making positions than <u>all</u> the previous Governors of California put together. I too have a dream, a dream that one day whatever is done to or for someone will be done neither because of or in spite of their race. We are all equal in the sight of God—we should be equal in the sight of man. By the way I was raised in poverty.

Sincerely,
Ronald Reagan

EUREKA COLLEGE

"I loved three things: drama, politics, and sports," Reagan wrote in his first autobiography.[23] *At Eureka College, each of these areas shaped his experience. Reagan's love of football paved the way for his entry into college. Impressed by his enthusiasm for the game, Eureka officials made arrangements to supplement the seventeen-year-old's*

$400 in savings with a partial scholarship and a dishwashing job at Tau Kappa Epsilon, or Teke House, the fraternity that Reagan pledged. He struggled on the football team but became a first-string guard during midseason of his sophomore year and continued in that position for the remainder of his college days.

Reagan's introduction to politics came during his first semester of college. Chosen to represent faculty and students at the strike rally to oppose Eureka President Bert Wilson's cost-cutting measures, Reagan gave his first speech late in the evening on November 28, 1928. The speech "was as exciting as any I ever gave," he later recalled. "For the first time in my life, I felt my words reach out and grab an audience, and it was exhilarating."[24] Reagan became swept up in a political controversy that received national attention.[25] In early December, Wilson resigned.

A few days after giving his first speech, Reagan attended a theater production of Journey's End with Margaret Cleaver, his high school and college sweetheart, and her parents. He was immediately drawn to the character of Captain Stanhope, a war-weary military man. "Once again fate intervened—as if God was carrying out His plan with my name on it," wrote Reagan. Later, Eureka's drama instructor decided to stage Journey's End and Reagan won the part of Captain Stanhope. "I was in heaven," he later recalled.[26] In the spring of 1930, Reagan was part of the Eureka College one-act production of Edna St. Vincent Millay's Aria da Capo, which won second place in a national competition at Northwestern University. Reagan was one of three actors to receive individual acting awards. "I guess that was the day the acting bug really bit me, although I think it was probably orbiting pretty close to me for a long time before that, even before Journey's End and my student plays at Dixon High."[27]

Reagan soaked in all that the small college of about 220 students had to offer. He participated in swimming, track, and the booster club; joined the staffs of the Pegasus, the campus newspaper, and the yearbook; and was elected president of the student senate for his senior year. In his letters, however, he most typically refers to football and his fraternity. Politics and acting would become Reagan's profession, but life lessons were learned and deep impressions made as a member of Eureka's football team.

In the years following his graduation from the Disciples of Christ–affiliated liberal arts college in 1932, Reagan remained committed to his alma mater. He served on the college's board of trustees, and during his governorship and presidency he gave major speeches at Eureka. He also remained in close contact with many of the friends he made during those formative years.

The letters below provide snapshots of Reagan's college days through his recounting of some of the lives and experiences that touched him and the lessons he learned there.

————————

Reagan sends a sympathy note to the wife of a 1926 graduate of Eureka College after the death of her husband. He mentions having seen recently two of his college football teammates, William Franklin Burghardt and Ray Holmes.

Mrs. Raymond Ranes
May 3, 1979 [28]

Dear Esther:

I have only just now learned of your loss and want you to know how deeply sorry I am. I know words can't be of much help at a time like this—I wish they could. We can only trust in God's mercy and know that he does have a plan for each one of us. I was in Eureka recently, and both Franklin Burghardt and Ray Holmes were there.* You would have been so proud and so would Doc to have heard them talking about what he had meant in their lives. He had the greatest effect of any human being on all that has happened to them. Just know how much so many of us wish we could help. Know that you have our deepest sympathy and that you are in our thoughts and prayers.

Sincerely,
Dutch

———

Reagan writes about the impact that Ralph McKinzie, his football coach at Eureka College, had on his life. McKinzie was known as Coach Mac.

Mr. Tom Cassidy
1979 [29]

Dear Tom:

I have just learned of the party and the recognition that you gave to Coach Mac. As one who played under him in a much earlier day, I just wanted to express my appreciation to all of you for what you did. He remains an unforgettable man in my life and I am happy that even though the years have passed, all of you have been permitted to know him. Perhaps you know this little anecdote, but, if not, I'll tell it.

Some years ago, when he retired, having reached the official retirement age at Illinois Northern, and returned to Eureka, one of the Illinois football players asked, "Is he going to Eureka to play or coach?" In my day, occasionally, he would decide in scrimmage to show one of the backs just how a certain play was run. I had the misfortune to go through from guard and try to nail him when he carried that ball. All I can tell you is he went through the entire varsity, came back, handed the quarterback the ball, and said, do it that way. I don't know whether anyone else touched him. But I did, and I hurt for a week!

Congratulations on what appears to be a good basketball season underway. I hope in the near future there will be another chance for me to get to Eureka and this time to finally be able to visit the house. I know this probably won't be seen

———

* William Franklin Burghardt and Ray Holmes were football teammates of Reagan's.

by you until you return from Christmas vacation, but, to all of you there, I hope your holiday season was everything you wished. Very best regards.

> Yours in the bond,
> Ronald Reagan

Reagan's most vivid experience with racism, one that he would recall throughout his life, took place during college. While traveling in Illinois, the Eureka College football team planned to stay in a hotel, but the manager told Coach Mac that the hotel did not accept coloreds. The coach said the team would stay elsewhere, but the manager said other nearby hotels had the same policy. Reagan, who had gone into the hotel while the team waited on the bus, was told by the coach that the team would sleep in the bus. Reagan objected: "Mac, if you do that it will be worse for them [the blacks]. They'll feel that everyone has been made uncomfortable because of them. Why don't you go out and tell them that you can only take part of the squad in here. Tell them that we're going to have to split up."[30] Reagan then invited his black teammates to stay with him, and Nelle and Jack welcomed their son's classmates, one of whom was William Franklin Burghardt, into their home.

Reagan corresponded with his friend Burghardt for many years.[31]

> Mr. William F. Burghardt
> Lanham, Maryland
> January 9, 1980[32]

Dear Burgie:

It was good to hear from you, and I thank you from the bottom of my heart for your generous contribution. Believe me, it will help and I'll do my best to see that you never have reason to regret it.

I got a kick out of your race for the mile relay team. I had never known of that. I'm sure Mac would remember it, though, because, for some strange reason, and maybe I'm wrong, I've always thought that our particular group in those few years at Eureka were kind of special to Mac.

I'm hot on the campaign trail these days. We'll be doing about six states in four days on a trip that starts day after tomorrow.

Maybe, someplace along the line, or trail, we'll get to your neighborhood, and we'll cross paths again. I hope so. It would be good to see you. In the meantime, have a good New Year and take care of yourself. I hope to see you one day soon.

> Best regards,
> Dutch

In the midst of his 1980 presidential campaign, Reagan stayed in touch with Coach Mac.

Coach Ralph McKinzie
July 31, 1980[33]

Dear Mac:

It was great to hear from you, and I appreciate more than I can say your generous words about me.

I know it's a long, hard road ahead. A little bit like doing the duck waddle the length of the field and back. I promise you I'll give it all I've got.

I'm glad you're going to be on the field again at Eureka this fall. It just wouldn't seem right to not have you there.

Please give everyone my best regards and, again, thank you for your good letter which I treasure.

Sincerely,
Dutch

Reagan writes about his friendship with Burghardt.

Miss Effie E. Porter
Chicago, Illinois
September 13, 1982[34]

Dear Miss Porter:

I'm sorry to be so late in answering your letter of July 12 but it takes a while before mail reaches my desk. This time it reached my desk while I was in California—so more delay.

I can't tell you how much I appreciate your letter and how much I'm in agreement with you about some of our so-called leaders. For some time now I've wondered whether many of those who've made a career of heading organizations, whatever the cause, don't really want the problems solved because then their jobs would be gone.

In those tough '30s you mentioned I wasn't too far from you. I was washing dishes in the girls dormitory of a small college in Illinois to get an education. I worked beside and played football beside a young black man from Greenfield Illinois—Franklin Burghardt. We remained close friends throughout the years until his death a year ago. He had gone on to be the athletic director of Morgan State University in Baltimore.

Bless you and thank you for writing me as you did. Believe me your letter continues to make [me] feel good because I read it over again every once in a while. Especially when I've been raked over the coals by Carl T. Rowan.*

Sincerely,
Ronald Reagan

---

* Carl Thomas Rowan was a nationally syndicated newspaper columnist.

Dan Gilbert, the president of Eureka College from 1977 to 1985, wrote President Reagan to say that 75 percent of the students supported him in a straw vote on campus. He wrote also that Warner McCollum, the new football coach, is "a class coach" who wants a winning team.

The Honorable Dan Gilbert
Eureka, Illinois
November 14, 1984 [35]

Dear Dan:

Thanks for your good letter and my thanks to all those students who gave me a vote. I'm very proud.

I was very pleased with the story you sent about Coach McCollum. In a day where the drift is the other way I think it's great that Eureka stays on course. Please give him my best regards and appreciation. He is in the mold of another Eureka coach, the one I played under—Ralph McKinzie.

Well it only took me four years to get through Eureka. It looks like I'll need eight to complete my present job.

Best regards,
Ron

President Reagan writes to Coach Mac's son and his wife.

Mr. and Mrs. Jim McKinzie
Sterling, Illinois
February 5, 1987 [36]

Dear Jim and Lenore:

Thank you very much for sending me Mac's letter and thank you for your own letter and good wishes. You wrote of the relationship between your father and me; I don't believe it is exclusive. Your father was a coach, but more than that he was a teacher and as such believed his job was not only to teach fundamentals of a game but fundamentals for later life. I once heard him say he didn't base his rating on games won or lost but on the record of the player in later life. What kind of man the boy had become.

In my own case I didn't do a good job of switching from lordly high school senior to lowly freshman. I've never told this before but I decided (in that first year) that the coach didn't like me and that's why I wasn't first string. I came back for year two with the determination that I'd force him to use me by learning and working so hard he'd have no other choice. He did test me. In scrimmage he moved me around to different positions—on the second team of course. I would dig in and act as if each position was the one I wanted to play. Then one day a disabling injury permanently removed the first string right guard spot and guess what? He put me there and I spent three years averaging all but three minutes of every game as right guard. He'd known all along what my problem was and he set out to cure it and did. With that realization came a warm feeling of appreciation and affection for Coach Mac—which I feel to this day.

Sincerely,
Ronald Reagan

In a letter to the president of Eureka College, Reagan expresses sorrow at the loss of his football coach, and encloses a check to be used for the college. Reagan also expresses his desire to see the college's athletic center bear the name of Ralph McKinzie. In 1970, the athletic center was named in honor of Reagan and his brother, and is still called the Reagan Center. The football field bears the name of Reagan's revered coach.

Mr. George Hearne
Eureka, Illinois
December 27, 1990 [37]

Dear George:

I hope Christmas was all that you and your family hoped it would be and that the New Year will be a happy one for Eureka and for you. A part of my heart will always be there "beneath the Elms." *

I'm so sorry that Mac didn't stay with us long enough to see his name bestowed on the Athletic Center. Please accept the enclosed for wherever it will do the college the most good.

My heartfelt regards to you and your family.

Sincerely,
Ronald

President Reagan sends a contribution to Eureka for its athletic center, and again writes that he would like the facility to be named for Coach Mac.

Mr. George Hearne
Eureka, Illinois
September 25, 1991 [38]

Dear George:

It was good talking to you yesterday and learning of the college's growth. I was also pleased to hear of the athletic center's progress. I hope the enclosed will help with the uncompleted part.

---

* "Neath the Elms" is the Eureka College slogan.

Has there been any decision about the name for the center[?] I recall when it was proposed that it be named for Coach Mac. I have to say I personally would favor such a recognition. He was so much a part of the college's history. I shall always remember that front page on the bulletin board in the administration building. It was from a Peoria paper and the headline read, "MacKinzie Beats Bradley 52 to Zero." Mac had been a player at Eureka then not a coach when he did that. He scored every point. The paper was on that board for all my four years.

Well that's enough of that. I will always love Eureka.

Best regards,
Ronald

———

Reagan thoroughly enjoyed living in a fraternity house, and writes that he would like to see the trend away from fraternity living reversed.

Dr. Paul Flipkowski
Late 1960s or 1970[39]

Dear Frater Flipkowski:

I've enclosed the autograph you requested and certainly wish you well in your project.

As the years have gone by the memories I have of the four years spent in the Teke house seem to grow brighter and richer. I know that today many schools (including Eureka) have brought fraternities into the dormitory and eliminated the fraternity house living I knew. It is a trend I regret. Perhaps it is a trend we can one day reverse—I hope so.

Yours in the bond,
Ronald Reagan

———

Kip Hayden was a Eureka College student and editor of the Pegasus, *the college newspaper. He asked Reagan for a "Back in My Day" essay about Eureka.*

Dr. Kip Hayden
Eureka, Illinois
1974[40]

Dear Kip:

You do me a great honor but at the same time scare me to death in asking for a letter about Eureka. I have long been a believer that anyone who talks across the generations in the context of "when I was your age" automatically makes himself one hundred and eight years old. Looking back my memory is very vivid (as yours will be) and I recall football "greats" of past years (like five or ten years past) returning to Eureka for homecoming. In my mind they were Neanderthals who couldn't possibly understand the modern game as we were playing it. Now you want me to be the Neanderthal and the years are far more than five or ten.

You opened one door with your proposal that suggestions about the *Pegasus* itself might be appropriate. I'll make one suggestion and if it is something you are already doing ignore it and forgive me for not being as familiar with the *Peg* as I should be. The suggestion—more newsy items about campus doings so that potential students and "old grads" can get a flavor of what college life day in, day out is like "neath the elms." I've always nursed a suspicion that students choose a college less on the curriculum outlined in the catalogue than on the general campus life they think is part of going to college.

And that brings me to my nostalgic, "back in my day" essay. Eureka has always been a small school in a small town atmosphere. I know in my day that was something of an itch you couldn't scratch. The nearby big schools, the University of Illinois etc. seemed to have a glamour that made us wonder if we weren't missing something by not being in a crowd and a big town. If that fits any who are still reading this please read on.

Looking back I can see we were the ones who were actually having a unique college experience that would live with us as a long and glowing memory. Oh sure—that long stretch between Christmas and spring vacation when the slush won't melt gets boring but it's just as slushy in the city. Later on the lilacs bloom in Eureka but they are hard to find on campuses that are mostly paved over.

In my job these past eight years I've been a part of big-time education as a regent of the University of California—all nine campuses and more than 100,000 students. All I've seen since has convinced me if I had it to do over again I'd still go to Eureka. Just being elbowed in a crowd as 27,000 students go milling between classes isn't necessarily where the action is.

One thing about Eureka, you can't remain anonymous. Students in the big assembly-line diploma mills can spend four years admittedly getting a good education but never stretching themselves outside of their chosen studies to discover if they could participate in a play, sing in the glee club, make a team or serve in a campus elective office. In a small college everyone is needed and there is no place to hide. If you make it in Eureka it's because your fellow students know you—not because they don't. And if you can make it under those circumstances you can make it anywhere.

You are having a unique experience that is getting harder and harder to find in academia. If we aren't very very careful it may one day be impossible to find. Live this experience while you can, the memory will be most precious. And help preserve it for others yet to come.

Someday if you ever are foolish enough to solicit another letter I'll tell you how we as a student body recruited new students for Eureka.

Best regards,
Ronald Reagan

Governor Reagan seeks support for Eureka College.

Mr. John Henry Altorfer
Peoria, Illinois
Circa 1967–1975[41]

Dear Mr. Altorfer:

I hope you won't think I'm presuming on our acquaintanceship by intruding on you with a request. I recall our meeting at Sam Harrod's house several years ago on the occasion of the Eureka College library dedication. Coincidentally Eureka College is the subject of my request.

In my present position I have become increasingly aware of the plight of the independent colleges in our land and even more convinced of the need for their survival. It would be a dark day indeed for academic freedom if all higher education rested with the state-run schools.

My interest is in the independent school in general and Eureka College in particular. I am personally indebted to Eureka for making it possible for me to get an education during those dark Depression years when I was totally dependent on the jobs and scholarships the college provided even though the school itself was almost equally destitute.

Now let me hasten to say I'm not soliciting funds. I suppose in a way I'm asking for flesh and blood—your flesh and blood. Eureka is in need of the kind of counsel and advice which a person like yourself can give. Will you meet with President Ira Langston of Eureka, your friend Sam Harrod and his son, Judge Harrod, at a time convenient for you? They have in mind an advisory council to the president they'd like to discuss with you. Forgive me if I presume too much. I have no right to be seeking a favor but will indeed consider it a great favor if you can find time for such a meeting. They are aware that I am making this request and will be getting touch with you shortly.

I hope our paths cross again soon.

Sincerely,
Ronald Reagan

During his 1980 presidential campaign, Reagan thanks his brother Neil "Moon" Reagan for being a generous financial supporter of Eureka.

Mr. Neil Reagan
Rancho Santa Fe, California
1980[42]

Dear Moon:

I'm sorry I can't be there to congratulate and thank you for what you've done over the years for our Alma Mater. Right now I'm out job hunting.

I know you had no idea this was going to take place, but all of you who are being recognized today are deserving of recognition and thanks from all who know and love Eureka.

It's hard to explain, isn't it, how four short years "neath the elms" could remain such an important part of our lives. I hope and pray it will be the same for those who are students there on this 125th anniversary as it was for those of us who were on the campus when the 75th anniversary was celebrated. (Some of the press would have it that I was there for the founding.) But if it is the same then, there will be a 175th occasion like this, a 200th and on into the future.

All it will take is the loyalty and devotion to Eureka that you have felt and shown over the years. Congratulations again.

Sincerely,
Ronald

––––––––

Due to his presidential campaign, Reagan had to resign from Eureka College's board of trustees.

Mr. S. S. Schneider
June 26, 1980 [43]

Dear Mr. Schneider:

Thank you very much for sending me my honorable discharge from the board of trustees and thank you very much for reading the message to the group and for the message. I'm grateful.

I realize that I really have been a member in name only for these several years but want you to know that I was always very proud at least to have my name listed as a trustee of Eureka College. My Eureka years still remain a very large and important part of my life.

Thanks for your good wishes. Best regards.

Sincerely,
Ron

––––––––

President Reagan thanks William Stephens and Opal Stephens, both graduates of Eureka, for making a contribution to the college.

Mr. and Mrs. William Stephens
Rock Island, Illinois
July 11, 1983 [44]

Dear Frater and Mrs. Stephens:

I've just learned of your generous gift to Eureka College and as a fellow alumnus and fraternity brother want you to know how grateful I am. The old school gave us all a sound foundation on which to build our lives. I commend you both for the special way you have chosen to remember our Alma Mater.

God bless you.

Yours in the bond,
Ronald Reagan

In a letter to the son of James Rosborough, a man who graduated from Eureka College in 1928, President Reagan sends his regrets about the death of J. Dan Benefiel, another 1928 graduate of the college.

Mr. R. D. Rosborough
Las Vegas, Nevada
June 19, 1984[45]

Dear Mr. Rosborough:

My brother forwarded your sad word about Dan. I had not heard of his death and was truly saddened as I know you were.

J. Dan was responsible for my becoming a Teke and indeed was most helpful in my getting work at Eureka which was necessary if I was to go to college. I knew your father also. Those Tekes of that class were frequent visitors back to the old brick house on Walnut Avenue.

You were kind and thoughtful to send me the word and I'm most grateful.

Sincerely,
Ronald Reagan

President Reagan agrees to hold in confidence Dan Gilbert's decision to resign as president of Eureka College. Gilbert resigned in 1985 and was replaced by George Hearne.

The Honorable Dan Gilbert
Eureka, Illinois
November 16, 1984[46]

Dear Dan:

Just a note to acknowledge your letter and the news of your resignation—which I shall hold in confidence.

Thanks for all you've done for Eureka College. I know you'll be missed.

My best to Linda.

Sincerely,
Ron

President Reagan sends a thank-you note to contributors to Eureka College.

Mr. and Mrs. Earle M. Jorgenson
Los Angeles, California
December 18, 1984[47]

Dear Marion and Earle:

Thank you very much for my Christmas gift. The little college (the oldest coeducational west of the Allegheny Mountains) lives in genteel poverty and recently faced quite a financial crisis.

When I was there I saw professors go months without paychecks and yet the school made it possible for me and others in those Depression days to get an education even though we had no money. They allowed me to defer tuition until I graduated and gave me a job to pay for my board. You have done a worthy deed and I'm truly more grateful than I can say.

Bless you both and we look forward to seeing you.

Love,
Ron

———————

President Reagan thanks two Eureka College donors for sending him a birthday greeting, and writes about the many jobs he had during college to defray expenses. His first job was washing dishes in his fraternity house. He later washed dishes in the girls' dormitory and taught swimming.

Mr. & Mrs. Paul Lightfoot
Roanoke, Illinois
February 6, 1985[48]

Dear Paul and Mildred:

What a happy surprise to hear from you after these many years. Thank you for your birthday greetings and good wishes.

Yes Paul I was in charge of the pool at the college and taught swimming. That was how I earned my board and room. I graduated from washing dishes in the girls dormitory to taking care of the pool.

Let me wish you both—a little in advance I know—a happy 50th anniversary. Please say hello for me to all those Eureka friends on one of your Friday night get-togethers.

Again thanks and best regards.

Ronald Reagan

———————

In 1975, Reagan began to send personal memorabilia to Eureka College. Toward the end of his presidency, he explains that his presidential library will be in California but he will continue to send mementos to Eureka. *

Dr. George Hearne
Eureka, Illinois
June 16, 1987[49]

Dear George:

This is a hard letter to write with the resolution by the trustees on the desk before me. Having lived half a century in California and planning to return there

———————

* In 1994, Eureka College began displaying its collection of Reagan memorabilia in a museum exhibit. This exhibit was made permanent in 2002 and is displayed in the Ronald W. Reagan Museum, located in the college's Donald B. Cerf Center.

when my term in office expires, I naturally wanted the library to be in close proximity to our home. It will not be associated with any particular institution but will be available to any and all for appropriate gatherings, seminars and such.

We've gone too far down the road now to make a change but believe me I bear a feeling of guilt as I read the invitation of the board and their well-reasoned arguments. Will you please convey my regret and my apology?

I have always intended (providing this meets with your approval), to provide artifacts, pictures and souvenirs of my time here that would be in the nature of a museum of some historical significance. As a matter of fact I've accumulated a considerable number of things which are in storage here designated as material for Eureka College and I continue to add to them.

Again forgive me and very best regards.

Sincerely,
Ron

———

President Reagan added the note below to a letter that was written and typed on his behalf to the president of his alma mater. He expresses concern about the college's proposal to build a museum and a conference center.

Mr. George A. Hearne
Eureka, Illinois
January 27, 1988 [50]

But George, having lived with Eureka's genteel and sometimes desperate poverty so long, I can't help but worry about the costly project you've proposed. If money in that amount can be raised are there not more valuable and urgent uses for it "neath the elms?" I'll be guided by your judgment on relative values but, want you to know I want what's best for Eureka.

I'm deeply grateful for your dedication to an institution so dear to my heart. Thanks for all you've done and continue to do for me and for Eureka.

Sincerely,
Ronald Reagan

———

From his post-presidency office in Los Angeles, President Reagan continued to reminisce about his college days.

President George A. Hearne
Eureka, Illinois
January 22, 1990 [51]

Dear George:

It was good to be with you on the 8th even if there wasn't much time for a visit. I'm so proud of Eureka and the progress it has made. Having been there back in the Great Depression days I meant it at the banquet when I said, "if I had it to do over again I'd go to Eureka." I've never for a moment regretted my choice of Eureka. I hope I can continue lending a hand. Maybe one of these days my travel schedule will allow me a stop "Neath the Elms." I hope so.

I appreciate hearing from you. Very best wishes to you.

Sincerely,
Ron

IOWA

Reagan offers here a detailed account of "a start in radio and a start in pictures," beginning with job hunting in the depths of the Depression. The man whose advice he took is Sid Altschuler, whose family spent summers in Dixon visiting his wife's parents.[52] Reagan goes on to tell about the interview in Davenport, Iowa, that gave him his start in radio, the move to Des Moines, how he got his Hollywood screen test, and his first contract with Warner Brothers.

Ron Cochran
May 12, 1980[53]

Dear Ron:

It was good to talk to you and to renew and refresh my memory of those old days in Iowa. Here is the information as per our phone conversation about the start in radio and in Hollywood.

When I graduated from college in 1932, the depths of the Depression, it was a time when, as you remember, the government was putting ads on the radio urging people not to leave home looking for work because there was none. Even though I had graduated with a degree in economics, I didn't know what I really wanted to do. But, in those Depression days, you thought basically of just getting a job.

I went back to my summer job of lifeguarding for that final summer after graduation to get some pocket money. During that summer, a man who usually came to the park with his family for summer vacation and who'd remained successful in spite of the Depression gave me what turned out to be some pretty solid advice. He had told me that he could help me get a job in one of several lines of business if I could tell him what I honestly wanted to do.

Finally, having to face up to it, I knew that I wanted something in the entertainment world. My two biggest joys through high school and college had been football, which I played for eight years, and dramatics. But in 1932 in a small town back in the Midwest, you didn't say out loud to someone you wanted to be an actor. So I told him that I had thought about radio and being a sports announcer. His advice was to start out touring the radio stations. He said I should tell them I believed in the future of radio and that I had a future in it myself and that I would take any kind of job simply to get inside the station. And then I would take my chances on achieving what I really wanted—the sports announcing end.

It was, as I said, good advice. I started hitchhiking and made Chicago, which was really a big radio center then, my first stop. I figured that if I started at the top and finally did hit one that would give me a job, it might be a little bigger than if I started at the bottom and went up. I was wrong, of course, and a very nice lady in a program department in about the fifth station I'd tried in Chicago told me I was wrong. She said that the major stations couldn't afford to take inexperienced help but that I should go out to what they called "the sticks" to the smaller stations in the smaller towns. And she repeated almost exactly what my mentor had said on the beach in the past summer that someplace along the line, I'd find a man who believed in the future of radio and who knew that he would have to bring along and develop new people—young people for the future.

Well, my journeys took me to WOC in Davenport. It was a 5,000 watt station and broadcast simultaneously on the same wavelength with WHO Des Moines— both stations owned by the same company. Of course, I learned all of this later. All I knew was Peter MacArthur, the program manager, had informed me that they had just hired an announcer the day before—a young fellow from the University of Iowa and where had I been because they had been holding auditions for days. This was too much for me after all the hitchhiking, and as I went out the door, I said, "How the hell does a guy get to be a sports announcer if he can't get a job in a radio station?" And down the hall I went to the elevator.

Fortunately, the elevator wasn't there, and as I waited, I heard a clumping down the hall. I looked around the corner, and it was Pete, who was badly crippled by arthritis and walked with two canes. He was thumping his way down the hall, and he was cursing in his Scotch brogue and saying, "Wait up for me you big bastard." And so I waited, and when he caught up with me he said, "What was that you said about sports?" And I said, "Well, I'd like to be a sports announcer someday." And he said, "Do you know anything about football?" I told him I'd played it for eight years. He said, "Do you think you could tell me all about a football game and make me see it as if I were listening on the radio?" And I said, "I think I could." He took me into a studio, put me in front of a microphone, and said, "Now I'm going to be in another room. You won't be able to see me, but I'll be listening, and when that red light goes on up there, you start broadcasting an imaginary football game."

Well, he left the studio, and I stood there and thought, well, I've got to be able to have names to call off if I'm going to pretend broadcast so I picked a game from the previous season that we had won in the last 20 seconds when a 65-yard run by our quarterback gave us a one-point victory. I knew all our own fellows' names, and I knew enough of the other team's names that I wouldn't have to fake and try to dream up some names. Then I decided to start the game—or the broadcast—in the fourth quarter, building up to that one play.

All of a sudden, the red light went on and I said, "Here we are in the fourth quarter of this game with the score . . ." I gave the score showing the other team a touchdown ahead of us, and I said, "a chill wind is whipping through the stadium" (we didn't have a stadium, we only had bleachers because Eureka College is a small school), "and the long blue shadows are settling over the field." Incidentally, I got a little superstitious about that expression and I never did a football broadcast thereafter without coming to that moment, even if it was a rainy day, when I would say this is the time—if the sun were shining—that the long blue shadows would be settling over the field.

Well, I came up to the moment when it was 20 seconds to go and we were on our own 35-yard line. I was right guard, and the right guard pulled out most of the time from the line and ran interference—led the interference, as a matter of fact. The play we called was an off-tackle smash with Bud Cole carrying the ball, and I was the key man in blocking in that I had to take the first man in the secondary to get him past that line of scrimmage. I missed my man on this play and I don't know how Bud ever shook loose, but he cut back to the left and ran down the sidelines 65 yards for the touchdown. In the reenactment I want you to know, I didn't miss that man in the secondary—I delivered an earth-shattering block that sprung Cole loose. Then, having announced the touchdown, I just grabbed the mike with both hands and said, "That's all."

Well, in a little bit, Pete came back into the studio where I was waiting and said, "Be here Saturday. You're broadcasting the Minnesota-Iowa game, and we'll give you $5 and bus fare." I had only been in a stadium of any size twice in my life—that is to be up in the stands. The rest of the time I was on the field. I had never been in a press box. But there I was on Saturday. It was a tryout, and Pete hedged his bets—he had a regular announcer from the studio who had done some special events broadcasting there with me. I did the first quarter, and then he had the other fellow do the second quarter. I did the third quarter, and as that quarter was coming to an end, a note came down from behind us. It was to the announcer, and it said, let him finish the game, which meant let me finish it. I knew I had the job. I did the rest of the season and, subsequently was hired for a staff job.

WOC and WHO were soon to become just WHO Des Moines and 50,000 watts—a key station for one of the major networks in the Midwest. And there I was, a sports announcer broadcasting Big Ten football and doing the home games of the Chicago Cubs and White Sox by telegraphic report and loving every minute of it.

In those days the Cubs did their spring training at Catalina Island. I was as far west in Des Moines as I had ever been in my life, and I had a yen to see the West. So, I persuaded the station to send me to spring training camp with the Cubs in return for which I gave up any vacation.

The first time I went out, I was instructed very carefully to contact Joy Hodges, who had started her singing career on WHO and who was then in Hollywood making some pictures and singing with one of the big-name bands. I did contact her, and she was very nice, and I now know, looking back, what an effort it must have been to give a few hours to someone from back home whom she didn't even know on the basis of a friend's recommendation. About my third trip out, something had happened that stirred a little bit of that show business yen I had once had.

Gene Autry was becoming popular as a musical Western star, and he had a great gimmick for building audiences. He would take a singing or musical group of country music or western type music from a station like ours and put them in one of his pictures. He did this throughout the country, using these acts as a publicity device when his picture played that particular area. WHO was on the circuit for him, and he hired a group known as the Oklahoma Outlaws. Knowing they were there making a picture, I couldn't resist going out to the studio before I went over to Catalina Island. I visited them on the set. They took me to other sets in the studio, and I met a few people who were working in other pictures there and then left to go on my way to Catalina.

But all the time I was covering spring practice, my mind was back in Hollywood and on those Oklahoma Outlaws who were there in a studio actually being motion picture performers. When we returned to Los Angeles for the usual exhibition games the Cubs played, we put up at the Biltmore, and Joy was singing in the Biltmore Bowl. The first evening I went down and sent a note back. She came out, and we had dinner together there in the Bowl. I told her about my experiences at the studio, and then I asked her how does someone get into this business of pictures? She told me she had an agent who was honest, who would tell me whether I should go back and be content to stay in the press box or whether there was a possibility and that he'd be truthful with me. Would I see him if she made a date? The next day, she called and said I had an appointment with him at 10 o'clock in the morning, and at 10 o'clock in the morning I was there. We talked for a while, and then I blurted out, "Joy told me you'd tell me the truth. Should I go back to Iowa and keep on broadcasting?" He answered me by picking up the phone and calling Max Arno, the casting director at Warner Brothers. He told him that he had someone that Max ought to see. So we climbed in his car and out to Warner Brothers we went. Max interviewed me and at one point asked me a rather strange question, I thought. He said, "Is that your real voice?" And I said, "Well it's the only one I've got." He then turned to the agent, Bill Meiklejohn, and said, have him here on Tuesday, and we'll shoot a screen test.

I couldn't believe it. It was as if someone had put together some enormous dream, and I was just walking through it. I later learned that the question about my voice was because Warners had a coming young star by the name of Ross Alexander, who, for some tragic reason, committed suicide, and evidently, my voice was somewhat similar to his. It was this that attracted Max Arno's attention.

On Tuesday, I arrived, I did a scene from [The] Philadelphia Story with one of the young contract actresses there, and then Mr. Arno explained to me that it might be a couple of weeks before Mr. Warner could see the screen test and, therefore, just stick around. I did then what turned out to be one of those lucky accidents. I said, "Well, there is no way I can stick around for a couple of weeks. I'm a sports announcer, the Cubs are leaving tomorrow to go back, and I'm going back with them. I've got a job to do." And it was only after we all got on the train the next day that I collapsed, and the dream was over, and I wondered, "What have I done? What am I doing here, I may have blown the chance of a lifetime."

I didn't realize that Hollywood was a place where everyone knocked down the doors trying to get in, and they weren't used to someone telling them that he had another job and couldn't wait around. It must have intrigued them a little. I got home, and the next day I was at the studio telling everybody there all the things that had happened to me. I had actually had a screen test, etc., and then a telegram arrived. They were offering a seven-year contract. I accepted by wire.

This was in April. I broadcast baseball and broke in a newly hired announcer and on June 1st, after driving from Des Moines to California in three days, I reported at the studio as per the contract. I was to put in 13 years at Warner Brothers, interrupted by four years in the service in WWII.

Well, there it is Ron. That's a start in radio and a start in pictures, and, as you said on the phone the other day, there is some kind of pattern or some kind of fate that affects our lives. When I look back now and think how easily I could have turned in different directions, I have to believe in that and I say a little prayer of thanks every night. My best to Beulah and thanks for being interested in doing this.

Best regards,
Ron

While he was the sports announcer for WHO, Reagan replied to a listener who was interested in broadcasts of the girls' basketball championship games. This is the only letter we have found from Reagan's years as a sports announcer in Iowa.

A WHO Listener
March 4, 1937 [54]

Dear Friend:

The State Tournament will be held in Des Moines March 18, 19 and 20. WHO will not broadcast any games but KSO and KRNT at 1420 and 1320 on the dial might do the finals.

Glad to hear of Ellis Veatch we were on the same football squad in college.

My periods of sports news are at 6:40 in the evening but will shift to either 9 or 9:15 May 1.

Thanks for your letter.

Sincerely,
Dutch Reagan

Joseph "Buzzy" Sisco was the mentally handicapped brother of the Sisco sisters, to whom Reagan wrote often. Here he tells Buzzy about announcing Cubs games from wire service reports and what he did when the wire went dead.

Mr. Buzzy Sisco
Healdsburg, California
December 24, 1985 [55]

Dear Buzzy:

Many years ago I was a radio sports announcer and used to broadcast by telegraphic report big league baseball games.

I would sit at a microphone in the studio and on the other side of a glass window a telegraph operator would receive from the ballpark in Morse code each play of the game. He would type the message as it came in and slip it under the window to me. For example his note to me would say—S one C. That meant the pitcher had thrown a called strike to the batter and I would describe it as if I were at the game seeing it happen.

Well I was doing a game between the Chicago Cubs and the St. Louis Cardinals. The score was tied, nothing and nothing in the ninth inning. A Cub player Billy Jurges was at bat. I saw my operator begin to type so I had the pitcher wind up and start his throw to the plate. Just then I was handed the slip of paper and it said: "the wire has gone dead." I had a ball on the way to the plate. The only thing I could think of that wouldn't get in the records was a foul ball so I had Jurges foul one down the back of third base.

My operator just shrugged and indicated he was getting no message from the ballpark.

There were several other stations broadcasting that game and I knew I'd lose my audience if I told them we'd lost our telegraph connections so I took a chance. I had Jurges hit another foul. Then I had him foul one that only missed being a home run by a foot. I had him foul one back in the stands and took up some time describing the two lads who got in a fight over the ball.

I kept on having him hit foul balls until I was setting a record for a ballplayer hitting successive foul balls and I was getting more than a little scared. Just then my operator started typing. When he passed me the paper I started to giggle—it said: "Jurges popped out on the first ball pitched."

I've waited a long time to tell that story. And didn't tell it until after I was no longer a sports announcer.

All the very best to you Buzzy. Give Miss Sam and Miss Bertha my very best regards.

Sincerely,
Ronald Reagan

In 1936 and 1937 Reagan arranged for the WHO radio station in Des Moines for whom he announced the Chicago Cubs games to pay his way to the Cubs spring training site on Catalina Island off the coast of California. It was from there that he got himself to Los Angeles and, eventually, Hollywood. This letter is about a September 2, 1968, article* in the Chicago Tribune *by Charlie Grimm, manager of the Chicago Cubs. Grimm claimed Reagan sent recordings ("platters") back to Des Moines to be played on the air. Reagan writes that he sent letters to be read on the air, not recordings. Paul Loyet was the chief engineer at the radio station while Reagan was its sports announcer.*

Mr. Paul A. Loyet
Circa September 1968 [56]

Dear Paul:

Thanks for the papers and the nostalgia but where did Charlie Grimm get those stories? You know I never sent any platters back—you guys got letters for Ed Reimers to read on the air. I seem to remember something about a drunken squabble and a one punch fight but the recipient was a smart bottomed young reporter named Jack Diamond who later turned up in Hollywood as a public man— way over on the left and it was my second year out there on Catalina. Anyway it was fun to read and to remember what really did happen.

Best regards,
Dutch

Monte Osburn was a high school junior who wrote a letter to President Reagan asking for his recollections of the Great Depression.[57]

Monte Osburn
Henderson, Texas
March 29, 1982 [58]

Dear Monte:

Thank you for your letter and for picking me for your interview. I'll do my best to give a picture of the Great Depression days.

Let me give you first the setting or perhaps I should say viewpoint from which I'll be replying to your questions.

I graduated from high school in 1928 and that autumn enrolled at Eureka Col-

---

* The article was an excerpt from Charlie Grimm with Ed Prell, *Jolly Cholly's Story: Baseball, I Love You* (Chicago: Regnery, 1968).

lege. My home was in a town of about 10,000—Dixon Illinois. Eureka College is a small liberal arts college one hundred miles south of Dixon.

Our family was of very modest means. My father had told my brother and me that if we intended to go to college, while he would try to help, we'd have to work our way. He managed a small shoe store. All of this of course is prior to the stock market crash that brought on the Depression.

Having heeded my father's words I had held summer jobs since I was fourteen years of age saving money toward the day. The last three summers including the one after graduation I was the lifeguard at a river beach in a park outside of Dixon. I received a needy-student scholarship for half my tuition at Eureka and a job waiting table in the fraternity I joined for which my meals were free. The job also included washing the dishes.

I think now I've answered your first and third questions. I graduated from Eureka in 1932, the very depths of the Depression. I had continued to lifeguard every summer and did so after my graduation to get some job-hunting money. My father's job had gone when the shoe store closed. He was in and out of work usually as a shoe salesman on straight commission, no salary. My mother got a job in a dress shop at fourteen dollars a week. On one of my years at college I shared my summer earnings with them to help pay the grocery bill.

How did the Depression affect me? Well it was a constant thing on everyone's mind. One fourth of the work force was unemployed and there was no such thing as unemployment insurance. My father finally got a job during the New Deal in charge of what we call welfare now but it was called "Relief" then and it wasn't spelled ROLAIDS.

Once a week the fathers of many of the kids I'd gone to school with would line up to go into the little office of the County Supervisor of Poor which my father shared with him. They'd receive something similar to today's food stamps plus whatever surplus farm products the government had bought—potatoes, fruit, etc.

My folks had taken a small apartment which was really just the upstairs of a home. When my brother and I were home from Eureka he slept on the couch and I had a cot on the upstairs landing. Those were changes because before we'd always lived in a house (rented) and had a bedroom for ourselves. I guess I've already answered question four about the change in life style.

But you wanted the Depression up to 1936. Well after the beach closed in the summer of '32 and I had my diploma I started hitchhiking around Illinois looking for a job. One day I crossed the Mississippi River into Iowa in my search. I'd decided I wanted to be a radio sports announcer but I was asking for any kind of job in a radio station—just to get on the inside.

That day in Davenport Iowa the man interviewing me got out of me the fact that I aspired to sports announcing. I forgot to tell you earlier I had played football in high school and college—varsity first string two years in high school and three years in college.

He asked me if I would broadcast an imaginary game for him. Calling on memory of our last games the previous season I did. He told me to be there Saturday. I would broadcast the University of Iowa vs. Minnesota game. I was to receive five dollars and bus fare.

That led to a job as announcer at WOC which in about a year and a half became WHO Des Moines, one of the major 50,000-watt stations in the country. I was able to send money home to my parents regularly and finally actually bought a car— a cheap one.

When I think back on those days (to answer question five) two things stand out. One was the drabness. For a time automobiles came only in black paint. If you saw any other color it was an old pre-Depression model. People went to movies (you could get in for a quarter) possibly because it was relief from the drab, dreariness of the Depression. But the other thing I recall is the human warmth. As in any kind of calamity people were closer together. There was a spirit of helpfulness and yes kindliness abroad in the land. But somehow you clung to the thought that one day somehow things would get better.

Eventually they did but not before 1936. World War II ended the Depression but that was hardly the way anyone wanted to see it end.

I hope this is of some help and I'm enclosing a booklet you might find interesting.

Best regards,
Ronald Reagan

POLITICS

Reagan's active interest in politics began early and he was for a long time a strong supporter of Franklin Delano Roosevelt.

Mrs. Russell B. Aitken
New York, New York
January 17, 1989 [59]

Dear Mrs. Aitken:

There are no words to properly thank you for giving me that letter. You are most kind and generous. My first vote was cast for FDR in 1932. I had just graduated from Eureka College and found a job in that terrible time of great unemployment.

Again my heartfelt thanks and very best wishes.

Sincerely,
Ronald Reagan

Reagan answers questions about the presidency and presidents he has known. He tells about the first time he saw a president—in 1936 in Des Moines, Iowa—and goes on to recount meeting President Truman and other presidents and campaigning for some of them.

Ronald E. Wade
September 4, 1979[60]

Dear Ron:

You asked me whether I thought the presidency had grown too weak as a result of Vietnam and Watergate. I believe the greatest blow to the power of the presidency has resulted from Vietnam. The world today has a belief that a president of the United States cannot respond to a crisis or emergency as presidents have in the past—some 125 times. There is a danger in this.

Naturally, we do not want to change the Constitution; we do not want a president to be able to declare wars without getting permission from Congress. But, there is a risk if the image persists that an American president would find it politically impossible to respond to some kind of emergency situation wherever it might be in the world.

Now, as to your other questions. The first president I ever saw was Franklin Delano Roosevelt from a distance of about 30 feet as he passed by in a parade in Des Moines, Iowa, in the 1936 campaign. He was riding in an open car, a luxury I'm afraid presidents can't afford any longer in this day and age. The first president I ever met was Harry Truman. I was a Democrat in those days and campaigned for him. He, George Jessell, and I rode together in an automobile to an evening rally at Gilmore Field here in Los Angeles. I introduced the President: George was the Master of Ceremonies for the evening. I later met and became acquainted with President Eisenhower. In fact I played golf with him on two occasions. I did not have the opportunity to meet John F. Kennedy. As governor of California, I did know and occasionally worked with President Johnson, President Nixon and Gerald Ford.

Indeed, I campaigned for the latter two.

If this isn't what you had in mind, please let me know and again, best regards.

Sincerely,
Ronald Reagan

Cal Williford was a young black aide in the 1980 Reagan presidential campaign. His mother writes to thank Reagan for her son's experience. Reagan replies with an explanation of some of the concerns that led to his becoming a Republican.

Lucinda Williford
San Pablo, California
Circa 1980[61]

Dear Mrs. Williford:

I can't tell you how much your letter meant to me. I'm truly grateful and very proud.

I guess we who call ourselves Republicans haven't done a very good job of explaining what it is we really want for the people. Maybe we've been so busy trying to fight against programs of the government because we don't think they'll solve the problem that we haven't taken the time to explain that we <u>do</u> want the problems solved.

I started out as a Democrat, casting my first vote for Franklin Delano Roosevelt in 1932. One of the things that disturbed me over the years was my party's indifference to the situation in the South, where blacks were denied their constitutional rights for so long. And, of course, the South was a one-party region, solidly Democrat. It seemed that Washington would do nothing to upset that situation. My first Republican vote was for Eisenhower and I didn't get around to becoming a Republican until 1962.

Well, you didn't write to hear me tell my life story. I want you to know how much all of us thought of Cal. He's a fine young man and you can take credit for that. He spoke of you often. If we added anything, it was only because the pattern had already been set. We saw him in every kind of situation and a campaign tour can offer just about every kind of situation. You would have been very proud of him. I can tell you he was liked by everyone who came in contact with him.

Again, thank you for a letter I shall treasure. Please give the regards of our son Ron, Mrs. Reagan and myself to Cal.

Sincerely,
Ronald Reagan

REAGAN'S ENGLISH AND
IRISH ROOTS

Reagan had always known that his mother was British. Nelle Reagan's father, Thomas Wilson, was Scottish; her mother, Mary Anne Elsey, was English. It was not until he became president that he knew anything about his father's heritage except that he was Irish. Burke's Peerage prepared a family tree for him. Reagan passed highlights along to his brother, Neil Reagan, nicknamed Moon. In June 1984, he and Nancy visited Ireland and especially the town, Ballyporeen, where his great grandfather was born and grew up, and they kept in touch with the distant relatives they met.

Mr. and Mrs. J. Neil Reagan
Rancho Santa Fe, California
October 28, 1981 [62]

Dear Bess and Moon:

It looks like Duke is doing well. He's a good man and I know you must be happy.

The enclosed pictures are of the hometown of our great grandfather. Please note the name on the pub—that has to be a first for a president.*

The little clipping indicates that the clan didn't start in Ballyporeen. Incidentally, the picture of "Cashel"—the ruins on the hill—that is where St. Patrick is supposed to have erected the first cross in Ireland.

Incidentally, we hail from one of the four tribes of Tara descended from the High King of Ireland—Cathair Mor in 200 A.D. It seems we were the defenders for a few centuries of the Gap of Glendine, a narrow pass in the Slieve Bloom mountains. Our motto was "The Hills Forever." Every now and then I'd like to take to the hills myself.

By the way our great grandmother was Catherine Mulcahy.

Mike Kinney dropped in on me the other day and today Louis Schuman came by.

Have to go now. Nancy sends her love.

Love,
Dutch

Lucy Conboy met Susan Baker, the wife of Reagan's chief of staff, James Baker, at a Washington event and later sent Mrs. Baker information about Ballyporeen. Mrs. Conboy had visited Ballyporeen with her grandmother, who had been born there; her cousin, Dermot Wall, still lived there. Mrs. Baker passed the information along to Reagan. Mrs. Conboy later met Reagan at a Washington reception honoring Claire Booth Luce where they chatted for some time about Ireland and their other mutual interest—horses. [63]

Mrs. Lucy L. Conboy
Washington, D.C.
May 23, 1984 [64]

Dear Mrs. Conboy:

Mrs. Baker passed on to me your comments on Ballyporeen and I just want you know how much I appreciate your kind thoughtfulness.

---

* Ronald Reagan Pub.

Nancy and I are looking forward eagerly to our visit to Ireland and your letter has added to our anticipation. Until coming to Washington I had no knowledge of my father's family line since he had been orphaned before he was six years old. The Irish government has seen to it that we now have the family tree. Your description of Ballyporeen has contributed greatly.

I don't know how much opportunity I'll have to get acquainted with individuals although I will be making a public appearance in Ballyporeen. I'll keep my eyes open for a Dermot Wall.

Again my thanks to you.

Sincerely,
Ronald Reagan

———

Patrick O'Regan was a distant Irish cousin of Reagan's.

Mr. Patrick J. O'Regan
Cork, Ireland
February 27, 1985 [65]

Dear Mr. O'Regan:

Our mutual friend Maureen O'Hara Blair has forwarded to us the gifts from the Reagan clan, Buttevant, North Cork, Delano, as well as your letter regarding the founding of the state of Oregon by Eugene O'Regan and the newspaper clippings. Thank you so very much and will you convey our thanks to the Reagan clan.

Mrs. Reagan and I are more grateful than words can express to have the walking sticks and the plaque as well as the information about my forebears. To have lived so long with no knowledge of my father's family and to now be so fully informed about my roots is an experience hard to describe. I only know I'm truly happy and grateful to you all.

Perhaps you would see that the clan received this photo of Nancy and myself with our gifts and the extra picture is for you with our heartfelt thanks.

Sincerely,
Ronald Reagan

———

Phil and Jo Regan were old friends of Reagan's from Hollywood. Phil Regan was an Irish tenor and movie actor who worked for a time for Warner Brothers and had been a New York City policeman. As a Democrat he supported Reagan in Reagan's first bid for the California governorship. Reagan remarks on the close relationship of people with similar names.

Mr. and Mrs. Phil Regan
Pasadena, California
April 22, 1987 [66]

Dear Jo and Phil:

It was good to talk to you the other day in California. Now we're back here in the Puzzle Palace on the Potomac and California seems too far away.

Thank you for the Irish songs. I'll be playing the tape tonight. By the way the government of Ireland did a family tree for me. I've never known anything about my father's family. He was orphaned when he was six years old. Well now I know and all us Reagans, Regans, Ragans and those with an O in front are cousins and the clan goes all the way back to Brian Boru.

Phil, I'm sending back the material on the ranch in case someone might be interested. I'm happy with the one we have and hope to be riding over it a while longer.

By the way J.L.* made another remark when he heard I was running for governor. He said; "No—Jimmy Stewart for governor, Ronald Reagan for best friend."

Best regards,
Ron

An article in the Dagur-Timinn, *a daily newspaper published in Reykjavik, Iceland, suggested that Reagan's ancestors were possibly Icelandic. The U.S. ambassador to Iceland sent Reagan the article. Reagan restates the facts about his Irish, English, and Scottish heritage.*

The Honorable Nick Ruwe
Reykjavik, Iceland
November 3, 1987 [67]

Dear Nick:

Howard Perlow delivered the translation of the article in *Timinn* regarding my (?Icelandic?) parentage. I thought you might like to have my comments in case of future questions.

First of all the story is without any foundation at all. My great grandfather on my father's side hailed from Ballyporeen, Ireland. The pub there is named after me and I've seen the church records and no I've never ordered them sealed.

But to be specific I was born in Tampico Illinois. Besides the local records I have an older brother who remembers my birth. He wasn't happy, he wanted a sister. There are a few people around who remember my birth. Of course most have passed on but I remember them and their relationship with our family.

Nick I'm amazed at the detail in that story and it makes me wonder. I know

---

* Jack Warner of Warner Brothers.

there are at least two Ronald Reagans in addition to myself. One was a policeman in Sacramento when I was governor. The second was an officer in the Army, WWII. I never met him but other officers who had crossed paths with him at Ft. Bennington said he portrayed himself as Ronald Reagan the actor. He wouldn't sign autographs—said the Army had ordered him not to.

Well enough of that. This R.R. is Irish, English and Scotch and made his first and so far only visit to Iceland at the invitation of General Secretary Gorbachev. As I said that's quite a family history the *Timinn* printed only it just ain't me.

Love to your lady and warmest regard,

Ron

CHAPTER TWO

Home and Family

R<small>EAGAN'S FAMILY</small>, *the one he was born into and the one he made, played an important role in his life. The family he was born into shaped his beliefs and character. The family he built gave him support and counsel as he fought his way up the political ladder.*

Of his two parents, Jack and Nelle, it was Nelle who was central to his upbringing. A deeply religious woman with a flair for acting, she helped to instill in him a faith in God that built in intensity as he grew older. When he landed an acting contract in Hollywood at age 26, she and Jack soon followed him to Los Angeles. She helped him with his budding movie career, answering much of his fan mail.

Reagan's father, Jack, was a shoe salesman who provided a decent, lower-middle-income life for his family, often moving as his job prospects changed. He was a good husband and father, but he suffered from a serious drinking problem. His alcoholic binges introduced an anxious uncertainty into the day-to-day family life, and Reagan was taught early that Jack was afflicted with a "disease" over which he had no control. Reagan's initial politics were those of his father—a Roosevelt supporter and a New Deal Democrat.

Jack died in May 1941 at the early age of 58, just after Reagan had turned 30. Jack saw his son make over two dozen movies, become a star, and marry Jane Wyman, but he never glimpsed the odyssey that would take him to the White House. Nelle remained close to Reagan until she was well over 70, saw him serve in the Army during World War II, watched his first marriage dissolve, his movie career fade away in the mid-1950s, and his life reemerge, phoenix-like, when he found and married Nancy Davis in 1952.

But Nelle's mind began to fail; she was committed to a nursing home in the late 1950s and died a few years later, in 1962, when she was 77 years old.

The person next closest to young Ronald Reagan was his brother, Neil (nicknamed

"Moon").* Born in 1908, Moon was a bit over two years older, and for many years was taller, better at sports, and better in school. But Reagan caught up with Moon and soon eclipsed him, both in height and accomplishment. Moon became a Republican shortly after World War II and strongly argued the virtues of free enterprise with his brother, who was still "a New Dealer to the core." † The two brothers remained close over the years, Moon rising to be a top executive of the McCann-Erickson advertising firm, but they were competitive and Moon seemed to have a glint of envy as Reagan's career soared. They stayed in touch all their lives, and Moon handled the advertising in Reagan's gubernatorial campaign in California, although he was not active in his presidential campaigns. He died in 1996 at age 88.

There were two strong women that were central in Reagan's family life. The first was his mother, Nelle, and the second was his wife, Nancy, whom he married in 1952.

He was married earlier to Jane Wyman. The marriage lasted eight years (1940–48) and then she left him, apparently more interested in pursuing a movie career than being a wife and mother. Reagan was stunned by her decision and was quite despondent for the next couple of years. Wyman fulfilled her goal, rapidly winning an Oscar and becoming one of Hollywood's most famous movie stars. Neither Reagan nor Wyman has ever talked about why the eight-year marriage came apart. But then Reagan met Nancy Davis. His despondency vanished and they were married on May 4, 1952.

For more than 50 years Nancy Reagan has been the central part of Reagan's family life.

A graduate of Smith College, she pursued an acting career. When Reagan married Nancy in 1952, she was a 30-year-old actress who had been in ten movies. It was her first marriage. From the beginning they were literally inseparable. Happily and openly in love, they operated as a team. She was his best friend and his most trusted counselor. As they built their home and ranch and had children, they both moved away from acting. Nancy became a full time wife and mother as Reagan moved on to television, public speaking, and his political career.

Nancy was a partner for Reagan throughout his public life. Highly intelligent, with a sixth sense for asking insightful, penetrating questions, she became the indispensable person who helped and supported him.

Ronald Reagan had five children. His first, Maureen, from his marriage to Jane Wyman, was born in 1940. His second child, Michael, was adopted by him and Jane Wyman in 1945. His third child, Christine, died the same day she was born in

---

* In high school Neil Reagan and a close friend on the football team were called "Moon" and "Mushmouth"—the names of the two lead characters in the Moon Mullins comic strip. Neil's nickname stuck and, from then on, the only person who called him Neil was his mother. (Ronald Reagan, An American Life, Simon & Schuster, 1990), p. 38.

† Reagan, An American Life, p. 105.

1947. When Jane Wyman divorced Reagan in 1948, the lives of the first two children were disrupted. Wyman won an Oscar in 1949 and skyrocketed to worldwide fame—and soon the two children, for whom she had custody, found themselves in boarding school. Michael was only five years old.

Reagan and Nancy's first child, his fourth, was Patricia Ann (Patti). Six years later, after two miscarriages, he and Nancy had their second child, a boy, Ronald Prescott (Skipper).

Unlike their parents, not one of the surviving four children received a college degree. By normal standards, they were successful, although they often followed a road different from that of their parents. While young, their relations with their parents were sometime strained, but as they grew older their parents seemed to gain more and more respect in their eyes.

Maureen was the most political of the children, even changing her registration to Republican before her father. She ran for the U.S. Senate in California in 1982 (and lost) and eventually became co-chair of the Republican National Committee. She died of cancer in 2001.

Michael turned out to be philosophically closer to his father than the other children. At one point he became a world-champion ocean boat racer, a decidedly dangerous occupation, and then moved on to become a highly successful, nationally syndicated radio talk show host.

Patti and Ron vied with one another for who was most independent and headstrong. At fourteen Patti, a beautiful, intelligent adolescent, tried to run off with the dishwasher at a private school she was attending. After dropping out of college she went to live with a member of the Eagles, a rock group. Her politics were far to the left of her father and she continually vented her views publicly, especially on nuclear weapons—much to the embarrassment of her parents. A talented writer, like her father, she also wrote a number of books detailing the personal trials of being a Reagan. But as the years passed and her father began his slide into the depths of Alzheimer's disease, she expressed fondness for him and became much closer to Nancy.*

Ron, like Patti, was gifted with many innate talents. Quick-witted, he could be charming and delightful. But after being accepted at Yale, he walked away after a few weeks and decided to become a ballet dancer. He succeeded brilliantly, becoming a member of the Joffrey Ballet. He left ballet and became a writer and television performer.

As Nancy summarized, "Every family has problems, and we were no exception. . . . What I wanted most in the world was to be a good wife and mother. As things turned out, I guess I've been more successful at the first than the second."†

The following letters give us some sense of Reagan's feelings about his parents and brother, his wife and children, and where he liked to live.

---

* Nancy Reagan, *My Turn: The Memoirs of Nancy Reagan* (New York: Random House, 1989), pp. 146–77.

† Ibid.

For over 50 years Reagan's home life revolved around his wife, Nancy. During that time, whether he was traveling to make movies or for General Electric, or in the California governor's office or the White House, he wrote letters to Nancy. Over 700 of these handwritten letters, notes, telegrams, and gift cards were saved by Nancy and many of them were published in her book, I Love You, Ronnie.* *The following letters are previously unpublished.*

This letter, written on Christmas Day after they had been married for 23 years, reveals a lot about how Reagan felt.

Nancy Reagan
Los Angeles, California
December 25, 1975 [1]

Dear Mommie:

The star in the East was a miracle as was the Virgin Birth. I have no trouble believing in those miracles because a miracle happened to me and it's still happening.

Into my life came one tiny "dear" and "a light shone round about." That light still shines and will as long as I have you. Please be careful when you cross the street. Don't climb on any ladders. Wear your rubbers when it rains. I love my light and don't want to be ever in the dark again.

I love you—Merry Christmas,
Your ranch hand

Helen Gurley Brown, the editor of Cosmopolitan, *asked Reagan to "do something absolutely wonderful for* Cosmopolitan, *its millions of girl readers, and for me"— "jot down . . . the nicest thing a girl ever did for me."*
So Reagan did.

Helen Gurley Brown
Cosmopolitan
New York, New York
May 28, 1971 [2]

The nicest thing a girl ever did for me was when a girl named Nancy married me and brought a warmth and joy to my life that has grown with each passing year.

I know she won't mind if I say the second nicest thing was a letter from a little fifth grade girl last week. She added a P.S. "You devil you." I've walked with a swagger ever since.

Ronald Reagan

---

* Nancy Reagan, *I Love You, Ronnie: The Letters of Ronald Reagan to Nancy Reagan* (New York: Random House, 2000).

Another Christmas letter from Reagan on official stationery, while he was governor of California, to Nancy.

Nancy Reagan
Sacramento, California
Circa 1967–73 [3]

To My Darling First Lady,
Obviously this isn't fur and almost as obviously it isn't a gold case—every one was fresh out. It is something for the one I love but a million of these couldn't express how much I love you nor would they be worth what you mean to, mean to, mean to (you're a broken record with me and I hope you just keep on in my life forever) me.

I love you,
Merry Christmas

Another simple love letter from Reagan to Nancy, with one added fillip—Reagan drew a heart around the word "heart" in his second sentence.

Nancy Reagan
Los Angeles, California
Circa 1970s [4]

Dear Mrs. Reagan:
Please forgive the borrowed stationery—we Fairies don't do much writing.
I am giving you a ♥heart —well actually you already have it. But I'm filling it with even more love ♥ and devotion (if that's possible). It will now be bursting at the seams and it's yours forever.

The Tooth Fairy

P.S. Your tooth was soooo! Big!

Governor Reagan's secretary relays a message that the Mission Inn in Riverside, California, would like him to accept the honorary chairmanship of the "Mission Inn Honeymooners." Here is Reagan's reply:

Governor Reagan's secretary
Sacramento, California
Circa 1967 [5]

We spent our wedding night there.
It's o.k. with me.

Ronald Reagan

Bill Bright, the president of Campus Crusade for Christ International in San Bernardino, California, knew Reagan's mother when she cared for people who were ill or in need. He passed along two letters that an old friend of Nelle, Phyllis Harris, wrote to Reagan, commenting that Nelle "was a saintly woman" and that he was not surprised that the president frequently mentioned her "because of the influence she had in his life in his younger years."

Mrs. Hugh Harris
Sierra Madre, California
January 9, 1985 [6]

Dear Mrs. Harris:

Thanks to Bill Bright I've received your recent letter and your long delayed letter of 1982. Thank you for both and for your very generous words and prayers.

You were very kind to tell me of your experiences with "Nelle." By the way did she ever tell you that my brother and I (after we'd grown up) called our parents by their first names? They seemed to like it.

I remember so well her ministering to the patients at Olive View.* I used to rent movies for her to take to them—that was before TV. And as far back as I can remember she regularly visited the jails back in our home town, Dixon Illinois. She truly lived a life of "doing unto the least of these." I like to think maybe she's still giving me a hand now and then.

Again my heartfelt thanks to you.

Sincerely,
Ronald Reagan

In 1984 Reagan's brother Moon and his wife Bess were trying to decide whether to drive up to Rancho del Cielo, Reagan's 658-acre ranch in the Santa Ynez Mountains, for Thanksgiving dinner, and also whether it would be worthwhile to attend Reagan's second inauguration in Washington, D.C.

Mr. and Mrs. J. Neil Reagan
Rancho Santa Fe, California
Circa November, 1984 [7]

Dear Bess and Moon:

Well fun time is over for us and we're back in our Potomac Puzzle Palace. It was good to see and be with you both if even for a short time.

I've enclosed the Santini † story although you've probably seen it already. I told

---

* After Nelle and Jack moved to California in 1937 to be with Reagan she began to minister to the tuberculosis patients at the Olive View Sanitarium.
† In May 1984 Maureen Santini was named the chief White House correspondent for the Associated Press (AP).

you she's among the unfriendlies and I think you can see she edited the two hours down to those things she thought would be the least helpful.

But Moon how could you call that graceful, gentle incline from the coast up to the ranch gate a "winding unpaved road?" Why even Queen Elizabeth enjoyed the drive—after changing from a "limo" into a four-wheel drive. She did (I'll admit) refer to the ride as "adventurous."

Seriously though there are a couple of points that made me conscious of being a little thoughtless. It is a 200 mile drive* and I hadn't figured that out until reading the interview. It is a h—l of a long way to go for a turkey dinner. Listen we love seeing you but believe me will understand if you should decide to phone your Thanksgiving greeting instead.

And on that subject we'll understand if you don't want to bother with the Inaugural. Believe me we wouldn't go if we didn't have to. We've made a few suggestions about omitting some of the trappings but don't know whether the Congressional committee who stages the thing will go along. We certainly won't blame you and indeed will understand if you decide not to make the trip. I wish tradition had it that we didn't have inaugurals for reelections—just put your hand on the Bible and take the oath.

If you do decide to skip it let us know so we can plan accordingly. If you do come we'll be glad to see you but will keep you out of reach of Miss Santini.

Love to you both.
Dutch

Reagan replies to a memo passed to him by his brother, arguing against executive privilege for the executive branch of the federal government.

Mr. J. Neil Reagan
Rancho Santa Fe, California
March 28, 1983[8]

Dear Moon:

Just a quick line to acknowledge your letter and the memo from your lawyer friend about executive privilege. I agree with much of what he said—indeed most of it. Particularly is he right about how you can be taken by surprise in this job when some[one] down in the bureaucratic ranks goes off the reservation.

I do differ in his almost blanket repudiation of executive privilege. A president has to use it to protect classified material having to do with national security. But there are some other areas. One has to do with the present EPA† hassle. First let me say the congressmen who are raising the stink have yet to offer anything

---

* It is actually about 240 miles from Rancho Santa Fe, California, to Reagan's ranch in Santa Ynez, and would take about four and a half hours without much traffic.
† Environmental Protection Agency.

but allegations and accusations.* They are in fact a lynch mob. When they first raised a holler we offered them almost 800,000 documents. We held back less than 100 on the advice of the Justice Department. These were papers that had to do with possible litigation between the government and various industrial concerns.

To make those papers public could prejudice the government's case in some instances or reveal evidence we were holding etc. Once the lynch mob succeeded in creating a public perception that we were hiding some wrong doing we had no choice but to find a way to make these documents available with whatever safeguards we could employ.

I'll be very surprised if they find anything and if they do I'll bet it would be way down in the ranks. The minute they started I ordered the FBI and the Justice Department to investigate every allegation. So far nothing.

Nancy sends her best. Love to Bess and have a nice trip.

Love,
Dutch

P.S. You were going to get me Gene Blome's address and phone number. I tried to call him to talk about the sculpture he sent us. It seems he's moved or something.

———

Reagan responds to a birthday gift from his brother and sister-in-law.

Mr. and Mrs. J. Neil Reagan
Rancho Santa Fe, California
February 22, 1983[9]

Dear Bess and Moon:

I've had to do a little detective work. A package arrived with a handsome (Kelly) green sport shirt which I'm looking forward to wearing as soon as the d—n snow melts back here—which it's doing.

As for the detective work—my only clue as to the donor was the knowledge that the package started its journey in La Jolla. Either there had never been a card or the card was lost in the procedures that take place for security reasons before I re-

---

* Anne M. Gorsuch, 38 years old, was a member of the Colorado House of Representatives when Reagan appointed her the administrator of the Environmental Protection Agency in 1981. A well-known conservative who had opposed some federal energy and environmental policies, she soon became a political target. In October 1982, John D. Dingell (D-Michigan), the powerful chairman of the House subcommittee on oversight and investigation of the Energy and Commerce Committee, issued a subpoena directing Gorsuch to deliver 35 documents which he believed contained information about official misconduct and political favoritism. President Reagan, acting on the advice of his White House counsel and the attorney general, instructed Gorsuch not to comply with the subpoena, claiming executive privilege. Within weeks the House, by a wide margin, voted Gorsuch in contempt of Congress. The political battle accelerated and, on March 9, 1983, Gorsuch resigned and gave Congress full access to all the documents requested. Gorsuch was never charged with any wrongdoing.

ceive anything. But my detective work was successful—so thank you very much for my very fine shirt. It really is handsome.

With this birthday I finally reached par (72) now the object of the game is to see how many strokes over par I can achieve.

Thanks again.

Love,
Dutch

One of his old neighbors in Dixon, Illinois, sent Reagan a school photo reminding him that his older brother Neil was once taller than he.

Mrs. Helen Lawton
Dixon, Illinois
December 19, 1983[10]

Dear Helen:

Thank you very much for the photo and for going to the trouble of having it enlarged. This was more than kind of you and I'm truly grateful. I'd forgotten there was a time when I was smaller than Neil. Since we've grown up I've always topped him a little but at that early age I guess his two years made a difference. I'm afraid about the only name I can add to those you've recalled is the gym teacher Kuhn standing down in front. I'm amazed that you found me. I believe I'm scheduled to be in Dixon in February for the opening.* I hope so.

Thanks too for your lovely Christmas greeting. I hope your Christmas was all you hoped it would be. I'm sure this will not arrive 'til after Christmas so I'll say Happy New Year. We're spending Christmas here in Washington and some of the family will be with us.

Again my heartfelt thanks.

Sincerely,
Dutch

In 1935 David Miller began to gather the stories of 72 elderly Native Americans who fought in the Battle of the Little Big Horn. Years later he wrote a book, Custer's Fall, *from the perspective of the Indians. The Reagans had recently returned from their trip to Ireland in June 1984.*

Mr. J. Neil Reagan
Rancho Santa Fe, California
June 21, 1984[11]

Dear Moon:

Just a quick line to let you know I got your letter and have arranged for the V.I.P. White House Tour. I can't do the book foreword for David Miller but I'll write and

---

* This refers to the opening of the Ronald Reagan Boyhood Home museum in Dixon, Illinois, in February 1984.

let him know. I'm sorry because I'm a fan of General George Armstrong Custer. The problem is it would be commercializing the office, etc.

I'm sorry to hear about your hand. You know I've been thinking about an operation after the election on that one bent finger of mine. It's not curled over as much as yours but you're giving me some second thoughts.*

Ireland was great. You can add "Mary Queen of Scots" to the family tree. They brought in a young man who is actually of our family line and it was a shock to all of us, there actually was a physical resemblance. All in all it was a great experience. I saw the book and the original handwritten record of our great, grandfather's baptism at age three days in 1829.

Nancy sends her love to you both as do I.

Dutch

In the early summer of 1954 Reagan starred with Barbara Stanwyck in the movie, Cattle Queen of Montana. *The picture was shot in Glacier National Park in Montana, and Reagan played an undercover army officer sent to track down Indian disturbances. Later he said making the film was "like playing cowboy and Indian."* †

When he addressed this letter to his daughter, Patti, she was 21 months old.

Patti Reagan
Pacific Palisades, California
July 12, 1954 [12]

Dear Patti:

I thought I'd better write and explain why you aren't finding me in the usual place these mornings. I had to come way up here to a beautiful place called "Glacier Park" in order to keep alive the myth that I'm a working man. This won't take too long and then I'll be home saying "Boo Patti" to you and "Deedee and Teddy and Saing".

This place is beautiful with granite peaks and lakes and glaciers—and contrary to what the studio told me it is rather cool. Therefore unless the weather changes I have all the wrong clothes with me. That isn't serious however because by tonight the wardrobe man will be here with my picture clothes and I'll wear them most of the time.

Incidentally we are way up on the continental divide near the Canadian border and they tell us it is not uncommon to see the northern lights. The altitude is such that if you walk and talk at the same time (a thing not entirely foreign to my nature) you have to pause for a few deep breaths.

There were no "Northern lights" last night but there was a big moon and a

---

* The two brothers had the same affliction, Dupuytren's contracture, a condition that pulls one or two fingers into the palm of the hand—usually requiring surgery to remedy.

† Anne Edwards, *Early Reagan* (New York: William Morrow, 1987), p. 451.

sky full of stars shining down on the glaciers and snow covered peaks. It was a beautiful night with a constant breeze that seems to have come from out among the stars and it seems at times that if you listen very carefully it will whisper secrets as old as time.

Pretty soon the moon and the stars and this breeze got together and filled me with a longing so great that it seemed I'd die of pain if I couldn't reach out and touch your Mommie. You aren't old enough to really understand what I mean but you will someday. Right now just imagine what you feel like when you want "num num" real bad and it isn't in sight and when you want to hold Teddy real tight—put this all together, double it and it is just a faint hint of how I feel.

Maybe it is a good thing to be apart now and then. Not that I have to be away from your Mommie to know how much I love her but a thirst now and then makes you know and remember how really sweet the water is.

I'm counting on you to take care of Mommie and keep her safe for me because there wouldn't be any moon or stars in the sky without her. The breeze would whisper no secrets and the warmth would go out of the sun. So you guard her very carefully and then you'll always have a pair of footsteps to follow, and if you follow her footsteps you'll grow up to be a sweet, lovely person just made for love.

This love is why we are apart right now. You see we want you to always be surrounded with love so you'll know how important it is. So now we taste of loneliness in order to share some of our love with you. We are happy to do this because you are very much a part of our love.

Just guard her and keep her safe till I come home—because I love her and you very much.

Daddy

P.S. My address here is St. Marys
Browning, Montana.

When Patti was 13 years old she went to the Orme School in Arizona. Founded in 1929, the coed school was located on a 40,000-acre working cattle ranch near Flagstaff. She turned herself in for breaking the rules of the school by smoking, and Reagan tries to persuade his 15-year-old daughter of the virtues of truth-telling.

Miss Patti Reagan
The Orme School
Mayer, Arizona
March 5, 1968 [13]

Dear Patti:

Yes—turning yourself in was the right thing to do and I'm sure you feel better for having done it. I'm sure you realize also that it was proper for the school to impose a punishment as they did. If we could pay for rule breaking just by confessing it there wouldn't be much law and order. In the Bible we can read where Jesus heard confessions and promised forgiveness but on the condition that we would go forth and not commit the sin again.

These are two issues here Dear Patti. One is the fact that for two years you broke not only school rules but family rules and to do this you had to resort to tricks and deception. Why is this of such great concern to the school or to me and your mother? The answer is very simple. We are concerned that you can establish a pattern of living wherein you accept dishonesty as a way of life.

Let's turn from you and translate it into someone else. Would you be happy if you weren't sure that I was quite honest? Would you be comfortable if you had to wonder whether you could believe things I said? Or if perhaps now you had to worry that maybe I was being dishonest in this job—that some day the paper would carry a story exposing me as a lawbreaker? You know the answer of course. But don't you see—compromising with truth no matter how trivial does something to us. The next time it serves our purpose we do it again and one day we find ourselves in trouble and we're not quite sure why or how.

Now issue number two—smoking itself. I'm sure I don't have to repeat all the reasons why it's bad for you. Science leaves us very little doubt about it anymore. Yes I know many adults continue to smoke but I don't know any <u>who don't wish they could quit</u>. That alone should tell you something—if they want to quit and can't that's pretty good proof that tobacco is capable of forming a habit stronger than human will power. Unfortunately women are more susceptible to habits than men and find them much harder to break or change. How many I've seen (among our friends) pregnant and told by the doctor that smoking during pregnancy would harm their baby—but the habit was too strong. You see it's very hard to do something wrong and just hurt yourself.

I enjoyed your poem although I read a touch of nostalgia. There is nothing wrong with that all our lives we build memories and the important thing is to build happy ones. I too will remember the ranch with nostalgia but with great warmth for the happy days spent there. You'll be part of those memories—sitting up on a big black horse (Baby) in front of my saddle—splashing in the pool (without bathing suit) at age three and getting your own first horse.

What keeps the memory from haunting us with unhappiness is if we have moved on to some things equally or more enjoyable. For example I built and loved a small ranch in the valley before you were born. I remember it happily but then came the ranch you knew—now there will be another ranch and so it goes. There was Baby, then Nancy D. and now it will be "Little Man." Life is to remember with pleasure and look forward with anticipation. Your poem will add to the pleasure of remembering when we must leave this ranch and thank you for it.

I must go now. I hope you'll accept and work out your hours without bitterness and with the intention of not repeating the act that brought them about. I hope too you'll continue to improve in your studies.

We are all looking forward to Easter vacation together at Bama Deedees and Bapas.* They were over here for our wedding anniversary yesterday. You'll probably quit writing poems if you think each one will bring on a four page letter from me. I promise not to do this often.

Love,
Dad

Soon after, he writes Patti again after receiving her grades in the mail.

Miss Patti Reagan
The Orme School
Mayer, Arizona
April 2, 1968 [14]

Dear Patti:

I know we'll be seeing you soon, so this won't be too much of a letter, but I did want to tell you your grades came, and not only were we thrilled and very proud of you, but even more so at the things your teachers wrote about your attitude towards your studies and about your ability and participation. We're very happy.

I've enclosed this page of the paper on Bonnie and Clyde, and I'm sure your reaction is going to be that I did it as a kind of "I told you so", but it isn't that at all. Knowing your interest in writing I thought that here was a great example of how a screen writer, wanting to make a successful and entertaining picture, used some of the truth and then used dramatic license where necessary to make his story successful. You can compare that to this story, where the author's purpose was completely different in that he wanted to write a factual account.

You'll see passages in here and recognize how, in some instances, they were truthful in the picture, but in others they altered the facts for dramatic purposes. You can even see the possibilities that they wanted to go in another direction. For example, suppose they wanted to make a hero of the Texas Ranger. Then he would have been the central figure, with a story written about his almost ruined career and his effort to reestablish himself, and then, of course, Bonnie and Clyde would have appeared as the villains.

At any rate, I think you'll find this most interesting now that you've seen the picture.

Again, though, we're very proud of you.

Love,
Dad

---

* Edith and Loyal Davis, her grandparents.

On a Wednesday night, June 5, 1968, in the kitchen of the Ambassador Hotel in Los Angeles, Sirhan Sirhan shot Robert F. Kennedy at point-blank range just after he had addressed his presidential campaign supporters. Kennedy died early the next morning at age 42. It shocked the nation. Reagan, then governor of California, writes to his daughter that same evening.

Miss Patti Reagan
The Orme School
Mayer, Arizona
June 5, 1968[15]

Dear Patti:

As you know, and as Mommie has told you, I've been in and out and up and down the state, so I'm a little late in answering your letter.

We still have some time about your question as to schools, so let me see what I can find out about everything around here with regard to that senior year.

I know you are concerned, as all of us are, about what happened here. It is a great tragedy, just as it was a great tragedy for his brother.* I've been here in the office all day, and feeling almost sick most of the time. Even though I disagree with him on political matters and even though I disapprove of him and his approach to these problems, I still feel very deeply the tragedy of this young man taken from his family in this way. I don't mean to make this sound so final, but the latest word we've been getting is one that the condition is very grave. Of course you'll know the answer by the time you read this as to how great the tragedy is or whether things are going to turn for the better.

In all of this sometimes one can learn why a certain course has been followed. There are many times when I have wondered why I'm doing what I'm doing.† Now is one of those moments when I'm grateful that I can be in a position to perhaps change things to see that we do start a return to sanity and law and order and turn away from this whole creed of violence that seems to be so prevalent in our land.

Isn't it strange, a few months ago our friend in Washington ‡ told me that she foresaw a tragedy for him before the election. She didn't know whether it would be in the nature of illness or accident, but that there would be a tragedy befall him.

I must run now.

Love,
Dad

---

* The assassination of John F. Kennedy, five years earlier.

† Reagan is now 57 years old.

‡ Probably refers to the psychic Jeane Dixon (1918–1997), who claims to have foreseen in 1968 that Robert F. Kennedy would never become president because of "a tragedy" in the Ambassador Hotel.

Ron Reagan was only eight years old when his father got him some personal photos of his then idol, Roman Gabriel, quarterback for the Los Angeles Rams in the National Football League. George Shuman was the photographer.

> Al Larson
> Long Beach, California
> January 17, 1967 [16]

Dear Mr. Larson:

You were very kind to send me the photos and I'm most grateful.

The Skipper has quite a case of hero worship for Roman Gabriel, so that picture is on his wall already.

Will you please tell George Shuman how much we both appreciate having the pictures.

> Best regards,
> Ronald Reagan

Founded in 1922, the Webb School was a college prep boarding school in Claremont, California. Reagan writes to his son, Ron, in his sophomore year, giving him fatherly advice and urging him to work harder on his grades.

> Ronald Reagan
> Webb School
> Claremont, California
> Circa 1972 [17]

Dear Son:

This letter may ramble a bit because it has to do with some concerns of mine. I suppose they are concerns every father has as he watches his son go through each year and period of life that he himself went through and remembers so much more clearly than you might think the opportunities he missed and the needless mistakes he made.

Some fathers get so uptight in their concern they wind up trying to relive their own youth by stage-directing their son's life. I hope by now I've convinced you this is not my intention or desire. Some fathers cop out and, under the pretense of being a 'pal,' don't set any ground rules at all, and thus avoid having to make any tough decisions. This I have no intention of doing.

These concerns have been on my mind for some time, and so has this letter. Now it has been triggered by your report card. You did fine in Ancient History— B+. You also had a B+ in English I, but an unsatisfactory effort. This makes the B+ less to be desired than a lower grade if the lower grade represented the absolute best effort of which you were capable. But then comes a lesser grade, a C- in French I, with a notation that, "The quality of work has diminished quite a bit." Again I say the C- would be all right with me if it represented your best try. This would be true also of the D in Algebra I, but the effort was rated unsatisfactory and the teacher's notation read, "Ron has been relying on last year too long—he'd better force himself to get to work or he'll be in trouble."

Everything in life has a price and our biggest mistakes are when we don't really ask the price before we make our choice. Do you remember our Christmas shopping and the jolt you had when you had the gift wrapped and then heard the price?

The "trouble" the algebra teacher mentioned is the price you pay for not forcing yourself to work at something that is less interesting than other things you'd rather do. For example, the price can be ineligibility for outside activities, including athletics. It can be cancellation of summer plans because you have to make up credits in summer school. It can be limitation of your choice of colleges because you don't meet the requirements of the ones you'd really like. It can even be taking five years to get through school instead of four, and actually it can be all of these, which is quite a price to pay for a little goofing off.

This period of the school year, whether it be high school or college, is the toughest. Don't ask me why, but it's always been true. This is when the excitement of fall and starting the new year seems a long way back and the summer an even longer way ahead. It's easy to get bored, to complain about everything and to think the school and everyone connected with it are out to ruin your life. This is when you have to remember the price for giving up and copping out. It's also the time when you build some character muscle to see you through real problems that come along later in life. And they do come along.

It's only a few years now (they seem many to you) until you'll be out of school and really beginning your life. All that has gone before and these remaining few years of school and college are "spring training" for the real season. When we are young we look at adults going about their day-to-day work and it all seems pretty dull and uninteresting. Believe me, that isn't so. I can't remember a time since graduation when I've been bored. Finding the thing you want to do and making a go of it is next in importance to finding the person you want to share your life with.

Here again what you do now affects the choices you have. When I was announcing sports I was happy and thought that was all I wanted out of life. Then came the chance at Hollywood and that was even better. Now I'm doing something that makes everything else I've done seem dull as dishwater when I look back. But without some of the things I had to learn in college and didn't particularly care about, without some of the chores I didn't like when I was doing the GE television show, I couldn't do and wouldn't have had the chance to do what I'm doing now.

We don't know what turns our life will take or what doors will open and there is nothing worse than to have such a door open and then learn you gave away your admittance ticket back in your school days.

The other day when we were talking about the POWs we spoke of self-discipline and how it saved their lives. There is an inner man within all of us we have to call on once in a while. Having the guts to do the nasty little boring tasks, sticking to them when we'd rather goof off, decides whether that inner man has enough muscle to be of any help when we need him.

Six months ago in the graduating class of the California Highway Patrol Academy there was a young man who led the class. He really wanted a career in the patrol and being top man in that class took a lot of doing, both in the brain and the muscle departments. A couple of weeks ago on the San Bernardino Freeway a drunk driver hit him and sheared his right leg off below the knee. Can you imagine what life looked like to him and his young wife? Oh sure, he'd get a pension, he wouldn't starve, but what would he do with his life besides sit on the front porch? Well, it won't be that way. He bought more than that with his willingness to put out at the academy. We are going to break the old rules and when he's up and on an artificial leg we are putting him back on duty as a patrolman. Now he has a double job—he has a chance if he makes it to open the door for others who suffer disabling injuries so they won't wind up in a rocker on the front porch. Think of the price he might be paying now if he'd decided to be just another kid "getting by" when he was in the academy.

Well, if you've read this far let me just wrap it up by telling you your mother and I have known many moments of great pride in you. We've also known moments of doubt in ourselves; times when we've worried as to whether we've made that inner man as strong as he'll need to be sometime later in life when you call on him for help.

Keep an eye on the price tag; some things are very expensive and you pay for the rest of your life.

Love,
Dad

Reagan replies to a writer's questions about his children.

Miss Anita Summer
Circa early 1975 [18]

Dear Miss Summer:

Enclosed is the eight-by-ten glossy you requested and the answer to your reader's question.

Only one of our children is at home, our son Ron now approaching 17, a junior in high school. Understandably he would be a little embarrassed by press attention. Our daughter Patti, 22, is aspiring to a musical career including the writing of music. My son and daughter, Mike and Maureen, are grown. Mike is doing very well in the boat business and Maureen is a very talented (I'm proud to say) hostess on radio and TV talk shows.

[letter incomplete]

An old friend tells Governor Reagan that a visitor to his home, Ruth Shelton of Honolulu, had seen Maureen, his daughter (now 28 years old), on television, and had "praised her poise and intelligence."

Mr. Laurence Beilenson
Beverly Hills, California
September 29, 1969 [19]

Dear Larry:

Just a line to thank you for your kindness in passing the word about Maureen.

It's amazing how easily you can lose track of the day to day activities of your fledglings once they take wing on their own. I was glad to hear about her.

Best regards,
Ron

Maureen was deeply involved in women's campaign activities and served a two-year term as co-chair of the Republican National Committee. Jeane Kirkpatrick was ambassador to the United Nations, and a neoconservative who had been a Democrat until the 1980s.

The Honorable Jeane Kirkpatrick
New York, New York
March 29, 1985 [20]

Dear Jeane:

I'm sorry I can't be with you in person but believe me my heart is there. Being a convert myself, let me say a heartfelt welcome and assure you the water is just fine on this side of the dam and I'm sure you'll be very happy among us Elephants. I can tell you we're more than happy to have you.

You are being hosted by the GOP Women's Political Action League at their first major function. Carla Hills, Nancy Reynolds* and my daughter Maureen came together on a very wonderful idea and all the others there tonight also thought it was a great idea. They have come together to raise money and provide support for women candidates for state and federal offices.

In 1984 our party had a net gain of ninety-five women legislators at state and federal level—a record. The goal is record numbers in '85 and '86. So you see, here

---

* Carla Hills was named secretary of the Department of Housing and Urban Development in 1975 by President Ford, becoming the third woman to hold a U.S. cabinet post. In 1989 she was named the U.S. trade representative by President Bush. Nancy Reynolds began working for Nancy Reagan as her press secretary after the 1968 Republican convention and became Nancy's chief assistant and friend for many years.

is a new world to conquer which is just what you did as a truly great ambassador to the United Nations.

Thank you and God bless you.

Sincerely,
Ronald Reagan

———————

Michael Reagan was 26 years old when he married his first wife, Julie, who was 18. Just before the wedding in Hawaii on June 13, 1971, he received this letter from his father, giving him advice on how to stay happily married. Michael's marriage lasted a year and then dissolved. He married again in 1975.

Michael Reagan
Manhattan Beach, California
June 1971 [21]

Dear Mike:

Enclosed is the item I mentioned (with which goes a torn up IOU). I could stop here but I won't.

You've heard all the jokes that have been rousted around by all the "unhappy marrieds" and cynics. Now, in case no one has suggested it, there is another viewpoint. You have entered into the most meaningful relationship there is in all human life. It can be whatever you decide to make it.

Some men feel their masculinity can only be proven if they play out in their own life all the locker-room stories, smugly confident that what a wife doesn't know won't hurt her. The truth is, somehow, way down inside, without her ever finding lipstick on the collar or catching a man in the flimsy excuse of where he was till three A.M., a wife does know, and with that knowing, some of the magic of this relationship disappears. There are more men griping about marriage who kicked the whole thing away themselves than there can ever be wives deserving of blame. There is an old law of physics that you can only get out of a thing as much as you put in it. The man who puts into the marriage only half of what he owns will get that out. Sure, there will be moments when you will see someone or think back on an earlier time and you will be challenged to see if you can still make the grade, but let me tell you how really great is the challenge of proving your masculinity and charm with one woman for the rest of your life. Any man can find a twerp here and there who will go along with cheating, and it doesn't take all that much manhood. It does take quite a man to remain attractive and to be loved by a woman who has heard him snore, seen him unshaven, tended him while he was sick and washed his dirty underwear. Do that and keep her still feeling a warm glow and you will know some very beautiful music. If you truly love a girl, you shouldn't ever want her to feel, when she sees you greet a secretary or a girl you both know, that humiliation of wondering if she was someone who caused you to be late coming home, nor should you want any other woman to be able to meet your wife and know she was smiling behind her eyes as she looked at her, the woman you love, remembering this was the woman you rejected even momentarily for her favors.

Mike, you know better than many what an unhappy home is and what it can do to others. Now you have a chance to make it come out the way it should. There is no greater happiness for a man than approaching a door at the end of a day knowing someone on the other side of that door is waiting for the sound of his footsteps.

Love,
Dad

P.S. You'll never get in trouble if you say "I love you" at least once a day.

The four-year-old son* of Michael Reagan sent President Reagan a birthday card on his 72nd birthday.

Cameron Michael Reagan
Sherman Oaks, California
February 10, 1983 [22]

Dear Cameron:

Thank you very much for your nice birthday card and your good wishes. I know you signed it yourself too and that's fine.

Would you please tell your Mother and Father I received their card. It was very nice. Give them my love and tell them I appreciated the message on the card. Be sure and tell them and it will save me having to write another letter.

Again thanks.

Love,
Grandpa
(The man on T.V.)

Reagan writes to Michael's newborn baby daughter, Ashley.

Miss Ashley Marie Reagan
Sherman Oaks, California
May 10, 1983 [23]

Dear Ashley Marie: †

Your grandmother Nancy and I want to welcome you into the world. We're happy you are here and while we haven't been able to meet you in person yet (our job makes such pleasures hard to come by) we look forward to meeting you.

----

* Cameron Reagan was born on May 30, 1978.

† When Ashley was born the Secret Service agents immediately gave her the code name reserved for her—"Raindrop." This was probably a derivative of Nancy Reagan's Secret Service code name "Rainbow."

I know you've made your mother and father very proud and happy as well as your "big" brother Cameron Michael. There is a picture of you being held by Cameron on my desk so we know you are very pretty.

This world you are now a part of can be a very wonderful and exciting place and you can make it even more so by being a part of it. Give our love to your mother, father and brother and don't grow up too fast.

> Love,
> Your grandfather—RR

Michael Reagan had been a world champion ocean boat racer in the 1970s. In 1983 he agreed to drive a Wellcraft Scarab boat in a 605-mile race from Chicago on Lake Michigan to Detroit on Lake Huron. The twelve-hour race was called "Assault on the Great Lakes."

> Michael Yedor
> Beverly Hills, California
> September 12, 1983 [24]

Dear Mr. Yedor:

Thank you very much for sending me the tape on Mike's "Assault on the Great Lakes." It goes without saying I watched it with great interest and pleasure. It was done with dignity and class and I might add excitement, when the boat was completely leaving the water as it came off those waves.

Please give my regards to Eric Sherman.* It's hard for me to realize *The Hasty Heart* † was 34 years ago. I imagine my memories are clearer than his.

Again thanks and best regards.

> Ronald Reagan

Reagan belatedly responds to an Easter greeting from Michael, and encloses $50 checks for Cameron and Ashley Marie.

> Mr. and Mrs. Michael Reagan
> Sherman Oaks, California
> May 5, 1984 [25]

Dear Colleen and Mike:

Thank you for our Easter greeting which caught up with us at trip's end. What with the trip and all Easter got away from us—we're sorry. Actually it didn't dawn on us til we boarded the plane for Hawaii and our first stop that it was Easter.

---

* Eric Sherman, the director of "Assault on the Great Lakes," was the son of Vincent Sherman, the director of the 1949 movie, *The Hasty Heart.*

† Reagan had starred in the movie *The Hasty Heart* (1949), considered one of his best movies.

The enclosed are for a belated Easter for Cameron and Ashley Marie. Give them a hug for us.

Love,
Grandma and Grandpa

Patti Reagan became an antinuclear activist in the 1970s and argued the issue with her father, as Reagan describes here. Karen Silkwood was an antinuclear activist who questioned alleged violations of health regulations in the Kerr-McGee nuclear company where she was a member of the Oil, Chemical and Atomic Workers Union. She was killed in a car crash in 1974 that some felt was suspicious; her death was litigated until 1986, and made famous in the 1983 film Silkwood.

Mr. William F. Buckley, Jr.
New York, New York
July 15, 1981 [26]

Dear Bill:

Thank you very much for your engineering of the delivery of the information on Karen Silkwood and the magazine to California. We took them to the ranch. Patti came, and we had a good long discussion.

I was able to lower the boom with the Karen Silkwood case. She went no further with that particular subject. She read the article but, then, of course, wanted me to read or meet with scientists of another view on nuclear energy. I told her that I had done all those things and had had those writings analyzed by my own advisers, and there was no need for me to meet with any of these people. She then, however, asked if I could arrange for her to meet with someone in the science field of my side. I have just signed Jay Keyworth to be my science adviser. I told him of my personal problem and asked if he knew anyone who might be willing to talk to her, and he volunteered and said that he would particularly like to do that because he's had great experience with students who share those views.

So, on her next trip to Washington—he'll be here by then—I shall get them together. I think my biggest problem is, believe it or not, her friendship and admiration for Jane Fonda and Tom Hayden. I told her bluntly I could not share those feelings because both, in my mind, were traitors to their country. I didn't really try to argue that point with her because I know there's nothing harder than driving a wedge between friends—and she believes they are friends.

Bill, I appreciated very much George Will's letter regarding Bob Bork. I am going forward on this first court appointment with a woman to get my campaign promise out of the way. I'm happy to say I had to make no compromise with quality. She is truly excellent, and I believe will make a fine Justice.* But, so far, the

---

* In 1981 President Reagan named Sandra Day O'Connor of the Arizona Court of Appeals as the first woman on the U.S. Supreme Court.

person highest on the list for the next appointment, which I hope will be soon, is Bob Bork. If you don't mind, I'm going to show Bill Smith, Ed, [*] and the others, George's letter, which brings up a human side not normally available when you are judging a man's qualifications. Let me say, in our search, we found no one superior to him.

Thanks again for all your help and congratulations on the wonderful job you're doing in Kabul.[†] As soon as you have that cleaned up, maybe Namibia?

Nancy sends her love and please give our love to Pat.

Best regards,
Ron

Helen Caldicott is an Australian physician, known for her antinuclear activism. The founder of Physicans for Social Responsibility, she influenced many people during the 1980s. She had become close to Patti Reagan in 1982.

Patti (Reagan) Davis
Circa December 1982 [27]

Dear Patti:

We've had to go to the Kennedy Center. As you know I've been in South America and only got in late last night when I discovered our meeting has been moved to 5:15 tomorrow afternoon. Had you been notified of this? If not can you let Dr. Caldicott know?

We'll meet downstairs in the library instead of the office—no interruptions there.

Patti I think we should keep this a personal private visit. I won't be saying anything to the press about it and I don't think you or the doctor should either. That way they can't get into any stories about family disagreements etc.

We'll see you later.

Love,
Dad

On May 22, 1983, a UPI story reported that Dr. Helen Caldicott said "she spoke with Reagan Saturday for an hour and 15 minutes." Caldicott "accused Reagan of believing that the United States could engage in a nuclear war against the Soviet Union and win."

Later, Reagan wrote that "Patti had told me Dr. Caldicott had promised that if I spoke to her [in 1982] she would say nothing publicly about the conversation."[‡]

---

[*] William French Smith was attorney general; Edwin Meese III was counselor to the president.

[†] In their long correspondence the standing joke between Reagan and Buckley was that Buckley was the "Ambassador to Afghanistan," living in the embassy in Kabul.

[‡] Reagan, *An American Life*, p. 566.

Patti (Reagan) Davis
May 23, 1983[28]

Dear Patti:

The enclosed appeared in today's *Washington Post*. It has caused quite a stir in the press. Of course no such conversation took place nor have I had any conversation with her since we met in December. And as you know her words about my believing we could win a nuclear war were never part of that visit in December (I don't believe such a thing). So her speech is a complete falsehood both as to having a conversation with me at all and as to the subject of the supposed conversation.

Patti it isn't easy to learn we've misplaced our faith and trust in someone. I know. I've had that experience—once with someone I thought was my closest friend. But when it happens we must be prepared to accept it and not shut our eyes to the truth.

There was a time in ancient days when a messenger bringing bad news was put to death. I hope you won't call for my execution. I'm afraid the doctor is so carried away by her cause she subscribes to the belief that the end justifies the means. Such a belief if widespread would mean the end of civilization.

Love,
Dad

Reagan sends a letter to some of his old friends as he nears the end of his two terms as governor of California.

Reverend and Mrs. Ben H. Cleaver
Cape Girardeau, Missouri
October 25, 1973[29]

Dear Friends:

I'm afraid as the children grew older we grew forgetful about keeping up on family photos.

Here is the last one taken. Patti is now 21, and Ron is a gangly (football playing) 15 with long hair I regret to say. The style or fad continues to flourish here on the coast. He's alright, though, and is a pretty rugged kid.

Thank you for your kind words and thoughts. Your letters always brighten the day.

About that decision—I figure whatever course has been planned for me will be made evident.

Love,
Dutch

In this letter to his favorite fan Reagan describes what his son, Ron—now 21 years old—is doing. Mel Thomson was governor of New Hampshire. William "Bill" Loeb was the publisher of the Manchester Union Leader. *The author of the book,* Here's the Rest of Him, *was Kent Steffgen.*

> Mr. and Mrs. Elwood H. Wagner
> Philadelphia, Pennsylvania
> June 5, 1979 [30]

Dear Lorraine and Wag:

You've had quite a time with our friends at *Spotlight*. It makes you wonder what kind of an editor he is to write the insulting, sarcastic letter that he wrote. My own informants in Washington tell me that the man running *Spotlight* can literally be described as a Nazi.*

You asked about my affirming support for Red China. I think what he must be referring to is a passage in a speech in which I said that probably all of us, maybe I should have said most, approve of the bettering of relations with mainland China. That was not the issue. The issue was the dumping of a long time friend and ally, the Republic of China on Taiwan, and I then added that we could have had everything we now have with Red China without betraying Taiwan.

As for Mel Thomson, I don't know just what the situation is there. Mel, last time I spoke to him, was as friendly as he has always been. His close friend, Bill Loeb, the publisher of the paper there, is a little worried that Mel somehow has gone off the track, not with regard to me, but with the idea that possibly it is time for a third party or something of that sort.

I think that *Spotlight* is basing most of its articles on that book called, *Here's the Rest of Him*, but I also believe the same author has now come out with a new book that is something of a rehash of the first.

I will look into the matter of the radio scripts. We've had some changes of personnel at the office. That might have accounted for it. We aren't doing reruns—I am continuing to come up with new ones every week.

Regarding the date for the declaration, we have no such date—we just know it's going to come sometime this fall.

And the ranch name is *Rancho del Cielo,* which means ranch in the sky. It was an old Spanish land grant—it's up at about a 2,400 foot level so we thought that name was kind of appropriate.

It's nice to hear about Sandy and Scott, give them my best. I am very familiar with the Ambassador East. It used to be the dining spot when you would come

---

* Willis A. Carto, who was born in 1926, founded and controlled Liberty Lobby, the organization that published *Spotlight*.

into Chicago by train from the west and leave that night for New York on the Century.

Patti is doing some singing and song writing and a little TV work. She has had bit parts on a couple of *Love Boat* shows, and Ron has a scholarship in New York. He is all wrapped up in dancing. The ballet kind, believe it or not. It all started a few years ago when he was playing football and basketball and that idea hit the athletic world that ballet was a great exercise for athletes. Even the pros were getting into it. It caught his fancy, and I hasten to assure you he is an athlete and all man, and he's working like the devil at this, knowing that possibly he waited and started too late in life, but he wants to give it a try.

Thanks again for taking on *Spotlight*, but don't look forward to converting them. I think they are beyond help.

All the best,

Ron

Ron and his wife, Doria, sent President Reagan a pair of moccasins along with a postcard featuring a photo of Reagan in the 1930s, posing for an art class naked save for a pair of white shorts. The students surrounding him have their brushes poised.

Mr. and Mrs. Ron Reagan
New York, New York
July 25, 1983 [31]

Dear Ron and Doria:

I'll bet I can make two or even three miles in these moccasins. Thank you very much.

But about that card—you should have heard me scream when that fellow with the brush touched me.

Should I try for a royalty from that card company or just shut them down for selling pornographic postcards? Truth is that isn't really me—I was never that young.

As for that card you sent your mother—I was gorgeous in a tux but ugly as sin in a dress. I've thrown the dress away. It didn't do a thing for me.

We're looking forward to seeing you at Camp David. You might say a prayer about the weather. We had 14 straight weekends of rain this spring and early summer.

Thanks again for my moccasins. I really do like them.

Love,
Dad

Reagan muses about what his ranch means to him as he gets ready to run for president in 1980.

> Mr. William Loeb
> Manchester, New Hampshire
> June 29, 1979 [32]

Dear Bill:

It was good to get your letter and to hear about Mel.* I will keep in touch. Your story about young Bush is very interesting and dovetails with a few other things we've heard from that direction.

It is, as you say, too early to be making any decisions about that †—one almost has to wait and see how the campaign shapes up. Of course, one also has to consider that it might not be my problem. I don't want to get in the frame of mind of President Dewey.

Nancy and I are looking forward to August and think it's pretty necessary in view of the pace we have been keeping. Some place along the line, a fella has to have time to sit on a hill and think, or maybe just sit on a hill. I'll be happier knowing you are going to keep the folks there busy while I'm sitting.

Rainbow ‡ sends her best and our regards to Nackey.

> Best regards,
> Ron

Recovering from the assassination attempt on his life Reagan muses about his ranch and allows that he owns guns, and likes to shoot—but only at targets and tin cans.

> Miss Kristine M. Smith
> Eatonville, Washington
> June 19, 1981 [33]

Dear Miss Smith:

Thank you very much for your letter. I think it is especially kind of you to write with the warmth that you did since you feel we have so little in common ideologically. I am most grateful and happy to tell you that I am fully recovered now and feeling just fine.

I have a feeling that if we had an opportunity to visit, you would find we aren't as incompatible as you might think. I grew up a New Deal Democrat but found later on that the party had taken certain courses I could not follow. Beyond that,

---

* Meldrim Thomson, Jr. was the governor of New Hampshire, 1973–79.
† The vice presidential nomination.
‡ Secret Service code name for Nancy Reagan.

while I like to shoot and have some guns, my shooting is done at targets and tin cans. I am not a hunter and never a trapper.

I do find a sympathy, coming from the West, with the sagebrush rebellion. I don't think it's right for the federal government to own as much as 80% of a state.

As for animals, we have four dogs and seven horses and rejoice in the fact that when we ride on our ranch, we see mountain lion and bear tracks every once in awhile.

Again, thanks and best regards.

Sincerely,
Ronald Reagan

Reagan apologizes to a neighbor of his California ranch for the press corps and helicopter noise disturbing her tranquility.

Mrs. Glen Hancock
Goleta, California
August 3, 1981 [34]

Dear Mrs. Hancock:

I tried to call you several times after receiving your letter of July 9, using the number on your stationery, but there was no answer. So I'll have to try and cover the points in your letter with this one.

I'm confused about one or two things you said. One is your reference to patrolling planes and 'copters as a nuisance. Actually, all we have are the helicopters that take our people back and forth at the end of their work shifts and, of course, those that bring us in, which has only happened three times in the more than six months I've been president. I wonder if what you might be talking about was a period when they used military helicopters to bring in some of the communication equipment and temporary quarters for security personnel, things which I'm afraid just go with the job.

You remarked about the expense. Let me point out that we are not having a western White House. But it is a fact, and one beyond my control, that there must be communication facilities for those times when I might be there. There also is permanent security, and on the basis of what happened March 30, I guess there is evidence that such security is needed. It is true that gravel was brought up there for a parking area for the security and communication vehicles, also for the area where the helicopters land. But everything that is brought in there in the line of buildings for communication equipment is temporary and will be removed by the government when I'm no longer president.

I'm sorry about the harassment you mentioned on the part of the press. I can assure you they harass me more than a little also. They are the free press and seem bound and determined to trail me and report on whatever may be going on.

I am also puzzled by your reference to my changing the flow of the watershed, both when I was Governor and now. I know of nothing that could be interpreted as doing that. We are drilling a new well, but that's because the well we've had barely provides water for domestic use.

Mrs. Hancock—I love the area and the canyon as you say you do. It is our home. We are selling our residence in Los Angeles. I don't believe I could meet the requirements of this job if I could not look forward to an occasional few days there on the mountain that I love so much.

As I said, I have no control over some of the necessities that now go with me wherever I go. Let me give you an example. Recently, Nancy and I were invited to a Sunday lunch at a home in Virginia about an hour away from the White House. I was totally surprised to find that even for that lunch that near to Washington, the Signal communications equipment I mentioned earlier had to be established at that place so whatever might happen in the line of an emergency in the world, I would be within instant communication.

I'm sorry for any inconvenience that has been caused you and hope you'll understand what I feel is my need to now and then get to our ranch and do the things I've always loved doing.

> Best regards,
> Ronald Reagan

Reagan describes the first lengthy time he has spent at his ranch since becoming president.

> Mr. and Mrs. John Otis Carney
> Coro, Wyoming
> September 15, 1981 [35]

Dear Otis and Teddy:

How wonderful it was to get your letter. Nancy and I both thank you so much for your prayers and for your generous words.

We've just come back from having about 20 days at our ranch. I don't mind admitting I'm having a little trouble getting back into the Washington routine. We rode every morning, and every afternoon there were a million things to be done.

We had a freak storm in the spring that dumped eight inches of wet snow on the ranch, and I think there must be ten thousand oak limbs and trees that were downed by that heavy snow. Although we couldn't use all that firewood in the next 20 years, most of our afternoons were spent with chainsaws, jeep, and trailer, cutting off the little limbs and saving the logs for firewood. We brushpiled the other and are waiting for the rainy season to burn it. We never had to say, "What will we do?" We knew those fallen limbs were waiting for us just any time.

Nevertheless, it was fun, and I enjoyed every scratch and bruise and sore muscle.

King City doesn't seem too far away from our ranch there in the hills so maybe our paths will cross. Certainly, the two of us hope so. And we'll be looking for the new book.

Nancy sends her love to you both and so do I and, again, thank you.

Sincerely,
Ron

A 15-year-old girl adopted a horse—half thoroughbred, half quarter horse—through a 4H program and was told that her horse's mother's name was "Ronnies Baby" and was once owned by Reagan. She wrote to ask, "Is this true?" and hoped Reagan might be able to tell her "from the horse's mouth."

Miss Melissa Garrett
Pembroke Pines, Florida
July 2, 1985 [36]

Dear Melissa:

Congratulations on your new mount. The picture shows she is a beauty.

I think I can straighten out the ownership situation of Ronnies Baby. For a time I was in the thoroughbred breeding business, raising and selling yearlings at the annual California Thoroughbred Breeders Association sale. In doing this the yearlings were sold without names so the new owners who bought them for racing could have that privilege.

Desilu Productions was actually Desi Arnaz and Lucille Ball who were into racing. They bought one of my yearlings and since we knew each other quite well probably named it after me—"Ronnies Baby." I remember the night they bought my filly. While the bidding was going on I mentioned to Desi that I thought she was worth more than what was being bid. The next thing I knew he topped the final bid and bought her.

Well, all the best to you and happy riding. As the enclosed shows, I'm still in the saddle. This one is an Anglo-Arab (half thoroughbred and half Arabian) named El Alamein.

Best regards,
Ronald Reagan

An old friend from Eureka tells Reagan about her family and farm, and how she heard a strange noise in her kitchen—and at 5:00 A.M. discovered a baby squirrel scampering on the top of the window drapes.

Mrs. Esther Ranes
Banner Elk, North Carolina
September 7, 1984 [37]

Dear Esther:

It was good to hear from you. Thank you for the kind words about my appearance in Dallas. You set me up for the whole week.

I enjoyed reading about your family and found myself envying your son the doctor who can combine the farm and his work. I wish I could do that with our ranch. Unfortunately the ranch is 3,000 miles from Washington.

You had quite an adventure with the squirrel. We've had that problem at the ranch with field mice. We learned they were sneaking in if we left the door open while we stepped outside even for a minute or two. Now we go in and out watching the floor and closing the door immediately.

Nancy sends her best as do I.

Sincerely,
Dutch

———

One of the things Reagan loved about his ranch were the wild animals. As this letter and the following one indicate, among them were bears and mountain lions.

Mr. Karl R. Mull
Santa Barbara, California
March 3, 1983 [38]

Dear Karl:

Sorry we didn't get to see you this time but thank you very much for the photos of our visitor's footprints. Back when we first got the ranch we were on the circuit of a bear, but no signs for several years until now.

I showed your photos to Prince Philip when he and the Queen were here. He heads up the international organization for the protection of wildlife. He was most interested.

I hope I get a glimpse of our bear one day, but not while on horseback—say just as I come around a sharp curve.

Again, thanks and,

Best regards,
Ronald Reagan

Miss Sam and Miss Bertha Sisco
Healdsburg, California
November 7, 1983 [39]

Dear Miss Sam and Miss Bertha and Buzzy:

I'm glad your predator was finally trapped. I know we have some but only because one of our dogs brought one in after a night's prowl. You asked about our other wildlife; well we're evidently on the travel path of a bear—it shows up periodically. One day one of our secret service agents was sitting up on a hill above our house and a mountain lion strolled by. The agent didn't know if that was commonplace or not so he just sat there. We also have wild cats, now and then coyotes but not too often—we're at about 2,400 ft. altitude.

Now just writing about it has made me homesick for the ranch and here I am off to Japan and Korea instead.

Best regards,
Ronald

———————

Reagan's ranch also had some rattlesnakes. He used to carry a pistol while riding, loaded with shot-shells, so he could kill any he ran into. But one day he got careless, as he explains to the Siscos, whose dog had been bitten.

Miss Sam and Miss Bertha Sisco
Healdsburg, California
July 15, 1987 [40]

Dear Miss Sam and Miss Bertha:

Well it was good to hear from you even if some of your news was unhappy. I know your distress at what happened to Dassy-Doo. I once had a dog bitten by a rattler while I was riding at the ranch. I killed the snake with a rock then rushed the dog to a vet and like in your case he recovered.

I have a feeling your problem right now is a result of the clearing of the nearby property. The same thing happened to us when we had a ranch near Malibu and there was a lot of clearing excavations for a sewer line through the adjoining land near our property line. My worst moment came when I sighted a rattler crawling toward some rocks and couldn't find a stick or stone handy. Being accustomed to always wearing high leather boots at the ranch I stomped on his head—then realized I was wearing sneakers that day. Someone must have been looking out for me.

Now, about Christmas; you are very kind but I just have to tell you we have no place for any more of your very handsome work. We both have and treasure the belts you did for us and our little ranch house is handsomely decorated with all the things you've so kindly made for us. You probably aren't aware or don't remember how many wonderful, carved leather works you have bestowed on us over the years. We love each and every one but honestly don't have a place for any more. We both thank you and wish you well in your memorial to dear Buzzy.

Thanks again.

Sincerely,
Ronald Reagan

CHAPTER THREE

Health and Personal Appearance

RONALD REAGAN IS *a big man—six feet, two inches tall, broad shouldered, almost 200 pounds, and built like a football tackle (which he was at Eureka College in the early 1930s). Until Alzheimer's disease set in, Reagan seemed to be unusually healthy, enthusiastically involved in many activities, and rarely sick.*

But if you look closely, his life was studded with serious illnesses and ailments that beset him throughout his career. He was near death as many as four times.

His first brush was bronchial pneumonia when he was seven years old. In 1918 there were no miracle drugs; penicillin was not discovered until 1929. He recalls little of that time, except that during his convalescence he had a bed full of lead toy soldiers lined up in battle formation. When he finally recovered his mother, Nelle, told him he "almost didn't make it."*

His second brush was in 1947 when he was 36 years old. Co-starring with Shirley Temple in a movie called That Hagen Girl, *he was suddenly struck with viral pneumonia, the kind miracle drugs didn't cure. For days he lay in the Cedars of Lebanon Hospital in Hollywood. It became so difficult to breathe he tried to give up and only a skillful nurse kept him breathing. He finally recovered, 17 pounds lighter, and spent many weeks where "the lightest effort brought on a shortness of breath."†*

Reagan's third and most serious brush with death was the assassination attempt on March 30, 1981. John Hinckley's bullet bounced off his car, flattened into the shape of a dime and penetrated his chest, barely missing his heart. He was rushed to the George Washington University Hospital in Washington, D.C., where his chest cavity

---

* Letter from Ronald Reagan to Frank Sullivan, January 25, 1988.
† Ronald Reagan, *Where's the Rest of Me?* (New York: Duell, Sloan and Pearce 1965), pp. 194–95.

rapidly filled with blood. The doctors saved him, barely. When he first came out of surgery he opened his eyes, saw the nurses dressed in white and turned to Nancy and asked, "Am I alive?"

His fourth time happened shortly thereafter. As he began to recover from surgery an infection, staphylococcus, set in. By that time security measures were so tight that no one outside the hospital learned of Reagan's second secret struggle to live. He survived, but the staph infection was a tightly held secret for many years.

Reagan had other ills, not life-threatening, but serious enough to take him out of action. In 1949, at age 38, he was blocked while running to first base in a benefit baseball game. His right thigh shattered in six pieces, and he was in traction in a hospital bed for many weeks. There was a long recovery period, with therapy. It was almost a year before he threw away his crutches and canes.

He had a number of operations: two for prostate problems, one in 1967 and one in 1987. No cancer was found. In 1985 he had major surgery for colon cancer, and a cancerous section of his intestine was removed.

Reagan's next health problem was Alzheimer's disease. He announced it in a handwritten letter to the nation on November 5, 1994—almost six years after he left office. We will never know for sure, but it appears that Alzheimer's did not strike until well after he left the presidency. Something did happen in Mexico six months after he left office that could have accelerated its onset.

On July 4, 1989, the White House put out a press release announcing that while horseback riding "at a private ranch in Mexico," Reagan's horse "bucked wildly several times on a rocky downhill slope and eventually stumbled."* Later reports indicate Reagan struck his head on a rock after the horse threw him.

On September 8, 1989—two months after striking his head—Reagan underwent surgery at the Mayo Clinic in Minnesota to relieve fluid build-up on his brain.† Holes were drilled into his skull to relieve the pressure on the brain. A massive contusion of the brain can impair perceiving, thinking, and remembering.

Edmund Morris, Reagan's selected biographer, later described it this way: "Everyone watching the Nixon funeral (on April 28, 1994) could plainly see that Ronald Reagan was in the preliminary stages of degenerative cognitive dementia. He . . . had known it, I suspect, ever since a riding accident in July 1989 had inflicted a massive contusion on his brain."

Nancy Reagan has said something similar:

"I've always had the feeling that the severe blow to his head in 1989 hastened the onset of Ronnie's Alzheimer's.

The doctors think so, too." ‡

---

* Marlin Fitzwater, *Statement on Ronald Reagan's Riding Accident,* The White House, July 4, 1989.

† Associated Press, September 8, 1989.

‡ Nancy Reagan, *I Love You, Ronnie: The Letters of Ronald Reagan to Nancy Reagan* (New York: Random House, 2000), p. 180.

Reagan had one other accident. Just as he was about to turn 90, after suffering six years of dementia, he fell in his Los Angeles home and fractured his hip. In ten days he was out of the hospital, and the doctors called his physical recovery "remarkable." But his brain was still broken.

In addition to disease, accidents, and attack he had some problems, common to many, with his eyesight and hearing. As a boy, he was seriously nearsighted, so much so he couldn't see the ball clearly enough to play baseball. He was forced to wear heavy eyeglasses until he switched to contact lenses, which he always wore for most of the rest of his life. The hearing in his right ear was damaged in 1939 while making a movie and seemed to get worse as he grew older. While president he received two new hearing aids.

Reagan worked purposefully at maintaining his health and personal appearance. He didn't smoke, although he did make an ad for Chesterfield cigarettes in 1948. He rarely drank hard liquor—sometimes a glass of wine, and then in careful moderation. He did not depend on pills, not even taking aspirin regularly. In addition to nicotine and alcohol, he stayed away from caffeine and seldom drank coffee, unless he was unusually tired before a major speech.

He exercised regularly. While on the road campaigning he used to bring along a small wheel with a short axle through its center. At night in his hotel room he would kneel on the floor, grasp the axle in his hands and roll it back and forth. He swore those isometric exercises kept his muscles in tone.* In the White House, after he was shot in 1981, he had a bedroom turned into a gym which he used every day. He marveled that he was able to add two inches to his chest measurement even though he was 70 years old.

In sum, he suffered many, if not more, of the afflictions that affect all of us but he seemed to shake them off easily. The letters in this chapter give us some insight into his feelings about health, accidents, sickness and aging, and how he presented himself to his public.

––––––––

Tressie Masocco was the alumni president of Eureka College. Over the years she kept in touch with Reagan, inviting him back to reunions and other special events. Reagan was 38 when he wrote this letter, near the peak of his movie career but just two months after he had broken his leg in a baseball game between comedians and leading men to benefit the City of Hope Hospital in Duarte, California. It was nearly a year before he walked without crutches or a cane, and his right knee recovered only about 85 percent of its normal bend.†

––––––––––––

* Discussion with Martin Anderson on campaign plane, 1980.
† Reagan, *Where's the Rest of Me?* pp. 213–15.

Tressie Masocco
Eureka College
September 22, 1949[1]

Dear Tressie:

Just a hasty line to thank you for your kind letter of August 20. It was good to hear from you and I'm happy about your new job as "Alumni President." I hope Eureka can weather the changeover from plenty of "G.I." students to the "need a job" kind without falling onto lean years, such as we knew.

I'm getting to be quite an artist at handling crutches but even that stage is coming to a close, I'm happy to say. Just for the record though—I wasn't sliding into first, I was beating out a bunt and the first baseman blocked me off the bag. Well everything is an experience—now I'm qualified to play an invalid if ever the script calls for such.

Again my thanks and best wishes to you always.

Sincerely,
Dutch

Reagan reassures a campaign contributor who has written to Nancy expressing his concerns about Reagan's health and endurance.

Mr. R.W. Hanley
June 1, 1979[2]

Dear Mr. Hanley:

I hope you won't mind my answering you directly, although your letter was addressed to Nancy. We both appreciate very much your concern and, incidentally, I appreciate this opportunity to thank you personally for your contribution.

It is true that my schedule for May and June has been much heavier than usual. Part of this is because so many of the speaking engagements are the type of lecture appearances I have been doing on a regular basis, and I am trying to get as many of those in that I can before campaigning must start, and I will no longer have an opportunity to address nonpartisan groups.

Let me reassure you I am in good health, and while the schedule is heavy, Nancy and I manage to get a few days in between time at the ranch where we ride and I do such pleasant tasks as building a fence and cutting next winter's wood supply. Actually, I have learned to manage these tours on the "mashed potato circuit" pretty well, but as you have advised, we are taking the entire month off in August, and most of this time will be spent at the ranch, and there will be no problems on our minds except ranch problems.

You were more than kind to write as you did, and as I said earlier, both of us are very grateful to you.

Best regards.

Sincerely,
Ronald Reagan

Since 1961 Reagan had corresponded regularly with William F. Buckley, the publisher of National Review. *Here he comments on a recent column Buckley wrote.*

> Mr. William F. Buckley, Jr.
> New York, New York
> November 24, 1979[3]

Dear Bill:

Tomorrow we're off like Jetsetters but before takeoff I had to tell you how much I enjoyed the column. I may put it on cards suitable for framing and hand them out to everyone under 40. Only one correction—that line about black coffee on the plane; it's Sanka* (that caffeine will kill you) with a touch of cream and a chemical sweetener outlawed by the FDA. I hope that doesn't change your mind about my Peter Pan qualities.

Again my thanks and a promise that some day I'll show you the picture we keep in the attic which keeps on getting older.

Nancy sends her love and from both of us to Pat.

> Regards,
> Ron

While traveling Reagan usually carried a dispenser of saccharin tablets. It looked like a fountain pen and he cherished it. He would hold it over his rare cup of coffee (or Sanka), push on the top, and a small saccharin pill would be ejected into the cup. The device was a "Me-Ta-Sweet" dispenser, from the Armont Drug & Chemical Company in Miami, Florida.

> Armont Drug & Chemical Company
> Panray Division
> Circa 1970s[4]

Gentlemen:

Some time ago I received in the mail one of your Me-Ta-Sweet dispensers. Being a user of saccharin, etc., I have found this dispenser most practical and convenient. It is also a conversation piece because I've yet to meet anyone who has ever seen it before and I've never found it on sale here in California. Could you tell me if it is sold in California and where?

Thank you.

> Sincerely,
> Ronald Reagan

---

* Sanka is a brand of decaffeinated coffee.

Reagan received many letters from his supporters advising him not to dye his hair and to wear less makeup in his television appearances.

Mrs. Lindquist
Circa 1970s[5]

Dear Mrs. Lindquist:

Thanks very much for your letter and for your generous expression of support. I am truly grateful. Believe me I appreciate also your interest in my appearance and do accept your suggestion in the spirit it was offered. But there is a problem—I don't have a makeup man or wear makeup and would have to dye my hair to have grey at the temples.

Actually, you are not the first who has assumed I used makeup, but the truth is I didn't even use it when I was in pictures and TV.

Pat Brown made a crack about it in 1966 during the campaign and then we were together on *Meet the Press;* he and the reporters were wearing makeup and I was the only one on the show without it.

I think time will take care of the grey hair. Last Friday I had a haircut and the barber told me it's getting pretty speckled on top.

Again thanks and best regards.

Ronald Reagan

Rudy Vallee was one of the country's top vocalists in the decade before World War II, a major star on stage, in film, and in broadcast radio. Born in 1901, he was almost 80 years old when Reagan ran out of tape while dictating a letter to him, and finished the letter by writing this fragment.

Mr. Rudy Vallee
Circa 1980[6]

Finish to Letter to Rudy Vallee (ran out of tape)

. . . and picked up cuttings to see if I'm using dye. The truth is the color is my own—no dye. My older brother has hair about the same color as mine. It must be genes or we're just lucky, I guess.

I do appreciate your wanting to help and hope I get to see your show. I think I really should say concert.

Nancy sends her best as do I, and, again thanks.

Sincerely,
Ron

Reagan's favorite riding boots were relatively expensive, and made by the Dehner Company in Omaha, Nebraska. A Dehner vice president watched a Barbara Walters interview with Reagan, noticed that his boots were "old dawgs," and sent a new pair.

Mr. Jeffrey W. Ketzler
Omaha, Nebraska
February 8, 1982 [7]

Dear Mr. Ketzler:

Thank you very much for my boots—handsome as all Dehner boots are. You were very kind, and I'm more grateful than I can say.

You were very perceptive in your TV watching—that particular pair of field boots are older than the Jeep Barbara found so scroungy. As you know, I've been a wearer of Dehner boots for the greatest share of my adult life. In fact, I only strayed once: I was in England in 1949 and had a pair made by Maxwell—then bootmaker to the King. I hurried back to Dehners.

Well, again, my heartfelt thanks to you. Please convey my thanks also and my regards to your father.

Sincerely,
Ronald Reagan

The executive director of the Reagan/Bush 1980 campaign in Pennsylvania sent Reagan an actuarial table to help him counter charges he was too old to be President.

Mr. Marc L. Holtzman
Circa 1980 [8]

Dear Marc:

Thanks very much for sending me the actuarial table. That was a fine idea and something I wish I had thought of myself. I'm delighted to have it.

These, of course, are actuarial averages for insurance purposes. You might be interested to know that just recently a study was released that people who do attain my age usually live considerably longer and more active lives than even insurance statistics indicate. So, who knows. Anyway, I'm enjoying it as it is and, again, I certainly thank you for all that you are doing in this campaign.

Best regards,
Ron

A supporter questioned the way Reagan ran his campaign in 1980 and whether the rumors were true that he could only campaign for three days at a time.

Mr. G.W. McCullough
Circa March 1980[9]

Dear Hank:

Forgive me for being so late getting back to you on your good letter. I appreciate your writing and the concern you felt, and now, of course, you know I was experiencing the same concern and feeling the organization had begun to come apart. I finally decided there had to be a change, and the change, I think, has been beneficial as is apparent in the last several primaries. We have a happy ship now. You can put those rumors that I can only campaign for three days to rest. I'm home for 48 hours and then on the road again. This time Wisconsin, Kansas, and a few other places, but I think the press traveling with us has decided that I can go the distance and hold the pace. We have just concluded one trip, non-stop for 20 days with no days off, and both Nancy and I are still feeling ready to go on the next one.

But, again, I appreciate your concern and understand why you are concerned and hope now you are as relieved as all of us are. Nancy sends her love.

Best regards,
Ron

Lorraine Wagner was one of Reagan's early movie fans and had written to him since 1946. Reagan, now 69 years old, assures her and her husband that the New York Times *article that discussed the possibility of senility if he was elected president was nothing to worry about, nor were the "bumps on the tendon" in his left hand.*

Mr. and Mrs. Elwood H. Wagner
Philadelphia, Pennsylvania
July 2, 1980[10]

Dear Lorraine and Wag:

It was good to get your letter although I was upset to hear about all the bad luck with the stolen cars and cameras, broken collar bones, etc. Please give my sincere sympathy to Sandy and to Scott.

I appreciated hearing all the asides which I never get to hear from the walk through the marketplace.* One goes away wondering, but you've reassured me that the trip was worthwhile.

Those lines about senility were not volunteered by me. They made it look that way, but a doctor who writes for *The New York Times* insisted on getting my entire medical history from all the doctors I've ever seen including those who give me my annual checkup. He then interviewed me on the plane, and he brought up the entire

---

* Reagan is probably referring to walking through a crowd of people, perhaps in a mall, shaking hands. The candidate rarely is aware of what those people are saying among themselves.

subject and asked me about what I would do and so forth.* The funny thing is he was a young doctor, but I think I'm in better shape.

Let me reassure you about those supposed blisters. I really don't have any. I don't know which photo you're speaking of, but what it probably showed that looked like blisters on my left hand is a kind of bum finger I have with a couple of bumps on the tendon.

I have to make this short. We're on our way to a ranch in Mexico for a few days where there are no phones. So, again, it was good to hear from you and thanks for all you're doing in my behalf.

Sincerely,

Ron

Reagan acknowledges what a doctor has noticed in a press photograph—that he has Dupuytren's contracture, a relatively common disorder that tends to pull the fingers, usually the fourth and fifth finger, into the palm.† The disease runs in families, is commonly found in older males of northern European descent and is known as Viking disease. Reagan's brother, Neil, also had it.

Dr. Sander Garrie

La Jolla, California

June 13, 1983 [11]

Dear Dr. Garrie:

Your letter of last January 31 took a very long time to reach my desk. I'm aware of some of the foot dragging by bureaucracy but have no explanation for this delay. I'm sorry.

I have to compliment you on your perceptiveness. Yes I do have a Dupuytren contracture on that finger. As Dr. Dupuytren pronounced—it must be inherited. My older brother has a little finger so afflicted.

Having been told of the nature of corrective surgery by Nancy's father, the late Dr. Loyal Davis, I've resisted. As you perhaps know, he was a neurosurgeon.

Thank you for writing and for your good wishes.

Sincerely,

Ronald Reagan

---

* "Reagan Vows to Resign if Doctor in White House Finds Him Unfit," Lawrence K. Altman, June 11, 1980, p. A1. At age 69 Reagan would be the oldest man inaugurated as President, and this article explores the possibility of his becoming senile. Reagan had waived the traditional patient-doctor confidentiality and "six of his doctors stressed that they had found no evidence of serious problems." According to Altman Reagan "appeared mentally sharp as he spoke." When questioned specifically about becoming senile Reagan replied, "If I were President and had any feeling at all that my capabilities had been reduced before a second term came I would walk away. By the same token I would step down also." Reagan added that he "had never consulted a psychiatrist and had never had plastic surgery."

† *Medical Diagnosis and Treatment,* edited by Lawrence M. Tierney, Jr., Stephen J. McPhee, and Maxine A. Papakakis, Appleton & Lange, 1994, p. 680.

When an 87-year-old Republican decides to run for mayor of Seattle, Washington, to demonstrate that he is "not washed up," Reagan, now almost 74 years old, congratulates him and explains his own philosophy of aging.

Mr. Thom never became mayor of Seattle.

Mr. Herbert Thom
Seattle, Washington
January 28, 1985[12]

Dear Mr. Thom:

Congratulations on your decision to enter the campaign. Obviously, I cannot express a preference for any candidate in a race that belongs to the people of Seattle but I certainly can express my opinion that age should not be a consideration or an issue. My own philosophy is that getting old is 15 years down the road from where we are now. Your record indicates that you have served our country well. Wasn't it Cicero who said, "If it were not for the elders correcting the mistakes of the young there would be no state?" *

Sincerely,
Ronald Reagan

One of President Reagan's oldest friends and supporters, Holmes Tuttle, asked Reagan to send a signed photo to a woman in San Diego, California, for her 100th birthday in 1984. The woman, Teresa Hardie, on hearing of Reagan's colon surgery in the summer of 1985, wrote to Tuttle that she had the same operation 30 years ago: ". . . tell him I have lived to be 100 and so can he: I hope."

Mrs. Teresa Hardie
San Diego, California
July 31, 1985[13]

Dear Mrs. Hardie:

Our friends the Tuttles made sure I received your message and the word of your own experience 30 years ago. Thank you so very much, you were more than kind to think of me.

---

* In a drawer in his desk in the White House Reagan kept a packet of about 100 index cards, 4 inches by 6 inches, that were found filled with quotations he had carefully written by hand. Assembled over a long period of time, the cards contained 339 quotations he had written in tiny letters barely over one-eighth of an inch high. They are uncommon quotations, taken from the writings of people that included Aristotle, Demosthenes, Abraham Lincoln, Teddy and Franklin Roosevelt, Lenin and Stalin, Lord Acton, James Madison, Bastiat, Confucius and Pericles, Dwight D. Eisenhower and John F. Kennedy, the Bible and Cicero. The Cicero quotation he was trying to remember when he wrote this letter was taken from his private collection, "Had there not been older men to undo the damage done by the young, there would be no state." Three months earlier, in the second presidential debate with Walter Mondale, the Democratic candidate, the first question reporter Trewhitt asked was: "as the oldest president in history" would he "be able to function?" Reagan's reply included this quotation.

I'm already feeling fine and while I won't be chopping wood for a while I expect to be on a horse in a few more weeks.

Do you know the most encouraging part of your message was to learn you've managed without popcorn for 30 years. I received the same orders you did—no popcorn, nuts etc. From now on. I happen to be a popcorn freak and will eat any given amount. I've been wondering what life will be like without it. You've reassured me that I'll be able to adjust.

Well again my thanks. Nancy sends her regards as do I.

Sincerely,
Ronald Reagan

In February of 1966 Reagan came down with a bad case of the flu that "dogged him for the next year and a half." By August 1967 his prostate gland had become infected and enlarged and painful—so he had a prostate operation. In the White House, when Reagan had an operation for colon cancer on July 13, 1985, a former member of his gubernatorial staff, Bill Orozco, wrote and congratulated him on his "remarkable recovery," and reminded him of his behavior after the 1967 operation:*

"I remember well your operation [in] August 1967—you had just come home from the hospital and you called me at your Governor's office in the old State Building—you had seen a very tragic story in the morning *Times* . . . a man had been shot and killed and $80 stolen from him. He had left behind a wife and 15 children! In spite of your very recent operation and in spite of being recuperating, you still had the compassion to grieve for that family. Remember?

You had me call Cap Weinberger, then Secretary of the Department of Employment, to find the older boys jobs. You had me call Bishop Ward to get the younger children into Catholic School, and to pay two or three months on the mortgage . . . and you asked me not mention to anyone that you were the benefactor!"

---

* Lyn Nofziger, *Nofziger* (Washington, DC: Regnery Gateway, 1992), pp. 83–85.

Mr. Bill Orozco
Los Angeles, California
August 14, 1985 [14]

Dear Bill:

What a surprise and great pleasure to get your nice letter and good wishes. You brought back a lot of warm memories and I thank you for your prayers and your generous words.

The Lord has been answering prayers because I feel just fine and the doctors are unable to explain my rapid recovery. We know what explains it don't we?

All the best to you and again thanks.

Sincerely,
Ronald Reagan

––––––

Reagan was at his ranch, high in the mountains above Santa Barbara, California, recuperating from his colon cancer surgery, when he wrote this letter to Dr. Schwegman, a colleague of Nancy Reagan's brother, Richard (Dick) Davis, who was a neurosurgeon.

Dr. Cletus W. Schwegman
Philadelphia, Pennsylvania
September 4, 1985 [15]

Dear Dr. Schwegman:

Thank you very much for your kind letter which caught up with me in California where I've been for a happy, health-building few weeks. I appreciate your good wishes and generous words.

Give my best to your colleague, my brother-in-law, Dick. Tell him his sister is resting up from three weeks of policing an unruly patient who wanted to do some strenuous farm work. We worked out a compromise, I got my way provided I was back in the ranch house at 4:00 P.M. every day.

Again, thanks.

Sincerely,
Ronald Reagan

––––––

Nackey Loeb, the publisher of the Union Leader *in New Hampshire, often wrote to Reagan, proffering advice. Dr. Gold was a controversial doctor who, since the mid-1970s, had become convinced that hydrazine sulfate, a cheap chemical used in industrial processes, could control and cure cancer.* Unfortunately, all the carefully designed

––––––

* American Cancer Society, 2002.

*large-scale, randomized clinical trials of hydrazine sulfate "did not show any improve-
ment in cancer patient survival, weight loss or quality of life."* *

*There is no record of this letter being sent after Reagan drafted it. After answering
Dr. Gold, Reagan replies to Nackey.*

Dr. Joseph Gold
Syracuse, New York
September 5, 1985 [16]

Dear Dr. Gold:

Our friend Nackey Loeb † forwarded your letter to me and I thank you for
your interest and your kindness. I'm afraid the press has been more than a little
overboard in their coverage of my recent surgery. The impression has been given
that I was suffering from cancer and surgery removed the cancerous tumor. A
more accurate account is that in a routine physical exam a polyp of the type
that can become cancer was discovered. It was still within the colon and self
contained but since I was in the hospital and already prepped—I told them to remove it. It had developed a few cancer cells we discovered but that was the extent of it.

I have just undergone the six-month checkup which included a CAT scan
among other things and was given a completely clean bill of health I'm happy to
say. I'm at 190 pounds which was my pre-operation weight and feel just fine. I will
inform our White House Dr. Burton Smith of your letter and the information
about hydrazine sulfate.

Again my thanks to you.

Sincerely,
Ronald Reagan

Mrs. William Loeb
Manchester, New Hampshire
September 5, 1985 [17]

Dear Nackey:

Nancy and I got your letters and we both thank you.

I'm happy to have the information about hydrazine sulfate and will keep it
on hand just in case. You know, Nackey, I think some of our friends (question
mark) in the press have created a false picture of my situation. They have portrayed
me as having suffered from cancer until I finally had surgery to remove it. I'm

---

* National Cancer Institute, "Cancer Facts," February 12, 2002.
† William and Nackey Loeb, the publishers of the *Union Leader* in New Hampshire, were old friends
of Reagan. In the mid-1980s Nackey Loeb took over the publishing duties and continued to write to
Reagan.

happy to say this wasn't the case. When I went in to have a tiny non-cancerous polyp removed they discovered a new polyp of the type that can become cancer if left alone. I said remove it. Yes it was found to contain a few cancer cells but it was totally enclosed and had not gone through the intestine wall.

Nevertheless, I'm glad to have the word you sent and will be ready if the need should ever arise. In the meantime I feel great and spent the last ten days at the ranch riding every morning and doing some chores, like tree pruning and wood stacking in the afternoon.

Nancy thanks you for your kindness and so do I.

Sincerely,
Ron

Marion Grimm was the widow of Charles Grimm, manager of the Chicago Cubs baseball team that Reagan reported on during their spring training in California in the mid-1930s.

Mrs. Charles Grimm
Scottsdale, Arizona
September 10, 1986 [18]

Dear Marion:

Thank you very much for your "get well" card and nice letter which I found waiting for me when I got back here after our time at the ranch.

I appreciate your concern but I'm sorry the press makes even a routine check sound like major surgery. Truth is I'm healthy as a colt and spent my time at the ranch riding every day and getting in a supply of firewood for the winter. But it was sweet of you to care.

Nancy sends her best as do I and thank you for your picture. You are lovely as always.

Sincerely,
Ronnie

In July 1986 Reagan noticed blood in his urine; the White House doctor diagnosed it as an "inflamed prostate." Because of the press of events, topped by the burgeoning Iran-Contra scandal, he postponed surgery until January 5, 1987. Specimens taken from the prostate showed no cancer.

Less than two weeks later, at age 76, he delivered his State of the Union address to the Congress as scheduled.*

In high school Reagan had written a long poem for his class yearbook; now, two

---

* Edmund Morris, *Dutch* (New York: Random House, 1999), pp. 589, 616, 618.

days after his prostate operation he wrote a short one for the staff of the recovery room at the National Naval Medical Center in Bethesda, Maryland.

> The Staff of the Bethesda Recovery Room
> Bethesda, Maryland
> January 7, 1987 [19]

To the staff of the Bethesda Recovery Room:

> I'm sorry I'm not a poet
> And the next few lines will show it.
> But whether poetry or prose,
> I hope my deep gratitude shows.
>
> Your card with its art
> Truly touched my heart
> And that of my roommate as well.
> With both of us you really rang the bell.

Now if the above needs translating I'll turn to prose. Thank you for a message we'll treasure and thank you for the Jelly Beans. But more than anything thank you for your generous words, your prayers and all that you are doing for our country.

God Bless you all.

> Sincerely,
> Ronald Reagan

Phil Regan was a Hollywood friend, a handsome, popular tenor singer of the 1930s and 1940s.

> Mr. and Mrs. Phil Regan
> Pasadena, California
> January 7, 1988 [20]

Dear Jo and Phil:

This is just a line (from the hospital no less) to thank you for your good letter, good wishes and prayers. You can tell Monsignor Connelly the prayers were answered. I'm out of bed and going back to the White House tomorrow. Every test and check came up with a clean bill of health. In fact, they (the doctors) were claiming my insides are much younger than my years. I blushed modestly and did an, "aw shucks routine."

Again, thanks. Nancy sends her best as do I.

> Sincerely,
> Ron

Helen Lawton is an old friend who lived next door to the Reagan family in Dixon, Illinois, as they struggled through the Depression in the early 1930s. She congratulates "Dutch" on his 76th birthday, and tells him how "great" he looked giving the State of the Union address so soon after surgery.

Mrs. Helen Lawton
Dixon, Illinois
February 10, 1987 [21]

Dear Helen:

Thank you for your greeting and good wishes on the 37th anniversary of my 39th birthday. It was good to hear from you and to bask in the warmth of your generous words.

My recovery has been free of pain or even reduced energy. Of course the doctor has imposed some limits for the all important six weeks following surgery.* Now I'm starting the sixth week and in a few days I'll resume my daily gym workout. The Lord has truly blessed me and I'm most grateful.

Well again thank you and very best regards.

Sincerely,
Dutch

Lorraine Wagner had been Reagan's pen pal since his acting days in the 1940s. She wrote in 1987 about appearing on a radio talk show, hosted by Les Kinsolving, and taking calls defending Reagan. She congratulated Reagan on his speech in Berlin where he called on Gorbachev "to tear down this wall," claimed that there was "much boredom" with the Iran-Contra scandal, and wondered if he was "still jumping hurdles," recalling the last time she saw him jump was "in 1951 in California."

Mr. and Mrs. Elwood Wagner
Philadelphia, Pennsylvania
June 25, 1987 [22]

Dear Lorraine and Wag:

Thank you for my Father's Day card and even more for your warm letter. It was good to hear from you. I was very interested in your adventure with Les Kinsolving and am most grateful for your setting him straight. I've heard there are a couple of books out that apparently were written out of complete imagination. Thank you for taking care of at least one of them.

You know Les was a White House correspondent for a while. Maybe he still is and is just doubling in brass. By the way with regard to taking horses over fences I regret to say—not anymore. We still ride but since we only get to the ranch a

---

* On January 5, 1987, Reagan had prostate surgery. No cancer was found.

few times a year and my long time favorite "Little Man" has gone to horse heaven I've decided it wouldn't be fair to the job I have. I used to feel that way when I was doing movies. While I was making one I wouldn't jump. It is a sport where accidents can happen to the best of riders and while I miss it I have to feel it wouldn't be right to have to cancel a summit meeting or such while some bones mended.

Thank you for your kind words about our present troubles. I think there is a kind of political lynching going on but my conscience is completely clear, so I'm not losing any sleep. Nancy sends her best to you both and so do I.

Sincerely,
Ron

A mother and father with 10 children, five of them adopted with handicaps, wrote to Reagan telling him of one adopted son, Vincent, who came to them from India two years ago. Vincent was hearing impaired in both ears, and felt awkward and self-conscious about wearing hearing aids—until he read that President Reagan also needed one, and then "he lit up like a Christmas tree . . . [and] would love to hear from you."

Mr. and Mrs. John Kuharski
Minneapolis, Minnesota
November 28, 1983 [23]

Dear John and Mary Ann Kuharski:

Thank you very much for your letter, your kind words and your prayers. More than that, thank you for what you are doing with your lives and for so many others. I've had some contact with other families like yours and know the love that fills your home and surrounds you.

I'm enclosing a note to Vincent. My ear problem is the result of a shooting accident—no wound—the gun just went off right by my ear.* Over the years the nerves in the inner ear deteriorated with the result, a loss of much of the hearing in that ear. I wanted you to know because it is my understanding that various types of hearing aids are designed for different types of deafness. Vincent would probably have to be examined to see if this inside the ear amplifier would solve his problem.

My note to him is aimed at encouraging him to accept his problem. I hope it will help. In the meantime the name of the company which makes mine is Starkey Labs Inc. 6700 Washington Ave., S. Eden Prarie, Minn. 55344.

Again thanks and God Bless You.

Sincerely,
Ronald Reagan

---

* In 1939 Reagan, then only 28 years old, was filming a movie called *Secret Service of the Air*, and another actor fired a gun loaded with blanks very close to his right ear, causing a significant loss of hearing in that ear. (Anne McDermott, CNN, Bel Air, California, January 23, 2001.)

Dear Vincent:

I've sent the name and address of the hearing aid company to your parents. Those of us who have hearing problems sometimes have to have different types of aids depending on what causes our problem.

I know how you feel about the aids you wear behind your ears but if that's the kind you need, wear them and be happy they help you hear.

When I was your age I learned I couldn't see as well as other people and had to have glasses. They weren't quite as common then as they've become in recent years. I was very self-conscious and embarrassed about wearing glasses but believe me I outgrew that and learned to be happy because with them I could see all the beauty I'd been missing. Now it's glasses and a hearing aid and I think I'm pretty lucky.

Best Wishes to you and God Bless You.

Ronald Reagan

The doctor who fitted Reagan with new hearing aids forwarded a letter from a "very good friend" who was the "the most outstanding ear surgeon" in France, and "one of your greatest fans." He asked Reagan to reply to him.

Dr. John House
Los Angeles, California
July 3, 1986 [24]

Dear John:

Your letter with the enclosure from Dr. Causse has just reached my desk. Yes I know you sent it on May 8th but apparently it went through the general mail process here which means it had to battle its way through a half million other pieces of mail. That must never happen again so here is a little secret. On the outside of the envelope if you write again add "c/o Kathy Osborne." Your letter will skip over the bureaucratic jungles and be on my desk the day it reaches Washington.

I've answered Dr. Causse's letter with an apology for my tardiness. Now as to your question. I assume you were asking about the new hearing aids designed to cut down on background noise? I wear them for affairs such as state dinners and such and they are a big help. For regular wear I'm using the small one I was fitted with. They are more comfortable than the larger ones and a little less conspicuous. So all in all I'm very happy with both sets and depend on them completely.

I look forward to seeing you.

Best regards,
Ron

For an article on rowing machines, the newspaper USA Today *wanted to know if President Reagan used a rowing machine, and if so, how often.*

Response for *USA Today* article
March 4, 1986[25]

No, I do a series of exercises—some just calisthenics as a warm-up to exercises with weights.

However—having been a lifeguard for seven years I recognize the benefits from rowing.*

RR

Mike Abrums was the man who changed one of the rooms in the White House living quarters into a gym for President Reagan and Nancy.

Mr. Mike Abrums
Los Angeles, California
January 17, 1989[26]

Dear Mike:

We've been saying goodbye to these rooms in the White House where we've enjoyed such pleasant living these eight years. I just have to write you about one room in particular. You are very familiar with it because you transformed it from a bedroom into a gym.

For eight years I have ended each working day with a visit to that room where I've done the sets of exercises you prescribed. Thanks to you I leave here in better shape than when I arrived even though I'm eight years older. Thanks to you I discovered that even after living three score and ten I could add muscle in place of flab.

And you know of course that Nancy shares in this and has been a regular user of the gym in the mornings as I have been in the evenings. We are both more grateful than words can say.

Thank you and God bless you.

Ronald Reagan

---

* As a teenager in Dixon, Illinois, Reagan worked as a lifeguard for six summers and saved 77 people from drowning.

CHAPTER FOUR

Old Friends

REAGAN HAD *very few really close friends in whom he frequently confided his personal thoughts and fears. In fact, there may have only been one: his wife, Nancy. There were no drinking buddies, and no one else he talked to frequently.*

His other friends fell into two broad categories.

First, there were the famous, well-known men and women that he got to know as a result of his acting and political careers—people like John Wayne and Frank Sinatra, Richard Nixon and George Bush, and Margaret Thatcher and Mikhail Gorbachev. These were basically working relationships, though some of them turned into warmer, more intimate friendships. Reagan's correspondence with them can be found in later chapters on his Hollywood days and foreign and national leaders.

But there were many other friends, some closer than others, who were virtually unknown to the public. Reagan met and stayed in touch with them as he rose to power and after he was in power. Some provided pleasant company, but others provided critical advice and counsel in both domestic and foreign policy. They were not members of his staffs, with whom he worked intimately, often on a daily basis. They were not members of his "kitchen cabinets" who provided him with financial support and counsel. They were just "friends," people he knew and trusted, people he respected, people he liked to hear from.

There were about 50 or so men and women in this category. He met them throughout his life and career, from Illinois to Iowa to the Bohemian Grove.

Most of the following letters were written by Reagan during the eight years he was president.

The only girl Reagan seriously dated in high school and Eureka College was Margaret Cleaver. Her father was the Reverend Ben H. Cleaver, an imposing figure in Dixon, Illinois. While Reagan respected his father, Jack Reagan was an alcoholic and the son and father had little in common. One of the surrogate fathers Reagan *often went to for advice was Reverend Cleaver* and, while the romance with Margaret did not continue after college, his relationship with the Reverend did.*

Here, Governor Reagan responds to one of the Reverend's letters more than 40 years after he stopped seeing Margaret.

The Reverend B. H. Cleaver
Cape Girardeau, Missouri
May 24, 1973[1]

Dear Friend:

Just a line between meetings to say how good it was to hear from you. Your letters always brighten my day. I also enjoyed the clipping and thank you for sending it along.

Those were wonderful years in Dixon. I know that time tinges things with gold, and having survived the sorrows and troubles they look smaller, but even so it was a wonderful time.

As for what is happening to our country right now—I can't say publicly but feel very deeply that we are witness to a lynching.[†] True, there was lawbreaking, even though of a kind we've come to associate with campaign activities, but to watch the "night riders" ignore the harm they are doing our nation in these troubled times makes me a little sick.

What a contrast to the men Nancy and I have been privileged to meet in these recent weeks—the returning POWs.[‡]

We've had dinners in our home, four in all, until we had entertained all the returning Californians. These men without exception have become stronger, kinder, gentler and more sensitive men because of their experiences. Many who had no particular faith before are today deeply religious. Man after man told us very simply he lived to come home only because of faith in God.

I try to think of them when I see the daily headlines.

Love,
Ronald

B. J. Fraser taught English and world history at North Dixon High School in the late 1920s when Reagan was a student. He was also the adviser to the Dramatic Club and urged Reagan to join. Fraser was another "surrogate father" whose counsel was sought by Reagan. Fraser encouraged his acting, later saying Reagan was "head and shoulders above" others in the Dramatic Club and that he possessed "a sense of presence on the stage." §

---

* Anne Edwards, *Early Reagan* (New York: William Morrow, 1987), p. 68.
† President Nixon's Watergate scandal.
‡ Returning American prisoners of war captured by the North Vietnamese in the Vietnam War.
§ Edwards, *Early Reagan*, p. 69.

As Reagan geared up for the 1980 presidential run, some 50 years later, he learned that Fraser was ill and wrote to him.

B. J. Fraser
Dixon, Illinois
March 26, 1979 [2]

Dear B. J.:

I have just learned that you have been ill and hospitalized. I hope that by the time this reaches you, all will be well and whatever was troubling you will be healed.

B. J., I am sitting here wondering about a great many things and remembering many—remembering Lowell Park, remembering the many talks you and I had, and wondering how that Lowell Park lifeguard wound up sitting here as I am with the plans going forward to run for the presidency. I don't know whatever led me to this or made it possible; it certainly was nothing I could foresee back in those Dixon days. But one thing I do know, that all of the good things that have happened to me, one B. J. Fraser had a great deal to do with it. You played a very important part in my life, and I shall be forever grateful. Now take care of yourself and get well soon and just know you have my gratitude for more than I can ever say.

Best regards,
Dutch

———

Helen Lawton lived next door to the Reagan family in Dixon, Illinois, and knew Reagan as a young boy. She wrote to Reagan, thanking him for sending a note and a photo, and sent him a copy of two letters his mother had sent to her. After telling Reagan how much she liked going to his first Inauguration, she explained why she would not accept his invitation this time, and wishes him the "very best through the coming days and years."

Helen Lawton
Dixon, Illinois
January 24, 1985 [3]

Dear Helen:

Just a very quick line to say thanks for the letters. You made the right decision on the inaugural. The only one in town who wasn't turned off by the cold was the fellow from Alaska who brought his dog sled team.

Wouldn't you know, 48 hours after the final event the sun was bright and the temperature was in the 40s.

Again thanks.

Sincerely,
Dutch

A friend from Reagan's days as a lifeguard at Lowell Park in Dixon, Illinois, sent him a November 18, 1963, copy of the Dan Smoot Report, _a right-wing newsletter, published from 1955 to 1971. The report was entitled "How Did Socialism Grow in the U.S.?"_

Mr. Light Thompson
Princeton, Illinois
January 9, 1985[4]

Dear Light:

You must have dug deep in the files to find that Dan Smoot report. I'm pleased to have it. We need to be reminded of how the little Red brothers and even the pink ones operate.

I wasn't surprised to see ADA (Americans for Democratic Action) and United World Federalists mentioned. Having been as you know a working Democrat I was a member of both—in on the ground floor. However by the time of Smoot's report I was long gone. I had learned after a brief time they were "fronts" for other causes. I recall that after my resignations I had to threaten legal action to get my name taken off their letterheads and membership lists. I suppose we should be charitable and assume that maybe some of the individuals he mentioned in his report had the same experience.

It's interesting to note that ADA actually started as a home for liberal Democrats who opposed the left-leaning Democrats who were gaining such power in the Democratic party. The "Lefties" didn't oppose it, they just quietly infiltrated and took it over.

Well thanks again and best regards,

Dutch

Ralph Tipton, a manufacturer of auto supplies in Illinois, became a friend of Reagan's in 1934 when he was a radio sports announcer in Des Moines, Iowa.

Mr. Ralph Tipton
Sugar Grove, Illinois
November 29, 1983[5]

Dear Tip:

It was good to hear from you and I enjoyed reading about the 25th.* That brought on some nostalgia. I was adjutant of the outfit that trained those combat camera crews. We had them with every outfit all over the world. I better stop or I'll be telling war stories and mine can't match yours because I never got off the ground or out of California.

---

* Tipton flew combat missions during World War II with the 25th Bomb Group of the Eighth Air Force.

Now about those bumper stickers—I won't be announcing a decision until sometime after the 1st of the year. Thanks for your offer.

I'm sure happy with the business upturn and share your feeling about Lee Iacocca.*

Best regards
Dutch

In 1926 a nine-year-old Bill Thompson watched Reagan save the lives of swimmers who got in trouble in the Rock River that flowed through Lowell Park in Dixon, Illinois.† He and his wife, Jean, stayed in touch with Reagan over the years and spearheaded a project to restore and preserve the home that Reagan grew up in.

Mr. and Mrs. William Thompson
Dixon, Illinois
June 28, 1982 [6]

Dear Jean and Bill:

Forgive a hurried note but it's getaway time for us—back to the ranch for a few days. Yes, send the prints. I'll be happy to autograph them. Be sure and include the names to go on each one.

You touched a memory mentioning "Honey" Glessner.‡ He was the all around–able to do anything fellow in the gang. Good looking too. That white canoe was beautiful. I used to send it out at Lowell Park and we split the money—50¢ an hour.

Incidentally please thank John Beier for the cap.

The tourist brochure is beautiful and I appreciate all the "fun" items.

About the hat—Nancy isn't a hat wearer but has just a few she must have for such things as meeting royalty and the Pope where it is required. Right now there are none she can call extra, but she is going to look.

Again thanks.

Best regards,
Dutch

In response to request for information on the Reagan family home, Reagan fills in a diagram the Thompsons provided with the names of who had which room. The Thompsons were restoring Reagan's childhood home.

---

* President of the Chrysler Corporation.

† Edwards, *Early Reagan*, p. 14.

‡ Honey Glessner was a friend of both Thompson and Reagan. He owned a white canoe that he let Reagan rent out to "young lovers."

Mr. and Mrs. Bill Thompson
Dixon, Illinois
November 2, 1982 [7]

Dear Jean and Bill:

First, with regard to the furnishings of the house and the plans—location of rooms, etc., I think I covered that in Peoria. Now, however, with regard to the snapshots which I'm returning for your use and records, yes, these seem to fit my memory. I know mother's great joy was in getting a "kitchen cabinet." The Morris chair belongs in the living room.

You two are very kind to do all you are doing, and to give up personal possessions for the old house. I'm afraid I can't be present at the show you are planning, but maybe that's best. A little twinge of actor's instinct suggests I shouldn't be. If, however, a taped message—either just sound or film would help, we can do that. Just let us know. And, again, I thank you for all you are doing, and I marvel at how you manage to find the time and energy.

Best regards,
Dutch

Garth Henrichs graduated from Eureka College several years before Reagan entered. One of Reagan's classmates, Dick Crane, married Henrichs's sister. Henrichs began corresponding with Reagan in early 1938, congratulating him on his first movie, Love Is on the Air. *Reagan's mother answered the first letters, but Reagan began writing his own letters in 1949 while confined to a hospital bed with a shattered thigh. Henrichs was the publisher of a small, patriotic monthly magazine (five inches by seven inches—32 pages) called* Sunshine, *which he began sending to Reagan.* Sunshine *contained short stories about the Constitution, the flag, and morality—including many quotations and sayings.*

In Henrichs's last letter he told Reagan that his old college friend, Dick Crane, was dying. Reagan writes to Crane and then thanks Henrichs.

Mr. Garth Henrichs
Litchfield, Illinois
August 15, 1949 [8]

Dear Garth:

Just a line from my "up-ended" position to say thanks for your letter and all the good wishes.

Maybe I'll learn someday that athletics were better left behind, "Neath The Elms" and henceforth, I should confine myself to mental gymnastics. At any rate, a thigh divided into about four pieces should teach me something.

Thanks for your kind invitation. I hope someday I can accept. Give my best to any of the gang you see and my very best to you and yours.

Sincerely,
Dutch

Garth Henrichs
Litchfield, Illinois
January 4, 1952[9]

Dear Garth:

Just a quick line between scenes to thank you for the Christmas greetings and the welcome news that your magazine will continue to come throughout the year.

It is very kind of you and I appreciate it more than I can say.

All the best to you throughout the year and again my thanks.

Regards,
Ronald

Mr. Garth Henrichs[10]
Litchfield, Illinois
January 19, 1955

Dear Garth:

Just a belated line to thank you for your Holiday greetings to wish you all the best in the year to come.

I hoped to get back to Eureka on some occasion during this Centennial year but this weekly television chore* for General Electric has complicated things travel wise.

Anyway I'll hope that some leeway in the schedule will permit a break.

Again, all the best to you.

Sincerely,
Ronnie

Garth Henrichs
Litchfield, Illinois
June 17, 1955[11]

Dear Garth:

Just a quick line before hopping a train for what I'm afraid will be my last trip for a while. Which gets me into my regret at not being able to accept your invitation to the Centennial.†

We've all been idle for some time out here due to this "third-dimension" business but it looks as if we'll all get underway now to catch up. I'm sorry to have to say no but as things are shaping up, late this summer and through the fall will find me really scrambling, thanks to some TV film commitments as well as the regular Movie chores.

---

* Reagan was hosting the *GE Theater,* a weekly television program, and was at the time unwilling to travel by airplane.

† Eureka College was founded in 1855.

Please give your board my regrets and say hello to Dick and Monte.* I hope your Portland trip can include Southern California as we would love to see you.

Best regards.

Sincerely,
Dutch

Mr. Garth Henrichs
Litchfield, Illinois
August 20, 1961 [12]

Dear Garth:

It was good to hear from you although you added to my feeling of frustration. I always feel this way when news of Eureka commencement begins to come in. Strange what a hold that little campus can have on us and how nostalgia sets in anytime someone says "I was back."

I certainly hope fate and GE will be kind next fall and I'll be on hand when you reach California. I'm looking forward to it.

All the best,
Ronnie

Mr. Garth Henrichs
Litchfield, Illinois
November 19, 1981 [13]

Dear Garth:

Thanks very much for your letter and for letting me know about Dick.† I had lost all track of him and so knew nothing about his illness. I've just written to him.

It was good to hear from you and about Eureka days in spite of the sad news. Again, my thanks and best regards.

Sincerely,
Ron

Mr. Richard Crane
Pompano Beach, Florida
November 19, 1981 [14]

Dear Dick:

I've just learned of your recent surgery. Garth let me know. Take care of yourself and please know you will be in my thoughts and prayers.

Tell Monte ‡ to remind you, if you get rambunctious, that "a surgeon's scalpel is five months long." And, while you're about it give her my love.

---

* Richard (Dick) Crane and his wife Monte, Henrichs's sister.

† Richard Crane, a college friend of Reagan's.

‡ Dick Crane's wife.

It's a long way back to Eureka days but I have to say those days are as fresh in my memory as if they happened last week.

Again the very best to you both.

> Sincerely,
> Yours in the Bond,
> Dutch

Peter MacArthur gave Reagan his first job in radio broadcasting. An immigrant from Scotland, MacArthur was in vaudeville until arthritis crippled him and he became the program director of WOC, a powerful radio station in Davenport, Iowa, about 180 miles west of Chicago. He joked that the letters WOC stood for "World of Chiropractic."* After MacArthur died Reagan stayed in touch with his wife, "Hup."

> Mrs. Peter MacArthur
> Lake Worth, Florida
> July 29, 1980 [15]

Dear Hup:

This is just a line as we begin to rev up for the campaign to say how good it was to get your sweet letter and read your kind words. It's a long way back to that first Iowa-Minnesota game I broadcast. But, somehow, I have a feeling that everything great that's happened started with Pete when he gave me that chance.

Nancy sends her love and so do I.

> Sincerely,
> Dutch

Mrs. MacArthur thanked Reagan for "a hand written letter and gift" and marveled about "the time you sacrifice to make me happy." Maxine, her niece, had recently died.

> Mrs. Peter MacArthur
> Lake Worth, Florida
> January 10, 1984 [16]

Dear Hup:

It was good to get your letter but I was sorry to hear about Maxine.

We had a pleasant few days in California and as always found California is not an easy place to leave. But here we are back in Washington and counting the days until we can manage another weekend or so out there.

---

* Ronald Reagan, *Where's the Rest of Me?* (New York: Duell, Sloan and Pearce, 1965), pp. 47–48.

I won't say take care of yourself because it sounds like you are doing that. Say hello to Dottie* and thank you for your prayers.

Have a happy 1984.

Love,
Dutch

————

Charles Grimm was the manager of the Chicago Cubs baseball team when Reagan announced their games and covered spring training in southern California. After "Charlie" died, Reagan remained friends with his wife, Marion. In 1987, Marion, who lived in Scottsdale, Arizona, had come back to Chicago for the summer to see friends and had nearly been killed when she rear-ended a truck while driving to Rockford, Illinois. She "cracked a bunch of ribs" but was doing fine and thinking of writing a book.

Mrs. Charles Grimm
Chicago, Illinois
July 6, 1987 [17]

Dear Marion:

Thank you for your kind words about Nancy and myself and your prayers. Just remember you are in our prayers too and please be careful in your driving. You scared us with that trip to Rockford.

We know how you feel about the absence of so many people we used to know. The ranks are thinning for those of us who are still hanging on. We just have to know they've gone through a door into that other place the Lord promised us, that place where there is no pain or sorrow. One day he'll open the door for each of us and we'll be together again with friends and loved ones. But it's up to him to decide when that happens. In the meantime we make new friends.

Nancy sends her best, as do I. We're looking forward to that book so don't give up on it.

Sincerely,
Ron

Mrs. Charles Grimm
Scottsdale, Arizona
September 17, 1987 [18]

Dear Marion:

I've tried to have this arrive just about with you on your return to Arizona. Yes, you certainly can mention that you have some letters from me.† We go back a long way to when the Cubs were Charlie's gang and winning pennants.

————

* Dottie, a friend, drove Mrs. MacArthur to the doctor.
† Regarding the book she is writing.

It was good to hear from you, and I thank you for your kind words. Nancy sends her best, as do I.

Sincerely,
Ronnie

———

Joy Hodges (Mrs. Gene Schiess) was a band singer who had appeared on WHO, the second radio station Reagan worked for. She went to Hollywood and appeared in minor acting roles for RKO. While covering the Chicago Cubs baseball team during spring training in 1937 in California, Reagan looked up Hodges, then 22 years old. Over dinner he acknowledged his desire to be in the movies, and she set up an appointment with agent Bill Meiklejohn that led to a seven-year contract with Warner Brothers.

Mrs. Gene Schiess
Katonah, New York
December 27, 1982 [19]

Dear Joy:

Thank you for your kind words about the Christmas show. I've always had a yen for show business—didn't you know? That's right, I told you that in 1937 and now look what's happened. And you started it all with an introduction to Bill Meiklejohn.

Joy, if ever you and Gene are going to be in Washington let me have a little warning time and I'd love to have you see the Oval Office. The reason I need the warning is because there is some character I haven't found yet who tells me by way of a daily schedule what I'm doing every 15 minutes all day.

I remember Christmas at Loew's State. On one Christmas a couple of years later she* sent us a gift and left in the box the card of the person who'd sent it to her.

Give Gene my best and I hope your holidays were merry and bright.

Sincerely,
Dutch

———

This is one of the earliest handwritten letters by Reagan. Anna Griffith was his housekeeper in the 1930s when Reagan worked as station announcer for WOC and WHO in Des Moines, Iowa. On December 24, 1937, from his new apartment in The Montecito building in Hollywood, Reagan sends a Christmas greeting and a gift.

———

* Louella Parsons.

Mable and Anna Taylor Griffith
Des Moines, Iowa
December 24, 1937[20]

Dear Anna and Mable: *

Just a note to thank you for your lovely gift which I did not wait until Christmas to open. And to enclose my small contribution to your Christmas—may it be a Merry one.

Happy new year and may it bring you much happiness.

Sincerely,
Dutch

———————

Roy Brewer, a liberal Democrat, was a labor leader in the Hollywood crafts union who fought alongside Reagan to prevent Communist infiltration of the Hollywood unions. Reagan respected Brewer, once describing him as "one labor leader who talked as much about labor's responsibility as he did about its privileges." Brewer remained close to Reagan and often gave him suggestions on labor matters.

Roy M. Brewer
Tarzana, California
May 20, 1983[21]

Dear Roy:

Just a line from—(believe it or not) Air Force One. I'm on my way back to Washington from a quick in and out to Miami. This plane is a better office than the Oval for catch-up.

Thanks for all the material you sent. I went through every page of it and have given it to Bill to absorb. My but it brought back a lot of memories. It also reminded me that nothing has changed—they are still under the bed.

Nancy sends her best.

Sincerely,
Ron

Roy M. Brewer
Tarzana, California
August 31, 1984[22]

Dear Roy:

It was good to get your letter and I'm passing some of your campaign suggestions on to the campaign staff and you'll be hearing from them.

I appreciated your thoughts and kind words about the convention.† There sure

———————

* Mable was Anna's daughter.
† The 1984 Republican National Convention.

is something revealing about the media contrast in commenting about Dallas as compared to San Francisco.

I share your feelings about Barbara Mahone, she's quite a gal. She will be with us at least part time in another slot but her situation with General Motors was too good to pass up.

As you know by now the Teamster flap has a happy ending. I was sure it would because J.P. got an apology to me right after the story broke. I have our gang looking into the Van de Water* case. What's been done to him is unforgivable.

Nancy sends her best—so do I.

> Sincerely,
> Ron

Victor Honig was Reagan's barber in California. In 1982 Reagan learned that Irene, his wife, was seriously ill, and he called them in the hospital to express his sympathy. Just before she died she wrote to Reagan asking for a note from him that she could place in their Masonic Bible.

> Mr. Victor Honig
> Palm Springs, California
> November 23, 1982 [23]

Dear Victor:

I received the lovely letter from Irene asking me to send a note signed by Nancy and myself that she could put in your Masonic Bible. Here is the note although I learned at the same time of her passing.

Victor I know there are no words that can ease your pain or be of help at such a time but Nancy and I want you to know how deeply sorry we are. You are in our thoughts and prayers.

It isn't given to us to understand the why of such things. We can only trust in God's infinite mercy and in his promise that we go on to a better life where there is no pain or sorrow. Believe in that and have faith in his wisdom and healing.

Please know you have our deepest sympathy.

> Sincerely,
> Nancy and Ronald Reagan

Laurence (Larry) Beilenson met Reagan when he served as counsel to the Screen Actors Guild. A graduate of Phillips Andover Academy, Harvard College, and the Harvard Law School, he was a prominent member of the Los Angeles bar and a student of history, law, and military science. During World War II he rose from the rank of private to

---

* John Van de Water was Reagan's first nominee to the National Labor Relations Board and was turned down by the Senate.

lieutenant colonel, and was a commanding American liaison officer with the Chinese army. He became one of Reagan's most trusted outside advisers. Perhaps his most important influence on Reagan came through his 1969 book, The Treaty Trap: A History of the Performance of Political Treaties by the United States and European Nations. *He argued that over the centuries "all major nations have been habitual treaty breakers."* Reagan was convinced.*

> Mr. Laurence Beilenson
> Los Angeles, California
> August 11, 1980 [24]

Dear Larry:

Just a quick line before taking off for the ranch to acknowledge getting all the letters now that I didn't get before plus your last one.

I have a note right here on my desk regarding the announcement to be. You can count on it. I had an opportunity to remind Fred about the TV things. At this point, he's really about the only contact I have left in the media.

Thanks again for everything. My people on the foreign scene are reading your manuscript now.

Again, thanks and best regards,

> Ron

> Mr. Laurence W. Beilenson
> Los Angeles, California
> January 15, 1985 [25]

Dear Larry:

Thank you very much for your letter and the *Wall Street Journal* article—I had missed it. Thanks for writing it.

Larry, I was impressed by your own volunteer efforts. After all our years of friendship this was the first I had known of your volunteering for the Russian-Finland conflict and for service in France long before Pearl Harbor. May I say my surprise was brief and almost immediately followed by the realization that this was what I would expect of the Larry Beilenson I know.

God bless you.

> Sincerely,
> Ron

———

Douglas Morrow was a screen writer and movie producer whom Reagan met in Hollywood. Intelligent and aggressive, he peppered Reagan with ideas and proposals.

---

* Laurence W. Beilenson, *The Treaty Trap* (Washington, DC: Public Affairs Press, 1969); Lou Cannon, *President Reagan: The Role of a Lifetime* (New York: Simon & Schuster, 1991), p. 296.

In 1979 Morrow set up a meeting for Reagan to be briefed on our nuclear missile defenses at NORAD*, and in his letters he told fascinating tales of climbing Mount Everest. As Reagan got deeper into his presidency the letters from Morrow became more demanding—including a request to go into space and some grandiose, nutty economic schemes. Reagan finally backed away from him; his last known letter to Morrow was on July 16, 1986. Morrow died in 1994 at age 81.

Mr. Douglas Morrow
Glendale, California
December 23, 1983 [26]

Dear Doug:

Now that I'm straightened out on your Mt. Everest outing (doesn't that sort of underplay it) I've put my NSC† adviser back on it. You'll be hearing from someone in his shop about dates etc.

Please don't advertise that you haven't made the climb yet. I've already had you up there and back to a couple of people now recovering from surgery. They were greatly encouraged to hear of your exploit. If they do find out you're doing it in March or thereabouts I'll tell them you are doing it again—it was so much fun the first time. As for the tax matters I've discussed your letter with Don Regan and asked that the matter be given another go round in light of the additional points you made.

I've also asked him to have his staff analyze the income tax refunds proposal. I share your view that additional savings for retirement should be encouraged. I am however not too sold on making it compulsory.

Nancy sends her best and from both of us to you and Margot‡ we hope your holidays were warm and happy.

Sincerely,
Ron

Mr. Douglas Morrow
Glendale, California
June 10, 1985 [27]

Dear Doug:

Just received your letter and have to say I don't have any answer on your request to go off into the wild blue yonder. The top man at NASA knows this has my approval but I think you understand why I can't make it an order. I've gone out of my way to let him know of my continued interest and will keep on doing that.

As for the Cleveland Clinic invitation, our scheduling people have it plus my

---

* North American Aerospace Defense Command.
† National Security Council.
‡ Doug Morrow's wife.

own recommendation that I do it. They can't finalize anything this far ahead but will keep in touch with the clinic people as the summer progresses.

Doug the tax measure on Social Security was arrived at by the bipartisan group that finally remodeled Social Security in 1983. When we came here the program was going bankrupt and would have become so by July of '83. I tried to get the situation corrected in '81 but our Democratic friends claimed there was no problem and then used the issue in the '82 election. Quite successfully I might add. Truth was Social Security didn't make it to July of '83. We had to borrow $17 billion to keep sending the checks. Then the Democrats (after the election) came around and volunteered to join in an effort to repair the system. Remember in 1977 they had increased the Social Security payroll tax, the largest tax increase in our history, and said it had made Social Security safe until 2050 at least—so it made it until almost 1983. There is no way we could have further increased that tax although the commission did accelerate the implementation of some of the installments. The tax on some not totally dependent on Social Security was just one of several steps which did make it fiscally sound. Our tax reform should do a lot to minimize the effect of the tax.

Give my regards to Margot.

Sincerely,
Ron

Mr. Douglas Morrow
Glendale, California
July 16, 1986 [28]

Dear Doug:

Wait up a minute. Money isn't the big delay on the shuttle, safety is. It's true I wanted to look into this private funding because it was coming up from several directions. As it turned out there would be a conflict with the private sector which is moving toward commercial launching of satellites.

Doug, Jim Fletcher was in yesterday with a full report. He has declared that the next shuttle launch can't be scheduled until the first quarter of 1988. The study of and testing of the solid rocket boosters is part of the problem. Added to this are safety features on the shuttles themselves which are being studied. Yes the money problem has to do with several hundred million to make a start but it's my understanding from Jim that this does not change that 1988 date.

I know this is a disappointment to you but unless I heard him wrong '88 is the scheduled time. Love to Margot.

Regards,
Ron

A. C. Lyles was a longtime executive of Paramount Pictures in Hollywood who produced 20 movies. A friend of Reagan's for over 50 years, he was appointed to the Presi-

dent's Advisory Council on Private Sector Initiatives in 1983, and functioned as a Hollywood liaison, getting celebrities to entertain at the White House. He once said that Reagan possesses "the most optimistic viewpoint I have ever known in my life." *

Mr. A. C. Lyles
Los Angeles, California
June 13, 1983 [29]

Dear A. C.:

It was a really happy time having you and Marf† here. But I have an uneasy feeling that I let the few minutes we actually had time to visit go by without properly thanking you for that wonderful film you produced.

Now I remember that Hollywood truism that you should never get in a scene with a child and there I was with a group. But I thank you. It's going to be harder for Tip (you know who)‡ to convince the citizenry that I eat my young.

Again my heartfelt thanks. Nancy sends her love and from both of us to Marf.

Sincerely,
Ron

Lyles sent Reagan a photograph of a rearing horse from the 1947 movie Stallion Road. *It was the first film Reagan made after World War II and a special favorite of his because of the horses. (His character discovers a cure for anthrax.)*

Mr. A. C. Lyles
Los Angeles, California
May 15, 1986 [30]

Dear A. C.:

I remember this rearing horse very well. We used him in the movie. Like all us performers, he'd reach for the sky whenever the director asked him to. Or, remembering Hollywood, perhaps I should say whenever the director <u>told</u> him to.

Thanks for sending the photo. I'm pleased to have it. You are, as always, very kind and thoughtful.

Nancy sends her love, and from both of us to Marf.

Sincerely,
Ron

P.S. Happy birthday A. C. or is it an anniversary of your 39th?

---

* Cannon, *President Reagan,* p. 179.
† A. C. Lyles's wife, Martha.
‡ Thomas P. (Tip) O'Neill, Speaker of the House of Representatives.

Barney Oldfield was the great nephew of the legendary racing car driver of the same name. He met Reagan on the set of Dodge City *on April 1, 1939. A press officer in World War II, he later worked for Warner Brothers and served as Reagan's publicist, developing a lifelong friendship. As a consultant for Litton Industries he often traveled to the Soviet Union, and exchanged letters with Reagan frequently on a wide variety of subjects.*

Oldfield had heard that Senator Pete Wilson recommended the Presidential Medal of Freedom for Jimmy Stewart,* a dear friend of Reagan. He sent Reagan a long article on Stewart that appeared in the Congressional Record on March 27, 1985. Oldfield died on April 26, 2003.

> Colonel Barney Oldfield
> Beverly Hills, California
> April 24, 1985 [31]

Dear Barney:

I've put my okay on Jimmy for the medal. Thanks for your piece on him. Here I am in Washington and have to get a story in the Congressional Record by way of California.

Your story on Jimmy was great and I learned something. I had never heard the story about his appearance at the Military Reception Center † in World War II.

Thanks again.

> Best regards,
> Ron

Oldfield told Reagan that Disneyland featured a recreation of the meeting of two old soldiers, one American and one Soviet, at the Elbe River in Germany in 1945, and passed on a joke that a high ranking Soviet official, Georgi Arbatov, ‡ asked him to tell Reagan.

He also thanked Reagan for the letter he wrote, at Oldfield's request, to a young

---

* James (Jimmy) Stewart was one of America's great actors. He died in 1997 at the age of 89.

† Jimmy Stewart enlisted on March 22, 1941, almost nine months before Pearl Harbor. He became a pilot and flew 20 flak-strewn missions against German targets, including Berlin. The day he enlisted a clerk asked him where he worked and how much he made. Stewart replied, "MGM in Culver City, California and $2,700 a week." The clerk didn't know who Stewart was and said, "bull." His honor impugned, Stewart gave the clerk the phone number of his payroll department. The clerk called and almost dropped the phone when he got the answer.

‡ Georgi Arbatov was one of the Soviet Union's top experts on the United States, and attended every summit meeting between the two countries from 1961 to 1991. This was the story he asked to pass on: "Negotiations (between nations) is like the couple which when he wanted to, she didn't; when she wanted to, he didn't; when they both wanted to, they didn't have a place—and then, when they finally got a place, they forgot how to do it."

lady, Becky, who was born with an incurable disease and asked to hear from President Reagan. She read the letter every day until she died on May 1, 1988.

Colonel Barney Oldfield
Beverly Hills, California
May 16, 1988 [32]

Dear Barney:

Thanks for all the news about the Elbe reunion. That was quite an emotional moment—not alone for them but for all of us who remember World War II.

I'm sorry however to learn about Becky even though I know she's in a place now where there is no pain.

I hope Arbatov does push the General Secretary into talking about Disneyland. I think a Russian Disneyland would be the high spot of his "glasnost"—once the people got a look at it. You can thank him for his story too, or if I see him first, I will. As you can well understand, we are already cramming for our coming visit, and doing so with mixed emotions.

Nancy sends her best, and from both of us to Vada,*

Ron

Ward Quaal was one of the top radio broadcasting executives in America, the president of WGN Continental Broadcast Company. He met Reagan when the future president was acting in radio commercials for the WGN radio station in Chicago. In 1967, after Reagan became governor of California, Quaal began to correspond with him.

In a February 9, 1983, letter Quaal reported to Reagan that as he "traveled across our lovely land" he felt the people were behind Reagan, and that "they wish him well."

Ward L. Quaal
Chicago, Illinois
February 10, 1983 [33]

Dear Ward:

It was good to hear from you. My heart was warmed by your report on what the good people out there are thinking and feeling.

I agree with you about the need for job training. There is no question but that part of our unemployment problem is structural—not just recession.

When you are next in Washington give Mike Deaver† here in the White House a ring and I'm sure (if I'm here) we can have that five minutes you mentioned.

Best regards,
Ron

---

* Barney Oldfield's wife.
† Michael Deaver was deputy chief of staff in Reagan's White House.

Quaal was given an October 1979 issue of Readers Digest *that contained an article on John Wayne written by Reagan, and called it a "truly splendid statement."*

> Mr. Ward L. Quaal
> Chicago, Illinois
> August 17, 1984 [34]

Dear Ward:

I don't often get "book reviews" on my writing—thank you very much. You were kind to write as you did and I'm most grateful.

I appreciate also your sharing with me the story of your luncheon with Duke. He was really quite a guy. I'm afraid there aren't many like him on the horizon—certainly not in Hollywood.

Love to Dorothy and Nancy sends hers to you both.

> Sincerely,
> Dutch

Charlton Heston, a well-known actor, longtime political activist from the civil rights movement to the present, and an outspoken Republican, was a close friend of Ronald Reagan. Like Reagan, he had been the president of the Screen Actors Guild (1966–1971).

Here Reagan replies to Heston's message that Reagan's speech to a Joint Session of Congress on April 27, 1983, discussing Central America "was superb. It addressed eloquently one of the major issues facing the West."

> Mr. Charlton Heston
> Beverly Hills, California
> May 10, 1983 [35]

Dear Chuck:

Just a line (somewhat tardy) to thank you for your letter and kind words. I'm most grateful. The battle goes on and there will be a struggle to win approval in the House of any meaningful help in Central America. We still have a few who can see no threat from the left—only from the right and you don't have to be very far right.

Nancy sends her best. Thanks again.

> Sincerely,
> Ron

Mr. Charlton Heston
Beverly Hills, California
February 12, 1986[36]

Dear Chuck:

Just a line to thank you for your letter and kind words. Also to let you know I ran a TV tape last night and saw you in another stellar role: you were narrating a one-hour exposé of how television distorted the war in Vietnam. It was just great and is something all Americans should see—but then we know TV will never help them see it.

Thanks again.

Sincerely,
Ron

George Murphy, for many years an actor and producer, was elected senator from California in 1964 and served one term. He was especially close to Reagan. In 1943 they co-starred in This Is the Army, *with Murphy playing Reagan's father. They were close allies fighting the attempted Communist takeover of some Hollywood unions in the 1940s, with Murphy as president of the Screen Actors Guild during the critical period 1944–1946. Reagan said that he owed "a great deal to this cool, dapper guy who had to deal with me in my early white-eyed liberal daze."* *

Senator George Murphy
West Palm Beach, Florida
May 3, 1979[37]

Dear Murph:

It was good to get your letter and to catch up on all the gossip and rumors. I appreciate your doing this very much.

While I am not going to declare until fall, the formation of the national committee has allowed us to go forward with organizing quite a crew in the field, and things are looking very good. I know where you are—there's a little Texas influence, and it's easy to hear a lot about Big John.† We have just done an in-depth poll which presents a somewhat different picture with Baker‡ next in line and John trailing him. I don't underestimate him. I know he can be a formidable candidate. He is a good campaigner. I assure you there will be no overconfidence in our camp. But things are holding up well.

Regarding our lady who got the bad deal in the State Department, she was an-

---

* Reagan, *Where's the Rest of Me?* p. 179.
† John B. Connally, former governor of Texas, and secretary of the treasury under President Nixon.
‡ Howard H. Baker, minority (Republican) leader of the United States Senate, 1977–1981.

swered and now is being contacted about a possible meeting in Washington when I am there before the end of this month. It wasn't Lyn * who didn't answer. He had evidently handed a message, if he received one, over to our office, and Mike Deaver told me that he did respond to the effect that when we had a chance to get to Washington, she would be contacted, and this will be the first time coming up toward the end of May. It looks like it's going to be an exciting time and a busy one. Of course, having gone around the track once, I have no illusions about how tough it can be.

Thanks again, Murph, for all you are doing in my behalf and for sending me all the news. Nancy sends her best, and we both hope to see you soon.

Best regards,
Ron

––––––

Reagan reports to George Murphy on the new makeup of his White House staff—Donald Regan was chief of staff and Patrick Buchanan was director of communications—and reassures Murphy about George Shultz, the secretary of state. Right after World War II Reagan had joined a few organizations that turned out to be Communist fronts, and later fought the Communist infiltration of the movie industry at the Screen Actors Guild—thus Reagan's comment about their experience with the "little red brethren."

The Honorable George Murphy
Palm Beach, Florida
March 13, 1985 [38]

Dear Murph:

What a pleasure it was to hear from you. I can only quote the Governor of North Carolina in what he said to the Governor of South Carolina—"It's a long time between drinks."

Thank you for your birthday good wishes and your generous words. I'm pleased to hear how you feel about our new setup here and I share your view. I too, think we have a good team, particularly with Don and Pat on board. † I think with regard to George S., ‡ there has been some press speculation not based on any facts. He's pretty solid and we agree the greatest part of the time. When we don't he's a good soldier and marches to my drum.

That sudden press outbreak about my liberal past is kind of funny. H—l,

––––––

* Lyn Nofziger.
† Donald T. Regan, and Patrick J. Buchanan.
‡ George P. Shultz

I told all that myself in my autobiography, *Where's the Rest of Me?* I also spread it around back when you and I were touring the mashed potato circuit. A lot of the younger set don't know how experienced you and I are with regard to the little red brethren.

Nancy and I hope we see you both soon. Let us know if you get back here among the Potomac puzzle palaces.

She sends her love and from both of us to Bette.

Sincerely,
Ron

The Honorable George Murphy
Cashiers, North Carolina
October 29, 1987 [39]

Dear Murph:

It was good to hear from you and I'm grateful for your generous words. By the time you get this I will have announced another nominee for the Supreme Court. I promise you he'll be as conservative as Judge Bork. There is no way I'd go for a touch of liberalism to win over the lynch mob. We'll see if they have the nerve to repeat their scandalous performance. I don't think they will. Of course, in the meantime, we have to face up to the loss of a nominee who was, in my opinion, the most outstanding candidate in 50 years.

We're now in a session to see if we can get the Congress to face up, once and for all, to their responsibility to lend a hand in solving the deficit problem.

Nancy sends her love and, from both of us, to that lovely gal of yours.

Sincerely,
Ron

P.S. Just announced—Our nominee will be Circuit Judge Douglas Ginsburg. He's a good friend of Bork and just as conservative.

Earl B. Dunckel was a newspaperman in Schenectady, New York, before he was hired by General Electric and became the "communicator" for the GE Theater. In August 1954 Reagan was selected to be the host of the GE Theater. Part of his job included visiting and speaking at 135 GE plants with 700,000 employees. Dunckel was assigned to travel around the country with Reagan and did so for two years.

Dunckel, a political conservative, became close to Reagan. He also discovered that Reagan did his own speechwriting. After Reagan was elected president, Dunckel said, "he is a very good writer. . . . I don't care how many speech writers they have over there at the White House, the end product is his. I'll bet any amount of money on that."

Dunckel was transferred to another position at GE in 1956, and eventually left the *company. He continued to stay in touch with Reagan through Reagan's governorship of California and his campaigns for the presidency.**

Mr. Earl Dunckel
Stamford, Connecticut
December 27, 1976[40]

Dear Earl:

Yours was a good letter, with sound advice. I'm convinced that J.F. † has decided he's running again in 1980, which explains his present party activism.

I share your view that, with or without Carter, we are in for an economic belly-ache. As for England, only a coalition government can avert the coming disaster and it will have to have the spirit that ennobled England in the "Battle of Britain." Don't worry about John Sears. He is a political technician, not an adviser on philosophy or policy. I intend to speak out, as you described it on what I believe is right for America.

Best regards,
Ron

Mr. E. B. Dunckel
Stamford, Connecticut
July 20, 1979[41]

Dear Earl:

Just a line between trips—the last one to Mexico and the next one, tomorrow, to Northern California. But this is in response to your letter.

Perhaps you know already, but we're tentatively set on an announcement date in early November. In the meantime, come August, I am going to vacation.

Of course you can be of help. You already have been, and please don't think there is any holding back on the part of Mike Deaver and Pete Hannaford. They understand our relationship and are as delighted as I am at anything you can do. I think your press contacts and your ability at detecting trend lines is an area where we certainly can use your help. Possibly, as I get closer to the day, we can settle on some specifics, but I am counting on you.

Best regards.

Sincerely,
Ron

---

* Edwards, *Early Reagan,* pp. 452–57.
† President Gerald R. Ford.

Mr. Earl Dunckel
October 16, 1979[42]

Dear Earl:

Just a quick line before I board a plane again. I've decided, incidentally, that I am not going to say I get on planes, I'm just going to say—I wear them.

Anyway, thanks for the material. I may be able to get it into a radio script before they come to an end, which they will do with my announcement. But, I share your concern and want you to know that over the past year or so, I have done several radio scripts mainly on the increasing knowledge about the danger of marijuana.* Something really has to be done.

Again, thanks and best regards.

Sincerely,
Ron

Judge William Clark was one of Reagan's closest friends and had worked with him since the mid 1960s.

Bohemian Club Membership Committee
San Francisco, California
February 22, 1982[43]

To the Bohemian Club Membership Committee:

I am pleased to recommend to you William Clark for membership in the Bohemian Club. I have known him and his family for many years and hold him in the highest esteem.

He served as my chief of staff for a time during my term as Governor of California. It was my pleasure to appoint him to the bench where he served with such distinction that I named him to the California State Supreme Court. He is now serving me as foreign policy adviser in charge of the National Security Council.

In each and every position that he has held he has performed in an outstanding manner. But I'm aware that you, in fulfilling your responsibility on the Membership Committee of the Bohemian Club, look for more than ability and success in business or profession.

With that in mind I can recommend William Clark to you with no reservation whatsoever. Let me paraphrase Will Rogers and say I've never met anyone who, after getting acquainted with Bill Clark, didn't like him and hold him in the highest regard. He will be of great service to Bohemia, and contribute to the warmth and camaraderie we value so highly.

Sincerely,
Ronald Reagan

---

* Reagan had given national radio broadcasts on the dangers of marijuana in May and August of 1979. His last radio broadcast before announcing he was running for president was taped on October 25, 1979.

Walter Annenberg, a media magnate, was one of the wealthiest persons in America; in 1989 he sold TV Guide *magazine and other holdings for three billion dollars. He was a well-known philanthropist, a political activist, and had been appointed ambassador to Great Britain by President Nixon. A longtime friend of Reagan's, he shared many of Reagan's views, contributed generously to Reagan's presidential library, and gave wonderful New Year's Eve parties at Sunnylands, his estate in California. Reagan and Nancy regularly attended these parties, and Reagan often played a traditional round of golf with George Shultz and others.*

The Honorable Walter Annenberg
Rancho Mirage, California
March 18, 1988 [44]

Dear Walter:

Happy 41st anniversary of your 39th birthday! I've been 39 years old 38 times now and still find it most enjoyable, especially when you consider the alternative.

Of course it's also a time for looking back, taking a trip down memory lane. I'm doing that right now, and you'd be surprised how many of the happier times have to do with a gentleman named Walter Annenberg.

The first, or should I say the earliest memory, has to do with a somewhat homesick, lonely performer on a train between Philadelphia and New York. I was the lonely performer. Then a porter delivered an invitation from a gentleman in the club car. You were that gentleman. You asked me to join you, lovely Lee and your friends. For the rest of the ride I was anything but homesick and lonely.

The memories continue, visits in Philadelphia, then beautiful Sunnylands and, yes, Winfield House in London. And always a kind and thoughtful host but more important a cherished friend.

Walter, there are no words to express how much Nancy and I treasure your friendship and the support you've given in our present occupation. During the holiday season when people say, "Happy New Year," we know it will be happy. We'll be with you and Lee in Sunnylands.

Happy Birthday and God Bless You.

Sincerely,
Ron

Annenberg, from time to time, would suggest policies and personnel to Reagan. They were not always accepted. In his January 17, 1986, letter Annenberg noted that he had read a Wall Street Journal *essay on the meaning of President Eisenhower's talk on the "military-industrial complex," and asks Reagan if it would "be politically acceptable and wise for our country to set into motion legislation to limit the profits of the so-called 'military-industrial complex.'"*

The Honorable Walter Annenberg
Rancho Mirage, California
January 24, 1986[45]

Dear Walter:

Thanks for the *Wall Street Journal* essay, I hadn't seen it before.

I'm not sure legislation limiting profits wouldn't open doors to further government controls on business in general, but I'll keep this in mind. In the meantime, we've made considerable progress contrary to the drumbeat of propaganda about the defense buildup. In the first place, I have a commission headed by Dave Packard that will be reporting in shortly on their study of everything having to do with defense—emphasis on procurement.

When we got here, we found there was little or no competitive bidding on contracts. That has been changed with the result that virtually every major weapon system is coming in ahead of schedule and under budget.

I'll keep my eyes and ears open with Ike's warning in mind. We're looking forward to seeing you both.

Love to Lee.

Sincerely,
Ron

In an October 23, 1987, letter Annenberg reminded Reagan of his previous support of Arlin Adams, a member of the Appeals Court in Pennsylvania, for the Supreme Court.

Ambassador Walter Annenberg
Radnor, Pennsylvania
October 29, 1987[46]

Dear Walter:

I received your letter and suggestion about Judge Arlin Adams too late. We had already decided on and notified Judge Ginsberg and this afternoon I announced his nomination.

You are so right about the character of the people who testified for and against Judge Bork. I had a complete list of them and the comparison was unbelievable. The shenanigans that went on to see that good witnesses didn't get on prime-time TV were disgraceful.

I'm off to join Nancy in Phoenix.

Again thanks and warmest regards,

Ron

William Wilson was a wealthy investment counselor in Los Angeles. A longtime friend of Reagan's, he often rode with him. Wilson and his wife Betty knew Reagan was look-

ing for a ranch in 1973 and drove him to see what would become Rancho del Cielo. The ranch covers 688 acres and sits on a plateau 2,250 feet above sea level.

In 1981 President Reagan named Wilson his personal representative to the Holy See (Vatican); in 1984 Wilson was named ambassador to the Holy See, serving until 1986.

Ambassador and Mrs. William Wilson
Los Angeles, California
February 5, 1984[47]

Dear Betty and Bill:

Thank you for my very handsome suede jacket. Believe me I won't wear it while chopping wood. It's really the best looking thing I have.

The only thing that could have been nicer is if you'd wrapped yourselves up and popped out when I opened the box.

Nancy sends her love and again thank you.

Sincerely,
Ron

————

In 1987 Wilson and his wife met in New York with Cardinal William Baum, the grand penitentiary for the Vatican.* They were told that he, the pope, and others in the Catholic Church were increasingly concerned that "the people of Europe are beginning to experience a spiritual fatigue leading to a moral fatigue." Wilson wrote Reagan that the Cardinal is doing "all in its power to provide the spiritual leadership," but that "the only source of secular leadership is the United States."

Ambassador William A. Wilson
Los Angeles, California
March 5, 1987[48]

Dear Bill:

Just a few lines about your letter of February 20. You realize of course that you'll be reading the words of a Protestant even though the son of a Catholic father. But I assure you that latter point means I haven't even a tinge of religious prejudice.

Bill I'm worried about two things having to do with the spiritual or moral fatigue the Cardinal mentioned. One is general and in my view has to do with a secu-

————

* In the Catholic Church the penitentiary is a tribunal in the Curia Romana, presided over by a cardinal (grand penitentiary), having jurisdiction over such matters as penance, confession, dispensation, absolution, and impediments, and dealing with questions of conscience reserved for the Holy See. The Curia Romana is the body of congregations, offices, permanent commissions, etc., that assist the pope in the government and administration of the church. The Holy See is the office of the pope.

larism that is so prevalent today. An example—sex education in our schools. Well-intentioned though it might have been it is taught in a framework of only being a physical act—like eating a ham sandwich. The educators are fearful that any references to sin or morality will be viewed as violating the church and state separation.

This has been carried into other things so that outside the home or church no values are being taught or emphasized.

With regard to the Catholic church itself, I believe there is a faction within the clergy that is out of step with basic moral tenets. When I spoke a few years ago at the Notre Dame commencement, a group of Maryknoll nuns came down from Chicago and picketed the campus in protest against my being there. A sizable number of that order are today supportive of the Communist government of Nicaragua.

On the Protestant side that division is also present in several denominations as well as the National Council of Churches. By contrast the very fundamentalist denominations who stick closely to the Bible are showing an increase in followers. Maybe there is a clue there for all of us, "Let's get back to the ten commandments."

Well that's enough of a lecture from me. Nancy sends her love to you both.

Sincerely,

Ron

William (Bill) Lane and Reagan were both members of a California riding club, Vistadores Rancheros. Lane sent Reagan a tape of a ceremony that took place on a Ranchero trek in 1955 celebrating its 25th anniversary, believing the tape "reflects some of the early pioneer spirit" that Reagan admires. Lane, the former publisher of Sunset *magazine, was appointed ambassador to Australia (1985–1988) by President Reagan.*

Mr. L.W. Lane, Jr.
Menlo Park, California
December 14, 1984 [49]

Dear Bill:

Thank you very much for sending me the tape. I look forward to hearing it. Of course it will add to the homesickness a Californian lives with during any absence from California. My own is compounded by enforced absence from the Grove and Rancheros.

I'm most grateful for your generous words about our economic situation. I'm determined that if our administration is to meet its destiny we must once and for all get control of government spending which has been totally out of control for decades past.

Have a Merry Christmas and a happy holiday season. Again, thanks.

Best regards,

Ron

Victor Krulak, a retired three-star Marine Corps general, was an old friend and Bo-hemian Grove campmate* of President Reagan. Krulak wrote for the San Diego Union *and frequently advised Reagan informally.*

> Lt. General Victor H. Krulak, USMC (Ret.)
> San Diego, California
> August 23, 1980[50]

Dear Brute:

I've just arrived home and found your letter of July 30th awaiting me. I haven't even had time to read your attached articles, but they're right by my bed, and I will be getting into them. Thanks very much for sending them. I know they'll contain some helpful information.

I missed being at the Grove very much. There is one thing to be said about this contest I'm in—win or lose, either way, I'm going to be able to get back to Owl's Nest † next year. I had fully intended to be there until, after the nomination, I discovered I might be an embarrassment to our fellow Bohemians because of the round-the-clock surveillance by the press. They camp down at my driveway these days.

Thanks for your good wishes and for your prayers and I hope I'll be seeing you soon.

> Sincerely,
> Ron

> Lt. General V. H. Krulak, USMC (Ret.)
> San Diego, California
> February 4, 1985[51]

Dear Brute:

Thanks for your letter and the item I can hang on my jacket. I keep looking down the road to the time I can wear it at Owl's Nest.

But once again my biggest thank you is for that "open letter column." I'm most grateful for what I know will be helpful. I like your title for our strategic defense initiative. I bristle every time our media friends (?) call it "Star Wars."

I enjoyed your book ‡ but was amazed to learn of the extent of the effort that was made to do away with the Marine corps. Thank the Lord they failed.

> Best Regards,
> Ron

---

* The Bohemian Club has 121 camps scattered throughout the redwood forest they use for two weeks in July; Krulak and Reagan were both members of one of the camps called "Owl's Nest," which had about 25 members.

† Reagan did not attend the Bohemian Grove encampments during his presidency because he would have had to bring with him many Secret Service agents.

‡ Victor H. Krulak, *First to Fight: An Inside View of the U.S. Marine Corps,* United States Naval Institute, Annapolis, Maryland 1984.

CHAPTER FIVE

Hollywood Years and Friendships

ON MAY 22, 1937, *Reagan drove away from Des Moines, Iowa, and began a new life. A country boy who grew up in Illinois, he had gone to work as a sports broadcaster after he left college. Now he had just been offered a seven-year movie contract with Warner Brothers, starting at $200 a week. He replied by telegram to his agent, Bill Meiklejohn: "Sign Before They Change Their Minds."*

He left Iowa in style, in a creamy beige, V-8 Lafayette convertible coupe. The almost 2,000-mile trip took three days—across Nebraska and Wyoming, down through Utah and Nevada and then across the California desert to Hollywood. He was 26 years old.

Reagan worked in Los Angeles for the next 25 years. He made movies, became a well-known star, served in the Army for four years during World War II, headed the Screen Actors Guild for eight years, performed a nightclub act at the Last Frontier Hotel in Las Vegas, and then moved into television as the host of the General Electric Theater. *It was an exhilarating time, a roller coaster ride that made him a celebrity, broke up one marriage, turned him into a skilled labor negotiator, and changed his politics.*

He arrived in Los Angeles as a handsome youngster, brilliant, cocky, and sometimes brash, a New Deal Democrat. When he left the entertainment business in the early 1960s he was middle-aged, but still handsome, tempered by his experiences, more subdued and deliberate, a confident, conservative Republican.

All together he acted in 53 movies. Thirty were made during his early career— from 1937 to 1941—as he quickly became one of the best-known stars in the business. His first was Love Is On the Air. *He appeared with Humphrey Bogart and Bette Davis and starred in* Knute Rockne—All American, Santa Fe Trail, International Squadron, *and* Kings Row.

At the end of 1940, Reagan was ranked by Warner Brothers as their top feature *player. By early 1941 he had joined James Cagney and Humphrey Bogart as a top star.* The Audience Research Institute predicted that "within three years Reagan would be among the top ten in ability to sell movie tickets." He was even ranked ahead of John Wayne. Later, in August 1941, Warner Brothers signed Reagan to a new three-year contract at $1,650 a week. A national Gallup poll in the middle of 1941 ranked Reagan in the top 100 movie stars in the country, albeit in 82nd place.†*

Reagan's movie momentum was stopped by the Japanese bombs that fell on Pearl Harbor in December 1941. Even though he was 30 years old, and married with one child, he went on active duty. He reported to Fort Mason, in San Francisco, on April 19, 1942, as a reserve office in the Army Cavalry. He was now 2nd Lieutenant Reagan. Rejected for combat duty because of dismal eyesight, he was put to work on training films used to identify enemy aircraft, and others to boost the morale of the troops. Reagan was discharged on July 11, 1945, as a captain.

The four years in the Army broke the momentum of his movie career. During the war years movie attendance increased over 50 percent, new young actors appeared on screen—and Reagan reached 34 years. He made some good movies after World War II—Stallion Road, Storm Warning, and Law and Order—but by the middle of the 1950s his appeal had faded.

By the end of the war, however, Reagan was far more interested in politics and the future course of the world. In 1947 he was elected president of the Screen Actors Guild, the labor union representing actors. He soon learned the art of negotiation and was re-elected, serving until 1952. He was later elected to another term from 1959 to 1960.

His union presidency was a time of bitter, often violent, labor strife. The Communist Party tried to infiltrate the movie industry and Reagan, almost by default, became one of its leading opponents. Reagan faced lies and even physical threats‡ which helped to make him an implacable enemy of Communism. In 1946 he obtained a license to carry a gun, and was "fitted with a shoulder holster and a loaded .32 Smith & Wesson" that he strapped on whenever he left his home.

As his politics changed (though still a Democrat he supported Eisenhower in 1952) he moved into the budding field of television—becoming the host of the General Electric (GE) Theater in 1954. He hosted a major national variety show for GE, and at the same time began to travel around the country visiting the 135 GE plants. During these visits he walked the factory floors, spoke to workers, answered their questions—and gave speeches, which increasingly took on a conservative political coloration.

By 1960, still nominally a Democrat, he was actively campaigning for Richard Nixon against John F. Kennedy. After his change from Democrat to Republican, Rea-

---

* Edmund Morris, *Dutch* (New York: Random House, 1999), p. 172.

† Stephen Vaughn, *Ronald Reagan in Hollywood* (New York: Cambridge University Press, 1994), pp. 36–37.

‡ On October 3, 1946, while doing a beach scene for the movie *Night Unto Night*, Reagan received an anonymous telephone call threatening to disfigure his face with acid so that he would never act again. (Stephen Vaughn, *Ronald Reagan in Hollywood*, p. 140.)

gan rarely acknowledged changing any of his policy views, claiming that the party had left him. The record shows little trace of any views that would have been compatible with the Democratic Party of the 1960s.

In 1962 he changed his party registration. Four years later he was elected governor of California.

During his time in Hollywood and on the GE Theater, Reagan met many famous people in the movie and entertainment business. Some he became close to, and many stayed in touch with him over the years. The letters, almost all written in post-Hollywood years, suggest that only a few became close friends (George Murphy, in particular), but his relations were warm with John Wayne and Frank Sinatra. Reagan also wrote to many of his fans, especially one lifelong correspondent, Lorraine Wagner.

A 22-year-old woman, Joy Hodges, opened the door to Reagan's movie career. In 1937 Reagan arranged to spend his month's vacation on Santa Catalina Island, California, covering the spring training of the Chicago Cubs. In exchange for giving up his vacation, WHO, his radio station in Des Moines, Iowa, paid for the trip. His true purpose was to explore the possibility of a movie career. In early March he met with Joy Hodges, who was singing with the Jimmy Grier Band at the Biltmore Bowl, and told her he wanted "to visit a studio" and then "admitted he wanted a movie test."

Joy called her agent, George Ward of the Meiklejohn Agency, and arranged the test. The night before, Joy rehearsed with him and later said, "I couldn't believe his ability to read a page and practically recite it back."

He passed the screen test, and on March 22, 1937, received a telegram with an offer of a seven-year contract with Warner Brothers.

In 1983 he wrote a tribute to Joy for her high school's 50th reunion.

East High Class of 1933
Des Moines, Iowa
April 25, 1983 [1]

To the East High Class of 1933:

I know you are holding your 50th reunion and I wanted to bring you greetings and warm regards on this occasion. I have a special feeling for the class of '33. I arrived in Des Moines a year or two after your graduation and a year or two after that I met a member of your class. I had to go to California to do it. I was sports announcing for WHO and had been sent to California to cover the Chicago Cubs spring training.

I also carried strict orders to contact a young singer and actress who had left WHO for Hollywood before I arrived. Everyone in the station insisted that I carry greetings to that young lady and tell her how much she was missed at WHO. Well I carried out those orders faithfully and then got carried away and confided to her that I nursed a secret yen for acting myself.

Now Joy (you see I know who is reading this message) I don't want you to get self-conscious but I have to explain why I feel the way I do about the East High Class of '33.

Joy Hodges listened to my story, gave me wise counsel and introduced me to someone who could open the magic door. A studio contract followed and I left the Cubs for Warner Brothers Studio and twenty-five years of acting.

Now you all know why I think you are very nice people and why I really wish I could be there with you. Have a wonderful time.

If I thought you remembered I'd sign this "Dutch." Maybe I'd better play safe and just say—

Sincerely,
Ronald Reagan

———

One of Joy Hodges's friends, another Iowan, was Hugh Sidey, the political and White House correspondent for Time *magazine. Joy sent President Reagan a June 9, 1988, letter she received from Sidey, in which he praised Reagan's performance at the 1988 summit in Moscow: "Not in my time have I heard such a series of fine speeches— defining his Presidency, his leadership, the USA. He did them superbly. . . . We are really going to miss this guy."*

Mrs. Joy Hodges Schiess
Katonah, New York
July 11, 1988 [2]

Dear Joy:

How good it was to hear from you and how kind you are. Thanks for your generous words.

You surprised me with that note from Hugh. First of all, I wasn't aware of your friendship and second, while he's always fair, unlike so many of his media mates, I didn't know he looked upon me so favorably. I'm most pleased because I have admiration for him.

There will be some things of course that we will miss when we leave here, but we are really looking forward to California and boots and saddles. I have a horse waiting for me at the ranch. I hope he's ready for a lot of riding.

Well, once again, it was great to hear from you and to stroll down memory lane a bit. Give Gene my best regards.

Sincerely,
Dutch

———

Reagan responds to an inquiry about the impact of his college days and tells about the extent of his formal training in acting.

Mr. Robert V. Iosue II
Gettysburg, Pennsylvania
June 20, 1982[3]

Dear Rob Iosue:

Thanks very much for your letter and your kind words. I'm happy if my remarks were of help to you.

As I look back on those college days I find the entire experience contributed to my education. It's true I was caught up in a number of extracurricular activities besides football. There was the drama club, and that certainly contributed to my earlier career in Hollywood. In fact, that was the only formal training in acting I ever had. But I got involved in student government also, as well as staging homecoming and putting out the yearbook. Again, as I say, looking back I realize all those things were part of my education.

Best of luck to you and hang in there.

Sincerely,
Ronald Reagan

———

Eddie Foy, Jr., played the role of Reagan's sidekick in four movies made in 1939 and 1940. His granddaughter, Dina Elizabeth, became interested in her background, and wrote to Reagan requesting any information or memorabilia that the President might have about Foy. Reagan remembers the names of the movies and the order in which he made them—his 11th, 13th, 17th, and 20th movies. Foy died in 1983 at age 78.

Ms. Dina Elizabeth Foy
Las Vegas, Nevada
December 21, 1987[4]

Dear Ms. Foy:

I'm sorry I don't have any memorabilia regarding movies I worked in with your grandfather. If it will help, however, let me tell you that he and I made four movies together at Warner Bros. Incidentally, the producer of those pictures was his brother Brynie Foy.*

The pictures were a kind of series based on the records of the U. S. Secret Service. They were *Secret Service of the Air, Code of the Secret Service, Smashing the Money Ring,* and *Murder in the Air.* We were great friends and enjoyed working together. He usually played a kind of comedy relief role and close buddy of "Brass Bancroft" † (me).

Please give your father my very best regards.

Sincerely,
Ronald Reagan

———

* "Brynie" was the nickname of Bryan W. Foy.
† Reagan's screen name in each of these four movies.

From time to time people would write to Reagan asking him about his movie career. The following two handwritten drafts were probably written in the 1970s in response to such requests.

In 1938 Reagan had parts in two movies with Humphrey Bogart—The Amazing Dr. Clitterhouse *and* Swing Your Lady. *In 1939 Reagan played in* Dark Victory, *which starred Bette Davis and Humphrey Bogart.*

Jim
Circa 1970s[5]

Dear Jim:

I was in several pictures with "Bogie" but all before World War II. At that time I was just starting and, while he was more or less established, he was not rated as a star and played almost villain parts. He was an easygoing, extremely friendly fellow who went out of his way to be helpful to a beginner like myself.

During the war, Warner Brothers was unable to get George Raft for *Casablanca* and as so often happens settled for Bogie because he was under contract. The rest is history. It was one of those magic blessings every actor dreams of. He became a top star and deservedly so but he remained the same unassuming, nice guy he'd always been.

Enclosed is the picture you requested. I don't have any "stills" of the two of us.

Best regards,
Ronald Reagan

Jack Brownlee
Eureka, Illinois
Circa 1970s[6]

Dear Jack:

Forgive me taking so long to answer your December letter but I've been trying to track down information which could be helpful to you regarding your film festival idea.

First let me say I'm honored you'd like to do this, and second I'm well aware of the time drag on some of those "indoor" weekends 'neath the elms.

My problem is that I have no personal collection of such films, and all the studios have disposed of their backlogs to distributors who service the TV market. My brother being with a large advertising firm* has been helping and thinks he's located a source for the films there in the Midwest, so you'll be hearing directly from him.

May I suggest, if it works out, a few films of mine that might suit your purpose.

---

* Reagan's older brother, Neil, worked for McCann-Erickson.

I do this in self-defense because all of us have some turkeys we'd like to forget. Pre-World War Two—Warner Brothers: *Brother Rat, Knute Rockne—All American, Kings Row* (this one has been named as one of the all time great pictures).* Postwar: *The Girl from Jones Beach, Voice of the Turtle* (this now appears under a different name due to some legality over title—but it's the only picture I did with Eleanor Parker), *The Hasty Heart, Working Her Way Through College* (a musical based on the stage classic *The Male Animal*), and *Storm Warning.*† From Universal: *Bedtime for Bonzo,* and *Louisa.*‡

I hope it all works out.

Best regards,
Ronald Reagan

Michael Palmer, a lecturer on motion pictures, has had repeated requests for a "lecture on Ronald Reagan's career in the entertainment world," and wanted Reagan's approval. He intended to lead up to a showing of the 1940 film Santa Fe Trail *in which Reagan portrays Lt. George Custer.*

Mr. Michael Palmer
Port Jefferson, New York
February 17, 1983 [7]

Dear Mr. Palmer:

Helene Von Damm delivered your letter. I have no objection to your doing what you proposed. Like anyone else who ever made pictures I made a few I'd rather not have shown again but *Santa Fe Trail* isn't one of them. Incidentally I was put in that picture as second lead to Errol Flynn the day after the Knute Rockne picture was sneak previewed.

I don't know what access to movie prints you have but *Kings Row* was probably the finest picture I ever made. Others that cause me no shame are *Voice of*

---

* *Brother Rat* (1938) was about the Virginia Military Institute; "brother rat" was the name cadets called each other. *Knute Rockne—All American* (1940) is a football story in which Reagan plays the legendary George Gipp ("The Gipper"). *Kings Row* (1942) was considered the most distinguished film of Reagan's acting career.

† *The Girl from Jones Beach* (1949) is about a beautiful school teacher who prefers to be admired for her brains; *The Voice of the Turtle* (1947) is about a soldier on leave who meets a beautiful woman; *The Hasty Heart* (1949) is about a Scottish soldier who is kept in a Burma hospital in 1945 after the war is over because he only has a month to live; *She's Working Her Way Through College* (1952) was an old-fashioned musical comedy; and in *Storm Warning* (1951), Reagan played the role of a prosecutor crusading to break up the Ku Klux Klan.

‡ *Bedtime for Bonzo* (1951) was a well-regarded comedy where Reagan played opposite a chimpanzee, which later earned him many jibes. *Louisa* (1950) was an unusual comedy where Reagan played a genial, middle-aged architect.

the Turtle, The Winning Team (the life story of Grover Cleveland Alexander)—well that's enough.

Good luck to you and best regards,

Ronald Reagan

One of Reagan's old fans sent him six bottles of thimbleberry jam, and three original letters Reagan's mother had sent to him. He also sent some George Gipp "memorabilia," saying the publicity Reagan gets about his movie role as Gipp reminded him of President Truman's long association with "The Missouri Waltz." He wondered if Reagan was still "interested in Gipp."

> Mr. Chet Sampson
> Hollywood, California
> May 22, 1986 [8]

Dear Chet:

It was good to hear from you. Thanks for the jam and for all the Gipp mementos and for those letters of my mother. You are very kind.

You wondered about Gipp and whether this might be a forgotten part of my past. Quite the contrary. He has remained very much a part of my life, indeed playing him was the role that moved me into the star category. Curiously enough, at political rallies during my last campaign there would always be signs out in the crowd referring to me as "The Gipper." And believe me, I liked that very much.

When you make that trip to Washington let the girls know your schedule in advance and a meeting will be arranged. It will be good to see you.

Thanks again.

> Sincerely,
> Ron

Hazelwood was an estate outside Dixon bought by Charles and Myrtle Walgreen in 1928; Charles died in 1939. Reagan caddied at Hazelwood while in college. He stayed there as a guest of Mrs. Walgreen on his September 14–16, 1941, visit with Louella Parsons, who was also from Dixon. In this letter—the only letter we have found from his years on active duty in the military—he thanks Mrs. Walgreen for sending him pictures of the trip.

> Mrs. Charles Walgreen
> June 7, 1942 [9]

Dear Mrs. Walgreen:

This is just a note and a very belated one to thank you for that beautiful book of pictures of our Dixon trip. You were very kind to think of it and perhaps you'll understand how much I appreciate it when I tell you that such things as that celebration are now very highly treasured memories because I'm on active duty in the army.

Having held a reserve officers commission for several years the party of December 7 soon resulted in a change of job for me.

Well one of these days we'll finish the job and then maybe who knows we'll meet again at Hazelwood. In the meantime I have the pictures & the memories.

Thanks again & Best to you always—

Sincerely
Ronald Reagan
2nd Lt. Cav.

_____

During the latter part of World War II, Reagan was stationed at the Army Air Corps installation in Culver City, California. One of his duties was director of administration. On July 7, 1945, he sent a report to Major (Robert) Carson informing him of the following violations—"At 2027 [10:27 p.m.] lights burning in Major Carson's office . . . floor littered with papers . . . cigarette trays full in script clerk and asst managers' offices." And with his report Reagan sent Carson a detailed doodle showing an office with an overflowing cigarette tray, Reagan standing in the open doorway pointing, and a soldier on his knees on the floor in the midst of piles of paper saying, "But sir! If I turn off the light, I can't find Major Carson."

Carson saved the old report and doodle, and sent them to Governor Reagan in Sacramento.

Mr. Robert Carlson
Los Angeles, California
December 10, 1969 [10]

Dear Bob:

It was wonderful to hear from you, and I appreciated getting back the sample of my doodling. Obviously I was never intended to be a cartoonist, but someplace in the divine scheme of things perhaps I was an adjutant* because what I'm doing now was always in the cards. It is a relief to have had a least a little experience with the paper clips and the paper shuffling.

Turn out the lights and pick up those cigarette butts.

I hope our paths cross again soon.

Best regards,
Ronald Reagan
Governor

_____

* An adjutant is a staff officer in the Army who assists the commanding officer and is responsible for correspondence.

Reagan's wartime duties during World War II chiefly involved wartime propaganda—from starring in full-length movies such as This Is the Army *to making shorter films that taught our troops how to recognize enemy aircraft or raised morale. These shorter films included titles such as* The P-51 Story, For God and Country, Jap Zero, Target Tokyo, Fight for the Sky: Air War over Germany, *and* The Rear Gunner.

On January 17, 1944, Reagan was a participant in a one-hour national radio broadcast to sell war bonds, playing a fatigued soldier in a foxhole on the front lines. The other participants included Henry Morgenthau, Jr., Secretary of the Treasury, General Dwight D. Eisenhower, Admiral Chester W. Nimitz, and Bing Crosby.

About 45 minutes into the broadcast Secretary Morgenthau says, "Your government is determined that final surrender will be complete and unconditional. We're going to be sure this time that the enemy lays down its ideas as well as its arms."

Reagan replies: "That brings up a point, sir. What's going to happen to the apes that started this thing . . . the Nazis and the Fascists and those little . . . yellow . . .

Secretary Morgenthau interrupts: "You'll find your answer in Russia . . . The Russians are removing some of the worst stains from the face of this earth . . . by stringing the ringleaders of hate up and letting them hang there until they are dead. That is the final assurance of the future of free men." *

On January 22, 1944, Secretary of the Treasury Morgenthau wrote to Captain Reagan in Culver City thanking him and saying "this was the most effective program of its kind since the beginning of the war."

Thirty-eight years later, Henry Morgenthau III, the eldest son of Morgenthau, sent President Reagan a reminder of that day.

> Mr. Henry Morgenthau III
> Cambridge, Massachusetts
> February 2, 1982 [11]

Dear Mr. Morgenthau:

Thank you very much for the photo you sent. I well remember that trip to New York for the Bond Drive. I hope you have received your copy. If not, I know it's on its way.

Again, my thanks and best regards.

> Sincerely,
> Ronald Reagan

---

* Transcript of radio broadcast—The United States Treasury Department, *Let's All Back the Attack,* Monday, January 17, 1944, 9:00–10:00 P.M., pp. 42–43.

The London Sunday Mirror _wanted to know where President Reagan was on VE day in 1945 and what his recollections were._

> Sunday Mirror
> London, England
> February 8, 1985 [12]

I hadn't realized how dim my recollection was of VE day until the question was asked. Strangely enough my childhood memory of Armistice Day in the First World War is more vivid.

I think perhaps the reason for this was that on VE day* I was at my post as adjutant of an Army Air Corps installation in Culver City California, where I'd been stationed for over two years. Naturally there was great happiness that the war in Europe had ended. But still the war went on in the Pacific and seemed destined to continue for quite a while since the bomb was still a secret and no one could guess what was soon to happen.

Ours was an installation under the direct command of Air Corps Intelligence so we were almost instantly involved in communications regarding the change to one front. In many ways though it was business as usual except for the great happiness that the killing had stopped in Europe.

> Ronald Reagan

A former teacher from Akron, Ohio, wrote to President Reagan about the showing of documentaries on the killing of 140,000 people by the atomic bomb dropped on Hiroshima on August 6, 1945. She argued that American children should be shown documentary films of the Japanese bombing of Pearl Harbor on December 7, 1941, so they would know all the facts.

> Virginia Sica
> Akron, Ohio
> September 26, 1985 [13]

Dear Virginia Sica:

Thank you for your letter of August 8th and forgive me for being so late in answering but your letter has only just reached me.

Believe me I understand your frustration, in fact I was pretty upset with all those "anniversary" programs about Hiroshima. You are right about horrors per-

---

* On May 7, 1945, General Alfred Jodl signed the unconditional surrender of German forces on all fronts, and the surrender took effect at 11:01 P.M. on May 8, 1945.

petrated by our enemies in WWII. In fact, the Japanese killed more people, innocent civilians, in the occupation of Nanking, China than the atom bombs killed in
Hiroshima and Nagasaki together.

I know there are some films that have been shown about Pearl Harbor but I
have some concerns about documentaries that might build up a hatred in our
young people toward the Japanese people. For the first time virtually in history, we
have buried our hatred and now find Japan and West Germany our firmest friends
and allies. We must remember that most of the people in those countries weren't
born or were mere babies when that war took place. Would it be right to impose the
sins of their fathers and grandfathers on them?

Would it not be better if our own media refrained from bashing us for what we
did in the war and spent more time telling how we helped rebuild the countries that
were once our enemies?

Again, let me say I know how you feel and have wrestled with my own anger.
Thanks again and best regards.

Ronald Reagan

---

*Chasen's was a world-renowned restaurant in West Hollywood that catered to movie
stars, famous writers, playwrights, actors, presidents, and royalty. It was started in
1936 by Dave Chasen and closed in 1995. Chasen's was Reagan's favorite restaurant;
he particularly liked their chili—also the favorite of John Wayne and Frank Sinatra—
which Reagan served at his Fourth of July ranch parties.*

Mrs. Maude Chasen
Los Angeles, California
November 15, 1984 [14]

Dear Maude:

Thank you for your kind letter. I was pleased to be able to participate even a little in honoring you.

Nancy and I look forward to picking up old and happy habits again like dining
at "Chasen's." I guess it will be a few more years before we can have that pleasure but
we have memories to keep us warm.

Nancy sends her love and so do I.

Sincerely,
Ron

---

*The art department of Polo Ralph Lauren was researching old magazines for design
ideas and came across a full page ad of Reagan in a "Mr. T" fashion shirt. It was
called "the Ronald Reagan shirt—an authentic Esquire 'Mr. T' fashion." Worn with
a turtleneck sweater, it featured a deep V-neck, came in six colors and cost $10.00.
The ad probably ran in the late 1940s.*

Mr. Thomas S. Duane
Miss Cheryl Wotasek
Miss Anne F. Keistof
New York, New York
March 10, 1986 [15]

Dear Mr. Duane and Misses Wotasek and Keistof:

Thank you very much for sending me the "Mr. T" ad and your kind letter. You really sent me back down memory lane. Believe it or not, this was the result of an idea I had at a time when I was much given to sports clothes and, especially, sweaters. I persuaded a fellow in the business to make me the garment pictured in the ad. The next thing I knew they were on the market. Let me add that I had no commercial connection or interest in their marketing and this is the first I ever knew of such ads.

I do know all this took place long before the Mr. T* on television. In the Hollywood "Golden Era" when you were under contract to a studio they owned all endorsement rights and used them to plug your pictures. That is the only explanation I can think of with regard to the ad. I was under contract to Warner Brothers for about 13 years.

Well, I'd better stop, before I give you the story of my life. Again, thanks.

Sincerely,
Ronald Reagan

———

Reagan writes to a friend from Eureka College just before he and his co-star, Patricia Neal, sail to England on the ocean liner Britannia *to make a new movie,* The Hasty Heart.

Sam Harrod
Eureka, Illinois
November 1948 [16]

Dear Sam:

Just a quick line before I get underway. The enclosed sample is fine and seems like a good idea. My signing them however will have to wait a few months as I leave the 15th to make a picture in London.

We'll be there about three months and will be staying at the "Savoy Hotel."

Best to you and give my regards to everyone.

Yours in the Bond,
Dutch

P.S. Say hello to Louise and remember I always told you to be a Democrat and be right.

———

* Laurence Tureaud, also known as Mr. T, was a star of NBC-TV's *The A-Team*, which aired from 1983 to 1987. He is famous for wearing a mohawk haircut and heavy gold chains.

The late months of 1948 were a bad period for Reagan. His first wife, Jane Wyman, had filed for divorce on June 29, 1948, and it would not become final until July 18, 1949. He had signed up to do the movie, The Hasty Heart, *only to discover he was to have the second lead and that the film was to be made over a four-month period in London. When he arrived in London it was damp, cold, and foggy. England was still under food rationing, and there was no central heating. Reagan was not a happy camper and writes an ironic letter to his legendary boss, Jack L. Warner, the studio executive.*

To the finder: Please see this letter reaches J. L. Warner
Burbank, California
December 1948 [17]

Dear J.L.:

I am putting this letter in a bottle and throwing it on the tide with the hope that somehow it may reach you. Perhaps my report of life here in this dismal wilderness will be of help to future expeditions.

You will recall with what light hearts we set out such a long time ago—optimistic about an ability to find and thaw the "frozen dollar." * If we could have know then what lay ("lay"—there's a word I no longer experience or understand) before us how different would have been our mood.

Our first glimpse of this forbidding land was almost as frightening as a look at *The Horn Blows at Midnight.*† There seems to be a heavy fog but it had the odor of cow dung and coal soot—fearing an explosion of this gaseous stuff, I ordered "no smoking." Better I should have ordered "no breathing."

The natives were friendly in a sort of "below freezing" way but were won over by gifts—mostly cash. We were quite generous in this inasmuch as it was YOUR cash. They speak a strange jargon similar in many ways to our language but *different* enough to cause confusion. For example—to be "knocked up" here refers in no way to those delights for which "Leander swam the Hellespont." ‡ It merely means to be awakened from a sound sleep by a native device somewhat like our telephone. Another instance of this language difference is the word "bloody." You could see a native cut stern to stern but to describe the spectacle as "bloody" would get you thrown out of a saloon in London. Mentioning a pain in my "fanny" (which is easy to get here) I was distressed to learn that even this standard American term has an opposite meaning. If I had what they call a "fanny" I could be Queen of England.

---

* In England, American films could be shown, but any profits had to remain in the country and could only be used there, i.e., they were "frozen dollars."
† A 1945 Jack Benny film that had received bad reviews.
‡ In Greek mythology Leander swam the Hellespont nightly in order to spend the night with Hero, his secret lover. Today it is called the Dardenelles, a strait between European and Asian Turkey, connecting the Aegean Sea with the Sea of Marmara. The strait was 40 miles long and one mile wide. Swimming it was considered an impossible feat until the poet, Lord Byron, accomplished the feat.

Another misleading term has caused me some distress. There is a cleared space near the center of the native capital called Picadilly Circus. I have gone there many times and have yet to see an elephant or an acrobat. In fairness I must admit how even there are some characters (mostly female) who seem to be selling tickets to something. They keep pulling my sleeve and saying "two bob, Governor."

One of the most interesting customs of the higher-class natives is something of a sport. They all wear red coats to chase some dogs which in turn are chasing a fox. I should add the natives are mounted on horses. This affair is mistakenly called "a fox hunt." I say mistakenly because the red object has nothing to do with the fox, they actually are doing this to muscle up the horses which are then served for dinner. I have been very lucky so far in that I have been able to avoid the horse and eat only the saddle and harness.

In connection with this let me write a word about English cooking. What they do to food we did to the American Indian. The average meal should go from "kitchen to can" thus avoiding the use of the middleman.

My strength is failing now, so I'll hasten to put this in the bottle before I'm tempted to eat the cork. We think of you as we sit around the campfire and what we think could curl your hair and make H.M.'s * horses seem backward. Come to think of it that might be an improvement.

Cheerio! (that is the native word for good by. It is spoken without moving the upper lip while looking down the nose).

Ronnie

P.S. Due to the fuel shortage we are keeping the fire alive with "frozen dollars"— (yours).

———————

Reagan discusses business with Jack Warner, the top executive of Warner Brothers studio.

Mr. Jack L. Warner
Burbank, California
May 3, 1950 [18]

Dear Jack:

I don't know anything about your difficulty with MCA † nor do I care to know, naturally it is none of my business. They have just notified me of my right to utilize the William Morris office—a right which I waived. Having been with MCA almost as many years as you and I have been together I don't feel that strangers can suddenly take over and represent my best interests.

I hope that where our relationship is concerned you will allow Arthur Park to

———————

* His Majesty.
† The Music Corporation of America (MCA), run by Lew Wasserman, was Reagan's agent.

negotiate in my behalf. Actually he is personally involved in the particular item of business I wish to discuss.

I know that you will recall our discussion some time ago with regard to *That Hagen Girl.** You agreed the script and role were very weak but asked me to do the picture as a personal favor which I gladly did. At that time you encouraged me to bring in a suitable outdoor script which you agreed to buy as a starring vehicle for me. I found such a property in *Ghost Mountain*† and the studio purchased it with me, through MCA, acting as go-between to close the deal with the author.

Of late there have been "gossip items" indicating you intend to star someone else in this story. Naturally I put no stock in these rumors—I know you too well to ever think you'd break your word.

However I am anxious to know something of production plans—starting date etc. in order to better schedule my own plans. Frankly I hope it is soon as I have every confidence in this story.

Sincerely,
Ronnie Reagan

In the 1970s Reagan comforts an old friend from Dixon, Illinois, whose aunt has just died, and he reminisces about the late 1920s, when they played bridge on winter evenings and swam in the Rock River at Lowell Park in the summer.

Florence
Illinois
Circa 1970 [19]

Dear Florence:

I was so sorry to hear about Aunt Vivian. I know there isn't anything I can say to help, but still she lived a rich, full life and a great many of us are better for having known her. I'm sure God had his reasons, and they were based on love and mercy.

You are so right about those carefree days in Dixon; what wonderful memories we all have, thanks in great part to her. I've been down the trail of memories since your letter came. She taught us how to play bridge on some wonderful winter evenings but mostly my memories are of sun and water and all of you at Lowell Park.

------

* Reagan was reluctant to make this movie because his co-star, Shirley Temple, was only 21 years old and looked younger, and Reagan was concerned the public would not like him becoming romantically involved with the former child star.

† A story about a Confederate cavalry detachment sent into California by General Robert E. Lee on a secret mission (Vaughn, *Ronald Reagan in Hollywood,* p. 223). But Warner Brothers eventually changed the name to *Rocky Mountain* and produced it in 1950 with Errol Flynn, co-starring Flynn's wife Patrice Whymore. Anne Edwards, *Early Reagan* (New York: William Morrow, 1987), p. 370.

Don't look back unless it is to bask in the warmth of precious memories. Be glad you have them, but also reach out for the days ahead. This she did better than anyone I know.

Sincerely,
Dutch

———————

In this earlier 1951 letter to Florence, Reagan gives her some lengthy advice on living after she loses her husband, arguing that both she and her son need a man in their lives.

Florence Yerly
Sycamore, Illinois
December 17, 1951 [20]

Dear Florence:

I have put off answering your letter of last September mainly because I was resisting the urge to "give advice." I know I shouldn't and that you have every right to tell me to mind my own business but now I'm going to play "old Professor" (of swimming probably) and speak my piece.

Your letter led me to believe you are embarked on a course which can only lead to unhappiness and a barren future and this is all wrong. You are young and very attractive and have a great deal to offer some worthwhile man and both you and your son need a man in your life or lives.

You spoke of your aunt and the "ideals" she gave you. It is high time you reviewed those teachings in the light; not of modern living; but of <u>modern knowledge</u>. I too was raised in a home where "ideals" similar I'm sure to yours were taught, by my Mother. Now I have the highest regard for her and for her teachings but I have had to go on from there and find a "code for living" in keeping with my conscience and knowledge of right and wrong. This does not mean casting her principles aside but rather it is building to meet my present needs on a foundation I learned from her. At the same time I have learned painfully that some "idealism" is in effect a flight from reality.

You say you believe there is <u>one</u> love in life for each of us—this is just <u>not</u> true. Can you believe that God means for millions of really young people to go on through life alone because a war robbed them of their first loves? Maybe you'll resent this Florence but I must say it—you have to look into your own heart and ask yourself if you really believe in <u>one love</u> now lost to you or if this is a shield behind which you hide because your past experience did not measure up to your girlhood dreams and now you <u>fear</u> men.

I will grant you that all of us grow up with a "moonlight and roses" outlook on romantic relationships and sometimes it comes hard to reconcile this dream with the actualities of <u>physical</u> contact. To show you how "over idealistic" my training was—I awoke to the realization (almost too late) that even in marriage I had a little guilty feeling about sex, as though the whole thing was tinged with evil.

A very fine old gentleman started me out on the right track by interesting me in the practices of, or I should say, moral standards of, the primitive peoples never exposed to our civilization—such as the Polynesians. These peoples who are truly children of nature and thus of God, accept physical desire as a natural, normal appetite to be satisfied honestly and fearlessly with no surrounding aura of sin and sly whispers in the darkness. By our standards they are heathens but they are heathens without degeneracy, sex crimes, psycho-neurosis and divorce.

I guess what I am trying to say is that I oppose the dogmas of some organized religions who accept marital relationship only as a "tolerated" sin for the purpose of conceiving children and who believe all children to be born in sin. My personal belief is that God couldn't create evil so the desires he planted in us are good and the physical relationship between a man and woman is the highest form of companionship.

If I can, I want to say all this to my daughter. I want her to know that nothing between her and the man she loves can be wrong or obscene, that desire in itself is normal and right. There is one other thing I think she should know. If some man she finds attractive or likable feels desire for her, like any parent, I hope she'll have the common sense and good taste not to be promiscuous or involve herself in casual affairs but (and this is equally important) I don't want her to be disgusted and convinced that his desire is an indication of moral decay and vulgarity. Of course a man feels desire for an attractive woman—nature intended that he should and something would be amiss if he didn't. A girl's judgment of this man should be based only on his respect for her wishes but don't ask him not to feel an instinct as much a part of him as hunger and thirst.

The world is full of lonely people—people capable of happiness and of giving happiness and love is not a magic touch of cosmic dust that preordains two people and two people only for each other. Love can grow slowly out of warmth and companionship and none of us should be afraid to seek it.

Now I'm going to seal this letter very quickly and mail it because if I read it over I won't have the nerve to sent it—

Merry Christmas and Much Happiness

Sincerely,
Dutch

Reagan's six terms as president of the Screen Actors Guild after World War II formed an indelible impression in his mind: the Communist threat was real, deadly serious, and dangerous. Here, in 1962, he shares information with the young publisher of National Review, *a conservative magazine destined to have a powerful impact on the intellectual debate in the United States in the last third of the twentieth century.*

William F. Buckley, Jr.
New York, New York
May 26, 1962[21]

Dear Bill:

Enclosed are the two pamphlets I mentioned. Needless to say Mr. Fagan's diatribe against me, Roy Brewer (now Vice Chairman of the Council Against Communist Aggression) and the SAG, is completely irresponsible and contrary to fact. As a matter of fact the Screen Actors Guild was able to function as a primary force against the Communist attempt at take-over in Hollywood (1947) because it was free of Communist domination.

Regarding the other pamphlet it speaks for itself. No mention of real "crackpots" like Fagan but the usual attempt to paint the Conservatives as extremists.

When you are through with them could I have them back for my own files?

Best regards
Ronnie

The White House legal office informed Reagan in 1985 that the Miami Herald *had just published an article based on FBI documents released in response to a Freedom of Information Act request. The documents included a list of "sponsors" for a Communist front organization, the Committee for a Democratic Far Eastern Policy, in 1946, and Reagan's name was on the list.*

Reagan writes this note on the White House memo.

Fred F. Fielding
Counsel to the President
March 4, 1985[22]

Fred—anytime you can give my story out. I was a liberal New Deal Democrat, and have told many times how, like others, I was fooled into supporting causes. It was the 1947–48 Hollywood strike that opened my eyes. I have some pretty good stories.

RR

In 1954, as Reagan's movie career was winding down and before he signed on with the General Electric Theater *in September, he tried being a nightclub performer in Las Vegas. On February 15, 1954, Reagan opened at the Last Frontier Hotel.*

Murphy James
Las Vegas, Nevada
April 9, 1983[23]

Dear Mr. James:

My nightclub appearance in Las Vegas 1954 was a one-time thing. The experience was a typical show business story. In that period Las Vegas had just burst out in its search for well-known names and of course Hollywood was a natural source.

At the same time Hollywood was in the doldrums. The government consent decree forcing studios to divest themselves of theatre ownership had slowed production down to a minimum. I had finally freed myself from a studio contract after 13 years and was freelancing. My agent (MCA) was pressing me to do a nightclub show even though I do not sing or dance. I kept on saying no.

Then one day they asked me to at least meet with them and talk about it. In the meeting that followed I made my usual case that I didn't sing or dance and asked what could I do in a nightclub? Their response was, "you do a lot of benefits don't you?" Well the answer to that was of course yes, because it was true of everyone in pictures. They pointed out that my "benefit routine" was usually as MC; that I would do a humorous monologue and then introduce others.

This was what they had in mind with a slight variation. My act would be "Ronald Reagan Presents." We would pick a couple of good acts and then material would be written calling for me to wind up the show in a routine with the feature act—in this case the Continentals. I was amazed at the kind of money they said could be earned in this setup.

We were booked for two weeks at the New Frontier and the show was a great success with a sellout every night. We had really selected top acts.

I learned that success is treated differently in Las Vegas. Opening night we received such an ovation that we responded with several encores. The next morning I was ushered into a management meeting where I was told to shorten the show and no more encores. I was told how much it cost the casino for every minute we kept the customers away from the gaming tables.

I did enjoy the experience and we did receive offers from top spots across the country but I didn't think it was what I wanted to do so my nightclub career was wrapped up in that two-week booking.

I hope this is of some use to you.

Sincerely,
Ronald Reagan

Later, in 1954, Reagan signed up with General Electric to be the "program supervisor" of their new Sunday-night television series, called the General Electric Theater. *The initial program was thirteen half-hour dramas. When Reagan was not producing shows he made personal appearances at GE factories across the United States. The television shows began on September 26, 1954.*

Over the next eight years, Reagan traveled to all 135 GE plants in 40 states and met with 250,000 employees. Two of the eight years were spent on the road, giving up to 14 speeches a day. The next three letters, written between 1955 and 1958, describe some of his traveling activity. The fact that Reagan did not fly complicated his travel plans.

Ira Langston was the president of Eureka College.

Ira W. Langston
Eureka, Illinois
August 15, 1955 [24]

Dear Dr. Langston:

I have already spoken to GE about "Homecoming" and we are doing our best to work it out. Be assured there is no lack of desire on my part.

The main difficulty to be overcome is that I must be in New York for the Sunday show and I am one of those prehistoric people who won't fly.

As I understand it now my visit to GE plants has me in Danville, Illinois that week. Now GE is checking to see what part of the weekend I could spend in Eureka and still get a train to reach New York some time Sunday morning.

I will keep in touch with you and let you know just as soon as they send me the information. In the meantime I will certainly be hoping.

Best regards,
Ronald Reagan

Lorraine and Elwood Wagner
Philadelphia, Pennsylvania
November 5, 1956 [25]

Dear Lorraine and Wag:

Just a quick line between "takes." We've been filming some commercials for GE for about a week so I'm hard put to get anything done.

That's quite a young man in that picture you sent. He'll keep you busy for some time to come. I don't have any snaps of Patti at hand but you'll get to see her in action this winter. We are doing some commercials on our new house* and she'll be in a couple of them. That's what we've been filming all last week.

Here I go—they are yelling.

Best,
Ronnie

---

* General Electric had furnished Reagan's home with every kind of electric device they made, and were filming commercials of the family using them.

Reagan describes Hellcats of the Navy, *a 1957 picture he co-starred in with his wife, Nancy. It was the only movie they made together.*

Mr. Wayne Davis
Circa 1968 [26]

Dear Mr. Davis:

I'm sorry to be so late in answering your letter and hope I'm not too late.

Some years ago Mrs. Reagan and I co-starred in a picture called *Hellcats of the Navy*. The title came from a WWII incident known as "Operation Hellcat," and the script was written from an admiral's account of that operation. It involved the entry into the Japanese sea by American submarines. Slipping through mine fields and sub nets they lay on the ocean floor until a predetermined time, then surfaced and in a single operation virtually wiped out the Japanese merchant fleet.

Well, that is enough about the picture. In making it we did all of our filming on a USN submarine stationed in San Diego. It was commanded by Captain Kelly (now commander of U.S. Naval forces in Taiwan). His executive officer was Commander L.M. Bucher.

We struck up quite an astonishing friendship with the Kellys and the Buchers and became very fond of them. Naturally we had a special concern and interest when the *Pueblo* was captured.*

I hope this is of some interest to you.

Sincerely,
Ronald Reagan

Lorraine and Elwood H. Wagner
Philadelphia, Pennsylvania
January 15, 1958 [27]

Dear Lorraine and Wag:

I really haven't time at the moment to write a letter but I wanted to get your "pic." off before it got mislaid on this heaped up desk of mine.

We know what you mean about Xmas. Of course now we are approaching the inevitable day when Santa is no longer believed and we hate to see it come. On the other hand I guess we can look forward to the second edition † bringing Santa back.

On my way to the studio now to do or die for GE. Thanks for sending the picture and best regards.

Sincerely,
Ronnie

---

* In January 1968 the USS *Pueblo*, an American spy ship, was attacked and captured by North Korean gunships. Commander L.M. Bucher was the captain of the *Pueblo*.
† Patti was now seven years old, and Ronald Prescott was due in four months.

In the spring of 1962, at the end of their eighth season, General Electric decided to discontinue the General Electric Theater, *and Reagan was beginning to have some political trouble in the production of his television shows.*

> Lorraine and Elwood Wagner
> Philadelphia, Pennsylvania
> June 3, 1962[28]

Dear Lorraine and Wag:

Hope the enclosed fills the bill. I stole it from a GE press kit but we won't be needing those anymore.

Your questions about the Marion Miller stories* call for a couple of answers. First it was a near impossible job to cram five years of espionage into thirty minutes. We just grabbed for some dramatic moments we could tie together. Second however at our own studio I had to fight right down to the wire to make the Communists villains. When I say "fight" I mean really that. On our producing staff the liberal view that communism is only something the "Right-wingers" dreamed up prevails and they literally resorted to sabotage to pull the punch out of the show. Two individuals including the director wanted to cut the whole scene about the little girl saying her prayers. Finally in a near knock-down drag-out—they admitted their objection was because they were atheists.

'Twas a merry time we had but I'd gladly do it all over again. Let me make one thing plain—none of this fight involved GE. They were all for doing an anticommunist story and knew nothing of the battle I was having out here.

Must run now and MC a Rotary convention.

> Best,
> Ronnie

In May of 1962, long before he runs for political office, Reagan assures a supporter that he is going to try "even harder" to get things right in Washington.

> Mrs. Van Wies
> May 2, 1962[29]

Dear Mrs. Van Wies:

I have some idea of what your heartache has been and still is and I assure you I'll keep trying even harder to see if one day soon we can have a government in Washington that will recognize its responsibility to its citizens.

---

* Marion Miller was the author of *I Was a Spy: The Story of a Brave Housewife* (Bobbs-Merrill, 1960). Miller was invited to join a Los Angeles society supposedly for the advancement of the foreign-born in America, and did not suspect it was a Communist-front organization. When she reported the society's sedition to the FBI, she was asked to remain in the organization as an informant.

I'm very sorry I can't do anything about dramatizing the POW article but you see *GE Theater* has been cancelled as of the end of this season. All our shows are completed now and we won't be producing any new ones.

My thanks to you for your wonderful letter and my prayers for a happy end to your great burden.

Sincerely,
Ronald Reagan

Reagan recalls the degree of intellectual freedom he had while traveling around the country speaking at General Electric plants.

William G. Clotworthy
June 16, 1980[30]

Dear Bill:

It was good to hear from you after too long a time, and I'm most grateful to you for bringing me word of the *Newsweek* interview. Thanks, too, for disappointing them in what I'm sure was a quest for a little dirty linen.

You know, Bill, I've always remembered *GE Theater* and Ralph Cordiner* for the very fact that in all those years of speaking at the various engagements they set up, they never once told me anything I should or should not say nor did they ever suggest a subject. My speeches were totally my own. With the attitude so many have about big business, I find, when I have occasion to tell this to someone, that they are very surprised.

Incidentally, I have an address on George Galen. It is 67 Park, Richland, Washington. Well, thanks again. Nancy sends her regards, and we both hope one of these days our paths cross again.

Sincerely,
Ron

The April 1960 issue of Playboy *magazine carried an article, "The Oscar Syndrome," by Dalton Trumbo—a screen writer who was a member of the Communist Party from 1943 to 1948. The first two-thirds of the piece were about Hollywood and the Oscars, but then it slid into a bitter denunciation of the "blacklist," likening it to a witch-hunt: ". . . in recent years we have had in this country—and not for the first time in our history—a problem of witches."*

Reagan read the article. He had known Trumbo during the attempted takeover of his union by Communists, and expressed his dismay at a dinner to Homer (Buzzy) Hargrove, an executive at Merrill Lynch, Pierce, Fenner & Smith who turned out to be a friend of Hugh Hefner, the editor and publisher of Playboy. *Hefner was an admirer*

---

* President of General Electric while Reagan was working for them.

of Reagan and was upset that Reagan was upset—and wrote him a detailed three-page typed letter on May 13, 1960, defending the publication of Trumbo's article. Hefner argued that "the gag of censorship, the intimidation of blacklisting, the attempt of any kind to quiet a voice with which you or I may not be in total agreement, is the first step toward tyranny, and is precisely what this country is fighting against and what all totalitarian nations, Communist Russia included, have always stood for."

On July 4, 1960, Reagan replies to Hefner in a handwritten, six-page letter* detailing his understanding of free speech. He also explains, for the first time, his political odyssey from New Deal Democrat to Republican.

On July 12, after receiving Reagan's letter, Hefner wrote to Hargrove, thanking him "for passing along Ronald's original reaction to our Dalton Trumbo piece." Hefner told him he "got an extremely meaningful, well thought out and friendly letter" from Reagan, and thought he had "made us a new friend."

Mr. Hugh M. Hefner
Playboy
Beverly Hills, California
July 4, 1960[31]

Dear Mr. Hefner:

I've been a long time answering your letter of May 13 and my selection of "The Fourth" as an answering date is coincidence plus the fact that holidays are "free time" days around our house.

Your letter has been very much on my mind and I question whether I <u>can</u> answer in a way that will make sense to you. First because I once thought exactly as you think and second because no one could have changed my thinking (and some tried). It took seven months of meeting communists and communist-influenced people across a table in almost daily sessions while pickets rioted in front of studio gates, homes were bombed and a great industry almost ground to a halt.

You expressed lack of knowledge about my views, political background etc. Because so much doubt has been cast on "anti-communists," inspired by the radicalism of extremists who saw "Reds" under every "cause" I feel I should reveal where I have stood and now stand.

My first four votes were cast for FDR my fifth for Harry Truman. Following World War II my interest in liberalism and my fear of "neo-fascism" led to my serving on the board of directors of an organization later exposed as a "communist front" namely the "Hollywood Independent Citizens Commission of the Arts, Sciences and Professions." Incidentally Mr. Trumbo was also on that board.

Now you might ask, "who exposed this organization as a 'front'?" It was no cru-

---

* Morris, Edmund, *Dutch: A Memoir of Ronald Reagan* (New York: Random House, 1999), pp. 235–37; Meroney, John, "Rehearsals for a Lead Role," *Washington Post,* February 4, 2001, pp. G8–9.

sading committee of Congress, or the DAR or the American Legion. A small group of board members disturbed by the things being done in the organization's name introduced to their fellow board members a mild statement approving our democratic system and free enterprise economy and repudiating communism as a desirable form of government <u>for this country</u>. The suggestion was that by adopting such a policy statement the board would reassure our membership we were liberal but <u>not</u> a "front." The small group who introduced this measure were such "witch-hunters" as James Roosevelt, Dore Schary, Don Hartman, Olivia De Haviland, Johnny Green and myself.

Leaders of the opposition to our statement included Dalton Trumbo, John Howard Lawson, and a number of others who have since attained some fame for their refusal to answer questions. I remember one of their group reciting the Soviet Constitution to prove—"Russia was more Democratic than the United States." Another said if America continued her imperialist policy and as a result wound up in a war with Russia he would be on the side of Russia against the United States. We suggested this "policy statement" was perhaps a matter for the whole organization to decide—not just the board. We were told the membership was—"not politically sophisticated enough to make such a decision."

When we resigned the organization went out of existence only to reappear later (minus us) as "Independent Citizens Committee of the Arts Sciences and Professions" in support of Henry Wallace and the Progressive Party.

The "seven months" of meetings I mentioned in the first paragraph or two refers to the jurisdictional strike in the motion picture business. There are volumes of documentary evidence, testimony of former communists etc. that this whole affair was under the leadership of Harry Bridges and was aimed at an ultimate organizing of everyone in the picture business within Mr. Bridges longshoreman's union.

Now none of what I've said answers your argument that "freedom of speech means freedom to disagree," does it? Here begins my difficulty. How can I put down in less than "book form" the countless hours of meetings, the honest attempts at compromise, the trying to meet dishonesty, lies and cheating with conduct bound by rules of fair play? How can I make you understand that my feeling now is not prejudice born of this struggle but is realization supported by incontrovertible evidence that the American Communist is in truth a member of a "Russian American Bund" owing his first allegiance to a foreign power?

I, like you, will defend the right of any American to openly practice and preach any political philosophy from monarchy to anarchy. But this is not the case with regard to the communist. He is bound by party discipline to <u>deny</u> he is a communist so that he can by subversion and stealth <u>impose</u> on an unwilling people the rule of the International Communist Party which is in fact the government of Soviet Russia. I say to you that any man still or now a member of the "party" was a man who looked upon the death of American soldiers in Korea as a victory for his side. For proof of this I refer you to some of the ex-communists who fled the party at that time and for that reason, including some of Mr. Trumbo's companions of the "Unfriendly 10."

Hollywood has <u>no blacklist</u>. Hollywood does have a list handed to it by millions of "moviegoers" who have said "we don't want and will not pay to see pictures made by or with these people we consider traitors." On this list were many names of people we in Hollywood felt were wrongly suspect. I personally served on a committee that succeeded in clearing these people. Today any person who feels he is a victim of discrimination because of his political beliefs can avail himself of machinery to solve this problem.

I must ask you as a publisher, aside from any questions of political philosophy, should a film producer be accused of bigotry for not hiring an artist when the customers for his product have labeled the artist "poor box office," regardless of the cause?

I realize I've presented my case poorly due to the limitations of pen and paper so may I ask one favor? Will you call the FBI there in Chicago, ask for the anticommunist detail, then tell him of our correspondence (show him my letter if you like) and ask his views on this subject of communism as a political belief or a fifth column device of Russia.

Now my apologies for having taken so long in answering your letter and my appreciation for your having taken the time and trouble to write in the first place.

Sincerely,
Ronald Reagan

In the early 1960s the demand for Reagan as a conservative speaker began to grow. A group of Republicans tried unsuccessfully to bring Reagan to Metairie, Louisiana, which was almost 2,000 miles from Hollywood, a three-day drive if you did not fly.

Linda West
Metairie, Louisiana
October 1, 1963 [32]

Dear Mrs. West:

The time has come I know when you must go ahead on a definite basis regarding your December 13 date. I am still completely helpless with regard to making a commitment and therefore feel I must just settle for a rain check and hope for a future opportunity.

Believe me I have clung to a hope that something would happen to make the trip possible but fate was against me. Actually I've never been in this exact situation before and I'm not sure I can explain it so that it will be understandable. Normally it isn't easy to pin a studio down too far in advance regarding production plans but there are fairly reasonable periods when a fairly accurate guess can be made. Unfortunately my studio (Universal) is under completely new ownership and management. For almost a year they have been constructing new stages, a fourteen-story administration building and dozens of other auxiliary buildings and evidently during all of this haven't kept an eye on production.

It was my hope that by this time I would be scheduled for a picture and could count on accepting invitations such as yours prior to its starting date or immediately following production. We rarely go from one right into another. Now however the studio has kept pushing back start of production until, as they put it, one of these days they'll have to pull the plug.

I've just concluded a meeting—trying to get some specifics as to dates and they confess they are helpless except to say "stand by we are trying to get under way as quickly as possible." They have been cooperative in letting me accept a few dates in the immediate vicinity where even if production did start they would only have to shoot around me for one day but they say it is impossible to let me tie myself for longer periods. As I probably explained to you before I don't fly so we are talking of several days round trip to "Metairie."

One of these days the buildings will be up—the new management will be combat tested and hopefully I'll be able to make plans more than a week ahead. In the mean time I can only thank you for your patience and the honor you offered me and hope (as I said before) there will be another chance.

Sincerely,
Ronald Reagan

In the 1970s Reagan was asked by a friend for his views on the issue of censorship in movies. This handwritten draft was found in his files.

George
Circa 1970s [33]

Dear George:

I'm flattered that you would ask me to comment on the subject of censorship. I'm not sure my contribution will be what you had in mind, but I'll be happy to try. Truth is I have some rather strong feelings about much of what is being offered on the screen and tube of late. Yes there have been some good and inspirational stories but even these are too often tarnished by dialogue laced with profanity and vulgarities to say nothing of the inevitable bedroom scene which leaves little to the imagination.

"Imagination"—that is what is missing in much of today's film fare. I'm speaking of the audience's imagination. A rule as old as the theater itself is that no scene on stage or screen can equal the audience's ability to imagine. The embrace followed by a fadeout or panning to the window curtains blowing in the evening breeze left it up to the audience to imagine what was going on. Today a pair of performers suggesting nudity if not actually nude—show them what's going on and they aren't nearly as good in the flesh as they were in the audience's minds.

As for the vulgar language, it has become a substitute for good writing. Sit through a screening of the older movies. Look at *Casablanca* again and you are reminded of how sparkling and bright the dialogue used to be. Now profanity or a blurted obscenity is an easy reach for a laugh or gasp.

What to do about it? Well one thing that must not be done is to open the door to government censorship. Anyone with the character to be a good censor would have too much character to be one. There is no place in our free society for government at any level to impose itself on the theater. This is true in spades of the federal government. It must never be allowed a role in story approval, production control or artistic judgment.

We have come to refer to the Hollywood of the late 30s and 40s as the "Golden Era." We might do much worse than go back to something that worked very well during that era—the voluntary production code. Let the industry itself adopt, as it did many years ago, a voluntary code of ethics and behavior based on good taste and simple morality. Who knows—we might see another "Golden Era" when pictures would once again be the major entertainment for the entire family.

Thanks again for asking me.

Sincerely,
Ron

Frank McCarthy, a retired brigadier general, was a producer for Twentieth Century–Fox. He pushed the idea of doing a film on General George S. Patton until Darryl Zanuck agreed. It was a spectacular success, winning Academy Awards for best picture, best actor (George C. Scott), and best director.

Reagan always wanted to play the role of General Patton, and never did.

Mr. Frank McCarthy
Beverly Hills, California
March 10, 1970 [34]

Dear Frank:

I tried to call the other day but you were out of town, so I decided to put on paper what I had intended to put on the phone.

Nancy and the Skipper* and I saw *Patton* Saturday night. I told you once I would hate anyone who ever played that role other than myself. Now I hate George Scott for proving that no one in the world but him could ever have played the part.

Frank, it is a magnificent piece of picture making and it says some things that very much need saying today. I have been greatly disturbed for some time over the pernicious and constant degrading of the military. This picture restored a great deal of balance. I don't know whether Patton would ever be the kind of man you'd want to take on a picnic, but I do thank God that when trouble came, there were men like him around. I'm really too full of the picture yet to make specific com-

---

* Reagan's 11-year old son, Ronald Prescott.

ments other than to say it has been many years since I have so completely lost myself in a picture and have actually forgotten, while viewing it, that it was a picture. It was so real.

I have long been an opponent, as you know, of vulgarity, obscenity, and profanity on the screen as we are seeing it in so many pictures. On the other hand, I've never believed that I was a total square and have never been opposed to the use of anything absolutely essential to the telling of the story. It did not offend me in the slightest that you had Patton talking as Patton talked. In fact, before going, I gave the Skipper quite a lecture on the man and the history surrounding him, and then told him that he would be hearing this kind of language which didn't make it right for him or me to use, but that this was a part of the man and his character. Therefore, we sat through the movie and I had no embarrassment whatsoever about the language. It definitely belonged.

Once again, just know that all of us were tremendously entertained and impressed, and loved every minute of the picture. Thank you for a real contribution to our nation at this time. Nancy echoes and seconds all of this.

Best regards,
Ron

Marie Windsor began her career as an actress in 1941 and made 76 movies; in 1954 she married Jack Hupp. She served as a director of the Screen Actors Guild (SAG) for 25 years and was a friend of Charlton Heston.

Edward Asner was elected president of the SAG in 1981, and frequently used the forum to air his political views, especially his opposition to Reagan's involvement in Central America. That activity, including soliciting contributions from Guild members to oppose Reagan's foreign policy, drew the attention of Charlton Heston and other conservative actors. They formed a conservative coalition, Actors Working for an Actors Guild (AWAG), and served as a "watchdog" on Asner—and were represented on the board of directors of SAG.

In 1981 the Guild's awards committee chose President Reagan to receive the annual Life Achievement Award, a great honor for an actor. Controversy ensued when the board's selection was prematurely revealed, and Reagan's award was withdrawn. No Life Achievement Award was given in 1981; Reagan was never chosen again.

Edward Asner resigned as president of SAG in 1985. In 2001 Edward Asner received the Life Achievement Award from SAG.

Mrs. Marie Windsor Hupp
Beverly Hills, California
January 12, 1982 [35]

Dear Marie:

Thank you very much for your letter and for all the clippings. I hadn't seen any of this except Chuck Heston's letter. Now I know a lot more about the whole affair.

Marie I've been upset by what's happening to our Guild for some time. This last is just a small facet of the problem. I've always been so proud of SAG. We didn't engage in partisan politics because we respected the fact that our members were not of one party or political persuasion.

We were always honorable in our negotiations. I remember every time we went in to renegotiate the contract we had a little reminder session. We reminded ourselves that "what we asked for must be good for actors, fair to the other fellow and good for the industry." I doubt such meetings will be held by the present Guild management.

Thank you again and thank you very much for your generous words about my present role. Nancy sends her love as do I.

Sincerely,
Ron

Reagan resents the personal attacks made on him by Ed Asner.

Mrs. Marie Windsor Hupp
Beverly Hills, California
March 11, 1982 [36]

Dear Marie:

It was good to hear from you, and thanks for the news stories. I've been more than a little upset about what's happening to our Guild. We saw this happen to some of our sister unions and guilds in years past, but somehow I never believed it could happen to SAG.

I don't mind being a target for loud mouth Asner personally, but I sure do resent what he's doing to an organization we all put a lot into, including love and loyalty. I remember once during contract negotiations Y. Frank Freeman told me he had opposed the formation of the Guild, but then he said he had come to realize it was the greatest force for good in the motion picture industry. I don't think anyone will say that now.

Nancy sends her best and give our regards to Jack.

Sincerely,
Ron

In the years after he left the entertainment industry, Reagan had occasion to write to old friends, or occasionally to write about them to others. What follows is a selection of letters to or about his most famous friends.

In his later years Reagan often attended lavish parties at the California home of Walter Annenberg, a billionaire and an old friend. A Reagan supporter from Virginia

was distressed to read that Reagan attended one party with the likes of Frank Sinatra
and Spiro Agnew.* He sent a mailgram saying, "My boy is keeping bad company."
Reagan, who by then had known Sinatra for over 35 years, defends his old friend.

Richard J. Neville
McLean, Virginia
Circa Fall 1976[37]

Dear Mr. Neville:

Thank you for putting your address on the mailgram thus giving me an opportunity to reply. I could say I was only one of 130 guests at the house of the former ambassador to England † who was recently knighted by the Queen of England. But that would be evasive even though true. So let me answer by stating that I have known Frank Sinatra and Barbara Marx ‡ for a number of years; I'm aware of the incidents, highly publicized, quarrels with photographers, night club scrapes, etc. and admit it is a lifestyle I neither emulate or approve.

However there is a less publicized side to Mr. Sinatra which in simple justice must be recognized. It is a side he has worked very hard to keep hidden and unpublicized. I know of no one who has done more in the field of charity than Frank Sinatra. His contributions to worthwhile causes are extremely generous but he goes beyond this. There are people on permanent payrolls, a small town high school whose band and ball team are uniformed (he was only in the town a few days and has never had reason to go back) there is medical care for people who he has only read about in the papers.

A few years ago a small town in the Midwest had suffered a terrible calamity; he went there on his own and staged a benefit to raise funds. All the expenses were paid out of his pocket, in addition to which he bought thousands of dollars worth of tickets himself and had them distributed to servicemen; and police and firemen.

While I was governor there would come to my attention cases where there was no suitable government program—I would call Frank as well as others of the same nature and they would organize a solution for the unfortunate people who needed help. Most of the time Frank would simply take it upon himself. Let me just finish by saying he would be very upset if he knew I'd told you these things.

I hope you'll pardon this handwritten note but I'm leaving on a camping trip and have no chance to get into the office.

Thanks again for letting me reply.

Sincerely,
Ronald Reagan

---

* Spiro Agnew, the former governor of Maryland, was President Nixon's first vice president and was forced to resign in 1973 because of corruption charges.
† Ambassador Walter H. Annenberg (1969–1974), who had a home in Rancho Mirage, California.
‡ Barbara Marx, Sinatra's fourth wife, married him in July 1976.

Later still, in the White House, Reagan corresponded with Sinatra on several occasions. In 1982 Sinatra sent Reagan tapes of the performance he and Perry Como gave at the White House to honor the visiting president of Italy, Sandro Pertini.

Mr. Frank Sinatra
Rancho Mirage, California
September 13, 1982 [38]

Dear Francis Albert: *

I'm writing this before we've even had time to run the tapes. As you know we've been ranching and just returned to find them here.

You were very kind and thoughtful (as always) to do this and we are both truly grateful.

That was a special night, one we remember with great happiness. When we met President Pertini in Italy he made it evident he too remembered the evening with warm pleasure.

Nancy sends her love and again our thanks.

Sincerely,
Ron

On September 12, 1983, the Los Angeles Times _ran a cartoon by Paul Conrad depicting a soldier pinned down behind a barricade as shells exploded around him, calling President Reagan on his walkie-talkie. When Reagan doesn't seem to understand him, the soldier says, "Well, tell him to turn up his hearing aid!"_

Reagan had recently been fitted for a hearing aid and Sinatra took umbrage at this slur on his old friend. He wrote to the Times _to criticize them for publishing "Conrad's viciousness and hatred," and suggested that his cartoons were "better suited to outhouse walls."_

Sinatra sent a copy of his letter to President Reagan.

Mr. Frank Sinatra
Hollywood, California
September 22, 1983 [39]

Dear Francis Albert:

Now I've seen the "strong letter" that follows. I know it came from your heart because that's what my heart has been saying about that poison pen artist for a long time. Thank you for doing what you did and for making me feel good all over.

Nancy sends her love and I join her.

Sincerely,
Ron

---

* When close friends addressed Sinatra personally it was "Francis Albert," not "Frank."

Sinatra dropped President Reagan a note with "a suggestion!" that he believed "to be a pretty good positive move politically"—appoint Tip O'Neill, the Democrat Speaker of the House, as ambassador to Ireland. He signed off advising Reagan to "stay well, stay strong, ignore the idiots . . . you know what you have to do. God bless, Francis Albert."

Mr. Frank Sinatra
Hollywood, California
May 27, 1987 [40]

Dear Francis Albert:

Thanks for your letter and I appreciate your suggestion. Problem is I'm afraid I can't do it. For one thing we have an Irish colleen in that job now who was for a time a congresswoman and then a member of my cabinet.* To replace her would be to bring her world down around her ears and I just haven't got the heart to do that.

Just between us even if that weren't so I'd have a problem with some of my people. Tip has joined that chorus back here that's bent on a lynching with me in the noose. He's been saying some pretty harsh things publicly.

Nancy sends her love and again I appreciate your taking the time and trouble to write as you did. In a couple of weeks we'll be in Italy—Venice and Rome.

Best regards,
Ron

In 1967, Reagan narrated a Decca record called "Freedom's Finest Hour," a documentary of America's struggle for independence in the years from 1765 to 1787. The script was written by Sam Thomas.

John Wayne
Circa 1967 [41]

Dear Duke:

I wouldn't do this if this man wasn't known to me. I'm sending his script on to you as he requested only because of the narration I did for him in "Freedom's Finest Hour" which he mentions in his letter.

---

* In March 1983, President Reagan appointed Margaret Heckler, an eight-term congresswoman from Massachusetts, as secretary of health and human services. In Reagan's appointment speech he referred to her as "an Irish colleen . . . the daughter of Irish immigrants." In 1985 she resigned her cabinet post to become U.S. ambassador to Ireland.

This was a documentary of the American Revolution told entirely in paintings. It was unbelievable the appearance of action he obtained in cutting from one painting to the other. Evidently this is what he has in mind with the western paintings he lists here.

Obviously he'd like to have Duke Wayne do the voice over. That's up to you— believe me no obligation as far as I'm concerned. I just thought you might like to see this.

Best regards,
Ron

Reagan got to know John Wayne during the difficult years when he was president of the Screen Actors Guild (1947–1952) and they remained close friends. On June 11, 1979, as Reagan was beginning to accelerate his drive for the 1980 Republican nomination for president, John Wayne died of lung and stomach cancer.

Unable to break a speaking commitment in Ohio, Reagan provided a short, personal story to the people who were going to honor Wayne on June 29th.

John G. Hagner
June 11, 1979 [42]

Dear John:

I can't tell you how sorry Nancy and I are that we will be unable to accept your invitation June 29th. Unfortunately, we will be in Cleveland, Ohio, where I have been booked to make a speech for quite some time. Please know that our hearts will be with you there in Lancaster. Please give our congratulations to Polly and Chuck.

And as for the man you are honoring posthumously, Duke Wayne, there are no words to tell of my love and respect for him. Let me just tell you one story about Duke.

It was some years ago when there was a time of great labor trouble in Hollywood. I was president of the Guild and the daily press would usually give me a pretty good going over. This was prior, of course to our eight years in Sacramento, so Nancy wasn't quite used to picking up the morning paper and reading some of the things that she read about me. Her morale was pretty low, and then one morning when it was particularly bad I had gone to a meeting. When I came home, I found out the phone had rung, and when Nancy picked it up, there was Duke. He just said that he thought she might be feeling pretty low, and he wanted to perk her up and to tell her things were going to be all right. Every morning from then on, those calls came—no matter what he was doing. And when there was a mass meeting over which I had to preside—Nancy was very upset. Again the phone would ring and there would be Duke saying would you feel better if I were there. She said,

Oh, yes. And that night he left a dinner party, and she walked in on his arm. He was still attired in dinner jacket and black tie.

I think I should add that in those days, we weren't well acquainted with John Wayne. Nancy had only met him a few times, but that was Duke. If he thought he could be of help—he helped. And he really helped. God bless him, he was what he always played—a real hero.

Again, our regrets and our very best to all of you.

Sincerely,
Ronald Reagan

In 1968 Governor Reagan was elected chairman of the Republican Governors Association for a two-year term. As chairman of the upcoming meeting in December Reagan importunes Bob Hope to appear.

Bob Hope
September 4, 1968[43]

Dear Bob:

I know you've been approached about our Republican Governors' Conference in December and it goes without saying your presence will make me a Gubernatorial Top Banana.

This gathering is a regular annual several-day meeting hosted by a different state each time so on present count it won't be around here again for 27 years. But my own personal reason goes beyond that. I've wanted for a long time a legitimate occasion for paying tribute to you on behalf of our state. I know this sounds a h—l of a lot like, "be my guest but bring your music," but even with an "honorary degree" you have to make a speech so I'll pretend I'm not self-conscious.

We have in mind inviting some special guests from the services, Vietnam veterans and of course some genial citizens to keep the whole thing solvent.

Now beyond all this let me just add that if it is impossible for you we'll still love you. Oh Nancy will probably be inconsolable for two or three years, I'll require psychiatric care and our children will probably be taken from us to be put in a foster home. Jesse Unruh* might even become governor.

Give our love to Dolores.

Best regards,
Ron

In the early days of the 1980 presidential campaign Reagan thanks Johnny Carson and his wife Joanna for their substantial campaign contribution.

---

* Democratic Speaker of the House of California

Mr. and Mrs. Johnny Carson
October 11, 1979[44]

Dear Joanna and Johnny:

Nancy and I just got off another airplane. Do you know we are on them so much I don't think we ride them anymore, I think we wear them. Anyway, we arrived home to find your very generous contribution. We both want you to know how very grateful we are. You make us very proud, indeed. We'll do our best to see that you never have reason to regret your kindness. We both hope we see you very soon. And again our heartfelt thanks.

Sincerely,
Ron

_____

The king and queen of Spain, Juan Carlos and Sofia, were guests at the White House on October 13, 1981. Ella Fitzgerald, considered by many the queen of jazz singers, entertained.

Miss Ella Fitzgerald
Beverly Hills, California
October 28, 1981[45]

Dear Ella:

Forgive me for being so late in telling you how grateful Nancy and I are for the wonderful evening you gave to all of us at the White House. We know the demands that are made on your time and talent. You were more than kind.

The King and Queen are both fans of American music and they were still talking about you when we put them in their car to return to Spain.

And why not—Nancy and I are still talking about you. Nancy sends her love and again from both of us, a heartfelt thanks.

Sincerely,
Ron

_____

Mickey Rooney, though only five feet, three inches tall, made 240 movies, and had eight wives. In 1939 Rooney became the top box-office draw in the country. Reagan invited Rooney and his wife to a White House dinner on June 12, 1985, and, at age 65, Rooney declined, writing "Damn it! It's always when I'm working, but thank goodness that I am."

Mr. and Mrs. Mickey Rooney
Hollywood, California
May 31, 1985[46]

Dear Jan and Mickey:

Sorry you can't make it June 12th but you have an ongoing rain check. While we'll miss you we're happy you are working 'cause that means pleasure for a lot of people.

Mickey I'll bet you don't remember the first time we met. The year was 1937 or thereabouts. I was new in Hollywood living in the Montecito apartments.* Someone had run over a dog in the street outside. You came in to look for a phone book so you could find the nearest veterinarian and take the dog to him. I figured this had to be a nice guy and I was right.

Nancy sends her best and so do I.

Sincerely,
Ronald Reagan

Jack Benny was one of America's most famous actors and comedians, known for his self-deprecating humor and for "never being older than 39." He died in 1974 at age 80. His adopted daughter, Joan, was writing a book about her father and wrote to Reagan, saying "I know that you and Dad were good friends, and I thought perhaps there was something in your personal relationship that could help me with 'What was Jack Benny really like?'"

Ms. Joan Benny
Beverly Hills, California
May 5, 1988 [47]

Dear Joan:

Nancy and I think it's wonderful that you are doing a book on your father and you are right, it is about a "nice, sweet, gentle man."

Joan I don't know whether we can be of help or not in the sense of anecdotes, but we can testify as to his warmth and kindliness.

My first meeting with your parents was in the middle '30s at radio station WHO Des Moines, Iowa. They were truly great radio stars with a national network show that was must viewing by all American families. I was a young sports announcer who could not possibly know that one day I would know them as personal friends.

I can't recall the particulars that brought them to Des Moines, but they were asked to do an interview on our station and I was the interviewer. They were the first truly great stars I had ever seen in person let alone met and I was awestruck. The memory that stuck with me was of an unassuming man who fit the definition of a true gentleman. "He always said and did the kindest thing."

Some years would go by and I would find myself in Hollywood, an actor under contract to Warner Bros. Studio and included in a ring of friends that also included the Bennys. The friendship grew and we were frequently in each others homes. From that close up view I saw a Jack Benny who was kind, generous and thoughtful of others. He took a personal interest in the welfare of those who made up the Jack Benny show. He gave of himself to worthy causes doing benefits whenever asked.

----

* The eight-story apartment building Reagan moved into when he went to Hollywood in 1937.

He was totally the opposite of the miserly role he played on the air or in motion pictures starring him. This man who made an entire nation laugh every week was the greatest audience for others, starting with his dear friend George Burns. But even nonperformers at the dinner table or in the living room telling a joke or passing a funny remark would be rewarded with Jack's warm and honest laughter. Never once did this truly great humorist take center stage at a social occasion. He was a truly great audience for fellow professionals as well as amateurs.

One anecdote. A dinner party at our house. Three or four of us including George Burns were standing together talking and Jack joined us. He spoke of a new comedian he'd seen in the East at some club. He was most enthusiastic and called the new comedian one of the funniest performers he'd ever seen. George interrupted him: "Jack," he said, "you think he's great because you are a sucker audience. We probably wouldn't think he was funny at all." Jack remonstrated, but George wouldn't be stopped. He said that he was going to do something with his cigar that he'd lighted and none of us would think it was funny but Jack would fall right to the floor laughing. Then he took his cigar and flicked ashes on his lapel and Jack ended up on his knees beating the floor as he laughed.

Joan, he was a much beloved man by all who were privileged to know him. God bless you for what you are doing.

Sincerely,
Ronald Reagan

Gene Autry was Hollywood's singing cowboy, appearing on radio, television, and the movie screen during the 1930s, '40s and '50s. When he died in 1998 he had vast real estate holdings and owned the Los Angeles Dodgers. While in Chicago in 1983 he found a reprint of a speech General Douglas MacArthur gave to the graduates of West Point in 1933. It reminded him of the problems Reagan was having getting his defense program approved by Congress—and Autry sent it to him.

Mr. Gene Autry
Los Angeles, California
July 21, 1983 [48]

Dear Gene:

Thank you very much for sending me the copy of the *Observer*.* That was my first year in radio and I had a lot of memories reawakened. I read it, every page.

You were right about the MacArthur speech, we are hearing the same chorus today. We call them "Peaceniks," he called them "Peace Cranks." They are kissing cousins.

Again thanks and best regards,

Ron

---

* The *American Observer* was a supplement in the *Chicago Tribune*. In 1983 the *Tribune* reprinted the July 6, 1933, *American Observer* to celebrate the 50th anniversary of the All-Star Game.

George Burns was one of the country's greatest comedians and a close and old friend of Reagan's. On January 31, 1983, after he had just turned 87, he thanked Reagan for a "thoughtful birthday wire" and added "I hope you get that Social Security thing straightened out. With my luck, when I get old and I'm supposed to collect there'll be nothing left." He died 13 years later.

Mr. George Burns
Hollywood, California
February 9, 1983 [49]

Dear George:

I just had to answer your letter knowing how concerned you are about Social Security. Now that I've reached the age of eligibility you can rest assured I've done something about it. I've made sure it will be on a solid basis for all you young fellows when your turn comes.

February 6 was my birthday—I finally made PAR-72 the hard way.

Nancy sends her love and so do I.

Sincerely,
Ronnie

Joe Pasternak, a producer of 83 movies, wrote Reagan that Universal Pictures once vetoed his decision to cast Reagan in a Deanna Durbin movie. Durbin had starred in 23 movies in the 1930s and 1940s. Pasternak jokingly added that if Reagan had been given the role, he would have become "a bigger star and our country might have lost a great president."

Mr. Joe Pasternak
Beverly Hills, California
July 22, 1987 [50]

Dear Joe:

Thanks for your letter and for that job of no casting you did back there at Universal. I probably wouldn't have thanked you if I'd known at the time but now that I'm in an eight-year run of the play deal, things do look a little different. Of course I'll be at liberty in about a year and a half. Maybe I could play the life story of Mickey Rooney, or am I too tall?*

Seriously, it was good to hear from you and I thank you for your generous words.

Best regards,
Ronald Reagan

---

* Mickey Rooney was 5'3" tall.

Kenneth Barrow, a London writer, had been authorized by Helen Hayes to write her official biography and asked Reagan if he would say something about "the qualities which made her such an exceptional talent and such an enduring star."

Mr. Kenneth Barrow
London, England
December 20, 1982 [51]

Dear Mr. Barrow:

I don't know if I have the words to do justice to Helen Hayes or to make a contribution worthy of your book.

No I never had the experience of working with her on stage or screen—I'm sorry to say—Yes I was acquainted with her as we all knew each other in that Hollywood of the golden era. I have come to know her better in these later years when we are both somewhat removed from that time and place.

She is ever and always a lady; a lady of warmth and kindness, as eternally feminine as she was when she captured the hearts of all who saw her on stage or screen.

What was her secret? Certainly it wasn't just theatrical artistry although she was a superb actress. There was more to it than that. There was beauty and an inner light that was Helen Hayes herself shining through every role she played.

Many, many years ago an American patriotic poem was set to music, to the noble strains of your anthem "God Save the Queen." Our American poem however lost much in the transposition because in order to fit the music it had to be badly phrased.

During World War II a great ceremony was held in Soldiers Field Stadium in Chicago. Helen Hayes was introduced to a crowd of 125,000. Looking so tiny down on the floor of that great stadium she recited that poem, the words that everyone in that crowd had sung hundreds of times. I think it was the first time we had ever heard the beauty of those words. The silence when she finished was I'm sure a greater ovation than any she had ever received.

Perhaps others could be effective in reading that poem but would anyone else think of it?

If anyone is looking for sheer enchantment tell them to run a Helen Hayes picture.

Sincerely,
Ronald Reagan

An author writing a book on Barbara Stanwyck asked President Reagan for his recollections. In 1949 Stanwyck and Nancy (Davis) Reagan were in the same film, East Side, West Side, *and in 1954 she co-starred with Ronald Reagan in* Cattle Queen of Montana.

Memo on Barbara Stanwyck
Washington, DC
December 1, 1981[52]

I had known Barbara Stanwyck for a number of years—not in any close friendship but as someone you saw at social events in Hollywood and, of course, like so many others I was an admirer of her work on the screen.

It was, therefore, a real thrill for me when I received a call from my agent that I had been offered the part playing opposite her in a picture called *Cattle Queen of Montana*. It was based on a real life character, a woman who drove a herd of cattle all the way from Texas to Montana and set up ranching there.

I'd heard many stories about Barbara and her professionalism on the set. She would come in on time every morning and with all lines for that day learned. There was no temperament, no insisting on prerequisites or trimmings usually associated with stardom. It was all business. She was there to make as good a picture as possible for the people who were going to pay to see it.

We did most of the picture on location in Glacier National Park.* I remember one day when the scene called for me to come riding out of the woods and Barbara was swimming out in a lake. The name of the location—Glacier National Park—will give you some idea of the temperature of the water. They had a double on hand to do this scene for her but Barbara, with her knowledge of screen technique, knew it would be a better scene if they could be actually seeing her face rather than just the figure of a double far removed from the camera. So, into the icy water she went. And, scenes don't just get filmed in a few minutes, there's always a reason for doing it over and sometimes over again. But not one whimper out of Stanwyck.

She rode when the scene called for that and rode well. And, when we had to run through the woods and dive over a log and turn and start blazing away at the bad guys, she dived over the log. She was a pro in her work, she was always a lady. She was kind to those she worked with and I didn't know anyone on the set that didn't like working there very much and that didn't feel a great warmth and loyalty toward her.

I'm proud and happy that in that golden era of Hollywood, I had a chance to work with her.

—————

Ray Mosely was a British author "writing the life of Cary Grant" who asked Reagan "to tell me anything you may care to about Cary for my book." Grant had died in 1986 at age 82.

—————

* In Montana, below the Canadian border.

Mr. Roy Mosely
Los Angeles, California
December 21, 1987[53]

Dear Mr. Mosely:

I have just received your letter and thank you for your generous words. You were most kind and both Nancy and I are truly grateful.

We are pleased to learn you are doing a book on Cary Grant. We did not know of his heroism in World War II but that's explainable. Cary was (off screen) modest and quite unassuming. He was definitely not the character he played so well on screen. We were great admirers of both Cary Grants and felt the warmest friendship for him as a person. As for the onscreen Cary I used to proclaim to all who would listen, that he should receive an Academy Award for never having done a poor or even routine performance.

We are both grateful that he was one of the entertainment world honorees in the Kennedy Center Awards during our time here.

Before our marriage Nancy was under contract to MGM. She did a screen test with Cary for a part in one of his pictures. The test narrowed down to her and another actress who was given the role. Nancy of course was disappointed. Cary took her to lunch at the studio cafeteria and very kindly talked away her disappointment and complimented her on her acting. He told her she did something many actors didn't know how to do. She listened to the other actor.

In later years after we were married Nancy was his dinner partner at a banquet. I believe I was toastmaster that night so we were all at the head table. It was shortly after the birth of Cary's daughter. He started to tell Nancy what this meant to him and he teared up. That was all Nancy needed to start her crying. There they were, facing the entire banquet crowd and both in tears.

One last item. Cary did a picture with Grace Kelly in which he wore some crew neck sweaters. I thought they were great. Nancy ran into him and told him how much we enjoyed the movie; she also told him how much I liked those sweaters. A day or two later a package arrived at our house, in it were two sweaters of the kind he'd worn in the picture. I still have them.

Well I can only add you are writing about a magnificent thespian, a true gentleman and a cherished friend. I wish you well.

Sincerely,
Ronald Reagan

Two authors writing a biography of Shirley Temple for G.P. Putnam's Sons asked Reagan for comments. Shirley Temple was the most popular and famous child star of all time. Reagan and Temple had co-starred in a film, That Hagen Girl, *in 1947 just after she turned 21, and had been friends ever since. She made 83 movies and then later held a number of government posts. President Nixon appointed her a U.S. dele-*

gate to the United Nations in 1969, President Ford appointed her ambassador to Ghana in 1974, and President Bush named her ambassador to Czechoslovakia in 1989.

Mr. and Mrs. Lester David
Woodmere, New York
April 12, 1982 [54]

Dear Mr. and Mrs. David:

As per our phone conversation here is the letter about Shirley Temple. I won't repeat the story about her dramatic scene as a child and then her composed curtsy to the director and crew on the set and her line—next week—"East Lynne." (This is just a reminder in case it's useful.)

Like every one else in America I loved Shirley Temple in those days when a Depression-haunted world forgot the drab, dreariness for a few hours in a neighborhood movie house, especially when a tiny golden-haired girl named Shirley Temple was on the screen. Her talent and ability were such that at one time rumors went around that she was much older than she was said to be and was somehow stunted in her growth. This was so patently ridiculous that little credence was given to it. But affection for her probably helped too. She was a beloved American institution and people wouldn't hold still for any attempt to deprecate her.

I never knew her in those years when she was a child star. We became acquainted when she was borrowed by Warner Brothers, and we co-starred in a picture called *That Hagen Girl,* somewhere around 1947.

It was a story of an older man and a young girl. But I believe you are interested in her as a person. Let me just say that she was totally unspoiled—with a delightful sense of humor. She was most likeable and in theatre language a real pro. She was also intelligent, well informed, with an interest in a wide range of subjects.

She was conscious of the fact that audiences were unwilling to let her grow up. She wanted very much to be accepted as an adult actress carrying on in the profession which had been hers for so long. I never let her know that having been a part of that audience, I wasn't quite ready either, and not so sure I wanted to be a party to presenting her to America for the first time as a young lady. But she was just that—a lady in every sense of the word.

I hope this is of some help.

Best regards,
Ronald Reagan

George Marshall was one of Hollywood's top directors for 50 years, making 150 films between 1916 and 1972. He was also president of the Screen Directors Guild (1948–1950). Writing a book on his life in pictures, Marshall asks Governor Reagan for "a few comments on your early acting experience" arguing that his book "would not be complete without some word from you."

George Marshall
Los Angeles, California
July 29, 1970[55]

(ran out of tape—here is the finish)

I'll always be grateful that I knew Hollywood in the "Golden Era" when it was big and brash and confident it could do anything—and usually did. It also was the Hollywood that became Mount Olympus for the world's theatrical great.

In that time the greatest pool of theatrical skill and talent that has ever been assembled anywhere was the community datelined "Hollywood." At the same time it was a place of friendship and warmth where the great helped the least.

And there was pride in craftmanship.

Sincerely,
Ronald Reagan

CHAPTER SIX

Governorship

RONALD REAGAN'S *rise to national political prominence began on October 27, 1964, when he gave a televised speech in support of Barry Goldwater, the Republican presidential candidate. Reagan made his usual arguments against big government and high taxes, but this time was different; instead of speaking to workers in a General Electric plant or to civic leaders at a banquet hall, Reagan was speaking to a national audience in the midst of a presidential campaign. He was a hit, and "the speech" (as it would be called) helped raise large sums for Goldwater. Soon thereafter, a group of wealthy businessmen in California, later known as Reagan's "kitchen cabinet," asked him to run for governor. In early January 1966, Reagan announced his candidacy. He won the governorship handily.*

California always has been a social laboratory and harbinger for the nation. What happens in the most populous (and diverse) state reverberates throughout the United States. No time was this more the case than during the late 1960s and early 1970s, the years Ronald Reagan was at the helm. Many of his policy decisions had long-term policy implications for California, and many others had national effects.

Governor Reagan took on everything. He worked to reduce the rate of the growth of the state budget and bureaucracy. He sought to revise the state's treatment plans for the mentally ill and its guidelines on eligibility for welfare assistance. On the strength of the apparent success of his welfare reform plan of 1971, Governor Reagan was asked to testify before the U.S. Senate Finance Committee on the Nixon administration's Family Assistance Plan (FAP). Reagan's arguments for returning welfare decisions to the states were a contributing factor in the defeat of FAP. As Reagan's eight years in Sacramento came to a close, Lou Cannon wrote: "Reagan had more impact on the domestic policies of the Nixon administration than any other governor, and his welfare policies are now widely copied by other states." [1]

Reagan took firm stands on many other issues. He became deeply embroiled in resisting unrest at the state's public colleges and universities. This was the era of intense activity at California's public colleges and universities by the Black Student Union, the Free Speech Movement, Students for a Democratic Society, the Third World Liber-

ation Front, and other organizations. Reagan's reactions to campus activities and his education policies made national headlines. So did his support for capital punishment. His tax-limitation measure, proposed to the voters as an amendment to the state constitution, was rejected at the polls but foreshadowed the tax revolt of the 1970s, including California's Proposition 13.

Immediately after he won the governorship in 1966, a New York Times headline captured the thinking of many Reagan supporters: "Reagan Emerging in '68 G.O.P. Spotlight After a Million-Vote California Victory."[2] Two years later, Reagan launched a brief "favorite son" candidacy for the presidency, but Richard Nixon won the Republican Party's nomination. Throughout the Vietnam War and Watergate, Reagan defended President Nixon. He made four missions abroad on the president's behalf. Reagan was easily reelected in 1970. In 1976, he launched his first all-out bid for the presidency. Four years later, Reagan won the presidency by a 10-percentage point margin. It is hard to imagine him winning the presidency without the wealth of political experience and national exposure he gained during his eight years as governor.

The letters below were written either during Reagan's governorship or before the presidency, as he looked back at that era.

POLITICAL CAMPAIGNS

The 1960s and early 1970s were formidable and formative years in Ronald Reagan's political career. Several discrete moments proved to be turning points for Reagan, California, and indeed the entire United States. In his first campaign for governor, the 55-year-old actor trounced Edmund "Pat" Brown, the two-term incumbent, on November 8, 1966, winning with a million-vote margin. He was immediately seen as a 1968 presidential contender and briefly ran as a "favorite son" candidate in the 1968 Republican race. Two years later, Reagan was reelected governor with a half-million-vote margin over Assemblyman Jesse Unruh. Reagan actively campaigned on Nixon's behalf in 1972. By the time he stepped down as governor in January 1975, Reagan was a seasoned political figure who was widely considered to be a future Republican nominee for president.

The letters below address Reagan's political campaigning, from his famous 1964 Goldwater speech to the 1974 gubernatorial election won by Jerry Brown, the son of Pat Brown.

———

In 1965, Reagan was mulling over the idea of running for governor of California and feeling pressure to make a decision, as he writes in the letter below. On January 4, 1966, he would announce his intention to seek the Republican Party's nomination for governor.

Mr. Light Thompson
Circa 1965[3]

Dear Light:

Just a hasty line to return your letter—I hope it will never appear in your scrapbook as—<u>from</u> a man who became president.

I'm still mulling the California governor thing with no answer as yet but have a feeling they are closing in on me.

Whatever happened to lying in the sun at Lowell Park?

Best,
Dutch

Eight months before he makes the official announcement, Reagan tells his longtime pen pal and her husband that he will run for governor.

Mr. and Mrs. Elwood H. Wagner
Philadelphia, Pennsylvania
May 1965[4]

Dear Lorraine and Wag:

I know it's confusing but think of it this way—no one can say "yes" he's going to run this early. So you say yes but you also say maybe. Of course there always is the chance that maybe will be the answer after all—if some unforeseen happening changes the batting order. Suppose for example our new Senator George Murphy[*] should say "I want in"—obviously he and I would be competing for the same support. This is only an example—I don't think he will and I'm fairly certain I will—run that is.

Best regards,
Ronnie

The prospect of a run for governor by Ronald Reagan drew national attention in 1965, and Reagan was at once labeled a political extremist. An April 11 article in the New York Times *described him as "the idol of the far-right wing of the [Republican] party," and reported that he and a member of the John Birch Society had delivered speeches at the same conservative convention.[5] Speculation about Reagan's affiliation continued throughout 1965 and 1966.[6]*

In the letter below, Reagan explains that his refusal to indict the John Birch Society is based on his belief that the greatness of the United States stems from the right of its citizens to hold wrong views as long as those views do not infringe on the constitutional rights of others.

---

[*] George Lloyd Murphy was elected to the United States Senate from California as a Republican on November 3, 1964.

Mildred Bell
North Hollywood, California
September 15, 1965[7]

Dear Mildred Bell:

I don't think I deserve your letter. I have answered the question over and over again in any number of press conferences with regard to the Birch Society—but where is the integrity of the press? Somehow the question still seems unanswered as far as the communication media is concerned.

It does not endorse political candidates and even if it did I would not seek its endorsement any more than I would appeal to any "block," groups, clubs, etc. I intend to state my philosophy, my beliefs and my approach to current problems with the hope that individual voters will subscribe to those views and support me. In that case they will be buying my philosophy—I'm not buying theirs.

This entire issue has been created by my repeating a facetious remark which I'd been told had been made by a former Republican congressman (now a Birch employee) with regard to all Republican candidates.

My refusal to indict this group has nothing to do with fence sitting but is because of my deep seated conviction that the greatness of our nation is our willingness to grant people the right to be wrong—so long as they do not infringe on the constitutional rights of others.

[letter incomplete]

On September 17, 1965, the Beverly Hills Courier *condemned Reagan's candidacy for governor based on a report that linked him to the John Birch Society:*

It has been established to the satisfaction of reasonable men that Ronald Reagan has disqualified himself from consideration as a candidate for governor of California.

Three responsible officials of the Republican Party have come forward to testify that Reagan, in a party council, had the highest praise personally for John Rousselot, a national officer of the John Birch Society. . . .

Reagan, according to three witnesses from his own party, reported to party strategists that Rousselot was ready either to offer an endorsement of Reagan's candidacy—or to come forth publicly with an official John Birch denunciation of Reagan, if that would be of greater help to Reagan at the polls.

This is simply shocking and disgraceful, and any newspaper with any gizzard will denounce it as an incipient fraud on the voters of California. Those who were a party to it should be drummed out of all parties and erased from public life.[8]

A week later, Reagan issued the following statement: "I have never been and I am not now a member of the John Birch Society, nor do I have any intention of ever becoming a member. I have never sought Birch Society support, nor do I have any intention of doing so should I become a candidate for public office. In my opinion those persons who are members of the John Birch Society have a decision to make concerning the reckless and imprudent statements of their leader, Mr. [Robert] Welch." [9]

———

Below is Reagan's reply to the editor of the Beverly Hills Courier.

The Editor
Beverly Hills, California
October 5, 1965 [10]

To the Editor:

In your September 17 issue you editorialize on the front page concerning some supposed arrangement I had with the Birch Society. This editorial purported to be based on fact indeed you used the line "It has been established to the satisfaction of reasonable men. . . ." You could have established the true facts by simply calling me but this you did not do. I state now your editorial was based on distortions and unfairly attacked me (and that is a mild term for the intemperate nature of your unsubstantiated attack).

I trust you will give this reply the same prominent treatment accorded your editorial. I have attached a copy of a statement making my position on the Birch Society clear.

Ronald Reagan

———

In this letter, Reagan continues to state that he disagrees with the leader of the John Birch Society.

Mr. and Mrs. Eitel
Circa the fall of 1965 [11]

Dear Mr. and Mrs. Eitel:

First let me apologize for the second letter soliciting support, please ignore it. I'm sure you can understand that duplications sometimes occur when lists of names are volunteered.

Now as to the main issue. Enclosed is a copy of my full statement and you'll note it does differ from the news accounts of what I'm supposed to have said. I have no doubt we possibly disagree on Mr. Welch but I have stated on a number of occasions that his facts are unquestioned but he adds those facts up to wrong conclusions. An example being the charge that the Communist advances during the Eisenhower administration and our obviously faulty foreign policy spelled deliberate intent on the part of the president.

I intend to campaign on my philosophy and my belief in our constitutional form of government. I will gladly accept the support of all who share that belief.

Sincerely,
Ronald Reagan

Reagan discusses how he came to hold public office and points to his speech for Goldwater as a turning point.

Judy
After January 1967 [12]

Dear Judy:

Sometimes I'm not quite sure how my change in occupations came about. As you perhaps gathered from my book I always did actively support causes and candidates I believed in. In the 1964 presidential campaign I did a lot of speaking in behalf of Senator Barry Goldwater the Republican candidate for president. One of my speeches was broadcast nationwide on TV and attracted the attention of party leaders in California. The following year a group of them asked me to become a candidate for governor.

This was an entirely new thought that had never entered my mind. In fact I was very much opposed to the idea and had no desire to hold public office. They persisted however and here I am.

This is the only public office I've ever held but it has been the most challenging and soul satisfying experience of my entire life.

I have retired from show business.

Hope this is a satisfactory answer. Good luck with your paper.

Sincerely,
Ronald Reagan

Reagan maintains that he never intended to be a serious candidate for the Republican nomination for president in 1968, but ran as a "favorite son," knowing that he was not ready to occupy the highest public office in the United States. This letter was most likely written in the fall of 1975 because he confides that he must now make a decision about his future in politics. On November 20, he announced his intention to seek the Republican nomination for the presidency.

Mrs. Packard
Circa the fall of 1975 [13]

Dear Mrs. Packard:

Thank you for your letter and for your expression of support. I am truly grateful. Let me however reply to your points about timing. The myth that I played "coy" in '68 and made a last-minute announcement is just that, a myth. I was persuaded by our California Republicans to be a favorite son candidate to prevent a bloodletting primary in California. I agreed on the understanding that my goal would be to bring back to California a still united delegation.

The last-minute change in Miami was by our delegation which announced they considered me an actual candidate. I never believed that a former actor who had only been a governor a matter of months could suddenly say he wanted to be president.

I realize I have a decision to make now—and I assure you the situation is now different. I'm not playing games but I need more information than is presently available. This is because my decision must be based on what is good for our country.

If the decision is yes, I'll be proud to have your support.

Thanks again,
Ronald Reagan

In the fall of 1971, Ronald Docksai, national chairman of the Young Americans for Freedom (YAF), launched a "Draft Reagan" movement. In the letter below, Reagan warns the YAF that he would publicly repudiate the organization if it suggested him for the presidency.[14]

Mr. Docksai
Williamsburg, Virginia
May 21, 1971 [15]

Dear Mr. Docksai:

I have just learned (from the press) of the plans YAF has for carrying on a presidential campaign in my behalf. While I am naturally proud that you hold me in such high regard, I still must ask with all the urgency I can express that you desist. To publicly repudiate any activity of YAF is not something I'm eager to do but, in this instance, I'll have no alternative if this effort continues.

Let me presume on some seniority in the cause which has united us and plead with you to reconsider your position on Vietnam. It has been my privilege as a governor to receive in-depth briefings on the war and the international situation. As a result, I'm in full support of the president's Vietnamization policy.

It is impossible to view Vietnam without taking into consideration where it fits in the gigantic chess came called the Cold War. The stakes in that game are no less than our very existence and only the president has access to all the facts necessary for each move.

We've come a long way since those pre-Goldwater days when there were so very few of us sounding the alarm. We've elected a president, but he is opposed by a hostile Congress determined to deny almost every request he makes. The great permanent structure of government, the bureaucracy, resorts to outright sabotage as part of the effort to put back in power those who will renew the "trip" this country was on for the eight New Frontier and Great Society years.

The move you've announced can only divide and destroy our chance to go forward. I am pledged to support the president and have told him I'll lead a California delegation to the convention in his behalf. I ask you to join me in this lest we awaken to find those who oppose our dreams and goals returned to power. Ours is an uphill fight against a combination of press and political forces who deny everything we believe in. We cannot afford division.

Sincerely,
Ronald Reagan

————

In a letter to Senator John Tower (R-Texas), Reagan writes that he is urging the YAF to join him in supporting President Nixon in the 1972 election.

Senator John Tower
Circa late 1971 [16]

Dear John:

I've enclosed my letter to YAF regarding their ideas about the '72 elections. As you can see, I not only turned them off but urged their support of the president. They replied instantly and in the affirmative.

I wish you had checked with me on this because there are too many people now trying to split our forces for us to be lending a hand in the same direction.

Sincerely,
Ron

————

The letter below was written during the 1974 gubernatorial campaign when Democrat Edmund "Jerry" Brown Jr., ran against Republican Houston Flournoy. Reagan is concerned about Brown's views on public employees going on strike, something he opposed, and calls the candidate unstable. Brown went on to defeat Flournoy with slightly more than 50 percent of the vote.

Mr. Bill Deming
1974 [17]

Dear Bill:

I'm afraid the press were a little overenthusiastic with that third party bit but thanks for the kind offer anyway. These are swift moving days and one wonders what each new day will bring.

I wish we could get some answers from young Mr. Brown to the questions you pose. He at least has answered one—yes he does believe in the right of public employees to strike.

It's tragic how close we are to having this "confused" and rather unstable individual in charge. And if it happens Republicans will have only themselves to blame.

Best regards,
Ron

OFFICE OF THE GOVERNOR

Reagan brought to the office of the governor both people and ideas that would be important to him for the remainder of his political career. Written during the early years of his governorship, the letters in this section are a small sample of Reagan's thinking about how government should be run, his requirements for making executive-level policy appointments, and his relations with staff.

Lyn Nofziger was Reagan's press secretary during his gubernatorial campaign, and Reagan appointed him director of communications in his new administration. Nofziger asked the governor-elect to write a letter to his wife and daughters to help persuade them to move from the East Coast to California.[18] Reagan's letter follows.

> Mrs. Lyn Nofziger
> McLean, Virginia
> November 1966[19]

Dear Bonnie, Sue and Glenda:

I know how disappointed you must have been when the election was finally over and done with and the one you've been missing these many months didn't come home. I'm sure you have some thoughts tending toward the swift elimination of a recently elected governor and I can't say that I blame you. However let me state my case and while it won't make you miss him less perhaps you'll understand better why he didn't come home.

You see part of this is his own fault. Without him I might very well not have been elected and there'd be no problem at all. Believe me it could have been a different campaign without his knowledge, experience and wise counsel. I owe him a great debt of gratitude and you even more for sharing him and for doing it in such a way that he was truly effective. The days ahead are frightening at best but they'd be impossible without him.

He's told me he'll be with you for Thanksgiving and I'll see that he's there for Christmas if we have to get a court order and have the sheriff run him out of California.

I'm so grateful to all of you—and your missing husband and father is of such help there are no words to really express my thanks. Just know that I do thank you from the bottom of my heart.

> Sincerely,
> Ronald Reagan

In this letter, Governor Reagan addresses the pay scales used for different categories of state employees. He notes that those in top positions at the University of California are paid more than the governor and other members of his administration.

Roger
After January 1967 [20]

Dear Roger:

I can't tell you how grateful I am for your letter and the thought prompting it. Your every paragraph will be on hand and considered before the final decision is made. There is no question about the thorns to be avoided in this one.

Let me point out, however, some of the factors, political and nonpolitical, on the other side. There can be no divorcing of this from the legislative pay raise. The jealousy involved in the separation of powers is such that a governor vetoing that one would render himself permanently impotent. At the same time the executive pay raise was created and sponsored by the Little Hoover Commission* and endorsed by the businessmen's task force. Both called attention to the problem of compensation extending down into the ranks of civil service where assistants and deputies are now virtually even in salary with bureau and department heads.

Actually, executive salaries in California state government run behind local and county government. While it is true we've been able to enlist many like yourself willing to serve out of a sense of duty and unselfishness, this does not cover the second and third level positions so essential to good administrations.

The matter of the constitutional officers is equally thorny. If those salaries are not brought into line prior to the 1970 election, a raise could not, under law, take place until 1975. An idea of how much out of line these salaries are can be gained from a comparison with the scale in force at the university. The president of the university and the next dozen positions are higher salaried than the top thirteen positions in state government including the governor. For example, the university treasurer is paid more than Ivy Baker Priest;† a chancellor receives more than the lieutenant governor. In fact, professors are on a higher scale by far than constitutional officers and cabinet members.

As you can see, this is tough one, but again I am most grateful to you.

Sincerely,
Ron

Ronald Reagan vows to use his veto power as governor to combat the gerrymandering of California that he says Democrats successfully completed. "My basic rule," Reagan said shortly after being elected president, "is that I want people who don't want a job in Government. I want people who are already so successful that they would re-

---

* Following legislation put forth by Milton Marks, a Republican assemblyman, in 1962, the "Little Hoover" Commission on California State Government Organization and Economy provided independent oversight of the functions of the state government. It drew its name from a federal commission chaired by President Herbert Hoover. In 1993, the Little Hoover Commission was renamed the Milton Marks Commission.

† Ivy Baker Priest was the California state treasurer from 1966 to 1974.

gard a Government job as a step down, not a step up." [21] *There is an inkling of this philosophy when he discusses his second lieutenant governor, Edwin Reinecke.*

Mr. Eling
After January 8, 1969 [22]

Dear Mr. Eling:

This is that personal reply you asked for and I'm delighted with the opportunity. If you think I have any quarrel with your views about a new kind of person in politics—not by a d—n sight. But we can't just shoot the last survivors of the "Last Hurrah" and run in some replacements. First we have to get ourselves in a position to have a fair crack at the polls.

Ten years ago the Democrats did gerrymander the state and some of the "hacks" you criticize are still around because they were given sure-thing districts. If we had won the opportunity to reapportion it was my hope we'd do it as it is supposed to be—districts created on the basis of geography and community of interest. I shall use my veto power to try and accomplish that.

By way of encouragement, let me say there are quite a few men up here now who fit the guidelines you described. They are successful men who honestly felt a call to duty—to serve and do something for state and country. One such signed that campaign brochure. Ed Reinecke, the lieutenant governor, sold out a very successful business he had built to go to Congress, that's why I appointed him lieutenant governor. He has no need of state employment, he could retire and live in comfort. The state has need of him.

Don't give up on us—we share your views.

Sincerely,
Ronald Reagan

ECONOMIC POLICY

The history of Proposition 1 and how Reagan assessed it is a window into his pre-presidential thinking about taxes and presaged his later policies. Proposition 1 was both a spending and a tax limitation measure. It sought to cap expenditures at the same percentage of state personal income that the state received as revenue in 1973 (estimated at 8.3 percent); the ratio would decline gradually to 7 percent. It also made it more difficult to raise taxes, requiring a two-thirds vote of the legislature, and called for returning the existing surpluses in excess of an emergency fund to the people. Provisions to safeguard against a shift of state taxes to local governments also were included.

Reagan introduced Proposition 1 in the spring of 1973 and had only seven weeks to obtain the nearly 400,000 signatures of registered voters needed to call a special election in November. Michael Deaver, the assistant to the governor and director of administration, headed an effort that garnered 900,000 signatures. Peter Hannaford, the director of a small public relations firm in northern California, was included in the group that Deaver recruited to help keep the momentum going for Proposition 1 until Election Day.[23]

The governor and his forces campaigned throughout the state, but their efforts were no match for the opposition, which included prominent Democratic legislators, the California Teachers Association, the California State Employees Association, the League of Women Voters, local boards, and many others. They argued that Proposition 1 would shift the tax burden from the state to local communities. Proposition 1 was defeated on November 6 by a 54–46 margin.[24]

Reagan took comfort in the belief that his effort was paving the way for future tax limitation measures. In a letter he wrote: "[W]e planted a seed and we won't stop now. A number of other states have picked up the idea and may implement it before California does. We'll keep on trying."[25]

He did keep trying. Through his nationally syndicated radio program and speeches in the late 1970s and in his two presidential campaigns, Reagan spoke often about controlling government spending and cutting taxes at the federal level. Reagan believed that the seed planted by his measure led Californians to approve Proposition 13, a property-tax reduction measure, on June 6, 1978.[26] *After substantial tax reductions and efforts to control spending during the first two years of his presidency, Reagan would write to the editor of the* American Spectator: *"It's always seemed to me that when government goes beyond a certain percentage of what it takes as its share of the people's earnings we have trouble. I guess a simple explanation of what I've been trying to do is peel government down to bare essentials—necessities if you will, and then set the tax revenues accordingly . . . I think we've learned government's wants are limitless."*[27] *Proposition 1, itself a constitutional amendment, prefigured Reagan's support for a balanced budget–tax limitation amendment to the Constitution in 1982. The amendment (a joint resolution) received the required two-thirds vote in the Senate but failed to obtain the required votes in the House of Representatives. The failure was not due to a lack of effort by the Reagan administration, which went all out for the amendment so closely tied to President Reagan's economic philosophy.*

Charles
Before November 6, 1973[28]

Dear Charles:

I'm afraid the news reporting between here and Texas has been a little distorted.

The sales tax increase was actually a tax shift. We passed legislation last year to substitute a penny of sales tax for some of the homeowner's property tax. The sales tax was to increase this July 1. In the meantime we have an $825 million surplus which I want to give back to the people. The Democrats in the legislature are, of course, opposed.

To return part of the surplus, I had asked them to delay increasing the sales tax six months and use $300 million to subsidize the property tax reduction. Forty-eight hours before July 1 they pretended to do this, but in reality sent me a bill they knew I'd have to veto—which I did. So the sales tax went up.

We have secured signatures to put the matter of tax reduction and the one-time rebate on the ballot, and I've called a special election for this purpose on November 6. If passed it will bring about a long term (15 years) gradual reduction of taxes and fix a limit in the state constitution of the percent of total income the state can take in taxes.

The battle on this is going to be a little bloody.

Best regards,
Ron

John
Before November 6, 1973 [29]

Dear John:

Thanks very much for the clippings and for your efforts in behalf of Prop 1. The campaign is a little more vicious than anything I've ever been in, but then I guess when you talk about shutting off the money supply you've touched a central nerve.

Maybe when this is over and I can stay on the ground longer than an hour at a time, we can say hello. My best to Carol and, again, thanks.

Sincerely,
Ron

Mr. Ben Biaggini
After November 6, 1973 [30]

Dear Ben:

Your letter regarding your meeting with Brian just arrived—thanks very much for seeing him.

And while I'm at it—thanks, again, Ben for all you've done on Prop 1. We didn't win, and I guess all of us have learned just how deeply entrenched are the forces of the government establishment. Frankly, though, I think it was only round one and we've planted some thoughts in people's minds.

We are working on some legislative proposals which will have some of our "statesmen?" squirming as their own words come back at them.

Again my heartfelt thanks.

Sincerely,
Ron

Mr. and Mrs. Clarence T. Bowman
After November 6, 1973 [31]

Dear Mr. and Mrs. Bowman:

Thank you so very much for your kind letter and for your support, also for the editorial.

We lost this time out, but we'll keep trying and with the support of people like you will eventually succeed. You might be interested to know that postelection surveys of the "no" vote reveal almost 70 percent thought they were voting against a tax increase. Our own polls in the closing days of the campaign showed our opponents were making headway with the false statement that Prop 1 would cause property taxes to go up. We just didn't have the resources to counter their advertising blitz with the truth.

Again thanks and best regards,
Ronald Reagan

———

Alex Kozinski and Marc McGuire were students at the University of California at Los Angeles and co-wrote an opinion essay supporting Proposition 1 in the campus newspaper, the Daily Bruin. *They wrote: "Far more is at stake than the few dollars which taxpayers may save. At stake is the chance to halt the growth of government by limiting its source of funds."* [32]

Mr. Marc McGuire and Mr. Alex Kozinski
After November, 1973 [33]

Dear Mr. McGuire and Mr. Kozinski:

I have read the article you authored for the *Bruin* in behalf of Prop 1 and want to thank you. May I also tell you I have some idea of the courage it took. I'm sure you have some lonely moments.

The election is over and Proposition 1 was defeated but hardly on the issue of whether government's size, power and cost should be limited. Our surveys (postelection) reveal that almost 70 percent of the no vote believed the widespread falsehood that Prop 1 would <u>raise</u> not lower their taxes. In short almost all of the voters "yes" and "no" were actually voting against higher taxes.

Prop 1 was the first round of a fight that will continue. I hope you'll continue to support the idea because you are correct that the real cost of the tax burden is individual freedom.

Again thanks.

Sincerely,
Ronald Reagan

Richard and Myrtle Owen
After November 6, 1973 [34]

Dear Richard and Myrtle:

Thanks for your good letter. You have figured the Prop 1 defeat out correctly. Our surveys show about 70 percent of the "no" vote actually believed they were voting against a tax increase.

We did everything we could legally to protest the false advertising and the use of taxpayer's funds in the campaign against Prop 1. We had no cooperation from the secretary of state's* office whatsoever.

I don't know whether the lawsuits brought by the citizens' commission are being pressed or not but we are continuing our fight to get an accounting.

Again thanks and stay ready, we aren't going to let this one battle be the war.

Sincerely,
Ron

In the next four letters Governor Reagan writes about various measures he has introduced to reduce property taxes.

Mrs. Day
After January 1967[35]

Dear Mrs. Day:

As you probably know, we've been frustrated for several years now in our every effort to reform taxes so as to reduce the burden on the homeowner. Believe me, I share your feelings. The homeowner's tax is the one glaring inequity in the California tax structure.

It is a local tax—locally assessed, collected and administered. The solution we've been attempting is to shift some of the tax to wider-based state taxes. The state would then reimburse local government for the reduction in the property tax. We insist, however, that if we do this we must limit local governments' right to increase the homeowner's tax. In our present proposal the control we suggest is to require a vote of the people in each district as to whether their property tax can be increased. We also intend to take some of the school costs off the property tax.

I assure you we are still striving to get this through the legislature. If we fail in that, I intend to take it to the people as a ballot measure in a special election called for that purpose.

Thanks for giving me the chance to comment and wish us well.

Sincerely,
Ronald Reagan

Walter
After January 1967[36]

Dear Walter:

Thanks for your good letter. I too enjoyed our meeting and look forward to more exchanges of this kind.

---

* Edmund G. "Jerry" Brown Jr., was secretary of state. He was elected governor of California on November 5, 1974, and was reelected on November 7, 1978. Brown was elected mayor of Oakland, California, on June 2, 1998, and reelected on March 5, 2002.

I'm much more optimistic about our tax reform. Since our meeting, the figures we've been able to put together indicate that the potential for homeowners reduction are even more than we'd hoped. It looks as if they'd scale from more than 40 percent in the lower price range to more than 25 percent in the highest priced houses for most of our 1,200 school districts.

But even with using some of the remaining property tax for school equalization everyone gets some relief. Another 185 districts will get 20 percent cuts or above, 43 will be above 15 percent and only five school districts will fall to about a 10 percent level of tax reduction.

We hope to present the entire plan on Tuesday—

Best regards,
Ron

Mrs. Fredrick A. Williams
Pacific Palisades, California
Circa 1971[37]

Dear Mrs. Williams:

I'm glad you wrote as you did. Hopefully I can straighten the record a bit. Many people are confused about the whole matter of local property taxes and believe the state is involved. Actually, property taxes are levied by cities, counties, school districts and a number of special districts such as street assessment, flood control, water, etc.

The county assessor is not an employee of the government but is a county official <u>elected</u> by the people of each county. Mr. Watson's present move is evidently based on his interpretation of the law.

For some time now I have been of the opinion that the property tax is too high and, indeed, is an outmoded, unfair method of raising revenue. For the last four years I have tried to persuade the legislature we should take over some of the burden at the state level by increasing statewide taxes such as the sales tax, so that we could reimburse local governments for reduction of the homeowners tax. I am still hopeful of getting their support, even though so far they have failed to agree on such a change in the tax structure.

Again, thank you for letting me comment, and I assure you we'll keep trying.

Sincerely,
Ronald Reagan

Mr. Strong
Circa 1971 or 1972[38]

Dear Mr. Strong:

One of the frustrations I have known in this job is the inability to reduce taxes. You ask why I have not done this and I could answer very simply that the Democratic majority in the legislature has constantly sought to increase the cost of government.

In only one of the five years have we had a Republican legislature. In that one year my budget as submitted to the legislature was approved with no additional spending requested. By contrast, in the other four years more than $800 million was added by the legislature, all of which I vetoed.

But this isn't the entire answer. We collect half a billion dollars in state taxes which we then give to the counties to fund a reduction in property taxes for homeowners. We have eliminated the personal property tax, and last year we gave a bonus of a 10 percent rebate on the personal income tax. This year we'll give a 20 percent rebate. All of these have been made possible by economies the Democratic legislators have largely opposed.

With regard to the schools, we are giving more than $500 million each year over and above what the schools were getting the year I took office.

The state gets only 18 cents out of your tax dollar. The federal government in Washington takes 65 cents, and the rest goes to cities and counties. I think you can see that any real tax relief must come at the national level. If we could cut state taxes 10 percent across the board it would only reduce your tax burden by one and eight-tenths cents on the dollar.

Thank you for giving me the chance to comment.

Sincerely,
Ronald Reagan

EDUCATION

The late 1960s and early 1970s were tumultuous years for universities across the United States, and California state colleges and universities saw their share of student and faculty unrest. In his inaugural address on January 5, 1967, Reagan promised to restore calm to the campuses: *

We are proud of our ability to provide this opportunity [a college education] for our youth and we believe it is no denial of academic freedom to provide this education within a framework of reasonable rules and regulations. Nor is it a violation of individual rights to require obedience to these rules and regulations or to insist that those unwilling to abide by them should get their education elsewhere.

It does not constitute political interference with intellectual freedom for

---

* Ronald Reagan was sworn in as governor of California on January 2, 1967, and his inaugural address was given on January 5.

the tax paying citizens—who support the college and university systems—to ask that, in addition to teaching, they build character on accepted moral and ethical standards.[39]

In his capacity as governor, Ronald Reagan served as president of the Board of Regents of the University of California. He engaged in fierce battles with university administrators and student organizations.[40] At the end of Reagan's second term in office, Lou Cannon, a Reagan biographer, assessed Governor Reagan's record on education:

His campaigns against campus violence revealed a strong streak of anti-intellectualism—once he accused universities of "subsidizing intellectual curiosity"—and he has made many enemies and few friends in the state's educational establishment. But the outlays for higher education in his administration have increased by 100 percent, one of the best showings in the nation.[41]

Eighteen days into his governorship, Reagan voted along with the majority of the Board of Regents to dismiss Clark Kerr, president of the University of California. Reagan wanted Kerr to step down but thought it would happen later.[42] Harry R. Wellman became acting president until January 1, 1968, when Charles J. Hitch took over as permanent president, a post he held until 1975.[43]

In this letter to the publisher of the Los Angeles Times, *Governor Reagan takes issue with an editorial that claimed "the Reagan Administration has mounted an attack on the University of California and its president, Charles J. Hitch." Reagan also disagrees with how an education writer characterized his interactions with Kerr and Hitch.[44]*

Mr. Otis Chandler
Los Angeles, California
Circa November or December 1972[45]

Dear Otis:

In the last meeting with you and your editorial board we discussed the matter of editorials regarding policies and programs of my administration. I suggested at that time that the answer to any question about the purpose or intent of such policies could be obtained by calling my office.

It is now a number of editorials later with no call ever having been made. This letter is prompted by the most recent editorial dealing with administration policy—the one of Friday, November 24, in which I was accused of making a "personal attack" on U.C. President Charles Hitch.

The entire editorial was not only based on a false assumption but compounding its unfairness was the fact that it was based on a supposed news story in the *Times* which was a total fabrication by your education writer Mr. Trombley. In his story he declared that a presentation by my finance director, Verne Orr, to the University Board of Regents <u>would be</u> an attack on President Hitch as part of an effort on my part to oust the president. Much was made of the fact that a previous finance director had appeared before the regents six years ago at approximately the time "Clark Kerr was fired."

A telephone call would have revealed that Mr. Trombley's story was outlandish fiction written before Mr. Orr even appeared, and obviously before Mr. Trombley could have known what Mr. Orr was going to say. It also would have revealed there was no need or justification for the self-righteous editorial which served no other purpose except to repeat the original falsehood.

There is no such plot on my part and, what's more, President Hitch does not believe there is any such plot.

The truth, of course, is far less exciting than the idea of conniving and plotting. The regents' audit committee invited Verne Orr to report the findings of the state auditors in their recent survey of the university. Incidentally, these auditors audit all departments and agencies of state government, not just the university.

Having Verne discuss the entire matter of the university budget with the <u>finance</u> committee of the regents was my idea, and I'm sorry I didn't think of it five years ago. It is time the regents and the people of California understand that the university has not been singled out for discriminatory treatment, but on the whole has fared as well or better than other segments of state government. Pertinent to this is the fact that 76 percent of the highest-salaried state employees are in the university.

As for the Clark Kerr episode, I think your writers have things a little out of sequence. I'm sure your mother could have told you, as she told me, that for two years prior to my becoming governor the regents had tried to persuade President Kerr to resign. Having been governor less than a month, I was attending my first regents meeting when Clark Kerr brought the matter to a head by demanding an immediate vote of confidence. The regents (none of whom were my appointees) rejected his ultimatum and his resignation followed.

Mr. Trombley's unfounded story and the follow-up editorial did a disservice to the university and to your readers by diverting attention from the facts and figures presented by Verne Orr. An even greater disservice was the concocted story of a nonexistent feud which can only disturb students, alumni, faculty and the citizens of this state at a time when the university is recovering from the rioting and vandalism of a few years ago.

Sincerely,
Ronald Reagan

The Santa Cruz campus of the University of California erupted into student protest during a Board of Regents meeting attended by Governor Reagan on October 18, 1968. Motivated by an experimental course on racism at U.C. Berkeley in which Eldridge Cleaver was invited to give guest lectures, Reagan introduced a resolution that would bar visiting lecturers from teaching courses unless they had appropriate academic credentials. On November 22, the regents adopted a resolution clarifying the authority of chancellors and deans in hiring faculty, and Reagan withdrew his proposal.[46]

Reagan writes to the father of a student who let him know that she objected to the behavior of her classmates during his appearance at the regents meeting in Santa Cruz.

Mr. Bing Russell
Thousand Oaks, California
October 23, 1968[47]

Dear Bing:

Last Friday, as you've no doubt seen in the news, I had a rather busy time at the University of California Santa Cruz. There is no need for me to go into the sad experience of seeing students on that beautiful campus rioting, threatening physical harm to the regents assembled there, and cursing the regents with profanity and unrepeatable obscenities. Enough to say—it happened.

But out of all this came one bright moment, at least for me. On the bus tour of the campus, students had been assigned to the busses as guides. I found myself seated beside one of the nicest, most ladylike young women one could hope to meet—your daughter. After hearing her good common-sense reaction to all that was going on, I finally had to ask how she had been able to maintain such a sense of values in the atmosphere so prevalent there. She stated very simply, "That's the way my mother and father raised me."

You must be very proud and you have every right to be.

Sincerely,
Ronald Reagan

San Francisco State College was besieged with antiwar and civil rights protests during the late 1960s. As the crisis atmosphere on the campus rose, President John Henry Summerskill announced that he would resign. His resignation was accepted in May 1968 and Robert R. Smith briefly replaced him. Samuel I. Hayakawa, a professor of English, was appointed acting president on November 26, 1968. Hayakawa was known as a law-and-order college leader.

Governor Reagan expresses confidence in Hayakawa* in the following letter.

---

* Hayakawa was appointed the permanent president by the board of trustees of the California State Colleges in a vote of 16 to 2 on July 9, 1968, and he held the position until 1973.

Roland Rich Woolley
Los Angeles, California
December 3, 1968[48]

Dear Roland:

Just a line to say thanks. Keep your fingers crossed—we may have found the man for San Francisco State.

I'm waiting for Bob Finch to drop the other shoe and tell us whether he's going to Washington or not so I can get busy on naming a lieutenant.*

Best regards,
Ron

––––––––

Governor Reagan congratulates the "Samurai Scholar," as Hayakawa was sometimes called, for his handling of the activities of the Students for a Democratic Society, a national youth organization formed in 1959 whose expressed goal was to make the American political system more directly responsive to all people.

Dr. [Samuel I.] Hayakawa
Circa fall 1968 or 1969[49]

Dear Samurai:

Thanks very much for the picture—it reveals heretofore hidden talents. It also indicates you have surmounted the problems and obstacles that proved insurmountable for your predecessors. Congratulations. Perhaps there will be a day when you and I can play catch on the campus while students pause to watch with affectionate smiles on their faces.

Seriously let me say how sensible and encouraging was the masterful handling of the recent incident involving the two dozen SDS members.

Again thanks and best regards,
Dutch

––––––––

After the tumultuous days at San Francisco State, Governor Reagan looks back and credits Hayakawa's firmness for restoring calm to the campus.

––––––––

* On December 11, 1968, president-elect Richard M. Nixon announced that he would appoint California's lieutenant governor Robert H. Finch as his secretary of health, education, and welfare. On January 8, 1969, Governor Reagan announced that Congressman Edwin Reinecke would be his new lieutenant governor.

Dr. Sam Hayakawa
After January 4, 1971[50]

Dear Samurai:

Alex* told me of your call and good wishes thanks very much. May I in turn wish you and your lovely wife the very best in the coming year.

I know I shouldn't do this but can't resist being an "I told you so." Do you remember our phone conversation one morning during those dark days of battle? You were tired and understandably so and you asked, "when will it end?" I said, "it is ending, you are winning and while you can't see it now, one of these days it will be gone. It will just fade away." Well it has. But it faded away because you faced them down. Do you know where we can get another dozen like you?

All the best,
Dutch

―――――――

The late 1960s were watershed years for protest movements at public colleges and universities in California. Striking students at San Francisco State College and U.C. Berkeley demanded ethnic studies departments and put forth a list of other grievances. At San Francisco State, faculty went on strike for higher wages and improved work conditions. Governor Reagan writes about the strikes at the campuses in the next two letters.

Mrs. Marquita Maytag
La Jolla, California
October 23, 1968[51]

Dear Marquita:

Quite a contrast between the afternoon by your pool and the day spent in the rarefied atmosphere of higher education. But take hope—they are arresting students at Berkeley. Maybe my ultimatum to President Hitch† did some good. I told him if there was a sit-in and he didn't throw them out I'd send in police to do it for him.

Actually this was to be a thank you note for that wonderful easy day in your beautiful home. It was a badly needed pause and did much to recharge the batteries. All of us are truly grateful.

Don't worry about the campus—we are going to win this one.

All the best,
Ron

―――――――

* Alex Sherriffs was Governor Reagan's education adviser.
† Charles J. Hitch was president of the University of California from 1968 to 1975.

The Honorable Jack Williams
Phoenix, Arizona
March 17, 1969 [52]

Dear Jack:

I'm off for the airport and will read your speech on the plane—and steal a bit of it here and there. The clipping I've already read, and some of that will be stolen, too. Thank heaven you carried on and delivered the speech; but then, knowing you, I'm not surprised. Our Mayor Alioto* of San Francisco (and liberal bent) got bluffed out of talking by such a demonstration at George Washington University. I'm convinced we win when we defy the little monsters as you did.

Out here at Berkeley and at San Francisco State the striking teachers called off their strike when it became apparent they were really cheating. They voted a strike and they picketed, but we found they were really taking turns and sneaking back into their classrooms so they wouldn't lose their jobs. Two days ago at Berkeley an outdoor rally was broken up by a thundershower, and now the students have called off hostilities while they take their quarterly exams.

We are still on the side of the angels, but a little clout here and there is in order—after all, the Lord took a club to the money changers in the temple.

Best regards,
Ron

On February 5, 1969, Governor Reagan imposed a state of emergency at UC Berkeley in response to student strikes. Later that month, National Guardsmen were called up to open the entrance to campus that was being blocked by a teaching assistants' strike. In May, the National Guard and highway patrol were used to keep order on campus as the university sought to wrest control of the university-owned People's Park from students and others who wanted to use the park for their own purposes. Bayonets, shotguns, and tear gas were used by the National Guard to control the riots. On June 2, 1969, Reagan declared that at 6:00 A.M. the following day the state of emergency was being lifted and the National Guard withdrawn.

The letter below is about the crisis at UC Berkeley.

Pete
After the spring of 1969 [53]

Dear Pete:

If you are quoted correctly by the press, I'm afraid you don't have the entire sequence of events in the Berkeley war.

Enclosed is a speech I gave, which was broadcast statewide. I'll vouch for all the facts, as we are preparing a complete, documented report on the incident.

---

* Joseph L. Alioto.

I'll agree, bayonets are not pretty, but they brought an immediate end to the hand-to-hand conflict that had prevailed.

Regards,
Ron

———————

In a question-and-answer session at a meeting of the California Council of Growers at Yosemite on April 7, 1970, Governor Reagan sought to enlist the support of alumni of the state university system in efforts to stop student unrest. He said that campus radical students should be told, "If it takes a bloodbath now let's get it over with."[54] *The "bloodbath" statement caught nationwide attention, and was interpreted as Reagan's desire to have a confrontation with students. The phrase was used against Reagan in his reelection campaign against Assemblyman Jesse Unruh.*[55]

In the next two letters, Reagan explains what he meant. In the last letter he also objects to the unionizing methods of Cesar Estrada Chavez, a Mexican-American labor leader who founded the National Farm Workers Association, which later became the United Farm Workers of America.

Mr. Dave Goble
April 14, 1980[56]

Dear Mr. [Goble]:

Thank you very much for writing as you did and for giving me an opportunity to state my case. The bloodbath line was used as a figure of speech. I probably could have come up with a better one than that, but it was not intended in any way to suggest that having a bloodbath on the campus in answer to the rioting that was taking place there. I was speaking to a gathering of mainly University of California graduates. The vice president of the university was on the dais with me. A question came from the audience about what these alumni could do to help the university in its trying time. This was during the period when Wheeler Hall was burned and when an attempt was made to set fire to the great university library.* In answering the question, I prefaced my answer by pointing out that traditionally the campus was a place where men and women of good will could disagree in a civilized manner and discuss their disagreements and differences without resorting to violence. I explained that the university administrators had in this tradition tried to discuss the differences with the dissenters. But as dissent grew into violence and rioting and the other things I've just mentioned, the university administrators were finally coming to the realization that the dissenters were going beyond dissent and did not want a reasoned discussion on their differences and they, the administrators, were in effect indulging in appeasement. I then said these administrators had come to

———————

* In the midst of a student strike on January 22, 1969, a fire swept through Wheeler Hall at the University of California at Berkeley. On March 9, 1970, a three-alarm fire destroyed part of the university's main library.

realize the error of their ways and now knew they had to deal directly with the violence. And that is where I used, as a figure of speech, the expression that they, the administrators, knew they were going to have to take their bloodbath by resisting the rioters with expulsion, suspension, etc. Of the entire press corps present, only one man went out and wrote a story implying that I was advocating a bloodbath on the campus. All the other members of the press recognized I was using a figure of speech to note the penalties (suspensions, expulsions, faculty dismissals, etc.) the administrators would have to exact to regain control of the campus from the rioters, who had resorted to violence in their protest activities.

[no signature]

Mrs. L. Johsens
After April 7, 1970[57]

Dear Mrs. Johsens:

I hope you won't mind my answering your letter. So much of it concerned me it just seemed more simple this way.

First let me thank you for giving us the chance to hopefully correct some misconceptions about my statements and views. That misconceptions exist is easily understandable in view of the manner in which some stories are reported.

The so-called "bloodbath" statement is a perfect example. I was asked a question from the floor about the campus situation. In my rather lengthy answer I made the following points (all of which went unreported by the press). 1. The radical revolutionaries were only a small fraction of the students. 2. The great majority are fine young people. 3. We should not become so angry at the few we vented our rage on the others. Therefore we should vote for the university bond issue on the June ballot. 4. The college administrators need our help. They have lived in an atmosphere where violence was unknown and were totally unprepared to deal with it. They have temporized trying to reason with the radicals but now must recognize they have to stand firm and "take their bloodbath."

Obviously in this context the term was a figure of speech and actually applied to the administrators not the students. The reporter who blew this out of all proportion couldn't have misunderstood. His act was one of deliberate distortion for the sake of sensationalism.

Now as to the grape strike—which is no strike at all. I was an officer of my union and six times president over a period of twenty-five years. In other words I believe in labor's right to organize. But Mr. Chavez is seeking to sign up the employees to a contract and thus organize a union by forcing the workers to join because he and management have agreed they must. True unionism is based on the workers themselves choosing a union or forming one and then negotiating a contract with management. So far the great majority of workers have shown no desire to join the union of Cesar Chavez. Their freedom of choice must be respected.

I hope this clarifies these points. Without the comfort and help of prayer I would find my job impossible to bear. In suggesting that I arrogated power to myself may I ask what I had to gain? My income as an actor was several times what it is now and I only had to work a few months out of the year.

Sincerely,
Ronald Reagan

_____

Reagan was upset by an article attacking his stewardship of the University of California, and drafted a point-by-point response, though he apparently thought better of sending it. A note on the letter says it was not sent.

Between 1967 and 1975

Alex—*

With regard to the attached article what would you say about a reply—(to the magazine) something like this—[58]

Your December issue carried an article by a "leading American scholar" who preferred to remain anonymous. It appeared under the heading, "Points of the Compass—Campus revolt: California's Balance Sheet."

While the author revealed much factual knowledge of the University of California and events of the past few years, I'm afraid his personal bias caused him to draw several wrong conclusions. This is regrettable because once again a voice is raised in such a way as to keep the deeply disturbed moderate faculty from coming to the aid of regents who in truth seek moderate goals and a restoration of true academic freedom.

On page 86 the author refers to my "conservative, repressive Board of Regents." Then he goes on for the balance of the page deploring the politicization of the campus by committed radicals (his own term) and portrays the faculty (moderate) as defending academic standards against pressure from the administration which "seeks to conciliate the militant students."

It is true on the following page the author frankly concedes the moderate faculty lets the situation ride rather than seek alliance with the regents because to do so would be to join up with "reactionaries." Then however he proceeds to strengthen the belief that we are indeed reactionaries.

At this point on pages 87 and 88 I am the victim of what I earlier referred to as personal bias and wrong conclusions. Specifically he repeats the old fallacy about "budget cutting" and then flatly states that I have privately expressed the view that "excellence in education as well as expensive basic research ought to be the function of the elite private universities." He "substantiates" this falsehood (and I flatly state, falsehood is the only appropriate term) with a line about un-

_____

* Dr. Alex Sherriffs was Governor Reagan's education adviser.

named educators and representatives of the press who think it's true and therefore of course it must be so.

According to him I want the public universities to provide low quality mass education and am attempting to bring this about through budget reductions. Also I want the universities to balance the radical faculty element by employing an equal number of conservative faculty members.

There is no point in my explaining once again the fiscal facts of life in state government and the priority we've given the universities in these times of limited resources. But two things must be said; one my view of what the University of California should do flatly refutes his charge about mass education. If it becomes impossible to take all applicants qualified by virtue of being in the top 12½ percent of their class then we should raise the qualification to only those in the top 10 or 9 or 8 percent. The University of California should remain a prestige institution providing top quality education. Second I do not believe in matching numbers of professors by giving political saliva tests. Professors whether liberal, radical or conservative should not impose their personal philosophy on students. They should return to the one time ethic of their honorable calling and by exposing students to all viewpoints teach them how to think not what to think.

In conclusion let me add one challenge to so-called moderate faculty members. So long as they are afraid to stand up and join us in treating with those on the campus who presently discriminate on political grounds, so long as one department head can silence a faculty member by threatening to withhold deserved promotion, recognition or assignment academic freedom does not exist and therefore cannot be threatened by regents or politicians.

The author concludes with a statement about a vicious cycle perpetuated by those (regents and politicians, I presume) who oppose radicals. It's possible he's confused an "inner circle" for a vicious cycle. An inner circle of selfish academics who are delighted to have the protection of a wall of moderates resolutely on guard against the venal, anti-intellectual establishment. Let me offer a proposition—the regents and politicians will back off completely if the silent, disenfranchised, moderate majority in the faculty will right what's wrong. They might start by admitting out loud something is wrong. That would be a "giant step forward" for academic mankind.

Angela Davis was a young African-American woman who by 1970 had risen to national prominence as a member of the Communist Party of the United States of America and a supporter of the Black Panther Party. In the spring of 1969, at age 25, Davis became a visiting assistant professor of philosophy at the University of California at Los Angeles. In the fall, she was dismissed by the UC Regents because of her affiliation with the Communist Party. A California court reinstated her, however, based on earlier decisions by the U.S. Supreme Court, which ruled that bans on employing communists were unconstitutional.

On June 19, 1970, Governor Reagan, along with a majority of the UC regents,
voted not to renew Davis's teaching contract for another year. At a press conference
after the vote, Reagan cited her speeches, "particularly on those campuses where there
was already trouble and dissension," as the reason for her dismissal. He added: "Aca-
demic freedom does not include . . . speaking to incite trouble on other campuses." [59]
In the letter below, Reagan discusses the dismissal of Davis.

Mrs. Liston
Circa fall 1969–1970 [60]

Dear Mrs. Liston:

Just a line to say I share your concern with regard to educators and their ability
to indoctrinate rather than teach.

Unfortunately the problem is complicated and grows more so. In the instance
of Miss Davis the University of California did terminate her position. The university had a rule expressly forbidding the employment of faculty members who were
members of the Communist Party. Now the Supreme Court has given a decision
that such rules are unconstitutional.

I assure you I am not deserting and will continue to expose and oppose communism in every way I can.

Sincerely,
Ronald Reagan

Governor Reagan writes that while the University of California Board of Regents
should be responsible for choosing top administrators, he would not want them to select
faculty.

John
After January 1967 [61]

Dear John:

This is just a quick line but tardy to acknowledge your good letter of January 3.
I didn't get back into the office until the 8th hence the lateness of my reply.

I'm in complete agreement with you about the regents and the delegating away
of authority where administration personnel are concerned. While I would not
want to see the regents attempt to hire professors I believe we are responsible for
the selection of chancellors and of course the president.

Faculty suggestions should be given consideration but not their present
weight. What we have is a situation wherein the university administration is beholden to its own employees not its employers.

I'll look forward to exploring this subject further with you.

Best regards,
Ron

In the next two letters, Governor Reagan provides figures showing increases in state aid for public education at all levels during his administration.

> Mr. John Christman
> Pacific Palisades, California
> After January 1967 [62]

Dear John:

Enclosed is the speech containing the figures you requested. In view of your remark as to the use you'd like to make of them here are some additional statistics.

We have increased the state aid for public education (kindergarten through grade 14) 118 percent while enrollment was going up 10.6 percent. The University of California's budget has been increased 106 percent as against an enrollment increase of 41 percent. And the state scholarship and loan fund is more than nine times greater than it was in 1967.

While on the subject of higher education it is interesting that 543 University of California employees including 100 administrators are in the above $35,000 salary class compared to only 26 in state government jobs.

Hope this helps.

> Best regards,
> Ronald Reagan

> Miss Dawson
> Circa 1972–1975 [63]

Check with Verne Orr*—maybe my answer should be more explicit about the actual budget problem she mentions.

> RR

Dear Miss Dawson:

I appreciate your writing and giving me a chance to comment on the problem of such concern to you.

There would be no point in getting into a discussion of the controversy over the merits of early preschool education. I'm sure you are aware that two schools of thought exist on this subject. But educational policy is the jurisdiction of the State Superintendent of Education and primarily local school boards and administrators.

In the last few budgets of this administration we have increased state support for public education more than any administration in the history of the state. There is no question that education has had the highest priority of any item in the

---

* Verne Orr was California's director of finance from 1970 to 1975.

budget. Having seen to that it is up to the education administrators to decide priorities between the various facets of education.

In 1971–1972 we appropriated $41.6 million for child development programs designed to serve preschool age children. In the current budget this has grown to $93.4 million. The program has more than doubled in three years.

I can well understand your position and your disappointment at not being funded. I hope you can understand mine.

You made a reference to movie actors and to the children of poor people and it seemed to me the inference was that I lacked understanding of the problems of poverty. If I'm wrong I beg your pardon. If not let me assure you I understand poverty very well and from personal experience. I grew up in poverty and know full well how blessed I have been. Between us perhaps one day we can bring our society a little closer to ending poverty.

> Sincerely,
> Ronald Reagan

SOCIAL POLICY

Reagan's conservative viewpoint on social policy issues was reflected in his decisions as governor. He supported capital punishment, stricter guidelines for welfare eligibility, and a mental health care system that gave more power to local facilities than to state hospitals. He opposed abortion as well as environmental policies that challenged the right to private ownership. Ultimately Reagan believed that government was at its best when it restored power and responsibility to the individual.

––––––––

Six months into his governorship, Ronald Reagan liberalized California's abortion law by signing the Therapeutic Abortion Act, which permitted termination of a pregnancy when the mental or physical health of the mother was endangered or when statutory rape had occurred. After the bill went into effect, there was a significant increase in the number of abortions performed in California.[64] In the next two letters, Reagan writes that this increase was due to medical professionals abusing the health-of-the-mother provision. He writes that if he had to do it again, he would make the legislation airtight.

> Mr. Robert L. Mauro
> St. Paul, Minnesota
> October 11, 1979[65]

Dear Mr. Mauro:

I hope you won't mind my writing you about a recent column of yours suggesting that I might be preparing to abandon my anti-abortion position and that

I signed a permissive abortion bill while I was governor.* I think there are two things I should make plain here.

First, my position is that interrupting a pregnancy means the taking of a human life. In our Judeo-Christian tradition, that can only be done in self-defense. Therefore, I will agree to an abortion only to protect the life of the prospective mother.

Now, with regard to the permissive bill I supposedly signed, let me give you the correct history of what took place early in my term as governor. A bill was introduced that was permissive, indeed was abortion on demand. Naturally, there was great controversy about this bill. The author finally sent word that he would amend his bill to anything the governor thought he could sign. Faced with this responsibility, I probably did more study and more soul searching on the subject than I had done on anything in my eight years as governor. I came to the conclusion, as I have already stated, that it could only be justified to save a human life. Then the matter of health—meaning the permanent damage to health of a mother if she went through with her pregnancy—was brought up. It seemed to me that the mother would have the right to protect herself from permanent damage just as she would be able to protect herself, even if it meant taking a life, from someone threatening her with mayhem, so I agreed to that provision. I thought there was adequate provision in the bill requiring responsible boards in the medical profession to declare that such permanent harm would follow the birth of the child. Perhaps it was my inexperience in government, but, like so many pieces of legislation, there were loopholes that I had not seen, and the thing that made the California abortion bill become somewhat permissive in nature was violation of the spirit of the legislation by the very groups who were supposed to police it. This was particularly true in the case of psychiatrists. If faced with the same problem today, I can assure you I would make sure there were no loopholes in the bill. Indeed, I have already written Congressman Hyde telling him of my support for his amendment.†

Again, please rest assured there is no way I could or would change my position with regard to my opposition to the permissive abortion that is taking place throughout our land.

Sincerely,
Ronald Reagan

---

* Robert L. Mauro, "Pro-Life View of Presidential Candidate Possibilities," *The Wanderer,* September 20, 1979.

† The Hyde Amendment was a federal law that limited the use of Medicaid funds for abortions. Eight months after Reagan's letter, the U.S. Supreme Court voted 5 to 4 to uphold the Hyde Amendment, declaring that congressional restrictions on federal funds for abortions did not violate the equal protection rights of poor women. See Linda Greenhouse, "Limit on Abortions Paid with Medicaid Upheld by Justices," *New York Times,* July 1, 1980. As president, Ronald Reagan put his name to an article and book about abortion. "Abortion and the Conscience of the Nation," *The Human Life Review,*" vol. 9, no. 2 (Spring 1983): 7–16; and *Abortion and the Conscience of the Nation* (Nashville: Thomas Nelson Publishers, 1984).

Mr. Al Matt
St. Paul, Minnesota
October 11, 1979[66]

Dear Mr. Matt:

I have just written a letter to Mr. Mauro regarding a column of his with regard to my position on abortion. I just wanted to let you know that, as I wrote to him, I have not changed my position. I am very much in favor of an amendment, if that is necessary, to curb the abortion on demand that we have in so much of the country. Very simply, my feeling is that an abortion is the taking of a human life and that can only be justified or excused in our society as defense of the mother's life—if her life is threatened by continuing the pregnancy. There is no way I could or would change my position.

Sincerely,
Ronald Reagan

———

Reagan oversaw one execution during his eight years as governor: on April 12, 1967, he refused clemency to Aaron C. Mitchell, who had been sentenced to death for killing a policeman. On June 29, he commuted the sentence of Calvin Thomas based on evidence that the death row inmate had severe psychiatric problems.[67]

In a historic decision on February 18, 1972, the California State Supreme Court ruled the death penalty illegal. Previous convicts such as Sirhan Sirhan and Charles Manson were ordered to serve life sentences. Shortly thereafter, a petition campaign was organized to create a constitutional amendment that would restore the death penalty in California. Governor Ronald Reagan and California Attorney General Evelle J. Younger were among its supporters. On November 7, 1972, Californians voted for Proposition 17, which reinstated capital punishment in California. On December 7, 1976, the California State Supreme Court struck down the capital punishment law. Chief Justice Donald Wright, whom Reagan appointed, wrote the opinion in favor of reversing the law.[68]

Mr. Johnson
After January 1967[69]

Dear Mr. Johnson:

I appreciate your letter and your giving me a chance to comment on what is undoubtedly one of the most difficult parts of this job.

Let me say first with regard to my mental attitude, as you put it, I certainly feel no hatred nor is my position on capital punishment motivated by some "eye for an eye" concept. It is true I believe we must retain capital punishment, and I believe there is backing for this in the Scriptures. However, this must be thought of in the light of a preventive to murder.

On my desk is a list of 12 murderers who were sentenced to prison and subsequently, having served their sentences, were released. They went on to murder 22 more victims.*

As governor, I cannot put my personal feelings above the law. If our system of justice, including all the courts of appeal, decree a man must die for a crime, I can only reverse that decision if evidence is presented later which indicates he is entitled to clemency.

Believe me, no part of a governor's job is approached more prayerfully than this one.

Sincerely,
Ronald Reagan

Reagan aggressively tackled welfare reform during his governorship. In 1970, he formed a welfare task force that by the end of the year submitted a report warning that unless the rapidly rising costs of welfare were checked through more effective eligibility measures, the state government would eventually be bankrupt. Reagan wanted to present the findings to a joint session of the legislature but was turned down. After transmitting his tax reform plan to the legislature in March 1971, he took his message directly to the people in speeches across the state. Finally, Assembly Speaker Robert Moretti came to the governor's office to declare a truce. Together Reagan and Moretti worked on legislation that stiffened eligibility standards but also sought to increase benefits for those in dire need. The legislature approved the welfare reform bill on August 11, 1971. When Reagan presented his welfare reform plan to the legislature in March 1971, the welfare rolls stood at nearly two and half million. In January 1975, the month he left office, the welfare caseload had declined by almost 400,000.[70]

In this letter, Reagan discusses his task force and his views on reforming welfare.

Charles Broskas
1970[71]

Send copy this reply and Mr. Broskas' letter over to Ned H.† for his info.

Dear Charles:

Once again our minds have been following the same trail. We've had a task force working on the whole welfare subject and all our explorations take us in one direction—and that certainly isn't toward the guaranteed income.

I am convinced that our answers lie in the proven rules of private enterprise

---

* In a speech on September 28, 1981, President Reagan placed the number of victims of the 12 murderers at 34 and said, "I think capital punishment in the beginning might have reduced that figure considerably."

† Ned Hutchinson was the appointments assistant to Governor Reagan.

and that the dole, except for the aged and disabled, should be eliminated and a government work force be instituted for the able bodied.

Thanks for your good ideas on this and

Best regards,
Ron

———————

Reagan boasts about the success of his welfare reform program in the next two letters.

Charles
After August 1971 [72]

Dear Charles:

Just a quick few words to say how pleased I am at the way things are working out for you in the new assignment. And also to add a thank you for the inspiring story about the young man in medical school. It makes you wonder how anyone can have an excuse for welfare, doesn't it?

Our reforms here are being sensationally successful, even though we've had to fight the bureaucracy all the way.

Best regards,
Ron

Ed
After August 1971 [73]

Dear Ed:

Thanks so much for my welfare plaque. I'm going to keep it as a reminder of what used to be.

You'll be happy to know that the downward trend in caseload continues as a result of our reforms. If the courts will get out of the way we'll move even faster.

I'm anticipating a great drop in November. By the end of September we had 19,000 fewer cases than in March.

Thanks again,
Ron

———————

Early in his governorship, Reagan put forth a proposal to address the fact that the number of patients in California's mental facilities had been steadily declining for years without a corresponding decline in the mental health care workforce. In a statewide television address on April 16, 1967, Reagan admitted that his proposal to eliminate 3,700 mental health positions and reduce the budgets of state mental hospitals was "perhaps the most emotional issue" of his first 100 days in office. Reagan ultimately abandoned the reduction plan but instituted a community treatment idea that returned patients to their communities by placing them in local facilities where they could begin the process of resuming a normal life. As a result, some state mental hospitals were closed.[74]

In the next four letters, Reagan explains his approach to mental health care, and defends his efforts against rumors and attacks. The first three letters are replies to citizens who wrote to Mrs. Reagan.

> Mrs. Hawkins
> After January 2, 1967[75]

Dear Mrs. Hawkins:

I hope you won't mind my answering your letter. Nancy showed it to me, and since it has to do with future developments in the field of mental health, it seemed best perhaps that I explain present policy.

For several years now the state has been underwriting county mental health care clinics in what has been a tremendously successful program. The patient population in our state hospitals has been reduced so drastically that we are able to close some hospitals entirely and reduce others in size. This does not mean, however, that we will eliminate the need for all hospitals. There will always be a need for custodial care for those patients who cannot participate in the local outpatient program.

I don't believe you have reason to be concerned. I know that sometimes employees in the hospitals pass on rumors and contribute to misunderstanding of what is planned, but the present program is not some budget-cutting measure. Instead we have actually increased our spending on mental health because the program is proving so successful.

Thanks for allowing me to comment and, again, let me say you have no cause for concern.

If you have any further questions please don't hesitate to write.

> Sincerely,
> Ronald Reagan

> Mrs. McKay
> After January 1967[76]

Dear Mrs. McKay:

Nancy gave me your letter and the paper outlining the PCC position. I hope you won't mind my answering your letter directly instead of passing the information onto Nancy and then to you.

First, thank you for writing and giving me a chance to clear the air of some very real misunderstandings and misapprehensions. The PCC paper is based entirely on a false assumption and, I fear, misinformation possibly from some of the hospital employees caught up in the rumor mill which is an ever-present part of government.

We have two plans—one for the mentally ill, which is presently in operation, and one for the mentally retarded, which is still on the drawing boards. This second plan is aimed at a long-range move from large institutions to smaller, more personalized hospitals closer to the homes of the patients. This in no way is a program aimed at eliminating hospital or custodial care—quite the contrary. The more localized hospitals will be run by the counties but totally financed by the state. Whenever practical, we will offer the present state facilities to the counties; otherwise, new facilities will be constructed.

Now, as I say, this is only in the planning stage; but the decision has already been made that it will be coordinated with the parents and with the communities.

With regard to the feared move to Patton,* the only basis for this rumor is the proposed transfer of some patients, namely, the type who cannot take advantage of the outdoor campus at Pacific. These would include some of the severely retarded [of] adult age who require custodial care and some of the multiple handicapped who are, for example bedridden. But no one will be moved without the parents' consent.

As for Pacific, we are installing several million dollars worth of portable air conditioning equipment to alleviate problems in the older buildings.

I hope this clears the air somewhat. Let me assure you these plans are not (as has been charged) some part of an economy scheme. They are based on what we believe is a progressive concept of better care for the patients and an end to the large impersonal type institution.

Sincerely,
Ronald Reagan

Mrs. Perez
After January 1967[77]

Dear Mrs. Perez:

I hope you won't mind my answering your letter to Mrs. Reagan, and please forgive my delay in answering. She showed me your letter and I thought perhaps I could respond directly to the points you raised.

First of all, there have been no cuts in the budget for either the mentally ill or the mentally retarded. We are at the highest staffing standards ever before reached in California. We reviewed the old staffing standards three years ago and set a goal to achieve new standards over a five-year period. For the mentally ill we've reached the goal two years ahead of schedule. For the mentally retarded we are on schedule.

Now this doesn't mean there isn't room for improvement, and it would be wonderful if we could do even better. There never is enough money to do all we'd like to do.

It is true, also, that sometimes a particular hospital will have a temporary lowering of personnel due to inability to fill staff vacancies, illness, etc. It is also true

---

* Patton State Hospital is a forensic mental facility based in San Bernardino, California.

that rumors get started among employees, then people like yourself become victim to the rumors, and your distress is understandable. I know of no plans to close Sonoma, and I do know that we are moving ahead on plans for improvement in the whole treatment and care of the retarded.

This whole business of so-called budget cuts began a few years ago when we increased the move to local health care centers for the mentally ill. Actually the move increased the budget and the program has been worth it. Some employees in those hospitals, however, resisted the move as a threat to their own positions. Most, however, see it for what it is—a vast improvement in treatment and care.

I appreciate your writing and hope you'll feel free to do it again any time you have something worrying you.

Sincerely,
Ronald Reagan

Mr. and Mrs. Elwood H. Wagner
Philadelphia, Pennsylvania
After January 1967[78]

Dear Lorraine and Wag:

I'm here in the house for a hot twenty minutes and then on my way to a meeting and back to Sacramento by way of San Francisco. But there was time to read your letter and get this quick note off.

I was sure I'd written about the tape but it must be one of those cases of thinking something and then believing it had been done. Tell Scotty I got it and enjoyed it and he has my thanks—also my apologies for not writing sooner.

You mentioned the mental health ruckus. It's just part of the general rebellion stirred up by some of the die-hards who resist any reduction in the size of government. Some years ago California started on a new concept of mental health care that has put us pretty much up front in that field. The old-fashioned concept was literally warehousing mental patients—putting them in mental institutions and leaving them there for life. Out here we are curing the curables and thanks to the new tranquilizer drugs doing a good job of getting our patients back into a normal life.

We have a number of local care centers and the released patients continue getting care and treatment while they go about their daily lives. These local centers are run by the counties with the state putting up most of the money. Incidentally we've added $6 million to the budget for these local centers this year.

Naturally this has had an effect on the hospitals. In 1960 we had a patient population of 36,000. [T]his year, thanks to our new concept it is down to 23,000. In the meantime though because government just does grow we increased hospital employees by more than 1,000. All we are doing is reducing employees this year to maintain the present ratio of 2 2/3 patients to 1 employee. Some of the head-shrinkers are upset because they'd like private rooms for each patient with the round-the-clock private nurses. That's about all there is to it which proves how easy it is to get a scream of pain when someone's pet program is stepped on.

Must run now—tell Scotty again how much I enjoyed the tape and thanks for all your letters in my behalf.

Best regards,
Ron

Reagan is concerned about striking a balance between environmental policy and the right to private ownership.

Mr. Bright
After January 1967 [79]

These two letters from Mr. Bright and Mr. Lane may have been answered by others if not here are replies.

Ronald Reagan

Dear Mr. Bright:

Thank you for your letter and for the information regarding the South Coast Regional Commission. I was pleased to have the facts you presented.

Possibly we have both been misled by press coverage. The TV news channels and the papers carried stories that seemed to indicate a bureaucratic tangle of the kind that is accepted as typical of government all too often. Tanks, pipes and machinery for purifying wastewater were shown and described as rusting away while Water Quality Control demanded their installation and the Coastal Commission refused permission for this to be done.

I did not rush to the press with this, but asked my staff to look into the matter. I'm sure you know that I have struggled to rid government of red tape and hidebound procedures.

On that same day, I did a question and answer session with a high school class (a regular weekly practice). These young people asked questions that revealed a tendency to believe California was in immediate danger of total destruction. We engaged in a philosophical discussion in which I attempted to show them that we had to strike a reasonable balance. A number of hypothetical examples were offered, and it is true I described what I'd read in the paper. In the discussion I said there were two extremes, both wrong—those who would cover the state with concrete in the name of progress and those who wouldn't let you build a house unless it looked like a bird's nest. In between I told them was the vast majority who wanted to achieve a commonsense balance.

By way of encouragement that the struggle to preserve the environment was not a lost cause I pointed out that 40 percent of the entire coastline was already in public ownership.

These sessions, unfortunately, are covered by the wire services. What was a philosophical rap session with some bright (but uninformed) young people was reported in the press as administrative policy.

I've made no secret of the fact (although this didn't come up in the discussion) that I am worried lest our concern with the environment seriously erode our traditional right of private ownership. I hope this is of concern to you also.

Again, thanks for your letter, and I regret the less than accurate reporting which victimized both of us.

Sincerely,
Ronald Reagan

TRIPS ABROAD

As governor, Reagan made numerous trips abroad, including four on behalf of President Nixon.* These trips included stops in several capitals in Asia and Europe and a visit to Australia. One tour involved especially delicate diplomacy: in October 1971, as National Security Adviser Henry Kissinger was preparing to visit the People's Republic of China, Reagan traveled to Taiwan to reassure Chiang Kai-shek of American support. Reagan discusses this mission and others in the letter below. The legislator to whom the letter is addressed is not indicated in Reagan's dictated draft.

Senator
June 1980 [80]

Dear Senator:

Thank you very much for your letter and for sending me the information about your recent visit to Europe. Thanks, too, for your kind words about me in all of your appearances and interviews while you were on this trip. I'm deeply grateful.

I am enclosing a copy of a speech I made recently on foreign policy. I think it responds to some of the fears that you yourself discovered about whether I am, some-

---

* In September 1969, Reagan traveled to the Philippines, making a stopover in Hong Kong. In October 1971, he traveled to Taiwan, Japan, South Korea, Singapore, Thailand, and South Vietnam. In July 1972, he traveled to Denmark, Belgium, France, Spain, Italy, England, and Ireland. In November and December of 1973, he traveled to Australia, Indonesia, and Singapore. See Reagan's gubernatorial calendar in his gubernatorial papers at the Ronald Reagan Presidential Library, and *An American Life* (New York: Simon & Schuster, 1990), pp. 186–87.

how, a kind of wild man who's going to start a war. In my present speeches, I have been trying to point out that while I want our defensive strength brought up to par, I want that because I believe our nation is the only one that can preserve the peace, and we can only do that if we have the strength to keep someone else from violating it. There have been four wars in my lifetime. I don't want to see another one. I do firmly believe, however, that if you have the means to defend yourself properly you won't have to use those means.

I wonder if many people in Europe remember or know that while I was governor, President Nixon asked me to represent him in meetings with the heads of six European nations and the NATO high command in Brussels. This was not a ceremonial visit. I was there to reassure our allies that Nixon's trip to China and then to Moscow did not mean that we were acting unilaterally and downgrading our NATO alliance.

I also went on three missions to Asia for him. On one of those, while Kissinger was arranging the final details for the visit to mainland China, I was in Taiwan meeting with Chiang Kai-shek to explain this did not mean an abandonment of our relationship with the Republic of China.

Two years ago, I met with Helmut Schmidt in Germany, a number of leaders, including the foreign minister in France, and renewed my acquaintance with Margaret Thatcher.

Well—I'm getting off the track. Again, I do want to thank you from the bottom of my heart for your kind words about me, and I'm very proud and happy to have your support. I hope our paths cross soon.

Sincerely,
Ron

REAGAN'S RECORD

As a governor, Ronald Reagan responded to the civil rights movement and the antiwar movement in ways that were consistent with his conservative philosophy. He also responded in ways that were perhaps surprising given the "conservative" or "right-wing" label attached to him. Reagan will not go down in history as a "civil rights governor," but he writes that he had a stronger record on hiring minorities to executive-level positions in the state government than was commonly known. His efforts to reduce the rate of growth of the government bureaucracy and to return budget surpluses to the people through reduced bridge tolls and other measures were policies in which he took great pride.

In the letters below, Reagan assesses, defends, and explains some of his policy decisions as governor.

Reagan writes that he followed his plan for appointing judges even though it was not officially adopted.

Bob

Circa 1974[81]

Send a copy of this letter to Ned H.

Dear Bob:

Just a line to say I'll look into the situation with regard to John.

Let me explain what we've done over these eight years and why some of our best friends and staunchest supporters have, from time to time, been disappointed about judicial appointments. In the '66 campaign I proposed a plan for taking the appointment of judges out of politics. After the election I tried to implement this but was unable to get legislative support. However, for eight years we have voluntarily followed the plan.

Very simply the plan calls for submitting names of all nominees for judgeships to a series of committees ranging from laymen in the community to the state bar board of governors. Appointment is made based on the rating by these committees.[82] We have never made an exception because to do so would, of course, make the plan unworkable from then on.

I don't know whether the ratings have come back on the particular district you're interested in but will look into it right away.

Let me say the times when our plan is most difficult are times like this when someone like yourself who has been so faithful and so unselfish is interested. I hope it will turn out that your wishes can be fulfilled. I know if not you'll understand. In the meantime please know how grateful I am for all that you've done and for your unfailing support.

Sincerely,

Ron

In his memoir, Reagan recounted a meeting with black leaders from the San Francisco Bay Area in which he was asked why he did not advertise the fact that he had hired more blacks to executive positions in state government than all previous California governors combined. His response was that it would be "cheap politics" to brag about placing people in positions for which they were qualified. "With that," Reagan remembered, "the whole atmosphere of the meeting changed. They said they thought I had been quiet about it because I was fearful of angering my more conservative white supporters."[83]

In the letter below, Reagan writes that he has hired many blacks but probably has not done enough to make it widely known.

Mrs. Ruth Cooley
Monroe, Louisiana
After January 1975 [84]

Dear Mrs. Cooley:

Thank you very much for your letter and for answering a question that has been bothering me. I was so impressed with Monroe and found the people so outstanding, but had noticed the absence of Negroes in the audience, and thought it was inconsistent with everything else about the community.

I am aware that a campaign has been waged to portray me as against the poor and the black, but this is the first time and place it has apparently been so effective. First of all, our welfare reforms did not deny help to any deserving person. As much as anything, they were designed to enable us to do more for those who truly needed help. California's welfare load was so widespread the state hadn't been able to meet the increased cost of living. There had been no increase in the grants from 1958 until 1971. We increased the grants by 43 percent. The people we took off the rolls were not particularly Negroes—quite the contrary. We found for example one county in which 194 county employees—mainly white—were drawing welfare too.

In my eight years more negroes were appointed to executive and policymaking positions in state government than had been appointed by all the previous California governors put together. You are absolutely right that our job is getting our story across.

Thanks again—let's keep in touch!

Sincerely,
Ronald Reagan

In the next four letters, Reagan looks back at his administration's record. He discusses reductions in the size of the government bureaucracy and the welfare caseload; budget surpluses that he returned to the people instead of using for more government expenditures; his mental health plan; and hiring minorities to positions of authority. In the third letter, Reagan notes that members of the press went to his barbershop only to find that he doesn't dye his hair.

Mrs. Carl N. Alderson
Sacramento, California
Circa July 1972 [85]

Dear Mrs. Alderson:

Just a line to thank you for your good letter and to say it was good to see you even if only for a brief wave. Sometimes those days you recalled in '65 and '66 seem a million years back, and yet in another way only yesterday.

I often wonder if I would have gone on if I'd known all I know now and still I have no regrets. This has filled my life more than anything I've ever done.

Hope our paths cross again—

Best regards,
Ronald Reagan

Mr. Jimmy Dixon
After January 1975 [86]

Dear Jimmy:

It was good to see you the other night even though it was a split second. Thanks for your most generous words.

The figures I gave on California if those were the ones you meant are as follows: The state was spending well over a million dollars a day more than it was taking in and had been adding an average of 5,500 new employees a year for eight years.

In welfare 16 percent of all the welfare recipients in the country were on the rolls in California. We went to the people and asked for the top people in the state to serve on task forces. About 250 gave an average of 117 days full-time going into 64 state departments and agencies and came back with 1,800 specific recommendations as to how modern business practices could be used to make government more efficient. We implemented more than 1,600 of those. Before the end of my first term welfare was so out of hand the caseload was increasing by 40,000 people a month.

We froze the hiring of replacements for employees who left state service and instituted our welfare reforms. When our eight years ended we had virtually the same number of state employees we started with. Due to our growth in population this meant some departments had absorbed a workload increase of 66 percent. The welfare reforms halted the 40,000 a month increase—we now have 400,000 fewer people on welfare.

We've increased the grants to the truly needy by 43 percent, saved the taxpayers $2 billion and were able to return an $850 million surplus as a one-time tax rebate. All told we've given $5.7 billion back to the people in rebates, tax cuts and even bridge toll cuts. We gave the new government a balanced budget for the first time since 1943 plus a $500 million surplus.

If there are any more figures you want let me know.

Given my best to Jeanne.

Sincerely,
Ron

Mr. Squires
May 5, 1979 [87]

Dear Mr. Squires:

I'm sorry to be so late in thanking you for your March 11 column, but it has only been brought to my attention in the last few days.

I appreciate your kindness in saying that I am in the mainstream of our party and that I am "an articulate and effective spokesman" for the philosophy of conservatism. You did, however, question whether I could (if given a chance) make such a philosophy operational. At the risk of seeming presumptuous, may I fill you in on some points with which you might not be familiar? It's understandable, I hasten to say, that you wouldn't have knowledge of happenings in California or that we did make such a philosophy work. I use the plural "we" because, as governor I had the help of some very fine people.

When I took office, California was insolvent and spending a million dollars a day more than tax revenues. In the eight years of our administration, we made the state solvent, attained a triple-A rating (Moody's) for California bonds and left the new governor a half-billion dollar surplus. We also returned $5.7 billion to the tax-payers in direct rebates and credits.

It wasn't all cut, squeeze, and trim, however. We increased support for public schools eight times as much as the increase in enrollment and increased the schol-arship fund for needy students by 9,000 percent. While reducing the cost of welfare $2 billion in three years, we raised, at the same time, the grants for the needy by 43 percent. They hadn't had a cost of living increase since 1958. Our reforms in the case of the mentally ill became a model for other states and even a few foreign countries. There were other accomplishments, but these few should reassure you that commonsense conservatism can be made to work.

One last point. You'll be pleased to know that a number of your colleagues (members of the capital press corps) made a number of trips to the barbershop where my hair was cut and discovered for themselves that I did not dye my hair. Now, happily, enough grey is showing to make such research unnecessary.

Again my thanks for devoting your column to me.

Sincerely,
Ronald Reagan

Mr. George Jessel
Circa the summer of 1979 [88]

Dear George:

It was good to talk to you the other day, and I'm deeply grateful for your offer to help. After thinking it over, I believe probably the best things that you as a Californ-ian might be able to say would have to do with some high points in my record as governor rather than trying to specify issues and my views on the problems.

For example: when I became governor, the state was virtually bankrupt, spend-ing a million dollars a day more than it was taking in. The deficit in the middle of the fiscal year when I took office was already in excess of $200 million. The number of state employees had been increasing for eight years by around 6,000 employees a year. After eight years in office, we left our successor a $500 million surplus. The state payroll was virtually the same size in numbers of employees as it was when we started, and in the eight years, we had returned to the taxpayers in tax rebates and credits $5.7 billion. Each year that we accumulated a surplus, we simply gave it back to the people with the exception of the final year in which you leave office before the end of the year. California's welfare load was increasing at 40,000 people a month.

We reformed welfare and changed that to an 8,000 per month decrease. Over a three-year period, we reduced the welfare rolls by almost 400,000 people, saved the taxpayers $2 billion, and were able to grant increases averaging 43 percent to the truly needy. They hadn't had a cost of living increase since 1958. The state income tax had begun at the first $2,000 of earnings. When we left office, that had been changed to exemptions from the income tax until you were making $8,000. At the same time, we increased state aid to local schools. Our bonds received a triple-A rating by Moody's for the first time in the history of the state.

I appointed more members of the minority communities to executive and policy-making positions than all the previous governors of California put together.

Unemployment, which historically has been higher in California than the national average, was lower than the national average during our terms in office, and the cost of living increase in California was lower than the national average.

George, I think that's enough for now. If I think of anything else, I'll jot it down and get it to you. Again, thanks for all that you're doing.

Best regards,
Ron

CHAPTER SEVEN

Running for Office

"*I*T SEEMS *to me we used to have a breathing spell for the people between elections when they could concentrate on the World Series and forget politics," Reagan wrote in early 1979. "I wonder if this constant campaigning hasn't contributed to the reduction in the percentage of people who go to the polls. Have we possibly just gotten them so fed up they have tuned out anything political?"* [1]

From at least the time he agreed to run for governor of California, Reagan never tuned out anything political. He took no breathing spells.

Ronald Reagan's immediate problem when he left the governorship in early January 1975 was making a living. He accepted a proposal to do a daily taped three-minute radio commentary and a weekly newspaper column. [2] *He was also sought after as a speaker—what he called the "mashed potato circuit." Peter Hannaford and Michael Deaver, two of Reagan's top aides during the governorship, formed a public relations firm to manage Reagan's schedule. To Deaver's amazement, Reagan turned down an offer from CBS Evening News, anchored by Walter Cronkite and with a 40 percent share of the evening news, to do a twice-a-week commentary because, Reagan said, "they won't tire of me on the radio."* [3] *His first commentary was taped January 23, 1975, less than three weeks after he left office.*

In November 1975 Reagan challenged President Gerald Ford for the 1976 Republican presidential nomination. Reagan lost the closely contested race but campaigned actively for Republicans, including Ford, in the general election.

In 1980 Reagan ran again. The Republican primaries were highly competitive, and Bush won the first contest, the Iowa caucuses. But Reagan was the front-runner from the beginning. When the votes were counted in the Illinois primary on March 18, Reagan was virtually assured the nomination. [4]

By then Reagan had served two terms as governor of California, where he had dealt with the complexities of domestic issues and the relationship between the federal and state governments. He was a skilled negotiator, having served seven terms as president of the Screen Actors Guild. From 1954 to 1962 he had traveled the country for General Electric, speaking to employees at their 135 plants and making countless speeches to local groups. He had also undertaken several foreign policy missions on behalf of Republican presidents.

Equally important, between the governorship and his announcement as a candidate for the 1980 Republican nomination—with a 10-month break while he was a candidate for the 1976 Republican nomination—he had been reaching some 20 million people a week on a wide variety of issues through his radio commentaries and newspaper columns. When he seemed to be nowhere, he was everywhere. Over those five years many people had come to know where he stood on a whole range of domestic, foreign, and national defense issues.

Reagan wrote by hand many letters between the time he left the governorship in early 1975 and his election as president in 1980—probably around 500 a year, including, in 1979 and the first eight months of 1980, over 800 dictated letters of which his secretaries' transcriptions have survived.

In his campaign correspondence Reagan keeps in touch with supporters, contributors, old friends, members of the press, policy advisers, politicians. He takes special care to explain his actions and decisions to supporters who ask or advise him to take a different course—to form a third party, to announce earlier, to adopt one or another strategy, or to make staff changes. He reassures those concerned that he is not sacrificing principle for political expediency. He writes to one supporter, "The only thing that makes this struggle worthwhile is the thought of being in the position to carry out those things I have believed in for so long."⁵ The correspondence reflects hard work and focus, and demonstrates that he was in charge of both the policy and strategy of his campaigns.

In 1985 Dennis Puleo, an ex-Marine who served in Vietnam, wrote that he regained his confidence in politicians and in government when Reagan ran in 1980. He had one question for Reagan: "At about what time in your life or career did you even slightly entertain the thought or dream of actually becoming President?"

Mr. Dennis Puleo
Center Ossipee, New Hampshire
March 5, 1985⁶

Dear Mr. Puleo:

Your letter has only just arrived at my desk so forgive the delay in answering. Thank you for your kind and generous words. I'm most grateful.

I'm sorry about the schedule changes in the Inaugural and hope they didn't spoil anything for you.

You asked at what time in my life did I even entertain the thought of the presidency. Well I can honestly say that throughout my years in pictures and TV the thought of public office never occurred to me. I always believed in paying my way, life had been good to me so I campaigned for people and causes I believed in. Then in '64 I went all out for Barry Goldwater. Late in the campaign I made a speech in his behalf on NBC TV. The speech rang a bell I guess and raised a lot of money etc. In '65 with the California governor's race coming up in '66 a group of Republicans called on me asking that I run against the incumbent Governor Pat Brown. The party was terribly split as a result of the '64 primary between Goldwater and Rockefeller, they cited my speech and said I could unite the party. I dismissed them out of hand. I was very happy in show business. They kept coming back until Nancy and I were worn down and thought maybe we did have a duty.

As governor I was asked to be a favorite son candidate for president to hold our California party together. I agreed on the condition that that was as far as it would go. I would not be a real candidate.

Well to shorten this down, the first time I ever thought of seeking the presidency was in 1976 because I felt Jerry Ford could not beat Jimmy Carter whom I'd known as a governor. In 1980 after four years of the Carter administration I decided to make the race again because I believed I could do some good. I can honestly tell you that until that 1965–66 period I had never thought of public office at all.

Sorry to be so long about it but that's the story. Please give my best to your wife.

> Sincerely,
> Ronald Reagan

THE 1976 RUN

Reagan considered his 1976 challenge to sitting president Gerald Ford carefully, evaluating, in his words from one letter, "whether I offer the best opportunity for victory." Although he announced an exploratory committee called Citizens for Reagan on July 15, 1975, he was not yet certain he would run. His formal announcement came on November 20, 1975.[7] He decided against running on a third-party ticket and pledged to support the Republican nominee whoever it might be. Reagan lost the first five primaries, but won the sixth in North Carolina on March 23, 1976.[8]

———

Ralph Tipton, an Illinois manufacturer, had been a friend since 1934 when Reagan was working as a sports announcer in Des Moines, Iowa.[9]

> Mr. Ralph Tipton
> Lisle, Illinois
> August 25, 1975[10]

Dear Tip:

Just a line to say thanks. Your bumper stickers are masterpieces, although I don't quite see myself on Mount Rushmore—no more room.

I hadn't heard about the YAF [Young Americans for Freedom] convention. Apparently, the news didn't get this far west.

Tip, I just can't make the early decision you suggest. For one reason, I have to be sure, or reasonably so, that I offer the best opportunity for victory. The principal consideration has to be that the Democrats do not occupy the White House. I think you'll agree we don't have the information we need to know that answer just yet. Let's put it this way—on a scale of one to ten (on going) I'm at about eight.

Again thanks.

Sincerely,
Dutch

After losing five primaries Reagan was urged to withdraw. Even before he won the North Carolina primary he was determined not to quit, but the victory in North Carolina was important in enabling him to raise the funds to stay in the race.

Miss Diem
1976 primary season[11]

Dear Miss Diem:

Thank you very much for your contribution and especially for your note. I am truly grateful.

I appreciate the football comparison; it's very apt. I've never believed the game is over 'til the final gun and I intend to stay in the present game all the way.

Again, my thanks and best regards.

Sincerely,
Ronald Reagan

When the primary season was over, neither Reagan nor Ford had enough committed delegates to win on the first ballot at the convention. Reagan approved a plan from John Sears, his campaign manager, to announce his proposed running mate early to try to get the support of uncommitted delegates in the Northeast. He chose Senator Richard Schweiker of Pennsylvania, who had a reputation as a liberal Republican. Meanwhile Jimmy Carter, Governor of Georgia, already had enough delegates for the nomination of the Democratic Party.

In this letter Reagan explains his choice of Schweiker to his staunch supporter and "buddy" Earl Dunckel, who traveled with Reagan on the General Electric tours during 1954 and 1955.[12] Reagan contrasts his choice with that of Barry Goldwater in 1964, who chose as his running mate William Miller, a conservative but unknown member of Congress who did not add to the appeal of the ticket.

Mr. Earl Dunckel
New York, New York
August 10, 1976 [13]

Dear Earl:

I'm about four answers behind and very late with this. I didn't get it until too late for your July 17 affair. I was in the wrong end of the country anyway, but I do appreciate the invitation.

Your suggestion about the secretary of state is a good one but, unfortunately, you can't do it under the new election laws. I hope you've recovered from the shock waves of what I did do.

Earl, as the campaign has gone on, I've come to realize we could have been on the way to winning a convention and losing an election. The Northeast states were sitting it out on the Republican side, ready to concede to Carter. I decided I couldn't go down the Bill Miller road Barry took. However, contrary to all the labeling that's going on, I found the senator in line with my views on defense, détente, abortion, amnesty, crime, bussing and gun control. He's also introduced a constitutional amendment to restore prayer and Bible reading in the public schools and he did support Goldwater in '64.

Ford can't win in November and Carter must not.

Regards,
Ron

————

Reagan's selection of Senator Schweiker as his proposed 1976 running mate concerned conservative supporters. Three years later it still bothered some of them. This letter, written after Reagan's announcement for the 1980 nomination, is a comprehensive retrospective on this decision. Paul Laxalt of Nevada was the only senator to support Reagan's 1976 candidacy. [14]

Mr. Kiesewetter
Circa November 15, 1979 [15]

Dear Mr. Kiesewetter:

Thank you very much for writing me and for giving me an opportunity to reply. I can understand your feelings in view of the appearance my action in '76 gave. Unfortunately, I had little time with the strategic problem facing us to make it clear to my own supporters that my action was not as it appeared—one of expediency. Let me outline the situation:

The primaries were over. The state conventions had been finished. The campaign had settled down to a hunt for uncommitted delegates. You'll recall a great many of such delegates found themselves with invitations to the White House for various State dinners, including one given for the Queen of England. I, of course, had no such opportunity.

In our delegate hunt to the Northeast, we had discovered that the leadership of our party in the main Northeast states had already written off the election as going to the Democrats. It was apparent they were only going to try and preserve their own little fiefdoms within the party. My great fear was that I might get the nomination and then lose the election. And this, on top of the 1964 Goldwater defeat, would set back the cause that I believe in for years to come, if not forever.

We came up with the idea of choosing as a running mate a candidate from the Northeast to try and get them back into the war. The decision to announce this early was to counter the other thing I mentioned, our kind of dead-in-the-water position, which could see us going to the convention already defeated. Obviously, we were limited as to Northeastern candidates.

The decision with regard to Senator Schweiker came only after hours and hours of meetings with him. He was Senator Laxalt's seatmate, and Paul had told me that he thought a meeting between us might prove surprising to both the senator and myself—and he was right. In spite of his liberal record, I learned that the senator had introduced a bill to restore Bible reading and prayer in the public schools. He was opposed to abortion on demand. He had run on a platform of being against gun control. He favored capital punishment, and his voting record was completely solid with regard to the need for more national defense. Then we got into the economic measures, and he frankly admitted that he had voted for a number of government programs which had been failures and had not solved our problems—programs which had to be called liberal. But also, he had come to the realization that he had been wrong, that these programs were not the answer, and that we had to turn to the private sector.

At one point in our long discussions, I told him I thought I was looking at myself 20 years ago because, in case you didn't know, I converted from being a New Deal Democrat to a Republican. And, it was precisely because I found I could no longer support the philosophy of the leadership of the Democratic Party. So I had not abandoned my belief, nor will I, that the man suggested for the second spot on the ticket should be one who would carry on the programs enunciated by the presidential nominee.

If you will check his voting record since '76 you will find it about 100 percent on our side. I did not convert him. He was undergoing that conversion at the time I made the choice. He is a deeply religious man with a fine family and great integrity, and my only regret is that so many people were not given the opportunity to understand that.

I hope you will reconsider your request to be removed from our mailing list.

Again, thank you for giving me a chance to explain the situation.

Sincerely,
Ronald Reagan

Reagan lost the nomination to Ford the night of August 18, 1976, by a vote of 1,187 to 1,070. Motioned to the podium by Ford at the convention after Ford gave his acceptance speech, Reagan spoke of the importance of preserving freedom and avoiding nuclear destruction and said: "This is our challenge. And this is why . . . we must go forth from here united, determined that what a great general said a few years ago is true. 'There is no substitute for victory.' " He got a standing ovation. Many delegates thought they had nominated the wrong man. On the plane ride back to California he autographed a convention ticket with the message "We dreamed—we fought & the dream is still with us." [16]

Reagan's letters after the convention remind supporters of the substantial influence Reagan delegates had on the Republican platform. He notes that he will be returning to his radio broadcasts and newspaper columns. On September 1, 1976, less than two weeks after the convention, he taped 12 radio addresses, including a retrospective on the campaign and convention and three commentaries comparing the platforms of the Democratic and Republican parties. In October he resumed his syndicated newspaper column, now twice weekly.

In post-convention letters Reagan also reminds supporters of his pledge to support the Republican nominee and notes that this is not the time for a third party. He encourages them to look forward to building a winning coalition based on the principles in the platform. Here are seven such letters.*

Miss Lani Schweiker †
McLean, Virginia
After the 1976 convention [17]

Dear Lani:

We were all happy to receive your letter and everyone in the family sends you a thank you and warm regards. Believe me, getting to know the Schweiker family was a happy experience for all of us. I told your father the other day when I called that, if and when you come west, please let us know.

Lani, we didn't achieve our goal but the race was worth the effort. We influenced the platform, we are listened to more than we were before and I'm sure we have caused the people to think about issues and problems more than they did before.

Please give the regards from all of us to your parents and brothers and sisters. We hope we'll see you again soon.

Sincerely,
Ronald Reagan

---

* Reagan had already considered and rejected the third-party idea, stating in a November 1974 press conference that "I am not starting a third party. . . . I do not believe the Republican Party is dead. I believe the Republican Party represents basically the thinking of the people of this country, if we can get that message across to the people. I'm going to try to do that." Quoted in Cannon, *Reagan*, p. 197.
† Senator Schweiker's daughter.

Mr. Philip W. Flannery
After the 1976 convention [18]

Dear Mr. Flannery:

I can understand your position and hope you'll understand mine. Throughout the campaign I pledged to support the choice of our party and feel honor bound to keep that pledge.

The party platform was largely written by people who supported me. It is based on the positions I took during the campaign. I shall campaign on that platform and consider Mr. Ford bound to that platform which expresses the will of our party's rank-and-file membership.

When November 2nd has come and gone, I'll do all I can to rally a new majority around the principles embodied in that platform.

Thanks for allowing me to comment.

Sincerely,
Ronald Reagan

Mr. Luke B. Schmidt
Dallas, Texas
After the 1976 convention [19]

Dear Luke:

How nice to hear from you and to have a chance once again to thank you for all you did in my behalf. Nancy adds her thanks also and her remembrance of Denton and Bowling Green.

Luke, I'm sure you must know that the third party vote was given serious consideration even before I announced for the Republican nomination. I said no only after great thought and study.[20] Then, when I entered the Republican race, I pledged my support of the ticket and feel bound by that pledge.

I believe now we must see that our candidates are held to the platform we had so much to do with writing. Then we must be ready in November, after the election, to reassess and mobilize the Democrats and Independents we know are looking for a banner around which to rally. To that end, I think I can be something of a voice and intend doing all I can to bring about a new majority coalition. Our cause is not lost and may even be more possible in the days ahead. Don't lose faith and don't think the war is over. I'm starting my five-day-a-week radio commentaries, newspaper column and speaking tours immediately.

Thanks again and best regards.

Sincerely,
Ronald Reagan

Mr. James A. Smith
Middletown, Virginia
After the 1976 convention[21]

Dear Mr. Smith:

First let me thank you for your mailgram but even more for all your help and support. I'm very grateful and very proud.

I understand how you feel but may I make a suggestion? We, and by we I mean so-called conservatives, are truly in the mainstream of American thought today. I am concerned that a third party movement now will only divide us, bring victory to the Democrats and lead to the charge that we are responsible for that victory.

If a Republican victory does occur based on our platform (and it is our conservative platform) then we can continue to build for the future. If we lose then I believe we should look at our party and see if the only answer isn't the one you suggest; a gathering together of a new coalition, bound together by common beliefs and philosophy.

Let me assure you, I intend to return to my daily radio commentary and news column and public speaking. I'll do my best to provide a voice for our philosophy and for such a movement.

Again, my thanks. Nancy wears a campaign button that proclaims, "Hangeth In There."

Sincerely,
Ronald Reagan

Mr. Russell Castle
Petersburg, Virginia
After the 1976 convention[22]

Dear Mr. Castle:

Even though you said not to answer, I feel I must acknowledge your good letter. Thanks, too, for the "five year plan." There is much to think about there.

I'm sorry I can't heed your suggestion about running on a third party ticket. In the first place, it is too late to get such a party on the ballot and, even if it weren't, I fear we would only succeed in dividing the ranks of those who share our philosophy. More important, however, I pledged at the beginning of this campaign that I would support the party's decision. I don't feel I can break that pledge.

After the election in November, however, I truly believe we should reassess our party and lay plans to bring together the new majority of Republicans, Democrats and Independents who are looking for a banner around which to rally.

Sincerely,
Ronald Reagan

Mr. Ron La Montagne
After the 1976 convention[23]

Dear Mr. La Montagne:

Thank you for sending me the copy of your letter to Mr. Ford and for your generous words. I know it sounds very self-serving for me to say I agree with your premise regarding our chances for victory in November.

My fear that he could not win, more than anything else, moved me to enter the race. I believe Carter is vulnerable, particularly if he is deprived of his anti-Washington issue.

Again, my thanks and best regards.

Sincerely,
Ronald Reagan

———

Edward Hickey had been Reagan's security chief in Sacramento and worked for him after he left the governorship and in the White House.[24]

Mr. Edward V. Hickey
Oxon Hill, Maryland
After the 1976 convention[25]

Dear Ed:

Nancy and I are both more grateful than we can say for a truly heartwarming letter. Thank you.

We are at peace with ourselves and believe the Lord must have something else in mind for us to do. I'm starting the radio programs right away and soon will be back in the papers with a column and, of course, there is always the mashed potato circuit. I'll be doing my best to see that the good Dr.* doesn't give away the Canal, Taiwan, or the rest of our military. It would have been easier the other way, but now we'll try by remote control.

Nancy sends her love and please give our best to Barbara and the boys. We both hope we'll see you soon.

Sincerely,
Ron

———

Reagan campaigned for Ford and other Republicans during the 1976 election season and would have done a 30-minute TV speech for Ford had he been asked. Gerald Ford lost the 1976 election to Democrat Jimmy Carter. The electoral vote was 297 to 240, but Carter got only 50.1 percent of the popular vote, Ford 48.0 percent.[26]

---

* Dr. Henry Kissinger, Ford's (and formerly Nixon's) secretary of state.

Mrs. Florence P. Moore
Idaho Falls, Idaho
November 2, 1976 [27]

Dear Mrs. Moore:

It is election day as I write this, hoping that Ford will be elected. It seems there has been a curtain of silence around my activities since Kansas City.* I've been in 25 states campaigning for the president and all of our ticket. I filmed a set of commercials ranging from five minutes to 30 seconds for the president, sent out a million letters soliciting support for him and issued a press statement urging support on election eve. To tell you the truth I had thought it might be helpful if I could do a second 30-minute speech in his behalf on TV but was not asked to do so. Under the new election laws all national TV must be ordered and paid for by the candidate.

Thanks very much for your kind letter and generous words. All we can do now is wait and pray. Whichever way it turns out we must continue fighting and working for the cause we believe in.

Best regards,
Ronald Reagan

Reagan tells his close friend George Murphy about a quick trip to Washington, D.C., where he met with President Gerald Ford, Vice President Nelson Rockefeller, John B. Connally, and Ron Nessen (a Ford aide) on December 9, 1976, about possible people to chair the Republican National Committee (RNC). Reagan attended a second meeting with Ford, Rockefeller, and Connally on January 5, 1977.[28] Although Reagan notes the grassroots support for Dick Richards of Utah, William Brock, former Tennessee senator, succeeded Mary Louise Smith as RNC chair in 1977 and served until 1981, when Richards got the job.

Senator George Murphy
Los Angeles, California
Circa late December 1976 [29]

Dear Murph:

Just a quick line to tell you how my quick in and out happened. My speaking trip was Atlanta Monday, Alabama Tuesday and Mississippi on Wednesday. On Friday, Mike got a call from Stu Spencer, asking if I'd come to a Monday meeting with John, Nelson and the president.† The president would call me if he was assured in advance I'd say yes. Mike told him of my trip and that I could come up from Mississippi for an afternoon meeting on Thursday. That was the last we heard until late

---

* Kansas City, Missouri, was the site of the 1976 Republican convention.
† "Mike" is Reagan aide Michael Deaver. Stuart Spencer had run Ford's 1976 campaign.

<u>Wednesday</u> afternoon, which meant a scramble to switch airline tickets, etc. Do you suppose they were hoping I wouldn't come?

Actually, the meeting wasn't very much.

I got the impression they didn't really have a candidate. I made the point there should be no hint or suspicion that we were choosing the chairman. They agreed and said we should just suggest the several names that came up as possibilities to the National Committee.

Murph, the biggest single block of support I can detect is for Dick Richards, the State Chairman of Utah—I don't mean support from Nelson or the President. He's a h—l of a guy and you and I could be very happy with him. His support is grass roots.

I'll keep you apprised—they want another meeting.

Best regards,
Ron

Reagan had turned down a 1974 feeler and a couple of approaches in early 1975 from Ford about serving in his cabinet or in another high-level post[30]—jobs that would have taken him out of the running for 1976. Nor did he want to chair the Republican National Committee, as he explains in this letter.

Mr. and Mrs. Bill Lockhard
Fort Worth, Texas
Circa late 1976[31]

Dear Mr. and Mrs. Lockhard:

Thank you for your mailgram and very generous words. You honor me greatly and I thank you.

Please believe I intend to do everything I can to rally our party around the principles enunciated in our platform and to see if we can't become a new majority.

I have to say, however, I believe I can be more effective without being party chairman. Under present party rules, the chairmanship is a full time, salaried job. This would mean giving up my five-day-a-week radio commentary which is on several hundred stations, as well as the weekly newspaper column which is syndicated nationwide.

Remaining independent, I'm in a position to speak out in both those channels for the things we believe in as well as against those things our opponents may try to do. As party chairman, I would not be allowed those forums.

But, again, I do share your concern and pledge you I intend to be as much a voice as I can be in rebuilding and expanding our party.

Best regards,
Ronald Reagan

THE 1980 RUN

Although Reagan was the last of the formal candidates* to announce for the 1980 Republican nomination, he formed an exploratory committee in March 1979 and was certain he would run months before his formal announcement on November 13, 1979.

He campaigned on two main issues: the need to improve the economic performance of the country and the need to improve national defense. Carter was vulnerable on both counts. Inflation was high and so was unemployment. Among other foreign policy problems, hostages were seized at the U.S. embassy in Iran on November 4, 1979, and the Soviets had invaded Afghanistan in December 1979.

Laurence Beilenson was an old friend of Reagan's with whom he corresponded frequently.

Mr. Laurence W. Beilenson
March 27, 1979 [32]

Dear Larry:

I'm a long time in getting back to you in response to your note but want you to know I've been out on that "mashed potato circuit." Either I am getting used to the food at the banquets or it has improved in quality. I actually find myself looking forward to the meal.

I agree with you about the major issues and am frightened to death about what I continue to see going on in Washington. I think I have those three assets you spoke of. I do believe in God and I certainly have a steadfast wife, and I think I have a sense of humor, although, it's getting harder to laugh at some of the things going on.

I appreciate your offer of help, and you can depend on it—I'll call on you.

Best regards,
Ron

Unlike the 1976 campaign, by the time Reagan's exploratory committee for 1980 was announced, he was certain he would run.

---

* The other candidates, in the order in which they announced, were Phil Crane of Illinois, Harold Stassen of Minnesota, Benjamin Fernandez of Los Angeles, John Connally of Texas, George Bush of Texas, Robert Dole of Kansas, John B. Anderson of Illinois, Larry Pressler of South Dakota, and Howard Baker of Tennessee. Lowell Weicker of Connecticut had already withdrawn. Jonathan Moore, ed. *The Campaign for President: 1980 In Retrospect* (Cambridge, Mass.: Ballinger Publishing Company, 1981), pp. 263–67.

Mr. Charles Broska
March 27, 1979[33]

Dear Charles:

Thank you very much for sending me the copy of your letter to Schlesinger.* Your ideas are sound, but may I make a suggestion. Conservation, of course, is a most helpful thing, and we should be practicing it, but I truly believe the answer to our energy problem is an energetic program of increasing our own supply, and this we have not done. I believe it could be done if the government would get off the back of the energy industry and turn it loose in the free marketplace. I not only believe that there is oil yet to be discovered but that there is enough oil left in the old wells that, at a proper price, could be brought to the surface through steam injection and other means that we could in several years be virtually self-sufficient.

With regard to me and the coming race, I think it is far too early to announce a candidacy. Indeed, I think we're wearing our people out by not giving them any rest at all between campaigns. On the other hand, I must conduct myself on the basis that I will be a candidate. As you know, we have a national exploratory committee at work. I expect to announce a decision in late summer or early fall, but, just between us, I know what the answer will be.

Best regards,
Ron

As early as March 1979, Reagan contends with criticisms of John Sears, his chief political strategist. Sears was viewed as responsible for the selection of Schweiker as Reagan's proposed 1976 running mate and some of Reagan's supporters were suspicious of him.

Mr. Harry T. Everingham
Arizona
March 29, 1979[34]

Dear Harry:

I've just returned from another speaking trip to find your letter awaiting me. Apparently, your first letter never made it through the mails because I didn't receive it, and I have to tell you that is not uncommon. In our particular area, we are having great trouble with letters not arriving where we sent them or letters not arriving. I'm glad you sent me the column and are giving me a chance to comment but first, with regard to your invitation for April 14, unfortunately, we will not be able to make our trip to Phoenix because of my scheduling so I'll have to take a rain check on your invitation.

Now as to the column. Harry, we are very much aware that there were short-

---

* James Schlesinger was secretary of energy from August 5, 1977, until August 1979.

comings and criticism, particularly of John Sears, as a result of the last campaign. On the other hand, we feel that he does have talents and something to offer in our campaign. The difference is that in '76 I honestly didn't know I was going to be a candidate, and, therefore, our organization was hastily put together with everyone being called upon to do more than their specialty. It is true that John went off on his own many times, and, in doing so, upset a number of people. That will not be true this time. He will be a part of the organization, but he will be doing only those things that he can do well, and he will not be in charge of the campaign.

I agree with you about Kevin Phillips's * ability as a journalist, but I feel that you should know that Kevin was one of a small group who tried to persuade me to go along with the third party movement in '76 and has been rather unforgiving of me for not doing that. Some of the conclusions he's drawn in his present column are not based on the facts. Let me assure you, no one is trying to soften my image, or move me from my deeply held conservative convictions. This, however, seems to be a general theme among some of the Eastern columnists, most of whom I don't think are exactly in my corner. They would like nothing better than to divide our ranks.

Now that we have announced our committee and are able under the law to go forward with organizing, things are being put together in good style, I can assure you. I don't know whether you have seen the list of names [of people who have endorsed the campaign]. It includes more than 250 nationwide, including many congressmen and senators. Such former Cabinet members as Bill Simon and Earl Butz are on the list as well as names that look like a who's who in the business world.

Again, thanks for giving me a chance to comment and my regrets at not being able to accept your invitation. I'll be in Phoenix next week speaking at Trunk and Tusk, but that will be my only opportunity this spring to get to Arizona.

Best regards,
Ron

Charles Wallen of San Mateo, California, was a friend of William F. Buckley—hence the reference to Bill and Pat (Buckley's wife) in this letter. Edmund G. "Jerry" Brown, Jr., was governor of California at the time.

Mr. Charles Wallen, Jr.
March 29, 1979 [35]

Dear Charles:

I have just come back from a speaking trip, and reading about Bill and Pat in your letter makes me very envious. I'm getting so I know the layout of every Holi-

---

* Author of *The Emerging Republican Majority* (1968). Phillips and other conservatives tried to persuade Reagan to run on a third-party ticket on June 16, 1975 (Hannaford, *The Reagans*, p. 67).

day Inn in America. I know Bill Loeb has talked about the possibility of not going into New Hampshire, but I think before any decision has to be made, we'll have a lot of polling done and know whether there is the possibility that he suggests. Frankly, I think it would have to be a pretty desperate situation to not go in. There could be a backlash in bypassing that traditional primary. I was delighted to read about the governor's appearance at your convention and how it turned out. You are absolutely right about him. It just seems unbelievable that he can get away with it as long as he has.

Thanks for your offered help. While I won't be declaring for a few months, we are organizing and getting prepared.

Best regards,
Ron

―――――

The Democrats would eventually nominate Jimmy Carter as their Presidential candidate, but in the summer of 1979 Senator Edward M. Kennedy (D-Massachusetts) was a possibility. Winfield Schuster was a Massachusetts textile executive who was acquainted with Nancy Reagan's parents, Loyal and Edie Davis, through visits in Arizona.[36]

Mr. Winfield Schuster
June 11, 1979 [37]

Dear Mr. Schuster:

Thank you very much for sending me the news article on Democratic fortunes in the New England primaries. I am delighted to have it. I must say that Senator Kennedy does remain an enigma in the coming race. I find myself believing that he truly would like to stay out of this race, waiting for 1984, but may be pushed into it if things continue to worsen for the president and if others, such as our own Governor Brown, should lead a challenge. I've had another wild idea I'll just give you for your consideration. I wonder if the senator might possibly offer himself as second on the ticket and then be positioned as heir apparent for 1984 if the president stays at all viable as a candidate but is in trouble and threatened by others. Whatever happens, it's going to be an interesting year coming up.

Again, thanks and best regards.

Ronald Reagan

―――――

The Pope visited his native Poland, a Communist-governed but mainly Roman Catholic country in Eastern Europe, June 2–10, 1979, and supported the anti-Communist Solidarity movement, which was already under way. Reagan responds to concern about the challenges of serving as president in difficult times, noting that the success of the Pope's visit to Poland was at least in part the result of the office he held.

Mr. Ed Langley
June 19, 1979 [38]

Dear Ed:

I can't tell you how much I appreciate your letter and your concern for me. It was good to hear from you after all this time, and as I say, I'm more than a little grateful for your concern.

I know the problems that would confront anyone in that office. I know, too, that we may be approaching a disaster point both economically and on the world scene, but Ed, someone has to do it. If this is what the Lord would have me do, then we will find that out, and maybe it should be someone who has no political ambition, who is at an age where he can do what he thinks should be done without worrying about the votes in the next election.

At any rate, my course is set, and while I am not making it public to the press, other than to say I will announce a decision in the fall, I know what that decision will be and I am going to go for it. If, as you say, a voice is needed, one thing must be said for that office: the voice from that podium is louder than that of anyone who just tries to raise his voice out there in the countryside. I share your feelings about what the Pope has done in that trip to Poland, but Ed, would his voice have been heard by so many, would he have inspired so many if he were not the Pope?

Again, my heartfelt thanks and best regards.

Ron

Mr. Winfield A. Schuster
July 25, 1979 [39]

Dear Win:

Thank you very much for sending me the additional material. It's most interesting how the "Chappaquiddick" story is breaking into the news these days. The recent happenings in Washington have all the appearances of a boat that is getting lower in the water, and someone has decided a few passengers have to be thrown overboard.

Thanks again and best regards.

Sincerely,
Ron

Reducing taxes was basic to Reagan's economic plan—although so were controlling spending and limiting government regulation. Reagan had long advocated tax reduction and simplification, and he supported the Kemp-Roth tax reduction legislation in 1978.[40] *A variant of it was enacted after he became president. Jack Kemp was a member of Congress from Buffalo, New York, popular with conservatives. Reagan wrote brief letters to him frequently.*

Mr. Jack Kemp
July 25, 1979[41]

Dear Jack:

Just a line to thank you for sending me not only your good letter but that fine presentation. You and I are certainly in agreement on the fact that wherever they have the courage to do it, proper tax reduction results in more prosperity for all, including government itself. You have a wealth of good research in that presentation, which I shall be referring to from time to time.

Thanks again and best regards,
Ron

———

Craig Stubblebine, an economist, was a member of the task force that advised Governor Reagan on tax and spending limitation measures. He sent Reagan occasional policy recommendations and other advice.

Mr. Craig Stubblebine
October 16, 1979[42]

Dear Stub:

Thanks very much for your letter and, as usual, I find myself in great agreement with all you had to say. Your first point, however, about making them love you, not just believe you, believe me—I agree with that. I think I gained that knowledge in show business, and out on the road I do my very best to establish a personal relationship—even with a crowd. It's easy for me, too, because the truth of the matter is I do like people.

Don't worry about confining yourself to a one-page memo as we did in Sacramento. I appreciate having your thoughts very much and will look forward to hearing from you.

Again, thanks and best regards,
Ron

———

Reagan announced for the presidency on November 13, 1979. The American people want, he said, "leadership that will trust and believe in their right to run their own lives and which will eliminate government roadblocks and unleash their great strength and energy."[43]

Reagan assures a supporter that he is receiving advice from competent people with military experience and people at the Hoover Institution, where Reagan was an honorary fellow. Reagan visited NORAD (the North American Aerospace Defense Command, responsible for warning the nation about incoming missiles) on July 31, 1979, with Doug Morrow and Martin Anderson.[44]

Mr. Roberts
Circa November 15, 1979[45]

Dear Mr. Roberts:

Thank you very much for your letter and for the contribution you mailed to the office. I am in complete agreement with you about the dangerous state of our nation. Let me assure you I am in regular contact with a number of our retired generals and admirals and now and then someone not retired. I am receiving information and help from people like Lieutenant General Daniel Graham, former head of military intelligence, Admiral Moorer, Admiral McCain, and a number of others. Recently I visited NORAD and had a most informative meeting. I also have access to all of the personnel at the Hoover Institution at Stanford by virtue of my own honorary membership in that group.

In the timing of the campaign, however, I don't believe I should deal in real specifics this early—it will come later. However, I am making my position perfectly clear in regard to the need for our country to be number one in defensive capability.

As for the bureaucracy you mentioned, I have given some specifics on that based on my experience in California's government where we turned a 75 percent growth in the bureaucracy over an eight-year period into a virtually dead-even position for eight years in spite of the fact that state population was increasing faster than any other state. One of the ways to reduce the federal bureaucracy would be to turn a number of programs, such as welfare, back to the states with no federal jurisdiction at all and, of course, to turn back with them the sources of revenue to fund them. As you might know, in California we reformed welfare and turned a 40,000 a month increase in case load into an 8,000 a month decrease over a three-year period. I'm convinced this can be done nationally.

Your last point about gold backing for our money has been one of great interest to me for some time, and I have asked a number of leading economists who have volunteered their help to look into this matter and get back to me with a plan as to how it could be accomplished.

Thank you again for your letter and please don't hesitate to write with any other questions you may have.

Sincerely,
Ronald Reagan

Caspar Weinberger was finance director in Reagan's California administration and served the Nixon administration as director of the Office of Management and Budget and secretary of the Department of Health, Education, and Welfare. He was to become Reagan's secretary of defense. Weinberger apparently wrote to Reagan about the hostages in the U.S. embassy in Iran seized November 4, 1979, in response to which Carter halted imports of oil from Iran and froze Iranian assets in the United States.

Later, Carter ordered a rescue effort that failed. The hostages would not be freed until the day Reagan was inaugurated as president.

Mr. Caspar Weinberger
Circa November 15, 1979[46]

Dear Cap:

No one has said it better. I've been holding my peace with frustration growing because I don't want to say anything to endanger those people, but you're absolutely right that there seems to be no use of the great power this [country] has to let those fanatics know that we could make things very unpleasant for them.

It took him a week to decide to stop buying oil. Now even the farmers are willing to give up a half-billion dollar market in protest, but the government says no. I'd give anything to know what our capacities are and what our options for some kind of forceful action are, but I guess you have to have the job first to find those things out.

Thanks very much for sending it to me. I'm going to see that all our people read your statement.

Best regards,
Ron

John Sears continued to be a contentious figure in the Reagan campaign; in Michigan the leadership of the Reagan campaign went to Republican Governor William G. Milliken rather than Jack Wellborn, who ran Michigan in 1976. Nevertheless, Reagan continued to defend Sears.

Mr. R. W. Hanley
Circa November 15, 1979[47]

Dear Mr. Hanley:

Thank you very much for your letter and for giving me a chance to comment on the problems you see in my campaign. First, however, let me thank you for your support and assure you that contributions sent to the return address on this letter will be all mine without having to be shared with any of the money raisers.

I know many people feel as you do about John Sears. On the other hand, I know that he is very well thought of, particularly in the Eastern half of the United States, and he is probably the best political pro in the business. All of this talk that he is trying to moderate my views or make me less conservative is just newspaper talk. No one is trying to change my position. What he is trying to do is heal the wounds in the Republican Party so that we'll not just win a nomination, if I am going to win it, but we'll have a united Republican Party with which we can win the election. He has gone to a great many people who were formerly for Ford and has persuaded some of them to join our campaign or at least to be neutral and not in opposition.

The incident in Michigan that you mentioned is one that has been very painful to me. I consider Jack Wellborn a good friend and will certainly be forever grateful for his help in '76. Our people are working right now to persuade him to change his mind and to be a part of the campaign. The disagreement occurred when we tried to point out the need to involve those Republicans in Michigan who did not support me the last time so that we could have more than 29 delegates out of the more than 80 that Michigan has and so that we would have a chance to carry Michigan in the general election. There is no question but the feelings there between the various factions are quite bitter. We hope that we can persuade them to move together and I very much want Jack in the campaign.

Again, let me assure you, I am not changing my positions one bit nor is anyone in my organization trying to change me. And, above all, anyone who comes aboard, whatever his label may be—moderate or whatever—will have to accept me as I am. I am not making deals. I never have, and I never will. Again, thanks.

Sincerely,
Ronald Reagan

H. R. Gross had been news director of WHO, the Iowa radio station where Reagan worked in the 1930s.[48] Gross represented the third district of Iowa in the U.S. Congress from 1949 to 1975. "Bob" refers to Governor Robert Ray of Iowa, a Republican.

Mr. and Mrs. H. R. Gross
After November 13, 1979[49]

Dear H. R. and Hazel:

Thank you very much for your letter and your kind words about my declaration. After all these years on the late, late show, it was kind of a shock to find myself on TV in prime time.

Let me assure you the stop in Des Moines was purely a gesture of goodwill. I sat too long with Bob at governors' conferences not to know that he and I are hardly soulmates.

I have a feeling you are probably concerned about the various press accounts and columns that I am somehow moderating my positions or trying to move over to collect a different kind of Republican. Believe me, it is purely press and probably an effort to snipe because I'm still out in front in the polls. I actually would be happier, I think, if I weren't. Riding point leaves you pretty exposed and subject to attack from all sides. Let me tell you two dear friends—I am not changing, have not changed and will not. There wouldn't be any point in seeking that man-killing job if I didn't do it with the idea of working for the principles I believe in. I have discovered out in the country on the trail that if there is any movement, it is the other way—that more Americans than anyone realizes are coming over to our positions.

Nancy sends her best and both of us wish you both a very Merry Christmas and the happiest of holidays.

Again, thanks,
Dutch

Reagan explains references to statehood for Puerto Rico in his announcement speech.

Prof. Allan D. Charles
Circa December 20, 1979 [50]

Dear Professor Charles:

Senator Laxalt forwarded your letter to me, and I am happy to have the opportunity of responding.

It is true I referred to Puerto Rico and statehood in my declaration of candidacy. I don't think it could be described as a "vehement endorsement," however. Having discussed a closer relationship with Mexico and Canada, I felt I should call attention to the rest of the Western Hemisphere and indicate, in so doing, that I was just thinking in terms of a "fortress America." But the position I stated is one adopted by the Republican Party nationally. That is, if Puerto Rico should vote to ask for statehood, we would grant it.

Puerto Rico is a U.S. territory and has been for most, if not all, of this century. My only other reason for mentioning this in my speech was the fact that with our attention to Iran and the Middle East, most Americans are unaware of what has been going on in the Caribbean islands. We are being ringed in there by islands, which, one after the other, have come under the influence of the Soviet Union by way of Castro. I believe this constitutes far more of a threat than most people realize—a threat to the security of our country. As you know, there is a Communist radical faction in Puerto Rico which has been trying to bring about independence from the United States. The Puerto Rican Republican Party has opposed this and has worked for statehood for many years. My declaration was simply that if the people of Puerto Rico voted for statehood, I would support legislation to grant this. I was not trying to show how "liberal" I am, for I am not.

I am a conservative and will not change my position to seek votes. There would be no purpose in running if I were willing to give up my own deeply held convictions.

Sincerely,
Ronald Reagan

M. Stanton Evans wrote an article for the October 27, 1979, issue of Human Events, *" 'Sears Factor' Is Troubling to Conservatives," arguing that John Sears was a liberal running a conservative's campaign. In a November 14 article distributed by the Los Angeles Times Syndicate, Evans suggested Reagan was moderating his views at the behest of his advisers.*

Mr. Edward Caffery
Late December 1979[51]

Dear Mr. Caffery:

Thank you very much for your mailgram and for giving me an opportunity to reply.

I, too, read Stan Evans' column and was concerned as you evidently are. So much so, in fact, that I called Stan. We have known each other for a number of years, and I think he jumped to conclusions because of some of the Washington press stories about my campaign.

Let me assure you I feel as you do about the vice presidency, and if it should fall to me to recommend a nominee, it would not be a liberal with any idea of balancing the ticket. I don't believe in "balancing the ticket." I believe the vice president should share the president's philosophy and views.

It is also untrue that I am moderating my positions or beliefs in any way in order to get elected. If I were willing to alter my positions, there would be no reason for me to seek that office. My only purpose in doing what I'm doing is to have an opportunity to put my beliefs into practice. I believe what I've always believed. I stand on the same principles I followed for eight years as governor of California, and there has been no change.

Again, thanks for letting me reply.

Sincerely,
Ronald Reagan

———————

Reagan explains the thinking behind his announcement speech for the 1980 campaign in this letter.

Mrs. F. M. Akers
January 9, 1980[52]

Dear Mrs. Akers:

Thank you for writing as you did and for giving me a chance to comment. I can understand your concern because I know the press has been distorting a great many things about the campaign, probably in their eagerness to have more of a contest than we seem to be having. I'm referring to the polls that have me out in front.

The press is going to get their contest because I don't take these early polls seriously. I believe in running scared. I think it's going to be a hard, tough race in our party, but maybe that's good for us.

I must say, I'm hard put to understand the mixed reactions to my announcement speech. My own feeling was that I had to remember it's a long way 'til next November. First, of course, it's a long way 'til next July and the convention, and I will be speaking throughout the country. Announcing my candidacy on nationwide television left me with the problem that I didn't want to say everything I'll be saying in the next few months there on TV and then have only to repeat myself to the hundreds of audiences I will be addressing in these coming months. I tried simply to point out the issues I would be addressing and to mention the one new idea—the North American Accord to intrigue a little press attention.

I have been surprised, however, at the diverse opinions. A number of people felt as you do about the speech, but, by contrast, as many others have been telling me it was quite outstanding. All I can say is, it wasn't easy. There was a temptation making that announcement to think I had to give the whole sermon, and yet, at the same time, as I've indicated I realized that I had to have something left to say in these coming months in which I will be followed daily by the national press.

With reference to Iran, I have been speaking out on that in speeches since, and will be doing so even more, but at that time, if you'll recall, all of us felt bound not to say anything that would create disunity or that would endanger our hostages. I don't think now, though, that we should be bound by that because I believe the weakness of the president's position is so evident and the various steps he has taken so obviously could have been taken in the first few days, not after waiting several weeks, that it is fair to point this out, and I will be doing so.

I do want you to know that Mr. Sears is not determining my policy. He is working in the field winning delegates—a task at which, I think, he is rather capable. But I am determining what policy will be and what it is that I will be proposing as government programs. And, I have not changed. The press stories to the effect that I am trying to change my image in order to win some other segment are absolutely false. I still believe the things I've always believed in and am campaigning on those issues.

Again, thanks, and best regards.

Sincerely,
Ronald Reagan

Reagan plays down the internal staff conflicts in his campaign—or more correctly, simply treats them as matters not to be discussed with outsiders. The efforts of John Sears, campaign manager, to gain complete operating control had resulted in Lyn Nofziger's move to a job outside the campaign structure, Martin Anderson's decision to be available to the campaign only part time, and Deaver's walkout on November 26, 1979 when Sears tried to make Reagan choose between Sears and Deaver.[53] All three were to return a few months after Reagan fired Sears on the day of the New Hampshire primary—before the votes were counted.

Reagan would later write more openly to G. W. McCullough (p. 81) that he had been worried that the campaign organization had begun to "come apart," had decided to make changes, and found the results beneficial. Paul Laxalt was the formal campaign chairman and a close friend and adviser of Reagan's, but did not run the campaign day-to-day. Sears was later replaced by William Casey.

Miss Ruthie Johnson
Office of Senator McClure (R-Idaho)
Washington, D.C.
Late December 1979 [54]

Dear Miss Johnson:

Senator Laxalt gave me a copy of your letter to him because he knew that I would want to respond to some of the points you made. I welcome the opportunity and am grateful to Paul and to you for giving me the chance to comment directly.

I can assure you that Ronald Reagan is not moderating his position in any way. There would be no point in running for that office if I were willing to do that. My only reason for seeking it is to be able to attempt the things that I have always believed in. Let me, in fairness, say also that no one is trying to change me or moderate my positions.

Probably Paul told you, but I will repeat it anyway so you'll know it's true. The news, particularly in some of the columns, that a power struggle was going on and that Lyn Nofziger, Mike Deaver, and Marty Anderson were all leaving my campaign because of Sears's pressure are untrue.

Lyn was performing a function in the campaign that was not particularly his specialty. Mike Deaver is the one who asked him, with my permission, to take another assignment. Lyn preferred not to do this and so left the campaign, but he has replaced me, at my request, as chairman of the Citizens for the Republic, our political committee which we formed in 1977. I had to resign as chairman in order to be a candidate.

Mike Deaver informed us last August that he could not stay past the November 13 declaration date and has left the campaign as a full-time staff member to return to the business he and Pete Hannaford have created and of which he serves as president, but he remains with us on a volunteer basis and is my representative to the executive advisory committee, which is chaired by Bill Simon, former secretary of the treasury.

Marty Anderson, who has been working on issues, has had to return part-time to the Hoover Institution at Stanford. He remains part-time with us, and Ed Meese who was my executive assistant while I was Governor, has come on board full-time to work with Marty. Perhaps I should explain that when I refer to Ed as my executive assistant it means he was my top administrative aide in Sacramento.

While it is too early to even think about the vice presidency, let me assure you that if I am the nominee, I will recommend to the convention someone who shares my views and philosophy so that those things upon which I run would be carried out in the event he had to take over.

Paul is the chairman of my campaign, and it is my campaign, and I am making the major decisions and all of the policy decisions. Let me assure you if I should be elected, I will be in charge of putting together my administration and it will be done as it was done in California. People will not be picked on the basis of reward for political contribution or service.

May I just point out that most of those who have been writing the stories that have so concerned you are not journalists who are sympathetic to my views or yours and certainly they are not trying to be helpful. I can only repeat that of the three men whose names have been mentioned, two are still with my campaign, and Lyn is in an all-important post in connection with that campaign as chairman of CFTR [Citizens for the Republic].

Again, thanks.

Best regards,
Ronald Reagan

Reagan decided not to debate the other Republican candidates in Iowa on January 5, 1980.* The Iowa precinct caucuses were held on January 21, 1980. George Bush, later to be Reagan's running mate, got 31.6 percent of the vote to Reagan's 29.5 percent. Reagan's defeat in Iowa called into question the campaign strategy of John Sears, who had discouraged Reagan from making much effort in Iowa.

Reagan's early guess, expressed in a March 27, 1979, letter to William Loeb, was that John Connally of Texas would be his most formidable opponent—"I am tending to think that when it comes down to the wire it will be Big John we will mainly be dealing with out of all the candidates announced so far. I may be wrong, but he is a formidable campaigner." That prediction turned out to be wrong.[55]

Mrs. Dan Dahle
January 5, 1980[56]

Dear Mrs. Dahle:

This is in reply to your letter of December 29th which just reached me, and I am answering it on that January 5th when the debate is taking place, and, of course, as you know, I'm not there. Believe me, I am filled with mixed emotions. I know, of course, that many people are going to resent my not going. On the other hand, I feel so strongly that Republican candidates should not campaign against each other but against the opposition. We should let the members of our party decide which one should carry the banner, and, then, all of us should unite behind that one. I just could not participate in something that was to be a debate.

I have appeared at conventions and spoken to the delegates, knowing that both before and after me at other sessions the other candidates were speaking. But the debate format requires, I think, the stressing of differences between us rather than those things that we, as Republicans, have in common. And this was my sole reason for refusing to debate.

We have fought so hard here in California to overcome factionalism in our party and to unite a party that was terribly torn apart that I just can't help feeling the way I do.

---

* George Bush, John Anderson, Robert Dole, and John Connally debated.

I will be in Davenport before you receive this letter. I am speaking there on the 7th and at Waterloo on the 10th. My son, as you probably know, has been in Iowa for a week. My daughter is going in a few days, and Nancy will be there, and I will be back on the 19th. I'm proud to have your support, and thank you for your blessing.

Sincerely,
Ronald Reagan

After losing the Iowa caucuses, Reagan decided to join future debates, although some people thought he risked more than he would gain. Others continued to worry that Reagan was moderating his views.

Mr. Keith Ferguson
Early February 1980 [57]

Dear Mr. Ferguson:

Thank you very much for your letter and for your advice. Under normal circumstances, I would agree with you completely. Unfortunately, since Iowa, I've had to change my mind. It was my decision not to debate in Iowa, not because I was the front runner, but because I felt it was divisive and could possibly return our Republican Party to those days when it was so factionalized. Apparently, we are more united and can afford to do these things because I have to admit I did not find the debate there divisive in any way. I, therefore, have agreed to debate in New Hampshire.

I don't think your statements about the other debates and how they were lost by front-runners agreeing to debate applies at this particular time. There was no way I could match George Bush's time and effort in Iowa because he started campaigning there eight months before I was even a candidate. He picked two or three early spots in order to gain momentum, and one of the others in which he also campaigned for the better part of a year was New Hampshire. I, therefore, believe the situation that you spoke of in my case is reversed, and there could be an advantage in doing what I am going to do. I do appreciate, however, your interest and support and your sound advice under any other circumstances except those which pertain at this particular moment.

Again, thanks and best regards,

Ronald Reagan

Lee Edwards, a conservative author of books and articles, wrote a long article favorable to Reagan titled "Ronald Reagan: A Leader for the 1980s." It was published as a Human Events *special supplement on January 19, 1980.*

Mr. Lee Edwards
Circa early February 1980 [58]

Dear Lee:

Thanks very much for sending the *Human Events* article, but thanks even more for writing it. We have sent copies to many of our chairmen and to all our surrogate speakers. I'm deeply grateful.

We have beefed up the New Hampshire effort and I have practically taken up residence there, as you suggested. I don't mind telling you I'm running scared. George has put practically as much time in New Hampshire as he did in Iowa and has a sound organization as well as momentum. I'll be debating there on February 20.

In other words, I was wrong about Iowa.

Again thanks and best regards,
Ron

Mr. John Reagan McCrary
New York, New York
Circa February 15, 1980 [59]

Dear Cousin Tex:

Your letter of January 22nd is not easy to answer, but I appreciate your writing and the pictures of my iceberg headquarters.

I've read all the Eastern press about my new image, that Sears is pulling the strings and I'm the puppet. On top of this I read how I'm coasting, riding above the fray. If seven states in four days is coasting, then I guess I am. The truth is that press treatment is phony and made out of whole cloth.

I made the decision not to debate in Iowa because I honestly thought it would be divisive. I was wrong—maybe all the years of preaching have paid off and the party is together. (Except I suspect there is an Eastern establishment determined to stop Reagan—this Reagan.)

Anyway, having realized my mistake, I am going to debate in New Hampshire and wherever else they go for that foolishness.

Tex, no one has been trying to moderate me. I'm saying the things and preaching the policies I've always believed in and I'm campaigning the way I choose to do it. I'm in charge.

Yes, Tex, it's possible I didn't hear the question at Greenbriar or the one at lunch with you and Charlie. I've had one bad ear since the late '30s when an actor shot a .38 off right beside my right ear. I imagine that would be seen now as a result of age by the same people who are putting out the garbage about puppets, etc.

I never thought the nomination was a sure thing [and] I don't think so now, but I'm going to fight like h—l.

All the best,
Ron

Fred Lennon was an Ohio industrialist and substantial contributor to Republicans. Lennon apparently indicated he would not support Reagan.

Mr. Fred Lennon
Circa February 18–29, 1980[60]

Dear Fred:

I returned home from a seven-state trip to find your letter awaiting me. Fred, I know how concerned people are. I know, also, that much of what they are concerned about is total fabrication by the press. I think we all realize now that we were influenced too much by the polls and should have spent more time in Iowa.

The debate idea was mine. I realize now it's a luxury I can't afford. But I have worked so hard and so long for party unity that, from the very first, I laid down the law that I would not engage in debates with other Republicans. I felt that it emphasized our differences rather than what we had in common. However, I'm not going to stand out there alone tilting at windmills so, I will be debating in New Hampshire as well as South Carolina and elsewhere if they decide to have them.

The fabrication from the press that I mentioned has to do with my positions and this talk that I am moderating my views. No one who has heard me speak any place on this campaign can say that. Last week, in Florida, I had four standing ovations in the middle of my speech and virtually the same thing in several other places where I made that speech. We have virtually doubled the time we are going to spend in New Hampshire and, of course, you know how well we did in Arkansas, and, actually, we were up against a plot that had been conceived to do the reverse. As you remember, in '76 I won the Arkansas primary by a tremendous margin. I would have again so they cancelled the primary and, as part of a "stop Reagan" movement, switched it to this present system. Here, Fred, I must give John Sears the credit. It was his strategy, and it was his fellows that went into Arkansas—I only appeared there once—and they carried the day for us to have the six actual delegates at the convention to Baker's four and Bush's one.

You mean a very great deal to the campaign, and I need you very much. I'm hoping and praying you will reconsider and give me a further chance.

Sincerely,
Ron

Reagan's outright rejection of the idea of John Anderson as his running mate was not only based on political philosophy. Anderson had stated that he would rather see Edward M. Kennedy (D-Massachusetts) as president than Reagan.[61] Anderson eventually ran as an Independent.

Mr. and Mrs. Robert G. Overbaugh
After March 11, 1980 [62]

Dear Bob and Cherie:

I'm sorry there wasn't time to get together and have a visit when I was in Illinois, but you saw the pace we were traveling so know how impossible it was.

I'm back in California now for a few hours and then will be on the road again. I appreciated your letter and your suggestions about the vice presidency. I haven't let myself even think of that yet. I'm going to wait until it is more certain that I might be the nominee. One thing I can say is it will not be John Anderson. He won't accept me as a president, I don't see why I should accept him as a vice president.

You asked about my brother, Moon. He lives out here in Rancho Santa Fe. He has retired from the advertising business so puts in most of his time on the golf course.

It was good seeing you and, again, thanks.

Best regards,
Ron

––––––––––

In this March 14, 1980, letter to William Buckley, Reagan still does not know whether Gerald Ford will enter the 1980 race. Reagan had beaten Bush better than 2 to 1 in the February 26, 1980, New Hampshire primary. Ford was viewed as the only possibility for stopping Reagan, and on March 1 Ford declared that he would entertain a request to run from the Republican Party, even though it was too late to enter most primaries.

The day after this letter was dictated Ford stated that he would not be a candidate (he had also said so on October 19, 1979). Reagan would win the Illinois primary decisively on March 18, 1980, with 48.4 percent of the vote to Anderson's 36.7 percent and Bush's 11 percent,[63] making it increasingly likely he would have enough delegates to win on the first ballot at the convention.

Mr. William F. Buckley Jr.
New York, New York
March 14, 1980 [64]

Dear Bill:

I thank you for your column on New Hampshire, and I thank you for your letter about the Johnson piece in the *Washington Post*. Now, hoping I won't seem ungrateful, I have a rare opportunity that I seldom have ever had to add to your store of information.

I guess my principal mistake with regard to the president and his statement in Poland was that I made it sound as if he spoke those words upon arriving and getting off the airplane. Bill, he actually did make that statement, but he made it the next day at a luncheon. Our records show that he again made very much the same statement again about our concept of human rights being preserved in Poland on a later occasion on the same visit. By later, I mean within 24 hours of the first statement. Anyway, you were good to take this matter up and provide me with the additional information.

I hope you're having a wonderful time there on the ski slopes. If you look up and see something familiar sailing through the air, it is me wafted aloft by the results in South Carolina, Georgia, Florida, and Alabama. I know I won't have that easy a time in Illinois. Anderson seems to have captured even the *Tribune*. Now, of course, we anxiously await the word from Mount Olympus as to whether there will be a Ford in my future. As I dictate this, he's in Washington talking to a group of congressmen who, from all I learn, are not at all happy about the prospect of his getting in the race. I hope he'll think it over and realize that what he's proposing and the way he's doing it could be very divisive and, once again, the Republicans would be trying to win a convention rather than an election.

Well, have fun and we're waiting for you to come back. Nancy sends her love.

Best regards,
Ron

William Casey took over the management of the 1980 campaign after Sears was fired. Reagan assures a supporter that Casey's membership in the Council on Foreign Relations (CFR) and the Trilateral Commission does not reflect his foreign policy views. Casey became director of the Central Intelligence Agency in the new Reagan administration. The OSS is the World War II Office of the Secret Service, the predecessor to the CIA.

Mrs. DeJuan Strickland
After April 25, 1980 [65]

Dear Mrs. Strickland:

Thank you very much for your letter and for your generous words. I am more than happy and proud to have your support. I share your views about the CFR and the Trilateral Commission. Let me reassure you about Mr. Casey. It is true that he is listed as a member of CFR, as is William Buckley. Mr. Casey was in the OSS during World War II—responsible for much of the military intelligence we needed in the Normandy invasion. He very frankly has joined CFR in order to be able to hear the visiting dignitaries and officials from other countries who are regularly invited to address that organization. That is his only reason as I'm sure it is Mr. Buckley's reason for his connection. I have every confidence in him and promise you there will be no compromise of principles.

Again, my thanks.

Very best regards,
Ronald Reagan

With the nomination locked up, Reagan took time to respond to people who questioned him on a variety of personal and political matters, as the next three letters demonstrate. Here Reagan clarifies how much he receives from his California state pension for Sister Mary Ignatius, who wrote to him frequently.

Sister Mary Ignatius, DMJ
Daughters of Mary and Joseph,
Los Angeles, California
June 5, 1980 [66]

Dear Sister Mary Ignatius:

Thank you very much for your good letter and for your generous words. It made me very happy to hear from you again.

I appreciated your suggestions and assure you that those who serve in my administration, if I am elected, will be people who believe in the things that you and I hold dear. As to the suggestion about my state pension, I think the gentlemen who spoke to you were ill-informed. My pension is $15,000 not $50,000. And right now it comes in very handy. I am probably the only candidate who had to give up all of his earning activities in order to be a candidate, so this has been a year with no revenue coming in. I had been earning my living through speaking engagements, radio programs, and newspaper columns. All of those, of course, had to be given up in order to be a candidate. You can tell the gentlemen, however, that I have made a decision that one of my first duties as president, if elected, will be to put a freeze on the hiring of federal employees to replace those who leave government service or retire.

Thank you again for your good letter and thank you for your prayers.

Sincerely,
Ronald Reagan

Dr. Fredrick W. L. Kerr
June 26, 1980 [67]

Dear Dr. Kerr:

I appreciate getting your letter and having the opportunity to reply. I assure you that I am going to name a vice president who will share my views and convictions. I also intend to follow the policy I had in California as governor of seeking people for cabinet positions and other high posts who you might say, don't want a job in government. These will be people who will have to step down to take such a job and will do so because of dedication and commitment.

I'm sorry you feel as you do about the unity dinners. I think the Republican Party is doing something no party has ever done in this regard, and that is to hold dinners throughout the country under the banner of the winner of the primaries.

All party candidates are attending, and we are dividing the proceeds in order to pay off the campaign debts.

I believe this has produced more unity than the party has ever seen. And, at the same time, it serves notice to others who might want to seek public office that the party will carry off its wounded, and not just urge people to seek office and then leave them heavily indebted if their campaign fails.

Obviously, this sharing will go to candidates with whom I'm in disagreement on various policy matters. It does not, however, in any way suggest that I will, as you put it, slide into an association with those whose views are opposed to mine.

Again, I thank you for your letter and thank you for your expression of support of me, and I assure you that I will do my utmost to put together an administration that will carry out the programs and policies I have been enunciating and in which I believe. There would be no way I could seek this office if I were willing to compromise my principles.

Again, thanks and best regards.

Sincerely,
Ronald Reagan

Mrs. Kay Starr
June 26, 1980[68]

Dear Kay:

How nice it was to hear from you and to receive your suggestions and your good wishes. Believe me, I have thought about the idea of a woman for vice president but have to tell you polls we've taken indicate, just as you said, that the people aren't quite ready for that yet. I don't understand it because I'm a big fan of Margaret Thatcher, the prime minister of England.

You were kind to write, and I hope our paths will cross again very soon.

Sincerely,
Ron

Richard Wirthlin, Reagan's pollster in 1980 and an important contributor to campaign strategy, sent Reagan a memo called "Strategy for the Doldrums"—what to do to maintain interest between the primaries and the convention. Wirthlin advised Reagan to seek former President Gerald Ford's input and counsel and, as a gesture that would attract Republicans who had not supported Reagan in the primaries, offer Ford the vice presidency.[69]

Reagan visited Ford at the office near Ford's Rancho Mirage, California, home on June 5, 1980. Reagan had heard that Ford considered Reagan responsible for Ford's 1976 loss to Jimmy Carter. Reagan reviewed the extent of his campaigning for Ford and other Republicans in 1976 and discussed the vice presidency. Ford expressed no in-

terest, but a Reagan-Ford ticket appealed to some Republican leaders because the ticket polled well against Carter-Mondale. It began to be seriously considered. Reagan tells about his June 5 meeting with Ford in these letters.

Mr. Richard Wirthlin
Circa June 12, 1980[70]

Dear Dick:

Just a line as I get on another airplane to thank you for sending the memo on the primaries. I'll keep my fingers crossed.

A week ago I did something that has been on my mind for some time. It has to do with your paragraph about Jerry F[ord]. I had a meeting with him and cleared the air about misunderstandings he had as to my campaign effort in his behalf in '76. I think it was a good talk and will have a good effect in the coming months.

Again, thanks and best regards,
Ron

Sam Devine was a Republican congressman from Ohio. Devine served on the House Select Committee on Assassinations; Reagan had served on the Commission on CIA Activities Within the United States.

The Honorable Samuel L. Devine
June 26, 1980[71]

Dear Sam:

I have just returned home from our meeting in Washington to find your good letter awaiting me. I'm sorry we didn't have an opportunity to visit and perhaps explore what you were writing about.

I have to tell you I am convinced from my meeting with President Ford a few days earlier that he is adamant in his position about the vice presidency. He brought the subject up and made it plain that he believed that he could be of greater service in his present capacity, helping in the campaign, than he could on the ticket. He brought up the matter of how it would look if he hastily reregistered in another state to meet the Constitutional requirement. He also brought up the matter of our similarities in age and felt that the post should be taken by someone who had a political future. At any rate, he brought up the subject and did convince me that there was no way that he would do that.

I appreciate very much your taking the time and trouble to write, and I certainly want to have your input and would be most grateful if you'd feel free to write anytime that you have a suggestion. I look forward to a meeting in the days ahead when we will have more time to exchange ideas than we had in this most recent trip.

Again, thanks and best regards,

Sincerely,
Ron

The Reagan campaign considered replacing William Brock of Tennessee, who was chairing the Republican National Committee, with someone more favorable to Reagan, but encountered opposition and instead installed Drew Lewis of Pennsylvania as a deputy to Brock.[72]

Mr. T. E. Stivers
Decatur, Georgia
July 2, 1980[73]

Dear Ted:

I'm finally getting around to answering your letters and just want to thank you for all you've done.

I was particularly pleased to hear how far you went in healing the wounds and at least smoothing over the cracks in the plaster regarding the National Committee, etc.

I believe we have the national headquarters situation in hand. I know how you feel, but I have to tell you when all the rumors started flying around about the chairman leaving, I think all of us at this end were amazed at how many of even our closest supporters were terribly upset and thought it would be a blow to unity. We have Drew Lewis in there now as deputy to protect our interests, and I really believe the situation is going to be all right. The young lady you mentioned, it was interesting to learn, is as unwelcome to the chairman as she is to the rest of us. I guess she's on her way out.

I appreciate also your input on the decision I have to make regarding the second spot. It really is a tough one, and there's no way that everyone is going to be pleased by this one, but I share your good opinion of the names that you put in. Rest assured I'm not going to do any ticket balancing. Please give my best to your good lady, and I hope I'll be seeing you soon.

Best regards,
Ron

Reagan was nominated on July 16, 1980, at the Republican National Convention in Detroit, Michigan. Enthusiasm for a Reagan-Ford ticket was increasing, and Reagan's advisers were negotiating with Ford's over his possible role in a Reagan presidency in an effort to get Ford to accept the vice presidential nomination. But when Ford did a television interview with Walter Cronkite about a co-presidency, Reagan demanded a quick decision from Ford. They met and agreed Ford should not be the vice presidential nominee; Reagan immediately called George Bush with the news that he had it. In a letter to William Loeb, Reagan wrote later that "I'm sure you know (just between us) that my heart was really in Nevada." He was referring to Paul Laxalt, senator from Nevada.[74]

Here Reagan explains the staff negotiations about a Ford vice presidency and the final decision.

Ambassador John Davis Lodge
August 18, 1980[75]

Dear John:

It was good to hear from you and to get your letter, and I appreciate your suggested statement about George, although I don't think there is any longer any flap.

I think you'd like to know that throughout that entire Ford situation in Detroit, Jerry was against it and told me so from the beginning. There was no bargaining with me or with him, but some people who felt strongly that he should do that were coming back to our people with various ideas and proposals that they thought might be used to persuade him to say yes. Each time, they indicated that they thought that if such a concession as they were suggesting were made, they were optimistic that he would say yes. Finally, when the situation was virtually out of hand on the convention floor with all the press speculation and so forth, I sent word through our people to those others that there was no way that I could give up my responsibilities with regard to cabinet appointments and so forth. I said I had to have an answer right away because the situation at the convention hall was out of hand.

Jerry, himself, came down and told me that he had not changed his mind at all, that he did not think he should ever do it, but that he was heart and soul behind me and would do everything he could to help me get elected, but that he just had a gut instinct that the other thing wouldn't work.

I had to confess by that time I was in complete agreement with him. And out of it all, I think, came an improvement in our relationship that erased any lingering feelings that he might have had with regard to '76. He said as much and so I think it all turned out for the best.

Nancy sends her best as do I and give our regards to Francesca.

Sincerely,
Ron

Reagan addresses in detail Ann Petroni's concerns about platform planks and agrees with her that the key issues for the campaign are the economy and foreign policy.

Mrs. Ann King Petroni
July 31, 1980[76]

Dear Mrs. Petroni:

Thank you very much for your letter and for giving me the opportunity to respond with regard to your concerns.

I, too, believe the campaign should focus on the basic and key issues of the economy and foreign policy. I realize there was a great news emphasis on those other matters at the convention. This was probably because those were the only areas in which we had the hint of disagreement and possible division.

With regard to the Equal Rights Amendment, we did have two groups which were on opposite sides. One wanted a definite plank in the platform opposing the amendment; the other, of course, wanted one supporting it. I believe we were very successful in getting a plank that emphasized our concern with equal rights for women without getting into the matter of whether this would be done by an amendment. It was a compromise which, like all compromises, was not completely pleasing to either of the two factions but was acceptable to all.

As to my own position, I am strongly for equal rights. I just don't happen to believe that the amendment is the best way to achieve this.

While I was governor, I supported, and signed into law, 14 statutes eliminating specific discriminations against women that were in the California legal code. If I am elected, I am pledged to establish liaison with the 50 governors to encourage and speed up similar actions in all the states as well as to exercise and overview the 19 federal laws eliminating such discrimination to make sure they are actively in force.

To put it briefly, my feeling about the amendment is that it is too rigid. It would eliminate those laws we now have which recognize the physical differences between men and women. These are legitimate laws which, for example, recognize that women in industrial jobs should be protected from having to lift weights that are beyond their strength and which could be injurious to them. Such laws could be cancelled out by the ERA.

On abortion, it is true that I believe we take a human life by interrupting a pregnancy. I also believe in a mother's right to defend her own life. The reference to abortion in the platform is only three sentences long. Again, let me point out that, in these matters, there were people very emotionally aroused and with strong views on both sides. I believe in each case the compromise was the best that could be arrived at.

Under the judiciary, there is only a single sentence. It says, "we will work for the appointment of judges at all levels of the judiciary who respect traditional family values and the sanctity of innocent human life." By its inclusion, this sentence also resolved what seemed to be a problem for a time that could lead to divisiveness.

Let me repeat, however, that, like you, I believe the major issues facing this country today include the threats to our economy and continued prosperity. On the international scene, of course, there is the threat of the Soviet Union with its present military superiority and our lack of any consistent policy which has brought us diminished respect throughout the world. Those issues plus the energy crisis are going to be a large part of my campaign thrust.

Again, I thank you, and if you have any further questions, please don't hesitate to drop me a line. I'll be very happy to answer any other questions you may have. I thank you for writing, and I thank you for your expression of support. Best regards.

Sincerely,
Ronald Reagan

———

Reagan reassures Blanche Seaver, a staunch conservative supporter and a large contributor to Republican campaigns, about George Bush and Bush's commitment to support Reagan's policies.

Mrs. Frank Seaver
July 31, 1980[77]

Dear Blanche:

It was good to hear from you, and I know you were disappointed that it wasn't Phil Crane in the second spot. Please believe that we did a lot of soul-searching and a lot of researching before any decision was made.

The biggest thing against Phil was the fact that in two years campaigning for the presidency he went down rather than up in attracting any following.

On the other hand, by the time we got to Detroit, there was a tidal wave rolling for Bush. Our own friends and supporters—good staunch conservatives like Strom Thurmond and Senator McClure and many others and friends like Holmes Tuttle, Justin Dart, and Jack Hume—were solidly behind him. Our surveys also showed that he was one of the only potential candidates who added to the ticket with regard to gaining votes. Nevertheless, before making the decision, I secured his promise that he supported my position on abortion and would stand behind the platform.*

I read very carefully the material you sent. I think we should recognize that George resigned from the Trilateral Commission some time ago. On the questions in the review of the news, there was one suggesting that he once opposed détente with Red China. The answer given is that, as our ambassador to the United Nations, he was instrumental in getting Red China into the U.N. But it is not true. I was in the middle of that whole affair. What happened was that while Kissinger was out of the country, other nations that had promised us they would not oust Taiwan broke those promises. The issue was brought up, and Red China entered the U.N. while Taiwan was thrown out. Our entire administration opposed this and was outvoted.

Rest assured, Blanche, that I know about the Eastern establishment and the Trilateral Commission, and I am not about to be taken over by them. We're going to try to do at the national level what we did here in California. We will also have a

---

* Reagan secured this commitment when he telephoned Bush with the good news. Martin Anderson was present when the call was made.

policy with regard to the Soviet Union that will be quite a change from the Carter policy.

Nancy sends her love, as do I, and again, thank you very much for your support.

Sincerely,

Ron

Reagan explains to his friend Ward Quaal why he agreed to debate John Anderson in the general election (Anderson ran as an Independent). As it turned out, Carter refused to join the debate with Anderson.

Mr. Ward L. Quaal
July 31, 1980 [78]

Dear Ward:

Thank you very much for your two letters and for sending the picture. Believe me, that brought back some warm memories.

Ward, I share your concern about Anderson and the debates. But when I answered that question, I didn't think I had any choice. It seems that Carter had expressed his refusal to debate Anderson, and, since the debates are going to be sponsored by the League of Women Voters, I responded that if they decided that Anderson, by virtue of the polls, was a viable, legitimate candidate, why, yes, if they included him, I would debate. Frankly I have a feeling by that time he won't be that kind of candidate and, therefore, will not be included. Like you, I have very little respect for the man.

Nancy sends her best. Give our regards to Dorothy, and we, too, hope we'll be seeing you one of these days soon.

Sincerely,

Ron

Reagan tells William Simon, former secretary of the treasury and a campaign adviser, that he doesn't consider it necessary to announce cabinet members in advance. Irving Kristol was editor of The Public Interest.

Mr. William Simon
August 11, 1980 [79]

Dear Bill:

Believe it or not, your letter of July 9th with the enclosure by Irving Kristol has just reached me.

Before I comment on Irving's suggestion, let me just say that I think all of us now are in complete agreement with what you had to say in Detroit that night. We were all carried away by the euphoria of what seemed like the dream ticket, and we hadn't done much thinking about what might follow after the election.

I must say that, from the very first, Jerry had those extreme doubts about doing it and never gave them up. By the time he came down to see me, I had changed my thinking, too, and I think the only good that came out of it was a relationship between him and me that is better than anything we've ever had.

Now, as to Irving's suggestion. I won't close my mind to possibly deciding sometime during the campaign to make early announcement of possible Cabinet members, but I feel now that it isn't a good idea. I think that he is concerned because of that flurry of press stories about supposed misstatements by me. Those stories have in the main stopped because they never were true. I don't claim to be the ultimate expert or last word on all matters, but I am not really as worried as he is about my handling of press questions. Frankly, I think with the counsel and advice that I have from all of you, I'm better equipped to answer them than the press is to ask them. I've learned, also, that the world doesn't come to an end if sometimes you have to answer a question by saying, I don't know the answer to that, but I'll find out.

I hope I'll be seeing you soon. Nancy sends her best as do I.

Sincerely,
Ron

———

Reagan's emphasis on foreign policy was a strong campaign theme; here he responds to issues raised by a supporter.

Mrs. Herbert A. Stade
August 23, 1980[80]

Dear Mrs. Stade:

First of all, on behalf of Nancy and me, thanks again for a lovely, but all too brief, time at your home. You were most generous to make your home available, and we are truly grateful.

I wish we hadn't been so rushed and I wish I had been able to read your letter before we left and that we could have talked over the problems you discussed.

I am very much aware of the situation in our military today and particularly in our Navy. In my speeches to the Veterans of Foreign Wars and the American Legion, particularly in the Legion speech, I took up the subject that you brought up in your letter about the need for us to have a realistic program of pay and benefits for our military to keep people in the service and make them want to follow careers there. I am particularly concerned about the Navy. I know what has been done to it under this administration, and I think I know how much must be done as quickly as possible to restore it to its proud place. Believe me this will be a top priority in my administration if I am successful and have an administration.

In my speech to the Legion, I reminded them that Admiral Moorer back in 1969 said that we needed a navy of 800 ships to meet our responsibilities in the three oceans. Today we have 415, and, as you discovered in San Diego, sometimes they can't put to sea because they don't have the manpower, or if they do put to sea, they don't have the ammunition and the equipment they need.

Incidentally, before coming home on Wednesday, I visited the Sun Shipbuilding Yard in Boston and spoke there to several thousand employees. I touched on the same subject. Not only do we need to build ships, but, as you yourself said, we need to see that men and women interested in a career in the service will find it rewarding and will enlist.

Nancy sends her very best and please give our regards to your husband and your family and tell them how very much we enjoyed meeting them and how much we hope our paths cross again soon.

Sincerely,
Ronald Reagan

September 1, 1980, was Labor Day, and the general election campaign traditionally begins the day after Labor Day. The European reaction to Reagan's candidacy was one of astonishment. In this letter of which only the typed version has been found, Reagan defends the idea that he does have some experience in foreign affairs, but turns down an invitation for a foreign visit during the campaign season.

The Right Honorable Lord Derek Pritchard
House of Lords
London, England
September 1, 1980[81]

Dear Derek:

How good it was to hear from you after this long time and to be reminded again of that most enjoyable visit we had in London. I am greatly honored to hear what you said about my appearance before the Directors Conference.

Thank you for your offer of hospitality and your generous invitation. I'm afraid any such visit, however, must be delayed. We have 60 campaign days ahead of us here and have ruled out a European visit because we're convinced our own press would simply treat it as trying to cover what they say is a lack of international experience. In other words, that I was trying to become an instant international authority.

Actually, while I do not claim that having seen the monkey, I can run the circus, I think I've had at least a little touch of such experience since President Nixon sent me once to Europe to visit the heads of state of six countries regarding particular problems, not just a ceremonial visit, and three times to Asia, including the time when Kissinger was making final arrangements in Peking for Nixon's first visit. And, I was on Taiwan explaining to Chiang Kai-shek the meaning of Nixon's trip. There then have been other visits on my own both when I was governor and just two years ago another trip to Asia and Iran. On some of these latter trips, I was a guest of the governments of those countries by invitation.

That still doesn't lessen my regret at having to turn down your kind invitation. I shall hope for an opportunity to make such a visit and hope that our paths will cross soon in the near future.

Again, a heartfelt thanks.

Sincerely,
Ronald Reagan

———

Reagan wrote, as far as we know, few letters during the general election campaign of 1980. He was elected the 40th president of the United States on November 2, 1980, by 489 electoral votes to Carter's 49. He won 51 percent of the popular vote to Carter's 41 percent. Control of the Senate switched to the Republicans with 53 Senate seats.

CHAPTER EIGHT

Core Beliefs

*R*EAGAN GREW UP *a Democrat. He talked politics and political philosophy with Republicans and Democrats over the years. Colleagues remember the discussions with H. R. Gross at WHO, George Murphy at the Screen Actors Guild, Barney Oldfield on Hollywood sets, Earl Dunckel on trains traveling the country to make appearances at General Electric plants, and with his father-in-law, Loyal Davis. His high school sweetheart's father, Reverend Cleaver, was perhaps the earliest adult whose political views he considered seriously other than those of his parents.*

After World War II he made efforts to bring about, as he says in his autobiography, "the regeneration of the world I believed should have automatically appeared."[1] He joined organizations whose avowed objective was to save the world from neo-Fascism. But it was his experiences with post–World War II Communist attempts to gain influence in Hollywood that convinced him of the dangers of communism and eventually led to his support for Republican candidates and his switch in party registration.

As early as 1952, in a commencement address at William Woods College in Fulton, Missouri, Reagan expressed his view that America is special: ". . . the great ideological struggle that we find ourselves engaged in today is not a new struggle . . . I, in my own mind, have thought of America as a place in the divine scheme of things that was set aside as a promised land." The first section of this chapter includes letters that recall these themes.

Reagan's opposition to appeasement of the Soviets demanded a strong military, and his letters in The Military section reflect the high regard with which he held that institution.

Other letters, in the Government and Governing section of this chapter, address a wide range of his basic convictions on the nature of government and its functioning. Letters in which he wrote about his Christian beliefs, the power of prayer, and life after death are in the Religion section.

The section on Reading, Writing, and Speaking includes letters in which Reagan wrote about what he was reading, his own writing, and his observations on the differences between the written and the spoken word.

AMERICA AND THE AMERICAN PEOPLE

Reagan believed that America was special, not only in its revolutionary republican founding but in the eyes of God—"a special place for people who wanted to be free," and "the golden hope of all mankind." His November 13, 1979, announcement for the presidency was his famous statement on the subject: "We who are privileged to be Americans have had a rendezvous with destiny since the moment in 1630 when John Winthrop, standing on the deck of the tiny Arbella off the coast of Massachusetts, told the little band of Pilgrims, 'We shall be as a city upon a hill.' " It was a theme he had used in his speech for Goldwater in 1964.

Reagan believed that democracy worked and he had confidence in the American people and their ability to make the right decisions if they were well informed. He also welcomed immigrants gladly.

Reagan responds to a letter asking about his religious beliefs and how they relate to the office he is seeking.

> Dorothy D. Conaghan
> Tonkawa, Oklahoma
> Circa 1976 [2]

Dear Dorothy:

Thank you for your letter and accept my apology about the earlier letter you mentioned. Evidently, it was lost in the campaign shuffle.

By coincidence, I am a member of the Christian Church and attended a Christian Church school, Eureka College in Illinois. Of course, that isn't an answer to the questions you asked. Yes, I do have a close and deeply felt relationship with Christ and believe I have experienced what you refer to as being born again.* I have come to realize that whatever I do has meaning only if I ask that it serve his purpose. This, in a sense, is an answer to your third question also for I believe that, in my present undertaking, whatever the outcome is, it will be his doing. I'll pray for understanding of what it is he would have me do.

I have long believed there was a divine plan that placed this land here to be found by people of a special kind and that we have a rendezvous with destiny. Yes, there is a spirit moving in this land and a hunger in the people for a spiritual revival.

---

* When questioned Reagan explained his born-again experience as his decision to be baptized in his early teens, which came after he read the book, *That Printer of Udell's*. Peter Hannaford, *The Reagans* (New York: Coward-McCann, 1983), p. 254.

If the task I seek should be given me I would pray only that I could perform it in a way that would serve God.

Sincerely,
Ronald Reagan

———————

Reagan wrote the following in response to a request for his views on national purpose from Kenneth Wells, president of the Freedom Foundation at Valley Forge.

Dr. Kenneth Wells
Valley Forge, Pennsylvania
Circa 1967–68[3]

A number of Americans from time to time have suggested the need for a national purpose as if somehow we are drifting aimlessly without purpose.

Perhaps their very suggestion is a measure of how far we've drifted from what has been our national purpose for 200 years. Their suggestion creates an image of a determined people marching in ranks dedicated to the completion of some program or project. But wasn't and isn't our national purpose the original cause which created us a nation? We brought forth a social structure to guarantee for the first time to each individual his right to control his own destiny. Our nation exists for one purpose only—to assure each one of us the ultimate in individual freedom consistent with law and order. God meant America to be free because God intended each man to have the dignity of freedom.

———————

Here Reagan writes to a young man about the importance of people taking responsibility for their government.

Philip
Undated pre-presidential[4]

Dear Philip:
Thanks very much for your generous words. I'm most grateful—pleased also at your interest in government.

You have touched on the very heart of the matter—people involvement. In recent years growing possibly from the Great Depression years when people were literally stunned by the collapse of the economy there has been a decline in political participation by the people. The Roosevelt era was characterized by a government takeover to an extent we've never known.

Personal initiative was our national characteristic. Organized labor was fragmented and had little power mainly because most Americans resisted joining anything that might restrict their individualism.

The pattern changed quickly. The year I graduated from college the government was running radio ads urging you not to leave home looking for work but to stay and wait for the government to help you.

Today so many things we once thought of as personal or private responsibility are now just accepted as government's job. With this in my opinion has grown the idea that we are incapable as individuals of affecting government. Thus the clichés—"there is no difference between the parties," "my vote doesn't count," "politicians are all alike."

I have learned that the people can influence government and that our system will only work if the people participate. But the people must be informed or rather inform themselves. Jefferson said the people will not make a mistake—if they have all the facts. If there is a weakness in our two-party system it is that we accept a party label as ours and then vote the label without questioning whether the party continues to represent our own philosophical beliefs.

I was a Democrat when the Democratic Party stood for states rights, local autonomy, economy in government and individual freedom. Today it is the party that has changed, openly declaring for centralized federal power and government sponsored redistribution of the individual's earnings.

You asked for some ideas; let me suggest that every government service should be weighed against the cost of that service in loss of personal freedom. We willingly give up our right to drive 90 miles an hour down a city street because we want safety for self and family. By the same token do we want government to have the right to censor films because some filmmakers lack good taste?

Government exists to protect rights which are ours from birth; the right to life, to liberty and the pursuit of happiness. A man may choose to sit and fish instead of working. That's his pursuit of happiness. He does not have the right to force his neighbors to support him (welfare) in his pursuit because that interferes with their pursuit of happiness.

I hope this is something of what you wanted.

> Best regards,
> Ronald Reagan

Although the 1970s were a time when Reagan was critical of government, he notes in this letter that much is right with America.

> Lenore Hershey
> Pre-presidential[5]

Dear Lenore Hershey:

In reply to your letter of May 21, here is why I still believe in and what I think is right about America.

Americans are, in their time of discontent, encouraged by doom and gloom criers who would have us believe our only salvation lies in becoming docile sheep for the government shepherd. I happen to believe government is not the solution to our problems—government is the problem.

It is true we have grievous troubles, but it's also true we are better off than any other people on earth. Ninety-five percent of our people have the daily minimum intake of nutrients essential to maintain health; 99 percent of our homes have gas or electric appliances in their kitchens; 96 percent have TV, and we own 120 million automobiles and trucks. That's on the material side.

There is a spiritual side. We are a generous people. We have shared our wealth more widely among our people than any society heretofore known to man. We support more churches and libraries, more symphonies and operas, and more nonprofit theaters than any other country. We publish more books than all the rest of the world put together. One third of all the young people in the world who are getting a college education are getting it in the United States and we have more doctors and hospitals, in proportion to population, than any other country in the world.

Now all we need is to be reminded of our destiny—that God intended America to be free; to be the golden hope of all mankind.

Ronald Reagan

Otis Carney was the author of plays and books. He sent a campaign contribution for the 1980 election.

Mr. Otis Carney
Paicines, California
November 1979[6]

Dear Otis:

Nancy and I were so pleased to get your letter, and before saying anything else, let me tell you of my heartfelt gratitude for your very generous contribution. I am deeply grateful.

You are so right in your letter as to what is important to the people today. While they talk about the real issue of inflation, energy, etc., they hunger for a spiritual revival to feel once again as they felt years ago about this nation of ours. There is a great sense of frustration. I have been speaking on this. I don't know whether word has reached you or not, but I have been using a quote in my talks from Tom Paine back in the dark days of the Revolutionary War when it didn't seem possible this nation could come into being. He told his fellow Americans, "We have it within our power to begin the world over again." I have tried to suggest that that might be the destiny for our party.

I envy you your visit to South Africa. I've had invitations to go there and have never been able to make it. I, too, am convinced that that must be the ally with which we line up in any world strategy that we are going to follow for our own security.

Nancy sends her love and please give our very best to your family. Again, thanks.

Best regards,
Ron

Miss Sandy Loftis
Scottsdale, Arizona
November 10, 1981[7]

Dear Miss Loftis:

Thank you very much for your letter of September 30. I'm sorry to be so late in answering but it does take a while for letters to reach my desk.

I appreciate very much your taking the time and trouble to write and tell me of that early experience. You reaffirmed what I myself deeply believe—that the people of this country can be depended upon to do what has to be done if government will give them the chance. We are starting here at the national level a program to increase voluntarism throughout the country in almost every area. So far it seems to be off to a fine start.

Again my thanks to you. Best regards,

Sincerely,
Ronald Reagan

The next two letters are to grateful immigrants. Petre Teodorescu immigrated from Communist Romania. The Meghjis had come to the United States in January of 1972 with "two suitcases and $350 between the two of us" and eleven years later had graduate degrees and owned their own home, but were most grateful that they could "go to bed at night without fear of that official pounding on the door."

Mr. Petre Teodorescu
Scottsdale, Arizona
February 4, 1983[8]

Dear Mr. Teodorescu:

Thank you very much for your letter and for your good wishes.

Sometimes those of us who were born in this country tend to take things for granted. It takes someone like you who has only recently come here to remind us how lucky we are. Like you, I dream of the day when all over the world people can know this freedom and escape from communist rule. I promise you, I shall do everything I can to preserve the freedom that you have found here.

Again, my thanks.

Sincerely,
Ronald Reagan

Mirza and Gulshan Meghji
Lilburn, Georgia
August 19, 1983 [9]

Dear Mirza and Gulshan Meghji:

Thank you very much for writing and sharing your experience with me and welcome to the United States. We are pleased and proud to have you as citizens. I'm glad you found friendship and hospitality here.

Your accomplishments in such a short time are truly outstanding and should be an inspiration to all our people. I hope we can always provide the peace you have found and that we can work toward spreading that peace to all the world.

Again my thanks and God bless you.

Sincerely,
Ronald Reagan

―――――――――

Dianne Roe wrote to protest the one-sided news coverage of the 40th anniversary of the dropping of the atomic bomb on Hiroshima. She tells Reagan about an American family who suffered at the hands of the Japanese during World War II. Myra Paradies, whose father was American, "lived in the Philippines with her husband and five children when the Japanese bombed Manila. She, her husband, and two of her children were captured and made to stand outside their home while the Japanese burned their house to the ground" while two daughters died in the burning house. Myra was shot but survived. Myra's brother, Don Johnson, was imprisoned in Manila with his wife, children, and parents, where some members of the family died; another brother was captured and tortured. "There were no protestors; no memorial funds were set up on behalf of Myra or other members of the Johnson family," Roe said. "None of the news media interviewed Americans who had been bombed, tortured, or mutilated."

Ms. L. Dianne Roe
Gales Ferry, Connecticut
September 27, 1985 [10]

Dear Ms. Roe:

I'm sorry to be so late in answering your letter, but it has only just now made its way to my desk. Thank you for writing as you did and for telling me the story of Myra and the Johnson family.

Like you I was disturbed by the one-sided editorializing that was carried on during the 40th anniversary of Hiroshima. I've become more and more conscious of an element in our land of people I call the "blame America first" crowd.

We have every right to stand tall. Our country is unique in all the world. A former prime minister of Australia said some years back, "I wonder if anybody has thought what the situation of the comparatively small nations would be if there were not in existence the United States—if there were not this giant country prepared to make so many sacrifices."

In the days following World War II, Pope Pius the XII said, "The American people have a great genius for splendid and unselfish acts. Into the hands of America God has placed the destinies of an afflicted mankind."

We have kept our rendezvous with destiny. Thank you again.

Sincerely,
Ronald Reagan

THE MILITARY

Reagan's respect for those who serve in the military was great. In the first letter he explains how as president he came to return their salute. He wrote many letters expressing his respect and pride. His letters to Dorothy Nuese are especially eloquent in expressing his own feelings about his responsibilities as commander in chief.

Mr. Samuel B. Chelmer, Jr.
Albany, Georgia
October 16, 1981 [11]

Dear Mr. Chelmer:

Thank you very much for your letter of September 25th. It was kind of you to write and I'm most grateful. I have to confess returning the salute to the military was a little difficult at first. I tried nodding and speaking but they would continue to hold the salute. I was bound by my own previous military experience where I knew I was not supposed to return a salute if I were not on active duty or in civilian clothes. My arm would stiffen every time, almost automatically coming up, and then I would control it—but as I say it bothered me. Then one day when I'd only been in office a short time I mentioned this to a four-star Marine general and told him that maybe there should be a regulation that the commander in chief could return salutes even though he was in civilian clothes. The general very quietly said, "Mr. President, I think if you did it no one would complain." It dawned on me what he was saying, and from then on I started returning the salute. I want you to know it gives me as much pleasure as it does those young men I'm saluting and as much pleasure as your letter gave me in acknowledging this.

Thanks again and best regards,

Sincerely,
Ronald Reagan

Reagan replies to Dorothy Nuese, who wrote that her son, Ted, had enlisted in the military. "Thank you for taking the time to listen to the passions of a mother's heart," she

wrote. "And, please, will you be especially careful with the country just now?" Reagan
wrote again almost two years later to inquire about her son.

Mrs. Dorothy Nuese
Laurel, Iowa
September 29, 1981 [12]

Dear Mrs. Nuese:

I can't tell you how much your letter of August 6 has meant to me. Let me apologize for being so late in answering, but it does take some time for mail to reach my desk through all the wheels of the bureaucracy.

I shared your letter with Nancy. She cried, and I had quite a lump in my throat. We're parents, too, and we understand what you expressed so eloquently.

You must have done a fine job of raising that young man, and I agree with you—the government is getting a good deal. I told Nancy that when our own left the nest, it must have meant we did something right, for, certainly, it would be wrong if they didn't want to try their wings and get out on their own.

There are those who believe that men in uniform are somehow associated with starting wars. That's like saying policemen cause crime. Your son has joined what I called the peacemakers. Keeping the peace is the most important problem we face. And I believe that because young men like your son are willing to put on the uniform and endure the rigors of military life, peace is more secure.

I will be as careful with the country as I can. God bless you! Warm regards,

Sincerely,
Ronald Reagan

Mrs. Dorothy Nuese
Laurel, Iowa
April 26, 1983 [13]

Dear Mrs. Nuese:

It has been quite a while since you sat in that empty bedroom writing me of your son's departure. I've often thought about him and you and wondered how he's getting along and if he's happy with the choice he made. I hope he is. I don't know which branch he chose.

It is a gray rainy day here in Washington and I've been reading your letter again. I don't mean to impose but if you could find the time to write and let me know about your son I'd be most grateful. If you'd send the letter to me at the White House in care of Kathy Osborne (my secretary) I'd get it right away.

Best regards,
Ronald Reagan

Mrs. Dorothy Nuese
Laurel, Iowa
May 23, 1983 [14]

Dear Mrs. Nuese:

Thank you very much for your letter—correction—letters. I did enjoy both and appreciate your writing. I'm pleased to know Ted doesn't regret his decision. Your concern about a "militaristic point of view" is understandable but may I offer another view? The paradox of military training is that young men are taught a trade which we hope and pray they will never use. It is important that they take pride in what they are doing. The terms are esprit de corps and morale. Those things are very important. The better they know their trade, the higher their morale, the better are our chances of maintaining peace. They are truly the keepers of peace by virtue of their willingness to man the ramparts and by hard-won skills.

Well I didn't intend to write a lecture but I am so proud of all the young men like Ted and yes the young women in uniform. But rest assured with that pride goes increased determination to do everything I can to prevent their ever having to go to war.

I appreciate your concern and understanding with regard to the news media and what it is like on my side of their cameras and notepads. Sometimes it seems they are less interested in legitimate news than they are in proving their knowledge and wisdom is superior than ours. The most frustrating thing is when I have the facts to prove them wrong but can not reveal those facts without endangering security or wrecking some plan we're engaged in.

Thank you again and I wish you every success in your writing. Give my regards to Ted.

Sincerely,
Ronald Reagan

––––––––

The U.S. Marines invaded Grenada on October 25, 1983. Ted was stationed in Arizona.

Mrs. Dorothy Nuese
Laurel, Iowa
November 3, 1983 [15]

Dear Mrs. Nuese:

It was good to hear from you and to have your approval. I'm so proud right now of those young Americans in uniform I could burst. It seems that I've had a lump in my throat for the last several weeks.

I'm sure you'll be interested to know that in the closely guarded sessions where our military chiefs were planning the Grenada missions (and they only had hours to do so) their top priority was to minimize casualties. And this they were doing with no prompting from us.

I will be as careful of our country as I can. I remember making you that promise two years ago. Having to order those young men of the Rangers, the 82nd Airborne and the Marines into a combat situation was the hardest thing I've had to do since I've been here.

Again thanks for your understanding.

Sincerely,
Ronald Reagan

"I am a Vietnam Veteran," Mark Smith wrote, "and I want to thank you for the revitalization of the American soldier's image under your administration. . . . It means a great deal to me Mr. President that my country does not look with such scorn upon us." Smith was unemployed when he wrote but had confidence that "in a nation as great as this" things would change.

Mr. Mark L. Smith
Kenosha, Wisconsin
November 8, 1982 [16]

Dear Mr. Smith:

I'm sorry to be so late in answering your good letter but it takes a while before mail reaches my desk. Thank you for your generous words and believe me I do have faith in our people.

I share your joy at the turnaround we've made with regard to the military. There is pride again in the uniform by those who wear it and those who see it. I have always believed that you who served in Vietnam fought as bravely and as well as any Americans ever have in any war. And your cause was a just and noble one. Yours was not a failure, the failure was in a government that asked men to die for a cause the government was afraid to let them win.

I hope by the time you receive this your employment problem has been solved. If not yet I know it will be because the economy has turned upward.

Thanks again for writing.

Sincerely,
Ronald Reagan

GOVERNMENT AND GOVERNING

In these letters Reagan discusses his political philosophy and addresses a wide range of topics on government and governing. A few of the letters touch on how his views changed over the years.

Reagan defends his own principles against a charge of expediency from a woman who criticized the California governor for supporting Republican President Nixon,

who was running for a second term in 1972. He defends Nixon's record and argues
against the third-party alternative. It was a choice he would make again for himself
in 1975.

Mrs. H. R. Younginer
Barstow, California
Circa early 1972 [17]

Dear Mrs. Younginer:

I gave up a career I loved—certainly an affluence I could never hope to match
in public life—all at the very time point when I could have both my career and the
leisure to enjoy my hobby and sport (ranching) which I loved as much as my career.
I don't say this to complain or to ask for special consideration but to suggest for
your consideration that my decision to do what I'm doing must have been based on
some deep-seated convictions about the course our nation was taking.

Does it seem rational that I would make such a sacrifice and then for political
expediency go against those convictions? When my present term is up, I've made it
plain I'll not seek another. I've also made it plain I want no federal appointment. I
intend to serve as governor God willing through these next three years.

My beliefs are the beliefs I held when I first ran for this office, when I campaigned for Barry Goldwater in 1964, and for the years previous to that when, as a
citizen, I traveled coast-to-coast speaking on behalf of conservative principles. Indeed, I chose to continue speaking even when it meant the loss of my television
show.

This nation has never been in greater danger. Yes, our defenses are approaching
second best to Russia—yes, inflation has virtually driven us from the world markets we must have. Yes, government has a permanent structure—a bureaucracy so
huge and firmly entrenched that it has the power to override the decisions of
elected representatives.

Richard Nixon didn't cause this—he inherited it. He also inherited a Congress
catering to the "peace at any price" syndrome. He asked for a defense weapon, the
ABM. It passed Congress by one vote in the Senate—the vote of the vice president
who broke a tie. And that was for only one ABM, not a whole defense system such
as the Russians have.

Look at the attitude of Congress, the sabotage of his efforts by the bureaucracy,
and the communications media which seldom sees any threat from the left but
never misses a chance to downgrade the military or business or even our country.

Yes, there are things I might have chosen to do differently, but I still believe the
president has the same conservative philosophy he always had. He is maneuvering
for elbow room both in the economic situation and on the international scene.

The other day someone who shares your present feeling sent me some quotes
from Theodore Roosevelt. I admire "Teddy" greatly and quote him often. But these
were all statements urging that we think of country first rather than loyalty to some

particular president. Well, I agree with that. But Teddy made these statements during the campaign when he broke with the Republican Party and ran for president on the Bull Moose ticket. He didn't win and the Republican president didn't win—we elected Democrat Woodrow Wilson.

I believe there is a better chance to advance my conservative principles with a Republican president, even though I disagree with some of what he does. I believe we have a better chance to elect a conservative president in 1976 if he doesn't have to run against an incumbent Democrat. I believe this country could very well cease to exist as a free nation if one of the present Democrat challengers should be in charge for these next four years.

Sincerely,
Ronald Reagan

Reagan answers a variety of questions about government, economic policy, and foreign policy asked by a Republican Air Force captain who believed that Reagan was too much on the side of big business. The oil depletion allowance was a tax deduction for oil producers for oil taken out of the ground.

Captain Wayne P. Spiegel
APO San Francisco, California
Circa 1975 [18]

Dear Capt. Spiegel:

I'm sorry to be so late in answering your letter but I've been out doing the banquet circuit and it only just caught up with me. I appreciate your writing and giving me a chance to comment on the problems you posed.

You express concern about our party or at least those of our party who are in government taking a big business approach and not caring enough for individuals. I see it somewhat differently. In my opinion, the problem is a <u>big government</u> approach, and that is strictly a Democrat philosophy which we as Republicans should oppose.

We have turned to government more and more (for answers that could better be provided in the marketplace) until we have shackled business and industry with so many restrictions, nitpicking regulations and punitive taxes we can no longer compete in the world market. Thus, we can't expand industry to provide the jobs our people need.

Remember, business doesn't pay taxes—it collects them for government but it must pass those taxes on as part of the cost of production. So they end up in the price of the product with the customer paying them. When we make businesses collect too many, we price them out of the market. None of the other leading industrial nations do as much of this to their industries as we do. Let me finish this point by giving an illustration. A farmer raises wheat. If he can't get enough for his wheat to pay the property tax on his farm, he loses his farm. The wheat goes into a loaf of bread and the buyer of the loaf ends up paying that property tax. More than half the price of a loaf of bread is made up of 151 taxes that have accumulated between the wheat field and the grocer's shelf.

Incidentally this answers your question about the oil depletion allowance. Cancel it and they have to charge more for gasoline. That tax break, by the way, encourages more exploration for new sources of oil, about 90 percent of which is done by independents who couldn't afford the risk without it.

Now let me offer some answers to your other questions. Why $300 million in aid to Vietnam? Well, for one reason, we gave our word when we withdrew our own forces that we would replace, bullet for bullet, weapon for weapon, whatever South Vietnam had to expend to resist if North Vietnam violated the cease fire. North Vietnam violated it 72,000 times in the first 12 months. Now Congress has put our country in the position of breaking our pledged word to an ally. The dominoes are beginning to fall. The Philippines, a nation that we created, now says, in effect, they can no longer depend on us, so they make overtures to Red China. Japan has opened negotiations with Hanoi. Henry Kissinger returns from the Middle East empty handed because suddenly no one there is sure they can trust us and war again seems imminent when only a few months ago the United States was able to end a war and bring them closer to peace than at any time in half a century.

Why don't we impose wage and price controls? Because they don't work and never have. Hammurabi tried them in Babylon 5,000 years ago and they failed. Emperor Diocletian imposed them on Rome and almost bankrupted the empire. They distort the natural market forces, create shortages and end up with black markets supplying the people's needs at bootleg prices. England had them in effect following the Napoleonic wars and if it hadn't been for smugglers the people would have starved. The controls of 1971 are part of what caused our troubles today.

The answer to gas rationing is much the same. The increased cost of gasoline (the marketplace at work) has already brought about a reduction in use. We could do more if our government would appeal to the people to voluntarily quit wasteful use of oil products. We waste more than Japan's total consumption. The American people never have failed when they've been called upon to lend a hand. Right now though Washington is so d—n busy trying to impose rules and taxes no one has thought to ask the people to help.

Your question about economically and ecologically sound automobiles. Don't look to government for the solution—government is the problem. We are the only country manufacturing automobiles that turned to "add ons," pollution devices to filter out the smog. Other countries let their automakers try to come up with more efficient, cleaner burning cars. Our smog devices lowered engine performance and increased gas consumption. Who is to blame? The auto industry told government they could clean up the motors but it would take longer than the deadline allowed by government. Their arguments were ignored so their only recourse was to the wasteful smog control devices.

Your last question—when is the legislative branch of government going to quit conducting "witch hunts" and get down to solving the problems of the land? The answer to that is when more of them begin to worry about the next generation instead of the next election. Also when the American people begin riding herd better than we're doing now. In a recent poll less than half the people could name their U.S. congressman and of those who could 86 percent couldn't name a single thing he stood for. Government by the people only works if the people work at it.

Again my apologies for being so late and my thanks for giving me a chance to comment. A few of the answers might cause a little heat in future discussions.

Best regards,
Ronald Reagan

During his last days as governor of California, Reagan writes to the Cleavers about his eight years as governor and his plans for the future. He recalls Cleaver's judgment on the New Deal during Roosevelt's first term as president.

The Cleaver Family
Cape Girardeau, Missouri
December 16, 1974 [19]

Dear Friends:

I was so sorry to hear about Mabel's accident. I hope she is getting along without too much pain or distress. Please give her regards from Nancy and myself.

These are nostalgic times for us as we make plans to move back to Los Angeles. The house and my office get a little more bare each day as things are moved in preparation for our final departure. These have been eight wonderful years: challenging, exciting and yet with a sense of accomplishment that is most inwardly rewarding. My plans are going forward so that I can devote full time to writing, using radio and traveling about the country speaking on the philosophy I believe in and what must be done if we are to save this system of ours that has provided so much for so many. I remember once, many years ago when I was an ardent New Dealer during the first term of FDR, you remarked that we could not spend our way into prosperity. I thought you were wrong at the time. Now, from hindsight, I realize that we took a turning back there in 1932 that has led to our present troubles. I watch the present administration in Washington with a certain unease. There are indications they are going to continue the same old shopworn government panaceas. I believe the time is too late for that.

I don't know what the future may hold for me, but as I say, I intend to hit the sawdust trail and speak out on the issues of the day for whatever that's worth or whatever help it might be.

From all of us to all of you, a very Merry Christmas and a Happy New Year. I hope that one day my sawdust trail will take me to where you are.

Love,
Dutch

Reagan replies to a writer who thought his radio broadcasts should be taken off the air.
He expresses hope that she will listen in the next few weeks. The five radio addresses
Reagan mentions are all written in his own hand; they were taped March 23, 1977, for
airing the following month.

> Ms. Jamie Harrison
> Fayetteville, Tennessee
> Spring 1977[20]

Dear Ms. Harrison:

I have been informed of your complaint about my broadcasts and your suggestion they be taken off the air. I'm sorry you feel that way and hope you won't mind
my writing a few words in my own defense.

It is true a great many of my commentaries have to do with government policies, bureaucratic bungling and what Cicero called "the arrogance of officialdom."
I don't believe this is evidence of a "closed mind" as you suggest, and I assure you it
is not because of lack of love for country. Quite the contrary.

I believe in this system and don't believe it has ever failed us. We have failed it
many times. When a national poll reveals that only 46 percent of the people can
name their U.S. congressman and of those who know the name 86 percent can't tell
you anything more about him (how he votes, what he believes etc.), we are not
practicing government by the people. And we are failing the system.

I began my citizenship as a New Deal Democrat and only switched parties
when in my opinion the leadership of my party departed from the democratic traditions of states' rights, free trade and individual freedom.

In my lifetime, I have seen the permanent structure of government grow in
size, power and cost. From 26 people employed in the private sector for every one
public employee, we have gone to a ratio today of only four-and-a-half to one.
What is of greater concern is that only 70 million Americans work and earn in the
private sector to support themselves and their families but, through their taxes, also
support 81 million Americans who are totally dependent on tax dollars for their
year-round living. In 1930 governments—federal, state, and local—took ten cents
in taxes out of every dollar earned. Today, they take 44 cents—two-thirds of it for
Washington.

As governor of California I saw bureaucracy from the inside. In the "war on
poverty" I saw the federal government implement a multibillion-dollar program
to give work to the unemployed. One instance in our state was the hiring of 17
unemployed laborers to work in our parks. Half the total budget for that project,
however, went for 7 administrators to oversee the 17. We carried out the most
comprehensive welfare reform ever attempted in this country and in three years
saved the taxpayers two billion dollars while at the same time increasing the
grants to the truly needy by 43 percent. Every step of the way we were opposed by
the bureaucracy at HEW in Washington. They continue to ignore the reforms

which the present Democratic governor of California says are still proving successful.

Yes I try to call people's attention to new projects by bureaucrats which will further erode our freedom and increase government cost. President Lincoln said it is possible to be loyal to government and still be critical of those in power. You will never hear me assail our system or the Constitution. Summing it up I guess what I want is the same freedom for today's young people that I knew when I was growing up. I remember an America so respected in the world that an American caught in a war or revolution in another land could pin an American flag on his lapel and walk through the combat zone in perfect safety, his protection that tiny symbol of our country.

I hope you'll listen at least for the next few weeks because I'm doing a broadcast about our great generosity. Another about the difference between ourselves and Russia as to what we give medals for, and three broadcasts about the government of Chile.

Thanks for signing your letter and giving me a chance to respond.

Sincerely,
Ronald Reagan

Reagan responds to a writer who apparently proposed that senators be elected in national elections.

Mr. Ivan T. Collier
Bryan, Texas
Undated pre-presidential[21]

Dear Mr. Collier:

I found your suggestion very interesting and yet as I turned it over in my mind it had a drawback—at least in my opinion.

If you'll recall until about 1914 senators were appointed by state governments to represent the state in its relations with the federal government. The House of Representatives was elected by the people to represent the people as a whole. This was part of the process of federalism I mentioned in my talk. Senators were literally officers of their respective states representing their state's interests in the federation.

By constitutional amendment this was changed and they were elected by popular vote. Whether intended or not this resulted in the Senate becoming, in effect, a part of the national government rather than state officers.

I'm inclined to believe that electing them on a nationwide basis would further reduce states' rights and centralize more power in Washington.

It was good to be with you the other night. I really enjoyed meeting all of you.

Sincerely,
Ronald Reagan

Reagan responds to a critique of his performance on a television program and comments, in this letter and the next, on the labels used to characterize political views.

> Father Liederbach
> Cleveland, Ohio
> Undated pre-presidential[22]

Dear Father Liederbach:

Sometimes on a show like the Donahue program—with questions coming from the host, the audience and by telephone—I'm the first to admit one goes home thinking of and regretting lost opportunities. It's a little like that rejoinder you think of after the argument is over and your adversary is far away.

I have often addressed my fellow Republicans on the need to escape a false image carefully nurtured over the years by opponents. In doing this I have deplored the use of labels. In the first place, they have different meanings to different people. And yet, today, the common usage of those labels has become so fixed it's virtually impossible to reverse the trends.

Today's conservative is, of course, the true liberal—in the classic meaning of the word. But it is today's so-called liberal who did the switch on these two words. He affixed the title conservative on those who opposed his affinity for centralized authority and a big government as the answer to all problems.

We Republicans do have a problem with labels. What do we do now that the leading polls indicate the majority of Americans (including Democrats and Independents) express a preference, whether they use the title or not, for the things called conservative. But those same polls say the title causing our party the most trouble is the word Republican. I don't know what we can do about that.

I very much appreciate your writing me and wish we could all discuss issues without the distortion created by doing so in the context of labels.

> Sincerely,
> Ronald Reagan

Reagan explains the sources backing his statements about political trends in the electorate.

> Miss Donna Mosher
> Norman, Oklahoma
> Late 1970[23]

Dear Miss Mosher:

The basis for my remarks have been a number of polls and surveys which indicate the conservatism of citizens when asked questions about the solutions to the major problems. These plus a few election results—such as the record-breaking

Republican landslide in 1972 when millions of Democrats obviously rejected the outspoken liberalism of McGovern as a candidate.

In 1964, when Goldwater ran for President, openly advocating conservatism, he was, in effect, bucking the trend. About 76 percent of the electorate believed the federal government was the best agency for solving our social and economic problems. Today, polls show that only 36 percent subscribe to that belief.

In 1972, the Political Science Department at Georgetown University polled the delegates to the Republican and Democratic conventions on their answers to the problems of crime, welfare, unemployment, etc. Naturally, the delegates were poles apart. But, when they polled the rank-and-file party membership of each party, they found the Democrats more in line with the Republican leaders (convention delegates) than with their own.

In January of 1975, Opinion Research of Princeton found 59 percent of union members favored "right to work" laws. With their families included, it was 62 percent. By similar majorities, they disagreed with union leadership on union participation in politics and thought their leaders were too powerful. On common situs [picketing], 57 percent were against such a bill. They believed a union should only be allowed to picket the contractor with whom they have a dispute—not the entire construction job.

The Communication Workers of America in Wyoming, a union very liberal, to say the least—some call it "left wing"—polled its membership on several issues and were completely surprised by the results. On gun control, 85 percent were against it; 74 percent against national health insurance; 91 percent favored the death penalty and 96 percent believed able-bodied welfare recipients should be made to work in return for their welfare grants.

I hope this will be of some help to you. Tell your father I, too, am concerned about our party's name. The problem, though, is that, under the new election laws, a change of name could be interpreted as a new party. In that case, there would be a question about eligibility for matching funds in 1980.

Best regards,
Ronald Reagan

Ben Shaw was the publisher of the Dixon Evening Telegraph.

Ben T. Shaw
Dixon, Illinois
May 10, 1979 [24]

Dear Ben:

Thanks very much for sending me your good editorial. As usual you have put your finger on a very real problem. The permanent structure of our government with its power to pass regulations has eroded if not in effect repealed portions of our Constitution.

I have been speaking particularly in my talks around the country about the 10th article of the Bill of Rights. The federal government is performing functions that are not specified in the Constitution and those functions should be returned to the states and to the people. Of course the tax sources to fund them should also be turned back.

Again my thanks to you and best regards,

Sincerely,
Ron

———

Reagan responds to a complaint about a campaign fundraising event for which ticket prices were high.

Mr. Dutton
November 1979[25]

Dear Mr. Dutton:

I appreciate very much your letter and your expression of support. I know how you feel with regard to the recent appearance in Boston of Dean Martin and Frank Sinatra, and yet I don't know that I have an answer to the problem that you mentioned. With the strict limitation on soliciting contributions now imposed on candidates by the government, raising sufficient funds to campaign is extremely difficult. One of the remaining loopholes by which money can be raised is the benefit performance by well-known entertainment personalities. With the seating limited to a theater and the limited time such personalities can give to benefit performances, one is forced to try to reap the harvest from those who can make major contributions. The alternative would be if the entertainer could donate several weeks of time and normal theatrical prices then could be charged for a long run of appearances and you would come out with approximately the same net contribution. Unfortunately, these people haven't the time to do it in this way.

As I said, I know I don't have a satisfactory answer for you and can only express my regret. I hope there will be an opportunity for you to see Dean in person, but I'm afraid it won't be possible at either a political or charitable benefit. On such occasions, the scaling of tickets is usually aimed at those who can contribute a rather sizeable amount.

On the other hand, maybe one day some sanity will return to government, and some of the more repressive campaign laws will be repealed. Experiencing them from the inside as a candidate, I can assure you they are not very helpful to the democratic process—namely in allowing the candidates to get their message to the greatest number of people.

Again, thanks for writing.

Best regards,
Ronald Reagan

H. E. Chiles was a Reagan supporter from Texas who wrote that the "financial plight" of the nation called for a declaration of emergency. By February of 1983 the economy was recovering from the recession and many economic indicators were turning up— and Reagan disagreed with Chiles.

Mr. H. E. Chiles
Fort Worth, Texas
February 10, 1983 [26]

Dear Eddie:

It was good to hear from you and I appreciate having the full quote you sent me. I've known of that quote but didn't have it in its entirety. It will be useful.

Your words about it being too late to play politics are right on target and I must say there are signs that our opponents are aware of that. There may be a little sounding off now and then but I believe we're going to have some unaccustomed bipartisanship on a number of matters having to do with the economy.

Eddie I don't believe the president has the power to declare an emergency short of war. One of our problems is the extent to which Congress has reduced presidential powers. This is particularly true in the budgeting process. I don't believe there is a state in the union with a budget system as Mickey Mouse as that of the federal government. What I wouldn't give to have a majority in both houses. Believe me I dream of making some fundamental reforms before I leave this place.

I'm greatly encouraged by the recent economic indicators, especially the increase in employment and the drop in the unemployment rate. Both housing, and autos have turned up. Now don't tag me as excessively optimistic or whistling past the graveyard. I'll keep my feet on the ground and we are tapping the private sector for input. Paul V[olcker] is cooperating. Granted we have a long way to go but I think the start has come.

Inflation averaged out at 3.9 percent for '82 but in the last three months it ran at an annualized rate of 1.1 percent. Real wages went up 1.8 percent for the year but again the last three months the annualized rate of increase was 3½ percent.

Again let me thank you for writing as you did and please let me have your ideas and your thinking.

Love to Fran.

Sincerely,
Ron

RELIGION

Behind Reagan's view of America as a special place was his religious faith. His letters make clear that he believed in the Bible, the power of intercessory prayer, and the existence of an afterlife.

Mrs. Warne
Circa 1967[27]

Dear Mrs. Warne:

I'm not sure I understand your definition of the terms you used so let me simply answer your questions in my own way.

I believe the Bible is the result of Divine inspiration and is <u>not</u> just a history. I believe in it.

I was raised in the Christian Church which as you know believes in baptism when the individual has made his own decision to accept Jesus. My decision was made in my early teens.

I hope this answers your questions.

Best regards,
Ronald Reagan

———

Reagan responds to a critique of one of his radio addresses, "Christmas," taped January 9, 1978. The commentary was a retrospective on the 1977 Christmas season in which Reagan lamented the tendency to minimize the divinity of Jesus and concluded that the effect of Jesus on the world is a miracle that cannot be explained "unless he really was what he said he was"—the promised Messiah, the Son of God.[28]

The Reverend Thomas H. Griffith
Shell Beach, California
March 1, 1978[29]

Dear Reverend Griffith:

I appreciate your taking the time and trouble to write as you did regarding my radio commentaries. It would seem, however, that we are epitomizing the theological debate I spoke of on the air. While I do not pretend to be a theologian, I do have a deep-seated religious belief and have frequent contact with theologians of some stature, including my own pastor, Donn Moomaw.

My difficulty in understanding your own view of Jesus does not come from a "limited Sunday school level theology." Perhaps it is true that Jesus never used the word "Messiah" with regard to himself (although I'm not sure that he didn't) but in John 1, 10 and 14 he identifies himself pretty definitely and more than once.

Is there really any ambiguity in his words: "I am the way, the truth and the life: no man cometh unto the Father but by me?" Then he said, "In my Father's house are many mansions. If it were not so, I would have told you. I go to prepare a place for you." In John 10 he says, "I am in the Father and the Father in me." And he makes reference to being with God, "before the world was," and sitting on the "right hand of God." [30]

I realize, of course, that you are familiar with these words of Jesus. These and other statements he made about himself, foreclose in my opinion, any question as to his divinity. It doesn't seem to me that he gave us any choice; either he was what he said he was or he was the world's greatest liar. It is impossible for me to believe a liar or charlatan could have had the effect on mankind that he has had for 2000 years. We could ask, would even the greatest of liars carry his lie through the crucifixion, when a simple confession would have saved him?

I could refer to the scores and scores of prophecies in the Old Testament made several hundred years before his birth (all of which were realized in his life). You, of course, could answer that, as a Jew he was aware of those prophecies. But, then again, wouldn't we be describing the act of a faker? Did he allow us the choice you say that you and others have made, to believe in his teachings but reject his statements about his own identity?

Again my thanks for your letter and for allowing me to state my case.

Sincerely,
Ronald Reagan

Reagan expresses his confidence that what happens—in this case, his loss of the 1976 nomination—is part of God's plan.

Mrs. Van Voorhis
Circa 1976 [31]

Dear Mrs. Van Voorhis:

Thank you and Jeff and Mr. Van Voorhis for your wonderful warm letter and Christmas greeting. It was good to hear from you although I'm sorry to hear Jeff hasn't been feeling well.

I appreciate your good wishes about the campaign but it's nice to have it over with. Toward the end it became a little muddier than it started and it started pretty messy. It was hard not to reply in kind.

Whether it is this job or whether it is early training from long ago now just becoming clear, I find myself believing very deeply that God has a plan for each of us. Some with little faith and even less testing seem to miss in their mission, or else we perhaps fail to see the imprint on the lives of others. But bearing what we cannot change, going on with what God has given us, confident there is a destiny, somehow seems to bring a reward we wouldn't exchange for any other. It takes a lot of fire and heat to make a piece of steel.

Merry Christmas to all of you and a Happy New Year.

Sincerely,
Ronald Reagan

Herman Kahn was a futurist and author of the book On Thermonuclear War; *he died on July 8, 1983. Armageddon is the location of the final battle between the forces of good and evil foretold in the Bible.*

Mr. and Mrs. Peter D. Hannaford
Los Angeles, California
February 10, 1983 [32]

Dear Irene and Pete:

Thank you very much for my birthday gift *Horses and Americans* *—I love it and will treasure it. Thanks too for your good wishes.

Pete I got the Herman Kahn article—very interesting and in many ways informative. Lately I've been wondering about some older prophesies—those having to do with Armageddon. Things that are news today sound an awful lot like what was predicted would take place just prior to "A" Day. Don't quote me.

Again thanks to you both.

Sincerely,
Ron

The Cleavers were the parents of Reagan's high-school sweetheart, Margaret; Helen was Margaret's older sister. Reagan often recounted learning to look up instead of behind him when faced with a difficult decision.

The Reverend and Mrs. Ben H. Cleaver
Cape Girardeau, Missouri
January 4, 1973 [33]

Dear Friends:

It was a joy to receive your Christmas greeting and good wishes for the years ahead, but most particularly, your generous words. Helen, if I'd been able to get that kind of grade from you in French, I wouldn't have needed an interpreter last

---

* The book was probably by Philip Duffield Stong (Garden City, NY: Garden City Publishing, 1946). It includes 103 illustrations from old prints and photographs. An earlier edition was published in New York in 1939 by Frederick A. Stokes.

summer in Paris. But then, I didn't deserve any better grade than I got and I worry about whether I deserve the grade you've all just given me.

One thing I do know—all the hours in the old church in Dixon (which I didn't appreciate at the time) and all of Nelle's faith, have come together in a kind of inheritance without which I'd be lost and helpless. During my first months in office, when day after day there were decisions that had to be made, I had an almost irresistible urge—really a physical urge—to look over my shoulder for someone I could pass the problem on to. Then without my quite knowing how it happened, I realized I was looking in the wrong direction. I started looking up instead and have been doing so for quite awhile now. My faith is unshakable, and because all of you were so much responsible, I thank you for a peace beyond description.

> Love,
> Dutch

Steve Bollinger died in 1984 while serving as assistant secretary for community planning and development in the Department of Housing and Urban Development (HUD). A letter of condolence from the President and Mrs. Reagan was read at his funeral. Paul Bollinger sent Reagan a draft of a letter Steve was writing to the president found in Steve's desk at HUD after he died. The letter expressed understanding of the difficulties of deciding to run for office when one's life was threatened, an experience Steve had had when running for local public office in Ohio.

> Mr. Paul F. Bollinger, Jr.
> Washington, D.C.
> July 17, 1984 [34]

Dear Mr. Bollinger:

Thank you very much for your letter of July 3rd. Thank you too for sending the draft of Steve's letter. It means a great deal to me. His loved ones have been in our thoughts and prayers.

The other day I read a verse—author unknown, which seemed to me a most comforting thought for those who have said goodbye to a loved one or friend.

The poet wrote of seeing a ship, all sails set, put out to sea. As he watched the ship grew smaller and smaller and finally was entirely out of sight. It was gone. But then he said somewhere else the ship was coming into view just as large and real as when he'd watched it sail away. It was not gone it had just gone to another place beyond our sight.

It was the poet's explanation of death. I'm sure Steve has gone to another place—the better place we've all been promised.

Thanks again.

> Sincerely,
> Ronald Reagan

The quotation from President Abraham Lincoln used in the following letter was one of Reagan's favorites, kept on a handwritten four-by-six-inch card in his desk. Sister Mary wrote to congratulate him on his reelection.

Sister Mary Ignatius, DMJ
Rancho Palos Verdes, California
November 26, 1984[35]

Dear Sister Mary Ignatius:

Nancy and I are deeply grateful for your warm letter and card congratulating us on having our option taken up. We are, as always, even more grateful for your prayers in our behalf. I believe in intercessory prayer and know I have benefited from it. I have, of course, added my own prayers to the point that sometimes I wonder if the Lord doesn't say, "here he comes again."

Abe Lincoln once said that he would be the most stupid human on this footstool called Earth if he thought for one minute he could fulfill the obligations of the office he held without help from one who was wiser and stronger than all others. I understand what he meant completely—and if that is mixing politics and religion then it is a good and proper mix.

Again, you have our heartfelt thanks.

Sincerely,
Ronald Reagan

READING, WRITING, AND SPEAKING

This section comprises a variety of letters that give an indication of Reagan's reading habits as well as his writing process. He describes his early reading in a letter to Helen Miller of the Dixon Public Library on page 7. As an adult Reagan read a wide range of books, newspapers, and magazines as well as the correspondence that arrived daily— in addition to the briefing papers and decision memoranda that constituted the routine documents of his jobs in government. He sent occasional copies of articles to cabinet members and staff with a brief note.

The library at Reagan's ranch included many books on the American West, California's natural and political history, and horse training and breeding. But it also included titles such as The Great Democracies *(Winston Churchill),* The Future of American Politics *(Samuel Lubell),* The Kennedy Promise: The Politics of Expectation *(Henry Fairlie),* Keynes at Harvard: Economic Deception as Political Credo *(Zygmund Dobbs),* Leaders and Battles: The Art of Military Leadership *(W. J. Wood), and* The Works of Epictetus *(Thomas Wentworth Higginson).**

---

* Inventory done by Young America's Foundation—Reagan Ranch, Santa Barbara, California.

*The abundance of handwritten drafts of radio addresses and speeches from the
1970s bears witness to Reagan's own claims in this correspondence that he was his own
primary speech writer, but a few letters, included here, elaborate. Even during his presidency drafts of many important speeches and addresses from the Oval Office exist in
his own hand.*

Reading

National Review *was founded by William F. Buckley Jr.; the first issue was published November 1955.*[36] *Reagan read it regularly from its founding through his presidency.*

*In its early years subscribers were asked for contributions to make up losses.
Reagan wrote this letter shortly after the* General Electric Theater *was cancelled.
Later that year Reagan was to become host of the television series* Death Valley
Days.

> William F. Buckley Jr.
> New York, New York
> June 16, 1962[37]

Dear Bill:

I'm a little concerned about addressing you so informally since JFK gave you
billing in his commencement address. An honorary degree yet! Frank Merriwell
must have turned over on the library shelf.*

Bill I did receive your earlier letter and should have written and told you
what now must be said. My interest has not waned and I'd be lost without *National Review* but at the same time I'm out of a job. Even though the *GE Theater* continues on through the summer (reruns) I've been sans income for a time
and will be until I'm rediscovered. Unfortunately I'm one of those who didn't get in
on the "gimmick" deals—it's always been straight salary with me—hence high
bracket.

Please consider me still a supporter but in theater parlance, "temporarily between engagements" (I write the word temporarily with fingers crossed—not an
easy task). I'll rejoin the ranks when I can.

> Best Regards,
> Ronnie

---

*In a May 23, 1966, letter William Vandersteel, president of the Ampower Corporation,
expressed confidence that Reagan could win the presidency in 1968 and enclosed a
pamphlet by Ayn Rand titled "Conservatism: An Obituary" written after the 1960*

---

* John F. Kennedy gave the commencement address and accepted an honorary degree at Yale on June
11, 1962. Frank Merriwell is the fictional hero of *Frank Merriwell at Yale* by Burt L. Standish.

presidential campaign. In the essay Rand argues that many conservatives are opposed
to statism but don't seem to realize the only good alternative is capitalism.*

William Vandersteel
New York, New York
May 23, 1966 [38]

Dear Mr. Vandersteel:

    Thanks very much for pamphlet. Am an admirer of Ayn Rand but hadn't seen
this study.

Sincerely,
Ronald Reagan

Richard G. Hubler, co-author of Reagan's first autobiography, Where's the Rest of Me?
*recommended a book on the fall of the Roman empire† after a Reagan speech on the
subject was criticized in* Time *(October 31, 1969). Reagan replies.*

Mr. Richard G. Hubler
Ojai, California
Late 1969 [39]

Dear Dick:

    I've obtained the book. Thanks for the tip and for your good letter. My speech
was based on some writings of Robert Strausz-Hupé so I figured it couldn't be
far off.

    Hey! How about that royalty check we just received? That was a happy surprise.

Best regards,
Ron

---

*Reagan writes to thank Henry Salvatori, a California supporter, for Harvard professor
Edward Banfield's book about problems of the inner cities.*

Mr. Henry Salvatori
Los Angeles, California
Circa August 1971 [40]

Dear Henry:

    At last I've gotten into the book *The Unheavenly City.* Thanks for sending it. I
haven't finished it yet, but am far enough to know I'm in agreement. We tend to

---

* The pamphlet was based on a lecture given December 7, 1960, at Princeton University and republished
in Ayn Rand, *Capitalism: The Unknown Ideal* (New York: New American Library, 1966), pp. 193–203.
† Hubler recommended Sir Samuel Dill's *Roman Society in the Last Century of the Western Empire* (second edition, 1899), Book III, chapter 2, pp. 245–81.

accept these charges and statistics without bothering to learn if they are really true.

I told the president the other day we ought to find out if the unemployment rate is really as bad as it's painted. I've done some study on this one and know the Department of Labor staffers can shade it up or down just in the manner they take the poll. Unemployment is not determined by a head count, but by a poll in some 30-odd selected districts.

Again thanks, and I hope we see each other soon. Love to Gracie.

Sincerely
Ron

Reagan thanks Blanche Seaver, a California supporter, for a subscription to the weekly conservative newspaper Human Events. *In 1983 he would call it "a paper I read regularly" in a letter to Sylvia Kinyoun (p. 598) in which he responded to her letter to the editor published in that newspaper.*[41]

Mrs. Frank R. Seaver
Los Angeles, California
During governorship[42]

Dear Blanche:

Nancy and I are so grateful for the subscription to *Human Events*. It was kind of you and we've already found it interesting and informative.

I hope we'll be seeing each other soon and again our heartfelt thanks.

Sincerely,
Ron

Allen Drury wrote novels about Washington politics. Two of his books, Mark Coffin, U.S.S.: A Novel of Capitol Hill *and* The Hill of Summer: A Novel of the Soviet Conquest, *were published in 1981.*

Mr. Allen Drury
Tiburon, California
July 15, 1981[43]

Dear Allen:

I have waited to answer your good letter of June 1 until I could complete reading your book.

First of all, let me thank you for that and for the inscription. It will go on the shelf in the White House library, but it took me a while to read it because most of my own personal reading is limited to that last brief period before the lights go out after I've done all the "homework" I bring home with me. Sometimes I've had to force myself to turn out the light. I enjoyed that book so much. You know, when I read all the others, I was, of course, an outsider in Washington. It was quite something to read this one here in the White House where I have the problems faced by the principal in your book. Nancy is now going to get a chance to read it, but I told her I had to read it first because I was learning how to be president. I very much feel you have come close to the truth as to what perhaps my problems will be.

Now, however, let me comment on the other reading; your letter, which I have just finished reading again. As you know, I have twice been a visitor to Taiwan, met with President Chiang and, before him, his father the Generalissimo. Some of the names you mentioned are familiar to me. I was, of course, greatly disturbed by the Carter move. I think it was unnecessary and that he could have obtained an improved relationship with the PRC [People's Republic of China] without betraying our longtime friend and ally. I am going to continue a policy of trying to improve relations with the PRC but in no way at the expense of Taiwan. I have taken steps not to downgrade but to increase the relationship between our two countries in that we have communication at high levels with the Taiwan commission, once the Embassy, here. The information you have given me in your letter is going to be most helpful to me, particularly with those diplomat types whose first instinct is to look for a way out.

Nancy sends her very best regards and, again, I thank you for your book and for your letter.

Sincerely,
Ron

Reagan thanks Jeffrey Hart for his book, When the Going was Good! American Life in the Fifties, *but notes that it takes time, given his other responsibilities, to get through a book. Tony Dolan was a White House speechwriter; Hart had worked on Reagan speeches in 1968.*

Mr. Jeffrey Hart
Hanover, New Hampshire
October 6, 1982 [44]

Dear Jeff:

A belated thank you for the book delivered by Tony Dolan. I should of course be able to give you a review but I'm not that far into it. I've learned in this job that reading a book is a longtime undertaking with frequent and lengthy interruptions. But I've gotten far enough to know I like it and I thank you. I did cheat a little and find my picture, but my reading is aimed at cover to cover, slow though my progress is.

Jeff, I hope you won't accept some of the press and media interpretations of my record as based on fact. I'm unchanged philosophically and with regard to my determination to accomplish what we set out to do.

Again thanks and I'll keep reading.

> Sincerely,
> Ron

———

The Baltimore Sun, *a Washington-area newspaper, inquired in June 1984 about the books Reagan was reading. He wrote out a list.*

Marlin Fitzwater, who became Reagan's press secretary on February 2, 1987, suggested to Reagan that he provide such information regularly, but the president declined. Political biographies were a favorite genre.[45]

> *Baltimore Sun*
> June 26, 1984[46]

The Rise of the Right
William Rusher

The Africans
By David Lamb

The Turning Point: Jefferson's Battle for the Presidency
Frank Van Der Linden

The Third World War
General Sir John Hackett

Dezinformatsia
By Richard Shultz and Roy Godson

———

Norman Sprague was a medical doctor and a donor to colleges and universities in southern California.

> Dr. and Mrs. Norman F. Sprague Jr.
> Los Angeles, California
> August 13, 1984[47]

Dear Erlenne and Norman:

Thank you very much for sending me the Louis L'Amour book. You can bet I'll read it. I'm a L'Amour fan and didn't know he'd done a non-Western. You were more than kind to think of me.

Thanks too for your kind words.

> Warmest friendship
> Sincerely,
> Ron

————

Reagan began his daily newspaper reading with the cartoons and may have checked out the astrology columns as well.

Mr. Jeff MacNelly
April 18, 1984 [48]

Dear Mr. MacNelly:

Thank you very much for your gift of an original cartoon. Believe me I shall treasure it always. You'd have no way of knowing this but I am a cartoon aficionado up to and including reading the complete comics every morning. Along with that comes the editorial page for the cartoons—not the editorials.

Again my heartfelt thanks.

Sincerely,
Ronald Reagan

Miss Belva Clement
April 14, 1980 [49]

Dear Miss Clement:

When I made the remark about jinxing the rest of my campaign, I suppose I was admitting that, from my years in athletics and as a sports announcer, I have some of the foibles that go with that activity—ballplayers having a lucky glove and that sort of thing. I just have a feeling that to say or indicate that you think you're going to win is kind of tempting fate.

With regard to your question about astrology, I have to tell you I don't know. I would not say that I am a great believer, and yet, at the same time, I cannot deny evidence that would indicate that there might be something to it. I guess the word from me is I am an agnostic where astrology is concerned. I don't believe I'm really superstitious.

Best regards,
Ronald Reagan

————

Calvin Coolidge, thirtieth president of the United States, was a favorite of Reagan's. Shortly after he took office Reagan hung Coolidge's portrait in the Cabinet Room.*

———————————

* Peter Hannaford, ed., *The Quotable Calvin Coolidge: Sensible Words for a New Century* (Bennington, Vermont: Images from the Past, 2001), p. vii.

Mr. James M. Huntley
White River Junction, Vermont
January 29, 1985[50]

Dear Mr. Huntley:

Thank you very much for sending me the copy of Calvin Coolidge's Christmas Greeting of 1927.* I'm delighted to have it. I happen to be an admirer of "Silent Cal" and believe he has been badly treated by history. I've done considerable reading and researching of his presidency. He served this country very well and accomplished much before speaking the words, "I do not choose to run."

Again, my thanks.

Sincerely,
Ronald Reagan

On March 5, 1982, Irina Ratushinskaya, a dissident Russian poet born in the Ukraine, was sentenced to seven years' hard labor and an additional five years of internal exile for "agitation carried on for the purpose of subverting or weakening the Soviet regime."[51] She and her husband were allowed to leave the Soviet Union for London in December 1986, just after the October 11–12, 1986, Reykjavik summit. She came to the United States in 1987.

The Reverend Dr. Richard Rodgers
Birmingham, England
November 12, 1986[52]

Dear Rev. Rodgers:

Thank you for sending me the book *No, I'm Not Afraid* by Irina Ratushinskaya. You were very kind and I'm most grateful.

Quite some time ago I received by way of our U.S. Information Agency a letter from a Soviet labor camp. It was handwritten and so tiny, (only 4 inches in width and three quarters of an inch from top to bottom) that it must have been interpreted by using a powerful glass. It was in Russian but an English version was provided by those who saw that the smuggled letter reached me. It was a letter congratulating me on my election. It contained 47 words plus the salutation and the signatures of 10 women prisoners. Accompanying it was a 4 inch by 4 inch handmade chart—the same tiny writing, the record of the hunger strikes by the ten women between August 1983 and through December 1984.

---

* The Christmas greeting read "To the American People: Christmas is not a time or a season, but a state of mind. To cherish peace and good will, to be plenteous in mercy, is to have the real spirit of Christmas. If we think on these things, there will be born in us a Savior and over us will shine a star sending its gleam of hope to the world.—Calvin Coolidge."

As I read Irina's book something prompted me to get out this letter. The ten signatories are the women Irina writes about in her book including herself of course. I'm sure you can understand what meaning the book has to me now. Thank you for your great kindness.

Sincerely,
Ronald Reagan

Writing

No handwritten draft has been found of Reagan's most famous pre-presidential speech—the one for Barry Goldwater on October 27, 1964, called "A Time for Choosing." But on June 22, 1966, Sue Ragland Diggle of Dallas, Texas, who had met Reagan on the movie set of The Winning Team *in 1952, wrote to tell him that she heard him make the Goldwater speech. "I don't know whether or not you wrote it," she said, "nor do I care, but it was the finest speech I ever heard and you delivered it magnificently." Reagan's handwritten note on Diggle's letter says simply: "I wrote it."* [53]

Reagan wrote an article for National Review *published in the December 1, 1964, issue about the Republican defeat in the election. "We lost a battle in the continuing war for freedom," he said, "but our position is not untenable."*

Mr. William F. Buckley Jr.
New York, New York
November 10, 1964 [54]

Dear Bill:

Just a line to apologize for the enclosed article as per your wire. I know longhand is a curse to editors but your deadline and the weekend are just too close together.

Hope this is o.k. but know definitely it isn't up to the high standards of *National Review.*

Nancy sends regards.

Sincerely,
Ronnie

Reagan describes his speechwriting to William Loeb.

Mr. William Loeb
Manchester, New Hampshire
Circa 1978 [55]

Dear Mr. Loeb:

Thank you so much for sending the inscribed calendar. Would you please convey my thanks to Jack Frost and tell him when the calendar is out of date I'll keep his drawings. They are magnificent.

I appreciate also your editorials and understand your criticism very well. In fact, I'm in agreement about speeches that are read.

Actually, I had no written copy and was working from handwritten notes which I had worked on during the plane trip and the drive over to New Hampshire. At the risk of sounding as if I'm building an alibi, my problem was new material and difficulty in seeing my notes in the light provided at the podium.

That really does sound like an alibi but unfortunately it is true. You know when you can take a speech on the road and use the same theme to audience after audience (and I've had that experience in years past) it is possible to achieve a great freedom from notes. You can also hone and polish the original draft.

In this job, though, it seems as if I'm always having to come up with a new speech on a different subject. The night before I left California I addressed a national convention of construction engineers. In Washington, two nights before New Hampshire it was the Touchdown Club, and by the end of the week the Alfalfa Club and the American Conservative Union.

Nancy gives me h—l because I won't get a speechwriter and just go with someone's canned product but I've been on the mashed potato circuit so long doing my own I just can't be comfortable with someone else's words.

Anyway, give my regards to Mrs. Loeb and again thanks to you. It was a pleasure visiting with you and I look forward to our paths crossing again.

Sincerely,
Ron

―――――――

Reagan turns down John McClaughry's request for a speechwriting job, stating that he usually digs up his own facts as well as doing the writing. Reagan used the Winthrop quotation mentioned in this letter in his November 13, 1979, announcement speech; Reagan's use of the same quotation in his handwritten draft of a radio address taped on August 7, 1978, does not capitalize "pilgrims."

John McClaughry was a writer from Vermont; he later served on Reagan's domestic policy staff, headed by Martin Anderson.

John McClaughry
After November 13, 1979 [56]

Dear John:

I guess you have caught me! I quoted exactly from the essay about Tom Paine so should not have trusted the essayist. I will drop freezing at Valley Forge and make it a little more accurate in the future.

As to the John Winthrop quote, you of course, and I suppose properly, capitalized Pilgrims. I had simply used pilgrims with a small "p" meaning any group of people who are embarked on a journey such as those who first came to this country. I just hadn't given thought to the fact that it might be translated to the particular group that were called Pilgrims among our Founding Fathers. I appreciate your catching me up on that, and I will simply refer to them as a little band of travelers or whatever from now on.

With regard to the speeches, John, I appreciate very much your offer although I don't know how much work there would be on the longer-term basis. You see for most of the years I have been speaking, I have been the speechwriter. I have always dug up my own facts and material and done my own speechwriting. Now and then in a campaign such as this, obviously, I cannot do it all myself so a number of people have from time to time volunteered or have been asked to do a kind of framework speech which I then have taken and made my own. This does not mean that I wouldn't welcome help in this regard. I would hate to impose upon you for a draft of a speech you've kindly offered knowing that there wouldn't be too many opportunities for future writing on a professional basis. Let me have someone in our group get in touch with you to talk about the issues we're stressing for Republican audiences—aiming at primaries, of course, and then whatever you decide, knowing all that I've told you, will certainly be all right with me. But again let me thank you very much for your kindness in volunteering to do this.

Best regards,
Ron

Reagan thanks a correspondent, a minister at St. Giles Presbyterian Church, for informing him about the identity of a speaker who encouraged the signing of the Declaration of Independence—Jonathan Witherspoon.

Dr. Alf Graham Taylor
Greenville, South Carolina
August 3, 1981 [57]

Dear Dr. Taylor:

I'm sorry to be so late in answering your letter, but the mail in the White House does not always get through the various channels to my desk in a hurry.

I want to thank you for your kind words about my statement on the 4th of July. I also want to thank you very much for the information about Dr. Witherspoon. I have used that full quote for a number of years under the impression that speaker was never named or known and even that he had entered the hall without anyone knowing who he was or how he got there. I am very pleased to have the more accurate information you have provided. If I use it again or, I think I should say when I do, I'll be pleased to now give full credit and recognition.

Thank you again for your generous words.

Best regards,
Ronald Reagan

Reagan, by his own admission, did not know how to type.

Miss Linda Cave
Undated pre-presidential[58]

Dear Linda:

Thanks for your good letter and congratulations on your grades. I'm happy I was a part of it.

Don't feel too bad about the typing—I can't even type, "Now is the time for all good men to come to the aid of the party." In fact I can't type at all.

Again thanks for using me as a subject and for your very nice letter.

Sincerely,
Ronald Reagan

Here Reagan comments on the differences between the spoken and written word.

Miss Cahill
Undated pre-presidential[59]

Dear Miss Cahill:

Thanks very much for sending me the transcript although, I'll confess, I hope no one else ever sees it in its raw state. I'm continually shocked (by this time I shouldn't be) to find how much we punctuate by inflection, gesture and expression in ordinary conversation. Then when it is transcribed in cold print, it appears almost incoherent with unfinished or broken sentences, interjections, etc.

Some years ago, a few unfriendly reporters used to print such verbatim paragraphs from President Eisenhower's press conferences. He, of course, read as virtually illiterate—when, in truth, his replies to questions, when heard aloud, made very good sense.

Even making allowances for all of this, I'm still not sure I was of much help to you. It was nice to see you and I wish you well with your undertaking.

Sincerely,
Ronald Reagan

CHAPTER NINE

Economic Policy

W HEN REAGAN *became president in January 1981, the economy was not in good shape. Inflation and unemployment were both high; so were interest rates. The consumer price index had increased 13.3 percent in 1979 and 12.4 percent in 1980. Banks were charging their best customers 20.5 percent for short-term loans, and the mortgage rate on a new home was over 13 percent. Unemployment was 7.4 percent of the labor force and economic growth was sluggish.[1] Price controls on energy had left people waiting in lines at gas pumps.*

Reagan moved immediately on his program for economic recovery—controlling spending, cutting taxes, reducing regulation, and lowering inflation.

A revised budget for fiscal 1982 with spending reductions in many programs and tax cut proposals was sent to the Congress.* A series of meetings was set up with the chairman of the Federal Reserve Board of Governors, Paul Volcker, to express support for a stable and sound monetary policy that would bring down inflation. On the deregulation front, Reagan decontrolled, by executive order, production prices of crude oil and refined petroleum products, setting in motion further decontrol of energy prices. He established a task force on regulatory relief and created an outside advisory board of distinguished economists, headed by George P. Shultz, that included Milton Friedman, Alan Greenspan, and Arthur Burns. All these actions took place during Reagan's first month in office.[2]

Restoring the economy was not easy, and it took time. The Federal Reserve, free to make its own decisions, followed a monetary policy that brought inflation down faster than expected and eventually resulted in declining interest rates, but unemployment increased, output fell, and deficits widened. Economists would later iden-

---

* A consequence of inflation was that the tax burden—the percentage of income paid in taxes—increased automatically every year as wage earners got raises to cover the increased cost of living unless Congress legislated tax "cuts." In fiscal 1981, when Reagan's tax cut had not yet taken effect, revenues were 20.2 percent of gross domestic product, well above the 1970s average of about 18.5 percent. This "bracket creep" was eliminated by 1985 through indexing the tax brackets.

tify August 1981 as the beginning of the recession and November 1982 as the low point. Reagan's top priority—increases in defense spending—contributed one-fourth of the $200 billion deficit of fiscal 1983,* but it was far from the only cause. Lower personal and business income meant less revenue and more spending for programs like food stamps and unemployment insurance than the administration (and other economic forecasters) had predicted at the time Reagan sent his program to the Congress.

Once recovery began, it continued for 92 months, until July 1990—the longest period of peacetime economic growth in the post–World War II period. From the trough in November 1982 until the month Reagan left office, 16 million new jobs were created; another 2 million were created by July 1990. Consumer prices increased 4.4 percent in 1988; unemployment was 5.5 percent of the labor force, having decreased steadily from its peak of 10.6 percent in the depths of the recession. Interest rates were above the lows they had reached in 1986 but continued to reflect lower underlying inflation; the prime rate was 10.5 percent. The federal budget was not in balance, but deficits were declining.[3] Stock market averages more than doubled.

"Reaganomics," as Reagan's economic program was at first pejoratively called, included spending control, tax cuts, deregulation, and a stable monetary policy. All were designed to increase long-term economic growth and jobs. Some people emphasized only the "supply-side" tax cuts, which focused on incentives for work, saving, and investment, and a few people even promoted the idea that tax cuts alone were all that was needed to revitalize the economy and balance the budget. But neither Reagan nor his advisers ever took that position.[4]

As these letters show, Reagan was thoroughly convinced that domestic spending needed to be controlled. Congress did not approve all the spending cuts Reagan requested. In his second term Reagan's economic concerns were to maintain the tax cuts and deal with the continuing problem of federal spending. Lower tax rates and simplification of the tax code were achieved with the Tax Reform Act of 1986, proposed by Reagan in May 1985. Reagan recognized that the deficit, with the economy fully recovered, was structural but he was unwilling to increase taxes or cut defense spending for the purpose of balancing the budget.

Reagan responds in these letters to questions about his economic program and to suggestions for change, as well as to many people who wrote to him about their economic problems.

––––––––––

During the 1980 campaign Reagan supported the Kemp-Roth tax bill to cut marginal tax rates (the tax rates on additional income earned) across the board. But spending control was also an essential part of the Reagan economic program, as he makes clear in this letter responding to Representative Clair Burgerner (R-California), who sent

––––––––––

* Fiscal 1983 began October 1, 1982.

Reagan the results of a poll on the economic preferences of his constituents. Jack Kemp was a congressman from New York; William Roth was a Republican senator from Delaware.

Congressman Clair Burgerner
1980[5]

Dear Clair:

Thanks very much for your good letter and for the results of your poll. I'm not surprised and want you to know that while I have been advocating the Kemp-Roth tax bill, I always preface it with the declaration that we must immediately start to reduce the size and cost of federal government to bring it down to a lesser percentage of our gross national product. I guess that means I agree with the majority of your people.

I think it is interesting that the two biggest points were to cut federal spending to eliminate the federal deficit and to cut spending and taxes simultaneously. Those two, totaling 77 percent I think, indicate the wisdom of the American people. I was under the impression that Jack had given up his single-minded approach on the tax bill and that it had been amended to include a reduction in spending. If that isn't so, at least I'm amending it that way because I think both are necessary. Much as people want lower taxes, I think it is true that they are hard to sell on the idea that those lower taxes alone would generate additional funds and solve our deficit problems.

Thanks again for writing me and for giving me this information. It will keep me on track.

Best regards,
Ron

A monetary policy that would steadily bring down the rate of inflation was a critical part of Reagan's economic policy. Reagan met with Paul Volcker, chairman of the Federal Reserve Board of Governors, January 23, 1981, at the Department of the Treasury and later, at the White House, on several occasions in 1981 and 1982. They discussed the economy but not the specific policies of the independent Federal Reserve. Nevertheless, Reagan's support for a monetary policy that would reduce inflation was clear and important.[6]

Paul Trousdale and Justin Dart were Reagan supporters from Southern California.

Mr. Paul Trousdale
February 22, 1981[7]

Dear Paul:

Justin passed your letter along to me, and I just want to thank you for your generous words. Thank you too for your suggestions. I have recently set up a program of meetings with the Federal Reserve Board and believe that we are going to work more closely together. I think we'll have interest rates coming down in the next few months. I agree with you that is the greatest stumbling block now to our economic recovery. The goal is to have a steady and reasonable growth in money supply instead of the roller coaster we've had over the last several years with wild surges and then equally wild cutbacks.

The other thing, of course, that we must do is lower the inflation rate and here I'm very optimistic because we have already exceeded our own expectations in that regard and all the signs are that it's continuing to go down. Lenders of course have had to factor in inflation in order to get any return on the money they loan. We are now in single digit inflation for the first time in a number of years and I believe it's going even lower.*

It was good to hear from you, and again my thanks.

Sincerely,
Ron

Reagan's economic program, sent to Congress on February 18, 1981, called for cutting marginal tax rates 10 percent each year for three years; he later agreed to only 5 percent for the first year. The program also included accelerated depreciation schedules for business to encourage investment in new plant and equipment and thus job creation. Congress added the indexing of tax brackets. Reagan disagrees with Charles Broska's idea of making scheduled tax reductions dependent on economic growth. Broska was a supporter from Southern California and president of the Shoreline Retirement Association. Jack Anderson was a syndicated columnist.

Mr. Charles J. Broska
Orange, California
June 9, 1981 [8]

Dear Charles:

Just a quick line between chores to answer your good letter, which was most welcome. Thanks for the kind words about my speech.

I don't know what to say about Jack Anderson. Frankly, he comes out with what he claims is surefire material but too many times I know from the position I'm now in, it is complete fiction. I guess there's no way of stopping him.

I appreciated your tax proposal about the 10 percent and tying the next two years to some level of economic achievement. We really did study such an alternative, but we're convinced that the business community would not have the

---

* The rate of inflation in the consumer price index was 8.9 percent for 1981, down from 12.4 percent the previous year.

confidence in the Congress to carry through on those other two increases that are necessary if this tax bill is to be what we want it to be and that is an incentive; a program to increase investment and productivity. We think three years are the minimum for people in business and others to be able to look ahead and say, I can plan knowing what is going to take place over the next three years. I have come down now to 5-10-10 and believe we have a good chance of putting together a coalition which will support this. It won't be easy and it'll be quite a fight, but we're going to fight.

Thanks again for your letter. Best regards.

Sincerely,
Ron

———

Deregulation was an important part of Reagan's economic program. The work of the Task Force on Regulatory Relief and review of new agency regulations by the Office of Information and Regulatory Affairs in the Office of Management and Budget slowed down the proliferation of new regulations and simplified others.*

Ms. Gertraude B. Crabb
Seattle, Washington
June 16, 1981 [9]

Dear Trudy:

Forgive me for the familiarity, but I felt so good about your fine letter and your approval of what we're trying to do that I just couldn't be formal. I hope deregulation hasn't been too hard on your business and I appreciate more than I can say your willingness to make a sacrifice and your belief that industry will be more efficient. We hope in the near future that we can make a great many unnecessary and burdensome regulations go away and have a task force working on that right now.

Thank you for your words of support. Best regards.

Sincerely,
Ronald Reagan

———

* During the Reagan administration significant deregulation, some of which began in the Carter administration, also occurred in transportation (trucking, rail, and air), telecommunications (the consent degree achieved in the AT&T antitrust case), financial institutions, and energy. Legislation proposed and passed in 1981 led to the profitability of Conrail, the government-owned freight railroad, and its subsequent privatization via a public offering in 1986.

Reagan's across-the-board income tax proposal was criticized as favoring the rich; he tried hard to counter this view. The across-the-board marginal rate cuts reduced taxes largely in proportion to the taxes paid.

Mr. John R. Gelsinger, Sr.
Woodbury, New Jersey
July 15, 1981 [10]

Dear Mr. Gelsinger:

Thank you very much for your letter of June 12. I can understand your concern regarding the tax proposal in view of the attacks that have been made on our proposal both by politicians and by the news media.

The charge that our tax program is not reaching the very people you are talking about is entirely false, and these attacks are pure demagoguery. Those Americans earning between $10,000 and $60,000 a year are paying 72 percent of the total income tax. Our proposal will give them 75 percent of the total tax rate reduction.

Our opponents are suggesting that the bulk of the tax cut be given to those down in the very bottom range and below $10,000 instead of evenly across the board to the entire middle class. We are opposed to this because we believe it is absolutely necessary to restore incentive to those people you yourself have mentioned who work and earn, pay their bills, send their children to school, support our government—the great middle class of America. They are the ones who, if given tax relief, will through savings provide the investment capital we need to restore industry in America. Our proposal also is going to wipe out the penalty in the income tax paid when husband and wife in the same family are both employed.* In addition, we are going to provide that money devoted to a personal retirement program, even for those presently in a pension program, will be income tax deductible.

I hope this gives you a better idea of what we're trying to accomplish, and, again, I thank you for writing.

Sincerely,
Ronald Reagan

The most important economic events of the summer were the passage of Reagan's budget proposals—both the spending control provisions in the Omnibus Budget and Reconciliation Act and the later passage of tax cuts (the Economic Recovery Tax Act).

---

* Reagan was an early proponent of eliminating the "marriage tax," which causes some married couples to pay more tax than the two would pay if single. The marriage tax remains a consequence of other tax provisions.

The House of Representatives approved the tax bill July 29, 1981. The recession that began in August 1981 and lasted for 16 months, until November 1982, reduced both individual and business income, and thus made tax collections lower than they would have otherwise been. Dollar revenues actually dropped in 1983. Reagan did not get all the spending reductions he requested of Congress.

Mr. Sam K. Farmer
Carthage, Missouri
July 15, 1981 [11]

Dear Mr. Farmer:

Thank you very much for your letter of April 21. I'm sorry to be so long in answering, but I do find my desk gets very deep in mail.

I appreciate very much your generous words and assure you that my creed is fight—not join them—and we're going to continue right down the line. We have secured passage in the House of our budget reductions; now comes the hardest part—the tax reduction program. But we are going to fight again. I believe it is absolutely essential that we have this program in order to restore the vitality to our economy.

Again, my thanks to you for your letter. I, too, enjoyed the friendship of General Bradley* and feel his loss greatly.

Best regards,
Ronald Reagan

Gordon Luce was CEO of a California savings bank. He sent with his letter a memo criticizing the lack of accountability of the Federal Reserve and reiterating Nobel economist Milton Friedman's view that the increase in the money supply should be steady and predictable. Reagan redirected Luce's memo to Murray Weidenbaum, who chaired his Council of Economic Advisers, with the message: "Do we really need the Fed?" It was a question Reagan had asked Volcker at their first meeting in January 1981.

Milton Friedman was a member of the President's Economic Policy Advisory Board. The board met with Reagan every few months to provide an outside perspective on the economy.

Mr. Gordon C. Luce
San Diego, California
July 23, 1981 [12]

Dear Gordon:

Thanks very much for your letter and for the observations about the Federal Reserve. I did spend my time in Ottawa telling the others, the Fed and high interest rates were not part of our economic package.

----

* General Omar Bradley died April 8, 1981.

I've passed your essay on to our economic types to see if they have an answer to whether the Federal Reserve is really necessary. Again, thanks.

Best regards,
Ron

———————

Reagan did not believe restoring vitality to the U.S. economy would be easy and considered additional spending reductions essential to restoring economic growth. As he often pointed out, however, they were reductions in the rate of growth of spending— federal spending continued to increase, not only for defense but for domestic programs as well.

Mr. Stephen I. Bloom
Cleveland, Ohio
September 29, 1981 [13]

Dear Mr. Bloom:

This is a belated reply to your letter of July 10. Forgive me for taking so long, but it takes a while for mail to get through the mill and reach my desk.

I just want to thank you for your kindness in writing but, also, for your understanding and your willingness to sacrifice in order to help correct our economic ills. We are proposing more cuts in government spending—not only for 1982 but for the two following years—in keeping with our original plan. I feel a little as if I'm promising blood, sweat and tears, but I believe we all must take a rather bitter-tasting medicine if we're to reverse the course of the last thirty-odd years.

Again, my thanks to you for your unselfish attitude and for your kindness in writing.

Sincerely,
Ronald Reagan

———————

The tax cuts passed in the summer of 1981 were scheduled to begin taking effect October 1, 1981; Reagan had originally wanted to make the first 10 percent cut (scaled back to 5 percent) retroactive to January 1, 1981, but had compromised on the starting date. By October the recession had begun, but the tax reductions had not. But even in October there was talk of delay. Lyn Nofziger, the director of communications in the White House, wrote a memo to Reagan opposing the delay; Reagan responded with a note, "I'm opposed to any delay in implementing the tax cut." [14] In October 1981 the rate on Treasury bills—securities the government sells to fund the deficit—dropped about a percent point from its level in September on three-month bills, six-month bills, and thirty-year bills.

The next two letters show Reagan's continuing concern with high interest rates and reflect his view that the problem is decades of irresponsible government spending, not the short-term policies of the Federal Reserve.

Mr. Eugene O. Perkins
Colorado Springs, Colorado
October 16, 1981[15]

Dear Eugene:

Thank you for your letter of September 28. Believe me, we are as concerned here about the high interest rates as you are. Indeed they are part of what makes our attempt to balance the budget and lower inflation more difficult. But those interest rates are caused by the need for government to go into the money market and borrow in competition with others to pay for the deficits we've inherited due to many years of fiscal irresponsibility in government. With government borrowing up to half of the available capital, interest rates go up if the old laws of supply and demand play their part. It is necessary for a lender to get not only an interest return on his money but to get back the loss of value of that money due to inflation over the years. It can't be blamed entirely on the Federal Reserve Board and even if that were the cause, that board is absolutely independent and no agency of government imposes controls on it. We are gaining in the inflation fight and just a few days ago we had the first drop in interest rates on the money the government must borrow to pay those deficits I mentioned. I want more than anything I've ever wanted to not only balance the budget as quickly as possible ending those deficits but then to make a start in paying off the national debt. I know it'll take a few generations to do that but at least I wish ours could make a start. Thank you again for your letter.

Best regards,

Sincerely,
Ronald Reagan

Although Reagan recognizes the independence of the Federal Reserve, he is familiar with the details of its policies and their consequences.

Mr. W. H. Hoyerman
Chicago, Illinois
November 10, 1981[16]

Dear Bill:

Your letter of October 19 really brought back some pleasant memories of our dinner in Lake Forest many years ago. I share your concern about what is happening and particularly the effect of the high interest rates.

Unfortunately, we can't relieve those, as we have in the past, by simply increasing the money supply. It was this roller-coasting of money that, in large part, coupled with high government spending, got us in our present fix. I will say, however, that a few weeks back the Fed did get inadvertently a little below its own target rate of increase. Then they were caught in the dilemma of how to get back to the proper rate without giving the wrong signal to the money markets, making it look as if we'd gone back to the earlier policies. They have overcome that now, and, as you can see, interest rates have been going down, slowly, but still going down. I believe this will continue and even increase in speed in the not too distant future.

The main battle still goes on with Congress. Even though we got our 35 billion dollar budget cut, that was only part of what's needed. We've told them that from the beginning. Now they're digging in their heels and it's going to take a real fight to get them to go the rest of the way, particularly for the years '83 and '84.

We are encouraged by the fact that inflation has dropped more than even we had anticipated, and this simply on the prospect of our program, without waiting for the program to even be put into effect. I'm very hopeful that, as the coming year goes on, we will see the effect of the tax cuts and the budget reduction. But we're also going to continue trying for more cuts to get government spending back down within its means.

Please give my best to Jan. And, again, thanks for writing.

Best regards,

> Sincerely,
> Ronald Reagan

"I wish to receive a response to this letter immediately, from President Reagan person-ally. . . . I demand to be heard," Bonnie Porter wrote. She believed he should experi-ence himself the sacrifices he was asking of others, and concluded with "You can't expect the Army to fight on the front lines if the captain is always in his tent."

Reagan responds to her complaints about many aspects of his economic program—tax cuts, social security, welfare, and his management of the White House—as well as a variety of unrelated issues: new dishes for the White House, selling planes to Saudi Arabia, and even his use of government transportation to get to Camp David.

> Mrs. Bonnie M. Porter
> Central City, Kentucky
> November 4, 1981 [17]

Dear Mrs. Porter:

Thank you for giving me the opportunity to address myself to your concerns. Your letter of October 1st has just reached my desk. You specified that you wanted to hear from me personally so here I am.

You asked how we could balance the budget by robbing the poor and giving to the rich. Well that isn't what we're doing. We are trying to reduce the cost of gov-ernment and have already obtained consent of Congress to reduce the budget by more than 35 billion dollars.

We are reducing tax rates across the board. This will give 74 percent of the relief to those who are presently paying 72 percent of the total tax, the average middle class American.

We are trying to do what you suggested—make able-bodied welfare recipients work at useful community jobs in return for their welfare grants. As governor of California I did this and it works very well. So far Congress doesn't like the idea.

We have not suggested reducing Social Security. We are trying to do what you suggested—removing those who are not disabled or deserving of grants they are presently getting.

We are not cutting back on school lunches for the needy. We are trying to quit providing them for those who aren't needy.

Now as to the White House, we aren't spending a penny of tax money. The government provides $50,000 for an incoming president to do what he will to the White House. We gave that money back to the government. We found, however, that the White House was badly in need of painting inside, the plumbing was so old there was danger of it giving way. Drapes and much upholstery was in need of re-covering and replacing, etc. Friends started a campaign to get donations to have this work done. It has all been completed without spending a single tax dollar.

The dishes were a donation by a trust and the company making them did so at cost. This is the way the White House has always been furnished. Beautiful antiques etc. have been gifts to the government. The last new china was in Harry Truman's time. There is a certain amount of breakage over the years. We're talking about china for state dinners when heads of government visit the United States and more than 100 people must be served. That is not the china we use for family meals.

Now for your other concerns; we are not going to increase the risk to miners, and yes, I've been down in a mine. As for black lung we are only trying to eliminate those cases where people are getting benefits who don't have black lung.

Selling planes to Saudi Arabia will run no risk of giving secrets away and it will provide thousands of jobs for American workers.

We don't take Air Force One to Camp David. The camp is only 20 minutes from the White House by helicopter. The helicopters have to fly a required number of hours every week to keep crew and machine in shape.

I hope this answers your concerns and I assure you this captain isn't in his tent when the fight is going on.

Sincerely,
Ronald Reagan

Reagan replies to a letter from the recording secretary of the United Steel Workers of America about trade policy for industries having difficulty competing in world markets and regulations that are hampering economic growth.

Mr. H. G. "Pete" Harmon
Fairfield, Alabama
November 10, 1981 [18]

Dear Mr. Harmon:

I'm sorry to be so late in answering your letter of September 25th but it takes some time for a letter to get to my desk.

You expressed concern about this nation's foreign trade policies and suggested they be restructured. We have found things that need to be changed and have made some changes in the interest of fairness. Where steel is concerned there is a triggering device whereby our government can take action in the event that foreign steel is being dumped on our market. Dumping is defined as selling at less than the cost of production with the foreign government subsidizing the producers' loss.

In the past few years this triggering device was not used even though there was evidence of dumping. We will use it.

The figures you gave me however regarding membership loss in Local 1013 over the last two decades must indicate to you that the problems of your industry are not something that just started last January.

We have let overseas competition get ahead of us in research and plant modernization not only in steel but in other industries as well. The result has been lost markets and thus unemployment, with all the personal tragedy that can bring.

I know we can't cure instantly what has been going wrong for so many years, but I believe our economic program will bring that cure. The Iron and Steel Institute has informed me that more than 20 major steel companies including U.S. Steel are embarking on more than five billion dollars worth of modernization and expansion, the biggest such move in the history of the industry. All this, the Institute says, has been made possible by our Economic Recovery Program, particularly the tax policies covering new equipment and plant modernization.

Now I know, as I said before, this will take time, but it will make us competitive in the world market again. I have been in modern steel mills in other countries, mills that were built after World War II with Marshall Plan help. I have also been in closed-down plants here in America in the last few years. Our competitors have been able to produce more steel per worker not because their workers are better but because their workers have better tools.

With regard to OSHA [Occupational Safety and Health Administration], we are not going to relax the safety standards aimed at reducing accidents. What we're trying to do is eliminate costly bureaucratic nonsense which helps no one except the bureaucrat who gets good pay for administering the nonsense. I'm thinking of such things as the man who was ordered to put separate men's and women's washrooms in his place of business. His only employee is his wife. At home they share the same bathroom.

As for Davis-Bacon,* I promised not to repeal it and I'll keep that promise, but like OSHA we have found administrative changes that are needed to save your tax dollars. Right now government is the biggest cost item in your family budget. It costs more than food, housing and clothing combined.

---

* The Davis-Bacon Act required that employees working under federal contracts be paid prevailing local wages.

Frankly, as an officer of my own union for more than 20 years—president six of those—I felt badly that Solidarity Day* was aimed at opposing our effort to cut government costs and your taxes. I wasn't surprised that the biggest share of the crowd was made up of federal employees. Let me assure you my highest priority is to see American workers back at work, making good money and keeping it.

Sincerely,
Ronald Reagan

Reagan argues in this letter that the recession was neither expected by the administration nor predicted by economic forecasters.

Mr. Homer R. Ayers
Goodlettsville, Tennessee
December 1, 1981 [19]

Dear Mr. Ayers:

Thank you for your letter. I'm sorry to be so late in my reply, but it does take a while for mail to reach my desk.

Since you wrote, interest rates have slowly begun to come down. There is no question that they have been responsible in large part for the recession we are now in. None of us here expected a great resurgence in the economy before 1982. Indeed we have predicted a soggy economy. We had not anticipated, however, the recession. And, as I say, I believe the high interest rates contributed to that. They have started down, however, and, of course, I know there will be a lull for a while because people are going to wait for them to go even lower before they borrow or seek a mortgage. But I am convinced that our plan, given a chance, is going to restore fiscal sanity to this country. It is a hard fight because many in Congress still cling to the old tax and tax, spend and spend theory that got us into our present situation.

I must be fair and say that while I believe the federal government played a part in the high interest rates, I think the marketplace itself and the law of supply and demand made its contribution with too much borrowing, both private and government, with a limited supply of capital. That's why I think as our tax program takes hold there will be an increase in available capital and thus interest rates will be further encouraged to drop. I believe we are going to see an improvement next spring or early summer. I wish I could say earlier than that, but I don't think that's possible.

---

* The AFL-CIO's September 19, 1981, Solidarity Day rally in Washington, D.C., attracted 260,000 participants including not only union members but groups representing women, minorities, the elderly, and the poor.

At any rate please be assured we are going to stick with our plan and continue to do battle with the Congress. In that regard, may I just say that your senator to whom you sent a copy of your letter, Howard Baker, has been a stalwart in this battle on the side of fiscal sanity. Thanks for writing as you did.

Sincerely,
Ronald Reagan

Reagan again links spending control and tax reduction; he also expresses his faith in the American people.

Mr. Ruben Betancourt
Plantation, Florida
December 1, 1981 [20]

Dear Mr. Betancourt:

Thank you very much for your letter. You didn't date it so I don't know how long you've been waiting for an answer. If it has been a long time, please forgive me but it takes a while for mail to get to my desk.

Please think nothing of your inability to respond to that fundraising letter from the Committee. I've had to say "no" many times myself in the past. But let me address myself if I can to the other things you said in your letter.

I know the problems are great, we are in an economic recession. We have been for too many decades spending above our means and taxing the people to the point that now our economy has slowed down. This is why I believe the answer is reduced government spending and reduced tax rates to allow the people to save and invest so there is capital for our industrial machine to rebuild itself.

I know, too, there is a crime problem. Indeed, I'm very much aware of that. But, may I tell you this also. Out in the country and all across this great land there are millions of Americans who want what you want, who are determined that we can be that kind of country again, and they give me the faith to keep on doing what I'm doing.

I have just answered a young black woman separated from her husband, four children, thirty-three years of age who is on welfare, but has managed to get herself a high school diploma, and now is setting out to get off welfare and be self-sufficient. Her courage and her faith in this country as expressed in her letter were such that my own faith was renewed, if that were necessary. Actually, I've never lost faith.

We have started here at the White House, a nationwide program to stimulate voluntarism. This country, before we began thinking that only government could do things for the people, had a proud heritage of the people themselves rallying together to meet needs, to solve problems, to do things that needed to be done. Well, we have appealed for a rebirth of that. We have a national committee going to work on it, and I'm beginning to get letters from all over the country from groups that have sprung into existence to do these voluntary things. I guess what I'm saying is, America is still filled with millions of good neighbors who, if you knocked at their door and needed help, would offer that help.

People like yourself are the backbone of this country, the great middle class, the unsung heroes who get up in the morning and go to work, send the kids to school, pay their bills, and, yes, if war comes, send their sons, or go themselves if they're young enough. And it's true, they are the people who have been hardest hit by the ill-advised government policies of the last few decades. They are the people we're listening to and trying to help. And recently, when our proposed budget cuts—the largest ever proposed in our nation's history—were before the Congress, the Congress heeded those people because by the hundreds of thousands they wrote and wired and telephoned through their congressmen and said that this was what they wanted.

So stay with it, don't give up. There are lots of us who feel as you do and are trying to do something about it, and I think we're going to get it done.

Sincerely,
Ronald Reagan

Reagan sympathizes with the plight of a farmer caught in the recession.

Mrs. Bill Casey
Anna, Illinois
December 1, 1981 [21]

Dear Mrs. Casey:

Thank you very much for writing as you did and giving me a chance to answer. Forgive me for being so late in responding but it does take time for mail to get through the mill and to my desk. Your letter has just reached me.

Mrs. Casey, having a ranch of my own, I do have some understanding of the problems you're talking about. I don't know of anyone who has been caught harder in the cost-price squeeze than the American farmer. You asked what is inflation—it really is just a plain case of our money becoming less and less because, over the years, they've turned on the printing presses at the mint and printed more money while we haven't made an increase in the things to buy with that money.

Our whole program is aimed at reducing that inflation which has caused the problems your son faces. We have made gains, we've reduced inflation by several percentage points in these ten or eleven months that we've been here. But, we have much farther to go. We have to bring inflation down to the point that interest rates also will come down, and we can do this by reducing government spending and reducing taxes, which we have just started to do.

The Congress is working on a farm bill. I have not seen it as yet, but I hope that it will offer some help in this situation.

Again, thank you for writing and best regards.

Sincerely,
Ronald Reagan

Reagan was considering transferring some programs to the states along with revenue sources to fund them—a proposal he had first made in 1975. The proposal sent to Congress following the fiscal 1983 budget called for the federal government to take over all responsibility for Medicaid in exchange for the states taking all responsibility for the AFDC (Aid to Families with Dependent Children) welfare program and food stamps; it also proposed turning other programs back to the states with revenue sources to fund them. Congress did not act on it.

Mr. James R. Nolan
Lenexa, Kansas
January 11, 1982 [22]

Dear Mr. Nolan:

Thanks very much for your letter of November 3rd and forgive my being so late with a reply.

We are continuing to plan further reductions in spending and we are not going to abandon our tax incentive program which I believe is essential if we are going to get the economy moving again.

It may be true that in the out years '83–84 etc. we may turn to some excise taxes but if we do it will be in connection with turning programs back to the states and local governments. In doing this we'll turn those increased excise taxes back to them also.

So far we have cut the increase in federal spending down from 17.1 percent in '80 and 14 percent in '81 to 9 percent for '82 and an estimated 6½ percent in '83. And this is with our increased defense budget which was so greatly underfunded in those years of high spending growth.

I believe our economic program will work but Congress must continue to co-operate in making the budget cuts for '83 and '84 that we are proposing.

Again thanks for your letter.

Sincerely,
Ronald Reagan

Arthur Burns was ambassador to the Federal Republic of Germany (West Germany). He served as chairman of the Council of Economic Advisers in the Eisenhower administration, chairman of the Federal Reserve Board of Governors in the Nixon adminis-

tration, and was a member of the President's Economic Policy Advisory Board in the Reagan administration. He wrote to express concern about the deficit and to recommend consumption taxes.

> The Honorable Arthur Burns
> Bonn, Germany
> January 12, 1982[23]

Dear Arthur:

Thank you very much for your letter and even more for all that you are doing.

We are continuing to labor over the budget as well as a plan that combines some consumer tax increases and a return of present federal programs to the state and local governments.

I believe in my budget message I'll be able to project a lower deficit as well as a probable upturn in the economy. We are definitely going to go after further spending reductions including the entitlement programs. I know our opponents will stage a battle but I believe we will have the people with us on this so we'll take on the fight.

You are absolutely right on the income tax etc. We will not retreat.

Again thanks and all the best.

> Sincerely,
> Ron

Victor Krulak wrote a column about the government spending that Reagan inherited from previous administrations.

> Lt. General Victor H. Krulak, USMC (Ret.)
> February 2, 1982[24]

Dear Brute:

Thanks very much for your letter but again as I do so often I thank you for that column. The open letter that you addressed to me but sent to the people. You said a lot of things that made me feel just fine. Back here I'm still battling of course against those who would have us forget the 40 years and think that all the troubles came about in the last four months. You set them straight in a masterful way and I'm most grateful. There's going to be an effort I know to whittle back on national defense but I will fight to the last pop gun before I give in on that. In fact I won't give in. They'll have to do it over my carcass, if that's possible.

Thanks again,

> Best regards,
> Ron

Reagan responds to the accusation that there is a "slice of life" with which he is out of touch. The Office of Presidential Correspondence in the White House handled many special cases of need, trying to find help for people in difficult circumstances, and Reagan saw some of these letters.

Mr. Kevin Weyl
San Francisco, California
February 11, 1982 [25]

Dear Mr. Weyl:

Thank you very much for taking the time and trouble to write as you did. I am most grateful.

You asked if I am in tune with the people who today are suffering, not alone in this recession, but as the result of years and years of distorted government policies that have wound down this great economic machine that has provided such good living for so many people. Yes, I think I am in tune. I was raised in poverty. I entered the workforce in the midst of the Great Depression which makes anything we've seen since look like happy days.

During the campaign, before I held this office, I did many of the things that you suggested. I could do them then even though they didn't play much of a part in getting votes. And, I did them for the very reasons that you suggested I do them—because of a personal concern and a desire to help those people. Unfortunately, that isn't as easy today as it was then. First, there is a great matter of security that makes it almost impossible to have that freedom. Second, there is just a plain lack of time if I'm to do the other things that I believe are necessary to get the wheels turning again. Still, I managed more contact than you can realize. Some of it was by way of Nancy, who is able to do these things more than I can. Also, by seeing that mail about particular problems comes to my personal attention, and then individual cases that come to me by way of people who know me and know that I do feel a concern. I know none of this sounds exactly what you had pictured—what you had in mind. But, I assure you one can't have been raised in poverty as I was and not still know the people I knew then and still have association and contact with those people.

The press has played the programs we're trying to institute as being aimed at the poor and the helpless and depriving them. I don't believe that is true. We are still spending more than we did the year before and we'll spend more next year than we do this year. But, we inherited a government that was increasing in cost—17½ percent a year. That's far and above the increase in revenues which is why we have a trillion dollar debt. All we've been doing is reducing that rate of increase and trying to get government back to where it spends within its revenues. And, at the same time, trying to get this great industrial machine moving again so the people who want them can have jobs so that we can take care of those who, no fault of their own, cannot provide for themselves. But the cuts we're making even in that increase are aimed at eliminating not the care of the needy, but the subsidies that have been going to the greedy.

I learned as governor of California, when we reformed welfare that no one in this country knows how many checks are going out, and the federal government had a tangle of regulations that prevented anyone from trying to find out who was cheating. We did find cheats. When you find one individual getting welfare under 127 different names and holding 55 Social Security cards, you know there is something wrong with the program. We're trying to correct that sort of thing. We have just recently found 8,500 Social Security recipients still receiving their checks and they've been dead for an average of seven years.

Do you think I don't miss the freedom to walk out the door and down the street and stop in at the corner drug store? Or, to stop the car and get out and get in a conversation with some people? Believe me, there is a feeling of claustrophobia in this job, along with all the perquisites that are supposed to make it so attractive.

Forgive me for going on this way, but your letter kind of touched a nerve. I just want you to know that I am aware of that slice of life you described, and am determined to do something about it.

Thanks again and best regards.

Sincerely,
Ronald Reagan

Lewis Lehrman was a New York executive and Reagan supporter who ran for governor in 1982.

Mr. Lewis E. Lehrman
New York, New York
February 22, 1982[26]

Dear Lew:

I know by now you're aware that I have decided against those who suggested higher taxes as a part of our program. But, I wanted you to know how very much I appreciated your letter of January 23rd. It made me more confident of my decision, and more comfortable. You were kind to write as you did, and I do appreciate it.

I have confidence in our program, and I wish I could convince people they should just have a little more patience. I'm getting tired of hearing that the program is a failure when the first and smallest phase of it only began on October 1st. I worry, at times, that the constant drum beat by the press might begin to affect people, and create a fear that I believe would be harmful to what we're trying to do.

Again, thanks and best regards.

Sincerely,
Ron

A citizen living at the Metropolitan Club in Washington, D.C., expressed concerned about the economy in early 1982 and sent Reagan an editorial arguing that he had

gone back on his campaign promise to balance the budget. Reagan reiterates his
commitment to that goal but explains the course of events and reminds the writer that
his top priority is rebuilding the nation's defenses. In a letter two months later he would
put it even more strongly: "I don't underestimate the value of a sound economy but
I also don't underestimate the imperialist ambitions of the Soviet Union. . . . I want
more than anything to bring them into realistic arms reduction talks. To do this they
must be convinced that the alternative is a buildup militarily by us. They have
stretched their economy to the limit to maintain their arms program. They know they
cannot match us in an arms race if we are determined to catch up. Our true ultimate
purpose is arms reduction."* [27]

Edward H. Sims
Washington, D.C.
March 22, 1982 [28]

Dear Mr. Sims:

Thanks very much for your letter and for the copy of your editorial. I appreciate your concern. May I, however, take issue with a line in the editorial that I have
gone back on my promise to balance the budget. That is still my goal. Unfortunately, the recession (and that has to be laid at the door of four decades of Democratic policy) changed our estimates dramatically. One change we are responsible
for—we lowered inflation faster than we anticipated and, since inflation is a source
of revenue for government, this reduced our estimated revenues which further
added to the projected deficit.

May I also point out that I have consistently and repeatedly stated that in our
perilous situation vis-à-vis the Soviets, if it came to a choice between balancing the
budget or rebuilding our defenses, I'd come down on the side of the latter.

But, I'm aware of the menace of the increased deficit. Our problem is, will our
opponents join in a bipartisan move to lower it, or will they sacrifice the national
good to have a 1982 campaign issue?

Thanks again.

Sincerely,
Ronald Reagan

———————

*Reagan responds to a telegram that says "you are so removed from the average family
it's hard to believe you understand our problems" by reviewing his own family and
school background.*

———————

* When Reagan announced the details of his economic program on September 9 in the 1980 presidential campaign the forecasts of the Senate Budget Committee and others showed large, growing surpluses
building to $182 billion by 1985. Reagan proposed to balance the budget by 1983, *unless* the cost of re-
building national defense precluded it. During 1981 forecasters revised their economic estimates
sharply downward.

Mr. Kenneth Loebker
Lawrenceville, Georgia
June 24, 1982 [29]

Dear Mr. Loebker:

Thank you very much for your wire of June 14 and for giving me a chance to reply. I can understand the perception you have of me in view of the image building done by so much of the press—false image building I might add.

You say I'm so far removed from the average family that I can't understand your problems. Mr. Loebker I read about myself and the stories that somehow I only like, understand and tolerate rich people and I get pretty frustrated.

I'm one of a family of four. My brother and I are all that are left—our parents died before any of this happened. We were poor and lived in a small town in Illinois. I worked my way through a small college in Illinois with a little help for playing football. In those days that meant they saw that you got a job washing dishes in the dining hall.

I've kept contact with all the friends I knew in those days. And now though it may be hard to understand I'm surrounded more on a daily basis with the same kind of people I always knew than I am with the so-called rich. The security detail, aides and staff and, to tell you the truth, our friends though successful now had backgrounds like my own.

You ask if there is some way that you and others could unite behind our programs—that you feel left out. I'm not sure I understand exactly what you mean. Believe me I want and need your support to get measures through Congress to reduce spending and taxes to help in the battle to get inflation and interest rates down. I'd like to hear from you and have your suggestions. To get a letter to me quickly address it to Mrs. Kathy Osborne here at the White House.

Again, thanks.

Sincerely,
Ronald Reagan

In this letter sympathizing with people in economic trouble because of the recession, Reagan looks forward to an improved economy. The end of the recession was still four months away.

Mr. and Mrs. Mac Stratman
Gunnison, Colorado
July 21, 1982 [30]

Dear Mr. and Mrs. Stratman:

I wish I could tell you there is some instant answer to your problem but there are no "quick fixes," for what ails our economy. Indeed "quick fixes," over the last 40 years have led to the present mess—a trillion dollar debt, the high interest rates which are torturing you, and the unemployment.

While interest rates have come down from the 21½ percent high of 1980 they haven't come down enough.* We are encouraged by the recent drop in the discount rate by the Federal Reserve † and have reason to believe it will slip another notch in the next couple of weeks. This will of course have an effect on interest rates. I am disappointed that interest rates haven't reflected the fact that we've cut the inflation rate more than in half. So far the financial markets seem to be fearful that we'll revert to higher government spending thus bringing back inflation, but we have no intention of doing that.

I hope and pray you can hang on because there is every sign the recession has bottomed out and while recovery won't be a sudden boom we can at least look forward to a improvement in the months ahead.

With very best wishes.

Sincerely,
Ronald Reagan

In the budget negotiations in 1982 Reagan traded increased taxes on business for promised spending cuts, but the tax increases were not nearly as large as the reductions enacted in 1981. Nevertheless, there were objections. Reagan explains the compromise to Alfred Kingon, editor of Financial World. *The compromise resulted in the passage of the Tax Equity and Fiscal Responsibility Act (TEFRA) on August 19, 1982; the spending reduction part of the bargain was not kept.*[31] *Kingon eventually worked as an aide to Don Regan when Regan became chief of staff in 1984.*

Mr. Alfred H. Kingon
New York, New York
July 28, 1982 [32]

Dear Al:

I can't quarrel with your editorial except that Bob Dole was only carrying out what had to be done in order to get the entire package of spending cuts etc. We cooperated to the extent of sending up a list of taxes we could not support and suggestions as to revenue measures that would be acceptable.

Very simply the tax bill is the price we had to pay for support on the whole program. We did get cuts in spending at a ratio of about $3 for every $1 of tax. That statement isn't quite accurate in that $31 billion of the $99 billion tax bill consists of better compliance in collecting taxes that are owed under present law and which are being evaded. That part of the bill is what we'd spoken of last year during the budget battle saying we'd attempt to correct it this time around.

---

* The prime rate was down to 15.5 percent by the end of July 1982.
† The discount rate was lowered from 12 percent to 11.5 percent in July 1982 and to 10 percent by the end of August. Overall inflation (as well as the consumer price index) was indeed about half of what it was when Reagan took office.

Let me recall to you that the forces now calling this *our* tax increase were moving heaven and earth to cancel our tax reductions. This headed them off. From '83 through '85 our tax cuts will amount to $408 billion so we stayed ahead of what they were trying to get.

I have your previous letter on my desk and no I haven't been told of what you told me in the letter. I intend to get into the subject you raised. Incidentally a thank you, very late, for all your help in the campaign and since the election.

You'll be hearing from us.

Sincerely,
Ron

Martin Feldstein, chairman of the Council of Economic Advisers, sent a memo to the president recommending a capital budget for the government. Don Regan was secretary of the treasury. David Stockman was director of the Office of Management and Budget (OMB).

Martin Feldstein
September 24, 1982[33]

Dear Marty:

Yes I believe this should be pursued. But you should coordinate with Don Regan, Dave Stockman and others as appropriate. OMB and Treasury have the lead responsibility in this area.

We had such a system in California. There of course it required a vote by the people for bond issues to cover capital investments.

Possibly it could be done at our level by congressional act.

Ron

Mrs. Robin Lisak wrote to oppose the TEFRA legislation to increase taxes on the grounds that having performed "major surgery" with the first tax cut, this was "hardly the time to return the patient to the operating table." Reagan attributes the cut in the prime rate by one of the nation's lead banks to passage of the legislation the day before and explains that total tax cuts still outweigh the increase.

Mrs. Robin E. Lisak
Chicago, Illinois
August 20, 1982[34]

Dear Mrs. Lisak:

I can't argue with much of what you say, indeed I'm in full agreement. You are right the signs are all favorable. Just a few minutes ago I was told Chase Manhattan

Bank had lowered the prime interest rate to 13½. Lowered interest rates are the answer to restoring our economy.

But I have to say, this move coming as it did, the day after the tax bill passed I believe is a reaction to the bill's passage. The money market has been waiting for a signal that Congress will continue what we started last year—cutting government spending, attacking the deficits and restoring fiscal sanity.

Now having said that let me explain the so-called tax increase. It is the price we had to pay to get Congress to go along with more spending cuts. Over the next three years spending will be reduced $3 for every $1 of the tax increase. Incidentally our tax cut passed last year will net the taxpayers $335 billion in tax cuts even after the $99 billion increases are collected in these next three years.

I thank you for writing as you did and appreciate your approval of what we've been doing (outside of the tax bill) and I'm grateful for your faith in our economic recovery program.

Sincerely,
Ronald Reagan

————

Reagan responds to a question from Arthur Laffer raised at a meeting of the President's Economic Policy Advisory Board, of which Laffer was a member. Gasoline taxes go into the Highway Trust Fund and are used for highway construction; the five-cent increase included, however, one cent for mass transit, a favorite program of Drew Lewis, secretary of transportation.

Professor Arthur Laffer
Rolling Hill Estates, California
January 24, 1983 [35]

Dear Art:

In trying to cover the range of subjects this morning in our meeting I left one out. You had mentioned the five-cent gasoline tax in discussing our tax increases. I intended and then overlooked commenting on that. I realize it is a tax and yet I would never have held still for that as part of a tax package simply to raise revenues.

Here is a brief history of how it came about. More than a year ago Drew Lewis came to [the] Cabinet with a very disturbing rundown on our deteriorating highways and bridges. He had some frightening figures on bridges that school buses refuse to cross without making the children walk across etc.

I was concerned but faced with our budget battle asked him to wait a year—which he did.

As you can imagine when he came back a year later his report was even more frightening. I agreed to the tax as purely a user fee for the purpose of restoring the system and that it would expire once that was done. If I'm still around I'll see that it does.* I'm not only against taxes—I never want to see a gasoline tax used for general revenue.

It was good to see you.

Best regards,
Ron

Jill Rathbun, mother of three and the wife of a member of the military with ten years' active duty, wrote to say that she was "deeply concerned over the military pay freeze action" to go into effect October 1, 1983. Reagan explains why it was necessary.

Mrs. Jill M. Rathbun
Wahiawa, Hawaii
March 15, 1983[36]

Dear Mrs. Rathbun:

Thank you for writing and for giving me a chance to respond. First let me say no one regrets the pay freeze more than I do—and yes I know you can say that's easy talk when it's hurting so many others. But believe me I know our people in uniform are not being paid what they deserve and we are going to continue trying to raise the scale. The freeze as you know is only for one year.

Faced with a deficit which could delay economic recovery we proposed a freeze for one year for all government employees and Social Security recipients. At first we intended to exempt the military. However there is a strong move in the Congress to massively reduce the defense budget. We had to go across the board if Congress was to give us the other savings we had to have.

With regard to the extravagances you mentioned I can only tell you there is a fresh wind blowing through the Pentagon and billions of dollars of savings have already been realized. But we are all agreed that as fast as we can we want to continue bringing military pay up to a fair level.

I am encouraged by the signs of economic recovery that may ease our deficit situation somewhat but in the meantime we are a long way from a balanced budget. And as you know many in Congress feel as they have in the past that defense should be the first place to cut. I promise I'll battle against that kind of false economy.

Please know a great many of your fellow citizens are very proud and grateful to you who are manning the barricades and defending our freedom.

Sincerely,
Ronald Reagan

---

* The Congress did not allow the gasoline tax to expire and has since enacted additional increases.

Reagan did not get all the spending cuts he requested of Congress.

Mr. H. E. Chiles
Fort Worth, Texas
April 26, 1983 [37]

Dear Eddie:

Thanks very much for your letter and for the copy of your mailgram. You bet I agree with it. I get so frustrated with those guys on the Hill who would hang the deficits around our necks while they refuse to give us the spending cuts we ask for.

If we had gotten the cuts we originally asked for the deficit in '83 (only our second budget) would be $40 billion less.

Love to Fran and I look forward to seeing you both.

Sincerely,
Ron

Public concern about the deficit was great enough that a "standby tax"—surcharges of 5 percent on personal and corporation income taxes and $5 on a barrel of oil—were being considered for 1985 and 1986 if expected revenues did not materialize. Feldstein supported the standby tax and sent a text of typical remarks he was making to the President for approval. Reagan replies.

Martin Feldstein
July 21, 1983 [38]

Marty I think there should be <u>more</u> emphasis on spending cuts. We should insist on spending cuts and entitlement reforms <u>before</u> we accept any tax increase. Whether intended or not I believe the memo gives an impression that we are thinking <u>first</u> of taxes. Incidentally I have only stated that the standby tax would take effect in <u>1986</u> and provided that in '84 and '85 we achieved the spending cuts we believe are essential.

RR

Bob Tyrrell, editor of The American Spectator, *sent Reagan an advance copy of a symposium on supply-side economics to appear in the November 1983 issue. "You have shifted the economic dialogue away from the statist hashish to incentives," he wrote. Reagan is appreciative but rejects the "supply-side" label and instead states his own economic principles. His view that the appetite of government for spending is unlimited is consistent with his support for a balanced budget tax limitation amendment to the Constitution (see p. 558).*

Mr. R. Emmett Tyrrell, Jr.
Bloomington, Indiana
October 6, 1983 [39]

Dear Bob:

Thanks for sending me the "preprint" and for your letter. I'm grateful for your kind words. I'm pleased too with the opinions of the "assembled sages."

You know Bob I'm not sure I really understood simon-pure "supply side" or that I agreed with every facet. It's always seemed to me that when government goes beyond a certain percentage of what it takes as its share of the people's earnings we have trouble. I guess a simple explanation of what I've been trying to do is peel government down to bare essentials—necessities if you will, and then set the tax revenues accordingly.

If we find then that we overdid on the tax cuts [then] adjust—but it will take a lot more evidence than I've seen to convince me adjustment is needed.

When the income tax amendment was being debated back there in 1913 one of its advocates declared the tax was necessary, "not for government's needs but for government's wants." Well I think we've learned government's wants are limitless.

Again thanks.

Sincerely,
Ron

––––––––

Laurence Beilenson, Reagan's friend from their SAG days, sent Reagan a copy of his article about Roosevelt's National Recovery Administration entitled "NRA: Blue Eagles, Sick Chickens" from the fiftieth anniversary issue of Daily Variety, *a newspaper of the entertainment industry. The issue carried a letter from Reagan on the front page.*

Mr. Laurence W. Beilenson
Los Angeles, California
November 7, 1983 [40]

Dear Larry:

Yes I have a copy of the *Anniversary Variety* but didn't get much beyond my letter so I'm pleased to have your article—thank you.

We are on the same track regarding an "industrial policy." Those who advocate such a thing would take us right back down the road of statism. The longer I stay here the more convinced I am that government no matter how well-intentioned is not qualified to run business and industry. When it sticks to its proper function it does very well—as say a rescue mission on Grenada.

Thanks again for writing the article and for sending it. Nancy sends her love.

Best regards,
Ron

Reagan expresses his disagreement with the economist Arthur Burns about the causes of high interest rates.

The Honorable Arthur Burns
Bonn, Germany
February 22, 1984[41]

Dear Arthur:

I'm very late in getting back to you please forgive me. I appreciate your sending me the roundup of views on our deficits.

While I deplore the deficits and am determined to get a handle on them, I can't accept their view that deficits are the cause of high interest rates.

Just recently I've seen a breakdown on deficit spending of the other industrial states (including U.K.—West Germany, Japan et al.) as a percentage of gross national product. In every instance their own deficits are above us in such a percentage but their interest rates are lower. At the same I note that while our deficits increased tremendously in the '82 and '83 years our interest rates were cut in half. I therefore have to challenge the assumption that deficits and interest rates are linked.

I'm convinced our problem is government spending as a percent of our national earnings and we must cut spending further than we have so far.

Didn't mean to get on a soap box. Thanks again and all the best to you.

Sincerely,
Ron

As recovery from the recession proceeds, Reagan acknowledges that the deficit is structural—recovery will not solve the problem. (In fact, deficits would finally disappear only in the years 1997–2001, primarily as a consequence of substantial reductions in defense expenditures.)

Mr. William D. Nielsen Jr.
Lorain, Ohio
March 19, 1984[42]

Dear Mr. Nielsen:

Thank you very much for writing as you did. Needless to say we are in great agreement. We can't turn to the "quick fixes" that have been the response to the cause of each succeeding recession.

I'm sure you know by now that we've made a proposal to the Congress for what I've call a down payment on the present deficit. This is of course only a start. Much more must be done in the next year or two to bring about structural reforms and get us once and for all back to a balanced budget policy. This will include securing passage of a Constitutional amendment to require balanced budgets.

Our down payment calls for some additional revenues but no change in tax rates. I've asked the Treasury Department to bring me a plan for overall tax simplification which could be taken up in '85. Some of the loopholes we presently propose closing would probably have been part of that simplification. We must not however yield to those who are demanding surtaxes and increased rates. The answer to our persistent economic problems is less government not more and certainly less redistribution of earnings.

Thanks again for your words of support.

Sincerely,
Ronald Reagan

Reagan agrees with Krulak that government overspending is the fundamental economic problem and questions the economic difference between taxing and borrowing as the means of financing that spending.

Lt. General Victor H. Krulak, USMC (Ret.)
June 14, 1984[43]

Dear Brute:

Thanks for your letter and the postcript. As usual your camp report resulted in a little homesickness.

Your column is right on. In London at the summit I think I convinced our friends and allies that our deficit had nothing to do with high interest rates. For one thing four of them have higher deficits as a percentage of GNP than we do, one is tied with us and one has lower. Our interest rates now are due to just plain fear that inflation will come back.

You are absolutely right that the problems are caused by government spending too much. I've asked several times what the difference is between borrowing or taxing. We're still taking the money from the people either way.

Thanks for your kind words about El Salvador. We'll keep slugging.

Regards,
Ron

William Rusher was the publisher of National Review; *his column on the accomplishments of the Reagan administration was published a few weeks before the 1984 election.*

Mr. William A. Rusher
New York, New York
November 29, 1984[44]

Dear Bill:

Well now that the smoke has cleared away and the shots are only an echo I can take pen in hand and thank you for that October 18 column of yours that William F. Buckley Jr. sent me.

You were just in time with that roundup of what's been accomplished. I was almost ready to vote for Mondale and you know who.

Seriously I do appreciate your generous words more than I can say and they did boost my morale. Bill we better brace ourselves, the flack will be flying when we go public with what we feel must be done to resolve this deficit problem. A lot of sacred cows are headed for the slaughterhouse.

Well again thanks. Nancy sends her love.

Best regards,
Ron

Reagan replies to a high school student whose teacher has told him that the United States has "seen its golden days and is now on its way down." Reagan compares the U.S. economic recovery to economic conditions in Western Europe and notes the success of the military buildup.

Mr. Paul E. Bulman, Jr.
Scituate, Massachusetts
September 26, 1985[45]

Dear Paul:

I know I'm kind of late in answering your letter but it takes a while before mail gets to my desk. I'm glad you wrote. I've heard the same things that Irish teacher said from some here in our country who always seem to blame America first for any and every thing. Well don't you believe him.

First on the economic side we've had the greatest and fastest recovery from recession over the past three years that we've ever had. In the last thirty-three months we've created more than eight million new jobs. We have more people employed than ever before. It's true that since 1979 we've reduced manufacturing jobs by 1,600,000. But we've added more than 9,000,000 new jobs to service industries and transportation alone. Just since 1982 some 2,000,000 new businesses have started in our country.

As for government spending, yes that's been out of line for 50 years and we must reduce our deficit but we're on the way to doing that. Our European friends haven't added one new job in more than ten years. We're trying to help them out of the recession they are still having with an unemployment rate that is two or three times the size of ours. In my last meeting with the leaders of those nations* they called what we are doing "the American miracle," and they asked me to tell them how we did it.

As for the military situation he was as far wrong as he was on the economy. It's true that when our administration started in 1981 our military had been allowed to slide downhill very badly. Today we are in better shape than we've been since World War II. Our new weapons systems are superior to just about anything in the world. Our Navy is being restored with new aircraft carriers and the Trident submarine. Airplanes, tanks, weapons of every kind are coming on line and our readiness has never been better. It's true the Soviets have more tanks and artillery and more men in uniform but remember they have to face not only the United States but all our allies, West Germany, England, France, Italy and so on.

You are right that ours is the greatest nation in the world. You young people are going to have things we never dreamed of just as we had it better than our parents before us. So stick to your dream and I wish you well in your plan to sign on for military aviation.

Best regards,
Ronald Reagan

Mrs. Schoper, the wife of a farmer and mother of three, wrote to President Reagan, "We're part of America that's dying. We're the part that still takes pies to sick neighbors . . . we're proof that working hard in America no longer pays off."

Reagan replies with empathy and specific information about the economic recovery.† He also mentions his tax reform proposal of May 1985, which became the Tax Reform Act (TRA) of 1986. This legislation lowered tax rates and eliminated various complex deductions.

Mrs. JoAnn Schoper
Jeffers, Minnesota
September 27, 1985[46]

Dear Mrs. Schoper:

Thank you for writing as you did. Perhaps I'm more understanding of your kind of farmer than you know. I started life in a small village in Illinois. It was a farm community existing to serve the needs of farmers. On Saturday the streets would be full of teams and wagons as the farmers from the surrounding countryside came to town to buy and sell. We in town were visitors, especially at threshing

---

* Reagan attended the meeting of the Group of Seven major industrial nations in Bonn, West Germany, in May 1985.
† The Consumer Price Index increased 3.8 percent in 1985—the fourth year it had been 4.0 percent or lower. Civilian employment in September 1985 was 107,519 thousand persons in comparison to the recession low of 98,979 thousand in December 1982.

time, to our farmer friends. In my family's case, our farm friends would pick us up in town because we couldn't afford any kind of transportation—horse and buggy or Model T.

Please Mrs. Schoper don't say your America is dying. Most Americans are still ready to lend a hand to a neighbor who needs help. Some 65 million Americans give time to volunteer causes just as you do.

Yes we give away surplus cheese, just as the government has welfare programs. But I've been trying to get government to help hardworking Americans like you and your family. We've brought inflation down from 13 percent to 2.5 percent for the last four months. Interest rates are less than half what they were five years ago and now I'm asking for a tax reform that will reduce your income tax sizably. Most important of all, we are trying to restore the economy so there will be a market for the things farmers produce. We have created eight million new jobs in the last 33 months.

Bless you, I know you aren't out for a free ride. We just want you to have more opportunity and a fair return for your work. Our goal, too, is to continue reducing interest rates.

Sincerely,
Ronald Reagan

Reagan explains why he would like to be able to veto specific items in the appropriations bills Congress sends him for signature.

Mr. James C. Schmidt
San Diego, California
April 27, 1987 [47]

Dear Jim:

It was good to get your letter and I appreciate your interest in our problems. Sometimes I wonder how they might look to me if I hadn't been a little conditioned by that mess we inherited in California.

Jim I'm going to keep on fighting for that line-item veto, but I'm afraid a trade as you suggested for a tax increase isn't the answer. With the Democrats back in charge in both Houses of Congress, there are too many of them just waiting for a crack in the dam to flood us with tax changes to pay for a pack of new spending ideas, not deficit reduction.

I'll keep on trying for the veto even if it's only for the next president, because you are right—it is the most essential tool to fiscal sanity. We are pushing for a whole new budget plan. You'd be amazed how Mickey Mouse the federal budget policy is. I doubt if any state would put up with it for five minutes.

Thanks again, and best regards.

Sincerely,
Ron

Charles Price was ambassador to Belgium from 1981 to 1983, and Ambassador to Great Britain from 1983 to 1989. Reagan reminds Price that taxes reduce the debt only if the budget is balanced.

The Honorable Charles H. Price
November 13, 1987[48]

Dear Charlie:

I'm late in answering your letter and will plead a hectic schedule plus some unscheduled events that upset my routine.

I appreciate your suggestions and want you to know a number of them are under consideration as we try to bring the Democrats in Congress into line. As you know I'm being very stubborn about new taxes that might adversely affect the economy. Our tax rate cuts have contributed to economic growth to such an extent that tax revenues are up $89 billion over what they were when the rates were higher. Our 1987 deficit was $73 billion less than in 1986.

Your suggestion of a tax just to reduce the debt is something I've had in mind for a time after we've balanced the budget. Get an amendment requiring a balanced budget from then on and pass a tax that could only be used to reduce that debt.

Well thanks again. Nancy sends her love and from both of us to Carol.

Sincerely,
Ron

Two of Reagan's reforms—the line-item veto and a balanced budget–tax limitation amendment to the Constitution—he did not achieve.

Mr. Philip J. Kruidenier
Des Moines, Iowa
November 23, 1987[49]

Dear Mr. Kruidenier:

Thank you for your October 16 letter. It has only just reached me, hence this late reply. You mentioned other letters. I'm afraid in the flood of mail that comes to the executive branch, much of it gets buried out there in the bureaucracy. In the future, if you should write, put the number 16690 on the front of the envelope.* That will get your letter directly to me.

I'm most grateful for your support and particularly so with regard to line-item veto. I've been preaching that ever since I've been here. Perhaps you know that gov-

---

* Any mail coming to the Reagan White House with the number 16690 on the envelope went directly to the president's personal secretary for Reagan's personal attention. Here he gives the code to a new correspondent whose letter has come to him through the selection of mail from the general public.

ernors in 43 states have that. I had it as governor of California. It truly would be of the greatest help in balancing the budget.

Let me tell you why the attack must be on the Congress itself and not on certain individuals—although I'm tempted many times to single out a few. The law requires the president to submit to Congress each year a budget for the coming year. Congress is then supposed to take that, change parts of it if they so desire, and vote on it. Since I've been president, not one of my budget proposals has ever been considered by the Congress. They've termed each one—dead on arrival and then packed all the appropriations into what they call a "Continuing Resolution." When this reaches me, I can't veto it without shutting the entire government down. See what line-item veto could do to change that?

You are right on a great many things including the Iran-Contra affair. As to your suggestions of things to do, I'll be doing them in this election year ahead. I do have one problem. I can go out making speeches (and I will) but much of the news media is on the other side. They will report that I made a speech and show it on television for about half a minute, but not the part where I make the points you want to hear.

Well, again my thanks to you for your generous words and support.

Sincerely,
Ronald Reagan

Reagan comments on the effects of his tax reform to Albert E. Schwabacher, a real estate investor from California.

Mr. Albert E. Schwabacher
San Francisco, California
July 13, 1988[50]

Dear Al:

I'm happy to hear you say our tax cuts are the real spark plug of our economic recovery. Those demagogs who scream our tax reform benefited the rich are talking through their hats. The top 1 percent ($100,000 a year and up) were paying 15.2 percent of the total income tax revenue in 1981. By 1983 when our tax plan was in place they were paying 20 percent of the total. The 21 percent who earned between $30,000 and $50,000 paid 50 percent. So the top 22 percent of all earners paid 70 percent of the total tax. And every year since, the total paid by the top earners has increased. Let me add there was a considerable reduction for those in the lower brackets.

Overall, of course, the lower tax rates resulted in an increase every year in total income tax revenues.

Nancy sends her love, and from us both to Cynthia.

Sincerely,
Dutch

———————

Milton Friedman reminded the president that an old Reagan speechline—"if we put the government in charge of sand, there'd be a shortage"—was true. The agreement on microchips—chips made of sand—between the United States and Japan had led to a shortage of microchips and a doubling of their price.

Dr. Milton Friedman
Stanford, California
September 13, 1988[51]

Dear Milton:

Forgive me for being so tardy in responding to your letter of July 25th but it sometimes takes a while for mail to make its way to my desk. In this case when it did get here I was out of town.

It was good of you to write as you did and I appreciate your bringing me up to date on the sand shortage. We were sorry you couldn't be here for the medal presentation but happy that you were recognized for your great contribution to our way of life.*

Nancy sends her very best regards and remember both of us to your lady. Again thanks for your letter.

Sincerely,
Ronald Reagan

———————

* Friedman was awarded the National Medal of Science on July 15, 1988.

CHAPTER TEN

Domestic Policy

R EAGAN CAMPAIGNED for the presidency on two primary issues—restoring the U.S. economy and restoring the nation's defense capabilities. These were his priorities in office as well. But he addressed a wide range of other issues, often with budget, economic, and foreign policy implications, both when campaigning and when in office. As Reagan says in one of these letters, "Sometimes it seems that I'm a juggler with at least fifteen balls in the air."

Federal spending for domestic programs—especially human resource programs such as health, welfare, and retirement—grew substantially through the 1960s and 1970s. By 1980 over 50 percent of federal spending was for such programs, more than twice the 1950s share. Just the opposite was the case for spending on national defense. Its share of federal spending declined over the same time period from over 50 percent to less than 25 percent.[1]

Social Security and Medicare had major budget implications. Together spending on these two programs was greater than that for national defense both when Reagan became president and when he left office. As national defense expenditures were reduced in the 1990s, outlays for the two programs would become twice the size of defense outlays.

Some of the issues on which Reagan wrote, such as abortion and school prayer, were considered part of the "new right" agenda. Reagan's correspondence reveals the consistency of his views on those topics over time and his sympathy with those who supported his views, but it also makes clear the higher priority he placed on his economic and national defense programs.

These letters offer a personal perspective on some of the many issues with which Reagan as candidate and officeholder dealt.

THE AIR TRAFFIC CONTROLLERS' STRIKE

The strike by the Professional Air Traffic Controllers' Organization (PATCO) in August 1981 and Reagan's firing of the strikers was a major event of Reagan's first year in office. Reagan's response to the strike was prompt and principled, the administration was well prepared, and Reagan did not back down on a difficult labor and economic issue. Of the 17,000 air traffic controllers, almost 13,000 struck. Reagan was on the record—specifically in a radio address taped May 25, 1977—that government employees do not have the right to strike.

Reagan announced the firing of the strikers on August 3, 1981, the day they went off the job, but gave them a 48-hour grace period to return to work. Reagan's action was considered a message to organized labor—a message he did not necessarily intend—and was also broadly interpreted as an indication that Reagan was tougher than anyone had thought.

In the first letter Reagan responds in sympathy to a woman whose son was fired, explaining why he cannot rehire the strikers. In the next letter he thanks one of the controllers who stayed on the job.

Mrs. Browning
Circa Sept 1981[2]

Dear Mrs. Browning:

I can understand your concern and your heartache. I can only hope that you will understand why it isn't possible for me to reinstate all those who went on strike. The law specifically prohibits public employees from striking. As you say, striking "is an inalienable right"—but not for government employees.

There is a difference. I was an officer of my union for some 25 years—president of that union for six terms. I led the union in the first strike it had ever engaged in. But even then I had to agree with FDR who proclaimed that public employment was different and that strikes against the people could not be tolerated.

When public employees began unionizing, organized labor at the highest levels supported their efforts only on the condition that they provide in their constitutions they would not strike. A strike is an economic contest between labor and management when negotiations have failed to resolve an issue. But governments can't shut down the assembly line. The services provided to the people, who in this case are the employers of all of us in government, must be continued.

Mrs. Browning, there are more than two million federal employees. What message would we be sending to all of them if we allowed a strike by one group or gave amnesty to them if they did strike? Believe me, there is no thought of punishment in what we are doing. There just is no way I can avoid enforcing the law. Let me recap what took place prior to the strike. I ordered our negotiators to point out to the PATCO representatives that a strike would mean the union members had to quit their jobs and we would have no alternative but to replace them. Concerned that the union officials had not notified the members of this, I withheld enforcement for 48 hours for the word to get around. Some controllers did report back for work in those 48 hours and, in fact, we kept the door open longer than that to make certain everyone had gotten the word.

The blacklisting you mentioned is a law that says federal employees who leave the government in this manner cannot reapply for federal employment for three years. I am trying to arrange a waiver of that law so that all the 12,000 can apply for whatever government jobs are available without waiting.

We have an obligation to those who did stay on duty and who have maintained flying schedules up to 75 or 80 percent of normal. At the same time however I do feel a very real sorrow for those who followed the union leadership at such a sacrifice. This is especially true of someone like your son who served our country in uniform. Please believe the plight of families such as that of your son is of great concern to me.

Sincerely,
Ronald Reagan

Mr. Jerry C. McMillan, ATCS
Atlanta, Georgia
September 29, 1981[3]

Dear Mr. McMillan:

Thank you very much for your letter of August 26. I can't tell you how much it brightened my day.

Let me thank you, also, for what you are doing so uncomplainingly. I am more grateful than I can say to all of you who are undergoing the hardships of added hours and added days of the week to keep our planes in the air.

I hope we can soon provide you with some relief to ease the burden. But, in the meantime, let me say not only am I deeply grateful, but our obligation is to you, and I certainly have no intention of weakening in the stand that I have taken with regard to those who chose to ignore their pledge. However, I did not know of the abuse that you were taking—the vandalism, threats, and so forth. I plan to see if there isn't something we can do to alleviate that or in some way offer protection.

Please convey my thanks to all of those there in the tower with you. Tell them how grateful we are for what all of you are doing.

Sincerely,
Ronald Reagan

THE VOLUNTEER MILITARY

"Cap, I would infinitely rather know that all of these men and women are here because they want to be, instead of being drafted and forced to be here," Reagan remarked to his secretary of defense, Caspar Weinberger, at a Pentagon ceremony on September 10, 1981.⁴ During his presidency Reagan improved military pay and benefits and morale to make the volunteer military more effective.

Reagan rejects Victor Krulak's call for a return to the draft. He and Krulak were both members of the Owl's Nest camp at the Bohemian Grove; Reagan notes he will miss their July encampment.

Lt. General Victor H. Krulak, USMC (Ret.)
San Diego, California
July 15, 1981⁵

Dear Brute:

I am sorry to be a month late in answering your letter, but just wanted you to know how homesick you made me when you told about all of you being there at Owl's Nest. I appreciated the snapshots very much. Thank you and all of Owl's Nest for the honor you are doing me this year.

I enjoyed your columns and must tell you I don't approve of the racetrack concept for the MX,* but I think I would like to continue the volunteer force and see if with some of the improvements we've made, we can't make it work as it used to. There are some very hopeful signs. We are getting a great flood of recruits, and many men who have served and left the service are coming back and re-enlisting. But more than that, there seems to be an upgrading in quality and a new morale and esprit de corps that have been lacking for some time. Anyway, let's try it for awhile and see if it doesn't work.

The other night we went to the ceremony out at the Marine Barracks here. It was a thrilling thing. It made you want to stand up and salute and sing the national anthem and anything else you could do. They were magnificent and when the very intricate performance of the drill team was over, I was amazed to discover that the bulk of them are in their first year of service and average between ages 18 and 19.

Well, Brute, again, say hello to everyone for me, and I'm going to spend a couple of very bad weekends in July wishing I were you-know-where.

Sincerely,
Ron

---

* The MX missile. In order to avoid first-strike vulnerability, it had been proposed that missiles be kept permanently mobile on specially built tracks.

Marjorie Fluor told the President she supported the military draft and hoped Rear Admiral Dwight Johnson of the Council for Inter-American Security, who was promoting a return to the draft by running a survey on conscription, would be able to report "positive" results to Congress. Fluor believed the draft would strengthen defense and reduce crime, drug abuse, and unemployment. Reagan disagrees.

Mrs. Marjorie Fluor
Santa Ana, California
February 9, 1983[6]

Dear Marjorie:

It was good to hear from you and I'm sorry about my own lack of writing. I'm afraid the days go by with me always thinking things will settle down. It's about time I guess for me to realize this is probably the regular pace and adjust to it.

Marjorie I don't know what the admiral and his organization are going to recommend but I have to say it won't accomplish the things you listed because we've already done that. When we came here there was no question but that our military was in a sad state and many people did think the draft was our only solution. That is no longer true. From a situation where we were only getting the castoffs of low intelligence and not even enough of those, in our volunteer military we now have a full enlistment with a waiting list. But we also have quality—highest level of average or above intelligence we've ever had; highest percent of high school graduates and up; highest reenlistment rate.

We have as many enlistees as we would require in a draft so as you were hoping we are already helping in reducing unemployment by about two million or more young people.

Best of all there is an esprit de corps—a spirit in the military we haven't had in years past. I'm so darned proud of them I could bust.

Well again it was good to hear from you. Nancy sends her love and we both hope our paths will cross one of these days.

Sincerely,
Ron

RACE RELATIONS

Reagan believed that he was brought up without bigotry or prejudice. He was proud of his record in fighting discrimination through employment opportunities and his appointments as governor. He believed in a growing economy and jobs rather than handouts that he felt demeaned recipients.

In these letters from the late 1970s and the presidency, Reagan addresses prob-

lems of Hispanics, native Americans, and blacks and regrets that his views and accomplishments are not better known and understood.

Lennie Pickard was an American Indian who worked in the field of education. Reagan thanks Pickard for his support, explains his approach to the minority community, and asks for Pickard's help in formulating policies on American Indians.

Mr. Lennie Pickard
August 6, 1979[7]

Dear Mr. Pickard:

I can't tell you how much I appreciate your fine letter and how grateful I am for what you are doing in my behalf.

First, let me address myself to the question of the black minority and what my position is, as well as how I feel we should approach them.

I realize there is a great lack of information about what I did as governor of California and it increases the farther east you go. As a result of this, I know that the minority community has an impression that I have little or no interest in their problems. When I became governor I discovered that after eight years of liberal Democratic rule in Sacramento, very little outside of rhetoric had been done for the minorities. The civil service regulations were such that it was virtually impossible for a black employee of state government to rise above the very lowest job levels. We got those rules changed. And even though we held down the increase in size of government during our eight years, we managed to change the balance and increase the percentage of black employees in state government to something comparable to their percentage ratio in our population. More importantly, however, there was a vast increase in the number who rose to supervisory positions. In addition to that, in those appointments I could make as governor, including judges and people in executive and policy-making positions, I appointed more blacks than all the previous governors of California put together.

My first few years as governor were during the period when people talked of long hot summers to come. We had had the Watts riots just prior to my taking office and racial tensions were very high. Without informing the press, I traveled up and down the state meeting with minority groups and leaders, sometimes in private homes, sometimes in headquarters they had in various community projects. I wanted to know firsthand what their problems were, what was on their minds, and what we could do to change things. The result was that when the riots broke out all over the country following the death of Martin Luther King, California was a state in which there was no disturbance at all. One somewhat radical leader is known to have passed the word down the state to cool it, that things were better in California.

Now I want to comment on how I believe we Republicans should approach the minority communities. I have been speaking all around the country and recently addressed the state conventions of Republicans in North Carolina, Virginia and Georgia. In each of those places, I said that our opponents, the Democrats, have for years appealed to the black community by offering handouts and making promises of greater handouts. We Republicans had not challenged them for that vote because we thought we would have to top their promises and that was against our philosophy. I said, I think we should go into those communities not because they're black or brown or any other color but simply because they are Americans as we are Americans and they have the same hopes and dreams and aspirations. They want to be treated as having dignity as individuals, they want better education for their children, they want jobs in the private sector with a future. And we should tell them that that is what our party has to offer. Not a no-growth policy but an equal chance for everyone. And I was gratified to find that literally I got a standing ovation in those southern states for advocating this. I received a similar reaction when I said the Democratic policy over the years of promising handouts had demeaned and insulted our fellow Americans in the minority communities.

I have recently returned from a visit with President Portillo of Mexico. I told him of my belief that we have been insensitive down through the years to our Latin American neighbors and that I would like to see a greater sensitivity on our part and the beginning of a program to create, literally, a common market situation here in the Americas with an open border between ourselves and Mexico. We had a very nice visit, and I'm sure that he knows I sincerely meant the things I had told him.

Now, Lennie, I come to the community of most interest to you. And I must confess that I need your help because I don't know the answers. As governor, I met many times with Indian groups and I discovered the difficulty was that we can't approach their problems as we do the others as simply a problem that is Indian versus white man because the Indians themselves still retain their tribal identification and properly so. Thus I would find myself trying to deal with one group and find that representatives of another tribe would come in with completely opposite viewpoints regarding their particular problem. One of the few opportunities I had to deal with one particular tribal policy that was successful was when the Army Corps of Engineers wanted to build a dam and flood Round Valley as part of the great California water project. Round Valley, a beautiful center of ranching and agriculture, had been given to the Modoc Indians a hundred years ago with the promise that they would be pushed no farther. This was theirs as long as the streams flowed and the grass was green. I vetoed the dam proposal because I said it was time that some of us started keeping the promises our grandfathers had made. Young Indians in a woodworking class made a very handsome plaque in appreciation and I treasure it very much.

I'll confess the Indian problem, or problems, seem very complicated to me, and

I don't know how to reconcile the desire to preserve the ancient ways, on the one hand and on the other, a desire to find a place as you obviously have here in our modern technological society. I believe our government has been tragically wrong down through the years and has played a big brother role to the detriment of the Indians for too long a time.

Very frankly, I would appreciate your own views on this matter. I hope our paths cross soon, and I look forward to being able to discuss these problems at greater length with you. Again, my heartfelt thanks for your letter and for what you are doing.

Sincerely,
Ronald Reagan

Reagan replies to beliefs that he is "the worst racist of the century" and wonders why his positions on many issues are not better known, given his five-day-a-week radio commentaries.

Tommy Thorson
Circa January 15, 1980[8]

Dear Tommy:

Thank you very much for your letter. I, too, am sorry there was no time for a visit because I think I could have put your mind to rest on a number of the issues you brought up.

First, let me say I feel as Lincoln did when he said he would be the most foolish man on earth if he thought he could face the job he had without feeling he had God's help. I believe very deeply in prayer and the power of prayer, and I could not have faced the responsibilities I did as governor, nor would I have the courage to seek the office of the presidency, if I didn't think I could call on and have the help of God.

You listed a number of things which you said your friends believed about me, and you wanted answers to them. The first was that I was the worst racist of the century. I wonder if they know that, as governor of California, I appointed more members of the minority community to executive and policy-making positions than all the previous governors of California put together. I also managed to make changes in the civil service laws so that minority members could rise to higher rank in civil service than they had previously been allowed to. Indeed, in spite of liberal Democrat administrations in California, the civil service rules were rigged against the minorities. I do not support the ERA. I am for equal rights for everyone and believe there still are discriminations against women in some of our laws, but I believe we could change the laws without a constitutional amendment. I am dead against the so-called equal rights for children, which would allow them to have a government-paid lawyer and sue their parents for whatever reason.

I am surprised at times that there is so much lack of knowledge about my positions. For several years except when I was running in '76 and now in the present campaign, I have had a five-day-a-week radio commentary on more than 300 stations nationwide. I took up virtually every subject mentionable and stated my views on those subjects, but I guess there were a lot of people who were not listening. Maybe, as the campaign goes on, there will be more awareness of where I stand on these various issues.

Thank you very much for your fine letter and perhaps one day our paths will cross again.

Sincerely,
Ronald Reagan

Willie Nunnery was a Wisconsin attorney.

Mr. Willie J. Nunnery
June 16, 1980[9]

Dear Mr. Nunnery:

Thank you very much for the note you handed me in Wisconsin. I'm sorry we didn't have time to visit.

I'm in complete agreement with what you said and am making an effort in my campaign to go after that vote that has been so taken for granted by Democrats. Personally, I believe that the Democrats have insulted our good American neighbors in the minority neighborhoods by constantly basing their approach on welfare handouts. You and I know that isn't the real need. That's why I believe Republicans can effectively appeal simply by stressing that our approach is an economy which can provide jobs, jobs with a future for every citizen. I've been encouraged in the recent primaries by those black citizens who have given me support. I'll confess I don't know what percentage of the citizenry they are, but, like you, I believe we must have them on our side, and we can do that by demonstrating that we're on their side.

Again, thanks and I hope our paths cross again soon.

Sincerely,
Ronald Reagan

In this letter Reagan makes clear his repudiation of the endorsement of the Ku Klux Klan and "everything the Klan stands for." Reagan's father, Jack, had not allowed his sons to see the film Birth of a Nation because it glorified the Klan.[10] In Storm Warning, filmed in 1949, Reagan played a reforming local police chief, Burt Rainy, who investigates the murder of a reporter investigating the Klan. A newspaper story quoted a let-

ter Reagan wrote to a friend while making the movie saying they were going to "lick the KKK. . . . Wouldn't Jack have been pleased!" [11]

Mr. Nathaniel J. Friedman
August 23, 1980 [12]

Dear Mr. Friedman:

Just a line to thank you very much for your letter to the editor of the *Los Angeles Times*. It was kind and generous of you to do this, and I am most grateful.

It wasn't until I left the South and was in New York that I learned the Klan had endorsed me. I immediately made it plain in a press conference that I do not want such an endorsement and that I repudiate it and everything the Klan stands for. I guess Mr. Young* didn't pay much attention to that.

Again, my heartfelt thanks.

Best regards,
Ron

Alonzo Smith was a black football player with whom Reagan played at Eureka. Wilfred "Tubby" Muller was another member of the team. Reagan writes that he shares Smith's view of the historically black colleges and universities and recalls his 1981 actions to increase federal assistance to them.†

Mr. Alonzo L. Smith
Jefferson, Texas
October 1, 1986 [13]

Dear Alonzo:

What a nice surprise to hear from you after all these years we've been away from "The Elms upon the Campus." We just had a fundraising dinner for Eureka last week. Did you know that Coach Mac, now in his 90s is still assisting the football coach at Eureka? He may outlast all of us.

I was pleased to be invited to meet with the black college and university presidents when they were here. Alonzo I've been able to lend a hand to the black college fundraising group and share your feeling about those schools. When I first took office I learned of a debt problem involving the government and Meharry Medical School that threatened to close the school down. We were able to take care of that

---

* Probably Andrew Young, syndicated columnist at the time and former U.N. ambassador in the Carter administration, who attacked Reagan's states' rights position as racist in an August 13, 1980, column in the *New York Times* and in speeches.

† Reagan issued Executive Order 12320 on September 15, 1981, designed to increase participation by historically black colleges and universities in federally funded programs. Reagan also increased federal funding by $9.6 million, an 8 percent increase, in part to solve the financial problem that threatened Meharry's survival.

situation. As you know, that black medical college has graduated half or more of all the black doctors in the country. Believe me I share your feeling about those schools and will do all I can to see that they continue doing what they have been doing so well for all these years.

Thank you for writing. It was good to hear from you. If you are talking to Tubby M. again give him my best regards.

Sincerely,
Dutch

————

Benjamin Hooks was executive director of the NAACP from 1977 to 1993. Kathy Osborne, Reagan's personal secretary, sent Reagan's draft of a letter to Hooks (the version printed here) to the staff for fact checking. The staff returned it with additional data and a recommendation that Reagan telephone Hooks instead of writing. But Reagan sent the letter. Hooks continued to publicly oppose Reagan and his policies.

Mr. Benjamin Hooks
Executive Director, NAACP
January 12, 1983 [14]

Dear Ben:

A short time ago you were quoted as having told the press that no administration in 30 years has "demonstrated as much determination as President Reagan to roll back hard-won gains of black Americans." You then described 1982 as the worst year in recent memory for blacks because of my budget policies.

Ben there are no facts to substantiate such charges and they are a distortion of the actual record as well as of my own position on these matters. The number of cases involving civil rights litigation were 753 for only nine months of 1982 as against 656 for all of 1980. In just eight months of 1982, $9.7 million in back pay and other monetary benefits was collected compared again to the full year 1980 when the figure was less than half that, $4.6 million.

The results of complaint processing for victims of discrimination show appreciable gains. The number of persons benefiting from EEOC's [Equal Employment Opportunity Commission] voluntary complaint settlements was 32,790 in the first six months of '82, a 53 percent increase over fiscal 1981 which includes three months of the Carter administration. The figures for investigations, settlements etc. show similar gains for our nearly two years here.

As for our budget cuts, economic policy etc. hasn't the lowering of inflation by almost two-thirds* been of help to blacks as well as to all others? Even people on welfare or at the poverty level of earnings have several hundred dollars more in purchasing power than they would have had if inflation had remained at the

---

* The consumer price index rose 12.4 percent in 1980, 8.9 percent in 1981, and 3.8 percent in 1982.

1980 level. Yes I know there is economic distress in the land and that black unemployment is exceptionally high.* But all the political demagoguery in the land can't hide the fact that this recession was caused by the high interest rates (the result of inflation) which prevailed in 1980 and much of '81. Our program was not yet in place when the bottom fell out. Now there are signs of recovery and I'm determined it will benefit everyone across the board. I hope that political prejudice will not keep you from really looking at our record and learning how unjustified your attack was.

Ben if only it were possible to look into each other's hearts and minds, you would find no trace of prejudice or bigotry in mine. I know that's hard for you to believe and that's too bad because together we could do more for the people you represent than either of us can do alone.

Prejudice is not a failing peculiar to one race, it can and does exist in people of every race and ethnic background. It takes individual effort to root it out of one's heart. In my case my father and mother saw that it never got a start. I shall be forever grateful to them.

Sincerely,
Ron

Mr. Richard A. Hernandez
California Republican Hispanic Council
Los Angeles, California
June 10, 1983 [15]

Dear Richard:

Thank you very much for making me an honorary member of the council. I am honored and proud. Please convey my thanks to your associates.

I can't tell you how good I feel about all that you are doing. For a long time I've believed that our Hispanic citizens with their love of family, their independence and self-respect would find themselves more at home with the Republican Party. With the California Republican Hispanic Council you have created the leadership which can show the way. We need you, not just your votes, but your active participation in party affairs, your input in party decisions and your ideas.

Again my heartfelt thanks.

Sincerely,
Ronald Reagan

On July 9, 1984, Reagan spoke to a group of newspaper editors, responding to a question about what would be done to attract black voters in the fall election. He noted the

---

* The black unemployment rate was 16.8 percent in March of 1983; white unemployment was 8.0 percent. By 1986 black unemployment was 10.7 percent; white unemployment was 5.5 percent. Between 1983 and 1986, black employment increased 18 percent and white employment increased 9 percent.

*administration's 1981 actions to aid black colleges and universities, emphasized the
economic recovery program and the jobs it was creating, and spoke of two programs
that he believed would be especially helpful to black youth, a two-step minimum wage
and enterprise zones. Neither program was moving in the Congress, where Democrats
wanted a bigger increase in the minimum wage.*

*Reagan received a July 10, 1984, letter[16] from Clarence Thomas, the chairman of
the Equal Employment Opportunity Commission and future Supreme Court justice,
thanking Reagan for hosting and attending a briefing for black appointees of the administration. Thomas noted the "perceived anti-minority views" of the administration and the hostility toward black appointees from other blacks. It was the view of the
black appointees that with the exception of opposition to quotas and bussing, "no positive or coherent policy exists."[17] The meeting was not open for press coverage. Reagan
telephoned Thomas in response to the letter.*

*These two letters express Reagan's frustration over accusations of bigotry and his
continued efforts in Congress to pass the programs he believed would be helpful to
minorities.*

Mrs. L. Smith
Los Angeles, California
August 29, 1984[18]

Dear Mrs. Smith:

I have no words to express my appreciation for what your letter meant to me.
Believe me you brightened my day considerably.

Nothing has frustrated me more in this job than the false image of bigotry that
has been fastened upon me. My parents, God rest their souls, brought my brother
and me up to believe that racial and religious prejudice were the greatest of evils.
We were opposing bigotry long before there was a civil rights movement. Being the
age I am in my younger days I knew at first hand the shameful period which thank
Heaven we've left behind us.

Well I'll heed your advice and not "overdefend" but please know how grateful I
am. God bless you.

Sincerely,
Ronald Reagan

Mr. Donald Wilson
Jersey City, New Jersey
January 28, 1985[19]

Dear Mr. Wilson:

Thank you for your letter. You'll never know how much it meant to me. I've been
frustrated by our inability to get our story through the wall of silence to the black
community. Right now we continue to try to persuade Congress to give us what we
call "enterprise zones." It is a program to use tax incentives to bring business and industry into depressed inner city neighborhoods to provide jobs and opportunity for

the people there. We're also battling to get a lower minimum wage for young people with no work experience so they can get that first job. The present minimum has priced them out of the job market. The Council of Black Mayors support this because black teenagers have the highest rate of unemployment in the land. We'll keep trying.

You are right also about how government programs have kept blacks in poverty, dependent on government handouts. I want to help them become independent.

Thank you again and very best wishes to you.

Sincerely,
Ronald Reagan

FEDERALISM

One of Reagan's basic convictions was that the federal government had grown too large and taken on responsibilities that properly belonged at the state or local level. Reagan first presented a proposal to return many federal programs to the states during the 1976 presidential campaign and often talked about the Tenth Amendment to the Constitution—"The powers not delegated to the United States by the Constitution, nor prohibited by it to the States, are reserved to the States respectively or to the people." Specific legislation for the federal government to take full responsibility for Medicaid (health care for the poor) in return for the states taking full responsibility for Aid to Families with Dependent Children (the basic welfare program) and food stamps, and a plan to return many grant-in-aid programs to the states along with the tax sources to fund them, was sent to the Congress in 1983. Congress took no action on that legislation, but during the Reagan years many federal programs were combined as block grants for the states to administer.

Mr. and Mrs. Fitzgerald
Fort Worth, Texas
Circa November 1980 [20]

Dear Mr. and Mrs. Fitzgerald:

Thank you for your wire. I want to share my thinking on some of the subjects you brought up. First of all, with regard to your suggestion of cutting expenses, I believe very definitely that government at the federal level is so filled with extravagance and waste that there can be sizeable reductions in spending. You are absolutely right about government labor. Today government labor averages about $4,000 a year, about the average for the private sector.*

---

* What Reagan means by "government labor" is unclear.

With regards to cities, towns, counties and states, I too favor an end to the present grant system, but I believe the federal government is in part responsible for their problems because it has not only usurped programs but tax sources to pay for them and then, in return for its grants, insists that local and state government spend the money on exactly the priorities laid down by [the federal] government but also the manner in which the money must be spent. There is great waste and extravagance in this system—to say nothing of the additional administrative overhead created by the federal government.

My own idea is that, in a planned and orderly manner, we should transfer many of these programs back to state and local government. Let those governments make those decisions as to whether they want to continue the programs but transfer back with them sources of taxation to pay for them. Don't just dump them on local government. I believe some programs would be retained in some areas—in others they would be found unnecessary. Overall, I think the reduction in administrative overhead would amount to a tremendous savings.

Regarding labor, you might be interested to know that when government employees first began to unionize, they sought and got the backing of organized labor but on one condition—organized labor insisted that those early government unions pledge not to strike. In recent years, that seems to have been forgotten, and we find government employees at every level striking whenever it suits their fancy. We should have a strict law that government employees are not allowed to strike. They can quit if they want to, but they can't strike.

Again, it was good meeting you and I hope this answers the questions you wrote in your letter.

Sincerely,
Ronald Reagan

Mr. and Mrs. Richard A. Stetson
Elmhurst, Illinois
February 10, 1982 [21]

Dear Mr. and Mrs. Stetson:

I appreciate your taking the time and trouble to send me a mailgram, but I believe I can't go along with your charge that I am trying to make fifty countries out of our fifty states. I am trying to restore the Tenth Amendment of the Constitution which very carefully spells out that all powers not specifically given to the federal government in the Constitution shall remain with the states and the people. Someplace in this last forty or fifty years we discarded, apparently, that part of the Constitution and handed the federal government tasks it is just not equipped to perform. And, the result today is not only our present recession, but a trillion dollar debt, inflation, high taxes, and high interest rates.

I was governor of a state, I know at firsthand the extravagance, the waste and the failure of so many of the federal programs that were imposed on our state. I know, too, how much better we could have performed some of those programs had it not been for the federal government usurping the authority. I am pleased to tell you that we have been meeting with governors and mayors, and working with them on how these functions will be apportioned. And, they are greatly enthused and believe that for the first time, they are going to have a chance to do the things that properly belong at their levels of government.

Thank you again.

Best regards,
Ronald Reagan

Congress enacted the National Maximum Speed Limit (NMSL) of 55 mph in 1974 in response to the energy crisis, but it was later justified as a safety measure. Not until 1987 was highway legislation enacted, over Reagan's initial veto on grounds of excessive spending, that allowed the states to increase the speed limit to 65 on rural interstates. The NMSL was abolished in 1995.

Mr. Robert S. Niccoles
Orinda, California
March 7, 1983 [22]

Dear Bob:

I sympathize and agree with your complaint. I too believe we should turn the speed laws back to the states where they belong. So far we just haven't been able to convince the troops in the Capitol it should be done.

Thanks for your words of support and best regards,
Ronald Reagan

SOCIAL SECURITY AND MEDICARE

Social Security (initially enacted in 1935) and Medicare (1965) were major expenditures in the federal budget. Congress repeatedly expanded Social Security eligibility and increased benefits between 1950 and 1972, when benefits were indexed to the consumer price index. Funded by a payroll tax on current workers, Social Security was ruled constitutional by the Supreme Court in 1937 as a welfare program but promoted to the public as contributory insurance. Benefits are based on formulas that allow payments far in excess of contributions, especially for those who retired before the 1980s. For later retirees, who have paid higher taxes, the program may not provide even a reasonable rate of return. As the population ages and more people receive benefits longer, the program eventually will run out of money unless taxes are increased or the benefit formula is made less generous. This is the actuarial imbalance of which Reagan speaks in these letters.

Medicare, which Reagan initially opposed, rapidly exceeded its predicted costs.

———

In this 1962 letter Reagan explains his position on the King bill, a forerunner of the Medicare legislation enacted July 30, 1965, to his longtime movie fan and pen pal. Reagan would later drop his opposition to Medicare as it became an entrenched part of the political landscape, but controlling costs was a major concern. (See page 578 for his first letter to Wagner on this issue.)

Lorraine Wagner
Philadelphia, Pennsylvania
August 16, 1962 [23]

Dear Lorraine:

A quick line from (as you can see) a little vacation with the kids.

Thanks very much for your letter to Drew Pearson. I think it is a masterpiece and I'm most grateful to you. I've been watching his column off and on since his blast at me and I honestly believe a case could be made that he is against America. Certainly he lends comfort and aid to the enemy.

Now about your own letter. Whatever the government provides it will be paid for by the people through taxes. The increase in Social Security taxes to finance the King bill will apply to all of us not just old people. I simply believe the other program administered at the state level can be more economical and efficiently managed than if we create a vast new government bureau in Washington. All history indicates this is what happens <u>every time</u> the federal government invades a new field.

With reference to the socializing of medicine and what it will mean to the freedom of doctors we must look beyond immediate bills which serve only as a foot in the door. Any remarks I've ever made along that line have referred to the ultimate once the program is started. To be blunt about it we can no more have <u>partial</u> socialism than a person can be "a little bit pregnant." I have a dozen quotes from socialists and socialist publications and backers of the King bill boasting that it is only designed to establish the principle so that socialized medicine can follow.

Well that certainly is enough of a lecture because here come the kids. Again let me say whatever your feelings may be about this particular legislation and there are certainly two sides to any question I'm truly grateful for your letter to Drew P.

Regards to Wag.

Sincerely,
Ronnie

*During the 1980 campaign, Reagan writes to a Russian-American professor and sup-
porter in response to questions on health insurance, Social Security, and the Soviet
threat.*

> Professor Vsevolod A. Nikolaev
> New York
> After November 13, 1979 [24]

Dear Professor Nikolaev:

It was good to get your letter and have the benefit of your thinking on some
very important subjects. I am most grateful for your generous words about my
speech on the 13th.

With regard to the vice presidency, if it should fall to my lot to recommend a
vice president, I assure you that it would be someone of my own persuasion.

Regarding national health insurance, you could reassure your student, Miss
Lee Catcher, that while I am opposed to socialized medicine, I have always felt that
medical care should be available for those who cannot otherwise afford it. I have
been looking into a program whereby government might pay the premiums for
health insurance for those who cannot afford it and, at the same time, make such
premiums for others a tax credit or deduction, preferably credit to encourage more
use of private health insurance. There is also the problem of insurance for those
catastrophic cases where the medical care goes on for years at a tremendously high
cost. I proposed a form of government insurance for that in California when I was
governor, but we couldn't get any legislative support for it. I do believe this is a particular problem which must be faced and where the government could have a hand.

Regarding Social Security, I have simply said that the government must do
something to resolve the actuarial imbalance which is going to have us finding the
well dry down the road a few years. I have, however, always insisted that the first requirement is that those people dependent on Social Security must be assured it will
not be denied them or taken from them.

I appreciate very much your views on the world situation and read them with
great interest. There can be no question that we must not minimize in any way the
threat to the free world by the Soviet Union.

And, last, but certainly not least important, may I thank you very much for
your generous contribution to my campaign. I hope you had a very happy holiday
season.

> Best regards,
> Ronald Reagan

*President Reagan was led to believe that his initial proposals to deal with the long-
term imbalance in Social Security would be at least considered by the Democratic
majority in the House, but once sent to Congress Democrats and Republicans alike*

refused to consider them. This politically sensitive program was ultimately addressed by a bipartisan commission.* In combination, dollar outlays for Social Security plus Medicare were larger than national defense outlays both when Reagan took office and when he left.

Mr. Austin Trimmer Jr.
Phillipsburg, New Jersey
July 24, 1981 [25]

Dear Mr. Trimmer:

I appreciate very much your concern with regard to Social Security and the unemployment situation.

Let me assure you our economic package is designed to stimulate the economy by reducing taxes and, hopefully, by increasing productivity so as to create more jobs and end the layoffs. I was encouraged recently when I received a report from fifteen of the major steel companies in this country. They are going to invest $3,200,000,000 in plant modernization and expansion, all on the strength of our economic package because they believe it will result in a return to increased productivity and prosperity.

If I may, let me explain the situation and what it is we were trying to do with Social Security. I have reneged on no pledge. I said during the campaign that we would do nothing to hurt those presently dependent on Social Security checks—that we would not pull the rug out from under those people so dependent. I did say that I would try to restore the integrity to the program. As it is now, the program without change will run out of money for paying benefits to the present recipients sometime late in 1982. Beyond that, however, there is a long-range actuarial imbalance which means that down the road in the next century, but within the lifetime of younger workers today, the program will be several trillion dollars out of balance.

Our proposal was intended to resolve both the short-term problem and that long-range imbalance. We did not, in any way, affect the benefits of those presently dependent on the program. We did make some changes of people who are presently receiving benefits to which they are not entitled. The point which concerns you, however, has to do with reducing the grants for those who retire early.

What the press never seemed to point out was that our plan called for reducing the percentage of total grant the early retiree could receive from 80 percent to 55 percent, but by working only one year and eight months longer, the early retiree could at some time, while he is still 63, take early retirement and get 80 percent of the full retirement benefit. Other points that were not made would have a greater effect for younger workers in that the present law calls for the Social Security tax

---

* Reagan announced the creation of the bipartisan National Commission on Social Security, to be chaired by Alan Greenspan, on December 16, 1981. The commission reported on January 15, 1983, and the resulting legislation was signed April 20, 1983.

and the amount of income subject to that tax to increase several times between now and 1986. Our plan called for eliminating those increases which are now more burdensome for most workers than the income tax and even reducing, after a few years, the present Social Security tax. This tax reduction alone to the beginning workers, the young person just starting in the labor force and working out to retirement age, would have meant $33,000 of additional income which he could put to better use for himself and his family.

In contrast the program Congressman Pickle* is suggesting would increase the age of retirement to 68. I don't know whether he would make a comparable increase in the early retirement age, but it would seem logical that such would happen, and remembering that one-year-and-eight-month-clause in our recommendation, I believe that his program would represent a greater hardship, besides which there is no suggestion of reducing the pay-roll tax.

It is possible that some people nearing age 62 and having made plans for early retirement would be caught in our proposal, and we are looking to see if we should change to a more phased-in feature giving some warning to people who are, as I say, approaching 62.

Let me add that under our plan we would solve both the short-range problem and the long-range actuarial imbalance.

You and I are in complete agreement with regard to the need to put the unemployed back to work so that they, too, are contributing to the Social Security fund, and I believe the economic program we are advocating will do just that.

I was president of my union for six terms. I served on the national board for more than two decades. I think I understand some of the problems of labor in America. I am shocked that the hierarchy of organized labor, so many of whom I know personally, are taking the attitude they are toward our plans to try and restore the economy. It is government's deficit spending, a debt now approaching a trillion dollars, that is responsible for the slowdown in our economy.

The answer to labor's problem is productivity that will make us competitive in the world market once again and bring prosperity for all. We cannot continue down the road of excessive government spending, taxes which are now taking more out of the worker's check than he must pay for food, housing, clothing and transportation. I will welcome any suggestion that will meet the problem we face of running out of Social Security funds in 1982. I don't know how any of us could even contemplate having to tell 34,000,000 people dependent on that program that the cupboard is bare.

Again, thank you for your letter and for giving me a chance to comment.

Sincerely,
Ronald Reagan

---

* Jake Pickle (D-Texas) was a powerful member of the House Ways and Means Committee, which had jurisdiction over Social Security.

Although Reagan thought Social Security legislation should have based payments on need, he was unwilling to propose eliminating benefits that people had been led to believe were theirs by right, as he explains to this writer.

Mr. Henry G. Newson
Charlotte, North Carolina
March 5, 1985 [26]

Dear Mr. Newson:

Thank you very much for your letter of January 28 which has only just arrived at my desk.

I appreciate your suggestion about Social Security and agree that there are faults in the system. The most obvious is that the program was created with no provision for a means test. In the effort to portray it as an insurance program the originators refused to limit it to people who would have no other way to provide for their retirement years.

Now our problem is that government has made a contract with the people and would be violating that contract if it said some who had contributed would no longer receive benefits. I've had an idea for a solution for some time but believe it should come from the recipients themselves. There is a fund in the U.S. Treasury Department made up of voluntary contributors to reduce the national debt. People with no need for their benefits could contribute them to that fund and get some return for their generosity in that their contribution would be tax deductible.

If in our tax reform proposal we are able to get a reduction in pay for government employees I intend to use the procedure I've just described. I've learned that presidents are prohibited by law from changing their salary so I intend to contribute a percent equal to the cut, to that fund.

Again thank you for your letter.

Sincerely,
Ronald Reagan

WELFARE

In his second term as governor of California, Reagan reformed the state's welfare system by tightening eligibility and reducing fraud, increasing work requirements, and increasing benefits.[27] Campaigning for the White House, Reagan denounced "welfare queens" and others who relied on the dole. But his fundamental commitment was to jobs and opportunity rather than a handout. The Family Support Act of

1988 was a major reform of welfare* that paved the way for the Welfare Reform Act of 1996.

H.R. 1 was Richard's Nixon's Family Assistance Plan proposed to Congress in 1969 while Reagan was governor of California. It incorporated a negative income tax. Reagan opposed it and helped to rally opposition. The plan was eventually defeated. Reagan's welfare reforms in California were a major success of his governorship and he considered them a model for the nation.

Circa 1971 [28]

Dear [addressee unclear]:

Thanks very much for sending me your address regarding H.R. 1. It goes without saying we are very much in agreement on the potential for evil in adding millions of new people to the relief rolls.

I am hopeful our own reforms in California may serve as an indicator of ways to break the welfare cycle during the delay the president has asked for in implementing reforms at the national level. I am encouraged to believe that the president has questions about the Family Assistance Plan. Certainly he was most helpful to us in our request that HEW † permit us to require welfare recipients to perform useful community service in return for their grants.

It seems to me the question of helping the working poor might be resolved better by giving them a tax break, allowing them to keep a greater percentage of their earnings rather than subsidizing them with an outright grant. I was struck recently by a case in Sweden's socialist society where an employed father earning $460 a month was allowed a $55 a month government allowance. His taxes average $139 a month. Common sense would suggest reducing his taxes $55 but that I suppose would be too unorthodox for the socialist mentality.

One last thought before this letter gets much too long. Since we instituted certain of our administrative reforms (but in my opinion mainly because of the public spotlight we focused on welfare) our 50,000 a month caseload increase has been reversed, and for four straight months we have reduced the caseload more than 25,000 a month.‡

Again thanks, and I hope we meet again in the very near future.

Sincerely,
Ronald Reagan

---

* See Andrew E. Busch, *Ronald Reagan and the Politics of Freedom* (New York: Rowman & Littlefield, 2001), pp. 160–61.

† HEW was the Department of Health, Education and Welfare, which later became the Department of Health and Human Services.

‡ The California caseload peaked at 2,459,800 in March 1971. Hannaford, *The Reagans*, p. 18.

Reagan sent his Secretary of Health and Human Services a copy of an article from the April 18, 1972 Wall Street Journal *by Paul Lancaster titled "Was the WPA Really So Awful?" The WPA was the Depression-era Works Progress Administration. Schweiker replied with a memorandum summarizing work requirements in various federal assistance programs and noting that states were forbidden to require work in exchange for unemployment insurance benefits.*

Secretary Richard S. Schweiker
February 1982 [29]

Dear Dick:

The attached is old but interesting. I'm not suggesting another WPA at this moment but there is food here for "workfare."

Why didn't unemployment insurance start out with something of a work requirement? It sure would end the "extended vacation" feature some have used it for.

Anyway just thought you'd find it interesting.

Ron

Irving Moulton, who called himself "a surviving business man," wrote to say, "Let's take a moment to say thanks to the millions of families in all walks of life who the last few years have survived and paid and will pay taxes April 15 without government help."

Mr. Irving R. Moulton
Perrysburg, Ohio
March 4, 1985 [30]

Dear Mr. Moulton:

Thank you for your letter of February 22nd and may I say, "right on." Since you wrote I've made a couple of speeches and done one of my Saturday radio broadcasts touching on the theme you so eloquently expressed in your letter.

Yes we have compassion for those who've tried and failed or who through no fault of their own must seek our help. But we can't impose unfairly on those who carry the load and make this country go and whose taxes pay the freight. For too long the forgotten American has been the citizen who sends the kids to school, goes to work, supports church and charity and pays taxes to keep the wheels turning. We'll keep on thinking of and caring for these Americans.

Again, thanks.

Sincerely,
Ronald Reagan

THE ENVIRONMENT

Reagan considered himself an environmentalist with a great love of nature and the outdoors, but thought many environmentalists had gone too far—"they wouldn't let us build a house unless it looked like a bird's nest."

Steven Hansch was the 13-year-old editorial editor of his junior high school newspaper, the Town Crier. *Hansch lived near the Reagans in Pacific Palisades and arranged to have his letter to Governor Reagan, in which he asked for comments on the environment, delivered through a security guard at the Reagans' home.*

Steven Hansch
Circa 1972[31]

Dear Steven:

Someone has written "there are three kinds of pollution—actual, hysterical and political." Hysterical pollution leads to political pollution with the result that all too often little or nothing gets done about actual pollution.

Young people today can become a great force for good in overcoming the mistakes of the past and insuring that their children will live in a cleaner world. The great need is for calm appraisal, recognition and evaluation of the real problem, and practical realism in solving it.

Let me give you some examples of hysterical pollution. A letter arrives on my desk signed by an entire schoolroom of eight-year-olds. They beg me to save them from smothering to death before they can grow up. Obviously they had been frightened into mailing such a letter by some adult who should know better.

Another letter, again from school children, expresses a belief that very soon all the redwood trees will have been cut down and replaced by plastic imitations.

Now let's look at the facts about both of these examples.

First, air pollution. Yes, we have problems in some areas, particularly our cities, but they are better than they were in the past. Martha Washington when she was the first lady of our land wrote a letter to her daughter about the terrible air pollution in Philadelphia. She said a majority of the city dwellers had eye infections from the smoke and gases in the air. Even Cicero in ancient Rome wrote of the joy in getting out in the country away from the poisonous atmosphere of the city.

Our problem today is caused largely by automobile exhaust. But not too long ago every home had a chimney belching coal smoke every hour of every winter day. We only discovered that autos were the cause of smog a few years ago, and now we are doing something about it. Today's autos are only about a third as polluting as the cars of just eight or nine years ago, and our regulations require the manu-facturers to virtually eliminate all pollutants by 1975.

In the meantime we have political pollution. A politician wanting to attract attention introduces a bill to ban all autos if they aren't 100 percent clean within an impossibly short time. He knows that his proposed bill would force every car and truck off the road, close down the manufacturers, put every oil station out of business and so on and on. Others have to rescue us from his demagoguery ei-ther by voting his bill down or by veto. He has made his splash, however, but in so doing has diverted the energies of those who are seriously trying to reduce air pollution.

The same thing happens with regard to the trees. California over the years has done one of the great outstanding jobs of preserving the great cathedral-like groves of redwoods. Almost 150,000 acres are now in our parks. Our lumber in-dustry cutting the less spectacular commercial redwoods is rapidly approaching what is called "sustained yield." This means cutting no faster than the trees can grow back. But once again our energies are diverted from the real task of improv-ing timber practices while we do battle with all sorts of unrealistic proposals. The plain truth is we can have a lumber industry providing wood for our home con-struction and furniture, and beautiful forests too.

In the November 24 issue of your *Town Crier* I was interested to read an article about the need to save our beaches for the enjoyment of all the people. All of us are dedicated to this goal and you should be encouraged by the true situation. Califor-nia has 1,050 miles of shoreline—more than 400 miles of which is already in public ownership. In March a commission created by the state will give us the findings of a two-year study of the coastline.

It is our intention to have the state, the counties bordering on the ocean and the seacoast cities come together in a united plan for all the coast. In the meantime we have had to fend off "coastline legislation" by politicians who know of the plans but who offer solutions without waiting for the study to be completed.

I suppose what I'm saying is—"find the facts." The problems of preserving our environment, the magic of this place we call California, are very real and require real solutions. We who are dealing with these problems at present need your help and we need to know that when you take over you'll be informed, determined and involved with actual, not hysterical or political, pollution.

Let me suggest that you can get factual information on our progress in solving these problems from our Department of Resources, State Capitol, Sacramento, California. We think California is showing the way to the rest of the country.

Thanks for giving me this opportunity to comment on this situation and again my commendation to you for your interest.

Sincerely,
Ronald Reagan

Reagan responds quickly and personally to a reader of a profile of the Reagans that suggested Reagan wasn't sensitive about the preservation of animal species.

Mr. Ewing

Circa 1970 [32]

Dear Mr. Ewing:

First of all we made no mention of our bar stools. The writer was in our home and observed them for himself.

Second, I share your concern about endangered species and about the killing of baby animals. It is true we have bar stools covered with cheetah skin but so far as I know it is not <u>baby</u> cheetah. What is more pertinent however is that the bar stools are more than twenty years old, dating back to a time when few of us were aware as we are now of the need to change our ways.

Thank you for writing and giving me a chance to set the record straight.

Sincerely,

Ronald Reagan

Reagan disagrees with this young woman's proposal, but notes progress is being made in air pollution.

Elizabeth

Circa 1967–1975 [33]

Dear Elizabeth:

Thank you for your letter and for your suggestions. I'm going to see that the proper agencies look them over.

I'm not pessimistic about the future and am even less so when I receive letters such as yours indicating that young Americans are now aware of our need to weigh our actions against their effect on the environment.

The tax incentive to reduce the number of automobiles I'm afraid could not be substantial enough to make enough of a reduction in the overall number of cars. We have and are, however, looking at similar ideas such as tax rates based on the polluting factors in various types of fuel.

Incidentally by way of encouragement, our efforts to clean up automobiles and stationary sources of air pollution are paying off. San Francisco has just announced a reduction of millions of pounds of pollutants each day, reducing smog back to the level of several years ago. In Los Angeles the 40 percent increase in population and consequent increase in automobiles has prevented such an improvement but still there has been very little increase in the amount of smog in spite of this great growth.

With the help of people like you we are going to preserve the beautiful environment of California.

Yours truly,
Ronald Reagan

Reagan objects to federal takeover of state lands.

Mr. Court McLeod
November 1979 [34]

Dear Mr. McLeod:

Thank you very much for your letter and for your words of support. I am truly grateful. Thank you, also, for expressing your concerns and giving me an opportunity to reply.

Before I take up the matter of the "trust lands," may I respond to your remarks about your own property tax situation. I am surprised to hear you say someone in my office in Sacramento wrote you and just said "tough luck." That certainly did not express my view nor characterize my staff. I had a number of letters of the same kind in those days as property taxes were skyrocketing. I always explained that the property tax was imposed locally, and the state could not just reduce or increase that tax.

I also explained that from the first day I was in office, I was trying to persuade the legislature, which, as you know, was Democrat, to pass legislation setting up a program whereby the state would subsidize local government in return for a reduction in the property tax, which is the only way that the state could have an effect on that tax. I tried throughout my first term and well into my second. One senator expressed to me the reason for my inability to get such a program. He said, "we're just not hearing from very many homeowners, and we're not going to do anything about it."

Finally, however, I did get a program which, at that time, when the average home price was $20,000, represented a 40 percent reduction in taxes. It also contained special relief over and above that for senior citizens. It wasn't as much as I would've liked, and it wasn't done in the way I would've liked to do it. It was not automatic—in other words, the individual had to understand the senior citizen rights and go in and apply for them. Naturally, there were many who never understood this even though we did our best to publicize the fact. But, when Jarvis came along with Prop 13, which dealt directly with those in charge of property tax—namely local and county government—I heartily endorsed it and argued throughout the campaign in its behalf.

Now, as to the trust lands, Alaska territory and the West, I too want land open space preserved for future generations, but I believe the federal government has been engaged in a land grab for a great many years. For example, just recently, the federal government, not satisfied with its holdings in national forests which can be enjoyed by people like you and me, has been changing millions of acres of this land to wilderness area. This means that unless you're able to put a pack on your back and hike in—to the woods with no trails, no vehicles allowed or roads, then you can't see all the public land.

When the original thirteen colonies became the United States, they, of course, had ownership of all the land within their boundaries. Indeed, the Constitution then stated and still does state that any states coming into the union subsequent to the 13 colonies would have the same right to territory as did those original colonies. The Constitution provides that the federal government is allowed to own land which it purchases only for the erection of forts, arsenals, dockyards, and other needful buildings. This, of course, then led to the inclusion of national parks, and no one of us denies the value of those national parks.

But states entered the union, and the country grew to the 100th meridian. Suddenly, the federal government was not so happy about giving up all that land to the states. They just violated the Constitution and held onto it, and then, in 1976, the Congress passed the Federal Lands Policy and Management Act which simply declared that the public lands would be retained in federal ownership. But, again, this law is contrary to the constitution.

Despite our great need for energy, the federal government has now seized upon 250,000 square miles of Alaska, which, under the terms of statehood, had originally been guaranteed to Alaska. This land is believed to be rich in possibilities for oil and natural gas, which does not mean that the wilderness would be destroyed or the open lands disappear. For many years, our national forests have been held on the basis of multiple use. Much of that land is open for leased grazing, some of it for lumbering, and some of it for minerals. But, basically, it is my belief that the people of the various states would have as much concern for the preservation of the beauty and the open space in their states as does the federal government. I just can't believe that a little elite group in Washington has a conscience and that the people themselves do not.

You mentioned the Santa Monica Mountains. Does it really require the federal government to make that decision and impose it on us or should it be the responsibility of all of us living in this city and in this country to determine what proportion of it we think should be preserved as open space. I believe that is a decision we can properly make. Well, those are my reasons for making the statement I did.

Again, I thank you for your letter and can heartily recommend that GE heating blanket because I've been sleeping under one for about twenty years now. It's just fine.

Best regards,
Ronald Reagan

James Watt was Reagan's first and prodevelopment, controversial, outspoken secretary of the interior.

> General Hal C. Pattison
> Fairfax, Virginia
> September 3, 1981 [35]

Dear General Pattison:

Thank you very much for writing as you did and for giving me an opportunity to comment with regard to your concern. I appreciate your generous words and the support you are giving to the party.

I have to say I believe our positions with regard to conservation have been wildly distorted and exaggerated. I do think there are some conservationists who have been rather extreme and would prevent us from meeting any of our needs for minerals, energy, etc. However, I, too, am a conservationist and a lover of the beauty of this country, and I assure you we are not going to allow it to be despoiled. I know Secretary of the Interior Watt is a conservationist and much of what he's supposed to have said or what he's doing is being quoted out of context and distorted. Please rest assured we will not return to poisoned air or water nor will we wipe out the beauty of this land.

Again, my thanks and best regards,

> Ronald Reagan

On February 25, 1982, Reagan established a property review board to explore selling excess federal land and buildings. Here he tells Laurence Beilenson why it isn't working.

> Mr. Laurence W. Beilenson
> Los Angeles, California
> September 5, 1985 [36]

Dear Larry:

Good to hear from you and I want you to know your *Wall Street Journal* essay is being widely circulated among my staff and cabinet. I'm glad to have your Adam Smith quote but must tell you there wasn't an environmental movement in his day. I get my brains kicked out for reducing the acreage of wilderness land that someone wants us to buy.

Seriously Larry I did have our agencies checking up on buildings and property the government owned and here and there some sales were made but they were chicken feed. First of all the bureaucracy is dug in on this and as FDR once said, "it is like punching a pillow—nothing happens." Mainly however congressmen have a built in resistance to any reduction of holdings in their respective districts. They are supported in this by environmentalists whenever open land is involved and of course that's where the big money is. Would you believe it—there is some national forest acreage in my ranch—totally surrounded by my property on all four sides and I'm trying to find a way to buy it?

I know this sounds like surrender on my part but not really. I'm still trying and will continue. Nancy sends her love.

Sincerely,
Ron

EDUCATION AND THE ARTS

Glenn Campbell was director of the Hoover Institution at Stanford University. Reagan appointed him to the Board of Regents of the University of California, on which he served for 19 years. As governor, Reagan was also a regent. He was also an honorary fellow of the Hoover Institution.

Dr. Glenn Campbell
Stanford, California
February 17, 1981 [37]

Dear Glenn:

I know that I'm saying thank you to your thank you, but it was so nice to get your letter.

It's been a long time, really, since we've ever had a chance to properly visit so I just felt like communicating. I know we've shared some meetings, but that isn't the same as in those old days when we were fellow regents. I miss that. I know this schedule back here [will], or at least I hope it will, settle down to something more normal. But, so far, it really has been busy. Sometimes it seems that I'm a juggler with at least fifteen balls in the air and one hand is tied behind my back. On the other hand, it feels good to really be dealing with some of the things we all talked about for so long.

Nancy sends her best and please give our regards to Rita.* Thank you both for all that you've done and for your offer of continuing help.

Sincerely,
Ron

* Campbell's wife, Rita Ricardo-Campbell, was also a fellow at the Hoover Institution and an expert on Social Security.

Reagan lets William Bennett, his second secretary of education, know his views of the National Education Association's (NEA) purpose. The NEA opposed Reagan's proposals on education.

The Honorable William Bennett
Department of Education
February 28, 1985 [38]

In a newsletter not too long ago of the NEA affiliate in Oregon: "The major purpose of our Association (NEA) is <u>not</u> the education of children, rather it is or ought to be the extension and/or preservation of our members' rights." This is it Bill.

R.R.

The National Endowment for the Arts was created in 1965. Although, as these letters indicate, Reagan would have preferred voluntary private sector funding for the arts, the agency's budget increased from $154.6 million in 1980 to $167.7 million in 1988. As a source of funding for the arts, agency funds are dwarfed by private contributions. It provided less than 2 percent of the amount provided by the private sector (80 percent from individuals) during the Reagan years and less than 1 percent in the late 1990s, when funds for the agency were sharply cut back.[39] Howard Richardson (1917–1985) was a playwright and performer.

Dr. Howard Richardson
New York, New York
September 29, 1981 [40]

Dear Dr. Richardson:

Thank you very much for your letter of July 1. I'm sorry to be so long in replying, but sometimes it takes a while for mail to reach my desk.

I am most grateful for your encouragement in what we are trying to do and hope that one day we will be able to return all support for the arts to the private sector and voluntary effort. I have always believed that is one of the distinctive American characteristics—assistance to good causes by voluntary effort.

It was good of you to write, and I am going to carry on with renewed strength.

Sincerely,
Ronald Reagan

Lois Albright, a musician, teacher, and conductor with the Viennese Operetta Company of America, wrote that she believes in "private enterprise for everything whether it is art or not art."

Miss Lois Albright
New York, New York
February 25, 1986[41]

Dear Miss Albright:

Your letter of January 20 has only just reached me so forgive the lateness of my reply. It does take a while for mail to make its way through the bureaucracy before reaching my desk.

Thank you for your kind and generous words. I'm most grateful. I must confess I'm somewhat in agreement with your views about our federal subsidies to the arts. I believe there is a place for government in encouraging art and in lending a hand to those who through no fault of their own are denied opportunity. On the other hand, like so many well-intentioned government programs there is no question but that we find ourselves paying (as you say) some to be lazy and some who make no contribution to the arts. We're trying to make some adjustments but as you can imagine we run into some roadblocks.

Incidentally we have the same problem with the needy. We are trying to limit our subsidies to the truly needy and remove from the rolls those who are not needy but are greedy.

Again, thank you for writing—I'm honored to receive a letter from one I so admire.

Sincerely,
Ronald Reagan

OTHER ISSUES

Reagan responded to letters on many other issues over the years—right to work, civil service pay, the Equal Rights Amendment, abortion, homosexuality, school prayer, gun control, the death penalty, immigration and refugees, and illegal drugs.

David Denholm was executive assistant to the president of Californians for Right to Work. Cesar Chavez's United Farm Workers union had been boycotting table grapes for years. Reagan was not initially an advocate of right-to-work laws, but later came to support them.

Mr. David Y. Denholm
Oakland, California
September 22, 1970[42]

Dear Mr. Denholm:

Thanks for giving me the opportunity to comment and state my views with regard to "Right to Work."

First, the circumstances under which I made my statement were chosen because not only my opponent, but some of his supporters in much of the labor press were so blatantly misstating my position. You and I are in agreement about many things with regard to the rights of rank and file union members which must be protected. At the same time, however, my own experience as a union member, officer, and several times president, has convinced me these matters can be corrected within the union shop framework (you'll note I didn't say closed shop).

My union, the Screen Actors Guild, is a classic example of democratic unionism. There is no compulsory assessment for political funds, there is a secret ballot on policy matters and the constitution provides that if ever 50 percent of the members plus one decide not to have a union, it shall be dissolved.

My position regarding Chavez is well known; the workers must be allowed to vote by secret ballot as to whether they should have a bargaining representative and who or what that representative should be. There can be no morality in either the boycott or in employers and Chavez signing contracts unless and until the workers themselves have voted.

I'm sorry we can't see eye to eye on the cause you so ably support, but here again my own experience reminds me of advantages that were taken in our industry of some of the Taft-Hartley clauses in its early version. Our problem perhaps will always be that among men of good will, a few can't resist the occasional loophole.

Again, thanks.

Sincerely,
Ronald Reagan

Reagan reworked his draft of this letter with great care; there are many deletions and insertions. A comprehensive overview of issues involved in civil service pay, the draft letter reflects the development of Reagan's thinking on this issue as well as a possible answer to a specific correspondent.

Draft on Civil Service Pay
Circa 1974[43]

Dear ——:

I know of no issue harder to resolve, or one that arouses more emotion, than that of proper pay scale for public servants. We swing between the token payment idea which makes public service a kind of philanthropy, and the other extreme of attempting to match pay scale to the responsibilities of the job. One leads to a near monopoly of public office by those who have wealth and can afford to give time and service, or the possibility of attracting men to government who take advantage of the power of office and are tempted to accumulate illicit wealth by selling favors.

At the opposite extreme is a salary scale commensurate to the job, and the danger of attracting inferior men incapable of earning a like salary in the competitive world of free enterprise. Remember, public office has drawbacks which lessen its attraction to many men of exceptional ability. There is the uncertainty of reelection, partisan assaults, constant criticism of motive and intent, and outright attempt at character assassination.

I confess I don't have a totally satisfactory answer, but lean very much toward the idea of salary and allowances, which make it possible for a dedicated individual to serve even though he has no personal wealth. If we want a man's best thinking applied to our community problems we should see that he is reasonably sure of being able to provide for his family and the education of his children.

It would be interesting to see a professional study of government positions, such as large industries undergo in establishing salary levels in their operations. Does a George Meany rate a salary for his admittedly responsible position nearly double that of a U.S. Senator representing a state with 20 million population? Should a president of a state university receive higher pay than the governor of that state?

In California we have undergone in recent years a change from a part-time legislature paid on a token basis to a full-time legislature with salary commensurate to the time and effort required by the job. It is unfair to speak of this complete transformation as just a pay raise. It is unfair also to refer to the salary adjustments of constitutional offices as a cost of living increase. Under our constitution, no such elected official can get a pay increase of any kind during the four-year term of his office. If, for example, no adjustment is voted during this present term to go into effect after the 1974 election, then the present pay scale will remain in effect until 1978.

The problem of inflation, in my opinion, is not caused by the salary scale of elected officials, but by excessive government spending for a variety of services not proper functions of government. At the federal level this has led to increasing the money in circulation, and consequently reducing its purchasing power.

[no signature]

Reagan explains his opposition to the Equal Rights Amendment (ERA) to a supporter who disagrees with him.

Luella Huggins
Altadena, California
February 5, 1979[44]

Dear Luella:

It was good to hear from you, and I was very interested in the undertaking you mentioned. By coincidence, during my years as governor I tried very hard for two things—unsuccessfully. One was in the field of organized labor where I wanted to do something by law that the Screen Actors Guild, which I once headed up, had done of its own free will: vote by secret ballot not only for officers but all policy affecting the guild. Naturally, the leadership of organized labor fought this and, with our Democratic legislature, was successful. The second thing is I don't believe there can be any justice whatsoever in allowing farm labor to strike at harvest time as they are presently doing in the lettuce fields. That isn't negotiating or a test of economic strength between management and labor; it is just sheer blackmail and unforgivable in a hungry world. I am glad to have your report and will have our people looking at it in the days ahead as well as, of course, my studying it myself.

Luella, I know you and I didn't agree on ERA, but again I think I should point out that I am not continuing to talk about it, I can't help but answer a question, and the only time I mention it is when I am asked in a press gathering or in a question-and-answer session with an audience. You and I are agreed on no discrimination by virtue of sex or anything else for that matter. I would support any statue that would eliminate any and all discrimination which does exist. It is only that matter of a constitutional amendment that I don't believe is needed or would be effective in some of the areas such as Social Security regulations which now discriminate against working wives. But I recognize what you say about this and the emotionalism of this issue and can only say that there is no way I can avoid answering a question on it.

Again, it was good to hear from you, and thanks for sending me the labor plan.

Sincerely,
Ron

Reagan addresses the use made of the abortion law passed in California and questions whether "bump and run" sex is preferable to monogamy. Reagan signed the Therapeutic Abortion Act (TAA) in 1967, six years before the Roe v. Wade *Supreme Court decision on abortion. It was one of the most liberal abortion laws in the United States.*

AB 1003 and AB 1004, which forbid any restrictions on a prisoner's access to an abortion beyond those of the TAA, were introduced by Democrat Yvonne Brathwaite of the California Assembly on March 1972.

Mrs. Stinson
Circa late 1972[45]

Dear Mrs. Stinson:

I hope you won't mind my answering your letter to Mrs. Reagan. Since it concerned legislation I thought perhaps this might be simpler.

First let me say I have signed AB 1004 and also AB 1003 by the same author. This latter bill grants inmates of our penal institutions the right to call in their own doctors to determine pregnancy and to continue with prenatal care.

I'm in agreement with you that the measures of our abortion law allowing a prospective mother to protect her own health (physical and mental) should apply to all. My quarrel is not with the law, but with the breakdown of the policing of the law, particularly by psychiatrists who permit abortions where there is no threat to the mother. This results in the taking of a human life simply for the convenience—not the protection—of the mother.

The problem of the unwanted child is a very real one and I cannot disagree that a solution must be found, particularly where abuse of the child is the result. However, I'm unable to agree that the state has a right to inject itself between parent and child and, in effect, say to the child "we'll help you bypass your parents in whatever their moral teaching has been." In a sense the state is putting an official stamp of approval on immorality. We can't continue to urge the reestablishment of the family as an answer to society's breakdown while we bypass the family when it suits our convenience.

The new age bracket for citizenship has already resolved this particular problem down to age 18. I question government's right to interfere at age levels below 18.

You cited the experience in some of the Scandinavian countries where child abuse is at a much lower level than in our own country. There are other facets, however, which should give us pause to think. Those same countries are seeing a vast increase in suicide, alcoholism, use of drugs and a kind of purposeless boredom among younger people. Is it possible that "bump and run" sex is a dead-end street compared to the age-old, time-tested concept of monogamy?

I appreciate your writing and what you are doing and wish there were more who shared your concern. Perhaps in spite of our disagreements between us we can at least move toward easing the problem, if not solving it.

Sincerely,
Ronald Reagan

Reagan explains his opposition to abortion.

Mr. Kenneth Fisher
Circa late 1970 [46]

Dear Mr. Fisher:

Thank you for writing as you did and for giving me the opportunity to respond. It is good to hear from you after this long time.

You and I are not in disagreement about the problems you brought up concerning the increase in teenage pregnancies and, I could add, the proportionate increase in VD. I do believe, however, you might have some incorrect statistics on the fate of the unwanted children. All of my information indicates there are literally millions of childless couples on waiting lists to adopt. One of my own sons was adopted and, if present law prevailed at time of his birth, might have been a victim of abortion instead.

Our disagreement apparently is on the solution to the problem of the increasing number of unwanted children. I believe we should treat more realistically with the erosion of moral standards, the spreading of a humanist philosophy and outright hedonism in our educational system, and [do] a better job of instruction in preventive measures.

Having had to face as governor the problem of abortion as a legislative proposal, I think I did more soul-searching and studying on the subject than anything else in my eight years. From all I learned, I am convinced that interrupting a pregnancy is the taking of a human life. I can support that only on the theory of self-defense—the right of a prospective mother to protect herself if her unborn child threatens her life or health. It is easy to refer to the unborn as a "fetus" but most medical doctrine recognizes the presence of a living human being whose personality traits, hair and eye color, and other characteristics have already been genetically determined.

If, with pregnancy, a window appeared in a woman's body so that she could look at her own child develop, I wonder at what point she would decide it was all right to kill it.

Well, again, thank you for your letter. I hope we can concentrate on our areas of agreement.

Best regards,
Ronald Reagan

Reagan defends his first appointment to the U.S. Supreme Court, Sandra Day O'Connor, to Republican Penny Pullen, who represented Park Ridge in the Illinois state legislature.

Representative Penny Pullen
Springfield, Illinois
September 30, 1981 [47]

Dear Representative Pullen:

I've received your letter of August 24th and appreciate very much your giving me the chance to comment on this situation. Let me first however thank you very much for all the help that you have given me on the campaign and for your support since 1964. I understand your concern about the court appointment, but please I ask you to believe that I feel as deeply as you do about the issue of abortion. I have not weakened in my belief that interrupting a pregnancy means the taking of a human life. Indeed the recent hearings in the Congress to establish if possible when life actually begins did nothing but strengthen my conviction regarding this taking of the human life. If experts of every persuasion were unable in those lengthy hearings to determine just when life began, then it seems to me they strengthened our case. If there is that much question, then simple humanity suggests that we opt for life until someone can definitely prove that life does not exist.

If there has been a mistake made in this appointment, then the mistake would be mine. I think perhaps you have the wrong impression of the people surrounding me. I am convinced that the cabinet we have put together, the senior staff members, etc. are of a caliber we haven't seen in government for some time. Almost without exception they made unbelievable sacrifices in order to serve. I gave a great deal of study before appointing Judge O'Connor. I am confident I made the right decision. As I said before, if I should be proven wrong, then the mistake is mine. Feeling as strongly as I do on the issue of abortion, does it seem likely that I would have been careless about this appointment? I appreciate very much your saying that in spite of this you would continue to support me. I hope you will have no reason to regret this.

Again thanks, and best regards.

Sincerely,
Ronald Reagan

Reagan explains the priority given to his economic programs.

Mr. Alan S. Quarterman
Lauderdale-by-the-Sea, Florida
February 10, 1982[48]

Dear Mr. Quarterman:

Thank you for your letter of December 14th and for giving me a chance to respond.

I am opposed to abortion, as you stated, and it does not reflect a lower priority in that we have not actively pursued legislation with regard to that subject. We must be guided by the leadership in the Congress with regard to when they feel they can get something and what our schedule of legislation must be. Their word to us was that our economic program had to take priority, and with the conflicting pieces of legislation that were being suggested on some of the social issues, including abortion, that we had to wait before we could push for some of those programs. Even now, the various anti-abortion groups are divided over two or three proposed pieces of legislation.

I think behind the scenes in committees, the congressional leadership is trying to sort out and determine which proposal they should go for. We are keeping in very close touch and, I assure you, that I will do all I can to rectify the situation we're now in.

Again, thanks for your letter.

Sincerely,
Ronald Reagan

Proposition 6 on November 1978 ballot in California provided for firing teachers who "advocate" homosexuality. Reagan issued a statement on September 24, 1978, in opposition and opposed it in a newspaper column.[49] The proposition probably would have passed had Reagan not opposed it.

Reverend Gay
Undated pre-presidential[50]

Dear Reverend Gay:

Thank you very much for writing me about Reverend Troy Perry and the Metropolitan Community Church. I was not aware of the use of my name and the office I hold. It was good of you to give me the chance to comment and, hopefully, to set the record straight.

In reply to your questions, I have never condoned homosexuality, and certainly do not support the abolition of criminal laws regarding sexual misconduct.

As for the indication of political support you cited (and, again, this was my first knowledge of the incident), every candidate is vulnerable to this sort of thing. Anyone can support any political candidate he selects and for whatever reason might be in his own mind. This is far different than support the candidate has asked for. You may be sure I never solicited such support.

A message was sent (a wire) over my signature to Reverend Perry on the dedication of his new building. This was a routine reply to what seemed to be a courtesy invitation. The invitation made no mention of the unusual nature of his congregation. Such a wire would be sent recognizing the success of any congregation that had acquired a place of worship. Such a wire would not have been sent had all the facts been known.

In answer to your fourth and last question, no, I am not supporting the movement to abolish or lessen the present laws concerning sexual conduct. I am deeply concerned with the wave of hedonism—the humanist philosophy so prevalent today—and believe this nation must have a spiritual rebirth, a rededication to the moral precepts which guided us for so much of our past, and have such a rebirth very soon.

Again, thank you for bringing this to my attention.

Sincerely,
Ronald Reagan

Reagan writes to an old friend and agrees with his analysis of the 1984 Democratic platform plank on sexual orientation.

Lt. General Victor H. Krulak, USMC (Ret.)
San Diego, California
October 30, 1984[51]

Dear Brute:

It was good to hear from you and the snapshot awakened a lot of happy memories. I'm glad you sent me your column, as always you hit the target. I haven't read the Democratic platform and wasn't aware of their position on "sexual orientation." You are right, that is political pandering of the most blatant kind. You know Brute I'm not one to suggest those people should be persecuted in any way but they are demanding recognition and approval of their lifestyle and no one has a right to demand that.

I'm out on the trail but my heart is in "the Grove."

Best regards,
Ron

This letter foreshadows Reagan's support for a school prayer amendment to the Constitution during his presidency.

Mr. Henri Lagueux
Circa June 1976[52]

Dear Mr. Lagueux:

Thank you for giving me the opportunity to comment regarding prayer in schools.

American tradition has long accepted God as being a part of our national tradition. Our country had something of a religious heritage in that our first settlers came here in search of freedom to worship. Our coins still bear the words, "In God We Trust" and our legislative bodies have chaplains as does our military.

Our Constitution prohibits any state religion or religious control of the state yet God is invoked several times in that Constitution. For many years virtually since the inception of public schools nonsectarian prayers were offered in schools. They were noncompulsory and certainly did not threaten our "separation of church and state."

I see no violation of anyone's right to freedom to restore such nonsectarian prayers in a noncompulsory manner. Those who don't care to pray can use the time for quiet meditation. It does seems unfair to me that one atheist could bring an action in court and impose her will on millions of families all over this land which in many official documents is described as "one nation under God."

Again thanks for letting me comment.

Sincerely,
Ronald Reagan

The Reagan administration supported a constitutional amendment to allow prayer in schools and such amendments were introduced in the Senate, but none was passed. Reagan describes the effort to Tom O'Brien, a real estate executive and fellow member of the Rancheros, a group that held annual horseback-camping trips.

Thomas O'Brien
Scottsdale, Arizona
March 22, 1984 [53]

Dear Tom:

Thanks for your letter and kind words. I don't intend to give up on school prayer and will be back again next year if not before.

Tom the tragedy here was one of perception. Believe it or not a number of senators honestly believed they were voting against something that would have the government mandating that schools had to have regular prayers. Actually our amendment said nothing of the kind. It specifically said the Constitution permitted prayer in schools and that no official could concoct a prayer.

Somehow though (aided by the liberal press) the debate raged about who would write the prayers, should the federal government have the right to order religion etc. I can't tell you how many senators—good guys—I tried to convince that they'd jumped to a false conclusion—with no success.

When we try again we're going to have to word the bill so it's completely clear we mean the Constitution to be neutral. Tom on another point—Ed Meese; there is no doubt this is a lynching of the innocent. The head lyncher is Senator Metzenbaum of Ohio who openly declared he was after him even before he found any of the things now being talked about.

Tom—I want you to know the VP has been as staunch a supporter of the administration as you could want. He carries a tremendous workload and is truly straight arrow.

Again thanks and best regards.

Sincerely,
Ron

Reagan opposed gun control even after an assassin tried to kill him but agrees here that there are appropriate actions that can be taken at the state level.

> Captain Leslie W. Teller
> Orange Park, Florida
> September 29, 1981 [54]

Dear Captain Teller:

Thank you very much for writing to give me your thoughts and observations on the subject of gun control and, also, our Crime Task Force.

I disagree in one principal respect. I believe that the problem belongs at the state level. I think there would be great problems with regard to enforcement at the national level.

May I just suggest what we have in California; a fifteen-day waiting period. Anyone buying a handgun must wait fifteen days while the state checks to see if he has a criminal record, etc. Moreover, we have passed some laws which I believe are probably more effective than gun control. Anyone convicted of a crime who had a gun in his or her possession at the time of the crime—regardless of whether the weapon was used—has five to fifteen years added to the sentence. Prison is mandatory; there can be no probation under that law.

Again, thank you for taking the trouble to write.

Best regards,

> Sincerely,
> Ronald Reagan

Reagan explains his support for the death penalty.

> Mr. Frick
> Circa 1972 [55]

Dear Mr. Frick:

Thanks very much for sending me your essays. I'm in great agreement with you regarding government spending and reduction of the size, power and cost of government.

Right now I'm engaged in a debate (struggle is a better word) to keep the legislature from enlarging government and increasing the state tax burden. We have frozen employment and reduced the office space required by government more than 20 percent.

On the issue of capital punishment, however, I have a contrary view. This is a difficult question, and my own view was not arrived at lightly. What do we do with the "lifer" who kills a guard or a fellow prisoner? He is already serving the maximum sentence unless we invoke the death penalty.

California leads the nation in its progressive prison reforms and rehabilitation, including such things as the marital visit. Still we have a senseless tragedy such as the recent San Quentin slaughter.

I have on my desk a list of 12 names—all served prison sentences in California for murder. Since their release, they have between them killed an additional 22 people. I am convinced after many years of study and soul-searching that the death penalty is a deterrent, and thus a measure of self-defense.

Thanks again for sending me your writings. I enjoyed reading them.

Sincerely,
Ronald Reagan

Reagan faced refugee crises from Haiti (at the start of his presidency), Vietnam (continuing from the late 1970s), and Cuba (the Mariel boatlift beginning in 1980). Here he discusses current policies regarding quotas.

Mr. Maurice W. Phillips
Minister of World Mission Support
Parkersburg, West Virginia
December 1, 1981 [56]

Dear Mr. Phillips:

Thank you very much for writing as you did. I understand your concerns about the Haitians coming to our door and our present position with regard to taking them in.

There is no change with regard to our taking in refugees who are fleeing, as the boat people did, from Communist conquerors or people fleeing the kind of dictatorship that we have seen in Cuba. The Haitians, however, are actually just coming to this country for economic betterment. I know something of what their lot is and I can well understand their wanting to come here. But, we have to have immigration quotas because that kind of immigrant is to be found in every corner of the world and there is no way that we could, without limit, take all who want to come here simply for the opportunity this country offers.

It is for this reason that we have moved with Canada, Mexico, and Venezuela on our Caribbean Plan. It is our hope that together these four nations, with the help of the private sector, can seek to alleviate the conditions that make so many people, particularly from the Caribbean states, want to come here. In other words, we're going to try to create an economic infrastructure in their countries so there will be opportunities and jobs and a decent living for the people. With this, we hope also will come the kind of social reforms that will make life more free, as it is here in our land, in those places where they do lack some of the democracy that we prize so highly.

We are continuing to take in the refugees from persecution. I'm sorry with regard to the Haitians that we can't take them all, but if we did, we would have no reason to have immigration quotas for a number of other countries. Please believe I am not unfeeling about this and do wish we could offer a haven for all.

Sincerely,
Ronald Reagan

———

While he was governor of California, Reagan penned a comment on an article about narcotics traffic: "The only answer is a generation of young people who will say 'no.' "[57] In 1985 Nancy Reagan launched her "Just Say No" to drugs campaign, which Reagan supports in this letter.

Mr. Richard G. Capen, Jr.
Miami, Florida
July 14, 1986[58]

Dear Mr. Capen:
    Thank you for sending me your column on drugs and thank you for writing it. You and I are in agreement on the need for a concerted national effort. At the federal level we've stepped up, as you know, our effort to limit the supply and vastly increased our seizure of drugs. At the same time we're aware the drug supply has increased at an even greater pace.
    It's apparent that Nancy has been on the right track. We must concentrate on taking the customer away from the drugs. The other way won't solve the problem. We are studying now how a nationwide effort can be mobilized. Whatever we come up with I know the news media will play an important role and I'm happy to know of your own interest and concern.
    Again thanks

Sincerely,
Ronald Reagan

———

Reagan often answered letters addressed to Nancy when they concerned policy, as he did actor Paul Newman's letter questioning his and Nancy's commitment to the antidrug campaign.

Paul Newman
1987[59]

Dear Paul:
    Having read your letter to Nancy I am compelled to write; first to reply to your suggestion that Nancy is less than dedicated to the antidrug campaign and second;

to inform you that my own commitment is not "campaign rhetoric." There has
been "rhetoric" over our proposed budget and it is pure political demagoguery.

Nancy has traveled tens of thousands of miles to virtually every part of this
country and to Europe and Asia motivated by her deeply felt devotion to the antidrug crusade. I believe she has done more and continues doing more than any
other single individual, particularly with regard to young people to whom she is totally dedicated.

Yes we have proposed a smaller appropriation for the drug program than we
had last year but it is bigger than the appropriation for 1986 which was bigger than
the one for 1985. Indeed we have increased the appropriation every year since we've
been in Washington. But the appropriation we've proposed for '88, it is true, is
smaller than the '87 budget and for a very good reason. Several hundred million
dollars were added to the '87 appropriation for one-time purchase of equipment
and facilities, radar balloons, helicopters, planes and such. Some of that money is
still being spent. This was as I say a one-time expenditure and had nothing to do
with ongoing program costs. May I say, those who have been loudest in their demagoguery have access to this information. It is they who are guilty of "campaign
rhetoric."

I'm sorry you removed yourself from the proposed antidrug film. It was a very
worthwhile effort and should not be sacrificed on the altar of partisan politics. I assure you our administration and my wife are dedicated to the nationwide crusade
against drug and alcohol use.

Sincerely,
Ronald Reagan

CHAPTER ELEVEN

The Cold War I: Ideology and Institutions

*T*HROUGHOUT HIS CAREER, *Reagan asserted that the political and ideological dimensions of the cold war were as important as the military contest. In a speech in Los Angeles on December 14, 1978, he declared: "The essential ingredients of any successful strategy designed to promote peace and to deter aggression include political, economic, and military and psychological measures. Too often we focus on the purely military aspects when we consider our own national security, and while we must always be certain that our guard is up and that we have a strong, viable deterrent force poised against any potential aggressors, this alone will not meet the requirements of the 1980s."* [1]

When he proclaimed on June 8, 1982, that "the march of freedom and democracy . . . will leave Marxism-Leninism on the ash heap of history," President Reagan was expressing a long-held belief that communism and the Soviet Union rested on a bed of sand because the system they proffered restricted freedom of speech, assembly, religion, and economic exchange, yet creativity and freedom are the engines of political and economic progress. Reagan believed that eventually the Soviet Union would crumble under its own weight. The guns-versus-butter trade-off would be central to the demise of the Soviet Union, but its opposition to freedom of all sorts would also be a central factor.

In Reagan's view, the United States had a role to play in hastening the Soviet demise. It should demand political opening within the Soviet Union and find ways to loosen the country's grip on the "people in the captive nations of Eastern Europe." [2] *The main way to achieve these goals, Reagan repeatedly declared, is through a show of American strength and resolve.*

He often wrote about the stringent institutional and societal requirements of fighting the cold war, and sometimes lamented domestic forces that hindered defense and foreign policy. He believed, however, that due to the nature of its political and eco-

nomic system as well as its special destiny to be a shining city upon a hill, the United States could effectively mobilize the military and nonmilitary means and the will to hasten the Soviet Union's demise. Reagan extolled the special destiny of the United States in a speech on February 15, 1975: "We did not seek world leadership; it was thrust upon us. . . . If we fail to keep our rendezvous with destiny or, as John Winthrop said in 1630, 'Deal falsely with our God,' we shall be made 'A story and byword throughout the world.' "[3] As the letters in this chapter show, Reagan firmly believed that the destiny of the United States included defeating totalitarianism.

The letters in this chapter address the economic, psychological, and political dimensions of fighting the cold war.

THE NATURE OF COMMUNISM
AND THE SOVIET UNION

In the two pre-presidential letters below, Reagan writes about the dilemma of selling wheat to the Soviet Union.

The Reverend David J. Holland
Circa mid-1970s[4]

Reverend David J. Holland:

Thank you very much for writing me and I'm happy you wrote to all those others.

By coincidence, I've just returned from the Republican Leadership Conference in Houston Texas where I spoke on the subject of your letter. I proposed a study to determine whether we were not indeed endangering our own safety and that of the free world by trading with the Soviet [Union]. I said also the study should include the moral problem involved; were we helping to keep the people of Russia and Eastern Europe enslaved? Such a study of course would have to involve our free world allies who are also trading with the Soviet Union.

There is no question but that the "cold war" was ended by Russia, not because of any change of heart, but simply as a change in strategy.

Again thanks and best regards.

Ronald Reagan

Mr. Ralph T. Johnson
Laguna Hills, California
Circa late 1970s[5]

Dear Mr. Johnson:

Thank you for your letter and generous words. I am in complete agreement about Panama, Cuba, etc. As for Russia, while we all hope for a world in which there will be friendship and peace, it has seemed to me that "détente" has been a one-way street.

I don't know whether Russia has a surplus of oil which could be used for barter. I'll have to look into that. My impression has been that Russia, too, was an importing nation. However, we have never exacted a proper return when we have bailed them out of an emergency, such as selling wheat when they've been unable to feed their own people.

Thanks again for your letter. If and when the occasion should call for it, I'll be proud to have your support.

Sincerely,
Ronald Reagan

The case of Ida Nudel, a Jewish Refusenik, was a cause that Reagan began championing more than a decade before she was granted a Soviet exit visa in October 1987. After he wrote the letter below he devoted a radio commentary, taped on November 30, 1976, to her confinement.[6]

Mrs. Alvin Turken
Beverly Hills, California
Circa November 1976[7]

Dear Mrs. Turken:

Thank you very much for your letter and the material on Ida Nudel.

I'm afraid a letter to President-elect Carter from me would not be very productive—politics being what they are—but I've already done some radio commentaries on this general subject and will continue to call attention to this continuing tragedy.

I agree with you about the Soviet susceptibility to public opinion. Maybe I can be of help in arousing public opinion by calling attention to the situation of Mrs. Nudel.

Thanks again.

Sincerely,
Ronald Reagan

By 1980 many Americans had stopped believing that the cold war would end. Yet as Reagan indicates to this supporter, he was committed to seeking the liberation of the Soviet bloc.

Mr. Severin Palydowycz
June 1980[8]

Dear Mr. Palydowycz:

May I thank you and all of your people for the most wonderful time that Nancy and I had with you at the festival in New Jersey. Our only regret is that we had to leave before the day was over. But your warmth, your hospitality, and your friend-ship have made a lasting impression on us, and you have given us a most happy memory.

Let me assure you that the problems outlined in the paper accompanying your letter will receive my attention. You are right when you say we must restore our prestige in the world. We must also keep alive the idea that the conquered nations—the captive nations—of the Soviet Union must regain their freedom. I re-member very well in the days of Hitler when some of our more liberal friends con-tinued to say we could not live in a world half-slave, half-free. They have been strangely silent in these decades since that war about the world that is still half-slave.

Again, our thanks to you and I hope our paths cross soon again.

Best regards,
Ronald Reagan

Following Pope John Paul II's visit to Poland in the spring of 1981, President Reagan writes about his view of the role of religion in the Soviet system. He writes also that he is developing his approach to foreign policy.

Mr. John O. Koehler
New York, New York
July 9, 1981 [9]

Dear John:

Forgive me for being so tardy in answering your letter, but I can only excuse myself on the press of business and a little traveling.

I can't tell you how much I appreciate your giving me all the information that you gathered. It adds a great deal to my knowledge of what is going on over there in the captive nations. I was particularly interested to read your comments about the resurgence of religion. I have had a feeling, particularly in view of the Pope's visit to Poland, that religion might very well turn out to be the Soviets' Achilles' heel. I've had some reports that it is even going on in an underground way in Russia itself.

I know I'm being criticized for not having made a great speech outlining what would be the Reagan foreign policy. I have a foreign policy; I'm working on it. I just don't happen to think that it's wise to always stand up and put in quotation marks in front of the world what your foreign policy is. I'm a believer in quiet diplomacy and so far we've had several quite triumphant experiences by using that method. The problem is, you can't talk about it afterward or then you can't do it again.

Please give Dorothy my very best regards and, again, thanks to you for a most informative letter.

Sincerely,
Ron

_____

Reagan sought to challenge the Soviet Union on an ideological level through the U.S. government-supported entities of Voice of America, created during World War II, and Radio Free Europe and Radio Liberty, created in the early years of the cold war. Based in Munich, Germany, Radio Free Europe broadcast in Eastern Europe and Radio Liberty was heard in the Soviet Union. The two entities merged in the mid-1970s and became known as RFE/RL.[10] President Reagan also strengthened the United States Information Agency (formerly known, as President Reagan refers to it below, as the United States International Communications Agency, or USICA). He appointed Charles Z. Wick as the director.

Mr. Barton L. Hartzell
Madrid, Spain
January 11, 1982 [11]

Dear Mr. Hartzell:

Thank you for your most interesting and informative letter and for your generous words.

I appreciate your suggestions regarding the ideological war. You'll be pleased to know that our International Communications Agency is under new management (Charles Wick) and we are going forward with all kinds of new plans using Voice of America—Radio Free Europe, etc. We are determined to <u>stop</u> losing the propaganda war.

Thanks again for your letter and sound suggestions.

Sincerely,
Ronald Reagan

_____

Reagan often contended, as he does here, that absent Soviet internal oppression, the Russian and American people would be friends. In an April 24, 1981, letter to Soviet General Secretary Leonid I. Brezhnev, Reagan wrote: "Indeed the peoples of the world, despite differences in racial and ethnic origin, have very much in common. They want the dignity of having some control of their individual destiny. . . . Government exists for their convenience, not the other way around."[12]

Mr. Bill Rieb
Rapid City, South Dakota
January 11, 1982 [13]

Dear Mr. Rieb:

Thanks for your letter and most interesting account of your travels through Russia. You confirm what I've always felt; that we and the Russian people could be the best of friends if it weren't for the godless tyranny and imperialist ambitions of their leaders. I said as much in a handwritten letter to Brezhnev last April while I was in the hospital. His reply was most disappointing.

Thank you again for writing and for your generous words.

Sincerely,
Ronald Reagan

In August 1982, a Canadian businessman sent President Reagan a 1927 newspaper article about the Soviet Union's world disarmament proposal to the League of Nations. In his letter, he wrote "this article . . . should only remind us all what kind of game the Soviet Union has been playing for a long time." [14]

Mr. Gordon Carpenter
Toronto, Canada
August 27, 1982 [15]

Dear Mr. Carpenter:

Thank you very much for sending me the newspaper story about the Soviet Union's arms proposal. One wonders what scheme they were hatching then or if at one time they really did consider such a thing. This of course was at a time when few if any nations had diplomatic relations with them if I remember correctly.

My thanks for your generous words. I'll try to be deserving of them.

Sincerely,
Ronald Reagan

Despite his ambivalence about selling wheat to the Soviet Union, Reagan contended that the grain embargo imposed by President Jimmy Carter in the wake of the Soviet invasion of Afghanistan in December 1979 hurt American farmers and was an ineffective means of addressing Soviet aggression. Reagan upheld his pledge by lifting the grain embargo on April 24, 1981.

Mr. Franciszek Lachowicz
Bridgeport, Connecticut
December 9, 1982 [16]

Dear Mr. Lachowicz:

Forgive me for being so late in answering your letter of November 11 but it arrived while I was away from Washington. I am just now catching up with my mail.

Let me assure you I feel as deeply as you do about the abuse of human rights of the people in the countries you mentioned. We are engaged in actions as a result that are hurtful to the Soviets. I lifted the grain embargo because no other free world nations would join us and we were therefore hurting only our own farmers.

We did have another thought in mind; the Soviets are facing grave economic problems, our sale of grain further drains them of hard cash.

We have also finally succeeded in getting our allies to join in an agreement that denies credit to the Soviet Union and restricts trade in high technology.

In the meantime we maintain contact and seek through quiet diplomacy to bring about changes. And, of course, we are negotiating with the hope of reducing the arsenal of nuclear weapons.

Our goal is peace and freedom for the enslaved people behind the "iron curtain."

Sincerely,
Ronald Reagan

Several months before the National Conference of Catholic Bishops would publish a widely discussed pastoral letter on war and peace, President Reagan not only takes issue with the bishops' call for a nuclear freeze but says that the Soviets have a slave system.[17]

The Reverend Stephen Majoros
Toledo, Ohio
March 15, 1983 [18]

Dear Father Majoros:

I can't tell you how much your letter meant to me. I'm sure the bishops supporting the "freeze" and unilateral disarmament are sincere and believe they are furthering the cause of peace. I'm equally sure they are tragically mistaken. What they urge would bring us closer to a choice of surrender or die. Surrender of course would mean slavery under a system that would banish God. I believe there is another way, the way we call peace through strength and it leads us away from the possibility of war.

Thank you for writing as you did.

Sincerely,
Ronald Reagan

Reagan often distinguished the Soviet political system from its citizens, but in this letter he disparages Russians themselves.

Mrs. A. S. Meyers
Greenbrae, California
December 7, 1983 [19]

Dear Betty:

Thanks very much for sending the story. It bears out a belief of mine that communism isn't the entire explanation for their conduct; they are just behaving like Russians.

It was good to hear from you. Nancy sends her best and we wish both of you a Merry Christmas and Happy New Year.

Sincerely,
Ron

―――――

In the fall of 1983, Senator William S. Cohen (R-Maine) introduced Suzanne Massie to National Security Adviser Robert "Bud" McFarlane. Then Massie, a scholar of Russian history and culture, met with Reagan in the Oval Office on January 16, 1984, to discuss her impressions of the Soviet Union and the state of bilateral relations. Reagan and Massie would meet many times,[20] and this letter reflects the conversations they had about religion and culture in the Soviet Union. As he mentions below, Reagan did not attend the funeral of Soviet General Secretary Yuri Andropov, who died on February 9, 1984. Vice President George Bush led the U.S. delegation. Reagan watched the procession on television and wondered how the suppression of religious freedom affected those living under Soviet rule at such a time.

Mrs. Suzanne Massie
Irvington, New York
February 15, 1984[21]

Dear Mrs. Massie:

I waited to answer your letter until after your return from the Soviet Union. In the meantime a great change occurred there. I dare to hope there might be a better chance for communication with the new leadership.

Watching scenes of the funeral on TV I wondered what thoughts people must have at such a time when their belief in no God or immortality is faced with death. Like you I continue to believe that the hunger for religion may yet be a major factor in bringing about a change in the present situation.

I hope your trip was all you wanted it to be.

Sincerely,
Ronald Reagan

―――――

In this letter, Reagan recounts his earliest meetings with Brezhnev and writes that the American and Russian people have a great deal in common.

Mr. and Mrs. Ronald D. Paton
Santa Ana, California
July 16, 1984[22]

Dear Mr. and Mrs. Paton:

I'm very late in answering your good letter of May 31 but only because it takes a while for mail to reach my desk. Thank you for sharing your friend's letter with me and for sharing the story of how you all came together. On your August vacation please give my regards to your friends. We have a few teachers here who should get the same treatment he gave the one over there and for the same offense.

You confirm something I wrote to Brezhnev when I was in the hospital (1981) after the shooting. It was a handwritten letter reminding him of our meeting back in '70 or '71 when he was visiting California. I almost described your own shipboard meeting in that I suggested that if a Russian family and an American family found themselves thrown together they would begin to get acquainted and discover how much they had in common. I even said they would agree to get together again. Then I asked him why governments couldn't do that. His answer was something less than satisfactory. But you have proven that people don't start wars. Only governments do that.

Thank you again and have a good time.

Sincerely,
Ronald Reagan

In an effort to leave the Soviet Union so that they could freely practice their religion, two Pentecostal families, the Vashchenkos and the Chmykhalovs, took refuge in the American embassy in Moscow in June 1978. A year later, Reagan wrote a radio commentary about their plight. As president he participated in "quiet diplomacy" with Soviet leaders to obtain their release. In the spring of 1983, Soviet exit visas were granted to the Pentecostals and they left the Soviet Union during the summer. Secretary of State George P. Shultz wrote that President Reagan's "own role in it [the release of the Pentecostals] had been crucial. I always felt it was significant that Ronald Reagan's first diplomatic achievement with the Soviets . . . was on an issue of human rights."[23] More than a year after their release, President Reagan received a letter from a young member of the Vashchenko family. She thanked him for his assistance and wished him well in his reelection bid.

Miss Liuba Vashchenko
Caldwell, Idaho
October 11, 1984[24]

Dear Miss Vashchenko:

Thank you very much for your kind letter. I can't tell you how happy I was when you were all released from our embassy and allowed to come to our country. I have refrained from commenting on the matter because we may have to employ the same means in others' behalf. We practiced a little quiet diplomacy and it succeeded.

I hope our paths will cross one day and I'm happy you are enjoying life here in our country.

Thank you for your good wishes.

Sincerely,
Ronald Reagan

Reagan reveals that he is mindful of the risks of sending a letter to Polish dissidents and asks that the president of Radio Free Europe/Radio Liberty orally convey his message to them.

The Honorable James L. Buckley
Munich, West Germany
March 4, 1985 [25]

Dear Jim:

Thank you very much for your letter of congratulations and for sending me that letter from our Polish friends. I know I can't answer them without putting their safety at risk. If you ever have a chance to relay an oral message, pass the word that I did receive their letter and that we will not forget them.

And while I'm doing thank yous, a very big one goes to you for what you are doing. You have my heartfelt thanks. God bless you.

Sincerely,
Ron

Seeking asylum, Miroslav Medved, a Soviet seaman, jumped overboard from the Mar-shal Konev, a Russian ship stationed near New Orleans, on October 24, 1985. Think-ing he was a stowaway, the local Immigration and Naturalization Service officers returned Medved to the ship. The State Department then intervened by demanding that American officials be allowed to interrogate Medved. Ihor Olshaniwsky, president of Americans for Human Rights in Ukraine, wrote to President Reagan to inform him of his organization's outrage at the handling of the case. President Reagan writes the note below on Olshaniwsky's message.

Note
Circa November 1985 [26]

I issued orders that if there was a problem getting him off the ship for question-ing—we should use armed force.* They were standing by. Under our interrogation with no Soviets present—he said he wanted to go back to Russia.

The day after Armand Hammer brought Soviet dissidents David and Cecilia Goldfarb out of the Soviet Union on his private jet, President Reagan thanks the American in-dustrialist for his intervention.

---

* In his memoirs, Secretary George Shultz writes: "A hurricane was building in the Gulf, and the notion of our officers trying to force their way on board the vessel in such weather was nightmarish, but we were prepared to do it. The idea of 'force' did not mean using weapons, but going aboard uninvited could be dangerous, so the INS and port authorities would carry arms." *Turmoil and Triumph,* p. 584.

Mr. Armand Hammer
Los Angeles, California
October 17, 1986[27]

Dear Armand:

I don't know how you did it but a big thank you from your countrymen on bringing the Goldfarbs out of the Soviet Union. It was truly a humanitarian deed and we are proud to have them in our country reunited with their family.

Again my heartfelt thanks and very best regards to Cecelia.*

Sincerely,
Ronald Reagan

On August 30, 1986, the Soviet Union charged the U.S. News & World Report *correspondent in Moscow, Nicholas S. Daniloff, with spying and arrested him. Although innocent of the charge, Daniloff was released on September 12 in a trade for Gennadi F. Zakharov, a Soviet scientific attaché arrested by the FBI on August 23 for paying for classified U.S. documents. In this letter to Nackey Loeb, publisher of the* Union Leader *(Manchester, New Hampshire), Reagan discusses the Daniloff case and his desire to have some Soviet dissidents freed as part of the exchange. After Daniloff and Zakharov returned to their respective countries, Soviet dissidents Yuri Orlov and his wife, Irina Valitova, and Viktor and Inessa Flerov were allowed to leave the Soviet Union.*

Mrs. William Loeb
Manchester, New Hampshire
October 17, 1986[28]

Dear Nackey:

I'm glad your two letters and editorials arrived on my desk at the same time. I enjoyed the one dated October 14 more than the October 7 mailing. I do agree however that your suggestion in the earlier letter about the news media creating a false message is true and I'm grateful for your prayers.

The column by Jim Finnegan was appropriately titled—"Lies, Lies, Lies"—because that's what it was.

Nackey of course we wanted Daniloff back. But we told the Soviet Union, everything, their spy, their invitation to a meeting etc. was on hold until Daniloff was freed. When they did that we then told them we'd do what presidents before me had done three times before in similar cases, exchange their guilty spy for Soviet dissidents. Our choice was Orlov and wife. By pleading no contest their spy acknowledged his guilt and we were saved months of trial while the Orlovs remained victims of Soviet cruelty.

Mr. Finnegan was off base again when he declared we were reneging on the So-

---

* Reagan most likely meant to refer to Frances, the wife of Armand Hammer.

viet intelligence agents we were sending home from the U.N. All 25 are now back in Moscow. There was never a question but that we were kicking them out.

Thanks again for your prayers and good wishes.

Sincerely,

Ron

In another letter to Suzanne Massie, President Reagan discusses meeting dissidents released from the Soviet Union.

Mrs. Suzanne Massie
Cambridge, Massachusetts
October 21, 1986 [29]

Dear Suzanne:

It was good to get your letter and your kind words. Your estimate of the Iceland affair is very reassuring. You mentioned their ability to wait. I'm wondering if things won't be on hold until after our election and possibly even after the West German elections in January.

They created another little haggling point with their ousting of five of our people from the embassy in Moscow and the consulate in Leningrad. Well we are going to respond in kind. They greatly outnumber us in their embassy here and their San Francisco consulate. We are going to reduce their majority shortly.

I've had quite an experience meeting with the Orlovs. I had a phone conversation also with Dr. Goldfarb but it wasn't very satisfactory. His voice was so weak I had trouble hearing him. I can only say I was aware he was thanking us and was happy to be here.

Nancy sends her best and again my thanks.

Sincerely,

Ronald Reagan

President Reagan congratulates a longtime friend on the publication of a book on the German pilot program for which Reagan wrote the preface. The proceeds from the sale of Those Wonderful Men in the Cactus Starfighter Squadron *were to go toward a scholarship for the Luftwaffe/U.S. Air Force International Friendship Foundation. President Reagan also suggests that the privileged class in the Soviet Union is resisting the reforms that Mikhail Gorbachev sought to impose.*

Colonel Barney Oldfield, USAF (Ret.)
Beverly Hills, California
June 1, 1987 [30]

Dear Barney:

Your two letters hit my desk at the same time—Monday June 1st. I was pleased to hear about those "Wonderful Men in the Cactus Starfighter Squadron." I'll have a word or two about that with Helmut Kohl in a few days. We'll be at the economic summit in Venice. The scholarship program sounds good—congratulations.

Your session with "my favorite film critic" sounds very interesting. He confirms what I have suspected, that the nomenclature is giving the general secretary some trouble as he seeks to streamline things. I know the feeling. We have a bureaucracy that reacts the same way.

Well all the best to your gal and thanks for the information.

Best regards,
Ron

In his speech before the annual convention of the National Association of Evangelicals in Orlando, Florida, on March 8, 1983, President Reagan spoke of "the aggressive impulses of an evil empire." Nackey Loeb's December 3, 1987, editorial, published a few days before the Washington Summit at which the intermediate-range nuclear forces (INF) treaty was to be signed, declared that "Ronald Reagan is promoting an agreement that will give communism the advantage, accompanied by a Hollywood show of smiles and handshakes with the leader of what the original Reagan called 'the evil empire.'" Loeb sent her editorial and a letter to President Reagan. Reagan writes back assuring the publisher that he has not changed his stripes.

Mrs. William Loeb
Manchester, New Hampshire
December 18, 1987 [31]

Dear Nackey:

Maybe we're even—I didn't enjoy reading those editorials you didn't enjoy writing. Nackey I'm still the Ronald Reagan I was and the evil empire is still just that. I wasn't talking about you or people like you when I spoke of "inevitable war." I did have in mind a few individuals who probably aren't aware or conscious of their feeling about inevitable war. Maybe I didn't make myself clear but I was talking about those individuals giving up on any effort to influence history and accepting permanent hatred and enmity as the only future for the two greatest superpowers. The probability of disaster is too great to accept that without making an effort.

We haven't weakened the western defense at all, quite the contrary. They are removing four warheads for every one we are taking out. But more important we still have thousands of tactical warheads on line that evens us up with their conventional weapon superiority. We won't bargain those away until and unless they agree to a reduction of conventional weapons. Incidentally their SS20's were targeted on every important city and seaport in Europe. Ports we'd need to reinforce our allies.

Nackey on the budget problems I'm aware that the Democrats have tagged me as responsible for the deficits but I counted on people like you to know the president can't spend a dime. We haven't had a budget since I've been here. Yes the law says I must present a budget every January. And every January the Congress throws my budget away and passes a "continuing resolution" with all the appropriations in that one resolution. If I veto, the government shuts down.

Yes I've asked for increases in defense spending. Rebuilding our national security was a must. Even Carter had projected a five-year military buildup to begin in 1982. Well the Congress cut my defense budgets by $125 billion. But at the same time they added $250 billion to my domestic budgets in those "continuing resolutions."

The problem is that for almost 60 years the House of Representatives has been solid Democrat except for four years—two in Truman's administration and two during Ike's.

Happy Holidays!

Ronald

President Reagan thanks a couple for sending him a translation of a prayer that was supposedly found on a Russian soldier killed in action during World War II. Some of the stanzas of the prayer capture Reagan's position on religious oppression in the Soviet Union: "Hear me Oh God, Never in the whole of my life have I spoken to you. . . . You know, from childhood on they've told me You are not . . . and yet, tonight, gazing up out of my shell hole, I marveled at the shimmering stars above me, and suddenly knew the cruelty of the lie." He recited the poem at the National Prayer Breakfast on February 4, 1988.

Mr. and Mrs. Gerhard P. Reinders
Appleton, Wisconsin
January 7, 1988 [32]

Dear Mr. and Mrs. Reinders:

Thank you very much for your kind letter, generous words and holiday greeting. And thank you too for the copy of that Russian soldier's prayer. It is deeply moving and makes one even more convinced that the most important human right being violated in the Soviet Union is the right to worship.

Nancy sends her thanks also and from both of us, very best wishes and regards.

Sincerely,
Ronald Reagan

On May 31, 1988, President Reagan was meeting with Soviet leader Mikhail Gorbachev at the Kremlin in their final summit. A reporter asked President Reagan whether he still considered the Soviet Union an "evil empire." He replied, "I was talk-

ing about another time, another era."[33] *In the next letters, written a few days after the summit, President Reagan again expresses the belief that a sea change is under way in the Soviet Union.*

> Mr. Armand S. Deutsch
> Beverly Hills, California
> June 7, 1988[34]

Dear Ardie:

It was great to get home and your letter made it even greater. Thank you for as always your generous words and wonderful way of raising my morale. We all felt good about the trip and then I read your letter and went into high gear.

Ardie this general secretary with his glasnost and perestroika has really moved the Russian people. We couldn't believe their friendliness and warmth. I'm talking about the people in the street—not the world of officialdom. Wherever we went they were massed on the curb, waving, smiling and cheering. And I'm convinced he is sincere about wanting to make a change. He'd have to be to take on the bureaucracy the way he has.

Well bless you both and love from both of us.

> Sincerely,
> Ron

The human dimension of the cold war was something to which Reagan gave considerable attention during his presidency. Here he replies to a letter from an American businessman who wanted President Reagan to know of an exchange he had in Belorussia before the Moscow summit. When a young man asked him if he would meet President Reagan at the upcoming summit, he responded: "No, I am just a businessman who has little to do with presidents and political matters." The 19-year-old responded: "Well, if you do meet him, please give him my best personal regards from Daniel Konstantinovich (himself) and tell him I think he will succeed in the efforts that bring him here."

> Mr. Max B. Flaxman
> Cranford, New Jersey
> June 7, 1988[35]

Dear Mr. Flaxman:

Thank you very much for your letter which unfortunately I did not get to read until after I left Russia. You were more than kind to write as you did and I'm sorry we didn't meet, sorry too that I couldn't acknowledge in person the kind words of Daniel Konstantinovich.

Nancy and I were both impressed, indeed overwhelmed by the warmth of our greeting by the people of Moscow who went out of their way to show their friendship. It just reassured me in my belief that people don't cause wars, governments do.

Again, my thanks and very best regards,

Sincerely,
Ronald Reagan

A few weeks after the Moscow summit, President Reagan writes to an old friend that glasnost, described by Mikhail Gorbachev in December 1984 as "an integral part of socialist democracy" and translated as "openness," [36] *is apparent in the Soviet Union and spreading throughout its republics.*

The Honorable George Murphy
Cashiers, North Carolina
July 8, 1988 [37]

Dear Murph:

It was good to hear from you and thanks for your kind review of our Moscow revels. I have to tell you we were surprised by the ordinary citizens, not the "nomenklatura." You can't believe how warm and friendly the ordinary people on the streets were. There was an enthusiastic laying on of hands, women were embracing Nancy and crying when she had to move on and there could be no doubt it was for real.

But that leads to something else; the people have of course heard of glasnost and evidently liked what they heard. Murph for the first time, I believe there could perhaps one day be a stirring of the people that would make the bureaucrats pay attention. The Estonians have demanded home rule and no one is shooting at them. In Leningrad a mob of 2,000 marched on the KGB headquarters and the KGB stayed inside. If glasnost was just showboating they may have to keep at least some of the promises or face a public they've never seen before.

On another subject you are so right about candidates Dukakis and Jackson.* Our campaign theme has to be one of revealing what they are really like. I'm glad to hear about Paul Harvey.†

I've passed the word about your protégé. By the time you get this the picture with John Preyer will probably have been taken.

Nancy sends her love as do I and to Bette also.

Sincerely,
Ron

---

* In 1988, Michael Dukakis and Jesse Jackson were campaigning to be the Democratic Party's presidential nominee.

† Paul Harvey is a well-known radio announcer based in Chicago, Illinois.

THE COLD WAR AT HOME

How, when, and where to fight the cold war were concerns of the first magnitude for the American people. Budget and resource requirements were always of central importance. In the letters that follow, Ronald Reagan grapples with these issues. Although he routinely recognizes, and sometimes laments, domestic forces that he thinks hinder defense and foreign policy, Reagan is usually optimistic about the country's capacity to mobilize itself against adversaries. In the years before his presidency, however, he expresses great concern about whether American leaders understand the requirements of maintaining superpower status.

Written before his presidency, this letter is typical of many statements Reagan made during the years following the United States's withdrawal from Vietnam. He held that government officials fail to understand that even in the face of the Vietnam debacle, the American people are prepared to increase defense spending substantially and to fight the cold war.

Mr. Imro I. Wood
Marion, Illinois
Circa late 1970s [38]

Dear Mr. Wood:

Thanks very much for your letter and sound suggestions. You and I are in great agreement. I shall continue trying to campaign on the issues and right now I'm convinced a major issue is the failure of our nation to maintain its strength in a very dangerous world.

The Russians perceive us as lacking in willpower. I believe it is a lack of understanding. Government has failed to keep the people aware of our true situation. I have found a great desire on the part of the people to support a program of military preparedness.

Thank you again for your letter and good wishes.

Sincerely,
Ronald Reagan

Five months before he announced his 1980 run for the presidency, Reagan writes that curbing government waste is not antithetical to a strong defense. This was one of the many ideas that Reagan consistently espoused throughout his political career.

Mr. Ross S. Williams
June 6, 1979 [39]

Dear Col:

Thank you very much for your letter of June 4th. I appreciate the information you sent. I assure you that while I am all out for an adequate defense posture, I have always felt that the military at the same time, like the civilian bureaucracy in government, must be reviewed for the very wasteful things of which you speak. We can have an adequate defense without the waste; indeed, it will be a better defense. Thanks again for taking the time and trouble to write. I am truly grateful.

Sincerely,
Ronald Reagan

In this pre-presidential letter to a U.S. senator, Reagan expresses his concern and skepticism about American military readiness and resolve as well as its position in the international system.

The Honorable Sam Nunn *
Washington, DC
1979 [40]

Dear Sam:

Thank you very much for your good letter and for sending me the copies of your two fine speeches. They made great, good common sense and hit upon angles that I'm sure were new to your audiences. Indeed, they were new to me. I'll probably do some cribbing as the days go on but will happily give you credit.

I'm in complete agreement with you that the question is whether we're prepared to compete with the Soviet Union in this arena. We must be or we'll just be another one of those great civilizations that slipped into the dustbin of history.

Again, thanks and best regards.

Sincerely,
Ron

The president of Smith College wrote to President Reagan to express deep concern about the purpose and direction of America's foreign and defense policies. In this reply, President Reagan contends that Soviet preferences and the nuclear freeze movement complicate his efforts to reduce nuclear weapons.

---

* Samuel A. Nunn (D-Georgia).

Miss Jill Conway
Northampton, Massachusetts
October 25, 1982[41]

Dear Miss Conway:

Thank you very much for your letter of September 21. I know you will be pleased to learn that we are proceeding along the very lines you proposed in our effort to make world peace a reality.

I am encouraged by my recent meetings with President Gemayel and King Hassan[*] and the representatives of the Arab nations. While it won't be easy a foundation has been laid that can lead to real negotiations in the Middle East.

I share your conviction that an answer must be found to the nuclear threat and am glad you support our effort to get mutual reduction of nuclear weapons. Our teams in Geneva are working very hard but I fear their efforts have been impeded by the nuclear freeze movement. Their Soviet counterparts have made no secret of their pleasure at the idea of unilateral restrictions on our part.

I am convinced that our own buildup is necessary if they are to continue to bargain in good faith. But let me assure you I share your view that our ultimate goal must be the elimination of nuclear weapons. We are also proceeding with plans along the line you proposed for increasing cooperation among the peoples of the world and greater understanding of man's potential for progress.

Again thank you.

Sincerely,
Ronald Reagan

President Reagan implies that the term "Vietnam syndrome" means a lack of appreciation of the sacrifices made by those who served in the war as well as a lack of understanding of the importance of the cause.

MSgt. Michael T. Henry
Keesler AFB, Mississippi
December 27, 1982[42]

Any address? If so—

Dear MSgt. Henry:

Thank you very much for your letter and for your poem. I assure you we share in common the concern you so eloquently express. I'm convinced our fellow Americans have left or are leaving behind the tragic Vietnam syndrome that haunted our land for so long. They are at last aware of your sacrifice and are beginning to realize how worthwhile the cause truly was.

---

[*] President Amin Gemayel of Lebanon and King Hassan II of Morocco.

Again my thanks—both for the poem and for what you've done for our country.

Sincerely,
Ronald Reagan

————————

Responding to a letter from a man who opposed the nuclear freeze movement, President Reagan declares, as he did numerous times in the late 1970s and during his 1980 presidential bid, that being strong is the way to avoid war.

Mr. Kenneth J. Hoover
Hammond, Indiana
December 27, 1982 [43]

Dear Mr. Hoover:

Just a line to thank you for your letter and the morale boost it gave me.

You are so right about what it would take to bring about an attack on us. I've known four wars in my lifetime. None of them came about because we were too strong.

Again thanks.

Sincerely,
Ronald Reagan

————————

President Reagan reports on a task force that was streamlining the Defense Department's procurement process.

Mr. Francis J. Kehoe
Paramus, New Jersey
December 27, 1982 [44]

Dear Mr. Kehoe:

Thanks very much for your good letter and for your warm words of support. I am most grateful.

I think you'll be happy to know we've started a campaign to weed out the non truly disabled who are abusing the VA system. We are beginning to have some success.

I have to say however I don't believe the situation in our defense buildup is as bad as the news media—and some congressmen would have you believe. We've had a citizen's task force made up of top people quietly working as volunteers in the DOD and the result has been a great many improvements in procurement etc. totaling billions of dollars in savings. We have already reduced our original five year budget for defense—voluntarily I might add—by $41 billion.

Again thanks for writing and rest assured we won't let up.

Sincerely,
Ronald Reagan

———

In a letter to President Reagan dated December 10, 1982, a Catholic priest said that he was a prisoner in a Siberian concentration camp for more than three years and knows that the Soviet government is untrustworthy. He also apologized for the American bishops' call for a nuclear freeze. President Reagan writes that he wishes the bishops could hear the priest's story.

The Reverend John Kmech
Chicago, Illinois
February 1, 1983[45]

Dear Father Kmech:

I can't tell you how much your letter of last month meant to me and how grateful I am. I'm sorry to be so late in answering but it sometimes takes a while for mail to reach my desk.

If only more people and yes if the bishops could hear and heed the words of someone like yourself who knows firsthand the godless tyranny of Soviet totalitarianism.

Thank you again for writing.

Sincerely,
Ronald Reagan

———

President Reagan proclaims that the nuclear freeze movement, including the freeze resolution introduced by Congressman Clement John Zablocki (D-Wisconsin) on January 3, 1983, is having a negative effect on his ability to reduce arms. He fears that the House will approve the resolution. It did so on May 4 in a vote of 278–149.

Ambassador Earl E. T. Smith
Palm Beach, Florida
March 17, 1983[46]

Dear Earl:

Thanks very much for your letter and I agree completely with your sum up of the situation.

I'm afraid by the time you get this the Democratic House will have voted Zablocki's resolution for a freeze. The letter writing promoted by the organized movement has had its effect. We've tried to counter with a substitute that would call for a freeze <u>after</u> we've had arms reduction, verifiable and down to equal levels.

There is a sense of "déjà vu" in this chorus over El Salvador with the same voices that gave us Cuba and Nicaragua.

Nancy sends her love and from both of us to Lesly.

Sincerely,
Ron

President Reagan acknowledges that many in the freeze movement have good intentions and want peace, as he does, but he disagrees with them on tactics and strategy.

Bishop Mark J. Hurley
Santa Rosa, California
April 19, 1983 [47]

Dear Bishop Hurley:

Thank you very much for your letter and generous words. Thanks too for the editorial you plan to write. I am most grateful. I can't help but feel if we had an opportunity to talk together we might find there were fewer differences between us than at times seem to be. I am sure for example we have no disagreement about the absolute necessity of achieving peace in the world. Possibly we only differ with regard to the path we take to reach our goal.

Again my heartfelt thanks for writing as you did and above all for your prayers.

Sincerely,
Ronald Reagan

President Reagan writes to a former prisoner of war who endorses his strategic defense initiative.

Mr. Paul Lazzaro
San Jose, California
April 19, 1983 [48]

Dear Mr. Lazzaro:

Thank you very much for your mailgram and your expression of support. You touched on something I've thought about many times; how different your life might have been, how many might not have died if our country had been prepared back in the '30s and '40s.

President Roosevelt was making the same pleas for adequate defense and meeting the same resistance in the Congress. I'll keep on pushing and I thank you again.

Sincerely,
Ronald Reagan

In June of 1983, a group of high school students chosen as Presidential Scholars visited the White House. During the visit, Ariela Gross, one of the students, gave Presi-

dent Reagan a petition supporting a nuclear freeze signed by 14 of the 141 Presidential Scholars. Reagan's instruction to his staff is written on the student's petition.

Note from students
June 16, 1983 [49]

No reply—<u>absolutely</u> no reply.

Ronald Reagan

President Reagan thanks a Catholic voter from Ohio for notifying his legislators that he supports the president's defense and foreign policies, and sympathizes with his distress over the American bishops' nuclear freeze posture.

Dr. Martin P. Harpen
Dayton, Ohio
June 21, 1983 [50]

Dear Dr. Harpen:

Thank you very much for your kind letter and generous words. I am pleased and proud to have your support. I'm glad that you are registering your feelings with your senators and Representative Hall.* If only more people would realize they can influence their elected officials by making their feelings known we'd solve a great many problems. I repeatedly say this but the press doesn't quote me on that subject, their excuse being that I've said it before.

You are so right about no agreement with the Soviets being better than a bad agreement. I've impressed this on our negotiators. I know how distressed you must be with the bishops' message on the freeze but I'm sure you are correct about the rank and file. Any number of priests have gone out of their way to tell me of their disagreement.

Again thanks for your letter. We'll keep trying.

Sincerely,
Ronald Reagan

Reagan tells a Vietnam veteran that the American government let servicemen down in the war in Southeast Asia.

---

* Senators John Glenn (D-Ohio) and Howard M. Metzenbaum (D-Ohio), and Congressman Anthony P. Hall (D-Ohio).

Mr. Robert L. Eastburn
Stanton, Delaware
July 17, 1984[51]

Dear Mr. Eastburn:

Thank you for your letter of May 31st and for sharing your thoughts with me. I appreciate your generous words and am sorry to be so late in responding.

You and all your comrades in arms did fight for freedom and for a truly noble cause. It is a cause that continues. You fought as well as any Americans have fought in our history and a new generation of Americans will have to be as willing to serve as all of you were. You did not lose a war, the war goes on. You were engaged in a battle of that ongoing fight for freedom and the battle was lost not by you who were fighting it but by political misjudgments and strategic failure in the highest levels of government.

Please take pride in what you did and let us all pledge that never again will this nation break faith with those who are fighting and dying for this nation and for freedom. God bless you.

Sincerely,
Ronald Reagan

CHAPTER TWELVE

The Cold War II: Politics, Arms, and Missile Defense

R ONALD REAGAN *argued that "military power . . . is the cement which makes national power effective in the diplomatic arena." He was particularly blunt in his major foreign policy speech of his 1976 presidential campaign: "Humanitarian impulses and benevolence are commendable and they have a place, but our strength and survival come first." In order to guarantee peace, the United States needed "to be second to none in military strength."* [1]

The letters in this chapter explain Reagan's views on the military dimension of the cold war and suggest that he was applying something like the logic of "Ockham's Razor" [2] *to policy issues, including U.S.–Soviet relations. In a letter written before he became president, he said: "I have long believed that our search for complex answers to many of our problems is, in truth, an effort to avoid obvious, simple answers because, though simple, they are hard."* [3]

Reagan had four core hypotheses about U.S.–Soviet relations from which he derived his strategies for fighting the cold war: (1) The Soviet economy is so weak at bottom that it cannot sustain a technology race with the United States; (2) The sole source of legitimacy of the Soviet Union in Eastern Europe is the Red Army's occupation. If it withdraws, the citizens of those countries will go their own way; (3) The American economy is so strong at bottom that it can sustain a technology race with the Soviet Union; and (4) The American people are prepared for substantial increases in defense spending if leaders clearly combine the military build-up with a preference for mutual cooperation with the Soviet Union.

In letters he wrote during his presidency, Reagan discusses how he implemented policy toward the Soviet Union. On July 9, 1981, he writes: "I know I'm being criticized for not having made a great speech outlining what would be the Reagan foreign policy. I have a foreign policy; I'm working on it. I just don't happen to think that it's wise to always stand up and put in quotation marks in front of the world what your foreign

policy is. I'm a believer in quiet diplomacy and so far we've had several quite triumphant experiences by using that method."[4] The temperature rose in U.S.-Soviet relations in 1983: the nuclear freeze movement continued to gather steam; the Strategic
Defense Initiative (SDI) and the "evil empire" speeches were delivered in the same
month; the United States deployed intermediate-range nuclear forces in Europe; and
the Soviet Union walked out of the nuclear weapons talks in Geneva. Yet, this was also
the year that quiet diplomacy had some tangible results. President Reagan worked privately with Soviet General Secretary Yuri Andropov to secure the release of the Pentecostal families who several years earlier had taken refuge in the American embassy in
Moscow. Reagan's public rhetoric sometimes belied his private efforts. This difference is
seen in his letters.

Reagan also discusses his foreign policy goals in his letters. In a letter dated June 28,
1982, he writes that his administration's "number one goal is to achieve a meaningful
reduction in armaments from strategic nuclear to conventional."[5]

The Strategic Defense Initiative, a plan to develop a defensive shield against nuclear weapons, was perhaps the most controversial weapons program of the Reagan
era. It was an important marker in the movement of the United States away from the
Anti-Ballistic Missile Treaty signed by President Richard M. Nixon and Soviet General
Secretary Leonid Brezhnev on May 26, 1972, and it paved the way for President George
W. Bush's decision to withdraw the United States from the treaty in 2001. Reagan's letters about SDI reveal his view about its influence on other military and political issues
in the cold war. He also declares that SDI "was my idea to begin with and we will deploy when it is ready."[6]

When Reagan became president, many believed that he did not want to engage in
nuclear arms negotiations with the Soviets, yet there were more superpower summits
in his presidency than in any other during the cold war. He met with Soviet General
Secretary Mikhail Gorbachev four times: (1) Geneva in 1985; (2) Reykjavik in 1986;
(3) Washington in 1987; and (4) Moscow in 1988. The signing of the intermediate-
range nuclear forces (INF) treaty on December 8, 1987, was one important marker
that an historic shift in superpower relations was taking place. A year later, while Reagan was still in office, British Prime Minister Margaret Thatcher declared: "We are not
in a Cold War now." Secretary of State George P. Shultz has observed that by the fall of
1988, "it was all over but the shouting."[7] In the letters below, Reagan discusses his view
of how military competition contributed to the political transformation that was
under way when his presidency ended in January 1989.

On June 18, 1979, President Jimmy Carter and Soviet General Secretary Leonid
Brezhnev signed the Treaty on the Limitation of Strategic Offensive Arms (known as
SALT II) in Vienna. Reagan opposed the treaty and said so in radio commentaries that
he wrote in the late 1970s. Perhaps his most comprehensive statement against the
treaty was made in a speech before the state convention of the California Republican
Party in San Diego on September 15, 1979. In his handwritten draft of the speech, Rea-

gan writes that "SALT II is not Strategic Arms Limitation, it is Strategic Arms buildup with the Soviets adding a minimum of three thousand nuclear warheads to their inventory and the United States embarking on a thirty-five billion dollar catch-up which won't be achieved until 1990 if then." [8]

In the next three letters, Reagan is emphatic about his opposition to U.S. Senate approval of the treaty and says that he is working to prevent it. The first letter is to Donald H. Rumsfeld, U.S. Secretary of Defense in the George W. Bush administration.

The Honorable Donald Rumsfeld
October 26, 1979 [9]

Dear Don:

Just a quick line between trips to thank you for your note regarding my pitch on SALT. I know you must feel as deeply as I do that passage of this treaty will be a serious blow to our security.

Thanks again, and I hope our paths will cross soon.

Regards,
Ron

Mrs. Ellen Garwood
Circa December 1979 [10]

Dear Mrs. Garwood:

Thank you very much for sending the wire and giving me the opportunity to comment. I can understand your concern in view of the recent press stories. Please be reassured those stories are completely inaccurate. Martin Anderson is still with us in the campaign, and Mike Deaver simply had to go for personal reasons from a full-time staff employee to a part-time volunteer position, but a very important one, in our campaign. I am with you with regard to the SALT II treaty. I'm doing everything I can to help get it defeated.

Best regards,
Ronald Reagan

Mr. Charles Burton Marshall
April 8, 1980 [11]

Dear Mr. Marshall:

I have heard from Dick Allen* about your response to my speech and the answer to the question regarding SALT that disturbs you. Dick has also told me of his invitation to you to join those who are providing me with needed input.

Believe me, you would be most welcome, and I would be honored if you felt that you could do that. May I clarify one thing on my answer to the question. I have

---

* Richard V. Allen was Ronald Reagan's foreign policy adviser during the 1980 presidential campaign and in 1981 was appointed assistant to the president for national security affairs.

given that answer a number of times and possibly I've grown careless in the wording. I don't really trust the Soviets, and I don't really believe that they will really join us in a legitimate limitation of arms agreement. What I was really trying to say and have said on several occasions was that the SALT II treaty should be returned to them and then, simply to prove to the world which nation truly wants peace, we should tell them we would be willing to sit at the table as long as it took to negotiate a legitimate reduction of nuclear weapons on both sides to the point that neither country represented a threat to the other, and I really meant the qualifier that we would be showing the country which really wanted peace because I'm quite sure the Soviet Union would never sit down with us at a table to negotiate such a legitimate agreement. I am deeply concerned about our precarious position at present and believe that we should be looking for the most likely deterrent and the one we could get on line the fastest before the window of opportunity becomes any wider for them.

Again, my thanks to you and my hope that you will become a part of our team.

Sincerely,
Ronald Reagan

In a note to one of his closest campaign advisers, Reagan gives a short assessment of a recent article by Georgi Arbatov, the director of the Institute of U.S. and Canadian Studies in Moscow. Colonel Barney Oldfield sent the article to Reagan and attached a letter Arbatov had sent to Oldfield. At the bottom of the page, Arbatov wrote: "P.S. Your old friend R. Reagan is making success." *

Mr. Edwin Meese III
Circa May 1980 [12]

Ed M.:

My friend sent this to me. Arbatov of course is the Soviet authority on the United States. He has a staff of 400. This is quite a view of us thru his eyes—written for *Pravda*.

Ron

Reagan sought the advice of some of the nation's leading experts on the Soviet Union and international relations during his 1980 presidential campaign. In this letter he recounts a conversation with University of Pennsylvania professor of political science

---

* In Arbatov's April 29, 1980, letter to Oldfield, he writes that his article appeared in *USA: Economics, Politics, Ideology.* The archival copy of Oldfield's letter to Reagan does not include a copy of the Arbatov essay. Arbatov most likely sent "U.S. Foreign Policy at the Start of the 80s," which appeared in the April 1980 edition of the journal.

and former diplomat Robert Strausz-Hupe. In 1981, President Reagan would appoint Strausz-Hupe ambassador to Turkey.

Mr. Bob Michel*
Circa late January 1980 [13]

Dear Bob:

 Just a quick line to thank you for sending me the transcript of your remarks on the floor. You said what needs to be said and said it forcefully. I believe we are in very perilous times. Not too long ago, Robert Strausz-Hupe told me he believed that if we didn't immediately do what you yourself have suggested, it is five minutes to midnight for the United States.

 Nancy sends her love. Please give our regards to the family.

Sincerely,
Ron

In this letter, Reagan criticizes President Carter's December 31, 1979, reaction to the Soviet invasion of Afghanistan a few days earlier. In a television interview, President Carter had said: "My opinion of the Russians has changed most drastically in the last week . . . this action of the Soviets has made a more dramatic change in my own opinion of what the Soviets' ultimate goals are than anything they've done in the previous time I've been in office." [14]

Professor Nikolaev
Circa January 1980 [15]

Dear Professor:

 Thank you very much for your good letter of January 5 with the wealth of information it contained. I am taking all of this up with our people out here and believe that you have summed up the situation in Iran very well. Our President's admission the other day that he at last believes that the Soviets are not to be trusted would be laughable, I think, if it were not so tragic. Even as he said it, he acknowledged that he would probably be willing to trust them in the near future when he will once again take up the SALT II treaty.

 Again, my thanks to you.

Very best regards,
Sincerely,
Ron

---

* Robert H. Michel (R-Illinois).

In the wake of the Soviet invasion of Afghanistan, the United States withdrew from the 1980 Moscow Olympics. Reagan had mixed feelings about boycotting the games as a sanction for the invasion of Afghanistan.

Mr. John P. Rodler
July 2, 1980 [16]

Dear Mr. [Rodler]:

Thank you very much for your letter and forgive me for being so late in responding, but I have been almost constantly out on the campaign trail. Let me say at this point again, however, how grateful I am for your contribution.

With regard to your suggestion about my position on the Olympics, I'm afraid I have already come to some change on that. I had hoped that enough of our allies and the free world would have recognized the hypocrisy of holding the Olympics in the Soviet Union. But since we are going it alone, I answered a press question the other day that I was having second thoughts and that I would have to stew a bit about whether we should penalize our own young people when no one else would join the boycott. I add, however, that since the Olympics were born to bring peace and discourage war, maybe we should stop the quadrennial lottery as to where the games should be held and have them permanently based in Greece where they started. This might serve to remind more of us of the original intent of the games.

Please give my very best to your wife and, again, my thanks to you for your letter.

Sincerely,
Ronald Reagan

"The United States is prepared to cancel its deployment of Pershing II and ground-launch cruise missiles," President Reagan announced on November 18, 1981, "if the Soviets will dismantle their SS-20, SS-4, and SS-5 missiles." He added that "[w]ith Soviet agreement, we could together substantially reduce the dread threat of nuclear war which hangs over the people of Europe. This, like the first footstep on the Moon, would be a giant step for mankind." Bilateral negotiations on intermediate-range nuclear forces began on November 30 in Geneva.

In the next two letters, President Reagan discusses the reasons why he will deploy Pershing II and cruise missiles in Europe if the Soviets do not dismantle their equivalent nuclear missiles.

Miss Virginia F. Adams
Charleston, West Virginia
April 21, 1982 [17]

Dear Miss Adams:

I appreciate the opportunity to respond to your concerns. I believe you have not been informed of my true position on nuclear weapons or the situation in El

Salvador. I can understand the latter because an effective world propaganda campaign of Soviet origin has been distorting the situation.

The Duarte government is the only moderate force standing between a far right group and the radical left guerrillas. These revolutionaries turned down every invitation to participate in the election and have instead threatened to kill those who vote. They have virtually destroyed the country's economy by blowing up power lines, bridges, transportation facilities and industries.

The government has brought about land reform and many social reforms. Our government which began supporting Duarte while Carter was president would not be in support now if those reforms had not been instituted.

With regard to nuclear weapons our country has made 19 proposals for the elimination or reduction of such weapons since 1946. Always the Soviets have been in opposition. Now I have proposed that we eliminate the intermediate-range nuclear weapons in Europe. Russia has 900 warheads targeting all of Europe, North Africa and the Middle East. Our allies have asked us to build and deploy in their countries comparable missiles as a deterrent. As a result of my proposal we and the Soviets are negotiating now in Geneva. So far they have said no to elimination of such weapons.

We are completing our studies now preparatory to negotiating a reduction of the strategic intercontinental missiles we and the Russians have aimed at each other.

The Soviets are ahead of us in number and power of such weapons. To have any chance of getting their agreement to a reduction we must convince them we will do what we have to do to match their strength.

We must reduce and hopefully eliminate nuclear weapons but we cannot do so unilaterally. The Soviet Union has the greatest offensive military power the world has ever seen.

Sincerely,
Ronald Reagan

Mr. Jay Harris
Lubbock, Texas
April 26, 1982 [18]

Dear Mr. Harris:

Thanks very much for your letter, which has reached me by way of Vice President Bush, and thanks for your generous words. I am most grateful.

In reply to your position paper let me say your suggestions are sound and we are proceeding along the lines of several of them. We are for example moving toward a summit meeting with Leonid Brezhnev and our team is in Geneva trying to negotiate a zero base in Europe for intermediate-range nuclear missiles. You are right about their SS 20's. Even behind the Urals they could reach every target area of Europe and the Middle East. If they dismantle we'll cancel the Pershings and Cruise missile deployment.

The on-site inspection will present a problem as will any method of verification. Since WWII our country has proposed arms reductions and even total elimination of nuclear weapons 19 times. Always the Soviet Union stopped short of agreement and in practically every instance verification was the stumbling block.

Your idea for helping the underdeveloped nations was the issue on the table at the Cancún Mexico conference. Some pretty good headway was made. Our Caribbean initiative embodies that same idea. Mexico, Canada, Venezuela and Colombia have joined us in that.

So far the Soviet Union has not joined in any of these undertakings. In all fairness it could be inability on their part. They are up against the wall economically, more so than at any previous time. It is my hope that this may make them more reasonable about arms reductions because their military buildup is the cause of their depression.

Again my thanks to you and best regards.

Sincerely,
Ronald Reagan

───────────

Joseph Coors, the head of Adolph Coors Company and an old friend of Reagan's, suggested that the President consider "modify[ing] any statements" against a nuclear first strike along the lines suggested by Edward Teller, a distinguished nuclear physicist. He also suggested that the word "bomb" connotes Hiroshima, and thus "neutron weapon" should be used. In his response, President Reagan agrees.

Mr. Joseph Coors
Golden, Colorado
April 22, 1982 [19]

Dear Joe:

Help! You didn't enclose the Teller letter. However you and I are on the same track with regard to the points you raised. There is no way we could assure the Soviets or our allies that we'd never make the first strike even though we know in our hearts we wouldn't.

I agree with you also about the "neutron bomb." I've tried using "warhead" and perhaps "weapon" is better but it isn't a bomb and that word does have a wrong connotation.

Incidentally rest easy about all the furor over a freeze. We can't go for that until there is a verifiable reduction to equality. I think the Soviets would be delighted with a freeze at the present levels.

It was good to hear from you. Give my regards to that lovely lady—my chairman. Nancy sends her best to you both.

Sincerely,
Ron

Insuring the survival of the MX, a highly accurate intercontinental ballistic missile (ICBM) with 10 multiple independently targeted reentry vehicle (MIRV) warheads, after a nuclear attack was a controversial defense policy issue during the Reagan administration. On October 2, 1981, Reagan announced that the United States would not base "the MX in the racetrack shelters proposed by the previous administration . . . [but] will complete the MX missile . . . and . . . deploy a limited number of the MX missiles in existing silos as soon as possible." Three days after his announcement, President Reagan reassured a nationally syndicated columnist that the MX will not be put on racetracks.

> Ann Landers
> Chicago, Illinois
> October 5, 1981 [20]

Dear Eppie:

By the time you get this you'll already know of our plans re—the MX. I appreciate your letter and your concern very much.

I assume part of your feeling about the MX was due to the ridiculous idea of running it around a racetrack with 4,600 silos. I've always been opposed to that. Our use of it will be to replace the aging Titans and some of the Minuteman missiles. The MX is a much more accurate missile with 10 warheads instead of 3.

Again thanks for writing. Nancy sends her love.

> Sincerely,
> Ron

"I believe . . . the Soviets won't really negotiate on arms reductions until we deploy the Pershing IIs and go forward with the MX," President Reagan wrote in his diary in the fall of 1983.[21] The belief that the MX was a bargaining chip was central to the president's national security planning and was reflected in many of his statements, including this letter to a well-known pediatrician and author.

> Dr. Benjamin Spock
> Rogers, Arkansas
> May 7, 1982 [22]

Dear Dr. Spock:

I'm afraid the experts you mention are not all that expert. We do not have strategic parity. In throw weight,—meaning destructive power the Soviets are far superior. They also are technologically superior in a number of other features.

We are going to engage them in negotiations to reduce nuclear weapons. This will be the 20th attempt by the United States to get such a reduction since WWII.

Always the Soviets refuse. I believe our intention to build the MX might offer an incentive to them to think of a mutual reduction in nuclear weapons.

[no signature]

Reagan explains his support for nuclear arms reductions talks.

Mr. John Matzger
San Leandro, California
May 11, 1982[23]

Dear Mr. Matzger:

Thank you very much for your letter and for your generous words about our economic recovery program. I'm most grateful.

With regard to the arms situation let me clarify something. I agree with you it wouldn't make sense to build up to parity with the Soviets and then propose a mutual reduction. I've studied the 19 previous efforts we've made since WWII to persuade them to join us in reducing nuclear weapons. I don't believe there will be a move on their part however so long as they have superiority and we are continuing to disarm unilaterally.

I'm sure you know that we are in negotiations now with them in Geneva regarding their intermediate-range nuclear missiles targeted on Europe. The negotiations were agreed to when we announced we would place Pershing missiles in Europe as a counter to their SS 20's.

Tomorrow I am announcing our invitation to the Soviets to join us in strategic nuclear arms reduction talks. I believe such talks will take place if they are convinced that the alternative is an arms race. A cartoon recently said it all; Brezhnev was speaking to a Russian general. He said, "I liked the arms race better when we were the only ones in it."

Again thank you for your good letter and sound suggestions.

Sincerely,
Ronald Reagan

President Reagan's views on nuclear policy are illuminated in this letter, which appears to be an unsolicited response to a column by Ann Landers. His handwritten draft, reproduced below, calls for the elimination of nuclear weapons, but the version that the president signed four days later was revised by the National Security Council staff and had a more muted tone. The NSC version states: "I've called for negotiations leading to major arms reductions, not limitations that only codify high levels. . . . I have . . . called for the reduction of the most destabilizing strategic elements, the ballistic missile warheads, by one-third in the first phase of negotiations on Strategic Arms Reduction. In the area of intermediate-range nuclear forces, I have also proposed the elimination of the most threatening systems, the land-based missiles."

Ann Landers
Chicago, Illinois
May 20, 1982 [24]

Dear Ann Landers:

I'm writing about your column of May 17 regarding the letter from "Terrified in D.C." I've had a few scares myself since I've been here but none of them radio-active.

Don't get me wrong. I'll take second [to] no one in my concern over the nuclear weapon threat—such a war is unthinkable. That is why I've called for negotiations leading to reduction—not limitation of nuclear weapons. Under the so-called limitation terms of "SALT II" both the United States and the Soviet Union could go on adding to the nuclear arsenals. We must have a true verifiable reduction leading to an eventual elimination of all such weapons.

We have to prove to the Soviet Union we are prepared to match them in such weapons or they won't even negotiate. Pretend to negotiate—yes. Make any head-way—no. They have such an edge on us now we have no choice but to rearm. As their superiority grows so does the danger of confrontation.

Ann we've tried 19 times since WWII to persuade them to join us in reducing or even eliminating nuclear weapons with no success. Wouldn't it be better if your readers sent that May 17 column to President Brezhnev?

Sincerely,
Ronald Reagan

———

Replying to a long letter from a Democrat who voted for him in 1980, President Reagan discusses his economic and defense policies. Although he does not present it in detail, Reagan declares that he has a grand strategy and mentions his goal of reducing nuclear and conventional weapons. The day after he wrote the letter below, the Strategic Arms Reduction Talks (START) began in Geneva. In contrast to the INF talks, which focused on intermediate-range nuclear missiles in Europe, the START negotiations were about long-range bombers and intercontinental missiles.

Mr. Irving S. Schloss
New Haven, Connecticut
June 28, 1982 [25]

Dear Mr. Schloss:

Thank you for writing and for giving me a chance to reply. I'm sorry to be so late in answering. But, now that I am let me say I disagree with your statement that current interest rates are the market's response to my policies. Perhaps to be exact I should say I disagree with your inference that I am—or my policies are—responsible for interest rates being too high. Yes they are too high, but they are about 20 percent lower than they were when I took office and for that I think my policies are responsible.

The previous administration brought interest rates from about 6½ percent in 1977 to 21½ percent in 1980; inflation from 4.8 percent to 12.4 percent; rate of increase in government spending to 17 percent a year even though it underspent on defense and left us the job of restoring our national security.

You suggest I should cut spending and defer the tax cuts. We have reduced the rate of increase in spending to half what it was and it will be further reduced in 1983. We have also reduced inflation from 12.4 percent to 3.7 for the last six months. The tax cuts are essential to get the economy going again just as a somewhat similar tax reduction by John F. Kennedy in 1963 stimulated the economy providing even higher receipts for government in spite of the reduced rates.

Since our 5 percent reduction last October the personal savings rate has increased to the point that the capital pool for investing will be up almost $300 billion over the next three years. As I recall taxes were increased some $300 billion between 1976 and 1980 and the deficits in that period totaled $318 billion. Incidentally some of the features of our tax program you criticized in your letter were not in our proposal. They were added on by Democratic members of the House and we had to accept them in order to get our program passed.

With regard to our spending on defense being simply a matter of throwing money at a problem while we have no global strategy to justify or direct our spending that is not the case. We have a definite and specific plan based on what we see as potential threats to our security in every area of the world. But in addition our number one goal is to achieve a meaningful reduction in armaments from strategic nuclear to conventional. Negotiations for this are now going on and I think I'm justified in saying the Soviets have come to the table only because they are convinced the alternative is an arms race they can't win. By the way in the "Camelot" of 1963 defense spending was 46 percent of the budget—in our '83 budget it is only 29 percent.

I share your feeling about high interest rates and their effect on recovery from the recession which apparently has bottomed out. It seems to me the money markets are holding back because they still aren't sure the government won't go in for the quick fix as it has seven times since WWII. In each case another recession followed with worse inflation. I'm hoping the present bipartisan budget resolution with its additional cuts in spending plus my veto of two spending bills in two days might send a reassuring message to those markets.

Again my thanks for writing.

Sincerely,
Ronald Reagan

In a memorandum to President Reagan, White House science adviser George A. Key-worth suggested that the president meet with Edward Teller to discuss Teller's idea of using a laser pump to direct the energy released by a nuclear blast. On the upper right-hand corner of the memorandum, President Reagan writes the following message to his assistant for national security affairs.

Judge William P. Clark
Washington, DC
July 29, 1982 [26]

Dear Bill:

We should take this seriously and have a real look. Remember our country once turned down the submarine.

Ron

President Reagan thanks Edward Teller for presenting his message to a scientific conference in Sicily.

Dr. Edward Teller
Stanford, California
October 25, 1982 [27]

Dear Friend:

Thanks for your good letter and my apology for being so late in answering. It has only just made its way through the government machinery to my desk.

Thank you too for carrying my message to the conference and for your presence there. If we keep on maybe one day the Soviets will see the light.

Best regards,
Ron

_Two months later, after calling the Soviet Union an "evil empire," Reagan tells a friend that his administration is having more contact with the Soviets than is known publicly. It was during this time that President Reagan was negotiating the emigration to the West of the two Soviet Pentecostal families._*

Mr. Paul Trousdale
Los Angeles, California
May 23, 1983 [28]

Dear Paul:

Thanks very much for your good letter and generous words. I'm sure you understand that I can't comment on the matter of '84. If I said no I'd be the deadest

---

* The story of the Pentecostal families is recounted in the discussion of the letter to Liuba Vashchenko in chapter 11.

lame duck around and if I said yes our opponents wouldn't cooperate on anything because it might help campaignwise.

Paul we have more contact with the Soviets than anyone is aware of and whether to have a meeting or not is on the agenda at both ends of the line.

Thanks again for the kind words and best regards.

Sincerely,

Ron

On January 3, 1983, President Reagan announced the creation of a Commission on Strategic Forces, to be chaired by former assistant to the president for national security affairs Brent Scowcroft. The mandate for the commission was to review American land-based intercontinental ballistic missiles and possible basing modes for the system. Three months later the commission recommended that 100 MX missiles be based in existing Minuteman silos. On May 24, the House of Representatives voted 239–186 to approve funding for research and development of the MX. The next day the Senate vote was 59–39. On June 10, President Reagan announced that the commission would be extended until January 3, 1984.

In this letter, President Reagan thanks former director of the Central Intelligence Agency Richard M. Helms for continuing to serve on the commission.

The Honorable Richard Helms

Washington, DC

June 10, 1983 [29]

Dear Dick:

Thanks very much for your letter and many more thanks for all your help. I saw you all out there on the lawn yesterday when I announced the "START" proposals. I'm sorry I couldn't stop and visit a bit but they really had me on a fast track. I know I'm taking advantage of you in asking the "Commission" to stay on for a time. That's what you get for doing such a fine job.

Again a heartfelt thank you.

Sincerely,

Ronald Reagan

On September 1, 1983, a Soviet interceptor shot down a Korean Airlines Boeing 747 and killed all 269 people on board. The next day, President Reagan described the shooting as a "barbaric act." On September 5, he repeated his earlier sentiment, but also stated that the superpowers needed to continue the nuclear weapons talks: "[W]e must not give up our effort to reduce the arsenals of destructive weapons threatening the world. Ambassador [Paul H.] Nitze has returned to Geneva to resume the negoti-*

---

* Paul H. Nitze headed the U.S. delegation to the INF negotiations from 1981 to 1984.

ations on intermediate-range nuclear weapons in Europe. . . . We are more deter-
mined than ever to reduce and if possible eliminate the threat hanging over mankind."
In the next three letters, President Reagan defends his punitive measures, such as re-
stricting Soviet airline flights to the United States.

In the midst of the INF and START negotiations in Geneva, President Reagan ex-
plains that he seeks reductions, not arms control and, mentions the shooting down of
the Korean airliner.

> Vice Admiral Marmaduke Bayne (Ret.)
> Irvington, Virginia
> September 12, 1983 [30]

Dear Admiral Bayne:

Thank you very much for writing as you did. Let me assure you our views on the Soviets and how to deal with them are in sync. And they are not "ultra conservative rantings."

I have never believed in any negotiations with the Soviets that we could appeal to them as we would to people like ourselves. Negotiations with the Soviets is really a case of presenting a choice in which they face alternatives they must consider on the basis of cost. For example in our arms reductions talks they must recognize that failure to meet us on some mutually agreeable level will result in an arms race in which they know they cannot maintain superiority. They must choose between reduced, equal levels or inferiority.

We will not let up on their guilt in this massacre and we intend to seek reparations in behalf of the victims.

Again my thanks to you and very best regards.

> Sincerely,
> Ronald Reagan

> Mr. and Mrs. Robert H. Adams
> Valley Center, California
> September 19, 1983 [31]

Dear Betty and Bob:

Thank you both for your letters and kind words. Nancy and I love you both and thank you.

Those people who would have us do more to the Russians don't offer very many specifics as to just what they'd have us do. The truth is we instantly reviewed every possibility and there were solid reasons why we didn't do things such as send their ambassador home. They'd send ours home and we don't think this is a time to be without eyes and ears in Moscow.

If you won't tell anyone I'll confide in you. Every night I stick pins in a Russian doll.

Again our thanks and our love.

> Sincerely,
> Ronald Reagan

Dr. John A. Lindon
Los Angeles, California
September 19, 1983 [32]

Dear Dr. Lindon:

I hope you won't mind my answering your letter to Mrs. Reagan since it concerned my response to the Soviet Union.

I can understand the frustration of those who want some kind of punishment imposed on the perpetrators of the Korean Airline massacre. No one is more frustrated than I am. Do you believe that I and my advisers from Secretaries of State and Defense, the Joint Chiefs of Staff and others in the National Security Council did not review every possibility? There were things that might have sounded good on the TV news but wouldn't have meant a thing in reality. Send their diplomatic people home? They would send ours home. And believe me this is no time for us to be without eyes and ears in Moscow.

I have great respect for George Will* but I think his endorsement of Mr. Rohatyn's† economic plan is unjustified. Mr. Rohatyn would impose suffering on the Polish people with the assumption that the Russians would have to come to their rescue. That assumes a generosity the Soviets do not have.

We have concluded agreements with our allies as of last summer to end their subsidizing of interest rates in trade with the Soviets. Last spring we helped them escape total dependence on the Soviets for energy. We also and at the same time secured an agreement shutting off high technology sales to Russia. These are some of the things now being suggested we do but we did them without waiting for something like this recent atrocity.

In reality this is not purely them versus us. It is the Soviet Union against the world and we intend to keep it that way. I assure you we have overlooked nothing nor will we.

Sincerely,
Ronald Reagan

In the fall of 1983, some of the Western European parliaments voted to deploy U.S. Pershing II and cruise missiles in their countries. In response, the Soviet delegation walked out of the INF negotiations and then refused to set a date for the next round of the START talks.

Writing to an old friend, President Reagan laments the view in the press that the

-----

* George Will has been a contributing editor to *Newsweek* since 1976.
† Felix George Rohatyn, a Democrat, was a prominent investment banker during the Reagan presidency. He served as President William J. Clinton's ambassador to France from September 11, 1997 to December 28, 2000.

*United States is blocking progress in bilateral relations, and predicts that after the 1984
presidential election, the Soviets will return to the negotiating table.*

Mr. Paul Trousdale
Los Angeles, California
May 17, 1984[33]

Dear Paul:

It was good to hear from you. Thanks for writing. You are so right. The Soviets
shoot down a plane, they walk out of the disarmament talks, boycott the Olympics
and the press asks, "why don't we do something?" Actually we have done everything
we could quietly to let them know the door is open. We do have one reservation. We
won't make some offer that would look as if we were rewarding them for walking
out. Just between us I think they are going to be this way until after the election.

Again thanks and best regards.

Ron

————

*On November 6, 1984, President Reagan was reelected in a landslide. He won 525 elec-
toral votes to Walter Mondale's 13, and took 59 percent of the popular vote. Less than
three weeks after the election, the superpowers announced that a meeting would be
held soon in Geneva to discuss setting an agenda for resuming nuclear arms negotiations. In this post-election letter, Reagan writes that although neither side wants war,
the United States must be cautious in arms talks because the Soviet Union is bent on
world domination.*

Mr. Stephan E. Speer
Wasco, California
December 18, 1984[34]

Dear Mr. Speer:

Thank you very much for your letter and your note. I'm sorry to be so late in replying but it does take a while before mail reaches my desk.

I share your concern about those who give in to the idea of war being inevitable. That in itself makes war more likely. I don't believe it is inevitable and I
also share your views on the horror of war. There have been four wars in my lifetime in one of which you fought. I don't want to see a fifth.

Let me assure you I have no higher priority than peace. I'm going to do everything I can to see if we can persuade the Soviets to join us in eliminating nuclear
weapons. We have to face this fact, the Soviet Union doesn't want war but it does
want to control the world and will use the threat of force to reach its goal. Which is
why we must not let down our guard. I think of our force as a deterrent to war.

Again thank you for your letter and for what you've done for our blessed
country.

Sincerely,
Ronald Reagan

The 13-month suspension of the nuclear arms negotiations came to an end in January 1985 when Secretary of State George P. Shultz and Soviet Foreign Minister Andrei A. Gromyko met in Geneva and agreed to resume the talks. Shortly thereafter President Reagan writes to a friend that he believes the Soviets were willing to resume negotiations because they needed to, and he expects the negotiations to lead to reductions in nuclear weapons.

Mr. Alan Brown
APO New York
January 22, 1985 [35]

Dear Alan:

Just a line to thank you for your letter of January 14. I feel as you do that the Soviets came to the table because they finally decided it was in their best interest to do so. I also believe that is our hope for reaching some agreement on arms reductions. They must be made to realize that the alternative will be an arms race which they can't win.

I have informed our negotiators in a meeting here today that they must not feel that an agreement of some kind is a necessity. They are there to secure a real agreement that is of mutual benefit and not to sign some kind of paper whether or not it is meaningful.

Nancy sends her best as do I.

Sincerely,
Ron

A month before his first superpower summit, President Reagan assures an old friend that he will not give away anything to his Soviet counterpart.

Lt. Gen. Victor H. Krulak, USMC (Ret.)
San Diego, California
October 15, 1985 [36]

Dear Brute:

Thank you for the column on *Time* magazine and friend Gorbachev.* I enjoyed it immensely. I wonder what I'd have to do to get such treatment from *Time* or several other magazines for that matter.

I'm looking forward to the meeting and hope that we can make some sense but I promise I won't give away the store. As a matter of fact I don't plan on giving anything away.

Best regards,
Ron

---

* *Time* published a special report on General Secretary Gorbachev in the September 9, 1985, issue.

A man whose father escaped from Eastern Europe during World War II gave Reagan advice about his upcoming summit meeting: "Let him [Gorbachev] know that we are a just and moral nation that will not stand for his brand of evil. Do not mince words with him. . . . Make it clear that we <u>will</u> have an operational space defense system. Let him know that as the bastion of 'liberty and justice for all,' we will not permit Soviet tyranny and expansion to continue unchecked." Reagan writes the note below on the letter.

> Mr. Paul Petry
> Tom Bean, Texas
> Circa late October 1985[37]

His last paragraph is exactly what I intend to do.

> RR

Three months before he would become the Soviet general secretary, Mikhail Gorbachev met British Prime Minister Margaret Thatcher in London. In what later became a famous assessment, she said: "I like Mr. Gorbachev—we can do business together."[38] President Reagan makes a similar appraisal after the three-day Geneva summit that began on November 19, 1985, but also reports that he stood by his convictions at the meeting.[39]

> Mrs. William Loeb
> Manchester, New Hampshire
> November 25, 1985[40]

Dear Nackey:

Thanks for your "Bon Voyage" editorial. We kept the faith. I must say my one-on-one meetings were most interesting. He is a somewhat different breed even though he solidly believes in their system. Some points were scored and we didn't concede anything.

> Thanks again,
> Ron

In the next two letters, President Reagan expresses surprise at General Secretary Gorbachev's reference to God during their private meeting at the Geneva summit.

> Mrs. Elsa Sandstrom
> La Jolla, California
> November 25, 1985[41]

Dear Elsa:

Thank you very much for your Thanksgiving greeting and your warm letter. You were more than kind and I'm deeply grateful for your generous words.

I think I was aware of all the prayers in my behalf particularly when I was alone with Mr. Gorbachev. Strangely enough in those meetings he twice invoked God's name. I think in our next meeting I may question him on that subject. My only reservation is the need to talk through an interpreter. It's not exactly like being alone.

Congratulations on your new assignment with the California Federation. They made a wise choice.

Nancy sends her love as do I.

Sincerely,

Ron

Mr. Alan Brown
APO New York
December 10, 1985 [42]

Dear Alan:

It was good to hear from you and I'm most grateful for your generous words—particularly about Geneva. I think they understand now that we view them realistically and are not so hungry to sign an agreement that we'll sign almost anything. All in all we were pleased with the outcome.

I wish he and I did not have to speak through an interpreter. He has aroused my curiosity—twice in our meetings he invoked the Lord's name and once cited a Bible verse.

Nancy sends her very best as do I and from both of us a Merry Christmas and Happy New Year.

Sincerely,

Ron

Here President Reagan remarks that General Secretary Gorbachev and his wife, Raisa, a sociologist, are staunch supporters of their political system, and says he holds no hope of converting the Soviet leader away from his philosophy. But Reagan also perceives that the new Soviet leader is "practical," and thus feels that Gorbachev will be willing to conclude bilateral agreements.

The Honorable George Murphy
Palm Beach, Florida
December 19, 1985 [43]

Dear Murph:

Thanks for your good letter and that most generous review of my performance in Geneva. I must say I enjoyed playing the part and the show did have something of a happy ending. Maybe I should say—"tune in next year for the second installment."

Seriously it was worthwhile but it would be foolish to believe the leopard will change its spots. He is a firm believer in their system (so is she) and he believes the propaganda they peddle about us. At the same time he is practical and knows his economy is a basket case. I think our job is to show him he and they will be better off if we make some practical agreements without attempting to convert him to our way of thinking.

I've turned the information on Frances Knight over to Jim Baker at Treasury. I'm sure he'll look into it. One thing I know about myself, having this job hasn't weakened my prejudice about the IRS.

You and your roommate have a Merry Christmas and a happy New Year. Me and my roommate send you both our love.

Sincerely,
Ron

Some details of President Reagan's private session with General Secretary Gorbachev at the Geneva summit are revealed in this letter to two friends.

Colonel and Mrs. Barney Oldfield, USAF (Ret.)
Beverly Hills, California
December 19, 1985[44]

Dear Barney and Vada:

Thank you for your letter and "wreath" of holiday greetings. Nancy and I hope the holiday season is all you want it to be.

Russia again! I can't keep up with your travels. Let me tell you how the movie bit came up at the summit. I had suggested to the General Secretary that we leave one of the plenary sessions and walk down to the lakeshore where there was a pool house complete with roaring fire. We were there for about an hour and a half for a one-on-one discussion. On the way down I told him to tell Arbatov all my pictures weren't B's. Arbatov had made a statement to the press and TV that I was just a B-movie actor. The General Secretary told me he had seen one of my pictures. He didn't remember the name but said I'd had my legs cut off. I told him it was *King's Row* and he said "yes that was it."

Shortly thereafter I invited him to come to the United States next year and he accepted. Then he invited me to Moscow in '87 and I accepted. Our people couldn't believe it had been that easy. They thought future visits would take long, hard negotiations.

Well knowing the post office I'll say I hope you <u>had</u> a Merry Christmas and Nancy does too.

Sincerely,
Ron

President Reagan provides Suzanne Massie with some impressions of General Secretary Gorbachev and the summit.

Mrs. Suzanne Massie
New York, New York
February 10, 1986[45]

Dear Mrs. Massie:

Thank you very much for your warm letter, your good wishes and your generous words. I was pleased to hear your views on the summit and the "man in the street" (Russian street) reaction.

I'm not going to let myself get euphoric but still I have a feeling we might be at a point of beginning. There did seem to be something of a chemistry between the General Secretary and myself. Certainly it was different than talking to Gromyko. Incidentally twice in our private conversation he invoked the name of God and once cited a Bible verse. This has stuck in my mind and stays a nagging question that won't go away. I hope nothing comes up to interfere with our next meeting which I hope will be in June.

Again my thanks and very best wishes.

Sincerely,
Ronald Reagan

By the time President Reagan writes this letter, two superpower summits had occurred but an arms reduction agreement had not been signed. Hopes were dashed at the second summit, held in Reykjavik, Iceland, on October 11 and 12, 1986, when President Reagan and General Secretary Gorbachev were unable to come to agreement on Strategic Defense Initiative research. In the next two letters, President Reagan contends that SDI and verification of an arms measure will not be sacrificed for the sake of concluding an agreement.

Lt. General Victor H. Krulak, USMC (Ret.)
San Diego, California
March 3, 1987[46]

Dear Brute:

It was good to hear from you and as usual to be rewarded by reading your column. You are right too about our friend's aim at SDI. I assure you I won't cave on that.

We're working on his latest proposal, which incidentally is what I proposed three years ago and again at Geneva and most recently at Reykjavik. I hope we can get together on it and will if he will meet us on verification. Without that there can be no deal.

Thanks for your encouraging words about what people are feeling when you get away from these puzzle palaces on the Potomac. You warmed my heart.

Sincerely,
Ron

Mr. Michael Suozzi
San Diego, California
March 23, 1987[47]

Dear Mr. Suozzi:

There are no words to properly thank you for writing as you did in your letter of February 27. I'm late in thanking you because your letter only reached my desk a few days ago but be assured it brightened my day. Nancy thanks you too for your generous words.

I was pleased also to get your article. I'm in great agreement with what you wrote. The Soviets and now the Sandinistas in Nicaragua have a sophisticated disinformation campaign going and many well-meaning Americans have been taken in by it.

Let me assure you we will not buy some agreement with the Soviets just to have an agreement. If we are to make progress in such things as arms reduction we will insist on full verification and of course absolute fairness.

Again thank you and God bless you.

Sincerely,
Ronald Reagan

———————

In an April 29, 1987 letter to President Reagan, William F. Buckley Jr., the editor of National Review, *wrote: "For the first time, I and my colleagues need to take very serious issue with you. It is all dramatically explained in the attached issue of* NR. *I have taken pains to see to it that the very first copy goes to you. You will discover in it the depths of our anxiety." In the issue of* National Review *titled "Reagan's Suicide Pact," President Richard M. Nixon and Secretary Henry A. Kissinger spoke "out jointly for the first time since . . . [leaving] office." They wrote: "If we eliminate American medium- and short-range forces in Europe without redressing the conventional imbalance, the Soviet nuclear threat to Europe will remain, and the gap in deterrence of conventional attack will be reopened."* In this letter, President Reagan reassures Buckley that he is committed to conventional force reductions.*

Mr. William F. Buckley Jr.
New York, New York
May 5, 1987[48]

Dear Bill:

Thank you for the early issue of *National Review.* I understand your "anxiety" and yes I have utmost confidence in our personal relationship.

————————————————

* Richard Nixon and Henry Kissinger, "A Real Peace," *National Review* May 22, 1987, pp. 32, 34. Also in this issue of the journal, Congressman Jack Kemp writes: "I agree that reducing offensive nuclear arms is a worthwhile goal. But in order to enhance security and peace, any agreement must include effective verification measures and compliance guarantees, and must also address the conventional imbalances of forces." Ibid., p. 30.

I do however believe the essays on possible arms agreements with the Soviets overstate the risks and understate my own awareness of the Soviet conventional weapon threat.

From the moment some six years ago (or thereabouts) when I went public with a zero-zero proposal on the INF I made it plain there would have to be a redressing of the conventional weapon imbalance. Later when I announced SDI I made it plain it should be based on the elimination of ballistic missiles and that I favored sharing it with everyone. I likened it to the outlawing of poison gas after WWI and the fact that we all kept our gas masks.

But closer to the point; my zero-zero proposal was blasted far and wide including by my then Secretary of State Al Haig. The theme was that zero-zero was so drastic I had destroyed any chance of getting an agreement with the Soviets. Well here they are proposing the same thing as if they thought of it first. I have not changed my belief that we are dealing with an "evil empire." In fact I warned the General Secretary in Reykjavik that his choice was to join in arms reduction or face an arms race he couldn't win.

Bill if we can get an agreement on both long-range and short-range missiles in both of which the Soviets have a sizeable edge we'll still have more than 4,000 nuclear warheads in Europe of the very short range including tactical battlefield weapons and bombs. Any reduction of these would have to be tied to conventional weapons on their side.

The most important thing is we intend to act with our NATO allies at every step.

I know you realize this is a personal letter and not a letter to the editor and it comes with warmest friendship. Love to Pat.

Sincerely,
Ron

The third superpower summit was a month away when President Reagan writes that America's firm stand has influenced General Secretary Gorbachev. The signing of an historic agreement to eliminate intermediate-range nuclear forces is expected to punctuate the summit meeting in Washington.

Lt. General Victor H. Krulak, USMC (Ret.)
San Diego, California
November 4, 1987[49]

Dear Brute:

Your readers here in the West Wing are as always enthusiastic about your two recent columns. And so am I. I think you are right about the General Secretary. This is about the third time our firm stand has brought about—as you put it, a blink.

Nancy is most appreciative of the message from you and my campmates and sends her heartfelt thanks. And again my thanks to you and best regards.

Sincerely,
Ron

―――――――

A few weeks after the meeting with General Secretary Gorbachev, President Reagan states that he has not given himself over to summit euphoria; he defends some of his statements about the Soviet leader and emphasizes the historic nature of the INF treaty signed on December 8, 1987.

Mr. John J. Tringali
Mill Valley, California
January 6, 1988 [50]

Dear Mr. Tringali:

I have only just received your letter of December 12th hence this tardy reply.

I'm afraid some of the confused media reporting has led you to some mistaken conclusions about our relations with the Soviet Union. I assure you I hold to the words of Demosthenes 2,000 years ago in the Athenian marketplace when he said; "What sane man would let another man's words not deeds tell him who is at peace and who is at war with him?" The treaty we have just signed calls for the destruction of the medium-range nuclear missiles. The verification provisions are the most stringent ever signed in an arms reduction treaty. I assure you we'll carry them out.

My remarks about Gorbachev and Afghanistan were intended to simply point out that he was not in a position in the Soviet government to have played any part in the invasion of Afghanistan. Also to point out that he inherited a great embarrassment. After eight years the massive Soviet military machine has been unable to overcome a handful of freedom fighters who are outnumbered and outgunned hundreds to one.

General Secretary Gorbachev is the first leader in the history of the Soviet Union who has agreed to destroy weapons they already have. All the others have agreed only to limits on how many more they'll build. He is also the first leader who has not reaffirmed the Marxian concept of a one-world Communist state. It will be interesting to see if he is still silent on that subject this June when he faces the Communist Party Congress.

As to the other important matters, human rights, regional conflicts etc. believe me they were a major part of our agenda and will continue to be.

I hope this eases some of your concerns.

Sincerely,
Ronald Reagan

Almost two months after the signing of the INF treaty, President Reagan reassures William F. Buckley Jr. about the agreement.

Mr. William F. Buckley Jr.
New York, New York
February 1, 1988[51]

Dear Bill:

Don't worry about the photographer, I've had him shot.

I still think we are on solid ground on the INF treaty based on our verification provisions and on the fact that Gorby knows what our response to cheating would be—it's spelled Pershing.

Bill hold your fire on Deaver.* Our information is that some of the usual press editing of his answers in an interview were slanted. We'll have to wait until we see his book.

We are both excited about your new undertaking and of course we will both be at liberty in the near future. Is there a juvenile character and an ingénue contemplated in your script—important roles of course? We'll be waiting for opening night and the movie version.

Nancy sends her love—so do I.

Ron

Henry Kissinger expressed deep concern about the implications of the INF treaty for the balance of power in Europe in a long essay in Newsweek.† *President Reagan counters the former secretary of state's charges in the letter below.*

Dr. Gerald B. Broussard
Oak Grove, Louisiana
February 15, 1988[52]

Dear Dr. Broussard:

Thank you for your letter of January 20th. I'm glad you support our INF treaty even though you have some reservations. I assure you we won't give away the store. I respect Henry Kissinger and consider him a good friend but in this instance do not believe he is fully informed. A nuclear war cannot be won and must never be

---

* Michael K. Deaver was the White House deputy chief of staff from 1981 to 1985.

† Henry A. Kissinger, "The Dangers Ahead," *Newsweek,* December 21, 1987, pp. 34–36, 41. See also Hedrick Smith, "The Right Against Reagan," *New York Times,* January 17, 1988, pp. SM 36–39, 72, 77, and Michael R. Gordon, "Kissinger Balks at Treaty on Strategic Arms," *New York Times,* February 24, 1988, p. A14.

fought. In such a war between the two great powers one has to ask if ever we launched those weapons at each other where would the survivors live? Over 100 Soviet citizens are still unable to return to their homes in Chernobyl and that power plant accident was less than the effect of one single warhead.

But you are right that we must always deal from strength and insist on verification of every agreement. In my meetings with the General Secretary I repeated several times a Russian proverb—"doveryai no proveryai"—"trust but verify."

Again thanks and best wishes.

Sincerely,
Ronald Reagan

At the summit in Moscow in the spring of 1988, President Reagan and General Secretary Gorbachev exchanged ratification documents on the INF treaty. In this letter, President Reagan expresses his pleasure with the summit.

Ms. Wilma Sullivan
Dallas, Texas
July 7, 1988 [53]

Dear Ms. Sullivan:

Thank you for your very kind letter and generous words. I'm most grateful. We were pleased with our Moscow meetings and believe we have improved relations between our two countries. I certainly hope so.

On our way back we made the overnight stop in England. That was a pleasure as always, tea with Queen Elizabeth, a good visit with Margaret Thatcher and overnight at the American embassy.

Again thank you for writing and God bless you.

Sincerely,
Ronald Reagan

MISSILE DEFENSE

In a speech he delivered on March 23, 1983, President Reagan told the American public that in "the search for ways to reduce the danger of nuclear war" his administration would "embark on a program to counter the awesome Soviet missile threat with measures that are defensive." He gave his assurance that research and development efforts in connection with the program would be consistent with the Anti-Ballistic Missile Treaty, an agreement signed by the United States and the Soviet Union in 1972 that limited both sides to deploying two ABM systems. President Reagan's strategic defense initiative, dubbed "Star Wars" by critics, was one of the most controversial defense policy issues of the Reagan presidency, and it continues to divide Democrats and Republicans to this day. Questions persist about how much President Reagan knew about missile defense and whether SDI was thrust upon him by others. Reagan addresses these issues in the following letters.

Reagan thanks his host, the commander of the North American Aerospace Defense Command (NORAD), for his tour of the Cheyenne Mountain complex.

General James E. Hill
Colorado Springs, Colorado
Circa August 1979 [54]

Dear General James E. Hill:

I can't tell you [how] much I appreciate your kindness and hospitality to all of us on our visit to "the mountain." You truly acted above and beyond the call and I'm most grateful.

All the way to Los Angeles we were talking about the briefing and what we had learned. I can assure you it will be most valuable to all of us in the days ahead. Please convey my thanks to all of those in your command who were so helpful.

I sincerely hope our paths cross again in the near future. Again thank you for an enjoyable, interesting and exciting experience.

Best regards,
Ron

The following letter is a response to a mailgram from the president of a Texas television station who informed Reagan that his station's computerized survey shows that the president's speech convinced 88 percent of those polled of the need for more defense spending.

Mr. McHenry Tichenor Jr.
Harlingen, Texas
April 18, 1983 [55]

Dear Mr. Tichenor:

Just a line to thank you for sending me the results of your poll. Thank you too for taking the poll. It was very kind of you to wire as you did. I'm especially grateful since some of the Eastern press insist the result was contrary to what your poll shows.

Best regards,
Ronald Reagan

Five days after President Reagan's speech on strategic defense, he received a ringing endorsement of his announcement from a retired Air Force general. President Reagan writes a thank-you letter that reflects the depth of his commitment to missile defense.

General John W. Vogt, USAF (Ret.)
Annapolis, Maryland
April 18, 1983 [56]

Dear General Vogt:

Thank you for your letter of a few weeks ago regarding defense against nuclear weapons. I am more than gratified to have your approval of my proposal, I am reassured.

You were kind to write as you did and I assure you I'll keep pushing as hard as I can on this.

Sincerely,
Ronald Reagan

The president of the Congress of Racial Equality (known as CORE) wrote to President Reagan on April 7, 1983: "We listened with great enthusiasm to the portion of your March 23rd speech that dealt with high energy beam technology, the technology of the 21st century. While no one can predict the ultimate uses of this technology, it seems to offer the first hope out of the mutual assured destruction (MAD) dilemma of nuclear armament. . . . We urge you to do everything in your power to help the Black community and other communities that do not normally directly involve themselves in these kinds of developments to do so. Please call on us, we are ready to help in any way we can."

In the upper right-hand corner of the African-American leader's letter, President Reagan wrote: "Give me a copy of this. RR." He then writes a reply.

Mr. Roy Innis
New York, New York
June 20, 1983 [57]

Dear Mr. Innis:

I'm sorry to be so late in answering your letter but it has only just reached my desk. Sometimes the wheels of bureaucracy can turn very slowly.

Thank you very much for your generous words. With regard to the idea of a defense against nuclear missiles I share your view of the mutual assured destruction policy, it makes no sense whatsoever. Hopefully a defense could result in real negotiations leading to the total elimination of nuclear weapons.

Mr. Innis I would like very much to cooperate with you in the educational and technological developments that will help all our people get as you say a "running start into the 21st century." If you don't mind I'd like to put a member of my administration in touch with you and again my thanks to you.

Sincerely,
Ronald Reagan

_____

Reagan comments on his religious beliefs, explains his expectations for the "Star Wars" program, and describes his view of Washington from the White House.

Mr. Patrick Mulvey
Whittier, California
June 20, 1983 [58]

Dear Mr. Mulvey:

Thank you very much for writing as you did. You brightened my day. I'm glad you are working as you are for our country.

With regard to a "Star Wars" defense system against nuclear weapons let me say the news media seems to be responsible for that descriptive term. Frankly I have no idea what the nature of such a defense might be. I simply asked our scientists to explore the possibility of developing such a defense. My thinking is that if such a defense can be found we could then move to get agreement on eliminating nuclear weapons completely. I agree with you that a so-called freeze at this time would certainly increase the chances of war.

You and I are in agreement also about our dependence on God. Without His help there is no way we can be successful. I have quoted those words from Second Chronicles many times.

You asked that I share with you what Washington looks like to me. My favorite view is from the so-called Truman balcony on the south side of the White House. You look down a vista of green lawn, then the parklike expanse called the Ellipse. The Washington Monument stands against the sky and then at the very end of the vista is the gleaming white-pillared Jefferson Memorial. It is truly inspiring.

Again my thanks to you and God bless you.

Sincerely,
Ronald Reagan

_____

In a letter to one of his closest friends, President Reagan compares SDI to the Manhattan Project, the program established by the United States to develop the atomic bomb during World War II.

Mr. Laurence W. Beilenson
Los Angeles, California
July 25, 1983 [59]

Dear Larry:

Thanks for sending me that clipping. It is true that in my announcement I said I was asking the scientific community to help and that I had no preconceived idea about what the nature of a defensive weapon might be but I share your view about the item you sent me.

Let me assure you we are meeting with a variety of people and are looking at the possibility of a crash effort à la "Manhattan Project." I've passed your suggested names on to our people.

Thanks again and best regards.

Ron

Reagan reiterates his belief that holding people hostage to the threat of a nuclear night-mare is not civilized and an alternative must be found.

Drs. Ivy Mooring and John Shelton
Los Angeles, California
November 1, 1984[60]

Dear Drs. Shelton:

Thank you very much for writing as you did and for the news about Terry. Thanks too for the article. I'm most grateful for your eloquent argument in my behalf.

I appreciate your suggestion about the "Star Wars" matter. That term was never mine, it was dreamed up by the press and now they saddle me with it. Actually I called for scientists to research and see if a defensive weapon against nuclear missiles could be found. But your suggestion of creating an umbrella-like image is very sound. I still believe if a defense can be found it is far more civilized than to continue relying on the threat of destroying millions of lives in retaliation for an enemy attack.

Nancy sends her best. Again thanks.

Sincerely,
Ronald Reagan

President Reagan writes to his close friend, author of a book on international treaty compliance that influenced Reagan's thinking, that SDI might very well be the program that ends the nuclear arms race.

Mr. Laurence W. Beilenson
Los Angeles, California
December 10, 1984[61]

Dear Larry:

Thanks very much for the article—"Watchtower." Having been a disciple for some time now of *The Treaty Trap*,[62] I recognized the quotes. I'm also determined that all our national security eggs will not be put in a "paper" basket. Just between us I have a suspicion the willingness of those other fellows to talk is born of their respect for our technology; they would like to head off our research on a defense against nuclear missiles. I happen to believe an effective defense weapon could bring closer the day when we could all do away with the nuclear threat.

Larry I think I can safely say there is nothing in our tax proposals that would worsen your situation.

Again thanks and warm regards,

Ron

In the next two letters to old friends, President Reagan implies that there must be something to SDI because it appears to be of great concern to the Soviets.

Lt. General Victor H. Krulak, USMC (Ret.)
San Diego, California
September 5, 1985[63]

Dear Brute:

Thank you for your two letters which reached me at the same time and for your columns. The one on South Africa has come in handy because we're huddling on that situation right now and as always your thoughts are to the point and sound as a dollar. The same goes for your essay on the Soviets and their hysteria over the SDI. I wonder why some of our own carping critics who claim SDI is an impractical wasted effort don't ask themselves, if it's no good how come the Russians are so upset about it?

Thanks for the word about Owl's Nest. I can't wait 'til I'll be lifting a glass with all of you.

Sincerely,
Ron

Colonel Barney Oldfield, USAF (Ret.)
Beverly Hills, California
March 17, 1986[64]

Dear Barney:

How right you were. Some of that cautious wording about Soviet shenanigans way back then made no sense at all. I'm still hoping we can get them to make at least a first step on the road to reducing nuclear weapons but not by giving up SDI. I think General Secretary Gorbachev has gotten the idea but maybe doesn't know how to get off the limb he's on.

I enjoyed your account of those good old NORAD days and the hometown story. I can't wait to see that picture. If and when we have that summit here in the U.S.A. I'm dying to show him things like stores where people don't stand in line, workers' homes with two cars in the drive etc. but it's frustrating because I know he will think we staged it just for him. After all isn't that what they do for us.

Nancy sends her best and regards to Vada.

Sincerely,
Ron

In a letter to President Reagan, Laurence Beilenson wrote: "When the history of your presidency is written, your greatest achievement in foreign affairs will be your SDI." President Reagan writes back and assures the former attorney for the Screen Actors Guild that SDI will not be a bargaining chip in arms reductions negotiations with the Soviets, and that he hopes SDI will lead to the elimination of nuclear weapons.

Mr. Laurence W. Beilenson
Los Angeles, California
August 1, 1986 [65]

Dear Larry:

It was good to hear from you and as always you are right on target. This place—this Capitol, leaks like a sieve. I don't know which is worse—the leak of a truth or the leak like the one you forwarded that is not based on fact. We will not allow SDI to become a bargaining chip. My own view is that we may be able to develop a defensive shield so effective that we can use it to rid the world once and for all of nuclear missiles. Then—since we all know how to make them we preserve SDI as we did our gas masks in the event a madman comes along some day and secretly puts some together.

Larry we haven't agreed to any artificial time restraints. We have a good idea of about how long research will take and are basing our proposals on that since research is within the restraints of the ABM treaty. We'll make no unrealistic long-time agreements reaffirming or pledging to observe the treaty.

You know, those people who thought being an actor was no proper training for this job were way off base. Everyday I find myself thankful for those long days at the negotiating table with Harry Cohen, Freeman, the brothers Warner et al.

Well thanks again. Nancy sends her love and so do I.

Sincerely,
Ron

In another letter to his longtime friend, President Reagan explains that a meeting with the Joint Chiefs of Staff was a key part of the genesis of SDI. He also reports on his discussion about SDI with General Secretary Gorbachev at the Reykjavik summit of October 11–12, 1986.

Mr. Laurence W. Beilenson
Los Angeles, California
October 16, 1986 [66]

Dear Larry:

It was good to get your letter and your confirmation regarding SDI. I wasn't aware that Sam Donaldson had said what he did about McFarlane and I question whether Mac [Bud] said such a thing.* Certainly he knew better.

Yes I've quoted from your books on a number of occasions and will continue to do so because they make such good sense. When I finally decided to move on what has become SDI I called a meeting of the Joint Chiefs of Staff. I said that until nuclear weapons there had never been an offensive weapon that hadn't inspired a defense all the way back to the spear and the shield. Then I asked them if in their thinking it was possible to devise a weapon that could destroy missiles as they came out of their silos. They were unanimous in their belief that such a defensive system could be developed. I gave the go-ahead that very day. The scientists working on this have achieved several breakthroughs and are quite optimistic, although they say we have several years to go. I have never entertained a thought that SDI could be a bargaining chip. I did tell Gorbachev that if and when we had such a system they would join us in eliminating nuclear missiles; we'd share such a defense with them. I don't think he believes me.

Well it was good to hear from you and thank you for the confirmation. Nancy sends her love.

Sincerely,
Ron

———————

In two more letters written shortly after the Reykjavik summit, which faltered on the disagreement about SDI, President Reagan states that he will not abandon missile defense.

Mr. J. H. Hume
San Francisco, California
October 16, 1986 [67]

Dear Jack:

Thank you for your kind message and generous words. As always you brighten my day. I hope we've put an end to all that talk about a "bargaining chip."

Nancy sends her love and from both of us to Betty.

Again my thanks.

Ron

———————

* Samuel A. Donaldson was a White House correspondent for ABC News during the Reagan presidency; Robert "Bud" C. McFarlane was the assistant to the president for national security affairs from October 1983 to December 1985.

Mr. William A. Cheek
Little Rock, Arkansas
November 17, 1986[68]

Dear William Alston (Cheek):

Your letter awakened a lot of memories of those days back on Cherokee Street. It was good to hear from you and I appreciate your words of support. Letters to the senators and congressmen will be a real help. Some of the people on the Hill are less than helpful with regard to SDI. Rest assured I'm determined to go forward with it and it won't be traded away.

Thanks again for writing. Best wishes and regards.

Sincerely,
Ronald Reagan

President Reagan writes that he will not allow the ABM treaty to impede SDI.

Mr. William A. Rusher
New York, New York
April 1, 1987[69]

Dear Bill:

It was good to hear from you and to hear your opinion of our writers. They are a good bunch and we work them like h—l.

Thank you for lending a hand in that advisory group. I'm grateful to all of you and look forward to future get-togethers. I'm sorry there wasn't a chance for you and I to visit. It's been "too long between drinks" as the governor of North Carolina said to the governor of South Carolina.

There was much good advice in that session and a number of suggestions we'll put in action. I still, however, have problems with the ABM treaty. For one thing our allies have a great concern about that. I can tell you though I will not let the treaty or anything else hold us back. If we agree to any times for deploying etc. they will be based on our own knowledge of when we believe we'll be ready which is still down the road a way.

Well hope I see you soon. Nancy sends her love. Again thanks.

Sincerely,
Ron

In the next two letters written during his final year in the White House, President Reagan boldly declares his commitment to SDI and reveals that SDI was his idea.

Fr. Daniel C. Sabatos
Brooklyn, New York
February 15, 1988[70]

Dear Father Sabatos:

I'm very late I know in answering your good letter of December 16 but sometimes it takes a while before mail reaches my desk. I have only just received your letter.

Let me assure you I'm in complete agreement with you on the matter of dealing with the Soviets. In our recent negotiations I repeated several times an old Russian proverb 'til the General Secretary was tired of hearing it—"doveryai no proveryai." It translates, "trust but verify."

You are right that the Soviets would like to trade us out of completing the SDI. I finally convinced them it was not a bargaining chip. There is no way that I will give up on trying to find and develop a defense against nuclear missiles.

Again my thanks to you and very best regards.

Sincerely,
Ronald Reagan

Dr. Robert Dick
Somerville, New Jersey
July 7, 1988[71]

Dear Dr. Dick:

Thank you for your letter of May 9 which I am only just now able to answer. It sometimes takes a while before letters reach my desk.

I want to assure you we are going to continue with our strategic defense initiative. It was my idea to begin with and we will deploy when it is ready. There are some who have suggested we deploy anti-ballistic missiles in the interim. That is the third stage of our plan, ABM's to pick off any warheads that might slip through the first two stages, which will destroy missiles as they come out of the silos and survivors in space.

We continue to face opposition in Congress to the plan and I fear the basing of the third stage now would be used as an excuse for canceling stages one and two. Even now they have made budget cuts that have set us back timewise. But rest assured we'll deploy as soon as we are able.

Thanks for writing.

Sincerely,
Ronald Reagan

CHAPTER THIRTEEN

The Middle East and Southwest Asia

B<small>Y THE TIME</small> he assumed the presidency in 1981, Ronald Reagan had been thinking, speaking, and writing about the Middle East for many years. He had also visited the region. He wrote about the Middle East for his nationally syndicated radio program.[1] In April 1978, he visited Iran and met with Mohammad Reza Shah Pahlavi. In the midst of his 1980 presidential campaign, Reagan declared his support for Israel: "Israel represents the one stable democracy sharing values with us in that part of the world, and they have a proven military capability that stands as a deterrent of further disruption and chaos. I think we should make it plain that we are going to keep our commitment to the continued existence of Israel."[2]

Reagan became deeply involved in Middle East and Southwest Asian crises as president. Cold war considerations dominated his involvement in the Soviet-Afghan war, and through military assistance to the Afghan rebels, he helped thwart Soviet designs. Reagan analyzes the geopolitical dimensions of America's involvement in the Middle East in some of his letters. In others he is concerned about the difficulty of trying to use diplomacy and military power in complex crises. He watched the negotiations between Israel and Lebanon his administration brokered give way to new rounds of fighting and stalemates. In Lebanon, initial success gave way to crushing disappointment and tragedy when 241 servicemen were killed by a truck bomb on October 23, 1983, and Arab-Israeli violence escalated during the first Intifada.

Under Reagan, the military used force more than once in the Middle East. Some of the instances included the projection of power during the war in Lebanon, and the exchange of fire with Iran in an attempt to maintain freedom of transit for vessels in the Persian Gulf.

The letters below represent Reagan's thinking about the Middle East before and during his presidency.

AFGHANISTAN

On December 25, 1979, the Soviet Union commenced a massive invasion of Afghanistan, and quickly installed a new regime in Kabul headed by Babrak Karmal, a former deputy prime minister of the country who was in exile in Eastern Europe. Six days later, President Jimmy Carter said: "My opinion of the Russians has changed most drastically in the last week."[3] On January 3, 1980, he asked the U.S. Senate to delay its consideration of the second strategic arms control treaty that he had signed at the Vienna summit with Soviet leader Leonid Brezhnev on June 18, 1979. The following day, President Carter announced a package of sanctions that included curtailing grain sales to the Soviet Union and withdrawing U.S. teams from the Summer Olympics in Moscow. He reaffirmed his threat of an Olympic boycott on January 20, when he declared that his country would not participate in the games unless Soviet forces pulled out of Afghanistan "within the next month." The following day he gave the State of the Union address and said that the United States would repel Soviet aggression and protect its interest in the Persian Gulf region through upgrades in military weapons, the establishment of a rapid deployment force, closer cooperation with allies, and a range of other measures.*

In the following letter, written around the time of President Carter's announcement, Reagan offers a different response. As president, Ronald Reagan would implement these suggestions. Writing to Soviet leader Mikhail Gorbachev on November 28, 1985, following their first summit, Reagan said: "One of the most significant steps in lowering tension in the world—and tension in U.S.–Soviet relations—would be a decision on your part to withdraw your forces from Afghanistan."[4]

Mr. Edward Langley
Circa January 1980[5]

Dear Ed:

It was good to hear from you, and I appreciate the opportunity to do a little clearing up with regard to the Russian grain. It is true I criticized the president's withholding of cattle feed while he sold grain for human consumption to the Soviet Union. I didn't think the Soviets were invading Afghanistan with livestock, but my criticism was too little and a futile gesture because the Soviets can get this feed-grain in other places. All we succeeded in doing was disrupting the commodities market, harming the agricultural industry here and yet posing no threat what-

---

* The boycott of the Moscow Olympics became official with the April 12, 1980, vote of the U.S. Olympic Committee. See Steven R. Weisman, "U.S. Olympic Group Votes to Boycott the Moscow Games," *New York Times*, April 13, 1980, pp. 1, 18.

soever to the Soviet Union. I was not criticizing the act of denying them grain but criticizing the fact that we were not taking all the other firm actions that we should. I believe the situation calls for an American presence in the Middle East—probably with air power, the supplying of arms to the Afghan freedom fighters by way of Pakistan, and, possibly, since we have a treaty with Pakistan, an American presence there in that country. I also would be willing to support a move to stage the Olympics in some other country. I would like to cancel them and have no Olympics at all, but, over and above everything else, this country openly and avowedly should start a crash program of military build-up. It is frightening to hear a man in the office of the presidency who has just discovered that the Soviets can't be trusted, that they've lied to him. Incidentally, speaking of that invasion, this too has a bearing—the motorized equipment came from the Kama River truck plant* which we helped build and which is run by American computers, and we did all of that on Russia's promise that they would not divert products from that plant to military use.

I hope this eases your mind. I realize that things do get distorted in the press. Again, it was good to hear from you.

Best regards,
Ron

THE FALL OF THE SHAH AND THE IRANIAN REVOLUTION

In the midst of the Iranian revolution and with the imminent return of Ayatollah Ruhollah Khomeini from exile in Paris, Shah Reza Mohammed Pahlavi and Empress Farah departed for Egypt on January 16, 1979. Six days later they traveled to Morocco. On June 10, the shah and his wife arrived in Mexico and later moved on to the Bahamas. President Carter allowed the couple to travel to New York on October 22 so that the shah could undergo treatment for cancer. The Iranians who seized the U.S. embassy in Tehran and took 66 Americans hostage on November 4 demanded the shah's return in exchange for the hostages.[6]

Mrs. Gullette
After November 4, 1979[7]

Dear Mrs. Gullette:

Thank you very much for your letter and for giving me an opportunity to reply. I can understand your reaction and your belief that the shah is unworthy of

---

* Located in Naberezhnye Chelny, the factory was built with American assistance in the 1970s with the understanding that the trucks would be used for civilian purposes.

sanctuary here in the United States. Certainly he has been treated to a demagogic going-over by many people and by some of the press. May I present a different side that I know not only from people in our government who have dealt with him over these last few decades but from personal observations because a year ago last April Nancy and I were in Tehran. I am quite sure that under his regime and under this one, the handling of criminals or people believed to be traitors is probably harsher than we in our own country would condone, but that is also true of virtually every other country in the Middle East. There are customs there which we frown upon but which are part of their culture and have been for some time. But looking beyond that, the shah set out to lift his people literally to the level of the people of America. When he was crowned, he said he did not want to be the ruler of his people if his people were poor. He set out to reform land holding. He gave to the peasants farm lands, beginning with his own personal, vast land holdings. He then, and perhaps this explains some of the hatred for him, gave to them the land holdings that were held by the Moslem priests—and these were even more extensive than his own. He freed women who had been bound in by the ancient traditions of their religion. When we were there, young women looking for all the world like American coeds were studying to be doctors, lawyers, teachers and so forth in the universities. All of them now have been ordered out of the university. It has been ruled by the present revolutionary government that women are not to be educated. It is true that he raised the price of oil, but this was at the suggestion of our own government, which knew it was the only way he could purchase the arms we were providing so that he could be a stumbling block to the southern push of the Soviet Union. In one of the moments of emergency in the Middle East when our Seventh Fleet was out of oil, he provided the fuel for the entire fleet at no charge to the United States. He forbade the Soviet Union to fly their military planes over Iran at the time of the Middle East crisis. Possibly he moved too fast, and yet when we saw the great apartment buildings and the low-cost housing for the poor that were being built, saw the streets where camels once were the beasts of burden filled with trucks and automobiles, we were convinced that he was sincere in his effort to improve life for his people. Incidentally, though a Moslem himself, he opened Iran up to freedom of worship and gave full rights to the various minorities—Christians and Jews— living in that country. I believe that, on balance our country had every moral reason and right to offer him sanctuary from the very beginning and not just as a patient after he became ill in Mexico.

Now, the statement I made, and the press did not see fit to print it so far as I can see, was that there was no added threat to our people in allowing him to stay if he chose to do that and his doctors felt he should because the Iranians had said that any effort to let him leave the United States would be considered an attempt to aid his escape and thus, even letting him go could possibly endanger our hostages. Our country has a rich tradition of offering sanctuary to political exiles, to refugees, and I am proud that we do have that tradition. I'm sure the shah made mistakes, as any ruler will but I don't believe that his regime could match this present revolutionary government for its bloodthirsty brutality.

Again, I appreciate your writing and allowing me to state my side of the case.

Sincerely,
Ronald Reagan

———————

Written after the Mexican Foreign Minister Jorge Castañeda's announcement on November 29, 1979, that readmitting the shah to Mexico was against the "vital interests" of his country,[8] this letter is another defense of the shah. Reagan also emphasizes that the United States should not negotiate with the captors because it could lead to blackmail, a principle violated during the Reagan administration's Iran-Contra dealings.

Mrs. Harold Stockton
Texas
After November 29, 1979[9]

Dear Mrs. Stockton:

I can understand your concern and certainly, I share your feeling about the 50 Americans who are being held and abused in our embassy in Iran. I did, however, say what the press indicated about offering refuge to the shah.

When Mexico announced they would not accept him back, the press asked me what we should do, and I said I thought the decision belonged to the doctors and the shah as to where he would go. Then I was asked what if the shah elected to stay here, and I said then that I thought he should be allowed to remain. The third question was, wouldn't this endanger the hostages' lives, and my reply was the Iranians have already taken care of this—they have told us there is greater danger to the hostages if we allow the shah to leave because they will construe that as the United States helping him escape.

I believe there is much more at issue than just a simple case of trading one man for 50. How would the United States appear to the world if we were willing to sacrifice a man who sought political asylum and who for 37 years had been the staunchest of allies to the United States? We, of course, would be giving him to a lynch mob in answer to their blackmail-type demands. Would any American ever be safe any place in the world again? It seems to me that our nation has always offered shelter to refugees or political exiles. In this case, as I say, the shah has a long record of friendship and service to the United States. For 37 years he kept Iran, with its 2,000 mile border on the Soviet Union, as a bulwark against Soviet expansion. He denied the Soviets, during the Middle East crisis, to fly military planes over Iran. At one particularly tense moment, when our Seventh Fleet in the Indian Ocean was virtually without fuel and unable to move in the event of an emergency, he fueled the fleet with Iranian oil and never sent us a bill. He did not join the other OPEC nations in the oil boycott in 1973. I believe we have much to gain by refusing to submit to blackmail. I don't know whether the president has availed himself of all of the options we might have for freeing the hostages, but I will not criticize him at this time because all of us should be concerned with the safety of those 50 Americans. We should say and do nothing that could possibly upset whatever negotiations are going on so in this instance I think all of us must remain united behind the administration in trying to win their freedom.

I appreciate your writing and giving me a chance to explain my position.

Best regards,
Ronald Reagan

On April 24, 1980, an American rescue mission sought to free the hostages in Iran. The next day, President Carter confirmed that the mission had been abandoned after three of the eight helicopters experienced mechanical failure. Of the 90-man rescue mission, five were injured and eight were left to die in the burning helicopters. Reagan reacts privately to an old friend and a former Republican U.S. senator from California.

Senator George Murphy
After April 25, 1980 [10]

Dear Murph:

It was good to hear from you, and your letter wasn't too long. It was just fine. I hope you do come to California to help knock off Cranston.* I expected him to campaign like a Republican—he always does. We have to expose his record, and maybe this time the PEOPLE WILL listen.

Things don't get better do they? As witness the bungled attempt in Iran. I'm glad we have men who will still volunteer and do tasks like that, but they deserve better than they are getting from this administration. Those eight helicopters were minelayers, and we only had 16 in the entire military.

Nancy and I have been on the road almost permanently for these last few months and are hoping the pace will let up soon. Of course it has to let up come June 3—the final primary day. By that time, I hope we have all that are required for the convention. Nancy sends her love, and we both hope we see you soon.

Sincerely,
Ron

More than four years after the fall of the shah, Reagan reflects on the changes that have occurred in Iran. He writes to a friend that he is sure that Iran was involved in

----

* Senator Alan Cranston (D-California).

the suicide bombing of the U.S. Marine barracks in Beirut, Lebanon, on October 23, 1983.

Lt. General Victor H. Krulak, USMC (Ret.)
San Diego, California
October 26, 1983 [11]

Dear Brute:

Your editorial was right on. Nancy and I were in Iran (to select one example) in 1978. Whatever the shah's shortcomings might have been, we saw land distribution, low-cost housing going up and young ladies at the university studying to be doctors and lawyers.

Today those young ladies are back in the black robes and covered faces of the long ago and are denied the right to be educated. And just between us there is no question in our minds but that the government of Iran was very much involved in the brutal slaying of our Marines.

Brute who do I make a check out to for the kitchen* and is it or is it not deductible so I can inform the fellow handling my affairs?

I won't be able to be at the club November 10th. I'll be on a trip to Japan and Korea.

All the best,
Ron

THE IRAN-IRAQ WAR

The historic enmity between Iran and Iraq resurfaced following the rise to power in 1979 of Ayatollah Ruhollah Khomeini, a Shia Muslim. Iraq possessed a Shia majority, but the government of Saddam Hussein and his Baath Party was dominated by Sunni Muslims. Hussein worried that the rise of Khomeini in Iran would cause Shia unrest in Iraq. Hussein also had a long-standing desire to take the Shatt al Arab waterway from Iran; he claimed it was Iraqi sovereign territory. In September 1980, a series of border skirmishes took place between the two countries, and on September 23, Iraqi troops invaded Iran. A bloody eight-year war ensued.

Perceptible changes in the political and military landscape of the Middle East were taking place around the period that Reagan wrote the letter below: President Jimmy Carter was brokering the Egypt-Israeli peace process, and as Egypt and Saudi Arabia

----

* Krulak wrote to his Owl's Nest campmates in early October 1983 with cost estimates for the camp's kitchen. Reagan was a member of this camp in the Bohemian Grove, the Bohemian Club's retreat in the redwoods of northern California.

were receiving American weapons, the Soviet Union was increasing its shipment of MIG-23 fighter bombers and other arms to Iraq and Syria. A February 15, 1978, New York Times article declared that "possibly the most unbalancing element in the current situation has been the transfer of advanced Soviet weapons to Iraq and Syria." [12]

Congressman Phil Crane
Washington, D.C.
February 20, 1978 [13]

Dear Phil:

It was good to get your letter and I very much appreciate your words about the Middle East situation. I'll admit to wondering just where Begin and Sadat * stand after that first round of spectaculars. I've had a feeling J.C. [Jimmy Carter] has been trying to look more involved than he really is—hoping perhaps that he might get some credit if a peaceful solution is achieved.

The military buildup in Iraq is alarming, and there has been no media mention of it to speak of. I hope I'll have a chance soon to talk with you about this.

Thanks very much for your letter, Phil, and for sharing your thoughts with me.

Sincerely,
Ron

Although it had declared neutrality in the Iran-Iraq war, the United States was never a disinterested party. At various times during the conflict, the United States tilted toward one side or the other. The United States became more explicitly involved in the war in early 1987 when Iran launched an offensive into Iraq near the Persian Gulf, and increased its mining of the area as it attempted to dominate the waterway. In the midst of these events, Kuwait sought protection for its ships and formally requested American naval escorts for its vessels in the Gulf. On May 17 an Iraqi missile hit the USS Stark, a Navy frigate that was stationed in the Gulf. Two days later, the Reagan administration announced that 11 Kuwaiti tankers would be reflagged and renamed and provided with naval protection. Tension in the Gulf rose in the next few months as several deadly skirmishes took place. Iran attacked both a Liberian and a Norwegian tanker on June 27. On July 22, the United States began escorting Kuwaiti tankers through the Persian Gulf. A coalition of nations was formed to provide naval protection for Kuwait in the Gulf, including the Soviet Union, Belgium, Great Britain, France, Italy, and the Netherlands sent minesweepers. The cooperation of all of these nations failed to prevent Iranian aggression; on October 16, an Iranian missile hit the Sea Isle City, a tanker under U.S. protection, while it was in Kuwaiti territorial waters. Three

---

* Israeli Prime Minister Menachem Begin and Egyptian President Anwar al-Sadat.

days later, the U.S. Navy attacked Iranian offshore stations in response. President Reagan describes the attack and his plans in a letter to a friend written 11 days after the strike.

Mr. Ward L. Quaal
Chicago, Illinois
October 30, 1987 [14]

Dear Ward:

At last an answer to your two letters of October 21. First as to Nancy—her recovery has been ahead of schedule from the time she came out of the recovery room.* She's doing just fine.

As to the second letter. You are right about our action in the Persian Gulf, the people are behind it. A poll just a few days ago gave evidence of that. The clipping is wrong. Yes the reply was low-key in a sense although our target was more than two old oil rig platforms. They were being used as radar and command and control bases tracking the shipping in the Gulf. But we have a list of targets we'll be using, tit for tat, if they strike again. Our love to Dorothy.

Sincerely,
Ron

The USS Vincennes *accidentally shot down Flight 655, a commercial Iranian airliner on July 3, 1988. Less than a month after Iran and Iraq agreed to a cease-fire under United Nations Security Council Resolution 598, Reagan writes about this incident as well as other crises that occurred during his presidency.*

Mrs. Lenore D. Lebow
Far Rockaway, New York.
August 25, 1988 [15]

Dear Mrs. Lebow:

I'm sorry to be so late in answering your letter of July 18 but it has only just now made its way through the bureaucracy and reached my desk.

First let me offer my heartfelt sympathy to you for the loss of your loved ones in the shooting down of the Korean Airliner 007.† We have told the Soviet leaders the fact that the plane was off course was no excuse for their savage and inhumane attack. We have reason to believe their savage deed was ordered by lower echelon military leaders and not the politburo in the Kremlin. But even so it was an unconscionable act of barbarism. And this has been told to those in top government positions.

---

* On October 17, 1987, Nancy Reagan underwent a mastectomy.
† September 1, 1983

However with regard to the USS *Stark* and the tragic loss of life, the missile was not fired by an Iranian plane. It was fired by an Iraqi pilot and was a case of mistaken identity. They have acknowledged and apologized for the error.

Now as to the reparations we have offered in the Flight 655 shoot down, the Iranian government will have no role whatsoever in the handling of the money. It is our intention to deal directly with the families of the victims and they are not all Iranians. The passengers who lost their lives were from a number of different countries. I think what we have proposed is the civilized thing to do and reveals the difference between us and the barbaric terrorism of some other countries.

With regard to retaliation may I point out we did retaliate when we had proof that Qaddafi was behind a terrorist killing.* Our planes attacked Libya with bombs and missiles and let it be known this would be our response to any further terrorism.

Again my sympathy for your great loss.

Sincerely,
Ronald Reagan

ISRAEL AND LEBANON

From its position in Jordan, the Palestine Liberation Organization (PLO) had engaged in border clashes with Israel over the West Bank. But in 1970, King Hussein's army expelled the PLO from Jordan in retaliation for PLO challenges to Hussein's control of the country. From its new position in Lebanon, the PLO infiltrated areas of Israel across the Lebanese border and carried out terrorist attacks against Israeli civilians.

The conflict between Israel and Lebanon was one of the first regional crises for which the Reagan administration sought to broker a resolution. In July 1981, the U.S. special emissary to the Middle East, Philip C. Habib, negotiated a cease-fire between Israel and the PLO. The agreement was adhered to until early June 1982 when Shlomo Argov, Israel's ambassador to Great Britain, was shot in London by the Abu Nidal terrorist group, which had split from the PLO in the 1970s. In response, Israel launched a full-scale invasion of Lebanon on June 6, 1982, and quickly pressed its way to Beirut.

Throughout the summer, the United States engaged in vigorous diplomacy. In early August, an agreement was reached: armed Palestinian fighters would withdraw from Beirut in exchange for their safe passage to Tunisia and other parts of the Arab world. On August 12, Israel agreed to a cease-fire. President Reagan announced on August 20 that 800 U.S. Marines would join a multinational peacekeeping force (MNF) in Lebanon to oversee the evacuation of the PLO and to ensure the safety of

---

* The headquarters and other facilities of Muammar Qaddafi, the leader of Libya, were bombed on April 15, 1986.

the civilians living in refugee camps. The forces arrived five days later. PLO Chairman Yasser Arafat departed Lebanon on August 30, and within two days most of the remaining Palestinian forces had left Beirut. The MNF began its withdrawal soon thereafter.

President Reagan sought to "seize the moment" of the PLO's withdrawal from Lebanon by introducing a Middle East peace plan. In a speech on September 1, 1982, he announced his "fresh start" initiative, which called for Palestinian autonomy in the West Bank and in Gaza, but required that the Palestinians enter into a formal association with Jordan. President Reagan declared that "the United States will not support the establishment of an independent Palestinian state in the West Bank and Gaza, and we will not support annexation or permanent control by Israel."

Two weeks later, on September 14, a shock wave was sent through the peace process: Lebanese President-elect Bashir Gemayel, a leader with whom Israel expected to have improved relations, was assassinated. Various groups in Lebanon immediately blamed each other.[16] Israeli troops reentered Beirut the following day, violating the August 12 cease-fire. On September 18, President Reagan, Secretary of State George Shultz, and other national security principals learned that Phalangist forces had entered the Sabra and Shatila refugee camps ostensibly to hunt down PLO fighters believed to be there. The Phalangists, a Christian Maronite political party and militia, had massacred Palestinian civilians, including women and children. President Reagan expressed "outrage and revulsion over the murders." In the midst of these events, the MNF leaders decided that their forces should reenter Lebanon. On September 21, Bashir Gemayel's brother Amin was elected president by the parliament composed of Christians and Muslims in a nearly unanimous vote. The MNF returned to Lebanon on September 29.

The Kahan Commission of the Israeli government investigated charges of malfeasance by Israeli officials at the Palestinian refugee camps and issued a report on February 8, 1983. The commission concluded that Defense Minister Ariel Sharon and other Israeli officials were indirectly responsible for the massacres at Sabra and Shatila. Three days later, Sharon resigned his post as defense minister.

The collision of diplomacy, politics, and bloodshed in Lebanon was particularly salient in 1983. On April 18, 63 people were killed when the U.S. embassy in Beirut was bombed. The following month, the Reagan administration brokered what became known as the May 17 Agreement between the Gemayel government and Israel. This accord required the withdrawal of Israeli troops from Lebanon along with the removal of Syrian forces. Syria did not participate in the negotiations and refused to remove its troops. The toll of the ongoing Lebanon conflict began to weigh on Menachem Begin. On August 28, he announced his intention to resign as prime minister. In September, the Israeli government announced the withdrawal of its troops from the Shouf Mountains, a strategic territory that overlooked Beirut International Airport, where the U.S. Marine barracks were located. Druze Muslim forces quickly gained control of the Shouf Mountains and began firing down on U.S. forces. U.S. naval guns returned fire on September 8 and, 11 days later, shelled Druze hilltop positions. In October, Yitzhak Shamir became the new prime minister of Israel.

The escalating violence in Lebanon caused many civilian fatalities, increased unrest, and led to further attacks on U.S. soldiers and diplomats in the region. On October 23, a truck-bomb attack killed 241 U.S. Marines and Navy personnel at their barracks. A similar attack was made against France's military installation where 59 people were killed. According to State Department reports, Hezbollah (the Lebanon-based Shiite Muslim "Party of God") may have played a major role in the April and October attacks on U.S. installations.[17] For the next few months, U.S. and Syrian forces continued to clash.

On February 6, 1984, President Reagan issued the following statement: "I call on the Government of Syria, which occupies Lebanese territory from which much of the shelling of civilian centers originates and which facilitates and supplies instruments for terroristic attacks on the people of Lebanon, to cease this activity." The next day, he announced that U.S. forces would be redeployed to ships off the Lebanese coast but also authorized them to use gunfire and air support against Druze and Syrian-dominated parts of Lebanon. The withdrawal of U.S. troops from Lebanon was completed by the end of the month. Under pressure from Syria and Lebanese Muslims, the Gemayel government announced on March 5 that it was abandoning the May 17 Agreement.

During Reagan's term as governor of California, he avows his commitment to the survival of Israel and defends the Nixon administration's policy toward the country.

Mr. and Mrs. Matus

After August 8, 1970[18]

Dear Mr. and Mrs. Matus:

I believe the United States is <u>and should be</u> committed to the preservation of Israel. I am convinced this is the policy of the Nixon administration. Indeed I have been informed this is so.

Let me sum up the Middle East situation as I believe it is and has been. Israel, outnumbered one hundred to one in the population of unfriendly surrounding nations, has held its own with the help of American military supplies. In addition, the U.S. presence in the area has kept the Soviet Union outside the Middle East, at least as an active participant. If ever the United States gave up that role, it wouldn't make much difference whether or not we supplied arms to Israel.

Since the cease-fire, the president has enlarged the role of the United States. He has moved boldly to befriend the Arab states and replaced the Soviet influence in those countries. I think the reaction of the Arabs has made it plain they were uncomfortable in their relations with Russia. This move puts the United States in a position of being able to influence the Arabs and act as an intermediary as a friend of both sides. Frankly, I believe it has been a brilliant policy, brilliantly carried out.

I don't recall the president's criticism of Israel's reaction to the terrorists' raids, so [I] won't comment specifically on that. Speaking generally, however, I think we must maintain credibility with both sides if we are to successfully eliminate Russia's troublemaking in that area.

To sum up and answer your questions, I feel the United States is morally bound to protect Israel's right to nationhood and I support that position without reservation.

Sincerely,
Ronald Reagan

———

In his reply to a letter from the president of the World Jewish Congress, Reagan seeks to allay any concerns that he opposes the Israeli government.

Mr. Edgar M. Bronfman
New York, New York
September 15, 1982 [19]

Dear Mr. Bronfman:

I can't tell you how much your letter means to me and how encouraged I am. Thank you for your kindness in writing and thank you for what you are doing and for your offer of help. I am most grateful.

I've been deeply disturbed by the inference in some newspapers that I'm conspiring to oust the present government of Israel. Such a thing has no place in my thinking at all. Indeed it is my hope that working together we can finally achieve peace and that Israel can live without fear of her neighbors. My every effort will be toward bringing that about.

Again my heartfelt thanks.

Sincerely,
Ronald Reagan

———

Reagan reassures a correspondent about mixed signals in his policy toward the Middle East.

Mr. William J. Lowenberg
San Francisco, California
December 27, 1982 [20]

Dear Mr. Lowenberg:

Let me assure you the press has a way of leaving out more than they include in their reports. All of us here are on the same course and it is one directed toward persuading Jordan to take the lead among the Arab states in coming to the negotiating table. It is true that publicly we at times have to say things to meet the other person's political needs at home. But first and foremost in all we do is concern for the security of Israel. Believe me we've made great progress and while there is still much to do our goal remains a just and fair peace.

Best regards,
Ronald Reagan

––––––––

President Reagan discusses a telephone call he made to Israeli Prime Minister Menachem Begin and the dilemmas faced by Philip C. Habib, the U.S. special emissary to the Middle East, during Israel's attacks on Lebanon.*

Mr. Robert M. Schrayer
Chicago, Illinois
August 27, 1982[21]

Dear Mr. Schrayer:

I'm afraid there is some confusion about my position or that of my administration with regard to the Lebanon situation. I believe you'll find Prime Minister Begin has expressed his belief that Israel has no better friend.

My call to him was because with the situation almost resolved our Ambassador Habib cabled that the bombardment—the heaviest of the war and which went on for 15 hours—had made it impossible for the negotiators to even meet. When I called, the prime minister told me he had already ordered a halt to the bombing. He called back 20 minutes later to tell me the artillery barrage had been called off.

Let me assure you we have no intention of forsaking our longtime friend and ally the state of Israel. We want the PLO out, Lebanon united as a nation, the northern border of Israel made safe and then continuation of the effort to bring peace to the Middle East.

Sincerely,
Ronald Reagan

––––––––

President Reagan writes to the editor of Commentary *to agree with his essay on the biased portrayal of Israel's role in the war in Lebanon.*

Mr. Norman Podhoretz
New York, New York
September 14, 1982[22]

Dear Norman:

Thank you for sending me the advance on your article "J' Accuse."[23] I read it with great interest and while at times I thought Israel overreacted to PLO forays in West Beirut, like you I was amazed at the one-sided reporting particularly on TV.

––––––––

* On September 7, 1982, President Reagan awarded Habib the Presidential Medal of Freedom for efforts in the Middle East.

No attempt was made to differentiate between civilian casualties and those that were PLO fighters. Your article will do much to straighten the record.

I am hopeful now that we can get on with the peacemaking as I'm sure you are.

> Best regards,
> Ronald Reagan

————

Reagan describes his meeting with Amin Gemayel, who had been elected president following the assassination of his brother, in this letter to one of the co-owners of the public relations firm that managed his affairs in the late 1970s.

> Mr. Peter D. Hannaford
> Washington, D.C.
> October 20, 1982 [24]

Dear Pete:

Now we're even—I've just met President Gemayel and had breakfast with him this morning. I'm very impressed with him. We are going to send some people to help him get organized.

I'm glad you are helping him. Like you I feel the Lebanese are a truly extraordinary people.

Nancy sends her best.

> Sincerely,
> Ron

————

Writing a few weeks before a terrorist attack killed 17 Americans at the U.S. embassy in Beirut, President Reagan tells a close friend that he believes U.S. efforts in Lebanon have been helpful. He writes also that the replacement of Ariel Sharon with Moshe Arens as defense minister is a positive step.

> Mr. Laurence W. Beilenson
> Los Angeles, California
> March 28, 1983 [25]

Dear Larry:

It was good to hear from you and I appreciate your concern. However I think the press did some out-of-context quoting and some guessing. I will say however there is a firm consensus that our country is and has been for a long time pledged to the continued existence of Israel as a nation. I've heard no contradiction of this in the State Department, Defense or the Congress or for that matter the press.

But with regard to what I said; I was talking about the Lebanon situation and our effort to persuade Israel, Syria and the PLO to get out and give the Lebanese a chance to reestablish sovereignty over their own land. Israel sees its northern border as vulnerable to forays by remnants of the PLO and wants to retain a military presence on Lebanon's side of the border. We have expressed a willingness to help Lebanon with our multinational forces until such time as Lebanon forces can demonstrate they are capable of guarding the border.

We've made considerable progress but haven't been able to get a sign-off.

Things have looked better the last few days with the change in defense ministers in Israel.

Nancy sends her best.

Sincerely,
Ron

———

Three days after the April 18 bombing of the U.S. embassy in Beirut, the nephew of one of the victims wrote President Reagan and said that he did not think his uncle's "life was lost in vain." Below is the president's reply.

Mr. John Welling
Wooster, Ohio
June 20, 1983 [26]

Dear Mr. Welling:

Thank you for writing as you did. Yes your uncle did give his life for his country and it was not in vain. It is up to all of us to be sure of that.

A number of years ago a president of this country declared that we have a rendezvous with destiny. In a world where terrorism spreads and the innocent die we must fulfill our destiny. If not us who? If not now when? Your uncle understood that. I know what a tragedy this must be for all of you who knew and loved him and you have our deepest sympathy. You also have my pledge to do all I can to see that what he believed in [is] carried on.

Sincerely,
Ronald Reagan

———

Seventeen days before the truck-bombing of the U.S. Marine barracks in Beirut, a Lebanese girl wrote President Reagan and said: "I think you should start showing the whole world, what the Marines can do. . . . It is terrible for us, innocent civilians (or aren't we?), to live in such a wretched state; take it from me, I am living in a country at war." In his reply, President Reagan expresses empathy for those living in the perilous circumstances that war brings.

Miss Patricia Nakhel
Beirut, Lebanon
November 28, 1983 [27]

Dear Miss Nakhel:

Thank you for your letter. I wish more people throughout the world could be made aware of the suffering of so many like yourself. As one of our famous generals in another time long ago said, "War is hell."

Patricia there have been four wars for our country in my lifetime. I served in one. I promise you we will do everything we can to end the bloodshed and terror that presently devastate your country.

You are in our prayers.

Sincerely,
Ronald Reagan

———————

President Reagan responds to his old friend's suggestion that the U.S. withdraw from Lebanon. A month later he would announce that U.S. forces in Lebanon would be redeployed offshore.

Mr. William F. Buckley Jr.
New York, New York
January 5, 1984 [28]

Dear Bill:

I hope your holidays in the Caribbean were as pleasant as ours in California. We really lucked out weatherwise, warm sun and no before-dawn phone calls.

I assume you are back in New York or did you go directly to Kabul?* That would be above and beyond the call of duty.

I'm not going to attempt a reply (in this letter) to your column. That will have to wait for a conversation time—glass in hand. I do have a reply may I hasten to say.

Bill the Middle East is a complicated place—well not really a place, it's more a state of mind. A disordered mind. But of course you know that without my telling you. I'm not being stubborn or too proud to admit to error. There has been progress precisely because the MNF is there. There could be instant chaos if a wrong or precipitate move is made. Withdrawal would be such a move. I could use all the clichés—"walking a thin line," "juggling with too many balls in the air," and so on and so on. The truth is most of the clichés would fit the situation. Let me just say, there is a reason why they are there.

Nancy sends her love and tell Pat we love her.

Sincerely,
Ron

———————

On January 30, 1984, a friend of President Reagan wrote to suggest the president make the following statement: "[A]s of today the U.S.A. is moving their Marines from Lebanon to U.S. ships off shore. If this act causes an additional threat of the takeover of Lebanon, by the Syrians, thousands of tons of TNT will respond from the sea." On Feb-

———————

* A reference to a running joke that Buckley served as ambassador to Afghanistan.

ruary 7, President Reagan announced that U.S. forces in Lebanon would be redeployed off shore, and on February 8 the U.S. battleship New Jersey *fired shells at Syrian-dominated positions near Beirut for more than nine hours.*

Mr. Paul Trousdale
Los Angeles, California
February 20, 1984 [29]

Dear Paul:

See. You made a suggestion about the troops in Lebanon and there they go—redeployed onto the ships. And a few tons of TNT were lofted onto the area occupied by the Syrians. Who says we don't listen to our constituents?

Seriously I appreciate your letter and assure you I understand your concern about that troubled part of the world. Sometimes I wonder if the Middle East was the cradle of the world's three great religions because they needed religion more than any other spot on earth.

Nancy sends her best as do I.

Best regards,
Ron

The parents of Sergeant Thomas G. Smith, USMC, wrote to President Reagan on August 22, 1984, almost a year after their son was killed in an attack on the U.S. barracks in Beirut, seeking assurance that their son did not die in vain.

Mr. and Mrs. Joseph K. Smith Jr.
Middletown, Connecticut
November 3, 1984 [30]

Dear Mr. and Mrs. Smith:

I'm terribly sorry to be so late in replying to your letter of August 22 but I have only just received it. It takes a while for mail to reach my desk and sometimes longer than other times depending on the overall mail flow. Please forgive me.

I know there are no words that can lessen your pain. I wish there were. But believe me those men aren't forgotten—by me or by the American people. And nothing has angered me more than those who for political purposes have charged they were not serving a worthwhile cause. Our Marines and all of you deserve better than that.

Their cause was peace and for the better part of a year they were succeeding in that cause. It was for that very reason the forces who don't want a just peace in the Middle East turned to acts of terrorism. First as you know, it was sniping, then mortar and artillery fire and finally the suicide bombing. The commanders who approved making the headquarters building a barracks did so because the building offered the best protection against artillery and small-arms fire.

Even now the possibility of a final peace in that tragic land exists only because of the presence of our Marines and their fellows in the multinational force during that year.

They had made possible the removal of 15,000 PLO radicals and stopped the full-scale war that was going on in the city of Beirut with thousands and thousands of innocent civilians maimed or killed. Only if we give up on trying to obtain peace will their sacrifice have been in vain. We will not do that.

I was present at Camp Lejeune for the memorial service last year and met the families of most of the men. There was another service this year at which General Kelly read a letter from me. I did not attend because I was sure the same people who have been using this tragedy for political purposes would accuse me of exploiting the event as part of the political campaign. Your son and his comrades deserve better.

Mr. and Mrs. Smith, I do understand your pain and sorrow. I am a parent myself, but more than that I am so proud of the young men and women who serve in our military and there is no greater burden in this office than having to make a decision that places them in danger.

I would be pleased to hear from you but to avoid the delay please send your reply in c/o Kathy Osborne—the White House. In that way your letter will reach me immediately.

Sincerely,
Ronald Reagan

———

Nearly two years after the Beirut bombing, a sergeant in the U.S. Marine Corps wrote President Reagan that although he initially felt remorse about surviving the blast while others were killed, he believed his purpose was to defend freedom. He wrote: "We accomplished our mission in Beirut, Lebanon, Mr. President, and so much more."

Sgt. Stephen E. Russell
Tarawa Terrace II, North Carolina
August 14, 1985[31]

Dear Sgt. Russell:

Thank you for your letter of June 25th and pardon my late reply. It takes a while for mail to reach my desk. I welcome this chance to express my appreciation for your service in Beirut. You are correct about accomplishing your mission; it was because you did, that the terrorists launched their all-out effort against you. You were not withdrawn because of failure but only because required defensive measures made continuation of your mission impossible.

Sgt. Russell the sense of guilt you say you felt is typical of combat. I first learned of it in WWII even though my service never included combat. It isn't given to us to understand the fortunes of war, why some are called upon to die and others spared. We must have faith in God's infinite wisdom and mercy. He alone decides and when we are spared it is because He has things for us yet to do.

Thank you for writing but more important, thank you for what you are doing. God bless you.

Sincerely,
Ronald Reagan

———

During his last year in office, President Reagan assures a Lebanese-American that the United States has not forgotten his homeland and is working to bring peace to Lebanon.

Mr. Asaad N. Karam
Nitro, West Virginia
January 6, 1988 [32]

Dear Mr. Karam:

Your letter has only just reached me, hence my tardy reply. Please know how much I appreciate your generous words.

Let me assure you we have not forgotten Lebanon and though our efforts are not as visible as was our sending of the military we continue to do all we can to bring peace to that troubled land. Sometimes diplomacy must be done quietly. Believe me we share your feeling about the tragedy that has struck your homeland and will continue to do all we can.

Again thanks for writing as you did.

Sincerely,
Ronald Reagan

MIDDLE EAST PEACE PROCESS

The Middle East peace process has always been plagued with intractable issues for which answers seem impossible. By the time Ronald Reagan assumed the presidency in January 1981, however, substantial progress had been made. The Arab-Israeli war of 1967 led to United Nations Security Council Resolution 242, the "territory-for-peace" measure that called upon Israel to return the occupied territories in exchange for security guarantees from its neighbors. Egyptian President Anwar Sadat and Israeli Prime Minister Menachem Begin signed "A Framework for Peace in the Middle East," and "A Framework for the Conclusion of a Peace Treaty Between Israel and Egypt" in Septem-

ber 1978 at Camp David. In March 1979, the two countries officially recognized each other and signed a peace treaty. The Lebanon war in the early 1980s had a corrosive effect on the peace process, but the Reagan administration sought to revive negotiations.

President Reagan enunciated his Middle East peace plan in a major address on September 1, 1982, as the evacuation of the PLO from Beirut was coming to a close: "While Israel's military successes in Lebanon have demonstrated that its armed forces are second to none in the region, they alone cannot bring just and lasting peace to Israel and her neighbors. The question now is how to reconcile Israel's legitimate security concerns with the legitimate rights of the Palestinians. And that answer can only come at the negotiating table." President Reagan reaffirmed his commitment to Israel, embraced the framework of U.N. Resolution 242, and endorsed the Camp David idea of having a five-year trial period of Palestinian self-rule in the West Bank and Gaza. The president called for "the immediate adoption of a settlement freeze." He then declared the centrality of Jordan to achieving Middle East peace: "It is the firm view of the United States that self-government by the Palestinians of the West Bank and Gaza in association with Jordan offers the best chance for a durable, just, and lasting peace."

A month after Egypt and Israel signed a peace agreement brokered by President Carter, Reagan criticizes the president's Middle East policy.

Mr. Richard James Whalen
April 17, 1979 [33]

Dear Dick:

Just a quick line between trips to thank you for the material you sent, particularly the analysis of the Middle East situation. It truly is frightening, and I found after I had read it that I couldn't keep from hearkening back to the Old Testament prophecies of the events that would foretell Armageddon. Maybe the United States couldn't head off what seems to be building up there, but surely we could have made a better try than this man has made.

Again, my heartfelt thanks and very best to your lovely partner.

Sincerely,
Ron

In this letter to one of the most famous Christian ministers in the United States, President Reagan links the selling of airborne warning and control systems (AWACS) to Saudi Arabia to making progress in the Middle East peace process.

The Reverend Billy Graham
Montreat, North Carolina
October 5, 1981 [34]

Dear Billy:

I'm so sorry to hear about Ruth. Please know that you both are in our thoughts and prayers. We hope that by the time you receive this her health is much improved.

Thank you very much for your statements about unilateral disarmament, I'm happy to have them on hand. They will be most useful in the days ahead for anything from AWACS to our disarmament talks with the Soviets.

I don't know how the AWACS matter will come out with the Senate but I do know that a refusal to allow the sale will set us back perhaps irretrievably in our Middle East peacemaking effort.

This is a very late reply to your good letter and I apologize. Nancy and I are so grateful for your prayers and your readiness to be of help. Please believe we offer that in return.

Give our love to Ruth and we hope we'll see you both soon.

Sincerely,
Ron

President Reagan responds to a letter from an official of the Union of Orthodox Jewish Congregations of America who expressed general support for the new Middle East initiative, but was concerned about the ability of the plan to protect Israel's rights in its own territory.

Mr. Fred Ehrman
New York, New York
October 25, 1982 [35]

Dear Mr. Ehrman:

I'm sorry to be so late in replying to your letter of September 29 but it takes a while for letters to reach my desk.

I appreciate your concern and recognize the problem you pose must be very much a part of the negotiations which will have to take place if we are to have peace in the Middle East. In my mind the negotiations to come will be on an exchange of territory in return for security. I've been encouraged by the attitude of the more moderate Arab states and believe they at last truly want peace.

I believe they will be concerned that practical safeguards are a necessary part of the solution. And of course it goes without saying that the United States will remain pledged to the security of Israel.

Best regards,
Ronald Reagan

Again, Reagan asserts his commitment to Israel.

Ms. Shirley I. Leviton
New York, New York
October 25, 1982 [36]

Dear Ms. Leviton:

I'm sorry to be so late in answering your wire. It takes a while before things make their way through the system to my desk.

I just want to assure you we do intend that negotiations should be within the framework of Camp David, and U.N. Resolutions 242 and 338.* This of course requires acceptance of Israel's right to exist as a nation. I have so informed a meeting of Arab leaders in a White House meeting. We have never and will never retreat from that position.

Sincerely,
Ronald Reagan

When President Reagan announced his Middle East peace plan on September 1, 1982, he called for "self-government by the Palestinians of the West Bank and Gaza in association with Jordan." King Hussein bin Talal of Jordan and PLO Chairman Yasser Arafat met in October to discuss the plan. In late November, in an apparent about-face, the PLO openly rejected the proposal. For its part, Jordan was reluctant about forming an association with the PLO.

In a speech at Tel Aviv University on October 30, 1984, Samuel W. Lewis, the U.S. ambassador to Israel, said that he felt the September 1 initiative was ill-timed. Lewis's remarks made national headlines in the United States and were interpreted as criticism of the Reagan administration's diplomacy in the Middle East. In a letter to President Reagan dated November 9, 1984, Lewis apologized for the embarrassment that his remarks caused and reiterated his support for the peace plan.

The Honorable Samuel Lewis
Tel Aviv, Israel
December 10, 1984 [37]

Dear Sam:

Thanks very much for your good letter and don't give the problem you mentioned a second thought. I've long since learned that several thousand miles' distance plus the press selectivity in reporting excerpts is insurance against getting exercised over anything I read under those circumstances.

---

* United Nations Security Council Resolution 338, adopted on October 22, 1973, sought to end the October war through an immediate cease-fire and called upon the parties to implement Resolution 242.

You know the truth is we thought we were off to a pretty good start on the September 1 plan and then Arafat had his second meeting with the king and did what seemed to be an about-face and everything went on hold. I appreciate all you've been doing.

Thanks again for your congratulations and good wishes.

Sincerely,
Ronald Reagan

CHAPTER FOURTEEN

Terrorism and the Iran-Contra Scandal

NICARAGUA was undergoing a revolution in 1979. In July, President Anastasio Somoza Debayle fled Nicaragua and the long reign of the Somoza dynasty came to an end as the Sandinista National Liberation Front (FSLN) took power. A resistance movement composed largely of peasants (later known as the Contras) quickly formed, and for the next decade Nicaragua would be besieged by a civil war. Presaging later U.S. policy, President Jimmy Carter cut assistance to the Sandinista regime.

Iran was also in a revolution in 1979. In January, as the country plunged deeper into political turmoil, Mohammad Reza Shah Pahlavi left Iran. The following month, Ayatollah Ruhollah Khomeini returned to Iran after living in exile. Later that year, the U.S. embassy in Tehran was seized and Americans were taken hostage. The Iranian hostage crisis dominated the last 444 days of the Carter presidency. On January 20, 1981, the day Ronald Reagan was sworn in to office, all 52 hostages were released from captivity.

Ronald Reagan at once interpreted the revolutions in Iran and Nicaragua in strategic terms. In 1979, he argued that in standing by as the regimes in the two countries unraveled, the Carter administration signaled to the world that it was prepared to leave long-standing friends in the lurch when trouble arose. He felt that geopolitical factors should compel American leaders to support friendly regimes in Iran and Nicaragua.[1] In December 1979, the Soviet Union invaded Afghanistan, a country on Iran's eastern flank. Iran and the Soviet Union shared a long border upon which the Soviets had military divisions poised to invade. In the Western Hemisphere, the Sandinista regime in Nicaragua was moving steadily toward the Soviet Union and Cuba.

As president, Reagan continued to make the case that Iran and Nicaragua were of the utmost strategic importance, and put forth measures in support of his analysis. In April 1981, the Reagan administration suspended economic aid to the Sandinistas, and by the end of 1982, it admitted that it was aiding the Contras. This support was challenged by congressional restrictions on aiding the resistance force imposed through several amendments introduced by Representative Edward Boland (D-Massachusetts).

Although it vowed to continue the neutrality stance in the Iran-Iraq War that President Carter had advocated, the Reagan administration engaged in strategic openings to both countries. In November 1984, diplomatic relations between the United States and Iraq were resumed after a 17-year disruption. Following the position he had taken when the shah lost power, President Reagan endorsed starting a political dialogue with Iran. In the summer of 1985, despite an existing U.S. embargo, President Reagan authorized Israel to sell American-originated arms to Iran.

Members of the national security team were in disagreement about the Iranian initiative. Secretary of State George P. Shultz and Secretary of Defense Caspar Weinberger opposed it. National Security Adviser Robert "Bud" McFarlane and other National Security Council (NSC) staffers supported the plan and oversaw the sale of TOW missiles to Iran through Israel later that summer and HAWK missiles in November. Additional deliveries were made in 1986. Following McFarlane's resignation in December 1985, Admiral John Poindexter, his replacement, continued the project. McFarlane and Poindexter were assisted by Lt. Colonel Oliver North, NSC deputy director for political-military affairs.

Peter Wallison, President Reagan's legal counsel during the ensuing Iran-Contra scandal after disclosure of the arms sales, writes that "the strategic elements [of an opening to Iran] were quickly discarded in favor of a flat-out effort to obtain the release of the hostages by shipping arms to Iran."[2] Between March 1984 and the summer of 1985, eight U.S. citizens in Beirut were kidnapped. One hostage, Jeremy Levin, escaped in February 1985, but the other seven remained in captivity. By mid-1985, when the shipment of arms to Iran began, there seemed to be no end to the hostage crisis. Trying to gain freedom for the Americans held hostage in Beirut had become an intractable issue and a proxy for the more expansive problem of international terrorism. The Reagan administration identified Iran as a key supporter of terrorist groups such as Hezbollah (the Lebanon-based Shiite Muslim "Party of God"), but the NSC staffers running the arms sales operation believed that Iran could facilitate the release of the remaining American hostages in Lebanon. Although some hostages were released during the operation of the program, others were taken. Yet Poindexter and North continued to transfer arms to Iran until the scheme was disclosed in November 1986.

On November 3, 1986, more than a year after the first arms shipment, Al Shiraa, a Lebanese magazine, reported that McFarlane had been on a secret mission to Tehran in an attempt to obtain assurance of an end to Iranian support for terrorism and to win the release of the U.S. hostages, again in exchange for further arms sales. The fact that the United States had secretly sold arms to Iran immediately created a firestorm in American politics. In a nationally televised address on November 13, 1986, President Reagan presented his version of the Iranian crisis and rationale:

For 18 months now we have had underway a secret diplomatic initiative to Iran. That initiative was undertaken for the simplest and best reasons: to renew a relationship with the nation of Iran, to bring an honorable end to the bloody 6-year war between Iran and Iraq, to eliminate state-sponsored terrorism and subversion, and to effect the safe return of all hostages. . . .

The charge has been made that the United States has shipped weapons to Iran as ransom payment for the release of American hostages in Lebanon, that the United States undercut its allies and secretly violated American policy against trafficking with terrorists. Those charges are utterly false. The United States has not made concessions to those who hold our people captive in Lebanon. And we will not. . . .

During the course of our secret discussions, I authorized the transfer of small amounts of defensive weapons and spare parts for defensive systems in Iran. My purpose was to convince Tehran that our negotiators were acting with my authority, to send a signal that the United States was prepared to replace animosity between us with a new relationship. . . .

[W]hy, you might ask, is any relationship with Iran important to the United States? Iran encompasses some of the most critical geography in the world. It lies between the Soviet Union and access to the warm waters of the Indian Ocean. . . .

[I]t is in our national interest to watch for changes within Iran that might offer hope for an improved relationship. . . .

Our interests are clearly served by opening a dialog with Iran and thereby helping to end the Iran-Iraq war. The war has dragged on for more than 6 years, with no prospect of a negotiated settlement. The slaughter on both sides has been enormous, and the adverse economic and political consequences for that vital region of the world have been growing. . . .

Since the welcome return of former hostage David Jacobsen,* there has been unprecedented speculation and countless reports that have not only been wrong but have been potentially dangerous to the hostages and destructive of the opportunity before us. . . .

Our government has a firm policy not to capitulate to terrorist demands. That no concessions policy remains in force, in spite of the wildly speculative and false stories about arms for hostages and alleged ransom payments. We did not—repeat—did not trade weapons or anything else for hostages, nor will we. Those who think we have gone soft on terrorism should take up the question with Colonel [Muammar] Qaddafi.† We have not, nor will we, capitulate to terrorists.

---

* On November 2, 1986, David P. Jacobsen was released from captivity in Beirut, Lebanon, after being held for nearly 18 months.
† President Reagan is referring to the U.S. air strikes on some of Qaddafi's headquarters in Tripoli on April 15, 1986, in retaliation for Libya's involvement in terrorism.

In a news conference on November 19, President Reagan reemphasized his position and took responsibility for the situation:

Our policy objectives were never in dispute. There were differences on how best to proceed. The principal issue in contention was whether we should make isolated and limited exceptions to our arms embargo as a signal of our serious intent. Several top advisers opposed the sale of even a modest shipment of defensive weapons and spare parts to Iran. Others felt no progress could be made without this sale. I weighed their views. I considered the risks of failure and the rewards of success, and I decided to proceed. And the responsibility for the decision and the operation is mine and mine alone. . . .

Bringing Iran back into the community of responsible nations, ending its participation in political terror, bringing an end to that terrible war, and bringing our hostages home—these are the causes that justify taking risks.

Policies related to Iran and Nicaragua became interconnected and led to the biggest scandal of the Reagan presidency. On November 25, 1986, Attorney General Edwin Meese III revealed that $10 to $30 million in Iranian payments for arms were transferred to the Nicaraguan Contras. Providing arms to the Contras was, at the very least, a violation of the spirit of the Boland amendments. President Reagan announced that he was appointing a special board that became known as the Tower Commission to undertake a comprehensive review of the NSC; that Admiral Poindexter was being reassigned to the Navy; and that Colonel North had been relieved of his White House duties. On December 2, President Reagan stated that he "welcomed the appointment of an independent counsel to look into allegations of illegality in the sale of arms to Iran and the use of funds from these sales to assist the forces opposing the Sandinista government in Nicaragua." President Reagan maintained that he was unaware of the Contra transaction.

For seven years, Lawrence E. Walsh, the Independent Counsel, would investigate the Iran-Contra affair. He oversaw the indictments of North, Poindexter, and Weinberger, among others. Some, like McFarlane, would plead guilty to misdemeanor charges. Those involved would receive suspended sentences or pardons, but as President Reagan writes in letters below, there was no doubt that the Iran-Contra affair marred the reputation of the United States.

The letters that follow show the consistency of President Reagan's public and private statements about selling arms to Iran, seeking the release of the hostages, and fighting terrorism.

TERRORISM

Found in a collection of pre-presidential letters from the 1960s and 1970s, this letter must have been written after Yasser Arafat became chairman of the Palestine Liberation Organization (PLO) in 1968.

Miss Lytle
Circa 1968–1980 [3]

Dear Miss Lytle:

Thank you for your letter and generous words. We are in agreement about many facets of the Middle East situation. I think the great difficulty is that there is so much right on both sides. The Palestinian question must be settled fairly. I am under the impression that Arafat has approved violence and terrorist activity. If I'm wrong about that, I stand corrected.

Sincerely,
Ronald Reagan

President Reagan's longtime correspondents worried about his safety while campaigning for reelection and lamented the need for barriers at the White House.

Mr. and Mrs. E. H. Wagner
Philadelphia, Pennsylvania
February 13, 1984 [4]

Dear Lorraine and Wag:

Thanks very much for your birthday greeting on the 34th anniversary of my 39th. And a heartfelt thanks for your generous and very kind words.

We had a wonderful (but brief) time in Dixon and Eureka and then on to the ranch which is always wonderful.

I share your view about the restrictions we are all under due to terrorist threats. I pray we can help bring back a more civilized world one day.

All the best—
Ron

Seven months after the attack on the U.S. barracks in Beirut, Lebanon, President Reagan writes that terrorist threats and intelligence reports about safety are the reasons he does not attend public church services in the capital.

Mr. Jerry Mueller
El Paso, Texas
May 31, 1984[5]

Dear Mr. Mueller:

Thanks for your kind letter and generous words, also your willingness to help. I'm most grateful.

I'll admit I was very frustrated when the press carried stories that I never had been a churchgoer and therefore was a hypocrite when I referred to God and his place in our nation's life.

We have always been churchgoers and would be now if it were not for the terrorist threats. We could handle the usual kind of kooky threat directed only against me. But the situation has changed as we saw in Beirut. Our intelligence now indicates the possibility of attack which could endanger a great many people.

We do not hold services in the White House. It has been tried in the past without much success. However it has been arranged that we can have communion there when we are in Washington. In addition we can occasionally go to church—sometimes when we are in other cities such as on Easter in Honolulu on our way to China; sometimes in Washington when we do it with no advance warning and without creating a regular pattern.

As I said, we miss going but prayer is very much a part of our daily life. Again thanks and God bless you.

Sincerely,
Ronald Reagan

---

*In a handwritten letter to President Reagan dated June 27, 1985, the governor of New York wrote: "As governor of a state of nearly eighteen million Americans all of them anguished over the plight of the hostages, I want to commend your handling of the situation and urge your continued restraint with firmness. We know that nothing you are charged with is more important than your agonizing responsibility here. We know how hard is the challenge to secure the safe return of our Americans without creating invitations to further terrorism." At the time of the governor's letter, seven Americans were in captivity in Lebanon.**

The Honorable Mario Cuomo
Albany, New York
July 5, 1985[6]

Dear Governor Cuomo:

Thank you very much for your kind letter of June 27. It was good of you to write as you did and I'm most grateful. I'm grateful too for so many who prayed

---

* As of January 1985, the following men were being held hostage: William Buckley, Martin Lawrence Jenco, Peter Kilburn, Jeremy Levin, and Benjamin Weir. Levin escaped in February. Terry Anderson was captured in March. David Jacobsen was captured in May. Thomas Sutherland was captured in June.

and to God for answering those prayers. Now we must go on 'til we have secured the freedom of the seven kidnap victims. They too must be brought home.

Again my thanks to you.

Sincerely,
Ronald Reagan

On October 7, 1985, four members of the Palestinian Liberation Front hijacked the Achille Lauro, *an Italian cruise ship in the Mediterranean Sea. They demanded the release of 50 Palestinians from Israeli jails, and on October 8 sent Leon Klinghoffer, a Jewish American passenger, to his death by throwing him overboard in his wheelchair after shooting him. The next day, the crew and passengers were released and the terrorists surrendered to the PLO under an agreement worked out with Egyptian authorities that gave them safe transport out of Egypt. The terrorists then boarded an Egyptian plane. On October 10, under instruction from President Reagan, U.S. F-14 Tomcats diverted the Egyptian plane to Sigonella, a NATO base in Sicily, Italy. U.S. forces were prepared to board the hijackers on an American plane and spirit them to the United States, where they would face felony charges. Following a standoff with Italian forces, the United States gave in to the Italian request to try the hijackers in Italy. The next day the Italian government charged the four hijackers with murder.*

On October 14, 1985, editorial by the publisher of the Union Leader *(Manchester, New Hampshire) endorsed President Reagan's action: "You are to be congratulated for courageous action in the war against terrorism. . . . At last, the evil forces of terrorism must reckon with our willingness to react to crimes against American citizens. . . . Our intelligence forces abroad, our military personnel, and our administration officials acted not only with courage but with discretion as well."*

Mrs. William Loeb
Manchester, New Hampshire
October 21, 1985[7]

Dear Nackey:

Just a quick line to say thank you for your "letter" editorial. I'm most grateful. I also feel fine and am grateful to the Lord for arranging things in the air over the Mediterranean. Our guys were great and all on about an hour's notice.

Best regards,
Ron

Captured in Beirut, Lebanon, on March 16, 1985, Associated Press bureau chief Terry Anderson would spend six years and eight months in captivity, longer than any other American held in the Middle East. More than a year into his captivity, Anderson's sister wrote to President Reagan saying that she knew that he was working toward the day when she and her brother would stand together on the White House lawn to celebrate his return to the United States.

Mrs. Margaret Peggy Say
Batavia, New York
November 26, 1986[8]

Dear Peggy:

Thank you very much for your kind letter and generous words. You truly brightened an otherwise dark day. Please be assured those hostages are never out of my mind. I'll never rest until their ordeal is ended and your letter has strengthened my resolve.

Again a heartfelt thank you.

Sincerely,
Ronald Reagan

Terry Anderson would not be released for nearly four more years when President Reagan wrote this letter to the hostage's sister.

Ms. Margaret Peggy Say
Batavia, New York
January 13, 1988[9]

Dear Peggy:

I'm very tardy in acknowledging your Christmas greeting but it has only recently reached my desk. I thank you and the Andersons for the beautiful card and I assure you we are praying for your loved ones. We are also doing everything we can and exploring every avenue to bring about their release. Don't mistake silence for abandonment or lack of caring.

I know there are no words that can lighten the grief you all feel or make the pain of those in captivity easier for them to bear. Just please know their plight is of great importance to us, they are not forgotten nor will they be.

Sincerely,
Ronald Reagan

Libya

U.S.–Libyan relations had been on a collision course throughout the 1980s. In December 1985, Colonel Muammar Qaddafi reportedly hailed as "heroic" the attacks at the El Al ticket counters at the airports in Rome and Vienna that killed 20 people, including five Americans. Members of Abu Nidal were believed to have participated in the at-

tacks, and officials in Washington argued that Libya aided the terrorists. The Reagan administration responded by severing economic ties with Libya on January 7, 1986. On March 24, Libya fired SA-5 missiles on U.S. aircraft as naval exercises took place in the Gulf of Sidra. In response the United States hit several Libyan patrol boats and an SA-5 base at Sitre, Libya. The crisis escalated when intelligence reports linked Libya to the bombing of a discothèque in West Berlin on April 5. Two people were killed in the attack and 155 wounded, including many Americans. On April 14, President Reagan announced the retaliatory measures he had approved: "Air and naval forces of the United States launched a series of strikes against the headquarters, terrorist facilities and military assets that support Muammar Qaddafi's subversive activities." There was a substantial reduction in Qaddafi's terrorist activities after the U.S. strike.

———————

The letters below were written over a span of four months. The first was written after the United States and Libya exchanged fire on March 24 and 25, 1986. The final letter was written in July after the U.S.–Libya crisis had subsided.

Mr. Ward L. Quaal
Chicago, Illinois
Circa April 1986[10]

Dear Ward:

It was good to hear from you—all three letters and the clippings. We haven't come around to the FCC situation yet but I appreciate your input on Mark and assure you it will be widely circulated before a meeting takes place.*

As for the *Tribune* editorials I find myself missing the old Colonel† more and more. This isn't the *Tribune* I grew up with back in Illinois.

They are so convinced we were out to attack Libya and thus should have been loaded with war correspondents. The truth is that particular exercise is an annual event and this was the seventh time we've held it in that same place. Each time we take groups of six reporters out on the command ship, one group at a time, rotating them back to shore every few hours. The last group had just been taken ashore when Qaddafi launched his attack and we responded.

I must confess I'm no happier about the second editorial about the constitutional amendment to balance the budget. Tom Jefferson at the Constitution's launching declared its one glaring omission was lack of a prohibition against the government borrowing.

———————

* In his letter to President Reagan, Quaal urged that Mark Fowler be reappointed chairman of the Federal Communications Commission. Fowler's term would expire on June 30, 1986. President Reagan reappointed Fowler, who served until 1987.
† Colonel Robert R. McCormick, legendary editor and publisher of the *Chicago Tribune* from 1912 to 1955 and a fervent conservative.

I'm with you on George Roche.* I'm totally opposed to that court decision that binds a college to federal controls if a student has a government grant.

Nancy sends her best and love to Dorothy from both of us.

Sincerely,
Ron

The Honorable Walter H. Annenberg
Rancho Mirage, California
April 21, 1986[11]

Dear Walter:

Thanks for your letter of April 9 and believe me I share your enthusiasm about Charles W[ick] † and the job he's doing. During our recent Libyan adventure he had a radio broadcast going night and day to the people of Libya telling them they were not our target.

I've taken up your proposal with Don R[egan].‡ Someone raised a question of protocol with reference to others of equal rank who might feel they too should be included. I assure you I'm checking this out. It seems like a good idea to me and I hope it can be done.

Nancy sends her love and from both of us to Lee.

Sincerely,
Ron

Mr. and Mrs. Hugh van Cutsem
Suffolk, England
May 22, 1986[12]

Dear Mr. and Mrs. van Cutsem:

Our mutual friend Ambassador Price** has forwarded your letter to me and I want you to know how very much I appreciate your writing. You are more than kind.

I know there are people in both our countries who disapproved of the action we took in Tripoli but I'm sure they lack understanding of what is at stake.

I shall be forever grateful to your prime minister for her courage and for the bond of friendship between us and between our two countries. You have just eloquently expressed that friendship. Thank you very much and God bless you.

Sincerely,
Ronald Reagan

---

* President of Hillsdale College in Michigan from 1971 to 1999, who refused federal funds rather than submit to guidelines such as Title IX on sex discrimination.

† Director of the U.S. Information Agency.

‡ Secretary of the treasury, 1981–1985; chief of staff to the president, 1985–1987.

** Charles H. Price II was the United States ambassador to England.

President Reagan replies to a letter from a U.S. Air Force sergeant who served at RAF Lakenheath, the U.S.-run military base in England at the time of the attack on Tripoli, Libya, on April 15, 1986. Great Britain was the only country to allow the United States to use its bases in preparation for the attack. President Reagan also writes some consoling words about Captain Fernando L. Ribas-Dominicci and Captain Paul F. Lorence, both killed in an exchange of fire.

MSgt. W. L. Austin, USAF
RAF Lakenheath, England
July 17, 1986 [13]

Dear Sgt. Austin:

Thank you very much for your letter of April 23rd and forgive the bureaucratic tangle that kept it from getting to my desk until now. I'm most grateful to you for your account of what took place at "Lakenheath" at the time of the Libyan mission. You have added to the great feeling of pride I had in the magnificent performance of those who flew the mission. And like you I pledge to do everything I can to see that men like Major Ribas-Dominicci and Captain Lorence will never be forgotten.

Again my thanks to you for writing and for what you and all the others in the 48th are doing for our country. Of all the things that make me proud in this position I hold, none can top my pride in the men and women in the uniform of our armed forces.

God bless you all.

Sincerely,
Ronald Reagan

A young Chinese man wrote President Reagan: "I am writing this letter to cry 'YES' to your RETALIATION against Libya. . . . This is your RIGHT and obligation." His letter was delivered by an American couple.

Mr. Liu Guangzhi
Zhongshan Guangdong, China
July 17, 1986 [14]

Dear Liu Guangzhi:

Thank you for your very kind letter which was delivered to me by Mr. and Mrs. Delahanty. They told me of their very enjoyable trip to the People's Republic of China and of your many kindnesses which added so much to their visit.

I recall my own visit to your country and particularly the pleasure I experienced in speaking to the students at Fudan University.* Thank you for your gener-

---

* President Reagan spoke with students at Fudan University in Shanghai, China, on April 30, 1984.

ous words about the action we took in Libya. We must all work together to bring an end to terrorism. We here in America value the friendship we have with the People's Republic of China and with the Chinese people.

Again thank you for your letter and my very best regards.

Sincerely,
Ronald Reagan

The Iran-Contra Scandal

Eleven days after he revealed that American weapons were being sent to Iran through Israel, President Reagan expresses disappointment that press reports have jeopardized an opening to Iran and efforts to free the American hostages in Iran.

Mr. William A. Rusher
New York, New York
November 24, 1986 [15]

Dear Bill:

I'm sorry I didn't get to see you at the dinner but they kind of rushed me in and rushed me out so there was no time for this rusher to look for another Rusher.

Anyway thank you for your column. It did buck the tide and for that I thank you. I'm really upset by what so many of your contemporaries have done. D——n it yes we sold them a few spare parts and weapons but the stake was a contact that could give us a chance at a relationship with Iran and we were succeeding. A plus on the side was return of three hostages and could have been five if the media hadn't blown our cover. I don't know if we can put it back together. If we can't it's a great loss for all the Western world.

Nancy sends her love. Again thanks.

Sincerely,
Ron

Mr. Paul Trousdale
Santa Barbara, California
November 24, 1986 [16]

Dear Paul:

Thank you very much for your more than kind letter. You brightened my day considerably. I've felt like I've been swimming in a pool of sharks and there's blood in the water. But I console myself with thinking this too will end because what we did was the right and sensible thing to do. My real regret is that the irresponsible press may have made it impossible to continue doing it. We won't know the answer to that for a while.

You are right about "Star Wars," I'm not about to give up on that.
Again thanks. Nancy sends her best.

Sincerely,
Ron

――――――

President Reagan offers a geopolitical argument for improving relations with Iran.

Mr. Robert H. Adams
Valley Center, California
Circa December 1986 [17]

Dear Bob:

I hope you are all well and sound and out of the hospital. Thank you for your letter, you brightened my day. I'm pleased to know you agree that we should be trying to establish a base for relations with Iran. Better us than the Soviets who have 27 divisions on the Iranian border.

Nancy sends her love from both of us to Betty. Again thanks.

Sincerely,
Ron

――――――

President Reagan reports to a friend that he has requested that an independent counsel investigate the Iran-Contra matter.

Mr. Jaquelin H. Hume
San Francisco, California
December 3, 1986 [18]

Dear Jack:

Thanks for your kind letter and warm words. I'm truly grateful. Thanks too for sending the copy of your letter to Jerry. I know it will be helpful to him.

I keep telling myself the lynch mob will move on to other fields. They better because I'm not about to let them tighten the rope around my neck. I think I've taken some steps that should speed the process—asking for an independent prosecutor etc. Actually there is no case and no laws were broken or even bent. They just don't want to believe I've told them the "whole truth and nothing but the truth."

Thanks again for your letter and your faith. Love to Betty.

Sincerely,
Ron

――――――

President Reagan expresses his belief that selling arms to Iran had been helpful in efforts to resolve the hostage crisis.

Mrs. Helen Lawton
Dixon, Illinois
December 3, 1986 [19]

Dear Helen:

Thank you for your Thanksgiving greeting and your good wishes. Thanks too for your prayers, Nancy and I are both grateful.

The worst thing about this press uproar is that it prevented the remaining hostages from being released. Well we'll just keep trying.

Again our heartfelt thanks and we hope your Thanksgiving was a happy one.

Sincerely,
Dutch

———————

In an address to the nation on December 2, 1986, President Reagan said that the independent counsel would investigate allegations that the money from Iranian arms sales was diverted to the Nicaraguan Contras. The next seven letters were written shortly after the president's address. In them, Reagan reiterates his public stance that although he knew about the arms sales to Iran, he did not know about the transfer of funds to the Contras.

Mrs. William Loeb
Manchester, New Hampshire
December 4, 1986 [20]

Dear Nackey:

It was good to hear from you. This is just a line to bring you up to date. Evidently my announcement on TV Tuesday December 2nd had something of an impact. Some have said it put a ring around the whole affair. Our own polls had begun to show a turnaround on the previous Sunday and by Tuesday afternoon were up several points after a tremendous nosedive. I think most telling was my request for an "independent counsel"—we used to call them a "special prosecutor." They are the same thing—just the title is different.

So far we have only the two individuals who knew about the money transfer and didn't tell me. If the investigation reveals there were others, they too will go. Nackey we had something good going that could have established a relationship with some responsible people in Iran. It is a distortion to suggest we were dealing with the Khomeini—we could never do that. In fact the people we were talking to were risking their lives. Now all the publicity has destroyed what we were trying to do and may have destroyed those people as well. The business of the money transfer was none of our doing and a complete surprise to us.

Again thanks for writing. Nancy sends her best.

Sincerely,
Ron

Mr. Philip B. Crosby Sr.
Winter Park, Florida
December 8, 1986[21]

Dear Mr. Crosby:

Thank you very much for your letter and words of support. I'm most grateful.

I appreciate also your suggestion about getting a list of questions from Congress and supplying answers. Right now however we have a problem with that. I have given the Congress and the press all the information we have. That's why we are bringing in a special investigator. There are things about which we don't have the answers. I approved the plan of entering into dialogue with those Iranian individuals. When the leak led to the press exposure I told them all I knew. The money problem was not known by me and was discovered by the attorney general in his investigation. He told me what he had found out at 4:30 on a Monday afternoon. On Tuesday morning I told the leaders of Congress and the press what I had learned. Now there will be a House committee and a Senate committee as well as the special counsel searching for whatever additional facts there may be.

Again my thanks and thanks for your prayers.

Sincerely,
Ronald Reagan

The Honorable George Murphy
Palm Beach, Florida
December 9, 1986[22]

Dear Murph:

It was good to get your letter and your reminders of other sharpies in days long ago. In our Hollywood adventure with infiltration and subversion you and I picked up a lot of knowledge the pundits and the politicos don't have.

This whole fuss today is mind-boggling. For two weeks or more the media is acting like they dug up the whole thing. I have to remind myself they got the whole story from me. When our own investigation turned up the alleged money transfer by way of a Swiss bank account I went to the pressroom instantly with Ed Meese in tow. I broke the story and Ed took their questions for an hour. Now they are acting like it was their story and when am I going to come clean.

Well there seems to be a weakening of their ardor. In fact I understand a few have indicated they don't know how to get off the subject gracefully.

Again thanks and love to Bette. Nancy sends her love.

Sincerely,
Ron

Mr. Laurence W. Beilenson
Los Angeles, California
December 10, 1986 [23]

Dear Larry:

This is to say thank you for two letters—the handwritten one and the letter of December 2nd. As always you make good sense and I'm grateful to you.

You know Larry this whole thing is hard to understand. I didn't try to do business with the Khomeini. I know he thinks I'm Satan. But it was others in his government who got word to us they would like to see if we couldn't establish a relationship leading to the future. With the strategic importance of Iran I couldn't pass up this opportunity. They asked for a token arms sale to prove our sincerity. Our reply was $12 million worth of spare parts and anti-tank missiles. We told them we'd like concrete evidence of their anti-terrorism and that could be their effort to persuade the kidnappers in Beirut to free our hostages. By the way countries in Western Europe have sold almost $3 billion worth of weapons to Iran and more than $7 billion worth to Iraq. Our Communist friends (?) sold about $5½ billion worth to Iran and $24½ billion worth to Iraq. I don't think our sale tipped the military balance.

A leak by a radical weekly in Lebanon blew the cover. Because of the threat to the people we were dealing with I begged the press to lay off. They didn't of course. But then our attorney general looked into the whole thing to make sure there were no "smoking guns" and he turned up the supposed transfer of funds. I immediately went to the press and told them everything we had discovered about that. Now for going on three weeks the press, with the facts I gave them are building a case that I'm covering up.

But you are right about the Contras. I'm convinced the case has become a battle between those who oppose helping the Contras and we who want to help. As this goes on I think I'll point out that you can't be against the Contras without being for the Communist government of Nicaragua.

Well I'm running on and better close. Again thanks. Nancy sends her love.

Sincerely,
Ron

Mr. Joseph F. Banashek
Churchton, Maryland
December 22, 1986 [24]

Dear Mr. Banashek:

Thank you very much for your letter. Your line of thought was right on target. We had been contacted by some individuals who were risking their lives in doing so but who were looking ahead to what will happen when the Khomeini is gone.

As for the hostages they were not ransomed. Their captors have a relationship with Iran. We had been asked by those who contacted us to prove our sincerity by arranging a military sale. We in turn told them they could prove their sincerity about being antiterrorist by using their influence to free our hostages. They did so and we would have gotten all of them if the story hadn't broken in the press.

Again thanks and best regards.

Ronald Reagan

Mr. Warren Murray
Medford, New Jersey
December 22, 1986 [25]

Dear Mr. Murray:

Thank you very much for your wire and for giving me a chance to explain what our purpose was in this Iranian situation. I share your feeling about the present ruler of Iran and the treatment of our citizens several years ago and doubt I'll ever be able to forgive those responsible. At the same time I can't find it in my heart to blanket indict all the people of Iran. Nancy and I were guests of the Shah in Iran shortly before his overthrow. We had an extensive tour of the country and met many fine people, some of whom were later executed by the present regime.

Iran is of great strategic importance in the Middle East. We had been contacted by some individuals who wanted to establish a base for renewed relations between our two countries. I'm sure they are anticipating a new regime to succeed the present ruler whose health is rapidly declining. At any rate they were taking a great risk in contacting us and in proving their opposition to terrorism by getting the release of some of our hostages.

The news leak in Beirut which precipitated the press furor here in America has of course halted the progress we were making and may have caused the death or imprisonment of some of those who had contacted us.

Only time will tell whether we can reestablish relations and continue our effort to bring about peace between Iran and Iraq.

Again my thanks to you for your understanding and support.

Sincerely,
Ronald Reagan

Lt. Colonel William Rossiter, USMC (Ret.)
Sylmar, California
December 22, 1986 [26]

Dear Bill:

What a warm wave of nostalgia you raised with your welcome letter. It was good to hear from you and I'm most grateful for your expression of trust in me in spite of the howl raised by the press lynch mob. They seem to forget that when the leak came from a source in Iran about our attempt to establish a relationship with reasonable elements in that country, I went on the air and told exactly what we were doing and why. Then when we discovered there was a possibility of some financial shenanigans I told the press what we had uncovered and that we were trying to uncover the details—(we still are)—but they accuse me of trying to cover up. Bill they wouldn't know what they know now if I hadn't told them and I still don't know any more than I told them.

Well enough of that. It's more fun to remember those days when we wore purple and white jerseys. Again it was kind of you to write. Give my regards to your wife and very best wishes to you both.

Sincerely,
Dutch

In the midst of the Iran-Contra crisis, President Reagan underwent prostate surgery. In the next two letters he mentions his health and his optimism about weathering the scandal.

Mrs. Charles Grimm
Scottsdale, Arizona
January 15, 1987 [27]

Dear Marion:

From both Nancy and myself a heartfelt thanks for your cards, letter and prayers. And I might add, your generous words of support.

Our holidays were happy. We spent New Year's in California. I even got in a couple of rounds of golf. Then it was back to Washington and the hospital. I'm happy to say there wasn't a hitch, all the exams came out A plus and the surgery was a success. I'm back at the office now and feeling fine.

The only sour note is as you yourself pointed out—the media. They are like a lynch mob looking for a victim. I know they've chosen me but I don't think they can get the rope around my neck.

Nancy sends her best—as do I.

Sincerely,
Ron

Dr. George Hearne *
Eureka, Illinois
January 16, 1987 [28]

Dear George:

I have just received your letter of January 7 and want you to know I'm deeply grateful for your kind words, good wishes and your prayers.

---

* George Hearne is president of Eureka College, President Reagan's alma mater.

The health problem is no problem. I'm back in harness with little or no discomfort or disability and the examination came out with a finding of nothing wrong.

You are right about my adventure with the media. It is frustrating beyond description to hear and read their daily intimations that I am covering some deep dark secret. I'm the one who told them what they know and am waiting to find out just what did happen between here and Iran. Hopefully the special prosecutor (now termed the independent counsel) will get the facts for us. In the meantime we are going forward with an agenda of the things we still want to get resolved in these next two years.

Again thank you for writing as you did. Please give my regards to Mrs. Hearne.

Sincerely,
Ron

A January 21, 1987, letter to the editor of the Washington Post *by John Cooper (former senator from Kentucky and ambassador to India, Nepal, and East Germany) stated that President Reagan acted within his constitutional authority in the Iranian crisis. President Reagan was given a copy of the letter, at the bottom of which he wrote: "Let me have this back. RR." He expresses his appreciation to the author in the following letter.*

The Honorable John Sherman Cooper
Washington, D.C.
February 9, 1987 [29]

Dear Senator Cooper:

I have just been given a copy of your letter in the *Washington Post* [of] January 21 and want you to know how grateful I am for your well-reasoned, common-sense response to the unfounded speculation which has characterized so much of the press reporting of the Iran situation.

When the press got wind of our effort to open a dialogue with certain Iranian individuals both in and out of government I immediately told them and the public what we had been trying to accomplish. When I subsequently learned there might have been some manipulation of funds, which was not part of our plan I made what information I had available. I am still waiting to learn if this was indeed true and what the particulars might be. In short I am not engaged in any cover-up, indeed I'm anxious to have the truth known and will help in any way I can to learn what the facts are and to make them known.

Again my thanks to you for bringing a touch of sanity to what has become a diatribe of unfounded charges and name-calling.

Sincerely,
Ronald Reagan

On February 26, 1987, the Tower Commission released its unanimous report find-ing that the Iran initiative had been conducted in a casual fashion with little in-teragency vetting and without the full knowledge and participation of President Reagan.[30]

On March 4, President Reagan gave an address to the nation about the Tower Commission's findings. He said:

For the past three months, I've been silent on the revelations about Iran. . . . The reason I haven't spoken to you before now is this: You deserve the truth. . . . I appointed a Special Review Board, the Tower board, which took on the chore of pulling the truth together. . . . I've studied the Board's report. Its findings are honest, convincing, and highly critical; and I accept them. . . .

A few months ago I told the American people I did not trade arms for hostages. My heart and my best intentions still tell me that's true, but the facts and the evidence tell me it is not. As the Tower board reported, what began as a strategic opening to Iran deteriorated, in its implementation, into trading arms for hostages. This runs counter to my own beliefs, to adminis-tration policy, and to the original strategy we had in mind. . . .

It's clear from the Board's report . . . that I let my personal concern for the hostages spill over into the geopolitical strategy of reaching out to Iran. . . .

The Tower board wasn't able to find out what happened to the money [diverted to the Nicaraguan Contras], so the facts here will be left to the continuing investigations of the court-appointed Independent Counsel and the two congressional investigating committees. . . . As President, I cannot escape responsibility.

The next five letters were written shortly after President Reagan's March 4, 1987, address.

The Honorable Walter H. Annenberg
Rancho Mirage, California
March 11, 1987[31]

Dear Walter:

Thank you for your letter and the editorial. I'd missed that one and am most happy to have it. Somehow the lynch mob seems to have ridden off into the sunset. Oh now and then you hear a faint yelp but I think they've lost their rope.

Nancy sends her love and give Lee a happy hug for me.

Sincerely,
Ron

Lt. General Victor H. Krulak, USMC (Ret.)
San Diego, California
March 19, 1987[32]

Dear Brute:

God bless you and thank you for that column. I'm writing this on the day of my press conference and I know the sharks are circling. By the time you read this you'll know whether they drew blood.

I thought you'd like to know that our pollster took two polls right after the 12-minute speech. The first was only with people who saw and heard the speech for themselves. Only 33 percent had an unfavorable reaction. The second was with people who only knew about the speech from what they read or heard in the media. More than 60 percent of those were unfavorable. I guess that tells us something.

Well again thank you.

Sincerely,
Ron

Mr. J. F. Fowls
Port Washington, New York
March 23, 1987[33]

Dear Mr. Fowls:

Thank you very much for your letter and your generous words. It was kind of you to write as you did and I'm most grateful.

You are right about the possibility of success up until the story broke in the press. The leak came from an Iranian official hostile to those we were dealing with and by way of a radical weekly paper in Beirut. I urged our press to hold off because of possible danger to the people we were dealing with but the pack was off and barking. There has been no word from some of those I mentioned and I fear the worst.

Again my heartfelt thanks to you.

Sincerely,
Ronald Reagan

The Honorable Julio P. Matheu
Guatemala City, Guatemala
March 23, 1987[34]

Dear Mr. Matheu:

My heartfelt thanks for your kind letter and generous words. I remember our meeting in 1982 and am more than happy to hear from you.

I am hopeful that perhaps we have put the Iran affair behind us and can now get on with matters of greater importance such as the CBI* program and our relationship with our Central and South American neighbors. I believe our own people have begun to realize how much the whole affair was blown out of proportion by our press.

Again my thanks to you and very best wishes.

Sincerely,
Ronald Reagan

Colonel Barney Oldfield, USAF (Ret.)
Beverly Hills, California
March 30, 1987[35]

Dear Barney:

Thank you for your good review of my go-around with the Fourth Estate. I must confess I really enjoyed it. I think we've really got this thing behind us although I'm still waiting to find out where that extra money came from and where did it go. We didn't ask for it. Our price was $12 million and we got that. It appears that some of the "go-betweens" on the Iran side maybe upped our price and skimmed some profit off the top. We must not forget everything was taking place in the Middle East.

Again thanks and best regards.

Sincerely,
Ron

Once again President Reagan tells a friend that he had no knowledge of the diversion of funds to the Contras.

Lt. General Victor H. Krulak, USMC (Ret.)
San Diego, California
June 17, 1987[36]

Dear Brute:

Thank you again! Your column on the Ayatollah is magnificent and puts the whole situation in focus as a number of our congressmen have been unable to do.

And you are right on about another segment of the Congress—that endless hearing with its litany of hearsay that would never be allowed in a courtroom. I will say however, the latest item—the memo supposedly written by North and intended for me which has been termed a smoking gun, was never given to me. I've never seen it and thus was clearly telling the truth when I said I did not know of

---

* The Caribbean Basin Initiative was the Reagan administration's economic aid program for the Caribbean region and Central America.

any Iranian money over and above the purchase price of the arms shipment. Today I had the pleasure of answering a shouted question from the press that "there ain't no smoking gun."

You know, even here in Washington the hearings are being ignored by more and more people even though they are on TV live hour after hour.

Well thanks again. You have a circle of fans here in the West Wing.

Sincerely,

Ron

Testifying before a congressional committee charged with investigating the Iran-Contra scandal, Admiral John Poindexter said: "Although I was convinced that we could properly do it [divert funds to the Contras] and that the President would approve it if asked, I made a very deliberate decision not to ask the President so that I could insulate him from the decision and provide some future deniability for the President if it ever leaked."[37] *President Reagan writes about Poindexter's July 15, 1987, testimony in the letter below.*

Mr. John R. Stevenson
Elmira, New York
July 16, 1987[38]

Dear Mr. Stevenson:

Your letter of June 16 has only just now reached my desk—hence this tardy acknowledgment. I'm sure you know that as of yesterday July 15, Admiral Poindexter's testimony confirmed that I have been telling the truth for the last seven months. I did not know there was additional money from the arms sale or that it was being diverted to the Contras. He was the one who kept this information from me.

I look forward to making a statement when the investigation is closed. Then those "two-thirds of the people" you mentioned will know I have not been lying.

Have a nice day.

Ronald Reagan

President Reagan replies to a letter from a woman who says that her admiration for him grows as she watches the congressional investigations on television.

Mrs. Margaret M. Brock
Los Angeles, California
July 30, 1987[39]

Dear Margaret:

Thank you very much for your letter and your generous words. As you can understand, living back here where the lynch mob is howling day and night it is wonderful to get messages such as yours. You remind us there is a great, big, real, country outside of Washington where real people live.

I think we're nearing the end of the bloodletting and the mob has failed in its effort.

Nancy sends her love and so do I. Thanks again and bless you.

Sincerely,
Ron

––––––––

President Reagan admits to a friend that the image of the United States has been hurt by the Iran-Contra affair, but he expresses confidence that the American people will see the scandal for the circus that it was.

Lt. General Victor H. Krulak, USMC (Ret.)
San Diego, California
July 30, 1987[40]

Dear Brute:

As usual you made me homesick with your mention of a breakfast at Owl's Nest. And as usual you gave my spirit a lift with your column. There is no question but that our image worldwide has been tarnished. I'm going to do everything I can to put the shine back on but only with practical and necessary programs and deeds—not make-up and theatrics. I'm certain of one thing, the American people helped by people like you are seeing this circus in its true light.

Your son was here in the Oval Office just the other day and we're proud to have him on board. He's a fine officer and human being and looks like his father.

Again thanks for the column. I'm circulating it as usual, here in the West Wing.

Sincerely,
Ron

––––––––

Six months after the release of the Tower Commission's report, President Reagan tells one of his old gubernatorial campaign advisers that the NSC has been reformed. He expresses frustration with misconceptions about his role in the Iran-Contra matter.

Mr. Stuart K. Spencer
Irvine, California
August 3, 1987[41]

Dear Stu:

Thanks very much for your helpful letter, and it is helpful. We're not too far apart on what should be said. I'll be able to say we have changed and are changing certain things. For example I appointed the Tower Commission to study the entire workings of the NSC. We have now reformed NSC according to their recommendations. We are also working with the Hill right now on intelligence and covert matters. That hasn't been easy because they really were out to have a lynching. Nevertheless I think we have something going there that will smack very much of bipartisanship.

I do think Stu that a couple of real misconceptions must be wiped out. They have been firmly planted in the public mind by constant repetition. I was not doing business with the Ayatollah, for example, but with individuals who could have been executed if they were exposed. Another is that I was not trading arms for hostages but as it developed Cap and George* were right when they argued that if our arrangement ever became known, it would look like trading. That's what happened.

Nancy sends her love.

Sincerely,
Ron

After a summer of televised congressional testimony on White House involvement in the Iran-Contra affair, President Reagan writes that the whole process led the lynch mob back to the statements he made when the Iranian initiative was first publicized.

Mr. Laurence W. Beilenson
Los Angeles, California
August 5, 1987 [42]

Dear Larry:

It was good to hear from you and I'm pleased and grateful for your words of support.

This has been quite a carnival back here and it had quite a lynch mob flavor. I knew every minute who was the intended lynchee. But somehow truth prevailed and now that the hearings are over I can talk again.

You know Larry when the leak about the covert operation brought all the press attention I was first to learn that somehow the arms sale had brought extra money which went into a Swiss bank account which had some connection with the Contras. Within 18 hours of learning this I met with the congressional leadership and after them the press and told them what I had learned. I also told them I was appointing a bipartisan commission and an independent counsel to look into the situation. Somehow that was overlooked and we had the eight-month circus which

---

* Caspar Weinberger, secretary of defense, and George Shultz, secretary of state.

in a way finally came up with what I'd already told them. The wondrous ways of Washington!

On another subject Larry I can't help but say the view of the Screen Actors Guild from 3,000 miles away is not very pleasant these days. I was always so proud of the guild and you had a lot to do with that but somehow that image is tarnished.

Well again, it was good to hear from you. Nancy sends her love.

Sincerely,
Ron

CHAPTER FIFTEEN

The Americas

U.S. RELATIONS with its neighbors were among the first foreign policy issues that Reagan addressed when he became a national spokesman on behalf of conservative ideas in the late 1970s. He consistently argued that the Soviet Union, through Cuba and on its own, sought to expand its influence in the Americas and was determined to undermine the position of the United States in the Western Hemisphere. He argued that Soviet and Communist infiltration could be countered most effectively through closer ties among all of the states from Canada down to Argentina and Chile. U.S. economic aid and support for democracy were essential to making the ties durable. In 1979, he proposed a North American Accord for Canada, Mexico, and the United States that would enhance economic and political cooperation.

Reagan's policies as president toward North and South America were consistent with the analysis he put forth in the 1970s. By his fourth month in the White House Reagan had cancelled economic aid to the Sandinista National Liberation Front (FSLN) in Nicaragua because of its assistance to rebels in El Salvador, a country the United States was supporting. Reagan was also supporting the Contras, the resistance force in Nicaragua, early in his presidency. Although the administration's policies toward Central America would be fiercely contested in the United States, and were sometimes blocked through legislation like the amendments put forth by Congressman Edward Boland (D-Massachusetts) that cut off aid to the Contras, President Reagan persisted in seeking ways to support forces he thought opposed communism and that could become democratic.

There was not much democracy in Latin America when Reagan assumed office in 1981; 13 of Latin America's major countries were considered free. By 1988, only two Latin American countries, Cuba and Suriname, were not free.[1] President Reagan was cautious in taking credit for the regime changes across the continent, but on February 20, 1986, while touring Grenada, a country to which the United States had sent forces more than two years earlier, he said:

[W]e are in a way all Americans in this hemisphere—from the North Slope of Alaska to the tip of South America, these are known as the Americas—and it's our birthright to live in freedom. It is our heritage. . . . Just in the last 5 years, Brazil, Argentina, Guatemala, Honduras, Bolivia, Uruguay, El Salvador, and, yes, Grenada have returned to democracy. Today 27 of 33 independent countries, countries with 90 percent of this hemisphere's population, are democratic or in transition to democracy. And we won't be satisfied until all the people of the Americas have joined us in the warm sunshine of liberty and justice.

President Reagan was criticized for putting geopolitics ahead of social and economic considerations in his policies toward Latin America. He responded that by supporting economic assistance measures like the Caribbean Basin Initiative and by promoting transitions to democracy, the United States was working to improve the lives of people all over the region. The letters in this chapter show him grappling with the political, social, and military dimensions of U.S. relations with its neighbors.

THE CARIBBEAN AND CENTRAL AMERICA

In November 1903, Panama declared its independence from Colombia and signed the Hay-Bunau-Varilla Treaty with the United States. The treaty granted the United States sovereign rights in a zone and surrounding area in which the United States would build and administer a canal. The canal opened in 1914. The United States was to defend the canal "in perpetuity . . . as if it were sovereign." Dissatisfaction with the status of the canal grew in Panama in the 1960s, and resulted in bilateral negotiations to revise the 1903 agreement. A declaration of principles, signed by U.S. Secretary of State Henry Kissinger and Panamanian Foreign Minister Juan Antonio Tack, was a product of the negotiations and set in motion talks that resulted in President Jimmy Carter and General Omar Torrijos Herrera, the leader of Panama, concluding two treaties to hand control of the canal over to Panama. The United States Senate ratified the Treaty Concerning the Permanent Neutrality and Operation of the Panama Canal on March 16, 1978, and the Panama Canal Treaty on April 18, 1978. The agreements went into effect on October 1, 1979.

Under the neutrality treaty, the United States retained the right to defend the canal against any interference that would violate the neutrality of the canal for use by ships. In case of an emergency, U.S. and Panamanian warships had the right to go to the head of the line. Beginning in 2000, defense and operation of the canal would be transferred to Panama.

When Ronald Reagan finished his second term as governor of California and turned his attention to speaking and writing about his views on national policy issues in January 1975, he became a prominent opponent of the negotiations on the Panama

Canal. In the late 1970s Reagan was declaring in speeches throughout the United States: "We bought it [the Panama Canal], we paid for it, it is sovereign U.S. territory and we should keep it."[2] *He expressed his opposition to the treaties throughout the 1970s. Reagan argued that the treaties were being concluded in the absence of a coherent Latin American policy by the United States; that the agreements did not ensure that ships from all nations would have unhindered passage through the canal; that the agreements might encourage Soviet interest in the region; and that under Panamanian control, the canal might not be available for American transit in a national security crisis.*[3]

Panama continued to be an important issue during Reagan's presidency, most notably during the grand jury indictments of General Manuel Noriega in 1988. In seeking ways to oust the Panamanian leader, President Reagan laid much of the groundwork for the U.S. invasion of Panama under President George H. W. Bush.

Written during the late 1970s when he was speaking extensively about his opposition to the treaties, the next three letters are consistent with Reagan's public declarations about the negotiations between the United States and Panama.

Bob
Washington, D.C.
Circa mid-1970s[4]

Dear Bob:

Thanks very much for the enclosures and information on the negotiations. I can't escape a feeling that we may be bailing out a dictator who could very well be ousted if he has to back down. And there are a half dozen American banks who could be holding an empty bag if a new regime in Panama refused to recognize the debt piled up by the general.

I've never taken a position that we shouldn't negotiate; only that we shouldn't do it under a threat of violence and we shouldn't negotiate our right to ownership of the canal or sovereign rights in the zone. We've modified the treaty in two previous negotiations but we've always refused to discuss ownership and sovereignty.

Incidentally, a committee in Florida, organized to oppose the giveaway, coined quite a slogan—"There is no Panama Canal—there is an American Canal in Panama."

Anyway, Bob, I think there is much to be gained by standing firm. Surely we should be aware of the sudden influx of Soviet personnel and money into Panama, the opening of a bank, etc.

Again thanks. I hope we'll see each other soon. Give my regards to your good wife.

Sincerely,
Ron

Senator Barry Goldwater
Circa late 1970s[5]

Dear Barry:

Your two letters arrived with the enclosures. I was happy to have the transcript of your debate in which you "done good." Sol* is a charming fellow but d—n it he's a smoothie and slides over some sticky points with what is considerably less than the truth.

As I said in my previous letter, I can understand why you couldn't know that like you I am for continued negotiations. I'm just against these particular treaties. But that wasn't very widely reported.

The memorandum you sent me is brilliant. I hope every senator has a copy of that one because the writer really exposed the frailty and ambiguity of these treaties.

Thanks again and best regards.

Ron

P.S. I'm enclosing a letter to the president sent by a solid citizen you may know. Thought you'd enjoy it.

Mr. Denison Kitchel
La Jolla, California
Circa late 1970s[6]

Dear Denny:

Enclosed [is] your magnificent manuscript and my heartfelt gratitude for having been allowed to read it. The next person to read it should be Jimmy Carter who is obviously getting his history from those middle echelon State Department types you described so well.

Denny may I bring you up to date a little on my own position? First of all I did not set out to make this an issue in last year's campaign. In fact while I knew the negotiations were going on I was confident they wouldn't get anyplace because of the 38 senators who had signed the pledge not to ratify the treaty. It never entered my mind to even mention the canal.

But, as you know, in New Hampshire you don't make speeches you go to town hall meetings and answer questions. I'll never forget the first meeting and the question from the floor about the canal. The audience looked at the questioner as if he'd announced the end of the world, then back at me as if to say, "what's he talking about." I told them about the negotiations and gave my own opinion as to what we should do. This experience was repeated time after time both there and in Florida

---

* Ambassador Sol M. Linowitz was one of President Carter's negotiators for the Panama Canal treaties. The other negotiator was Ambassador Ellsworth Bunker.

until it did become an issue—made so by the people. Then in Texas Jerry* made the great mistake of trying to deny it and the feathers hit the fan.

Well to get back to my position; I've never advocated slamming the door. I believe there is much we can do to correct things that are wrong and improve relations with Panama without bailing out. I've even kicked around the idea in my own head that possibly we could internationalize the canal; form a quasi-governmental corporation including every country of North and South America as partners participating in the ownership and protection of the canal. This would take care of the sovereignty issue because Panama as a partner would be providing the land (for a fee) and we would have provided the canal. So far this is just brainstorming but I'm greatly impressed by your own conclusions that we are presently on a wrong path but with a little courage there is a right path to accomplish what needs to be done.

Again my thanks to you and start the presses! We need this book now.

Nancy sends her best and give our love to May.

Sincerely,
Ron

On February 4, 1988, General Manuel Noriega, the leader of Panama, was indicted by federal grand juries in Florida for violating racketeering and drug laws. Despite an American promise not to extradite him, Noriega refused an offer of asylum in Spain. On April 8, President Reagan invoked the International Emergency Economic Powers Act of 1977, freezing all Panamanian assets in the United States and prohibiting payments to the government of Panama. The Reagan administration was unable to persuade Noriega to leave power. In December 1989 President George H. W. Bush ordered an invasion of Panama. Noriega surrendered and was brought to the United States to stand trial for drug trafficking, money laundering, and racketeering. He was convicted and given a 40-year prison sentence in 1992.

In the third paragraph of the letter below, President Reagan writes that the United States was supporting domestic opposition to General Noriega and would continue to do so. In the typed letter that apparently was sent, this paragraph was altered and the sentence about supporting Panamanian opposition to Noriega was deleted.

1SG Timothy O. Masterson, USA
APO Miami, Florida
Circa May–June 1988 [7]

Dear Sergeant Masterson,

I'm sorry to be so late in answering your letter of May 13. It seems as if it sometimes takes a while before mail makes its way to my desk. I have only just received your letter.

----

* President Gerald R. Ford.

Sergeant Masterson I share your opinion of the men you lead. Nothing in this job of mine makes me more proud than I am of the men and women in uniform in our military today. We've never had better. At the same time nothing has frustrated me more than the situation in Panama which you wrote about.

Let me explain a bit of what we're up against. First with regard to the indictment the U.S. Attorney got from a Miami grand jury; under the constitution of Panama a Panamanian cannot be extradited from Panama. We want the present military dictator out of Panama and we're willing to drop the indictment if he'd leave the country. We instituted some measures we thought would arouse the civilian opposition to organize against him. That didn't happen although there seemed to be a start but it faded away. We're not through yet and will continue our efforts.

Yes I considered what you have suggested and don't think I wouldn't like to. Unfortunately we have a situation with all of our Latin American friends. We haven't been able to call them friends very long. Dating back to an earlier time they have memories of "The Great Colossus of the North." We've made great progress in changing that image and they are grateful for our help and friendship but they still let us know they don't want our help if it means action by our military—anything but that.

I know your frustration and share it but can only say we haven't given up.

Thanks for writing and best regards.

Sincerely,
Ronald Reagan

The United States was involved deeply in the revolutionary change that swept through Central America in the late 1970s and 1980s. El Salvador and Nicaragua were at the center of U.S. policy toward the region. In El Salvador, on October 15, 1979, reform-oriented junior military officers overthrew the government of General Carlos Humberto Romero. The junta of three civilians and two military personnel pledged a transition to democracy and economic and social reforms, but was unable to bring order to the country. On December 4, 1980, four churchwomen of the American Roman Catholic Church were murdered near San Salvador. The next day, the Carter administration temporarily suspended economic and military aid to El Salvador. A few days later a new government was formed under the leadership of Christian Democrat José Napoleón Duarte. In January 1981, the Carter administration resumed delivery of military aid to El Salvador amid charges that Cubans and Nicaraguans were providing arms to antigovernment forces in the country. During the second month of Reagan's presidency, the State Department announced that the United States would send $25 million in military aid and 20 more advisers to El Salvador. Aid to the country would increase substantially during the Reagan administration.

The assassination of Pedro Joaquín Chamorro, the editor of La Prensa *and a* *prominent political moderate, on January 10, 1978, invigorated the Nicaraguan insurgent movement led by the Marxist-oriented Sandinistas. The Carter administration responded by supporting multilateral mediation efforts. On July 17, 1979, the Sandinistas overthrew the regime of Anastasio Somoza Debayle. As the Sandinistas consolidated power, the Carter administration was unable to build a relationship with the new regime or foster a more moderate anti-Somoza coalition in the country. The Reagan administration, however, was quick to take measures against the Sandinistas. On April 1, 1981, it cancelled $15 million in economic aid to Nicaragua in response to Sandinista support for the rebels in El Salvador. In May 1982, Nicaragua signed a $166 million aid package with the Soviet Union. In the fall, the Reagan administration admitted to providing modest support for the resistance forces in Nicaragua. On December 8, Congressman Edward Boland (D-Massachusetts) placed an attachment on the spending bill, which prohibited military operations in Nicaragua. In the years that followed, the Reagan administration would run afoul of restrictions on aid to the Contras put forth by Boland. This would lead to the Iran-Contra scandal, which constituted the diversion of profits from arms sales to the Iranians to support the Contras.*

In the following letters Reagan discusses the Carter administration's policies toward the Central American countries, seeks to elucidate his own policies during his White House years, and laments domestic opposition to his efforts.

A month before the Sandinistas were to overthrow the Somoza dynasty, Reagan replies to a letter from the last U.S. ambassador to Cuba.[8]

> The Honorable Earl E. T. Smith
> Palm Beach, Florida
> June 29, 1979[9]

Dear Earl:

Just a line to acknowledge your letter and to thank you for the attached article.

You are absolutely right about Nicaragua. It just seems to be a repeat of history: first in Cuba and then very much like a repeat of what we did in Iran. For someone who wanted to spread sunshine on the earth, he sure is creating a lot of tragedy.

Nancy sends her best and give our regards to Lesly.

> Sincerely,
> Ron

Throughout the late 1970s Reagan repeatedly charged that the Carter administration lacked a long-range strategy toward Latin America and had stood idly by as Communist forces infiltrated the Caribbean and Central America. In a letter he wrote before *assuming the presidency, Reagan makes these points and also invokes the Monroe Doctrine as a guide for U.S. foreign policy toward the region.**

Mr. Thomas D. Graham Sr.
1980 [10]

Dear Mr. Graham Sr.:

I was happy to receive your letter and to know that you had received mine in spite of that lengthy delay. You and I have something in common—I, too, was a Democrat and felt in 1962 that my party had left me. Well, actually, I felt that way a few years earlier but didn't get around to reregistering until '62.

You asked three questions and I am happy to answer all three. (1) No, my cabinet will not be composed of members of the eastern establishment. I am going to look for people who don't want a job in government but for whom such a job will actually be a step down—people who will be willing to sacrifice in order to serve their country. (2) I have no connection whatsoever with Nelson Rockefeller† or eastern bankers. (3) I believe that this administration has very dangerously allowed a Communist buildup both in the Caribbean and in Central America. I think it is time for us to adopt a long-range policy with contingency plans for what we will do in the event of certain emergencies. It should be aimed at strengthening our alliances here in this hemisphere to the point that we once again present the united front in defense of freedom. In other words, we need a return to something like the Monroe Doctrine.

I thank you very much for your willingness to support me and am very proud to have that support.

Sincerely,
Ronald Reagan

In 1982, the year Reagan wrote this letter, his administration had substantially increased economic and military assistance to El Salvador.

Reverend F. Andrew Carhartt
Boulder, Colorado
March 12, 1982 [11]

Dear Reverend Carhartt:

I can understand your concern about the situation in Central America and yes even your misunderstanding of what we are trying to accomplish there at the request of the El Salvadoran government.

---

* The doctrine expressed by President James Monroe in 1823 warned against European interference in the Americas and declared the United States the hemispheric hegemon.

† A four-term governor of New York State, Nelson A. Rockefeller unsuccessfully sought the Republican nomination for president in 1960, 1964, and 1968. He served as President Gerald Ford's vice president from 1974 to 1977.

I have no way of knowing the reliability of your informants but I do know that a very sophisticated worldwide propaganda campaign has been at work for a long time. May I point out that the Carter administration was convinced of the need to give economic aid and military supplies to the government of El Salvador and we are continuing that policy on the basis of the information we have.

Reverend Carhartt I'm sure you must realize that the person holding the job that is now mine has access to facts that are known to only a very few specialists whose job is to obtain facts upon which a president can determine policy. I am completely convinced that what we are doing is not only in the best interest of the United States but of the free world as well.

We have no intention of sending American combat forces there. You spoke of the lesson of Vietnam. In my view the immorality of Vietnam was asking young men to fight and die for a cause our government had no intention of winning.

Sincerely,
Ronald Reagan

In a letter dated March 1, 1982, a concerned Republican loyalist wrote to President Reagan: "We made a mistake in Nicaragua and we are about to make the same one in El Salvador. We should not get involved in supplying weapons to a government that to all but the very naïve is corrupt and a human rights violator. . . . We were wrong to supply Somoza in Nicaragua. . . . Al Haig [the secretary of state] is a Good Man, but not right 100 percent of the time, only 99 percent. We can't keep an unpopular Government in power by virtue of the arms we send them."

Mr. Peter M. Rosenberg
Tampa, Florida
March 31, 1982 [12]

Dear Mr. Rosenberg:

Thanks for your letter and for your support. I am most grateful.

May I beg to differ on one or two points in your letter. If memory serves me correctly the Carter administration did not support the Somoza regime in Nicaragua but let it fall because of its record on human rights among other things. It fell to our administration to establish relations with the new revolutionary government which we did. This was done even though Castro and a Soviet representative were present at the inaugural and proclaimed Nicaragua to be the first Communist state on the American mainland.

We provided a sizeable grant in aid to the new government. But then withheld a large portion of it when the radicals threw out their own partners in the revolution and did indeed make their government totalitarian. The government had promised us it would not deliver Cuban and Soviet weapons to the guerillas in El Salvador. We discovered they were in constant violation of that pledge. This triggered our shut-off of funds.

Support economically of El Salvador had begun under the previous administration because of the moderate nature of the Duarte government. While it is true there is a far-right fringe down there the guerillas are supported, trained and armed by Cuba and the Soviet Union.

I think yesterday's election proved our contentions that the guerillas do not have the sympathy of the people and that the Duarte government does have their confidence.

Since the press has hinted at so much that isn't true let me assure you we have no plans, or thought of sending combat forces anywhere in the world.

Again thanks for your letter.

Sincerely,
Ronald Reagan

President Reagan thanks a columnist and friend for his column defending the administration's policy toward El Salvador.

Lt. General Victor H. Krulak, USMC (Ret.)
San Diego, California
March 29, 1983 [13]

Dear Brute:

Thank you for your column and for sending it. I'm grateful to the few of you in the world of journalism who are countering the drumbeat of propaganda against El Salvador and our defense buildup.

I believe we are operating within the principles you laid down. Our economic help is three times greater than our military aid. As you know we trained three battalions here and all of them comprise the backbone of the government forces.

Thanks again and I miss Owl's Nest.

Sincerely,
Ron

In January 1983, the Reagan administration announced that it was lifting the ban on arms sales to Guatemala imposed by the Carter administration. U.S.–Guatemala relations are mentioned in the handwritten version of the letter to Robert R. McMillan, which is produced below, but this section is deleted in the version typed on White House stationery.

Mr. Robert R. McMillan
New York, New York
June 21, 1983 [14]

Dear Mr. McMillan:

Thank you very much for your letter regarding Central America. We are in complete agreement about the absolute necessity of providing military and economic aid not only to El Salvador but to other countries there as well.

We are having problems with some in Congress who refuse to see any relationship between what is going on there and our own national security. I am however encouraged that we may be able to do better. Last Friday I met with a group of congressmen just returned from a fact-finding trip to El Salvador and Nicaragua. They are converted totally to the need for us to do more and are convinced the revolution is aimed at all of Central America. Maybe with their help we can get some action.

By the way we are presently training several Guatemalan officers and have a request in Congress for additional funding so we can increase the number. We have not made any public statements about this because of a request by the government there that we not do so.

It's an uphill fight but we must have more success than we've had in letting the American people know what the stakes are. We need more public support than we've had.

Best regards,
Ronald Reagan

On May 25, 1983, rebels in San Salvador killed Lt. Commander Albert A. Schaufelberger, the U.S. military adviser to the government of El Salvador. The next day a friend of Schaufelberger's wrote to President Reagan. He characterized his friend as a great soldier and American and enclosed a copy of a postcard that Schaufelberger had sent him. "There are some signs of an ongoing war," Schaufelberger wrote, "but the overwhelming impression is that life goes on. . . . Barring something stupid by the U.S. Congress, the government forces should win—they're improving every day."

Mr. James F. Wright
Carmel, California
June 21, 1983 [15]

Dear Mr. Wright:

Unlike you I had never met Al Schaufelberger but I share your sorrow. I knew of him of course and his record—one of the best, and I feel a great sense of rage at the cowardly terrorists who took his life. You are right, our way of life is under attack and we cannot falter in the fight but I bleed for those fine young Americans who man the ramparts.

I phoned Al's mother and father and to you his friend I offer my heartfelt sympathy.

Sincerely,
Ronald Reagan

In a speech before the Organization of American States* on February 24, 1982, President Reagan announced the Caribbean Basin Initiative. The plan increased economic assistance and tax incentives for U.S. investment in Central America and the Caribbean and expanded duty-free entry of the region's exports for up to 12 years.

> Mr. Gary A. Anderson
> Chandler, Arizona
> June 24, 1983 [16]

Dear Mr. Anderson:

Thank you for your letter, your generous words and your suggestions. We see eye to eye on a number of issues. You'll be pleased to know that our Caribbean plan which we're waiting for Congress to pass is aimed at improving the economy and widening trade with 28 countries in the Caribbean and Central America. About three-quarters of our help to El Salvador is nonmilitary and aimed at helping improve the living standard of their people.

We are also engaged in a worldwide effort to teach the developing nations about democracy, how it works and how to practice self-rule. We are also expanding an exchange system among students. I know many of those things don't get much press attention and that's too bad.

I'm very sorry to hear about your illness. You will be in my thoughts and prayers. Again my thanks for your letter and very best wishes. God bless you.

> Sincerely,
> Ronald Reagan

During the visit of Pope John Paul II to El Salvador on March 6, 1983, Provisional President Álvaro Magaña Borja announced that his country would hold elections in 1983 instead of 1984. Three months later, President Magaña met with President Reagan at the White House to discuss the upcoming presidential elections, government and judicial reform, the military situation in El Salvador, and the Contadora Initiative to seek resolution of the crises in Central America. [17]

In the letter below, President Reagan provides his impression of Marina de Magaña, the wife of the president of El Salvador, and recounts what she said about meeting the pope.

---

* Formed in 1948, the Organization of American States is a regional organization whose mission is to promote peace, security, territorial and political sovereignty of member states, and to foster collaboration among them. As of 1983, the year of Reagan's letter, membership included 31 states from North and South America.

Colonel Barney Oldfield, USAF (Ret.)
Beverly Hills, California
July 7, 1983 [18]

Dear Barney:

I'm glad you met Mrs. Magaña. She was here with her husband—the president on a visit just recently. I was very impressed with both of them. She is so warm and outgoing and left a letter which was heartwarming.

Just outside the Oval Office she hugged me and said she loved the Pope and me but couldn't hug the pope.

Congratulations and thanks for what you are doing with that foundation. Things like that are what will really win the wars in Latin America. I like doing it through the OAS.

My best to Vada.

Ron

———————

In a letter dated July 28, 1983, Ezra Taft Benson, president of the Mormon Church's Council of Twelve Apostles, wrote to President Reagan and recounted his experience in Cuba as secretary of agriculture during the Eisenhower administration. He reported that during the trip President Fulgencio Batista told him that Fidel Castro was a Communist. He also wrote: "This entire situation, I believe, could have been avoided in Cuba and Central America had we reaffirmed the courageous policy of President Monroe. . . . To the Mormon people all of North and South America is Zion. In other words, it's a choice land, choice above all other lands."

President Reagan agrees that the Western Hemisphere is Zion, but says that he has learned not to invoke the Monroe Doctrine in discussions with leaders in the region.

The Honorable Ezra Taft Benson
Salt Lake City, Utah
August 4, 1983 [19]

Dear Friend:

Thank you very much for [your] letter and for your generous words. I'm most grateful. Believe me I keep very much in mind the memory of those days when so many were hailing Castro as a liberator. I sometimes wonder if powerful papers like the *New York Times* can ever find it within themselves to front page an admission that they made a tragic mistake. That of course brings up the question of whether it was a mistake in their eyes or whether they approve of the final result.

There is however one thing I must say to you with regard to the Monroe Doctrine. On my visit with the leaders of several South and Central American countries I eased into that subject somewhat gingerly. Without exception they rejected the use of the term. Apparently it is interpreted as "big brother" doing for them what they are unable to do for themselves. There is no question about their wanting help but it must come under a different title which recognizes them as partners not dependents.

I'm encouraged by gains we've made in winning their confidence and friendship and I intend to keep building on these gains. I too believe these continents stretching from the South Pole to the North Pole are Zion.

Thank you again for writing as you did.

Sincerely,
Ron

Reagan replies to the former head of the Reagan for President Oregon State Committee who wrote to say that former secretary of state Henry Kissinger's appointment to head a bipartisan commission on Central America gave the impression that Kissinger would be in charge of the State Department.[20] She added that some Oregon voters were uneasy about the appointment.

Mrs. Diana Evans
Salem, Oregon
August 4, 1983[21]

Dear Diana:

Thanks for your letter and I appreciate very much your concern. I was aware when the appointment was made that flack would be flying. We didn't make the decision lightly. I say, we, because all of us here including the secretary of state, Judge Clark, Jeane Kirkpatrick and others really round-tabled this. A lot of attention was given to what the reception would be abroad as well as at home.

This commission will not be involved in our Central American policy. Its mission is to come up with a long-range plan for our relations with our neighbors to the south and how we can help in eliminating the economic and social problems that contribute to their unrest. Considering all these things I believe we made a right choice.

Thank you for writing as you did, I'm truly grateful. I promise you we'll keep things in line.

Nancy sends her best.

Sincerely,
Ron

The presence of 55 U.S. military trainers in El Salvador elicited a great outcry of opposition from those who opposed the Reagan administration's Central America policy. And yet, Reagan writes, the policy suggestions of a Democratic legislator received little critical attention. In the letter below, President Reagan points out the double standard.

General Andrew P. O'Meara, USA (Ret.)
Arlington, Virginia
August 18, 1983 [22]

Dear General O'Meara:

Thanks very much for your letter and for your commonsense suggestion. I must admit it is frustrating to see a Senator Dodd* able to actually claim he would send in armed forces and still be hailed as a peace advocate while I'm a warmonger because we have 55 trainers in El Salvador.

General I am faced with a problem however much I might agree with your suggestion. Our friends to the south have let me know in no uncertain terms they need our help, our trainers, our weapons but we must not send our armed forces. The old memories of "gunboat diplomacy" are still with them. On his most recent visit President Magaña told me they must do the job with their manpower.

Again my thanks to you and very best regards.

Sincerely,
Ronald Reagan

In March 1979, Maurice Bishop led a coup that ousted the Prime Minister Eric Gairy and suspended Grenada's constitution. After rejecting a leadership challenge from Bernard Coard, his Marxist-oriented deputy, Bishop was placed under house arrest on October 13, 1983. On October 19, supporters freed Bishop, but he was soon brutally killed by his opponents. On October 21, the Organization of East Caribbean States, along with Jamaica and Barbados, decided to intervene if the United States would help.† The request was formally made to the United States the following day, and President Reagan promptly decided to send a military force to evacuate nearly 1,000 American medical students and to help restore order to the island. President Reagan was also concerned about the security implications of the situation in Grenada. The government of Grenada claimed that the airstrip being built with the help of Cuban workers and military personnel was for tourism. American overhead photography showed, however, that a 10,000-foot runway capable of receiving heavy cargo aircraft was being constructed. President Reagan and his national security team speculated that the So-

---

* Senator Christopher Dodd (D-Connecticut).
† At the time of the Grenada crisis, the membership of the OECS included the following: Antigua and Barbuda, Grenada, Montserrat, St. Kitts-Nevis, St. Lucia, St. Vincent and the Grenadines, and Dominica. The organization voted unanimously for the intervention. Grenada did not vote because its government had dissolved.

viet Union and Cuba might be planning to use Grenada as a new base in the Caribbean for launching subversive activities in Central and South America.

Together with countries from the Caribbean, U.S. military forces intervened in Grenada on October 25. The mission was a success. Two days after the intervention the American medical students were returned to the United States. Lives were lost during the mission. Several dozen Cubans and Grenadians as well as 19 Americans were killed. On November 9, the Grenadian governor general Sir Paul Scoon appointed an interim government. On December 3, 1984, Herbert Blaize was elected prime minister.

In the following letters, President Reagan discusses various aspects of the operation, including the deliberations and preparations of his cabinet and the Joint Chiefs of Staff, and considers the reaction of the American media and public to the intervention.

An American medical student evacuated from Grenada sent President Reagan a mailgram: "I extend to you my most sincere thanks for the action taken on our behalf in rescuing us from the potential hostage situation that existed in Grenada. The very fact that I am here today with my family proves that you accomplished your primary objective of saving the lives of Americans living there. I can reassure you that what my eyes saw actualized your insight into the grave effects that the completion of the airstrip would have had upon the free world."

Six days after the intervention, President Reagan replies.

> Miss Rosemarie Classi
> Ozone Park, New York
> October 31, 1983 [23]

Dear Miss Classi:

Thank you very much for your wire. I can't tell you how much it meant to me to learn of your willingness to endorse the action we have taken. There seems to be a concerted effort on the part of much of the media to downgrade the need for our rescue mission, which they insist on calling an invasion.

I share your feeling about those young men of the 82nd Airborne and the 75th Rangers. Our country can be very proud. Let me tell you it was a long night here in Washington as we waited for word that you were all safe.

Again thanks.

> Sincerely,
> Ronald Reagan

Responding to a letter of support from the American ambassador to Switzerland, President Reagan writes that after the operation, documents and weapons were found that linked Grenada to the Soviet Union and some of its allies around the world.

The Honorable John Davis Lodge
Bern, Switzerland
November 17, 1983 [24]

Dear John:

It was good to hear from you and I'm most grateful for your generous words.

You are absolutely correct in what you are saying about Grenada. The people met our troops with open arms, flowers and fruit. We brought home a treasure trove of documents—Soviet, Cuban, Libyan and even North Korean plus enough Soviet and Cuban weapons to fill an airplane hangar at Andrews Air Force Base.[25]

The people here have approved the operation by an overwhelming majority.

Nancy sends her best and from both of us love to Francesca.

Sincerely,
Ron

President Reagan writes that the fate of the American medical students in St. George's, Grenada, was the main reason for his administration's decision to intervene.

Morris Alpert, M.D.
Bay Shore, New York
November 28, 1983 [26]

Dear Dr. Alpert:

Thank you very much for your letter of October 29. I'm sorry to be so late in answering but it sometimes takes a while for mail to reach my desk.

It was kind of you to write as you did and your generous words did much to counter the criticism we've received from some.

The students of St. George's were our first and main concern and we're grateful to God for his help in making our mission a success.

Thanks again.

Sincerely,
Ronald Reagan

In his reply to a member of the Freedom of Information Committee, President Reagan explains why he initially restricted press coverage of the Grenada mission.

Mr. Bill Seymour
Morgantown, West Virginia
November 28, 1983 [27]

Dear Mr. Seymour:

I'm sorry to be so late in answering your letter of October 27 but it takes a while for mail to reach my desk, particularly so when a trip to Asia is factored in. Thank you for giving me a chance to respond to the press criticism regarding our rescue mission in Grenada.

First let me say I have not retreated from my belief in a free press and I share your own view about its importance to our way of life. But let me point out a few facets of the Grenada operation that seem to have been overlooked. From the time I received word of the request from the six Caribbean nations that we help them take action we gave our military chiefs only 48 hours to put a plan into action. We knew that with six other governments involved the risk of a leak was very great. There was the risk of Cuban action, Cuba being much closer, which could have left us with an outright invasion against a sizeable military force. Even short notice to the press regarding coverage would greatly increase the risk of a hostage situation.

I gave no order regarding the press. My order was that there be no interference with the commanders in the field. We had given them a hard task with only a scant measure of intelligence information. I understand that many of them have since stated, it was the first time in years that a campaign was carried out without civilian overview. And some added, "it was the first time in years we've been successful."

On the second day a press pool team was taken to Grenada from Barbados. This was enlarged on the third day and again on the fourth and then full press coverage was allowed with transportation provided by the military and permission given to those who wanted to provide their own. A top priority of the entire operation was to minimize casualties.

I hope this information reassures you about my position. If you have further questions I'd be pleased to answer them.

Sincerely,
Ronald Reagan

Reagan replies to a letter of support from the father of a sergeant with the 82nd Airborne Division that was sent to Grenada.

The Reverend Gene Skipworth
Zanesville, Ohio
November 28, 1983 [28]

Dear Reverend Skipworth:

Thank you very much for your kind letter. I share your pride in Sgt. Yale Skipworth and all of his companions in the 82nd Airborne, as well as those splendid young men in the other military forces who went into Grenada.

I hope all our fellow citizens are aware of the quality of young men and women in uniform. I can't see them without getting a lump in my throat. Wherever they are in the world they are a proud symbol of what is good in our land.

In saying this let me associate myself with your feelings about our duty in the world and your abhorrence of violence. Nothing in my present job is more difficult than ordering these fine young Americans into a situation where their lives are at risk. I am hopeful that their very quality and spirit will warn possible adversaries not to attempt violence. They are in truth the peacekeepers of the world.

Again thanks and best regards.

Sincerely,
Ronald Reagan

In a letter to a friend, President Reagan muses over the foreign policy double standards he sees applied to Central America by some Americans.

Mr. Alan Brown
APO New York
December 14, 1983 [29]

Dear Alan:

It was good to hear from you and may I say your letter got here quicker than much of our domestic mail from much closer locales.

I was more than happy to learn of the grassroots support abroad for our Grenada rescue mission as well as our situation in Central America. As for some of the unfriendlies I'm amazed how much they get away with. For example they automatically lean toward the rebels in El Salvador and against those in Nicaragua. The difference is that in El Salvador the government has elections and is trying to be democratic while in Nicaragua the government has embraced Castro* and the Soviets.

You know Castro and the Nicaraguan government have both claimed over and over that Cuba only has 200 military advisers in Nicaragua. Now without any apology both have announced that 1,000 of that 200 are returning to Cuba. It reminds one of the chorus girl whose salary was $50 a week and she sent 200 of it home to her folks.

Well again thanks for your good letter. Nancy sends her very best as do I.

Sincerely,
Ron

On April 6, 1984, the Wall Street Journal *revealed that the Central Intelligence Agency had been secretly supporting the mining of Nicaraguan harbors. The Senate on April 10 and the House on April 12 passed nonbinding "sense of Congress" resolutions*

---

* Cuban leader Fidel Castro Ruz.

stating that the United States should stop funding the mining. The day after the House resolution was passed, President Reagan replies to a letter from an American doctor living in Honduras. He writes that some in the U.S. Congress want to use the mining as a reason to cut off support for the Contras.

> Edward W. Capparelli, M.D.
> Cauquira, Honduras
> April 13, 1984 [30]

Dear Dr. Capparelli:

I'm sorry to be so late in answering your good letter of March 1st. It often takes a while before mail makes its way to my desk.

I'm most grateful to you for writing as you did and your letter will be most helpful in dealing with Congress which in my view is behaving very irresponsibly. I will protect your privacy however rest assured.

We're facing a near rebellion by Congress because of the harbor mining. At least some are using that as an excuse to shut off funding.

We'll fight as hard as we can to head them off. Your letter points up so eloquently the real need and the moral justification for continuing to help those oppressed people.

Thank you again for writing but also for the noble work you and Mrs. Capparelli are doing. Give her my warm regards.

> God bless you,
> Ronald Reagan

Reagan responds to a supporter the day before the Salvadoran President-elect José Napoleón Duarte met with members of the U.S. House of Representatives.

> Mrs. Josephine Pulvari
> Alexandria, Virginia
> May 21, 1984 [31]

Dear Mrs. Pulvari:

I'm sorry I never received your letter of November 19 last year but I'm glad you saw that I got a copy. My belated thank you for your holiday wishes and for your generous words. Incidentally I now know we were born in the same year.

You wrote about the weapons we captured on Grenada. We put them on display in an airplane hangar. But I'm afraid it didn't seem important to many members of the press.

I've just had a meeting with President-elect Duarte of El Salvador. He's speaking to the Congress tomorrow. Maybe he can make them understand how important it is that we stop this Soviet-Cuban march on Central America.

Again my thanks to you for all that you are doing.

> Sincerely,
> Ronald Reagan

A week after President Duarte's trip to Washington, President Reagan declares that El Salvador wants democracy.

Mrs. Jane Graham
Lafayette, Colorado
May 30, 1984 [32]

Dear Mrs. Graham:

I'm sorry to be so late in replying to your letter of March 21st. Sometimes it takes a while for letters to reach my desk. Please accept a belated but heartfelt thanks to you and your husband. I can't tell you how happy I was to hear from you and to learn of your change of mind about the "freeze" and "Central America."

With regard to the first we can all support that once we've persuaded the Soviets to join us in reducing the number of weapons to an equal and verifiable level. As for Central America I believe the election of President Duarte is a good sign that El Salvador truly wants real democracy.

Thank you again and very best regards.

Sincerely,
Ronald Reagan

In the next letter, President Reagan thanks one of the authors of Grenada: The Untold Story _for sending him the book.* The authors reported that the Soviet bloc supported a weapons buildup in Grenada and that Soviet-Grenada contacts were more extensive than most of the world, including the people of Grenada, knew before the U.S. intervention._

Mr. Gregory W. Sandford
American Embassy Berlin
APO New York
January 8, 1985 [33]

Dear Mr. Sandford:

I've just written a letter to your partner Richard and am writing to you to express my gratitude for the book on Grenada and for your generous inscription.

I've only been able to read the prologue but eagerly look forward to reading your entire account. As I told Richard, I think you both should know that when our people were telling our allies no decision had been made it actually had. I was so

---

* Gregory Sandford and Richard Vigilante, _Grenada: The Untold Story_ (Lanham, MD: Madison Books, 1984).

fearful of leaks which could increase the risk to our men that I clamped the lid on. Actually I gave the order for the operation immediately upon receipt of the request from OECS. That was about 3 a.m. when I was awakened in Augusta and told of the message.

Again my heartfelt thanks for your gift but more importantly for writing the book.

Sincerely,
Ronald Reagan

———

President Reagan shares memories of his visit to Costa Rica on December 3 and 4, 1982.

Mrs. Elizabeth G. Bredow
Doylestown, Pennsylvania
March 4, 1985[34]

Dear Mrs. Bredow:
Thank you very much for your letter of February 20. It was kind of you to relate your experience in Costa Rica and I'm most grateful.

I have very vivid memories of my visit there. I was greatly impressed by the pride the people have in their democracy. It was evident in the incident that was related to you. The audience obviously wanted the individual who interrupted my speech to sit down and be quiet but they would not do anything to interfere with what they saw as his democratic right.

Well again my thanks to you and best regards.

Sincerely,
Ronald Reagan

———

President Reagan thanks a friend and columnist for his essay in support of his policy on Central America and says that the Sandinista regime in Nicaragua is supporting a sophisticated propaganda campaign in the United States that is influencing some members of Congress.

Lt. General Victor H. Krulak, USMC (Ret.)
San Diego, California
March 11, 1985[35]

Dear Brute:
Thanks very much for your column it was medicine for what's going on back here. There is a sophisticated lobbying job going on here aimed at Congress and supported by the Sandinistas. It really is a well-funded operation involving profes-

sional lobbyists and I'm afraid too many in Congress are listening. Why is it so hard for some to only see threats from the right, never the left.

Bless you and keep at it.

Sincerely,
Ron

On March 1, 1985, members of the Nicaraguan opposition met in San José, Costa Rica, and offered a cease-fire plan that entailed mediated talks by the Bishops Conference of the Roman Catholic Church and internationally observed elections. On April 4, President Reagan endorsed the plan and asked the U.S. Congress for $14 million to be used for economic and humanitarian purposes in Nicaragua. He pledged to restrict the funding to nonmilitary purposes if the Sandinistas accepted the peace plan. This letter was written the same day.

The Honorable Earl E. T. Smith
Palm Beach, Florida
April 4, 1985 [36]

Dear Earl:

Believe me I agree with "the former Ambassador to Cuba," that Nicaragua is Cuba all over again. But try to convince a majority of the Congress of that—including a goodly number of Republicans.

The pro-Sandinista lobby on the Hill is almost as sophisticated an operation as I've ever seen. I have to say though that this time the secretary of state is on the side of the good guys. Our problem is the Congress. Tip O'Neill is influenced by someone in one of the religious orders and gets vehement about our hostility to the Sandinistas.

We're announcing a proposal this afternoon appealing for negotiations between the Contras and the government with the church on hand as a participant. This is the result of our efforts to get funding for the Contras. We've been told by our own people there is no way we can get a straight up or down vote on money for the Contras so we're making the money part of this whole proposal.

Believe me Earl we're as solid on this issue as we can be and you are right that Nicaragua is nothing but a Soviet-Cuban base on our mainland.

Nancy left for California this a.m. and thank heaven I follow her tomorrow. Love to Lesly.

Sincerely,
Ron

In a letter to President Reagan, two Nicaraguan exiles living in Costa Rica asked that President Reagan continue to press the United States Congress to provide economic aid to their homeland. They also said that the Soviet Union was attempting to dominate Nicaragua.

Mr. Fuad Farach and Mr. Alvaro Solórzano
San José, Costa Rica
May 20, 1985 [37]

Dear Mr. Farach and Mr. Solórzano,

Forgive me for being so late in answering your letter of March 25th. It has only just reached me. I appreciate very much your description of what has taken place in Nicaragua. I shall see that our Congress is informed also.

Let me assure you I shall continue doing everything I can to see that support is given to those who are fighting for freedom in your land, indeed in all of Central America. We must not permit the Communist bloc to get a foothold on the mainland of the Americas.

Thank you again for your kindness in writing.

Sincerely,
Ronald Reagan

———

By 1986, the United States Congress had passed several Boland amendments placing various restrictions on military aid to the Contras. On March 11, 1986, President Reagan directly challenged the congressional restrictions and asked that money be released for military support of the Contras. He said: "I've asked the Congress to vote them [the Contras] $100 million in aid of already appointed funds, a modest amount when compared to what the Soviets are providing the Sandinistas. . . . The Soviet bloc gave the Nicaraguan Communists over $500 million in aid. But last year we provided the freedom fighters with less than $27 million in boots and Band-Aids. What happened? The freedom fighters have been battered. You can't defend yourself against Soviet helicopter gunships with bedrolls."

An old friend from California wrote President Reagan on the day he made the request, congratulating him on his stance toward the Contras.

Mr. Henry Salvatori
Los Angeles, California
March 17, 1986 [38]

Dear Henry:

Thanks for sending the editorial. I hadn't seen it and it sure brightened my weekend. Thanks too for your generous words.

I've been meeting with congressmen and senators both Republican and Democrat trying to get them to see why we have to send help to the Contras. I really don't know where we stand as of now but I'm saying a prayer. I can't understand the reluctant ones, the issue is so clear-cut.

Nancy sends her love and from both of us to Gracie.

Sincerely,
Ron

Shortly after the United States intervened in Grenada, documents were found and published that showed Soviet involvement in the country. Reagan continued to use the captured documents to bolster his position. He does so in the next letter to a friend.

Lt. General Victor H. Krulak, USMC (Ret.)
San Diego, California
April 21, 1986[39]

Dear Brute:

Bless you and thank you. Your column really tells the story and I hope it does get to the people on the Hill. A number of them have bought the Sandinista disinformation line hook, line and sinker and I'll bet only a few have ever looked at *The Grenada Papers* since the State Department published the book.[40] Brute if we had secretly come upon documents signed by people like Gromyko and Ogarkov* (among others) and someone had leaked them they'd be on most of the front pages in America. But here are hundreds of documents we've willingly offered to the public and as far as I know only one journalist, a fellow named Krulak has seen their importance and their worth.

God bless you,
Ron

A Franciscan priest in El Salvador wrote President Reagan to encourage him to continue to work for peace in his country and throughout the world, and to let him know that he was praying for his success. President Reagan sent $250 to the priest and wrote "contribution" on the memo line of the check.

The Reverend Flavian Mucci, OFM
San Salvador, El Salvador
July 17, 1986[41]

Dear Father Mucci:

I'm sorry to be so late in answering your letter of last April, but it has only just reached my desk. It sometimes takes a while to make its way through the bureaucratic tangle. Thank you for writing as you did and for telling me of what you are doing. Thank you too for your prayers; you will be in mine. I promise too that we will continue trying to help peace come to El Salvador.

On behalf of all Americans, thank you for your untiring effort and God bless you.

Sincerely,
Ronald Reagan

---

* Soviet Foreign Minister Andrei Gromyko and Soviet Chief of the General Staff Nikolai V. Ogarkov.

More than two years after the U.S. intervention in Grenada, President Reagan traveled to the island. During his February 20, 1986, speech to the citizens of St. George's he expressed gratitude for Grenada's reentry into "the ranks of free nations" and announced an expansion of the Caribbean Basin Initiative that would make it easier for Caribbean textiles to be sold in U.S. markets. In this letter to a friend, President Reagan discusses how he was received in Grenada.

Colonel Barney Oldfield, USAF (Ret.)
Beverly Hills, California
July 17, 1986[42]

Dear Barney:

Thanks for telling me about your trip to Saint Lucia. I still find the Bermuda Triangle spooky. Why didn't that fellow tell you what they saw too much of when they were flying too low?

Thanks too for sending me the copy of George [Foreman]'s speech. You remember I knew him back when I was governor. I'm really impressed with what he's done for himself. That was a masterful address. You can be proud of Litton's part in that.*

Incidentally with regard to Grenada, I had occasion to go there recently. What a pleasure that was. There were no "Yankee Go Home" signs there but an awful lot of Yankee come back signs. They really welcomed us.

Best regards,
Ron

In the next two letters, President Reagan says that the Sandinistas hide the real situation from those who tour Nicaragua, and he knows that there is no freedom whatsoever in the country.

Dr. James Campbell
Clarinda, Iowa
October 20, 1987[43]

Dear Dr. Campbell:

Forgive my tardiness in replying to your message of August 10. Due to travel among other things your message has only recently come to my attention.

---

* In his letter dated July 7, 1986, Barney Oldfield wrote: "I was there [in Saint Lucia at the Inter-American Symposium for the Handicapped] with George Foreman, the former heavy-weight champion and Olympic Gold Medalist, who said he wanted to talk about a 'self-inflicted handicap' about which he knew a great deal—the handicap of a limited education. He exhorted parents to send their kids to school. The Right Honourable John Compton, the Prime Minister, told me it was the most important speech ever made in Saint Lucia!" Oldfield's letters typically were typed on the stationery of Litton Industries, a company in Beverly Hills, California, to which he was a consultant.

Thank you for your words. I have been trying to communicate that some of our people, however well intentioned, were treated to a "guided tour" in Nicaragua and did not see the country as it actually is. Obviously we in government have facts and information denied those who visit and are shown what the Sandinistas want them to see. This includes a little cluster of churches who portray religious freedom because that is what they are told to do. In the main, there is not religious freedom in Nicaragua. Indeed, there is no real freedom of any kind.

Again my thanks to you.

Sincerely,
Ronald Reagan

Mr. W. Robert Stover
Walnut Creek, California
October 20, 1987 [44]

Dear Mr. Stover:

Thank you very much for your letter and forgive my late reply. Your letter has only just now caught up with me, possibly due to some travel on my part.

I know the people I met with are sincere and truly believe they saw the real Nicaragua on their visits there. I have been trying to point out, by way of Donn,[*] the extent to which the Sandinistas have created a kind of "Potemkin Village" where they can show visitors what they want them to see. I hope we can make them aware of how much more information we have without revealing and thus destroying our sources

Again my thanks for your letter.

Sincerely,
Ronald Reagan

President Reagan thanks an American dentist for providing his services to Hondurans and for supporting his policy on Central America.

Dr. Ollie H. Scheideman, D.D.S.
Yuba City, California
October 21, 1987 [45]

Dear Dr. Scheideman:

I'm sorry to be so late in answering your letter but what with my travels and all it evidently got stuck in the bureaucratic process and has only just reached me. First let me express my appreciation and admiration for what you were doing on your trip to Honduras. Thank you too for your generous words.

---

[*] The Reverend Donn D. Moomaw was the pastor of the church President Reagan attended in Los Angeles, California.

Let me assure you I will not retreat from our position of helping the Freedom Fighters in Nicaragua. It is true there are those in Congress who are determined that we should abandon the fight but with the help of people like yourself I'm convinced we can win.

Again my thanks and best regards.

Ronald Reagan

NORTH AND SOUTH AMERICA

One of Ronald Reagan's themes from the time he emerged as a spokesman on national policy issues in the late 1970s to the end of his presidency was the importance of improving economic, political, and security ties between North and South America. Reagan primarily viewed the region through the cold war lens of U.S.-Soviet competition and wanted to block Soviet and Communist encroachments anywhere in the Western Hemisphere. The letters below illustrate the consistency of his geopolitical views.

Reagan also proposed closer cooperation among the countries of North America in his statement announcing his intention to join the 1980 presidential race. On November 13, 1979, he said: "[T]he key to our own future security may lie in both Mexico and Canada becoming much stronger countries than they are today. . . . It is time we stopped thinking of our nearest neighbors as foreigners."[46]

Reagan discusses his commitment to strengthening relations among the North American countries in the next two letters.

Dr. Philip Smith
1979[47]

Dear Dr. Smith:

Thank you very much for your good letter and for your generous words about Nancy and me. You are absolutely right that she is a great asset in what we are trying to do. Incidentally, she sends her greetings and best wishes.

I can understand your concern about my supposed strategy in view of the numerous press accounts that have me somehow trying to change my spots. Please believe this is purely press and possibly because I appear to be the front-runner in the polls. They have to have something to say. No one is trying to change me and certainly I would have no reason for running if I had to give up anything that I truly believe in.

I'm sorry you found the announcement speech lacking but let me just give a word of explanation. I have been out on the speaking circuit virtually since I left the Governor's office and of course was during the '76 campaign year. In this last year,

I have been speaking all over the country to Republican groups and therefore, am on record specifically with regard to issues ranging from taxation to energy to national defense and SALT II. My concern was that the announcement speech had to do something different from the speeches the press have heard me making throughout this last year.

About the only new program I had in mind and have had for some time was the idea of better relations between Canada, Mexico and our own country. As a matter of fact, a few months ago on my own, I went down to Mexico and met with the president there. We had a very good meeting and I felt him out about the idea I expressed on November 13. I am speaking now as I have for the past year again on the specific matters of taxes, the inflation fight, government regulations and so forth. I was glad to hear what you had to say about Ohio and assure you we won't make the same mistakes we made last time. I really want to campaign there and hopefully win your state.

Again, thanks and best regards from both of us.

Sincerely,
Ron

Mr. Frank J. Barboni
1980[48]

Dear Mr. Barboni:

Thank you very much for the note you handed me the other day. I appreciate your suggestions and, as you know, agree very much with you about strong ties with Mexico and Canada and agree also that the American people want the United States back together again. I appreciate your kind words and your taking the time and trouble to write the note that you did.

Best regards,
Ronald Reagan

In a letter dated February 22, 1983, Kathy Manace, a woman born in Toronto, Canada, who had moved to San Francisco in 1974 with her husband wrote to President Reagan: "In the United States, we found a country where the individual is still the most important element in the social and political structure, yet a country where the unity of such individuals in pursuit of common goals has provided a continuing strength."* In his reply, President Reagan writes of the bond between Canadians and Americans.

---

* Reagan wrote this on the letter: "Can I have this back? RR"; "Kathy [Osborne] maybe we should check with Anne [Higgins] to make sure that they don't answer the original. This is the copy that was sent to Mike D. [Deaver]. The original may be somewhere in the mail. RR". Dennis Bark, then deputy director of the Hoover Institution, attached Manace's letter to his own letter to Deaver dated March 3, 1983. He requested that Manace's letter be given to President and Mrs. Reagan.

Mrs. Kathy Cole Manace
San Francisco, California
March 14, 1983 [49]

Dear Mrs. Manace:

I can't tell you how much your letter has meant to me. In these times of economic distress and worldwide trouble when native born Americans sometimes cynically downgrade our country, you remind us of how much we have to be thankful for.

Believe me you have strengthened the traditional bond of friendship between Canadians and Americans—certainly as far as I'm concerned. I'm very proud you have become a citizen of the United States. And I'm overjoyed at your choice of party. Welcome.

God bless you.

Sincerely,
Ronald Reagan

During the 1980 presidential campaign, Reagan discusses the bracero program, which from the 1940s to the mid-1960s allowed Mexicans to work in the United States on a temporary basis. He also recalls a meeting in Mexico City with President José López Portillo.

Mr. Lewis Leman
1980 [50]

Dear Mr. Leman:

Thank you very much for your letter and thanks for what you are doing in my behalf. I am turning your letter over to my research people. Like you, I believe we must resolve the problem at our southern border with full regard to the problems and needs of Mexico. I have suggested legalizing the entry of Mexican labor into this country on much the same basis you proposed, although I have not put it in the sense of restoring the bracero program. Before announcing my candidacy, I went to Mexico City and met with President Portillo. We had a good meeting, and I told him that if I should be successful, I would want to discuss our mutual problems with him and solicit his views.

Thank you again for your good letter and sound suggestion.

Best regards,
Ronald Reagan

In another letter written during the 1980 presidential campaign, Reagan expresses his belief that Mexico is a Communist target.

Commander Lewis S. Hayes
June 16, 1980[51]

Dear Commander:

Thank you very much for your letter—for all the information—and for your suggestions. Like you, I am terribly disturbed about what is happening to our neighbors in the south. I believe, also, that the last domino in Latin America is intended to be Mexico. I am delighted to have all the information you sent and certainly will give it a great deal of thought and consideration.

Again, my thanks and best regards.

Ronald Reagan

Reagan replies to a letter about a resolution adopted by the general board of the Church of the Brethren on October 28, 1974. The resolution declared that the regime of Major General Augusto Pinochet "was not instituted by the free choice of the Chilean people."[52]

Mr. Ralph E. Smeltzer
Washington, D.C.
Circa January 4–June 6, 1975[53]

Dear Mr. Smeltzer:

Thank you for writing and giving me a chance to comment on the resolution adopted by the board of the Church of The Brethren. You realize of course you have me at a disadvantage because as a member of the commission I can give no interim opinion or progress report.* By the same token however would it not have been better judgment to await the commission's report before taking such a step?

I do take issue with some of the suppositions contained in the resolution. There is every reason to believe the present regime in Chile has the support of the majority and certainly there have been many reports exposing as false the charges of torture. The sentence describing the KGB† as not spying on us belies the fact that Russia has vastly increased her espionage and subversive activities particularly in the United States.

---

* Ronald Reagan was a member of President Ford's commission to investigate the activities of the CIA, known as the Rockefeller Commission. This letter is dated between January 4 and June 6, 1975, because these are the inclusive dates of the commission's activities. See *The Nelson Rockefeller Report to the President by the Commission on CIA Activities* (New York: Manor Books, 1975).

† The Committee for State Security was known as the KGB. The Soviet Union's main security organization, the KGB was responsible for overseas intelligence operations and guarding the country's borders.

Frequent charges are made but seldom substantiated that we are interfering in the internal affairs of other countries, but all the evidence indicates those countries are already being interfered with by the Soviet Union. For an example Portugal. In the face of this then are we interfering or are we helping a friendly people resist interference?

Sincerely,
Ronald Reagan

Between November 30 and December 4, 1982, President Reagan toured Brazil, Colombia, Costa Rica, and Honduras. He promised aid to the countries and sounded the alarm about "foreign support for terrorists and subversive elements" in Central America.[54] The last two letters are President Reagan's reflections on his trip.

Ms. Mary Louise F. Masin
Temple Hills, Maryland
December 27, 1982[55]

Dear Ms. Masin:

Thank you very much for your kind and may I say informative letter. I agree with you about the importance of the Spanish language. I am of the generation that had to take a couple of years of French in high school because it was the official language of diplomacy. But here we are in the Western Hemisphere where Spanish is the language of all but three countries.

I am determined to develop a relationship between ourselves and our neighbors to the south. On my recent trip I made very sure that I didn't appear to be proposing a plan—we've done that before. I asked them what our differences were and how they thought we might resolve those differences. I received some sound answers.

These two great continents have known more peace than any other area of the world and from pole to pole we worship the same God. Believe me I won't let up on this task.

Thank you again for your letter and your prayers.

Sincerely,
Ronald Reagan

Padre John Tupper
Sao Paulo, Brazil
December 27, 1982[56]

Dear Padre:

Thank you very much for your letter which only reached me after my return from Brazil. I didn't have an opportunity to do some of the things you suggested and am afraid I wouldn't have even if I'd had your suggestions before the trip. They had a very full schedule for me. However I do believe that I was fortunate enough to get more of a view and sense of Brazil than just that of officialdom.

I can say also that I really did go to listen. I've felt for many years that no matter how well-intentioned our efforts in the past, we were the great colossus seeking to impose our plans on them. This time I asked them what were our differences and how did they think we could resolve them. The response was most rewarding. Incidentally my impression was that President Figueiredo * truly does want democracy and better opportunity for the people.

Thank you for your prayers and your blessing.

Sincerely,
Ronald Reagan

---

* João Baptista Figueiredo was president of Brazil.

CHAPTER SIXTEEN

The International Scene

*I*N TERMS OF *foreign policy, by the time Ronald Reagan stepped down as president in January 1989 he was best known for confronting communism, for reaching a substantial arms-reduction agreement with the Soviet Union, for executing an aggressive policy toward Central America, and for earning a mixed record on Middle East strategy, tarnished primarily by the bombing of American military personnel stationed in Lebanon and by the Iran-Contra scandal. Above all, however, Ronald Reagan was thought of as a Cold Warrior.*

The letters in this chapter provide a somewhat different picture. Reagan discusses a wide range of issues, beginning before his presidency: his role in helping the United States forge a closer relationship with the People's Republic of China (PRC) during the Nixon administration; his developing position toward southern Africa; and his view of the state of American intelligence operations in the 1970s, for starters. During his presidency, Reagan writes about making hard decisions, such as his visit to the German military cemetery at Bitburg. During his presidency, Reagan developed programs of action on a wide variety of international issues.

SOUTHERN AFRICA

In the midst of the 1976 Republican primaries, on June 2, Reagan responded to a hypothetical question about Rhodesia by saying that "in the interest of peace and avoiding bloodshed," the United States might consider sending troops to the southern African country. Shortly thereafter, a Ford campaign television and radio spot declared: "Governor Reagan couldn't start a war. President Reagan could."[1] Reagan refutes the claim in the letter below.

Ed
After June 1976[2]

Dear Ed:

Thanks for your letter and the material. Apparently, my message (unless I'm on TV myself as in the speech) isn't getting circulation. I've never advocated armed intervention in any of the troubled areas of the world.

And, number two—Ford was only echoing (and not completely) me on the inheritance tax. I came out first but I advocated an exemption in the neighborhood of $200,000.

Best regards,
Ron

In his reply to one of his defense policy advisers during his 1976 (and later 1980) presidential campaigns, Reagan writes that he is working on a radio commentary about African politics, and lacks confidence in what the "secretary" is doing on the continent. In a radio broadcast script titled "Rhodesia" that was taped on February 2, 1977, Reagan wrote: "Our former Secretary of State [Henry Kissinger], on his mission to Africa, had persuaded the governments of Rhodesia and Great Britain and a number of African nationalist leaders to agree to a plan for a temporary government of Rhodesia while a transition to majority rule took place. . . . Now Rhodesia's Prime Minister Ian Smith has announced his government will no longer attend the meetings. Why? . . . Very simply the African nationalists, once they arrived in Geneva, conveniently forgot that they had agreed in advance to every detail of the Kissinger proposal."[3]

Lt. General Daniel O. Graham
Circa early 1977[4]

Dear General:

Thank you for sending me the copy of *Soviet World Outlook** it will be most useful. I'm already at work on a radio script regarding the African situation.

I'll confess I'm terribly alarmed by what is going on there and have no confidence in what the secretary is doing. There is an odor of appeasement, possibly heightened by the political season and the need for dramatics.

I look forward to getting the other issues and again my heartfelt thanks.

Sincerely,
Ronald Reagan

---

* *Soviet World Outlook* was a monthly report about Soviet affairs published by the Center for Advanced International Studies at the University of Miami.

In 1976, the Ford administration helped broker negotiations between Rhodesian prime minister Ian Smith and black nationalists that ultimately led to Robert Mugabe becoming the prime minister of the independent Republic of Zimbabwe on April 18, 1980. By supporting the Geneva talks between the minority government and such nationalists as Robert Mugabe and Joshua Nkomo in Rhodesia, Reagan felt the United States was aiding the rise of an anti-American regime.

> Mr. James McLaughlin
> Nanuet, New York
> Circa fall 1978 [5]

Dear Mr. McLaughlin:

I understand and share your anger and frustration on all of the subjects you mentioned. I am particularly upset and ashamed for our country over our treatment of Prime Minister Smith, who I will be meeting with probably before you receive this note.*

It is far too early to make any formal declaration of candidacy but barring the unforeseen it is very possible that I'll be making such a statement at an appropriate time.

Thank you for writing.

> Sincerely,
> Ronald Reagan

During the first year of his presidency, Reagan declares his opposition to apartheid and his support for Namibian independence from South Africa. He disagrees with the tactics of the South West Africa People's Organization (SWAPO), a Namibian independence group, and of the Soviets and Cubans in the region.

> Mr. Quentin R. Dawkins
> Hyde Park, Massachusetts
> October 20, 1981 [6]

Dear Mr. Dawkins:

Thank you for writing and telling me of your concern about South Africa and our policies. Let me assure you of one thing: I am as opposed to apartheid as I know you are. I know there are many people in South Africa who want to change in that. It is my belief that in working with them we can bring about that change just as we brought about a very necessary change in our own country.

May I offer a different view about some of the points you raised with regard to the recent invasion. Angola has Cuban troops based there in great numbers and those troops have a number of Soviet advisers, technicians and other people with

---

* During Smith's October 1978 visit to the United States, he met with Reagan.

them. SWAPO, I don't think, can be compared to our own American Revolution. It has been retreating into Angola for shelter and then crossing the border into South-west Africa (Namibia) where it commits terrorist acts against men, women and children. The goal is not only to free Namibia from South African rule, but also to give it a chance to start with a constitution that protects all the tribal groups in Namibia and does not just turn rule over to one group.

We strongly believe that violent acts work against the peace process in the area, and oppose all such actions. We do not believe that singling out one party in the violence is either honest or conducive to bringing the violence to an end. All the provocative and violent actions and forces must be exposed to international condemnation, including a condemnation of the Soviet Union and Cuba for pouring arms, advisers and regular troops into this troubled area. Illustrative of this, on the recent South African raid several Russian military advisers were killed and one was taken prisoner. This prisoner has told his captors of the extensive Soviet military involvement in this area.

I assure you that we are seeking a peaceful solution to Namibia's crisis and the explosive situation in Angola.

Sincerely,
Ronald Reagan

———————

President Reagan agrees with a woman who has written him saying that she does not support the anti–South Africa demonstrations in the United States and considers the Republic of South Africa to be a stable government in a strife-ridden region.

Ms. Joan Joyce Sellers
Camarillo, California
January 28, 1985[7]

Dear Ms. Sellers:

Thank you very much for your letter and good wishes and for sharing your views about South Africa. All of us find apartheid repugnant but so do many people in South Africa. We are working quietly to persuade and to help the South African government improve the situation there and we've had some real success.

You are right about the importance to us and the free world of South Africa as a trade partner. Indeed our own national security is at stake. I'm sure we can be of greater help to the disadvantaged blacks in South Africa by continuing our present policy than by taking to the streets in demonstrations.

Again my thanks to you.

Sincerely,
Ronald Reagan

———————

On January 16, 1985, the Reagan administration said it hoped to provide President Samora M. Machel of Mozambique with $1 million in nonlethal military aid. On

September 19, President Reagan met with him in the White House and promised U.S. aid in an attempt to pry Mozambique away from the Soviet Union. Several weeks later, Reagan responds to an old friend who wrote: "American financial support for the Communist government of Mozambique is incomprehensible to your most stalwart conservative supporters." Reagan had criticized the Carter administration for engaging with Machel on the ground that Mozambique violated human rights.[8]

Mr. Henry Salvatori
Los Angeles, California
October 15, 1985[9]

Dear Henry:

Sorry to be so late in answering your letter of October 3rd, but things have been a little hectic back here.

Henry I can't go into great detail about the Mozambique situation for reasons which I'm sure you'll understand but there are sound reasons for what we are doing. We are not alone. Some of our allies are following the same course. We have good reason to believe the present leader is available and that it's worth a try. The opposition forces are not exactly freedom fighters, indeed some are getting rather rich. South Africa has already cancelled its support—such as it was.

As for our recent visitor, that was part of the scenario and I have to say things went rather well. Still, don't worry, I'm not diving off the high board until I'm sure about the water in the pool.

On the Angola matter, yes we have room to move now that the "Clark Amendment" is out of the way* but we're a little handicapped by budget considerations. You are right however about the opportunity.

Nancy sends her love and from both of us to Gracie.

Sincerely,
Ron

The departure of the Portuguese from Angola in the mid-1970s occasioned the onset of civil war as three parties fought to control the country. The South African–backed National Union for the Total Independence of Angola (UNITA) was one of the parties who sought to wrest control from the ruling Popular Movement for the Liberation of Angola (MPLA). On January 30, 1986, President Reagan met with Jonas Savimbi, UNITA's leader, in the White House.[10]

---

* Since 1976, the Clark Amendment had barred U.S. aid to warring factions in Angola. The U.S. Senate repealed the Clark Amendment on May 15, 1985, and the House voted for its repeal on July 11. President Reagan signed a foreign aid bill that put the repeal into effect on August 8.

Mr. Henry Salvatori
Los Angeles, California
February 12, 1986 [11]

Dear Henry:

Thank you for your generous words about the State of the Union message, I'm most grateful.

You'll be pleased to know I had a fine meeting with Savimbi. He's a very impressive person. What a shame the Congress turned Jerry Ford down when he asked for weapons and supplies for Savimbi back when the leadership for Angola was up for grabs. They were still in that Vietnam syndrome so we wound up with a Communist government.

I promise you I'll keep close watch on the Mozambique situation. Nancy sends her love and from both of us to Gracie.

Sincerely,
Ron

P.S. I dictated the above on the plane—now we're at the ranch and proud owners of a brand new compressor. Henry thank you very much and thank Gracie. We have the best-equipped ranch in California.

———————

A famous African-American entertainer wrote a short wire to President Reagan on June 13, 1986: "As my friend and as my president, please do something about South Africa."

Mr. Sammy Davis Jr.
Beverly Hills, California
June 24, 1986 [12]

Dear Sammy:

My friend I have your wire and want you to know we are doing all we can about the tragic situation in South Africa but are as frustrated as you are with our lack of progress.

Sammy it is a much more complex problem than it appears on the surface. The Botha regime* is trying and has made a number of changes for the better. However there is an opposition party in that government which opposes the things he has done and makes it difficult for him to attack the ultimate problem of apartheid. It's a little like our own situation wherein the opposition party, a majority, in one house of Congress can throw roadblocks in our way.

Some of the things proposed here such as all-out sanctions and disinvestment

———————

* South African Executive President Pieter W. Botha.

by American firms in South Africa would hurt the very people we are trying to help and would leave us no contact within South Africa to try and bring influence to bear on their government.

The American-owned industries there employ more than 80,000 blacks. And their employment practices are like they are here with no discrimination. An American minister named Sullivan, a black himself, created an employment policy which the American employers adopted and which is very different from the normal South African customs.* Sanctions such as the Congress have passed would wind up eliminating thousands and thousands of jobs in the South African–owned mines and industries, and in addition would find us shooting ourselves in the foot. For example chrome which is essential in our steelmaking comes from South Africa. The only other source is the Soviet Union. I'm sure you can see what that would do to us. Not only would we be at the mercy of the Soviets we would be helping a nation that violates human rights as much or more than any other. Incidentally one of the products we buy from South Africa and which isn't available anywhere else is essential in the manufacture of the catalytic converters on our automobiles.

Now Sammy I don't want you to read this as putting such things before the great moral issue involved in apartheid. Believe me I see apartheid as an evil that must be eliminated. We must continue our efforts to bring this about. But we have a better chance of doing so if we maintain contact than if we pick up our marbles and walk away. You have my promise, we won't let up.

Best regards,
Ron

In the summer of 1986, both U.S. legislative chambers voted to impose economic sanctions against South Africa. The next three letters were written in the midst of the congressional deliberations.

Mrs. Mary R. Morgan
New York, New York
July 7, 1986 [13]

Dear Mrs. Morgan:

Laurence † delivered your letter. I appreciate your kind words and share your concern over the situation in South Africa.

---

* Minister Leon Howard Sullivan first issued a "Statement of Principles of U.S. Firms with Affiliates in the Republic of South Africa" in March 1977. He amplified the principles several times in the late 1970s and 1980s. See Leon Howard Sullivan, "The Statement of Principles" (Philadelphia: International Council for Equality of Opportunity Principles, 1984).
† Laurence Rockefeller.

I know an effort is being made to portray our position as one of callous disregard for the plight of the blacks in that country. I realize, of course, that some of this is political partisanship but at the same time that many sincerely concerned people are unaware of what we are doing. To tell the truth that is understandable because we have to be rather quiet if we are to be helpful.

Some of the measures that are being suggested such as the resolution approved in the House of Representatives would hurt the very people we seek to help.* They would also leave us completely estranged and with no possible chance of influencing the South African government. As you know we have employed some sanctions against South Africa but only those which would not impose economic hardships on the mainly black workers.

We also feel that closing down American-owned businesses there would only result in the unemployment of some 80,000 blacks. As it is those American firms have used a policy conceived by a black clergyman in our country, Reverend Sullivan,† with regard to employee relations. It is based on our own nondiscriminatory practices here at home.

We continue to press the South African government to move toward elimination of apartheid and to enter into discussions and negotiations with responsible black leaders. We have not hesitated in citing the immorality of present practices.

I appreciate very much your writing as you did and giving me the chance to comment. Nancy and I are so grateful for the warm hospitality we enjoyed at Pocantico Hills. Our schedule in the celebration would have been intolerably hectic if it weren't for the restful beauty of Kykuit.‡

Sincerely,
Ronald Reagan

Mr. Earl W. Schultz Jr.
Wheaton, Illinois
July 17, 1986[14]

Dear Mr. Schultz:

I have only just received your letter of June 18—hence this tardy reply. It sometimes takes a while for mail to find its way to my desk.

---

* On June 18, 1986, the House of Representatives approved legislation requiring U.S. citizens and companies to divest themselves of South African holdings. An exception was to be made for items of strategic importance designated by the U.S. president.

† Minister Leon Howard Sullivan.

‡ This letter is to Mary Rockefeller Morgan, who hosted the Reagans at the Rockefeller estate, Kykuit, at Pocantico Hills, New York, following the Reagans' participation in the centennial celebration at the Statue of Liberty on July 3, 1986.

Thank you for writing and for sending me the copy of your letter to the secretary of state.* Let me assure you I agree with just about all that you had to say. The situation in South Africa is not a simple problem of two races but indeed is one of tribal divisions and customs. I want very much for us to be of help in resolving these problems and bringing an end to apartheid without destroying all that has been created in that country.

Sincerely,
Ronald Reagan

The Honorable George Murphy
Cashiers, North Carolina
August 11, 1986[15]

Dear Murph:

It was good to hear from you even if accounts of the Grove make me homesick and more than a little envious. You know like you, I wanted another of the Senate candidates on our side but have to say that the nominee's voting record is not bad with regard to supporting my positions. He'll be a h—l of an improvement over the present senator †, and I'd join you in deep-sixing him and the playboy from Massachusetts.‡

We're in sync about South Africa. I have some recent figures on black resistance to punitive sanctions. The majority are well aware they would be the first to suffer and many of their leaders flatly declare that the radicals who do want them, want them because of the chaos they would bring. And, of course, they would be ready to seize power with the help of the Red Brethren.

Nancy and I are off in a few days for the ranch and three weeks of riding and country living. Nancy sends her love and from both of us to Bette.

Sincerely,
Ron

On September 26, 1986, President Reagan vetoed the bill to impose sanctions on South Africa. Three days later, the House of Representatives voted 313–83 to override the veto. The Senate overrode the veto with a vote of 78–21 on October 2, and the sanctions bill became law. Almost a year after the passage of the bill, President Reagan laments the outcome.

---

* Secretary of State George P. Shultz.
† Representative Ed Zschau challenged Alan Cranston, who won a fourth term to the United States Senate in 1986.
‡ Senator Edward Kennedy (D-Massachusetts).

Mr. John Kehoe
Sacramento, California
August 10, 1987 [16]

Dear John:

You have been busy since your Washington visit. I'm glad to read your observation about South Africa. I wish my veto of the sanctions bill had been upheld. It's too bad the *New York Times* thinks it is secretary of state and has such an effect on the rest of the media.

Congratulations on your first grandchild. Being a grandparent is fun—all the pleasure of parenthood without the responsibility.

My best to your gal and Nancy sends her best.

Sincerely,
Ron

ASIA

Cambodia

Reagan began speaking against the atrocities committed by the Khmer Rouge in Cambodia in the late 1970s.[17] As president, he sought to comfort two Cambodian refugees living in the United States who wrote to him about the inhumane conditions in their homeland.

Ty Tim Hel and Eng Sun Hel
Joliet, Illinois
August 27, 1982 [18]

Dear Friends:

Thank you very much for your letter of June 14. I'm sorry to be so late in answering but your letter for some reason has only just reached my desk.

I'm happy that you have found friends and freedom here in our land. I hope with all my heart that your homeland will one day be free of the cruel conquerors who have brought so much suffering to Cambodia. Many of us are doing our best to see that Cambodia is not forgotten.

Thank you for your generous words and kind Father's Day wish. God bless you.

Sincerely,
Ronald Reagan

The People's Republic of China and Taiwan

Ronald Reagan was deeply interested in and involved with Sino-American relations for many years. He first visited Taiwan in October 1971. Three years after he stepped down as governor, Reagan again traveled to Taiwan and declared his opposition to the Carter administration's efforts to normalize relations with the People's Republic of China. On December 15, 1978, President Jimmy Carter announced that United States relations with the PRC would be normalized on January 1, 1979, and the United States would notify Taiwan of its intention to withdraw from the Mutual Defense Treaty of 1954. In a January 15, 1979, letter to a couple in Taipei, Reagan revealed that he would use his nationally syndicated radio program to influence the U.S. Congress to oppose President Carter's policies. On February 10, Reagan urged conservatives to support Senator Barry Goldwater's (R-Arizona) court challenge to President Carter's termination of the U.S.–Taiwan defense pact.[19]

While the Reagan administration supported Taiwan, U.S.–PRC ties deepened during the 1980s. An August 17, 1982, joint communiqué with the PRC stated that the United States would not "carry out a long-term policy of arms sales to Taiwan." In late April 1984, President Reagan traveled to the PRC, making his first trip to a Communist country. When asked about Taiwan during an interview with Chinese television representatives on April 28, he said: "We don't believe that it would be right to cast aside longtime old friends in order to make new friends. But we will do anything we can to encourage the peaceful solution of this problem by the peoples of China."

The letters in this section reflect two decades of Ronald Reagan's thinking about and involvement with Sino-American relations.

Dr. Yung Wei
Circa late 1960s or 1970s[20]

Dear Dr. Wei:

Thank you very much for your letter and for sending me your article on Taiwan. I haven't read it as yet but have it on my bed stand and intend doing so.

I am very concerned about our foreign policy and the seeming obsession with détente. I feel we must continue our alliance with the Republic of China on Taiwan and never give anyone the impression that we are weakening in our pledge to defend it.

Thank you again and best wishes in your new work at the Institute of International Relations. I would enjoy hearing from you.

Sincerely,
Ronald Reagan

This letter was written shortly after Reagan returned from a trip in 1971 to Taiwan and other Asian countries on behalf of the Nixon administration. He was sent to reassure allies of U.S. commitment to them even though an opening to the PRC would be taking place.

Mrs. Frances Cooke
La Canada, California
Circa December 1971 [21]

Dear Mrs. Cooke:

I appreciate your telling me your position and thus giving me the chance to reply.

I have no disagreement whatsoever with the statements relative to the evil of communism contained in the articles by Congressman Schmitz and Senator Richardson.* I am aware of the Communists' determination to communize the world, and agree they have not retreated one inch from that position. But may I suggest there is in each article an assumption that is not verified? Both men, and I know them well and like them very much, have assumed that the president no longer shares this belief in and understanding of the danger of communism.

There is no basis for believing this and therefore assuming that Taiwan is doomed or that we will abandon old friends such as President Chiang Kai-shek.† As a matter of fact President Nixon has told me directly that if the Red Chinese should go adventuring and attempt the takeover of Taiwan they would have to fight the United States.

Now may I sketch in something of the situation as inherited by the president. We no longer have the nuclear superiority we had under Kennedy and which was frittered away by Kennedy and Johnson. We are close to the point at which an ultimatum by Russia would see us with no choice but surrender or die. Right now China and Russia are at odds with each other. There are 140 Russian divisions on the Chinese border. When two of our enemies are angry at each other—it is hardly to our advantage to buddy up to the stronger of the two.

At the moment President Nixon is fighting desperately to improve our defense posture in the face of tremendous congressional opposition. He won the ABM issue by one vote (Vice President Agnew's) in the Senate.‡

The Democratic position is in favor of even more disarmament. I'm sure that a

---

* John George Schmitz (R-California) and Hubert Leon Richardson, a Republican state senator in California.

† Chiang Kai-shek, also known as Chiang Chung-cheng, was the Chinese Nationalist leader. He and the Nationalist regime were driven off the mainland in 1949 and established their government on Taiwan. Chiang died in 1975.

‡ On August 6, 1969, Vice President Spiro T. Agnew cast the tie-breaking vote in the United States Senate on behalf of the development of the Safeguard anti-ballistic missile system. "Even though the margin of victory was razor thin," President Richard Nixon later wrote, "the vote established that America was still prepared to maintain its military strength." Richard Nixon, *The Memoirs of Richard Nixon* (New York: Simon & Schuster, 1990), p. 418. In this letter, Reagan paints a much gloomier picture about America's military strength and diplomatic resolve during those years.

new Democrat president would visit Peking and I'm sure he would go to negotiate the liquidation of Taiwan.

Thanks again for letting me comment and please accept my belated "Thanksgiving wishes."

Sincerely,
Ronald Reagan

In a letter to a former assistant attorney general, Reagan writes that he supports the legal challenge to the termination of the 1954 defense agreement with Taiwan introduced by Senator Barry Goldwater and other legislators on December 22, 1978. On December 13, 1979, the Supreme Court ruled that President Carter's action could stand.

Mr. Norman Littell
Circa late 1979 [22]

Dear Norman:

Thank you very much for your good letter and sound advice and suggestions.

I agree with you regarding the right of the president to revoke a treaty as he did with Taiwan. Since you wrote, of course, the judge has been overruled, but I understand that the group sponsoring this move is appealing to the Supreme Court. I hope they will use some good judgment. I share your admiration for Taiwan. I have been there twice—once to meet with Chiang Kai-shek as the representative of then President Nixon. The second time, after I was out of the governor's office, I met with his son, now the president of the Republic of China. More should have been made of the fact that the Communist People's Republic on the mainland started at virtually the same time the Republic of China started on Taiwan. Taiwan was a desolate waste due to the bombing by our B-29's. Comparing the two countries and what they have done is probably the greatest sermon in behalf of free enterprise anyone could ask for. I didn't know the part you had played in that, but from the information that you sent, I see that you helped draft the blueprint that made this success possible. You must be very proud.

You were very kind to send the invitation regarding the Sulgrave Club, but I'm afraid we're quite a considerable group wherever we go. Secret Service has been assigned to us so even a trip to the corner drugstore is a four-car caravan.

I was interested in your comment about Kennedy and what he is doing. Looking at that and looking also at the manner in which the president is using the power of the incumbency and tax dollars to further his own effort makes us realize our opponents are still of the same stripe they've always been. Isn't it strange how much they can get away with that we couldn't.

Again, thanks.

Best regards,
Ron

In the next two letters, one to Sam Yorty, the mayor of Los Angeles in the 1960s, and the other to an old friend, presidential candidate Ronald Reagan corrects press reports of how he would like to see U.S. representation in the PRC and Taiwan. In his reply to the mayor, he also informs Yorty that Taiwanese leaders are quietly keeping in touch with him.

Mayor Sam Yorty
August 18, 1980[23]

Dear Sam:

Thanks very much for your letter. I appreciated getting the word about the foreign minister. Through a roundabout way, our friends on Taiwan are keeping in touch with me, and they have expressed their confidence in me and my friendship for them and don't want me to make China an issue because, as they put it, they look forward to my being president.

I have always felt that, while the press called my statement one of advocating diplomatic recognition, that would be impossible since both Chinas insist that they are the real China. No, what I had in mind was, if I'm in a position to do so, making the private foundation liaison office on Taiwan an official one as our liaison office in Peking was official until recognition came, and we made it an embassy. Right now, it is my understanding that our people on Taiwan must meet with government officials of that country in cafés or clubs. They cannot go to a public office. And the same is true in Washington, where their people must meet our government officials in the same way and cannot actually visit them in their offices. I think you have put a word on it which I won't use until I get there. But the word is de facto.

Best regards,
Ron

Mr. Earl B. Dunckel
Washington, D.C.
September 2, 1980[24]

Dear Earl:

It was good to hear from you and to get your two letters packaged into one. I only had one question from the press about the Polish strike and I simply stated that I didn't believe it was our place to intervene in a purely domestic affair and that I hope the Soviet Union felt likewise.*

I was pleased to get the tip about Pakistan. I'm passing that on to our people to

---

* On August 13, 1980, Polish workers seized the Lenin shipyard at Gdansk. They demanded the right to form an independent union and for Lech Walesa to return to the union ranks. He had been dismissed in 1976 after a strikers' riot.

see if they can learn anything about it. They have some pretty good information sources.

I agree with you that my position on Taiwan is one that would be popular with the people. I have to believe this whole fuss was deliberately orchestrated by the administration. My last mention of Taiwan and improving our relations with them to offset Carter's betrayal of them, was in answer to a question by a Chinese back in May in Ohio. No fuss was raised then. There were a couple of columns that tried to portray me as wanting a two-China policy or diplomatic relations, when all I meant was to have the liaison office operate in Taiwan the way it operated in Peking before we had an embassy there. But suddenly, as the campaign gets under way, the whole China press comes out with a great furor. Well, my position is I'm not backing away one inch from where I stand on that because I don't think the mainland Chinese have any intention of giving up their relationship with us. Right now their concern is the Soviets. But I agree with you. We cannot go too far in trusting them. They don't like us any better than the Russians do.

I too have been annoyed by these unidentified staff members who are supposedly saying things and I honestly have to believe there aren't any—that this is just another one of those press tricks of wanting to say something so they attribute it to an unknown source.

It's funny you should mention about trying to pick out in advance what the press will attack and taking care of it in advance. We ourselves have decided now that we should go through every speech and try to pick out what the not-too-friendly press is going to use out of this as their lead line. At the same time, however, I am not going to be defensive and, even more important, I'll be damned if I'm going to let them press me into being cautious. I've been making speeches too long to change now.

Nancy sends her best and we both hope we see you soon.

Sincerely,
Ronald Reagan

During the first year of his presidency, Reagan writes that he is maintaining contact with Taiwan and that the Taiwanese understand the nature of U.S.–PRC relations.

Mr. John F. McIntyre Jr.
West Chester, Pennsylvania
July 9, 1981 [25]

Dear Mr. McIntyre:

I'm glad you wrote as you did and have allowed me the opportunity to speak to your concern.

Please have no fear; my attitude with regard to Taiwan has not changed, and they are aware of this. I keep in contact, and they know what we must do with regard to the People's Republic, but they know also that we are going to maintain the relationship that we have had in the past and that I have supported and endorsed during the campaign. I have personally visited Taiwan on two occasions and met with the President and other high government officials there and, as I said before, we do maintain a contact. Taiwan is a longtime friend and ally, and I will not be a party to tossing her overboard.

Again, thanks for giving me the opportunity to comment. Best regards.

Sincerely,
Ronald Reagan

———

A former Republican congressman from Minnesota wrote President Reagan to express his support for Taiwan, and attached letters from each of the five former U.S. ambassadors to Taiwan. The ambassadors supported selling weapons to Taiwan and the Taiwan Relations Act of 1979, which asserted that the United States would "provide Taiwan with arms of a defensive character, and . . . resist any resort to force or other forms of coercion that would jeopardize the security . . . of the people of Taiwan."

The Honorable Walter H. Judd
Washington, D.C.
May 18, 1982 [26]

Dear Walter:

Thank you very much for your letter and for sending me the messages from the retired ambassadors. I'm happy to hear that you are on the mend.

I hope you know that regardless of the press stories, I have not and will not change my position on our longtime friend Taiwan. It is true there are those in certain circles who think we must trade one China for another but I don't subscribe to that. I'll be tactful and try to improve and maintain the relations with the People's Republic of China started by R[ichard] N[ixon] but there will be no lessening of our relationship with our friends on Taiwan.

I'm dropping a line to each of the ambassadors to that effect. Take care of yourself and again thanks.

Sincerely,
Ron

———

Reagan writes to a friend who recently had visited Taiwan.

Mr. John Morley
Laguna Hills, California
December 22, 1982 [27]

Dear John:

Just received your good letter and the report on your trip. I'm happy to know that President Chiang Ching-kuo has confidence in my friendship for him and for

Taiwan and that he feels friendship for me as well. Please thank him for his message to me.

I remember with great pleasure our meeting and before that being guests in his father's home in 1972.* Please assure President Chiang that my feeling for the Republic of China remains unchanged and while we will continue to seek accord with the People's Republic of China it will not be at the expense of our friends on Taiwan.

I'd appreciate it also if you would deliver the attached photo to him on your next visit.

Sincerely,

Ron

President Reagan defends his April 1984 trip to the People's Republic of China, declares his commitment to allies around the world, and mentions his November 1983 trip to South Korea.

Mr. Joseph Becallo
West Monroe, New York
May 30, 1984 [28]

Dear Mr. Becallo:

I appreciate your writing and giving me a chance to straighten out what appear to be some misconceptions. Our policies are not designed to import, "slave labor goods," as you suggest in competition with our own workers.

Trade is a two-way street. We are an exporting nation and when we develop trade relations with other countries we create jobs here. Right now our trade is out of balance largely because our dollar is so strong in comparison to foreign money that too many of them can't afford to buy from us.

Mainly however I'd like to reply to your objections about the China trip. The leaders of China today it is true are practicing socialism but they are not the leaders who carried on the killings and persecution of their people. There has been a significant change with the death of those earlier dictators. China is embarked on economic changes that in many ways are beginning to look like our own free enterprise. They have a long way to go but we can help them get there sooner.

We can do this without slighting any of our friends like Taiwan, South Korea, South Africa and Israel. We will not forsake Taiwan. I recently visited South Korea and they are becoming one of our foremost trading partners. We are working closely with South Africa to bring about independence for Namibia and elimination of the Cuban troops in Angola. Israel presently receives more help from us than any other nation in the world.

Best regards,
Ronald Reagan

---

* Reagan was actually in Taiwan in October 1971.

Japan

In this reply to an old friend, President Reagan discusses his recent meeting with Prime Minister Yasuhiro Nakasone. The leaders agreed to reduce the trade imbalance between their countries.

> Mr. Laurence W. Beilenson
> Los Angeles, California
> May 19, 1987 [29]

Dear Larry:

Kathy [Osborne] shared your letter with me and your op-ed piece. I'm glad an op-ed column doesn't make you a journalist. Right now I have a less than charitable view of them, at least those here inside the beltway. The *Register* credited you with being an author and I agree. They could have added a darn good one.

I just have to reply and share some information that will hopefully reassure you that I haven't gone downhill from my days as SAG* president. I refuse to do another, "Play it again Sam." We've made some progress with our friend Prime Minister Nakasone's help. He's lost some political points at home because of his solid relationship with us but he hasn't wavered. We will lift the sanctions only when and if the violators return to observing the terms of our agreement.

On the general scene and again thanks to the prime minister we've made some other gains on opening their markets even though we still have quite a way to go. Another plus was getting them to raise the value of their underpriced "yen." But best of all we have improved the military situation, the price they pay for expenses of our forces based there, increase in the range guarded by their fleet etc. And there have been sizeable financial aid contributions to third world countries including the Philippines.

Some of these things we keep quiet about so as to protect our friend Nakasone. I hope we don't lose him in the coming elections. He truly has been a friend.

Now when do we take on the producers again? Or should I say, how are we going to restore the SAG to what it once was? Nancy sends her love and so do I.

> Sincerely,
> Ron

---

* Screen Actors Guild.

Thailand

Reagan discusses his October 1971 trip to Thailand as a representative of the Nixon administration. He also discusses Thailand's importance in the U.S. policy of containment designed to deter Soviet expansionism.

Mrs. Toffton
1974[30]

Dear Mrs. Toffton:

You've asked a complicated question with regard to our presence in Thailand. Incidentally, Thailand was one of the countries I was asked to visit as a representative of our government about three years ago. Apparently, our presence there is part of the strategy of containment just as NATO* is in Europe. Containment, of course, means discouraging aggression by the Communist bloc.

There is an economic factor involved also. Our being in Thailand is of financial help to the local economy as well as a factor in Thailand's own defense.

Those you saw demanding "Yankee go home" probably represented a faction who would not be concerned if the Red Chinese were occupying the bases now held by Americans. During my visit I was apprised of subversive activities particularly in the northern part of Thailand which indicated infiltration by Communist forces. I was also told that our presence meant economic stability that would be lessened considerably if we withdrew.

I agree with you, however, that we should do more than we have to curb waste and certainly we should not collaborate with fraud and graft as we have in so many nations.

Also, we should never, never fail to stand by any American whose rights are unjustly violated.

I don't know if this answers your question but hope it will be helpful.

Sincerely,
Ronald Reagan

The Vietnam War

Throughout his political career, Ronald Reagan supported the United States' involvement in the Vietnam War and defended President Nixon's policies toward Indochina. He explained his views in a January 15, 1980, letter: "I supported the mining of Haiphong Harbor and the bombing of Hanoi [in 1972] enthusiastically and was, in-

---

* Eleven western and southern European countries and the United States officially formed the North Atlantic Treaty Organization on April 4, 1949, for the purpose of collective security as hostilities with the Soviet Union were on the rise.

deed, considered a hawk because I have continued to say that the only immorality of the Vietnam War was that our government asked young men to die in a war that the government had no intention of winning." [31] *The two letters below, one written during his years as governor and the other during his presidency, show the consistency of his viewpoint on the United States' failed war in Indochina.*

Mr. Robertson
After January 1969 [32]

Dear Mr. Robertson:

I have just returned from the National Governors Conference in Washington and found your good letter awaiting me on my return.

First let me thank you for your generous words and the honor I feel that you would consider me for that very high office. Whatever the future holds for me I shall ever be grateful for the support people like you have given me these past several years.

While we were in the capital we were briefed by the president on the international situation and I must say he was very frank with regard to his plans for the future and the goal he seeks. There is no doubt all of us feel bitter about the inhumanity of the enemy we've been fighting. I think the president shares that feeling. But over the long haul a lasting peace in all of Southeast Asia is more important than the punishment we'd like to mete out.

The president is not swayed by any mawkish, forgive and forget sentiments. He is however willing to undertake a long-range plan of stabilization and with cool calculation believes repairing the war damage is essential to that plan.

I think we should support him in this even though it means swallowing a healthy desire to kick our tormentors in the teeth. Ever since WWII we have stumbled from one crisis to the next. Now we have someone who apparently knows where he's going and I think we should give him a crack at it.

Again thanks and best regards,
Ronald Reagan

Mr. Todd L. Thornton
Columbus, Ohio
May 27, 1987 [33]

Dear Todd Thornton:

I'm sorry to be so late in answering your letter of March 10. It sometimes takes a while for mail to reach my desk, your letter has only just made it.

Thank you for writing as you did. I'm most grateful and I'm happy to share your viewpoint—yours and Karen's. Please give her my regards and tell her how right she is to feel the way she does.

When after almost a decade of fighting in Vietnam we signed the Paris Peace Accords to end the war between South Vietnam and the Communist government of North Vietnam we withdrew our forces.* We had helped the South Vietnamese put together an army of half a million men. We believed this army with the tanks, helicopters and artillery we left them could defend their country if North Vietnam violated the peace treaty and attacked. We promised that if this happened we'd provide the fuel and ammunition for the things we left behind.

Well the North Vietnamese did violate the treaty and attacked as soon as our forces left South Vietnam. When our president asked Congress for money to keep our pledge the Congress flatly refused.† Just as they are refusing to help the Contras now. The South Vietnamese army retreated, abandoning the things we'd left for them and today the Communist forces of North Vietnam have taken not only South Vietnam but Cambodia and Laos as well.

We must not allow this to happen in Nicaragua. The Sandinistas have a disinformation network that has many Americans confused about what's at stake so just keep on preaching the gospel about Central America.

Again thanks.

Sincerely,
Ronald Reagan

EUROPE

Federal Republic of Germany

The human, political, and social costs of war came alive for Reagan when he visited the Federal Republic of Germany.[34] *In letters that serve as reflections about his trips there, he discusses the Holocaust and the success of the Allies' opening of the western front at Normandy on June 6, 1944. He sometimes refers to the artificiality of the division of Europe as exemplified by the Berlin Wall. Although he speaks of the pain that war inflicted on the Germans, he also believes that the German people are overcoming the horrors of the past. At the Brandenburg Gate on June 12, 1987, President Reagan declared: "I find in Berlin a message of hope, even in the shadow of this wall, a message of triumph."*

---

* Signed on January 27, 1973, the Paris Peace Accords called for a cease-fire.
† The U.S. Congress denied President Gerald R. Ford's request to send aid to South Vietnam, which fell to North Vietnam on April 30, 1975.

—————

Eight years before he would implore General Secretary Mikhail Gorbachev to "tear down this wall," Ronald Reagan was writing that the West should have torn it down and prevented its completion.

Mr. Arthur A. Kimball
Circa 1979–1980 [35]

Dear Mr. Kimball:

Thank you very much for your letter, and I assure you I am heartily in accord with all that you had to say. I not only was a visitor in behalf of President Nixon in Taiwan, but, after leaving the governor's office, I visited again and had a fine meeting with the new president there and, of course, am acquainted with all of those you met with and mentioned in your letter.*

I agree with you about the lost opportunity in Berlin when we could have knocked down and prevented the completion of the wall with no hostilities following. I agree, also, there was no need to betray Taiwan in order to improve our relations with mainland China. We could have had the latter without doing the former. Let me assure you that if I do succeed in winning the presidency, I will make it very plain from the first that my goal is to restore relations with Taiwan. I have the greatest admiration for what has been accomplished there in that brave country and the warmest regard for the people of Taiwan.

Thanks again for your letter and best regards,
Ronald Reagan

—————

The American who commanded the 82nd Airborne Division in the D-Day assault on June 6, 1944, and who had a distinguished career in the Army sent President Reagan a thank-you note for mentioning him in his Normandy address in France on June 6, 1984.

General M. B. Ridgway, USA (Ret.)
Pittsburgh, Pennsylvania
July 16, 1984 [36]

Dear General Ridgway:

It was good to hear from you but no thanks was needed. I was proud to have the opportunity to acknowledge your presence and your truly great service to this blessed land of ours.

—————

* Ronald and Nancy Reagan traveled to West Germany in the fall of 1978. They were accompanied by Richard V. Allen and his wife, Pat, and Peter Hannaford and his wife, Irene. See Peter Hannaford, *The Reagans: A Political Portrait* (New York: Coward-McCann, 1983), pp. 189–90.

If I could I'd make a trip to Normandy a part of our schoolchildren's education. It was a moving experience for Nancy and me. We can only imagine what it was for you who had been there on that day 40 years ago. God bless you.

Sincerely,
Ronald Reagan

Ronald Reagan's second visit to West Germany as president occurred in the spring of 1985. His itinerary included a visit to the military cemetery at Bitburg and the concentration camp at Bergen-Belsen. Many Americans opposed having their president visit Bitburg because SS storm troopers were buried there. Despite the uproar, President Reagan decided not to "back down and run for cover." [37] *Following the annual G-7 meeting held in Bonn,* * *he visited Bitburg and Bergen-Belsen.*

President Reagan ended his May 5 remarks at the concentration camp by saying that the Holocaust cannot happen again: "[R]ising above all the cruelty, out of this tragic and nightmarish time, beyond the anguish, the pain and the suffering for all time, we can and must pledge: Never again." Later that day at Bitburg President Reagan acknowledged that he had received many letters of both support and outrage at the fact that he had accepted the invitation to visit a German military cemetery. He explained his decision: "The evil war of Nazism turned all values upside down. Nevertheless, we can mourn the German war dead today as human beings crushed by a vicious ideology."

Years later, Reagan assessed his tour of the war sites: "I have never regretted not canceling the trip to Bitburg. In the end, I believe my visit to the cemetery and the dramatic and unexpected gesture by two old soldiers [American General Matthew B. Ridgway and German General Johannes Steinhoff clasped hands] from opposing sides of the battlefield helped strengthen our European alliance and heal once and for all many of the lingering wounds of the war." [38]

The next four letters were written at the height of the controversy over Bitburg.

Mr. Jesse A. Zeeman
Washington, D.C.
April 23, 1985 [39]

Dear Mr. Zeeman:

I'm sorry to be so late in answering your letter of March 30th. I've been away as you know so it wasn't brought to my attention until a few days ago.

Believe me I can understand your feeling of outrage and yes that of Mr. Rosensaft but let me say in my own defense that the media presentation of this whole episode is a gross distortion of fact. I'll try to put the matter in proper perspective.

---

* The G-7, a group of leading industrial democracies, met on May 2–4, 1985. The G-7 members were Canada, France, Germany, Italy, Japan, the United Kingdom, and the United States.

I will be in West Germany as a guest of the government at the time of the 40th anniversary of VE Day. Chancellor Kohl approached me some time ago as to what might be a proper observance of that day. I expressed the opinion that it was time for the world to view the day as one of gratitude that we have achieved friendship and 40 years of peace between erstwhile enemies. Of the seven nations represented at the economic summit three were enemies of the other four in WWII. Now we meet annually as allies.

Some time later he asked me to be a guest of his government for a state visit following the summit. He outlined a schedule which included our joint visit to the Bitburg cemetery on our way to a church service with our American troops. At about this same time I was told a West German political figure had asked me to pay a visit to Dachau. I felt that for me to do this on my own while a guest of the government would be taken as an affront to the people of Germany and at odds with the spirit of reconciliation the chancellor was trying to achieve. Frankly I suspected the invitation had a political motive. I'm afraid I didn't explain this very well when the question was asked in the press conference.

Only a short time ago when the media blitz reached Germany did I learn there had been some mix-up or confusion and that the Dachau visit was part of the official itinerary. I, of course, immediately accepted.

Mr. Zeeman my feelings about the Holocaust can be summed up in the words I've used a hundred times; "we must never forget and it must never happen again." Since I've been president we have regularly hosted gatherings in the East Room of survivors of the Holocaust. I'm more pleased than I can say that the visit to a concentration camp will be a part of the official program.

In a few days from now and prior to my trip I'll be attending a ceremony here honoring survivors of the Holocaust.

Thank you for giving me a chance to explain and to respond to Mr. Rosensaft's article.

Sincerely,
Ronald Reagan

Judge Joseph A. Zingales
Bedford, Ohio
April 26, 1985 [40]

Dear Judge Zingales:
I have just received your letter of April 16 and will probably be in Europe by the time you receive this. I want you to know how very much I appreciate your kind thoughtfulness in writing as you did.

These have been trying days for one who feels as deeply as I do about the inhumanity of the Nazi period. The Holocaust must never be forgotten and must never happen again. My purpose in accepting the chancellor's invitation was to emphasize that fact.

I hope the words I'll utter on the occasion will make plain that I'm not asking forgiveness for those who perpetrated the monstrous crime only remembrance so as to ensure it will never happen again.

Thanks again for an act of kindness I shall always remember.

Sincerely,
Ronald Reagan

Dr. Erwin T. Jacob
Tel Aviv, Israel
April 29, 1985 [41]

Dear Dr. Jacob:

My heartfelt thanks to you for your letter. You were more than kind to write as you did and I'm truly grateful.

This whole situation with regard to my coming visit has been most distressing, especially so since I feel and have felt for 40 years that the Holocaust must never be forgotten and such a thing must never happen again. I hope when I am at Bergen-Belsen, I'll be able to say something that will explain my reason for going there and correct the press distortions so widespread at the moment.

Again my thanks to you.

Sincerely,
Ronald Reagan

Mr. Michael Carowitz
Ann Arbor, Michigan
April 29, 1985 [42]

Dear Mr. Carowitz:

I hope you won't mind my answering your letter to Nancy. She is most grateful for your generous words about her activities. She passed your letter on to me because of the concerns you'd expressed about my coming visit to the cemetery in West Germany.

I too am an admirer of the late Scoop Jackson * and endorse everything he said to you in his letter. While I will be making my first visit to a camp—Bergen-Belsen, I had early exposure to the horror of those places. In WWII I was adjutant of an Air Corps post directly under Air Corps intelligence. One of our tasks was putting a film report together for the General Staff in the Pentagon. We received the first film taken by combat crews when our forces overran a number of the camps, Auschwitz, etc. None of us who worked on that report will ever forget the horrors we saw—the living and the dead.

I say with all my heart—this must never be forgotten and it must never happen again. Chancellor Kohl of Germany asked me to join him on this 40th observance of the war's end not to honor the dead in the cemetery but to point up that we erst-

---

* Senator Henry M. Jackson (D-Washington) died on September 1, 1983.

while enemies—now close allies who have lived in peace for 40 years, are united in our determination that the Holocaust will never be repeated. It seems to me this is a worthwhile and morally right thing to do. Thank you for giving me a chance to explain.

Sincerely,

Ronald Reagan

The next three letters were written shortly after President Reagan's trip to West Germany, defending the visits to the two World War II sites.

Mrs. Shirley Norwood McNamara

Wellesley, Massachusetts

May 15, 1985 [43]

Dear Mrs. McNamara:

I hope you won't mind my answering your letter to Nancy. She asked me to give you her regards but that since your letter concerned me and our recent trip she'd let me respond.

First let me express my sympathy for your great loss. I know there are no words that can ease the pain. I wish there were.

In accepting the West German government's invitation to join in an observance of the end of the war my only purpose was to recognize these 40 years of peace in which our one-time enemy has become a friend and ally at the same time it has admitted to the evil of the Hitler era. I learned that not only have they maintained the concentration camps with museums showing the full extent of their horror; they bring schoolchildren to them every year and impress on them that Germany must never allow such things to happen again.

I'm enclosing copies of the two speeches I made, one at Bergen-Belsen and then the one later in the day at Bitburg where our forces are based with the Germans on the NATO line. These explain what our purpose was in going there.

I appreciate very much your writing as you did and so does Nancy. I hope the enclosed scripts can lessen your concern which I fully understand.

Sincerely,

Ronald Reagan

Judge E. J. Houston

Ottawa, Canada

May 20, 1985 [44]

Dear Judge Houston:

Thank you very much for your kind letter. I am most grateful for your kind and generous words. They mean a great deal to me especially in view of your own wartime experience.

It seems to me we achieved something most unusual 40 years ago. Back through history wars were settled in such a way they planted the seeds for the next war. The hatreds and rivalries remained. Not this time. Here it is four decades later and our erstwhile enemies are our staunchest friends and allies.

Again my thanks to you and very best regards.

Sincerely,
Ronald Reagan

Colonel Barney Oldfield, USAF (Ret.)
Beverly Hills, California
May 20, 1985 [45]

Dear Barney:

Thanks very much for all your encouraging words and for all the history. I especially liked that high-level inspection and watering down of the dragon's teeth.

Barney I felt from the start that I was doing the morally right thing and I'm even more sure now. I've received some of the most moving letters (some of the other kind too) they are from veterans with stories to tell that put a lump in your throat. They think I did the right thing too.

I'm enclosing copies of my speeches—the morning talk at Bergen-Belsen and the afternoon one at Bitburg Air Force Base.

Thanks again and best to Vada.

Sincerely,
Ron

———

Lisa Zanatta Henn is the daughter of Private First Class Peter Robert Zanatta, who was among the first wave of troops to storm the beaches of Normandy on June 6, 1944. He survived the invasion, but had died by the time President Reagan mentioned him and his daughter during his D-Day speech in France on June 6, 1984.

Mrs. Lisa Zanatta Henn
San Mateo, California
May 22, 1985 [46]

Dear Lisa:

Thank you very much for your kind letter. It was kind of you to write as you did and you warmed my heart.

I've heard from a number of veterans who like your father had stories to tell about moments in the war when deeds of human kindness momentarily bridged the gap between enemies.

One thing that made me want to do the trip was the knowledge that in these 40 years since VE Day the Germans have become our friends and allies and have never asked us to forgive or forget the Nazi evil. Indeed they take their schoolchildren to the concentration camps and show them the horror of the Holocaust. They do it so such a thing can never happen again.

I've enclosed my speech at Bergen-Belsen and the one later in the day at our airbase in Bitburg.

Again my heartfelt thanks.

Sincerely,
Ronald Reagan

NATO and the Western Alliance

On April 4, 1949, 11 European countries and the United States formed the North Atlantic Treaty Organization (NATO), a collective defense organization in which the member states agreed "to safeguard the freedom, common heritage, and civilization of their peoples, founded on the principles of democracy, individual liberty, and the rule of law."[47] Greece and Turkey joined in 1952, and the Federal Republic of Germany joined in 1955. Difficulty with the Soviet Union was the main reason the organization formed and continued to deepen. Throughout the cold war, NATO was the United States's most important political and security alliance.

In these letters, Ronald Reagan writes about some issues within NATO, problems between NATO and the Soviet bloc, and U.S. relations with individual NATO members.

NATO has always been concerned about the potential for conflict between members on the grounds that such clashes would undermine the cohesiveness and effectiveness of the alliance. The long-standing disagreement between Greece and Turkey over the status of Cyprus is one such example. A pro-Greek military junta overthrew Cypriot President Mikhail Khristodolou Mouskos Makarios III on July 15, 1974. Five days later Turkish forces invaded, and on February 13, 1975, proclaimed a Turkish Cypriot state in the northern sector of the island. Negotiations between Greece and Turkey about the status of Cyprus began in 1975.

In this reply to his 1966 opponent for the Republican nomination for governor of California, Reagan writes that the Ford administration glanced sideways as events were unfolding on Cyprus.

Mr. George Christopher
San Francisco, California
Circa early 1976[48]

Dear George:

Thanks very much for all you did in New Hampshire, Massachusetts and Florida. I have been saying pretty much what was contained in the column you sent; that we closed our eyes first at the "Junta's" plot against Makarios and then looked the other way when Turkey moved. I've also called for the removal of Kissinger.

Again, my heartfelt thanks and I'll keep swinging.

Sincerely,
Ron

In a letter to his chief of staff when he was governor and 1980 campaign adviser, Reagan writes that the United States should have intervened between two NATO members in the crisis over Cyprus.

Mr. Ed Meese
1979 or 1980[49]

Ed—this I think is urgent. I can't recall exactly what I said in '76 but it was to the effect that we had been derelict in not intervening with two NATO allies involved in this tragic dispute. I know the importance of Turkey as an ally but a great injustice is being done to the displaced Greeks and I believe we should do something about them.

Ron

Although most leaders in Western Europe would eventually support the treaty on intermediate-range nuclear forces (INF) signed by President Ronald Reagan and Soviet General Secretary Mikhail Gorbachev in Washington on December 8, 1987, some expressed concern that the agreement would lead to a lessening of extended deterrence, the nuclear and conventional umbrella the United States provided them through NATO. At a NATO summit in Brussels on March 2 and 3, 1988, President Reagan sought to reassure his alliance partners of the United States' commitment to mutual security.[50]

In the letter below, President Reagan thanks an old friend for his words about the NATO summit.

Colonel Barney Oldfield, USAF (Ret.)
Beverly Hills, California
March 14, 1988[51]

Dear Barney:

Thanks for your letter re the NATO summit. I appreciated reading the history you provided and particularly Ike's role in getting it under way.

Barney I think a miracle has taken place and we can take a bow for it. In all those past wars the victors set peace terms that laid the foundation for the wars to follow. This time Uncle Sam played a role. There was something called the Marshall Plan and we applied it to allies and the defeated enemies alike. Only one (and it was an ally) the Soviet Union went its own expansionist way. As for the rest, 40 years of peace. And it looks like we might make it for another 40.

Our press tried to play down what was accomplished with terms like "papering over" divisions etc. Truth is there was and is real unity amon[g] the 16.

Best regards,
Ron

Northern Ireland

In a letter to the American ambassador to Great Britain, British citizen P.J. Hawksley-Cooke wrote that the United States opposed terrorism more vigorously in the Middle East than it did in Northern Ireland, yet the Irish Republican Army (IRA) received funds from some Bostonians and the Libyan leader Muammar Qaddafi. In his reply to Hawksley-Cooke, Ambassador Charles H. Price II defended the Reagan administration's record on terrorism. Price then sent a copy of the exchange to President Reagan, whose reply is below.

The Honorable Charles H. Price II
London, England
February 25, 1986[52]

Dear Charlie:

Thanks for your letter and the enclosed correspondence re the IRA. Your reply to Mr. Hawksley-Cooke was right on. We know there are some of Irish heritage who contribute to the terrorists in Northern Ireland but they are more than matched by those who preach the opposite. The Irish ambassador as well as quite a few of our citizens including many from Boston such as Speaker Tip O'Neill take to the speaking circuit to plead for no contributions.*

Love to Carole.

Ron

FOREIGN AID

As the United States accepted a position of global power after World War II, foreign assistance at once became a major part of its foreign policy. President Reagan often remarked that the extension of assistance to former wartime adversaries, such as Italy and West Germany, showed that the United States was not an aggressive great

---

* Margaret Mary Heckler was the American ambassador to Ireland from 1985 to 1989. Thomas P. O'Neill was the Speaker of the U.S. House of Representatives from 1977 to 1987.

*power, and that it used nonmilitary means to encourage peace, prosperity, and se-
curity.*

————————

*Written during his second term in the White House, the next two letters are examples
of President Reagan's thinking about American aid abroad.*

> Mrs. Arthur Shane
> Nutley, New Jersey
> September 30, 1985 [53]

Dear Mrs. Shane:

I'm sorry to be so late in answering your letter of August 2nd but it takes a while
for mail to reach my desk and I've only just received your letter. I'm glad you wrote
and sent the clipping about Mr. Castro and his effort to persuade our Latin neighbors to welch on their debts.* He wasn't successful I'm happy to say. Incidentally
those debts are not owed to our government but to banks and lending institutions
here and in Europe mainly.

May I say with regard to our foreign aid, it has two purposes. One is to help
them provide their own military security which is less expensive than our having
to provide it. The other is [to] help these lesser developed countries get their
economies going so they can be better customers of ours. Much of what we give
comes back to us in trade and helps provide American jobs.

You are right about our deficit spending though. Eliminating excessive
spending and eliminating the annual deficit is our primary goal and we can accomplish that by eliminating wasteful programs that are doling out money to
those who have no real need at the same time we continue to provide for those
who must have help. Then like you I dream of starting to make payments on the
national debt.

Again thank you for your letter.

> Sincerely,
> Ronald Reagan

> Mr. Edwin E. Post
> East Haven, Connecticut
> May 30, 1986 [54]

Dear Mr. Post:

Your letter of April 17 has finally reached me. It sometimes takes a while for
mail to get to my desk and this was particularly true in light of my recent trip to
Asia.

————————

* On July 26, 1985, at the celebration of the 32nd anniversary of the Cuban revolution, Cuban leader
Fidel Castro urged Latin American nations to refuse to pay their international debts.

I appreciate your sending me the article on our expenditures in behalf of foreign countries.* In the past, long before I ever thought I'd be doing what I'm doing now I did a lot of public speaking. Frequently my subject was the waste and extravagance connected with foreign aid. I'm pleased to tell you we've taken steps in these last five years to eliminate waste and fraud with some success.

But I've studied very carefully the article you sent me and let me point out something having to do with the time period, 1946–1971. Back in 1946 you may recall we created the Marshall Plan to help rebuild the war ravaged nations both friend and enemy.† Just picking out the nations listed in the article, helped by this plan accounts for more than half the total spending.

I don't think we can or should ignore the great benefit provided by that plan. Today three of our staunchest allies, West Germany, Italy and Japan were our enemies in WWII and we've known 40 years of peace.

We continue to have a foreign aid program today. Its purpose is to help developing countries build an economic structure so as to reduce poverty and misery and resist the overtures of the Soviet Union which is bent on an expansionist policy in an effort to make the whole world into a single Communist state. Also much of that aid is to help those countries have a defense capability of their own which is less costly than if we had to provide that defense with our own forces.

But please be assured we continue to search for ways to eliminate unnecessary spending both at home and abroad.

Thanks again for your letter.

Sincerely,
Ronald Reagan

INTELLIGENCE

In the post–Vietnam and Watergate era, U.S. legislators began to investigate the activities of American intelligence agencies to see whether they operated within the spirit and letter of American law. On January 4, 1975, President Gerald R. Ford created a commission to investigate whether the Central Intelligence Agency had "exceeded . . . [its] statutory authority."[55] *Ronald Reagan was appointed to the commission. Headed by Vice President Nelson A. Rockefeller, the commission submitted its report to the president on June 6, 1975. Two months later, Reagan taped a radio commentary about the commission for his nationally syndicated program: "My own reaction after months*

---

* "U.S. Foreign Aid: History's Most Awesome Giveaway," *New Haven Register,* October 31, 1971.
† Secretary of State George C. Marshall enunciated the economic recovery plan for Europe that bore his name in 1947, not 1946. He did so during his commencement address at Harvard University on June 5.

of testimony and discussion during the investigation of the CIA is 'much ado about—if not nothing at least very little.' "[56]

———————

The following pre-presidential letters express Reagan's view that many of the restrictions on the intelligence agencies jeopardize national security.

Mrs. Richard E. Duffy
Circa mid-1970s[57]

Dear Mrs. Duffy:

Thanks very much for your letter and for what you have done on my behalf. I'm most grateful.

Regarding my position on the issues you mentioned—whether it is necessary to reinstate both the House and Senate committees might be questionable but certainly one of them should be. I also believe we must stop this insane restriction of both the FBI and the CIA. We are flying blind at a time when we need both agencies capable of conducting counterespionage. Hand in hand with this goes an increased defense capability.

Again thanks and best regards,

Ronald Reagan

Mr. E. Spencer Garrett
Greenwich, Connecticut
Circa mid-1970s[58]

Dear Mr. Garrett:

Your letter of January 17 has just been delivered to me—which says something about bureaucracy.

Please be assured I'm in agreement with you about the need to keep an effective counterintelligence force alive and well in our land. Frankly, my concern is with the congressional committees now investigating the CIA. I have little faith in their objectivity.

Best regards,
Ronald Reagan

Mrs. Blanche Seaver
Los Angeles, California
Before June 6, 1976[59]

Dear Blanche:

Once again, and as always, I am in your debt. Those young people went out on their own with regard to the radio show and I must confess to mixed emotions. I'm proud, of course, of what they decided to do but, on the other hand, have concern about all the people like yourself who have done so much now are being asked by them to do more. Anyway, you know how grateful I am.

About the CIA commission—have no fear. I'm not a recipient of any favors nor would I be under any circumstances. Actually when the president asked me to be on the commission, I accepted because I feel there are those in Washington who would like to destroy the CIA and the FBI, just as they did the House Committee on Un-American Activities. We need the CIA as we need a strong military and I figured it was my duty to help if I could.

Thanks again and Nancy says from her too.

Love,
Ron

Mr. John Spence
Baltimore, Maryland
Circa mid-1970s[60]

Dear Mr. Spence:

Thank you for your letter. I read the clippings as you suggested, but am afraid I have trouble believing that either of the columnists can be totally objective on this subject.

I do not believe the CIA or any of our other intelligence agencies is in the business of trying to dictate what form of government other countries will have. The CIA exists to protect us from the aggression of others who would install their form of government on the United States. Their function is counter-intelligence which means the thwarting of enemy spies with hostile intent against our country.

Sincerely,
Ronald Reagan

CHAPTER SEVENTEEN

The Oval Office and Reelection

R ONALD REAGAN was the first president to serve two full terms in office since Dwight D. Eisenhower.

President Reagan followed the priorities he had laid out as a candidate—improving the economy and rebuilding national defense, as indicated in Chapter 7. His first year in office was marked by the assassination attempt on March 30, 1981, and by passage of tax and budget legislation that reduced taxes, increased defense spending, and controlled domestic spending—and by the beginning of a recession that would reach its nadir in November of 1982.

In 1983 the economy began to recover, and Reagan's 1984 campaign ads expressed the economic revitalization and renewed confidence in the country with the slogan "It's morning again in America." On his decision to run for a second term, Reagan quoted Lincoln: "Wasn't it Lincoln who said, 'having put the hand to the plow, it's no time to turn back'?"

Reagan brought with him to the White House many people who had worked with him in Sacramento when he was governor of California, after the governorship, and during campaigns, including Ed Meese, Mike Deaver, Lyn Nofziger, Martin Anderson, and Richard Allen.

James Baker III, who had run George Bush's campaign for the presidency, became chief of staff. Deaver was deputy chief of staff and Meese was counsellor to the president. They became known as the troika. Nofziger was assistant to the president for political affairs; Martin Anderson was assistant to the president for policy development; and Richard Allen was national security adviser. It was a strong team but not one free of internal politics or disagreements on what was possible and what was not—in politics, in economics, or internationally.

Peter Hannaford, who with Deaver had handled Reagan's affairs after he left the governorship, did not join the administration. William P. Clark, who had been with Reagan in Sacramento, served as deputy secretary of state until he became national security adviser when Allen resigned in January 1982. Two long-time Reagan associates headed cabinet departments: Caspar Weinberger as secretary of defense and William

French Smith as attorney general. Many other cabinet secretaries Reagan knew only slightly.

By 1985 most of the people who knew Reagan well from the governorship or campaigns had become heads of cabinet departments or had left for the private sector.

In these letters Reagan accepts resignations. He responds to people concerned about the running of the White House and the reelection campaign and explains his management style. He responds to people concerned about who is advising him and their internal disagreements, people recommending campaign strategy, and people commenting on his performance.

To outsiders—even those correspondents like George Murphy with whom he seems most unguarded—he defends both staff and policy resolutely, always assuring writers that he is in charge and doing all he can to change policy. To still other friends and to some people he has not met, he explains campaign strategy or tactics or comments on major events like the Challenger *tragedy or his D-Day anniversary speech at Normandy.*

Jack Hume was a supporter and friend of Reagan's from the time he ran for governor of California. Reagan wrote few letters mentioning the March 30, 1981, assassination attempt, usually referring to it as "the unfortunate incident" or "my little shooting episode." He was released from the hospital April 11.

Mr. and Mrs. Jaquelin H. Hume
San Francisco, California
April 27, 1981[1]

Dear Jack and Betty:

How good it was to get your letter—although we envied you, having to cancel the trip to California and Mexico ourselves because of the unfortunate incident. We continue to be persistently homesick and I've decided California is a very hard place to leave. But again, let me say how much we appreciated your letter and your generous words.

They tell me I'm well ahead of schedule in my recovery, and I must say, I'm feeling better every day. But I will agree with those doctors who say that a lung injury is the most painful.

The truce is over here in Washington. We're back in the fight now to get our economic package and wouldn't you know, we're having more trouble with some Republicans than we are with the Democrats.

Nancy sends her love, as do I, and to both of you again, a big affectionate thank you.

Sincerely,
Ron

Mr. James K. Edwards
Sacramento, California
September 13, 1982 [2]

Dear Mr. Edwards:

Kathy gave me your note and I'm delighted to hear you are out of the hospital and on the road to recovery. Take care of yourself and don't overdo.

When I left the hospital after my little shooting episode someone told me to remember a surgeon's scalpel is five weeks long. It was good advice.

Give my regards to Mrs. Edwards.

Sincerely,
Ronald Reagan

Reagan wrote this note, recalling the day of the assassination attempt on his life, for a USA Today *story on James Brady, who had been Reagan's press secretary. Brady was also hit by John W. Hinckley Jr. and was permanently injured.*

About Jim Brady
July 17, 1984 [3]

After the shooting in March of '81 my lowest moment came when they wheeled a stretcher by mine and I was told it was Jim Brady and that his chances were slim. Jim the unflappable, the generous, the witty, the one who had become such a trusted friend. It was the first I knew others had been shot and I really started praying.

I thought I knew and appreciated all Jim's good qualities before that day but new ones were revealed in the months that followed, the greatest of which was courage.

Ronald Reagan

Reagan defends his nomination of Sandra Day O'Connor, the first woman who would serve on the Supreme Court, to Harold Brown, a professor of theology.

Mr. Harold O.J. Brown
Deerfield, Illinois
August 3, 1981 [4]

Dear Mr. Brown:

Thank you very much for your letter of a few weeks ago and for giving me the opportunity to comment.

First, let me say I have called to the attention of our scheduling people your request with regard to the book and I hope this can be worked out.

Now, with reference to the choice I have made for the Supreme Court, let me just say some things you probably already heard in your conversation with Ed Thomas, although I have not talked to him about that. Mrs. O'Connor, I think, has been the victim particularly of one vindictive person in Arizona who launched the crusade against her even before the public announcement of her nomination. I saw some of this individual's original charges, including one that supposedly Mrs. O'Connor was opposed to my running for office as a candidate for president. I called Senator Goldwater about this, and he hit the ceiling. He told me that she hadn't spoken to him for a month in 1976 because he came out for President Ford instead of me. I think this was typical of most of the things that have been brought up against her.

Let me explain how things can be distorted with one example. As a state senator back in the early '70s, she is charged with having voted against a bill that would have prevented the university hospitals from giving abortions. The true situation is that she as a senator voted for a bill to rebuild the university football stadium. Over in the House, they added an amendment regarding abortions in the university hospitals. But the constitution of Arizona says that no amendment can be attached to a bill unless the amendment has to do with the body of the bill. Obviously, the hospital amendment had nothing to do with a football stadium so the Senate, with her vote included, had to turn down this amendment. She has assured me that she finds abortion personally abhorrent. She has also told me she believes the subject is one that is a proper subject for legislation. She cannot, as a candidate for nominee for the Court, go beyond such statements because anything she says in advance of appointment could later be used to disqualify her from hearing certain cases on the basis of being biased or prejudiced.

My position has not changed. I consider the unborn child a living human being, and an abortion is the taking of a human life. This, in my view, can only be justified, as it always has been within our tradition, in defense of the mother's life. I appreciate your giving me this opportunity to respond, and I hope that the truth will eventually triumph. I have full confidence in Mrs. O'Connor, in her qualifications, and in her philosophy.

Best regards,
Ronald Reagan

David Stockman, director of the Office of Management and Budget, told inside stories about the budget process and the economic program to William Greider of the Washington Post *at a series of 18 breakfast meetings, supposedly with the understanding that Greider would write a book about it later. Greider's article, "The Education of David Stockman," was published in the December 1981 issue of* The Atlantic, *but became available in Washington, D.C., on November 10. Greider quoted Stockman as claiming that the tax cuts were a Trojan horse for "trickle-down" economics designed to benefit the economy by reducing taxes on high-income earners. The quotation was right but the claim was false. The story was politically damaging and reduced Stock-*

man's effectiveness in working with members of the cabinet to reduce their proposed budgets. Edwin Meese and Michael Deaver thought Stockman should be fired, but James Baker supported Stockman and Reagan decided to keep him on.

Mr. Justin Dart
Los Angeles, California
December 7, 1981 [5]

Dear Jus:

Thanks very much for sending the information on Don Rice.* We'll keep it on file.

Jus, we've never had a chance to visit about Dave Stockman so let me just briefly lay it out. The writer (an admitted liberal) is a longtime friend of Dave's and they've argued (like you and I used to when I was a Democrat) about their philosophical differences.

Being long time friends, Dave agreed to give him progress reports on the building of the economic program with the understanding they were off the record, not for quote or attribution, and that once the program was in place his friend (?) would do an article on the birth of the economic plan.

Well his friend (an assistant editor of the *Washington Post*) called him and said he was doing the article and using quotes. When Dave told him this was a violation of their understanding, the reply was that the "off the record" only applied to the *Washington Post.*

If you read the article carefully, you see that Dave's quotes were not the damning part, it was the writer's interpretation.

Dave came to me and tendered his resignation—saying he wanted to spend his time publicly repudiating the charges in the article that I didn't believe in the program and was deliberately misstating the case to the people. I refused his offer to resign.

Jus, the whole thing has faded here and he is completely rehabilitated on the Hill. In the recent battle that led to my veto, the senators and House members were totally dependent on him and his figures.

I've had any number of letters from the Congress expressing their happiness that I'd kept him on. I think the appearances he's making are part of his desire to make sure no lingering suspicion remains that we were insincere about our program. One thing sure—you can bet he's no longer a friend to that journalistic prostitute he once trusted.

Hope to see you soon, and hope you are feeling better. Love to Punky.

Sincerely,
Ron

---

* Dart recommended Don Rice, President of RAND, as a replacement for Stockman.

———

Lyn Nofziger was assistant to the president for political affairs in the White House and had been Reagan's press secretary during the governorship and in campaigns. Here Reagan responds to Nofziger's letter of resignation.

Mr. Lyn Nofziger
January 4, 1982[6]

Dear Lyn:

You know this comes with mixed emotions. Yes I accept your resignation—but no I'm not happy about it. Maybe I should say, "wait 'til I get my hat and I'll go with you."

Thanks for all you've done and thanks for your generous words. Nancy and I wish you and Bonnie happiness and success in all you undertake. Just remember, you may be out of the administration but you are still in our lives 'til the end of the road.

Warmest regard,
Ron

———

Reagan explains his view of cabinet government to George Champion of the Chase Manhattan Bank, who urged Reagan to ensure that his staff and appointees support his program. The Eagle Forum was a conservative activist organization founded by Phyllis Schlafly in 1972 with branches in many states and local newsletters of the same name; Champion's sister Sara Andrews ran the Champaign County, Illinois organization.

Mr. George Champion
New York, New York
March 24, 1982[7]

Dear George:

Thank you very much for your good letter and for sending me the *Eagle Forum* with your sister's very generous words. I intend to write her and express my appreciation, not only for that one article but for all she is doing for the cause.

George the press here in Washington and to a great extent the [*New York*] *Times* seem bent on portraying our administration as divided and me as standing alone. Believe me that is not the case. Maybe they get that idea from the way I like to work. I use the cabinet and staff as a kind of board of directors. I want all the input I can get and the different viewpoints. From all of this, I make my decisions. Once that is done, I can assure you, we go forward united. But you are absolutely right about the bureaucracy. It not only resists, it sabotages what we're doing when it can.

Again my thanks and best regards.

Sincerely,
Ron

Clymer Wright was a conservative political activist and former newspaperman from Houston, Texas.

Mr. Clymer L. Wright, Jr.
Houston, Texas
May 18, 1982[8]

Dear Clymer:

I've just received a copy of your letter with the attached news articles and must tell you I'm very distressed. Yes there is undermining of my efforts going on and yes there is sabotage of all I'm trying to accomplish. But it's being done by the people who write these articles and columns not by any White House staff member and certainly not by Jim Baker.

Some in the media delight in trying to portray me as being manipulated and led around by the nose. They do so because they are opposed to everything this administration represents. I could show you similar stories with only the name changed. Stories in which other staff or cabinet members are named instead of Jim Baker. Don't join that group Clymer—you are helping them with their sabotage.

Clymer I'm in charge and my people are helping to carry out the policies I set. No we don't get everything we want and yes we have to compromise to get 75 or 80 percent of our programs. We try to see that the 75 or 80 percent is more than worth the compromise we have to accept. So far it has been.

There has not been one single instance of Jim Baker doing anything but what I've settled on as our policy. He goes all out to help bring that about. I'm enclosing an article in this week's *U.S. News and World Report*. It is an interview with Paul Laxalt who remains as solid in his convictions as he has always been. Please note his comment regarding Jim Baker.

Sincerely,
Ronald Reagan

The 1982 midterm elections were held at the depth of the recession; the Republicans would have only 165 seats instead of 192 in the House, but picked up one Senate seat, giving them 54.

Ward Quaal, an innovator in radio and television broadcasting, was the retired president of Chicago's WGN Broadcasting Company. He and Reagan exchanged frequent letters. WGN was the top radio broadcaster in the Midwest when Reagan was first looking for a job in radio; WGN turned him down.

James Watt was Reagan's first (and controversial) secretary of the interior, who had called Indian reservations "a failed experiment in socialism" as a critique of government policies encouraging dependency.

Mr. Ward L. Quaal
Chicago, Illinois
February 25, 1983 [9]

Dear Ward:

Thanks very much for sending the Ron Hendren script. Maybe he means well but you know this is an example of how successful the media and groups with an axe to grind can be in image making. The actual record of the Department of Interior under Jim Watt is possibly if not probably better than it has been for many, many years.

I've obtained the transcript of what Jim Watt actually said regarding the Indians and he was actually pointing out government's faults. Indian leaders who sounded off on him after hearing the press version did an about face when given his verbatim statement.

Thanks again and best regards,

Ron

What Reagan didn't write himself in the late 1970s (e.g., many of his newspaper columns) was often drafted by Peter Hannaford, one of the two principals of Deaver & Hannaford, Reagan's public relations firm. Hannaford did not go into the administration, but kept in touch with Reagan.

Mr. Peter D. Hannaford
Washington, D.C.
July 25, 1983 [10]

Dear Pete:

Thanks very much for the Pasadena tear sheet. I'm sending it over to Margaret Heckler* in case she missed this story. By the way here's one for you—a conversation piece for one of those moments when there's a pause. A county in Pennsylvania decided to do some cross-checking on computers to review their welfare lists. They came up with seven fugitives, escapees from prison, all drawing welfare and 32 inmates in state prison getting regular checks.

Nancy sends her best. Thanks again.

Sincerely,
Ron

Reagan announced on January 19, 1984, that he would run for reelection; Nancy had tried to persuade him not to run, but he was determined to do so.[11] Reagan had no serious Republican opposition.

---

* Margaret Heckler was secretary of health and human services from 1983 to 1985.

The speech on which Quaal complimented Reagan was his January 25, 1984, State of the Union address to a joint session of Congress.

> Mr. Ward L. Quaal
> Chicago, Illinois
> February 20, 1984 [12]

Dear Ward:

It was good to get your letter and I thank you for your generous words about the speech. I have to tell you I've faced a lot of audiences as you know but that "joint session" does make for a slight case of nerves before and after. This makes your words very welcome indeed.

I'm glad too that you approve my decision about running. Wasn't it Lincoln who said, "having put the hand to the plow, it's no time to turn back"?

Nancy sends her love and from both of us to Dorothy.

> Best regards,
> Ron

———

Edwin Meese III was Reagan's top aide in Sacramento and counsellor to the president in the White House. Reagan nominated him as attorney general on January 23, 1984. [13] Reagan assures Frank Whetstone, long-time Republican delegate hunter who wrote to recommend people who could replace Meese as counsellor, that Meese will continue to advise him.

> Mr. Frank A. Whetstone
> Cutbank, Montana
> February 27, 1984 [14]

Dear Frank:

It was good to hear from you. I'm sorry about the delay in answering but it takes a while before mail reaches my desk.

Frank I'm not sure who is engineering this operation that subjects you and others to all the phone calls. I realize, of course, that people like yourself are sincerely concerned but you shouldn't be.

I'm not replacing Ed because he'll be as near at hand as he's always been. I have a cabinet operating similar to the way we ran things in California and as attorney general Ed will be in those meetings as he is now. His job has been one of counseling and advising when I need someone to bounce things off of. He'll still be doing that. We've worked together for too many years for me to change now.

Frank I'm not being manipulated by people who are out to change my beliefs. If there were any such trying I'd kick their fannies out of here. I've lived too long with my beliefs to change now and no matter what those hacks in the press say, I make the decisions and will continue to do so.

I appreciate your writing and your support. Give my best to your gal.

Sincerely,

Ron

Reagan replies to a letter given to him by campaign consultant Stuart Spencer; the letter recommended "new ideas," especially a ballot initiative to require a balanced budget. Reagan defends his record and notes the failure in Congress of the constitutional amendment to balance the budget. The Reagan administration made a serious effort on such an amendment in 1982. The Senate passed a proposed amendment (S.J. Res. 58) on August 4, 1982, by 69–31; a similar amendment was, with considerable effort, brought to the floor for a vote in the House of Representatives on October 1, 1982, but it failed to get the required two-thirds majority to send it to the states for ratification.

Mr. S. J. Malek

Anaheim, California

March 26, 1984 [15]

Dear Mr. Malek:

Stu Spencer shared your letter (March 12) with me and I hope you won't mind my addressing some of the issues you raised.

I share your feeling about the promise we've heard in the Democratic primaries about "new ideas." I do however disagree that voting Republican or Democrat is "a waste of time" and means voting for more of the same. Mr. Malek I believe that what we've been attempting here in these three years represents new ideas after half a century of a policy based on big government with ever increasing interference in the lives of the people.

Granted we have not made the total overhaul that is needed but with the House of Representatives dominated by the party which for 50 years or so promoted the big government policy we've only gotten a portion of the changes we seek. Had we followed the budget projections of the preceding administration the deficit would be $191 billion bigger than it is.

You suggest direct vote of the people on some of our major issues. Under our Constitution that is not possible at the federal level. For two years I've been trying to get the Congress to approve a constitutional amendment requiring a balanced budget. So far no success. There is another way however to change the Constitution and that is for the states to call for a constitutional convention. Right now only two more states have to approve in order to have such a convention and there the people would have a voice.

That gentleman [Speaker of the House Tip O'Neill] you quoted as calling me a liar after my speech cannot, I assure you, substantiate his charges. Along with the Republican leadership in both houses of Congress we have laid out a program to start reducing the deficit by $150 billion over the next three years. This is only a first step and we intend to go further but it will take the people leaning on their congressmen to get it done.

We have so far cut the "rate" of increase in federal spending in half, reduced the federal payroll by tens of thousands of employees, eliminated regulations that once took 300 million man-hours of paperwork by our citizens and yet have only gotten half of what we asked for.

As for education, we have a bill before the Congress seeking tax credits for parents sending children to independent schools.

For 15 months we've averaged reducing the unemployment rolls by 300,000 a month.

Thanks for giving up the golf game.

Best regards,
Ronald Reagan

Reagan explains why he is civil to House Speaker Tip O'Neill in spite of personal attacks.

Mr. Jerry Granat
Hewlett, New York
May 31, 1984 [16]

Dear Mr. Granat:

Thank you for writing as you did and for giving me a chance to reply. I understand your concern. I've never quite been able to accept rival lawyers in a trial having lunch together during a recess.

I don't think you've seen me embracing or being embraced by Speaker O'Neill recently. And yes I find some of his personal attacks hard to forgive. He's an old line politico. Earlier in my term and before recent events he explained away some of his partisan attacks as politics and that after 6 p.m. we were friends. Well that's more than a little difficult for me to accept lately.

But Mr. Granat there are certain things I cannot do if I'm to carry out my responsibilities. I can't publicly refuse to be civil nor can I show anger and resentment. What we say to each other when the cameras aren't turning or the press listening in is a different matter.

I am responsible for the death of any man in uniform in the pursuit of his duty because I assign that duty. It has to be the most difficult burden for any president. But please don't think refusing to stoop is turning the other cheek.

Sincerely,
Ronald Reagan

William Rusher was publisher of National Review. *Ed Meese was investigated for various ethical violations during the time he served in office, but no charges were ever brought.*

> Mr. William A. Rusher
> New York, New York
> April 9, 1984 [17]

Dear Bill:

Month after month goes by and I gratefully accept and read cover to cover the issues of *National Review* you so kindly provide. And those months go by without a thank you from me I'm ashamed to say.

Please know I'm grateful and I thank you especially for this last one with the note regarding the editorial about Ed Meese.

He's taking a bum rap as so many others have at the hands of our permanent lynch mob. Now they list him as just one of a long list of culprits without ever acknowledging that virtually everyone on that list was cleared of any wrongdoing. To the lynchers accusation is proof of guilt.

In my nightly prayers I have to ask forgiveness for what I've been thinking about those villains all day. It's not an easy thing to do.

Nancy sends her best and her thanks too.

> Sincerely,
> Ron

June 6, 1984, was the fortieth anniversary of the Allied invasion of Europe in World War II. Reagan's commemorative speeches were brief but eloquent. In one he quoted General Omar Bradley: "Every man who set foot on Omaha Beach that day was a hero."

> Mrs. Omar N. Bradley
> Los Angeles, California
> June 25, 1984 [18]

Dear Kitty:

Thank you for your lovely letter and very kind words. You make me very proud indeed.

I can't describe the emotions that stirred within me as that day went on in Normandy. With all the horror war brings, if it has a purpose perhaps it is that men then reach their noblest heights. Certainly that was shining through the horror on that day in June forty years ago.

You were so kind to write as you did. I'll be forever grateful. Nancy sends her love as do I.

> Sincerely,
> Ron

The Democrats nominated Walter Mondale as their standard-bearer on July 19, 1984, after Mondale's long primary battle with Senator Gary Hart of Colorado. Mondale's running mate was Geraldine Ferraro, a member of Congress from New York.

Paul Trousdale, a real estate developer in Southern California, was a Reagan supporter and frequent correspondent. The issue of Social Security was still the untouchable "third rail" of American politics.

Mr. Paul Trousdale
Los Angeles, California
August 16, 1984 [19]

Dear Paul:

Just a line to thank you for your letter and your suggestion regarding the well-heeled receiving Social Security. I'm going to take this up with our crew.

As for using the program's shortcomings as a campaign issue I have a problem. The Democrats have been very successful in painting me as wanting to throw the senior citizens out in the snow. It's a subject I just can't touch in the campaign. But the other suggestion is a darn good one.

Nancy sends her best—as do I.

Sincerely,
Ron

Reagan's old friend from Hollywood volunteered to try to set the record straight on statements of Claude Pepper, Democratic representative (and former senator) from Florida, known by his opponents as "Red" Pepper. Pepper styled himself a defender of the elderly and protector of Social Security against the supposed threats of the Reagan administration.

Senator George Murphy
Palm Beach, Florida
September 10, 1984 [20]

Dear Murph:

It was good to get your sum-up of the convention and your approval. I don't know of anyone with a better background for doing that. I share your feeling about the media. I don't think they've ever let their bias hang out more.

I'm glad you are going to clean up after Red P[epper]. I couldn't believe my ears the other day when I heard that Mondale stated flatly as a fact that after the election I was going to cut the Social Security benefits. He's lying in his teeth. They were just as dishonest in the '82 campaign and then when it was over admitted we had been right all along that the program would be broke by July of '83.

They joined us in a bipartisan team I asked for and we got legislation that saved Social Security for as far as we can see into the next century. I can't believe they are at it again.

Nancy sends her love as do I to both of you.

Stay well and vocal and as a great cavalry general said, "Ride to the sound of the guns."—Pepper's pop guns.

Regards,
Ron

————————

The movie star Charlton Heston had served on the board of the Screen Actors Guild with Ronald Reagan and was a good friend who campaigned for Reagan in 1984.

Charlton Heston
Beverly Hills, California
Circa October 26, 1984 [21]

Dear Chuck:

I know something of the schedule you've been keeping on my behalf and just want you to know I'm more grateful than I can say.

My conscience is eased a bit because I've been out in the hustings myself since Congress left town. I've been on several campuses these past few days and can't get over the enthusiasm of young America. They are so gung-ho I get a lump in my throat. They are a far cry from those flag burners back in the '60s.

Nancy sends her love and we both send you a heartfelt thank you.

Sincerely,
Ron

————————

Reagan debated Mondale, the 1984 Democratic candidate, twice during the general election season, on October 11 and October 21. He did a poor job in the first debate, concentrating too much on facts and figures defending his record, but came back strong in the second.

Mrs. William Loeb
Manchester, New Hampshire
Circa October 26, 1984 [22]

Dear Nackey:

Your letter was so right and I hope the second debate made up for it a little. I have no one but me to blame for the first one. I've been hearing all those phony figures of his and looked to that first debate as a time to rebut. I had crammed like for a final exam and knew I was flat when the debate started. In sports they call it leaving your fight in the locker room.

Thanks for your good letter and bless you.

Sincerely,
Ron

Mondale had said in his July 19, 1984, acceptance speech to the Democratic convention that "Mr. Reagan will raise taxes, and so will I. He won't tell you. I just did." The federal budget deficit was a major concern to the voting public, but so were taxes, and Reagan finally took full advantage of Mondale's promise.

Mr. Ward L. Quaal
Chicago, Illinois
October 30, 1984 [23]

Dear Ward:

It was good to hear from you and I want you to know your suggestion about removing the gloves has been heeded. I've been beating him over the head on taxes as well as his record with regard to national defense. His record as a senator reveals that he voted 16 times to increase taxes. He also endorsed deficits as essential to prosperity and urged that they be increased.

I'm also pitching for our Senate and House candidates.

Nancy sends her love and from both of us to Dorothy.

Sincerely,
Ron

Reagan won reelection November 6, 1984, by 525 electoral votes to Mondale's 13, losing only Minnesota, Mondale's home state, and the District of Columbia; he won 58.8 percent of the popular vote.

Mr. Alan Brown
New York, New York
Circa October 26, 1984 [24]

Dear Alan:

It was good to hear from you and thanks for you generous words. With "President" Dewey in mind I refuse to let myself take anything for granted. You'll probably know the outcome by the time you receive this so I'll just assume your prayers are continuing.

As I write this November 6 is only twelve days away and the pace has been pretty hectic. Mr. M. is getting rather caustic and to tell the truth I've dished out a few jabs in response.

Nancy sends her best and again a heartfelt thank you.

Sincerely,
Ron

Susan Baker, the wife of Reagan's first chief of staff, James Baker, had been reluctant to come to Washington. She wrote Reagan on February 12, 1985, about her husband after

Baker traded jobs (announced January 8, 1985) with Don Regan, who had been secretary of the treasury. "Jim has told more people than I can recount," she wrote, "that no matter how tough his job was in the White House it was always a joy to work for you."

Baker had run George Bush's 1980 campaign and was viewed with suspicion by Reagan loyalists. In a March 13, 1985, note for an article in the Washington Post, *Reagan wrote about Baker. "He was totally supportive of all that I've tried to do, and we get along just fine. He saw that everyone had a fair hearing when there were differences on various issues and my only complaint was that he kept longer hours in the office than I'd promised Susan (Mrs. Baker) he would."* [25]

Mrs. James A. Baker III
Washington, D.C.
February 13, 1985 [26]

Dear Susan:

I can't tell you what your letter means to me. I've remembered many times how I promised you that I'd try to send everyone home at reasonable hours and how often I saw Jim putting in those sixteen hour days. I've nursed my guilt for four years wondering if I shouldn't ask your forgiveness. Now your wonderfully kind and generous words have been more than forgiving. Thank you and bless you.

It goes without saying that Nancy and I have been and are so grateful to you both for the sacrifice you've made and the help you've been. We're glad you are only changing desks. God bless you.

Sincerely,
Ron

Victor Krulak was a retired Marine who wrote columns for the Copley News Service; Reagan often passed them around at staff meetings in the·White House. Krulak and Reagan were both members of Owl's Nest camp at the Bohemian Grove, the Bohemian Club's retreat in the redwood forests of northern California. Security as well as time prevented Reagan from attending encampments while he was president.

At the time the letter was written, Regan was Reagan's chief of staff; Jim Baker was secretary of the treasury; Shultz was secretary of state; and William C. "Bud" McFarlane was his national security adviser.

Lt. General Victor H. Krulak, USMC (Ret.)
San Diego, California
March 26, 1985 [27]

Dear Brute:

You made me homesick with your note about the Grove and your work weekend. But then you made me happy with your column—as you always do.

I see that your work gets wide circulation here in the West Wing. It's a h—l of a place for an old ex-cavalryman. I'm surrounded by former Marines; Don Regan, Jim Baker, George Shultz, Bud McFarlane, and the list goes on and on.

Thanks again and best regards,

Ron

David Fischer served Reagan as a personal aide in 1978 and 1979 and during the presidency; James (Jimmy) Kuhn was his replacement. Reagan's personal aide and his secretary—first Helene von Damm and, as of September 1, 1981, Kathy Osborne— went with Reagan on virtually all trips, including those to his Rancho del Cielo home in California and to Camp David.

The Honorable David C. Fischer
Washington D.C.
April 1, 1985 [28]

Dear Dave:

I've always known this day had to come, indeed there were times I felt I should urge it on you. In not doing that I was just plain selfish. We traveled countless miles on the mashed potato circuit, the campaign trails, and the chores having to do with this present job, and you made all those miles seem shorter and easier. In the miles yet to come, I'll probably find myself looking over my shoulder for you and then I'll remember. My emotions too will be mixed as you say yours are. But while one will be a sense of loss at not seeing you, the other will definitely be a warm and friendly wish for happiness and success in all your endeavors. Nancy joins me in this.

There are no words to completely express our gratitude. Just know that you, Kathy, Tiffany, Lindsey and Jennifer will always be in our hearts.

Sincerely,
Ronald Reagan

Joe Coors headed the Coors Brewing Company. He was a longtime supporter of Reagan and other politicians who shared his political philosophy. Reagan reassures him about a staff change.

Mr. Joseph Coors
Golden, Colorado
July 11, 1985 [29]

Dear Joe:

It was good to hear from you and it was a pleasure to see Holly the other day even if it was only a quick hello.

I'm afraid our friends on the Hill have jumped to a conclusion and think the "sky is falling." Constantine Menges is a good man and a top authority on Latin American matters. He's not being ousted, he's being moved up to an assignment where his qualities will be better used than they have been in a more or less routine staff assignment.

I appreciate your sending me the letter you received, I didn't know they were doing that and I'll try to head them off before they embarrass themselves.

Nancy sends her best as do I and again thanks.

Sincerely,
Ronald Reagan

Michael Deaver was the last of the "troika" of Meese, Baker, and Deaver to leave the White House. Other longtime Reagan advisers and aides had also gone on to other jobs in the government or the private sector.

Michael Deaver
May 10, 1985 [30]

Dear Mike:

You know I've accepted your resignation orally but suppose I have to put something down on paper—after all this is Washington. The only place I haven't accepted it is in my heart and there I never will.

I've come to the conclusion that Nancy and I will both agree you will bodily leave the West Wing. You will no longer bear a government title. You will not actually handle such things as schedule, trips etc. But that's as far as we go. You will continue to be a part of our lives. We will have concern one for the other and refuse surgery that would in any way remove you from a relationship that is part of our life support system. In return we will continue to be eternally grateful.

Sincerely,
Ron

Reagan writes to George Murphy about his November 19–20, 1985, summit with Mikhail Gorbachev of the Soviet Union, reassuring Murphy about his advisers and his (Reagan's) ability to identify those who are not supportive. "Cap" is Caspar Weinberger, secretary of defense. Reagan notes that Richard Perle (later to serve at the Department of Defense in the George W. Bush administration with Secretary Donald Rumsfeld) was part of the negotiating team at the Geneva summit with Gorbachev. Roy Brewer was an anticommunist lawyer in Hollywood who continued to send Reagan information about the activities of people like Gus Hall (chairman of the American Communist Party). Robert Morris was former chief counsel for the U.S. Senate Internal Security Subcommittee.

Senator George Murphy
Palm Beach, Florida
November 25, 1985 [31]

Dear Murph:

Well we're home at last and I must tell you that sitting at that table in Geneva was a lot like those old days across the table from the studio heads in Hollywood. Turns out that was pretty good training.

We didn't go there concession-minded and we stayed that way. Murph, I have to say George Shultz has quietly done some housecleaning without conducting a purge. Our team was solid as a rock and no one was trying to budge me out of my stubborn tracks. As a matter of fact they were urging me on. I'm sure some of those other elements are still in the woodwork waiting for us to go away but all in all the level I'm dealing with seems pretty solid. Incidentally that press stuff about a feud is just their same old witch hunting. Cap's man Perle was one of our team in Geneva. Now don't worry that I've lost my bearings, I can still spot those other types and I'm always watching for them. I'll look forward to getting those "Morris" notes.

I've been keeping in touch with our old friend Roy Brewer and he comes up with some darn good information. Some of the old names like Gus Hall are still mounting the rostrum in California.

Please give Bette our best. Nancy sends her love.

Sincerely,
Ron

John Howard was president of a small conservative think tank, the Rockford Institute, in Illinois. He sent Reagan an essay he wrote about the Challenger *accident. The space shuttle exploded on January 28, 1986, just 73 seconds after launch. Its seven crew members included one civilian, teacher Christa McAuliffe. Reagan spoke briefly to the nation from the Oval Office that night, postponing the scheduled State of the Union address until February 4.*

Dr. John A. Howard
Rockford, Illinois
February 5, 1986 [32]

Dear John:

Thanks for sending me your eloquent commentary. It was most fitting and appropriate. These have been difficult times back here. Meeting with the families as we did was, as you can imagine, an emotional experience, indeed heartbreaking. In phoning them before our meeting, every family said through their tears—the program must be continued.

Again thanks.

Sincerely,
Ron

The 1986 midterm elections returned control of the Senate to the Democrats; a 53–47 Republican majority became a 55–45 minority. The Democratic majority in the House increased by five, although the number of Republican governors increased by eight. But the Democratic Senate majority jeopardized presidential nominations that would probably have succeeded earlier.

Senator George Murphy
Palm Beach, Florida
November 18, 1986 [33]

Dear Murph:

It was good to hear from you and as always your letter was meaty and full of fuel for thought.

There is no question as to where the press comes down—on us at every chance they get. But Murph I don't see this election as a setback to what we've been trying to do. As a matter of fact several of the Senate races were conducted with no controversy over issues. I went in and campaigned for Senate candidates on the issue of what we've accomplished and what we wanted to continue to do. The Democratic candidates never argued back. Indeed some of them were out on the trail echoing what I said. It was like punching a pillow.

You are right about that California race. Our candidate* didn't seem to be able to present a clear choice. He couldn't deliver a Rockne-between-halves speech and fire up the team. This one did disappoint me because you and I both know what A.C. [Alan Cranston] really is and I was dying to get rid of him. Well the world goes on and we'll keep fighting.

Nancy sends her love and from both of us to Bette.

Sincerely,
Ron

Reagan explains here that he does not discourage people who want to leave his administration.

Senator George Murphy
Palm Beach, Florida
February 2, 1987 [34]

Dear Murph:

It was good to get your letter and I thank you. You are also right about the feelings we both have with regard to the journalistic lynch mob.

---

* Ed Zschau, House Republican from California's Silicon Valley, was the 1986 Republican candidate for the Senate; he lost to Senator Alan Cranston (D), elected for a fourth term.

I share too your admiration for Pat B[uchanan]. I think he'll soon be returning to private life and I can only wish him well with a grateful heart. I think it's great that some of those who came on board and were of such help are now being rewarded with great opportunities on the outside. There is no way I'll try to hang on to them or even to regret their going to a just reward.

Well I'm feeling great and am glad you are too. Nancy sends her love and from both of us to Bette.

Sincerely,
Ron

The report of the Tower Commission on the Iran-Contra affair, which involved trading arms for hostages and the diversion of funds to the Nicaraguan Contras, was scheduled for release February 26, 1987. Don Regan, then chief of staff, had agreed with the president to announce his resignation after the report came out, but on the day of its release he heard on a newcast that the president had already offered the job to Howard Baker, former senator from Tennessee. He talked briefly with the president but left the White House immediately. Nevertheless, the President wrote him a gracious letter. Regan later wrote that "I had seen many such letters, so I knew that someone else had written it for him," but the draft is in Reagan's hand. Don Regan died on June 10, 2003.

The Honorable Donald T. Regan
February 27, 1987 [35]

Dear Don:

In accepting your resignation I want you to know how deeply grateful I am for all that you have done for this administration and for our country. As secretary of the treasury you planted the seeds for the most far-reaching tax reform in our history. As chief of staff you worked tirelessly and effectively for the policies and programs we proposed to the Congress.

I know that you stayed on beyond the time you had set for your return to private life and did so because you felt you could be of help in a time of trouble. You were of help and I thank you. Whether on the deck of your beloved boat or on the fairway; in the words of our forefather; "May the sun shine warm upon your face, the wind be always at your back and may God hold you in the hollow of his hand."

Sincerely,
Ronald Reagan

Congressional House and Senate committees continued to investigate the Iran-Contra affair, finally concluding that Reagan had not known about the diversion of funds to the Contras in advance but should have.[36] CNN (Cable News Network) covered the

hearings extensively. Margaret Heckler had been appointed ambassador to Ireland in
1985.

Although Reagan suggests he is vetoing many bills, he actually vetoed one less bill
in the 1987–88 years than he did in 1985–86. *

> The Honorable Margaret Heckler
> Dublin, Ireland
> June 17, 1987 [37]

Dear Margaret:

Your kind message and generous words arrived by way of Fred and Helen and I thank you from the bottom of my heart.

It was good to hear from you. I hope all goes well with you there on the "ould sod." I think CNN will be looking for new programming pretty soon. People over here are getting a little bored with the hearings and believe it or not Dick Wirthlin's polling is showing a definite upswing in our favor. It won't surprise you I know to learn that partisanship is booming up on the Hill now that I only have a year and a half to go. I sit at my desk with veto pen in hand.

Nancy sends her best as do I and again thanks.

> Sincerely,
> Ron

———

Reagan addressed the nation on the Iran-Contra affair August 12, 1987; in a March 4,
1987, address he had said, "A few months ago I told the American people I did not trade
arms for hostages. My heart and my best intentions still tell me that's true, but the facts
and the evidence tell me it is not." Here he looks at the history of congressional investi-
gations of presidents and suggests political motivation.

> Senator George Murphy
> Palm Beach, Florida
> July 21, 1987 [38]

Dear Murph:

Thanks very much for your good letter and call to arms. You are completely right about what's going on up on Capitol Hill. I'm waiting my turn. I won't comment publicly on this 'til the inquisition is all over, but when it is I'll go nationwide.

Murph isn't it strange, the Democrats have had a majority in both houses of the Congress for 46 of the 50 years from 1931 to 1981. Republicans had the Congress for two years during Truman's Presidency and two years during Ike's two terms. I

———

* Reagan vetoed 15 bills in 1981–82; 24 in 1983–84; 20 in 1985–86; and 19 in 1987–88. Overrides were respectively 2, 2, 2, 3. (U.S. Congress, Senate, Secretary of the Senate, *Presidential Vetoes, 1789–1988.* S. Pub. 102–12, 103rd Congress, 2nd session, Washington, D.C., U.S. Government Printing Office, 1992.)

had one house [the Senate] Republican for six years and now am back to a Democratic majority in both houses. In all these years no Congress ever investigated a Democratic president. But every Republican president was investigated, Ike for the Sherman Adams affair, Dick [Nixon] for Watergate, Jerry [Ford] for CIA and now my own lynching. Well so far they haven't gotten the noose around my neck and they won't because I've been telling the truth for these last eight months. It's fun now to see them and the press trying to get back off the limb they've all been out on.

I envy you the visits to the Grove but then the day I can join you is coming closer.

Love to Bette.

Sincerely,
Ron

Robert Bork, a distinguished legal scholar and member of the U.S. Court of Appeals for the District of Columbia, was nominated for the Supreme Court on July 1, 1987.* The confirmation proceedings were protracted and contentious. The nomination was defeated in the Senate 58–42 on October 23, 1987.[39] *The Democratic majority in the Senate made it more difficult for Reagan to confirm appointments and sustain vetoes.*

Morton Blackwell
October 21, 1987[40]

Dear Morton:

Thanks for your letter of September 30 and for your help on the Bork matter. As you must know by now we never had any intention of asking him to back away. In fact I personally let him know we'd be with him whatever his decision might be. When he decided to stay in I let him know we were happy with his decision.

Morton I think there was a distortion of our position as to his philosophy. We never portrayed him as an Earl Warren type nor did we ever use the word moderate. It's possible some might have used that term in repudiating the charge that he was some kind of radical but not any of us here in the administration to my knowledge.

Maybe we were overconfident in view of the quality of our witnesses compared to those opposed; Chief Justice Burger, seven former attorneys general for both Democrat and Republican presidents, nine deans of prestigious law schools, the endorsement of the American Bar Association. By the way two † of the four ABA board members who voted against him work for Senator Biden.

---

* Reagan's first appointment to the Court was Sandra Day O'Connor in 1981. When Chief Justice Warren Burger resigned in 1986, Reagan chose William Rehnquist, a member of the Court, as chief justice and nominated Antonin Scalia to the vacant seat. Scalia was the first Italian-American to serve on the Court.

† Corrected to "one" in the final version of the letter.

Well perhaps by the time you receive this it will be all over—I hope not—but if so, I assure you I'll come back with a nominee as much like him as I can get.

Again thanks and best regards.

Ronald Reagan

When the Bork nomination failed, Judge Douglas Ginsburg was nominated, but withdrew nine days later after admitting he had smoked marijuana while a professor at Harvard Law School. On November 11 Reagan nominated Anthony Kennedy, who was confirmed unanimously on February 3, 1988.

Mr. Alan Brown
APO New York, New York
November 20, 1987[41]

Dear Alan:

Nancy and I thank you for your generous words and your condolences.

On the matter of Judge Ginsburg however I think you've been victimized by press accounts that have distorted the situation in the interest of sensationalism.

The judge is really a fine man and would have made an excellent justice of the Supreme Court. He was overwhelmingly approved by the Senate committee little more than a year ago for the Court of Appeals and has actually been approved for government positions four times.

Alan the FBI in their examinations ask questions that would require answers as to whether an individual has ever been arrested for such things as drug possession, drunk driving etc. I don't think they ever ask if someone has "smoked a joint" anymore than they'd ask if someone had ever been drunk. They do ask if one has a drinking problem or is on drugs.

Ginsburg's use of pot was such a long time ago thing and then only a limited experiment, it never occurred to him to volunteer word of it. What happened was that a man who had known him in college went to the press with it. That man was organizing a liberal group to oppose him in the Senate hearing. When Ginsburg was faced with it he promptly acknowledged it, called it a mistake he regretted and that he should never have done it. I'm sure there are a great many of his generation who feel the same way. Withdrawing his name from the process was entirely his own doing.

Nancy sends her love and again our thanks to you.

Best regards,
Ron

Donald Regan's book, For the Record: From Wall Street to Washington *(New York: Harcourt Brace Jovanovich, 1988), revealed that Nancy had consulted an astrologer in her concern about Reagan's safety and held Nancy responsible for Regan's dismissal. It was published April 1, 1988.*

Mr. Philip Kruidenier
Des Moines, Iowa
May 17, 1988 [42]

Dear Mr. Kruidenier:

Just received your letter of May 12 and am most grateful for your kind words. It was good of you to write as you did and you brightened our day.

It gets frustrating at times when the media joins in as they have on this latest fuss. What is so frustrating is that the things they dwell on and pick over are for the most part absolutely false. Believe me, I've never made decisions based on astrology, crystal balls or reading tea leaves. And Nancy never fired anyone.

Well again my heartfelt thanks to you and very best regards.

Sincerely,
Ronald Reagan

In 1984 the president wrote to a friend that "the Vice President [George H.W. Bush] has been as staunch a supporter of the administration as you could want. He carries a tremendous work load and is truly straight arrow." [43]

The Republicans nominated Bush as their presidential candidate in 1988. He chose Dan Quayle, Republican senator from Indiana, as his running mate. Bush ran against Massachusetts governor Michael Dukakis, whose running mate was Lloyd Bentsen, Democratic senator from Texas. Bush would win with 426 electoral votes to 111 for Dukakis; he would get 53.4 percent of the popular vote.

Mr. Ward L. Quaal
Chicago, Illinois
August 4, 1988 [44]

Dear Ward:

I'm sure you know by now that I let the plant closing measure become law without my signature. It still had features that were harmful to business but a veto would have been overridden so I did a compromise between reality and my personal distaste. Incidentally, this was the first time I have done what I did, here or in eight years as governor.

I'm happy to hear how you feel about the vice president and I'm going to do all the campaigning I can in his behalf.

Love to Dorothy and Nancy sends hers too.

Sincerely,
Ron

Reagan writes to a Hollywood friend about George Bush.

Mr. Robert Stack
Los Angeles, California
August 2, 1988[45]

Dear Bob:

Thanks for your good letter and your generous words. I'm most grateful. I'm also happy to hear you'll man the ramparts for George Bush. He's really a top man and has played a major role in everything we've done. I share your opinion of those two characters on the other side.

I'm glad we're going to be neighbors. Nancy and I are looking forward to our new home and California. Nancy sends her very best and give our regards to Rosemarie.

Sincerely,
Ron

Reagan comments here on the debate between the vice presidential candidates, Quayle and Bentsen, and Bentsen's policy switches after his nomination.

Colonel Barney Oldfield
Beverly Hills, California
October 13, 1988[46]

Dear Barney:

I enjoyed your report on Korea and the Olympics and was glad to get your October 6 letter which meant you were safely home.

You were right about the debate—it was really a press conference with the questioners stacked against Quayle. It seems to me a debate would be asking each man the same questions so there could be a comparison of where each stood on particular issues.

You know Barney I wonder what it says about a man who is able to do a 180° turn simply to become candidate for the vice presidency. Bentsen voted with us every time on military aid to the Contras when he was being a senator not a candidate. Then came another vote just after he was chosen by Dukakis. Without any hesitation he voted against such aid.

Well again—welcome home.

Ron

George P. Shultz served as Reagan's secretary of state from July 16, 1982 until the end of Reagan's second term in office.

Secretary George Shultz
December 1, 1988 [47]

Dear George:

These are bittersweet days. Yes there is California to look forward to but there are also separations, partings with those who have been friends and teammates in a great undertaking.

Accepting your resignation is one of those bittersweet moments. You have served above and beyond the call of duty. You have been key to all we've accomplished on the international scene and thanks to all you've done we leave the ship of state in calmer waters than it was when we came aboard.

Nancy and I cling to one thought as we part, you and Obie will be in the same state with us and changing jobs does not mean a change in our friendship.

Thanks for all you've done for our beloved country and God bless you both.

Sincerely,
Ronald Reagan

President Reagan writes about preparing to leave the White House.

Mr. William A. Rusher
New York, New York
January 17, 1989 [48]

Dear Bill:

I'm late with this but didn't get it until my return from California. Since reading it you've been in our prayers. We're happy to get the word from you that you are on the recovery road and will be coming to California. I'll be getting my mail at my new office (Put office address and phone.)

It's four days 'til private citizenship again. We've been in a tornado of packing the accumulation of these years. It's a bittersweet time with all the goodbyes and such but it's coupled with our love for our California home.

But now let me close with a big thank you for that column. I should say those columns. I've been grateful and proud to have your support over the years and now this summing up that you did I will treasure.

Nancy sends her love and from both of us every good wish for your return to full health and vigor.

Sincerely,
Ron

On January 19, 1989, Colin Powell, Reagan's national security adviser, wrote, "For the last time allow me to say thank you. Thank you for what you did for our country and thank you for letting me be part of it all. It has been the experience of my life!" [49]

On the occasion of Colin Powell's retirement from the military in 1993—he was then chairman of the Joint Chiefs of Staff in the Department of Defense—Reagan recalls Powell's national security briefing on Reagan's final day in office. Powell later served President George W. Bush as secretary of state.

General Colin Powell
Washington, D.C.
September 30, 1993 [50]

Dear Colin:

Nancy and I are so sorry we can't be with you today at your retirement ceremony. I am sure it must be a little bittersweet and yet there must be tremendous anticipation for all that lies ahead.

I too remember vividly your coming into the office on that last day with your report: "The world is quiet today, Mr. President." It doesn't seem possible that so much time has passed.

Nancy and I are eagerly looking forward to seeing you and Alma here on November 9th at the Library. You have both been dear friends to us. We traveled the world together and witnessed extraordinary changes taking place around the globe. Through it all, you've always occupied a special place in our lives and our admiration has grown with each passing day.

God bless you, Colin and we'll see you soon.

Sincerely,
Ron

Reagan's last day in the Oval Office was January 20, 1989. He left in the desk a tablet of cartoonist Sandra Boynton's stationery with the legend "DON'T LET THE TUR-KEYS GET YOU DOWN" for incoming president George Bush, with this note: [51]

Dear George:

You'll have moments when you want to use this particular stationery. Well go to it.

George I treasure the memories we share and wish you all the very best. You'll be in my prayers. God bless you and Barbara. I'll miss our Thursday lunches.

Ron

CHAPTER EIGHTEEN

The Media

RONALD REAGAN, *like many politicians, had a mixed view of the media. On one level he saw it as a powerful and necessary part of a free society that did far more good than harm. He also liked many of the reporters, editors, and columnists who formed the ranks of the national press corps. On September 21, 1976, after he narrowly lost the Republican presidential nomination to President Ford, Reagan said to his national radio audience:*

Over the long several months and thousands of miles you get pretty well acquainted [with the press corps]. I saw the rough side of their work, the long hours when the day was done for me but they were still filing stories. In some instances with a special feature their producers or editors had called for their work went on through the night yet there they were on the bus or plane the next morning ready for the day's work ahead.

I have to say their treatment of me was fair. They were objective, they did their job and their pain was real when a shot or a paragraph was cut in the home office that lessened the objectivity of what they had done. Most important we parted friends and I'm richer for their friendship.

But on another level, with day-to-day, laser-like reporting on him, an emotional reaction often took over. These letters reveal a man who was acutely sensitive to what was being written and said about him.

When a reporter praised him and lauded what Reagan had done he was undeniably pleased and grateful, and he often wrote to say so. Sometimes he telephoned. Looking forward to future press coverage, he clearly believed in using the "carrot."

When the reporting was reasonably objective in his view, even if it was critical, he accepted it, took some lessons from what it said, and moved on.

But he could also use the "stick." If he felt the words were not true or were misleading or politically biased he did not hesitate to respond directly. Sometimes he did it in person, sometimes he telephoned, but he also wrote. When Reagan felt wronged he could respond strongly, smothering his critics with fact and argument, and sometimes skewering them with sharp wit.

————

In 1961 Reagan gave an 11-minute talk on the dangers of socialized medicine* and urged citizens to write their congressmen and senators to oppose a particular bill. But the talk was more than this; it included the seeds of the political philosophy he spelled out when—five years later—he ran for governor of California.

He gave permission for his talk to be distributed by the Women's Auxiliary of the American Medical Association as part of a 33 rpm phonograph recording. He begins the recording by saying, "It must seem presumptuous to some of you that a member of my profession (acting) would stand and attempt to talk to anyone on serious problems that face the nation and the world."

What he said was controversial and in this letter he writes back to his longtime pen pal, expressing his anger over a column written about his talk by Drew Pearson, one of the most famous columnists of the time. He adds a postscript about his future.

> Lorraine and Elwood H. Wagner
> Philadelphia, Pennsylvania
> July 13, 1961 [1]

Dear Lorraine and Wag:

I have a few minutes between shots so will attempt some kind of answer to your letter. You asked about Drew Pearson's article[†] and I'm just mad enough at that joker to remind you, FDR, Truman and Ike all called him a liar publicly. His story was dishonest except that such a record is available through medical associations and I made it. One of his "leg men" called me from Washington so Drew had the story correctly and cannot plead ignorance.

One paragraph of a talk I've been giving deals with the way socialized medicine can come about by gradual or "foot in the door" stages. The AMA asked if they could use a recording of that part of my speech. I <u>was not hired</u> by them nor did GE even know I was doing it. Very simply I'm in favor of helping those who need help. In the last session of Congress before this one we adopted a measure introduced by Senator Kerr (Democrat) and Congressman W. Mills (Democrat) known as the "Kerr-Mills" bill. This provides federal funds to the states to furnish medical care for the aged. The bill isn't actually working yet having only been passed eight months ago. Now I'm in favor of this bill—and if the money isn't enough I think we

———

* LP Record, *Ronald Reagan Speaks Out Against Socialized Medicine* (Chicago: American Medical Association, 1961).

† Pearson, Drew, "Hollywood Star vs. JFK," Drew Pearson Papers, Lyndon B. Johnson Library and Museum, Austin, Texas, draft column, June 17, 1961.

should put up more. However the groups lobbying for the "King" bill* won't even wait to see if the Kerr-Mills bill will do the job. They want a compulsory health insurance program tied on to Social Security for all senior citizens whether they need it or not. These people are so wild eyed and uninformed they told Congress the cost of nursing home care under their bill would only come to $9 million a year. A few weeks ago they said they were a little wrong it might run to as much as $200 million a year but they'd settle for $100 million the first year. The congressman who originally wrote the bill said "If we can get this passed it will be a foot in the door and we can expand it after that." The *Socialist* magazine says it is the first step they must have to bring about eventual socialized medicine. That is my story—I am not opposed to providing medical care for those who really need it and can't pay for it but I do not believe in compulsory health insurance through a government bureau for people who don't need it or who have incomes or even a few million dollars tucked away.

Attached is a copy of the wire I sent Pearson. Incidentally you won't find the threat of socialism spelled out in the bill—it never is. It comes about through the rules and regulations the Department of Health, Education and Welfare puts into effect to administer the bill.

Well that's my story.

Best,
Ronnie

P.S. I've been asked to run for governor and, while I'm highly honored I don't think I'm right for the part.

After Barry Goldwater was soundly beaten by Lyndon B. Johnson in the 1964 presidential contest many Republicans, impressed with Reagan's role in the campaign, began to think about him for higher office. By early 1965 the political left took notice and word soon got to Reagan that Jessica Mitford† had been commissioned to write a major article on him for Esquire *magazine.*

William F. Buckley, the publisher of National Review, *asked about it and, on February 24, 1965, received a letter from Harold Hayes, the managing editor of* Esquire. *Hayes told Buckley they had "assigned the piece to Mitford," but that they wanted to be "fair-minded" because it was a "controversial assignment," and would withhold judgment until they saw what she wrote. Buckley apparently shared the letter with Reagan.*

---

* H.R. 4222 was introduced in the House of Representatives by Cecil R. King (D-California) on February 18, 1961. It provided "for payment for hospital services, skilled nursing home services, and home health services furnished to aged beneficiaries under the old-age, survivors, and disability insurance program."

† Jessica Mitford, the author of *The American Way of Death,* an exposé of the funeral industry, was known for her left-wing political views.

The following four letters from Reagan discuss the article's journey as it was turned down by Esquire *and finally published in the November 1965 issue of* Ramparts,* *a well-known magazine of the political left.*

William F. Buckley Jr.
New York, New York
March 12, 1965 [2]

Dear Bill:

Here it is. I won't say I told you so I'll just dig a foxhole.

By d—n he † makes himself sound pretty noble too doesn't he?

No time for a letter I'm catching a train.

Again thanks,
Ronnie

————————

Reagan tells one of his fans, Lorraine Wagner, about the upcoming article by Mitford and she apparently writes to the editors of Esquire *magazine.*

Mrs. Elwood Wagner
Philadelphia, Pennsylvania
April 8, 1965 [3]

Dear Lorraine:

Just have time for a line more or less between trips. I don't know how you find time to do battle in my behalf the way you do but I am truly grateful.

With regard to the Mitford gal, she did try to see me and I refused to talk to her. I know with her background that she intends to do a hatchet job and I won't give her the opportunity for direct quotes which would give her story a kind of dignity and authenticity. This way her attack will be from across the street and I can answer back. As to her background before communism, she and her sisters were evidently in the English pro-Nazi group and there have been many news stories about her sister being one of Hitler's girl friends.

This is about all I have time for with packing to do, so again thanks for taking on the editors, and all the best.

Sincerely,
Ronnie

————————

* A radical left-wing magazine of the 1960s.

† Reagan is apparently referring to Harold Hayes of *Esquire* magazine.

Reagan gives Lorraine an update on the pending Mitford article. He cautions her to be careful with the letters she has been sending out, and returns one of the letters "with a correction I think you should make."

Mr. and Mrs. Elwood H. Wagner
Philadelphia, Pennsylvania
May 27, 1965 [4]

Dear Lorraine and Wag:

Here I am again between speaking trips, none of which I hastily and regretfully say will bring me to Philadelphia.

First let me say yes, I would be most happy to sign any books you send and will return them of course.

I can't tell you how much I appreciate your story of the young woman who didn't think I could be of help in the Charity campaign. It's another example of how far we've all gone in accepting labels without bothering to check them out. Incidentally, we are all waiting for the other shoe to fall now. The June *Esquire* is out and Miss Mitford's article did not appear. None of us knows whether this means cancellation or just holding it up until it can do more harm.

I'm enclosing the letter you have been sending out, with a correction I think you should make. Not that everything you said wasn't true, it was, but I've had some pretty good lessons from the lawyers involved in okaying my book, about how little the truth can help you if someone wants to get nasty in a lawsuit. I doubt that there will be any problem with regard to your personal letters, but even so in any future ones you just will have covered yourself better if you make the changes I suggested, and of course now we must change the June date although I don't know what to say now, unless some place along the line I can find out what their plans are.

I got quite a kick out of Mr. Burke's letter. He was not one of my staunch allies in those GE days, and not too long ago I heard that the now retired president of GE has said he never favored canceling the show, and believes it was a great error. Must get along now. Again thanks and best regards.

Sincerely,
Ronnie

Reagan fills Lorraine in on the final disposition of the Mitford article. Her article reviews Reagan's just-published book, Where's the Rest of Me? *and suggests that, "Perhaps there is really not much to find behind the two-dimensional Reagan of the screen." She accuses Reagan of "enthusiastically endors(ing)" the "witchhunt" that led to the "wholesale blacklisting and brutal wreckage of careers" in Hollywood, quotes an old Army buddy, Irving Wallace, that Reagan is "a man who parrots things—shallow and affable," and attacks Reagan's wife Nancy as "a lovable scatter-brain."*

Lorraine and Elwood H. Wagner
Philadelphia, Pennsylvania
November 1965[5]

Dear Lorraine and Wag:

The Jessica Mitford story finally came out in a magazine called *Ramparts*. It seems *Esquire* read it and decided it was <u>too vicious</u> for them. It really doesn't matter because most of *Ramparts* readers are so left they already don't like me.

It's all I thought it would be so I'm glad *Esquire* backed out.

Best,
Ronnie

By early 1969 demonstrations against the Vietnam War had become violent on many campuses, and Governor Reagan had taken steps to halt the campus disorder. The Beaver *was the college paper of the American River College, a large two-year college located in Sacramento, California. An editorial in* The Beaver *attacking Reagan had been reprinted in the Sacramento Bee, one of the largest papers in northern California.*

Bob L. Crane, Editor
The Beaver—American River College
Sacramento, California
March 27, 1969[6]

Dear Mr. Crane:

An editorial from your paper *The Beaver* was recently reprinted in the *Sacramento Bee*. I know better than to expect the *Bee* to give me an opportunity to explain my position but am hopeful that you as editor of *The Beaver*, where the editorial first appeared, will allow your readers to see my reply.

You correctly state my position in that I have been and am critical of those who have so lost faith in the people that they want to turn to an ever growing government for the answer to most, if not all, the problems besetting our citizens. But then you charge me with violating my own philosophy in that I seek to take over and control those educational institutions which have been the scene of tumultuous disorders. Apparently your opinion is based on some partial statements of mine, a lack of knowledge of other statements and a certain amount of misinterpretation. Let me hasten to say this is easily understandable because widespread circulation of some of my statements has been accompanied by an almost total lack of circulation of others.

Rather than reply to your editorial point by point, let me just state as briefly as possible my position. I believe in as much local autonomy as possible for educational institutions as well as community governments. Further, it is my conviction that only the college and university administrations can bring campus disorders to a halt and secure a permanent end to this type of disruption. Power to do this is already available to academic administrators.

Government on the other hand is responsible for the protection of people and property. At no time have state forces (California Highway Patrol and/or National Guard) been sent to a campus unless requested. Indeed they cannot be sent except on the request of local authorities.

To suggest that police on the campus in response to a call from campus administrators is the cause of violence rather then the result is just not borne out by the facts. At Berkeley, Wheeler Hall was fire bombed, students were beaten for trying to go through picket lines, a dozen buildings were vandalized and explosive bombs were found. As a result, the police, and subsequently state forces, were called for when the university administration asked that I declare a state of emergency. This hardly lays me open to a charge of perverting my authority. You might ask what the charge would have been if I had refused the chancellor's request for help.

It seems to me that under my oath I am duty bound to make available all the force at my command to protect the freedom and the rights of the people. One of those rights must certainly be the right of a teacher and a student to learn without fear of violence or threat of violence.

There can be no academic freedom if any group serves notice it will halt the educational process for everyone unless its demands are met.

If I have misunderstood your position or you don't understand mine, I'd be delighted to discuss this matter with you.

Sincerely,
Ronald Reagan

In October 1967 Reagan attended his first annual National Governors Conference. Hosted that year by Nelson Rockefeller, it was held on the cruise ship USS Independence (nicknamed the "Ship of Fools" by the media) which sailed from New York City to the Virgin Islands. It was a critical time in the Vietnam War and President Johnson's representative on board the ship was Price Daniels, a former governor of Texas. A radiogram from the president to Daniels with instructions to line up governors to support Johnson's Vietnam policies was delivered by error to Reagan's quarters. Bill Clark, Reagan's chief of staff, showed it to Lyn Nofziger*, Reagan's press secretary, who copied the document before it was returned to Daniels. Later that day they leaked the document to several reporters.

The story exploded, and Reagan was quickly accused of "stealing" the president's radiogram and releasing it to the press. In his reply to the New York Times *Reagan makes it clear that, while he will not present himself as a candidate for the presidency*

---

* Lyn Nofziger, *Nofziger* (Washington, DC: Regnery Gateway, 1992), pp. 85–87.

at the 1968 Republican convention, he has no intention of issuing a "Sherman-like"
statement that he would not accept the nomination if offered.

> The Editor, *New York Times*
> New York, New York
> Circa October 1967[7]

To: The Editor, *New York Times:*

On October 21st you editorialized to the effect that I was guilty of something less than noble conduct for reading a radiogram message mis-diverted to me and addressed to someone else. You used the word "intercepted" to create an impression I had in some way stolen the message and falsely charged me with "gleefully distributing copies to press and delegates." You of course know this is an outright distortion of fact.

As you well know a Xerox copy of the radiogram was delivered to me during a business session along with other messages. The radiogram was sealed in an envelope addressed to me as were the other messages. All of this was part of a regular distribution and many other governors were handed similar envelopes.

Since most of our messages reached us first in the original typing I assumed the Xerox copy was intended for distribution and that other governors were being handed the same message. This assumption was further strengthened by the belief so many of us had that the Vietnam resolution was inspired by and of great interest to the White House. It was only in the closing lines where suggestions for "arm twisting" some of my fellow Republican governors were made that I realized the copy was not intended for my eyes.

Do you suggest that I had no responsibility to warn my colleagues of the pressure that was about to be applied? An out of context statement regarding the coming Republican Convention has resulted in a misunderstanding of my position. I do not believe the nomination is locked up for any candidate and I do believe it will be an open convention.

My name will be placed in nomination. Obviously at that time I can be considered a candidate by delegates so inclined.

I am well aware of, greatly honored by, the activities in my behalf. While it would be impossible for me to present myself as a candidate prior to the convention I have never subscribed to the Sherman statement, indeed it is my belief that any citizen's response should be the direct opposite.

> Sincerely,
> Ronald Reagan

Skyline College is a community college located in San Bruno, California. In this letter Reagan brings to one student's attention several errors she made in a story in the campus newspaper about his speech to the Commonwealth Club in San Francisco.

Editor, *Skyline College Press*
San Bruno, California
Circa February 1978[8]

To the Editor:

In your issue of January 30, 1978 Kim Marcus wrote a story about my recent appearance before the San Francisco Commonwealth Club. Will you please convey to her my thanks for knocking a year off my age. I'm truly grateful.

At the same time, however, she did manage to touch a nerve when she described my face as "applied with heavy amounts of pancake makeup." I didn't wear makeup when I was in movies and doing television.

Please tell Miss Marcus I wore no makeup at the Commonwealth Club (I'm allergic to it). In the interest of press integrity tell her she has a standing invitation to do a "white glove" test on my face the next time she's assigned to cover an appearance of mine!

Thank you,
Ronald Reagan

P.S. About the lack of young people at the meeting—the Commonwealth Club invited 400 high school students to another meeting room in the hotel and I answered their questions for an hour following the luncheon.

———

In the December 15, 1975, issue of New York *magazine Richard Reeves, a syndicated columnist and prolific author, analyzes the upcoming race between Reagan and President Ford for the 1976 Republican nomination for president. While he doubts Reagan can beat any Democrat in November in the general election, he believes— unlike many—that Reagan is a formidable candidate, saying he "may be the best public speaker in America." Reeves considers him a "solid citizen" and "smarter" than Ford, and even predicts (wrongly) that Reagan will win the nomination. Reagan likes the article.*

Mr. Richard Reeves
New York, New York
Circa December 15, 1975[9]

Dear Mr. Reeves:

This just a line to thank you for your article in the December issue of *New York*. I'm aware that our viewpoints may differ, indeed you so indicated, but I appreciate your fairness. Perhaps one day our paths will cross and who knows we may discover our differences are not so terribly great.

I look forward to a meeting and in the meantime thanks again.

Sincerely,
Ronald Reagan

In this early 1979 letter Reagan discusses a number of political strategy matters with the publisher of the Union Leader *in Manchester, New Hampshire, one of his strongest supporters in the media.*

Mr. William Loeb
Manchester, New Hampshire
February 12, 1979 [10]

Dear Bill:

Just arrived home from the blizzards and 25 degrees below weather of Montana and North Dakota to find your three letters awaiting me. I know by now that you have received my letter about how the election turned out there. I know you had a hand in it, a good hand, and it was just great.

I appreciate all this information you have provided and can assure you it is most helpful to me and our team. Let me just respond to one thing about John Sears. We are well aware of his shortcomings as well as his talents and know that last time we gave him the ball without very much of a game plan. It's going to be very much different; he will be a part of the organization. But the head man is definitely Paul Laxalt, and John will be doing those things we think he does well, but not a solo job with all of us wondering what happens next.

Bill, I wasn't tiptoeing around you in that last campaign. Mel had told me that he was going to stay kind of arm's length because of possible repercussions in certain circles. I was well aware of what you were doing in my behalf and figured that my job was to go out and see if I couldn't round up some of those others that were beyond the circle. And you were absolutely right; you did do the job that gave us those 8,000 votes where we needed them.

You are also absolutely right about the idea of a balanced ticket. I must confess there is a corner way down inside of me that thinks it's wrong for one man to dictate who the second man on the ticket will be. For a long time now, I have watched this tradition grow and have wondered if the convention shouldn't have much more to do with it than it does. Maybe something like FDR used to do when he would approve a list of acceptables for the convention. If I did that, believe me my list would consist of people who were heart and soul with my philosophy.

I was most interested in your visit with Jeff Bell. He looms very large in a column by Evans and Novak on that same subject, only the scene was Florida where apparently he is urging a Kemp campaign. We'll just have to see what happens. My own hunch is that Jack will stew and stew and then maybe not even try for the Senate but just stay in that nice safe spot he has. Maybe it was football, but he does play the percentages.

My best to Nackey, and I hope we'll be seeing you soon. Rainbow sends her regards.

Sincerely,
Ron

Reagan complains about the duplicity of a 60 Minutes *television crew involved in a Dan Rather interview of Reagan that aired on January 27, 1980, and the lack of press coverage of his policy statements on inflation, energy, and foreign policy.*

Mr. Jay W. Stream
San Luis Obispo, California
Circa February 1980[11]

Dear Jay:

I'm late in answering your good letter of February 11th, but we've been campaigning for twenty straight days. We're due out again in forty-eight hours so I'll hurry my reply.

First of all let me say you were not at all presumptuous, and I'm grateful for your sound suggestions and the kind interest in my fortunes that prompted your letter.

As you know there have been some drastic changes in our organization, and I'm campaigning in the style that suits me and which I've always enjoyed. I'm meeting informally with the people on a question and answer basis.

On the *60 Minutes* matter, no one on our team can be blamed. The scene was shot in my office—one hour of tape from which they took fifteen minutes, the shots you saw. The camera remained in its same position as far away from me as Dan's camera was from him. They did their trick with lenses. I was really shocked when I saw the show. Other cameramen on the tour have indicated we were had.

Incidentally, we have quite a stable of pro-footballers out on the road as surrogate speakers now. And Nancy breaks off from the tour frequently to campaign on her own—very successfully, I might add.

I must say I'm amazed, though, at how little the press has revealed that I am speaking on the issues and offering specific answers to inflation, energy, and the foreign policy failures of the administration. The national press traveling with us has heard me go at these subjects day after day, and still the columnists write that I'm not dealing with the issues. It's d—n frustrating.

Well, enough of my complaints. Your letter was right on, and I'm most grateful to you. Nancy sends her best and give our love to Wayne.

Sincerely,
Ron

William Raspberry is a Pulitzer Prize–winning columnist for the Washington Post. *Reagan had recently attended a luncheon with the newspaper's editorial board. He thanks Raspberry, one of the few black columnists in the national press corps, for a resulting column on welfare.*

Mr. William Raspberry
Washington, D.C.
Circa July 1980 [12]

Dear Mr. Raspberry:

I have just read your column on welfare and the comparison between your lawyer friend and myself. I want to thank you for a very fair and very objective commentary.

As you can imagine, the person on the answering end at one of those editorial board luncheons goes away wondering what kind of impression he's made or how his answers were accepted by those doing the questioning. I don't know about others, but for me it is impossible to have any idea of what the verdict might be. Needless to say, your column brightened my day considerably.

I hope there will be an opportunity sometime in the near future when you and I can have a visit about the problems touched on in your column. I have long felt that, in many ways, black Americans and white are more the victims of welfare than the beneficiaries. My dream is the welfare program that will measure its success by how many people were enabled to leave welfare—not by how many we add to the rolls each year. I recognize the need to care for those who, through no fault of their own, must depend on the rest of us. But our goal should be salvage—not permanent bondage under the benevolent hand of the case worker.

Again, my heartfelt thanks and very best regards.

Sincerely,
Ronald Reagan

William Loeb alerted Reagan to a December 5 column by Holmes Alexander, a well-known conservative writer who was critical of what Reagan has been doing and saying.

Mr. William Loeb
Manchester, New Hampshire
Circa December 1979 [13]

Dear Bill:

Thanks very much for your letter and for sending me Holmes Alexander's column, although I can't say that it made for enjoyable reading. Yes, there is no one in between us, and I see all the letters that you send me. But I have taken advantage of your kindness when you have suggested so often not to bother answering because I am just about permanently on the road now.

I can't believe I'm boring the electorate if I can judge by the evidence of the reception to my speeches, including that in Nashua, nor do I think I'm taking it easy on the Carter administration. As you put it so well, I have been saying that Carter's lack of foreign policy—his weakness—created the situation now where 50 Americans are held hostage. I have also been saying that anything he has done so far to correct this could and should have been done in the first 24 hours. I am advocating specifically an across-the-board tax cut a la the Kemp-Roth plan, changes in the business tax to increase productivity, and cancellation of the inheritance tax and the tax on interest on saving accounts. You would be surprised at the audience reaction particularly to the statement about the inheritance tax. I get almost a standing ovation. Anyway, I'm going to write Holmes because his column regarding my announcement is so at odds with columnists like John Chamberlain and Jack Kilpatrick that I'm hard put to understand what his objections are.

Again, thanks and forgive me for not answering more often. Nancy and I just came back from another seven-state, four-day trip and are due out again the first of the week on another one. Give our love to Nackey.

Sincerely,
Ron

The conservative columnist Holmes Alexander wrote an open letter to Reagan on December 5, 1979, critical of his announcement speech on November 15, recalling his earlier choice of Richard Schweiker as his running mate in 1976 as "expediency" and questioning Reagan's position on a variety of issues.

Holmes Alexander
Circa December 1979 [14]

Dear Holmes:

I have only recently seen your column of December 5th. I'm on the road so much that I'm afraid I miss a great many things. Since you wrote it as a letter to me, I felt I should reply.

First of all, I appreciate all your kind words about our previous meeting and your opinion of me based on that meeting and infrequent meetings since. I wish there could be another one. I think possibly that, if we sat face-to-face again, you'd find there hasn't been much of a change, if any, and certainly not in the things I believe and in the things that I want to accomplish.

You say that in '76 I yielded to temptation and chose expediency instead of principle when I selected Dick Schweiker as my running mate. My choice was not because of any desire, as they say, to balance the ticket—well, in one way to balance it, and that was geographically. I had gone to the East to try to win over uncommitted delegates after the primaries and state conventions were over. I found in the great Northeastern states almost unanimously that our Republican leaders had written off these areas in the coming election and were convinced they would be won by the Democrats. Their only interest in the election was, as so many of them put it, to try and hang on to what they already had. I believe what some of them meant was to hang on to their only little fiefdoms.

I know the label that Dick carried. I know that it was justified by his voting on economic issues. But I made my choice only after long hours of discussion with him. I found I was talking to a man who, as I said once in our conversations together, reminded me of myself 20 years ago when, as a New Deal Democrat, I made my change. On the social issues, we had no disagreement. Dick, like myself, was opposed to abortion on demand, in favor of capital punishment, and had a well-nigh impeccable record with regard to national defense issues. He had introduced a constitutional amendment to restore prayer and Bible reading in the schools and had run successfully on a platform against gun control. When we began discussing the economic issues, he opened up, explained his previous positions, and said he now realized that things he had voted for did not cure the problems he had hoped to solve. He said he had returned to a belief that private enterprise was the way to solve those problems.

Unfortunately, the strategic decision to break with tradition and announce my choice early prevented me from contacting and explaining to supporters—even my closest ones—this information about him and the fact he had undergone this change himself and was certainly undergoing it before we met. I confirmed this in conversations with Paul Laxalt, who had been his seatmate for two years and who had told me that he thought Dick and I would both be surprised about each other if we had a talk. Now, of course, if you look at his voting record since '76, the ACU* rating is 87 percent.

With regard to my announcement speech, Holmes, I'm a little bewildered. You, and I must admit, some others, have assailed it as some kind of bland pabulum. On the other hand, such compatriots of yours as Jack Kilpatrick, John Chamberlain, and others have hailed it as brilliant and a masterpiece. Personally, I put it someplace between. Here was my problem: I know that I have ahead of me a long, long trail of almost daily speeches. I know there will be many more opportunities to speak on television. I couldn't, as the young preacher said at his first sermon, put the whole load in that announcement speech and then find myself only able to repeat what those who viewed me on television had already heard and seen.

Please believe me when I tell you the idea of a North American accord has been mine for many, many years. I have seen presidents, both Democrat and Republican, approach our neighbors with pre-concocted plans in which their only input is to vote "yes." Some months before I declared, I asked for a meeting and crossed the border to meet with the president of Mexico. I did not go with a plan. I went, as I said in my announcement address, to ask him his ideas—how we could make the border something other than the locale for a nine-foot fence. It was a good meeting, and I think he was honestly surprised to hear a Gringo saying the things I had said. As for Puerto Rico, I simply felt I had to add something in that speech lest the rest of Latin America think I was writing them off and concentrating only on our immediate neighbors.

---

* American Conservative Union.

To answer some of your other questions in your letter to me, I have always spoken well of our sending the Marines to the Dominican Republic. I supported the mining of Haiphong Harbor and the bombing of Hanoi enthusiastically and was, indeed, considered a hawk because I have continued to say that the only immorality of the Vietnam War was that our government asked young men to die in a war that the government had no intention of winning. While I have refrained from answering those questions about what I would do about the hostages if I were in the White House—because of the fear of endangering them—I have not hesitated to criticize the lack of foreign policy of this administration and to point out that the situation was created by President Carter's vacillation, which made possible the capture of our embassy and our fellow citizens in the first place.

The one place, Holmes, where I can't go along with you is in regard to attacking the other Republican candidates. I've labored too long in the vineyards trying to put this shattered Republican Party together to start violating my own 11th commandment—thou shalt not speak ill of another Republican. I believe we have the party more unified than ever in our history, and I'm going to continue to run against the Democratic record and explain those things I would do differently, i.e., the Kemp-Roth tax bill, remodeling the tax on business and industry to restore incentive, cancellation of tens of thousands of unnecessary regulations to increase productivity to where we once again can compete in the world market, to reduce the percentage of the people's earnings that the government is taking and to get spending back within the limits of government revenue.

I advocate returning to the states and local communities such programs as welfare and public education and returning with them the tax sources, not federal grants, to pay for them. I am stressing the need for a crash buildup of our military strength to the point that no one will dare do what they have been doing in the three years of this administration. We should establish a presence in the Middle East, and we certainly should be shipping arms to those freedom fighters in Afghanistan.

I hope our paths cross soon. It would be good to talk to you again, and, as I said earlier, I appreciate the kind words you also had to say about me in your letter.

Best regards,
Ronald Reagan

bcc: Loeb

On July 2, 1980, the National Association for the Advancement of Colored People (NAACP) met in Miami. An invitation for Reagan to address the convention had been sent to Republican National Headquarters. Apparently Reagan was unaware of the invitation, had made plans to be in Mexico, and found out about the invitation while the meeting was in progress. Senator Ted Kennedy, who spoke at the meeting, was critical

*of Reagan, and the press reported that Reagan had apparently ignored the NAACP's
invitation.*

Mr. William Loeb
Manchester, New Hampshire
July 2, 1980 [15]

Dear Bill:

Just a quick line before taking off for a few days in the country. My that sounds
strange to me after what we've been through, but, anyway, I wanted to thank you for
sending me that poll by Bill Long. That is cheerful news. I hope it's that way, say
along about late October.

You can bet I'm going to hang on to that blue-collar vote if it's humanly possible. I just had an experience today, though, that shows how delicate everything is. I
only learned within the last few hours that an invitation had been sent to me to
speak at the NAACP in Miami. The invitation had been sent to the Republican
National Headquarters. I don't know why or how, but I just learned of it within the
last hour. I will be in Mexico. I called Mr. Hooks and explained to him, and I'm sure
I convinced him that this had happened and that I certainly would never leave
them without a reply of any kind which is what they thought had happened. Of
course, it's already in the press, not my explanation, but the fact that I had apparently ignored their invitation. He is satisfied, and I am sending a wire which he requested stating what happened. But it just shows what we have to watch out for
every second. And, of course, you find yourself wondering if you were sabotaged
or did someone just slip up, or was it the mails. Anyway, we're trying to get the truth
out now.

Nancy sends her best. Give our regards to Nackey and best best regards.

Sincerely,
Ron

---

*After a year in office Reagan compares the press in Washington, D.C., to the Illinois
press with an old friend from Eureka.*

Mr. Sam Harrod III
Eureka, Illinois
February 4, 1982 [16]

Dear Sam:

Just a quick line to thank you for your note and for sending the column.

You are right, what we're getting from the press is dictated by ideology. But, if
you think it's bad out there, you ought to have to get up every morning and start the
day with the *Washington Post* and the *New York Times*.

Again, thanks.

Yours in the Bond,
Dutch

Bill Breisky, the editor of the Cape Cod Times *in Hyannis, Massachusetts, wrote an opinion column after attending a White House briefing and luncheon along with a few dozen other editors from the Northeast. First he thanked President Reagan for his hospitality, but then asked several questions including: "Who can assure us that it would be inconceivable, even impossible, for the United States to launch a preemptive nuclear strike against Russia?" and "What would happen . . . if you told Mr. Brezhnev that, as a peace gesture, we were going to cut, say, $20 billion from our fiscal '83 defense budget?"*

Bill Breisky, Editor
Cape Cod Times
Hyannis, Massachusetts
April 26, 1982 [17]

Dear Mr. Breisky:

I'm replying (although I'm quite tardy in doing so) to your column entitled, "Thank you Mr. President." And may I say thank you for your kind words.

You also had some questions so here are some answers. Your first one was about education and how we could make sure that all children had equal opportunity to get an education. I believe the answer to that is in a public school system that started at the local level when virtually all education was by way of private and or church supported schools. Then came the tax supported state colleges and universities. And finally the system of two-year colleges supported at the local level. In California there are more than 90 of these. Now and in very recent years we have in addition to this great public education system, loan and scholarship programs at state and federal levels. Our budget proposal for 1983 calls for $7 million in grants and loans.

There was a question about how high a level of unemployment and interest rates the people could tolerate. The interest rates must come down to a fair return for the lender. At present he must charge an interest rate covering that plus the loss in value of his money over the period of the loan due to inflation. We have lowered inflation from 12.4 percent to 4½ percent for the last six months. Interest rates have come down about 20 percent but that isn't enough. Inflation must be eliminated.

As for unemployment, so long as one person able and willing to work remains unemployed the rate is too high.

What guaranty do we have that the United States won't launch a preemptive nuclear strike against the Soviet Union? Look at the record. There have been four wars in my lifetime. The United States didn't start one of those. After WWII when we were the only nation with the "nuclear bomb," we offered to turn everything to do with nuclear power over to an international body. I have proposed negotiations to eliminate intermediate range nuclear missiles in Europe and such negotiations are underway in Geneva. We are planning for negotiations to start reducing the strategic weapons.

Now and last—what you call "record" defense spending was reduced so much that we created a window of vulnerability vis-à-vis the Soviet Union. Maybe our budget is "record" compared to those of the previous administrations but only in such a comparison.

Less than 30 percent of our '83 budget proposal is for defense. In 1962 JFK's budget for military spending was 48 percent of the total budget. We are spending on defense an amount equal to 6 percent of the GNP, JFK spent 9 percent. I only picked the single year—1962 as an illustration but it was typical of the peacetime military spending.

I hope this answers the questions you didn't have a chance to ask. I assure you we are striving to reduce the deficit and hope one day to eliminate it and inflation as well.

Sincerely,
Ronald Reagan

—————

Alfred Kingon, the editor-in-chief of Financial World *and an early Reagan campaign supporter from New York, wrote a bullish editorial for his July 1, 1982, issue arguing that "Prosperity is just around the corner, but it's a difficult corner to turn." He sent an advance copy to Reagan.*

Mr. Alfred H. Kingon
New York, New York
June 25, 1982 [18]

Dear Al:

In all the turmoil of the reception last evening, I don't know whether I saw you or not or whether you weren't there. That's an awful confession to make but those receptions become a blur of hands and faces with someone tugging at your back to turn around. Forgive me.

I had hoped if we did have a chance I could thank you for your letter and that editorial. I have Don Regan * looking at it right now. I know the income tax system has become so complex it is turning people away from government more angry at the complexity than they are at the tax itself.

I think we have to stay with our present tax cut plan lest people think we've lost faith in it, but while we do we can study the flat rate idea.

With the budget resolution passed and a veto of a spending bill sustained can't we see a little drop in the interest rates? This is becoming an obsession with me but I'll try not to picket a bank.

Best regards,
Ron

—————————

* Secretary of the treasury.

By the middle of 1982 the economy was still in bad shape and Reagan was having nearly as much trouble with the conservative media as he was with liberals. In this letter he replies to Nackey Loeb, who had succeeded her husband as publisher of the Union Leader. *She had sent Reagan a column by Jeffrey Hart, a professor of English at Dartmouth College. Hart had worked for Reagan during his brief presidential campaign in 1968.*

Mrs. William Loeb
Manchester, New Hampshire
June 28, 1982 [19]

Dear Nackey:

How good it was to hear from you even if you did give me a polite spanking. From you I'll take it and like it.

Nackey, my old friend Jeffrey Hart based his column on some misinformation plus the image that is being created of me as being packaged and delivered by staff and aides who won't let me think for myself. First let me clear up the "misinformation." Solzhenitsyn was definitely invited to the luncheon but didn't want to be a part of the group we'd invited. For what reason I don't know. As for the "off the record" ruling on my remarks our guests had asked that our discussion be off the record—no press coverage.

Now back to the image making, that seems to be not only a theme of the liberal pundits but of the so-called "new conservatives" including some of my old friends from *Human Events* etc. It just isn't true. I'm not turning my back on Taiwan and other than a few state department types no one is trying to push me that way. Maybe my speech at the U.N. will also indicate I'm not soft on Russia. And none of our gang tried to talk me into giving up our tax cuts even though for a time half the columnists were saying they were on a near daily basis.

Maybe a few events in the last couple of days will further substantiate my claim that I'm being me. I just hope being me can accomplish all that needs to be done.

I tried a meeting with some of those conservatives I mentioned, John Lofton, Stan Evans, Alan Ryskind et al. and gave them chapter and verse on what the actual record is but it didn't do much good.

Again—it was <u>good</u> hearing from you and I thank you for sending Jeffrey's column. I hadn't seen it.

Best regards,
Ron

Sol Polk, the president of a large retailing firm near Chicago, wrote to President Reagan on November 12, 1982, telling him that, in spite of the "doom and gloom reports about the American economy," he is convinced by economic indicators that "we aren't as bad off as we keep telling ourselves we are."

Reagan agrees and on July 8, 1983—eight months later—it was announced by the National Bureau of Economic Research that the economic recession officially ended in November 1982.

Mr. Sol Polk
Melrose Park, Illinois
December 27, 1982 [20]

Dear Mr. Polk:

I guess this calls for one of those "small world" remarks. Thank you for your letter but even more for the morale boost it gave me. I had just read a different kind of letter from an Illinois businessman who is on the edge of caving in.

I share your outlook and have been heartened by the evidence of increase in private sector initiatives plus the widespread voluntarism and good works in this Christmas season. I am more than a little upset by the constant drumbeat of doom and gloom we are getting from the news media. They could create a recession if we didn't already have one and certainly they are doing nothing to help us out of one.

Again my thanks to you for what you are doing and what you plan to do. Let's spread the word.

Sincerely,
Ronald Reagan

————

The wife of a Marine major who tested new military equipment informed President Reagan that a question by reporter Sarah McClelland on "wasteful military equipment" at a recent news conference was off base, and suggested he call her husband for confirmation.

Mrs. Donald T. Mize
Dale City, Virginia
March 15, 1983 [21]

Dear Mrs. Mize:

Thank you very much for your letter. I'm sure the drumbeat of false propaganda must be even more frustrating to you and your husband than it is to me. May I just say that from getting around the country and from the mail I receive I know the overwhelming majority of Americans are as proud as I am of our military forces.

For the life of me I don't understand the voices raised in what I must call our liberal press whining about the defense budget and criticizing virtually every aspect of the military. They don't speak for the American people and they aren't going to have their way.

Please give your husband the Major my regards and my thanks for what he is doing for all of us.

Sincerely,
Ronald Reagan

Nickie McWhirter, a reporter for the Detroit Free Press, *writes an article dealing with a developing scandal enveloping Reagan's head of the Environmental Protection Agency, Anne M. Gorsuch (Burford). McWhirter concluded that Burford, who eventually resigned, was forced to leave in a "feeding frenzy." Reagan thanks McWhirter for her article.*

> Ms. Nickie McWhirter
> Detroit, Michigan
> March 28, 1983 [22]

Dear Ms. McWhirter:

I have just been presented with a copy of your March 11 column in the *Free Press*—the column on Anne Burford, and I want to thank you. May I make just one correction: Anne wasn't fired nor would I ever have asked for her resignation. She resigned because she believed the EPA just wouldn't be allowed by the "frenzied feeders" to function unless she did.

You stand almost alone among your contemporaries in recognizing that all of the attack so far has consisted of allegations and accusations with no proof of wrongdoing. Almost totally obscured by the "feeding frenzy" is the fact that under Anne's guidance the EPA was doing a fine job. I've asked her to accept another appointment in our administration. She is a gallant lady.

Thank you for a real civics lesson. In my book you and "Mary Lou" both should go to the head of the class.

> Sincerely,
> Ronald Reagan

Reagan agrees with one of his supporters on the problem of unnamed White House aides and other unnamed sources cited in press reports.

> Mr. Victor L. Austin
> New York, New York
> June 28, 1983 [23]

Dear Mr. Austin:

Thank you more than I can say for your kind letter and generous words. Those stories quoting unnamed aides or White House sources I'm afraid are in truth the imagination of the writer and yes they can get your goat. But a letter like yours does a lot to set things right.

Again my thanks and best regards,

> Sincerely,
> Ronald Reagan

One of the many thousands of letters sent to the president was used by Paul Harvey on his radio news show, and was heard on over 1,200 radio stations. In the letter, a policeman from Chicago argues that Reagan's policies are "good for everyone—not just white males," and that minority groups are upset because Reagan has "not done anything special for them." After seeing the transcript that was broadcast Reagan writes the policeman a letter, thanking him.

Detective Garland Conway
Louisville, Kentucky
October 20, 1983 [24]

Dear Officer Conway:

Thank you very much for your letter and your generous words. I'm truly grateful.

You did a masterful job of summing up a very real problem. I can't help but wonder if some of those loud complaining "leaders" of special interest groups aren't moved by purely selfish reasons.

If they ever acknowledge that the situations which brought their organizations into existence have now been solved, their jobs are no longer necessary. So they have to keep them stirred up and angry at someone.

Again my heartfelt thanks.

Sincerely,
Ronald Reagan

A 57 year old woman, who supported Reagan for governor and president, writes to the editor of Human Events *that she has become disillusioned—accusing Reagan of supporting "multi-billion-dollar tax bills. . . . world communism through trade and the World Bank. . . . (and) deficit spending." She concludes by saying "I feel betrayed," and will not support him because he "espouses a weak America and a strong Soviet Union."*

In this long letter Reagan attempts to persuade her that she is mistaken.

Mrs. Sylvia Kinyoun
Thousand Oaks, California
November 3, 1983 [25]

Dear Mrs. Kinyoun:

I read your letter to the editor in the October 29 issue of *Human Events**—a paper I read regularly. With the constant drumbeat of criticism by much of the

---

* Kinyoun, Sylvia Mrs., letter to the editor, *Human Events*, October 29, 1983, page 19.

press I can understand why you might have a distorted view of what I have done or not done. There is a political bias—whether they will admit it or not—in much of the press and it can hardly be described as in my favor.

First with regard to your letter let me thank you for the support you gave to me as governor and now as president. I hope I can prove to you I haven't changed in my beliefs. I do not support large tax increases. We passed the biggest tax cut in our nation's history but the so-called tax increase that followed was to straighten out some "goodies" which had been added by Congress and went beyond what we had asked for. Fully a third of the increase was not an increase at all but measures to better collect taxes already owed and which were being evaded because of various loopholes. But let me tell you what the majority in Congress promised if I'd support that tax increase; there would be $3 in spending cuts for every $1 of added revenue. I regret to tell you, the Congress has not kept that promise.

Let me just say about the World Bank;—these international funding agencies are useful in keeping world trade going by helping the new developing countries get on their feet and remain as customers of countries like our own.

As for deficits believe me I want to get back to a balanced budget and tried to persuade (without success) Congress to support a constitutional amendment requiring that. Half the present deficit is the result of the recession. That will come down as recovery continues. The other half is structural. It is built into the automatic increases built into so many programs by Congress. We have only gotten about half the spending cuts we asked for. If Congress had given us the rest, the present deficit would be $40 billion less than it is.

Congress is also the problem with regard to the departments of energy and education. The leadership on both sides of the aisle will not move on this.

Mrs. Kinyoun, on the Korean airline massacre some of the actions that were suggested we've already taken. We persuaded our allies last spring to stop sales of high technology to the Soviets and also to stop trade with them based on low interest credit. We cancelled several things that were desired by the Soviets and that were in the works. I'll admit even so to being frustrated because there is so little we can do short of shooting at them.

I'm very proud of the improvement we've made in our military strength and there will be no "weak America." I think we showed off some of that improvement in Grenada.

Forgive me for burdening you with this long letter but I felt you deserved a reply.

Sincerely,
Ronald Reagan

Victor "Brute" Krulak, a retired three-star Marine Corps general, was an old friend and Bohemian Grove campmate* of President Reagan. Wounded and rescued by PT boat skipper John F. Kennedy in World War II, Krulak was the President of the Copley News Service, wrote a syndicated column, and frequently advised Reagan informally.

Lt. General Victor H. Krulak, USMC (Ret.)
San Diego, California
November 21, 1983 [26]

Dear Brute:

Thanks for the report on the camp meeting and double thanks for the fine column.

You know Dick Nixon said a good and proper thing regarding the comparison of press coverage of WWII and Grenada. He said: Things were different then; the press was on our side.

Best regards,
Ron

General Winn was the commander of the North American Air Defense Command Combat Operations Center located in Cheyenne Mountain in Colorado. Winn retired in July 1978, one year before Reagan visited the facility, which can detect a nuclear missile attack. Winn warned in a letter to Reagan that "totalitarian rule is growing despite the absence of any successful socialist model," and that "terror, especially in the nuclear age, is the only legacy of failed Marxism." He also worried about dissent within Reagan's staff. Reagan's response blames the media for misreporting on some of Winn's issues.

Brigadier General David W. Winn, USAF (Ret.)
Colorado Springs, Colorado
June 10, 1984 [27]

Dear General Winn:

Thank you very much for your insightful letter and wise words. I am writing this as I return from the summit in London.†

In spite of the usual slanting and inaccuracies of the media, who consider such meetings failures unless there is friction or a feud to write about, the meeting on the

---

* Krulak and Reagan were both members of Owl's Nest, a camp with about 25 members that is one of 121 camps scattered throughout the redwood forest used every summer for two weeks by the Bohemian Club.

† Economic summit held in London in June 1984.

whole was good and worthwhile. There was consensus on some of the issues you raised in your letter with regard to the anti-freedom forces in the world; more realism than in some past summits.

Indeed it was easier to achieve consensus there than in Washington with some of the factions in Congress. General Winn I believe that again the media has exaggerated supposed differences within our administration. It is true I encourage presentation of all facets but there is no compromise with principle on my part nor has such been urged upon me.

I'm most grateful for your letter and strengthened by the points you made with such eloquence and logic. Thank you and God bless you.

Sincerely,
Ronald Reagan

A couple of months before the 1984 election Reagan was asked to do a "pre-broadcast voice check" for his weekly radio address to the nation. He playfully spoke into his microphone: "I am pleased to announce I just signed legislation which outlaws Russia forever. The bombing begins in five minutes." Someone in the media overheard him say it, and leaked it. Walter Mondale intoned that bombing Russia was no joking matter and some of the European press talked about the president's "instability" and "trigger happiness." Malcom Forbes wrote a quick reply in his magazine telling Reagan's critics they were "more of a joke by far than Reagan's mike-test quipping."

Mr. Malcolm S. Forbes
New York, New York
August 21, 1984 [28]

Dear Mr. Forbes:

Just a line to say how pleasant it was to see at least once in print some understanding of what can happen in a pre-broadcast voice check. Thank you very much.

Granted I shouldn't have said it even though I was sure I was saying it only to the several people who know me well and with whom I work. The damage if any was due to the worldwide press dissemination. I had no idea the line had been opened to the press HQ for a line check. Well—I'll go back to counting from now on.

Thank you again.

Sincerely,
Ronald Reagan

The author of seven books on the presidency, Hugh Sidey wrote a regular column for Time *magazine. After Reagan was reelected in 1984, Sidey wrote that he had gained* *remarkable stature, saying that the question now is "not whether Reagan will be different but whether the world may make some adjustments to him. The polls in Europe show a marked increase in respect for Reagan. . . . the needle in the national compass may spin, but Reagan is fixed and steady as true north."* *

Mr. Hugh Sidey
Potomac, Maryland
November 29, 1984 [29]

Dear Hugh:

Just another fan letter. This time with reference to your *Time* column in the November 26 issue. I'm trying not to get a swelled head but you are making that a difficult task.

Thank you for your kind and generous words. I'll try my best to be deserving of them.

Nancy sends her best.

Sincerely,
Ron

———

Reagan responds to one of Paul Harvey's radio newscasts and fills him in on upcoming meeting that Harvey is scheduled to have with the head of the American Red Cross.

Paul Harvey
Chicago, Illinois
June 21, 1985 [30]

Dear Paul:

Thank you very much for, "Mr. President, Spare My But." You made my day and that goes for our top staff people. I gave them copies. You certainly helped our tax reform campaign also.

Paul I understand you have just had or are slated to have a meeting with our leader of Red Cross. He told me of your concern about Red Cross seemingly refusing to help in the hostage situation. This was another press error. We never asked the Red Cross to intervene nor will we. They have been most helpful in the ways they are set up to help—contact with the hostages to see they are being properly cared for etc.

Well again my heartfelt thanks to you.

Warm regards,
Ronald Reagan

---

* Sidey, Hugh, "Using the Tried and True," *Time* magazine, November 26, 1984, p. 40.

Reagan writes that he has been subjected to Soviet propaganda when Izvestia, *the official news organ of the Supreme Soviet, omitted some of his answers in his interview with its journalists on October 31, 1985.**

Mr. George Montgomery
Los Angeles, California
November 12, 1985 [31]

Dear George:

Thank you for your letter and for the photos. Sculpturing has always been an unknown art to me, now I have some inkling of how it's done and I find it fascinating.

You are right about the Russian people and how little they will be allowed to know. I have just received the *Izvestia* interview I did with four reporters. The parts of my answers they omitted did in many instances actually change the meaning of what I had said.

Nevertheless I'm looking forward to the meeting and continue to hope that maybe we can reduce some of the distrust between us.

Nancy sends her best and again thank you.

Sincerely,
Ron

On December 6, 1985, the Orange County Register *in southern California carried an editorial charging that the Reagan administration had not slowed federal spending and that "conservatives" have no real interest in slowing the growth of goverment.*

The Editor, *Orange County Register*
Santa Ana, California
February 4, 1986 [32]

Dear Mr. Editor:

On December 26th a *Register* editorial stated that "contrary to popular mythology" we had not slowed the rate of federal spending in our years here in Washington. Then citing 1984 figures and those for the first five months of '85 you had the rate of growth in spending triple the rate under the previous administration. Your conclusion was that if we are conservatives then conservatives have no interest in cutting back government.

---

* "Remarks in an Interview with Representatives of Soviet News Organizations, Together with Written Responses to Questions, October 31, 1985," *Public Papers of the Presidents, Ronald Reagan, 1985* (Washington, DC: USGPO, 1988), volume I, 1331–42. For an English translation of the *Izvestia* interview see "Reagan Interviewed by Soviet Journalists," *The Current Digest of the Soviet Press* 37 (November 27, 1985): 1–20.

I have debated as to whether I should reply and my final decision was that I should—hence this letter.

Between 1977 and 1981 the average rate of growth in total federal spending was 13.5 percent nominal, or 4.5 percent adjusted for inflation. By comparison the average rate of growth between 1981 and 1985 was 8.7 percent nominal or 3.9 percent in real terms. The figures are quite different if you separate out defense. In the Carter years defense grew at an average rate of 3.9 percent in real terms vs. 7.1 percent during my first term. For domestic spending it was 3.7 percent under the previous administration vs. 1.2 percent in my first term.

True there was a single-year upsurge between '84 and '85. Part of that was increased payments to farmers through the Commodity Credit Corporation, an increase in defense spending in outlay terms and a one-time write-off in federal housing loans.

And of course there was an increase in interest payments on the national debt which will be true every year until we balance the budget. In general however the rate of growth in federal spending has been reduced considerably and government is smaller by some 78,000 employees on the domestic side.

I hope that conservatives in Orange County know that we are going to continue trimming down the government monster.

Sincerely,
Ronald Reagan

One of Reagan's oldest friends, a strong financial supporter, sent him a copy of a letter to the editor of the New York Times *that criticizes the way the government reports on the monthly unemployment figures.*

Mr. Armand S. Deutsch
Los Angeles, California
June 25, 1986 [33]

Dear Ardie:

Thank you for sending me Paul Manheim's letter to the *New York Times*. I get so d—n frustrated when the monthly unemployment figures come out and are reported as unemployment increases when there is a higher percentage of the potential work force employed than ever in our history. What was it Disraeli said; "there are lies, d—n'd lies and statistics." Paul has a little of Disraeli in him.

I'm with you on Zschau.* Of course I had to be neutral in the primary, but now we all have to get behind him and make him a senator.

Love to Harriet.

All the best,
Ron

---

* Ed Zschau was running against Alan Cranston in 1986 for the Senate seat in California. Zschau lost.

Nackey Loeb offered the President some advice: "introduce Rex (the Reagan's dog) to a good dog trainer." She felt that "it is hard on Nancy's image to see her being pulled around," and added that she was sure "it is hard on her arm as well."

> Mrs. William Loeb
> Manchester, New Hampshire
> July 2, 1986 [34]

Dear Nackey:

I wish there were editorials like yours and columns like Mel's in every senator's district. What we are seeing in this Manion case* is another lynching in which some senators are trying to bring down a better man than themselves. And of course as always there are some deluded souls who believe the falsehoods of the lynchers and go along with the mob.

Nackey our dog situation is one of youthful exuberance, on the part of the dogs—not us. We were well along in training Lucky before she took residence at the ranch but even so she forgot her lessons when the helicopter (which meant Camp David) was on the lawn. Now we're doing a repeat—in spades. Rex is still only a pup and when that chopper comes in he just tunes us out. I think he believes "Marine I" is his personal dog basket.

You know there is always a crowd on the south lawn, not just the press, both when we leave and when we return and Rex does get excited with the clapping and waving, etc. I have a sneaking feeling he'll still be doing this when we take our final liftoff in January 1989. From then on he better quiet down because there will be horses in his life.

Again thanks for the clippings.

> Sincerely,
> Ron

Reagan responds to a letter from an old Hollywood friend, Nedda, the wife of Joshua Logan. Logan directed such films as South Pacific *and* Bus Stop. *Nedda Logan includes a clipping about Ed Asner from the* New York Post.

---

* On February 21, 1986, Reagan nominated Daniel A. Manion, the former deputy attorney general of Indiana to the U.S. Court of Appeals for the Seventh Circuit in Chicago, Illinois. He was opposed by such liberal groups as "People for the American Way," who charged that Reagan was packing the court with right-wing judges. After a tough political fight Manion was confirmed by a single vote, cast by Vice President Bush, and received his commission on July 24, 1986.

Mrs. Josh Logan
New York, New York
July 3, 1986 [35]

Dear Nedda:

Just a hasty line before diving into that celebration in New York. We have a schedule that looks like it should be for three weeks not three days.

Thank you for your nice letter and for that clipping about Mr. Asner.* What's that old line "if you lie down with lice you get lousy?" I thought he just had a thing about me—now I can see he has a thing about our whole system.

Nancy and I are sorry to hear about Josh's ill-health and hope he'll cut it out of the picture. Nancy sends her love to you both and do so I. Again our thanks.

Sincerely,
Ron

Andrew Heiskell, the chairman of Time Inc., sent a letter to Nancy Reagan complaining about the decline in charitable giving caused by her husband's tax-cutting policies. Heiskell enclosed a copy of a lecture on this matter given by John Chancellor, the former network news anchor for NBC television. Nancy gave the letter to her husband.

Mr. Andrew Heiskell
New York, New York
September 23, 1986 [36]

Dear Andrew:

I hope you won't mind my answering your recent letter to Nancy and forgive me for being so tardy in doing so. I can only plead the merry-go-round I've been on for the past several weeks.

I think John Chancellor's August 26 lecture was way off track. I know many concerned about charitable giving expressed a fear that our income tax cuts from 70 percent to 50 percent would result in fewer contributions but that hasn't happened. Nor do I think it will happen as a result of the further reduction in tax reform. Last year private giving reached an all-time high of almost $80 billion and corporate giving has increased over the last few years. This also holds true for those who volunteer their time and service.

I'm sure there are individuals here and there whose generosity is based on the

---

* Ed Asner was best known as the actor who portrayed Lou Grant in *The Mary Tyler Moore Show* on television in the 1970s. He served as president of the Screen Actors Guild (1981–85), was a liberal political activist, and had a poor opinion of Reagan.

percentage of tax deduction, but overall the figures indicate that Americans in the main are motivated by generosity.

Let's keep our fingers crossed. Nancy sends her best as do I.

Sincerely,

Ron

———

Paul Trousdale, a successful real estate developer, was one of Reagan's California friends. Here Reagan commiserates on Trousdale's views of the press after one of Reagan's press conferences.

Mr. Paul Trousdale
Los Angeles, California
March 23, 1987 [37]

Dear Paul:

Thanks very much for your letter and your kind words about me and your proper words about our friends (?) in the media.

Someone sent me a clipping from an Illinois paper. It carries quotes going back to 1858 in the press of that time about Lincoln. One paper called him everything from a thief to a gorilla. But when he was shot the same paper went into a mix of crocodile tears and a eulogy about this "great and good" man.

I hope I can avoid such a change of heart by today's press, considering the price. Nancy sends her best.

Sincerely,

Ron

———

Charles Grimm was the manager of the Chicago Cubs baseball team when Reagan was covering the games for WHO radio* in the 1930s. Grimm's wife wrote to President Reagan, incensed by the way the media was treating him.

Mrs. Charles Grimm
Scottsdale, Arizona
March 30, 1987 [38]

Dear Marion:

Thank you for your kind letter and generous words. I am most grateful. You are so right about the media, they seem to be in business not to report the news but to make it by attacking whoever is in charge. Just between us, I handle it by pretending I'm on the mound pitching and they are out in the right field bleachers.

———

* WHO was an NBC radio affiliate in Des Moines, Iowa, a powerful station that broadcast throughout the Midwest.

Next time you see Tom, give him our best regards. Nancy and I have known him for a long time. And when and if you make that trip to Washington, let us know. In case they have me out of the country on May 7, let me say Happy Birthday now.

Again, my thanks for your kindness and your prayers.

Sincerely,
Ron

Nackey Loeb wrote to Reagan about "the unfair way in which the media has been treating" him with regard to the Iran-Contra scandal, and muses as to whether the Founding Fathers anticipated the politics of scandal.

Mrs. William Loeb
Manchester, New Hampshire
June 17, 1987[39]

Dear Nackey:

Your letter and editorial were what I consider a warm and happy welcome home. I assure you I'll be making use of that 1980 news report.

You are so right about the other events that somehow didn't ring any bells here inside the beltway. What can we do to get some better direction in some of our schools of journalism? I've heard some disturbing things lately about indoctrination being the general rule rather than "who, what, when, where" that once was taught.

Nancy sends her best and we both thank you.

Sincerely,
Ron

CHAPTER NINETEEN

The Critics

MOST OF THE LETTERS *that Reagan wrote did not involve responding to critics, but some did. Reagan's critics were a varied lot. Most were concerned citizens who wrote him about a particular policy. Some of their concerns were based on inaccurate, incomplete, or incorrect information, but others simply disagreed with Reagan's true policies.*

Every four or five weeks Reagan would be given a stack of letters, usually around 30, chosen from the thousands that poured into the White House every day. Most of the letters were selected by his correspondence staff, headed by Ann Higgins. The letters tended to reflect the current issues that were dominating the news, and overall they were supposed to be a sampling of what was on people's minds. Some of these letters were friendly, even laudatory, but others were intensely critical of his person and his policies. Reagan had begun this practice while he was governor of California. His replies were usually detailed.

Some of the letters came from Democrats, who objected to his policies. Some came from conservative supporters who felt he was not pursuing certain policies with enough vigor. Perhaps the toughest letters to answer came from the mothers and fathers of young men and women who had died after being ordered into battle by Reagan. There were also letters from old friends, who spoke directly and frankly; these letters he seemed to cherish, even though some of them stung. His replies tenaciously defended what he had done or what he was doing. Usually the tone of his letters was calm, often sympathetic, but on occasion his anger flared and he could not resist taking a swipe at some of his tormentors.

Most of the people who knew Reagan thought he was amiable and easygoing. Even with old friends and staff he rarely argued or disagreed. When criticized in person he seldom pointed out the errors or inaccuracies in the critic's argument. But in his letters he was unusually direct and candid, even when it seemed unlikely he would convert his critic.

On January 23, 1976, just as the presidential campaign was heading into the primary elections, the Los Angeles Herald Examiner *editorialized that Reagan was refusing to discuss specific issues or state his positions on the key problems facing the nation. Reagan writes a blistering response.*

The Editor, *Los Angeles Herald-Examiner*
Los Angeles, California
Circa January 1976[1]

To the Editor:

I am at a loss to understand your editorial of January 23rd. You charge that as a candidate I have refused to discuss specific issues or to state my position on the problems facing our nation.

I agree with your statement that the voters have a right to hear a candidate's position on the issues and problems he would face if he succeeded in winning the office he seeks. But then you go on with your declaration that I have been above the fray and have indulged in bland generalities. Possibly you've been on a ski vacation somewhere in the mountains or out of the country for several weeks.

If you don't mind I'd like to bring you up to date at least with regard to my campaign speeches, press conferences and broadcasts. I have—One; given (repeatedly) a complete, detailed account of the changes I would try to bring about in the federal tax structure, including the elimination of two specific taxes;—the income tax on interest from savings accounts and the federal inheritance tax which threatens the continued existence of the family owned farm and business.

Two; I have called for the return to states and local governments programs the federal government has usurped and which it has proven incapable of managing—beginning with welfare.

Three; I have specified that federal tax sources to fund these programs should be transferred with them and have given examples of how this could be done.

Four; I have given examples of federal regulations that reduce productivity and increase inflation and have called for their cancellation.

Five; On the energy crisis I have discussed government's part in creating that crisis and recommended measures to solve it.

Six; International affairs—I have made definite proposals with regard to Afghanistan, the Middle East, Soviet aggression, SALT II and our defense needs.

There have been other subjects on which I've been pretty explicit but these will give you an idea of what you've missed.

Welcome back from where ever you were.

Ronald Reagan

During the 1976 campaign Reagan argued that the United States should keep the Panama Canal. He lost the election, and also lost that argument when in 1977 President Carter signed the Panama Canal Treaty, transferring control of the canal to the Republic of Panama. Here Reagan responds to the argument that we were only leasing the Canal Zone.

Mr. Ronald A. Reed
West Los Angeles, California
1976[2]

Dear Mr. Reed:

I'm afraid the encyclopedia is wrong in this case. I know there has been confusion for many years because of the annual payment and in some circles the belief has grown that we do indeed lease the Canal Zone. The Hay-Bunau-Varilla treaty makes it explicitly clear that we have sovereignty over the Zone and there is no mention of leasing. Our Supreme Court upheld our sovereign right in a 1907 decision. Incidentally in addition to the payments to Panama and Colombia the United States bought in fee simple every bit of private property from each individual owner in the Zone.

Best regards,
Ronald Reagan

The Ford-Rockefeller wing of the Republican party never forgave Reagan for challenging President Ford in 1976. Many felt then—and still do—that Reagan and his supporters gave only tepid support to Ford in the general election and thus were responsible for Jimmy Carter winning the presidency. In this letter a frustrated Reagan tries to explain to an angry Ford supporter how much he campaigned for Ford and how united the Republican Party was.

Mr. Ervine F. Smith
Pacific Palisades, California
Circa November 1976[3]

Dear Mr. Smith:

I realize no words of mine can change a mind as evidently set as yours. Let me just say that, back in the middle of the primaries, the Republican senators, as a group, unanimously passed a resolution offered by Senator Percy of Illinois declaring that my campaign had done more to revitalize the Republican Party than anything in the last twenty years. All but two of those senators were supporting President Ford.

Following the convention, virtually the entire Republican congressional delegation sent me a letter of thanks for the way I conducted my campaign. Every signer was a supporter of the president.

In the six weeks of the campaign following Kansas City, I campaigned in twenty-five states, did a series of TV commercials at the president's request, a thirty-minute TV speech and over a million letters were sent out over my signature, soliciting financial support for the president. I'm sure you must have worked for his election but, I assure you, I did all that I could possibly do and those who had supported me rallied around the president. The party was more united in this campaign than in any I've ever seen. At least that's what President Ford told me when he called the day after the election to thank me.

Very truly yours,
Ronald Reagan

In January 1977 Reagan had given one of his national radio broadcasts on the lack of liberty in Panama. He had also argued that it was difficult to negotiate with General Omar Torrijos, the Panamanian dictator, when he threatened violence. This position was a rare disagreement with William F. Buckley, Jr., who sent Reagan a National Review _column arguing that Panama had a strong economic stake in keeping the Canal open, that they would negotiate a reasonable settlement with the United States and, after making it clear that "we have a right to stay in . . . then get out," that the United States should act "while the initiative is still, clearly, our own."_

William F. Buckley, Jr.
New York, New York
January 27, 1977 [4]

Dear Bill:

I'm now square with the world—unless the enclosed bounces.* Forgive this mismatched stationery and the scrawl—things are a little hectic at the moment.

I appreciate getting your columns although for the first time (it must be) we are in disagreement about the conclusion. Incidentally I had read your article about the young banker's visit to Cuba. In fact I did one of my broadcasts† on that one, giving you and _National Review_ appropriate credit. I've also done a broadcast on the lack of civil liberties in Panama.

Bill I'm in favor of negotiations to smooth the friction etc. but feel that the general put us in an untenable position when he said "or else." ‡ The "or else" was of course violence if we did not give in to his demand. Then Henry§ gave credence

---

* This was probably a check for the renewal of his subscription to _National Review_.
† Ronald Reagan, "Cuba," November 16, 1976, in _Reagan In His Own Hand_, edited by Kiron Skinner, Annelise Anderson and Martin Anderson (New York: Free Press, 2001), p. 195.
‡ Reagan felt that to agree with Buckley's position would be tantamount to giving in to a threat. Although Reagan had high respect for Buckley, he disagreed with him on a number of issues, such as compulsory national service.
§ Henry Kissinger.

to this when he publicly stated or inferred that was the reason why we had to negotiate.

How do we negotiate now without appearing to be acceding to a demand?
Nancy sends her best and give Pat our love.

Regards,
Ron

———————

The Spotlight *was a weekly tabloid with a reputation of being right-wing and anti-
Semitic that had been published by the Liberty Lobby since 1975. It focused on "con-
spiracies" of both the left and the right, and Reagan was often in its gun sights, charged
with "moving leftward." Kent Steffgen, author of two books attacking the "liberal"
Reagan,* Here's the Rest of Him *(1968) and* The Counterfeit Candidate *(1976), had
long argued that Reagan was promoting "backdoor socialism."* Spotlight *published a
four-page article drawn from these books and included a large ad for* The Counterfeit
Candidate *in their December 4, 1978, issue. A Reagan supporter sent Reagan the clipping.*

Mrs. Buford S. Craig
Burbank, California
December 6, 1978[5]

Dear Mrs. Craig:

Thank you for writing and for enclosing the clipping from *Spotlight.* I had not
seen it. The author of that book is well known to me but not by me. To my knowledge we have never met and I'm hard put to understand his motive. His first book
was totally false and proven so by the record. I'm sure this recent version is the
same.

You asked if the statements in the clipping were true: for example did I appoint
large numbers of Rockefeller supporters to state offices and did I support him for
president?

I was Barry Goldwater's state chairman in 1964 when we defeated Rockefeller
in the California primary. I never supported Rockefeller for president in 1968 or
any other time. As for a Reagan-Rockefeller ticket in 1976, I chose my running
mate* before we even got to the convention, and Rockefeller led the New York delegation for President Ford.

The other charges in his sales pitch for his book are equally false, and the record
of my eight years as governor proves this. He† charges me with "back door socialism" in tax matters. Actually I returned to the people in tax rebates of state surpluses and tax credits $5.7 billion. I opposed forced bussing, the ERA, abortion

———————

* Senator Richard Schweiker from Pennsylvania.
† Kent Steffgen.

on demand, socialized medicine and those other things he mentioned. During my eight years, we passed 41 anti-crime bills to make things tougher on criminals, and I favor the death penalty.

Kent Steffgen—(whoever he is) is an unmitigated liar.

Again, I thank you for bringing this to my attention. Please write if you have any further questions.

Sincerely,
Ronald Reagan

One of the reporters covering Reagan in the 1979 campaign was Margaret Warner, who wrote about politics and government for the San Diego Union *newspaper and later joined the* News Hour *on PBS. Reagan took umbrage at one of her stories that implied he had an "imperial candidacy." He also defended his loss to President Ford in the 1976 New Hampshire primary.*

Margaret Garrard Warner
San Diego Union
San Diego, California
October 1979[6]

Dear Miss Warner:

I read your article regarding my visit to the Republican State Convention a few weeks ago. Normally I take for granted the right of a journalist to express his or her own opinion in reporting a story and rarely do I do what I'm doing now—which is attempt a rebuttal.

Forgive me for making an exception with regard to your story. I'm afraid someone has given you a great deal of misinformation about the 1976 New Hampshire campaign. Possibly because of that you then viewed happenings in San Diego through a somewhat distorted glass.

In 1976 I was assigned Secret Service protection as was every other candidate, Democrat and Republican. They performed their duty in a low-key, unobtrusive manner as they are trained to do and there was never an incident or complaint to my knowledge by anyone about them making me inaccessible.

We traveled in two busses because of the national and local press accompanying us as we averaged visiting twelve to fourteen towns a day. In each town it was very much a personal kind of campaigning, one on one with questions and answers not speeches. Sometimes I stood on the running board of a fire engine, once on a stack of feedbags out in the snow etc.

I alternated riding in the two busses and between towns gave time for any and every kind of interview. The national press was very cooperative and recognized the necessity of granting local press first chance—which we did. Actually you know I won New Hampshire as far as the number of votes received. I lost by less than

1,500 but 6,000 of my votes were thrown out because they voted for all nineteen of the Reagan delegates on the ballot. They were supposed to vote for only sixteen.*

In San Diego it is true our schedule was crammed and hectic but that was hardly our choice. We had but part of an afternoon and evening with many people who had good reason to seek appointments. It is true Jim Lake shut off one question after he had signaled the end of the press conference but isn't that customary? Would it have been fair to let one reporter have an added question without giving others the same opportunity?

As for the meeting with the young people by the pool, as you know the day was extremely hot and I was told they'd been waiting out in that heat for more than an hour. Mr. Kane the *Time* reporter had been told there could be no one-on-one interview on the trip because we had already had to refuse others. He was told a later meeting would be arranged.

If there is an "imperial candidacy" in this political season I assure you it is not mine. I wouldn't know how to act in such a thing.

Sincerely,
Ronald Reagan

Reagan replies to a hawkish citizen who has received a Republican fundraising letter that included a policy questionnaire. After apologizing for the nature of the questionnaire, he launches into a long discussion of his policy views.

Mrs. Doris Murphy
March 14, 1980 [7]

Dear Mrs. Murphy:

Thank you for writing and giving me a chance to reply and, hopefully, correct some possible misunderstandings.

I have to admit that the fundraising letters are usually done on a kind of assembly line basis. True, they bear the signature of the candidate, but maybe they don't, because of their purpose, say things exactly the way the candidate has been saying them. For that I apologize. But may I tell you some of the things that I have been saying throughout this country.

I don't think of the voters as voters. They are people. And I have to tell you something else. I find it most stimulating and even inspiring to meet the people of this country as you meet them during a campaign. You learn all over again what a truly great people they are. And my complaint—possibly the reason I'm running—

---

* The ballot listed 19 possible delegates for Reagan, but only 16 could be elected. If a voter voted for more than 16, and many ardent Reagan supporters did, *all* their votes were disqualified. If only 16 delegates had been listed on the ballot it would have been impossible to disqualify votes, and Reagan would have won the 1976 New Hampshire primary.

is that government is robbing the most independent people who ever lived of that independence and taking away from them their right to control their own destiny. Yes, this country is of the people, by the people, and for the people and what we need today, is more by the people. You asked if we are not all responsible—don't we have a democracy? Well, probably we are all responsible to the extent that we tend to be apathetic or to go our own way with our own affairs and not look too closely at government. But we truly are not a democracy, we are a republic. We have decided from our very beginning that rather than direct democracy, we would choose people to represent us to do those government functions as they felt best with a certain amount of guidance from the people and correction by the people if those representatives go too far afield from what it is the people want. I have no disagreement with you about the manner in which we have followed wars with a mismanaged peace which very often did lead to the next war, and I believe that we're probably doing the same thing and have been for sometime.

Now, may I turn to a few of your notes on the questionnaire? First, the one asking if we trust Mr. Carter's ability to judge and assess accurately the military and political intentions of Soviet leaders? I think the answer to this is, no, and I believe we can assess accurately. We have seen him on television declare that the presence of the Soviet brigade in Cuba is unacceptable and then destroy the credibility of this nation by doing nothing about it.

With regard to the question of Afghanistan and your own observation of what we could do about it, it was the president who uttered the sternest of warnings to the Soviets when their troops were poised on the Afghanistan border and told them there would be serious consequences if they crossed that border. Again, our credibility is compromised because they crossed the border and nothing was done. Should a leader utter such threats if he knows he cannot respond if his threat is ignored?

I agree with your response to question four—that we don't believe the Soviets will observe the provisions of SALT II unless there is on-site inspection and, since there isn't, I recommend we should return the SALT II treaty to them and tell them we are not going to sign it. You are right that they have achieved military superiority. I don't believe this country was in as dangerous a situation the day after Pearl Harbor as it is today. We must immediately find and start building an effective deterrent because peace is our policy and national security.

I find myself in disagreement regarding the neutron warhead. I am looking for ways to prevent war. The massive Russian armored forces poised on the eastern approach to the historic invasion routes to the West could be neutralized not by dropping the neutron warhead, but the threat of it. I am not interested in a war where we have to fight those tanks. I'm looking for weapons that would be so much of a deterrent that the enemy will not attack. I believe we have to start building up our Navy again because we are a maritime nation. Yes, it will take time, but, at the moment, we are building ships for the Navy at a lower rate than just replacement for those which are being retired because of age.

We agree about the draft. I think that we can bring our military up to strength and, if we try, build an active reserve force without resorting to the draft.

And you and I agree about the situation in Iran. The failure of his foreign policy resulted in the Iranian government falling to the revolutionaries to begin with, and he did have plenty of warning and failed to take any action to prevent the taking of the hostages.

I don't believe the National Committee of the Republican Party sent the questionnaire out with the idea that you were going to have to pay to express your opinion. This idea of a questionnaire has been rather successful, not only in raising funds for the party but in bringing to focus what the positions of the party should be on a number of issues. I believe that a political party is nothing more than a group of people who are brought together by their sharing of a common viewpoint on major issues. It doesn't mean that we all agree on everything, but we have a common approach to government. In this case, the Republican Party's approach is, and I believe should be, a reduction of the power and the size and the cost of government and the return of more local authority and autonomy and more individual freedom to the people. Again, I thank you for letting me respond.

Sincerely,
Ronald Reagan

———————

A woman from New York City, clearly distraught, writes to Reagan with a list of complaints. She believes that "supply-side economics" may kill the "poor and elderly," and that perhaps "that is its purpose." She suggests that Reagan spend less time on his "personal needs, such as long vacations, shorter hours, fashion, parties and being the head of a royal family."

Dorothy Walton
New York, New York
November 4, 1981 [8]

Dear Miss Walton:

I'm glad you provided me with a return address so I can respond to your letter of September 2nd. Incidentally, forgive me for being so late in answering. With the hundreds of thousands of letters that come in each month it takes a while for one to reach my desk.

You expressed worry about "supply side" economics. I don't know who gave it that title but we're really talking about common sense. Runaway inflation, high interest rates and unemployment didn't start with this administration. They are the result of almost 40 years of deficit spending and excessive taxation. Our national debt has now reached a trillion dollars.

I know we can't cure all that at once but we have to start and that means reducing taxes that are stifling the economy and cutting back on government spending. Our program just went into effect October 1st so it can hardly be blamed for our troubles. The truth is inflation is falling and so are interest rates. I believe our program will work.

Now with regard to my working habits, I can understand why you would have some wrong ideas in view of some of the ridiculous falsehoods that pop up in the news.

This president doesn't have a nine-to-five or nine-to-three schedule, nor does he have a five-day week. I take the elevator up to the living quarters in the White House with reports, briefings, and memorandums for which there is no reading time during the day. I spend my time until "lights out" trying to absorb all of that. The same is true of the weekends—when I'm not attending a summit conference or making a speech somewhere.

The air controllers were warned well in advance that the law specifically prohibits federal employees from striking. In addition, they had each signed a written oath that they would not strike. May I remind you FDR (whom I supported) declared that public employees could not be allowed to strike.

Now it is true I went to California for roughly three weeks, but the Congress had gone home as they always do at that time of year. I was still president, however, and there was never a day that I did not have meetings with cabinet members and staff and, of course, the reading went on as usual.

You referred to the incident of the planes and my not being awakened. That isn't exactly correct. I was awakened at 4:30 A.M. when full information had finally been received. I wasn't awakened earlier because early bulletins were too sketchy and provided no information that might require a decision by me. But being called at 4:30 A.M. is hardly a case of letting me sleep the night through for fear of disturbing me.

I assure you I am not the head of a "royal family" and our program and my effort is aimed at helping the poor because they are hit hardest by inflation.

Thanks again for letting me respond.

Sincerely,
Ronald Reagan

Reagan replies to a federal employee with 30 years' experience, who bitterly complains about being "reviled, humiliated, and ridiculed in public" by Reagan and others in his administration.

Mr. J. P. Fox
Woodbridge, Virginia
November 4, 1981[9]

Dear Mr. Fox:

Thank you for writing as you did and for giving me a chance to respond.

How do I say and make you understand that my criticism of, quote, bureaucrats, unquote, is not aimed at you or the thousands of employees like you?

I have stated many times that the majority of government workers are conscientious, proud of what they are doing and are indeed good public servants. Unfortunately, such lines are seldom if ever quoted so you have no way of knowing they were spoken.

I'm sure you will agree from your years of service there are those—most often in positions of some authority whose top priority is maintaining the status quo. It is these I refer to in the tone that has caused your resentment. I can cite cases of deliberate sabotage of policy changes, new furniture at year's end to use up the budget, etc.

All of this I experienced as governor and still see it as president. But, in both jobs I was always aware of the other—the hardworking, efficient and, yes, patriotic employees.

I apologize for not saying this more often in an effort to get it quoted, and thank you again.

Sincerely,
Ronald Reagan

In the late winter of 1982 the U.S. economy was in the middle of an economic recession that had begun seven months before President Reagan took office, and did not end until November 1982. In March 1982, to most citizens the economy looked bleak. Reagan's proposal for an across-the-board tax cut of 30 percent had passed as only a 5 percent reduction for the first year. But more tax reductions—10 percent a year for the next two years—were on the way, as well as a sharp reduction in the top rate. Here Reagan tries to explain his economic and other policies, even though there is not yet evidence they are working.

Mr. Lee F. Jones
Cadillac, Michigan
March 22, 1982 [10]

Dear Mr. Jones:

I couldn't help but answer your letter even though from its tone I know no statement of facts as they really are can alter your evident bias. Your complaints as listed in your first paragraph, (except for the income tax cut) can hardly be laid at the door of this administration. Indeed the price of gas has come down since we've been here and the postal service is an autonomous corporation created by Congress a few years ago.

Yes, your income tax cut (5 percent as of October 1) was minuscule, particularly since your Social Security tax increased in January due to a measure passed by the previous administration. May I point out your tax cut would have been 10 percent, retroactive to January 1, 1981 but the Democratic majority in Congress refused to pass that. However our program does call for a 10 percent cut in July and another 10 percent in 1983.

By the way, we have reduced inflation to the point that last year the purchasing power at the poverty level was increased $255 and at a $20,000 income that would be about $750. Inflation which was 12.4 percent is now running at 4.5 percent.

As for educational cutbacks they can't amount to much since all federal aid to education totals less than 10 percent of total education cost and we haven't reduced that sizably. As for your son's college prospects it is true we are trying to set a family income level above which college loans are denied. We found many well-to-do people taking such low interest loans and reinvesting those loans in U.S. treasury bills for which the taxpayers were paying an interest rate double and even triple the interest on the college loan.

You spoke of your service in Vietnam and three purple hearts. Believe me that is service above and beyond the call. In my view the tragedy and yes immorality of that conflict was asking young men to do what you did and others to die for a cause our government had no intention of winning. I have pledged to do everything I can to see that never happens to any other generation of young Americans.

Obviously you don't see the need for our defense buildup but I found (when I took office) half our planes grounded for lack of spare parts, ships that couldn't leave port, and only a three weeks' supply of ammunition. I believe the road to peace requires a buildup to deter the Soviet Union and then realistic negotiating with them to bring about a legitimate reduction of arms by both countries.

One last line—you cite the partisan attacks alleging that I'm dedicated to helping the rich. Can you find one fact to support that? Oh yes! The 70 percent income tax rate on unearned or investment income was reduced to 50 percent. That was not proposed by us in our tax bill. It was added by a Democratic member of the Democratic-controlled House Ways and Means Committee, and again was part of the price we had to pay to get our economic program adopted.

I'm enclosing your letter to me because just possibly you'd rather not have it in the files which are now public property.

Sincerely,
Ronald Reagan

A conservative, who had donated more than $1,000 to the Republican Party, urges Reagan to back off his tax cut and slash up to $20 billion from defense spending in order to reduce the deficit and prevent the Democrats from winning in the fall elections. He is particularly concerned about the election prospects of Congressman John Hiler (R-Indiana) and Senator Richard Lugar (R-Indiana).

Mr. William B. Riblet
Elkhart, Indiana
April 5, 1982[11]

Dear Mr. Riblet:
I'm sorry to be so late in answering your letter of February 12. It has only just reached my desk.

I can understand your concern about the deficit and the coming elections. Let me assure you the situation with regard to the budget is not as it appears by way of the media. There is a little matter of getting the cooperation of the Democratic majority in the House. There is more going on than is visible on the surface. You'll be pleased to know we have a task force of top-level businessmen who are going to look at the Defense Department, and others as well, to see where modern business practices can bring about savings.

Our goal must be to send a message that will give confidence to the money markets to bring interest rates down. Actually, it is a lack of confidence in government that is keeping them high. We have inflation now for five months at less than a 4½ percent rate—they just aren't ready to believe it will stay down. It is all important now that we show government spending will be further reduced.

I share your high regard of Congressman Hiler and for Senator Lugar. Thank you for your help and support.

Sincerely,
Ronald Reagan

Richard Viguerie, a well-known conservative activist who specialized in raising money through direct mail, was never friendly to Reagan. His "open letter" to President Reagan in the July 1982 issue of the Conservative Digest *accused him of "détente with liberals," arguing that "most of your major appointments are not conservatives," recommending a number of policy initiatives including investigating the "widespread use of illegal drugs in the media," and urged him to ask "the American people . . . to make sacrifices." Reagan fired back with both guns. But the letter was never typed or sent; after it was written Reagan slashed the draft with a large "X" and wavy lines. He never responded to Viguerie.*

Mr. Richard A. Viguerie
Falls Church, Virginia
August 17, 1982 [12]

Dear Richard:

I had already seen the magazine and given my opinion of it to John Lofton.

It is difficult for me to believe you wrote in friendship as you say you did because the charges of betrayal are without foundation. In your "open letter" you ignore the fact that I am promoting school prayer, a balanced budget amendment, anti-abortion, and tuition tax credits as I said I would. We have and are moving ahead on crime, illegal drug use and quality education. Indeed we have succeeded in virtually closing down the flow of drugs into the country by way of Florida. We did it with an unprecedented use of federal forces including the military in cooperation with local and state forces.

Our record of appointing women, blacks and Hispanics to meaningful government positions is possibly better than any previous administration at this point.

I'm not going to go through your letter point by point but I have to ask myself why you've made no effort to ask for my reasoning behind some of the decisions you take issue with. And I must be honest and tell you I don't believe I am guilty of dividing and, yes, destroying the conservative movement at the very moment it has the greatest opportunity to reshape government philosophy it has ever had. But someone is.

If there is a setback in conservative fortunes it will be the *Conservative Digest* not my administration that brings it about.

Ronald Reagan

———

Reagan replies to a woman whose husband has been forced by the poor economy to work in Florida, leaving her alone in Ohio. While having voted for Reagan she accuses him of being "very wealthy" and not thinking "of people like me—not rich, not poor— worth nothing except to each other."

Mrs. Gail E. Foyt
Dayton, Ohio
August 20, 1982 [13]

Dear Mrs. Foyt:

I'm sorry to be so late in answering your letter of July 7 but it has only just reached my desk.

I wish I could tell you there is some instant answer to the economic problems besetting us but I can't. However it is my strong belief that we are on the right track and the economy is turning up.

I hope and pray by the time you receive this your own situation is improved and that you are or soon will be united with your husband.

Mrs. Foyt your sentence with regard to my not being able to understand the real world touched a tender nerve. I grew up in poverty, although in a small midwestern town you didn't think of yourself as poor. Maybe because the government didn't come around and tell you, you were poor. But I do understand very well what you were saying. I've been making speeches for about 30 years on the fact that the forgotten men and women in America were those people who went to work, paid their bills, sent their kids to school and made this country run.

You said you'd pray for me and I'm grateful. I have a great faith in prayer and I intend to pray for you.

Sincerely,
Ronald Reagan

A Republican insurance agent from South Dakota accuses Reagan of "thinking like a Democrat," wasting billions on foreign aid and raising the gas tax. The Surface Transportation Act of 1982 raised the tax on gasoline from four cents a gallon to nine cents, a 125 percent increase in the federal tax. One cent of the increase went to mass transit and four cents to highways. Foreign aid was just over $9 billion a year at the time.

Mr. Lyle V. Frey
Mitchell, South Dakota
December 27, 1982 [14]

Dear Mr. Frey:

May I take issue with you on your suggestion that I'm beginning to think like a Democrat? I guess I've probably—in years passed—made more speeches than anyone about extravagances in foreign aid. But that was when we were buying Haile Selassie* a million-dollar yacht, sawmills for a country that had no trees and paving a highway in a land where there were no automobiles.

Let me assure you foreign aid as we are handling it today is very much in line with our national security needs. In some instances it substitutes for a military presence we would have to otherwise maintain.

As for the highway tax—we had put that off for more than a year now but finally could not wait any longer. We have an emergency situation with regard to our national highway system and a great many bridges, any one of which has the potential for a tragic disaster. We feel that a gas tax as a user fee to fund necessary repairs was a fair way to solve the problem. I assure you I will never approve such a tax as just a part of general revenue raising.

Thanks for writing and giving me a chance to respond.

Sincerely,
Ronald Reagan

Reagan responds to a telegram from a man who "canvassed, campaigned, voted and donated money" to Reagan, and now, despite acknowledging that Reagan is "making headway" on the economy, wants him to cut defense spending and balance the federal budget if he hopes "to be reelected."† The budget deficit was $74 billion in 1980, had risen to over $125 billion in 1982, and was expected to climb to over $200 billion in 1983.

---

* Emperor of Ethiopia (1930–74)
† Mr. Norton's telegram was sent on January 25, 1983. While the economic recession officially ended in November 1982, the announcement by the National Bureau of Economic Research (NBER) that it was "officially" over was not made until July 8, 1983. While signs of economic recovery were evident in early 1983 the recession did not "end" until the NBER said it did.

Mr. Mike Norton
New Orleans, Louisiana
February 8, 1983 [15]

Dear Mr. Norton:

Thanks for your wire. I can understand your concern about both the deficit and the defense budget. There has been a drumbeat of propaganda against defense spending aided and abetted by much of the media.

I do not believe I'd be meeting my responsibility as president if I gave in to that. We have reduced the defense spending we first proposed in 1981 by $58 billion and have now agreed to $55 billion more over the next five years. Much of this was made possible by the reduction of inflation and management improvements. Defense is now only 29 percent of the total budget. Under Presidents Eisenhower and JFK it was nearly 50 percent.

We can't achieve arms reductions agreements with the Soviets unless we maintain a level of strength that gives them an incentive to negotiate.

Sincerely,
Ronald Reagan

A political supporter, whose children waved American flags at Reagan's limousine when he left for Washington, complains about the increase in payroll taxes. The payroll tax rate (combined Old Age and Survivors Insurance and Disability Insurance) for both employee and employer grew from 10.1 percent in 1978 to 10.7 percent in 1981 to 10.8 percent in 1983. However, the base salary that was taxed more than doubled from $17,700 in 1978 to $35,700 in 1983. This sharply increased the progressivity of the tax for higher income workers.

Mr. Phillip N. Robinson
Pacific Palisades, California
February 8, 1983 [16]

Dear Mr. Robinson:

I appreciate your letter and am grateful for having had your support. I believe however there may be some misunderstanding about the Social Security taxes.

In legislation adopted during the previous administration (1977) a package of Social Security payroll tax increases was adopted. It amounts to the biggest tax increase in our history and calls for further increases from 1985 to 1990. At the time the president said we had solved the fiscal problem of Social Security to at least 2015. If you'll recall in late 1981 I called attention to the fact that Social Security would be broke by July 1983 unless some action was taken. No action was taken, the temptation to use Social Security as a political football in the '82 election was too tempting.

I called for a bipartisan task force to present a plan aimed at restoring the fiscal integrity of Social Security. I believe the tax increase you referred to in your letter is the schedule of tax increases between '85 and 1990 which were passed in 1977. It is true that we acceded to moving them up to 1984. In return for that one year acceleration however an income tax credit will be given for that first year.

No one is truly happy with the compromise solution but compromise was the only alternative with the "House" in Democratic hands. There are two other tax changes in the package but I must confess I don't feel as bad about those. Present Social Security recipients are receiving much more than they ever paid in. We are asking that single individuals who have $20,000 income <u>not</u> including Social Security benefits and couples with $25,000 be required to pay income tax on their Social Security benefits. I see this as a step at least toward correcting a mistake in the program—there should have been a means test from the beginning. I find that I am eligible for Social Security. I am refusing to take it.

The other tax change has to do with the self-employed. They presently pay 75 percent of the total payroll tax of employee and employer. They will be asked to pay 100 percent but will get an income tax deduction for the employer half just as employers do now.

I hope you can understand the necessity of compromise in this highly politicized issue. I assure you my basic goals have not changed. Right now I'm faced with a Democratic effort to cancel the 10 percent income tax cut scheduled for July 1st and the indexing of that tax beginning in 1985. I shall fight to the end to prevent that happening and can use all the support I can get.

Best regards,
Ronald Reagan

———

Married at the time of this letter to actor Cliff Robertson, Dina Merrill was a well-known actress who knew the Reagans. Daughter of E. F. Hutton, the stockbroker, and Marjorie Merriweather Post, a member of high society, Dina wrote to Reagan about her concern about the administration's policies regarding the treatment of women and blacks.

Mrs. Cliff Robertson
New York, NY
February 10, 1983 [17]

Dear Dina:

Your interview in *Womens Wear Daily* (February 3) was brought to my attention. This was the first I'd known that you had written me because I never received the letter. Evidently we have to blame the postal service for this one. I had a complete check made of our mail department and there is no record of your letter ever having arrived. This isn't the first time this has happened I'm sorry to say. Maybe it's sabotage, I should have a code name.

If you were quoted accurately in *WWD* you are concerned about our policies regarding treatment of women and blacks. Dina, nothing has frustrated me more than the unfounded propaganda on this subject. Our record with regard to blacks is probably better than any previous administration in responding to civil rights complaints, directing government contracts to minority owned businesses, appointment to executive positions in government etc.

On the matter of equality for women, we have a task force that has been combing regulations and laws for any trace of sex discrimination. We've made considerable progress with those things we can change administratively and are proposing and have proposed bills where legislation is required. We have secured the cooperation of all 50 states in doing the same thing at their level. And of course I'm sure you know our record with regard to high level appointments in government.

Well enough of that. I really set out to explain I hadn't received your letter. Nancy sends her best and we both hope our paths will cross again before too long.

Sincerely,
Ron

---

*A minister in the Church of Jesus, who served in Air Force intelligence for a number of years, sent a telegram imploring Reagan to stop denigrating those who wanted an agreement between the United States and the Soviet Union to freeze the production and deployment of nuclear weapons. The nuclear freeze movement was launched in 1980 in Brookline, Massachusetts, by Randall Forsberg when she wrote a four-page manifesto entitled, "Call to Halt the Nuclear Arms Race." Over the next two years support grew in the United States, culminating in a large demonstration of nearly half a million people in New York City on June 12, 1982. Walter Mondale and many other Democrats supported the idea of a nuclear freeze in the 1984 election.** *

Reverend Robert E. Kent
Independence, Missouri
April 18, 1983 [18]

Dear Reverend Kent:

Thank you for writing and for giving me a chance to respond. First let me say there apparently isn't as much difference between us as you seem to think. I am totally dedicated to negotiations leading to legitimate and verifiable reduction of nuclear weapons by all nations and the two superpowers in particular. I hope and pray that once such reductions begin we could one day see an end to all such weapons.

Some things however have changed since you left the service. We do not have parity—quite the contrary. And we no longer excel in accuracy. The bulk of our weapons are more than 15 years old. The bulk of theirs are less than five years old. They outweigh us in megatonnage four to one.

---

* Adams, David, *The American Peace Movements* (New Haven, CT: Advocate Press, 1985), Chapter 6.

I have stated many times the overwhelming majority of people in the nuclear freeze movement are sincerely motivated and want peace. I join them in that. All I ask is that we negotiate a reduction first to where we do have parity—then we freeze. To freeze now adds to the risk of war because we <u>are</u> inferior to them in such weaponry. It is our willingness to modernize our forces that has brought them to the negotiating table.

I'm sure you realize that in my present position I have access to all the information available on this subject, in fact more than is available to almost anyone else. I make my judgements based on those facts. Again I assure you I want peace. There have been 4 wars in my lifetime. I want also the total elimination of all nuclear weapons.

Sincerely,
Ronald Reagan

Reagan writes back to a 38-year-old man, the president of a small welding shop in Pennsylvania with six employees, who has given up hope and believes "America is dying." Two weeks after Reagan replied, on July 8, 1983, the National Bureau of Economic Research announced that the recession had actually ended in November 1982.*

Mr. R. Richard Anderson
Oreland, Pennsylvania
June 24, 1983 [19]

Dear Mr. Anderson:

Forgive me for being so late in answering your letter of April 7. Sometimes it takes quite a while before letters reach my desk. I hope you are still hanging in there because I have to disagree that our land is dying.

You are 38 years old. Just by coincidence when I was 38 years old at exactly this time of year I was lying in traction in a hospital with my thigh broken in six places. I had been scheduled to start a picture three days after I went in the hospital and being a freelance actor I was moaning about the loss of revenue because they put another actor in my part and went ahead without me. But my mother had always told me "everything happens for the best." The picture I didn't make was a colossal failure and my being in it wouldn't have changed that.

Mr. Anderson I know you are in a particularly hard hit area and it must be hard not to get discouraged when as on your bicycle ride you see so many signs of the recession. But by hanging on you've spared a half dozen families from disaster. I've been all over this country and you'd be surprised how many people are doing the same thing.

Now the signs of recovery are picking up, more so than in any other land. I

---

* Statistical Abstract of the United States, "Business Cycles Expansions and Contractions," 1995, page 561.

know if you read the *Inquirer* you don't see much to cheer you up but frankly I don't believe some of the press is in tune with what is going on.

You say more laws and regulations are making it harder on business. I have to disagree. Yes there are some guys in Congress who are trying to do that but there are a lot of us getting in their way. In these one and a half years we have reduced regulations to the point that American business has been saved 300 million man hours of government-required paperwork and we're not though yet. July 1st you get another 10 percent cut in the income tax. Yes Congress or some in Congress want to cancel that. Well if they try I'll veto it and I know my veto will be upheld. We're going to have that tax cut.

I wish I could tell you all that is happening in the country with people banding together to do things we'd begun to think only government can do. All over there is the neighborly spirit we once knew years ago. I even had a class of fifth graders send me a letter with $187.00 they'd raised on their own to help reduce the national debt. More than 100 Marines stationed overseas wrote to tell me they'd go without a cost of living raise if it would help the country.

I pray things are better for you and I hope you will hang in there. As the song says "There's a great day coming."

Best regards,
Ronald Reagan

The owner of a small meat market in New Jersey threatens that unless the economy recovers soon he and the other four voting members of his family will vote for a president who can help them.

Mr. Thomas S. Fogliani
Tenafly, New Jersey
June 28, 1983 [20]

Dear Mr. Fogliani:

I understand how you feel and believe me I feel as you do about taxes but can I put in a word for myself?

I'm sure you know that Social Security after years of abuse was faced with going broke by July of this year if something wasn't done. We were finally able to get the Democratic leadership in the Congress to join in a bipartisan effort to straighten things out. The result was a compromise. On our side we wanted to find some way of restructuring the program to protect all those now on Social Security but without raising taxes. The other side led by the Democratic leadership in the Congress wanted to solve virtually the entire problem with additional taxes.

Naturally we had to come down somewhere in the middle. The case made for making the self-employed pay both employer and employee tax was that otherwise they would receive full benefits for only half payment. We did however insist that the employer share be made an income tax deduction as it is now for regular employers. We managed to win that point. I'm sorry we couldn't do better. Give my regards to Sylvia, Thomas, Robert and Ronald. I hope I still have you all in my corner.

Sincerely,
Ronald Reagan

———————

Reagan responds to a critic, a probation officer who called him "ill advised, misinformed, and generally living in a dream world" and likened him to Hitler. The writer complained of Reagan's attitude toward "trouble makers" in school, and for talking about "getting the disruptors" out of the classroom. He argued that they are "children . . . who because of environmental conditions, and immaturity, made very poor decisions for themselves."

Mr. Byron W. York
Murphysboro, Illinois
September 6, 1983 [21]

Dear Mr. York:

You say you considered writing to me for two years before you finally did, thinking it would be a "worthless exercise." Well I've considered responding for almost three months* for the same reason. I doubt that any words of mine can change a mind so opinionated as yours.

You have never met me. You are in a position to have some knowledge of the media image building that takes place in the world of politics and yet you are confident that you can understand my thinking, or as you put it the thinking of those who tell me what to think. And all of this because I suggested that teachers in a classroom are possibly not the best way to cope with physical assault, mayhem and rape in the classroom.

Mr. York I have the highest regard for the intelligence of the American people and have been most outspoken in my criticism of those in the entertainment field and politics who look down and talk down to them. A president is not as lonely and isolated as you are so sure he is, nor is he surrounded by inferiors as you suggest. He is indeed usually surrounded by dedicated and unselfish people who have made considerable personal sacrifice in order to be of service to their countrymen.

You say you did many of the things I did when you were young and became self-supporting at a relatively young age. Yes I did all that—21 years before you did it and while a great, historic depression gripped the world. According to you we differ in that I didn't benefit from my experience as you did and don't remember as much as I should or I remember it incorrectly.

I assure you I have lived in and not above the world for 72 years as you say you

———————

* It was actually two months.

have for 51. I hope that in your present work you have more tolerance than you've revealed in your letter.

Sincerely,
Ronald Reagan

———

David "Mick" Staton, a Republican, was elected to Congress from West Virginia in the same year that Reagan was elected president. Eleven months after being defeated in his reelection bid in 1982 he wrote a letter to Reagan that began with the sentence: "Quit groveling, Mr. President."

Mr. Mick Staton
Charleston, West Virginia
September 30, 1983 [22]

Dear Mick:

Forgive my tardy answer to your letter of August 25. It sometimes takes a while before letters get to my desk.

I'm sure you can understand if I take exception to your charge that I have been "groveling." On the other hand I can understand why you would have such a misperception in view of the general tone of the press in reporting on anything to do with me or my administration; such reporting invariably based on those unnamed sources they claim to be quoting.

Let me deal first with the matter of the International Business Women's Convention* here in Washington. About twelve hundred women, most of them from other countries arrived at the White House for a tour that had been arranged and confirmed. Then some bureaucratic bungle saw them turned back at the gate. When I learned about this I called the president of the American group (who had arranged the visit) to see if there was any way we could reschedule the tour. Unfortunately that was impossible.

Mrs. Madenwald was so depressed and embarrassed about having to apologize at the next morning's meeting that I asked if I could apologize instead. I don't think, under the circumstances that could be called groveling. She was almost tearful in expressing her gratitude. So next morning I was there and couldn't have asked for a warmer welcome. I received a standing ovation when I finished. Mrs. Madenwald was most gracious which makes it hard for me to understand how within an hour of our parting she could have released to the press such a vitriolic attack. I received a wire of apology from the international president of the group and as I say the members made me most welcome.

———

* The International Business Women's Group was formed in the early 1980s by a small group of business women who wanted a regular forum to exchange ideas, and to support business women in difficult cultural environments in countries around the world.

As for Ansel Adams*—yes I was disappointed that he would go to the press. I've long admired his art and when I was told he disapproved of me I invited him and his wife over for a visit. In the visit I learned what you apparently know that philosophically he and I are on different wave lengths.

As for Barbara Honegger,† she didn't even know what was in the report she signed. It carried word of about 25 laws we've already changed. While I don't support ERA or abortion on demand I also don't support inequality based on gender. As governor I had state laws that discriminated changed and set out to do the same with federal laws over two years ago.

You say you want a president who is dedicated to serving all the people. Well, doesn't that include addressing an organization which invited me to speak and which also invited the vice president? Now we weren't well received but you'd be surprised at how many sought us out later to apologize for the organization and to express their appreciation for coming. Would we be doing the job if we only spoke to those who agreed in advance with what we were going to say? That's like preaching to the choir.

Mick I'm still promoting the things I believe in and campaigned on and will try to convince the unbelievers. Remember I was once a member of the other party and became a convert. I think others can be converted too.

Sincerely,
Ronald Reagan

———

Mel Thomson, the governor of New Hampshire (1972–1978), was a powerful political force in the state. In late 1983 he wrote a condescending letter reminding Reagan that he has forgiven his "political derelictions and shortcomings over and over again," and that Reagan's list of "failed opportunities is long and tragic." Thomson's letter ends by threatening to oppose Reagan in New Hampshire if he runs for reelection. Reagan is not amused and replies with a long seven-point letter refuting the charges.

———

* Ansel Adams was one of the country's greatest photographers and an ardent environmentalist. He met with Reagan for 50 minutes in July 1983. Reagan had liked his photography, but Adams thought Reagan had little interest in protecting the environment. Adams later wrote to David Kennerly, a former White House photographer, that the meeting was "very discouraging," that talking to Reagan was "like confronting a stone wall." He added that when he left he had "a sinking feeling that this country is in very poor hands." The next morning he went public with his criticism of Reagan, which was broadcast around the world. Ansel Adams died nine months later, on April 22, 1984.

† Barbara Honegger was secretary to Martin Anderson in the White House in 1981–82. After Anderson left in April 1982 she became involved in women's rights issues, and was critical of Reagan. Later she moved on to conspiracy theory and wrote a book (*October Surprise*, Tudor Publishing Company, New York, 1989) charging that the Reagan-Bush campaign in 1980 had struck a deal with Iran to hold the American hostages captive until Reagan was elected.

Governor Meldrim Thomson Jr.
Orford, New Hampshire
October 3, 1983[23]

Dear Mel:

You asked me to accept your letter in the spirit in which it was written. We've known each other too long for me to do anything but that. I was pleased to see you the other day and wish our meeting could have been long enough to take up and discuss all the issues raised in your letter. Since that wasn't possible I'll try to take them in the order you listed them.

First the matter of so-called trilateralists; Mac Baldrige is as solid a conservative as anyone could find as is George Shultz.* Both were top recommendations of the talent hunters I'd put together during the transition and that team had virtually every top backer of conservative causes in the history of the conservative movement—Holmes Tuttle, Jack Hume, Joe Coors† etc. Henry Kissinger has no permanent place in the administration. He is chairing a bipartisan study group which meets a congressional demand as a price for getting the support we must have for our effort in Central America.

Second: The departments of energy and education. Mel we have been absolutely unable to get congressional support for their elimination and that includes even our staunchest allies on the hill. We intend to keep it on the agenda but in the meantime we have made substantial improvements. Let me just touch on energy. Total energy efficiency has increased every year we've been here. Domestic oil production is a million barrels a day over the Carter administration's estimates. In '77 we imported half our oil. It's now down to a quarter. We produce nearly 90 percent as much energy as we consume. Our strategic petroleum reserve has been tripled and we have minimized federal control and involvement.

Third; We talked about China so I won't dwell on that except to say we have definite restrictions on the level of technology we make available. And as I said, we have not retreated one inch in our relationship with Taiwan.

Fourth; On the Panama Canal I'm not aware of any legal ground on which we could base a claim to take it back. We have done much to improve the relationship there and eliminate the hostility that prevailed at the time of the negotiations.

Fifth; The balanced budget. Mel deficits aren't made in the White House. They are made in the chambers of Congress. Have you thought of how big the deficit would be without our economic plan? I can tell you how much smaller it would be if Congress had given us all the spending reductions I tried for. This year's deficit alone would be $40 billion less. Each year I come back asking more reductions in what they want to spend. What is needed more than anything else is what many of

---

* Malcolm Baldrige was secretary of commerce; George Shultz was secretary of state.

† Homes Tuttle, Jacquelin Hume, and Joseph Coors were old friends from California, part of the "kitchen cabinet" that had supported Reagan since he first ran for the governorship in 1966.

us had as governors—line-item veto. I intend to keep working at getting that but in the meantime my '84 budget proposal would have put us on a solid road of declining deficits leading to a balance a few years down the road. I'm still battling for it and am closer than I was a few months ago.

Sixth; I have reduced the taxes on the so-called poor as well as improved their lot by changing inflation from more than 12 percent to less than 3 percent.* As for IMF, † Mel you used the right word in our talk—"perception." The perception that IMF is a giveaway or a bank bailout is totally false. The $8.4 billion contribution (so called) is not a budget item nor does it add to the deficit. It's like a deposit in a bank and we have full drawing rights on it. In fact the two largest users of IMF funds have been England and the United States. When money is loaned to other nations we get our share back plus interest. At the same time it is the only institution which can impose economic reforms on extravagant countries as a condition for borrowing.

Seventh; Mel as I told you, about the Korean plane massacre, ‡ there were grandstand plays we might have made such as Carter's grain embargo but they wouldn't really punish the Soviets. And how would pushing Poland into bankruptcy, as some have suggested, hurt the Russians? It would actually hurt the Polish people and they are as innocent as the victims in the plane. Believe me we reviewed every option and are still doing so.

The other points you closed your letter with, (immigration for one)—Mel we have lost control of our borders. I don't know whether the legislation § will pass or not but I believe I should sign it if it does. It is a very complex issue with our agriculture dependent on migrants, several million people as residents undetected and a dozen other facets.

As for the Monroe doctrine—don't think that wasn't on my mind. But I've learned even our best friends in Central and South America would turn on us. It has much of the gunboat diplomacy aura around it. We're making progress in the Hemisphere but it has to be on a partnership basis not the "big colossus" of the North giving orders.

---

* In 1983 some changes in the way the costs of home ownership are measured reduced the inflation rate slightly from 4 percent to 3 percent.

† International Monetary Fund.

‡ When a Korean 747 airliner, Flight 007, carrying 269 people, wandered off course over the Soviet Union and was shot down on September 1, 1983, with no survivors, the Soviets at first denied any knowledge of it. But the United States had secret intelligence intercepts that proved the Soviets did it deliberately, and the passengers included a U.S. congressman. At first the CIA refused to reveal what it knew for fear of compromising our intelligence operations, but Secretary of State George Shultz insisted. Faced with proof they had done it, the Soviets still maintained that they thought the huge Boeing 747 was an American "spy plane."

§ A controversial immigration reform bill, sponsored by Senator Alan Simpson (R-Wyoming) and Congressman Romano "Ron" Mazzoli (D-Kentucky), passed the Senate but was defeated in the House. It would have established "employer sanctions," making employers responsible for not hiring aliens.

On the national holiday you mentioned, I have the reservations you have but here the perception of too many people is based on an image not reality. Indeed to them the perception is reality. We hope some modifications might still take place in Congress.*

Finally; as for Lebanon, that situation is only one facet of the whole Middle East problem. Mel is there any way the United States or the Western world for that matter can stand by and see the Middle East become a part of the Communist bloc? Without it our West European neighbors would inevitably become Finlandized and we'd be alone in the world. As it is we're not alone in Lebanon. We are part of a multinational force because those nations recognize their stake in the Middle East.

In the world today our security can be threatened in a number of places far distant from our own shorelines. I'm not trigger happy and I don't want a war. Whatever I do it is based on my belief that certain actions offer a chance to forestall war. And those beliefs are based on full access to all the intelligence information available.

Well—there, and I hope you'll take this in the spirit in which it is written. Nancy sends her best and from both of us to that lovely lady of yours.

Sincerely,
Ron

The letter that Reagan answers below was sent to his oldest child Maureen by the woman who had been her old Sunday School teacher and who was deeply concerned about the threat of nuclear war and American aid to Central America. Maureen asked her father to reply.

Mrs. Laurence M. Clark
Redland, California
December 14, 1983 24

Dear Mrs. Clark:

I hope you won't mind my answering your letter to Maureen. She allowed me to do this because she thought I could better respond to the concerns you expressed. She asked that I tell you she remembers you very well and sends you her very best regards.

Mrs. Clark I'm aware that a great deal of image making has gone on about me. That is to be expected with regard to anyone in this position but in my case much of it has been entirely contrary to what I believe and to what my goals and purposes really are.

Would it surprise you to know I share your horror of nuclear weapons and am

---

* Mel Thomson was opposed to creating a legal public holiday in honor of the Reverend Martin Luther King, but the bill to do so passed the House by a vote of 338–90 on August 2, 1983.

convinced there must never be a nuclear war? I know this brings up a question with regard to our program of modernization of our nuclear forces. Very simply the answer to that is, for some years back the only defense against these weapons has been a deterrent. An earlier Democratic administration named it the MAD policy—mutual assured destruction. We must admit it has prevented a major war in Europe for some 40 years now but it is a terrible threat hanging over the world.

In recent years the Soviet Union has engaged in the biggest military buildup in history both in conventional forces and in nuclear weapons. They now have superiority and are continuing to increase their margin. We still have a deterrent capacity but must replace our aging missiles with some comparable to theirs or face the reality of facing in the near future a surrender-or-die ultimatum.

Because of our change in policy the Soviet Union has grudgingly joined in disarmament talks with us to a greater extent than at any time since WWII. My hope indeed my dream is that if we can once start down the road of reducing on both sides the number of missiles they will be convinced of the wisdom of eliminating all such weapons. The United States has tried to interest the Soviets in arms control some 19 times since WWII without success. I believe we've caught their attention this time* because they are convinced we'll rearm to match them if they don't consider joining in a planned reduction.

As for Central America, 75 percent of all our aid has been in economic and social reforms. Only 25 cents out of each dollar has gone to military aid. The great economic inequalities in many of those countries have made them ripe for subversion. We want to help correct this but I assure you we are not planning any military actions there. A very definite planned assault by Cubans as proxies of the Soviet Union is aimed at the Western hemisphere. It must be stopped if we are to have peace.

Forgive me for going on at such length. I hope I have eased some of your concerns.

Sincerely,
Ronald Reagan

---

* When the Soviets shot down the Korean passenger plane with 269 people on board on September 1, 1983, it reaffirmed Reagan's conviction the Soviet Union was an evil empire. See Ronald Reagan, *An American Life* (New York: Simon & Schuster, 1990), p. 582. On October 10, 1983, Reagan watched a videotape of the movie *The Day After*, which portrays the city of Lawrence, Kansas, being wiped out in a nuclear war with the Soviet Union. A few days later he was briefed by the secretary of defense, Caspar Weinberger, on our plan in the event of a nuclear attack. Reagan then went on the offensive; he gave the go-ahead to speed up research on the Strategic Defense Initiative, his "Star Wars" plan, and prepared to put Pershing II nuclear missiles in Europe and aim them at the Soviets. On November 23, 1983, the first Pershing II missile was deployed in West Germany. The Soviets walked out of all negotiations dealing with nuclear missiles, saying they would never return while the Pershing II missiles were in place. Nonetheless, six weeks later, Ambassador Anatoly Dobrynin of the Soviet Union met with George Shultz and agreed to begin a serious and private dialogue on nuclear missiles.

*On October 23, 1983, a terrorist truck bomb killed 241 U.S. Marines and Navy per-
sonnel as they slept in their barracks in Beirut, Lebanon. Stationing the U.S. military
there was a controversial policy opposed by many of Reagan's advisers, including Secretary of Defense Caspar Weinberger, but Reagan and others were convinced it was
necessary in order to keep peace in Lebanon and the rest of the Middle East. After the
terrorist attack pressure mounted to remove our troops and, after a meeting of the
NSPG* on February 7, 1984, three and a half months later, President Reagan agreed
to redeploy the troops from Lebanon to ships stationed offshore. On December 9, 1983,
the family of a Marine who was scheduled to return to Lebanon in February 1984 had
written to Reagan and asked a simple question: "Why?"*

> John Staley and Family
> Charlotte, North Carolina
> February 16, 1984 [25]

Dear Mr. and Mrs. Staley, Wesley and Kevin:

I'm sorry to be so late in answering your letter of December 9 but sometimes it
takes a while for letters to reach my desk.

I will try to answer your one-word question—"Why." But first let me say I do
understand the "personal and private anxieties of a parent." You know of course
that I am a parent myself but more than that I have a personal feeling about those
splendid young men in uniform, among them your son and brother. There is nothing in my job so difficult as issuing the order that sends those young men into situations where they are endangered. There is nothing so heartbreaking as the calls
I've made to wives and parents who've lost husbands and sons.

As to your question, our national security is involved very directly in the Middle East. Indeed the security of the free world is at stake there.

In September of 1982 I proposed a plan for peace in the entire area carrying on
the process started at Camp David under the last administration. Before the negotiations could really get started the blowup came in Lebanon. In reality the Arab
world and Israel were all involved—the very nations we were trying to bring to the
peace table.

It was essential that Lebanon be helped to regain control of its own territory
and that the foreign forces fighting there be removed.

We and our allies, the British, French and Italians, sent in a force to help preserve stability while a government was reestablished and a Lebanese military was
organized.

For the better part of a year this multinational force contributed to very real
progress. I wish you could see letters of the kind I've received from Lebanese people

---

* National Security Planning Group, which usually included the national security adviser, the vice president, the secretary of state, the secretary of defense, the head of the CIA, and key White House staff.

blessing us for bringing order and normal living to their land. The PLO terrorists were removed. The Israelis began a withdrawal and meetings started to bring about internal peace in Lebanon.

Because progress was being made those who don't want a stable Lebanon began, last fall, the terrorist attacks on the multinational force and we know the tragedies that followed.

We immediately began studying how we could redeploy our forces and still help bring about peace.

As you know now we are placing our men on the vessels offshore and I have authorized firing back when we are fired upon. While there is still a chance for peace we must not give up. Our presence there is necessary if there is to be such a chance. However if your son and brother is in the replacement detachment I'm sure he will remain on board ship and not be stationed in Beirut as before.

I realize this is a sketchy reply to your question. I hope it gives you some understanding of the importance of our presence there.

Sincerely,
Ronald Reagan

————————

A former member of the U.S. Public Health Service, who was in El Salvador for two years in the late 1970s, is intensely critical of Reagan's Central American policy, charging him with "the worst form of political demagoguery," and saying his "policies bring dishonor to the American system." Reagan felt that the growing Communist presence in Central America posed a threat to the United States, and that "Communist penetration of the Americas"* had to be stopped.

Mr. Robert S. Lawrence
Weston, Massachusetts
May 31, 1984 [26]

Dear Mr. Lawrence:

Thank you for including your return address in your letter of May 10. I appreciate the opportunity to reply to your statements which while well intentioned do not present a factual account of either the situation today in El Salvador or Nicaragua.

It is true that El Salvador was supportive of repressive and violent forces even after the coup which overthrew a military dictatorship. But there were those in that coup who wanted true democracy. One such was for a time chosen to be president but was never allowed to serve. José Napoleon Duarte was imprisoned, tortured and exiled. He is now the president-elect of El Salvador.

There have been three elections in 26 months. Bipartisan teams of observers

————————

* Reagan, *An American Life,* p. 479.

from our country have been in El Salvador for each of those elections and they have been unanimous in their praise of the people who voted in spite of death threats by the guerrillas. Guerrillas I might add who are trained and supplied by Cuba, the Communist bloc countries and the Sandinista government of Nicaragua.*

Of course the duly elected government of El Salvador beset by powerful guerrilla forces has not entirely gotten a handle on the right-wing radicals assailing that government from within. But they have made tremendous strides and will make more under the newly elected president.

Mr. Lawrence our democracy is 200-plus years old but I remember a time in this century when citizens could be lynched without any arrests being made. Don't you think it's understandable that a new democracy can't do everything in less than a decade? They are trying.

As for Nicaragua the Sandinista government is pure totalitarian and has committed genocide against the Miskito Indians.† The Contras assailing that government is led in large part by people who were part of the revolution that overthrew Somoza. All they want is the democracy they fought to have. The Sandinista group denied them a place in government and to this day has never kept one of the promises made to the Organization of American States whom they asked for help during the revolution.

The archbishop of San Salvador has been quoted as calling for removal of our forces. He has denied this and states that he wants us to stay. The bishops of Nicaragua at risk of their lives have called on the Sandinista government to keep its promises and stop persucuting the Nicaraguan people.

Yes you are right that Central America needs economic help and social reforms. Our legislation before Congress asks for an $8 billion five year program to

---

* In the August 25, 1980, edition of the Mexican magazine *Proceso,* Cayetano Carpio, a principal leader of the Salvadoran guerrillas, said:

"The process of revolution in Central America is one. The triumphs of one and the triumphs of the other . . . Guatemala will have its hour. Honduras its own. Costa Rica will live in a brilliant moment. The first note was heard in Nicaragua . . .

"Nicaragua had become its base, all of Central America its target. El Salvador was first on the list. In 1980, at Cuban direction, several Salvadoran extremist groups were unified in Havana and established their operational headquarters in Managua. Cuba and its Soviet-bloc allies provided training and supplies, which began to flow clandestinely through Nicaragua to El Salvador to fuel the armed assault." See George Shultz, *Turmoil and Triumph* (New York: Charles Scribner's Sons, 1993), p. 286.

† For many years Nicaragua has had unresolved ethnic problems with the Miskito Indians, an indigenous tribe who live on the eastern, Caribbean side of the country. In a May 9, 1984 speech President Reagan described his understanding of what the Nicaraguan government was doing: ". . . there has been an attempt to wipe out an entire culture, the Miskito Indians, thousands of whom have been slaughtered or herded into detention camps, where they have been starved and abused. Their villages, churches and crops have been burned." See Lou Cannon, *President Reagan: The Role of A Lifetime* (New York: Touchstone, 1991), p. 366.

do just that. Only about 20 percent is to provide military support. You can't institute economic reforms while you are defending yourself against a powerful, well-armed hostile force.

We support the 21 points of the Contadora group.* We continue to appeal to the guerrillas in El Salvador and the Sandinistas to negotiate a peaceful settlement in both countries. So far the guerrillas have refused and so have the Sandinistas. The government of El Salvador and the Contras in Nicaragua have joined us in seeking a peaceful solution. We are not militarizing Central America.

And in addition to the doctors and teachers you identify as Cubans in Nicaragua there are also several thousand Cuban military there in addition to some PLO, Bulgarians and others. We have 55 military instructors in El Salvador.

Sincerely,
Ronald Reagan

On May 9, 1984, Reagan gave a nationally televised speech from the Oval Office explaining his Central American policy. Written the same day the speech was given, a letter to Reagan charges him with "misrepresentation" and "half truths," and ends by asserting that what was "heard tonight gives me little reason to hope that your administration will contribute significantly to the solution of those problems."

Mr. Harry A. Ide
Ithaca, New York
May 31, 1984[27]

Dear Mr. Ide:

There were no misrepresentations or half truths in my speech. I can, however understand why you might think so since your letter reveals your acceptance of the worldwide propaganda put forth by the Cuban and Soviet disinformation network.

The radical right-wing forces in El Salvador which admittedly would have a totalitarian government every bit as repressive as the one the guerrillas are fighting to have do operate without governmental sanction. Indeed the duly elected government (three elections in 26 months) has made tremendous strides in curbing their

---

* In the early 1980s Mexico, joined by Colombia, Venezuela, Panama, and five other Central American countries sought a regional solution to the problems of Central America. They called themselves the Contadora process, named for the island off the Pacific coast of Panama where the meeting first took place in early 1983. In September 1983 they issued a "Document of Objectives" which became known as the "twenty-one points." The points included "democratic representative and pluralistic systems that will guarantee . . . fair and regular elections . . . reduction of current stock of weapons . . . [and preventing] the use of their own territory by persons, organizations or groups seeking to destabilize the Government of Central American countries . . ." (see Shultz, *Turmoil and Triumph*, pp. 401–402).

activities. D'Aubuisson* had his chance in a free and open election and he was rejected by the voters—more than 80 percent of the electorate voted even though the guerrillas had told them, "vote today and die tonight." Were we a perfect democracy for all of our 200 years? What about lynchings with no arrests being made more than 100 years after we had adopted our constitution?

Why is it that every murder is purported to be the work of the so-called death squads? The guerrillas a couple of years ago boasted openly they had killed more than 10,000 of their countrymen.

In Nicaragua I'm sure some of the Contras are former members of the National Guard. They would be executed if they tried to live as citizens under the Sandinistas. Most of the leadership of the Contras is made up of men who were part of the revolution against Somoza. When victory came they were denied a place in government. The Sandinistas, who a few years ago joined the PLO in declaration of war against Israel, seized total control and with Cuban and Soviet help have established a totalitarian government on the Cuban and Soviet pattern. I think there are other reasons behind Mr. Pastora's† reluctance to align himself with the Contras.

Nicaragua now has a military greater than that of all Central American nations combined. The government has declared its revolution is not bound by any national boundaries.

We do support the Contadora process and its 21 points. There have been criticisms from time to time by some in that process but still we have a good relationship. We continue to seek a negotiated peace and the government of El Salvador and the Contras support us in this. Only the guerillas and the Sandinistas refuse. We were providing financial aid to the Sandinista government for some time after I took office as my predecessor had. Then it became clear the Sandinistas were supplying arms to help overthrow the government of El Salvador. In fact the guerrillas headquarters is in Nicaragua about 20 miles from the capital.

Incidentally the persecution of the Miskito Indians has not ceased. Thousands upon thousands are herded into concentration camps under deplorable conditions.

We have legislation before Congress for an $8 billion five-year program to help Central American countries establish viable economies and social reforms. Less

---

* Roberto D'Aubuisson became a leader of a military faction in El Salvador who feared a Marxist takeover of the country in the early 1980s. He was linked to death squads who targeted those suspected to be part of the Marxist insurrection, and was backed by wealthy landowners and businessmen. In 1982 he was elected president of a new Constitutional Assembly. He ran for president of El Salvador in 1984, but was defeated by José Napoleón Duarte. D'Aubuisson died on February 20, 1992. (*New York Times,* February 21, 1992.)

† Eden Pastora was a Sandinista hero of the revolution that overthrew the dictator, Anastasio Somoza, in July 1979, and was known as "Commandante Zero." Opposed to Soviet and Cuban advisers, he became a leader of the Contra "Freedom Fighters."

than a quarter of that amount is to provide help to their security forces so such a program can be implemented.

Thank you for giving me a chance to reply.

Sincerely,
Ronald Reagan

_____

In late April 1984 Reagan traveled to the People's Republic of China, where he signed numerous cooperation agreements on nuclear proliferation, economic matters, and cultural exchanges. He also gave a speech in the Great Hall in Bejing. Later it was revealed that certain parts of his speech dealing with democracy and free enterprise were censored in the Chinese media, as was a quotation from Abraham Lincoln: "No man is good enough to govern another man without the other's consent."*

A New Hampshire woman writes and savages Reagan for his speech, calling him "plain stupid," saying that "the U.S. and Reagan" represent "the greatest threat to the whole world today," not the Soviet Union. She ends by accusing Reagan of taking "daily zzzz's" (naps).

Miss Joan Roberts
Portsmouth, New Hampshire
May 31, 1984[28]

Dear Miss Roberts:

In reply to your letter of April 27th I can understand how you have a misperception about my speech in China, there was a certain amount of distortion in the press accounts. Actually there was no "incident" worthy of a press story. Relations with the Chinese leaders were and are on a sound friendship basis.

The theme of their remarks and mine was one of recognizing the differences between us but emphasizing how many things we had in common. In my speech I made no criticism of their system or philosophy but in the context of getting to know each other better I sketched the basics of our system so they could understand where we were coming from. At the same time I contrasted them and ourselves with the country which has 56 divisions poised on their border. (We only have 17 divisions in our entire Army.) I also mentioned that country's expansionist policies which have them promoting the conflict in Vietnam and Kampuchea † on China's southern border. All of these things had been discussed with my hosts and we were in agreement.

I believe some bureaucrat at a lower echelon took it upon himself to edit out those few lines possibly because of the impending visit of a Soviet diplomat. He incidentally canceled his visit, probably because of China's movement of troops to

_____

* Joseph Bosco, "Let the US speak to the Chinese," *Commentary,* August 14, 2001.
† Cambodia, located between Vietnam and China, was then under the control of the genocidal Khmer Rouge, a Communist group that slaughtered millions during its reign of terror.

the Vietnam border. By the way, my line about the "greatest threat to peace in the world today" was a repeat of what Premier Zhao had said to me.

Well you see your letter did get to me and I don't take daily zzzz's. That's another distortion by the press. I'm enclosing your letter just in case you'd prefer to have it in someone else's possession.

Sincerely,
Ronald Reagan

———

The following three letters from President Reagan to Norman Lear are part of an exchange that took place in the middle of 1984, just before the presidential election campaign began in earnest. A former radio and TV writer, Lear went on to become one of America's best-known TV producers. In 1981 he retired from television and founded "People for the American Way," a liberal lobby group.

On May 7, 1984, Lear wrote to President Reagan expressing his concern about the separation of church and state, and accusing him of becoming "Evangelist-in-Chief." Reagan responded on May 22, arguing that the First Amendment is only to ensure there is "no official state church," and not to "make freedom of religion into freedom from religion."

On June 15, Lear responded with a four-page essay, going into detail on a number of issues and telling Reagan he is sending a copy of his letter "to other citizens." Reagan replies again on June 25. Lear replies with a third letter on July 19, challenging Reagan's analysis, and ends by writing, "Perhaps we must simply agree to disagree."

Reagan drafts a third letter on July 27 asserting there should be "no law against prayer in school," and agrees with Lear that "we do have the right to disagree." He ends by asking, "Is it OK if I utter a prayer of thanks for that here in this public housing I live in?"

The third letter, however, is never sent, as Lear prepares to make public his private correspondence with Reagan. On September 6, the New York Times *published excerpts (about 30 percent) from the first five letters. The October issue of* Harper's *published almost complete versions of the five letters, save for couple of quotes from the Reverend Billy Graham and Paul Weyrich, a conservative activist.*

Reagan's third letter went into the White House files, and there was no more correspondence with Norman Lear.

Mr. Norman Lear
People for the American Way
Washington, D.C.
May 22, 1984 [29]

Dear Norman:

I appreciate your writing (May 7) and giving me a chance to set some things straight. First let me say that until I read your letter I was unaware of any "Christian Nation Movement," and I certainly do not support the notion that any group of citizens is to be accorded special standing "because they practice any religion."

I do believe the First Amendment is being somewhat distorted or misinterpreted by some who would, by government decree, make freedom _of_ religion into freedom _from_ religion. The First Amendment plainly is to ensure that in this nation there shall be no official state church. The amendment says the government shall not establish religion but it also just as plainly says the government shall not interfere in the practice of religion.

But isn't the government doing the latter when it decrees that a child cannot ask a blessing before lunch in the school cafeteria—particularly when we remember the child is compelled by law to attend school?

It is true I've addressed a number of religious groups—always by their invitation. Some have been Protestant, some Catholic, some Jewish and some have been conferences or conventions of representatives of all religions. Usually I've expressed my views on matters ranging from the right of a child to pray in school—if the child wants to do this—to tuition tax credits to correct the injustice of a parent supporting two school systems while only using one, and to my belief that abortion on demand is the taking of a human life unless and until someone can prove the unborn child is not a living being.

Norman, maybe we're coming to the same concern from opposite viewpoints, namely the threat to individual freedom. I believe that Madalyn Murray O'Hair, who brought about the anti-school prayer decision, was imposing her atheism on those of us who believe in God. The goal of our nation must always be the ultimate in individual freedom consistent with an orderly society.

Now, having said this, let me also say that I approve of the references to God in the Declaration of Independence, the inscription "In God We Trust" on our coins and engraved on the wall in the Capitol Building. I believe history shows that every great civilization that has ended up in history's dustbin did so after forsaking their God or Gods. At the same time, I believe in every American's right to worship whatever God or Gods he or she chooses or no God at all. I also believe, however, that the God of Moses and His Son admonished us to go into all the world and spread their word. But those who hear must decide for themselves as to accepting that word.

Well, I've gone on long enough, but let me just close by saying that I believe I have a responsibility to speak out for decency and the basic moralities without which there can be no civilization or personal freedom.

Sincerely,
Ronald Reagan

Mr. Norman Lear
People for the American Way
Washington, D.C.
June 25, 1984 [30]

Dear Norman:

I won't attempt to respond to the quotes you listed in your letter not knowing the context in which they were uttered. It does seem to me, though, that people of any persuasion urging their associates to participate in political activity is pretty much what democracy is all about. And I say this even though I'm sure I would disagree with the course they might be suggesting we follow.

But in mentioning one you referred to me as lobbying for government-mandated prayer readings. That is how the school prayer amendment was defeated. Its opponents made the argument that we were advocating mandated prayer. We were doing nothing of the kind; to the contrary, we opposed mandated prayer. We wanted nothing more than recognition that the Constitution does not forbid someone from praying in school if they so desire.

Norman, my father moved around a lot in search of better opportunities. As a result, I attended six different schools in the eight years of elementary school. There was never one in which there was prescribed prayer yet we knew we could if we wanted to. You asked about the case I mentioned of a child not being allowed to say grace in the school cafeteria. Without looking it up I believe the locale was Mississippi and it was children not child. The school authorities thought they were required to forbid the practice. Evidently some parents made a case of it and the courts upheld the school authorities.

I am not using this office as a pulpit for one religion over all others, but I do subscribe to George Washington's remark regarding high moral standards, decency, etc. and their importance to civilization and his conclusion that to think we could have these without religion as a base was to ask for the impossible.

Obviously, when I'm addressing an audience who share my own religious beliefs—indeed, a religious group—I see nothing wrong with talking of our mutual interests. I can recall no instance where I have ever tried to proselytize others or impose my beliefs on those of other faiths. Madalyn Murray O'Hair demanded and got denial of anyone's right to pray in a school. I simply ask that they be allowed to pray if they so desire—and that prayer can be to the God of Moses, the man of Galilee, Allah, Buddha, or any others.

I said I would not take up the quotes of the clergy you brought to my attention, but isn't it possible those quotes were defensive rather than aggressive? Possibly they were in response to such statements as made in *The Humanist* by Paul Kurtz: "Humanism can not in any fair sense of the word apply to one who still believes in God as the source and creator of the universe. Christian Humanism would be possible only for those who are willing to admit that they are atheistic Humanists. It surely does not apply to God-intoxicated believers."*

Then there is the statement by John J. Dunphy (same magazine) that the battle for humankind's future will be waged and won in the public school classroom and the new faith of Humanism will replace the "rotting corpse of Christianity."

---

* Kurtz, Paul, ed. *The Humanist Alternative* (Buffalo: Prometheus Books, 1973), p. 177.

Believing that both of us are arguing for individual liberty, I have to call to your attention that it is Humanist doctrine that "we must relinquish some of our liberties and that religious values are overridden by what government determines is the general welfare or in the public interest."

Well, I've gone on too long. It was good to hear from you.

Sincerely,
Ron

Mr. Norman Lear
People for the American Way
Washington, D.C.
July 27, 1984[31]

Dear Norman:

I'll have to be brief as I'm on my way to California to open the Olympics and then thank Heaven to go to the ranch.

I still think we're missing connections somewhere. The court decision regarding the cafeteria prayer did happen recently in a southern state not New York. A second incident that now will be taken care of by the equal access bill had to do with a group of students holding a Bible discussion at recess on the school grounds. They were told they'd have to stop.

As to whether a school would have a programmed, organized prayer that should be left up to local school districts. Frankly I can't see that happening. It never did in any schools I attended even though at that time there was no rule against it. All I asked is that the Constitution be observed to the extent of saying there is no law against prayer in school.

But you are right—we do have the right to disagree. Is it OK if I utter a prayer of thanks for that here in this public housing I live in?

Best regards,
Ron

Dr. Joseph Giordano was the head of the trauma team at George Washington University Hospital that gave President Reagan emergency treatment after he was shot in the chest on March 30, 1981. On September 23, 1984, Dr. Giordano published an article in the Washington Post, *accepting credit for saving the President's life, but criticizing him for being critical of "government social programs"—some that helped make Giordano's medical career possible, such as "low-interest government loans" and "generous federal funding for bio-medical research," and others like "Head Start . . . housing for the elderly . . . Social Security . . . Medicare . . . and civil rights legislation."*

Giordano, an American of Italian descent, felt that civil rights legislation had

*"aided Italian Americans and other ethnic and racial groups by making discrimina-
tion not only illegal but also socially unacceptable.*

Dr. Joseph M. Giordano
Washington, D.C.
September 25, 1984 [32]

Dear Dr. Giordano:

I read your article in the *Washington Post* (Sunday September 23) and felt I had
to write to you with reference to your concern about federal programs.

Believe me I can understand your concern but hope I can also reassure you.
There has been a steady drumbeat of political demagoguery duly reported in the
press that we have slashed away at essential social programs in our cost-cutting efforts.

The truth is we have done no such thing. We are spending 37 percent more on
food programs for the elderly and the needy than was being spent in 1980. Social
Security has been put on a sound fiscal basis and the average couple receives $180 a
month more than they were getting. As for needy students and I was one of those
myself, about 40 percent of all full-time college students are receiving some form of
federal aid, loans, grants etc.

We do have a problem with Medicare. The trust fund faces the same kind of imbalance social security faced a year or two ago. We are recommending some
changes affecting the providers more than the patients but certainly nothing that
will deny needed care.

As for civil rights that too has been kicked around for political purposes. Our
record of enforcement including cases brought against those who discriminate, re-
dress for those discriminated against, etc. surpasses that of any previous administration since the bill was passed in the early '60s.

I owe you too much to let you go on believing the current propaganda.

Best regards,
Ronald Reagan

---

*The daughter of an old acquaintance from Dixon, Illinois, sends a letter telling Reagan
about the book* Reagan's America *by Gary Wills.**

Marion Foster
Dixon, Illinois
February 24, 1987 [33]

Dear Marion:

It was so good to get your letter and take a walk down memory lane. You were
more than kind with your generous words of support and I thank you from the
bottom of my heart for all you've been doing over on Hennepin Avenue.

---

* Wills, Gary, *Reagan's America* (New York: Doubleday, 1987).

I haven't read Gary Wills' book but have seen some supposed quotes in a review that bothered me a little. These were quotes of his statements, not those of anyone he'd interviewed. I've come to believe too many press people fancy themselves as psychologists. They claim to know the innermost thoughts of someone whom they've never been closer than in the crowd at a press conference. One has proclaimed that I'm only reading lines I spoke in a movie.

Marion, I think those of us who grew up in our time and place have been blessed with some true values and an appreciation for common sense.

I had a run-in, back in the '60s, when I was governor of California, with some students in those days of campus riots. They had asked for a meeting with me. One of them started off with a diatribe about my generation. He said it was impossible for us to understand our own children. He claimed that we didn't grow up as they had in a world of instant electronic communication, journeys to the moon, jet travel, nuclear power, etc. When he paused for breath I told him, "yes it was true we didn't have those things when we were their age—we invented them." They changed the subject.

Sometimes I feel sorry for these youngsters today. I wonder if we have failed to give them something of what we all received. On the other hand, I have to say these high school and college students I've met today are considerably different than those in the '60s, so maybe the world will do alright.

Well again thank you for writing as you did and please give my love to your mother. Tell her Dutch said hello.

Sincerely,
Ronald Reagan

CHAPTER TWENTY

Reaching Out

R EAGAN *reached out to people in many ways. He wrote to congratulate on a birth-day or anniversary, to regret an invitation, to thank someone for a gift, to sympathize on the loss of a loved one, and to help—sometimes with a contribution.*

THE SISCO SISTERS

Reagan corresponded with the Sisco sisters—Bertha and Samueline ("Sam")—from 1972 until at least 1987 and also wrote to their mentally handicapped brother, Joseph "Buzzy" Sisco. The Sam Sisco collection, offered at auction September 15, 1999, included almost 100 typed and handwritten letters, doodles, and photographs.*

Sam and Bertha Sisco first reached Reagan with a request for assistance from the State of California on October 6, 1972. Reagan admired their desire to be independent and their pledge to take care of their brother, and made an effort to find state programs to help them in addition to the funds to which Buzzy was entitled. But he also helped personally. "I am looking into the possibility of the rocking chair you mentioned and believe I can find one. [He did—he sent his own rocking chair.] In the meantime perhaps the enclosed will help buy a few of the things which give him pleasure." [1]

The Siscos made engraved leather goods to help support themselves, and Reagan admired their art and skills. He bought or received as gifts from them belts and other items. He showed their work to friends and owners of stores who might carry it. Although the Siscos seemed to impose on Reagan's good will, they wrote colorful letters about the life on their farm that he probably enjoyed. He sometimes replied with stories of his own.

---

* Joseph "Buzzy" Sisco, born February 25, 1929, died in 1984; Bertha Sisco, born in 1913, died December 16, 1998. Samueline Sisco was born in 1927. The Sam Sisco Collection was offered by California Book Auction Galleries of Butterfield & Butterfield (Sale 7036Z). The letters in this chapter and elsewhere in this book are from handwritten drafts in the Ronald Reagan Library.

Reagan writes to James O'Kelley, president of the Robert Scholze Tannery in Chattanooga, Tennessee, about the possibility of a barter arrangement—Scholze leather for the Sisco sisters' finished goods—and explains how he came to correspond with them.

Mr. James L. O'Kelley
Circa 1976[2]

Dear Mr. O'Kelley:

I hope I'm not being too forward in writing you on a matter that has to do with your business. If so and if you choose to ignore this letter believe me I'll understand.

While I was governor of California I had an opportunity to help two maiden sisters with a problem concerning their younger brother. Briefly he is a forty-three-year-old mentally retarded individual. They promised their dying mother they would take care of him and have all these years. Their principal source of revenue is their state grant to care for their brother. I won't bother you with details of the problem concerning him but I was able to resolve it and this began a correspondence which continues to this day. More than that however they have sent me gifts including a belt and a guest book for our ranch which are the finest examples of the ancient art of Spanish leather engraving I've ever seen.

They want very much to be self-dependent so I managed to get them some clients for their leather engraving by simply displaying these gifts. Some of my ranching friends were willing to pay $100 or more for a belt (without buckle) their work is so distinctive. The book is a masterpiece, personalized and with horses and riders pictured in a way I've never seen in leather engraving. Now they tell me they can duplicate a western painting such as a Remington or Russell in leather. They of course see this engraving talent as a way by which they can be self-sustaining. Incidentally I showed my belt to several dealers in Los Angeles who sell Western gear and without exception they priced it at $150.

Now the reason for this lengthy letter (if you've stayed with me thus far). It seems they have attracted some clients—among them the Lake Charles Art Gallery in Louisiana. They have no capital to purchase the leather they need. In a letter to me they wrote and I'll quote, "the only leather in the United States that's worth a hoot is at Robert Scholze Tannery. In our day we've used leathers from every tannery in the United States and even overseas. Scholze is by far the very, very best."

The upshot was they sought my advice as to whether I thought they could propose a barter deal for rolls of your leather. I haven't answered them but decided to write you instead. I know nothing of your business—whether an example of their art could be useful in any way or whether you personally might be interested in something like the book I described or one of their paintings carved in leather or whatever. They have done saddles, boots, etc. Again I can only say I've never seen anything to match what they can do. Their names are Miss Sam and Bertha Sisco, P. O. Box 148, Healdsburg, California 95448—phone 707-433-5379.

Forgive me if I've been presumptuous but in this day of eager freeloaders I've been impressed with their desire to make it on their own. And greatly impressed by their talent.

Sincerely,
Ronald Reagan

———

Reagan thanks the Siscos for one of their leather works, encloses a check, and explains why he cannot make a larger investment in their business. The Lake Charles Art Gallery in Louisiana became a Sisco client.

Miss Sam and Miss Bertha Sisco
Healdsburg, California
Circa 1976[3]

Dear Miss Sam and Miss Bertha:

Again, I have to say how much you surprised me with that magnificent book. I thought I'd seen the acme in the guest book you made but you continue to surpass yourselves. I'm also most grateful for the inscription—I hope I can live up to it.

The book was presented to me in your behalf on the campaign plane and immediately circulated for signatures by all aboard. I'll watch for an opportunity to show it to Wayne Newton if ever our paths cross, as well as others I think might be interested.

Now the hard part. I'm enclosing a little something (I wish it could be more) hoping it will help with the leather. I can't make the investment you offer, much as I'd like to. I know there have been stories about how well off I'm supposed to be but they are exaggerations, to say the least. Now that I am a candidate, my earnings have stopped altogether and this will hold until I either get the job or lose and can go back to the radio program and speaking engagements. Meanwhile, I'll do everything I can to display your magnificent art hoping that one day the right door can be opened.

Tell me, would it help if I dropped a line to this Mr. Roddy in Lake Charles, Louisiana, telling him my own feeling about the things you've done? I'll wait until I hear from you.

Sincerely,
Ronald Reagan

———

Reagan writes to Stanley Marcus, owner of department stores, about carrying the leather goods the Siscos make.

Mr. Stanley Marcus
Dallas, Texas
Circa 1976[4]

Dear Stanley:

Forgive me for presuming on our brief time together at the [Bohemian] Grove. You'll recall I spoke of the two ladies who do the remarkable leather work (Spanish engraving). They did the ranch guest book for me—quite a conversation piece—as well as some belts, hatbands, etc.

They have written me asking if they could send some things of that kind for you to put in the store on consignment as a way of determining if there is a market for their art. They proposed that if this meets with your approval, they be told where and how to address the shipment. Their addresses are: Miss Sam and Miss Bertha Sisco, P.O. Box 148, Healdsburg, California 95448.

As I told you at the Grove, they are rather unforgettable characters who came to my attention while I was governor. Their leather work is beyond anything I've ever seen.

I was sorry my stay at the Grove was so short and hope our paths will cross again soon.

Best regards,
Ron

The Siscos wrote about a brother's mare that took 12 and a half months to foal and their own problems: "We had our Arab mare bred twice and both times got nothin' . . ." Reagan advises them on how to write a contract for the services of a stallion.

Miss Sam and Miss Bertha Sisco
Healdsburg, California
February 27, 1984[5]

Dear Miss Sam and Miss Bertha:

Just a line to say I hope the photos of me with some of your fine art work have arrived by now. If not let me know.

I never had any of the foaling problems with our mares (when we had mares) that you describe I'm happy to say. All were delivering around the normal 11 months.

If you ever decide to try remember to make the stallion contracts read "no fee unless there is a live foal." That means a foal that after delivery, stands and nurses. From then on you are on your own.

Our few days at the ranch were great. The weather was beautiful and we rode every day.

Best regards,
Ronald

"Say you know you've never asked us to make our fine Vice President Bush one of our leather belts, do you think he would like one?" the Sisco sisters wrote on August 30, 1984. "We would sure like to make him one, just give us his waist measurement, initials he wants on belt tip and if he likes horses we'll give him horses, or if he would rather just have a design, say wild roses or acorns let us know. . . . Dar-Si-Ah [their Doberman] either stepped on a rock or stuck her foot in a hole. . . . Dr. McCrystle operated on her for 2 ½ hours." "You should see Dr. McCrystle's reception room at his hospital," the letter goes on. Veterinarian David McCrystle's reception room was decorated with photographs of Nancy and Ronald Reagan and letters from the president.

> Miss Sam and Miss Bertha Sisco
> Healdsburg, California
> September 14, 1984[6]

Dear Miss Sam and Miss Bertha:

I was sorry to hear about Dar-Si-Ah's latest accident but happy to get the word that Dr. McCrystle did his usual magnificent work. I've just dropped him a line.

With regard to the VP and a belt I have to tell you I'm not inclined to believe that's his style. He's a boater not a horse person like us. He's out on the ocean in a speed boat every chance he gets. Let me also say he's a great partner and vice president.

Now about me and Christmas—remember last year's gift was to be for two years. So it is our coming gift just delivered a little early.

My secretary will send some campaign buttons as soon as she can locate them. I understand the ones with pictures are a little hard to come by so it may take a while, but she'll do her best to find some.

Best to Buzzy.

> Sincerely,
> [no signature]

Buzzy died in 1984, but the sisters continued to work on a memorial for him and sent Reagan a poem in his memory. Reagan sent them $100. They continued to write to Reagan after he left the presidency, but later replies were staff-written.

> Miss Sam and Miss Bertha Sisco
> Healdsburg, California
> November 23, 1987[7]

Dear Miss Sam and Miss Bertha:

It was good to hear from you, and we both had a lump in our throats as we read your poem. It is truly beautiful. We thank you.

Knowing my schedule, may I make this our Christmas message? We wish you both a Merry, Merry Christmas and a Happy New Year!

The enclosed is in memory of Buzzy, to you who cherished and loved him so. God bless you both.

Sincerely,
Ronald

CHARITY AND HELPING PEOPLE

Reagan was brought up to believe in tithing—contributing 10 percent of his income to charity. "Would the Lord consider His share as being His, if I gave it to my brother to help him through school?" Reagan asked the minister in Davenport, Iowa, where in 1933 he had been hired for $100 a month as a staff announcer for the WOC radio station. The minister said the Lord would, so Reagan's brother "Moon" got $10 a month.[8]

Reagan often tried to help people in difficult circumstances in a variety of ways— usually by trying to do what they asked. Sometimes he tried to find a job for someone; sometimes he instructed his staff to follow up on whatever government assistance might be available; sometimes he sent a check; sometimes he arranged a meeting. His inclination to help was strong enough that his staff considered him a soft touch. On one letter he wrote, "Although my contributions to major charities have been made already, please accept the enclosed check as a token of my appreciation for what Mary and her associates are doing." He added a note for the staff that said "So I'm a sucker—RR."[9]

Early in his presidency Reagan established a task force on private sector initiatives. "The possibilities are limitless," he said, "for what we can take over that government has once been doing."[10] Reagan himself sent checks to individuals and contributed to diverse charitable causes in amounts of $50 to $1000 and in larger amounts to Eureka College.

These letters are examples of his responses to requests for help or contributions and his encouragement of voluntary private action.[11]

Reagan explains to a correspondent that his tax returns don't reveal all his charitable contributions because some of them are not tax deductible.[12]

Jack B. McConnell, M.D.
Basking Ridge, New Jersey
January 11, 1982 [13]

Dear Dr. McConnell:

I'm sorry to be so late in answering your letter of last October but believe it or not it has just reached my desk.

I understand your criticism regarding what seems to be my failure to contribute proportionate to my income. I was raised to believe in tithing—giving one tenth (as you do) and I try to do that. However a goodly share of what I give is not deductible for tax purposes and therefore doesn't show up in the press disclosures of my tax returns. I have chosen to help certain individuals I believe are deserving and obviously can't make that public.

You are right however that I can set an example to encourage others so I'll have to find a way around my problem without abandoning those who have come to depend on me.

I thank you for your letter.

Sincerely,
Ronald Reagan

Greg Brezina founded Christian Families Today, a faith ministry, in 1980, after 22 years in professional football, 12 of them with the Atlanta Falcons. The Bible verse Reagan mentions reads, "If my people, which are called by my name, shall humble themselves, and pray, and seek my face, then will I hear them from heaven, and will forgive their sin, and will heal their land." Reagan encourages voluntary action to address some of the nation's problems.

Mr. Greg Brezina
Fayetteville, Georgia
October 25, 1982 [14]

Dear Greg:

It was good to see you last night and I appreciate very much your letter. I have long believed that the American people are hungry for a spiritual revival. I also believe there are evidences that such a revival is taking place. It is true that we can still see pornography, drug use, profane and obscene language commonly used etc. But there are other signs, increased membership in the more fundamental religions where social gospel has not replaced the Bible. All over the country parents are uniting in groups to reclaim their children from drug addiction. There is a program at work in the military which has had fantastic success in the last year in reducing particularly the use of marijuana.

Greg I could go on with a litany of the private sector initiatives we're encouraging which have brought literally millions of people into voluntary good works replacing government projects. Let me assure you that II Chronicles 7:14 is ever present in my mind. My daily prayer is that God will help me to use this position so as to serve Him.

Teddy Roosevelt once called the presidency a bully pulpit. I intend to use it to the best of my ability to serve the Lord.

Again my thanks to you and God bless you.

Sincerely,
Ronald Reagan

Reagan made frequent contributions to Eureka College, his alma mater. The itemized contributions on his tax returns show over $40,000 given to Eureka from 1981 through 1987. Here he expresses pleasure with the news from the president that Eureka College is doing well. [15]

President Daniel D. Gilbert
Eureka, Illinois
July 8, 1983 [16]

Dear Dan:

Your letter made me a little homesick. I could share even at this distance the atmosphere, the feeling that seems to be so peculiarly Eureka. I don't know how to explain it but there is a Eureka spirit. Maybe it's because the old school has stubbornly maintained tradition. Didn't someone once say something about tradition being the glue that held civilization together?

I'm delighted with all the good news. There have been times in these last 50 years when it seems as if the college "neath the elms" might not make it but somehow it always did.

God bless you all.

Sincerely,
Ron

Reagan contributed to the Randy E. Cline Memorial Fund from his personal account. Cline was killed in the Grenada rescue mission, which began October 25, 1983.

Mr. Philip Kirby
Cloverdale, Indiana
December 5, 1983 [17]

Dear Mr. Kirby:

I understand that you have started or are starting a college scholarship fund for the yet-to-be-born child of Sgt. and Mrs. Randy Cline. First let me commend you for this action and commend too the people of Cloverdale who I know will express their sympathy to the family and their appreciation for the sacrifice Randy made for all of us.

Sgt. Cline was one of the Rangers who lost their lives in the Grenada rescue mission. I wish every one could have met with the rescued medical students as I did and hear their praise of our men in uniform. There was no doubt in their minds that the threat to their lives was very real and they owe their lives to brave young Americans like Randy Cline—"Greater Glory Hath No Man."

Again my thanks to you.

Sincerely,
Ronald Reagan

On December 3, 1984, a disastrous gas leak at a Union Carbide plant in Bhopal, India, killed over 2,000 people and injured many more. Robert Macauley of AmeriCares spoke to Mother Teresa on December 12, 1984, and wrote to Reagan about their conversation. She said, "Bob, please ask President Reagan to pray for us on December 16th"—the day Union Carbide was scheduled to neutralize the remaining poisonous methyl isocyanate in its chemical plant. She also told Macauley that vitamins were among the critical needs in both Calcutta and Bhopal.

Mr. Robert Macauley
New Canaan, Connecticut
December 19, 1984 [18]

Dear Bob:

It was good to hear from you and please tell that wonderful lady Mother Teresa I did pray on December 16 and a number of days before and after. Truth is I try to remember to pray in her behalf frequently.

The enclosed is to help a bit in getting her those vitamins she requested.

Best regards,
Ronald Reagan

Reagan replies to a severely disabled young man, Peter Aviles, from Caldwell, Idaho, whose dream was to meet a U.S. president he had read about. Reagan met briefly with him May 30, 1985. He lived in Dorothy Todd's home.

Mr. Peter Aviles
Caldwell, Idaho
January 28, 1985 [19]

Dear Peter:

Thank you for your letter. I can understand your interest in history—I'm something of a history buff myself although my main interest is in the history of our American West. As some historian put it, it was the most unusual march of empire in world history. It wasn't led by the military but by settlers who bet their lives and the lives of their families as they opened up the West in the face of hardship and hostile Indians.

If you are going to be in or near Washington at any time let me know and we'll see if we can't arrange that handshake. Write me, but on the envelope put, "Attn: Kathy Osborne." That way the letter will get to me without any delay.

As you can imagine there are times when I'm not in Washington. For example in February I'll be away from the 13th until the 18th. In March I'll be in Canada the 17th and 18th. In April away from the 5th to the 15th. And the economic summit conference in Germany will have me out of the country from the 1st of May 'til possibly the 10th and that's as far ahead as I know my schedule.

Please give my best regards to Mrs. Todd and if you like show her this letter.

Best regards,
Ronald Reagan

———

Lorrie Ackerman was the 13-year-old president of her Girl Scout Cadette troop. She wrote to thank Reagan for canceling the January 1985 Inaugural parade because of the extreme cold. Reagan sent $50 with his letter.

Lorrie Ackerman
Kensington, Maryland
March 4, 1985 [20]

Dear Lorrie:

Thank you very much for your kind letter. I had some misgivings about my decision, thinking of all those who would be disappointed. A letter like yours helps to make me feel I made the correct decision and I thank you for being so kind and taking the time and trouble to write.

Your Cadette troop 1541 sounds like a real active group with some achievements to be proud of. I wish you well on your plans for a trip to Europe. I've enclosed a small contribution for your fundraising campaign. After all us presidents have to stick together.

Best regards,
Ronald Reagan

———

Reagan sent a contribution for the building fund of Bel Air Presbyterian Church, to which he belonged in California. Donn Moomaw was the minister of the church.

Mr. Donn D. Moomaw
Los Angeles, California
March 16, 1985 [21]

Dear Donn:

It was good to hear from you and to learn of the exciting plans for Bel Air. Will we be able to find our way around when everything is completed? The enclosed is just a little something on account. I don't know if you have a particular title for the building fund so I just made this out to the church, as you can see, but it is for the new construction.

Thank you again for coming to the Inaugural. As for the West Coast Reagans, that one particular problem with the adverse publicity and all seems to have been resolved by that meeting we had some months back. Score another for prayers being answered.

Nancy sends her love, and from both of us to all your family.

Sincerely,
Ron

———————

The House of Hope was a children's refuge started by a faith ministry. The article mentioned in the letter said, "Mr. President, Your vision of America is the accurate one." Reagan enclosed a check with his reply. He had just returned from his May 27 Orlando visit.

Mr. and Mrs. Kelly McDonald
Orlando, Florida
May 28, 1985 [22]

Dear Mr. and Mrs. McDonald:

On my recent visit to Orlando I read Charley Reese's column in the *Sentinel* about Sara Trollinger and her friends starting the movement that led to the establishment of the House of Hope. And of course I read of your own involvement in this fine undertaking.

It is an inspiring and heartwarming story and all of you who have contributed to its success deserve a thank you from all Americans. Please accept the enclosed as a token of my appreciation and admiration. God bless you.

Sincerely,
Ronald Reagan

———————

Christopher Edley, president of the United Negro College Fund, wrote to thank President Reagan for his telephone message during the "Lou Rawls Parade of Stars" show on December 28, 1985, a fundraising telethon. Edley apologized for an on-air phone interview with the Reverend Jesse Jackson, which had followed Reagan's message; Jackson had claimed that Reagan exploited the occasion. Reagan's call had been "eagerly sought," Edley said.

Mr. Christopher F. Edley
New York, New York [23]
January 24, 1986

Dear Mr. Edley:

Thank you very much for your kind letter. I'm truly grateful. Have no concern about the telephone interview that followed my part on the telethon. I'm honored to have been a part of the show and will continue to support the United

Negro College Fund. It's a great organization dedicated to a fine and deserving cause.

Again my thanks to you.

Sincerely,
Ronald Reagan

————

Phyllis Cole was a constituent of Carlos Moorhead, member of Congress from Illinois, who apparently brought her problem to Reagan's attention.

Mrs. Phyllis Cole
Morrison, Illinois
July 9, 1986 [24]

Dear Phyllis:

I've just learned that you are having some health problems. I hope they will soon be a thing of the past. You'll be in my thoughts and prayers until they are.

Phyllis I know you've been helping your granddaughter Lara at the University of Illinois. Having worked my way through Eureka I know something of the problems she faces. Would you care to tell me her situation? There might be something I could do with regard to some of the student aid programs. If you care to write me just address it to me here at the White House and on the envelope write "Attn: Kathy Osborne." That will bring it to my desk immediately.

Again—take care of yourself and all the best.

Sincerely,
Dutch

SYMPATHY

Reagan wrote many letters of condolence in his own hand. These letters are characteristic both in the sentiments they expresses—that no words can lessen sorrow, that God has a plan for each of us, and that death is a new beginning—and in their focus on the particular situation.

————

Reagan writes in sympathy to Bob Hope about his brother George, who died in June 1969.

Mr. Bob Hope
North Hollywood, California
September 2, 1969 [25]

Dear Bob:

It seems as though sometimes one is asked to bear more than his share.

Nancy and I have just learned of your brother George's passing and want you to know how deeply sorry we are. You continue to be in our thoughts and prayers.

Give our love to Delores and again our deepest sympathy.

Sincerely,
Ron

———————

Mrs. Gilpatrick was a friend of Maureen Reagan's; she had recently lost her daughter, whom the Reagans had met.

Mrs. Gilpatrick
Wianno, Massachusetts
Circa 1970s[26]

Dear Mrs. Gilpatrick:

My daughter Maureen has just told me of your tragic loss. Mrs. Reagan and I enjoyed knowing your daughter and want you to know how much we share your sorrow. Words of course are of little help at such a time but please know you have our deepest sympathy.

We never face moments like this without wondering why such things happen and of course there is no answer. We can only trust that God in his infinite wisdom does have a plan for all of us and though it isn't given to us to understand, we must have faith in His mercy.

Again, our sympathy—you are in our thoughts and prayers.

Sincerely,
Ronald Reagan

———————

Doris Collins wrote just before the first anniversary of the October 23, 1983, bombing of the Marine barracks in Beirut in which her son, James Ray Cain, U.S. Navy hospi- talman, was killed. She said, "As a mother of one of the young men who was killed, I personally do not feel that you 'owe anyone an apology,' and I support you 100 per- cent." Whether the Marines "died in shame" had become an issue in the 1984 election campaign.

Mrs. Doris Collins
Gardendale, Alabama
October 30, 1984[27]

Dear Mrs. Collins:

I have no words to tell you how very much your letter meant to me. My heart has ached for all of you who bear such a burden of sorrow and then to have the added pain of someone telling you the sacrifice your loved ones made was for no reason.

Mrs. Collins there was a reason and a cause. The cause was peace and your son and those other fine young men died because the enemies of peace knew they were succeeding. Now your letter comes and with all you have to bear you express concern for me. I have asked, with regard to men like your son, where do we find such men? Now I ask where do we find such women as you?

God bless you and from the bottom of my heart I thank you.

Sincerely,
Ronald Reagan

"Uh oh," said Michael J. Smith, pilot of the Challenger, *73 seconds after takeoff. It was the last transmission from the exploding space shuttle. Reagan telephoned the families of the crew of the* Challenger *and later met with them. Smith's wife, Jane, found a quotation on his dresser that she sent to Reagan. Reagan had the quotation reproduced calligraphically and sent it to the family.* Both he and Nancy signed the handwritten letter.*

Mrs. Michael J. Smith
Circa February 1986 [28]

Dear Jane:

You were more than kind to give us the quotation Mike left with you. Nancy and I are deeply touched and grateful.

Believing as we do that Mike has reached that "new beginning," we send you and Scott, Allison, and Erin his words to remind you that he wants above all else that you should find happiness. We share his wish with warmest friendship and affection for all of you.

Nancy and Ronald Reagan

Elizabeth Glaser contracted AIDS from a blood transfusion in 1981 while she was pregnant and before the disease had been identified. Her daughter was born with AIDS and died in 1988. Mrs. Glaser herself, a founder of the Pediatric AIDS Foundation, died in 1994.

Mrs. Paul Glaser
Santa Monica, California
August 29, 1988 [29]

Dear Mrs. Glaser:

We've been trying to call you with no success, hence this letter. Nancy and I want you to know you are very much in our thoughts and prayers. We know there

---

* "For man, there is no rest and no ending. He must go on—conquest beyond conquest; this little planet, and its winds and ways, and all the laws of mind and matter that restrain him. Then the planets about him, and, at last out across the immensity of the stars. And when he has conquered all the depths of space and all the mysteries of time—still he will be but beginning." [H. G. Wells screenplay, *Things to Come*, 1936]

are no words that can lessen your sorrow—how we wish there were—but please know you have our deepest sympathy.

We can only trust in God's infinite wisdom and mercy knowing he has received your daughter in that other world where there is no pain or sorrow and where one day we shall all be joined with those we love for evermore.

We are moving in every way we can and as fast as we can to find answers to the terrible scourge that brought such sorrow to you and to so many others. You will continue to be in our prayers.

God bless you.

Sincerely,
Ronald Reagan

CHAPTER TWENTY-ONE

The Lighter Side

R EAGAN WROTE *many letters to children and young people. He replied both to individual letters and to collections of letters he received from school children.*

Some letters came to him from children of people he knew well. Others were hand-delivered by people with whom he met. Still others came from the sample of mail from the general public Reagan received every few weeks from his staff. Reagan answered these letters as he did others, usually drafting his replies on a yellow pad.

Reagan's responses are always appropriate to the age of the children to whom he writes. When he writes to teenagers, he treats them as adults. He often gives advice— usually in the guise of a story about his own experience. He always supports parents, but he readily agrees when children claim that their teachers have distorted an issue.

The Children's Unit of the White House Correspondence Office considered it important to communicate directly with children—and thus their parents—especially on policies on which the children's teachers might disagree with the administration.[1] The staff took its lead from the president.

Even on the lighter side, when writing to children or engaging in humor with adults, Reagan gets a point across. His humor often has bite as well as wit. He appreciated one-liners and was always looking for stories or jokes to make a point in a less than totally serious way. He trades stories in some of these letters.

CHILDREN

Reagan did not realize he needed glasses until he was in high school, when he discovered that his brother could read highway signs but he could not. He tried on his mother's glasses and was amazed at the world he saw.[2] He advises his young correspondent to wear her glasses until she's ready for contact lenses.

Miss Rachel Virden
Dallas, Texas
November 23, 1983[3]

Dear Rachel:

Thank you for your letter. Have a happy birthday on June 13th. Rachel I know how you feel about glasses. I have been nearsighted all my life and when I was young I felt as you do about wearing glasses but I wore them. Being able to see clearly was more important. Now maybe seeing me on TV or my picture in the paper you wonder where my glasses are. I'm wearing them—contact lenses. Wear your glasses now and in a few years when your eyes have reached their full size you might look into the idea of contacts. It's very simple and easy to wear them. I've been wearing them all my adult life. But in the meantime don't deny yourself the joy of being able to see things clearly.

Again thanks for your kind letter.

Best wishes.

Sincerely,
Ronald Reagan

———————

Andy, a seventh grader, wrote: "Today my mother declared my bedroom a disaster area. I would like to request federal funds to hire a crew to clean up my room."

Andy Smith
Irmo, South Carolina
May 11, 1984[4]

Dear Andy:

I'm sorry to be so late in answering your letter but as you know I've been in China and found your letter here upon my return.

Your application for disaster relief has been duly noted but I must point out one technical problem; the authority declaring the disaster is supposed to make the request. In this case your mother.

However setting that aside I'll have to point out the larger problem of available funds. This has been a year of disasters, 539 hurricanes as of May 4th and several more since, numerous floods, forest fires, drought in Texas and a number of earthquakes. What I'm getting at is that funds are dangerously low.

May I make a suggestion? This administration, believing that government has done many things that could better be done by volunteers at the local level, has sponsored a Private Sector Initiative program, calling upon people to practice voluntarism in the solving of a number of local problems.

Your situation appears to be a natural. I'm sure your mother was fully justified in proclaiming your room a disaster. Therefore you are in an excellent position to launch another volunteer program to go along with the more than 3,000 already underway in our nation—congratulations.

Give my best regards to your mother.

Sincerely,
Ronald Reagan

———————

First-graders sent Reagan an Easter greeting delivered in person by Chris, a classmate of theirs with muscular dystrophy. They asked him about the presidency: "Do you work a lot? Is it hard to be a President?"

Ms. Kitty Grund's First Grade Class
Brewster Elementary School
Rochester, Michigan
April 6, 1983[5]

Dear Members of [Ms. Grund's First Grade Class]:

Thank you very much for your letters and for your giant Easter greeting. Thanks too for the jar of jelly beans and yes I do like jelly beans.

Chris brought all these things and told me about all of you. I know why you like him so much. I like him too.

You asked some questions in your letters. What is the White House like? It is a very beautiful, big house almost 200 years old. It really is the people's home. It belongs to all Americans.

One of you asked if a president has a lot to do. Yes in fact a president takes a lot of homework home from the Oval Office every day. And one of you said your mother was upset about taxes. We're all upset about taxes but there will be a cut in taxes as of July first which I persuaded the Congress to pass because taxes were too high.

There are many people who need our help in these troubled times. Shannon I'm glad your church is giving food to the poor. We are making some progress in helping people get jobs but it is slow work.

You live in a wonderful country and I'm sure you know that. We'll try to keep it that way for you until you are grown up and able to take over. So study and learn so you'll be ready.

Once again thank you for your letters and presents.

Sincerely,
Ronald Reagan

Students at the John Sipley School sent brief messages to the President.

> Mr. Ed Roweau
> John L. Sipley School
> Woodridge, Illinois
> March 16, 1983[6]

Dear Mr. Roweau:

Thank you very much for your kind letter and please extend my thanks to Miss Mahon, Mrs. Kolak and all of your students for their generous words.

They also had some questions: yes I have plenty of jelly beans, my favorite sport now is riding but my real love is football which I played in high school and college. Heather I do like my job. Angela and Maria I like pork chops too but my real favorite is macaroni and cheese.

Thank you all again and best regards.

> Sincerely,
> Ronald Reagan

Dallas was a third-grader whose mother worked for Alaska state senator Arliss Sturgulewski.

> Dallas Hargrave
> Juneau, Alaska
> March 14, 1984[7]

Dear Dallas:

Thank you for your letter. Senator Sturgulewski saw that I got it.

Your life sounds very interesting what with bears and eagles so near at hand. And of course the fishing.

Tell Heidi that while they don't let me sell Girl Scout cookies, believe it or not the Girl Scouts came to the White House and made me an honorary Girl Scout. So now you know at least one of the things that happens to a president.

You asked if I like being president, well it's a lot of office work and meetings to try and solve problems, but yes I like it. It's good to think you are able to help people and our country.

Then sometimes you have a pleasant meeting with people like the senator. We had lunch in the State Dining Room in the White House.

Please give my regards to your mother and father and Heidi. Again thanks for your very nice letter.

> Sincerely,
> Ronald Reagan

Reagan makes an effort to help Courtney Justice, a second-grader, with her report on the White House. Courtney wrote that she and her sister were friends of Ashley and Cameron Reagan, Michael Reagan's children, and had visited the White House with her parents and the Michael Reagans during the second Inaugural. Courtney found three books in the library about the history of the White House but, she wrote the President, "it is very hard to find stories about you."

> Miss Courtney Justice
> Sierra Madre, California
> April 29, 1987[8]

Dear Courtney:

It was very nice of you to write as you did and both Mrs. Reagan and I are most grateful for your letter. And please thank your sister for coloring that picture for us.

I hope I'm not too late with regard to your report on the White House. According to the Constitution the president is the chief executive officer of the government (that's like being the head of a big business concern) and is the commander in chief of all the armed forces. The president is responsible for our national security.

As president it was my job to select the people [who] would make up what is called my cabinet. They each have the title of secretary except the head of the Department of Justice whose title is attorney general. The vice president is also a member of the cabinet. Some of the others are secretary of state, secretary of defense, secretary of agriculture, secretary of health and human services etc. There are more but that will give you the idea.

You asked what do I do? Well the days can be pretty full. At 9 a.m. every morning Monday through Friday I meet with my chief of staff, his assistant and the vice president. We go over things that are scheduled for the day, problems we may be having with regard to action by the Congress, requests for me to appear and make speeches and on and on.

Then at 9:30 on a normal day, my national security advisor and his top assistant come in with the latest information regarding foreign affairs. He leaves me with a leather folder containing about a half hour's reading on worldwide matters.

Throughout the day memorandums come to my desk, papers and laws that have to be signed or refused by me and of course mail. The president has a few thousand people in government who are appointed by him and there are always some who are retiring and have to be replaced so there are meetings with staff to do that.

I've enclosed a page for the month of May from what is known as an advance schedule. That means it isn't complete. There will be changes and additions for each day. Every evening I get a corrected and final schedule for the next day plus information on the various appointments and meetings for that day. All of that is my bedtime reading.

Of course there are occasional trips. For example in June I will go to Italy for a meeting with the leaders of six other countries and then a one-day stop in Germany. I hope this gives you an idea of what the president does. Of course there are happy times too such as getting a nice letter from a little girl named Courtney.

Best regards,
Ronald Reagan

Reagan tells a fourth-grader what he read when he was in fourth grade.

Jeff
During the 1970s[9]

Dear Jeff:

I can't remember many of the books I read in fourth grade, but a few do stand out in my memory. One was *Robinson Crusoe;* another was a book called *Pirates of the Spanish Main;* and one I read over and over again was called *Northern Trails.*

This last one was not a story like the others but was a book about the wilderness of Alaska and northern Canada. I think more than anything else this book planted in me a love for nature and the outdoors.

Let me just say one thing to you about books and reading. Don't let TV keep you from developing the habit of reading. Reading is a magic carpet and you can never be lonely if you learn to enjoy a good book.

Someday when you are grown up and find yourself alone in a city on a business trip or riding across country on a plane, you'll discover the hours fly if you have something to read. This is true for those days when the flu bug has you down in bed, or even on a vacation when you just feel lazy.

Thanks for your letter and very best to you.

Sincerely,
Ronald Reagan

A fifth-grader wrote, "When I was in the fourth grade, my teacher had the class write you a letter saying that we disagreed with your budget cuts in education. My mother found the letter I wrote and got mad. Then she explained to me why the budget cuts were necessary. . . . Now I understand and I know not to write anything that is not my own idea." One of the effects of Reagan's education budget was, supposedly, that the children would have no books. Reagan's replies to such letters were as much for the parents as the child.

Jason Alexander Tolson
Landover Hills, Maryland
October 25, 1982[10]

Dear Jason:

I'm sorry to be so late in answering your letter but it takes quite a while for mail to reach my desk. I want to thank you for writing as you did. Please tell your mother

I agree with her about what you had been persuaded to do by your teacher. By the way have all the bad things you were told would happen, no books etc. happened?

Thank your mother too for her understanding of what we're trying to do to make things better. And again thank you.

Sincerely,
Ronald Reagan

An eighth-grader wrote that the schools are trying to "brainwash us kids to tell our parents to have a nuclear freeze."

Miss Mary J. Rickey
Portland, Oregon
December 6, 1982 [11]

Dear Miss Rickey:

Thank you very much for your letter and for sending me the material you were given in school. I agree with you this is a shameful thing to do. We all know the horror a nuclear war would bring—that's why we are doing our best to prevent such a war while at the same time we are trying to negotiate a reduction of nuclear weapons with the Soviet Union.

The material you sent is designed to frighten people and to do so for only one purpose—to sell the nuclear freeze idea which at this time would increase the chance of nuclear war. It is true the Soviets favor a freeze because they have a greatly superior nuclear force compared to ours. A freeze would be fine and we could all support it if first we get a reduction in weapons to where we are even.

Thank you again and give my regards to your parents.

Sincerely,
Ronald Reagan

Reagan writes to a boy whose older brother David was, according to a note from the boy's teacher, Joyce Ann Munn, "the last Marine to be identified from the Beirut tragedy." The Marine barracks in Beirut, Lebanon, were truck-bombed on October 23, 1983, killing 241 military personnel.*

Mr. Kenneth Randolph
Siloam Springs, Arkansas
March 15, 1984 [12]

Dear Kenneth:

I'm sorry to be so late in answering your letter but with half a million letters coming to the White House every month it takes a while before a letter finally reaches me.

----

* David M. Randolph of Siloam Springs, USMC LCPL (Lance Corporal), was killed in Beirut on October 23, 1983; he was 19 years old.

Kenneth I can understand your sorrow about David's death and your bitterness. He and so many others were victims of a vicious act of terrorism. It was a terrible tragedy and one we must never forget. There is nothing harder for a president to do than to send our splendid young men like your brother into situations where their lives are in danger. Our Marines were in Lebanon to help bring about an end to senseless killing that has been going on for years. The kind of people responsible for the killing of our men have been killing men, women and children in the city of Beirut. David and the others were killed because those fanatic barbarians were afraid our Marines were going to be successful in their mission. Our Marines including your brother believed in their mission and that it was worthwhile. They were there to try and bring peace.

You have my deepest sympathy and you are in my prayers. Please give my regards to Miss Munn and thank her for her note.

Sincerely,
Ronald Reagan

————————

An 11-year-old suggested that Reagan rename his dog "Deficit" so he could say "Down Deficit" and finally "Deficit's gone!"

Stephan M. Lieske
La Canada, California
March 4, 1985 [13]

Dear Stephan:

Thanks very much for your letter and your suggestion about a name change for our dog Lucky. I've thought it over and have decided to keep calling her Lucky. You see I'm doing my best to make the deficit go away but I don't want her (our dog) to go away. If I'm lucky we'll eliminate the deficit but we'll still have Lucky. You'd like her she's only six months old and a lot of fun.

Best regards,
Ronald Reagan

————————

Reagan wrote quite a few "welcome to the world" letters to newborns, like this one to Joanne and Bill Drake's daughter, born May 3, 1994. Joanne Drake was the chief of staff of Reagan's post-presidential office.

Caitlin Drake
May 4, 1994 [14]

Dear Caitlin:

Start eating these jellybeans now and you'll grow up to be a good Republican!

Ronald Reagan

Christopher, the son of Rick Burt, U.S. ambassador to West Germany, wrote to the president, ". . . since you were kind enough to write me when I was born, I wanted to write to give you an update. . . . I am now 10 months old."

Christopher Burt
American Embassy
Bonn, West Germany
February 15, 1988 [15]

Dear Christopher:

Thank you for your letter wishing me a happy birthday. I'm a little early in wishing you a happy first birthday but the next two months will go by quickly for both of us.

I'm most grateful for the kind things you had to say about me. Thanks for your generous words. Thanks too for telling me of how you've learned to appreciate our country and have seen the difference between freedom and those not so free places. One day you'll be able to tell your contemporaries who haven't had your experience how really lucky they are.

That Yankee uniform you are wearing in the picture took me back a few years. I was once a radio sports announcer and broadcast many games in which the Yankees were playing and most of the time winning. You wear it well.

Please give my warmest regard to your parents. They are doing a wonderful thing for our country and we are all very proud of them. Tell them Nancy sends her love—they'll know who she is. As a matter of fact she held you and hugged you when you were younger.

Well again—have a happy birthday in a couple of months and very best wishes.

Sincerely,
Ronald Reagan

Reagan welcomed immigrants to the United States gladly. Here he responds to a telegram dated September 2, 1982, from a nine-year-old who writes, "As a Lebanese immigrant to the United States of America I do thank you, Mr. President, for your beautiful speech about my country." Reagan's address to the nation on U.S. policy in the Middle East was given the day before. "The Lebanon war, tragic as it was, has given us a new opportunity for Middle East peace," he said. "We must seize it now and bring peace to this troubled area so vital to world stability while there is still time . . . and we can now help the Lebanese to rebuild their war-torn country."

Rosie Djinguezian
Los Angeles, California
October 25, 1982[16]

Dear Rosie:

Thank you very much for your telegram and for your prayers. Mrs. Reagan thanks you also and we both welcome you to our and now your country. We'll keep on trying to bring peace to Lebanon and the Middle East.

I met the new president of Lebanon Amin Gemayel a short time ago. He is a fine man.

Again thanks.

Sincerely,
Ronald Reagan

YOUTH

Reagan visited Purdue University in Indiana on April 9, 1987. Here he answers questions from freshmen, sophomores, and juniors printed that day in the school newspaper, the Purdue Exponent.

Editor, *Purdue Exponent*
April 28, 1987[17]

To the Editor:

I have only just received the April 9 issue of the *Purdue Exponent.* I found the questions on page seven of the six students who responded to your query as to what one question they would ask me if given the chance. I'm sorry there was no opportunity for them to ask or me to answer.

I was so warmly received on your campus and so greatly impressed by all that I saw and heard I thought the least I could do was answer those questions.

Sharon Cania asked if I thought the relationship between the United States and the Soviet Union would ever get better. I have to say Sharon I believe there is reason to believe it will. In my talk with Gorbachev in Geneva I told him our two countries didn't mistrust each other because we had weapons. We had weapons because we mistrusted each other and reduction of arms would follow if we worked to eliminate the causes of our mistrust. Today we are both talking reduction of arms and this is the first Soviet leader who has ever volunteered to destroy deployed weapons. I think there is reason to hope.

Shawn Baskett asked if I was squeamish about having my "innards" displayed on national TV. Yes Shawn I was. I realize a great deal of privacy is sacrificed when you take this job but there should be some limits. I guess what I resented most was the attempt to make the whole thing look more serious than it really was.

Mark Peters asked what could be done to stop the spread of communism in the Philippines. Well first there must be no hesitation in using force to disarm and subdue the communist bands who are using violence to impose their way on the people of the Philippines. At the same time there must be an education program to make the people realize that communism is anti-freedom and rules always by a totalitarian dictatorship. At the same time the government of the Philippines must show the people it is trying to bring about democracy and equal opportunity for all.

Tammy Gatlin asked if I thought my loss of popularity over the Iran affair will hurt the Republicans in the upcoming elections. Well Tammy not if the truth—all the truth finally comes out and is given fair treatment in the press. Very simply we were approached by Iranian representatives who claimed they wanted to establish a better relationship looking toward the day when there will be a new government in Iran. Iran is a nation of 50 million people in a most strategic position in the Middle East. Apparently those Iranians had misrepresented themselves. So we had made a mistake but it was no scandal. I hope the voters will keep in mind that by '88 the Republicans will have only had a majority in both houses of Congress for four of the last 58 years and one house, the Senate, for six years. The Democrats will have dominated both houses of Congress for 48 years and one house for an additional six.

Carol Gloyd wanted to know if I would run for a third term if the Constitution allowed it. Carol I can't really answer because I've always believed the people let you know whether you should run or not and since I've been 39 years old 38 times now they might have some hang-ups about me serving another term. I will tell you this though; I will support doing away with the 22nd Amendment for future presidents. Why should the people be denied the right to vote for anyone they want and for as many terms. The president and the vice president are the only federal officers who are elected by all the people and now they are the only ones with a limit on how many times they can serve. I think the 22nd Amendment limits the people's democratic rights.

Jerry Ryzewski wanted to know why I continue to make financial cutbacks which result in less fortunate students being unable to "go for further education." Jerry I'm afraid there has been some misunderstanding about our student aid programs. It is true we have made some changes because it was discovered that grants were going to students whose families were in income brackets above a level that would qualify them for aid. We have shifted some grants to loans and in some instances eliminated the interest subsidy. Actually the total financial support for education—federal state and local—is higher than it has ever been and 42 percent of all college students in the country are receiving some form of federal help. The changes we've made are intended to direct more aid to the neediest students and away from those less needy.

Again my thanks for a wonderful day on your campus.

Sincerely,
Ronald Reagan

———————

Scott Osborne, a high school senior, was the son of Reagan's personal secretary in the White House, Kathy Osborne. He wrote that he planned to go to college and study architecture, but "if I don't accomplish that, I'll probably end up in construction starting out as a construction superintendent and eventually work my way up to a partner in the company." Reagan offers career advice and responds to Scott's postscript, which said: "I'd just like to say one thing. If at age 18 we're old enough to vote and to fight for our country in the event of a war, we should be able to drink."

Mr. Scott Osborne
Fair Oaks, California
January 28, 1985 [18]

Dear Scott:

I have your letter and was very happy to hear from you. Your mother keeps me posted on your progress and your intention to study architecture. I think that's great but don't be surprised if you undergo a change of mind or for that matter more than one in the years ahead. I majored in economics and then wound up a sports announcer and later an actor.

I don't say this to suggest in any way your choice isn't the right one, it's just that in these next few years you'll be exposed to a number of new viewpoints and you should follow your own instincts. Architecture is a fascinating profession and a happy marriage between art and practical construction.

Scott I shouldn't do this but I have to argue with you a bit on your postscript about age 18 and the right to drink. Forgive me but voting and soldiering are different than starting in on what we have to recognize is actually a form of drug. Now don't think I'm a hypocrite, I enjoy a cocktail now and then before dinner and have a taste for a good dinner wine. I also recall feeling exactly as you do now and looking back I realize the Lord must have been watching over me. At that age (about 18) getting drunk seemed like the thing to do, the point of drinking. Then before something too awful happened (although there were a few near scrapes) I realized that I was abusing the machinery, this body, we only get one you know. But more than that I had an example to look at. My father was an alcoholic, I loved him and love him still but he died at age 58 and had suffered from heart disease for a number of years before his death. He was the victim of a habit he couldn't break.

Forgive me for playing grandpa—but think about it a little. Become an archi-

tect or if you change your mind—whatever and we'll celebrate your graduation
with a champagne toast and I'll furnish the wine.

All the best to you.

Sincerely,
Ronald Reagan

Reagan responds to high school juniors who created a budget for the government distributed as follows: education, 5 percent; trade, 2 percent; payroll, 14 percent; welfare, 14.5 percent; Social Security, 14.5 percent; and national defense, 49 percent.

Miss Michelle Paris
Rocklin, California
August 29, 1984 [19]

Dear Miss Paris:

Thank you very much for your letter and for sending me the budget you and
your fellow directors [of the budget project] created. And if you have the chance
please give my compliments and thanks to those others whose names were on the
budget.

Now I assume the budget was for the federal government. If that is true then
your 5 percent figure would be too high because while the federal government gives
some support to education, our schools get their main support from state and local
governments.

Your payroll figure recognized that payroll is one of the major costs of government. This is also true for welfare. I agree with you that we should do more to put
able-bodied recipients into useful community projects. As governor of California
we obtained permission to do this in 35 counties as an experiment. It was very successful.

You are right about Social Security. Last year we corrected some fiscal shortcomings in the program which had it facing bankruptcy. Now it is self-sustaining.
The Social Security payroll tax pays for Social Security entirely.

Now we come to national defense and I agree with your justification for why it
must be well funded. Back through our history defense normally did take about
half the budget because our national security is the primary function of the federal
government.

I'm happy to say now however our defense budget is down to less than 30 percent of the federal budget and we are rebuilding and maintaining our defenses adequately. This doesn't represent so much a reduction as an increase in recent years
of the social programs such as Social Security, welfare, etc.

Well again thanks for writing and my compliments on the job you did.

Sincerely,
Ronald Reagan

Theresa Accaso, 15 years old, attended Villa Angela Academy in Cleveland, Ohio. She sent the president a newsletter about nuclear war she had gotten at school; she was frightened. "The whole world could be completely blasted all over the universe in just a matter of minutes," she wrote. "Won't you ask for freeze talks?"

Miss Theresa Accaso
Euclid, Ohio
February 14, 1984[20]

Dear Miss Accaso:

Thank you for writing as you did and for giving me the chance to reply to the "S.T.O.P. [Student/Teacher Organization to Prevent Nuclear War] News" * and its so-called fact sheet which I found somewhat lacking in facts.

There is no question about the horror of nuclear war. I believe with all my heart that a nuclear war can never be won and must never be fought. The problem confronting us is how to prevent such a thing from ever happening. In that regard I have to point out a president of the United States has access to all the relevant facts and more information than the authors of the fact sheet can possibly have no matter how well intentioned they are.

Let me give you a fact; the Soviet Union has a definite superiority today in nuclear weapons. We have asked them to join us in negotiations to reduce the number of such weapons and I've even proposed eliminating them altogether. In the meantime we have had to modernize our own force to reduce their superiority and thus give them some reason to negotiate a reduction. It is true they proposed the nuclear freeze but that was to freeze us into a position of inferiority making it possible for them to attack with no risk to themselves.

I won't try to refute every so-called fact in the paper you sent me although I assure you I can. As an example take the first two items—that beginning in December '83 we plan to deploy hundreds of nuclear missiles in Europe and that the world will be only six minutes from nuclear war.

It is true we are going to deploy Cruise and Pershing II missiles in Europe. In 1979 (before I was president) our NATO allies asked us to do this and our government agreed. It's taken until now to have such missiles available. What the fact sheet didn't say was that the Soviets had and have about 1,300 nuclear warheads targeted on all of Western Europe, all capable of hitting the European cities in six minutes or less. The missiles we are just beginning to put in place are a deterrent to indicate that a Soviet attack could result in unacceptable damage to them also. The paper also does not show that I have invited the Soviets to join in disarmament talks to eliminate such weapons or to at least reduce the number. The Soviets so far have insisted that our NATO allies should have no missiles but they are willing to reduce their own warheads to somewhere between 800 and a thousand.

---

* Vol. III No. 2, October 1983.

Another item as an example, we are building 100 MX missiles. The paper says the Soviets will try to catch up. We are the ones trying to catch up. The Soviets have hundreds and hundreds of new missiles bigger and more powerful than the MX. We at present have nothing to match them. Again we are trying to build a deterrent.

I hope you will look farther than S.T.O.P. for information to help you arrive at a decision. In the meantime let me again say, my most cherished goal is peace and the elimination of the nuclear threat hanging over the world. I must be frank and say I am disappointed that teachers—no matter how well intentioned would resort to such one-sided tactics and impose such misinformation on students.

Thank you again and God bless you.

Sincerely,
Ronald Reagan

Matthew Solari, age 16, asked President Reagan why a moment of silence in school violates the constitutional separation of church and state.

Matthew Solari
Brigantine, New Jersey
September 21, 1984 [21]

Dear Matthew:

Thank you very much for your letter and your generous words. Thanks too for your kind words about Nancy. She was very pleased and sends you her best regards.

With regard to your question about prayer in school I'll try to explain. For 180 years there was no restriction regarding prayer. Anyone was free to pray if he or she so desired. Then a woman named O'Hair, an atheist brought a suit in behalf of her son charging that prayer in school violated the constitutional separation of church and state. The case reached the U.S. Supreme Court which handed down a ruling in her favor thus outlawing prayer in school. It's an interesting note that her son now grown up has become a Christian and disagrees with his mother.

We have been trying to get legislation to change that court decision and allow voluntary prayer in school with the local schools and communities in charge. Just recently the House of Representatives passed a bill allowing silent prayer and also permitting students in religious groups the use of classrooms for meetings after school hours the same as other clubs and organizations. This latter "equal access" bill is now law. The Senate did not pass the silent prayer bill believing we should have full right of prayer oral as well as silent.

I hope this answers your question. I agree with you, the ban on prayer in my view was a violation of our constitutional rights and we'll keep trying.

Best regards,
Ronald Reagan

Mike Pepa's family was shocked when U.S. Steel in Gary, Indiana, shut down the entire shop where Mike's father worked. Mike was 14; his sister Chrissy was 11. "The way you could help me is send my sister (or me) a letter from you. Tell her it's not so bad, you're trying to help," Mike wrote.

Mike Pepa
Crown Point, Indiana
October 20, 1982 [22]

Dear Mike:

Thank you very much for your letter. Please give my regards to your mother and father. I have a hunch they are pretty proud of their son.

I'm sorry about the shutdown and hope your father will soon be back on the job. I know from personal experience how he feels. I wish I could tell you and him there is an instant cure for what ails our country. I can't do that, of course, but I do think we are seeing the beginning of an upturn. Things are going to get better.

Please tell Chrissy that. Tell her also that a lot of the gloomy talk on the TV news is just that—talk. When I see and hear them I get angry many times myself knowing how little they really know about what's going on.

Thank you again and God bless all of you.

Sincerely,
Ronald Reagan

Reagan responds to a number of questions from a 14-year-old boy whose father, Major James H. Schaefer Jr., was one of the eight men burned in the failed rescue attempt to free the hostages in the U.S. embassy in Tehran, Iran, on April 24–25, 1980.

Mr. Mike Schaefer
Quantico, Virginia
January 11, 1982 [23]

Dear Mike:

You didn't take up my time and I'm glad you wrote. You must be very proud of your father and you have every right to be. And I'll keep on trying to rebuild our defensive strength to what it should be.

You asked about Air Force One. It really is a great plane equipped for comfort on flights of any length and manned by a magnificent crew.

With regard to Iran I have always felt we could have done more to prevent the revolution there and that the hostage matter was badly handled. We should have brought our people home when the revolution took place without waiting for them to be taken hostage.

I am in full support of the space shuttle and feel we must continue our exploration of outer space.

Again thanks for writing and best regards,

Ronald Reagan

Cyndi Davis wrote to question expenditures on space programs.

Cyndi Davis
During governorship[24]

Dear Cyndi:

Thanks for letting me comment regarding the space program and its value to our country and to mankind.

Many special-interest groups have been attacking our exploration of space on the basis of how much could be done to provide needed social welfare reforms with that money. Sometimes it makes me wonder if this isn't the same kind of opposition Columbus ran into when he was trying to raise money for the exploration that led to the discovery of America. Man's great yearning to explore the unknown should not be curbed because he can't tell in detail all he hopes to find.

No one denies that we should do all we can to correct the causes of human misery. It isn't necessarily true, however, that spending more money will accomplish that end. Our proposal to reform welfare was made because the money presently going to welfare is being inefficiently used and is not serving the people it is supposed to help.

Remember too the money for the space program isn't spent on the moon. It pays the wages of tens of thousands of people all over the United States who make the equipment. If the space program were cancelled, these people would be unemployed and in need of welfare.

Just one last point—look how many people are better off, how much better the world is because of the voyage of Columbus. Can we say for sure that exploring space may not create such great benefits for mankind?

I hope this helps you in your thinking on this subject.

Best regards,
Ronald Reagan

Reagan replies to a thank-you note he received after speaking to a Stanford University journalism class.

Miss Smith
Pre-presidential[25]

Dear Miss Smith:

You were very kind to take the time and trouble to write as you did and I'm most grateful. It might interest you to know that you are the first student of all the journalism classes I've met with who ever wrote such a letter. Please know that you brightened my day considerably. I've always had an optimistic outlook and you've made it easier to continue that way.

These are apt to be hectic and confusing times, particularly for young people. You are constantly beset by voices demanding an end to any and all established values, not necessarily because something better is at hand, but simply because the old should be replaced by something. If you'll forgive my rewarding you for your kindness with some unsolicited (and probably unnecessary) advice—search for the truth always—see if there is another side to every issue.

Again, thanks. I hope our paths cross again in the near future.

Sincerely,
Ronald Reagan

Reagan answers a question from a young man on how to lead a happy life.

Brad Rumble
Circa 1980[26]

Dear Brad:

Thank you very much for your kind letter and good wishes. I am deeply grateful.

Your question is a broad one, and almost a frightening one, but I'll try to answer. An important factor in a happy life is to choose an occupation you enjoy. Don't be upset if right now you can't decide what you'd like to do to earn a living. I couldn't make up my mind on that until after I had graduated from college—yet things turned out all right.

Someone once said; "Life begins when you begin to serve." I have put it in a different way, namely that we should all pay for the good things that life brings us. By this I mean be willing to lend a hand in civic, charitable or other causes that make our society better. If you look around you'll see adults who are willing to serve on hospital boards, help in charity drives, serve in their church, or in political party work.

Having mentioned church let me add my own deeply held belief that true success and happiness—especially happiness—can only come from letting God be a part of your life.

Start thinking now, (and don't be in a hurry), about the lines of work that might reward you with work you'd enjoy and begin participating in extracurricular activities in school, church, club or what have you. Find those things that give you a feeling of purpose and usefulness.

I'm sure there are better answers to your question but this is the best I can do.

Again thanks for writing and best regards,

Ronald Reagan

Reagan responds to a request from a writer putting together a book on how people have overcome setbacks and tragedies in early life. He recalls early events in his own life that seemed tragic at the time but turned out not to be so.

> Miss Elena Kellner
> Los Angeles, California
> July 20, 1979 [27]

Dear Miss Kellner:

Thank you very much for your letter and for wanting to include me in your book.

There have been major setbacks of the kind you described in my life, moments of tragedy, and yet, I don't know that I have an experience that would fit the pattern that you have described in your question. Let me explain. I guess my mother gave me a greater faith than I knew but I have realized it as the years have gone on. I was taught from the very beginning and accepted the idea that when all else fails, you then turn to God and put it in his hands. In connection with that faith, she also convinced me that when things happen that we can't understand or that seem as terrible setbacks, we must try to believe that everything happens for a reason and for the best and if we simply deal with it and trust in God, there will come a time when we will understand why that particular thing happened, and we will discover that because of it, something better resulted.

Let me give one example that was not a great tragedy but, at my particular age and at that particular time seemed so: I got out of college in the depths of the Depression in 1932. The government was putting announcements on the radio urging people not to leave home looking for work because there was none. I had decided that I wanted to get into radio, and I had decided that what I wanted to be in radio was a sports announcer. I didn't listen to the government announcements. I went hitchhiking around the Midwest simply asking at radio stations for a job, a job of any kind so that I could get in the studio and then would take my chances with working up to sports announcer. Finally, after weeks of this, I hitchhiked my way home, arriving in a downpour of rain.

My mother told me that a new Montgomery Ward store had opened in our small home town and was looking for someone known to the people in town for having had athletic experience to manage the sporting goods department.

This wasn't radio, of course, or sports announcing. But remember, it was 1932 and it was a job. Wet and bedraggled as I was, I went right down and was interviewed for the manager. I must have looked like a bum, and I realized I wasn't going over very well. The next day I found that a local high school athlete of more recent vintage had been given the job. It was a very low moment, but again, that faith that my mother had given me was sustaining.

The next day, I hitchhiked out again, 75 miles in the opposite direction, where there was another radio station, walked in, stated my case and was told they had just hired a young man to break in as an announcer the day before.

This was a little too much for me, and on the way out the door, I mumbled, "how does a guy ever get to be a sports announcer if he can't get a job in a radio station?" I reached the elevator. But before it arrived at that floor, the program director I'd been talking to, a wonderful old Scotsman, crippled with arthritis hobbling on canes, caught up with me, and said, "what is that you said about being a sports announcer?" And I told him of my ambition. He asked me if I knew anything about football. Well, I'd played the game for eight years—through high school and college. The upshot of it was I was given a tryout. I broadcast a Big Ten football game for the station and that began my career in radio. As you can see, I look back on that Montgomery Ward job and understand very well why I didn't get it. But down through the years, there have been other moments, some of tragedy.

There were only four in our family—my mother and father, my brother and I. My brother and I had never known grandparents. All of them had died before we were born, so you can imagine when my father died of a heart attack, it literally was the first experience with death for any of us. It was a very traumatic experience. But again, I have to say that faith that I mentioned was there. And all through my life, when those moments have come, when I've felt as if I have gone my limit and can do no more, I have turned and asked God to help. And somehow, he always has.

I don't know if this can be of any help to you. But it's the best I can do with regard to your questions. Again, it was good to hear from you and thanks for asking.

Best regards.

Sincerely,
Ronald Reagan

HUMOR

Reagan used humor for many purposes and it suffused much of his writing. In a few of these letters Reagan tells a story with a set punch line, but most often his humor pops up when least expected—as a comment on some aspect of his job or a perspective on what he is doing—just as his spontaneous one-liners suffused his personal conversation.

In the first letter Reagan uses humor to enliven an otherwise routine apology.

Reverend Doyle Daugherty
Commack, New York
March 11, 1982[28]

Dear Reverend Daugherty:

I've just received a news clipping regarding the campaign solicitation you received addressed to Mr. God. I thought perhaps I should offer an explanation to you. I've already spoken to God about it.

I hope both He and you will understand that while the letter bore my signature such letters are the product of a computer. The Senate campaign committee has permission to use my name in its fundraising so I hadn't seen or known of this letter until the clipping arrived.

Reverend Daugherty I've asked God for a great many things—particularly since getting this job—but never for a campaign contribution. Maybe I'll ask for help in correcting a greedy computer. At least the computer has raised its sights considerably; the only other experience of this kind was hearing from a lady whose prize show horse had received such a letter.

I've already asked God's pardon, I hope I have yours.

Sincerely,
Ronald Reagan

Snoopy, a character in the long-running comic strip Peanuts, *decided to run for president. Reagan replies to the author of the comic strip. Skipper was an early nickname for Reagan's son Ron.*

Mr. Charles M. Schulz
August 11, 1980 [29]

Dear Charles:

How good it was to hear from you after much too long a time. The new candidate in the race will certainly keep me from being overconfident. If I'd only known of his political ambitions, I might have persuaded him to run on the ticket with me as vice president.

The little cartoon strip I've enclosed belongs to our housekeeper, Anne. And she has prevailed upon me to ask if you would autograph it for her. She has kept it all these years—30 of them.

One of these days, with all the traveling we are doing, I hope that our paths will cross again. It's been too long.

Nancy sends her best, as do I. Skipper, who now insists he has outgrown that name, is in New York, but I know he'll be pleased to know you remembered him.

Anything you can do to talk Snoopy out of running will be appreciated. How would he feel about a cabinet post?

Best regards.

Sincerely,
Ron

William Freeman wrote to complain about irresponsible government spending. He described himself as a working man.

Mr. William J. Freeman
Norfolk, Virginia
April 5, 1982 [30]

Dear Mr. Freeman:

Thank you for your letter of February 10. I'm sorry to be so late in answering. You were kind to write as you did and I'm grateful.

You are correct in your description of what happens in Washington when you try to shut off the government money machine. It's a little like getting between the hog and the bucket.

Let me reassure you however about our friends on Taiwan. We will not desert them and have taken steps to rectify some of what was done in 1979.

Again thanks and best regards.

Sincerely,
Ronald Reagan

Reagan advises the son of a friend on marriage.

Mr. M. Scott Ayres
Roanoke, Virginia
June 6, 1983 [31]

Dear Scott:

Your father told me of your coming marriage. I hope you won't mind my offering congratulations. Your father has been more than kind in his helpfulness to me. Thanks to him I'm still able to get in the saddle in these times when I can't get to our ranch.

I wish you a lifetime of happiness and can assure you marriage is the best way to achieve that. Thomas Jefferson said, "Happiness in the married state is a blessing to be desired above all others." Now I didn't hear Jefferson say that but I know he's right. Ignore all the cynical jokes about marriage, a man can't be complete without it. It's worth working at and the more you work at it the more happiness you'll have.

Congratulations and best wishes.

Sincerely,
Ronald Reagan

Judy Cassell sent Reagan a puppet that talked when its strings were pulled—to use, she said, "when you don't want to be quoted." Helene von Damm, Reagan's former per-

sonal secretary, was working in the White House Office of Presidential Personnel and would become ambassador to Austria on June 22, 1983.

Judy Cassell
Eugene, Oregon
March 15, 1983 [32]

Dear Judy:

Thank you very much for my puppet—we have become fast friends. I'm trying to teach it to take over a press conference for me.

I'll give Helene your message and may I say I share your high opinion of her.

Again my thanks to you and best regards.

Sincerely,
Ronald Reagan

Reagan writes to the author of the Dick Tracy *comic strip.*

Mr. Chester Gould
October 16, 1981 [33]

Dear Mr. Gould:

Thank you very much for my "original Dick Tracy" cartoon. Thank you more however for your words (via Dick) of encouragement. They mean a great deal to me when there are so many Monday morning quarterbacks sounding off on Friday night.

You should know that Dick Tracy and I are old friends. I am a comic strip reader from way back and still consider it a major crisis if I have to start a day without them. I rarely do.

Again my heartfelt thanks. I won't weaken any more than Dick would turn crooked.

Best regards,
Ronald Reagan

On one occasion Reagan had some fun with his presidential powers. While he was at a luncheon at James Kilpatrick's country home on May 31, 1981, the White House signal operators, who were always with the president, tried to reach Kilpatrick's son Christopher, serving in the Navy on the USS Pratt. *When Reagan found out only the president could make such a call, he made it, and Christopher, who had been at sea for 40 days, was able to talk to his wife, who was at the luncheon. Christopher wrote to thank the president: "The dust has not quite settled from last night's radio call . . . No one knew who "White House" was and why they might call* Pratt. *In seconds the light dawned . . . It was as if God called the Vatican and only wanted to speak with a particular altar boy."*

> QM2 Christopher Kilpatrick
> At sea on the USS *William V. Pratt*
> July 9, 1981 [34]

Dear Christopher:

I've received your letter, thanks to your father, and want you to know how much I enjoyed it, although I am a little worried about possibly upsetting Navy routine.

Maybe your father has explained how the call came about but in case he hasn't let me do so. It seems our signal operators, who are as close at hand as the Secret Service, boasted to your father that they could reach anyone in the world almost instantly. When he told them to try you they came up empty because you were at sea. One of them then said only the president could make that call.

Nancy and I had met your very charming wife and I just decided if I could make that call then the call would be made. Frankly it was more fun than I usually have in this job. Anyway I'm glad you two were able to talk to each other.

Please tell your shipmates how grateful we here at home are for all that you are doing in our behalf. We're proud of all of you and I assure you your parents and your wife are proud of you.

Again thanks for your letter and very best regards—

> Ronald Reagan

George Eccles was a Salt Lake City banker; his brother, Marriner, chaired the Federal Reserve from 1936 to 1948. George Eccles died in 1982.

> Mr. and Mrs. George Eccles
> Salt Lake City, Utah
> November 28, 1981 [35]

Dear George and Lolie:

I learned from Doug about the unfortunate illness that kept you from making the China trip. I'm truly sorry and hope there will be another opportunity. Above all I hope that you are recovered and feeling fit—that's more important than any trip.

I'm sitting here waiting out the long afternoon 'til 5 p.m. when the Senate votes on the AWACS sale to Saudi Arabia. At the moment the count looks about even. One undecided senator told me he was going to pray for guidance. I told him if he got a busy signal it was me in there ahead of him with my own prayer.

Well again I hope and yes pray that you are once again enjoying good health.

> Best regards,
> Ron

Ralph Tipton, an Illinois manufacturer, met Reagan when he was a sports announcer in Des Moines, Iowa. The Moonlight Inn, later closed, was a bar in Des Moines. Raymond Moley was an FDR brain-truster.

Mr. Ralph M. Tipton
Downers Grove, Illinois
December 10, 1984 [36]

Dear Ralph:

Thanks for sending the newspaper story, I enjoyed seeing the happy family. Jonathan looks like quite a fellow. Do you suppose he'll turn out better for not having experienced a "Moonlight Sun"?

Thanks too for all your help in the campaign. If we need an alibi for Minnesota try this one. When Kefauver beat Adlai Stevenson in the Minnesota primary, Raymond Moley, when asked to explain it by the press said; "Have you ever tried to tell a joke in Minneapolis?"

By the way I've got you topped on that 1973 klunker. I'm driving a 1963 Jeep at the ranch and a 1953 Ford tractor. Fun isn't it? Well thanks again and have fun.

Best regards,
Dutch

LeRoy Prinz was a Hollywood choreographer. Every Day's a Holiday *and* St. Louis Blues, *filmed during the late 1930s, are among his credits. He died September 15, 1983.*

Mr. LeRoy Prinz
Los Angeles, California
August 11, 1983 [37]

Dear LeRoy:

Your daughter, Lee Barker, wrote me about your illness. LeRoy, you can't do this to me. I was counting on you to teach me how to do a timestep. All those years at Warner Brothers and I never learned.

Of course in the job I have now maybe I should learn a highkick. There are plenty of targets back here I could practice on.

Seriously old friend, you'll be in our thoughts and prayers. Take care of yourself. Nancy sends her very best regards as do I.

Sincerely,
Ron

Reagan didn't tell his favorite jokes to television audiences because he thought too many people would hear them for him to be able to use them again. Here he writes down a few he used frequently with smaller groups.

Barney Oldfield often sent Reagan jokes and humorous stories; Reagan some-
times used them at the beginning of daily staff meetings. Reagan wrote the first letter
here shortly before the Reagan-Gorbachev summit in Reykjavik, Iceland, on October
11–12, 1986.

Colonel Barney Oldfield
Beverly Hills, California
October 6, 1986 [38]

Dear Barney:

I haven't been there yet, but just having finished *Red Storm Rising* by the author
of *Red October*. I think I know every square foot of Iceland. If you haven't read it, it's
worth the effort.

Here's my latest from the Soviet Union to reward you for the stories. It's night-
time, a soldier calls to a citizen walking by and orders him to halt. The citizen starts
running, the soldier shoots him. Another citizen asked the soldier why he did that.
The soldier replies—"curfew." "But it isn't curfew time yet," the citizen says. "I
know," said the soldier, "but he's a friend of mine. I know where he lives. He
couldn't have made it." I'm assured this is a story the Russians are telling each other.

Thanks again and best to your lady.

Ron

Colonel Barney Oldfield
Beverly Hills, California
April 26, 1988 [39]

Dear Barney:

Thanks for the two new jokes, I'll be telling them almost immediately. I may
not tell them to Gorbachev but then he's probably heard them.

He does have a sense of humor though. I told him two guaranteed Russian
jokes and got two belly laughs in return. One had to do with the American telling
the Russian he can go into the Oval Office, pound the president's desk and say: "Mr.
President, I don't like the way you are running our country." The Russian replies: "I
can do that." American: "You can?" Russian: "I can walk into the General Secretary's
office, pound the desk, and say: "Mr. General Secretary, I don't like the way President Reagan's running his country." Have you heard that one?

The other one needs hearing. I'll save it and tell you the next time we see each
other.

Again, thanks, and best regards.

Sincerely,
Ron

Reagan and William F. Buckley had a long-running joke that Buckley was serving as
the ambassador to Afghanistan during the Reagan administration. "I am willing to

accept reappointment as your secret emissary to Afghanistan," Buckley wrote after Reagan was reelected in 1984.

> Mr. William F. Buckley Jr.
> New York, New York
> December 10, 1984 [40]

Dear Bill:

Of course you'll continue in Kabul, your sentence has four more years to run and no time off for bad behavior. I appreciate your kind words about my letter but I don't know Latin—that was just my poor writing and a certain weakness in spelling. Do you suppose that's how Latin got started in the first place?

I was glad to get your input on Van [Galbraith]. Some of our gang thought he wanted a return to private life. Actually we haven't gotten into either of those posts yet. I'm scheduled to meet with Jeane in the coming week.* So far we've been living and dreaming budget cuts and tax reform. In addition to that we've just been given a 10-week-old pup. It's an unbroken (house wise) sheep dog. May I say that while she's cute as a Cabbage Patch doll she adds an unexpected complication to White House living. How do you teach a puppy to scratch an elevator when she wants out?

Nancy sends her love and to Pat from both of us.

> Sincerely,
> Ron

The Werblins sent the President a book called The Compleat Horse *for his birthday. David "Sonny" Werblin was chief executive officer of the Madison Square Garden Corporation and one-time owner of the New York Jets.*

> Mr. and Mrs. David A. Werblin
> New York, New York
> February 19, 1987 [41]

Dear Leah Ray and Sonny:

You made my day with your birthday wishes and that magnificent book. I have not cooled off on horses at all even though in my present job I spend too much time with only a part of the horse. But then I take off for the ranch and there is an entire horse waiting to be ridden. Bless you both and thank you. Nancy sends her love.

> Sincerely,
> Ron

---

* Jeane Kirkpatrick was serving as ambassador to the United Nations; Buckley recommended Evan Griffith Galbraith as her sucessor. Reagan appointed Vernon Walters.

Reagan writes to Theodore Hild, who was managing the Illinois survey of historical sites for the state's Department of Conservation. Reagan was born in an apartment on the second floor of 111 S. Main Street, Tampico, Illinois. The first floor may have housed a bakery at the time rather than a bank.

> Mr. Theodore Hild
> Springfield, Illinois
> May 1973 [42]

Dear Mr. Hild:

Thanks very much for the photos—I'm delighted to have them.

Perhaps my birthplace will be harmful to the Republican image though. For Lincoln it was a log cabin and here I am born over a bank.

Thanks again.

> Sincerely,
> Ronald Reagan

Joan Roll was a movie fan of Reagan's. She began writing to him in 1948. Many replies, although signed "Ronald" or "Ronnie," were written by Reagan's mother or Neil Reagan's wife, Bess. But Nelle's mental faculties failed in the late 1950s, and here Reagan takes up his own pen to thank Roll for a Westinghouse radio entertainment system she had gotten at a bargain price while working there. Reagan was travelling for General Electric and hosting the television program GE Theater at the time, and his home was a showcase for GE products.

> Miss Joan Roll
> Pittsburgh, Pennsylvania
> December 31, 1956 [43]

Dear Joan:

Just a line to thank you for your very handsome Xmas gift (even if it is Westinghouse). You really shouldn't have done it but even so Nancy and I are very grateful and have a place all picked out for it. We won't let GE know but we are already enjoying it.

Again our thanks and very best wishes for a Happy New Year.

> Ronnie

Reagan comments with some chagrin on the education crisis (see Chapter 6) that confronted him when he took office as governor of California in these two letters to Repub-

lican governors also elected in 1966. Spiro T. Agnew later served as Richard Nixon's first vice president but resigned in disgrace.

Governor Spiro T. Agnew
Baltimore, Maryland
January 1967 [44]

Dear Ted:

I guess we are both discovering a new world about now. It will be good to see you again and compare notes.

Having been hung in effigy five times already I'm beginning to feel experienced.

Best regards,
Ron

———

New Mexico's governor wrote humorously to Governor Reagan for economic help: "Now do me a favor—send me a factory—preferably a large one."

Governor David F. Cargo
Sante Fe, New Mexico
April 1967 [45]

Dear Dave:

Would you settle for some demonstrators—large and unkempt?

Ron

———

Whenever Governor Reagan left the state of California, his lieutenant governor became acting governor, able to sign and veto bills. Reagan would send the lieutenant governor a form letter with the dates of his departure and return. Only the signature "Ron" and the postscript, which was different each time, were handwritten.

The Honorable Robert Finch
Lieutenant Governor
State Capitol
Sacramento, California [46]

Dear Bob:

This is to notify you that I plan to be absent from the State beginning at —— on ——, returning —— at ——.

Section 10 of Article V of the Constitution provides that the powers and duties of this office devolve upon the Lieutenant Governor during the Governor's absence.

I want to assure you that my office and staff are at your service during my absence.

Sincerely,
Ron
RONALD REAGAN
Governor

February 10, 1967
P.S. Solve something—<u>anything</u>

April 26, 1967
P.S. I've changed my mind—<u>don't</u> let anything happen.

June 20, 1967
P.S. Remember to put the date on all the bills you sign—it saves the girls from having to put them back in the typewriter. The savings on "ribbons" is incalculable.

November 1, 1967
P.S. In case of trouble you'll be right on the border and I recommend crossing it.

October 24, 1967
P.S. Home two days and found the pace too quiet—try to stir things up a bit and I'll come home.

November 28, 1967
P.S. You've been on a boatride—you should know the ride I've been getting! Anyway I'm going down to "Mory's" (the place where Louis dwells) and find out how Frank Merriwell did it.

January 15, 1968
P.S. This isn't a duplicate—it just means I'm spoiling your peace of mind for part of Saturday.

January 26, 1968
P.S. Solve everything by noon.

January 26, 1968
P.S. Just in case you didn't get everything done by noon.

May 10, 1968
P.S. You get to stay in gay mad Sacramento and I have to sweat out four days in Honolulu.

May 17, 1968
P.S. I'll try to drop in again soon if you'll promise to have everything cleaned up.

June 12, 1968
P.S. This is what I dig—running over to Tulsa when things are slow.

July 17, 1968
P.S. Veto anything that costs more than $2.

September 17, 1968
P.S. As you've no doubt heard there is a campaign for something or other going on.

CHAPTER TWENTY-TWO

American Leaders

THE CORRESPONDENCE *between Ronald Reagan and some of America's leading political figures is much more cautious and routine than Reagan's letters to family,
friends, constituents, and pen pals, yet it speaks volumes about the evolution of his political career. Reagan sought President Dwight D. Eisenhower's advice during his 1966
gubernatorial campaign, but was endorsed by the 34th president only after he secured
the Republican primary. During his presidency, Reagan would reply favorably to President Gerald R. Ford's suggestions regarding appointments to his administration. The
most interesting Reagan letters related to Ford were written to others in the late 1970s.
In these letters, Reagan negatively assesses Ford's performance as president as well as his
aspirations to return to office. Letters to Senator Barry Goldwater and Secretary of State
Henry Kissinger are friendly but cautious. Goldwater unwittingly launched Reagan's
political career; Reagan called for the firing of Kissinger in his 1976 presidential bid.*[1]

*There is a substantial body of correspondence between Reagan and President
Richard M. Nixon. It, too, is cautious but friendly. The correspondence found in the
National Archives begins in 1959; letters in the files of the Nixon Library, the Reagan
Library, and Reagan's post-presidency office continue until a few months before
Nixon's death on April 22, 1994. The letters show Vice President Nixon taking notice in
1959 of his fellow Californian's oratorical skills and public appeal as a spokesman for
General Electric. Reagan in turn supported Nixon's presidential bid in 1960. Four
years after Nixon failed to become governor of California, he supported Reagan's gubernatorial bid. Relations were strained during Reagan's brief "favorite son" campaign
to become the Republican Party's nominee for president in 1968. Nixon won the nomination and the presidential election and was supported by Reagan during some of his
darkest days in the White House. President Nixon provided advice about strategy during Reagan's 1980 campaign and throughout Reagan's presidency. President-elect Reagan sent artful and brief responses. In correspondence after Reagan left Washington,
the two men wrote primarily about home and family, but they also continued to discuss the major foreign policy issues facing the United States.*

It has been said that relations between Reagan and President George H. W.

Bush were very cool when the baton was passed in January 1989. The letters do not erase this impression, but they do show a kind and friendly correspondence during and after President Bush's White House years.

Barry Goldwater

As Reagan reached the halfway point in his first term as president, Senator Goldwater offered to help with the upcoming reelection campaign.

Senator Barry Goldwater
Washington, D.C.
January 17, 1983[2]

Dear Barry:

Lyn* has told me of your letter to him and your offer of help if signals are "go" for '84. Also your belief that I should.

While this isn't the time to make such a decision I want you to know you've made me very proud and I'm truly grateful.

Nancy sends her love. Again thanks.

Ron

Three days after Vice President George Bush defeated Governor Michael Dukakis in the presidential race, Senator Barry Goldwater wrote President Reagan and said: "I just wanted you to know . . . that I have appreciated your Presidency, I think you have done one hell of a good job. You started the country on a new route, one it should not have deviated from in the first place. I hope, during the course of time, that we might have the pleasure of seeing each other, together with your wonderful Nancy. In the meantime, just know you have the undying thanks of this old American, and you always will." President Reagan sends a note of appreciation to the senator.

Senator Barry Goldwater
Scottsdale, Arizona
November 21, 1988[3]

Dear Barry:

Just received your nice letter and I thank you for your generous words. They mean a lot to me.

As you can imagine I'm looking at January 20 with mixed emotions. There is of course anticipation about getting back to California and the ranch but then some regret because of things we didn't get done here.

I hope our paths will cross and Nancy joins me in this. She sends her love and from both of us warmest regard.

Again thanks—

Sincerely,
Ron

---

* Franklin (Lyn) Nofziger was special assistant for public affairs to President Reagan in 1981–82.

Lady Bird Johnson

The wife of the 36th president of the United States sent President and Mrs. Reagan a thank-you note for the 1985 holiday card they had sent her: "I am thinking . . . of the responsibilities you bear for your country, and I want you to know, I am among the many Americans who wish you Godspeed in all you do." President Reagan sends a cordial reply.

Mrs. Lyndon B. Johnson
Stonewall, Texas
January 27, 1986[4]

Dear Lady Bird:

Thank you for your kind letter and generous words. Nancy and I were both touched by your letter and we both are grateful for your prayers and good wishes. You will be in our prayers as well.

Again our thanks and best wishes.

Sincerely,
Ronald Reagan

Thomas H. Kean

In addition to writing to foreign leaders, former U.S. presidents, and members of Congress, President Reagan corresponded with other American leaders such as state governors. This letter is a reply to the governor of New Jersey, whom Reagan mentioned in his State of the Union address on January 25, 1988. In the speech, Reagan spoke about the governor's commitment to education.

The Honorable Thomas H. Kean
Trenton, New Jersey
February 1, 1988[5]

Dear Tom:

Thank you for your kind words about my speech. I meant what I said about you because you have done and are doing a great job. You have turned your state around and made it a shining example of fine government.

Best regards.

Ron

P.S. Just as I was preparing to sign this note, I learned of your mother's passing. Nancy joins me in sending you deepest sympathy on your loss.

Henry A. Kissinger

In a letter to Henry Kissinger, then the assistant to the president for national security affairs, Governor Reagan argues that awarding a government contract to produce

F-5 fighter aircraft to Northrop, a California-based company, would help California's economy. In making the suggestion, he admits that he is changing his tune about the B-1 bomber, which is still a few years away from production. In November 1970, Northrop beat out Lockheed Aircraft Corporation, LTV Aerospace Corporation, and McDonnell Douglas Corporation for a billion-dollar contract to make fighter jets that the United States would provide to Southeast Asian allies.[6]

> Dr. Henry A. Kissinger
> Washington, D.C.
> Circa 1970[7]

Dear Henry:

I appreciate your calling and understand why (at last) direct contact was inadvisable.

With regard to the "Fighter" contract let me reiterate the points about its importance to California. This has been the main production for Northrop and is the building block upon which they are able to stay in business for such subcontracting as frames for other aircraft.

Without this "building block" <u>seven plants</u> in the Los Angeles–Long Beach area will close. These plants incidentally have some of the highest ratios of minority employment in all of California industry. Aerospace is about 35 percent of the state's manufacturing and our unemployment is already far above the national average.

I do not believe this is the problem with LTV. Because of the A-7 program they are not faced with layoff problems or plant closings.

Now lest you think I'm greedy—had I known there was a question about the Northrop plane when I urged the B-1 my tune might have been different. Actually to get B-1 and lose this would result in a net loss of employment in the industry here.

I stress these factors because I've been told the quality of the planes is no longer an issue. If so then I must repeat the socioeconomic elements (and for that matter the political) weigh heavily in California's favor.

The whole of southern California will be affected by this and I have to say far more than the B-1, because the employment will be affected immediately whereas the B-1 production is a couple of years in the future. Nevertheless the B-1 announcement was heavy print and headlines all over the state.

Please don't think I'm overboard on this—it isn't really that important—but I have a yellow monk's robe and a can of gasoline it if doesn't go through.* Do you think the Lincoln Memorial would be a good place for a BBQ?

> Best regards,
> Ron

---

* Reagan is referring to the fact that some monks engaged in self-immolation as a protest against the Vietnam War.

Governor Ronald Reagan sends a copy of a famous speech by General George S. Patton Jr. to National Security Advisor Henry Kissinger. Patton delivered the message to the U.S. Third Army on June 5, 1944, before the units landed in Normandy.

Dr. Henry A. Kissinger
San Clemente, California
July 28, 1970[8]

Dear Henry:

It was good seeing you last night—my mind is busy but my lips are sealed.

Enclosed is the Patton speech made to his Third Army before it left England to cross the channel. The scene has been described to me as the thousands of men [were] seated on a hillside.

Best regards,
Ronald Reagan

This letter is from a collection of undated correspondence from the 1970s in Reagan's private papers. It could have been written after Henry Kissinger's July 31, 1979, U.S. Senate Foreign Relations Committee testimony on the second strategic arms control treaty (SALT II), signed by President Jimmy Carter and Soviet General Secretary Leonid Brezhnev on June 18, 1979. In that testimony, the former secretary of state suggested that Senate support for the treaty be tied to substantial increases in military spending. Reagan took a harsher stand, arguing that the Senate should not ratify the treaty on the grounds that it "is not a strategic limitation. It is a strategic buildup." He thanks Kissinger for sending him the critique of SALT II.[9]

Dr. Henry A. Kissinger
Washington, D.C.
After July 31, 1979[10]

Dear Henry:

Thanks so very much for sending me your critique on SALT II. As usual it's brilliant and most helpful.

It was fun being with you the other night and I'm getting laughs with one or two of your lines—but I give you credit for them.

Nancy sends her best and we both send regards to your Nancy.

Again thanks.

Sincerely,
Ron

During the first month of his candidacy for the 1980 Republican presidential nomination, Reagan states that he considers Henry Kissinger a casual friend but would not have him serve as an adviser during his campaign.

Dr. W. C. Huyler
After November 13, 1979[11]

Dear Dr. Huyler:

Thank you very much for your letter and for giving me the opportunity to comment. I know Henry Kissinger, of course. While he was a White House adviser, I was briefed by him four times on occasions when the president asked me to represent him on trips abroad—three times to Asia and once to seven countries in Europe. On all of these trips, I met with the heads of state of the various countries.

I would describe my relationship with Henry as that of a casual friend, but I can assure you I would not choose him as an adviser, and I have been critical of his performance as secretary of state. Apparently, the press, or at least some element of it, in looking around for new stories, has speculated or suggested that he might be advising me on foreign policy. This is absolutely not true. I have a number of well-known and very capable people, some connected with the Hoover Institution at Stanford, who are helping in the field of foreign policy. Henry Kissinger is not one of them, nor will he be.

Again, thanks and please give my regards to Mrs. Huyler. I appreciate your continued support.

Sincerely,
Ronald Reagan

PRESIDENTS

Dwight D. Eisenhower

Three days after Ronald Reagan defeated George Christopher, a former mayor of San Francisco, in the competition to be the Republican nominee in California's gubernatorial race, he writes President Dwight D. Eisenhower to thank him for his campaign advice. On June 15, 1966, the 34th president officially endorsed Reagan and said that if Reagan won, "you can bet" he would become a possible Republican presidential contender.[12]

President Dwight D. Eisenhower
Gettysburg, Pennsylvania
June 10, 1966[13]

Dear Mr. President:

Now that the shouting has died (at least for a while) I want to thank you for your invaluable advice and suggestions. I realize of course this was offered within the framework of neutrality and was born of your great interest in and devotion to the cause of Republicanism.

Nevertheless my TV appearances profited by a reduction in verbiage and the resulting slower pace drew some appreciative comments. Thanks to you the creative society was described more understandably as a "do things" society.*

Most of all however I'm deeply grateful for your willingness to share your time, thoughts and philosophy with me.

I know you'll be happy to learn that party unity in California is becoming a reality. Pledges of support are coming in from campaign workers and chairmen in the Christopher camp.

Nancy joins me in thanks and best wishes and we both hope you'll give our regards to that member of your family who did hint she wasn't completely neutral—we love her.

Again thanks and best regards.

Sincerely,
Ronald

Gubernatorial candidate Ronald Reagan writes that he and President Eisenhower are in agreement that hyphenating names based on cultural heritage divides Americans. He suggests the Republican Party encourage Americans to abandon this practice.

General Dwight D. Eisenhower
Gettysburg, Pennsylvania
July 22, 1966 [14]

Dear General:

Nancy and I and the children are beachcombers (now only two days left). We've been soaking up sand, seawater and sun for two weeks now. The rest has been wonderful but there is a strong temptation to forget I'm due back on the campaign trail.

Freeman* called and read your letter to me with the very sound advice and suggestions—some of which are already being put into action. I am in complete agreement about dropping the hyphens that presently divide us into minority

---

* During his campaign against George Christopher, Reagan gave his "Creative Society" speech at the University of Southern California on April 19, 1966. In that speech, he discussed at length his rejection of Lyndon Johnson's Great Society, and explained his alternative. "[T]he basis of the Creative Society," he declared, was the "government no longer substituting for the people, but recognizing that it cannot possibly match the great potential of the people, and thus, must coordinate the creative energies of the people for the good of the whole. . . . This means the Creative Society must return authority to the local communities—give them the right to run their own affairs. The people in San Francisco know better than anyone in Sacramento where a freeway in San Francisco should go." Speech found at the Ronald Reagan Presidential Library, Simi Valley, California.

* There are several letters at the Dwight D. Eisenhower Library between Freeman F. Gosden and President Dwight D. Eisenhower during Reagan's gubernatorial campaign. Gosden, the former co-creator and co-star in the radio serial "Amos n' Andy," assessed support for Reagan throughout California.

groups. I'm convinced this "hyphenating" was done by our opponents to create voting blocks for political expediency. Our party should strive to change this— one is not an Irish-American for example but is instead an American of Irish descent.

Once again I'm indebted to you for giving me the benefit of your thinking and experience.

Nancy sends greetings and please give our regards to Mrs. Eisenhower.

Again thanks—

Sincerely,
Ronald

Reagan writes that Republicans are providing Edmund "Pat" Brown, his Democratic Party challenger and the incumbent governor, with ammunition against him.

President and Mrs. Eisenhower
Gettysburg, Pennsylvania
Before November 1, 1966 [15]

Dear President and Mrs. Eisenhower:

The weekend is over and the peaceful ease of El Dorado seems very far away tonight. As a matter of fact I'm not sure we can ever afford to remember it as we return to active combat on the political front.

Governor Brown has just appeared on TV assailing Republicans in general and me in particular. Unfortunately his ammunition was provided by Republicans and one wonders if we'll ever learn.

Nancy and I enjoyed being with you both so very much and it goes without saying the golf match was for me a memorable occasion. You may have been concerned with some golf shots that went off course but you hit home with some sound philosophy I'll long remember.

Freeman relayed your thoughts and suggestions by way of Holmes* Sunday afternoon and I'm deeply grateful to you. As I told you I'm working on a speech designed to make plain what are my fundamental beliefs. If you wouldn't think it presumptuous I'd like to submit it to you once it takes shape and have the benefit of your judgment.

Nancy has just been on the phone to Dr. Davis and Edith and they as well as Nancy send you and Mrs. Eisenhower their best as do I.

Sincerely,
Ronnie

---

* Holmes Tuttle, a member of Reagan's California "kitchen cabinet."

Richard M. Nixon

New York Postmaster Robert K. Christenberry sent Vice President Richard M. Nixon a copy of a speech by Ronald Reagan, host and program supervisor of the General Electric Theater. *In May 1959, Reagan delivered a speech titled "Business, Ballots, and Bureaus" at a General Electric meeting at the Waldorf Hotel in New York City.**

Vice President Richard Nixon
Washington, D.C.
June 27, 1959[16]

Dear Mr. Vice President:

You were very kind to write me about my talk and I feel honored that you took the time to read it. I am grateful too for the reassurance your letter gives me in continuing to speak on such a controversial matter.

"General Electric" has had me touring quite a bit in the past few years and I have been speaking on this subject in every section of the country. I might add, the subject and material are my own, General Electric has never suggested in any way what I should or should not say.

During the last year particularly, I have been amazed at the reaction to this talk. Audiences are actually militant in their expression that "something must be done." The only adverse opinion in the last two years was an editorial in a local "teamster union" paper which I accept as further evidence that sound thinking is on our side.

In several instances this talk was broadcast and here too the reaction as evidenced by mail was unanimous in support of "sound economy." I am convinced there is a groundswell of economic conservatism building up which could reverse the entire tide of present day "statism." As a matter of fact we seem to be in one of those rare moments when the American people with that wisdom which is the strength of democracy are ready to say "enough." Such a wave of feeling marked the end of the "Capone era." Prohibition was ended in the same way with people (even those who opposed drinking) deciding that the wrong method had been tried.

Well I'd better stop or you'll have another "speech" to read.

Again, my thanks to you and very best wishes—

Sincerely,
Ronald

During the Vice President's trip to the Soviet Union, Richard Nixon and Soviet Premier Nikita S. Khrushchev had an impromptu public exchange about the merits of

---

* The speech actually attached to the Nixon-Reagan correspondence is Reagan's 1961 address titled "Encroaching Control."

their political systems at a hall in Moscow where the American National Exhibition was under construction. That exchange on July 24, 1959, became known as the "kitchen debate" because part of the dialogue occurred in a model American kitchen. On August 1, Nixon spoke to the Soviet people in a televised address. He said that if Premier Khrushchev continued to try to spread communism around the world, the people of the Soviet Union would "continue to live in an era of fear, suspicion and tension." [17]

In the letter below, Reagan congratulates Nixon for speaking bluntly in the Soviet Union. Nixon replied to the letter less than three weeks later. He wrote: "There is probably nothing quite as heartwarming after a trip like the one we have just completed as receiving a letter such as yours upon our return. . . . I was most interested to have your thoughts on the ideological struggle, and in my opinion your analysis of the nature of the basic conflict between the Free World and the Communist bloc is exactly right. Certainly all Americans need to recognize as clearly as you do the fundamental dishonesty of the phrase 'peaceful co-existence' as interpreted and practiced by the Reds. Because of your interests, I thought you might like to have the enclosed copies of some of my recent speeches in which I discussed this in more detail."

> Vice President Richard Nixon
> Washington, D.C.
> September 7, 1959 [18]

Dear Mr. Vice President:

I just wanted to add my voice to those congratulating and thanking you for what you did and said on your recent trip. One thing in particular has long needed saying, namely that "Communism or Marxism is the only system with aggression advocated as an essential part of its dogma."

As the cold war continues I'm sure many people lose sight of the basic conflict and begin to accept that two nations are foolishly bickering with some justice and right as well as wrong on each side. This "tolerant" view ignores of course the fact that only "Communism" is dedicated to imposing its "way and belief" on all the world. This is in direct contradiction to our belief (so forcefully expressed by you) that people should be allowed to choose for themselves.

It was almost startling to hear you say this directly to the Russian leaders because I suddenly realized it was a truth seldom if ever uttered in diplomatic exchanges.

Knowing that "questions" are the best form of argument and debate I would like to see us, in the future, answer their charges of "imperialism" by asking over and over again, "Has Russia abandoned the Marxian precept that Communism must be imposed on the whole world?"

Only when their answer to that question is affirmative can we truly believe in "coexistence." Until such time "coexistence" means "don't do anything while I steal your house."

Again my thanks to you for the great step you took in starting us back to the uncompromising position of leadership which is our heritage and responsibility.

Mrs. Reagan joins me in every good wish to you and your family.

Sincerely,
Ronald

Reagan writes that he hopes to see the vice president at the Rose Bowl Parade. Former Miss America Bess Myerson and Reagan were hosting the event for ABC-TV on January 1, 1960, in Pasadena, California.

Vice President Nixon replied six days later: "As you can imagine, the Pasadena Committee has me pretty heavily scheduled that day but I shall be on the lookout for you because I, too, would enjoy the opportunity of a visit if we can work it into the day's activities."

Vice President Richard Nixon
Washington, D.C.
December 11, 1959 [19]

Dear Mr. Vice President:

I have just learned you and your fine family will be an important part of the Rose Parade, New Year's Day. It seems I'll be talking about you as I am broadcasting the description of the parade for ABC-TV. I hope there will be an opportunity some time during the many activities to talk to you as well. At any rate we shall look forward to seeing you.

Nancy joins me in wishing you all the best for the holiday season.

Sincerely,
Ronald

On the same day that Senator John F. Kennedy (D-Massachusetts) gave his speech accepting the nomination at the Democratic National Convention in Los Angeles, California, Reagan writes Vice President Nixon, who would run against Kennedy in the general election, with some thoughts about Kennedy's speech and the Democratic convention.

Vice President Richard Nixon
Washington, D.C.
July 15, 1960 [20]

Dear Mr. Vice President:

I know this is presumptuous of me but I'm passing on some thoughts after viewing the convention here in Los Angeles.

Somehow the idea persists that someone should put an end to the traditional demonstrations which follow each nomination. True they once had their place when their only purpose was to influence the delegates within the convention hall.

Now however TV has opened a window onto convention deliberations and the "demonstration" is revealed as a synthetic time waster which only serves to belittle us in what should be one of our finer moments. One has a feeling that general gratitude would be the reward for anyone who would once and for all declare the "demonstration" abandoned.

Starting with the opening speech and continuing through all the speeches until Kennedy's acceptance speech I thought the Democrats could pick up some campaign money by selling the collection of addresses as, "talks suitable for any patriotic occasion with platitudes and generalities guaranteed." I do not include Kennedy's acceptance speech because beneath the generalities I heard a frightening call to arms. Unfortunately he is a powerful speaker with an appeal to the emotions. He leaves little doubt that his idea of the "challenging new world" is one in which the federal government will grow bigger and do more and of course spend more. I know there must be some shortsighted people in the Republican Party who will advise that the Republicans should try to "out liberal" him. In my opinion this would be fatal.

You were kind enough to write me and comment on the "talk" I had given and which you had read. That is why I'm presuming on your busy day with these thoughts. I have been speaking on this subject in more than 38 states to audiences of Democrats and Republicans. Invariably the reaction is a standing ovation—not for me but for the views expressed. I am convinced that America is economically conservative and for that reason I think someone should force the Democrats to publish the "retail price" for this great new wave of "public service" they promise. I don't pose as an infallible pundit but I have a strong feeling that the 20 million non voters in this country just might be conservatives who have cynically concluded the two parties offer no choice between them where fiscal stability is concerned. No Republican no matter how liberal is going to woo a Democratic vote but a Republican bucking the giveaway trend might re-create some voters who have been staying home.

One last thought—shouldn't someone tag Mr. Kennedy's bold new imaginative program with its proper age? Under the tousled boyish haircut it is still old Karl Marx—first launched a century ago. There is nothing new in the idea of a government being Big Brother to us all. Hitler called his "State Socialism" and way before him it was "benevolent monarchy."

I apologize for taking so much of your time but I have such a yearning to hear someone come before us and talk specifics instead of generalities. I'm sure the American people do not want the government-paid services at "any price" and if we collectively can't afford "free this and that" they'd like to know it before they buy and not after it is entrenched behind another immovable government bureau.

You will be very much in my prayers in the days ahead.

Sincerely,
Ronnie Reagan

Reagan asks Nixon to autograph a photo for a film director. When Reagan wrote this letter, he was still a spokesman for General Electric, although the work was coming to an end, and Nixon was campaigning to be governor of California.

Mr. Richard Nixon
Beverly Hills, California
March 26, 1962[21]

Dear Dick:

The enclosed picture is of you and "friend." The friend is our neighbor the director Henry Koster. He asked our help in getting the photo autographed.

If you'd be so kind as to sign, seal and drop in the mail he'd be grateful and so would we.

Best to Pat,
Ronnie

Four years after Nixon lost his bid to unseat California Governor Edmund "Pat" Brown, Reagan would run against, and defeat, the two-term incumbent. Nixon and Reagan had remained in contact, and Nixon began giving Reagan advice on the campaign. Here Reagan briefly mentions his battle against three contenders in the upcoming Republican primary: former mayor of San Francisco George Christopher, United States Senator Thomas Kuchel, and former governor Goodwin J. Knight.

Mr. Richard Nixon
New York, New York
May 7, 1965[22]

Dear Dick:

It was good to hear from you and I assure you there will be no first blows or even second, struck by me. Just between us I wish the other boys would get the idea. So far, Kuchel, Christopher and Knight have tee'd off with some rather below the belt quotes.

But you have my promise—I'll speak no evil (except about Democrats) and I'll act like I hear no evil, but that will test my acting ability.

Nancy sends her best and please give our regards to Pat.

Sincerely,
Ronnie

As Nixon geared up for his presidential campaign, he wrote to Reagan. In his letter dated August 4, 1967, he addressed the July 24, 1967, column by Rowland Evans and Robert Novak that attributed criticism of Reagan to the Nixon camp: "Like many other columns on Richard Nixon by Evans and Novak, this one is fabricated from whole cloth. Neither I nor my personal staff have had anything to do with the brace of them for the past two years. Parky [Dr. Gaylord Parkinson, chairman of Nixon's national campaign] denies that he has talked to them, and has no idea who the 'Nixon insider' could be who made the alleged comment, 'Let Ronnie have the kooks.' " This comment was said to represent a Nixon campaign strategy to unload party extremists on Reagan, who was rumored to be considering his own presidential campaign.

In his reply, Reagan writes that he was not surprised by such reports, and indeed expects more. He also writes that he enjoyed meeting with Nixon at the Bohemian Grove, the campground of a San Francisco men's club. In a highly publicized meeting at the Grove during the weekend of July 23, 1967, Reagan and Nixon discussed Republican Party unity in light of the upcoming presidential election.[23]

The Honorable Richard Nixon
New York, New York
August 16, 1967[24]

Dear Dick:

Thanks for sending me the column. I'm quite sure the pace of this sort of thing will step up in the days ahead. I think it is very important that all of us on our side keep reminding ourselves and each other that we shouldn't believe any quotes unless we hear them first hand. I'm always reminded of the Hollywood days and how the people in our business would read the gossip columns and your first reaction was always how dishonest they were about yourself, but two paragraphs later you're believing every word when they talk about someone else.

It was a pleasure being with you at the Grove. Nancy sends her best, and please give our regards to Pat.

Sincerely,
Ron

Reagan congratulates Nixon on winning the New Hampshire and Wisconsin primaries in the spring of 1968, and reassures Nixon that he is only running a favorite son campaign.

Mr. Richard Nixon
New York, New York
April 10, 1968[25]

Dear Dick:

Congratulations on your excellent showing in New Hampshire and Wisconsin. It's truly good of you to take the time to write and I greatly appreciate hearing from you.

708 REAGAN: A LIFE IN LETTERS

I'm especially happy to know you understand the touchy position I'm in at this time maintaining a neutral stand while running as California's Favorite Son.

My wish, like yours, is to have a united Republican Party behind our candidate in November.

Sincerely,

Ron

In late 1973 Nixon's Watergate problems were increasing. "I would appreciate hearing from you by return wire," William F. Buckley wired Reagan on November 6, 1973, "whether National Review *should counsel the president to resign." "Send wire," Reagan instructed his staff.*

Mr. William F. Buckley Jr.
New York, New York
November 6, 1973 [26]

HELL NO

RONALD REAGAN

President Nixon wrote a letter to Reagan the day after Reagan lost the nomination to President Ford at the Republican Convention in Kansas City, Missouri. Nixon said: "Having won a few and lost a few I can say that winning is a lot more fun! But you can take pride that in losing you conducted yourself magnificently. The millions who saw and heard you on TV during the convention had to conclude—even if they in some cases did not agree with your philosophy—that you were an eloquent and persuasive advocate of your point of view. . . . As you concluded your eloquent statement at the end of the convention—Pat turned to me and said: 'Ronald Reagan, in defeat, was as great as he was in victory. And throughout the convention Nancy was beautiful, intelligent—and—most important of all—a real lady.' "

Reagan thanks President Nixon and says that the Northeast state delegations influenced by Nelson Rockefeller had contributed to his defeat.

President Richard Nixon
San Clemente, California
August 27, 1976 [27]

Dear Mr. President:

Thank you for your very heartwarming letter and generous words. And please tell Pat how much we both appreciate her kind words. We hope and pray she is fully recovered.*

---

* Pat Nixon suffered a stroke in July 1976.

Nancy and I are at peace with ourselves and are enjoying a freedom we haven't known for some time. We remember with pleasure that where delegates had freedom to vote we did well. Defeat came in those three Northeast states where the party structure controlled the vote and I suspect "Rocky" controlled the party structure.

But that's all past. I'm starting my radio commentary soon and possibly a newspaper column so I'll be doing business at the same old stand and for the same old cause.

Nancy sends her best and we both hope we'll see you soon.

Again our heartfelt thanks.

Sincerely,
Ron

In one of his first appearances after resigning the presidency on August 9, 1974, President Nixon sounded the alarm in a speech in Hyden, Kentucky: "At a time when aggressive dictatorships are stirring up covert subversive action all over the world, the United States should strengthen our CIA to counter their activities. When they are increasing aid to aggressive acts, the United States should increase its aid to counter them." [28]

Ken Khachigian, a White House speechwriter during the Nixon presidency and later a speechwriter in the Reagan administration, sent Reagan a copy of Nixon's July 2, 1978, speech. Reagan sends a note of thanks to President Nixon.

President Richard Nixon
San Clemente, California
July 14, 1978 [29]

Dear Mr. President:

Thanks very much for having Ken Khachigian send me the copy of your address in Hyden Kentucky. I enjoyed reading it, but more than that, it said things that truly need to be heard today.

I'm concerned as I know you are by a foreign policy that seems to have us at sea without rudder or compass.

Nancy sends her best and please give our regards to Pat.

Again thanks—

Sincerely,
Ron

Shortly after Reagan's May 14, 1979, television interview with Bill Moyers, President Nixon wrote the following brief note: "I thought you would be pleased to know that the reports on your TV interview with Bill Moyers have been sensational. You have elated your friends and have struck fear into the hearts of your opponents in the media!"

President Richard Nixon
San Clemente, California
May 31, 1979 [30]

Dear Mr. President:

Thank you very much for your note regarding the Moyers broadcast. I appreciate your generous words.

I was surprised at how easy and enjoyable the interview was. While I met him once at a dinner party in New York I certainly couldn't say I knew him. Naturally I was aware of his connection with LBJ so was prepared to be on guard but as it turned out there was no reason for concern.

Nancy sends her best and please give our love to Pat.

Again thanks.

Sincerely,
Ron

On November 4, 1980, Ronald Reagan won the presidency by a 10 percentage-point landslide. Seven days later, President Nixon sent the president-elect an 11-page memorandum. In the single-spaced typed document, President Nixon wrote: "As one who has been there and who seeks or wants absolutely nothing except your success in office, I would like to pass on to you some candid observations based on past experience and on intimate knowledge of some of the people you are considering for major positions. . . . As you know, I believed before the election that, while foreign policy was to me the most important issue of the campaign, the economic issue was the one which would have the greatest voter impact. Now I am convinced that decisive action on the inflation front is by far the number one priority. Unless you are able to shape up our home base it will be almost impossible to conduct an effective foreign policy. Consequently, I would suggest that for at least six months you not travel abroad and that you focus the attention of your appointees, the Congress and the people on your battle against inflation. . . ."

In a section of his memorandum titled "Personnel Guidelines," the former president wrote: "There has been a lot of press speculation about whether you should appoint Nixon-Ford people or new people to top posts. I have very strong views on this issue. Based on the foregoing analysis you cannot afford on-the-job training for your Secretaries of State and Defense. However, in all other positions you should put in your own team unless you conclude that someone who served in the past is indispensable for your needs now." He went on to recommend Alexander M. Haig, his own White House chief of staff, for secretary of state, and John B. Connally, a former gover-

nor of Texas and one of the presidential contender in the 1980 Republican primaries, for defense.

The president-elect writes an artful reply.

President Richard Nixon
November 22, 1980[31]

Dear Mr. President:

Forgive this handwritten note but I've found a few minutes of quiet and want to keep them that way.

There are no words to thank you for all your kindness and help through these final campaign weeks and now in your election day letter and your sound advice of November 17.

I followed your advice regarding those last campaign days although I couldn't manage to get all the rallies indoors. But I did stick with the proven campaign speech and the polls kept going up a point or two each day.

I can't thank you enough for the guidelines you gave me on personnel and the cabinet meeting suggestion—this will be done.

Nancy is so grateful and proud of your letter to her. She sends her love and from both of us to Pat.

Again thanks and warm regards.

Ron

—————

In his March 15, 1982, letter, President Nixon wrote: "Our grandson, Christopher, was three years old yesterday. When playing with his dog, they knocked over and broke a vase. He looked up at Tricia and said: 'Don't worry, Mommy, Reagan will fix it!' This shows he was born with good political intuition and that he had the right kind of parental and grand parental influence."

President Reagan sends a friendly reply.

President Richard Nixon
New York, New York
March 18, 1982[32]

Dear Mr. President:

Thank you for your kind letter. I should say letters because I didn't answer your last one before this one came.

Nancy and I were delighted to hear about Christopher—please don't disillusion him just yet. It's nice to think someone believes you can fix anything. Of course you may have a budding "standup comic" there who will be the Johnny Carson of his day.

I appreciate very much your encouraging words and I will "stay steady in the buggy."

Monday and Tuesday of this week I was in Alabama, Tennessee and Oklahoma addressing their state legislatures. All three of course are predominantly Democrat and yet they seemed to be enthusiastic in their support of what we're trying to do.

You once suggested that getting out of Washington to meet the real people was a good antidote for what goes on here. You were right. I've been out on a couple of speaking junkets getting the *Post* and the *Times* out of my mind.

Nancy sends her love and from both of us to Pat.

Again thanks.—

Ron

Four days after attending funeral services for ABC-TV news anchor Frank Reynolds, President Reagan writes President Nixon about the sadness that he and Nancy feel. He also writes about the ongoing crisis in Lebanon.

President Richard Nixon
New York, New York
July 27, 1983[33]

Dear Dick:

Thanks for your very nice letter and thanks for sending us the letter from Frank. We were very fond of Frank and Henriette. It was a shock for us to learn that he had cancer and was suffering pain as far back as '76 when we first met him in New Hampshire in the primary there.

Evidently his closest associates knew nothing of that and certainly no one ever heard him complain. The funeral had us both fighting to control our tears and we didn't succeed too well. Would that there were more like him in his profession. Fair and compassionate he was.

I'll be meeting the foreign and defense ministers of Israel tomorrow for a talk about Lebanon. I hope we can persuade them to define their planned deployment as just one phase of their agreement to withdraw. That might possibly give us a little leverage on Syria. Then again—being the Middle East maybe it wouldn't make any difference at all.

Nancy sends her best to you both. My love to Pat.

Warmest regard,
Ron

In this thank-you note, President Reagan mentions that he is looking forward to making a public statement about the Iran-Contra affair. On March 4, 1987, he would speak to the nation about the scandal and the recommendations of his bipartisan board, the Tower Commission, on how to restructure the National Security Council. In the note below, he also mentions criticism he has endured by Chris Wallace, the chief White House correspondent for NBC-TV.

President Richard Nixon
New York, New York
Before March 4, 1987[34]

Dear Dick and Pat:

Just a line to thank you for your good wishes and kind words. It was good to hear from you.

I have a feeling we're getting closer to when I can go public and straighten out some of the distortions that are now so prevalent.

The other night I saw Chris Wallace having me over the hill and having to get directions to the bathroom. I may challenge him to an arm wrestle.

Nancy sends her love and so do I—to you both.

Sincerely,
Ron

————

In his August 16, 1988, letter about the presidential election, President Nixon wrote: "It will be close but if he [George H. W. Bush] can make ideology the issue it could mean 4 more years of the Reagan Revolution." President Reagan replies that he has been campaigning on behalf of Bush and that he thinks Massachusetts Governor Michael S. Dukakis, the Democratic nominee, would be a disaster as president.

The Honorable Richard Nixon
New York, New York
September 12, 1988[35]

Dear Dick:

This should have been on its way weeks ago. My only excuse is—the ranch and some California campaigning for three weeks that sort of closed my mind to other things.

Thank you for your generous words. Both of us thank you and please express our appreciation and regard to Pat.

I'm going to do all I can to help George. I feel deeply that "the Gov." would be a disaster.

Warmest regards,
Ron

————

On October 28, 1989, President Nixon arrived in the People's Republic of China for an unofficial visit. In meetings with Chinese officials, Nixon discussed American reactions to the massacre in Tiananmen Square that occurred in June and the subsequent crackdown on political opposition and protest in the country.

Upon his return, President Nixon forwarded to President Reagan a copy of the memorandum he had sent to six senators and congressmen about his trip to China. He also wrote that his wife "thought Nancy and you were outstanding" on ABC-TV's 20/20. The program aired on November 17, 1989.

> The Honorable Richard Nixon
> Woodcliff Lake, New Jersey
> November 30, 1989 [36]

Dear Dick:

Thanks for sending your memo on Sino-American relations. Believe me I feel far better informed on the subject than I've ever been. And I'm sure your visit had an impact and has served to help our relations.

Tell Pat thanks for her kind words about *20/20* and give her our love.

Warm regards.

> Ron

––––––––

In reviewing President Nixon's book, In the Arena, *on May 30, 1990, the* Wall Street Journal *stated: "He obviously was delighted with* Newsweek's *'He's Back' cover following his speech to publishers. . . . [T]he speech worked to ingratiate himself with the beautiful people at the expense of the Reagan foreign policy."*

The following day, President Nixon sought to correct this impression in a letter to President Reagan: "My speech before the Publishers was not an attack on the Reagan Administration, but on the contrary was a strong defense before a skeptical audience of your policy of aid to the Contras. I am enclosing a copy of the speech I made on that occasion for your personal files."

> President Richard Nixon
> Woodcliff Lake, New Jersey
> June 8, 1990 [37]

Dear Dick:

Thank you for your letter and for that fine speech. And thank you for correcting the *Journal.*

I'm surprised at the effectiveness of the Sandinistas' disinformation program. They must have outside help. One day a slick paper magazine turned up on my desk in the Oval Office. It was cover-to-cover propaganda and contained a card telling readers how to use it to provide a subscription for their senator or congressman. The magazine was published in Berkeley, California.

As you know the Sandinistas have managed to enlist a number of religious groups for their cause, among them is the National Council of Churches. I'm afraid the recent election isn't safe from subversion.

Well you were very kind to come to my rescue and I'm deeply grateful. Nancy sends her love and both of us do to Pat, bless her soul.

Warmest regard

> Ron

This letter is most likely about Richard Nixon's book Seize the Moment: America's Challenge in a One-Superpower World.

President Richard Nixon
Woodcliff Lake, New Jersey
January 22, 1992 [38]

Dear Dick:

So next year you will be celebrating the 41st anniversary of your 39th birthday. Well next month I'll be celebrating my 42nd anniversary of that birthday.

Dick I've just recently completed my reading of your latest book which you sent me. I have to tell you I found it fascinating and your approach to what our policy should be was brilliant. Every page I turned revealed a mind superior to any and all who are in high places trying to resolve the great problems of the world today. Believe me I'm keeping your book close at hand and will use it when I'm faced with taking a position on any of the great problems facing us in these days. My heartfelt thanks to you.

Nancy sends her warmest regard as do I. And from both of us—love to Pat. Again my thanks.

Ron

Two days before Nixon's eighty-first birthday and four months before his death, President Reagan sent this letter.

The Honorable Richard Nixon
Woodcliff Lake, New Jersey
January 7, 1994 [39]

Dear Dick:

Happy Birthday, young fellow! It's hard to believe that a couple of kids like us are "maturing" so rapidly. . . . I mean so well!

Nancy and I want to send you our best as you celebrate yet another remarkable year. Surely 1993 had some low points, but Dick, you've led an extraordinary life and have been so richly blessed. Believe me, your many friends are certainly thankful for you!

By the way, my roommate and I are disappointed that we won't be able to join you on the 20th of this month for the event at your library. You were so kind to include us in your "reunion" of sorts and I hope it's a resounding success.

Let's get together soon before another birthday rolls around!

Sincerely,
Ron

Gerald R. Ford

During the 1976 Republican primaries, Reagan vociferously challenged U.S.–Soviet détente as practiced by President Gerald R. Ford. Here, he is blunt about President Ford's foreign policy.

> Mr. Edwin J. Gray
> San Diego, California
> Circa spring 1976[40]

Dear Ed:

Just a line, before hitting the trail again, to thank you for your letter. You'll be happy to know we are all on the same wavelength. I am taking Mr. Ford on, nose-to-nose regarding our foreign policy which frankly scares me to death. We are second to the Soviets now and getting more so.

Will you tell Gordon I got his letter and thank him for the information. It fits what we have been gathering.

> Best regards,
> Ron

Reagan defends himself against the charge that he did not energetically support Ford's 1976 presidential campaign.

> Mr. Ralph Tipton
> Lisle, Illinois
> Fall 1976[41]

Dear Tip:

Your letter [was] received and I can't wait to take my TV tuner out for a ride.

I think our people really did the work for Ford and were the backbone of his campaign. I'm awestruck when I hear some of his underlings complaining about me. I was in 25 states, did a series of national TV ads (in addition to the TV speech) and put out more than a million fundraising letters.

Tip, have a happy holiday season. Nancy and I wish you all a Merry Christmas and a Happy New Year.

> Sincerely,
> Dutch

In his reply to a professor of Russian heritage teaching in the United States, Ronald Reagan gives his assessment of President Ford's presidential aspirations and possibilities in the presidential election of 1980.

Professor Vsevolod A. Nikolaev
Circa 1979–1980 [42]

Dear Professor Nikolaev:

Thank you very much for your letter and for sending the copy of the letter by former President Ford. I believe you'll find that letter was for the purpose of raising funds—not for any campaign he might be considering but for the national Republican Party. As a matter of fact, they have invited me to write such a letter a little later in the year for the same purpose. I truly believe that President Ford is not a candidate in the sense of running in the campaign. I do believe he has thought that possibly, with 10 Republican candidates, there might be a standoff with no one getting enough votes to be nominated, and in such a case, the convention might turn to him as someone who could carry the support of the majority. I'm inclined to believe that will not take place at the coming convention. More recently than his broadcast, the polls have been leaving him out and only polling with regard to those of us who are announced candidates. But, I do thank you for your letter and thank you for sending me his letter, which I had not seen.

Best regards,
Ronald Reagan

Reagan wrote the next three letters during his presidency. He responds favorably to President Ford's recommendations of candidates for various posts in his administration.

President Gerald R. Ford
Rancho Mirage, California
April 19, 1983 [43]

Dear Jerry:

Just a line to let you know we've followed up on your recommendation of Colonel Lousma. Ron Mann of our personnel department has had a meeting with him and is greatly impressed and shares your own feelings about him.

The ambassador situation is very tight right now. We may have to put him on a presidential board until something opens up. We'll keep after it.

Nancy sends her best to you and Betty as do I.

Sincerely,
Ron

President Gerald R. Ford
Rancho Mirage, California
March 29, 1985 [44]

Dear Jerry:

Thanks for your letter of March 20 and your input on Bill Cramer. I share your high regard for him and have put his name into the hopper. I have to tell you the list is long and is a veritable "Who's Who." We're going to review every nominee as thoroughly and honestly as we can.

Again thanks. Nancy sends her best and give our regards to Betty.

Sincerely,
Ron

President Gerald Ford
Rancho Mirage, California
March 24, 1988[45]

Dear Jerry:

In answer to your letter of March 16 J. Willard Marriott Sr. is one of the nominees for the Medal of Freedom. The names haven't been sent to me yet but I assure you he'll have my approval. I share your feeling for him and appreciate your letter very much. Thanks for your welcome input.

Nancy sends her best and our regards to Betty.

Sincerely,
Ron

George H. W. Bush

In this letter, President Reagan seeks his successor's approval before committing to two meetings with President Gorbachev. Following the second summit between President George Bush and President Mikhail Gorbachev, the Soviet leader met with President and Mrs. Reagan on June 4, 1990, in San Francisco in the midst of a busy tour of the San Francisco Bay Area. Four months later, President and Mrs. Reagan traveled to Moscow. In a speech before the Supreme Soviet on September 17, President Reagan addressed "the reformulation of the relationships in your union." He advised: "Differences can be resolved in ways that are fair to all, but reason must prevail over passion if there is to be a climate conducive to the settlement of disagreements."[46]

President George Bush
Washington, D.C.
December 22, 1989[47]

Dear George:

I received the attached invitation from President Gorbachev to visit the Soviet Union. My inclination is to accept for a trip in early May. However, before offering any response I wanted to run it by you.

As you know, I previously invited President and Mrs. Gorbachev to visit California. I would like to renew this invitation to them to visit after your summit in June. Please let me know if this makes sense to you.

Nancy joins me in sending our very best wishes to you and Barbara for the Holidays.

Sincerely,
Ron

P.S. Thank you for my books—I shall treasure them. And thanks for the report on the summit and your handling of the *Time* magazine attack.[48]

President Reagan tells President Bush that their friendship has been important to him over the years.

President George Bush
Circa early 1990s [49]

Dear George:

Just a quick line to tell you that Walter Annenberg told me about your letter to him re the Ullmann* article. I just want you to know how grateful I am for your warm words about our relationship. George our friendship means a great deal to me and I hope we can stand above potential troublemakers. Your letter assures me that we can. You have my heartfelt thanks and my friendship always.

Sincerely,
Ron

---

* President Reagan is most likely referring to an article written by Owen Ullmann, a writer for Knight-Ridder newspapers.

CHAPTER TWENTY-THREE

Foreign Leaders

SPANNING *several decades, Ronald Reagan's correspondence with foreign leaders provides a unique window on his intellectual and operational style and policies. His preferred style of diplomacy was personal; for example, correspondence with members of the family and entourage of the shah of Iran reveal a relationship that started well before Reagan became president and continued through his presidency. Reagan is distinctly open and sometimes unguarded in letters to and about the leaders of America's closest allies in the West; he formed lasting personal relationships with several of his counterparts. Many of his letters to allies do not appear to have been put through the interagency process of drafting and redrafting by staff at the Department of State and the National Security Council; President Reagan spoke for himself. He encouraged stronger Western cooperation and expressed appreciation to allies who worked toward that goal.*

Reagan's personal approach to leaders of rival nations such as the Soviet Union was different. Letters to Soviet heads of government were routinely reviewed and commented upon by advisers and staff, but President Reagan was in full command of the diplomatic pouch. All of these letters reflect ideas he presented in conversations, meetings, speeches, and writings throughout his political career. Sometimes Reagan's own draft became the final letter. This appears to be the case in Reagan's April 1981 letter to Soviet General Secretary Leonid Brezhnev, written shortly after Reagan was shot. Reagan's intellectual imprint on all of this correspondence is unmistakable. We present a few of these letters, and explain the process by which they were drafted based on a close study of declassified documents in the Heads of State–USSR files at the Reagan Library, and based on interviews with some of the Reagan administration officials who worked on U.S.–Soviet relations.

There are a few letters to and about Soviet and Russian officials after Reagan left the White House in January 1989. These letters typically reflect nostalgia for the cooperation that was achieved in the 1980s and an abiding commitment to making sure that common ideals prevail in both countries.

In a concluding section of his memoir titled "Understanding Ronald Reagan," Sec-

retary of State George P. Shultz wrote: "Critics said Ronald Reagan read too many letters and not enough briefing books. I often wished he would spend more time on the briefing books, mastering details more fully and following up more aggressively on the management of foreign policy. But the letters buoyed him up and also gave him a continuing sense of contact with the people."[1]

CANADA

Following a summit conference of the leading industrial democracies in Ottawa, Canada, President Reagan sends a thank-you note to his host.

The Right Honorable Pierre Elliott Trudeau
Ottawa, Canada
August 3, 1981[2]

Dear Pierre:

Just a line to tell you how very grateful I am for your note and for the recording by our mutual friend, Robert W. Service. I am answering before I've even had an opportunity to play it, but I look forward to doing that very quickly. You were more than kind to send this, and I assure you I shall treasure it.

Let me also again thank you for all the great hospitality you and your countrymen gave us at the summit. I think it was most successful and, in large part, due to your handling of all of the meetings, including the informal dinner meetings.

Again, my heartfelt thanks and best regards.

Sincerely,
Ron

EGYPT

After his crackdown on religious and political opponents, religious fundamentalists assassinated Egyptian President Anwar el-Sadat. The next day, President Reagan writes a condolence letter to Sadat's wife on behalf of himself and Nancy. In the letter, he fondly remembers meeting with President Sadat at the White House two months earlier.

Mrs. Jihan Sadat
Cairo, Egypt
October 7, 1981[3]

Dear Jihan:

We know there are no words that can ease the burden of grief you bear. How we wish there were. Just know that we share your sorrow and pain.

True, our meeting was brief. But in that short time, we came to feel a deep and abiding friendship for you both.* That is not surprising because the world had already found a place in its heart for Anwar and all that he represented. A statesman, yes, but also a warm, kindly man of courage and vision.

We can only trust in God's infinite mercy and wisdom as he did and pray for understanding and healing.

We will try to carry on the great effort for peace Anwar so nobly began, but we shall miss him more than words can say.

Please know how deep is our sympathy for you and your family and know that you are in our thoughts and prayers.

We are sending the album of your visit here but also this picture which shows, we believe, his very soul.

God bless you and keep you,
Nancy and Ronald

FRANCE

Three days after President François Mitterrand participated in the Statue of Liberty centennial celebration in New York Harbor, President Reagan writes to thank the leader of France for his visit and to ask a favor on behalf of Billy Graham, a renowned evangelist. Reagan also cites a Reader's Digest *article that reports that a genealogist has found that he is distantly related to Mitterrand.*

President François Mitterrand
Paris, France
July 7, 1986 [4]

Dear François:

Just a line to say how good it was to see you here for Miss Liberty's birthday celebration. It was very kind and generous of you to make the trip and I thank you on behalf of all Americans.

Now may I impose on you further? One of our most prestigious religious figures, the world renowned Reverend Billy Graham is holding a crusade this September in Paris in the new Bercy Sports Stadium. We have been close friends for many years. Our Ambassador Rodgers † will be speaking to you about a possible appointment with Reverend Graham while he is there. I would be most grateful

---

* President Reagan and President Sadat met at the White House on August 5 and 6, 1981, to discuss alternatives for making progress on the Camp David agreements signed by Sadat and Israeli Prime Minister Menachem Begin in September 1978.

† Joe M. Rodgers, United States ambassador to France from 1985 to 1989

if you could find time to see him. The ambassador has all the information about dates etc.

Now, and having nothing to do with the above request, I must share with you an item I just read on my way home in one of our prestigious magazines, the *Reader's Digest,* July issue page 148. It says that British genealogists in 1984 traced my family back to connection with Riagain, kin to the Irish King Brian Boru and this made me a cousin to, among others, President François Mitterrand.* So our recent get-together was something of a family reunion.

All the best to you.

Sincerely,

Ron

GREAT BRITAIN

In February 1983, Queen Elizabeth II and Prince Philip, Duke of Edinburgh, set sail on the royal yacht, H M Y Britannia, for a five-nation tour of the Caribbean and North America that included a visit to California. Heavy rain and high winds prevented a scheduled horseback ride on March 1 at the Reagan's ranch in Santa Barbara County, but the royal guests were still able to visit Rancho del Cielo. On March 4, the Queen and Prince Philip hosted a small gathering to celebrate the Reagans' 31st wedding an-niversary aboard the Britannia in San Francisco Harbor.

Her Majesty Queen Elizabeth II
London, England
March 15, 1983 [5]

Your Majesty:

We miss you. I know your visit to our West Coast became a harrowing, tempest-tossed experience but through it all your unfailing good humor and gra-ciousness won the hearts of our people.

In two weeks we'll be back at the ranch you only got to see for a few moments when temporarily the fog lifted. I'll be trying a new saddle for which I thank you. We are having our card from the *Britannia* crew framed. And we are hoping that one day in the not too distant future you'll return to our shores when the sun is shining and the skies are blue. In other words, in good riding weather.

Thank you again for your many kindnesses and for a most memorable experi-ence. Please give our very best regards to His Royal Highness.

Sincerely,
Ronald Reagan

---

* Dale Van Atta, "The Joys of Ancestor-Hunting," Reader's Digest 129 (July 1986): 144–48.

In his reply to a letter from a distinguished historian of Soviet Russia, Reagan recalls meeting Margaret Thatcher and says he holds her in high regard. Reagan was first introduced to Thatcher on April 9, 1975, when he met her at the Houses of Parliament during a trip to London, where he gave a speech on the Soviet threat before the Pilgrims of Great Britain.

Dr. Robert Conquest
Escondido, California
After spring 1975[6]

Dear Dr. Conquest:

Thank you for your letter and, most especially, for your column. You are very generous and kind to me and I am grateful.

I appreciate your suggestion about the months ahead and intend to roundtable this with my associates. Incidentally, I'm in solid agreement with your "P.S." I well remember my meeting with Margaret Thatcher and have nothing but the highest respect for her.

Again, thanks and I hope we'll see each other when you come to California.

Sincerely,
Ronald Reagan

On May 3, 1979, Margaret Thatcher of the Conservative Party was elected prime minister of Great Britain. Charles Joseph Clark of Canada's Progressive Conservative Party was elected prime minister on May 22. Reagan writes that he is pleased by the election results in both Great Britain and Canada. He also recalls his April 1975 and November 1978 meetings with Thatcher.[7]

Ms. Luella Huggins
Altadena, California
September 4, 1979[8]

Dear Luella:

It was good to hear from you, and I certainly can understand your frustrations about the letters you get asking for contributions. You know, of course, that in direct mail anymore your name is in a computer and just comes spilling out from that unfeeling machine.

Luella, you have done everything you should do, and please, just toss any other letters that come in the wastebasket. The computer will never know the difference.

And, while I'm at it, thank you very much for your contribution; you were very kind to do this, and I'll try to see that you never have reason to regret it. I'm certainly in agreement with you about the world situation and what must be done in our own country. I've been greatly encouraged by the election results in England,

Canada, etc. And, like you, I believe we should follow suit here. I have had the privilege of two meetings with Margaret Thatcher and can tell you I was convinced from the first meeting that she should be England's prime minister. I know she will make a great one. She has courage and great intelligence.

I'll try to make your slogan come true.

Again, thanks and best regards.

Sincerely,

Ron

On April 28, 1983, the day after President Reagan addressed a joint session of Congress about Central America, Peter Hannaford, a longtime associate, wrote to congratulate the president on his speech. He also noted that while in England, he and his wife had dinner with Ed Reed, one of Reagan's friends from Des Moines, Iowa. Hannaford also observed that Prime Minister Thatcher was "leaving her opponents in the dust."

Mr. Peter D. Hannaford
Washington, D.C.
May 3, 1983 [9]

Dear Pete:

Thanks very much for your kind words about the speech. The returns on it reflect a better reception than some of our columnists are willing to concede. Of course the real test will be in Congress.

Thanks too for sending me the Thatcher interview. She continues to be my favorite head of state. And you ran into Ed Reed. I haven't seen him in years.

Nancy sends her best and give our regards to Irene.

Sincerely,

Ron

Replying to a letter from the American ambassador in England, Reagan expresses concern that the opposition to Prime Minister Thatcher's policies by moderate Conservative Party leaders could have disastrous consequences for Great Britain.

Ambassador Charles H. Price II
London, England
May 23, 1985 [10]

Dear Charlie:

Just a line to acknowledge your letter of March 25th which, believe it or not I have only received since my return from Europe.

I'm with you on our girl Margaret. If they turn away from her they may very well have thrown away their last chance.

As for the other article—on one Ambassador Price—I'm in complete agreement with the author, "Price is right for Ron."

Nancy sends her love and from both of us to Carole.

Sincerely,
Ron

In preparation for its April 15, 1986, attack on Libya, motivated by that country's support of terrorism, the United States sought logistical support from Great Britain and France. France refused the use of its airspace. Prime Minister Margaret Thatcher, however, granted use of British air bases. British public opinion polls showed that there was substantial opposition both to her decision and to the U.S. attack. Thousands of demonstrators in Great Britain, Italy, Sweden, and West Germany held marches and burned American flags to show their opposition to the American action. President Reagan writes that Thatcher was courageous.

Mr. Jack Lunzer
London, England
April 23, 1986 [11]

Dear Mr. Lunzer:

Thanks to our mutual friend Walter Annenberg, I have received your message and am most grateful to you for your generous words. It was kind of you to write as you did and having your approval brightens my day.

May I say all of us here are beholden to Prime Minister Thatcher for her courage. The bond between our two countries is something we cherish.

Again thanks.

Sincerely,
Ronald Reagan

In a letter to President Reagan, a British citizen wrote that a Socialist victory in the upcoming elections in the United Kingdom would harm Anglo-American relations. He also said that President and Mrs. Reagan were successfully shouldering the burdens that come with occupying the White House. Less than five months later Margaret Thatcher was returned to office for a third time.

Mr. Andrew McTurk Cook
Sheffield, England
January 27, 1987 [12]

Dear Mr. Cook:

Your kind letter has finally reached me—hence the delay in answering. Thank you for writing as you did and thank you for your generous words. I'm most grateful.

While it wouldn't be fitting for me to comment on the upcoming election in your country I must say I have the greatest respect and admiration for your prime minister. She is a tower of strength in our economic summit meetings and has contributed greatly to the international stability that prevails in the Western world.

Again my thanks to you and very best regards.

Sincerely,
Ronald Reagan

During his first year back in California after his presidency, Reagan writes to Prime Minister Thatcher.

Margaret and Denis Thatcher
London, England
September 20, 1989 [13]

Dear Margaret and Denis:

How nice of you to write and thank you for your good wishes. They have come true. I'm feeling just fine to the surprise of a few doctors. Nancy and I are back in California and enjoying a normal life.

Nancy sends her love and so do I. As always it was a great pleasure to hear from you. I'm not going to miss too many things but assure you I'll miss our economic summits.

All the best to you.

Sincerely,
Ron

Less than a month before he would write to the American people about his Alzheimer's disease, President Reagan sends a birthday greeting to Margaret Thatcher.

Prime Minister Margaret Thatcher
London, England
October 13, 1994 [14]

Dear Margaret:

Across the miles I hope you'll feel the warm wishes and blessings we send on the occasion of your birthday. What a wonderful opportunity to celebrate you and your lifetime of accomplishments and tell you how much you have meant to us through the years.

How blessed I have been to celebrate so many of life's special moments with you. Your life has certainly been full . . . just count your blessings that it hasn't been as long as mine! It's been a wondrous journey, Margaret, and I pray that the coming years will be equally rewarding and joyful.

Happy Birthday on this special day. It's special because it's your day. Nancy joins me in sending our love and best wishes to you and Denis.

Fondly,
Ron

IRAN

President Reagan thanks Empress Farah Pahlavi, the widow of Mohammad Reza Shah Pahlavi, who had died more than four years earlier, for a letter and a gift. He also fondly recalls his visit with her in Iran in April 1978, less than a year before the shah fell from power and left Iran.

Her Majesty Farah Pahlavi
Greenwich, Connecticut
December 26, 1984 [15]

Your Majesty:

Thank you for your very warm and gracious letter and for your gift. Nancy and I are delighted to have that beautiful and magnificent book. We remember with great pleasure our meeting in California and especially your warm hospitality on our visit to Iran. We pray that one day there will once again be that Iran which we knew for such a brief but pleasant time.

Please give our regards to your children and our very best wishes. I am working on that passport matter and will get back to you on it.

Again thank you.

Sincerely,
Ronald Reagan

———

President Reagan tells Princess Fatemeh Pahlavi that the United States betrayed her brother, the shah of Iran. Reagan is referring to President Jimmy Carter's decision not to support the shah in 1978 and 1979 as Iran plunged into a crisis that forced the leader to depart Iran and never return.

Her Royal Highness Fatemeh Pahlavi
London, England
November 15, 1987 [16]

Your Royal Highness:

Thank you very much for your cable. I am most grateful for your kind words, good wishes, and your prayers in my behalf.

Your brother, the late shah was a true friend of my country and as it turned out, a friend betrayed. I hope one day justice can be done.

Again my heartfelt thanks to you and warmest regard from both Nancy and myself.

                                        Sincerely,
                                        Ronald Reagan

Ronald Reagan had known Ardeshir Zahedi, the Iranian ambassador to the United States from 1959 to 1961 and from 1973 to 1979, for many years when he became president on January 20, 1981. A typed letter dated August 29, 1978, from Reagan to William Loeb, a newspaper publisher, mentioned Zahedi: "I'm so glad that you like the ambassador. Ardeshir Zahedi is really a good friend, but more important, a good friend of this country. I've known him quite a few years. He was educated in America and during the riotous sixties, he actually, on his own, went out on the campuses and dared the wrath of the dissidents by making speeches about what a wonderful country America was and how much it has done for other countries in the world."[17] Four months before the letter was written, the Reagans met with Zahedi in Iran.

Loyal to the shah, Zahedi departed Iran when the shah did in January 1979. He took up residence in Switzerland, where President Reagan writes to thank him for a gift.

                                        The Honorable Ardeshir Zahedi
                                        Montreux, Switzerland
                                        June 26, 1984 [18]

Dear Ardeshir:

Bill Smith delivered your gift to us and Nancy and I want you to know how very grateful we are. You were very kind and thoughtful but then you always are.

We were happy to hear from Bill that you are in good health and spirits. We miss you. And we both know how you must bleed for what is being done to your homeland. You are in our thoughts and prayers.

Nancy sends her love and we both wish you all the very best. Again thanks.

                                        Sincerely,
                                        Ron

President Reagan thanks the former Iranian ambassador to the United States for a birthday gift, and recalls his visit to Iran in April 1978.

                                        The Honorable Ardeshir Zahedi
                                        Montreux, Switzerland
                                        February 9, 1987 [19]

Dear Ardeshir:

Thank you very much for my beautiful birthday gift. I am a great admirer of Boehm sculptures and will treasure this magnificent piece. Thanks too for your most generous words. I am most grateful. We talk of you often, recalling those embassy parties and your hospitality in offering your home to us on our trip to your homeland in a happier time.

Nancy sends her love and again my heartfelt thanks.

Sincerely,
Ron

ISRAEL

Shimon Peres was the first Israeli opposition leader to receive an invitation to the White House from an American president. On April 24, 1980, Peres and President Jimmy Carter met and discussed the Labor Party leader's proposal to return to Jordan heavily populated areas of the West Bank.[20] Two months later, in the midst of his presidential campaign, Reagan replies to a letter from Peres.

The Honorable Shimon Peres
Jerusalem, Israel
June 26, 1980[21]

Dear Mr. Peres:

Thank you very much for sending me your article. I have read it with great interest and assure you that you have contributed a great deal to my understanding of the many problems in the Middle East crisis. You were kind to do this, and I'm most grateful.

Sincerely,
Ronald Reagan

JAPAN

In midterm elections held on November 4, 1986, the Democrats regained control of the United States Senate with a 54-seat margin. Although the Republican Party did not win a majority of governorships, it gained several states, and thus narrowed the Democrats' margin. The day after the election, President Reagan told White House staff that together they would "complete the revolution that we have so well begun."[22] A few days later, in a reply to the prime minister of Japan, * *Reagan writes of the elections.*

---

* Ronald Reagan first met Yasuhiro Nakasone in April 1978 while visiting Japan. Nakasone was a backbencher in the Japanese government at the time. See Peter Hannaford, *The Reagans: A Political Portrait*, page 163, and a May 27, 2003, memorandum to the authors by Richard V. Allen.

His Excellency Yasuhiro Nakasone
Tokyo, Japan
November 18, 1986 [23]

Dear Yasu:

Thank you very much for your letter and for your kind words of support. Yes we were disappointed with the outcome of our Senate races but the election of so many state governors was of great importance. In our system governors rank higher than senators so we know the outcome was not a rejection of our policies.

I agree with you that we must continue to strengthen the ties between our two nations and I'm grateful to you for all you have done to further that cause.

Nancy sends her warm regards and from both of us to Tsutako.

Sincerely,
Ron

On March 6, 1987, Prime Minister Nakasone wrote to President Reagan to congratulate him on his televised address on the Iran-Contra scandal. He said the speech, delivered two days earlier, "was well received in Japan, as in the United States." He added: "It was a superb shot from the rough which caught the green right at the pin!"

His Excellency Yasuhiro Nakasone
Tokyo, Japan
March 12, 1987 [24]

Dear Yasu:

Secretary Shultz has just delivered your letter to me and I thank you very much. Of course your comparing my speech to some good golf shots reminded me of how much I miss those California golf courses while I'm sitting here in the cold weather of Washington. But you and I will continue to work closely together I assure you. I look forward with great pleasure to seeing you at the summit.

Nancy sends her very best and give our warm regards to Tsutako.

Sincerely,
Ron

Shortly after stepping down as prime minister of Japan, Yasuhiro Nakasone sent President Reagan a book of photographs titled "Ron & Yasu: In the Footsteps of the Japan–U.S. Leaders, 1982–1987."

The Honorable Yasuhiro Nakasone
Tokyo, Japan
February 11, 1988 [25]

Dear Yasu:

What a happy surprise! Your letter and the album were delivered to me today and Nancy and I haven't stopped going through it since it arrived. What happy memories it brings back. Memories of our effort in behalf of a better relationship between our two countries, but more important, memories of a wonderfully warm friendship that will be with us always.

Thank you for a gift we shall cherish. Nancy sends her love to Tsutako and you and so do I.

Warmest regard,
Ron

MEXICO

Eight days after meeting President José López Portillo in Mexico City to discuss U.S.–Mexico relations, and four months before announcing his intention to seek the Republican Party's nomination for the presidency, Reagan inquired about Mexico's interest in buying F-5E military aircraft from Northrop, a California-based aircraft company. During Reagan's first year as president, Mexico purchased F-5 Tiger II fighter jets from Northrop.

President José López Portillo
Mexico City, Mexico
July 25, 1979 [26]

Dear Mr. President:

I want to thank you very much for your kindness in giving me time on my recent visit to Mexico City. You were very generous, and I am most grateful. I shall continue to work for the kind of relationship between our two great countries that we discussed.

If it should be the Lord's will that I attain the office I am presently seeking, let me assure you I will be asking for another meeting to discuss and hopefully implement the kind of fair and open relationship that should exist between us as neighbors.

In the meantime, may I be so presumptuous as to mention another matter which I did not think should be brought up in the brief time we had together. I am aware that some time ago your government made an inquiry of ours about obtaining delivery of the F-5E Northrop fighter plane. Since I am a Californian, I, of course, am very familiar with the Northrop Company and with that aircraft. I believe the situation is presently on hold at your government's request. I have taken keen interest in the F-5E aircraft and followed closely the activities in Washington on the provision and support of this fine airplane. In this regard, I feel that if the government of Mexico is still interested and should request a letter of offer from the United States government, that such a request would receive an affirmative reply. For whatever it is worth, I happened to have learned that Northrop could make almost immediate delivery, which, I'm sure, would mean a lower price than if the planes had to be constructed at the ever increasing rate of inflation in our land.

Forgive me if I am out of line in bringing this matter to your attention. I have no connection with Northrop and only mean to be helpful if your government is still interested in this aircraft.

Again, my thanks to you and my sincere hope that one day in the near future, we will have another opportunity to discuss cooperation between our two nations.

With warmest regards,

Sincerely,
Ronald Reagan

After he was elected president, Ronald Reagan was given a white Arabian stallion by the president of Mexico. El Alamein was being trained at a horse farm in the Santa Ynez Valley. By the time President Reagan wrote the letter below to thank President José López Portillo for a new belt, El Alamein had been moved to Reagan's ranch near Santa Barbara.

President José López Portillo
Mexico, D.F.
June 24, 1982 [27]

My Dear Friend:

Forgive me for being so tardy in thanking you for the magnificent belt our mutual friend the Governor of Baja* presented to me on your behalf in Houston, Texas. You were most kind and thoughtful to do this and I am truly grateful.

In a few days I'll be going to our ranch where I shall proudly wear my new belt. I never cease to be amazed at the beautiful needlework on the belt and on that saddle that accompanied El Alamein. I don't know how it is accomplished but it is wonderful to behold.

El Alamein is handsome as ever and will be waiting for me at the ranch.

Again my heartfelt thanks and warm regards.

Sincerely,
Ron

THE PHILIPPINES

In a letter dated November 7, 1972, the San Francisco consul general of the Philippines wrote Ronald Reagan and enclosed "vital documents on the declaration of Martial Law in the Philippines." In his reply, Reagan thanks him for the documents and recalls

---

* Roberto de la Madrid.

meeting with President Ferdinand E. Marcos. The meeting occurred in September 1969 when Reagan represented President Richard M. Nixon at the opening of a new cultural center in Manila.

> Consul General Trinidad Alconcel
> San Francisco, California
> November 7, 1972 [28]

Dear Consul General Alconcel:

Thank you very much for the documents you sent. I have found them most informative and interesting.

I remember our visit to the Philippines and my meetings with President Marcos with great pleasure, and hope the troubles besetting your land will soon be ended.

> Again thanks and best regards,
> Ronald Reagan

SOUTH KOREA

On October 26, 1979, South Korean President Park Chung Hee was shot and killed by the head of South Korea's intelligence agency. Reagan expresses his regret in a letter to Paik Too Chin, the Speaker of South Korea's National Assembly. He mentions meeting President Park during his trip to South Korea in October 1971 and exchanging letters with him over the years.

> Dr. Paik
> South Korea
> 1980 [29]

Dear Dr. Paik:

Thank you very much for sending the essay by Professor Ahn. I was most interested in what he had to say and certainly hope that his plea for unity will be heeded by all your people. I know what a traumatic experience the tragedy of President Park's assassination must have been for all of you. May I say that I felt a sense of personal loss myself even though my meeting with President Park took place several years ago. We have on occasion exchanged letters, and I felt a friendship for this remarkable man. The free world has lost a friend and fighter for all that we hold dear.

Nancy and I are most grateful for your Christmas greeting. Please accept our best wishes to you and to Mrs. Paik for the merriest of holidays. I hope our paths will cross again in the not too distant future.

> Sincerely,
> Ronald Reagan

THE VATICAN

On June 6, 1987, President Reagan visited Pope John Paul II at the Vatican, and then traveled to Venice for a summit of the leading western industrial nations. In a reply to a friend, he praises the pope, and says that the western allies have grown closer.

Mr. Phil Regan
Pasadena, California
June 25, 1987 [30]

Dear Phil:

Just a line to thank you and Jo for your kind letter, good wishes and prayers. Our summit was a complete success but you'd never know it from the press accounts. Actually we got everything we went for and the relationship with our six allies has never been closer.

Let me assure you the pope is still Catholic and let me add, still a truly great human being. Our visit is something I'll long remember.

Nancy sends her love and from both of us to Jo.

Sincerely,
Ron

SOVIET UNION/RUSSIA

Reagan recalls the circumstances under which he met Georgi Arbatov, the director of the Soviet Union's Institute for the U.S. and Canadian Studies.

Colonel Barney Oldfield, USMC (Ret.)
Beverly Hills, California
March 12, 1984 [31]

Dear Barney:

I don't know too many people outside diplomatic circles who are pen pals with a regular in Politburo circles. We're trying to engage them in some dialogue right now. If he asks about me tell him I don't eat my young. I met him once when I was governor.* Nancy and I were taking a walk in Washington. He came out of the em-

---

* In correspondence with the authors in May 2003, Peter Hannaford wrote that Reagan's first meeting with Arbatov was probably in the summer of 1977.

bassy and evidently recognized me because he waited by his car 'til we came by and then introduced himself.

Nancy sends her best and from both of us to Vada.

Thanks again.

Sincerely,
Ron

Soviet General Secretary Konstantin Chernenko died on March 10, 1985. The next day, President Reagan went to the Soviet embassy in Washington, D.C., to pay his respects and sign a book of condolences. Below is the note he wrote.

Note of condolence
Washington, D.C.
After March 10, 1985[32]

My condolences and sympathy to Chairman Chernenko's family and to the Soviet government and people in this time of bereavement. Let us rededicate ourselves to ensuring a lasting peace between our countries.

In his reply to a birthday greeting from Soviet leader Mikhail Gorbachev, Reagan, now retired and living in Los Angeles, California, reminisces over their first summit, held in Geneva in November 1985.

His Excellency Mikhail Gorbachev
Moscow, USSR
March 1, 1990[33]

Dear Mikhail:

Thank you for your warm words about my birthday and your more than generous references to the part I played in our mutual effort to bring about improvement in Soviet-American relations.

I too have warm memories about our meetings beginning with that first meeting in Geneva. I'm happy that you too are committed to interaction between our two countries. I believe between us we can make a contribution to world peace and the brotherhood of man.

Nancy joins me in this and in the warmest wishes and greetings to Raisa and yourself. Let us keep in touch.

Sincerely,
Ron

Kathy* can we get this off to M. Gorbachev? typed of course.

---

* Kathy Osborne worked as an assistant to Reagan from his governorship through his first few postpresidential years.

On June 12, 1991, Boris Yeltsin was elected president of the Russian Federation, and on December 25, Mikhail Gorbachev resigned as president of the disintegrating Union of Soviet Socialist Republics (USSR). In a letter to his longtime pen pal, Reagan states that he has written both the former leader of the USSR and the Russian president. Still calling it the "Soviet Union," Reagan writes that he thinks the country is working toward freedom.

Mrs. Lorraine Wagner
Philadelphia, Pennsylvania
January 3, 1992 [34]

Dear Lorraine:

Forgive me for this short reply to your heartwarming letter. I'm grateful to you for writing as you did but right now I'm trying to catch up (after the holidays) with a desk loaded with paper—none of which can compare to your wonderfully warm letter.

I've just addressed a letter to Mikhail Gorbachev and another to Boris Yeltsin. I'm really optimistic about what's going on in the Soviet Union. My letters were in reply to letters from each of them. I think the Soviets are really working to become free as we are.

Nancy sends her best regards as do I and to the family. As you can see I've just switched pens. The other one gave up.

Love,
Ron

SOVIET LEADERS

Reagan's first letter to Leonid Brezhnev of the USSR, the handwritten draft of which was not located until the summer of 2003, established his foreign policy vision and may mark the beginning of the end of the Cold War.

Ignoring his State Department advisers and much of his National Security Council staff, Reagan took charge and superimposed his own philosophy on the administration with this letter. Reagan thought his advisers were too strident toward the Soviet Union, and believed that calm but tough negotiations, backed by overwhelming military power, would change the minds of the Soviet leaders.

Ronald Reagan first met a leader of the Soviet Union on June 23, 1973, in San Clemente, California.[35] Reagan was governor of California, Richard Nixon was president of the United States, and Leonid Brezhnev was the general secretary of the Soviet Union.

"When we met," Reagan would later remind Brezhnev in 1981, "I asked you if you were aware that the hopes and aspirations of millions and millions of people through-

out the world were dependent on the decisions that would be reached in your meetings." This basic idea—the importance of the decisions made by U.S. and Soviet leaders in meeting the hopes and aspirations of the people they represented—was a
recurrent theme in Reagan's personal outreach to Soviet leaders in both handwritten
correspondence and personal meetings.

Reagan's other recurrent theme was his effort to ensure Soviet leaders that the
United States had no territorial ambitions and no aggressive or offensive intention.
This he considered to have been demonstrated by U.S. restraint after World War II,
when the United States was in a unique position of power—the only country with nuclear weapons and the only major country not devastated by World War II.

Reagan emphasized these two themes when he met with Anatoly Dobrynin, Soviet
ambassador to the United States, on February 15, 1983, again when he wrote to Soviet
leader Yuri Andropov, and yet again in a brief postscript to a letter to Konstantin Chernenko, who had succeeded Andropov in the top Soviet position. They were the main
thrust of the talking points Reagan prepared for his meeting with Soviet foreign minister Andrei Gromyko in September of 1984.

And when Reagan and Gorbachev met informally at their first summit before the
formal sessions began, Reagan again chose to talk about the importance of what the
two of them did. As he later described it: "Here we were, I said, two men who had been
born in obscure rural hamlets in the middle of our respective countries, each of us poor
and from humble beginnings. Now we were the leaders of our countries and probably
the only two men in the world who could bring about World War III. At the same time
we were possibly the only two men in the world who might be able to bring peace to the
world." [36]

Reagan's personal communications with Soviet leaders in letters and meetings reflect his inclination to deal with people directly and his confidence that in a one-to-one
relationship he could be effective and convincing. "Both of us have advisors and assistants," he would later write Gorbachev, "but, you know, in the final analysis, the responsibility to preserve peace and increase cooperation is ours." [37]

Reagan's Geneva summit meetings with Gorbachev in 1985 were not his first successful experience at personal communications with leaders of other governments.
Reagan's third economic summit meeting with leaders of the largest industrialized
states in May 1983 was extremely successful because Reagan called for a change in the
rules—no pre-written communiqués and more time for the leaders to talk directly to
each other, with translators and note takers in another room. Margaret Thatcher,
Great Britain's prime minister, passed him a handwritten note saying "Thank you for
your superb chairmanship." [38] Reagan's first meeting with a Communist head of state
was with Premier Zhao Ziyang of the People's Republic of China, in January 1984,
with whom he developed considerable rapport. Reagan responded to strong words with
firmness about the Taiwan Relations Act. He went to China in April 1984, where he
had successful meetings with Zhao, the general secretary of the Chinese Communist
Party Hu Yaobang, and Deng Xiaoping. [39]

―――――――

On March 6, 1981, less than six weeks after Ronald Reagan was inaugurated, he received a letter from Leonid Brezhnev, head of the Soviet Union, reiterating existing Soviet policy. The Department of State and the president's National Security Council (NSC) began work immediately on a reply for Reagan to sign, and several drafts went back and forth between State and NSC. The president even approved a March 26 memorandum from Richard V. Allen, his national security advisor, returning a draft to State for a rewrite because Richard Pipes, NSC's Russian expert, advised that it was "undiplomatic" and deserved "more careful thought" given that it was "the first formal exchange of correspondence between the heads of state of the United States and the USSR."[40] But on March 30, the day the president was shot, Brezhnev's letter had not yet been answered.

On April 18, 1981, a week after he was released from the hospital and still recovering from the attempted assassination, Reagan sat in the White House solarium and drafted his own letter to Leonid Brezhnev on a yellow pad. In his personal diary Reagan wrote, "Don't know whether I'll send it, but enjoyed putting some thoughts down on paper."[41] Reagan sent his draft to Richard V. Allen, who had it typed as the president wrote it. Allen then tried to combine the president's draft with the State Department draft, but the president was not satisfied. On April 22 he wrote in his diary, "Won part of the battle with the bureaucrats—they drafted a letter to Brezhnev along usual lines, but included major parts of mine. We sent it back for a rewrite including more of mine."[42]

In the end the drafts were not combined—instead, both letters were sent. On April 23 Reagan wrote by hand his four-page letter to Brezhnev on his presidential stationery, a letter virtually identical to the typescript of his draft except for the order of the paragraphs and a few suggestions from Allen. "I . . . sent the letter largely as I had originally written it," Reagan would write later. On April 24 he also signed the more formal typed letter drafted by State and amended by the National Security Council. Secretary of State Alexander Haig took both letters to the Soviet embassy for delivery to Brezhnev.[43]

Here is the text of Reagan's first draft of the handwritten letter.

> General Secretary Leonid Brezhnev
> USSR
> April 18, 1981 draft[44]

My Dear Mr. President:

I regret and yet can understand the somewhat intemperate tone of your recent letter. After all we approach the problems confronting us from opposite philosophical points of view.

Is it possible that we have let ideology, political and economical philosophy and governmental policies keep us from considering the very real, everyday problems of the people we represent? Will the average Russian family be better off or even aware that his government has imposed a government of its liking on the people of Afghanistan? Is life better for the people of Cuba because the Cuban military dictates who shall govern the people of Angola?

In your letter you imply that such things have been made necessary because of territorial ambitions of the United States; that we have imperialistic designs and thus constitute a threat to your own security and that of the newly emerging nations. There not only is no evidence to support such a charge, there is solid evidence that the United States when it could have dominated the world with no risk to itself made no effort whatsoever to do so.

When WWII ended the United States had the only undamaged industrial power in the world. Its military might was at its peak—and we alone had the ultimate weapon, the nuclear bomb with the unquestioned ability to deliver it anywhere in the world. If we had sought world domination who could have opposed us?

But the United States followed a different course—one unique in all the history of mankind. We used our power and wealth to rebuild the war-ravaged economies of all the world including those nations who had been our enemies. May I say there is absolutely no substance to charges that the United States is guilty of imperialism or attempts to impose its will on other countries by use of force.

A decade or so ago, Mr. President, you and I met in San Clemente, California. I was governor of California at the time and you were concluding a series of meetings with President Nixon. Those meetings had captured the imagination of all the world. Never had peace and good will among men seemed closer at hand.

When we met I asked if you were aware that the hopes and aspirations of millions and millions of people throughout the world were dependent on the decisions that would be reached in your meetings.

You took my hand in both of yours and assured me that you were aware of that and that you were dedicated with all your heart and mind to fulfilling those hopes and dreams.

The people of the world still share that hope. Indeed the peoples of the world despite differences in racial and ethnic origin have very much in common. They want the dignity of having some control over their individual destiny. They want to work at the craft or trade of their own choosing and to be fairly rewarded. They want to raise their families in peace without harming anyone or suffering harm themselves. Government exists for their convenience not the other way around.

If they are incapable, as some would have us believe of self-government, then where in the world do we find people who are capable of governing others?

Mr. President should we not be concerned with eliminating the obstacles which prevent our people from achieving these simple goals? And isn't it possible some of these obstacles are born of government aims and goals which have little to do with the real needs and wants of our people?

It is in this spirit, in the spirit of helping the people of both our nations, that I am proposing to lift the grain embargo with the hope that we can enter into negotiations for renewal of long-term grain sales to benefit the people of our two countries for several years to come.

————

Reagan later drafted a letter to Brezhnev about Anatoly Shcharansky, a Soviet dissident exiled to Gorky, and the seven Pentecostal Christians who had taken refuge in the U.S. embassy in Moscow. Although the National Security Council had already prepared a draft, Reagan used virtually none of it, adopting only the basic organization of the letter.[45] Reagan did not make public his human rights efforts, but he and his secretary of state continued their efforts. The Pentecostals left the embassy on April 12, 1983, and were allowed to leave the Soviet Union in the next few months.[46] Shcharansky was allowed to return to Moscow in December 1986. The Brezhnev letter to which Reagan refers was dated May 25, 1981, and is the reply to Reagan's two letters of April 24. The NSC characterized it as "conciliatory in tone but unbending in substance."[47]

General Secretary Leonid Brezhnev
USSR
June 16, 1981 draft[48]

My Dear Mr. President:

I'm sorry to be so long in answering your letter to me and can only offer as an excuse the problems of settling into a routine after my hospitalization. I ask your pardon.

I won't attempt a point by point response to your letter because I agree with your observation that these matters are better discussed in person than in writing. Needless to say we are not in agreement on a number of points raised in both my letter and yours.

There is one matter however which I feel I must bring to your attention. All information having to do with my government's practices and policies past and present is available to me now that I hold this office. I have thoroughly investigated the matter of the man Shcharansky an inmate in one of your prisons. I can assure you he was never involved in any way with any agency of the U.S. government. I have seen news stories in the Soviet press suggesting that he was engaged in espionage for our country. Let me assure you this is absolutely false.

Recently his wife called upon me. They were married and spent one day together before she emigrated to Israel assuming that he would follow shortly thereafter. I believe true justice would be done if he were released and allowed to join her.

If you could find it in your heart to do this the matter would be strictly between us which is why I'm writing this letter by hand.

While on this subject may I also enter a plea on behalf of the two families who have been living in most uncomfortable circumstances in our embassy in Moscow for three years. The [Vaschenko] family and the [Chmykhalovs] are Pentecostal

Christians who feared possible persecution because of their religion. Members of that church in America would, I know, provide for them here if they were allowed to come to the United States.

Again as in the case of Shcharansky this is between the two of us and I will not reveal that I made any such request. I'm sure however you understand that such actions on your part would lessen my problems in future negotiations between our two countries.

Sincerely,

[no signature]

Yuri Andropov succeeded Brezhnev as leader of the Soviet Union on Brezhnev's death in November 1982. Reagan and his secretary of state, George Shultz, were working on increased communications with the Soviets. Shultz had arranged for Reagan to meet privately with Soviet Ambassador Anatoly Dobrynin February 15, 1983; the meeting lasted two hours and they discussed a wide range of issues—START (Strategic Arms Reduction Talks), INF, Afghanistan, Poland, and human rights, including the Pentecostal Christians living in the U.S. embassy in Moscow. On June 26 the Soviets announced that one of the families could leave and, shortly thereafter, the other. Reagan kept his word not to crow.[49]

Reagan wrote personally to Andropov on July 11, 1983, in response to a July 4 greeting from Andropov. He wrote his own draft, according to George Shultz, while at Camp David, where Reagan spent July 8–10. William P. Clark, Reagan's national security adviser, wrote a memorandum to Reagan dated July 9 recommending a substitute for "the last paragraph in your draft," which Reagan adopted with some changes.[50] Clark noted on July 13 that Shultz had read and liked the letter.[51]

General Secretary Yuri Andropov

USSR

Circa July 8, 1983 draft[52]

I appreciate very much your letter pledging an "unbending commitment of the Soviet leaders and the people of the Soviet Union to the cause of peace, the elimination of the nuclear threat and the development of relations based on mutual benefit and equality with all nations."

Let me assure you the government and the people of the United States are dedicated to the cause of peace and the elimination of the nuclear threat. It goes without saying that we seek relations with all nations based on "mutual benefit and equality." Our record since we were allied in WWII confirms that.

Mr. Secretary General don't we have the means to achieve these goals in the meetings we are presently holding in Geneva? If we can agree on mutual, verifiable reductions in the number of nuclear weapons we both hold could this not be a first step toward the elimination of all such weapons. What a blessing this would be for the people we both represent. You and I have the ability to bring this about through our negotiations in the arms reduction talks.

Yuri Andropov died on February 9, 1984, and was replaced by Konstantin Chernenko.

Reagan received a letter from Chernenko, the new head of the Soviet Union, dated March 19, 1984, on which he (Reagan) wrote, "I think this calls for a very well thought out reply and not just a routine acknowledgment that leaves the status quo as is." The Department of State drafted the reply, which focused on countering the Soviets' arguments about an alleged U.S. "threat," reaffirmed the U.S. commitment to arms control and U.S. flexibility in the search for agreement, and expressed willingness to consider a non-use of force undertaking if the Soviets agreed to confidence-building measures the United States proposed.[53] Reagan signed the seven-page typed letter and then added a postscript in his own hand that had been drafted by Robert C. McFarlane, his national security advisor, to reflect views McFarlane had often heard Reagan express in meetings with staff and visitors.[54] Chernenko's subsequent reply said, "I, of course, took note of the pledge of commitment to the lessening of tensions between our countries made by you in the handwritten addition to your letter."[55]

His Excellency Konstantin Ustinovich Chernenko
USSR
April 16, 1984[56]

. . . .

P.S. Mr. Chairman

In thinking through this letter, I have reflected at some length on the tragedy and scale of Soviet losses in warfare through the ages. Surely those losses which are beyond description, must affect your thinking today. I want you to know that neither I nor the American people hold any offensive intentions toward you or the Soviet people. The truth of that statement is underwritten by the history of our restraint at a time when our virtual monopoly on strategic power provided the means for expansion had we so chosen. We did not then nor shall we now. Our common and urgent purpose must be the translation of this reality into a lasting redirection of tensions between us. I pledge to you my profound commitment to that goal.

Reagan's first handwritten letter to Gorbachev followed their first summit in Geneva on November 19–20, 1985. The letter was drafted by Jack Matlock of the NSC on guidance from Robert C. McFarlane but was, McFarlane says, "clearly the president's idea. We discussed it before leaving Geneva to come home and it was important to him to maintain the momentum that he created in his sessions with Gorbachev there."[57] The letter expresses the same themes Reagan had developed in his earlier letters to Soviet leaders. As those who worked for him became familiar with his thinking and how he wanted to proceed, they were able to write drafts that more readily met with his approval.

Gorbachev replied on December 24, 1985, with a long handwritten letter of his own characterized by the Department of State as informal and very much Gorbachev's own style—plain and direct. Reagan replied to that letter by hand on February 16, 1985.[58]

General Secretary Mikhail Gorbachev
USSR
November 28, 1985[59]

Dear General Secretary Gorbachev:

Now that we are both home and facing the task of leading our countries into a more constructive relationship with each other, I wanted to waste no time in giving you some of my initial thoughts on our meetings. Though I will be sending shortly, in a more formal and official manner, a more detailed commentary on our discussions, there are some things I would like to convey very personally and privately.

First, I want you to know that I found our meetings of great value. We had agreed to speak frankly, and we did. As a result, I came away from the meeting with a better understanding of your attitudes. I hope you also understand mine a little better. Obviously there are many things on which we disagree, and disagree very fundamentally. But if I understand you correctly, you too are determined to take steps to see that our nations manage their relations in a peaceful fashion. If this is the case, then this is one point on which we are in total agreement—and it is after all the most fundamental one of all.

As for our substantive differences, let me offer some thoughts on two of the key ones.

Regarding strategic defense and its relation to the reduction of offensive nuclear weapons, I was struck by your conviction that the American program is somehow designed to secure a strategic advantage—even to permit a first strike capability. I also noted your concern that research and testing in this area could be a cover for developing and placing offensive weapons in space.

As I told you, neither of these concerns is warranted. But I can understand, as you explained so eloquently, that these are matters which cannot be taken on faith. Both of us must cope with what the other side is doing and judge the implications for the security of his own country. I do not ask you to take my assurances on faith.

However the truth is that the United States has no intention of using its strategic defense program to gain any advantage, and there is no development underway to create space-based offensive weapons. Our goal is to eliminate any possibility of a first strike from either side. This being the case, we should be able to find a way, in practical terms, to relieve the concerns you have expressed.

For example, could our negotiators, when they resume work in January, discuss frankly and specifically what sort of future developments each of us would find threatening? Neither of us, it seems, wants to see offensive weapons, particularly weapons of mass destruction, deployed in space. Should we not attempt to define what sort of systems have that potential and then try to find verifiable ways to prevent their development?

And can't our negotiators deal more frankly and openly with the question of how to eliminate a first-strike potential on both sides? Your military now has an advantage in this area—a three to one advantage in warheads that can destroy hardened targets with little warning. That is obviously alarming to us, and explains many of the efforts we are making in our modernization program. You may feel perhaps that the United States has some advantages in other categories. If so, let's insist that our negotiators face up to these issues and find a way to improve the security of both countries by agreeing on appropriately balanced reductions. If you are as sincere as I am in not seeking to secure or preserve one-sided advantages, we will find a solution to these problems.

Regarding another key issue we discussed, that of regional conflicts, I can assure you that the United States does not believe that the Soviet Union is the cause of all the world's ills. We do believe, however, that your country has exploited and worsened local tensions and conflict by militarizing them and, indeed, intervening directly and indirectly in struggles arising out of local causes. While we both will doubtless continue to support our friends, we must find a way to do so without use of armed force. This is the crux of the point I tried to make.

One of the most significant steps in lowering tension in the world—and tension in U.S.–Soviet relations—would be a decision on your part to withdraw your forces from Afghanistan. I gave careful attention to your comments on this issue at Geneva, and am encouraged by your statement that you feel political reconciliation is possible. I want you to know that I am prepared to cooperate in any reasonable way to facilitate such a withdrawal, and that I understand that it must be done in a manner which does not damage Soviet security interests. During our meetings I mentioned one idea which I thought might be helpful and I will welcome any further suggestions you may have.

These are only two of the key issues on our current agenda. I will soon send some thought on others. I believe that we should act promptly to build the momentum our meetings initiated.

In Geneva I found our private sessions particularly useful. Both of us have advisors and assistants, but, you know, in the final analysis, the responsibility to preserve peace and increase cooperation is ours. Our people look to us for leadership, and nobody can provide it if we don't. But we won't be very effective leaders unless we can rise above the specific but secondary concerns that preoccupy our respective bureaucracies and give our governments a strong push in the right direction.

So, what I want to say finally is that we should make the most of the time before we meet again to find some specific and significant steps that would give meaning to our commitment to peace and arms reduction. Why not set a goal—privately, just between the two of us—to find a practical way to solve critical issues—the two I have mentioned—by the time we meet in Washington?

Please convey regards from Nancy and me to Mrs. Gorbachev. We genuinely enjoyed meeting you in Geneva and are already looking forward to showing you something of our country next year.

Sincerely yours,
Ronald Reagan

CHAPTER TWENTY-FOUR

Pen Pals

T HE 13-YEAR-OLD *was struck by Ronald Reagan's performance in* Brother Rat *in 1943 and she wrote to him. Lorraine Makler was young and insecure, living in suburban America. Ronald Reagan was handsome, married, and famous, a star living in Hollywood. He replied, and over the next 50 years Lorraine would receive approximately 150 letters from Reagan.*[1]

In the mid-1940s, Lorraine became the president of the Philadelphia chapter of Reagan's fan club. She stood out among the several hundred members of the international fan club because she relentlessly inserted herself into Reagan's life and he didn't seem to mind. Wagner corresponded with Reagan from his Hollywood days through to his post-presidential years. She wrote about the major personal and policy issues he faced and confided in him about her own life. She also closely followed what was being written and said about her pen pal and then took action. Lorraine defended Reagan in letters to editors of national magazines and newspapers that carried unfavorable articles on him. Throughout Reagan's career, Lorraine's letters appeared in the Philadelphia Bulletin, Philadelphia Inquirer, Newsweek, Time, *and some of the Los Angeles–area newspapers. In addition, Wagner frequently called Philadelphia talk-radio shows to defend her pen pal.*

Ronald Reagan married Nancy Davis on March 4, 1952, three months before Lorraine married Elwood Wagner, a sailor in the Navy and a member of the Reagan fan club over which she presided. From mid-1952 on, Lorraine addressed her letters to "Ron and Nancy" and Reagan usually addressed his to "Lorraine and Wag." Reagan wrote most of the replies but Nancy Reagan wrote to Lorraine as well. Members of Lorraine's family also corresponded with the Reagans. One of the letters below is President Reagan's reply to a letter from Sandy, the Wagners' daughter.[2]

A second pen pal came into Reagan's life after he became president. On March 12, 1984, President Reagan introduced himself to Rudolph Lee-Hines during a question-and-answer session with students at Congress Heights Elementary School in southeast Washington, D.C. He said, "I want to have a student from here be a pen pal, and we'll exchange letters. And I understand that the young man who's going to do this is

Rudolph Hines. Where is Rudolph Hines? He doesn't know this yet." Rudolph came forward and the president continued: "[T]he idea is that you and I will kind of exchange letters with each other. You write and I'll answer you, or I'll write and you'll answer me. . . . And maybe you can tell me some of the things that are going on here, and maybe sometimes in my letters, I'll complain about what's going on at the White House." This pen-pal relationship continued to the end of Reagan's presidency.[3]

The official pen-pal relationship began for two reasons. At age five and in kindergarten, Rudolph distinguished himself as a good reader in the Writing to Read program, a national IBM project that taught students how to read using computer software. In the fall of 1983, President Reagan and his cabinet began participating in Partnerships in Education, a government initiative to encourage the private sector to become more involved in education. President Reagan took this charge seriously, and when Congress Heights Elementary School, later renamed Martin Luther King, Jr. Elementary School, was chosen as a White House partner, the school's principal, William Dalton, designated Rudolph to be the president's pen pal. Rudolph was chosen because of his excellent reading skills and because Dalton felt that he could write letters with minimum help from adults.[4]

Rudolph's nickname is traditionally spelled R-U-D-Y, but he and President Reagan agreed in their correspondence that the president would use two Ds. Reagan addressed his letters to Ruddy.

There was something eerily similar about the early years of Ronald Reagan and Rudolph Lee-Hines as expressed in their correspondence. Reagan wrote letters about his Huck Finn–type adventures as a child. Ruddy had his own Huck Finn adventures and described them in letters to President Reagan. Ruddy also wrote to the president about acting, friendship, summer camp, schoolwork, and learning how to ride a horse. Reagan drew from his own boyhood experiences to advise and counsel his pen pal on his activities.

President Reagan's relationship with Rudolph went beyond the written word. Because the White House had adopted Rudolph's school, students at Martin Luther King, Jr. Elementary School made field trips to the White House, occasionally joined groups welcoming President and Mrs. Reagan upon their return from a trip, and had school visits by White House staffers, many of whom volunteered as tutors and participated in school activities. President and Mrs. Reagan visited the school several times. On January 15, 1986, President Reagan spoke at Rudolph's school. He began his remarks by mentioning his "pen pal, Rudy Hines." Mrs. Reagan visited the school in 1984 and 1986. When the Reagans traveled to Washington in November 1989 for the unveiling of their portraits at the White House, they returned to MLK Elementary School.[5]

Reagan's correspondence and interaction with Lorraine and Rudolph has some similarities. In letters to both, he showed flashes of humor when discussing criticism of him. He responded to their letters dutifully and seemed to enjoy the continuity of the relationships. Lorraine and Rudolph were invited to the White House several times; Lorraine attended both inaugurations and Rudolph attended the second inauguration.

Reagan had other pen pals. For instance, from the 1940s to the early 1990s he corresponded with Zelda Multz, the third president of the international fan club dedicated to Reagan's acting career.[6]

A selection of correspondence to Lorraine is reproduced below; some of his other letters to her appear elsewhere in this book. A few of Reagan's letters to Zelda and all of his extant correspondence to Ruddy, with the exception of a few short notes, are included in this chapter.

LORRAINE WAGNER

On February 26, 1951, Time reported that master of ceremonies Ronald Reagan gave "a diatribe against the 'irresponsible press' of Hollywood" at a banquet at the Beverly Hills Hotel held by Photoplay magazine. The June 1951 issue of Motion Picture, which was released by mid-May, carried "An Open Letter to Ronald Reagan" signed by the editors of the magazine. The letter said: "According to newspaper reports, the Screen Actors Guild, of which you are president, plans this summer to launch a campaign to prevent fan magazines from running any stories about the private lives of established film stars. You implied that such stories might be all right for young actors on their way up, but that, once a person becomes a star, the only news that should be published about him ought to be stories which the star himself considers acceptable." The editors accused Reagan of having a double standard; he allowed the press into his home and life when he was happily married to Jane Wyman but did not want press coverage of his divorce.

Reagan defended himself in a letter dated May 21, 1951, to the editors of Motion Picture. He denied all of the charges against him made by the magazine, including a report that he was planning a campaign to prevent press coverage of the lives of stars. He stated that SAG was "unalterably opposed to censorship." Concerning his personal life, he wrote: "As for the family or private life stories I permitted in 1941 and 1943, experience has led me to believe this was a mistake. The selling of motion pictures should not be based on the private lives of the people employed in them. No industry should entrust the merchandising of a billion dollars' worth of product to the frailties of human nature." Reagan asked that his letter be printed in Motion Picture. In a reply to Reagan, Maxwell Hamilton, editor of the magazine, defended himself but did not agree to publish Reagan's letter.

Lorraine Makler entered the fray with a letter to Hamilton dated July 3, 1951. She wrote that the public wants substantive news instead of sensational stories, and defended Reagan and other actors against intrusive reporting. In his response to Makler, Hamilton reported that he was prepared to publish both sides of the correspondence if Reagan felt that his magazine was being unfair to him. Lorraine continued her defense of Reagan in a lengthy second letter to Hamilton dated July 24, 1951.

The next two letters relate to the controversy.

Miss Lorraine Makler
Philadelphia, Pennsylvania
July 12, 1951 [7]

Dear Lorraine:

I'm balancing this and a magazine on my knee before going into a meeting but I wanted to get off a quick line to say I'm glad I'm not Maxwell Hamilton.

Seriously I'm really grateful to you for championing my cause—actually it is the cause of all actors. Your letter is so "on the nose" I'm taking it to our "Motion Picture Industry Council" to show them how different the "voice of our public" is from the nagging voices of our "gossiping buzzard brigade."

Again my heartfelt thanks and sincere regards always—

Ronnie

P.S. It is now a few days later and I have received your letter and the copy of Mr. Hamilton's. I am enclosing the letter he wrote to me—whenever you finish send it or a copy back because I am building a file on Mr. Hamilton.

You will remember I told you he had sent a three-page letter explaining why *Motion Picture* could not print my answer to their open letter and that this three-page letter was as dishonest as their original attack? This is the letter and while it is very clever I still stand on my charge that it is thoroughly dishonest.

Hamilton consistently employs an old debating trick—that is to answer your letter by assuming that you said something other than you intended. You of course are supposed to reply defending yourself and attempting to clarify your stand which draws you away from his original falsehood and serves the double purpose also of getting you on the defensive.

In his own letter to you for example his last paragraph holds the "stinger." He assumes that you have charged him with Communist sympathies. You did nothing of the kind—you cited my anti-Communist record and urged that because of it I deserved some consideration. Mr. Hamilton is trying to get you to reply stating that you didn't intend to accuse him of any such thing. He also charges that you are planning on printing only my side of the story (ignoring the fact that his side was printed in *Motion Picture*) also forgetting that in your letter you told him you were reprinting <u>his</u> letter <u>and my answer</u>. Of course he wants my answer and then a <u>second</u> answer from him.

And the <u>big lie</u> in his letter to you is in paragraph three in which he states he told me they would be "delighted to publish both sides of the argument." Look his letter over carefully—you'll find <u>no such offer.</u> You will find in the last line of paragraph one a clear statement that they <u>won't print my reply.</u>

In keeping with his regular practice—paragraph one charges me with criticizing the use of an open letter. So he defends "open letters" as a journalistic device. Did I attack "open letters" or did I attack falsehoods contained in an open letter? That's pretty obvious—I <u>wrote an open letter</u> myself. In the same paragraph he justifies his action by quoting the *L.A. Daily News*—he does this again in paragraph three and assumes that having read something in the papers it was true. Well that was the basis for my "squak"—if he had checked with me he would have learned that I had been misquoted in those publications and I hadn't named a fan magazine as he charges.

Paragraph two quoting "Tom Brady" is completely off base. My story with Brady was that the Screen Actors Guild was going to put a stop if possible to studios pressuring actors into publicity gags when the actor felt it was bad for him careerwise.

It goes on in this vein all the way through. His charge that he can show you stories that I censored! Of course he can. But he doesn't explain that the only stories I get (or any actor) to censor are interviews in which we are being quoted. Well if his "interviewer" has me "saying" things I didn't say in the interview certainly I change them—this is certainly my privilege.

Paragraph five about "Tony Curtis" is pretty funny. He admits that five movies and twelve minutes on the screen resulted in a flood of fan mail so the studio starred him—then he says the fan magazines did the trick. The fan mags started yelling for stories after the public saw him and said "tell us about him."

Paragraph six really gets down to what Mr. Hamilton has been mad about for three years. His idea of the "background" of news is a personal quote from me on a subject I don't even discuss with close friends.

Well there it is Lorraine—the whole mess including his letter to me. Frankly I think his "open letter" and my reply are a complete story only you have hit him with his lies exposed and he's trying to cover up. Anyway you have most of the facts—as many as I can think of and I have faith in your good judgment. In writing to him may I remind you of something my Pop once told me—"There is one kind of contest you should never get into with a skunk."

Don't hesitate to write me about anything that bothers you.

> Best always,
> Ronnie

Miss Lorraine Makler
Philadelphia, Pennsylvania
August 8, 1951 [8]

Dear Lorraine:

Just a quick word before I hop a train—it seems I'm appearing at the "Soap Box Derby" in Akron Ohio.

I think you have really written Mr. Hamilton's obituary and packed him away for keeps. Even if he should answer (which I doubt) I don't think he can say anything which would require any further reply from you.

With regard to your questions; in an "off the record" discussion with several people I did mention or clarify what I meant by "irresponsible press." However I have never mentioned the name of any individual or publication to the press and the stories quoting me as doing so are completely false.

Now as to the "Producers Association." This is the organization responsible for our voluntary censorship code. They set the rules for themselves in order to keep the screen clean and in good taste. Along with this they prescribe a code of ethics governing advertising (Howard Hughes at RKO* doesn't obey this code but they can't help that).

They have no authority over anything written about Hollywood except that in an effort to keep publicity on a higher plane they have told all those "reporters" who want entrée to the studios that they must conform to the code as established by them. If someone does get out of line they can't keep him from writing—they can only refuse him future studio cooperation. It is because we the actors feel this group hasn't set a high enough standard that we are going to (in our negotiations) tell them of our problems.

Must catch that train now. Again from the bottom of my heart thanks. You have been a champion without equal.

> Best,
> Ronnie

On November 11, 1962, ABC-TV aired "The Political Obituary of Richard M. Nixon." The program consisted of an interview with Alger Hiss, a former State Department official who was convicted of perjury for stating that he did not participate in a Communist espionage ring. Congressman Richard M. Nixon had led the House Un-American Activities Committee's investigation of Hiss in 1948. Hiss spoke to ABC about the former vice president: "My impression of him as an investigator was that he was less interested in developing the facts objectively than in seeking ways of making a preconceived plan appear plausible. . . . This feeling grew increasingly throughout the hearings. . . . I think that he was politically carried along. Whether the initial motivation was political, I certainly don't think that he was unaware of the political boost, the political soaring up into outer space that the hearings and the subsequent trial provided for him."[9]

Reagan defends Nixon in this letter.

> Mrs. E. H. Wagner
> Philadelphia, Pennsylvania
> November 20, 1962[10]

Dear Lorraine:

Just a quick line to answer your letter re the ABC show.

I don't think straight news reporting should be edited or censored. For example, out here ABC taped an interview with a newspaper editor about the Hiss broadcast, but then edited the tape in such a way that the broadcast appeared favorable to Hiss when actually it had gone the other way. Fortunately, having a newspaper the editor was able to tell his side the next day. However, I don't think

---

* Howard Hughes was a film producer and billionaire who owned RKO Pictures during the late 1940s and the early 1950s.

the Hiss broadcast comes under the banner of news reporting. It was a plain case of allowing a convicted perjuror and spy to attack a man who had served as vice president of the United States. In my opinion ABC was guilty of the worst possible taste and your local station was completely right in refusing to carry the broadcast.

My best to Wag.

Sincerely,
Ronnie

Ronald Reagan's first autobiography, Where's the Rest of Me? The Ronald Reagan Story, *was published in 1965. He writes about the circumstances that led to that book.*

Mr. and Mrs. Elwood H. Wagner
Philadelphia, Pennsylvania
July 25, 1963 [11]

Dear Lorraine and Wag:

I just have time for this hasty line before taking off for a few days, but did want to answer the question about the book.

I am afraid it is autobiographical. The publisher wanted it that way in order to get at the story of the Screen Actors Guild and some of the Communist assault on Hollywood.

Have no time for more, but did want to answer about my literary epic. Am glad I only have one life to write about because it's really a chore.

Best regards.

Sincerely,
Ronnie

*Reagan thanks Wagner and her husband for Christmas gifts but asks that in the future they make contributions to charity instead.**

Mr. and Mrs. Elwood Wagner
Philadelphia, Pennsylvania
January 2, 1964 [12]

Dear Lorraine and Wag:

On behalf of all of us our thanks for your wonderful and thoughtful gifts.

The Skipper † is very large with the crayons and keeps me busy sketching animals for him to color. Patti was of course thrilled with her gift, and I'm not just

---

* Wagner replied that she and her husband would like to continue sending gifts because their division of labor—Lorraine choosing the gifts and Elwood packaging them—was something that her husband cherished. The two couples continued to exchange gifts for years. Telephone interview with Lorraine Wagner on March 27, 2003.

† Skipper was the nickname for Ronald Prescott Reagan, Ronald and Nancy's son. He was born on May 28, 1958.

being polite. She is constantly raiding my desk for pencils so now we're both happy, and of course your gifts to us which go with the tray and the other things, are much appreciated.

Now, however, I want to offer a proposition and I would love to have your frank view on this. I think I mentioned this last year, but then we all went ahead and did what we've always been doing. Nancy and I every once in a while feel so guilty. Perhaps that isn't the right word, but you know what we mean. So much good fortune has been ours that we feel we should do more and receive less. Now, how would you feel about an agreement that whatever you were going to do for us and we were going to do for you at Christmas, that we instead contribute in your names the same amount to charity, or to someone with a greater need, and consider that our exchange of gifts? Please let us know your honest thinking about this as the idea is no good unless it's mutual.

Again our thanks to you and all our best wishes for the coming year.

Sincerely,
Ronnie

———

In several cases that were heard in 1962 and 1963, the U.S. Supreme Court declared the official reading of prayer in public schools unconstitutional. On April 22, 1964, a Wall Street Journal *article noted: "Perhaps the loudest din falling on Congressional ears these days is not calling for civil rights or anti-poverty legislation but clamoring for prayer—public school prayer, that is. Far from subsiding as last year's Supreme Court decision outlawing required school prayer and devotional Bible reading grows more distant, pressures on Congress to initiate counter-action have been steadily expanding. Local and national campaigns on behalf of a Constitutional amendment to 'put God back in the schools' have flooded the Capitol with supporting mail and petitions (one of them almost three miles long)."* [13]

Reagan discusses his positions on Republican presidential candidate Senator Barry Goldwater as well as prayer in public places.

Mr. and Mrs. Elwood Wagner
Philadelphia, Pennsylvania
June 16, 1964 [14]

Dear Lorraine and Wag:

Just a quick line as I try to catch up in the lull between our primary campaign and the convention. Now I'm sure you realize I respect anyone's right to their political beliefs. My only complaint with regard to my choice, Barry, is that a concerted campaign has been made to keep people from knowing where he really stands, and many people are confused by what his opponents say he stands for. Just make sure that your opinion is based on something other than these false charges and then in the good old American way, it's just a case of each of us backing his own choice and all of us accepting with good grace the outcome.

With regard to the Prayer Amendment I don't believe a test case would work. No law has been passed. We have only an interpretation by the Supreme Court based on a test case, so the Court of course would render the same decision in any new test. The Constitution says, Congress shall make no law with regard to religion, either endorsing or restricting it. Well I used the wrong term there, "endorsing." The Constitution is pretty explicit that Congress shall do nothing to create a state church. Our Congress has made no such law so what is affecting us today is an interpretation by the Court that in itself assumes the power of law, and in my opinion violates the Constitution in that it restricts religious practice by refusing to allow a child to say a prayer while on public property. The suggested amendment is really in the nature of a clarification so that the Constitution would spell out that we could pray voluntarily, any place and at any time. Frankly I am for it and hope it passes because this Court has gone a long way toward taking over the functions of Congress with regard to making laws.

I have no way of knowing if or when we can get East. I am hopeful of doing some campaigning, but even that is indefinite until I know whether I'll be working or not. Maybe I'll just have to depend on you telling us about the Fair, although we do have a great desire to see it. But then I've learned one thing about this business, nothing is certain and things can change on short notice.

Best regards.

Sincerely,
Ronnie

For the first time in its 55-year history, the National Association for the Advancement of Colored People (NAACP) formally took a stand on a presidential candidate when a resolution opposing Barry Goldwater was adopted at its annual convention in June 1964.

Two weeks before the Republican National Convention in San Francisco, California, Reagan defends Goldwater against the charge that he opposes civil rights.

Mr. and Mrs. Elwood Wagner
Philadelphia, Pennsylvania
July 2, 1964 [15]

Dear Lorraine and Wag:

I know I probably sound like a stuck record with this idea about Barry's being misquoted, and yet the assault against him has now reached such a point of desperation that there seems to be no conscience whatsoever with regard to ignoring things he has actually said. For example on the civil rights issue he did his best to explain that he was for civil rights but against obtaining civil rights at the cost of invading certain basic rights of all citizens of both races. I don't know whether you know this, but I think you should, that curiously enough Barry has a fantastic record of personal involvement in behalf of Negroes long before he ever got in politics. As a businessman in Phoenix he was aroused when he discovered that a Negro orchestra leader had been denied service in the airport café. Until that time he had not known there was any discrimination practiced at the then new airport. Before he stopped he had desegregated the airport, desegregated the National Guard, I believe the first state where this was accomplished, desegregated the schools in Arizona and was the first employer to hire a Negro secretary. The NAACP made him an honorary member.

All of this they seem to have forgotten. He didn't confine his work to just this particular racial problem. His efforts in behalf of the Indians in Arizona have made him the most beloved white man on the reservations. He is the only life member of a Mexican American Legion Post, and this happened as the result of his work to get a better break for Mexican Americans. Just one incident involved the preventing [of] deportation of a Mexican, now an American citizen, after liberal Senator Chavez of New Mexico* and two governors had refused to even hear the man's story.

Well enough of this, I'll answer any and all questions but in the meantime am enclosing two booklets. The one by the senator explains itself, the other I have found to be the most complete compilation of the subversive record in this country. The man who authored it is completely reliable and I guarantee it will be interesting reading, but frightening. May I just say I think it's wonderful of you to keep an open mind but also to make such an effort to find out the facts on all sides. I wish there were more of you and less people operating on just plain prejudice.

Best regards.

Sincerely,
Ronnie

P.S. If I'm overdoing the pitch just holler and I'll lay off.

In a question-and-answer session on July 10, 1964, at the Republican Convention, Goldwater said that he supported giving the supreme commander of the North Atlantic Treaty Organization (NATO) authority to use tactical nuclear weapons in the event of a Soviet attack on Europe, but wanted the American president to maintain control of long-range nuclear weapons.[16] Reagan speaks briefly to this issue in writing his pen pal.

Some of the attitudes and policies toward the United Nations and foreign assistance that Reagan would put forth during his presidency are seen in this 1964 letter. He also continues to defend Goldwater's civil rights record, and declares his own opposition to the civil rights legislation under consideration by the U.S. Congress.

---

* Senator Dennis Chavez (D–New Mexico). Chavez was appointed to the United States Senate in 1935 and remained in that post until he succumbed to cancer on November 18, 1962.

Mr. and Mrs. Elwood Wagner
Philadelphia, Pennsylvania
August 4, 1964 [17]

Dear Lorraine and Wag:

I'll have to take this point by point.

First, with regard to the man who challenged that Barry was not an honorary member of NAACP. The man is right as of now. Barry was given an honorary life membership because of his contributions in Arizona to the cause of civil rights, but he returned that membership not too long ago when the NAACP launched an all-out attack against him. He felt it was the only honorable thing to do since they seemed to have changed their minds about him. I can well understand your point, or your concern that the legislation should be passed and then changed later. However, I think you'll find that historically it is much more difficult to undo a bad law, or modify it after it's passed, than it is while the legislation is still in the talking stage. I personally believe that the present civil rights bill is purely an emotional bill based on political expediency. You will find that many of the things the bill supposedly does are already covered by law, and that the problem has been unwillingness to enforce existing laws. The main point that caused concern in the present legislation and was I think responsible for the way Barry voted, was the dangerous precedent now established that a man is guilty when charged and must prove his innocence. As we all know, one of the great advances in human relationships under our Constitution was the idea that a man is innocent and his guilt must be proven by the state beyond the shadow of a doubt. Under this new bill any individual can charge the proprietor of a café, or bar, or hotel, or an employer with discrimination, and the man accused is guilty as charged until and unless he can prove the charge is false. I personally believe the danger in this far overshadows the evil we are trying to correct.

Now regarding your other points. I'm afraid the present administration and even the previous one, have given lip service to NATO, but they've made no effort to correct some of the problems that are causing our European allies great concern and which have kept some of those allies from contributing their prescribed share of manpower and resources. One of the touchiest is America's reluctance to allow our allies any partnership with regard to decisions over nuclear weapons. The U.N. question is too complicated I'm afraid for me to go into in great detail, but basically it has to do with the need for reorganization. No one, including Barry, suggests locking the door and closing up shop, but no one in the beginning even contemplated a U.N. in which some 60 new and very much uneducated nations such as the new African states, with a total population between them less than that of the United States, could outvote the United States 60 to one. This has been coupled with a tendency lately to violate the U.N. constitution and interfere directly with the internal affairs of various states. Again we come to the matter of precedent. On the basis of what we did in Africa, the U.N. could today actually demand the right to move into the South and take action on our racial problems.

On the point of economic assistance or showing people what to do, you are right that this is the purpose of the Peace Corps, but this is at a very local level of showing individuals how to do practical things in their everyday lives. I think Barry's point with regard to foreign aid is aimed at a bigger or higher level of national policy, for example pointing out that our great prosperity and wealth was the result of free, private investment, without government cartels, controls and the state monopoly now practiced in so many countries.

Well that's enough of lecture. Now to answer a happier question, our ranch is in the Malibu hills between the coast highway and the Ventura freeway, the nearest town Agoura. That should locate it pretty well in case you read news of fires, and believe me I hope you don't.

All the best.

Sincerely,
Ronnie

Reagan discusses Goldwater again and suggests ways to combat intolerance. He reveals that he once resigned from a country club that barred membership based on religion.

Mr. and Mrs. Elwood Wagner
Philadelphia, Pennsylvania
September 8, 1964 [18]

Dear Lorraine and Wag:

First of all happy to hear you had such a nice vacation, and even happier that it took you past a pretzel factory. We are enjoying the pretzels very much—thank you.

I'm afraid the campaign is heating up to the point that I'm unable to find too much time for our philosophical discussions. Barry is due here in town today and I'm on the reception committee as well as the MC for the rally tonite. I know one thing, we are not in disagreement at all about injustice or the need to do something for people who are the victims of injustice, but aren't we toying with a very great danger, namely that of deciding the end justifies the means. Once we accept this, regardless of how noble the end, we have opened the door for almost every kind of mischief. I can't help but feel that someplace along the line we have decided to substitute law for individual responsibility. In other words sort of like the clergyman who gets discouraged trying to teach people to be good, and says, "From here on I'll just order them to be good and never mind their soul's salvation." Take for example an apartment house. Rather than pass a law that says to the proprietor he cannot manage his property, doesn't the real responsibility lie with the individual tenants of the apartment building saying, if this building has rules discriminating against people because of race or religion I won't live there. Sometimes it seems to me that a lot of well-meaning people who feel strongly about intolerance don't feel strongly enough to stand up and be counted as individuals to make a fuss, so they feel a law can remove this responsibility from them and thus they can have what they want without having to take an individual stand.

I don't want to sound smug but some years ago I faced this decision with regard to a country club that barred membership to one group on the basis of religion. I resigned and stated my reason for resigning. It was quite a bombshell, but you'd be surprised what a follow-up effect there was and how many people decided that it was their individual responsibility also.

Well, I do have to get busy so again thanks for the pretzels, and now I'm off campaigning.

Sincerely,
Ronnie

P.S. This will sound like outright politicking but I wish you could know this guy Barry as I have known him over the years. He is a truly humble man and utterly incapable of doing an unkind or dishonorable thing.

After several months of corresponding with Reagan about Goldwater, Lorraine reversed her position and gave her support to the Republican presidential aspirant. President Lyndon B. Johnson defeated Goldwater in a landslide victory in 1964.

Mr. and Mrs. Elwood Wagner
Philadelphia, Pennsylvania
November 5, 1964 [19]

Dear Lorraine and Wag:

I'm not going to try to write a long letter. As you can imagine we are kind of snowed under winding up this campaign, and frankly getting ready to continue the fight.

I did, however, want to tell you what a thrill it was to get your letter regarding your decision. I don't agree that you have been brainwashed. I do agree that you kept an open mind, looked at both sides and made a personal decision in the finest example of the tradition of our democracy. If we are to continue having freedom it will be because of people like yourselves and not those who are just blindly going down the road, voting on the basis of who makes the most attractive promise. This was only one battle and the war will go on because keeping freedom is a continuous process.

Bless you, and best regards.

Sincerely,
Ronnie

Although Reagan's fan club had disbanded many years earlier, Wagner continued to defend her pen pal in letters to editors of newspaper and magazines. She also received solicitations as a result of having supported Goldwater.

Mr. and Mrs. Elwood H. Wagner
Philadelphia, Pennsylvania
July 6, 1965 [20]

Dear Lorraine and Wag:

As usual it was good to hear from you and I never cease being amazed at the letters you manage in my behalf, but now about the letter of solicitation you received.

You have your own problems there and your own candidates to support. I couldn't understand how you received such a letter, until I discovered the committee for its first mailing used a list of Goldwater contributors. I won't promise not to turn in the names of the others you gave me, but I really mean you are to feel no obligation and the letter was sent without my knowledge. I would say you have already served above and beyond the call of duty.

Best regards.

Sincerely,
Ronnie

Reagan answers Lorraine's question about a filming incident.

Mr. and Mrs. Elwood H. Wagner
Philadelphia, Pennsylvania
July 26, 1965 [21]

Dear Lorraine and Wag:

First of all it's true that a saber came my direction and nicked me, but I've probably been cut just as bad shaving. Actually it could have been quite serious in that I was tied to a post and the saber was supposed to have gone past my ear and embedded itself in the post. They cooked up a mechanical aiming device for the thrust but the saber cut itself a new track and caught me on the point of the shoulder, fortunately on top of the shoulder bone so that it just nicked me, bounced off and went on into the post. Had it been a little lower, where it could not have bounced over, I would have been punctured.

About the newspaper here, we have two and I'll give it some thought as to which one might give the best accounts, but you have plenty of time because there will probably be no official declaration until some time this winter.

Now about your friends. I have gone down the schedule and believe it or not I'm in the opposite ends of the state at every stage. When they are in Los Angeles I will be in the northern end of the state contacting party leaders in the so-called smoke-filled rooms. Please tell them how sorry I am and point out to them that this is kind of an abnormal situation for me. Our number here is GRanite 2-2332.

Best regards.

Sincerely,
Ronnie

Reagan confides that he will run for governor of California.

Mr. and Mrs. Elwood H. Wagner
Philadelphia, Pennsylvania
December 24, 1965 [22]

Dear Lorraine and Wag:

I won't take time between politics and holidays to make this much of a letter, but just wanted to tell you I'll be making the big announcement on statewide television here on January 4. From then on I guess it'll be for real.

I hope you all had a happy Christmas and Hanukkah.

Nancy sends her best wishes.

Best regards,
Ronnie

P.S. The above was written before your last letter arrived. I'm returning your two letters for mailing or whatever you decide. First on Ed Sullivan I wrote to him and told him how Guild records indicate I wasn't even in California during the period I'm supposed to have received a letter. Anyway he has the facts now so we'll see what he does. Certainly your letter would do no harm but on the other hand he may be on the way to apologizing already.

On the other—I'd say mail it although Zel is correct. There is no doubt the writer is not on my side yet I must say he showed great signs of trying to be fair and his bias only slipped out in a kind of "double meaning." A letter of yours could be pretty good punishment though because so many people took his story at face value and thought he was being nice to me. It must drive him a little crazy to think he actually ended up helping me when that wasn't his intention.

Four days after he won the Republican Party's nomination for governor of California, Reagan discusses Lorraine's letter writing on his behalf.

Mr. and Mrs. Elwood H. Wagner
Philadelphia, Pennsylvania
June 11, 1966 [23]

Dear Lor and Wag:

I won't try to write much of a letter, because we are off to Arizona for a few days to pick up Patti.

The score is in, and of course it's far above anything we had expected. Now, the real job begins. I appreciate not only your good wishes but all that you have been doing with regard to the letters. As a matter of fact, we reprinted and used as a headquarters display, the Crocker editorial, based on your letter to him quoting my letter to Sandy. So you see you were in the campaign after all.

Again, thanks and all the best.

Sincerely,
Ronnie

––––––––

A month after winning the governorship of California, Reagan recognizes that there is more to the state's problems than he knew when he was running for office.

Mr. and Mrs. Elwood Wagner
Philadelphia, Pennsylvania
December 8, 1966[24]

Dear Lorraine and Wag:

Just a quick line from a very busy whirl—the only thing I've found busier than the campaign—what happens afterward—to thank you for your good words and kind messages. Each day I learn more of the problems confronting us and discover things I wish I'd known during the campaign. I didn't say half enough.

I haven't much time, but I will answer one question. Yes, Peanuts was in the picture with us, and it was a lot of fun working with him.

All the best to you.

Sincerely,
Ron

––––––––

Less than a month into his governorship, Reagan finds humor in his growing conflict with the state's colleges and universities.

Mr. and Mrs. Elwood H. Wagner
Philadelphia, Pennsylvania
January 18, 1967[25]

Dear Lorraine and Wag:

For obvious reasons I won't try to make this much of a letter, but did want you to know I received yours and the clippings, and am most grateful.

I think I must be a success already. I've been "hung" on two college campuses in effigy, which since it happened in the first week in August, it does give me an edge over some other governors who have managed to have this done sometime later in their terms.

This is going to be a busy life. Again thanks, and best regards.

Sincerely,
Ronnie

In late October 1967, the National Governors Conference was held on a ship that sailed to the Virgin Islands. Reagan discusses a syndicated columnist, Marianne Means, who wrote about him and Mississippi Governor Paul B. Johnson.

Mr. and Mrs. Elwood H. Wagner
Philadelphia, Pennsylvania
November 9, 1967 [26]

Dear Lorraine and Wag:

Nice to hear from you, and you are right about the trip. The ocean was there, but it wasn't quite as restful as it could have been.

About the phone interviews, I just leave that to the Press Department. Evidently there are so many requests from around the nation they've had to adopt a rule on that, but I didn't know it at the time. I just don't overrule them when they feel the need for something like that.

I have seen this Marianne Means letter before. It's kind of a form she's sending out, so she must be getting a lot of mail. Now the truth is that yes, Governor Johnson and I were two of the 50 governors at the White House Conference. I met some, not all. I don't even recall whether he was one. The picture she claims to have shows us in the whole group, being photographed on the steps with the president. Actually, we were not side-by-side. A curious coincidence—on shipboard this time I went over to a table after having someone point out Governor Johnson to me and then made a mistake and held out my hand to the wrong man. In other words, I didn't even remember what he looked like. When the story first broke in her column I immediately contacted Governor Johnson to tell him what I was answering. I have a letter from him confirming we never had any such conversation. And just between us, he claims that at the party she mentions where she interviewed him, he recalls being introduced to her on the dance floor, but he doubts that she was in shape to remember him.

I have to run now. Some more meetings.

All the best,
Ron

In the fall of 1967 Governor Reagan's administration informed Dr. Lester Breslow that he would not be reappointed Director of Public Health, a post to which Governor Edmund G. Brown had appointed him in 1965. [27]

Mr. and Mrs. Elwood H. Wagner
Philadelphia, Pennsylvania
February 15, 1968 [28]

Dear Lorraine and Wag:

It was good to hear from you, and I certainly appreciate all the overheard comments about the press conference. As you can imagine, I sometimes have a great curiosity as to what the ladies and gentlemen of the press are really saying and thinking after those press conferences.

I enjoyed hearing, too, about the office work and the typical bureaucratic hang-up. I suppose this is one of the things that is getting me a little sniping here, because we've been digging those things out and getting rid of them. A great many employees love it, but there are those supervisor types who just hate anyone who changes the old routine.

About your uncle and his note, my statement about dropping Dr. Breslow was the kindest thing I could say after he had violated what was an agreement for his benefit. We gave him the chance to resign and accept an offer with no question cast against his ability. We were even going to deny that he'd been dropped. He would simply be leaving to take the position, which happens to be professor in charge of a department in the University of California, a position he now holds.

It was he who ran to the press to plant the idea that he had been railroaded, once he was secure in the other job. It was sort of like in the divorce, saying mental cruelty to hide the real reason, when I said it was just our mutual philosophical differences.

It is true that the doctor has spent his entire life in government service, and while I don't mean to imply there is something wrong with that, his entire approach to the many problems in our Welfare situation was always to go for more government instead of less. In other words, if our Medicaid is breaking down, then enlarge it, all the way to socialized medicine, as if that would cure the problems we already have. Please assure your uncle that my philosophy about medical care for the poor can be stated very simply—no one in this country should be denied medical care because of a lack of funds, and no one will be denied such help in California.

In reality, the issue with our Public Health doctor was simply one of my right to institute the programs that I believe in, and thus my right to appoint the team members who will implement them. If the people don't approve then they get rid of me at the next election. But I don't believe I should be forced to try and put into effect my programs with the past governor's appointees doing their best to see that they don't work.

Well, that's enough for now. Back to work.

It was good to hear from you.

Regards,
Ron

Reagan discusses his thinking on social and tax policy during his second year as governor.

Mr. and Mrs. Elwood H. Wagner
Philadelphia, Pennsylvania
May 31, 1968[29]

Dear Lorraine and Wag:

I'm off for Los Angeles, so will get to the questions right away.

We have a bill in the legislature to give to the counties one-half cent in sales tax, which they must use in place of an equal dollar amount of property tax. However, our Assembly, still dominated by Democrats, is trying to kill the bill with unacceptable amendments. Their only reason has to be that it's an election year and they don't want us getting credit.

Actually, the answer to property tax lies with a committee I have working on a program of complete tax reform. First we must have a suitable source of revenue, broader based than just the property owners and geared to our economy so that it keeps pace with economic growth and inflation. In my book this is something like the sales tax. Then we must rule out taxing property to pay for welfare and education. Property should pay taxes for those services which property actually receives, such as fire protection, street maintenance, sewers, water, garbage etc.

On the welfare centers, this one goes way back. My predecessor hastily opened 13 multiple service centers where welfare recipients could go and find all services under one roof. It was supposed to be an experiment, but the centers opened on the basis of where they'd benefit his campaign the most.

By the time we came along we learned that four centers were handling 94 percent of the load and the others shared 6 percent between them. Also, contrary to the original idea, they hadn't reduced the other welfare offices one bit, just duplicated the already existing services.

We closed all but the four and really made them a practical experiment. They proved successful because we expanded them to include such things as Fair Employment Practice Commission, State Labor Office, and even exams for Civil Service. We now have six working very successfully, and there will be more as we find areas where they can better substitute for the existing but scattered agencies.

The law says that welfare recipients who are able-bodied must be willing to accept harvest jobs from the farmers or go off welfare. Since Wirtz ruled out our braceros* we've had a harvest problem every year with whole crops left to rot in the fields. Remember, we are the number one farm state in the Union. Last year we even had to make prison labor available to harvest, and of course we've used the federal law regarding welfare workers.

Now the Danish official: he was a lawyer and in no way connected with Denmark's mental health program. He never contacted his consul here, and they were

---

* Under the braceros program, Mexican nationals were allowed to work on U.S. farms if the farm owners could certify that they could not find enough domestic workers to harvest their crops. Reagan is referring to Secretary of Labor W. Willard Wirtz.

embarrassed by his sounding off the way he did. His hostess was a woman who has attacked California's mental health program for years, even under Brown.

California is spending more per patient than any major state in the field of mental health, but what is more important, we are number one in the percentage of patients who are returned to normal living. We have actually increased the ratio of nurses to patients and are considered the outstanding state in mental hygiene.

We have a feeling out here (I do definitely) that welfare is a failure. The aim of welfare should be to salvage people and make them able to take care of themselves. We can't do all we'd like to do because of federal restrictions, but we have started a pilot program in one city—Fresno. We've put all the welfare programs into one package under one director, and we've set it up to take welfare recipients in one end and carry them through screening, analysis of their problems, basic education if that's needed, job training, and finally independence by the way of jobs in private industry. In America today there are 458 different welfare and poverty programs, and the only result seems to be more people on the dole, not less.

That's the story. Now I'm off to Los Angeles.

All the best,
Ron

The friendship between Reagan and Wagner grew from that of a star and his fan to a politician and a supporter and then into something warmer. Here he suggests ways to help Wagner's elderly cousin in New York, and sympathizes about their mutual friend and former president of Reagan's international fan club, Zelda Multz, whose mother has died.

Mr. and Mrs. Elwood H. Wagner
Philadelphia, Pennsylvania
December 2, 1968 [30]

Dear Lorraine and Wag:

Just a quick line before I take off for another Governors' Conference, and, I might add, a belated answer to your earlier letter. This is the first chance I've had to get to my personal correspondence.

Yes, our good friend Charlie Conrad has been reelected, I'm happy to say, and we now have a majority in the Assembly.

I particularly wanted to get this answer to you about the case of your elderly cousin. It is very difficult to know how each state and locality handles these problems. I could give you the answer for California but not for New York. So I've done the best I could. Attached is a whole list; depending on his neighborhood, you can find the name of the person you should contact.

Must run now. It was good to hear from you, although I was terribly sorry about the news of Zelda's mother.

Sincerely,
Ronnie

───────────

In early 1969, Southern California experienced the worst flooding in over 30 years. President Richard M. Nixon declared the state a disaster area in late January, and allocated millions in federal funds for rebuilding. Reagan reports that his house and ranch escaped disaster. He also says he will try to discreetly help his friend with troubles with the Internal Revenue Service.

Mr. and Mrs. Elwood H. Wagner
Philadelphia, Pennsylvania
March 24, 1969 [31]

Dear Lorraine and Wag:

I know it's a long time since January 30th, and your letter has been on my desk, without answer, all that time. But then, as your letter indicated, I don't have to tell you that things have been going on out here.

Actually, we were most fortunate, personally, in the floods. Our home is apparently on solid rock, and all things considered, the ranch area came through just fine. We may learn, I'm afraid, if we're going into a wet cycle, that a lot of California has been built in the wrong place.

I was very interested in your story about the Internal Revenue Service. This is one good thing about the recent election. At least now, learning of things like this, I can pass the word to people who might be interested in doing something about it. It will always be done discreetly, have no fear.

It's a Monday morning and I'm hard at it. So I won't take any more time except to say thanks and best wishes.

Sincerely,
Ron

───────────

As he prepares to run for reelection as governor, Reagan gives his views on welfare, the Vietnam War, and Cesar Chavez, the Mexican-American labor organizer.

Mr. and Mrs. Elwood H. Wagner
Philadelphia, Pennsylvania
October 7, 1969 [32]

Dear Lorraine and Wag:

I didn't mean to leave you in suspense, it's just that it's too early to commit as to whether you're running or not because to do so means you lose all that free television time.

You are right that I meant welfare is the most serious problem domestically. Vietnam of course is in a class by itself. Crime, basically, is the problem of local government and beyond that, state government. I think the Nixon administration has done a great deal through the Justice Department to remove some of the inhibitions that have been interfering with local law enforcement, and this basically is what we should count on from them. But welfare is getting to be not just an economic problem, but one of philosophy and morality. We're getting like ancient

Rome where being poor has become a career as they organize and demand their rights—so called. They become a potent factor as they did in Rome with politicians becoming demagogues in order to win their support.

On the Vietnam question, I can't help but feel that behind the scenes there are some power plays being worked and that Nixon has no intention of going on with the talking while our men are being killed beyond a certain point. I think he is giving every opportunity for the peace talks to work, but at a point in the not too distant future we'll deliver an ultimatum to Hanoi.

I'm sorry to hear about the Rabbi upholding the boycott. There has probably been more confusion and outright deception of good people on this one than on anything else. This is not a legitimate labor move. The farm workers in California are more protected and have higher pay and better working conditions than anywhere in the world. We are a model in that particular sense.

Chavez is attempting by blackmail to create a union without giving the workers themselves an opportunity to choose whether they want one or which one it should be. Thousands of Mexican-Americans in California are in opposition to Chavez and they are to be found working in the vineyards, making good money and utterly opposed to joining his union. Frankly, I'm a little disgusted with the clergy of every denomination who without making any effort to learn the truth, are continuing to consider this a kind of holy crusade.

Must get back to work now; I've been away too long.

Best regards,
Ron

In the midst of his reelection campaign, Reagan writes about his challenger, Assemblyman Jesse Unruh and the former mayor of Los Angeles, Sam Yorty. He also presents his views on gays serving in public office. Reagan had some experience addressing homosexuality in public life. During his first year as governor, two men were dismissed from his staff for allegedly participating in a homosexual ring.[33]

Mr. and Mrs. Elwood H. Wagner
Philadelphia, Pennsylvania
April 16, 1970[34]

Dear Lorraine and Wag:

It was good to hear from you, and I've put your letter to Boyarsky* in the mail. I assumed that's what you wanted. I hope it scorches him good. It was a good letter, you certainly had most of the points right. You just have to assume he doesn't care for our philosophy.

In that connection, you asked why should a suspected homosexual represent a risk in state administration. I agree with you that the national viewpoint is one, of

---

* Bill Boyarsky wrote for the *Los Angeles Times*.

course, based on the security risk—the possibility of blackmail or extortion using this information to get government secrets. Such a thing, of course, is not a threat at the state level, but I think we have to recognize they are still outside the law. While many people are suggesting more open recognition and a change in the laws, their tendencies do have them in violation and, therefore, if exposure comes, there would be a reflection on government.

I didn't see Anderson's column attacking Yorty, but it doesn't surprise me. Yorty is trying for a faction of the Democratic Party that is more moderate. Unruh, on the other hand, is lining up all the extremely left radical groups and this of course would endear him, I should think, to Anderson.

I don't know why my name was omitted from the Vietnam gift organization unless someone here simply notified them that now that I'm in this office, I have restrictions as to the use of my name.

There are two newspapers I could suggest for campaign coverage. One would be the *Los Angeles Herald Express,* and I think just addressing that to Los Angeles, California, should reach them. The other would be the *Santa Monica Outlook.* And, again, I think that paper could be reached by simply addressing Santa Monica, California.

About the other address you wanted, the address of my headquarters, a statewide headquarters has opened in Los Angeles. The address is 1250 North Western Avenue, Los Angeles 90029.

I have to get back to work now but, again, it was good to hear from you.

Best regards,
Ron

Governor Reagan writes that the Fresno Bee, *published by the McClatchy family, is a socialist newspaper that has targeted him.*

Mr. and Mrs. Elwood H. Wagner
Philadelphia, Pennsylvania
May 8, 1970 [35]

Dear Lorraine and Wag:

Just a quick line as the pace grows hotter to answer your question about Patti. She graduates this June.

As to the other question about the enclosed editorial, you can assure your friend that the paper he's reading and will probably read as a resident of Fresno is the *Fresno Bee.* That paper is published by a family who inherited the paper from the founder. In his will he specified the paper must support all programs leading toward government ownership. In other words, the paper's philosophy is socialist. This particular paper, because of that, probably carries on the most uninterrupted, the hardest, and the most dishonest campaign against me and my administration of any publication outside the *Daily Worker.* The matter of the will is not just conversation. I have actually seen a copy of the clause that specifies that this paper had to endorse such a policy.

Best regards,
Ron

Reagan defeated Assemblyman Jesse Unruh in his reelection bid on November 3, 1970, but the voters turned Republican Senator George Murphy out of office in favor of Congressman John V. Tunney, a moderate Democrat.

Mr. and Mrs. Elwood H. Wagner
Philadelphia, Pennsylvania
November 25, 1970 [36]

Dear Wag and Lorraine:

You've almost had more of the California campaign than I've had. I can assure you of one thing—when we were sitting inside the president's bulletproof car listening to the rocks bounce off, if it had been a show staged by me I'd have used a double.

Our campaign got a little messy and there were times I thought of hitting back but now I'm glad I didn't—I think. Tunney was pretty dishonest about Murphy and sad to say he got away with it.

That gal who did the welfare cheating (staged) did a great job. We've had a task force working on this whole mess and hope we can finally begin to get some light shed on it. Would you believe an $11,000 a year schoolteacher getting welfare legally in the summer months because of financial hardship in not being paid for those two months? Her hardship was due to making a down payment on a new house. All of our economies these past four years have gone down the drain—all of it used to pay the increases in welfare. This year we've had a 31 percent increase in the number of people on the Aid to Dependent Children program.

Well back to work.

All the best,
Ron

This letter is about the headlines of the day. Some, such as the trial of Charles Manson for the Tate-LaBianca murders, were gruesome.

Mr. and Mrs. Elwood H. Wagner
Philadelphia, Pennsylvania
April 23, 1971 [37]

Dear Lorraine and Wag:

Thank you for your good letter and for the fascinating article on Governor Shafer.* Let me just say, you are not too far wrong, and I share your opinion. We are

---

* Raymond P. Shafer, the Republican governor of Pennsylvania from 1967 to 1971.

proceeding with our private legal assistance program on an experimental basis in one or two areas.

As for the Manson trial, I think the appeals will go on for years. I agree with you about their deserving the death sentence.

I'm going down the line taking your questions here. The trial was very costly and, yet, I don't know whether it exceeded in cost the expense of the Sirhan trial.*

I did do the column you read. It even appeared in the *New York Times*, although I was interested to see when they printed it, they explained at the bottom of the column that I was the governor of California.†

The things you've read about court decisions out here on welfare do not apply to our reform proposals, but to some of the things we tried to do administratively, so we could give a cost of living increase to the really needy. The decision was simply a technical one that we must do this through legislation.

I think the Calley affair‡ is one of the most complex problems we had. It should have been settled in Vietnam. At the risk of oversimplification, let me say I think we must accept that some men become brutalized by war. There is no way to know in advance who those men will be. When it happens, you remove the man much as you would remove him for combat fatigue and treat it as a problem of emotional disturbance. There is no question that he did wrong. On the other hand, the people we're fighting against, and even those on our own side, have a different standard than ours. They both practice a great cruelty among themselves. Unfortunately, the press, in all these years, has never played up as they did in World War II the savagery and the atrocities performed even on our own men. Not since the Indian wars have we fought an enemy who sent women and children onto the battlefield armed with knives to torture the wounded. You haven't read this in newspaper accounts, but there are many soldiers who can tell you frightening experiences of this kind. It does, somehow, make more understandable the willingness of a man to kill supposedly noncombatant women and children. He is not a hero, but on the other hand, I'm not sure he should be treated as just a wanton criminal. I think he must be viewed as a man who probably could have gone through life without committing a single crime until we exposed him to the brutalizing force of war.

I must close now. It was good to hear from you.

Best regards,
Ron

---

* Sirhan Bishara Sirhan murdered Robert F. Kennedy on June 5, 1968 in Los Angeles while Kennedy was campaigning to be the Democratic Party's presidential nominee.
† Ronald Reagan, "Welfare Is a Cancer," *New York Times*, April 1, 1971, p. 41.
‡ Lt. William Calley was convicted of murder for a massacre in My Lai, a South Vietnamese village, in 1968. He was sentenced to life in prison, but appeals led to his release in 1974.

In the spring of 1971, Governor Reagan announced the creation of the California Ecology Corps, which was formed mainly as a vehicle for conscientious objectors to the draft to serve the state. Meanwhile Lorraine continued to write letters-to-the-editor on Reagan's behalf.

Mr. and Mrs. Elwood H. Wagner
Philadelphia, Pennsylvania
June 17, 1971 [38]

Dear Lorraine and Wag:

I've just arrived home from my short eastern trip to find your letter awaiting me.

First of all, my phone number here at the office, and I'm easy to find, is (916) 445-2843.

I was briefly in Boston for the one speech and the next night in Manchester, New Hampshire, and then on my way home.

The conscientious objectors project you asked about has come about because some of our honor camps where juvenile offenders have been housed and used in firefighter projects in our forest lands now have to be closed. Our rehabilitation system is working so well we no longer have the offenders to man the camps. Since COs have to put in two years of work in some kind of community project, we are going to man those camps as ecology centers doing things that need doing in the forests as well as fighting the fires with conscientious objectors.

As for your other question about Liberty Lobby, I have always thought it was a little far out.

Question five, we did find there were loopholes in the regulations which permitted some welfare help to strikers and we have closed those loopholes.

Thanks for your letters to Art Buchwald and to the Editor. I never cease to wonder where you find the time and energy to take them on but you always do so in a top-grade manner. I have to close now because, believe it or not, after one day back here I'm off to a speech in Fresno.

Warm regards.

Sincerely,
Ron

At the Western Governors Conference at Jackson Lake, Wyoming, in July 1971, Republican Governor Thomas Lawson McCall of Oregon said that Governor Reagan had given President Nixon "more anguish than anyone else—Republican or Democrat" because of his criticism of welfare policy. McCall added: "I would hope the Governor of California would really come out foursquare for reelection of the president and not hold him hostage" to his views on welfare reform.[39] Reagan writes that McCall apolo-

gized. On July 16, 1971, President Richard M. Nixon announced that he would visit the People's Republic of China. Reagan says that this is a part of a geopolitical plan but does not have kind words for the "Red Chinese."

> Mr. and Mrs. Elwood H. Wagner
> Philadelphia, Pennsylvania
> August 3, 1971 [40]

Dear Lorraine and Wag:

I thought you'd be interested to know the first person I met when I arrived in Wyoming was Governor McCall, and his first sheepish word was "Sorry." He's just a fellow who can't resist getting his name in the papers.

I can understand your concern about the president and Red China, but honestly don't believe it should be upsetting. First, I think the president is very realistic and hard-nosed about the Red Chinese, but sometimes things have to be done, for example in negotiating the end of a war, which cannot be explained openly until the game is all over.

As to the situation in the U.N., the truth is, the United States can no longer hold down the majority who want to admit Red China. Behind the scenes we have succeeded, however, in making it necessary to have a two-thirds majority to oust the Nationalist Chinese. So by backing away on our resistance of the first, we have pretty well guaranteed the continuation of Taiwan in the U.N. At the same time, we are pretty sure the Red Chinese will not accept a seat under those terms.

Personally, I think the Red Chinese are a bunch of murdering bums. I think the president probably believes the same; but in the big chess game going on, where Russia is still head man on the other side, we need a little elbow room. It was very interesting to note the other day how little attention was paid to the fact that the North Vietnam negotiator from Paris showed up in Peking.

Now I must get back to my own war with the legislature.

> Best regards,
> Ron

This long letter is full of policy analysis, Hollywood talk, discussion about horses, and a brief update on Maureen and Michael, Reagan's children from his first marriage.

In 1971, Reagan was deeply involved in welfare reform. A month before he wrote the letter below, the California legislature passed a welfare reform bill that bore many aspects of the tax reform plan he had submitted in March. As the legislation was being debated in the spring, a Superior Court judge ruled in favor of the California Welfare Rights Organization, which sought to prohibit Reagan's administration from removing thousands of families from welfare. Reagan writes about an approaching challenge from the welfare organization.

The governor calls George Lester Jackson a hardened criminal. Jackson, a San

Quentin prisoner, was killed on August 21, 1971, in an attempted escape that took the lives of several inmates and guards. Jackson was one of the Soledad Brothers, and was linked to Angela Davis, whose teaching contract at the University of California at Los Angeles had been voted down a year earlier by Governor Reagan and a majority of the University of California Board of Regents.

By the time Jackson was killed, Davis had been in prison for almost a year on the charge of owning some of the guns used in the Marin County Courthouse shootout that left George's younger brother, Jonathan Jackson, and several others, including Judge Harold J. Haley, dead.

Mr. and Mrs. Elwood H. Wagner
Philadelphia, Pennsylvania
September 8, 1971 [41]

Dear Lorraine and Wag:

It was nice to get your letter, although I am constantly amazed at your awareness of California problems.

The story about the racehorse was most interesting. It occasionally happens, but isn't commonplace. Unfortunately, the news story was wrong about the little fellow running someday in a race. Since the identity of the father is unknown, he can never be registered as a thoroughbred, eligible for racing. At any rate, things like this can happen. As a matter of fact, I took the original Tar Baby from *Stallion Road* over a 5'3" jump and discovered two days later she had been in foal more than eight months.

You asked if I were satisfied with our welfare reform. Yes, although the Welfare Rights Organization is, of course, going to challenge us in court on almost every part of it, and in these times you never know what the judge will decide.

I share your disgust about the news coverage of the San Quentin slaughter. Jackson was a hard-bitten, violent criminal who engineered what was nothing less than a massacre. I wish some of those bleeding hearts could have had to make the phone calls I made to the widows of the guards.

You really threw one at me with that cash-flow problem of withholding. The answer very simply is we are behind as a result of the previous administration. In other words, your idea would work if we had the lump sum cash from say the April tax collection and then could prorate it out to pay the bills for the following months. But because of those past sins, we have borrowed the money in advance and each lump sum that comes in is used to pay off the borrowing. There is no way to get the several hundred million dollars ahead that we would have to do to start a cash-on-the-line program of the kind you suggested. I had even hoped that if we got withholding, and once got on a cash basis, that perhaps as time went on we could relax it and give people the choice of withholding or maybe quarterly installment paying or not paying until the end of the year. I must say, however, I have noticed a change out here in the public opinion polls, probably brought about by the increased use of credit cards. Four years ago the majority of our people were opposed to withholding. Today a sizable majority just simply agrees it would be a convenience for them, and they would like to have it.

I know what you mean about the movie mags. It's just another reflection of the breakdown of the industry. Once upon a time the motion picture industry literally had a phone number. We on the Guild could get on the phone and in a short time have a meeting concerning industry problems with the leaders of the entire industry. Today it is scattered hundreds and hundreds of independent producers—too many of them out for a fast buck—and no real cohesive force. I am beginning to see the first little signs that TV might be loosening the bars a little so they can begin showing some of this modern crop of obscene movies. I will be ready to join an organized holler if they do.

I don't think Maureen is in line for a wedding, but Mike was married recently to a very nice girl and seems very happy.

Best regards,
Ron

The Wagners and the Reagans continued to exchange gifts almost 30 years after Lorraine first wrote to Reagan.

Mr. and Mrs. Elwood Wagner
Philadelphia, Pennsylvania
December 30, 1971 [42]

Dear Lorraine and Wag:

Thanks so much for our handsome mail coach with its very first-class load—the decanter and glasses.

Believe me it will prove useful. If I'd been a teetotaler those guys in the legislature would have driven me to drink. Now I can take the ride in style.

Nancy joins me in our thanks and our hope that yours have been happy holidays.

Have a good new year,
Ron

Negotiations to end the Vietnam War were stalled, and Reagan took a hard line on the issue.

Mr. and Mrs. Elwood H. Wagner
Philadelphia, Pennsylvania
April 24, 1972 [43]

Dear Lorraine and Wag:

On reading the opinion held of me in the prison back there, I'd better not visit any prisons, and if I do, I'd better keep my back to the wall.

The book you asked about, *The Creative Society,* is actually a collection of speeches and statements that was put together. The publisher is Devin-Adair Company of New York.*

I think the Vietnam offensive you mentioned is pretty plain proof of what the enemy has always been like. This is obviously his answer to the president's offer of a peace plan. Now, I believe we have to bring him to the negotiating table, not by promising to quit bombing, as Johnson did 18 times, but by carrying on the bombing until he hurts so badly he has to come to the table. Actually, the president has no choice. This is the only way to protect the less than 100,000 men we still have there, and who are awaiting transportation home.

I know you'll have a most interesting session with your brother-in-law.

Best regards,
Ron

In July 1972, Governor Reagan traveled to Denmark, Belgium, France, Spain, Italy, England, and Ireland as a representative of the Nixon administration. A few days before he attended the Republican National Convention in Miami Beach, Florida, Reagan thanks the Wagners for a gift and tells them about his tour of Europe.

Mr. and Mrs. Elwood H. Wagner
Philadelphia, Pennsylvania
August 16, 1972 [44]

Dear Lorraine and Wag:

Just a line before getting off to Washington and Miami to thank you for our Snoopy—He's my hero, so we are delighted to have him.

You are right about the trip—it was exciting and we had some tourist time in spite of all the business. We toured castles and cathedrals and even cruised along the Italian coast for a weekend.

It was good to hear every European leader I met with talk about this president being the first one who was really approaching the problem of peace in a realistic, practical manner. It sounded better than those "Yankee Go Home" lines we used to hear about.

Again, thanks.

Best regards,
Ron

Saint Patrick's Day in 1973 witnessed car bombings and shootings in Northern Ireland.

---

* Reagan gave a speech titled "The Creative Society" during his 1966 gubernatorial campaign. In 1968, a collection of this and other speeches was published under the same name.

Mr. and Mrs. Elwood H. Wagner
Philadelphia, Pennsylvania
March 20, 1973 [45]

Dear Lorraine and Wag:

Thanks for the greeting on St. Patrick's Day. I hope before the next one they'll find an answer to the foolish and tragic killing on the Emerald Isle. Right now another saint is needed.

You asked about the card. From my own observation the personally written letter does carry more weight, although in Washington they are impressed by numbers. The effect of hearing that 50,000 pieces of mail came in on one side of an issue affects congressmen who don't bother to check whether they were form letters or not.

Your story about the orders on tax returns for flood victims is very interesting. I am convinced that administrations and even Congress are sabotaged many times by an upper level of the bureaucracy. In our own welfare reforms we had to watch some departments that would carry out the reforms in such a way as to make them appear unworkable. They didn't mind victimizing innocent and deserving welfare recipients in their attempt to create an impression that we were being destructive and unkind. Like you, the people carrying out the orders weren't to blame, but somewhere above them an executive was shorting out administration policy.

As for my recent announcement, I think I'd go crazy trying to be a legislator. There is some missionary work to be done out on the banquet circuit and I may just hit the trail again.

Best regards,
Ron

In 1967, Robert G. Baker, a former protégé of Senator Lyndon Baines Johnson, was convicted of fraud, grand larceny, and tax evasion. Convicted in the 1960s in a grain storage swindle, Billie Sol Estes was said to have the backing of Johnson. Reagan compares these scandals to Watergate. This letter also includes a discussion of Serrano v. Priest, *a landmark case in which California's Supreme Court ruled that using funds from local property taxes to fund public education was unconstitutional.*

Mr. and Mrs. Elwood H. Wagner
Philadelphia, Pennsylvania
June 22, 1973 [46]

Dear Lorraine and Wag:

I share your frustration about the tragedy in Ireland, even more so since our recent visit to that very lovely, warm, and friendly country. It's hard to reconcile what we saw with what's going on.

I also share your frustration about Watergate. I have to tell you it is not hard for me to accept that this could have gone on without the president's knowledge. Just judging it by my own much smaller shop. If my staff wanted to keep something of this kind from me, it would be very easy for them to do so. You have to be dependent so much on staff who not only stand between you and a multitude of things you don't have time for, but you have to depend on them also for the information on other matters. You are absolutely right that in the world of politics this really, taken in perspective, is not as serious as things where graft and corruption were involved, such as the Bobby Baker case or the Bill Sol Estes case. Then, of course, looking back over the several years to 1960, there now is very much documentation for the charge that the 1960 election was stolen outright, mainly in Chicago, St. Louis, and Dallas, Texas. As for bugging, John Roosevelt has publicly stated that his father started it. He says FDR had practically everyone in Washington bugged. On the other hand, that doesn't make this right. A little group of individuals, we're not sure how many yet but we'll learn it from the court trial, did a very stupid and criminal thing, and I'm sure they're going to be punished. Right now most of what we're hearing before the Senate committee is hearsay that would be inadmissible in a court of law. I still have confidence that when the smoke clears we will find the president was not involved.

You mentioned the Christopher smear in my campaign. I hope you realize that was in the primary and the smear came from my opponent, Pat Brown.* His team thought Christopher would be harder to beat in the election than I would, so they knocked him out of the primary, or tried to, with their smear so they could have me as an opponent. I've wondered what their second thoughts might be.

No, the POWs were not bitter, but most patriotic and most supportive of what the president has been doing in the war. The Serrano case has not come to trial yet and, yes, we have gotten all the petitions signed so that our measure will be on the ballot for a tax reduction.† It will not reduce government services.

I can't tell you about the Lou Cannon book.‡ I never read it.

Best regards.

Sincerely,
Ron

In late November and December 1973, Governor Reagan traveled to Australia, Indonesia, and Singapore. He reports on that trip and discusses the defeat of Proposition 1, a tax-limitation measure he put before the California voters in a special election on November 6, 1973.

---

* Reagan is referring to George Christopher, his Republican challenger in the 1966 primary for governor, and Edmund "Pat" Brown, the Democratic incumbent he faced in the general election.
† Governor Reagan is referring to Proposition 1.
‡ Lou Cannon, *Ronnie and Jesse: A Political Odyssey* (Garden City, New York: Doubleday, 1969). This book chronicles Reagan's 1970 reelection campaign against Assemblyman Jesse Unruh.

Mr. and Mrs. Elwood H. Wagner
Philadelphia, Pennsylvania
February 8, 1974[47]

Dear Lorraine and Wag:

Once again I'm off on a little errand in Texas, but wanted to get at least a short reply off to your letter.

You mentioned the "ugly American" tag—we found no trace of it. As a matter of fact, the Japanese have replaced us in that regard. Their expansion in trade and investments has given them a high visibility. We were warmly greeted and received.

By the way, we may have lost Proposition 1 in the election, but we won it in "the Advocates" debate.* All the talk about the complicated form on the ballot was typical of their campaigning. Under California law the exact legal wording must appear on the ballot and even the simplest statute looks pretty formidable when you have to see it in its legal form.

Tell your friend from Sterling, Illinois, she must mean my cousin. (he was old enough to be an uncle) His name was Charles Smith.

Your uncle, who says Proposition 1 favored the well-to-do, has been victimized by the falsehood that property taxes would have to go up and they do hit the low earner harder. Actually, we had a provision preventing a property tax increase unless the people themselves voted to increase them. The measure only put a limit on the percent of total earnings the state could take. Any change in taxes—which could be raised or lowered within that limit was left in the hands of the legislature as it is now.

I enjoyed your exchange with Ms. Kubany.

Best regards,
Ron

––––––––––

Reagan was busy starting a new life after having been governor of California for eight years, from 1967 to 1975. After his governorship, he continued to write Lorraine about policy issues. He does so in this letter.

Mr. and Mrs. Elwood H. Wagner
Philadelphia, Pennsylvania
July 17, 1975[48]

Dear Lorraine and Wag:

Just a line before another trip starts. No need to answer the gal—she works for a consumer agency and it's just a case of bureaucracy defending itself. Most of my information has come from studying the bill and the debate in Congress about it. Very simply, it will create a fantastically powerful super agency.

Isn't it funny—under my administration in California, we were the first state to

* *The Advocates* was a PBS-TV public affairs show broadcast in the late 1960s and 1970s.

have a consumer agency and it became a model for other states. The truth is we don't need a federal agency.

Best regards,
Ron

In January 1975, Reagan began a nationally syndicated radio program, titled Viewpoint, *as well as a newspaper column. He also worked on his new ranch near Santa Barbara.*

Mr. and Mrs. Elwood Wagner
Philadelphia, Pennsylvania
August 28, 1975[49]

Dear Lorraine and Wag:

Just a quick line to say I've gotten on the matter of *Viewpoint* and your station. I can't imagine what happened. I wonder if someone at the station is fooling the program director. Anyway, it's being checked into.

Your story about the schools should be an indication of how far we've gone down the road to "1984." Now and then I think back to my own younger days and realize how impossible such things would have been—for that matter even just a few years ago.

I think we did hear from the people about Florida and the convention but couldn't fit it in.

Yes, there is as much work at the new ranch and we're doing most of it ourselves and that's why I'm ending this letter because I'm off to the ranch.

Best regards,
Ron

Reagan writes the Wagners about his life—giving speeches around the country, increasing the reach of his radio program, and living on his ranch. He also notes that he still writes his own speeches but has help on research from staff. A month later he announced his intention to seek the Republican Party's nomination for the presidency.

Mr. and Mrs. Elwood H. Wagner
Philadelphia, Pennsylvania
October 22, 1975[50]

Dear Lorraine and Wag:

Just a quick line before boarding the plane for New York. I'll try to cover everything in your good letter but may miss a point or two in my haste. By the time you get this, of course, I'll have been in and out of Philadelphia. It is really an in and out this time—arriving just in time for the lunch and off to Yale right after.

First, thank you very much for all you've done with the talk shows. It's wonderful how one voice with the courage to speak up can turn things around. Bless you and thanks again.

About the radio show—I just can't figure it. I inquired and all we can figure is the sponsor must have dropped out and the station didn't want to carry it on the chance of picking up another. We've just closed a deal in which "Mutual Network" has picked it up and is making it available to their more than 600 stations.

On the ranch—they really have twisted that. In California, we have a law designed to encourage the preservation of open space and farm land. All it does is tax farm land as farm land, not possible subdivision property, if the owner signs a 10-year contract with the county that he won't use it for subdivision. If he breaks the contract, he is charged retroactively for higher taxes. The ranch we bought was already—and had for years—been under the "Williamson Act," as the law is called. We are going to run cattle just as the previous owner did. The minute we bought he place, a couple of cranks began digging into everything, as to whether we'd given "favors" as part of the purchase price. Well, we only bought it last December, a few weeks before I left office and there was no hanky-panky.

I'm still writing my own speeches, although I do have staff help now on research. The TV debate was edited down from more than two hours actual debate to a one hour show.* I haven't seen it, although I'm inclined to believe that in this case I was treated fairly.

I'm at the airport so must close. Again, thanks and give the kids (grown up kids) my best.

Sincerely,
Ron

Reagan congratulates Sandy, the Wagners' daughter, on graduating from high school and writes about his wins and losses in the 1976 Republican primaries. He defeated President Gerald Ford in California's primary on June 8.

Mr. and Mrs. Elwood H. Wagner
Philadelphia, Pennsylvania
June 14, 1976 [51]

Dear Lorraine and Wag:

First please congratulate Sandy for me. I should do half as well. You both must be very proud.

Speaking of proud—I'm very proud of all that you do in my behalf. I try to add it up and it comes out to twenty-three and one-half hour days. And all I can do is say thanks.

---

* In her letter dated October 14, 1975, Wagner mentions a televised debate between Ronald Reagan and Ralph Nader, the consumer advocate. The debate aired in Philadelphia, Wagner's hometown, on October 12.

California really outdid our greatest expectations with a win even greater than the '66 gubernatorial race. We won all but two counties and they were close. Incidentally, they were two counties I never have carried.

Tell Ken Boehm* thanks and to stay in there and fight. This challenging of delegates is standard now with the Ford people. They railroaded both the Arkansas and Kansas conventions in a shameless manner and caught us by surprise. Then came Missouri and we were ready. They challenged 395 state delegates but on Saturday morning were forced to withdraw the challenge. It was a real head-to-head contest. Ford was there with all the pomp and panoply of his office. I was there minus the p & p. We actually won a clean sweep of all 19 delegates but our people thought they should give up one to their governor (for Ford) and I agreed. It's a battle now for each single delegate so we'll go after the undecided or the shaky committed. If you know of any let us know. We just picked up three more in Ohio on a recount. In another district there is a delay because of some ballot boxes that had been tampered with.

I'll have to go now—Iowa is next. Again thanks and my best to Sandy.

Sincerely,
Ron

Even though Reagan lost the Republican nomination to President Ford, he continued to be involved in the presidential campaign. In this letter, he thanks the Wagners' daughter, a college freshman and supporter.

Miss Sandy Wagner
Indiana, Pennsylvania
October 26, 1976[52]

Dear Sandy:

If memory hasn't grown too dim, I know you must be having a few readjustment pains. Your experience must be more trying than mine because I chose a small college and you are in a sizeable university. Still, some things are the same; heavier assignments, no one to tell you to study and a kind of "here I am on my own and I don't know whether I like it" feeling.

Believe me, it gets better. It's sort of like putty; the more you work at it, the better it gets.

I'm out on the road campaigning as much as I was during the primaries. I have to swallow hard now and then but I keep telling myself that we can at least hold our man to the platform and it is a good platform we can all believe in. Carter disturbs me more than a little. I have a deep-seated feeling that he is a real phony.

---

* Kenneth Boehm was the Pennsylvania state chairman of Citizens for Reagan, the campaign organization for Reagan's presidential run in 1976, and a talk show host in Philadelphia.

Sandy, I know of all you did in my behalf and I'm grateful. Don't think it was all wasted. Between us, we made some people aware of the issues for the first time. We just have to keep at it—like those assignments you're getting.

All the best,
Ronald Reagan

Reagan is skeptical about the Trilateral Commission, a private organization formed in 1973 by Japanese, European, and North American leaders to enhance cooperation among industrialized democracies and to promote their international leadership.

Mr. and Mrs. Elwood Wagner
Philadelphia, Pennsylvania
Circa 1977 or 1978[53]

Dear Lorraine and Wag:
Just a line and some information on "Trilateral." Yes I'm catching a plane again. This time though for a weekend at the Bohemian Grove.

I was interested in your comment on Jeffrey St. John.* Our paths crossed a few days ago in Washington. I very much fear he is a little paranoid and thinks I've sold out to the bad guys.

I'm glad you liked Gloria Toote.† I think she's great. Please send Reverend Floyd's ‡ address to me. We'll put him on a mailing list.

Your concern about the trilateral commission is shared by many—including me. I've enclosed a packet that gives some background as well as a few eyebrow-lifting remarks by a commission member. Naturally it isn't a research piece which digs down deep but it's obvious that Trilateralists believe there is an elite which should guide the affairs of men.

All the best,
Ron

Upon returning from his second trip to Europe after his governorship, Reagan writes to the Wagners. He expresses satisfaction with the outcome of the midterm elections and regret that Eugene (Sonny) Kane was defeated in his bid for a congressional seat representing a Philadelphia suburban area.

---

* Jeffrey St. John was a columnist and television commentator.
† Gloria Toote, an African-American Republican attorney in New York, supported Reagan during his 1980 presidential campaign. In 1983, President Reagan appointed her vice chairman of his Advisory Council on Private Sector Initiatives.
‡ Reverend Theodore Floyd was a frequent caller to radio talk programs in Philadelphia. He and Lorraine Wagner often called programs to defend Reagan and his policies.

Mr. and Mrs. Elwood Wagner
Philadelphia, Pennsylvania
December 6, 1978 [54]

Dear Lorraine and Wag:

We've just returned from a brief trip to Europe—meeting with the bigwigs there and picking their brains to find out how Americans look from across the water—and found your good letter and newspaper story, how about that.

I am enclosing a card which will hopefully take care of future press conferences. Thanks for all your kind words; it was good to see you.

I am sorry that Sonny Kane didn't make it. We had pretty good luck with a lot of the candidates I campaigned for—I guess we just can't win them all. Basically, I thought it turned out to be a good year for Republicans. We've strengthened ourselves in the state houses, added some congressmen and senators, and, all in all, kind of pushed the opponents over to our way of thinking in certain areas. So, maybe the old ship of state will keep on chugging along.

I hope the enclosed card will do the job. Give our regards to—I can't say the children anymore—those fine young people of yours and have a Merry Christmas and Happy New Year.

All the best to you both.

Sincerely,
Ron

———

The December 4, 1978, issue of the Spotlight, *a far right publication, carried an article titled "The Voice of a Conservative, the Record of a Liberal." In the letter below, Reagan addresses some of the issues raised in the article and in a book by Jack W. Germond and Jules Witcover. Reagan explains why on July 28, 1967, he signed a measure supported by Republican Assemblyman David Donald Mulford that prohibited the possession of loaded weapons in areas where it would be illegal to use such a weapon. Reagan also corrects the charge that he supported Nelson "Rocky" Rockefeller's presidential candidacy and tells the story of why he did not become President Gerald Ford's running mate in 1976.*

Mr. and Mrs. Elwood Wagner
Philadelphia, Pennsylvania
February 5, 1979 [55]

Dear Lorraine and Wag:

I never cease to be amazed at the letters you turn out in my behalf; they are masterpieces and must cause some discomfort when the recipients get them.

As for Germond and Witcover, I think their book had a number of inaccuracies born mainly of the press habit of simply deciding what they think you are thinking and then writing the story accordingly. You are absolutely right about *Spotlight* and the gentleman who runs that show. He is, according to my informants in Washington, truly a neo-Nazi. I don't know what I could add to what you said to him—you did him up brown. But just so you will have a clear conscience about your letter, let me say that story is based on the book which was done back early in my term as governor and is totally dishonest. If I answered it point by point, this letter would become a book, but let me give you just two examples: He says I claim to be opposed to gun control but, as governor, signed an extremely restrictive gun control bill infringing on the rights of law-abiding citizens. He even mentioned the bill by name: the Mulford Bill. Well, it is true that I did sign such a bill, but I hardly think it was gun control. The Black Panthers had invaded the legislative chambers in the Capitol with loaded shotguns and held these gentlemen under the muzzles of those guns for a couple of hours. Immediately after they left, Don Mulford introduced a bill to make it unlawful to bring a loaded gun into the Capitol Building. That's the bill I signed. It was hardly restrictive gun control.

[He] charges me with great secret support for Rocky. I wonder how he explains that I was Goldwater's chairman in California, and we carried that state for Barry against Rocky. Those are just two samples, and the rest of the story is in line with that.

You asked about our trip to Europe. Well, I can assure you that the national leaders I met in England, France, and Germany could not hide their concern about us and what we are doing over here. They are extremely concerned and want the solid dependable United States, including the solid, dependable dollar that they once knew. They are very fearful, and I'm afraid that if we don't begin showing some muscle soon, they are going to begin making overtures to the Soviet[s] in a feeling of self-defense.

Now, to get back to the book and your question about the vice presidency. The two staffs had agreed that the winner at the convention would call upon the loser. Our people had told the Ford staff that there shouldn't be any talk of the vice presidency if he had anything of that kind in mind. They knew my position, of course, but, to tell you the truth, they wanted to be able to talk to me afterward and see if such an offer were made, whether my position was a sound one. That was the only reason for barring talk of it the night before. It was around one o'clock in the morning when Ford got to my suite at the hotel. What [was] later said on the TV show was that half of the leadership of the party, including my own supporters and the president, came to me on the basis that this was necessary to save the party and win the election. But Nancy and I both knew that would be virtually impossible to say no to. As a matter of fact, the very next morning my supporters and 29 state chairmen did come to see me asking permission to talk to the president about my being on the ticket in order to strengthen the chances of victory. Before they had gone very far in their approach, the phone rang, and it was Ford telling me he had chosen Dole. So Nancy and I never actually had to face whether we would do it or not, and obviously Ford had no intention of offering it to me. Frankly, I think the Lord was watching out for us because I really didn't want it and would have only done it, I guess, under the circumstances I described where I would have been afraid that my conscience would have haunted me had I refused.

Well, I just returned from another speaking trip. This one took me to Montana and North Dakota where it's 30 degrees below zero. I'm glad to be back.

Best regards and thanks again and give my regards to Sandy and Scott. That Sandy is going to outsmart all of us with that 3.6 grade point average.

Sincerely,
Ron

The Wagners visited Reagan in the Oval Office during his last year as president.

Mrs. Lorraine Wagner
Philadelphia, Pennsylvania
June 16, 1988 [56]

Dear Lorraine:

Please have no regrets about your visit to the Oval Office. It was just great to see you again and have a chance to get started down memory lane. The only regret is that as always these days my visits can't be long enough.

Give my very best to Wag and the family.

Once again—it was great seeing you.

Sincerely,
Ron

Reagan sends a holiday greeting during his first post-presidency year.

Mr. and Mrs. Elwood H. Wagner
Philadelphia, Pennsylvania
December 27, 1989 [57]

Dear Lorraine and Wag:

You are ahead of me. Don't ask me how I've gotten so far behind but the schedule has me on my way to someplace or from someplace most of the time.

Anyway—Nancy and I hope your holidays were all you wished them to be and ours were better because of your warm greeting. Give the family our best and thank you both.

Sincerely—
Ron

In 1990, President Reagan continues to provide the Wagners with updates on his activities.

Mr. and Mrs. Elwood H. Wagner
Philadelphia, Pennsylvania
June 30, 1990 [58]

Dear Lorraine and Wag:

Well! what a happy Father's Day greeting you gave me and I thank you from the bottom of my heart. Yes we were at the Warner celebration and it really was a journey down memory lane. It was a magnificent show both film and live. Actually it was typical of how Hollywood used to do things—big and glittering.

Thank you again—your greeting was "one for the Gipper." Nancy sends her best.

Sincerely,
Ron

ZELDA MULTZ

Ronald Reagan thanks Zelda Multz, the former president of his international fan club, for sending him gifts and informs her of the status of his radio program and newspaper column, which were nationally syndicated between 1975 and 1979.

Miss Zelda Multz
Brooklyn, New York
Circa 1975 or 1976 [59]

Dear Zelda:

Thank you very much for our calendar and memo books. They go to the ranch where they'll put an end to scattered notes on torn pieces of paper and even paper napkins. Bless you!

I'm off on a little speaking jaunt—(no politics, at last). The radio program is up to 181 stations and growing and about 100 newspapers for the column.

Nancy sends her best and again we both thank you.

Best regards,
Ron

President Reagan reminisces about Dixon and Eureka. On February 6, his 73rd birthday, he toured the Illinois towns of his youth.

Miss Zelda Multz
Brooklyn, New York
February 27, 1984 [60]

Dear Zelda:

It was good to hear from you and I appreciate your good wishes on the 34th anniversary of my 39th birthday. Thanks too for the news story. I hadn't seen that one.

Going back to Dixon and Eureka (all on the same day) was really fun. I wish there had been a little more time but even so it was a warm trip down nostalgia lane. The arch and the Nachusa tavern all looked the same as when you saw them.

Somehow the rooms in our old house seemed smaller than I remembered them. Thanks again.

Sincerely,
Ron

This is Reagan's final letter to Zelda.

Mrs. Zelda Multz
Brooklyn, New York
Between 1989 and 1994[61]

Dear Zelda:

Here I am—day after my birthday and receiving your wonderfully warm message. Your card expressed the hope my day is happy. Well it is and your letter alone could make me happy and has added greatly to this day.

You have my heartfelt thanks and you have helped make this a happy day for me.

It's a day I shall not forget. And Zelda is a name I'll always remember.

Bless you—
Ron

RUDDY HINES

In a letter dated April 3, 1984, Ruddy enclosed a photograph of himself and thanked President Reagan for a picture the president sent him of Mr. and Mrs. Reagan and their dog. He told the president that his hobbies were "painting and watching golf," and added, "I like to read and write too. At recreational reading time, the children pull out the rugs and read the newspaper. Some of my classmates even take off their shoes." His teacher, Mrs. Brenda Williams, Ruddy explained, would put 50 points on the board and would take one away each time a student broke a rule. His classmate Melinda drew a picture that "had a sailboat on the water and the sun was out." Ruddy said that he enjoyed his tour of Air Force One with Mr. Dalton, the principal of Congress Heights Elementary School.

Rudolph Hines
Washington, D.C.
April 9, 1984[62]

Dear Rudolph:

Thank you for your letter and for sending your picture. I'm glad to have it.

You said one of your hobbies was painting. That's fine and it's something you can get a lot of pleasure from throughout your life. I didn't paint when I was your age but I liked to draw cartoons and still do. What I do now is called doodling and usually is done when I'm in a meeting of some kind. I've enclosed a few from a recent meeting.

You also mentioned reading and that is good. Rudolph if you get in the habit of reading stories for pleasure you'll never be lonely. Sometimes I worry that TV is going to rob young people of the great pleasure there is in a good book. When I was only a little older than you I had a library card and used to take out books from the public library in the small town where we lived. To this day when I have to take a trip I make sure to have a book along.

I think Mrs. Williams' idea about the 50 points is a good one. We all need to keep score on ourselves to measure how we are doing. Melinda's picture must have been very pretty the way you described it.

On Wednesday the 18th of April Mrs. Reagan and I have to start on our trip to China. We'll be in California for a couple of days, then stop in Hawaii overnight and further on spend a day and night on the island of Guam. All of this is to help us readjust to the difference in time when we get to China. Otherwise we'd be all turned around because when it's noon here it's midnight there. If there is a map around you might look for Hawaii and Guam.

The trip is to meet with the government leaders of China and see how our two countries can become better friends. We'll be back on May 2nd. We're going on that plane you visited—*Air Force One.*

Well Mrs. Reagan says hello and please give our regards to Mrs. Williams and your classmates.

Sincerely,
Ronald Reagan

Less than two weeks after returning from his first visit to a Communist country, President Reagan replies to a letter from Ruddy and encloses photographs from his trip with detailed handwritten captions. Next to one photograph of him and Nancy, President Reagan wrote: "This is the Great Wall—built more than 2,000 years ago to keep the barbarians from the North from invading the kingdom."

Rudolph Hines
Washington, D.C.
May 11, 1984 [63]

Dear Rudolph:

I returned from our China trip to find your letter awaiting me. I thank you for your kind words about my doodling. Sometimes I erase a line I've been careless in drawing but not very often. No—Mrs. Reagan doesn't draw and I'm afraid we didn't have contests to see who could draw best. Sometimes I doodle with a pen if one is handy.

I'm glad to hear you enjoy reading. I can't give you a comparison of my levels when I was your age because we had a different kind of grading system. I was better at reading than at math. But your levels sound great. Keep it up.

Our trip to China was fantastic. There was a lot of hard work but some time also for sightseeing. I've put some notes on the back of these pictures to explain them.

Best regards,
Ronald Reagan

A month after traveling to the People's Republic of China, President Reagan toured Ireland, the United Kingdom, and France. Eight days after his return, he describes his trip to his pen pal.

Rudolph Hines
Washington, D.C.
June 18, 1984[64]

Dear Rudolph:

It was good to hear from you and to learn what you've been doing. The pictures of China and these were taken by our White House photographers.

Ireland was a wonderful experience. I had never known anything about my father's family. He had been orphaned before he was six years old. But when I became president the government of Ireland did some research and learned that my great grandfather came from a village in Tipperary County, Ireland named Ballyporeen.

I went to the church where he was baptized in 1829, 155 years ago. They showed me the old church book with the handwritten record of his baptism written in 1829.

There are only 350 people living in the town but there were several thousand the day I was there. We flew on to Dublin the capital of Ireland after the homecoming in Ballyporeen. I made a speech there to the Dail—that's what they call their Congress.

Then we flew on to London England for the meetings I was to have with the leaders of England, France, Canada, West Germany, Japan and Italy. But before they got under way we went across to France for the observance of the 40th anniversary of D-Day. That was the day (June 6th 1944) when our Allied forces stormed the beaches in World War II. It was the turning point of the war as we went on to defeat the Nazis and free Europe.

At Omaha Beach there are 9,360 of our soldiers buried in a cemetery, each grave marked by a white marble cross.

Many veterans of that battle had returned for the ceremony as well as families of some of the dead. It was an emotional experience for all of us.

Back in London we had three days of meetings discussing problems of trade and international affairs. The last night we were invited to a dinner by the Queen of

England at Buckingham Palace. And the next day *Air Force One* brought us back to Washington. It's always good to get home even though our trip was interesting and worthwhile.

Incidentally a few days before we took that trip I flew out to Colorado Springs where I met some of our Olympic athletes at the Olympic training center. Our Air Force Academy is also there and I was there for the graduation ceremony.

Well as I say it's good to be home.

Best regards,
Ronald Reagan

Ruddy wrote President Reagan about his experiences at summer camp. In his reply, President Reagan describes his summers as a child in Dixon, Illinois, as well as his most recent vacation at Rancho del Cielo, *his ranch near Santa Barbara, California.*

Rudolph Hines
Washington, D.C.
August 22, 1984 [65]

Dear Rudolph:

Thank you very much for the pictures. You are quite a photographer. I really enjoyed your work.

I'm glad you had such a good time at camp and especially glad you learned how to swim. For seven summers during my high school and college years I was a lifeguard at a park in my home town (Dixon Illinois). We swam in the Rock River which in many ways was like the Potomac here in Washington. It's a great and healthy sport and I still enjoy it.

We're just back from our vacation. We had two weeks at our ranch in California. We rode horseback every morning and then in the afternoon did the things that needed doing around the ranch. Once upon a time I would have called it work but after sitting [at] a desk all year it seems like fun.

We built an addition to the patio which meant going out with a Jeep and trailer and finding flat stones. We laid them in a bed of sand then dumped dry cement dust on them and swept it into the cracks between the stones and wet it down with a hose. When the cement hardened we had a nice stone floor all cemented in tight.

Then we cleaned up a stretch of woods pruning out the dead limbs and trees. We sawed the heavier limbs up for firewood and piled the smaller stuff up to burn this winter. We have a rainy season in California and a dry season and you have to wait for that rainy season to do any outdoor burning. This time of year a bonfire could start a forest fire.

Of course there were still some things to do that go with my job, reports, meetings, phone calls and signing laws passed by Congress. I managed to get most of that done in the early morning or in the evening so I still had time for the fun things.

Well vacation is over and now it's time for the convention and then the campaign. Mrs. Reagan and I are off to Dallas.

Thanks again for the photos. I've enclosed a few taken at the ranch on our vacation.

> Best regards,
> Ronald Reagan

Ruddy invited the Reagans to his house for dinner. In his letter of invitation, he wrote, "You have to let us know in advance so my mom can pick up the laundry off the floor."[66] The Reagans accepted the invitation and arrived at Ruddy's house on September 21, 1984. Ruddy cut short the dinner so that he could attend a Michael Jackson concert. Almost two months later he wrote President Reagan: "I'm sorry I couldn't write to you sooner and send you some pictures of me. I have been busy with 'Test Taking Skills' and trying to get A's in my subjects. I'm trying to make the 'Honor Roll' again this year. . . . The Michael Jackson Concert was great! . . . I see you on TV. I am hoping you will be President again. I know it's hard work. I hope we will always be Pen Pals." His postscript: "I'm going to be Mr. T for Halloween. I'll send some pictures of me as Mr. T."

> Rudolph Hines
> Washington, D.C.
> November 4, 1984[67]

Dear Rudolph:

It was good to hear from you and to learn that you are trying for the "Honor Roll." I'm proud of you and I know your mother and father must be. I'll look forward to those pictures of you as Mr. T.

I've been out campaigning, but now that's coming to an end—I'm happy to say. Right now I'm doing this letter on *Air Force One* somewhere between Chicago and California. So far, today, I've been in Milwaukee, Wisconsin, Rochester, Minnesota, St. Louis, Missouri, and Chicago, Illinois. Now we're headed for Sacramento, California where we'll start the day tomorrow. Then we'll go to Los Angeles and San Diego. That winds it up. We'll vote in California and wait for the election returns. Of course, by the time you get this you'll already know whether I won or not. Right now I won't let myself think about that.

Mrs. Reagan and I enjoyed our evening with you and your folks very much. We're both glad you had a good time at the concert. You are right about her, she probably would have jumped at the fireworks.

Well, I've got to get back to some homework I have to do so I'll close.

> Best regards,
> Ronald Reagan

On the same day, President Reagan thanks Ruddy's mother for her letter and admits that he will be uptight on election night.

Ms. Stephanie H. Lee
Washington, D.C.
November 4, 1984 [68]

Dear Ms. Lee:

Thank you for your letter and generous words. Nancy and I are both grateful. We enjoyed very much our visit. I've just done a letter to my pen pal [Ruddy Hines] and as I told him I was doing the letter on *Air Force One* on our way to California for the last day of campaigning and the election. Well that's where I'm doing this one also. No matter what the polls say I'll be a little uptight until Tuesday night.

I appreciate your good wishes. And of course hope you get your wish. It's my wish too.

Nancy sends her very best and asked me to tell you how much she enjoyed meeting you.

Again our thanks and very best regards.

Sincerely,
Ronald Reagan

President Reagan congratulates Ruddy on his grades, gives him some acting tips, and says he looked good as Mr. T.

Rudolph Hines
Washington, D.C.
December 10, 1984 [69]

Dear Rudolph:

Congratulations on those nine B's and on your campaign to turn them into A's.

Now about that acting job—take it from an ex-actor there are ways to help with your lines. One way is when you are walking, lying in bed awake or just sitting around, try to mentally recite your lines. Don't say them aloud—just think them and see if you can remember them. That of course won't take the place of actually saying and rehearsing them. It will be added to that. I'm betting on you, you'll do just fine.

Your Thanksgiving sounds great. Ours was nice too, we went to the ranch and started the day with a horseback ride, then home for turkey.

Thanks for the pictures, you make quite a Mr. T.

Your Pen Pal,
Ronald Reagan

Before departing for California for the holidays, President Reagan thanks Ruddy for his Christmas gift.

Rudolph Lee Hines
Washington, D.C.
December 26, 1984[70]

Dear Ruddy:

I'm on my way to California for New Year's but had to drop you a line to thank you for my Christmas gift. I can't tell you how happy I am to have that book on Western movies. I just happen to be a fan of Westerns. In fact when I was making movies I always wanted to be in more Western movies than I ended up doing.

Thank you again. Please give my regards to your parents and I hope you had a very Merry Christmas.

Sincerely—Your Pen Pal,
Ronald Reagan

After receiving an invitation to President Reagan's second inaugural, Ruddy had some questions. He wrote: "What is an (inauguration?) What do you do? Is it parties, concerts and parades? Or is it something else? Do you have to study for it? Does the inauguration take a long time? My mom said that this is a very special time for you and that the whole country will be watching. Is that true? What will Mrs. Reagan be doing? Does she have to study too? I will be reading about it in the newspaper." President Reagan answered four days after he was inaugurated again.

Rudolph Hines
Washington, D.C.
January 24, 1985[71]

Dear Rudolph:

Just received your letter and was glad to hear from you. You asked some questions about the inaugural but maybe now that it's over you already have the answers. Just in case you missed a few I'll answer anyway.

The inauguration is the swearing in of the president. Once elected or reelected as I was your term begins at noon on January 20th with you taking an oath to uphold the Constitution and fulfill the duties of the presidency.

This year the 20th fell on Sunday, the first time since Eisenhower's inaugural. So I had to take the oath on Sunday but repeated it on Monday for the public. I told some of our congressmen that maybe we should change the Constitution so that when the 20th was a Sunday the president would still be president until Monday noon.

Over the years traditions have built up so that a big entertainment takes place the night before. Ours was at the Convention Center with Frank Sinatra in charge. Then on inaugural day there is a parade. Ours was canceled because of the cold. On inaugural night there is a big party. That custom started back in 1789 when George Washington became president. Now our country has become so big we had to have 11 of them. Nancy and I showed up and made an appearance at all 11. This was the 50th inauguration in our country's history.

I mentioned the cold and canceling the parade; this was the coldest inaugural day we've ever had and the first time the outdoor events had to be canceled. Let me tell you how cold it was; upstairs in the White House there is a big potted plant in front of the window we open at night for fresh air when we go to bed. This time I only opened it about two inches. In the morning the plant was dead. It had frozen.

I'll look forward to hearing about the science fair and hope you succeed in the rocket launch. Please give our regards to your folks.

Best wishes from your pen pal.
Ronald Reagan

––––––––

President Reagan is pleased about Ruddy's good grades. He tells him more about the American tradition of inaugurating presidents and encloses photographs of himself and Nancy at the inauguration.

Rudolph Lee Hines
Washington, D.C.
March 6, 1985 [72]

Dear Rudolph:

I was pleased to learn of your grades. I have to tell you, you are doing better than I did. And while you didn't win at the science fair, an honorable mention isn't bad.

You asked about why the inauguration wasn't held on Sunday. It has always been a tradition that the inaugural programs, the parade and all should not be held on the Lord's day, interfering with church services. The reason I had to be sworn in on Sunday though was because under the law I would no longer have been president after noon Sunday. There would have been 24 hours with no president of the United States. Just between us I don't see why we can't amend the law to read that when January 20th falls on a Sunday the president's term is extended 24 hours to noon Monday.

I've enclosed some photos of inaugural events with notes on the back as to what they are.

Please give your Mom and Dad my very best regards. Nancy sends hers also.

Sincerely,
Ronald Reagan

Following a trip to view the Life *magazine exhibit at the Smithsonian, Ruddy sent a postcard to his pen pal: "I love the picture of the gaboon viper's skeleton. Mom said it was gross." President Reagan replies in a letter written a week after meeting in Canada with Prime Minister Brian Mulroney to discuss acid rain.*

Rudolph Hines
Washington, D.C.
March 25, 1985 [73]

Dear Rudolph:

Got your card and it was good to hear from you. I know we're both busy but I was pleased to learn of your visit to the Smithsonian. We're so lucky to live in a city where there is such a great museum.

We were in Canada for a summit meeting with their government leaders. It was quite a shock to find ourselves back in winter. The snow drifts were several feet high and it was really cold.

Give our regards to your folks.

Sincerely,
Your Pen Pal,
Ronald Reagan

On April 15, 1985, President Reagan visited the Ringling Bros. and Barnum & Bailey Circus at the D.C. Armory to lend support to the Safe Kids program, which finger-printed children and provided parents with safety documents in an attempt to address the problem of missing children. Ruddy met President Reagan at the circus and was fingerprinted.

In a letter to President Reagan, Ruddy wrote: "It was good to see you at the circus. I wasn't feeling well that day but I had a good time. Thanks again for the 'whistle.' It blows real loud." He also wrote about school activities, learning French, and a prob-lem with a friend: "I have learned if you hurt a friend they don't like you as well as be-fore. I called my best friend, Raymond [Tucker], a bad name because I was very mad at him. I didn't mean to say it. I told him I was sorry, but it hasn't been the same. What do you think I should do? I hope things get better between us." President Reagan offers words of advice.

Rudolph Hines
Washington, D.C.
April 23, 1985 [74]

Dear Ruddy:

It was good to hear from you and to be with you at the circus. I thought you were pretty quiet that day and I'm glad to know the reason and also glad to know you are alright now.

I'm sorry to hear about your problem with Raymond. You did right in telling him you were sorry. Maybe you need to do a little more if he's still acting not so friendly. Go to him when you can talk quietly without others around. Tell him good friends aren't easy to come by and that you want to be his friend. Tell him you were upset and not thinking straight when you called him what you did but you didn't mean it and you want him for your best friend.

Thanks for the pictures I really enjoyed them. You brought back some memories for me. I used to be in school plays—also some pageants and plays in Sunday school.

Stick with that French. I didn't do as well as I should have in French and I sure was sorry when I found myself in France. I could manage a little but I realized for the first time how wonderful it would be if I could make myself understood in their language.

Speaking of languages we are off to West Germany April 30th for what's called an economic summit. I don't know a word of German.

Well give my best to your folks.

Sincerely,
Ronald Reagan

Ruddy wrote, "We [he and Raymond] are friends again like before because we talk and play together again." He described a trip to Atlantic City with his mother and godmother: "My mom played the slot machines that you put quarters in, but she said it's too easy to lose your money. She played for only a minute. My godmother said that some people stay for hours. I don't think I could do that." Ruddy wrote about his upcoming school play and the cast party the parents would host. He also asked how President Reagan traveled.

Rudolph Hines
Washington, D.C.
Circa June 1985 [75]

Dear Rudy:

Congratulations on your award and I'm happy to learn that you and Raymond have patched up your differences and are back on good terms. I'm proud of you.

Sorry about the weather in Atlantic City but it sounds as if you had a good time anyway. Your Mom is right about those slot machines. You know they are called, "one-armed bandits." You can find lots better things to do with a quarter than to give it to the "bandit."

I know by the time you get this your play will have taken place and the party for the cast as well. I hope it was a success and that you all had a good time.

Enclosed is a little something for your birthday. It is a book mark so you won't lose your place when you put a book down. Have a happy birthday and thanks for inviting me to your party. Unfortunately my schedule won't let me be there and I'm really sorry. But you have a happy birthday and a wonderful vacation.

Oh—I almost forgot you asked me about our trips and where we stayed. The only time we slept on *Air Force One* was on the way to Germany last month. It took most of the night to get there. On trips around the country here we stay at hotels. I guess you get used to answering the questions and having your picture taken but it would be nice sometime to just go unnoticed. The only place that happens though is on the ranch and we'll have a few days there next month.

Your Pen Pal,
Ronald Reagan

———————

On September 1, 1985, Ruddy wrote: "It has been a long time since my last letter to you. I have waited to write until after your vacation at the ranch. My mom said your vacation was long overdue and I was not to worry you with a million questions. I know I ask a lot of questions sometimes but I hope you don't mind." President Reagan responds with answers to Ruddy's questions.

Rudolph Hines
Washington, D.C.
September 9, 1985[76]

Dear Ruddy:

It was good to hear from you and to hear about your vacation trip. Thank you very much for our gift. Nancy joins me in this, we both think the glasses are lovely with those beautiful ring-necked pheasants on them. I assure you we'll use them with great pleasure.

Don't worry about asking questions, feel free to ask them anytime. About the one on riding—when I was in high school and college I spent my summers as a life-guard at a river beach in my home town. The man who took care of the park had a horse for pulling some of the equipment he used in keeping the park cleaned. Sometimes at the end of the day he'd ride the horse bareback (no saddle) down to the beach. One day he teased me into riding the horse and before I knew it I liked riding. Later when I was a sports announcer near an Army cavalry post I became a reserve officer in the cavalry.

Riding is a wonderful sport and a very healthy sport. An old cavalry saying is, "nothing is so good for the inside of a man as the outside of a horse." It's only natural to be afraid at first of a horse but that goes away as you begin to ride. You asked me about learning karate and how to breach the subject to your parents. Ruddy, being a parent myself I can tell you your parents are the best friends you'll ever have. The best way is to simply talk it over with them. The decision they make will be based on what they think is best for you right now. Listen to them and accept their decision knowing they have your best interest at heart. I can recall some turn-downs by my parents when I was young. At the time I was pretty upset and thought my parents were wrong but as time went by I usually looked back and decided they had been right.

By the way Ruddy parents worry and are sorry they can't spend more time with their children, it's just that life gets a little complicated, what with making a living and all.

Thanks again for our beautiful gift and happy school days. The enclosed is a little going to school gift.

Sincerely,
Ronald Reagan

President Reagan answers more of Ruddy's questions.

Ruddy Hines
Washington, D.C.
October 28, 1985[77]

Dear Ruddy:

Well it was good to hear from you and I'm glad school is going so well and that you like your teacher. Good luck with the karate lessons.

I ride on weekends up at Camp David. I tried Rock Creek Park once but so many Secret Service agents had to go along and the concern about security was so great it didn't seem worth it. I'll just keep on doing it at Camp David and of course at our ranch when I can get to California. I'll be there this Thanksgiving for a few days and riding every day.

You asked about the presidential seal. It remains the same for each president but can only be used as the seal for whoever is president and while he is holding that office.

I've met the photographer Ansel Adams. He does specialize in scenic photos and has covered many if not all of our national parks.

It was good to see you in the Rose Garden. I hope the pamphlet on the Royal coat of arms gave you the information you wanted. I had it on my desk to be sent with this letter but when I saw you out there I hadn't finished this letter so I figured I'd hand it to you.

My best wishes to your folks.

Your Pen Pal,
Ronald Reagan

Speaking at the Martin Luther King Jr. 1986 celebration at Ruddy's elementary school, President Reagan talked about the racial discrimination his college football teammate, William Franklin Burghardt, faced on the field while playing against "a fellow that was filled with hatred and prejudice." Burgie, as Reagan nicknamed his friend, stood his ground and played the game, injured by the white player. "[H]e didn't play dirty;

he played clean. . . . And by the middle of the fourth quarter his opponent, playing dirty with all of his dirty tricks, was literally staggering. And his coach had to send in a substitute for him." The player then said to Burgie: " 'I just want you to know you're the greatest human being I've ever met." The player then "turned and left the field." After President Reagan visited Ruddy's elementary school, Ruddy wrote: "It was good to see you again and my friend Raymond said that he would never wash the hand that you shook again. My mom and some of her friends told us about the days of Martin Luther King and other stories like the story of your football friend. I hope I never meet anyone who would hurt me just because I am a different color."

Ruddy wrote that he hoped President Reagan liked the birthday cake he and his aunt made. He also talked about the explosion of the space shuttle Challenger, *which occurred on January 28, 1986: "My mom asked me if I had any questions or feelings about the accident. I told her that I thought it was sad that all the families would not have any place to go, like a cemetery, to say goodbye. My folks say that pioneering people often took chances with death so that the rest of us could do what they did without fear or without harm."*

Rudolph Lee Hines
Washington, D.C.
Late February 1986 [78]

Dear Rudolph:

It was good to get your letter and to hear about those grades, keep it up. You know we have something in common—I didn't do well in science either but like you I kept trying. We have to do that.

I'm just now settling back after my birthday. We all enjoyed the cake very much, thank you and Aunt Gilley. My biggest and best birthday present was a tractor for the ranch. We had a tractor I'd been using for 33 years and it was getting harder and harder to keep it going. Well 31 of our friends got together and bought a second-hand tractor that's quite a bit younger than the one we had. I can't wait to get to the ranch and have a ride on it—maybe even do a little work with it.

I shared your feelings about the shuttle tragedy. I think most everyone in the country was saddened. Your folks are right about the debt we owe to those who have pioneered in our country. Each of the families of those who lost their lives told me we must keep the space program growing, that their loved ones would want it that way.

Well I'm off to Grenada for a meeting down there. I'll be back the same day which means a lot of hours in the air.

Give my regards to your folks.

Sincerely,
Ronald Reagan

On April 3, 1986, Ruddy wrote: "It's Easter break—finally! This is one of my favorite times of the year. . . . I went to early Mass at our church and then helped my grand-

mother and aunt Delores prepare a family brunch. . . . It has been so warm these past few days that we tried several times to visit the Cherry Blossoms. The tourists were so heavy that we were unable to do more than drive past."

Rudolph Hines
Washington, D.C.
April 22, 1986 [79]

Dear Rudolph:

I'm glad to hear about your Easter break. Out in California we read and heard about the wonderful weather you were having. Ours was nice but not quite as summery as what you were having back here.

We went to church on Easter at a little country church down in the valley. Then every day for the rest of the week we had a horseback ride, usually in the morning. In the afternoons we cleared some of the riding trails that had gotten overgrown. All in all, it was a good time and a nice change from the Oval Office.

The end of this week will see us on our way to the island of Bali and Japan. On Bali we'll have meetings with some of the leaders of Indonesia, Malaysia, Singapore, the Philippines and some other Asian governments. They are joined in an organization called ASEAN.

From there we'll go to Tokyo for the annual economic summit with the leaders of England, France, Italy, West Germany, Canada and Japan. It will be a busy time. We have a lot to talk about including terrorism and what we can do about it. We'll be back in Washington May 7th. Since the time difference is 12 hours, I think we'll have a little trouble with jet lag.

Best regards.
Your Pen Pal,
Ronald Reagan

Ruddy was among the guests who greeted President and Mrs. Reagan at the White House when they returned from the G-7 summit in Tokyo. President Reagan describes the trip in this letter to his young friend.

Rudolph Lee Hines
Washington, D.C.
May 12, 1986 [80]

Dear Ruddy:

It was good to see you at the White House when we returned from Japan. That was quite a trip. We were in the plane actually flying, a total of 38 hours and gone a total of 13 days. Two of the flights were over fourteen hours each.

On the way out we stopped overnight in Los Angeles and two nights in Honolulu. This was to help us adjust to the time change which totaled 13 hours. While we were in Bali and Japan it was daytime there when it was night in Washington. It does get you a little mixed up as to sleeping. You can change your clock but you can't change that inner clock in each of us that tells us when to get sleepy.

You know there is a line known as the international dateline out in the Pacific Ocean. It is where yesterday [or] tomorrow and today meet. For example going to Bali we left Hawaii about 10 a.m. Monday morning and that afternoon as we crossed the dateline it became Tuesday. Coming home from Tokyo we left there at noon Wednesday crossed the dateline and arrived in Washington at two o'clock that same afternoon, although we'd been flying 14 hours with a one-hour stop in Alaska to refuel. We'd flown through the night and seen the sunrise but it was still Wednesday. You can get a little confused.

The trip was worthwhile. On Bali we met with the president of Indonesia, a country of 165 million people on 13,600 islands spread over 3,000 miles of ocean. We also met with the foreign ministers of five other Asian countries. All those countries are important trading partners of ours and we had a lot to talk about.

In Tokyo we met with heads of state of Japan, England, Germany, Italy, Canada and France. We are all allied and meet each year to discuss our mutual problems. I think it is wonderful that three of those countries now our good friends were our enemies in World War II.

Now all I have to do is get readjusted to sleeping on Washington time which isn't easy.

Give my regards to your folks and all the best to you.

Sincerely,
Ronald Reagan

On June 12, 1986, Kathy Osborne, President Reagan's secretary, sent a note to President Reagan: "Would you like us to come up with a gift item for Rudolph for his birthday? We've got new presidential key chains, and we've got a great set of three books; the first inaugural, the second inaugural, and the White House? Let me know if you want me to do something about the birthday." President Reagan responded: "Yes on the gifts and I'd make it the books."

On July 30, 1986, Ruddy wrote: "Half the summer has gone by and I still have not properly thanked you and Mrs. Reagan for my birthday gifts. My mom is pretty mad at me because she said it shows poor manners. I apologize for my lateness in not letting you know how much I enjoyed the books. I was so surprised to see myself and my school in a book. I showed all my friends and they thought it was 'hip.' " Ruddy asked if President Reagan was going to California for the summer and expressed the hope that his parents would take him to the Expo in Canada.

In his reply, President Reagan writes that he will visit his ranch and will enjoy the recess of the U.S. Congress.

Rudolph Hines
Washington, D.C.
August 14, 1986[81]

Dear Ruddy:

I'm sorry to be so late in answering your letter, it has only just reached me. Maybe that's because of some of the traveling I've been doing.

It sounds like you've had quite a summer and accomplished a great deal. I was glad to hear about that horseback riding. That's been my sport for many years now, and I would hate to ever have to give it up. It's a great, healthy exercise, in addition to being a lot of fun.

By the time you get this, we'll be in California on our ranch and riding every day. We get a few weeks off because the Congress is taking a recess 'til after Labor Day. I won't miss them a bit.

I hope you get that trip to Canada and the Exposition. I haven't run into anyone who has been there, so I can't answer your questions about it.

Give my regards to your folks and, again, it was good to hear from you.

Sincerely,
Your pen pal,
Ronald Reagan

———

In a letter dated September 8, 1986, Ruddy wrote: "Welcome back! Hope you and Mrs. Reagan enjoyed your stay at the ranch. . . . My friend Raymond [Tucker] didn't come back this year because he moved away and goes to another school." Ruddy also wrote that he could not find anything to play with because his belongings were packed so that his apartment could be painted.

President Reagan sympathizes with Ruddy. He also writes that he is determined to seek the release of Nicholas Daniloff, an American journalist taken into custody by the Soviet Union on August 30, 1986, on a spy charge. He writes about his admiration for Martin Luther King Jr. and mentions that he knows Coretta Scott King, the widow of the slain civil rights leader. President Reagan had found himself immersed in a controversy three years earlier, however. At a news conference on October 19, 1983, he responded to a question about whether he thought King had been associated with Communists:

"We'll know in about 35 years, won't we? No, I don't fault Senator [Jesse] Helms' sincerity with regard to wanting the records opened up. I think that he's motivated by a feeling that if we're going to have a national holiday named for any American, when it's only been named for one American in all our history up until this time . . . we should know everything there is to know about an individual. . . . I also recognize there is no way that these records can be opened, because an agreement was reached between the family and the government with regard to those records. And we're not going to turn away from that or set a precedent of breaking agreements of that kind. . . .

"I would have preferred a day similar to, say, Lincoln's birthday, which is not technically a national holiday, but is certainly a day reverenced by a great many people in our country. . . . [B]ut since they seem bent on making it a national holiday, I believe the symbolism of that day is important enough that I'll sign that legislation when it reaches my desk."

Two days later, President Reagan called Mrs. King and offered his apologies.[82] On November 2, 1983, President Reagan signed the legislation making King's birthday a national holiday in the presence of the King family at the White House.

Rudolph Hines
Washington, D.C.
September 26, 1986[83]

Dear Rudolph:

Well it was good to get your letter and hear about your summer. You are right the summer does seem as if it went by in a hurry. Our big summer event now is the three-week visit to our ranch when the Congress has a recess.

We have a horseback ride every morning then in the afternoon I get at the ranch chores that have piled up. This time it was three oak trees that had fallen and had to be cut up and the logs split for firewood.

I'm luckier than you about that painting business. Our ranch house needed touching up so we arranged to have it done after we came back to Washington. Of course we may have a few problems with finding things when we get back there for a few days next month. I hope not.

You'll like bowling. I haven't had time lately but always enjoyed it. I hope you get your trip to Atlanta and to visit the place Martin Luther King Jr. knew so well. He was a great man we must always remember. I never knew him personally but do know his widow Mrs. King. She is a lovely lady.

As you've seen in the news I'm sure, I'm having a few problems with the Soviet Union. They are holding one of our journalists Nick Daniloff hostage. My number one duty is get him back and I won't rest until he's safely back here in the United States.

Well happy fourth grade and give my regards to your folks.

Sincerely,
Your Pen Pal,
Ronald Reagan

In his letter of October 27, 1986, Ruddy asked about President Reagan's second summit with Soviet General Secretary Mikhail Gorbachev in Reykjavik, Iceland. He also informed the president that his mother was going to have her gallbladder removed. His postscript said, "Mom said I could have her gallstones to do a science project. What do you think?"

President Reagan replies two days after the midterm election.

Rudolph Hines
Washington, D.C.
November 6, 1986[84]

Dear Ruddy:

Just got back to Washington and found your letter awaiting me. I've been out campaigning for our candidates though 22 states and wound up in California.

Ruddy I think we made great progress in Iceland and now our arms negotiating teams are continuing to meet in Geneva Switzerland. We'll have a better idea of our chances in a few days. Secretary of State Shultz is meeting with the Soviet foreign minister* in Vienna in a few days.

Iceland was something of a different world but the people are very nice and very friendly. They are also proud of their country and their way of life.

It's true that the only trees are in and around the city. They have been brought into the country and planted by the people. There are no trees natural to Iceland. There is plenty of green grass for the raising of sheep, cattle etc. It is studded with black volcanic boulders and ridges on the low hillsides. This time of year daylight is only five hours long and yes it does seem strange to be in darkness at about 3:30 in the afternoon. Our flight there was about six hours long.

Your trip sounds interesting and fun. Thanks for my "worry stone." Now that the election is over I think I'll make use of it.

I'm sorry to hear about your mother's operation and hope everything went well and that she's recovering nicely and without much pain. Please tell her for Nancy and me that she's in our thoughts and prayers. She's right about the stones—they would be quite a project. How many in the class could match that?

All the best to you.

Sincerely,
Ronald Reagan

Reagan sends holiday greetings and congratulates Ruddy for participating in a school play.

Rudolph Hines
Washington, D.C.
December 18, 1986[85]

Dear Ruddy:

Well hello my fellow actor. I'm glad you found acting fun, I know I always did even though I was making my living doing it.

I'm happy the Thanksgiving day was so enjoyable. Mine was too. We went out to our ranch. The weather was beautiful, we rode horses every day and our

---

* Eduard Shevardnadze.

family came to the ranch for Thanksgiving Day and yes we stuffed ourselves on turkey.

Please give my regards to your folks and wish them a Merry Christmas and a Merry Christmas to you.

Sincerely,
Ronald Reagan

————————

Four days after prostate surgery, President Reagan catches up with Ruddy.

Ruddy Hines
Washington, D.C.
January 9, 1987[86]

Dear Ruddy:

I'm a little late with this but Nancy and I want you to know how much we appreciate the beautiful scarfs we found under our Christmas tree. Please thank your mother and tell her how much we admire her handiwork.

We left for California right after Christmas and had New Year's with friends in the desert at Palm Springs. I had my annual golf game. Hadn't played since last New Year's in the same place. Then the day after we got back here I went into the hospital. Everything turned out fine and I'm back at the White House catching up.

Again our thanks to you and your mother.

Sincerely,
Ronald Reagan

————————

Two days before he would address the nation on the Iran-Contra scandal, President Reagan starts a letter to his pen pal with a little humor about his memory.

Rudolph Lee-Hines
Washington, D.C.
March 2, 1987[87]

Dear Ruddy:

It was good to hear from you Pen Pal, and please thank your mother for her note and tell her not to worry at all about forgetting the stamp. As some of the newspapers would have you believe, forgetting is what I do best.

Our busy times seem to come at the same time. I'm faced with a couple of speeches plus a lot of work with Congress on the budget and some other matters. Your projects for [the] science fair sound great and I wish you well.

The bowling sounds great. I never did very well at that sport although I enjoyed it. Back when I was about your age I made a little spending money setting up the pins at the YMCA bowling alleys. I think you have better scores now than I ever made.

Now I'll get back to my speeches. All the best to you in the tournament and regards to your mother.

Sincerely,
Ronald Reagan

In a March 23, 1987, letter, Ruddy informed Reagan that he won second prize at school for his science project and first prize in the regional competition. He also wrote: "I have a second pen pal. He's Japanese. . . . He's in the 4th grade and he likes soccer and video games. He wrote to me in Japanese and someone who understands the language had to translate his letter for me. . . . I wrote back to him and asked if he could write to me in English. Their language is very difficult to understand. Do you know any Japanese?" He also wrote about flying his kite in the warm weather.

Rudolph Lee-Hines
Washington, D.C.
April 3, 1987 [88]

Dear Ruddy:

Well congratulations on the success of your science project. I have to tell you I never did that well in science when I was in school.

As for your other pen pal Yuki, no I don't know any Japanese. It will be interesting to see if Yuki begins responding in English. It's my understanding that the Japanese schools emphasize learning English and that it's a requirement for high school graduation.

Your kite sounds like a 747 of kites. I only saw a few minutes of the kite flying on the TV news. Of course the shots were too far away to identify anyone so I'll never know if I saw your kite. But it sounds like you had a good time.

We'll be leaving for California Thursday April 8th for a couple of days in Los Angeles and then nine days at the ranch. We're really looking forward to it. We haven't been to the ranch since Thanksgiving. You'll enjoy Williamsburg it's part of our national history and has many places of great interest.

I'm sure your grandmother will enjoy Hawaii. It's hard to pick out any one place to see. She'll find it enjoyable wherever she goes.

Have a good vacation yourself.

Sincerely,
Ronald Reagan

Following a western economic summit meeting in Venice and a visit with Pope John Paul II at the Vatican, President Reagan describes his trip. He also congratulates Ruddy on his activities and excellent grades and sends birthday greetings as well. Kathy Osborne, President Reagan's secretary, also wrote Ruddy on June 25, 1987: "Dear Ruddy,

The president asked me to send you the enclosed set of books for a belated birthday gift.
I will also be sending you, in a few days, a packet of photos taken during our trip to Italy.
With best wishes, Kathy Osborne." [89]

Ruddy Lee-Hines
Washington, D.C.
June 25, 1987 [90]

Dear Ruddy:

It was good to hear from you and your mother was right. I appreciate your support as a friend very much.

Our trip to Italy was busy but at the same time interesting. As you know we were in Venice and it's unusual and exciting to be in a city where almost all the streets are canals and you travel by boat wherever you go. Yes the pope speaks English and a half dozen other languages for that matter. We had a good visit. He'll be visiting our country next year.

Now though let's talk about you. Second in the bowling league is pretty good and getting a new bike is super. But topping everything are those grades. Do you want to know something? I never in all my school years had a card with six A's and three B's and on top of that five certificates for science fair, spelling bee and computer excellence. Congratulations and keep it up.

And a belated Happy Birthday!

My very best regards to your folks.

Sincerely,
Your Pen Pal,
Ronald Reagan

A month after the third U.S.-Soviet summit was held in Washington, Ruddy informed
his pen pal about school and bowling. He wrote about the summit: "Congratulations
on the success of the U.S./Soviet summit. Hopefully, after a while, there'll be no need
for summits. Does Mr. Gorbachev have any hobbies like us? Does he have any children?
Does he speak any English at all or does he need an interpreter all the time? It must be
pretty hard to get eye to eye with someone else speaking your words for you."

Rudolph Lee-Hines
Washington, D.C.
January 22, 1988 [91]

Dear Ruddy:

How nice to hear from you. We really enjoyed the goodies and tell your mother thanks. I'm going to turn this place upside down until I find the book. Sometimes the bureaucracy gets in the way.

Congratulations on your grades. I'm sorry I can't be of help on the science fair. I have to confess I didn't do very well in science when I was in school.

Yes and congratulations on your bowling score. I did some bowling when I was your age, at the YMCA in Dixon but I never scored 134.

I don't have many answers to your questions about Gorbachev's family or his hobbies. We never got around to that kind of conversation, possibly because all our talk had to be through interpreters. You are right, it would be better if he could understand our language or of course if I could talk Russian.

Just between us (on another subject) I was rooting for the Redskins even though in my job I'm not supposed to take sides. I think it's going to be quite a Super Bowl.

Good luck in your play about Martin Luther King Jr. He was a great man.

My best to your mother.

Sincerely,
Ronald Reagan

CHAPTER TWENTY-FIVE

Back to California

WHEN REAGAN'S *airplane headed back to California it was as if a giant switch had been thrown. The phones were silent. The staff of hundreds was gone. Most of the press now turned to the next president. Reagan was once again a private citizen. There still was Secret Service protection, but the risk of an attack was greatly diminished.*

Reagan observed one symbolic marker: "One person was notably absent: the military aide, the person who, since twelve noon on January 20, 1981, had been at my side with the information I would need in the event of a nuclear strike.* No longer could Reagan ignite Armageddon.

There is little evidence that Reagan missed Washington, the immense power, the intense attention, the glory. He had Nancy and his beloved ranch. He settled in and soon was immersed in his memoir, written with the assistance of Robert Lindsey, former San Francisco bureau chief of the New York Times, *and published by Simon & Schuster in November 1990.*

Reagan did a little traveling. He flew to London in June 1989 and gave the annual Winston Churchill Lecture. The next day he was knighted by Queen Elizabeth. On July 21 Reagan was inducted into the Cowboy Hall of Fame in Oklahoma. In October he flew to Japan to receive Japan's highest award, the Grand Cordon of the Supreme Order of the Chrysanthemum, and gave two speeches. On November 15 Reagan went back to the White House for the unveiling of his official presidential portrait.

Something else happened during his first year out of office. On July 4, while vacationing in Mexico at the ranch of Bill Wilson, Reagan was bucked off a horse while riding a rocky trail. He fell about 15 feet, and struck his head on a stone when he hit the ground. At first his injuries seemed minor, just some bruises. But he had taken a sharp blow to his head and as the weeks passed the seriousness of his condition worsened.

---

* Reagan, *An American Life*, p. 725.

Reagan flew to the Mayo Clinic in Rochester, Minnesota, and was diagnosed as having swelling of the brain. He underwent an operation in which holes were drilled in his skull to relieve the building pressure and he was discharged after one week. Nancy Reagan and others are convinced that that blow to his head in Mexico was the beginning of his slow slide into the dark mists of Alzheimer's disease.

Over the next three years Reagan was active, but his traveling and speaking engagements gradually slowed down.

In early 1990 he gave videotaped testimony in one of the Iran-Contra trials, a total of seven hours. Later that year he spoke at the dedication of the Nixon Library and birthplace in Yorba Linda, California. In September he took a 10-day trip to Europe—visiting the site of the Berlin Wall, addressing the Polish Parliament in Warsaw, visiting with Soviet President Gorbachev and addressing the International Affairs Committee of the Supreme Soviet in Moscow, and meeting with Pope John Paul II in the Vatican. In December, he flew to England and spoke to the Cambridge Union Society in Cambridge.

In 1991, Reagan stayed much closer to home. On November 4, he dedicated the Ronald Reagan Presidential Library in Simi Valley, California.

In 1992 Reagan entertained Mikhail Gorbachev at Rancho del Cielo, spoke at the Republican National Convention in Houston, Texas, and gave one campaign speech for President Bush in Orange County, California. In December he made his last trip to Europe and talked to the Oxford Union Society at Oxford University in England.

In 1993, Reagan's schedule slowed considerably. On January 15 he flew back to the White House and received the Medal of Freedom from President Bush. On May 15 he gave the commencement address at The Citadel in South Carolina.

In 1994 Reagan gave his last scheduled speech in February at a birthday party in his honor that was held in Washington, D.C. In April, he and Nancy attended the funeral of former President Richard Nixon. On November 5, 1994, age 83, he wrote and made public the letter announcing that he had Alzheimer's disease.

All in all, it has been a quiet ex-presidency, far from the active post-presidential career of Jimmy Carter, or even the writing and traveling of the late Richard Nixon. After the onset of Alzheimer's, despite a continuing physical strength that allowed him to recover from a broken hip suffered in 1991, he disappeared from public view, his mind steadily slipping into the darkness of the quiet disease that has no cure.

The following letters reveal steady contact with old friends, until 1994.

On Reagan's last day in office he received a letter from a man he had been corresponding with regularly for 30 years—former President Richard Nixon. Nixon told Reagan he had "eight great years in the White House" and that "Politics is a roller coaster and you ended right at the top!"

According to his files, the first letter Reagan wrote, as a new private citizen, was this reply to Nixon—eleven days after Reagan returned to California.

Richard Nixon
Woodcliff Lake, New Jersey
January 31, 1989 [1]

Dear Dick:

Your letter caught up with us here in California. In fact I'm in our new office from which I can see the blue Pacific.

Thank you for your generous words and warm good wishes. Nancy and I are most grateful and give our very best wishes to Pat and of course to you.

As you well know we're having to learn or I should say re-learn a lot of simple things like turning off the lights, etc. Just learning to find the light switches was a chore after living in that public housing on Pennsylvania Avenue.

Again our thanks to you and warmest regard.

Sincerely,
Ron

––––––––

Reagan thanks Prime Minister Margaret Thatcher for his visit with her at 10 Downing Street during his trip to London.

The Right Honorable Margaret Thatcher, M.P.
London, England
June 26, 1989 [2]

Dear Margaret:

Nancy and I returned home with so many lovely memories of our trip to Europe, but most special is that of our visit with you at #10 Downing. We were sorry to have missed Denis, but it was wonderful to be able to spend time with you and Mark.

While our trips to Europe will be less frequent now that I am a private citizen, it is our hope that your travels will bring you out our way so that we can return your kind hospitality.

Again, Margaret, it was lovely seeing you. Nancy joins me in sending much affection and warmest regards to you and Denis.

Sincerely,
Ron

––––––––

Nine days after his accident in Mexico Reagan replies to his pen pal of 40 years, and explains what happened.

Lorraine Wagner
Philadelphia, Pennsylvania
July 13, 1989 [3]

Dear Lorraine:

Thank you very much for your letter and for all those "tear sheets" as the press calls them. Most of all, thanks for my Fathers Day card with its warm message.

Now as to the horse episode—I didn't fall off. Something spooked him (he was one of the Mexican ranch horses not one of mine) and he erupted. I was bucked off. I've some sore bruises but it's a miracle I broke no bones. I came down from about 15 feet and landed on my back on hardpan covered with stones. But know your letter and all those clippings made it all worthwhile. I can say it again it was a nice trip down memory lane—for a while I forgot my black and blue spots.

My warmest regard to Wag and say hello to Scott and Sandy.

Bless you,
Ron

From his first days as a teenager Jim Rogan's political hero was Ronald Reagan. After finishing law school in 1983 he engaged in private practice and then began his own political career—the California state assembly (1994–96), Congressman from California (1997–2001) and then Undersecretary of Commerce for Intellectual Property (2001—). After Reagan left the White House, Rogan wrote to him explaining why he had followed Reagan's course and left the Democratic Party.

James E. Rogan
Los Angeles, California
August 3, 1989[4]

Dear Jim:

I haven't the words to properly describe how impressed I am both with your letter and your article. Thank you for sharing your life with me in the letter and for giving such an account of what has actually happened to the political parties in our land in your article.

Like you I left the Democratic Party and like you I don't believe we changed. We still support the same beliefs we always had but the party leadership set off on an entirely different course. It is this that you so eloquently explained in your article. It is the best and most complete exposition I have seen of the philosophical reversal of the Democratic Party.

Your essay should be the basis for freeing up Democrats who are discontented but still not aware of how far their party leadership has turned from what they as individuals believe. After dealing with a Democratic majority in the House of Representatives for eight years, a majority they've had for 55 of the last 59 years, I can't help but think our very safety requires that your exposition be widely distributed. I want you to know that I'll be quoting from your essay on my own mashed-potato circuit lectures.

My very best to Christine* and again my thanks to you.

Sincerely,
Ronald Reagan

----

* James Rogan's wife.

In a letter to George Hearne, president of Eureka College, Reagan demurs from asking his old friend, Walter Annenberg, to contribute to the college.

> Dr. George Hearne
> Eureka, Illinois
> August 23, 1989[5]

Dear George:

I'm sorry I can't be of help with Walter Annenberg. He's very much involved with the fundraising for the Presidential Library right now and I must say has been most generous in his own giving. This rules out any persuasion by me.

I hope to be able to make a contribution of some size before the year is out and will try to hurry it up—I'm talking about Eureka not the Library. I'll know more when I come back from our trip to Japan.*

> Best regards,
> Ron

Eight days after undergoing surgery at the Mayo Clinic in Minnesota to relieve fluid pressure on his brain caused by the horseback riding accident in July, President Reagan writes a childhood friend about the accident and his health. He also writes that he is resuming normal activities.

> Helen Lawton
> Dixon, Illinois
> September 16, 1989[6]

Dear Helen:

I've just received your lovely card and the Lord did hear your prayer. We're home in California now. I did some yard work this morning and I feel just great. Naturally I have to be careful until my head is healed so riding is a little way down the road but not too far.

God has been very good to me. The riding incident was actually a miracle. I landed on my back from a height of about 15 feet on a hard surface covered with rocks and all I suffered were some bruises.

Again, Helen—thanks. It was good to hear from you.

> Sincerely,
> Dutch

Reagan writes to the young daughter of Kathy Osborne, his longtime personal secretary in the White House who was now working in Reagan's California office.

---

* Reagan earned $2 million for the speeches he gave in Japan in October 1989.

Meshelle Osborne
Santa Monica, California
December 14, 1989[7]

Dear Meshelle:

As you can see, I'm taking care of your mother. By writing this myself I'm saving her from having to type it.

Congratulations on your tennis. I played a little when I was your age but then football, track and swimming got in the way and now it's horses—so no tennis for me.

Your mother keeps all of us on track and doing what we should. You can be very proud of her. I don't know what we'd do without her. And incidentally she's very proud of you.

Nancy sends her very best to you as do I. And we wish you the merriest of Christmases and a Happy New Year.

Hope to see you soon.

Love—Your Buddy,
Ron

During the Reagan presidency many high-fashion clothes designers lent Nancy Reagan dresses and gowns to be worn at public events. Many of them were expensive, costing thousands of dollars, and in early December 1989 the Internal Revenue Service began an investigation to determine whether back taxes were owed on any of the borrowed clothing. On December 21, 1989, Richard Nixon writes to Reagan telling him that he and his wife Pat think "the IRS investigation on Nancy's gowns was about the most unfair and ridiculous activity of that biased organization we have ever heard of," and that "most people regard this as being a very cheap shot."

President Richard Nixon
Woodcliff Lake, New Jersey
January 4, 1990[8]

Dear Dick:

My heartfelt thanks for your letter. It couldn't have come at a better time. Believe me I share your view of the IRS bureaucrats and regret that I couldn't make a dent in them. You know in my first year an agent spent six months in the office handling my affairs, going back into my returns for the last several years before I took office.

As you imagine Nancy is quite upset. Your kind letter helped. We both hope your holidays were all you wanted them to be.

Nancy sends her thanks and warmest regard.

So do I. Love to Pat.

Sincerely,
Ron

In the January 9, 1990, San Diego Union, Edward Fike, the editor of the editorial page, wrote a column arguing that "history will deal kindly with . . . Reagan's many triumphs."

Edward L. Fike
San Diego, California
January 23, 1990[9]

Dear Edward Fike:

Thank you very much for your letter and a great many thanks for your column. Thank you for writing as you did. I'll be forever grateful for your generous words. I don't get many chances to collect editorials but I'll treasure yours.

Nancy joins me in a heartfelt thank you.

Sincerely,
Ronald Reagan

Reagan and Gorbachev maintained their relationship for several years after Reagan's presidency.

Mikhail Gorbachev
Moscow, USSR
Circa February 1990[10]

Dear Mikhail:

Thank you for your warm words about my birthday and your more than generous references to the part I played in our mutual effort to bring about improvement in Soviet–American relations.

I too have warm memories about our meetings beginning with that first meeting in Geneva. I'm happy that you too are committed to interaction between our two countries. I believe between us we can make a contribution to world peace and the brotherhood of man.

Nancy joins me in this and in the warmest wishes and greeting to Raisa and yourself. Let us keep in touch.

Sincerely,
Ron

Reagan receives a valentine card from his old pen pal and comments on the video-taped testimony he gave in the Iran-Contra trial of John Poindexter on February 16 and 17 in Los Angeles.

Lorraine and Elwood H. Wagner
Philadelphia, Pennsylvania
March 4, 1990 [11]

Dear Lorraine and Wag:

Forgive this brief note as an answer to your good letter. My excuse is—I'm off on another speaking trip. Thank you for writing as you did. Nancy and I loved your valentine.

My interrogation on the Poindexter case was at worst a few hours of boredom. I had to say, "I can't recall," to so many questions—like what I did on "November 26, 1986." I was tempted several times to reply by asking the lawyer—"where were you three years ago last Friday?" But I didn't.

Things are rather busy out here what with my speaking engagements and all. Some times I seem to be busier than I was in Washington. But all in all we're enjoying ourselves and it's great to get to the ranch as often as we do a few days each month.

Again thanks to you both and regards to the family.

Sincerely,
Ron

In March 1990 Walter Annenberg's foundation gave a $50 million challenge grant to the United Negro College Fund.

Walter Annenberg
Rancho Mirage, California
March 13, 1990 [12]

Dear Walter:

We got off the phone before I had a chance to tell you how wonderful it is for you to be so generous to the United Negro College Fund, so I'm writing this note to tell you that what you have done is one of the single greatest acts of generosity I have ever known. Generosity is nothing new for you—I know—but your support of that great organization is very special and will do so much good where it is needed.

Walter, there are no words that can adequately express the kindness and compassion that are at the center of your character. You embody all that is good about our country. I consider it a blessing to have you as my friend.

Nancy joins in sending our love to Lee.

Happy Birthday!

Ron

On July 19, 1990, Reagan gave an address at the dedication of the Richard Nixon Library in Yorba Linda, California. Two days earlier, Nixon met with Reagan in his Century City office and the Nixons had dinner at the Reagans' home in Bel Air.

Richard Nixon
Woodcliff Lake, New Jersey
June 5, 1990 [13]

Dear Dick:

Your letters arrived and we're looking forward to seeing you and Pat in Yorba Linda. I've told our people to see what can be done with regard to a visit here at the office. You know some of my speaking engagements are booked way in advance but don't appear on my schedule very far in advance. I'm sure it can be worked out and you'll be hearing from us soon.

Nancy sends her love and from both of us to Pat.

Ron

In May 1990 Reagan postponed a planned trip to Europe, following the discovery of intestinal adhesions that were caused by his 1985 cancer surgery. Reagan assures the Wagners that he is fine and tells them about his June 4 meeting in San Francisco with Mikhail Gorbachev, who was still general secretary of the Soviet Union.

Lorraine and Elwood H. Wagner
Philadelphia, Pennsylvania
June 9, 1990 [14]

Dear Lorraine and Wag:

The media as usual made a fuss out of proportion to the facts. My health is fine. It's true we postponed our Europe trip until September. The reason was that I had some symptoms of possible adhesions due to that surgery back a few years in Washington. The doctor wanted me to go on a liquid diet while I went through a series of X-rays. Everything has turned out fine and I feel great. As for my hand it has healed nicely. Actually it was one finger and it did get bashed pretty good—no golf for a few weeks, but I'm back on the course and my finger has healed.

My visit here with Gorby was short but as usual good. He's having some problems back home with the zealots who don't want to tone down communism. I hope he wins. He's trying to bring into being some of what we have. I hope he has his way.

Thank you for the "Reagan Record" pictures. I'm glad to have them but tell me—was I ever that young?

Well Nancy sends her best and from both of us—

Warmest Regards,
Ron

Reagan tells his pen pal some private thoughts about his recent trip to Germany, Poland, and Russia.

Lorraine Wagner
Philadelphia, Pennsylvania
October 26, 1990 [15]

Dear Lorraine:

I can only answer your great letter with this note. They have me in and out of town so much I hardly have time to write.

Let me tell you our trip to Germany, Poland and Russia was amazing. In all three countries the people on the street would actually applaud and cheer for the U.S.A. And this would include high-ranking government officials. They are definitely on their way to democracy and free enterprise.

I can understand your caution and believe me I agree but I've based my opinion on deeds not words, and the deeds are actually visible. In every meeting with Gorbachev I'd hand him some names of dissidents and tell him I was interested in those people. In every case in only a matter of days those people would be allowed to emigrate.

You are right about the line-item veto. All over our country when I mention it our people stand up and cheer. The Democratic majority in the Congress refuse to hear of it but we must have it. As a governor I had it and used it 943 times without being overridden once. We have to lean on our Democratic Congress and make them see the light.

Give my regards to Wag and to both of you from Nancy.

Regards,
Ron

In August 1989, Simon & Schuster announced that they had hired Robert Lindsey, the West Coast bureau chief for the New York Times, *to help Reagan with his memoirs. Lindsey, a talented writer, was with Reagan "every step of the way."* * *After the book was published in 1990 Reagan thanks him.*

Robert Lindsey
Carmel, California
November 25, 1990 [16]

Dear Bob:

I'm ashamed of myself for not writing this sooner. The book is out, finished and a success and very largely due to you. I couldn't have done it without you and I'm eternally grateful.

---

* Ronald Reagan, *An American Life* (New York: Simon & Schuster, 1990), p. 7.

It was great working with you, an experience I'll always remember, especially those days across the desk from each other with the tape machine running. A lot of people have gone out of the way to praise me for the book and every time it happens I say a silent thank you to a fellow named Robert Lindsey.

Again my heartfelt thanks and God Bless you. Nancy joins me in this.

Sincerely,
Ron

On December 11, 1990, Nixon sent Reagan a copy of his new book, In the Arena, *in which he called Reagan "a good actor who became a great politician."* Knowing that Reagan had just finished writing his own autobiography, Nixon wrote: "I'm glad the book . . . is finally behind me . . . we both know how much fun these books are to write!"*

The Honorable Richard Nixon
Woodcliff Lake, New Jersey
January 4, 1991 [17]

Dear Dick and Pat:

Nancy and I hope the holidays were all that you hoped they would be. Thank you for your good wishes. We had the family for a Christmas dinner and as usual spent New Years at the Annenberg place in Palm Springs.

Dick you are so right about that writing a book business. Believe me I don't want to even attempt another one.

Nancy sends her best and so do I.

Sincerely,
Ron

Reagan responds to a series of questions posed by his pen pal, Lorraine Wagner, just after his 80th birthday.

Lorraine Wagner
Philadelphia, Pennsylvania
February 16, 1991 [18]

Dear Lorraine:

Thank you for your letter and all the generous words about things we did and didn't do. Thanks too for the summary card which will help me cover all the points.

---

* Richard Nixon, *In the Arena: A Memoir of Victory, Defeat and Renewal* (New York: Simon & Schuster, 1990), p. 265.

With regard to the Dixon visit, it came about because I was on a speaking tour in the area and could spare a day and overnight in Dixon. There was no special event except that when I got there a schedule of outdoor appearances had been worked out by the home folks including an appearance at the high school. All in all it was a most heartwarming couple of days.

Now as to some questions. If I mentioned Armageddon in my lifetime it was accompanied by the Bible prophecy that no man would know of its coming but certain signs and events would precede its coming. Many Bible students have called attention to those signs—wars fought to no conclusion, natural disasters, earthquakes, storms, volcanic eruptions etc. that would increase.

Next question—was my administration responsible for decision not to use neutron bombs. That is part of SDI*—to come up with a defense against nuclear missiles that would render them useless. At the same time we started negotiating limits and reductions of such weapons. There is the INF† treaty where the Soviets and us agreed to eliminate such weapons. We are negotiating with the Soviets trying to get a mutual reduction of "strategic" nuclear missiles.

You are right about "Desert Storm" kindling patriotism. Yesterday I was at BYU‡ in Provo, Utah and Salt Lake City. In both towns virtually every house had flags in their windows and even the trees were wrapped in yellow ribbons. And yes the Patriot missile§ is an offshoot of SDI.

As for our Presidential Library and Museum in Simi Valley it isn't scheduled to open until November. The building is virtually completed but it will take several months to install all the exhibits.

As for Question 11—Bush** does communicate by phone at times. Also we exchange notes and last week he sent one of his appointees out here to see me.

Now as to Gorbachev, I still believe he wants reforms that will bring about private ownership of land and private enterprise. The problem is with the bureaucracy. They don't want to give up their privileges and they are blocking him at every turn. I don't know if he can win or not.

Well thanks again for your letter. Nancy sends her best and give our regards to Wag.

Love,
Ron

---

* The Strategic Defense Initiative.
† Intermediate Nuclear Forces.
‡ Brigham Young University.
§ The Patriot is an Army surface-to-air missile defense system. It defends against aircraft, cruise missiles, and short-range ballistic missiles.
** President George H.W. Bush.

Kitty Kelley's Nancy Reagan: The Unauthorized Biography *was published in early 1991. The 603-page book was considered scurrilous by the Reagans, and they were convinced the author had invented many of her sources.*

> The Honorable Richard Nixon
> Woodcliff Lake, New Jersey
> April 11, 1991 [19]

Dear Dick:

A big thank you for your letter and thank Pat also. Nancy and I are truly upset and angry over the total dishonesty of Kitty Kelley and her book. We haven't found one person she names as her sources who has ever known her or been contacted by her. Believe it or not one she named was the minister of our church—Reverend Donn Moomaw. He has written a denial for the church bulletin. Your letter will help me keep Nancy from worrying herself sick. She is Kelley's main victim and is very upset.

You and Pat are very kind and thoughtful and we love you for it.

Again our heartfelt thanks.

> Ron

Martin Anderson directed policy research for Reagan's 1976 and 1980 presidential campaigns, served as his economic and domestic policy adviser in the White House and as a member of the board that built his Library in California. This letter is an example of why no records exist for many of the letters Reagan wrote after he left office. After writing a letter like this he would seal it in an envelope, write the addressee's name on the outside, hand the envelope to a secretary who would insert it into a larger envelope and add a label containing the typed name and address.

> Mr. Martin Anderson
> Portola Valley, California
> May 3, 1991 [20]

Dear Marty:

I just wanted to tell you how grateful I am for your long time support and friendship, and for all your help on my Presidential Library. I'm pleased that you will be continuing on the board until the Library opening in November and I look forward to continuing to stay in touch.

My heartfelt thanks and warmest personal regards.

> Sincerely,
> Ron

R. (Bob) Emmett Tyrrell was the editor of The American Spectator, *a national political magazine.*

Mr. R. Emmett Tyrrell Jr.
Great Barrington, Massachusetts
May 10, 1991 [21]

Dear Bob:

Thank you very much for your letter of April 26. I'm truly pleased by your generous words. And Nancy thanks you for your P.S. She has been rather low because of the totally false fiction of Kitty Kelley. It's amazing how many of K.K.'s so called informants have written or called to say they've never met or spoken to K.K.

I'm deeply grateful to you for your proposal to set the record straight on my administration. You might be surprised at the actual figures that rebut the charges of the anti-RR intellectuals. If they can be of any use to you let me know.

Believe it or not I'm rereading my diaries* because my memory needs help. When I left the governorship I was amazed at my lack of recall of all that had happened. When I became president I decided to keep a record of each day's happenings I'm not sure they would outdo the book I've already done but I'm continually amazed at how many things I'd forgotten.

Well again my thanks. Nancy sends her best—as do I.

Sincerely,
Ron

Reagan's pen pal sent a copy of her rebuke to Kitty Kelley and asked him two more questions about meeting Queen Elizabeth and free trade.

Lorraine Wagner
Philadelphia, Pennsylvania
May 31, 1991 [22]

Dear Lorraine:

There are no words to properly thank you for your letters,—the one to us and one to that K.K. character. Just know that Nancy and I are more grateful than we can say. Nancy sends her love and so do I. You'll be happy to know that scores of people among the thousand K.K. cites as her informants have made contact with us and told us they've never had any contact at all with her. Incidentally we have word that her book is not selling and is piling up in the bookstores.

---

* Every night while he was president, and sometimes during the day, Reagan wrote about daily events in his diary. The result was four leatherbound volumes whose total length was approximately half a million words (Morris, Edmund, *Dutch: A Memoir of Ronald Reagan,* Random House, New York, 1999, p. 662). Reagan's diaries have not yet been published. Nancy Reagan also kept a diary during her White House years.

Enough of her, here is my answer to your two questions. Yes, we had a very pleasant get-together with the Queen in Miami, Florida. This included a dinner on their yatch—I know I've misspelled that—I should just call it "boat."

Second question—"how will the free trade policy make more jobs in America?" I'm convinced there will be an increase in trade both ways, which will result in more jobs on both sides of the border. Mexican workers will be able to buy more because they'll have more money. I don't have all the specifics but I do know there has been a lot of study and not just by government bureaucrats but by the business community here.

But most important right now is to tell you how deeply grateful Nancy and I are for your wonderfully kind and generous words. And how much we admire how you put K.K. in her proper place. Give our regards to Scott and the family and again our heartfelt thanks.

> Love,
> Ron

For one full year, between August 1991 and August 1992, Reagan's files indicate that the only person to whom he wrote personal letters was his pen pal Lorraine Wagner and her family. He seemed to thoroughly enjoy reading their letters and wrote to them six times over the course of the year.

> Lorraine and Elwood H. Wagner
> Philadelphia, Pennsylvania
> August 19, 1991 [23]

Dear Lorraine—Wag and Family:

We received and enjoyed your letter. I'm answering it but don't think I can match it for news and information and your photo.

I understand your reporting on being active since your retirement. I've been surprised at how busy I am. It seems at times I'm more active than when I was in office. Part of that of course is my schedule of speeches. I'm on the "mashed potatoes" circuit most of the time.

You wrote of Kathy*—she moved to Sacramento because of her mother's illness and her children are in school, there. We miss her but know she's doing the right thing. Dottie† as you know replaced her here in our office and she's doing a great job.

I'm glad you like Ron's‡ show. We've been seeing it and we think he's doing a good job. I hope he succeeds with it because he needs to find something solid.

---

* Kathleen L. Osborne was Reagan's personal secretary in the White House and had returned to California with him.
† Dottie R. Dellinger had worked in the White House Visitors Office, and became Reagan's executive assistant in California.
‡ Reagan's son, Ronald P. Reagan, was then the moderator of a television talk show.

We'll I'm getting back to work and Nancy and I wish you well and appreciate your letter very much.

All the best and God bless you.

Ron

Lorraine Wagner
Philadelphia, Pennsylvania
February 11, 1992 [24]

Dear Lorraine:

Thank you for your letter and your generous words. I'm not sure I deserve them but I sure enjoy reading them. Let me first answer your questions about Linda Chavez.* She was on our "Equal Opportunities" commission.

I think your feeling about the election is correct. I don't believe I should take sides in the primaries, only in the general election. However I personally hope Bush † will be the next president.

If you are considering a visit to the Library come vacation time I think you'll enjoy it. The people who made up the Foundation ‡ did a magnificent job. I've visited a number of presidential libraries, many of them on university campuses. I have to tell you none of them match the one we have here in Simi Valley.

Well again—it was good to hear from you and I thank you. Nancy sends her regards and from both of us to Wag.

Sincerely,
Ron

Lorraine and Elwood H. Wagner
Philadelphia, Pennsylvania
February 18, 1992 [25]

Dear Lorraine and Wag:

On top of my birthday letter comes a valentine—thank you both for that and for your letter. I'm pleased that you added up our years of friendship. It's been a happy 48 years.§ And that makes it more than half my lifetime.

Nancy sends her thanks and warm regards. All the best to both of you.

Warmly,
Ron

---

* Linda Chavez was the White House director of public liaison (1985) and the chairman of the National Commission on Migrant Education (1988–1992). She is the president of the Center for Equal Opportunity.

† President George H. W. Bush.

‡ The board of directors of the Reagan Presidential Foundation oversaw the fundraising and construction of the Ronald Reagan Presidential Library.

§ Their correspondence began in 1944.

Lorraine and Elwood H. Wagner
Philadelphia, Pennsylvania
March 9, 1992 [26]

Dear Lorraine and Wag:

Thanks for your letter and good wishes on our 40th anniversary.* Having said that I think I owe you some history. I'll begin with Moon and Bess's † bonfire. Yes there was a big fire that raged through Bel Air destroying many homes. They managed to save theirs but it was damaged severely. They later moved to their present locale.

Now on the matter of real estate. George and Barbara ‡ came to our house for tea on his recent campaign trip to Los Angeles. The story about us hanging paper on our gate is outrageous fiction. Our house has a high wire fence upon which is a canvas cover. It was there when we bought the place and remains there in response to the Secret Service because it keeps the house and us from being open to view from the street.

Now I come to the "speech." § I was still in show business and had no thought of getting into politics. Not being able to sing or dance, when I did personal appearances I made speeches. I wrote them myself and was out on the circuit much of the time. During campaign years I went out on the speaking tour in behalf of people I believed should be elected. "The speech" as you termed it was one I'd been delivering for appearances at fundraisers for presidential candidate Barry Goldwater. Here in California the Republican Party was split down the middle. The Republican leadership asked me if I would make my speech (and it was mine written by me) on national radio if they bought the time on NBC. I said yes and did the speech. It was very successful and raised $8.5 million for the Goldwater campaign.

Well after the campaign those same Republican leaders called on me and asked if I would run for governor of California in the coming campaign. I had never given a thought to public life for myself. I was happy to be in show business. They kept after me 'til Nancy and I were having trouble sleeping. I thought they were crazy. Finally I told them if they'd make it possible to accept all the speaking invitations I was getting in California I'd come back and tell them who should be running for governor and I'd campaign for him. After a few months I discovered the people wanted me to be the candidate. Nancy and I talked it over and I gave in. I was a victim of "the speech."

It was entirely mine. After I was elected governor and later as president I found out you no longer had time to write your own speeches. So I worked with the

---

* The Reagans were married on March 4, 1952.
† Reagan's older brother and his wife.
‡ President Bush and his wife Barbara.
§ A national fundraising speech Reagan gave for Barry Goldwater in 1964.

speechwriters and gave them copies of my previous speeches so they could learn my style and it's been that way since.

George Bush was a darn good vice president for me and didn't just sit on the sidelines. He played a major role in every thing we were doing. I think he should be the new president for a second term.

Well that's enough history or maybe too much. If so—forgive me.

Nancy sends her very best as do I.

Blessings on you and again thanks,

Ron

Lorraine Wagner
Philadelphia, Pennsylvania
August 6, 1992[27]

Dear Lorraine:

As usual you warmed my heart with your letter and the sun seemed brighter. I share your feeling about the importance of the coming convention and I hope I can help Bush. He must win when you look at the others in the race.

I feel as I did when I was there. We must end this century-old rule of the House of Representatives. I can't tell you the eight years of uphill fight I had with the Democratic Congress. This is Bush's problem now and we must find a way to give a Republican president a Congress that is on his side. I truly believe that Bush's problem is one of constant opposition by the "House." Remember I had eight budgets put on the shelf by a Democratic Congress. They declared every one "dead on arrival."

Well enough of this. We obviously are on the same team and I'm happy to share the battle with both of us on the same side. Thank you for your letter and very best regards.

God bless you.

Ron

Gerald Ford was born on July 14, 1913. Reagan sends him a birthday greeting on his 80th birthday. Richard Nixon's wife Pat had died on June 22, 1993, and both Ford and Reagan attended her funeral in Yorba Linda, California.

Gerald Ford
Rancho Mirage, California
July 14, 1993[28]

Dear Jerry:

So I hear today is the big day when you join the small but illustrious group of octogenarians. It's quite a club and we welcome you as our newest member!

In all seriousness, Nancy and I want to send our best to you on your big day. It was a pleasure seeing you and Betty recently in Yorba Linda. Although the occasion was sad, I hope the four of us will have the opportunity to get together under happier circumstances soon.

Please give our love to Betty. Happy 80th Birthday . . . and many more!

Sincerely,
Ron

On July 30, 1993, Reagan gave President Nixon and his children a private tour of Reagan's new library in Simi Valley. When Nixon wrote with thanks he added that he looked forward to seeing the Reagans at Le Cirque, a well-known Manhattan restaurant. In September the Reagans had lunch with the Nixons in New York.

Richard Nixon
Woodcliff Lake, New Jersey
September 29, 1993 [29]

Dear Dick:

As always, it was wonderful seeing you in New York last week. It was unquestionably one of the highlights of our trip, and we're still talking about how nice it was to catch up with you over a long lunch. We hope you are continuing to watch the developments in the health care battle* closely. We are glued to CNN and are amazed by it all. Please give our love to your beautiful family, and let's get together again very soon.

Warm regards,
Ron

At the end of 1993, former President George Bush wrote Reagan a long, personal letter telling him about the "wonderful family Christmas" in Houston, although most of his children were "nesting at their own houses." George W. Bush was in the governor's mansion in Austin, Texas. Bush told Reagan that his book in progress, on foreign policy, which he co-authored with Brent Scowcroft, "is one slow piece of work," and that "a basic problem may be that neither Brent nor I is too hot a writer. We may turn to a 'ghost.' "

George Bush
Houston, Texas
January 4, 1994 [30]

Dear George:

Thank you for your letter of December 28. I have to confess, I just can't compete with your "self typing." I have a hard enough time with a pen, let alone a typewriter. I hope you won't mind that I "dictated" this letter.

---

* In 1993 President Clinton proposed a controversial national health care plan, spearheaded by his wife, Hillary. The plan was eventually defeated.

Glad to hear that you and yours enjoyed a busy Texas holiday season. As usual, the holidays seemed to fly by—I was barely finished with my pumpkin pie and we were already packing up the decorations for next year. Nancy and I made a quick trip to Walter Annenberg's New Year's and a little golf. As you know his place is so beautiful, but I'm getting tired of spending my vacation in his sandtraps!

It sounds as if your library is moving right along. I can only tell you that for me, it has been tremendously rewarding to watch it all come together. You must be feeling as I did before the dedication—like an expectant parent, waiting for the baby to be born. It won't be long before you're off and running too!

I think of you often, George—especially on Thursday around lunchtime*— and I do hope that our paths will cross soon. In the meantime, please give our best to Barbara and try not to work too hard.

Sincerely,
Ron

Reagan turned 83 on February 6, 1994, and was honored by a large, formal birthday party in Washington, D.C. Margaret Thatcher was one of the speakers at the dinner.

Margaret Thatcher
London, England
February 8, 1994 [31]

Dear Margaret:

How do I begin to thank you for sharing my 83rd birthday celebration with Nancy and me in Washington? "Thank you" seems inadequate when trying to express my overwhelming gratitude!

Your presence at last week's gala was clearly my most treasured birthday gift and I shall always remember your dignified tribute and powerful message. As you know well, I don't often display my emotions publicly, but throughout your speech I had a lump in my throat the size of a golf ball. I was touched beyond words and your explanation of our unique friendship echoed my sentiments perfectly.

Throughout my life, I've always believed that life's path is determined by a Force more powerful than fate. I feel that the Lord brought us together for a profound purpose, and that I have been richly blessed for having known you. I am proud to call you one of my dearest friends, Margaret; proud to have shared many of life's significant moments with you; and thankful that God brought you into my life.

Please express my warmest thanks to Denis and may God bless you always.

Sincerely,
Ron

---

* Reagan established the practice of having lunch with his vice president every Thursday while they were in the White House.

Joanne Drake, Reagan's chief of staff in California, had just become the mother of a baby girl, Caitlin, in 1994.

> Joanne Drake
> Los Angeles, California
> May 4, 1994 [32]

Dear Joanne:

Congratulations on the birth of your daughter, Caitlin!

She is truly a blessed little girl to have been given you for her mother. Enjoy this time of discovery. Nancy and I send our thoughts of joy to you and Bill.

> Fondly,
> Ronald Reagan

After a tough California primary fight in June 1994, Republican Governor Pete Wilson's Democratic opponent in the general election was Kathleen Brown, the daughter of one former Democratic California governor, Pat Brown, and the sister of another, Jerry Brown.

Reagan supported Wilson, who thanked Reagan in a March 14 letter for his "introductory remarks at the California Republican Convention." Pete Wilson won the governorship in November.

> Pete Wilson
> Sacramento, California
> June 8, 1994 [33]

Dear Pete:

Congrats on last night's victory!

I'm more convinced than ever that there will <u>never</u> be a "Brown III" in California. There's no stopping you now, Pete.

My best to Gayle,

> Sincerely,
> Ron

Reagan sends greetings to former President Bush on his 70th birthday, June 12, 1994.

> George Bush
> Houston, Texas
> June 12, 1994 [34]

Dear George:

Happy Birthday, young fellow! I know this is a big one for you. It's hard to believe that a couple kids like us are "maturing" so rapidly . . . I mean so well!

Heck, at seventy you're practically still a kid. I began a new career at your age . . . what have you got planned?

I know it's been a busy year and I pray the upcoming one will bring you continued fulfillment and happiness!

Nancy joins me in sending our very best wishes on your special day.

Sincerely,
Ron

Four months before Reagan announced that he was suffering from Alzheimer's disease, he writes to his old friend, now 86 years old, thanking him for a large contribution to the Reagan Library.

Walter Annenberg
Wynnewood, Pennsylvania
July 7, 1994 [35]

Dear Walter:

I cannot begin to find the words to express my gratitude for your generous gift to the Presidential Library. I am deeply touched by your selfless gesture, another striking example of your tender heart and deep affection for America.

Walter you and I have been around America for a very long time. One day soon the Lord will call us home and thoughts of this world will no longer cloud our minds. In the meantime, however, we must see to it that our great nation stays the course and our days are spent with meaning and purpose. I believe you are doing just that—each and every day—through your singular efforts in education, the arts, and in charitable circles from coast to coast. And long after you're gone, the lamp of knowledge will burn brilliantly in the minds of young Americans everywhere. Walter, this will be your legacy, one which will forever endure the passage of time.

Thank you for your friendship over the years. Nancy and I send our love to Lee.

Sincerely,
Ron

This is the last letter Reagan sends to President Ford, congratulating him on his 81st birthday.

Gerald Ford
Rancho Mirage, California
July 14, 1994 [36]

Dear Jerry:

Happy Birthday, young fellah! Hard to believe it's that time of year again—I'm just glad it's you and not me. As you reflect on all the things in your life for which you should be grateful, include among them the fact that you're still not as old as I am!

Nancy and I hope your birthday is a special one. Enjoy the day and please give our love to Betty.

Sincerely,
Ron

In 1994 the Simi Valley–San Fernando Valley Freeway (Route 118), which passes close to the Ronald Reagan Presidential Library, was renamed the Ronald Reagan Freeway. One person who played an instrumental role in the renaming was Willie Brown, the powerful Democratic speaker of the California State Assembly. An old friend and political foe of Reagan, he was a member of the Assembly while Reagan was governor. In 1996 Willie Brown became the mayor of San Francisco.

Willie Brown
Sacramento, California
September 6, 1994[37]

Dear Willie:

I couldn't let a day go by without thanking you for all you did to make the Ronald Reagan Freeway a reality. I'll admit that while people have "tried to drive over me" for years, this is the first time I will actually welcome it!

Please know how touched I was by the gesture and that I shall always be grateful for the relationship we have shared through the years.

Sincerely,
Ron

Reagan's farewell letter to the public.

My Fellow Americans
Los Angeles, California
November 5, 1994[38]

My Fellow Americans:

I have recently been told that I am one of the millions of Americans who will be afflicted with Alzheimer's disease.

Upon learning this news, Nancy and I had to decide whether as private citizens we would keep this a private matter or whether we would make this news known in a public way.

In the past Nancy suffered from breast cancer and I had my cancer surgeries.

We found through our open disclosures we were able to raise public awareness. We were happy that as a result many more people underwent testing. They were treated in early stages and able to return to normal, healthy lives.

So now, we feel it is important to share it with you. In opening our hearts, we hope this might promote greater awareness of this condition. Perhaps it will encourage a clearer understanding of the individuals and families who are affected by it.

At the moment I feel just fine, I intend to live the remainder of the years God gives me on this earth doing the things I have always done. I will continue to share life's journey with my beloved Nancy and my family. I plan to enjoy the great out-doors and stay in touch with my friends and supporters.

Unfortunately, as Alzheimer's disease progresses, the family often bears a heavy burden. I only wish there was some way I could spare Nancy from this painful ex-perience. When the time comes I am confident that with your help she will face it with faith and courage.

In closing let me thank you, the American people for giving me the great honor of allowing me to serve as your president. When the Lord calls me home, whenever that may be, I will leave with the greatest love for this country of ours and eternal optimism for its future.

I now begin the journey that will lead me into the sunset of my life. I know that for America there will always be a bright dawn ahead.

Thank you, my friends. May God always bless you.

Sincerely,
Ronald Reagan

Following President Reagan's announcement to the American people that he had Alzheimer's disease, letters of sympathy poured into his office in Los Angeles, California. He then penned a final thank-you note. It was handwritten on his office sta-tionery, professionally copied, and sent to thousands of well-wishers.

Dear Friend
Early 1995 [39]

Dear Friend:

Nancy and I are deeply grateful for your kindness following the announcement of my illness. Individuals like you give us the courage and inspiration to move for-ward. With your prayers and God's grace, we know we will be able to face this latest challenge. May God bless you.

Sincerely,
Ronald Reagan

Reagan could not resist one last political stroke. Nine days later he writes to Haley Barbour, the chairman of the Republican National Committee from 1993 to 1996. The Republican Party had just won the House of Representatives for the first time in decades and Newt Gingrich was about to become Speaker of the House.

Haley Barbour
Washington, DC
November 14, 1994[40]

Dear Haley:

Congratulations on a great job for the Republican Party. I couldn't be happier with the results of the election. And please don't count me out! I'll be putting in my licks for Republicans as long as I'm able.

Sincerely,
Ronald Reagan

A NOTE ON METHODS

In 1996 and 1997, in Ronald Reagan's private papers at the Reagan Library, Kiron Skinner discovered handwritten drafts of his speeches and letters along with drafts of commentaries for Reagan's nationally syndicated radio program in the 1970s. A selection of some 200 radio addresses were published by the editors in 2001 in *Reagan, In His Own Hand: The Writings of Ronald Reagan that Reveal his Revolutionary Vision for America.* The research and editorial decisions entailed in the present volume are considerably more complex. The letters in this book have been carefully vetted to ensure that they are Reagan's own work (with a few exceptions noted). They have been edited only for consistency of spelling and abbreviations.

Authenticity of Reagan Letters

The authenticity of letters written by presidents of the United States is often in question. All modern presidents have signature machines—autopens—that can reproduce a genuine signature flawlessly. Most letters "signed" by our modern presidents were written by staff and signed by a machine or a secretary attempting to replicate the president's signature. Many letters personally signed by a president were drafted by a member of his staff able to write a letter that would meet with his approval.

Reagan had an unusual—if not unique—habit for a president; he often wrote a handwritten draft that was then typed by a secretary, and signed by him. Sometimes he simply wrote and sent a handwritten letter directly. Approximately 80 percent of the letters in this book are handwritten drafts by Reagan himself. Another 15 percent were dictated by Reagan, and for the remaining four percent, though we have not found a handwritten draft, we have examined the circumstances of the letter carefully and are confident of its authenticity. The Index of Letters notes whether the letter was found in handwritten, dictated, or typed form.

During Reagan's days as an actor in Hollywood and host of *GE Theater,* his eight years as governor of California, his eight years as president, and the years before and after the presidency, hundreds of thousands of letters were sent out over his signature. We have ignored this vast quantity of staff–generated correspondence and nonetheless discovered over 5,000 genuine Reagan letters, written or dictated over a period of 70 years. We have chosen 1,100 of them that we consider of special interest and significance.

The letters are presented as Reagan drafted them. We have used standard spelling and expanded abbreviations, but we have not changed punctuation except for occasional clarification and to standardize the salutation and closing; Reagan rarely used any punctuation in drafts after either one. We have not usually included Reagan's occasional marginal notes about where to find an address or to whom to send a copy.

At times when drafting both speeches and letters, Reagan discarded a first draft and wrote a second one.

The letters as sent sometimes differed in minor ways from what Reagan wrote, but his secretaries (e.g., Kathy Osborne in the White House) confirm that he always read and signed the final version of any letter he drafted or dictated himself. The differences occurred for several reasons. For letters citing data, the White House staff was often asked by the president's personal secretary Kathy Osborne (and earlier Helene von Damm) to check facts. Osborne also asked the National Security Council or the Secret Service to clear letters that she thought might contain national security or personal security information. Occasionally a phrase or sentence was deleted or changed.

Reagan rarely dated anything he wrote. The dates on the letters are the dates on the final typed versions, when we have them; the dates on which Reagan's dictation was first typed by a secretary; or estimated from the information in the letter or the archives (e.g., pre-presidential) in which the letter was found.

On handwritten drafts, we have used the text Reagan drafted. Dictated letters were sometimes lightly edited by staff, and here we have included staff editorial changes as it is not possible to tell whether changes are corrections of the secretary's transcription or actual editing. Such editorial changes were never substantive. Anne Higgins, who was in charge of the White House Office of Correspondence, and her assistant in the Children's Unit, Constance Mackey, both note that typists were not allowed to change the president's drafts.

Reagan's Hollywood Fan Mail

Some handwritten letters signed "Dutch," "Ron," "Ronnie," or "Ronald Reagan" were excluded from consideration for the book because they are in his mother's handwriting.

Soon after Reagan reported to Warner Bros. Studios June 1, 1937, he had a seven-year contract in hand and invited his parents, Nelle and Jack, to join him there. They arrived, according to Nelle's best friend Marion Foster, in mid-September 1937, not long after his first picture was released.

"Fan mail had started to arrive and was becoming a problem," Reagan wrote in *Where's the Rest of Me?* "I cooked up an idea that turned out to be not only good for him [Jack], but of great value to me. I turned this assignment over to him, and it became in reality a regular job in which he had a pass to the studio, working with the mail department. He took charge of ordering the necessary photos and stationery and, in short, set up a system for handling what would turn out to be thousands of letters."

Reagan doesn't mention that his mother, Nelle, was enlisted to actually answer the mail, and she began doing so almost immediately. She wrote in Reagan's name not only to movie fans like Lorraine Wagner but to old friends of Reagan's from Eureka College and Des Moines, Iowa, signing the letters "Dutch," "Ron," or "Ronnie." Between 1945 and March 1951, for example, Lorraine received at least 11 letters written by Nelle but signed with Reagan's name. Nelle also answered two letters to Garth Henrichs of Eureka; several to Joan Roll, another movie fan; and several to a friend from Des Moines, his former housekeeper Anna Griffith. Nelle also wrote letters as herself, signing her own name. At one time or another, however, all of these correspondents also received letters written and signed by Reagan. Reagan eventually took over the correspondence to Lorraine and others for two reasons: it went beyond discussion of his roles in movies and began to be involved with issues, and his mother became, at the age of 57 or 58, senile and unable to help.

Nelle's work on her son's behalf was unearthed by Herman M. Darvick, an autograph dealer, who noticed the similarity of the handwriting on fan membership cards and letters Reagan's mother, Nelle, wrote in her own name, and published an article in *Pen and Quill* (18.1 Jan./Feb. 1985) about the differences in their handwriting. Darvick found evidence that Nelle also answered some of Jane Wyman's correspondence (Wyman was Reagan's first wife). Reagan separately told Martin Anderson that as an actor he received many letters from gays, and that his mother answered them.

A recent collection of fan letters, published by the recipient, Mary Joan Roll-Sieffert (Joan Roll), includes letters to Joan from Nelle herself, letters in Nelle's hand signed "Ronald," letters to Joan from Bess Reagan (the wife of Neil Reagan, Ronald's brother), and letters in Bess's hand signed Ronald—as well as a few letters that appear to be genuine Reagan letters. Thus, Reagan's fan mail was something of an extended-family enterprise. The letters Reagan wrote himself are often thank-you notes for gifts, and unlike Nelle's letters, not one of them promotes his movies. One of the letters signed "Ronald" but in Nelle's hand notes that Reagan's mother and sister-in-law help him with fan mail by writing addresses on envelopes and postcards.

Another collection of Reagan fan mail, to fan club president Zelda Multz, has recently been offered for sale, with the dealer's caution that some may be signed by a secretary or autopen. Handwritten drafts of one letter to Joan Roll (then Joan Sieffert) and three to Zelda Multz exist in the archives we have consulted for this book.

REFERENCES, SOURCES, AND INTERVIEWS

Letters from three major sources are included in this book: (1) Closed collections at the Ronald Reagan Presidential Library and other libraries and archives; (2) Open collections at the Reagan Presidential Library, the Richard M. Nixon Library and Birthplace, the Young America's Foundation Reagan Ranch Center, and other libraries and archives; and (3) Letters that are privately held. A few letters from published sources are also included. The abbreviations used in the endnotes to designate the sources of the letters are noted here in parentheses.

Of the letters in the book, approximately 42 percent are from closed collections, 2 percent from privately held collections, and 56 percent from open collections. Closed collections are not open to scholars or the public without special permission.

Many interviews in person or by telephone were conducted as part of the research for this book. Some of the interviews are cited in the book, but others were used only for background purposes or to confirm a source. The list of the people interviewed, both those cited in the book and those from whom the authors received background information but have not cited the person in a footnote or endnote, are listed below. Also included are people with whom we corresponded by letter, fax, or electronic mail.

The authors have created an archive of letters from the sources listed below. Their collection will eventually be open to the public at the Hoover Institution Archives.

Archival Collections

RONALD REAGAN PRESIDENTIAL LIBRARY

Open Collections

Executive Secretariat of the National Security Council, Heads of State-USSR (NSC HOS-USSR). This is a collection of declassified correspondence between President Reagan and the leaders of the Soviet Union—Leonid Brezhnev, Yuri Andropov, Konstantin Chernenko, and Mikhail Gorbachev.

Nancy Davis Reagan Collection (NDR). This collection includes over 700 items—letters, greeting cards, and gift cards—sent or given by Ronald Reagan to Nancy Davis Reagan. This collection was given to the Reagan Presidential Library after Nancy Reagan published many of the letters in her book, *I Love You, Ronnie: The Letters of Ronald Reagan to Nancy Reagan.*

President's Daily Diary. This is the journal of Reagan's meetings and telephone calls during his presidency. Used for reference.

Presidential Handwriting File Series II (PHF Series II). The Presidential Handwriting File comprises six series. Series II includes hand-drafted responses to correspondence as well as notations the president made on documents sent to him. Documents in this file are available to the public.

Closed Collections

Ronald Reagan Gubernatorial Papers (RRGC) Originally held at the Hoover Institution Archives, this collection of Reagan's governorship papers contains a set (Boxes 1–6) of Reagan's handwritten letters and notes.

Office of Administration—Anne Higgins Correspondence—Mail Samples. The seven storage boxes contain the periodic reports on the mail coming into the White House and samples of letters from the general public selected for the president. Used for reference.

Presidential Handwriting File Original (PHF Original). Most of the letters in this collection written during Reagan's presidency are available to the public as PHF Series II. The original file also includes documents that have remained closed for reasons of privacy or executive privilege.

Pre-Presidential Papers (PPP). This collection is designated to include material about and by Ronald Reagan from 1921 to 1980. It includes high school and college essays, personal correspondence written during the governorship (1967–1975), and writings from the period between the governorship and the presidency (1975–1980).

Audio-Visual Collections PR011 321001 (PR011 321001 Audio). This collection comprises letters dictated by President Reagan from the beginning of his presidency until February 1982, copies of the letters as sent, and often the secretary's first transcription of the dictation. Of 265 letters, 21 have been made available to the public through requests under the Freedom of Information Act.

Presidential Personal (PHF Series VI PP). This collection contains many letters that have not been made public because they are personal papers not related to the duties of the president. Documents in this collection handwritten by the president or including handwritten notes have been designated as part of Series VI of the Presidential Handwriting File.

Presidential Political (PHF Series VI PL). This collection contains letters that have not been made public because, like the Presidential Personal papers, they are considered unrelated to the duties of the president. Handwritten documents from this collection have been designated part of Series VI of the Presidential Handwriting File.

1980 Reagan-Bush Campaign Files (Campaign 1980). Boxes 914–19 and 921–24 include correspondence and staff memoranda. Box 923 includes transcripts of over 800 dictated letters.

OFFICE OF RONALD REAGAN

Closed Collection

Office of President Reagan (post-presidency) (RR-VP). This set of letters, handwritten between 1989 and 1995, was made available to the authors by the Office of Ronald Reagan.

CHURCHILL COLLEGE ARCHIVES

Closed Collection

Collection of Margaret Thatcher. Churchill College Archives. Letters between Reagan and Thatcher that Thatcher has saved are in this collection.

DWIGHT D. EISENHOWER PRESIDENTIAL LIBRARY

Open Collection

Dwight D. Eisenhower: Papers, Post-Presidential, 1961–1969, File Folder. "RE," Box 33, 1966 Principal File Series (DDEL). This file contains three 1966 letters from Reagan to Eisenhower.

EUREKA COLLEGE

Open Collection

Eureka College Archives. Some of Reagan's college classmates have donated original letters or copies of their letters to the Eureka College Archives. A few letters are also available in the Eureka College Museum.

Closed Collection

Eureka College President's Office. Copies of letters kept in the president's office were made available to the authors by special permission.

GEORGE C. MARSHALL LIBRARY

Open Collection

Frank McCarthy Collection.

HOOVER INSTITUTION ARCHIVES

Open Collection

Ronald Reagan Subject Collection (RRSC). This collection contains some of Reagan's letters, speeches, and writings at various points in his political career. Used for reference.

Closed Collections

Citizens for Reagan (CFR). This collection mainly contains Reagan's writings and other documents about his activities during the late 1970s. Used for reference.

Deaver and Hannaford (DH). This collection is similarly constituted to the Citizens for Reagan files. Used for reference.

NATIONAL ARCHIVES AND RECORDS ADMINISTRATION

Open Collections

Richard M. Nixon Presidential Materials, Staff, NSC files. National Archives, College Park, Maryland (NARA-Nixon). There are some letters from Ronald Reagan to Richard Nixon and Henry Kissinger in this set.

Pre-Presidential Papers of Richard M. Nixon, General Correspondence (series 320). Mr. and Mrs. Ronald Reagan file. National Archives Pacific Region, Laguna Niguel Office (NARA PR-LN). This collection includes correspondence between Nixon and Reagan from 1959 to 1962.

THE RICHARD NIXON LIBRARY AND BIRTHPLACE

Open Collection

Pre-Presidential Papers Series 501.1 and 501.105 (RNLB). This series contains Nixon-Reagan correspondence between 1963 and 1968.

Closed Collection

Ronald Reagan Special File. (RNLB). This series contains Nixon-Reagan correspondence between 1974 and 1994.

PLAYBOY ARCHIVES

Playboy Archives. Correspondence between Hugh Hefner and Ronald Reagan in 1960 is included in these archives (closed).

SEELEY G. MUDD MANUSCRIPT LIBRARY, PRINCETON UNIVERSITY

Policy and Public Service Papers of James A. Baker, III. The Baker Collection includes the draft of President Reagan's first handwritten letter to Brezhnev.

WARNER BROTHERS ARCHIVES

Open Collecton

Warner Brothers Archives (WBA). The Ronald Reagan Legal File at University of Southern California contains a 1950 letter from Reagan to Jack Warner.

YALE UNIVERSITY LIBRARY

Closed Collecton

William F. Buckley Jr. Papers. Manuscripts and Archives. Yale University Library. The Buckley papers contain correspondence between Buckley and Reagan from 1962 through Reagan's presidency.

YOUNG AMERICA'S FOUNDATION: REAGAN RANCH CENTER ARCHIVES

Open Collection

Lorraine Makler Wagner Collection (LMW RRanch). This collection includes approximately 150 letters from Reagan to Wagner as well as letters from Nelle Reagan, Nancy Reagan, and others.

Anne Volz Higgins Collection (AVH RRanch). This extensive collection of Reagan letters includes many duplicates of materials from several collections in the Reagan Presidential Library.

Private Collections

Many people provided us with one or more letters from their private collections. Individuals whose letters are used in this book are listed below:

Martin Anderson	Robert Lindsey
Walter Annenberg	Zelda Multz
Roy Brewer	Bonnie Nofziger
William P. Clark	Kathleen Osborne
Earl B. Dunckel	John L. Robertson
Edward Fike	James Rogan
Sam Harrod III, Sam Harrod IV, and	Mabyl Griffith Taylor and Charles Taylor
Andrew Harrod	R. Emmett Tyrrell
Donald Kaecker	Stephen Vaughn
Helen Lawton	Jim Zabel

Letters from Published Sources

About a dozen letters from published books, journals, and auctions are used in this book. The previously published books of collections or selections from Reagan's correspondence include two books of selected letters written during his governorship and edited by his personal secretaries (Davis and von Damm) and one collection put together by a fan (Roll-Sieffert). One letter was obtained from a journal that printed a facsimile and another from an auctioneer who provided a facsimile of the letter sold on a Web page.

Kathy Randall Davis, ed., *But What's He Really Like?* (Menlo Park, California: Pacific Coast Publishers, 1970). (KRD)

Mary Joan Roll-Sieffert, *The Real Ronald Reagan: A True Humanitarian.* (Ontario, Canada: Epic Press, 2003).

Helene von Damm, *Sincerely, Ronald Reagan.* (New York: Berkeley Publishing, 1980). (HVD). This collection is an expanded version of the earlier edition published by Green Hill in 1976.

Interviews and Correspondence

People with whom the authors did formal interviews or communicated by telephone, letter, or electronic mail (often more than once) include:

Richard V. Allen	Biff Henley	Richard Pipes
James A. Baker III	Anne Volz Higgins	Charles Price II
Lynn Beer	Raymond S. Holmes	Nancy Reagan
Georgiana Bollman	Donald Kaecker	Nancy Clark Reynolds
William P. Clark	Teresa Kennell	Junius Rodriguez
Chris Collins	Victor H. Krulak	Jack Shelley
Lucy Conboy	James Kuhn	Katherine C. Shepherd
James K. Coyne	Helen Lawton	George P. Shultz
William Dalton	Stephanie Lee	Samueline Sisco
Herman Darvick	Rudolph Lee-Hines	Patsy Skidmore
George Davison	Robert C. McFarlane	Stuart Spencer
Dorothy Dellinger	Connie Mackey	Craig Stubblebine
Chuck Donovan	Ron Marlow	Mabyl Griffith Taylor
Joanne Drake	Sharleen Volpe Martin	William C. Thompson
Earl B. Dunckel	Suzanne Massie	Loesje Troglia
M. Stanton Evans	Jack Matlock	Helene von Damm
Lindy Fekety	Ramona Moloski	Ellis R. Veatch II
Milton Friedman	Zelda Multz	Lorraine Wagner
Marlin Fitzwater	Barney Oldfield	Steven Welch
Steven Hansch	Kathleen Osborne	Cathy Wildenradt
Peter H. Hannaford	Monte Osburn	Sara Willen
Kip Hayden	Jim Ostroff	William A. Wilson
Jerry Heller	Steve Parrott	Richard Wirthlin

NOTES

The following abbreviations are used in the Notes:

AVH RRanch	Anne Volz Higgins Collection, Young America's Foundation, Reagan Ranch Center Archives, Santa Barbara, California
Campaign 1980	Reagan-Bush 1980 Campaign Files, Ronald Reagan Library
CFR	Citizens for Reagan Collection, Hoover Institution Archives
DDEL	Dwight David Eisenhower Library
DH	Deaver and Hannaford Collection, Hoover Institution Archives
HVD	Helene von Damm, ed., *Sincerely, Ronald Reagan* (New York: Berkley Books, 1980).
KRD	Kathy Randall Davis, ed., *But What's He Really Like?* (Menlo Park, California: Pacific Coast Publishers, 1970).
LMW RRanch	Lorraine Makler Wagner Collection, Young America's Foundation, Reagan Ranch Center Archives, Santa Barbara, California
NARA-Nixon	Richard M. Nixon Presidential Material. National Archives, College Park, Maryland.
NARA PR-LN	Pre-Presidential Papers of Richard M. Nixon, General Correspondence. Mr. and Mrs. Ronald Reagan file. National Archives Pacific Region, Laguna Niguel Office.
NDR	Nancy Davis Reagan Collection, Ronald Reagan Library
NSC HOS-USSR	Executive Secretariat of the National Security Council, Heads of State-USSR, Ronald Reagan Library
PHF Original	Presidential Handwriting File-Original, Ronald Reagan Library
PHF Series II	Presidential Handwriting File Series II, Ronald Reagan Library
PHF Series VI PL	Presidential Political, Presidential Handwriting File Series VI, Ronald Reagan Library
PHF Series VI PP	Presidential Personal, Presidential Handwriting File Series VI, Ronald Reagan Library
PPP	Pre-Presidential Papers, Ronald Reagan Library
PR011 321301 Audio	Audio-Visual Collections, PR011 321301, Ronald Reagan Library
RNLB	Richard Nixon Library and Birthplace
RR-VP	Ronald Reagan Personal Correspondence, Office of Ronald Reagan (post-Presidential)

RRGC	Ronald Reagan Gubernatorial Papers, Ronald Reagan Library
RRSC	Ronald Reagan Subject Collection, Hoover Institution Archives
SV	Collection of Sam Vaughn of Ronald Reagan–Cleaver correspondence.
WBA	Warner Brothers Archives

INTRODUCTION

1. Interview with Nancy Clark Reynolds, May 3, 2003.
2. Michael Deaver is quoted in "White House Pen Pal," *Newsweek,* March 22, 1982.
3. Interview with Lindy Fekety, April 25, 2003.
4. Interview with Chuck Donovan, May 6, 2003.
5. Interview with Nancy Clark Reynolds, op. cit.
6. Interview with Kathy Osborne, a personal secretary to Reagan for several years of his gover-norship and for most of his presidency, May 27, 2003.
7. Interview with Helene von Damm, May 23, 2003. The authors have found a substantial body of Reagan's handwritten letters and other drafts in a closed section of the gubernatorial files of the Reagan Library.
8. Handwritten letters from these years are found in PPP Box 20 and dictated letters in Campaign 1980 boxes.
9. Higgins periodically provided President Reagan with a detailed "Mail Volume Report." The report would include the amount of mail that the president, first lady, and White House staff received for a given period, and it would include the numbers of letters opposed to and in support of a set of policy issues.
10. Interview with Anne Higgins, April 14, 2002.
11. Ibid. There are many copies of the sealed envelopes in the archives. The notes vary on these copies of the envelopes that have been saved. For instance, some envelopes have the note "sealed presidential" written on them, while others have a note stating "sealed handwritten presidential."

CHAPTER ONE: THE EARLY YEARS

1. Ronald Reagan, *Where's the Rest of Me? The Ronald Reagan Story* with Richard G. Hubler (New York: Duell, Sloan & Pearce, 1965), p. 17.
2. Audio available on Eureka College Website, www.eureka.edu.
3. Letter to Kenneth J. Bialkin, undated, during presidency, PHF Series VI PL/PP1.
4. The Don Kaecker Collection.
5. PHF Series VI Box PP4.
6. AVH RRanch.
7. PHF Series VI Box PP2.
8. Harold Bell Wright, *That Printer of Udell's: A Story of the Middle West* (Chicago: The Book Supply Co., 1903).
9. PHF Series II Box 8 Folder 119.
10. The Canadian title was *Songs of a Sourdough.* See Robert W. Service, *Songs of a Sourdough* (Toronto: William Briggs; London: Fisher Unwin, 1907), and *The Spell of the Yukon and Other Verses* (New York: Barse & Hopkins; Philadelphia: E. Stern & Co., 1907).
11. PHF Series VI Box PL/PP1.
12. Letter to Dallas O. Baillio, undated pre-presidential, PPP Box 20 Folder A-C.
13. PR011 321301 Audio. Reagan got borrowing privileges at the Dixon Public Library on December 20, 1921. Anne Edwards, *Early Reagan: The Rise to Power* (New York: William Morrow, 1987), p. 53.

14. PHF Series II Box 1 Folder 2. The text here is the handwritten draft. A final version including a story about the signing of the Declaration of Independence was published in *Parade*, "What July Fourth Means to Me," June 28, 1981, p. 7.

15. PHF Series VI Box PL/PP1. Reagan wrote about Christmas for the December 1981 issue of *Harper's Bazaar*, but the article was not used.

16. PHF Series VI Box PP2.

17. Campaign 1980 Box 923 Dictation.

18. Edwards, *Early Reagan*, pp. 53–54, 73–74, 249–50.

19. PHF Series VI Box PP1.

20. PHF Series II Box 13 Folder 202.

21. PHF Series II Box 8 Folder 105.

22. AVH RRanch.

23. Reagan, *Where's the Rest of Me?* p. 6.

24. Ronald Reagan, *An American Life* (New York: Simon & Schuster, 1990), p. 48.

25. "Students Strike at Eureka College," *New York Times*, Nov. 29, 1928, p. 23.

26. Reagan, *An American Life*, p. 58.

27. Reagan, *An American Life*, p. 58.

28. Campaign 1980 Box 923 Dictation.

29. Campaign 1980 Box 923 Dictation.

30. Quoted in Kiron K. Skinner, Annelise Anderson, and Martin Anderson, *Stories In His Own Hand: The Everyday Wisdom of Ronald Reagan* (New York: Free Press, 2001), p. 36. See also Ronald Reagan *Where's the Rest of Me?* p. 64, and *An American Life*, p. 52, and Lou Cannon, *Reagan*, pp. 37–38. Raymond Holmes, a member of Eureka's football team in the early 1930s, discusses the incident in "Ronald Reagan and Segregation in The Midwest," unpublished essay, March 1, 2001, Alumni Office, Eureka College. The facts of the incident vary slightly in these accounts.

31. Henry Allen, "The Saga of Burgie and Dutch," *Washington Post*, March 7, 1981, p. C1, and Alan Donovan, "Dr. William Franklin Burghardt, 69, Dies," *Washington Post*, August 11, 1981, p. B4.

32. Campaign 1980 Box 923 Dictation.

33. Campaign 1980 Box 923 Dictation.

34. PHF Series II Box 4 Folder 50.

35. PHF Series VI Box PL/PP1 Legal.

36. PHF Series VI Box PP3.

37. Eureka College President's Office.

38. Eureka College President's Office.

39. PPP Box 20 Folder E–F.

40. PPP Box 20 Folder G–H.

41. PPP Box 20 Folder A–C.

42. Campaign 1980 Box 922 Folder 9-1.

43. Campaign 1980 Box 923 Dictation.

44. PHF Series II Box 7 Folder 90.

45. PHF Series II Box 9 Folder 130.

46. PHF Series II Box 10 Folder 148.

47. PHF Series II Box 2 Folder 153.

48. PHF Original.

49. PHF Series II Box 18 Folder 291.

50. PHF Series II Box 19 Folder 319.

51. Eureka College Archives.

52. Reagan, *Where's the Rest of Me?* pp. 42–45.

53. Campaign 1980 Box 923 Dictation.
54. Collection of Jim Zabel.
55. PHF Series II Box 14 Folder 214.
56. Telephone interview with Monte Osburn, February 19, 2003.
57. RRGC Box 3.
58. PHF Series VI Box PL/PP1.
59. PHF Series II Box 21 Folder 345.
60. Campaign 1980 Box 923 Dictation.
61. PPP Box 20 Folder W.
62. PHF Series VI Box PP1.
63. Telephone interviews with Lucy Conboy, December 10, 2002, and February 3, 2003.
64. PHF Series II Box 9 Folder 128.
65. PHF Series II Box 11 Folder 168.
66. PHF Series VI Box PP3.
67. PHF Series II Box 19 Folder 310.

CHAPTER TWO: HOME AND FAMILY

1. NDR Box 5.
2. NDR Box 6.
3. NDR Box 5.
4. NDR Box 1.
5. RRGC Box 2.
6. PHF Series VI Box PP2.
7. PHF Series VI Box PL/PPL.
8. PHF Series II Box 6 Folder 74.
9. PHF Series II Box 5 Folder 71.
10. PHF Original.
11. PHF Original.
12. NDR Box 6.
13. NDR Box 6.
14. KRD p. 37.
15. KRD p. 80.
16. RRGC Box 4.
17. HVD pp. 124–27.
18. PPP Box 20 Folder S.
19. Campaign 1980 Box 914.
20. PHF Series II Box 12 Folder 176.
21. HVD pp.121–23.
22. PHF Original Legal.
23. AVH RRanch.
24. PHF Original Legal.
25. PHF Series VI PP Box 2.
26. RR-VP.
27. NDR Box 6.
28. NDR Box 6.
29. Eureka College Archives.
30. Campaign 1980 Box 923 Dictation.
31. PHF Original Legal.

32. Campaign 1980 Box 923 Dictation.
33. PR011 321301 Audio.
34. PR011 321301 Audio.
35. PR011 321301 Audio.
36. PHF Series II Box 13 Folder 191.
37. PHF Series VI Box PL/PP.
38. PHF Series II Box 5 Folder 22.
39. PHF Series II Box 7 Folder 103.
40. PHF Series VI Box PP4.

CHAPTER THREE: HEALTH AND PERSONAL APPEARANCE

1. Eureka College Archives.
2. Campaign 1980 Box 923 Dictation.
3. William F. Buckley Jr. Papers. Manuscripts and Archives. Yale University Library.
4. PPP Box 20 Folder P.
5. PPP Box 20 Folder L.
6. Campaign 1980 Box 922 Folder 9-1.
7. PHF Series II Box 5 Folder 69.
8. Campaign 1980 Box 923 Dictation.
9. Campaign 1980 Box 923 Dictation.
10. Campaign 1980 Box 923 Dictation.
11. PHF Series VI Box PP1.
12. PHF Series II Box 11 Folder 163.
13. PHF Series II Box 13 Folder 195.
14. PHF Series II Box 13 Folder 198.
15. AVH RRanch.
16. PHF Series VI Box PL/PP1 Legal.
17. AVH RRanch.
18. PHF Series VI Box PP3.
19. PHF Series VI Box PP3.
20. AVH RRanch.
21. PHF Series VI Box PP3.
22. PHF Series II Box 18 Folder 292.
23. PHF Series II Box 8 Folder 106.
24. PHF Series II Box 16 Folder 246.
25. PHF Series VI Box PL/PP1.
26. AVH RRanch.

CHAPTER FOUR: OLD FRIENDS

1. Eureka College Archives.
2. Campaign 1980 Box 923 Dictation.
3. PHF Series II Box 11 Folder 161.
4. PHF Original.
5. PHF Series II Box 8 Folder 107.
6. PHF Series II Box 3 Folder 43.
7. PHF Series VI PL/PP1.
8. Eureka College Archives.

9. Eureka College Archives.
10. Eureka College Archives.
11. Eureka College Archives.
12. Eureka College Archives.
13. PHF Series II Box 1 Folder 14.
14. PHF Series II Box 1 Folder 14.
15. Campaign 1980 Box 923 Dictation.
16. PHF Series II Box 8 Folder 112.
17. PHF Series II Box 18 Folder 293.
18. AVH RRanch.
19. PHF Series II Box 5 Folder 63.
20. Collection of Mabyl Griffith Taylor and Charles Taylor.
21. PHF Original Legal.
22. PHF Series VI Box PL/PP1.
23. PHF Series II Box 4 Folder 57.
24. Campaign 1980 Box 923 Dictation.
25. PHF Series II Box 2 Folder 159.
26. PHF Series II Box 8 Folder 110.
27. PHF Series II Box 13 Folder 187.
28. PHF Series II Box 16 Folder 249.
29. PHF Series II Box 6 Folder 85.
30. AVH RRanch.
31. PHF Series II Box 12 Folder 179.
32. PHF Series II Box 20 Folder 227B.
33. PHF Series II Box 5 Folder 70.
34. AVH RRanch.
35. PHF Series II Box 6 Folder 83.
36. PHF Series II Box 15 Folder 226.
37. Campaign 1980 Box 923 Dictation.
38. AVH RRanch.
39. AVH RRanch.
40. PPP Box 21.
41. Campaign 1980 Box 923 Dictation.
42. Campaign 1980 Box 923 Dictation.
43. PHF Series II Box 2 Folder 28.
44. PHF Series II Box 19 Folder 319.
45. PHF Series II Box 14 Folder 219.
46. PHF Series II Box 19 Folder 310.
47. PHF Series II Box 8 Folder 114.
48. PHF Series II Box 18 Folder 282.
49. PHF Series II Box 10 Folder 152.
50. Campaign 1980 Box 923 Dictation.
51. PHF Series II Box 11 Folder 165.

CHAPTER FIVE: HOLLYWOOD YEARS AND FRIENDSHIPS

1. PHF Series VI PL/PP1.
2. PHF Series II Box 20 Folder 332.
3. AVH RRanch.

4. AVH RRanch.

5. PPP Box 20 Folder I–L.

6. PPP Box 20 Folder A–C.

7. PHF Series VI Box PP1.

8. PHF Series II Box 15 Folder 240.

9. Sold by University Archives of Westport, Connecticut (www.universityarchives.com), Stock #23729-001. The envelope, sold with the letter, was used by the seller to date the letter. Since Reagan went on active duty in January 1942 and was promoted to first lieutenant a year later, the only June 7 on which he was a second lieutenant occurred in 1942.

10. Campaign 1980 Box 915 Folder 1–2.

11. PR011 32101 Audio.

12. PHF Series VI Box PP2.

13. PHF Series II Box 13 Folder 203.

14. PHF Original Legal.

15. AVH RRanch.

16. Collections of Sam Harrod III, Sam Harrod IV, and Andrew Harrod.

17. WBA, as quoted in Anne Edwards, *Early Reagan* (New York: William Morrow, 1987), 366–68.

18. WBA.

19. PPP Box 20 Folder E-F.

20. Collection of John L. Robertson M.D. The letter was bought by dealer Herman Darvick in person from the recipient, Florence Yerly (then Florence Welch), and sold to collectors Bob and Marg Cantor. The Cantors subsequently offered it for sale through Christie's, but the reserve price of $17,000 was not met. The Cantors later sold the letter to Robertson at the reserve price.

21. William F. Buckley Jr. Papers. Manuscripts and Archives. Yale University Library.

22. PHF Series II Box 18 Folder 172.

23. PHF Original Legal.

24. Eureka College Archives.

25. LMW RRanch.

26. PPP Box 20 Folder D.

27. LMW RRanch.

28. LMW RRanch.

29. AVH RRanch.

30. Campaign 1980 Box 923 Dictation.

31. *Playboy* Archives.

32. Hoover Institution Archives, Hoover Institution Records, Box 994, 1954–1964.

33. PPP Box 20 Folder G-H.

34. Frank McCarthy Collection, Box 9, Folder 14, George C. Marshall Library, Lexington, Virginia.

35. PHF Series VI PL/PP1.

36. PHF Series II Box 2 Folder 30.

37. *Manuscripts,* Volume XXXVIII—Number 3, Summer 1986.

38. PHF Series II Box 4 Folder 50.

39. PHF Original.

40. PHF Series II Box 18 Folder 290.

41. PPP Box 20 Folder D.

42. Campaign 1980 Box 923 Dictation.

43. KRD p. 104–105.

44. Campaign 1980 Box 923 Dictation.

45. PHF Series II Box 1 Folder 12.
46. PHF Series II Box 13 Folder 187.
47. PHF Series VI Box PP4.
48. PHF Series II Box 7 Folder 91.
49. PHF Series II Box 5 Folder 70.
50. PHF Series VI Box PP4.
51. PHF Series II Box 4 Folder 60.
52. PR011 321301 Audio.
53. PHF Series II Box 19 Folder 313.
54. PHF Series II Box 3 Folder 35.
55. RRGC Box 2.

CHAPTER SIX: GOVERNORSHIP

1. Lou Cannon, "The Reagan Years," *California Journal* 5 (November 1974): 360; Peter Hanna-ford, *The Reagans: A Political Portrait* (New York: Coward-McCann, 1983), pp. 23–24, and Marjorie Hunter, "Nixon Affirms Welfare View After Reagan Hints Shift," *New York Times,* February 2, 1972, p. 34.
2. Gladwin Hill, "Reagan Emerging in 1968 Spotlight," *New York Times,* November 10, 1966, p. 1; see p. 29 for headline noted in the text.
3. PHF Series VI Box PP/PL1. The date on this letter is unknown, but a note on the upper right-hand corner says "1960's? 1965?".
4. LMW RRanch.
5. Gladwin Hill, "California Rivals Jockey for Race," *New York Times,* April 11, 1965, p. 59.
6. See for example Lawrence E. Davies, "Reagan Assesses Political Future," *New York Times,* July 25, 1965, p. 52; and Gene Blake, "Welch Claims Birch Members Helped Reagan Win Election," *Los Angeles Times,* December 8, 1966.
7. RRGC Box 6.
8. "Ronald Reagan Exits Right," *Beverly Hills Courier,* September 17, 1965.
9. "Statement of Ronald Reagan Regarding the John Birch Society." September 24, 1965. See the John Birch Society files in the Gubernatorial Papers at the Ronald Reagan Library.
10. RRGC Box 6.
11. RRGC Box 5.
12. PPP Box 20 Folder I–L.
13. PPP Box 20 Folder P.
14. For a brief discussion of Reagan's disapproval of Docksai's movement see David Brudnoy, "Conservatives and 1972," *New Guard* 11 (December 1971): 14–16. See also "Reagan Candi-dacy Backed," *New York Times,* May 23, 1971, p. 8.
15. PPP Box 20 Folder D, and Helene von Damm, *Sincerely, Ronald Reagan* (Ottawa, Illinois: Green Hill Publishers, 1976).
16. PPP Box 20 Folder T.
17. PPP Box 20 Folder D.
18. Lyn Nofziger, *Nofziger* (Washington D.C.: Regnery Gateway, 1992), pp. 57–59.
19. Lyn Nofziger, *Nofziger.* The authors obtained a copy of Reagan's handwritten letter from Nofziger.
20. PPP Box 20 Folder R.
21. Quoted in "An Interview with Ronald Reagan," *Time,* November 17, 1980, p. 36.
22. PPP Box 20 Folder E–F.
23. Deaver devoted much of his time to the Proposition 1 campaign.

24. This review of Proposition 1 is based on the analysis found in Lou Cannon, *Reagan* (New York: G. P. Putnam's Sons, 1982), p. 189; Peter Hannaford, *The Reagans: A Political Portrait,* pp. 19–25; Lewis Uhler, *Setting the Limits: Constitutional Control of Government* (Washington, D.C.: Regnery Gateway, 1989), pp. 115–16, 177; and Kiron K. Skinner's interview with Milton Friedman at the Hoover Institution, Palo Alto, California, on December 4, 2002.

25. The undated letter is addressed to William C. Vondrasek, PPP Box 20 Folder V.

26. Ronald Reagan, *An American Life* (New York: Simon & Schuster, 1990), p. 207.

27. Letter to R. Emmett Tyrrell Jr., is found in PHF Series II Box 7 Folder 99.

28. PPP Box 20 Folder A–C.

29. PPP Box 20 Folder I, J, K, L.

30. PPP Box 20 Folder A–C.

31. PPP Box 20 Folder A–C.

32. Mark McGuire and Alex Kozinski, "For the Tax Initiative," *Daily Bruin,* November 2, 1973, pp. 5 and 7.

33. PPP Box 20 Folder K.

34. PPP Box 20 Folder O.

35. PPP Box 20 Folder D.

36. PPP Box 20 Folder W.

37. PPP Box 20 Folder W.

38. PPP Box 20 Folder S.

39. Gubernatorial Papers. Ronald Reagan Library.

40. For a recent review of some of Reagan's interaction with the UC campuses, see a memoir by the president of the University of California who was dismissed by the Board of Regents during Reagan's first month as governor. Clark Kerr, *The Gold and the Blue: A Personal Memoir of the University of California, 1949–1967,* volume 2 (Berkeley: University of California Press, 2003), pp. 283–302.

41. Lou Cannon, "The Reagan Years," p. 360.

42. The accounts differ on the firing of Kerr. See Lou Cannon, *Reagan,* p. 149; Clark Kerr, *The Gold and the Blue,* vol. 2, pp. 293–96.

43. The University of California Board of Regents unanimously voted to appoint Charles Hitch president on September 22, 1967, but Hitch did not assume the position until January 1, 1968. See Gladwyn Hill, "Charles Hitch, Economist, Named President of U. of California," *New York Times,* September 23, 1967, p. 30, and "U. of California President," *New York Times,* January 2, 1968, p. 23.

44. William Trombley, "Orr Will Address Regent Unit; Move to Oust UC's Hitch Seen." *Los Angeles Times,* November 14, 1972, pp. 1 and 26; and "Reagan's Attack on UC and Hitch," *Los Angeles Times,* November 24, 1972, p. 6, part II.

45. PPP Box 20 Folder A–C.

46. Ron Moskowitz, "Regents Foil 'Takeover' by Reagan," *San Francisco Chronicle,* October 19, 1968, p. 1; Wallace Turner, "Reagan Rebuffed on Cleaver Issue," *New York Times,* October 19, 1968, p. 35; Lance Gilmore, "UC Regents Back Hitch; Rebuff Governor on Cleaver Lectures," *San Francisco Chronicle,* October 20, 1968, p. A4; and the September 20, October 18, and November 22 , 1968 minutes of The Regents of the University of California.

47. PPP Box 20 Folder R. A facsimile of Reagan's handwritten version of this letter is also found in Kathy Randall Davis, *But What's He Really Like?* (Menlo Park, California: Pacific Coast Publishers, 1970), pp. 42–43.

48. PPP Box 20 Folder W.

49. PPP Box 20 Folder G–H.

50. Campaign 1980 Box 915 Folder 2–3.

51. PPP Box 20 Folder M & Mc.

52. Campaign 1980 Box 915:2–1.

53. PPP Box 20 Folder P.

54. Quoted in Peter Hannaford, *The Reagans: A Political Portrait* (New York: Coward-McCann, 1983), p. 19.

55. See Wallace Turner, "Reagan Remark a Campaign Issue: 'Bloodbath' Comment Fuels Oratory in California," *New York Times*, April 19, 1970, p. 43.

56. Campaign 1980 Box 923 Dictation.

57. PPP Box 20, Folder I–L.

58. RRGC Box 4.

59. William Trombley, "Regents Refuse to Renew Miss Davis' UCLA Contract," *Los Angeles Times*, June 20, 1970, p. 1.

60. PPP Box 20 Folder L.

61. PPP Box 20 Folder I–L.

62. PPP Box 20 Folder A–C.

63. PPP Box 20 Folder D.

64. Keith Monroe, "How California's Abortion Law Isn't Working," *New York Times*, pp. SM 10.

65. Campaign 1980 Box 923 Dictation.

66. Campaign 1980 Box 923 Dictation.

67. Kathleen Teltsch, "Bitter Controversy Persists in the State Two Years After Partial Abolishment of Capital Punishment," *New York Times*, May 10, 1967, p. 34, and "U.S. Hearing Held on Coast Over Staying 58 Executions," *New York Times*, June 30, 1967, p. 17.

68. See Earl Caldwell, "California Court, in 6-1 Vote, Bars Death Sentences," *New York Times*, February 19, 1972, pp. 1 and 8; "A Death Penalty is Petition's Aim," *New York Times*, March 19, 1972, p. 63; Tom Wicker, "Death Again in California," *New York Times*, November 12, 1972, p. E11; and Wallace Turner, "Coast Court Upsets Death-Penalty Law," *New York Times*, December 8, 1976, p. 21.

69. PPP Box 20 Folder I–L.

70. See Anthony Beilenson and Larry Agran, "The Welfare Reform Act of 1971," *Pacific Law Journal* 3 (July 1972): 475–502; Hannaford, *The Reagans*, pp. 17–18; Marjorie Hunter, "Nixon Affirms Welfare View After Reagan Hints Shift," *New York Times*, February 2, 1972, p. 34; William E. Pemberton, *Exit with Honor: The Life and Presidency of Ronald Reagan* (Armonk, New York: M. E. Sharpe, 1998), pp. 79–80; and Reagan, *An American Life*, pp. 188–91.

71. PPP Box 20 Folder A–C.

72. PPP Box 20 Folder A–C.

73. PPP Box 20 Folder E–F.

74. Quoted in Lawrence E. Davies, "Reagan Vows Economy Won't Cut Mental Services," *New York Times*, April 17, 1967, p. 29. See also Cannon, "The Reagan Years," p. 362, and Lawrence E. Davies, "Reagan Disputed on Mental Care," *New York Times*, April 16, 1967, p. 48.

75. PPP Box 20 Folder G–H.

76. PPP Box 20 Folder M.

77. PPP Box 20 Folder P.

78. LMW RRanch.

79. PPP Box 20 Folder A–C.

80. Campaign 1980 Box 923 Dictation.

81. PPP Box 20 Folder A–C.

82. Reagan describes the way in which he appointed judges in *An American Life*, pp. 174–75.

83. *An American Life*, p. 183.

84. PPP Box 20 Folder A–C.

85. RRGC Box 105.
86. PPP Box 20 Folder D.
87. PPP Box 20 Folder S.
88. Campaign 1980 Box 923 Dictation.

CHAPTER SEVEN: RUNNING FOR OFFICE

1. Letter to William Loeb, March 27, 1979, Campaign 1980 Box 923 Dictation.
2. Efrem Zimbalist suggested the idea to Reagan, noting that Harry O'Connor, a radio syndicator, might be interested. He was. Peter Hannaford, *The Reagans: A Political Portrait* (New York: Coward-McCann), 1983, p. 53.
3. Michael Deaver tells this story on *Reagan In His Own Voice*, (Kiron K. Skinner, Annelise Anderson, and Martin Anderson, eds. (New York: Simon & Schuster Audio, 2001). Deaver and Peter Hannaford were on Reagan's staff in Sacramento and formed a public relations firm in 1975 with Reagan as their main client.
4. Lou Cannon, *Reagan* (New York: G. P. Putnam's Sons, 1982), p. 258.
5. Letter to Mr. Biller, circa November 15, 1979 (Campaign 1980 Box 923 Dictation).
6. PHF Original.
7. Cannon, *Reagan*, p. 200.
8. Cannon, *Reagan*, p. 214.
9. Susan Bailey, "Someday He'll Show Letter from Reagan," *Portsmouth Herald*, circa December 1984. A copy of the article is in PHF Series II Box 10 Folder 151 at the Ronald Reagan Library.
10. PPP Box 20 Folder O. Date and place from HVD p. 191.
11. PPP Box 20 Folder O.
12. Earl B. Dunckel, "Ronald Reagan and the General Electric Theater, 1954–55," an oral history conducted in 1982 by Gabrielle Morris, Regional Oral History Office, The Bancroft Library, University of California, 1982, pp. 25–26, and RRGC Box 4, Reagan note on December 28, 1975, letter from Dunckel.
13. PPP Box 20 Folder D and collection of Earl B. Dunckel.
14. Cannon, *Reagan*, p. 231.
15. Campaign 1980 Box 923 Dictation.
16. Collection of Martin Anderson.
17. PPP Box 20 Folder S.
18. PPP Box 20 Folder E–F.
19. PPP Box 20 Folder S.
20. Reagan met on June 16, 1975, with a group who wanted him to run as an independent, including Richard Viguerie, Howard Phillips, Paul Weyrich, and Kevin Phillips (Hannaford, *The Reagans*, pp. 67–68). Viguerie was a critic; in a November 17, 1983, letter (PHF Series II Box 7 Folder 104) Reagan thanked his good friend, Roy Brewer, for answering a recent Viguerie attack: "Thank you for your response to Viguerie it was great. You know this so-called conservative has never been for me. Back in '76 he and a few of his ilk had me to a secret meeting in which they pushed for me running on a third party ticket. I told them I was going to run as a Republican and that what they proposed just didn't make sense. That did it for me—I became the enemy. In 1980 they were for Connally. But you told him off in great style—Thanks."
21. PPP Box 20 Folder S.
22. PPP Box 20 Folder A–C.
23. PPP Box 20 Folder L.
24. Hannaford, *The Reagans*, p. 157.

25. PPP Box 20 Folder G–H.

26. Theodore H. White, *America in Search of Itself: The Making of the President 1956–1980* (New York: Harper & Row, 1982). One electoral vote was cast for John Hospers in Virginia.

27. PPP Box 20 Folder M.

28. The dates of the meetings with Ford and the attendees are from the index to the President's Daily Diary, Gerald R. Ford Library, as reported by archivist Helmi Raaska.

29. PPP Box 20 Folder M.

30. Cannon, *Reagan,* p. 195. Hannaford (*The Reagans,* pp. 55, 63) reports other Ford offers of employment to Reagan.

31. PPP Box 20 Folder L.

32. Campaign 1980 Box 923 Dictation.

33. Campaign 1980 Box 923 Dictation.

34. Campaign 1980 Box 923 Dictation.

35. Campaign 1980 Box 923 Dictation.

36. RRGC Box 2, Winfield Schuster letter of April 4, 1969, and Reagan draft reply.

37. Campaign 1980 Box 923 Dictation.

38. Campaign 1980 Box 923 Dictation.

39. Campaign 1980 Box 923 Dictation.

40. Hannaford, *The Reagans,* pp. 182–83.

41. Campaign 1980 Box 923 Dictation.

42. Campaign 1980 Box 923 Dictation.

43. Campaign 1980 Box 949.

44. Martin Anderson, *Revolution* (New York: Harcourt Brace Jovanovich, 1988), pp. 80–81.

45. Campaign 1980 Box 923 Dictation.

46. Campaign 1980 Box 923 Dictation.

47. Campaign 1980 Box 923 Dictation.

48. Anne Edwards, *Early Reagan* (New York: William Morrow, 1987), p. 142.

49. Campaign 1980 Box 923 Dictation.

50. Campaign 1980 Box 923 Dictation.

51. Campaign 1980 Box 923 Dictation.

52. Campaign 1980 Box 923 Dictation.

53. For their own accounts, see Anderson, *Revolution,* pp. 328–31; Michael K. Deaver with Mickey Herskowitz, *Behind the Scenes* (New York: William Morrow, 1987), pp. 85–91; and Lyn Nofziger, *Nofziger* (Washington, D.C.: Regnery Gateway, 1992), pp. 233–41.

54. Campaign 1980 Box 923 Dictation.

55. Letter to William Loeb, Manchester, New Hampshire, March 27, 1979, Campaign 1980 Box 923 Dictation.

56. Campaign 1980 Box 923 Dictation.

57. Campaign 1980 Box 923 Dictation.

58. Campaign 1980 Box 922 Folder 9-5.

59. Campaign 1980 Box 922 Folder 9-5.

60. Campaign 1980 Box 923 Dictation.

61. Cannon, *Reagan,* p. 258.

62. Campaign 1980 Box 923 Dictation.

63. Jonathan Moore, ed. *The Campaign for President: 1980 in Retrospect* (Cambridge, Mass.: Ballinger Publishing, 1981), pp. 265, 269–70, 282.

64. Campaign 1980 Box 923 Dictation.

65. Campaign 1980 Box 923 Dictation.

66. Campaign 1980 Box 923 Dictation.

67. Campaign 1980 Box 923 Dictation.

68. Campaign 1980 Box 923 Dictation.

69. Interview by Annelise Anderson with Richard Wirthlin, February 5, 2003. Wirthlin's memo advised that ". . . at least one direct visit between you and Ford prior to the convention would be very much in order." Elizabeth Drew, *Portrait of an Election: The 1980 Political Campaign* (New York: Simon & Schuster, 1981), p. 368.

70. PPP Box 20 Folder W. Reagan's visit to Ford is reported in Cannon, *Reagan,* p. 262.

71. Campaign 1980 Box 923 Dictation.

72. Hannaford, *The Reagans,* pp. 259–60.

73. Campaign 1980 Box 923 Dictation.

74. Letter to William Loeb, July 29, 1980, Campaign 1980 Box 923 Dictation.

75. Campaign 1980 Box 923 Dictation.

76. Campaign 1980 Box 923 Dictation.

77. Campaign 1980 Box 923 Dictation.

78. Campaign 1980 Box 923 Dictation.

79. Campaign 1980 Box 923 Dictation.

80. Campaign 1980 Box 923 Dictation.

81. Campaign 1980 Box 923 Dictation.

CHAPTER EIGHT: CORE BELIEFS

1. Ronald Reagan, *Where's the Rest of Me? The Ronald Reagan Story* with Richard G. Hubler (New York: Duell, Sloan & Pearce, 1965), p. 140.

2. PPP Box 20 Folder A–C, dated 1976 in Helene Von Damm, *Sincerely, Ronald Reagan* (New York: Berkley Publishing, 1980), p. 88.

3. KRD p. 87.

4. PPP Box 20 Folder P.

5. PPP Box 20 Folder G–H.

6. Campaign 1980 Box 923 Dictation.

7. PR011 32101 Audio.

8. PR011 32101 Audio.

9. PHF Series II Box 7 Folder 94.

10. PHF Series II Box 13 Folder 203.

11. PR011 321301 Audio.

12. PR011 321301 Audio. The incoming letter was quoted in Eleanor Clift and Thomas M. DeFrank, "Letters from the President," *Reader's Digest,* September 1983, p. 50.

13. PHF Series II Box 6 Folder 81.

14. PHF Series II Box 6 Folder 84.

15. PHF Series II Box 7 Folder 102.

16. PHF Series II Box 4 Folder 56. Smith's letter is dated September 19, 1982.

17. PPP Box 20 Folder X–Z.

18. PPP Box 20 Folder A–C; PPP Box 20 Folder G–H.

19. SV. Typed only.

20. PPP Box 20 Folder G–H. The radio addresses mentioned in the letter were called "Chile I," "Chile II," "Chile III," "Charity," and "National Review." See Kiron K. Skinner, Martin Anderson, and Annelise Anderson, eds., *Reagan, in His Own Hand* (New York: Free Press, 2001), Appendix, for the listing of Reagan's radio addresses from 1975 to 1979.

21. PPP Box 20 Folder A–C.

22. PPP Box 20 Folder L.

23. PPP Box 20 Folder M.

24. PPP Box 20 Folder S and PPP Box 22.

25. Campaign 1980 Box 923 Dictation.

26. PHF Series II Box 5 Folder 70.

27. KRD p. 57.

28. PPP Box 14.

29. PPP Box 20 Folder G–H. Typed copy in PPP 3.

30. The biblical quotations are, respectively, from John 14:6, John 14:2, John 14:10, John 17:5, and, as one specific case of many, Mark 16:19.

31. PPP Box 20 Folder V.

32. PHF Series II Box 5 Folder 70.

33. SV. Typed only.

34. PHF Series II Box 10 Folder 135.

35. AVH RRanch. The version of the Lincoln quotation Reagan uses can be found in Elton Trueblood, *Abraham Lincoln: Theologian of American Anguish* (New York: Harper & Row, 1973).

36. Lee Edwards, *The Conservative Revolution: The Movement That Remade America* (New York: Free Press, 1999), p. 80.

37. William F. Buckley Jr. Papers. Manuscripts and Archives. Yale University Library.

38. RRGC Box 5.

39. RRGC Box 2.

40. RRGC Box 2.

41. PHF Series II Box 7 Folder 107.

42. RRGC Boxes 1 and 4.

43. PR011 321301 Audio.

44. PHF Series II Box 4 Folder 52.

45. Interview with Marlin Fitzwater by Annelise Anderson, January 3, 2003.

46. PHF Series VI PP2.

47. PHF Series II Box 10 Folder 137.

48. PHF Series II Box 9 Folder 125.

49. Campaign 1980 Box 923 Dictation.

50. PHF Series II Box 11 Folder 164.

51. Irina Ratushinskaya, *No, I'm Not Afraid,* translated by David McDuff (Newscastle upon Tyne, England: Bloodaxe Books, 1986), p. 11. George P. Shultz, *Turmoil and Triumph: My Years as Secretary of State* (New York: Charles Scribner's Sons, 1993), pp. 745–49, reports her release and describes his prior negotiations with Eduard Shevardnadze about her and other dissidents, refuseniks, and political prisoners.

52. PHF Series II Box 17 Folder 263. The letter was actually mailed November 17, 1986, after Anne Higgins sent it to the National Security Council for review to determine whether any of the details in the letter would endanger the women who signed the smuggled letter.

53. RRGC Box 5.

54. William F. Buckley Jr. Papers. Manuscripts and Archives. Yale University Library.

55. PPP Box 20 Folder L.

56. Campaign 1980 Box 923 Dictation.

57. PR011 321301 Audio.

58. PPP Box 20 Folder A-C.

59. PPP Box 20 Folder A-C.

CHAPTER NINE: ECONOMIC POLICY

1. Data from the *Economic Report of the President* (Washington, D.C.: United States Government Printing Office, 1982), Tables B5, B31, B55, B67. Various issues of this annual publication were used in this chapter for other similar data on unemployment, interest rates, and inflation. Data on the budget are from *Budget of the United States Government: Historical Tables* (Washington, D.C.: United States Government Printing Office, 2003). Data on business cycle troughs and peaks are from the National Bureau of Economic Research and is published in the *Statistical Abstract of the United States Government* and on the bureau's Web site.

2. Executive Order 12287, issued January 28, 1981, decontrolled prices and allocations of crude oil and refined petroleum products. Reagan addressed the nation on the economy on February 5, 1982. The President's Economic Policy Advisory Board was announced on February 10, 1981, and formally created by executive order on March 2, 1981. Reagan sent his revised budget and tax reduction proposals to the Congress on February 18, 1981, and addressed a joint session of Congress on the program for economic recovery that evening. Martin Anderson, adviser to the president for policy development, set up the President's Economic Policy Advisory Board and was its executive secretary. His account in *Revolution* (New York: Harcourt Brace Jovanovich, 1988), pp. 261–71, is the most detailed account of the board available.

3. The following table shows spending (budget outlays) as a percentage of gross domestic product (GDP) for major budget categories, receipts, and the budget deficit, for the year before Reagan took office, his first year in office, 1983 (the worse recession year), 1986 (when the defense buildup was at its maximum in relation to the economy), and his last year in office.

PERCENTAGES OF GDP

Spending	1980	1981	1983	1986	1988
National defense	4.9	5.1	6.1	6.2	5.8
Human resources	11.5	11.8	12.4	10.9	10.6
Net interest	1.9	2.2	2.6	3.1	3.0
Other (net)	3.3	3.1	2.4	2.3	1.8
Total Spending	21.6	22.2	23.5	22.5	21.2
Receipts	18.9	19.6	17.4	17.5	18.1
Difference (Deficit)	-2.7	-2.6	-6.1	-5.0	-3.1

In sum, Reagan increased defense spending by about one percentage point of GDP, but it was on a declining path by 1988; he reduced spending on human resources (health, education, welfare, social security, and so forth) by about one percentage point. Interest on the federal debt increased. Taxes were, in Reagan's final year, higher in relation to the economy than the average for the 1970s.

4. William A. Niskanen, *Reaganomics: An Insider's Account of the Policies and the People* (New York: Oxford University Press, 1988), pp. 18–19, defines "supply-side economics" as "the application of microeconomic theory to the effects of fiscal policy on the incentives to work, save, and invest and on the allocation of resources in the economy." It is not, he goes on to say, new economic theory and "does not conclude that a general reduction of tax rates would increase tax revenues, nor did any government economist or budget projection by the Reagan administration ever make that claim. . . . Supply-side economics does not address the effects of government borrowing; specifically, it does not provide a basis for con-

cluding that deficits do not matter." Niskanen was a member of the Council of Economic Advisers in the Reagan administration. See also Anderson, *Revolution*, pp. 141–63, for a discussion of supply-side economics that concurs with Niskanen. Both books provide detailed information on Reagan's economic views and policies.

5. Campaign 1980 Box 923 Dictation.
6. In addition to the January 23, 1981, meeting, Reagan met with Paul Volcker in 1981 on May 18, June 16, and December 14; and was present at a dinner honoring him on July 18, 1987 (memorandum from the archivist Greg Cumming, RRL). Lou Cannon, *President Reagan: The Role of a Lifetime* (New York: Simon & Schuster, 1991), p. 273 notes a meeting on February 15, 1982. Others present at these meetings included, often, Edwin Meese, James Baker, Donald Regan, David Stockman, and Martin Anderson. See Anderson, *Revolution*, pp. 249–53 for greater detail. Reagan appointed Alan Greenspan chairman of the Federal Reserve Board in August 1987. Greenspan met with Reagan as a member of the President's Economic Policy Advisory Board, but not as chairman of the Federal Reserve Board.
7. PR011 321301 Audio.
8. PR011 321301 Audio.
9. PR011 321301 Audio.
10. PR011 321301 Audio.
11. PR011 321301 Audio.
12. PHF Series II Box 1 Folder 6.
13. PR011 321301 Audio.
14. PHF Original. Nofziger sent a copy of his memorandum, dated October 18, 1981, to Edwin Meese, James Baker, Michael Deaver, Martin Anderson, and David Stockman.
15. PR011 321301 Audio.
16. PR011 321301 Audio.
17. PHF Series II Box 1 Folder 12.
18. PHF Series II Box 1 Folder 13.
19. PR011 321301 Audio.
20. PR011 321301 Audio.
21. PR011 321301 Audio.
22. PHF Original Legal.
23. PHF Series II Box 2 Folder 24.
24. PR011 321301 dictation tapes. "Here we are," Krulak wrote in his January 14, 1982, column ("An Open Letter to President Reagan"), "puffing and straining under a load of taxes and national debt that has been heaped on us over maybe 30 or 40 years, and they seem to expect you to wave a wand and make it all go away." Collection of Victor H. Krulak.
25. PR011 321301 Audio. The typed letter says "prerequisites" instead of "perquisites" and is a transcription error.
26. PR011 321301 Audio.
27. PHF Series II Box 2 Folder 31.
28. PHF Series II Box 3 Folder 37.
29. PHF Series II Box 3 Folder 42.
30. PHF Original Legal.
31. Niskanen, *Reaganomics,* p. 77; see pp. 76–79 for details about TEFRA.
32. PHF Original Legal.
33. PHF Series II Box 4 Folder 51.
34. PHF Series II Box 4 Folder 48.
35. PHF Series II Box 5 Folder 66.
36. PHF Series II Box 5 Folder 73.

37. PHF Series VI Box PL/PP1.
38. PHF Series II Box 7 Folder 91.
39. PHF Series II Box 7 Folder 99.
40. PHF Series VI Box PP1.
41. PHF Series II Box 8 Folder 117.
42. AVH RRanch.
43. PHF Series II Box 9 Folder 130.
44. PHF Original.
45. PHF Series II Box 13 Folder 202.
46. PHF Series II Box 13 Folder 203.
47. AVH RRanch.
48. PHF Series II Box 19 Folder 311.
49. PHF Series II Box 19 Folder 312.
50. PHF Series II Box 20 Folder 332.
51. PHF Series II Box 21 Folder 336.

CHAPTER TEN: DOMESTIC POLICY

1. In the federal budget, "human resources" includes all spending for programs in these functions: education, training, employment, and social services; health; medicare; income security; social security; and veterans benefits and services. See Executive Office of the President, Office of Management and Budget, *Historical Tables, Budget of the United States Government* (Washington, D.C.: U.S. Government Printing Office, annual), especially Table 3.1, for further detail.
2. PHF Series II Box 1 Folder 17.
3. PR011 321301 Audio. ATCS is a federal job category for air traffic controllers.
4. Caspar Weinberger, *Fighting for Peace: Seven Critical Years in the Pentagon* (New York: Warner Books, 1991), p. 51.
5. PR011 321301 Audio.
6. PHF Series II Box 5 Folder 70.
7. Campaign 1980 Box 923 Dictation.
8. Campaign 1980 Box 923 Dictation.
9. Campaign 1980 Box 923 Dictation.
10. Ronald Reagan, *Where's the Rest of Me?* (New York: Duell, Sloan & Pearce, 1965), p. 8.
11. Quoted in Anne Edwards, *Early Reagan* (New York: William Morrow, 1987), p. 398. See Steven F. Hayward, *The Age of Reagan: The Fall of the Old Liberal Order 1964–1980* (Roseville, California: Prima Publishing, 2001), pp. 694–700, for further details on attacks on Reagan as racist and his repudiation of endorsement by one Klan chapter.
12. Campaign 1980 Box 923 Dictation.
13. PHF Series II Box 16 Folder 259.
14. PHF Series II Box 5 Folder 66.
15. PHF Original Legal.
16. PHF Series II Box 9 Folder 133.
17. For an overview of the Reagan administration's missteps on matters such as the Bob Jones University case that contributed to the perception of insensitivity on race matters in spite of Reagan's basic absence of prejudice, see, e.g., Lou Cannon, *President Reagan: The Role of a Lifetime* (New York: Simon & Schuster, 1991), pp. 519–25.
18. PHF Series II Box 10 Folder 141.
19. PHF Series II Box 11 Folder 162.

20. Campaign 1980 Box 923 Dictation.
21. PR011 321301 Audio.
22. PHF Original Legal.
23. LMW RRanch.
24. Campaign 1980 Box 923 Dictation.
25. PR011 321301 Audio.
26. PHF Series II Box 18 Folder 172.
27. Reagan negotiated effectively with the Democratic legislature to develop and pass the California Welfare Reform Act of 1971.
28. PPP Box 20 Folder S.
29. PHF Series II Box 2 Folder 28.
30. PHF Series II Box 12 Folder 171.
31. PPP Box 20 Folder S. The story of how Hansch got his letter to Reagan is from electronic mail from Hansch to Annelise Anderson, May 31, 2003.
32. PPP Box 20 Folder E–F.
33. PPP Box 20 Folder E–F.
34. Campaign 1980 Box 923 Dictation.
35. PHF Series II Box 1 Folder 6 and PR011 321301 Audio.
36. PHF Original.
37. PR011 321301 Audio.
38. PHF Series II Box 12 Folder 170.
39. Budget figures for the National Endowment for the Arts are available from the agency. For private giving, see Center on Philanthropy at Indiana University, *Giving USA* (Indianapolis, Indiana: American Association of Fundraising Counsel Trust for Philanthropy, 2002). They estimate total private charitable giving in 2001 at $212 billion, of which $12.14 billion, or 5.7 percent, was for the arts.
40. PR011 321301 Audio.
41. PHF Series II Box 15 Folder 229.
42. PPP Box 20 Folder D (draft) and collection of Roy Brewer for a copy of the letter as sent.
43. PPP Box 20 Folder A–C.
44. Campaign 1980 Box 923 Dictation.
45. PPP Box 20 Folder D.
46. PPP Box 20 Folder E–F.
47. PR011 321301 Dictation tapes.
48. PR011 321301 Audio.
49. The text of the newspaper column is printed in Peter Hannaford, *The Reagans: A Political Portrait* (New York: Coward-McCann, 1983), pp. 185–86.
50. PPP Box 20 Folder G–H.
51. PHF Original Legal.
52. PPP Box 20 Folder L.
53. PHF Series II Box 9 Folder 122.
54. PR011 321301 Audio.
55. PPP Box 20 Folder E–F.
56. PR011 321301 Audio.
57. RRGC Box 4.
58. AVH RRanch.
59. PHF Series II Box 17 Folder 276.

CHAPTER ELEVEN: THE COLD WAR I

1. The speech is found in RRSC Box 3 Folder RR Speeches 1978.
2. Reagan made this statement in appearances in Michigan on May 13, 1976. See CFR Box 40 Folder Presidential Campaign 1976. Policy Statements. . . . Speeches, Press Releases. April 23, 1976, to May 31, 1976. CFR Box 109 Folder RR 1976 Speeches, Statements, Press Releases, Press Manifesto. 6-3.
3. Reagan's speech is reprinted in *Human Events* (March 1, 1975).
4. PPP Box 20 Folder G–H.
5. PPP Box 20 Folder S.
6. Kiron K. Skinner, Annelise Anderson, and Martin Anderson, eds., *Reagan, In His Own Hand: The Writings of Ronald Reagan that Reveal his Revolutionary Vision for America* (New York: Free Press, 2001), pp. 144–45.
7. PPP Box 20 Folder W.
8. Campaign 1980 Box 923 Dictation.
9. PR011 321301 Audio.
10. On July 4, 1994, President William Clinton accepted Czech President Vaclav Havel's invitation to move RFE/RL to Prague.
11. PHF Series II Box 2 Folder 23.
12. NSC HOS-USSR Box 38. The letter is reproduced in Chapter 23.
13. PHF Series II Box 2 Folder 23.
14. See "Russia Urges Total World Disarmament," *Toronto Daily Star,* November 30, 1927, p. 1.
15. PHF Series II Box 4 Folder 49.
16. PHF Series II Box 4 Folder 60.
17. *The Challenge of Peace: God's Promise and Our Response: A Pastoral Letter on War and Peace* (Washington, D.C.: United States Catholic Conference, July 8, 1983).
18. PHF Series II Box 5 Folder 73.
19. AVH RRanch.
20. Telephone interview with Suzanne Massie on December 2, 2002. See also the Presidential Daily Diary, Ronald Reagan Library.
21. PHF Series II Box 8 Folder 116.
22. PHF Series II Box 9 Folder 134.
23. George P. Shultz, *Turmoil and Triumph: My Years as Secretary of State* (New York: Scribner, 1993), p. 171. Later in a letter to Soviet leader Konstantin Chernenko, Reagan wrote that he was "touched by that gesture and in my view, it showed how quiet and sincere efforts could solve even the most sensitive problems in our relationship." See his *An American Life* (New York: Simon & Schuster, 1990), p. 597. For Reagan's radio commentary see Skinner et al., *Reagan, In His Own Hand,* pp. 177–78.
24. PHF Original.
25. AVH RRanch.
26. PHF Series II Box 13 Folder 207.
27. PHF Series II Box 16 Folder 261.
28. PHF Series II Box 16 Folder 261.
29. PHF Series II Box 16 Folder 261.
30. AVH RRanch.
31. PHF Series II Box 19 Folder 313.
32. PHF Series II Box 19 Folder 316.
33. Lou Cannon, "Russians, Reagan: A Sizing Up. 'It's Better to See Once Than to Hear 100 Times,' " *Washington Post,* June 1, 1988, p. A1.

34. PHF Series II Box 20 Folder 328.
35. PHF Series II Box 20 Folder 328.
36. Quoted in Thomas Parrish, *The Cold War Encyclopedia: The Complete Guide to the Most Important Conflict of Our Time* (New York: Henry Holt, 1996), p. 115.
37. PHF Series II Box 20 Folder 331.
38. PPP Box 20 Folder W.
39. Campaign 1980 Box 923 Dictation.
40. Campaign 1980 Box 923 Dictation.
41. PHF Series II Box 4 Folder 54.
42. PHF Series II Box 5 Folder 62.
43. PHF Series II Box 5 Folder 62.
44. PHF Series II Box 5 Folder 62.
45. PHF Series II Box 5 Folder 68.
46. PHF Series II Box 2 Folder 74.
47. PHF Series II Box 6 Folder 80.
48. PHF Series II Box 6 Folder 80.
49. PHF Series II Box 6 Folder 85.
50. PHF Series II Box 6 Folder 72.
51. PHF Series II Box 10 Folder 135.

CHAPTER TWELVE: COLD WAR II

1. See Reagan's statements in the 1960s and 1970s in CFR Box 35. Reagan's February 10, 1976, foreign policy speech at Philips Exeter Academy is in CFR Box 40 Folder Presidential Campaign 1976. The final quote in this paragraph is from a January 7, 1976, stump speech. See PPP8 Folder (RR Speech)—Stump—1/7/76.
2. The essence of William of Ockham's (1285–1347) methodological principle of parsimony is a basis toward simplicity in designing theories. See Marilyn McCord Adams, *William Ockham,* vol. 1 (Notre Dame, Indiana: University of Notre Dame Press, 1987), p. 156.
3. This undated pre-presidential letter to Professor Dan McLachlan Jr., is found in PPP Box 20 Folder M.
4. The letter is addressed to John O. Koehler and is found in PR011321301 Audio. It is reproduced in Chapter 11.
5. See the June 28, 1982, letter addressed to Irving S. Schloss. PHF Series II Box 3 Folder 43. The letter is reproduced in this chapter.
6. See the July 7, 1988, letter addressed to Robert Dick. See PHF II Box 20 Folder 331. The letter is reproduced in this chapter.
7. See Don Oberdorfer, "Thatcher Says Cold War Has Come to an End," *Washington Post,* November 18, 1988, p. A1, and George P. Shultz, *Turmoil and Triumph: My Years as Secretary of State* (New York: Charles Scribner's Sons, 1993), p. 1131.
8. For radio commentaries about SALT II see Kiron K. Skinner, Annelise Anderson, and Martin Anderson, eds., *Reagan, In His Own Hand: The Writings of Ronald Reagan that Reveal his Revolutionary Vision for America* (New York: Simon & Schuster, 2001), pp. 75–91. Reagan's handwritten draft of his SALT II speech is found in Campaign 1980 Box 924, and the typescript of the speech is in CFR Box 104 and RRSC Box 3. Peter Hannaford writes that Richard V. Allen assisted Ronald Reagan with the draft of the speech. See Hannaford's *The Reagans: A Political Portrait* (New York: Coward-McCann, 1983), p. 207.
9. Campaign 1980 Box 923 Dictation.
10. Campaign 1980 Box 923 Dictation.

11. Campaign 1980 Box 923 Dictation.

12. Campaign 1980 Box 919 Folder 6-1.

13. Campaign 1980 Box 923 Dictation.

14. "Transcript of President's Interview on Soviet Reply," *New York Times,* January 1, 1980, p. 4.

15. Campaign 1980 Box 923 Dictation.

16. Campaign 1980 Box 923 Dictation.

17. PHF Series II Box 2 Folder 33. Reagan's handwritten version presented here has the same substantive content as the typed version that was apparently sent, but the two versions have slightly different wording.

18. PHF Series II Box 3 Folder 35.

19. PHF Series II Box 3 Folder 35.

20. PHF Series II Box 1 Folder 10.

21. Ronald Reagan, *An American Life* (New York: Simon & Schuster, 1990), p. 586. See also "Statement on Deployment of the MX Missile," *Public Papers of the Presidents, 1982* (Washington, D.C.: U.S. Government Printing Office, 1983), pp. 1502–03.

22. PHF Series II Box 3 Folder 36.

23. PHF Series II Box 3 Folder 37.

24. PHF Series II Box 3 Folder 40.

25. PHF Series II Box 3 Folder 43.

26. PHF Series II Box 4 Folder 48.

27. PHF Series II Box 4 Folder 54.

28. PHF Original Legal.

29. PHF Series II Box 6 Folder 85.

30. PHF Series II Box 7 Folder 96.

31. PHF Series II Box 7 Folder 97.

32. PHF Series II Box 7 Folder 97.

33. PHF Series II Box 9 Folder 127.

34. PHF Series II Box 11 Folder 154.

35. PHF Series II Box 11 Folder 160.

36. PHF Series II Box 13 Folder 205.

37. PHF Series II Box 14 Folder 208. A typed version of President Reagan's note was not found in the Presidential Handwriting File, and thus it is not known if the president's note was typed and sent as a letter to Paul Petry.

38. Philip Revzin, "London Visit by Kremlin No. 2 Prompts Thatcher to Say: 'I Like Mr. Gorbachev,'" *Wall Street Journal,* December 18, 1984, p. 38.

39. In her pre-summit editorial for the Manchester, New Hampshire, *Union Leader,* Nackey Loeb writes that President Reagan "must not speak in the voice of those who want peace at any price—those who would compromise out of fear. . . . The American people have twice elected Ronald Reagan because they feel he best represents their beliefs. If talk he must with the Soviets, let Ronald Reagan never forget that he is speaking for Americans." November 15, 1985.

40. PHF Series II Box 14 Folder 209.

41. PHF Series II Box 14 Folder 209.

42. PHF Series II Box 14 Folder 211.

43. PHF Series II Box 14 Folder 213.

44. PHF Series II Box 14 Folder 213.

45. PHF Series II Box 14 Folder 224.

46. PHF Series II Box 18 Folder 281.

47. PHF Series II Box 18 Folder 283.

48. PHF Original.
49. PHF Series II Box 19 Folder 311.
50. PHF Series II Box 19 Folder 315.
51. PHF Series II Box 20 Folder 320.
52. PHF Series II Box 20 Folder 322.
53. PHF Series II Box 20 Folder 331.
54. PPP Box 20 Folder G–H.
55. PHF Series II Box 6 Folder 79.
56. PHF Series II Box 6 Folder 78.
57. PHF Series II Box 6 Folder 86.
58. PHF Series II Box 6 Folder 86.
59. PHF Series II Box 7 Folder 91.
60. PHF Series II Box 10 Folder 146.
61. PHF Series II Box 10 Folder 150.
62. Laurence W. Beilenson, *The Treaty Trap: A History of the Performance of Political Treaties by the United States and European Nations* (Washington, D.C.: Public Affairs Press, 1969).
63. PHF Series II Box 13 Folder 199.
64. PHF Series II Box 15 Folder 233.
65. PHF Series II Box 16 Folder 252.
66. PHF Series II Box 16 Folder 260.
67. PHF Series II Box 16 Folder 260.
68. PHF Series II Box 17 Folder 264.
69. PHF Series II Box 18 Folder 285.
70. PHF Series II Box 20 Folder 322.
71. PHF Series II Box 20, Folder 331.

CHAPTER THIRTEEN: THE MIDDLE EAST AND SOUTHWEST ASIA

1. See Kiron K. Skinner, Annelise Anderson, and Martin Anderson, *Reagan, In His Own Hand: The Writings of Ronald Reagan that Reveal his Revolutionary Vision for America* (New York: Simon & Schuster, 2001), pp. 212–18.
2. *Time* (June 30, 1980).
3. "Transcript of President's Interview on Soviet Reply," *New York Times,* January 1, 1980, p. 4.
4. NSC HOS-USSR.
5. Campaign 1980 Box 923 Dictation.
6. The shah left a New York hospital on December 2, 1979, and was granted sanctuary in San Antonio, Texas. Two weeks later he traveled to Panama, and then entered an Egyptian military hospital on March 24. He died in Cairo, Egypt, on July 27, 1980, and was buried there two days later.
7. Campaign 1980 Box 923 Dictation.
8. Alan Riding, "Mexico Bars Return of Shah as Doctors Finish Treatment; U.S. Sues Iran in World Court," *New York Times,* November 30, 1979, pp. A1, A19.
9. Campaign 1980 Box 923 Dictation.
10. Campaign 1980 Box 923 Dictation.
11. AVH RRanch.
12. Drew Middleton, "Israel's Eroding Might," *New York Times,* February 15, 1978, p. A1. See also Marvine Howe, "Arab Foes of Sadat Plan to Meet Again Before Mid-January," *New York Times,* December 29, 1977, p. 7.
13. PPP Box 20 Folder A–C and typed from PPP Box 2 RR Correspondence c. 1978.

14. AVH RRanch.

15. PHF Series II Box 20 Folder 334.

16. George P. Shultz writes: "No one knew who had placed the bomb that killed him [Bashir Gemayel]. Lebanese Christians blamed the Palestinians; Palestinians blamed Israel; others claimed it was an inside job." *Turmoil and Triumph: My Years as Secretary of State* (New York: Charles Scribner's Sons, 1993), p. 101.

17. See Appendix B of *Patterns of Global Terrorism* (Washington, D.C.: Department of State, Office of the Coordinator for Counterterrorism), May 21, 2002, and David Lamb, "The World; Hezbollah Feeling the Squeeze; International Pressure on Syria and Iran to Sever Terrorist Ties Threatens the Support that the Lebanese Militants Rely On," *Los Angeles Times*, May 3, 2003.

18. PPP Box 20 Folder M. This letter was written during the Nixon administration. Reagan uses the term "cease-fire," but it is not entirely clear if he is speaking about the cease-fire of August 1970 as the war of attrition came to a close or the cease-fire, followed by disengagement agreements, of the October war, which began in 1973. Both conflicts took place during the Nixon administration.

19. PHF Series II Box 4 Folder 50.

20. PHF Series II Box 5 Folder 62.

21. PHF Series II Box 4 Folder 49.

22. PHF Series II Box 4 Folder 50.

23. Norman Podhoretz, "'J' Accuse," *Commentary* 74 (September 1982): 21–31.

24. PHF Series II Box 4 Folder 53.

25. PHF Series II Box 6 Folder 75.

26. PHF Series II Box 6 Folder 86.

27. PHF Series II Box 8 Folder 106.

28. PHF Series II Box 8 Folder 110a.

29. PHF Series II Box 8 Folder 117.

30. PHF Series II Box 10 Folder 146.

31. PHF Series II Box 13 Folder 198.

32. PHF Series II Box 19 Folder 316.

33. Campaign 1980 Box 923 Dictation.

34. PHF Series II Box 1 Folder 10.

35. PHF Series II Box 4 Folder 54.

36. PHF Series II Box 4 Folder 54.

37. PHF Series II Box 10 Folder 151.

CHAPTER FOURTEEN: TERRORISM AND THE IRAN-CONTRA SCANDAL

1. See some of Reagan's 1979 newspaper columns found in CFR Box 106.

2. Peter J. Wallison, *Ronald Reagan: The Power of Conviction and the Success of his Presidency* (Boulder, Colorado: Westview Press 2002), p. 172.

3. PPP Box 20 Folder L.

4. PHF Series VI Box PP2.

5. PHF Series VI Box PL/PP1.

6. PHF Series II Box 13 Folder 192.

7. PHF Series II Box 13 Folder 206.

8. PHF Series II Box 17 Folder 266.

9. PHF Series II Box 19 Folder 317.

10. PHF Series II Box 15 Folder 235.

11. PHF Series II Box 15 Folder 236.

12. PHF Series II Box 15 Folder 240.
13. AVH RRanch.
14. PHF Series II Box 16 Folder 249.
15. PHF Series II Box 17 Folder 266.
16. PHF Series II Box 17 Folder 266.
17. PHF Series II Box 17 Folder 266.
18. PHF Series II Box 17 Folder 267.
19. PHF Series II Box 17 Folder 267.
20. PHF Series II Box 17 Folder 268.
21. PHF Series II Box 17 Folder 268.
22. PHF Series II Box 17 Folder 269.
23. AVH RRanch.
24. PHF Series II Box 17 Folder 271.
25. PHF Series II Box 17 Folder 271.
26. PHF Series II Box 17 Folder 271.
27. PHF Series II Box 17 Folder 274.
28. PHF Series II Box 17 Folder 275.
29. PHF Series II Box 17 Folder 277.
30. *The Tower Commission Report: The Full Text of the President's Special Review Board* (New York: Bantam Books and Times Books, 1987).
31. PHF Series II Box 18 Folder 282.
32. PHF Series II Box 18 Folder 283.
33. PHF Series II Box 18 Folder 283.
34. PHF Series II Box 18 Folder 283.
35. PHF Series II Box 18 Folder 284.
36. PHF Series II Box 18 Folder 291.
37. David E. Rosenbaum, "Admiral on Stand," *New York Times,* July 16, 1987, pp. A1, A11.
38. PHF Series II Box 18 Folder 294.
39. PHF Series II Box 18 Folder 297.
40. PHF Series II Box 18 Folder 297.
41. PHF Series II Box 18 Folder 298.
42. PHF Series II Box 18 Folder 299.

CHAPTER FIFTEEN: THE AMERICAS

1. Raymond D. Gastil, *Freedom in the World: Political Rights and Civil Liberties, 1980* (New York: Freedom House, 1980), and *Freedom in the World: Political Rights and Civil Liberties, 1986–1987* (New York: Greenwood Press, 1987).
2. See Reagan's speech on December 13, 1975 in Houston, Texas. CFK Box 103 and RRSC Box 1.
3. Reagan's views on the Panama Canal treaties are presented comprehensively in articles, interviews, speeches, and statements during the 1970s. See his September 8, 1977 Senate testimony. A draft in Reagan's own hand is found in Campaign 1980 Box 924. See also "Reagan on the Canal," *Newsweek,* September 19, 1977, p. 50; Ronald Reagan, "The Canal as Opportunity: New Relationship with Latin America," *Orbis* (Fall 1977): 547–63; and the text of Reagan's February 8, 1978, remarks on CBS-TV following President Carter's fireside chat on the Panama Canal treaties. The text is found in CFR Box 104 Folder Reagan Speeches 1978, and RRSC Box 3 Folder RR Speeches 1978.
4. PPP Box 20 Folder G-H.

5. PPP Box 20 Folder G-H.

6. PPP Box 20 Folder K.

7. PHF Series II Box 20 Folder 331.

8. Earl E. T. Smith served as ambassador to Cuba from 1957 to 1959, the revolutionary period in which Fidel Castro rose to power. On June 15, 1982, President Reagan announced that he was appointing Smith to the Presidential Commission on Broadcasting to Cuba.

9. Campaign 1980 Box 923 Dictation.

10. Campaign 1980 Box 923 Dictation.

11. PHF Series II Box 2 Folder 30.

12. PHF Series II Box 2 Folder 33.

13. AVH RRanch.

14. PHF Series II Box 6 Folder 88.

15. PHF Series II Box 6 Folder 72.

16. PHF Series II Box 6 Folder 87.

17. See Lydia Chavez, "Pope Makes Plea of Reconciliation for Salvadorans: President Tells Him at Airport that Election Will Be This Year Instead of in 1984," *New York Times*, March 7, 1983, p. A1. Elections in El Salvador were actually held on March 25, 1984. On May 6, 1984, a runoff election was held between the Christian Democrat José Napoleón Duarte and the Republican Alliance candidate Roberto D'Aubuisson. Five days later, the Central Elections Council announced that Duarte was the winner with 53.6 percent of the vote. The Contadora process began in January 1983 as a regional attempt to resolve the crises in Central America. Colombia, Mexico, Panama, and Venezuela, the "Core Four," led negotiations to promote democracy and arms reductions in Guatemala, El Salvador, Honduras, Nicaragua, and Costa Rica. The United States and Cuba were not formally a part of the Contadora process, but played an important outside role. Although not ultimately successful, Contadora paved the way for the "Esquipulas process," headed by Costa Rican President Oscar Arias, which resulted in accords that encouraged democracy and peace in the region.

18. AVH RRanch.

19. PHF Series II Box 7 Folder 92.

20. On July 19, 1983, President Reagan announced that he was forming a National Bipartisan Commission on Central America to be chaired by Henry A. Kissinger. The commission was officially established on August 4, and was terminated after it submitted its final report on January 11, 1984.

21. PHF Series II Box 7 Folder 92.

22. PHF Series II Box 7 Folder 93.

23. PHF Series II Box 7 Folder 101.

24. PHF Series II Box 7 Folder 104.

25. For an assessment of the documents and weapons found after the intervention in Grenada see Paul Seabury and Walter A. McDougall, *The Grenada Papers* (San Francisco: Institute for Contemporary Studies Press, 1984), and *Lessons of Grenada* (Washington, DC: Department of State, February 1986), Department of State Publication 9457.

26. PHF Series II Box 8 Folder 106.

27. PHF Series II Box 8 Folder 106.

28. PHF Series II Box 8 Folder 106.

29. PHF Series II Box 8 Folder 109.

30. PHF Series II Box 9 Folder 124.

31. PHF Series II Box 9 Folder 127.

32. PHF Series II Box 9 Folder 128.

33. PHF Series II Box 11 Folder 158.
34. PHF Series II Box 12 Folder 170.
35. PHF Series II Box 12 Folder 173.
36. PHF Series II Box 12 Folder 177.
37. PHF Series II Box 12 Folder 184.
38. PHF Series II Box 15 Folder 233.
39. PHF Series II Box 15 Folder 236.
40. *The Grenada Documents: An Overview and Selection* (Washington, DC: Department of State and Department of Defense, 1984).
41. AVH RRanch.
42. PHF Series II Box 16 Folder 250.
43. AVH RRanch.
44. AVH RRanch.
45. AVH RRanch.
46. A copy of Reagan's statement on November 13, 1979, is found in DH Box 7 Folder Announcement November 13, 1979. See also Robert Lindsey, "Reagan, Entering Presidency Race, Calls for North American 'Accord,'" *New York Times* November 14, 1979.
47. Campaign 1980 Box 923 Dictation.
48. Campaign 1980 Box 923 Dictation.
49. PHF Series II Box 5 Folder 72.
50. Campaign 1980 Box 923 Dictation.
51. Campaign 1980 Box 923 Dictation.
52. "Resolution on the CIA and Third World Countries." The resolution is held at the Church of the Brethren Washington Office.
53. PPP Box 20 Folder S.
54. The quote is in Steven R. Weisman, "Reagan Denounces Threats to Peace in Latin America," *New York Times,* December 5, 1982, pp. 1, 18. See also Warren Hoge, "Reagan Begins His Latin Tour in Cordial Brazil," *New York Times,* December 1, 1982, pp. A1, A12.
55. PHF Series II Box 5 Folder 61.
56. PHF Series II Box 5 Folder 63.

CHAPTER SIXTEEN: THE INTERNATIONAL SCENE

1. Ellen Hume, "Reagan Clarifies Remarks on Rhodesia," *Los Angeles Times,* June 4, 1976, p. 12; and Jon Nordheimer, "Ford, in Ad Shift, Describes Reagan as Peace Threat," *New York Times,* June 6, 1976, pp. 1, 31.
2. PPP Box 20 Folder E–F.
3. Quoted in Kiron K. Skinner, Annelise Anderson, and Martin Anderson, *Reagan, In His Own Hand: The Writings of Ronald Reagan that Reveal His Revolutionary Vision for America* (New York: Free Press, 2001), p. 180. For Kissinger's assessment of his diplomatic activities in southern Africa see his *Years of Renewal* (New York: Simon & Schuster, 1999), pp. 985–1016.
4. PPP Box 20 Folder G–H.
5. PPP Box 20 Folder M.
6. PR011 321301 Audio.
7. PHF Series II Box 11 Folder 163.
8. See Skinner et al., *Reagan, In His Own Hand,* pp. 186–88.
9. PHF Series II Box 13 Folder 205.
10. See "No Aid Offer Seen as Reagan Meets Angola Rebel," *New York Times,* January 31, 1986, p. A6; R.W. Apple, Jr., "Red Carpet for a Rebel, Or How a Star is Born," *New York Times,* Feb-

ruary 7, 1986, p. A16; Steven V. Roberts, "House Panel Said to Ask Reagan to Rethink Aid for Angola Rebels," *New York Times,* February 8, 1986, p. A3; and Gene I. Maeroff, "No Aid, Savimbi Says," *New York Times,* February 8, 1986, p. A3.

11. PHF Series II Box 14 Folder 225.
12. PHF Series II Box 16 Folder 244.
13. PHF Series II Box 16 Folder 247.
14. PHF Series II Box 16 Folder 249.
15. PHF Series VI Box PP3.
16. PHF Series II Box 18 Folder 300.
17. For three radio commentaries about Cambodia that Reagan wrote in 1977 see Skinner et al., *Reagan, In His Own Hand,* pp. 36–41.
18. PHF Series II Box 4 Folder 49.
19. For the schedule of Reagan's trip to Taiwan see "Master Schedule," Hoover Institution Records, Box 1005, Folder Foreign Travel. For his speech in Taiwan on April 21, 1978, see Ronald Reagan, "The American Citizen Views the Republic of China: Taiwan vs. The People's Republic of China," *Vital Speeches* (July 1, 1978). See also Richard Halloran, "Carter's Recognition Step Draws Applause and Anger," *New York Times,* December 16, 1978, p. 10. In a January 15, 1979, letter to Dr. and Mrs. C. F. Koo of Taipei, Taiwan, Reagan wrote: "Just this morning, I taped fifteen commentaries, and five are on the subject of China. I reiterate that we have betrayed not only the people of Taiwan but the people of the mainland who must have been dreaming that one day they might be free. . . . The reason for this series of five coming on as they will now in the next few weeks is because I was waiting for Congress to return. Since I am on a station that is widely listened to by the people of Washington, I wanted to build some pressure to see if Congress wouldn't stand firm against the President's decision." PPP Box 22 Folder RR Chron January 79. See also "Carter's Vow on Taiwan Is Demanded by Reagan," *New York Times,* February 11, 1979, p. 9. A Reagan 1980 campaign circular titled "Ronald Reagan Speaks Out on the Issues" has a section on Taiwan in which President Carter's decision to break relations with Taiwan is attacked. See Deaver and Hannaford, Box 4, Folder RR—General—Position Papers 1980.
20. PPP Box 20 Folder W.
21. PPP Box 20 Folder A–C.
22. Campaign 1980 Box 923 Dictation.
23. Campaign 1980 Box 923 Dictation.
24. Campaign 1980 Box 923 Dictation.
25. PR011321301 Audio.
26. PHF Series II Box 3 Folder 39.
27. PHF Series II Box 5 Folder 61.
28. PHF Series II Box 9 Folder 128.
29. PHF Original.
30. PPP Box 20 Folder T.
31. This letter was written to Holmes Alexander. A typed version is in the archives. RRSC Box 3, Folder RR Correspondence 1980.
32. PPP Box 20 Folder S.
33. PHF Series II Box 18 Folder 290.
34. Ronald Reagan's first visit to the Federal Republic of Germany was in November 1978. Richard Allen, who was traveling with Reagan, has reported that during a visit to the Berlin Wall, Reagan said: "We have to find a way to knock this thing down." Allen provided the authors with this information in a May 27, 2003, memorandum.
35. Campaign 1980 Box 923 Dictation.

36. PHF Series II Box 9 Folder 134.

37. Reagan wrote these words in his April 4–14, 1985, diary entry, which he cites in *Ronald Reagan, An American Life* (New York: Simon & Schuster, 1990), p. 377.

38. Reagan, *An American Life*, p. 384.

39. PHF Series II Box 12 Folder 179.

40. PHF Series II Box 12 Folder 180.

41. PHF Series II Box 12 Folder 180.

42. PHF Series II Box 12 Folder 180.

43. PHF Series II Box 12 Folder 182.

44. PHF Series II Box 12 Folder 184.

45. PHF Series II Box 12 Folder 184.

46. PHF Series II Box 12 Folder 185.

47. The founding members of NATO were: the Kingdom of Belgium, Canada, the Kingdom of Denmark, France, Iceland, Italy, the Grand Duchy of Luxembourg, the Kingdom of the Netherlands, the Kingdom of Norway, Portugal, the United Kingdom, and the United States. The NATO charter is reproduced in Edward H. Judge and John W. Langdon, eds., *The Cold War: A History Through Documents* (Upper Saddle River, New Jersey: Prentice Hall, 1999), pp. 50–52. Spain joined NATO in 1982, and the Czech Republic, Hungary, and Poland joined in March 1999. In November 2002, the following states began accession talks with NATO: Bulgaria, Estonia, Latvia, Lithuania, Romania, Slovakia, and Slovenia.

48. PPP Box 20 Folder A–C.

49. Campaign 1980 Box 919 Folder 6-31.

50. See Julie Johnson, "At NATO Parley, Reagan Reassures," *New York Times*, March 2, 1988, p. A10; and James M. Markham, "For NATO, Reassurance: Nuclear Deterrence Affirmed by Reagan," *New York Times*, March 4, 1988, p. A6.

51. PHF Series II Box 20 Folder 324.

52. PHF Series II Box 15 Folder 230.

53. PHF Series II Box 13 Folder 204.

54. PHF Series II Box 15 Folder 241.

55. See the preface to *The Nelson Rockefeller Report to the President by the Commission on CIA Activities, June 1975* (New York: Manor Books, 1975).

56. Quoted in Skinner et al., *Reagan, In His Own Hand*, p. 121.

57. PPP Box 20 Folder D.

58. PPP Box 20 Folder W.

59. PPP Box 20 Folder S.

60. PPP Box 20 Folder S.

CHAPTER SEVENTEEN: THE OVAL OFFICE AND REELECTION

1. PR011 321301 Audio.

2. PHF Series II Box 4 Folder 50.

3. PHF Series II Box 10 Folder 136. According to published accounts Reagan did not learn of Brady's condition until after his own surgery.

4. PR011 321301 Audio.

5. PHF Original.

6. PHF Series II Box 2 Folder 21.

7. PHF Series II Box 2 Folder 32.

8. PHF Series II Box 3 Folder 39.

9. PHF Series II Box 5 Folder 71.

10. PHF Series II Box 7 Folder 91.
11. Nancy Reagan with William Novak, *My Turn: The Memoirs of Nancy Reagan* (New York: Random House, 1989) pp. 264–65.
12. PHF Series II Box 8 Folder 117.
13. Meese was not confirmed by the Senate until February 23, 1985; he was investigated for ethics violations but the case was dropped.
14. PHF Series II Box 8 Folder 118.
15. PHF Series II Box 9 Folder 122.
16. PHF Series VI Box PL/PP1.
17. PHF Series II Box 9 Folder 123.
18. PHF Series II Box 9 Folder 131. (Michael Barone is mentioned in Lou Cannon, *Ronald Reagan: The Role of a Lifetime* [New York: Simon & Schuster, 1991], p. 511, as considering the campaign over with this speech.)
19. PHF Series II Box 10 Folder 138.
20. PHF Series VI Box PL/PP1.
21. PHF Series VI Box PL/PP1.
22. PHF Series VI Box PL/PP1 and AVH RRanch.
23. PHF Series II Box 10 Folder 145. Mondale's acceptance speech is quoted in Cannon, *Ronald Reagan*, p. 511.
24. PHF Series VI Box PL/PP1.
25. PHF Series II Box 12 Folder 173.
26. PHF Series II Box 11 Folder 166.
27. PHF Series II Box 12 Folder 176.
28. PHF Series II Box 12 Folder 177.
29. PHF Series II Box 13 Folder 193.
30. PHF Series II Box 12 Folder 182.
31. PHF Series II Box 14 Folder 209.
32. PHF Series II Box 14 Folder 223.
33. PHF Series VI Box PL/PP1.
34. PHF Series II Box 17 Folder 276.
35. PHF Series II Box 18 Folder 289. Regan's belief that the letter was drafted by someone else is stated in Donald T. Regan, *For the Record: From Wall Street to Washington* (New York: Harcourt Brace Jovanovich, 1988), p. 374.
36. William E. Pemberton, *Exit with Honor: The Life and Presidency of Ronald Reagan* (Armonk, New York: M.E. Sharpe, 1997), p. 191.
37. PHF Series II Box 18 Folder 293.
38. PHF Series II Box 18 Folder 296.
39. Cannon, *Ronald Reagan*, p. 809.
40. PHF Series II Box 19 Folder 306.
41. PHF Series II Box 19 Folder 311.
42. PHF Series II Box 20 Folder 327B; Regan, *For the Record.* Nancy's own account is given in Nancy Reagan, *My Turn.*
43. Letter to Tom O'Brien, March 22, 1984, PHF Series II Box 9 Folder 122.
44. PHF Series II Box 20 Folder 334.
45. AVH RRanch.
46. PHF Series VI Box PL/PP1.
47. AVH RRanch.
48. PHF Series II Box 21 Folder 345.
49. RR-VP.

50. RR-VP.
51. RR-VP.

CHAPTER EIGHTEEN: THE MEDIA

1. LMW RRanch.
2. William F. Buckley Jr. Papers. Manuscripts and Archives. Yale University Library.
3. LMW RRanch.
4. LMW RRanch.
5. LMW RRanch.
6. PPP Box 20 Folder A–C.
7. Campaign 1980 Box 917.
8. PPP Box 20 Folder S.
9. PPP Box 20 Folder R.
10. Campaign 1980 Box 923 Dictation.
11. Campaign 1980 Box 922 Folder 9-1.
12. Campaign 1980 Box 923 Dictation.
13. Campaign 1980 Box 923 Dictation.
14. Campaign 1980 Box 923 Dictation.
15. Campaign 1980 Box 923 Dictation.
16. PR011 321301 Audio.
17. PHF Series II Box 3 Folder 38.
18. PHF Series II Box 3 Folder 43.
19. PHF Series II Box 3 Folder 43.
20. PHF Series II Box 5 Folder 63.
21. PHF Series II Box 5 Folder 73.
22. PHF Series II Box 6 Folder 75.
23. PHF Series II Box 6 Folder 88.
24. PHF Series II Box 7 Folder 101.
25. PHF Series II Box 7 Folder 102.
26. PHF Series II Box 7 Folder 104.
27. PHF Series II Box 9 Folder 130.
28. PHF Series II Box 10 Folder 138.
29. AVH RRanch.
30. PHF Series II Box 13 Folder 189.
31. PHF Series II Box 14 Folder 208.
32. PHF Series II Box 14 Folder 221.
33. PHF Series II Box 16 Folder 245.
34. PHF Series II Box 16 Folder 246.
35. PHF Series II Box 16 Folder 246.
36. PHF Series II Box 16 Folder 258.
37. PHF Series II Box 18 Folder 283.
38. PHF Series II Box 18 Folder 284.
39. PHF Series II Box 18 Folder 291.

CHAPTER NINETEEN: THE CRITICS

1. Collection of Martin Anderson.
2. PPP Box 20 Folder R.

3. PPP Box 20 Folder S.
4. William F. Buckley Jr. Papers. Manuscripts and Archives. Yale University Library.
5. PPP Box 18479.
6. PPP Box 20 Folder X–Z.
7. Campaign 1980 Box 923 Dictation.
8. PHF Series II Box 1 Folder 12.
9. PHF Series II Box 1 Folder 12.
10. PHF Series II Box 2 Folder 31.
11. PHF Series II Box 2 Folder 33.
12. PHF Series II Box 4 Folder 48.
13. PHF Series II Box 4 Folder 49.
14. PHF Series II Box 5 Folder 63.
15. PHF Series II Box 5 Folder 69.
16. PHF Series II Box 5 Folder 69.
17. PHF Series II Box 5 Folder 70.
18. PHF Series II Box 6 Folder 79.
19. PHF Series II Box 6 Folder 88.
20. PHF Series II Box 6 Folder 88.
21. PHF Series II Box 7 Folder 95.
22. PHF Series II Box 7 Folder 98.
23. PHF Series II Box 7 Folder 99.
24. PHF Series II Box 8 Folder 109.
25. PHF Series II Box 8 Folder 116.
26. PHF Series II Box 9 Folder 129.
27. PHF Series II Box 9 Folder 129.
28. PHF Series II Box 9 Folder 129.
29. Presidential Records, Ronald Reagan Library.
30. PHF Series II Box 9 Folder 131.
31. PHF Series II Box 10 Folder 136.
32. PHF Series II Box 10 Folder 144.
33. PHF Series VI Box PL/PP1.

CHAPTER TWENTY: REACHING OUT

1. Letter quoted from Campaign 1980 Box 915:2–4; story about rocking chair from Helene von Damm, ed., *Sincerely, Ronald Reagan* (New York: Berkley Books, 1980), p. 132.
2. PPP Box 20 Folder O.
3. PPP Box 20 Folder S.
4. PPP Box 20 Folder M.
5. PHF Series II Box 8 Folder 118.
6. PHF Series II Box 10 Folder 143.
7. PHF Series II Box 19 Folder 312.
8. Ronald Reagan, *Where's the Rest of Me?* (New York: Duell, Sloan & Pearce, 1965), p. 55.
9. Letter to Mrs. Coulombe, circa 1967–74, PPP Box 20 Folder A–C.
10. President Reagan met on September 21, 1981, with representatives of the private sector engaged in volunteer work and created a task force on private sector initiatives on October 14, 1981.
11. In addition to the contributions mentioned in the letters in this chapter, Reagan contributed to the George Gipp Recreation Area in Laurium, Michigan (PHF II 17:262), and

also to such diverse recipients as the St. Vincent's School of Santa Barbara, a training center for developmentally disabled children; the National Foundation for Cancer Research in 1986; the Alice Faye Christmas Fantasy, December 10, 1987, at the Joslyn Cove Communities Senior Center in Rancho Mirage, California; the Horatio Alger Association in New York City, December 10, 1987; and Project Children in 1987 and 1988 to sponsor a child from Northern Ireland to come to America for summer vacation (AVH RRanch). No systematic record of his contributions or the recipients exists, and we have not seen his cancelled checks or check registers, if indeed they still exist.

12. Reagan's tax returns for 1981 through 1983 and 1985 through 1987, released to the public during the presidency, show average charitable donations of about 5 percent of adjusted gross income. The 1984 tax return was not seen by the editors.
13. PHF Original Legal.
14. PHF Series II Box 4 Folder 55.
15. In addition to Eureka College, the other specifically itemized contribution on Ronald and Nancy Reagan's tax returns during the presidency is to Northwestern University Medical School, where Nancy's father was on the faculty.
16. AVH RRanch.
17. PHF Series II Box 8 Folder 108.
18. PHF Series II Box 2 Folder 155.
19. PHF Series II Box 11 Folder 162.
20. PHF Original.
21. AVH RRanch.
22. PHF Series II Box 12 Folder 186.
23. PHF Series II Box 14 Folder 219.
24. PHF Series II Box 16 Folder 247.
25. RRGC Box 2.
26. PPP Box 20 Folder G–H.
27. PHF Series II Box 10 Folder 145.
28. Collection of Kathleen Osborne.
29. PHF Series II Box 20 Folder 335.

CHAPTER TWENTY-ONE: THE LIGHTER SIDE

1. Interview with Connie Mackey, May 2, 2002.
2. Ronald Reagan, *Where's the Rest of Me?* (New York: Duell, Sloan & Pearce, 1965), p. 19.
3. PHF Series VI Box PP1.
4. PHF Series II Box 9 Folder 126. Fred Ryan, who worked for Michael Deaver, flagged Smith's letter as "the unique request of the week."
5. PHF Series II Box 6 Folder 76.
6. PHF Series II Box 5 Folder 73.
7. PHF Series II Box 9 Folder 120.
8. PHF Series II Box 18 Folder 288. This letter is an example in which the letter the recipient receives differs from the letter the president drafted; Courtney is sent a schedule for an average day instead of an advance schedule, which would be a potential security risk to the president if made public. In spite of such occasional changes, the president always saw and signed the final letter (interviews with Connie Mackey and Kathy Osborne).
9. PPP Box 20 Folder I–L.
10. PHF Series II Box 4 Folder 54.
11. PHF Series II Box 4 Folder 59.

12. PHF Series II Box 9 Folder 120.
13. PHF Series II Box 12 Folder 170.
14. RR-VP.
15. PHF Series II Box 20 Folder 322.
16. PHF Series II Box 4 Folder 54.
17. PHF Series II Box 18 Folder 288.
18. PHF Series II Box 11 Folder 162.
19. PHF Series II Box 10 Folder 141.
20. PHF Series II Box 8 Folder 115.
21. PHF Series II Box 10 Folder 143.
22. PHF Series II Box 4 Folder 53.
23. PHF Series II Box 2 Folder 23.
24. PPP Box 20 Folder D.
25. PPP Box 20 Folder S and HVD pp. 159–60.
26. Campaign 1980 Box 922 Folder 9-3.
27. Campaign 1980 Box 923 Dictation.
28. PHF Series II Box 8 Folder 119.
29. Campaign 1980 Box 923 Dictation.
30. PHF Series II Box 2 Folder 33.
31. PHF Series II Box 6 Folder 85.
32. PHF Series II Box 5 Folder 73.
33. PHF Series II Box 1 Folder 11.
34. PHF Series VI Box PP2.
35. PHF Series II Box 1 Folder 12.
36. PHF Series II Box 10 Folder 151.
37. PHF Series II Box 7 Folder 93.
38. PHF Series II Box 16 Folder 259.
39. PHF Series II Box 20 Folder 327A.
40. PHF Series II Box 10 Folder 151.
41. PHF Series II Box 17 Folder 279.
42. RRGC Box 1.
43. Mary Joan Roll-Sieffert, *The Real Ronald Reagan: A True Humanitarian* (Belleville, Ontario, Canada: Eric Press, 2003), pp. 88–89 (facsimile on p. 88). Letters from Bess Reagan to Joan (pp. 103–04 and 106–07) tell of Nelle's senility.
44. RRGC Box 3.
45. RRGC Box 3.
46. RNLB.

CHAPTER TWENTY-TWO: AMERICAN LEADERS

1. For instance, while Reagan was on the campaign trail in Illinois on March 10, 1976, Reagan said: "I think the first step [toward revising U.S. foreign policy] is to replace Dr. Kissinger with a new Secretary of State." See CFR Box 102 Folder 5–15 Press Releases, 1975, 1976.
2. AVH RRanch.
3. PHF Series II Box 21 Folder 341.
4. PHF Series II Box 14 Folder 219.
5. AVH.
6. Dana Adams Schmidt, "Northrop Gets Contract for Jet to Be Sold to Allies in Asia," *New York Times,* November 21, 1970, p. 12.

7. NARA-Nixon.

8. Campaign 1980 Box 915 Folder 2-2.

9. For a review of Kissinger's criticism of the SALT II treaty see Karen Elliott House, "Kissinger Advocates Linkage of SALT to Huge Increases in Military Spending," *Wall Street Journal*, August 1, 1979, p. A1, and Charles Mohr, "Kissinger Suggests Senate Link Treaty to More Arms Funds," *New York Times*, August 1, 1979, pp. A1, A6. For Reagan's thinking on SALT II see his speech before the Republican State Central Committee in San Diego on September 15, 1979. It is found in CFR Box 104 Folder 1–6 RR Speeches 1979, and RRSC Box 3 Folder RR Speeches 1979.

10. Campaign 1980 Box 917 Folder 4-1.

11. Campaign 1980 Box 923 Dictation.

12. David S. Broder, "Eisenhower Meets Reagan and Backs Him for Governor," *New York Times*, June 16, 1966, pp. 1, 30.

13. DDEL.

14. DDEL.

15. DDEL.

16. NARA PR-LN.

17. Osgood Caruthers, "Nixon Tells Russians End of Fear Depends on Khrushchev Tactics: Allies Back U.S. Visit by Premier," *New York Times*, August 2, 1959, pp. 1, 24.

18. NARA PR-LN.

19. NARA PR-LN.

20. NARA PR-LN.

21. NARA PR-LN.

22. RNLB Collections.

23. Lawrence E. Davies, "Nixon and Reagan in Informal Talks," *New York Times*, July 24, 1967, p. 14.

24. RNLB.

25. RNLB.

26. RRC Box 1 RRGC.

27. RNLB.

28. Jo Thomas, "Nixon, Hailed in Kentucky Town, Stresses the Need for U.S. Strength," *New York Times*, July 3, 1978, pp. 1, 7.

29. RNLB.

30. RNLB.

31. RNLB.

32. RNLB.

33. RNLB.

34. RNLB.

35. RNLB.

36. RNLB.

37. RNLB.

38. RNLB.

39. RNLB.

40. PPP Box 20 Folder G–H.

41. PPP Box 20 Folder T.

42. Campaign 1980 Box 923 Dictation.

43. PHF Series II Box 6 Folder 79.

44. PHF Series II Box 12 Folder 176.

45. PHF Series II Box 20 Folder 326.

46. Concerning President Gorbachev's visit to the San Francisco area in June 1990, see R. W.

Apple, Jr., "Gorbachev Urges Major Changes In the World's System of Alliances," *New York Times,* June 5, 1990, pp. A1 and A16. "Reagan, on a Visit, Warns Soviets Not to Let Revolt Get Out of Hand," *New York Times,* September 18, 1990, p. A6.

47. RR-VP.

48. The "P.S." is the only part of this letter that is handwritten. It is handwritten on the typed version that is found in the private papers of Ronald Reagan.

49. RR-VP.

CHAPTER TWENTY-THREE: FOREIGN LEADERS

1. George P. Shultz, *Turmoil and Triumph: My Years as Secretary of State* (New York: Charles Scribner's Sons, 1993), p. 1135.

2. PR011321301 Audio.

3. PHF Series II Box 1 Folder 10.

4. PHF Series II Box 16 Folder 227.

5. PHF Series II Box 5 Folder 73.

6. PPP Box 20 Folder A–C.

7. For a review of these trips see Peter Hannaford, *The Reagans: A Political Portrait* (New York: Coward-McCann, 1983), pp. 64 and 188.

8. Campaign 1980 Box 923 Dictation.

9. PHF Series II Box 6 Folder 82.

10. PHF Series II Box 12 Folder 186.

11. PHF Series II Box 15 Folder 237.

12. PHF Series II Box 17 Folder 275.

13. The collection of Margaret Thatcher.

14. RR-VP.

15. PHF Series II Box 11 Folder 156.

16. PHF Original Legal.

17. PPP Box 4 Folder L.

18. PHF Series II Box 9 Folder 132.

19. PHF Series II Box 17 Folder 277.

20. Terence Smith, "Peres Tells Carter of West Bank Plan," *New York Times,* April 25, 1980, p. A3.

21. Campaign 1980 Box 923 Dictation.

22. Bernard Weinraub, "Reagan Vows to Finish his 'Revolution,'" *New York Times,* November 6, 1986, p. A29.

23. PHF Series VI Box PL/PP1.

24. PHF Series II Box 18 Folder 282.

25. PHF Series II Box 20 Folder 321.

26. Campaign 1980 Box 923 Dictation.

27. PHF Series II Box 3 Folder 43.

28. RRGC Box 1.

29. Campaign 1980 Box 923 Dictation.

30. PHF Series II Box 18 Folder 292.

31. PHF Series II Box 8 Folder 119.

32. PHF Series II Box 12 Folder 173.

33. RR-VP.

34. LMW RRanch.

35. Anatoly Dobrynin. *In Confidence: Moscow's Ambassador to America's Six Cold War Presidents (1962–1986)* (New York: Random House, 1995), p. 282.

36. Ronald Reagan, *An American Life* (New York: Simon & Schuster, 1990), p. 636. Reagan's remarks to Gorbachev are also summarized in Don Oberdorfer, *The Turn: From the Cold War to a New Era: The United States and the Soviet Union 1983–1990* (New York: Random House, 1995), p. 144, and in the official U.S. Department of State memorandum F96-087#56 in the Ronald Reagan Library. Reagan's talking points for his meeting with Gromyko are printed in Kiron K. Skinner, Annelise Anderson, and Martin Anderson, *Reagan*, eds., *In His Own Hand* (New York: Free Press, 2001), pp. 496–98.

37. NSC HOS-USSR Box 40 8591143-8591239, handwritten letter to General Secretary Gorbachev, November 28, 1985.

38. PHF Series II Box 6 Folder 84.

39. Interview with George P. Shultz, March 18, 2003. See Shultz, *Turmoil and Triumph*, for details on the Williamsburg summit (pp. 352–53) and Reagan's meetings with Chinese leaders (pp. 395–97).

40. Letters from Soviet Leaders often took four to six weeks to answer. Reagan's approval of the March 26, 1981, memorandum from Richard V. Allen recommending that the formal letter be sent back to the Department of State for redrafting is in NSC HOS-USSR Box 37 8100630. State also revised the draft in early April to reflect a strongly worded U.S. "hot line" cable about possible USSR military intervention in Poland and the Soviet response to that cable (NSC HOS-USSR Box 38 8190199-8190201).

41. Quoted in Edmund Morris, *Dutch: A Memoir of Ronald Reagan* (New York: Random House, 1999), p. 437. On April 21, 1981, Reagan wrote in his diary, "I should know today whether my letter to Brezhnev has passed inspection by the striped pants set." *Personal Diary of President Ronald Reagan,* quoted with permission of the Ronald Reagan Presidential Foundation (RRPF).

42. The April 22, 1981, diary entry is from the *Personal Diary of President Ronald Reagan,* quoted with permission of the RRPF. In addition to the diary, accounts of the drafting of the April 24, 1981, letter to Brezhnev are given in Michael K. Deaver, *Behind the Scenes* (New York: William Morrow, 1987), pp. 262–63, Reagan, *An American Life,* pp. 267–271, and Richard V. Allen (letter to Annelise Anderson, August 21, 2002), although Deaver gets the date wrong. Allen recalls that the president had his yellow-pad draft hand-carried to Allen at the NSC. Allen's attempt to combine the two drafts is in NSC HOS-USSR Box 38 8190202-8190303 dated "Rev. 4/22/81." In his final handwritten letter Reagan adopted a few suggestions from Allen, including the sentence "Perhaps this decision will contribute to creating the circumstances which will lead to the meaningful and constructive dialogue which will assist us in fulfilling our joint obligation to find lasting peace." (NSC HOS-USSR Box 38 8190204-8190205. Allen's edits on PRESIDENT'S ORIGINAL.) Allen is also certain that the Department of State never saw Reagan's handwritten draft (although they probably saw Allen's attempt to combine the two drafts). Both Deaver and Reagan are convinced that State saw Reagan's draft, but the draft they saw may have been an earlier effort of Reagan's to draft a letter to Brezhnev; Haig told Lou Cannon that "very early on" Reagan drafted a letter to Brezhnev on a weekend at Camp David and showed it to Haig the following Monday morning; Haig claims to have persuaded Reagan not to send it. See Lou Cannon, *President Reagan: The Role of a Lifetime* (New York: Simon & Schuster, 1991), p. 301. By March 30, 1981, Reagan had spent four weekends at Camp David, including the weekend after Brezhnev's letter arrived on March 6, 1981. "When I told him I was thinking of writing a personal letter to Brezhnev," Reagan says in *An American Life* (p. 270), "he was reluctant to have *me* actually draft it."

43. "Attached is script of letter I wrote to Brezhnev by hand," Reagan wrote in his diary on April 23, 1981 (*Personal Diary of President Ronald Reagan,* quoted with permission of the RRPF).

Quotation about sending it "as originally written" from Reagan, *An American Life*, p. 271. Secretary of State Alexander Haig delivered the letters to Soviet Ambassador Anatoly Dobrynin April 25, 1981. "Haig brought me not one but two letters from Reagan," Dobrynin wrote. "The first was a formal reply . . . the other was written in Reagan's own hand. . . . Haig had received it from Reagan himself at the same time he was handed the formal reply." Dobrynin, *In Confidence*, p. 492. Richard Pipes of the NSC, who edited State's draft of the formal letter, recorded in his journal that Allen told him on April 24 that "Both letters went. . . . the president's letter on top of yours." Letter from Richard Pipes to Annelise Anderson, November 2, 2002. The final handwritten letter to Brezhnev reflects the April 21, 1981, decision to lift the grain embargo, several word changes, and Allen's suggestion quoted in the above note. All changes can be traced in the NSC documents cited. Reagan quotes the final text in *An American Life*, pp. 272–73; a copy of the final handwritten letter is in NSC HOS-USSR Box 38 8190204-8190205. Dobrynin (*In Confidence*, p. 492) later wrote regarding the handwritten letter, "I found that it was animated by the classic idea of America's invariable goodwill in international affairs."

44. The handwritten original is located in the Policy and Public Service Papers of James A. Baker III, Seeley G. Mudd Manuscript Library, Princeton University. A typescript labeled PRESIDENT'S ORIGINAL exists in NSC HOS-USSR Box 38 8190204-8190205. A second typescript with a few word changes by Richard V. Allen and corrections of typist's errors is labeled SLIGHTLY REVISED. These documents are untitled and undated. Reagan referred to his April 24, 1981, letter when he edited a November 16, 1981, State Department draft of a later letter to Brezhnev (a reply to an October 15, 1981, letter to Brezhnev): "Dick—I felt it should be shortened so forgive my slashing. Also I tried to give it something of the tone of my first letter.—Ron" (NSC HOS-USSR Box 37 8106607).

45. The NSC draft of June 8, 1981, is available in NSC HOS-USSR Box 37 8103356-8105534.

46. Shultz, *Turmoil and Triumph*, p. 170. The Soviets allowed the Vashchenkos to leave their village in June and the Chmykhalovs in July 1983. The long-term grain agreement was concluded on July 28 and signed on August 25, 1983 (p. 281).

47. NSC HOS-USSR Box 38 8190204-8190205, Memorandum for the President from Richard V. Allen, May 28, 1981, "Leonid Brezhnev's Letter of March 28, 1981."

48. NSC HOS-USSR Box 37 8105534.

49. Shultz, *Turmoil and Triumph*, pp. 164–65, 167–71.

50. Collection of William P. Clark, July 9, 1983, to Mr. President, Subject "Your Reply to Andropov." The replacement for the final paragraph reads:

> *Mr. General Secretary, you and I share an enormous responsibility for the preservation of stability in [the] world. I believe we can fulfill that mandate but that to do so will require a more active level of exchange than we have hitherto been able to establish. We have much to talk about with regard to the situation in Eastern Europe, South Asia and particularly this hemisphere as well as in such areas as arms control, trade between our two countries and other ways in which we can expand east-west contacts. Historically our predecessors have made better progress when communicating has been private and candid. If you wish to enage in such communication you will find me ready. I await your reply.*

51. Collection of William P. Clark, handwritten note dated July 13, 1983: "George [Shultz] read & liked letter. We agreed Art [Arthur Hartman, U.S. ambassador to the Soviet Union] should take it in—he, however, suggested other options. Dob [Dobrynin] goes in to see George Friday morning & then to Moscow. George says it's too late for him to go to Moscow. wpc." Dobrynin, *In Confidence*, p. 530, reports that the letter was delivered by the American ambassador in Moscow on July 21.

52. Collection of William P. Clark. A copy of the final handwritten letter to Andropov is in NSC HOS-USSR Box 38 8290913-8391032.

53. Reagan's comment is in NSC HOS-USSR Box 39 8401238. The letter was drafted in accordance with NSDD 137, issued March 31, 1984, which requested that "a letter to Chernenko be drafted focusing on START and INF—the flexibility we have shown to date, our readiness to reopen talks anytime, anywhere, etc.—and refuting Soviet allegations about the U.S. threat." April 6, 1984, Memorandum for the president from George P. Shultz, "Response to Chernenko's March 19 Letter," NSC HOS-USSR Box 39 8490236-8490448.

54. Electronic mail from Robert C. McFarlane to Annelise Anderson, May 2, 2003.

55. NSC HOS-USSR Box 39 8490695.

56. NSC HOS-USSR Box 39 8490236-8490448.

57. Electronic mail from Robert C. McFarlane to Annelise Anderson, May 2, 2003.

58. NSC HOS-USSR Box 40 8591293. The February 16, 1985, letter to Gorbachev was drafted by Jack Matlock of the NSC.

59. NSC HOS-USSR Box 40 8591143-8591239.

Chapter Twenty-four: Pen Pals

1. Many of the early letters to Lorraine were written by Reagan's mother Nelle because she answered fan mail on his behalf. Within a few years, however, Reagan was writing to Lorraine in his own hand. His earliest letters to Lorraine were typically handwritten, but beginning in the 1960s much more of his correspondence was typed. In a letter dated July 11, 1963, Reagan explained to Lorraine why his letters were less frequently written by hand: "Reason for the typing. I have a girl helping because I'm working on a book." He was referring to his first autobiography, *Where's the Rest of Me?* During the late 1970s, when the advertising firm Deaver and Hannaford managed Reagan's activities, and during his presidency, Lorraine received typed and handwritten letters. Given that some of the letters during this period were written by his staff, we have included mainly letters for which a handwritten draft exists.

2. Telephone interview with Lorraine Wagner on March 27, 2003.

3. Reagan's letters to Ruddy were typed, but the captions on photographs were in Reagan's handwriting. In an interview with Kiron K. Skinner on December 6, 2002, in Arlington, Virginia, Stephanie Lee, Ruddy's mother, said that she has kept President Reagan's letters to Ruddy. She has typed copies of Reagan's letters. The handwritten drafts of those letters are found in private and open files at the Ronald Reagan Library. In a few instances, only the typed version has been found in the archives. As Stephanie Lee noted in a September 21, 1984, interview for the *Washington Post,* Reagan's typed letters sometimes included marginal notes written by hand. Lee told Skinner that there was some correspondence between Reagan and Ruddy after the presidency. The authors did not find this correspondence in letters given to them by Reagan's post-presidency office in Los Angeles, California.

4. Martin Weil and Lawrence Feinberg, "Rudolph's Red-Letter Day: Reagan Surprises Pen Pal with Dinner Visit," *Washington Post,* September 22, 1984. In Kiron Skinner's interview with William Dalton, Stephanie Lee, and Rudolph Lee-Hines, it was explained that Rudolph wrote his own letters, sometimes typed them on a computer, and that Mr. Dalton or his teacher would make grammatical corrections but the content of the letters was fully Rudolph's. Interview on December 6, 2002, in Arlington, Virginia.

5. Donnie Radcliffe, "The Reagans, Hanging in There," *Washington Post,* November 16, 1989.

6. Zelda Multz was the third president of the international fan club dedicated to Reagan's acting career. Arlene Polito and Terry Sevigny were the first and second presidents, respectively.

Lorraine Wagner provided Kiron K. Skinner with this information in a telephone interview on March 27, 2003. Only a few of Reagan's letters to Multz are in the open and private files at the Ronald Reagan Library. Two of the letters in the archives and a letter in Multz's possession are reproduced in this chapter. The Multz-Reagan correspondence is for sale through University Archives (www.universityarchives.com).

7. LMW RRanch.
8. LMW RRanch.
9. Peter Kihss, "Hiss Holds Nixon Was Opportunist," *New York Times*, November 12, 1962, pp. 1, 23.
10. LMW RRanch.
11. LMW RRanch.
12. LMW RRanch.
13. Joseph W. Sullivan, "Pressure is Mounting to Nullify High Court Ban on School Prayer," *Wall Street Journal*, April 22, 1964, p. 1.
14. LMW RRanch.
15. LMW RRanch.
16. "Excerpts From Goldwater Remarks at G.O.P. Platform Session," *New York Times*, July 11, 1964, p. 8.
17. LMW RRanch.
18. LMW RRanch.
19. LMW RRanch.
20. LMW RRanch.
21. LMW RRanch.
22. LMW RRanch.
23. LMW RRanch.
24. LMW RRanch.
25. LMW RRanch.
26. LMW RRanch.
27. Lawrence E. Davies, "Reagan Dropping Health Director," *New York Times*, December 27, 1967, p. 73.
28. LMW RRanch.
29. LMW RRanch.
30. LMW RRanch.
31. LMW RRanch.
32. LMW RRanch.
33. See Lou Cannon, *Reagan* (New York: G. P. Putnam's Sons, 1982), pp. 132–38, and Lyn Nofziger, *Nofziger* (Washington, D.C.: Regnery Gateway, 1992), pp. 74–82.
34. LMW RRanch.
35. LMW RRanch.
36. LMW RRanch.
37. LMW RRanch.
38. LMW RRanch.
39. Wallace Turner, "An Outspoken Governor," *New York Times*, July 13, 1971, p. 14.
40. LMW RRanch.
41. LMW RRanch.
42. LMW RRanch and PPP Box 20 Folder W.
43. LMW RRanch.
44. LMW RRanch and PPP Box 20 Folder W.
45. LMW RRanch.
46. LMW RRanch.

47. LMW RRanch and PPP Box 20 Folder W.
48. LMW RRanch and PPP Box 20 Folder W.
49. LMW RRanch and PPP Box 20 Folder W.
50. LMW RRanch.
51. LMW RRanch.
52. LMW RRanch and PPP Box 20 Folder T.
53. LMW RRanch.
54. LMW RRanch.
55. Campaign 1980 Box 923 Dictation.
56. LMW RRanch.
57. LMW RRanch.
58. LMW RRanch.
59. PPP Box 20 Folder M.
60. AVH RRanch.
61. Collection of Zelda Multz.
62. PHF Series VI Box PP2.
63. PHF Series VI Box PP2.
64. PHF Series VI Box PP2.
65. PHF Series VI Box PP2.
66. Jim Ostroff, "Sincerely Ron," *Life,* November 1988, p. 204. This story was also recounted in Kiron Skinner's interview with William Dalton, Rudolph Lee-Hines, and Stephanie Lee on December 6, 2002, in Arlington, Virginia.
67. PHF Series VI Box PP4 and PHF Original Legal.
68. PHF Original Legal.
69. PFF Series VI Box PP2.
70. PHF Series II Box 11 Folder 156.
71. PHF Series II Box 11 Folder 161.
72. PHF Series II Box 12 Folder 172.
73. PHF Series II Box 12 Folder 175.
74. PHF Series II Box 12 Folder 179.
75. PHF Series VI Box PL/PP1.
76. PHF Series II Box 13 Folder 200.
77. PHF Series II Box 13 Folder 207.
78. PHF Series VI Box PL/PP1.
79. PHF Series II Box 15 Folder 237.
80. PHF Series II Box 15 Folder 238.
81. PHF Series VI Box PP3.
82. See Francis X. Clines, "Reagan's Doubts on Dr. King Disclosed," *New York Times,* October 22, 1983, p. 7. The date of the telephone conversation is confirmed in the Presidential Daily Diary, Ronald Reagan Library.
83. PHF Series VI Box PP3.
84. PHF Series II Box 17 Folder 262 and AVH RRanch.
85. PHF Series II Box PP3.
86. PHF Series II Box 17 Folder 273.
87. PHF Series II Box PP3.
88. PHF Series VI Box PP3.
89. PHF Series VI Box PP4.
90. PHF Series VI Box PP4.
91. PHF Series II Box 19 Folder 318.

CHAPTER TWENTY-FIVE: BACK TO CALIFORNIA

1. RNLB.
2. Collection of Margaret Thatcher, Churchill College Archives.
3. LMW RRanch.
4. Collection of James E. Rogan.
5. Eureka College Archives.
6. Collection of Helen Lawton.
7. Collection of Kathleen Osborne.
8. RNLB.
9. Collection of Edward Fike.
10. RR-VP.
11. LMW RRanch.
12. Collection of Walter Annenberg.
13. RNLB.
14. LMW RRanch.
15. LMW RRanch.
16. Collection of Robert Lindsey.
17. RNLB.
18. LMW RRanch.
19. RNLB.
20. Collection of Martin Anderson.
21. Collection of R. Emmett Tyrrell.
22. LMW RRanch.
23. LMW RRanch.
24. LMW RRanch.
25. LMW RRanch.
26. LMW RRanch.
27. LMW RRanch.
28. RR-VP.
29. RNLB.
30. RR-VP.
31. RR-VP.
32. RR-VP.
33. RR-VP.
34. RR-VP.
35. Collection of Walter Annenberg.
36. RR-VP.
37. RR-VP.
38. RR-VP.
39. Collection of Helen Lawton.
40. RR-VP.

ACKNOWLEDGMENTS

ᴛɪoɴs have been raised about how Ronald Reagan rose to power,
governed, how he felt about things like religion, family and Holly-
Mᴀt kind of man he was. Hundreds of books have been written in an at-
lve this puzzle. And, undoubtedly, hundreds more will be written as
ᴠs continue to examine the record.

until we unearthed the massive trove of his personal letters, no one sus-
ᴅ that Reagan himself would provide the answers. These personal, private
ᴇrs—the heart of this book—tell the story of how Reagan did what he did, and
what kind of man he was, in his own handwritten words.

Many people were part of what we called the "Reagan project," which found the
letters in dozens of different places, catalogued and analyzed them, and then tried
to place them in historical context.

The key person in making this happen was Nancy Reagan, who opened Ronald
Reagan's private correspondence to us. Nancy had not read all of the letters that sat
in those sealed archival and storage boxes, and she realized they were Reagan's private thoughts, not meant for publication. But she has known him intimately for
more than 50 years and was confident that whatever we found, it would be the genuine Reagan. She told us simply, "I just want people to know who Ronnie is." With
the exception of letters that dealt with personal financial matters or with medical
examinations, we had free rein to select and publish. Moreover, Nancy graciously
answered many of our questions and helped us identify some of the people to
whom he wrote.

In 2000 Nancy published a book of the love letters Reagan had written to her
over many decades, *I Love You, Ronnie.** Our book, *Reagan: A Life in Letters,* of
1,100 of his other letters, opens to the public another substantial body of private
communication of a former president.

Joanne Drake, President Reagan's chief of staff in California, played an instrumental role in providing access to his papers. In addition, drawing on the many
years she spent with Reagan, she provided us with advice and ideas on many aspects
of the project.

---

* Nancy Reagan, *I Love You, Ronnie* Random House: New York, 2000, 189 pages.

A special acknowledgment goes to Mark B\.son, the executive director of the Ronald Reagan Presidential Foundation. Mark h\.\.een an integral part of the Rea- gan project since its inception and has been insti\.ental, together with Joanne Drake, in facilitating our access to the private papers o\.\.ald Reagan that are kept in the vaults of the Ronald Reagan Presidential Librai\.imi Valley, California. Besides expanding the activities of the library over the pa\.ears, including the coming display of *Air Force One,* Mark has provided valu\.idance in many ways.

George P. Shultz, the Thomas W. and Susan B. Ford Distingu\.\.ow at the Hoover Institution, has given us strategic counsel on the Reagan p\.\.ng the four years we have worked on it. Drawing on his long, close associa\.\.\.\. gan as his secretary of state, Shultz wrote a Foreword for our book tha\.\.fa- with additional insight into Reagan's character. It underlines the importa\.\.fa- derstanding Reagan by tracing the trajectory of his national security and ec\. policies. In addition, Secretary Shultz secured two valuable collections of lette\. this book—letters that Reagan wrote to Margaret Thatcher and to Walter Ann\. berg.

We especially want to acknowledge the role of our editor at Free Press, Bruce Nichols. He has worked with us since the spring of 2000 when we began our first book, *Reagan, In His Own Hand.* With great skill, judgment, and dedication he has patiently worked with each of us throughout this project. His good sense and good humor were indispensable as we analyzed over 5,000 handwritten letters and se- lected 1,100 finalists; at times his firm hand was crucial in navigating us through the shoals of sustained collaboration. He was particularly helpful as we organized and shaped the structure of the book. Bruce is a great editor.

The other key people who worked with Bruce Nichols provided invaluable help. Casey Reivich and Christopher Litman, his assistants, fielded many questions that arose as we worked on the book. Cassie Dendurent worked diligently on pub- licity, and Carol de Onís, the copyediting supervisor, skillfully guided us through the jungles of copyediting a 1,000-plus page manuscript.

Anne Hawkins, our agent in New York, has consistently been of great help at every step of this book, just as she was on our earlier books—*Reagan, In His Own Hand, Stories in His Own Hand,* and *Reagan in His Own Voice.* We value her coun- sel and judgment, and especially the encouragement she has always offered us at critical times.

We wish to acknowledge with special gratitude the funding that was provided by supporters of the Hoover Institution. A major grant in support of the Reagan project and the efforts of the Hoover Institution to make it possible came from the late Barton A. Stebbins of Laguna Beach, California, and his trustee, Donald W. Crowell of San Marino, California. Mr. Stebbins, who died in 1999, held Ronald Reagan in the highest regard, both as a person and as an inspirational leader. He "would have been deeply honored by the opportunity to help underwrite the com- munication of this powerful message about the man who changed our world for the better, in public ways and, as this book shows, in so many private and personal ways," said his trustee, Mr. Crowell.

Tad Taube of Woodside, California, a longtime Overseer of the Hoover Institution, was one of the first to recognize the importance of understanding Reagan's character and leadership style, and he provided generous support in the early stages of the project. Taube was joined by the Honorable L. W. "Bill" Lane Jr. of Portola Valley, California, an old personal friend of Reagan's, who also provided support and counsel.

Kiron Skinner would like to thank the John M. Olin Foundation and its executive director, James Piereson, and Dean of Humanities and Social Sciences at Carnegie Mellon University, John Lehoczky, for funding some of her research for this book.

The scholarly resources of the Hoover Institution and Stanford University, and the strong, consistent support and counsel of the director of the Hoover Institution, John Raisian, were vital to the project. We had a support staff of five research assistants and secretaries that made it possible to identify, analyze, and keep track of thousands of handwritten letter drafts from many sources.

An important part of the Hoover Institution support came from Elena Danielson, the Assistant Director for Library and Archives. Most notable was her assistance in finding the extensive handwritten Reagan material that was part of his gubernatorial papers, which were originally donated to the Hoover Archives and later given to the Reagan Presidential Library. Special thanks go to Linda Bernard, the deputy archivist, and Carol Leadenham, the reference archivist; two archivists who worked on the collection earlier and are now retired, Molly Sturgis and Pruda Lood; and reference librarian Molly Molloy.

The administrative staff was vital to the effective functioning of the project and we especially want to express our appreciation to Associate Director Richard Sousa, Bill Bonnett, Helen Corrales, Craig Snaar, Kelly Doran, Frank Coronado, Claudia Hubbard, Karen Kenlay, Deborah Ventura, Celeste Szeto, and Dan Wilhelmi. We also wish to recognize Noah Corwin and Jeremy Weis, technicians at Central Computer Systems, who built some of our computers and kept them operating.

One of the most difficult aspects of writing this book was not so much locating Reagan's handwritten letters (although in many case that did require quite a bit of ingenuity), but rather in keeping track of the letters we did find. Each handwritten draft that we considered to be important was initially copied on acid-free paper, carefully typed, and inserted into our computer database. Then each letter in the database was entered into a spreadsheet that gave key information about each letter: the recipient, the date, a brief description of the contents, and so forth. Often there were incoming letters that Reagan had answered, and they were filed with Reagan's reply. Altogether, about 5,000 letters were placed into our tracking system.

Allison Asher was the director of the Reagan project, with the responsibility of supervising the construction of the database and letter spreadsheet. She did a superb job for all of the co-authors. As the project progressed and the number of letters mounted, the database became increasingly important in our analytical work. Without it we would have found it almost impossible to sort, analyze, and select as we did. In addition, Allison provided invaluable ideas and recommendations regarding many of the letters.

Leslie Johns directed the work of our Reagan project taking place at Carnegie Mellon University. She tirelessly researched issues raised in Reagan's letters and was assisted by a team of researchers including Suneal Chandran, Kaiting Chen, Lela Gibson, Tim Lo, and Lara Panis.

Bill Bishop, Gail Dickey, Amy Patterson, and Rosa Stipanovic of Carnegie Mellon University provided administrative and computer assistance.

Lillie Robinson, assistant to Martin Anderson, Heather Campbell, research assistant to Annelise Anderson, and Nicole Saulsberry, research assistant to Kiron Skinner, spent considerable time on the project doing library research and tracking down people and documents. The delicate work of reading Reagan's handwritten drafts and accurately understanding and typing their contents into the computer database was all done by Allison Asher, Heather Campbell, Nancy Cloud, Lillie Robinson and Karen Walag. Allison Asher, Heather Campbell, Lillie Robinson, and Susan Schendel also worked on proofreading. Other research assistants who worked with us included Lydia Anderson, Nikhil Iyengar, Sergei Kudelia, Steve Missildine, Alex Porfirenko, Natasha Porfirenko, and Maria Sanchez.

The three co-authors spent a good deal of time with the archives of the Ronald Reagan Presidential Library. Our experiences confirmed that presidential libraries are collectively a great scholarly asset, making possible studies of the U.S. presidency that would otherwise be impossible. The staff of the Reagan Library—from the director, Duke Blackwood, and the deputy director, John Langellier, to the archivists and the support staff—were uniformly helpful. They were all professional and well-informed and made every effort to aid us in our research. They were also very nice men and women to work with. We would especially like to express our thanks and appreciation to the professional archivists—Diane Barrie, Greg Cumming, Mike Duggan, Sherrie Fletcher, Cate Sewell, and Steve Branch (audio-visual)—and to archival technician Meghan Lee.

Archivists and curators of other institutions also provided us with expert assistance, including: Susan Naulty, archivist at the Richard Nixon Library and Birthplace in Yorba Linda, California; Marilyn Fisher, curator at the Young America's Foundation Reagan Ranch Center Archives; Anthony Glass, Eureka College archivist; Valerie Yaros of the Screen Actors Guild; Paul Wormser of the National Archives and Records Administration (Pacific Region); Helmi Raaska of the Gerald R. Ford Library; David J. Haight of the Dwight D. Eisenhower Library; Anne Shaw of the Regents of the University of California; Noelle R. Carter of the USC Warner Brothers Archives; Joanne Smith of Lawrence Livermore National Laboratory; Mike Timonis of the George C. Marshall Library; Françoise Djerejan of the James A. Baker III Institute for Public Policy at Rice University; Allen Fisher at the Lyndon B. Johnson Library and Museum; and Paul Neuhaus of the Hunt Library at

Carnegie Mellon University. Our thanks also to photographers Brian Forrest and Thomas R. DuBrock.

While writing this book, we conducted numerous interviews with people who were knowledgeable about the process of Reagan's letter writing or who were frequent correspondents. They include Richard V. Allen, James A. Baker III, William Dalton, Dorothy Dellinger, Chuck Donovan, Joanne Drake, Earl B. Dunckel, Lindy Fekety, Marlin Fitzwater, Peter. H. Hannaford, Biff Henley, Anne Volz Higgins, Victor H. Krulak, James Kuhn, Helen Lawton, Stephanie Lee, Rudolph Lee-Hines, Connie Mackey, Ron Marlow, Sharleen Volpe Martin, Suzanne Massie, Barney Oldfield, Kathleen Osborne, Jim Ostroff, Nancy Reagan, Nancy Clark Reynolds, Katherine C. Shepherd, George P. Shultz, Patsy Skidmore, William C. Thompson, Loesje Troglia, Helene von Damm, and Lorraine Wagner.

People we interviewed or with whom we corresponded about specific letters or events include Richard V. Allen, Lynn Beer, Georgiana Bollman, William P. Clark, Chris Collins, Lucy Conboy, James K. Coyne, Herman Darvick, George Davison, M. Stanton Evans, Milton Friedman, Steve Hansch, Kip Hayden, George Hearne, Jerry Heller, Raymond S. Holmes, Donald Kaecker, Teresa Kennell, Ron Marlow, Robert C. McFarlane, Jack Matlock, Ramona Moloski, Zelda Multz, Monte Osburn, Steve Parrott, Richard Pipes, Charles Price II, Junius Rodriguez, Jack Shelley, Samueline Sisco, Stuart Spencer, Craig Stubblebine, Mabyl Griffith Taylor, Ellis R. Veatch II, Steven Welch, Cathy Wildenradt, Sara Willen, William A. Wilson, and Richard Wirthlin.

We also want to thank those who offered general advice and counsel at various steps in this long project. They include: Arnold Beichman, Michael Boskin, Bruce Bueno de Mesquita, George H.W. Bush, Robert Conquest, Helene von Damm, Otto Toby Davis, Robyn Dawes, Peter Duignan, David Eisenhower, Paul S. Fischbeck, Baruch Fischhoff, Leslie Gelb, Edwin J. Gray, Alan Greenspan, Frank E. Grizzard, Steve Hayward, Robert Hessen, Tera Hunter, Steven Klepper, L.W. "Bill" Lane Jr., Edwin Meese III, Allan Meltzer, Don Meyer, Anita Naranjo, Lyn Nofziger, Charles Palm, Rita Ricardo-Campbell, Condoleezza Rice, Peter Robinson, James Sanders, Maureen Sanders, Thomas Schwartz, Ellana Schwartz, Thomas Schwartz, Steven Schlossman, Byron R. Skinner, Gloria V. Skinner, Ruby A. Skinner, Mark Skousen, Tad Taube, John Taylor, Darrell M. Trent, Joe W. Trotter, Stephanie Wallach, and Lowell Wood.

We would like to express our profound thanks for those who gave us copies of Reagan's letters from their private collections. We were pleasantly and continually surprised at how many people had received letters from Reagan—and had saved them. Every person we asked was happy to provide us with copies of the letters in their collections, and many of them were used in this book. We expect that the list of people known to have Reagan letters will grow dramatically in future years, but those we have identified include: Richard V. Allen, Martin Anderson, Walter Annenberg, Roy Brewer, William F. Buckley Jr., William P. Clark, Joanne Drake, Earl B. Dunckel, Edward Fike, Milton Friedman, Julian Gingold, Andrew Harrod, Sam

Harrod III, Sam Harrod IV, Anne Volz Higgins, Raymond S. Holmes, Philip H. Jones, Donald Kaecker, Kent Kaiser, Victor H. Krulak, Helen Lawton, Robert Lindsey, Ron Marlow, Donn D. Moomaw, Wilfred and Lola Muller, Zelda Multz, Bonnie Nofziger, Kathleen Osborne, Thomas L. Phillips, John L. Robertson, James Rogan, Nancy Reagan, Nancy Clark Reynolds, Mary Joan Roll-Sieffert, Nick Sarantakes, Jack Shelley, Mabyl Griffith Taylor, Margaret Thatcher, William C. Thompson, R. Emmett Tyrrell, Stephen Vaughn, Lorraine Wagner, and Jim Zabel.

As the book neared completion, a number of people were kind enough to read part or all of the draft manuscript and provide us with useful comments and criticism. They include: Kenneth Adelman, Richard V. Allen, Lou Cannon, William P. Clark, John Cogan, Joanne Drake, Laurie Eisenberg, Milton Friedman, Peter Hannaford, Charles Hill, Ron Marlow, Suzanne Massie, Robert C. McFarlane, William Ratliff, Nancy Reagan, George P. Shultz, and Peter Wallison.

INDEX OF LETTERS

Key: H = Handwritten   D = Dictated   T = Typed

INDEX

Calley, William, 771
Cambodia, 524, 535, 641*n*
Cambridge Union Society, England, 811
Camp David, 301, 302, 451, 565, 799
Campbell, Glenn, 356
Campbell, James, 507–508
Canada, 509–511, 721, 724, 725, 796, 801, 802
Cancún Mexico conference, 403
Cania, Sharon, 672
Cannon, Lou, 106*n*, 109*n*, 168, 185, 638*n*, 778
Cape Cod Times, 593
Capen, Richard G., Jr., 370
Capital punishment, 169, 197, 199–200, 218,
    368–369, 590, 614
Capparelli, Edward W., 501
Cargo, David F., 691
Carhartt, F. Andrew, 489–490
Caribbean Basin Initiative (CBI), 477, 483, 493, 507
Caribbean Plan, 369
Carnahan, Mel, 68
Carney, John Otis, 70
Carney, Mrs. John Otis, 70
Carney, Otis, 259–260
Carowitz, Michael, 539–540
Carpenter, Gordon, 377
Carson, Joanna, 158
Carson, Johnny, 158
Carson, Robert, 131
Carter, Jimmy, 116, 215–217, 374, 434
    Egypt-Israeli peace process, 438, 439, 452
    foreign policy, 251, 284, 377, 400, 402, 433, 456,
        457, 483, 485*n*, 488, 525, 527, 529, 588, 611,
        616, 617, 728
    Iranian hostage crisis, 231–232, 437, 591
    1976 campaign and election, 222, 225, 245, 611,
        782
    1980 campaign and election, 225, 228, 254
    post-presidential career of, 811
    SALT II (Treaty on the Limitation of Strategic
        Offensive Arms of 1979), 397, 698
Carto, Willis A., 66*n*
Casablanca (film), 128, 151
Casey, Mrs. Bill, 306–307
Casey, William, 236, 243
Cassell, Judy, 684–685
Cassidy, Tom, 15
Castañeda, Jorge, 436
Castle, Russell, 221
Castro, Fidel, 234, 490, 494, 500, 545
Catalina Island, 29, 30, 33
Catcher, Lee, 344
Catholic Church, 120, 378, 504
Cattle Queen of Montana (film), 51, 163, 164
Causse, Dr., 91

Cave, Linda, 291
Center for Advanced International Studies,
    University of Miami, 516*n*
Central Intelligence Agency (CIA), 243, 500, 512*n*,
    546–548, 571, 633*n*, 709
Challenger accident, 550, 567, 661, 800
Chamberlain, John, 589, 590
Chamorro, Pedro Joaquín, 487–488
Champion, George, 554
Chancellor, John, 606
Chandler, Otis, 185
Chappaquiddick, 229
Charles, Allan D., 234
Charles (last name unknown), 179, 200, 201
Charters, Alexander, 11
Chase Manhattan Bank, 314–315
Chasen, Dave, 134
Chasen, Maude, 134
Chasen's restaurant, Hollywood, 134
Chavez, Cesar Estrada, 191, 192, 358, 359, 767, 768
Chavez, Dennis, 756
Chavez, Linda, 825
Cheek, William A., 430
Chelmer, Samuel B., Jr., 262
Chernenko, Konstantin, 736, 738, 743
Chernobyl, 422
Chiang Ching-kuo, 284, 527, 530–531
Chiang Kai-shek, 206, 207, 253, 284, 526, 527
Chicago, Illinois, 3–5
Chicago Cubs, 29–33, 87, 102, 125, 607
Chicago *Tribune,* 464
Chile, 482, 512
Chiles, H.E., 275, 317
Chmykhalov family, 380, 741–742
Chris (last name unknown), 665
Christenberry, Robert K., 702
Christian Church. *See* Disciples of Christ
Christian Families Today, 654
Christman, John, 196
Christopher, George, 542–543, 699, 700, 706, 778
Chuck (last name unknown), 157
Church of the Brethren, 512
Churchill, Winston, 280
Cicero, 83, 83*n*, 270, 350
Citadel, The, South Carolina, 811
Citizens for Reagan, 215, 782*n*
Citizens for the Republic, 237, 238
Civil rights and race relations, 12–13, 16, 207, 208,
    212, 331–340, 625–626, 646, 756–758
Civil service pay, 176–177, 359–360
Clark, Bill, 583
Clark, Joseph, 724
Clark, Mrs. Laurence M., 634–635
Clark, William P., 117, 408, 495, 549, 742

ABOUT THE EDITORS

KIRON K. SKINNER is an assistant professor of political science at Carnegie Mellon University and a Hoover Institution research fellow. Her articles have appeared in *The Wall Street Journal* and *National Interest*. She earned her Ph.D. from Harvard University. **ANNELISE ANDERSON** has been a senior research fellow at the Hoover Institution since 1983. In 1980 she was a senior policy adviser to the presidential campaign of Ronald Reagan, and from 1981 to 1983 she served as associate director for economics and government with the Office of Management and Budget. She earned her Ph.D. in economics from Columbia University. **MARTIN ANDERSON** is the Keith and Jan Hurlbut Senior Fellow at the Hoover Institution. After serving as a special assistant to Richard Nixon, he was a senior policy adviser to the 1976 and 1980 presidential campaigns of Ronald Reagan and served as chief domestic and economic policy adviser under President Reagan. He is the author of six previous books, including *Revolution* (1988) and *Imposters in the Temple* (1992). He earned his Ph.D. in industrial management from the Massachusetts Institute of Technology.

RONALD REAGAN Sept. 30 - 1993

Dear Colin

Nancy & I are so sorry we can't be with you today at your retirement ceremony. I am sure it must be a little bittersweet and, yet, there must be tremendous anticipation for all that lies ahead.

I too remember vividly your coming into the office on that last day with your report: "The world is quiet today, Mr. President." It doesn't seem possible that so much time has passed.

Nancy and I are eagerly looking forward to seeing you and Alma here on November 9th at the Library. You have both been dear friends to us. We travelled the world together and witnessed extraordinary changes taking place around the globe. Through it all, you've always occupied a special place in our lives and our admiration has grown with each passing day.

God bless you, Colin and we'll see you soon,

Sincerely
Ron

General Colin L. Powell,
USA - Chairman of the
Joint Chiefs of Staff
The Pentagon - Wash. D.C. 20318